THE
HEBREW
BIBLE

VOLUME 2

PROPHETS

THE
HEBREW
BIBLE

VOLUME 2

PROPHETS

NEVI'IM

A TRANSLATION WITH COMMENTARY

ROBERT ALTER

W. W. NORTON & COMPANY

Independent Publishers Since 1923

New York   London

For information about permission to reproduce selections from this book, write to Permissions, W. W. Norton & Company, Inc., 500 Fifth Avenue, New York, NY 10110

For information about special discounts for bulk purchases, please contact W. W. Norton Special Sales at specialsales@wwnorton.com or 800-233-4830

Manufacturing by LSC Communications Crawfordsville
Book design by JAM Design
Production manager: Julia Druskin

ISBN: 978-0-393-29249-7

W. W. Norton & Company, Inc., 500 Fifth Avenue, New York, N.Y. 10110
www.wwnorton.com

W. W. Norton & Company Ltd., 15 Carlisle Street, London W1D 3BS

4 5 6 7 8 9 0

For Jonas, Judah, Amos, and, especially, Michael,
dear friends now gone whose presence
in my life made a difference in all this.

About the Author

Robert Alter's translation of the Hebrew Bible, the magnificent capstone to a lifetime of distinguished scholarly work, has won the PEN Center Literary Award for Translation and the Koret Jewish Book Award. His immense achievements in scholarship ranging from the eighteenth-century European novel to contemporary Hebrew and American literature earned Alter the Robert Kirsch Award for Lifetime Achievement from the *Los Angeles Times*. A member of the American Academy of Arts and Sciences and the American Philosophical Society, Alter is Emeritus Class of 1937 Professor of Hebrew and Comparative Literature at the University of California, Berkeley.

Contents

Introduction to the Hebrew Bible

I. THE BIBLE IN ENGLISH AND THE HERESY OF EXPLANATION

Why, after so many English versions, a new translation of the Hebrew Bible? There is, as I shall explain in detail, something seriously wrong with all the familiar English translations, traditional and recent, of the Hebrew Bible. Broadly speaking, one may say that in the case of the modern versions, the problem is a shaky sense of English and in the case of the King James Version, a shaky sense of Hebrew. The present translation is an experiment in re-presenting the Bible—and, above all, biblical narrative prose—in a language that conveys with some precision the semantic nuances and the lively orchestration of literary effects of the Hebrew and at the same time has stylistic and rhythmic integrity as literary English. I shall presently give a more specific account of the kind of English I have aimed for and of the features of the Hebrew that have prompted my choices, but I think it will be helpful for me to say something first about why English translations of the Bible have been problematic—more problematic, perhaps, than most readers may realize.

It is an old and in some ways unfair cliché to say that translation is always a betrayal, but modern English versions of the Bible provide unfortunately persuasive evidence for that uncompromising generalization. At first thought, it is rather puzzling that this should be the case. In purely quantitative terms, we live in a great age of Bible translation. Several integral translations of the Bible have been done since the middle of the twentieth century, and a spate of English versions of individual biblical books has appeared. This period, moreover, is one in which our understanding of ancient Hebrew has become considerably more nuanced and precise than it once was, thanks to comparative Semitic philology aided by archaeology, and also thanks to the careful reanalysis of the formal structures—

syntax, grammar, morphology, verb tenses—of biblical Hebrew. One might have expected that this recent flurry of translation activity, informed by the newly focused awareness of the meanings of biblical Hebrew, would have produced at least some English versions that would be both vividly precise and closer to the feel of the original than any of the older translations. Instead, the modern English versions—especially in their treatment of Hebrew narrative prose—have placed readers at a grotesque distance from the distinctive literary experience of the Bible in its original language. As a consequence, the King James Version, as Gerald Hammond, an eminent British authority on Bible translations, has convincingly argued, remains the closest approach for English readers to the original—despite its frequent and at times embarrassing inaccuracies, despite its archaisms, and despite its insistent substitution of Renaissance English tonalities and rhythms for biblical ones.

Some observers have sought to explain the inadequacy of modern Bible translations in terms of the general decline of the English language. It is certainly true that there are far fewer people these days with a cultivated sensitivity to the expressive resources of the language, the nuances of lexical values, the force of metaphor and rhythm; and one is certainly much less likely to find such people on a committee of ecclesiastical or scholarly experts than one would have in the first decade of the seventeenth century. There are, nevertheless, still some brilliant stylists among English prose writers; and if our age has been graced with remarkable translations of Homer, Sophocles, and Dante, why not of the Bible?

Part of the explanation, I suspect, is in the conjunction of philological scholarship and translation. I intend no churlish disrespect to philology. On the contrary, without it, our reading of the Bible, or indeed of any older text, is no better than walking through a great museum on a very gloomy day with all the lights turned out. To read the Bible over the shoulder of a great philological critic, like Abraham ibn Ezra (1092–1167), one of the earliest and still eminently worth studying, is to see many important things in fine focus for the first time. There is, however, a crucial difference between philology as a tool for understanding literary texts and philology as an end in itself, for literature and philology work with extremely different conceptions of what constitutes knowledge. To be fair to the broad enterprise of philology, which has included some great literary critics, I use the term here as shorthand for "biblical philology," a discipline that, especially in its Anglo-American applications, has often come down to lexicography and the analysis of grammar.

For the philologist, the great goal is the achievement of clarity. It is scarcely necessary to say that in all sorts of important, but also delimited, ways clarity is indispensable in a translator's wrestling with the original text. The simplest case, but a pervasive one, consists of getting a handle on the meaning of particular terms. It is truly helpful, for example, to know that biblical *naḥal* most commonly indicates not any sort of brook, creek, or stream but the kind of freshet, called a *wadi* in both Arabic and modern Hebrew, that floods a dry desert gulch during the rainy months and vanishes in the heat of the summer. Suddenly, Job's "my brothers betrayed like a *naḥal*" (Job 6:14) becomes a striking poetic image, where before it might have been a minor puzzlement. But philological clarity in literary texts can quickly turn into too much of a good thing. Literature in general, and the narrative prose of the Hebrew Bible in particular, cultivates certain profound and haunting enigmas, delights in leaving its audiences guessing about motives and connections, and, above all, loves to set ambiguities of word choice and image against one another in an endless interplay that resists neat resolution. In polar contrast, the impulse of the philologist is—here a barbarous term nicely catches the tenor of the activity—"to disambiguate" the terms of the text. The general result when applied to translation is to reduce, simplify, and denature the Bible. These unfortunate consequences are all the more pronounced when the philologist, however acutely trained in that discipline, has an underdeveloped sense of literary diction, rhythm, and the uses of figurative language; and that, alas, is often the case in an era in which literary culture is not widely disseminated even among the technically educated.

The unacknowledged heresy underlying most modern English versions of the Bible is the use of translation as a vehicle for *explaining* the Bible instead of representing it in another language, and in the most egregious instances this amounts to explaining away the Bible. This impulse may be attributed not only to a rather reduced sense of the philological enterprise but also to a feeling that the Bible, because of its canonical status, has to be made accessible—indeed, transparent—to all. (The one signal exception to all these generalizations is Everett Fox's 1995 American version of the Torah. Emulating the model of the German translation by Martin Buber and Franz Rosenzweig [begun in 1925, completed in 1961], which flaunts Hebrew etymologies, preserves nearly all repetitions of Hebrew terms, and invents German words, Fox goes to the opposite extreme of other modern versions: his English has the great virtue of reminding us verse after verse of the strangeness of the Hebrew original, but it does so at the cost of often being not quite English and consequently of becoming a text for study rather than a fluently readable version that conveys the stylistic poise and power of the Hebrew.) Modern translators, in their zeal to uncover the meanings of the biblical text for the instruction of a modern readership, frequently lose sight of how the text intimates its meanings—the distinctive, artfully deployed features of ancient Hebrew prose and poetry that are the instruments for the articulation of all meaning, message, insight, and vision.

One of the most salient characteristics of biblical Hebrew is its extraordinary concreteness, manifested especially in a fondness for images rooted in the human body. The general predisposition of modern translators is to convert most of this concrete language into more abstract terms that have the purported advantage of clarity but turn the pungency of the original into stale paraphrase. A good deal of this concrete biblical language based on the body is what a linguist would call lexicalized metaphor—imagery, here taken from body parts and bodily functions, that is made to stand for some general concept as a fixed item in the vocabulary of the language (as "eye" in English can be used to mean "perceptiveness" or "connoisseur's understanding"). Dead metaphors, however, are the one persuasive instance of the resurrection of the dead—for at least the ghosts of the old concrete meanings float over the supposedly abstract acceptations of the terms, and this is something the philologically driven translators do not appear to understand. "Many modern versions," Gerald Hammond tartly observes, "eschew anything which smacks of imagery or metaphor—based on the curious assumption, I guess, that modern English is an image-free language." The price paid for this avoidance of the metaphorical will become evident by considering two characteristic and recurrent Hebrew terms and the role they play in representing the world in the biblical story.

The Hebrew noun *zeraʿ** has the general meaning of "seed," which can be applied either in the agricultural sense or to human beings, as the term for semen. By metaphorical extension, semen becomes the established designation for what it produces, progeny. Modern translators, evidently unwilling to trust the ability of adult readers to understand that "seed"— as regularly in the King James Version—may mean progeny, repeatedly render it as offspring, descendants, heirs, progeny, posterity. But I think there is convincing evidence in the texts themselves that the biblical writ-

---

* The symbol ʿ represents the Hebrew consonant *ayin,* a glottal stop that might sound something like the Cockney pronunciation of the middle consonant of "bottle," in which the dentalized *t* is replaced by a gulping sound produced from the larynx.

ers never entirely forgot that their term for offspring also meant semen and had a precise equivalent in the vegetable world. To cite a distinctly physical example, when Onan "knew that the seed would not be his," that is, the progeny of his brother's widow should he impregnate her, "he would waste his seed on the ground, so to give no seed to his brother" (Genesis 38:9). Modern translators, despite their discomfort with body terms, can scarcely avoid the wasted "seed" here because without it the representation of spilling semen on the ground in coitus interruptus becomes unintelligible. E. A. Speiser substitutes "offspring" for "seed" at the end of the verse, however, and the Revised English Bible goes him one better by putting "offspring" at the beginning as well ("Onan knew that the offspring would not count as his") and introducing "seed" in the middle as object of the verb "to spill" and scuttling back to the decorousness of "offspring" at the end—a prime instance of explanation under the guise of translation. But the biblical writer is referring to "seed" as much at the end of the verse as at the beginning. Onan adopts the stratagem of coitus interruptus in order not to "give seed"—that is, semen—to Tamar, and, as a necessary consequence of this contraceptive act, he avoids providing her with offspring. The thematic point of this moment, anchored in sexual practice, law, and human interaction, is blunted by not preserving "seed" throughout.

Even in contexts not directly related to sexuality, the concreteness of this term often amplifies the meaning of the utterance. When, for example, at the end of the story of the binding of Isaac, God reiterates His promise to Abraham, the multiplication of seed is strongly linked with cosmic imagery—harking back to the Creation story—of heaven and earth: "I will greatly bless you and will greatly multiply your seed, as the stars in the heavens and as the sand on the shore of the sea" (Genesis 22:17). If "seed" here is rendered as "offspring" or "descendants," what we get are two essentially mathematical similes of numerical increase. That is, in fact, the primary burden of the language God addresses to Abraham, but as figurative language it also imposes itself visually on the retina of the imagination, and so underlying the idea of a single late-born son whose progeny will be countless millions is an image of human seed (perhaps reinforced by the shared white color of semen and stars) scattered across the vast expanses of the starry skies and through the innumerable particles of sand on the shore of the sea. To substitute "offspring" for "seed" here may not fundamentally alter the meaning but it diminishes the vividness of the statement, making it just a little harder for readers to sense why these ancient texts have been so compelling down through the ages.

The most metaphorically extended body part in biblical Hebrew is the hand, though head and foot are also abundantly represented in figurative senses. Now it is obvious enough, given the equivalent usages in modern Western languages, that "hand" can be employed figuratively to express such notions as power, control, responsibility, and trust—to which biblical Hebrew adds one meaning peculiar to itself, commemorative monument. But most modern translators substitute one or another of these abstract terms, introducing supposed clarity where things were perfectly clear to begin with and subverting the literary integrity of the story. In the two sequential episodes that end with Joseph's being cast into a pit—the first is a dry cistern, the second an Egyptian prison, but the two are explicitly linked by the use of the term *bor* for both—the recurrently invoked "hand" is a focusing device that both defines and complicates the moral themes of the story. Reuben, hearing his brothers' murderous intentions, seeks to rescue Joseph "from their hands." He implores his brothers, "Lay not a hand upon him," just as, in the other strand of the story, Judah says, "Let not our hand be against him." E. A. Speiser, faithful to the clarifying impulse of the modern Bible scholar's philological imagination, renders both these phrases as "do away with," explaining that it would be illogical to have Reuben, or Judah, say "Don't lay a hand on him," since in fact the counsel proffered involves seizing him, stripping him, and throwing him into the pit. But in fact this alleged illogic is the luminous logic of the writer's moral critique. Reuben pleads with his brothers not to lay a hand on Joseph, that is, not to shed his blood (this is the phrase he uses at the beginning of his speech), but neither his plea nor Judah's proposal is an entirely innocent one: although each urges that the brothers lay no hand on Joseph, there is a violent laying on of hands necessitated by the course of action each proposes. Even more pointedly, once Joseph is headed south with the caravan, those same fraternal hands will take his ornamented tunic (the King James Version's "coat of many colors"), slaughter a kid, dip the garment in the blood, and send it off to Jacob.

The image of hands holding a garment belonging to Joseph that is turned into false evidence brilliantly returns at the climactic moment of the next episode involving him, in Genesis 39. When Joseph flees from the lust of his master's wife, "he left his garment in her hand" because she has virtually torn it off his back in trying to effect her reiterated "Lie with me" by seizing him. In her accusation of Joseph, she alters the narrator's twice-stated "in her hand" to "by me," implying that he disrobed deliberately before attempting to rape her. But the narrator's cunning deployment of repeated terms has conditioned us to zero in on these two pivotal words, *wayaʿazov beyad,* "he left in the hand of," for in the six initial framing verses of the story, "hand" appears four times, with the last, most significant occurrence being this summary of the comprehensiveness of Joseph's stewardship: "And he left all that he had in Joseph's hands" (39:6). (Hebrew idiom allows the writer to use "hand" in the singular, thus creating an exact phrasal identity between the figurative reference to the hand in which the trust of stewardship is left and the literal reference to the hand in which the garment belonging to the object of sexual desire is left.) The invocation of "hand" in chapters 37 and 39—the story of Judah and Tamar lies between them—forms an elegant A B A B pattern: in chapter 37 hands are laid on Joseph, an action carried forward in the resumptive repetition at the very beginning of chapter 39 when he is bought "from the hands of the Ishmaelites"; then we have the supremely competent hand, or hands, of Joseph, into which everything is placed, or left, and by which everything succeeds; then again a violent hand is laid on Joseph, involving the stripping of his garment, as in the episode with the brothers; and at the end of the chapter, Joseph in prison again has everything entrusted to his dependable hands, with this key term twice stated in the three and a half verses of the closing frame. A kind of dialectic is created in the thematic unfolding of the story between hand as the agency of violent impulse and hand as the instrument of scrupulous management. Although the concrete term is probably used with more formal precision in this particular sequence than is usually the case elsewhere, the hands of Joseph and the hands upon Joseph provide a fine object lesson about how biblical narrative is misrepresented when translators tamper with the purposeful and insistent physicality of its language, as here when "hand" is transmuted into "trust" or "care." Such substitutions offer explanations or interpretations instead of translations and thus betray the original.

There are, alas, more pervasive ways than the choice of terms in which nearly all the modern English versions commit the heresy of explanation. The most global of these is the prevalent modern strategy of repackaging biblical syntax for an audience whose reading experience is assumed to be limited to *Time, Newsweek,* the *New York Times* or the *Times* of London, and the internet. Now, it is often asserted, with seemingly self-evident justice, that the fundamental difference between biblical syntax and modern English syntax is between a system in which parallel clauses linked by "and" predominate (what linguists call "parataxis") and one in which the use of subordinate clauses and complex sentences predominates (what linguists call "hypotaxis"). Modern English has a broad array of modal and temporal discriminations in its system of verbs and a whole armament of subordinate conjunctions to stipulate different relations among clauses. Biblical Hebrew, on the other hand, has only two aspects[*] (they are probably not tenses in our sense) of verbs, together with one indication of a jussive mode—when a verb is used to express a desire or exhortation to perform the action in question—and a modest number of subordinate conjunctions. Although there are certainly instances of significant syntactic subordination, the characteristic biblical syntax is additive, working with parallel clauses linked by "and"—which in the Hebrew is not even a separate word but rather a particle, *waw*[†] (it means "hook"), that is prefixed to the first word of the clause.

The assumption of most modern translators has been that this sort of syntax will be either unintelligible or at least alienating to modern readers, and so should be entirely rearranged as modern English. There are two basic problems with this procedure. First, it ignores the fact that parataxis is the essential literary vehicle of biblical narrative: it is the way the ancient Hebrew writers saw the world, linked events in it, artfully ordered it, and narrated it, and one gets a very different world if their syntax is jettisoned. Second, rejection of biblical parataxis presupposes a very simplistic notion of what constitutes modern literary English. The implicit model seems to be, as I have suggested, the popular press, as well as perhaps high-school textbooks, bureaucratic directives, and ordinary conversation. But serious writers almost never accept such leveling limitation to a bland norm of popular usage. If one thinks of the great English stylists among twentieth-century novelists—writers like Joyce, Nabokov, Faulkner, and Virginia Woolf—there is not one among them whose use of language, including the deployment of syntax, even vaguely resembles the workaday simplicity and patly consistent orderliness that recent translators of the Bible have posited as the norm of modern English. It is also well to keep in mind that literary style, like many other aspects of literature, is constantly self-recapitulative, invoking recollections of its near and distant literary antecedents, so that modernists like Joyce and Faulkner sometimes echo biblical language and

---

[*] Instead of a clear-cut expression of the temporal frame in which actions occur—past, present, future, past perfect, and so forth—aspects indicate chiefly whether the action has been completed or is to be completed.

[†]The modern Hebrew pronunciation is *vav*, with the vowel sounding like the short *a* in a French word like *bave*, with which it would rhyme.

cadences, and a mannered stylist like Hemingway, in making "and" his most prominent connective, surely has the King James Version of the Bible in mind. And in any event, the broad history of both Semitic and European languages and literatures evinces a strong differentiation in most periods between everyday language and the language of literature.

The assumption of biblical philologists that parallel syntax is alien to modern literary English is belied by the persistent presence of highly wrought paratactic prose even at the end of the twentieth century and beyond. A variety of self-conscious English stylists in the modern era, from Gertrude Stein to Cormac McCarthy, have exhibited a fondness for chains of parallel utterances linked by "and" in which the basic sentence-type is the same structurally as that used again and again in biblical prose. What such a style makes manifest in a narrative is a series of more or less discrete events, or micro-events, in a chain, not unlike the biblical names of begetters and begotten that are strung one after another in the chains of the genealogical lists. The biblical writers generally chose not to order these events in ramified networks of causal, conceptual, or temporal subordination, not because hypotaxis was an unavailable option, as the opening verses of the second Creation story (Genesis 2:4–5) clearly demonstrate. The continuing appeal, moreover, for writers in our own age of this syntax dominated by "and," which highlights the discrete event, suggests that parallel syntax may still be a perfectly viable way to represent in English the studied parallelism of verbs and clauses of ancient Hebrew narrative.

Since a literary style is composed of very small elements as well as larger structural features, an English translator must confront the pesky question of whether the ubiquitous Hebrew particle that means "and" should be represented at all in translation. This is obviously not a problem when the *waw* simply connects two nouns—as in "the heavens and the earth"—but what of its constant use at the beginning of sentences and clauses prefixed to verbs? The argument against translating it in these cases is that the primary function of the *waw* appended to a verb is not to signify "and" but to indicate that the Hebrew prefix conjugation, which otherwise is used for actions yet to be completed, is reporting past events (hence its designation in the terminology of classical Hebrew grammar as "the *waw* of conversion"). It is far from clear, as modern Bible scholars tend to assume, that the fulfillment of one linguistic function by a particle of speech automatically excludes any others; on the contrary, it is entirely likely that for the ancient audience the *waw* appended to the verb both converted its temporal aspect and continued to signify "and." But, seman-

tics aside, the general practice of modern English translators of suppress-
ing the "and" when it is attached to a verb has the effect of changing the
tempo, rhythm, and construction of events in biblical narrative. Let me
illustrate by quoting a narrative sequence from Genesis 24 first in my own
version, which reproduces every "and" and every element of parataxis, and
then in the version of the Revised English Bible. The Revised English Bible
is in general one of the most compulsive repackagers of biblical language,
though in this instance the reordering of the Hebrew is relatively minor.
Its rendering of these sentences is roughly interchangeable with any of
the other modern versions—the Jerusalem Bible, the New Jewish Publication Society, Speiser—one might choose. I begin in the middle of verse 16,
where Rebekah becomes the subject of a series of actions.

> And she came down to the spring and filled her jug and came back up. And
> the servant ran toward her and said, "Pray, let me sip a bit of water from your
> jug." And she said, "Drink, my lord," and she hurried and tipped down her
> jug on one hand and let him drink. And she let him drink his fill and said,
> "For your camels, too, I shall draw water until they drink their fill." And she
> hurried and emptied her jug into the trough, and she ran again to the well to
> draw water and drew water for all his camels.

And this is how the Revised English Bible, in keeping with the prevailing assumptions of most recent translations, renders these verses in what
is presumed to be sensible modern English:

> She went down to the spring, filled her jar, and came up again. Abraham's
> servant hurried to meet her and said, "Will you give me a little water from
> your jar?" "Please drink, sir," she answered, and at once lowered her jar on
> her hand to let him drink. When she had finished giving him a drink, she
> said, "I shall draw water also for your camels until they have had enough."
> She quickly emptied her jar into the water trough, and then hurrying again
> to the well she drew water and watered all the camels.

There is, as one would expect, some modification of biblical parataxis,
though it is not so extreme here as elsewhere in the Revised English Bible:
"And she let him drink his fill" is converted into an introductory adverbial
clause, "When she had finished giving him a drink" (actually in consonance
with the otherwise paratactic King James Version): "and she hurried" is
compressed into "quickly"; "and she ran again" becomes the participial

"hurrying again." (Moves of this sort, it should be said, push translation to the verge of paraphrase—recasting and interpreting the original instead of representing it.) The most striking divergence between these two versions is that mine has fifteen "and's," corresponding precisely to fifteen occurrences of the particle *waw* in the Hebrew, whereas the Revised English Bible manages with just five. What difference does this make? To begin with, it should be observed that the *waw*, whatever is claimed about its linguistic function, is by no means an inaudible element in the phonetics of the Hebrew text: we must keep constantly in mind that these narratives were composed to be *heard*, not merely to be decoded by a reader's eye. The reiterated "and," then, plays an important role in creating the rhythm of the story, in phonetically punctuating the forward-driving movement of the prose. The elimination of the "and" in the Revised English Bible and in all its modern cousins produces—certainly to my ear—an abrupt, awkward effect in the sound pattern of the language, or to put it more strictly, a kind of narrative arrhythmia.

More is at stake here than pleasing sounds, for the heroine of the repeated actions is in fact subtly but significantly reduced in all the rhythmically deficient versions. She of course performs roughly the same acts in the different versions—politely offering water to the stranger, lowering her jug so that he can drink, rapidly going back and forth to the spring to bring water for the camels. But in the compressions, syntactical reorderings, and stop-and-start movements of the modernizing version, the encounter at the well and Rebekah's actions are made to seem rather matter-of-fact, however exemplary her impulse of hospitality. This tends to obscure what the Hebrew highlights, which is that she is doing something quite extraordinary. Rebekah at the well presents one of the rare biblical instances of the performance of an act of "Homeric" heroism. The servant begins by asking modestly to "sip a bit of water," as though all he wanted were to wet his lips. But we need to remember, as the ancient audience surely did, that a camel after a long desert journey can drink as much as twenty-five gallons of water, and there are ten camels here whom Rebekah offers to water "until they drink their fill." The chain of verbs tightly linked by all the "and's" does an admirable job in conveying this sense of the young woman's hurling herself with prodigious speed into the sequence of required actions. Even her dialogue is scarcely a pause in the narrative momentum, but is integrated syntactically and rhythmically into the chain: "And she said, 'Drink, my lord,' and she hurried and tipped down her jug. . . . And she hurried and emptied her jug into the trough, and she ran again to the well to draw water and drew water for all his camels." The parallel syntax and the barrage of "and's," far from being the reflex of a "primitive" language, are as artfully effective in furthering the ends of the narrative as any device one could find in a sophisticated modern novelist.

Beyond these issues of syntax and local word choice lies a fundamental question that no modern translator I know of has really confronted: What level, or perhaps levels, of style is represented in biblical Hebrew? There is no reason, I believe, to be awestruck by the sheer antiquity of the text. If biblical Hebrew could be shown to reflect a pungent colloquial usage in the ancient setting, or a free commingling of colloquial and formal language, it would be only logical to render it with equivalent levels of diction in modern English. As a matter of fact, all the modern translators—from Speiser to Fox to the sundry ecclesiastical committees in both America and England—have shown a deaf ear to diction, acting as though the only important considerations in rendering a literary text were lexical values and grammatical structures, while the English terms chosen could be promiscuously borrowed from boardroom or bedroom or scholar's word hoard, with little regard to the tonality and connotation the words carried with them from their native linguistic habitat.

Whatever conclusions we may draw about the stylistic level of biblical Hebrew are a little precarious because we of course have no record of the ancient spoken language, and if, as seems likely, there were extracanonical varieties or genres of Hebrew writing in the ancient world, the vestiges have long since crumbled into dust. Did, for example, the citizens of Judah in the time of Jeremiah speak in a parallel syntax, using the *waw* consecutive, and employing roughly the same vocabulary that we find in his prophecies, or in Deuteronomy and Genesis? Although there is no proof, my guess is that vernacular syntax and grammar probably differed in some ways from their literary counterparts. In regard to vocabulary, there is evidence that what we see in the canonical books would not have been identical with everyday usage. First, there is the problem of the relative paucity of vocabulary in biblical literature. As the Spanish Hebrew scholar Angel Sáenz-Badillos has observed in his *History of the Hebrew Language* (1993), the biblical lexicon is so restricted that it is hard to believe it could have served all the purposes of quotidian existence in a highly developed society. The instance of the poetry of Job, with its unusual number of words not found elsewhere in Scripture, is instructive in this regard: the Job-poet, in his powerful impulse to forge a poetic imagery that would represent humankind, God, and nature in a new and even startling light, draws on highly specific language from manufacturing processes, food preparation, commercial and legal institutions, which would never be used in biblical narrative. The plausible conclusion is that the Hebrew of the Bible is a conventionally delimited language, roughly analagous in this respect to the French of the neoclassical theater: it was understood by writers and their audiences, at least in the case of narrative, that only certain words were appropriate for the literary rendering of events.

There is evidence, moreover, that people in everyday life may have had different words for many of the basic concepts and entities that are mentioned in the Bible. This argument was persuasively made by the Israeli linguist Abba ben David in his still indispensable 1967 study, available only in Hebrew, *The Language of the Bible and the Language of the Sages*. Ben David offers a fascinating explanation for one of the great mysteries of the Hebrew language—the emergence, toward the end of the pre-Christian era, of a new kind of Hebrew, which became the language of the early rabbis. Now, it is widely recognized that this new Hebrew reflected the influence of the Aramaic vernacular in morphology, in grammar, and in some of its vocabulary, and that, understandably, it also incorporated a vast number of Greek and Latin loanwords. But what is puzzling is that rabbinic Hebrew also uses a good many indigenous Hebrew terms that are absent from the biblical corpus, or reflected only in rare and marginal biblical cognates. The standard terms in rabbinical Hebrew for sun and moon, and some of its frequently used verbs like to look, to take, to enter, to clean, are entirely different from their biblical counterparts, without visible influence from any of the languages impinging on Hebrew. Where did these words come from? Ben David, observing, as have others before him, that there are incipient signs of an emergent rabbinic Hebrew in late biblical books like Jonah and the Song of Songs, makes the bold and, to my mind, convincing proposal that rabbinic Hebrew was built upon an ancient vernacular that for the most part had been excluded from the literary language used for the canonical texts. This makes particular sense if one keeps in mind that the early rabbis were anxious to draw a line between their own "Oral Torah" and the written Torah they were expounding. For the purposes of legal and homiletic exegesis, they naturally would have used a vernacular Hebrew rather than the literary language, and when their discourse was first given written formulation in the Mishnah in the early third century C.E., that text would have recorded this vernacular, which probably had a long prehistory in the biblical period. It is distinctly possible that when a ninth-century B.C.E. Israelite farmer mopped his brow under the blazing sun, he did not point to it and say *shemesh,* as it is invariably called in biblical prose texts, but rather *ḥamah,* as it is regularly designated in the Mishnah.

There is, of course, no way of plotting a clear chronology of the evolution of rabbinic Hebrew from an older vernacular, no way of determining how far back into the biblical period various elements of rabbinic language may go. It is sufficient for our effort to gauge the level of style of the Bible's literary prose merely to grant the very high likelihood that the language of the canonical texts was not identical with the vernacular, that it reflected a specialized or elevated vocabulary, and perhaps even a distinct grammar and syntax. Let me cite a momentary exception to the rule of biblical usage that may give us a glimpse into this excluded vernacular background of a more formal literary language. It is well-known that in biblical dialogue all the characters speak proper literary Hebrew, with no intimations of slang, dialect, or idiolect. The single striking exception is impatient Esau's first speech to Jacob in Genesis 25: "Let me gulp down some of this red red stuff." Inarticulate with hunger, he cannot come up with the ordinary Hebrew term for "stew," and so he makes do with *ha'adom ha'adom hazeh*—literally "this red red." But what is more interesting for our purpose is the verb Esau uses for "feeding," *hal'iteini.* This is the sole occurrence of this verb in the biblical corpus, but in the Talmud it is a commonly used term with the specific meaning of stuffing food into the mouth of an animal. One cannot be certain this was its precise meaning in the biblical period because words do, after all, undergo semantic shifts in a period of considerably more than a thousand years. But it seems safe to assume, minimally, that even a millennium before the rabbis *hal'it* would have been a cruder term for feeding than the standard biblical *ha'akhil.* What I think happened at this point in Genesis is that the author, in the writerly zest with which he sought to characterize Esau's crudeness, allowed himself, quite exceptionally, to introduce a vernacular term for coarse eating or animal feeding into the dialogue that would jibe nicely with his phrase "this red red stuff." After the close of the biblical era, this otherwise excluded term would surface in the legal pronouncements of the rabbis on animal husbandry, together with a host of vernacular words used in the ancient period but never permitted to enter the canonical texts.

All this strongly suggests that the language of biblical narrative in its own time was stylized, decorous, dignified, and readily identified by its audiences as a language of literature, in certain ways distinct from the language of quotidian reality. The tricky complication, however, is that in most respects it also was not a lofty style, and was certainly neither ornate nor euphemistic. If some of its vocabulary may have reflected a specialized literary lexicon, the language of biblical narrative also makes abundant use of ordinary Hebrew words that must have been in everyone's mouth from day to day. Just to mention the few recurrent terms on which I have commented, "hand," "house," "all," and "seed" are primary words in every phase of the history of Hebrew, and they continue to appear as such in the rabbinic language, where so much else is altered. Biblical prose, then, is a formal literary language but also, paradoxically, a plainspoken one, and, moreover, a language that evinces a strong commitment to using a limited set of terms again and again, making an aesthetic virtue out of the repetition. It should be added that the language of the Bible reflects not one level of diction but a certain range of dictions, as I shall explain presently.

What is the implication of this analysis for an appropriate modern English equivalent to ancient Hebrew style? The right direction, I think, was hit on by the King James Version, following the great model of Tyndale a century before it. There is no good reason to render biblical Hebrew as contemporary English, either lexically or syntactically. This is not to suggest that the Bible should be represented as fussily old-fashioned English, but a limited degree of archaizing coloration is entirely appropriate, employed with other strategies for creating a language that is stylized yet simple and direct, free of the overtones of contemporary colloquial usage but with a certain timeless homespun quality. An adequate English version should be able to indicate the small but significant modulations in diction in the biblical language—something the stylistically uniform King James Version, however, entirely fails to do. A suitable English version should avoid at all costs the modern abomination of elegant synonymous variation, for the literary prose of the Bible turns everywhere on significant repetition, not variation. Similarly, the translation of terms on the basis of immediate context—except when it becomes grotesque to do otherwise—is to be resisted as another instance of the heresy of explanation. Finally, the mesmerizing effect of these ancient stories will scarcely be conveyed if they are not rendered in cadenced English prose that at least in some ways corresponds to the powerful cadences of the Hebrew. Let me now comment more particularly on the distinctive biblical treatment of diction, word choice, syntax, and rhythm and what it implies for translation.

The biblical prose writers favor what we may think of as a primary vocabulary. They revel in repetition, sometimes of a stately, refrainlike sort, sometimes deployed in ingenious patterns through which different meanings of the same term are played against one another. Elegant synonymity is alien to biblical prose, and it is only rarely that a highly specialized term is used instead of the more general word. Here is a characteristic biblical way of putting things: "And God made the two great lights, the great light for dominion of day and the small light for dominion of night, and the stars" (Genesis 1:16). In addition to the poised emphasis of the internal repetitions in the sentence, one should note that the primary term for a source of light—*ma'or,* transparently cognate with *'or,* the light that is divided from the darkness in 1:4—is placed in the foreground. In fact, there are half a dozen biblical synonyms for "light," suggesting a range roughly equivalent to English terms like "illumination," "effulgence," "brilliance," and "splendor," but these are all reserved for the more elaborate vocabulary of poetry, whereas in prose the writer sticks to the simplicity of *'or* and *ma'or,* and everywhere it behooves a translator to do the same with English equivalents.

Some biblical scholars might object that my example is skewed because it is taken from the so-called Priestly source (P), which has a stylistic predilection for high decorousness and cadenced repetitions. But the stylistic difference in this regard between P and the two other conjectured source documents of the Pentateuch, designated J and E, is one of degree, not kind. Thus, when the second version of the Creation story, commonly identified as J's, begins in Genesis 2:4, we do get some greater degree of specification in the language, in keeping with the way creation is here imagined. Instead of the verbs "to create" (*bara'*) and "to make" (*'asah*) that accompany God's speaking the world into being in chapter 1 we are given the potter's term "to fashion" (*yatsar*) and the architectural term "to build" (*banah*). These remain, however, within the limits of a primary vocabulary. The nuanced and specialized lexicon of manufacturing processes one encounters in the poetry of Job and of Deutero-Isaiah is firmly excluded from the stylistic horizon of this narrative prose, though the subject might have invited it.

The translator's task, then, is to mirror the repetitions as much as is feasible. Let me cite one small example, where I learned from my own mistake. When Joseph's brothers recount to Jacob what happened on their first trip to Egypt, they say, in the English of my first draft, "The man who is lord of the land spoke harshly to us and accused us of being spies in the land" (Genesis 42:30). (The verb "accused" is also used in the New Jewish Publication Society translation.) On rereading, I realized that I had violated the cardinal principle, not to translate according to context. The Hebrew says, very literally, "gave us as spies," "give" in biblical usage being one of those all-purpose verbs that variously means "to set," "to place," "to grant," "to deem." I hastened to change the last clause to "made us out to be spies" because "to make," with or without an accompanying preposition, is precisely such a primary term that serves many purposes and so is very much in keeping with biblical stylistic practice.

What is surprising about the biblical writers' use of this deliberately limited vocabulary is that it can be so precise and even nuanced. Our own cultural preconceptions of writers scrupulously devoted to finding exactly the right word are associated with figures like Flaubert and Joyce, who meticulously choose the terms of their narratives from a large repertory of finely discriminated lexical items. Biblical prose often exhibits an analogous precision within the severe limits of its primary vocabulary. There are, for example, two paired terms, masculine and feminine, in biblical Hebrew to designate young people: *na'ar/na'arah* (in this translation, "lad" and "young woman") and *yeled/yaldah* (in this translation, "child" and "girl"). The first pair is somewhat asymmetrical because *na'ar* often also means "servant" or anyone in a subaltern position, and sometimes means "elite soldier," whereas *na'arah* usually refers to a nubile young woman, and only occasionally to a servant girl. Though there are rare biblical occurrences of *yeled* in the sense of "young man," it generally designates someone younger than a *na'ar*—etymologically, it means "the one who is born," reflecting a development parallel to the French *enfant*.

With this little to work with, it is remarkable how much the biblical writers accomplish in their deployment of the terms. In the first part of the story of the banishment of Hagar and Ishmael (Genesis 21), Ishmael is referred to consistently as "the child," as was his infant half brother Isaac at the beginning of this chapter. The grief-stricken mother in the wilderness says to herself, "Let me not see when the child dies." From the moment God speaks in the story (verse 17), Ishmael is invariably referred to as "the lad"— evidently with an intimation of tenderness but also with the suggestion that he is a young man, *na'ar*, who will go on to have a future. In the elaborately parallel episode in the next chapter that features Abraham and Isaac in the wilderness, Isaac is referred to by man and God as "the lad," and the term is played off against "the lads" who are Abraham's servants accompanying him on his journey, and not his flesh and blood ("And Abraham said to his lads, 'Sit you here with the donkey and let me and the lad walk ahead'").

In the story of the rape of Dinah (Genesis 34), she is first referred to as "Leah's daughter"—and not Jacob's daughter, for it is Leah's sons, Simeon and Levi, who will exact vengeance for her. The initial designation of "daughter" aligns her with both "the daughters of the land" among whom she goes out to see, and Shechem, Hamor's son ("son" and "daughter" are cognates in Hebrew), who sees her, takes her, and rapes her. After the act of violation, Shechem is overcome with love for Dinah, and he implores his father, "Take me this girl [*yaldah*] as wife." Speaking to his father, then, he identifies—tenderly?—the victim of his own lust as a girl-child. When he parleys with Dinah's brothers, asking permission to marry her, he says, "Give me the young woman [*na'arah*] as wife," now using the term for a nubile woman that is strictly appropriate to betrothal negotiations. After the brothers stipulate their surgical precondition for the betrothal, the narrator reports, "And the lad [*na'ar*] lost no time in doing the thing, for he wanted Jacob's daughter." Suddenly, as the catastrophe of this gruesome tale becomes imminent, we learn that the sexually impulsive man is only a lad, probably an adolescent like Dinah—a discovery that is bound to complicate our task of moral judgment. And now Dinah is called Jacob's daughter, not Leah's, probably because that is how Shechem sees her, not realizing that the significant relationship is through her mother to her two full brothers who are plotting a terrible retribution for her violation.

It should be clear from all this that a translation that respects the literary precision of the biblical story must strive to reproduce its nice discrimination of terms, and cannot be free to translate a word here one way and there another, for the sake of variety or for the sake of context. It must be admitted, however, that some compromises are inevitable because modern English clearly does not coincide semantically with ancient Hebrew in many respects. The stuff from which the first human is fashioned, for example, *'adamah,* manifestly means "soil," and it continues to have that meaning as it recurs at crucial junctures in the story of the Garden and the primordial banishment. But, alas, *'adamah* also means "land," "farmland," "country," and even "earth," and to translate it invariably as "soil" for the sake of terminological consistency (as Everett Fox does) leads to local confusions and conspicuous peculiarities. To take a more extreme example, a term that has no semantic analogue in English, the Hebrew *nefesh,* which the King James Version, following the Vulgate, often translates as "soul," refers to the breath of life in the nostrils of a living creature and, by extension, "lifeblood" or simply "life," and by another slide of association, "person"; and it is also used as an intensifying form of the personal pronoun, having roughly the sense of "very self." In the face of this bewildering diversity of meaning, one is compelled to abandon the admirable principle of lexical consistency and to translate, regretfully, according to immediate context.

Finally, though many recurring biblical terms have serviceable English equivalents (like "lad" for *na'ar*), there are instances in which a translation must make another kind of compromise because, given the differences between modern and biblical culture, the social, moral, and ideological connotations of terms in the two languages do not adequately correspond. Consider the tricky case of verbs for sexual intercourse. In English, these tend to be either clinical and technical, or rude, or bawdy, or euphemistic, and absolutely none of this is true of the verbs used for sex in the Bible. In Genesis, three different terms occur: "to know," "to lie with," and "to come into." "To know," with one striking antithetical exception, indicates sexual possession by a man of his legitimate spouse. Modern solutions such as "to be intimate with," "to cohabit with," "to sleep with," are all egregiously wrong in tone and implication. Fortunately the King James Version has established a strong precedent in English by translating the verb literally, and "carnal knowledge" is part of our language, so it is feasible to preserve the literal Hebrew usage in translation. (There is, I think, a good deal to be said for the general procedure of Tyndale and the King James Version in imitating many Hebrew idioms and thus giving the English a certain Hebraic coloration.) "Lie with" is a literal equivalent of the Hebrew, though in English it is vaguely euphemistic, whereas in Hebrew it is a more brutally direct or carnally explicit idiom for sexual intercourse, without, however, any suggestion of obscenity.

The most intractable of the three expressions is "to come into" or "to enter." In nonsexual contexts, this is the ordinary biblical verb for entering, or arriving. "To enter," or "to come into," however, is a misleading translation because the term clearly refers not merely to sexual penetration but to the whole act of sexual consummation. It is used with great precision—not registered by biblical scholarship—to indicate a man's having intercourse with a woman he has not yet had as a sexual partner, whether she is his wife, his concubine, or a whore. The underlying spatial imagery of the term, I think, is of the man's entering the woman's sphere for the first time through a series of concentric circles: her tent or chamber, her bed, her body. A translator, then, ought not surrender the image of coming into, but "come into" by itself doesn't quite do it. My own solution, in keeping with the slight strangeness of Hebraizing idioms of the translation as a whole, was to stretch an English idiom to cover the biblical usage: this translation consistently renders the Hebrew expression in question as "come to bed with," an idiom that in accepted usage a woman could plausibly use to a man referring to herself ("come to bed with me") but that in my translation is extended to a woman's reference to another woman ("come to bed with my slavegirl") and to a reference in the third person by the narrator or a male character to sexual consummation ("Give me my wife," Jacob says to Laban, "and let me come to bed with her").

Biblical syntax, beyond the basic pattern of parallel clauses, provides another occasion for what I have called a slight strangeness. The word order in biblical narrative is very often as finely expressive as the lexical choices. In many instances, the significant sequence of terms can be reproduced effortlessly and idiomatically in English, and it is a testament to the literary insensitivity of modern translators that they so often neglect to do so. Here, for example, is how the narrator reports Abimelech's discovery of the conjugal connection between Isaac and the woman Isaac had claimed was his sister: "Abimelech . . . looked out the window and saw—and there was Isaac playing with Rebekah his wife" (Genesis 26:8). The move into the character's point of view after the verbs of seeing is signaled by the so-called presentative, *wehineh* (rather like *voici* in French), which in this case I have represented by "there" but usually render as "look" (following the King James Version's "behold" and so deliberately coining an English idiom because the biblical term is so crucial for indicating shifts in narrative perspective). What follows "and there" is the precise sequence of Abimelech's perception as he looks out through the window: first Isaac, then the act of sexual play or fondling, then the identity of the female partner in the dalliance, and at the very end, the conclusion that Rebekah must be Isaac's wife. All this is perfectly fluent as English, and modern translations like the Revised English Bible, the New Jewish Publication Society, and Speiser that place "wife" before Rebekah spoil a nice narrative effect in the original.

But biblical syntax is also more flexible than modern English syntax, and there are hundreds of instances in the Hebrew Bible of significant syntactical inversions and, especially, emphatic first positioning of weighted terms. Syntactical inversion, however, is familiar enough in the more traditional strata of literary English, and if one adopts a general norm of decorous stylization for the prose of the translation, as I have done on the grounds I explained earlier, it becomes feasible to reproduce most of the Hebrew reconfigurations of syntax, preserving the thematic or psychological emphases they are meant to convey. The present translation does this, I think, to a greater degree than all previous English versions.

God repeatedly promises the patriarchs, "To your seed I will give this land" (e.g., Genesis 12:7), pointedly putting "your seed" at the beginning of the statement. Less rhetorically, more dramatically, when Hagar is asked by the divine messenger in the wilderness where she is going, she responds, "From Sarai my mistress I am fleeing" (Genesis 16:8), placing Sarai, the implacable source of her misery, at the beginning of the sentence. Still more strikingly, when Jacob is told by his sons that Simeon has been detained as a hostage in Egypt and that the Egyptian regent insists Benjamin be brought down to him, the old man begins his lament by saying, "Me you have bereaved" (Genesis 42:36). It is profoundly revelatory of Jacob's psychological posture that he should place himself as the object of suffering at the very beginning of his utterance (and again at the end, in a little formal symmetry). Normally, biblical Hebrew indicates a pronominal object of a verb by attaching a suffix to the verb itself. Here, however, instead of the usual accusative suffix we get an accusative first-person pronoun—*'oti*—placed before the verb, a procedure that beautifully expresses Jacob's self-dramatization as anguished and resentful father continually at the mercy of his sons. The "me" urgently needs to be thrust into the ear of the listener. Many translations simply suppress the inversion, but to put it decorously as "It is I" (Everett Fox) or paraphrastically as "It is always me" (New Jewish Publication Society) is to dilute the dramatic force of the original.

The sharpness and vividness of biblical style are also diluted when it is represented in English, as virtually all the versions do, by a single, indifferent level of diction. As I noted earlier, there seems to be nothing genuinely colloquial in the prose used by the narrator; but there is a palpable variation between passages that are more cadenced, more inclined to balanced structures of terms and elevated language, like the narrative of the Flood, and looser, more stylistically flexible passages. There are many instances, moreover, of single word choices that pointedly break with the stylistic decorum of the surrounding narrative, and for the most part these are fudged by the sundry English translations. When Hagar and Ishmael use up their supply of water in the wilderness, the despairing mother "flung the child under one of the bushes" (Genesis 21:15). The verb here, *hishlikh,* always means "to throw," usually abruptly or violently. This is somewhat softened by the King James Version and Fox, who use "cast." The Revised English Bible is uncomfortable with the idea of throwing a child and so translates "thrust." Speiser and the New Jewish Publication Society Bible altogether disapprove of spasmodic maternal gestures and hence dissolve "flung" into a gentler "left." In all such manipulation, the violence of Hagar's action and feelings disappears. When Laban berates Jacob for running off with his daughters, he says, "What have you done, ... driving my daughters like captives of the sword?" (Genesis 31:26). All the English versions represent the verb here as "carrying away" or some approximation thereof, but *nahag* is a term for driving animals, and is used precisely in that sense earlier in this very chapter (verse 18). To translate it otherwise is to lose the edge of brutal exaggeration in Laban's angry words. In the throes of the great famine, the destitute Egyptians say to Joseph, "Nothing is left for our lord but our carcasses and our farmland" (Genesis 47:18). Most English versions use "bodies" instead of "carcasses," with a couple of modern translations flattening the language even more by rendering the term as "persons." But the Hebrew *gewiyah*, with the sole exception of one famous mythopoeic text in Ezekiel, invariably means "corpse" or "carcass." What the miserable Egyptians are saying to their great overlord is that they have been reduced to little more than walking corpses, and he might as well have those. This sort of pungency can be conveyed if the translator recognizes that the Hebrew does not operate at a single bland level and that literary expression is not inevitably bound to decorous "logic."

These last two examples were taken from dialogue, and it is chiefly in dialogue that we get small but vivid intimations of the colloquial. Again, these are eliminated in the flat regularity of conventional Bible translation. When God rebukes Abimelech for taking Sarah into his harem, the king vehemently protests that he has acted in good conscience: "Did not he say to me, 'She is my sister'? and she, she, too, said, 'He is my brother'" (Genesis 20:5). The repetition of "she, she, too" is a stammer or splutter of indignation clearly indicated in the Hebrew. In some English versions, it disappears altogether. The King James Version turns it into a rhetorical flourish: "she, even she herself." Everett Fox, because of his commitment to literalism, comes closer but without quite the requisite feeling of colloquial mimesis: "and also she, she said." The seventeen-year-old Joseph reports the first of his dreams to his brothers in the following manner: "And, look, we were binding sheaves in the field, and, look, my sheaf arose and actually [*wegam*] stood up, and, look, your sheaves drew round and bowed to my sheaf" (Genesis 37:7). The language here is surely crafted mimetically to capture the gee-gosh wonderment of this naïve adolescent who blithely assumes his brothers will share his sense of amazement at his dream. The presentative *hineh* ("look") is the conventional term dreamers use to report the visual images of their dreams, perhaps partly because it readily introduces a surprising new perception, but here Joseph repeats the term three times in one breathless sentence, and the effect of naïve astonishment is equally expressed in his redundant "arose and actually stood up" (the Hebrew adverb *gam* most often means "also" but fairly frequently serves as well as a term of emphasis or intensification). The point is that the adolescent Joseph speaking to his brothers does not at all sound like the adult Joseph addressing Pharaoh, and a translation should not reduce either dialogue or narrator's language to a single dead level.

In the range of diction of the biblical text, the complementary opposite to these moments of colloquial mimesis occurs in the poetic insets. Most of these in the Torah are only a line or two of verse, though Genesis and Deuteronomy conclude with relatively long poems, and Exodus incorporates the Song of the Sea as Numbers does Balaam's oracles. Now, it has long been recognized by scholarship that biblical poetry reflects a stratum of Hebrew older than biblical prose: some of the grammatical forms are different, and there is a distinctive poetic vocabulary, a good deal of it archaic. No previous English translation has made a serious effort to represent the elevated and archaic nature of the poetic language in contradistinction to the prose, though that is clearly part of the intended literary effect of biblical narrative. The present translation tries to suggest this contrast in levels of style—through a more liberal use of syntactic inversion in the poetry, through a selective invocation of slightly archaic terms, and through the occasional deployment of rhetorical gestures broadly associated with older English poetry (like the ejaculation "O"). I wish I could have gone further in this direction, but there is a manifest danger in sounding merely quaint instead of eloquently archaic, and so the stylistic baggage of "anent" and "forsooth" had to be firmly excluded.

Two minute examples will illustrate how these discriminations of stylistic level are made in the Hebrew and how they might be conveyed in English. The enigmatic notice about the Nephilim, the human-divine hybrids of the primeval age, concludes with these words: "They are the heroes of yore, the men of renown" (Genesis 6:4). This line could conceivably be a fragment from an old mythological poem; more probably, it reads in the original as a kind of stylistic citation of the epic genre. The clearest clue to this in the Hebrew is the word "they," which here is *hemah* rather than the standard *hem*. This variant with the extra syllable is in all likelihood an older form: it occurs four times more often in poetry than in prose, and even in prose is often reserved for rather ceremonial gestures. There is no English variant of "they" that is similarly marked as poetic diction, and my translation compensates by using "of yore" instead of the phrase "of old" adopted by the King James Version and by most later English versions. In the next chapter, the unleashing of the Deluge is reported in this line of verse, with emphatic semantic parallelism and four Hebrew accents against three in the two halves of the line: "All the well-springs of the great deep burst, / and the casements of the heavens opened" (7:11). In order to convey a sense that this is poetry, beyond the mechanics of typography, a translator of course has to create a good deal of rhythmic regularity, but there remains a problem of diction. The Hebrew word represented by "casements" is 'arubot. It is a rare term, occurring only a few times elsewhere in the Bible, and it clearly means "window" or "window-like niche." The decision of several different modern translators to render it as "sluices" or "floodgates" has no philological warrant and is a conspicuous instance of translation by context. "Windows" in the King James Version is on target semantically but not stylistically. The occurrence of a cognate of 'arubot in Ugaritic poetry, several centuries before the composition of Genesis, is further indication that the term is poetic and probably somewhat archaic for the later Hebrew audience. "Casements," with its echoes of Keats and of Shakespeare behind Keats, seemed like a happy solution to the problem of diction. Though not all shifts in stylistic level in the Hebrew can be so readily represented by English equivalents, a translation that tries to do justice to the richness of the Hebrew must aim for some approximation of the nuances of diction in the original.

The most pervasive aspect of the magic of biblical style that has been neglected by English translators is its beautiful rhythms. An important reason for the magnetic appeal of these stories when you read them in the Hebrew is the rhythmic power of the words that convey the story. The British critic A. Alvarez has aptly described the crucial role of rhythm in all literary art: "the rhythm—the way the sounds move, combine, separate, recombine—is the vehicle for the feeling. . . . And without that inner movement or disturbance, the words, no matter how fetching, remain inert. In this way at least, the dynamics of poetry—and probably of all the arts—are the same as the dynamics of dreaming." I know of no modern English translation of the Bible that is not blotted by constant patches of arrhythmia, and the result is precisely the sense of inertness of which Alvarez speaks. The King James Version, of course, has its grand rhythmic movements—cultivated people around 1611 clearly had a much firmer sense of expressive sound in language than has been true of recent generations.

But these rhythms are more orotund, less powerfully compact, than those of the Hebrew, and in fact there are far more local lapses in rhythm than nostalgic readers of the King James Version may recall.

The final arbiter of rhythmic effectiveness must be the inner ear of the sensitive reader, but I would like to show that there is a vital dimension of biblical prose that translation has to engage by quoting a couple of verses in transliteration and then in three English versions, together with my own. In regard to the transliteration, it should be kept in mind that we have an approximate notion, not an exact one, of how biblical Hebrew was originally pronounced. There is some question about vowels in particular because vowel-points were added to the consonantal texts by the Masoretes—the Hebrew scholars of sixth- to tenth-century Tiberias who fixed the text of the Bible, with full punctuation, standard since then—more than a millennium after the texts were composed. There was, however, a continuous tradition for recitation of the texts on which the Masoretes drew, and anyone who has listened to the Masoretic Text read out loud can attest to its strong rhythmic integrity, which argues that its system of pronunciation was by no means an arbitrary imposition. Here is the narrative report of Noah's entering the ark as the Deluge is unleashed (Genesis 7:13–14). (Acute accents are used to indicate accented syllables. *W* is used for the letter *waw* [pronounced as *v* in modern Hebrew but as *w* in biblical times], especially to distinguish it from *bet* without *dagesh*, pronounced as *v*. *Ḥ* indicates a light fricative [something like Spanish *j*]; *kh* represents a heavier fricative, like the German *ch* in Bach.)

> 13. *Be'étsem hayóm hazéh ba' nóaḥ weshém-weḥám wayéfet benei-nóaḥ we'éshet nóaḥ ushlóshet neshéi-vanáw 'itám 'el hateváh. 14. Hémah wekhol-haḥayáh lemináh wekhol-habehemáh lemináh wekhol-harémes haromés 'al-ha'árets leminéhu wekhol-ha'óf leminéhu kól tsipór kol-kanáf.*

The Hebrew rhythm unfolds in groupings of three or four words marked by three or four stresses, usually with no more than one or two unstressed syllables between the stressed ones, and the sense of the words invites a slight pause between one grouping and the next. The overall effect is that of a grand solemn sweep, a sort of epic march, and that effect is reinforced in the diction by the use of *hémah* instead of *hem* for "they" at the beginning of the second verse.

Here is the King James Version:

13. In the selfsame day entered Noah, and Shem, and Ham, and Japheth, the sons of Noah, and Noah's wife, and the three wives of his sons with them, into the ark; 14. they, and every beast after its kind, and all the cattle after their kind, and every creeping thing that creepeth upon the earth after his kind, and every fowl after his kind, every bird of every sort.

The first of the two verses (up to "into the ark") is nearly perfect. I envy the freedom of the King James Version to follow the Hebrew syntax and write "entered Noah," an inversion feasible at the beginning of the seventeenth century but a little too odd, I am afraid, at the beginning of the twenty-first. But in the second verse rhythmic difficulties emerge. The repeated "after its kind," with its sequencing of a trochee and an iamb and its two stresses, is an ungainly equivalent of the Hebrew *lemináh*; "every creeping thing that creepeth upon the earth" is a whole mouthful of syllables in exchange for the compactness of the Hebrew; and "every bird of every sort" falls flat as a final cadence (apart from being inaccurate as a translation).

Here is E. A. Speiser's version of these two verses—a version, to be sure, intended to be accompanied by a philological commentary, but one that helped set a norm for recent Bible translations:

13. On the aforesaid day, Noah and his sons, Shem, Ham, and Japheth, Noah's wife, and the three wives of his sons had entered the ark—14. they as well as every kind of beast, every kind of creature that creeps on earth, and every kind of bird, every winged thing.

The initial phrase, "on the aforesaid day," is an ill-starred beginning in regard to diction as well as to rhythm. Something as mechanical as the list of the passengers of the ark is divided up in a way that undercuts its rhythmic momentum: at best, one can say that this version has intermittent moments of escape into rhythm.

Everett Fox, the most boldly literal of modern Bible translators, does a little better, but his attention to rhythm is by no means unflagging.

13. On that very day came Noah, and Shem, Ham, and Yefet, Noah's sons, Noah's wife and his three sons' wives with them, into the Ark, 14. they and all wildlife after their kind, all herd-animals after their kind, all crawling things that crawl upon the earth after their kind, all fowl after their kind, all chirping-things, all winged-things.

The first short clause, with the courageous inversion of verb and sub-ject, rings nicely in the ear. But the simple deletion of the "and" between Shem and Ham collapses the rhythm, and Fox's grouping of the list is not much better rhythmically than Speiser's. As in the King James Version, the decision to use "after" four times introduces a series of unwelcome extra syllables, and rhythm is virtually lost in "all herd-animals after their kind, all crawling things that crawl upon the earth after their kind."

Here is my own version, far from perfect, but meant to preserve more of the phonetic compactness of the Hebrew and to avoid such glaring lapses into arrhythmia:

13. That very day, Noah and Shem and Ham and Japheth, the sons of Noah, and Noah's wife, and the three wives of his sons together with them, came into the ark, 14. they as well as beasts of each kind and cattle of each kind and each kind of crawling thing that crawls on the earth and each kind of bird, each winged thing.

Biblical Hebrew, in sum, has a distinctive music, a lovely precision of lexical choice, a meaningful concreteness, and a suppleness of expressive syntax that by and large have been given short shrift by translators with their eyes on other goals. The present translation, whatever its imperfec-tions, seeks to do fuller justice to all these aspects of biblical style in the hope of making the rich literary experience of the Hebrew more accessible to readers of English.

II. ON TRANSLATING THE NAMES OF GOD

The God of Israel is referred to through a variety of names in these texts, and it is by no means self-evident how to render the names in English. The most difficult of them is the Tetragrammaton, YHWH. Modern bib-lical scholarship has agreed to represent this as "Yahweh," but there are problems with using that form in translation. The original Hebrew texts of the Bible were entirely consonantal, vowel-points having been added well over a millennium after the original composition of the texts. Because by then the Tetragrammaton was deemed ineffable by Jewish tradition, it was revocalized to be pronounced as though it read *'adonai*, LORD. The confidence of biblical scholarship that the original pronunciation was in fact Yahweh may not be entirely warranted. (See the comment on Exodus

3:14.) In any case, "Yahweh" would have given the English version a certain academic-archaeological coloration that I preferred to avoid, and it would also have introduced a certain discomfort at least for some Jewish readers of the translation. I rejected the option of using "YHWH" because it cannot be pronounced whereas the dimension of sound seemed to me vital to the translation. I have therefore followed the precedent of the King James Version in representing YHWH as the LORD, the last three letters in small uppercase to indicate that, like 'adonai, it is an anomaly, a substitution for another name.

The other most common designation of the deity is 'elohim, a word that is plural in form (perhaps, though this is far from certain, a plural of "majesty") but that is generally treated grammatically as a singular. "God" is the natural English equivalent, but in some contexts, where the generic character of the name seems prominent, I have rendered it with a lowercase g as "god," and when the name is treated as a plural, especially when the narrative context involves polytheism, I have translated it as "gods." Three other names for the deity, all borrowed from the Canaanite pantheon, occur in these books—El, Elyon, and Shaddai. Especially in poetry and at narrative moments of high solemnity, the writers appear to play on the archaic resonances of these names, and so for the most part I have given them in their Hebrew form, for in the particular contexts in which they typically appear a touch of linguistic archaeology seemed to me entirely appropriate.

Admittedly, any of the choices I have described may be debatable, but in all of them my aim has been to name the deity in English in ways that would be in keeping with the overall concert of literary effects that the translation strives to create.

III. ABOUT THE COMMENTARY

My original intention when I set out to translate Genesis in the mid-1990s had been simply to provide brief translator's notes. Puns, wordplay in the sundry naming-speeches, and other untranslatable maneuvers of the Hebrew needed to be glossed. The reader also had to be informed, I felt, of the occasional junctures where I adopted a reading that varied from the Masoretic Text, the received Hebrew text of the Bible. Similarly, it seemed proper to offer some explanation for translation choices that were likely to surprise either the general reader or the scholarly reader, or both. In some instances, such a choice reflects a proposed new solution to a crux in the Hebrew text. More often, it is an effort to represent a more precise understanding of the Hebrew than previous translations have shown (e.g., the tree of knowledge is "lovely to look at," not "lovely to impart wisdom"; Pharaoh puts a "golden collar" around Joseph's neck, not a "gold chain"). And most pervasively, the little surprises in the translation are attempts to find English equivalents for the nuances of implication and the significant changes of diction in the Hebrew that have not been much regarded by previous translators. Finally, since this translation is, within the limits of readable English style, quite literal—not out of fundamentalist principle but in an effort to reproduce some of the distinctive literary effects of the original—when the interests of English intelligibility compelled me to diverge from a literal translation, I have alerted readers to the divergence and given the literal sense of the Hebrew words in a note. And beyond all such considerations of word choice and level of style, I thought it necessary to offer succinct explanations of some of the ancient Near Eastern cultural practices and social institutions that are presupposed by the narratives, for without an understanding of them it is sometimes hard to see exactly what is going on in the story.

This last category of explanation is, of course, standard fare in modern Bible commentaries, where it is sometimes dished out in very large portions, and it is admittedly intended here as an aid for the relatively uninitiated. But as I got caught up once again in this endlessly fascinating text, it struck me that there were important features that by and large had been given short shrift in the modern commentaries. In fact, a good many of my observations on stylistic choices already shaded into a discussion of the literary vehicle of the biblical narratives, and this was the point at which the tightly cinched annotation I had originally intended began to loosen its bonds and reach out to commentary. There were whole orders of questions, it seemed to me, that had been neglected or addressed only intermittently and impressionistically by the modern commentators. Where are there detectible shifts of stylistic level in the Hebrew, and why do they occur? What are the reasons for the small poetic insets in the prose narratives? What are the principles on which dialogue is organized, and how are the speakers differentiated? Where and why are there shifts from the narrator's point of view to that of one of the characters? What are the devices of analogy, recurrent motifs, and key words that invite us to link and contrast one episode with another?

How is the poetry formally constructed? And do these books, granted their composite origins, exhibit overarching thematic and structural unities or lines of development?

On all these challenging questions I have surely not said the last word. Rather I have aspired to say some helpful first words in a commentary that I have sought to hold to modest proportions. Clearly, there is no way of separating a literary illumination of the biblical text from a confrontation with philological issues, on the one side, and, perhaps more indirectly, with historical issues, on the other. In any case, the exploration of the Bible as literary expression is the central focus of this commentary, and I would hope it would be of interest to everyone, from reader at large to scholar, who is drawn to the imaginative liveliness, the complexities, the stylistic vigor, and the sheer inventiveness of these splendid ancient stories and poems and legal and moral discourses.

Introduction to Prophets

This middle unit of the traditional tripartite division of the Hebrew canon, which is the largest of the three, comprises two very different sets of materials. The first, designated the Former Prophets for somewhat confusing reasons that will be explained below, is in fact a set of narratives, purportedly historical (Joshua, Judges, and the early chapters of Samuel) or substantially historical (much of Samuel and Kings).

The second large set of texts is a collection of prophecies in the proper sense of the term. These Prophetic books, although they incorporate some narrative materials, are by and large hortatory, much of them cast in poetry. The nature of the collection will be outlined in the section on the Prophets in this introduction. Because the two large blocks of texts were thought of as one set of "Prophetic" books, the traditional practice was to run them together with no formal dividing line between the end of Kings and the beginning of Isaiah and all that follows. This practice will be maintained here.

THE FORMER PROPHETS

To many readers, the rubric "the Former Prophets" may be puzzling. Some will not recognize it as the designation of a part of the Bible with which they are familiar. Some will wonder which prophets are involved, for the figures we usually think of as prophets like Jeremiah and Ezekiel are nowhere in evidence, and Isaiah has only a late walk-on appearance toward the end of 2 Kings. Then, the question poses itself: Former to what? Or even, what did they do after they stopped being prophets?

This conventional English title is a literal translation of the Hebrew *nevi'im ri'shonim*. The founders of Jewish tradition seem to have thought of the first of these two units as Prophetic literature because they imagined it as having been composed by various of the so-called writing prophets. This is not a view in any way embraced by modern scholarship. More plausible grounds for calling this sequence of narratives the Former Prophets is that, from Samuel onward, figures identified as prophets keep popping up, for the most part to frame the narrative with prophecies of doom. (This is not true for Joshua and Judges. The sole exception is Deborah in Judges 4, who is called a "prophet-woman," 'ishah nevi'ah, but she is not shown exercising that vocation.)

Biblical scholars, since the work in Germany by Martin Noth in the middle of the twentieth century, have adopted a more precise though less pronounceable designation for the large narrative from Joshua and Judges to Samuel and Kings: the Deuteronomistic History. In the late seventh century B.C.E., a major revolution in the religion of ancient Israel was effected when, in the course of renovation work on the Temple in the reign of King Josiah, a long scroll was purportedly discovered (see 2 Kings 22–23); it was referred to as "this book of teaching," sefer hatorah hazeh. Most scholars since the early nineteenth century have concluded that it was a version of Deuteronomy and surmise that it was actually composed around this time by reformers in Josiah's court. It put forth a new insistence on the exclusivity of the cult in the Jerusalem temple, vehemently polemicized against the use of any image or icon in worship, and proposed a system of historical causation in which the survival of a given king and of the covenanted people was strictly dependent on their loyalty—above all, cultic loyalty—to their God. All this was cast in language that highlighted certain formulaic phrases—"to love the LORD your God with all your heart and with all your might," "to keep His statutes, His commands and His dictates"—and in a distinctive rhetoric that, unlike other biblical prose, favored long periodic sentences and the oratorical insistence of anaphora, that is, emphatic repetition.

At the same time that Deuteronomy proper (which would acquire some additional layers when it was edited in the Babylonian exile only a few decades after its initial promulgation in 621 B.C.E.) was exhorting the people to follow what it deemed to be the right path, writers in this same circle sought to make sense of the history of the nation in the revelatory light of the new reforming book. A religious intellectual—it may actually have been a whole group, but for convenience's sake, scholarship refers to him schematically as the Deuteronomist—who was swept up in Josiah's reforms set out to assemble a more or less continuous version of the national history from the conquest of the land to his own time, covering roughly five centuries. This first Deuteronomistic historian does not envisage the destruction of the southern kingdom (the northern kingdom of Israel had disappeared a century earlier, in 721 B.C.E., at the hands of the Assyrians) or of the cutting off of the Davidic dynasty, so it is plausible to date him to the late seventh century B.C.E. Then, in the view of most scholars, a second and more or less final edition of the Deuteronomistic History was executed in the Babylonian exile after 586 B.C.E., probably just a few decades later (it contains as yet no vision of a return to Zion), incorporating an account of the devastation of the kingdom of Judah and the humiliation, mutilation, and exile of its last king

An elusive question about this entire chain of books is what exactly was the role played by the Deuteronomist in their composition. Some scholars are inclined to speak of him as the "author" of the history, a writer who utilized older textual and perhaps also oral materials but edited them and reworked them freely according to his own ideological bent. I find this view implausible. The Deuteronomist clearly drew on a wide variety of preexisting texts, some of them probably preserved in royal archives, from annals to folktales and legends to the most artfully articulated historical narratives He punctuated these disparate materials, especially in the Book of Kings, with formulaic assertions, often reminiscent of the language of Deuteronomy, of his own interpretation as to why particular historic events happened as they did. But there is abundant evidence that the old stories resisted the pressure of his insistent interpretation, showing their own view of things, and that for the most part he did not feel at liberty to tamper with the literary documents he had inherited.

Let me cite one central instance. Nearly a third of the Former Prophets is devoted to the story of Saul and David (1 Samuel 8 through 2 Kings 2). As a literary composition, this story manifestly antedates the Deuteronomist, perhaps even by as much as three centuries. It also happens to be one of the greatest pieces of narrative in all of Western literature. Biblical scholars have a lamentable habit of referring to it as "royal propaganda," and also of breaking it down into purportedly disparate sources in a fashion that does violence to its powerful continuities of style, image, motif, and character. Although David is clearly represented as divinely elected king in this narrative, he is also seen quite strikingly in all his human weakness, in his relentlessness, and in his moral ambiguity—hardly a figure of royal propaganda. And in regard to the issue of historic causation, events here are the consequence of human actions—in the preponderance of these stories, there is nothing miraculous and no divine intervention. When the aged king is dying, he calls Solomon to his bedside and instructs him to use his "wisdom" to get rid of two men against whom David has a score to pay off, and who also might well threaten Solomon's throne. This final gesture, worthy of a mafia chieftain, was evidently too much for the Deuteronomist, and so he inserted before David's hit list a whole swatch of dialogue, in which David, deploying an uninterrupted pastiche of Deuteronomistic phrases, piously enjoins Solomon to walk in God's ways and keep His commands. What the editor did not feel free to do was to change the inherited text or delete the parts of it he found objectionable.

This combination of tendentious editorial framing with an assemblage of disparate narrative texts from different periods and probably different regions of the country has been a source of debate and perplexity among scholars. General readers, on the other hand, may be grateful for the extravagant heterogeneity of these books. Each has its own distinctive character. The first half of Joshua is an account of conquest and destruction, enlivened by the tale of Rahab and the two spies and the fall of Jericho; the second half is a mapping out of the tribal territories in which the supposedly conquered land now appears far from fully conquered. Judges comprises a series of episodes of martial derring-do in the sundry struggles of the tribes with the surrounding peoples, and it includes the unforgettable cycle of stories about the Herculean folk-hero Samson. After the anarchic period recorded in Judges, Samuel recounts the founding of the monarchy in the long continuous story, which is the artistic pinnacle of these books, of David from brilliant youth to the sad infirmity of old age. It is in Samuel, as the German scholar Gerhard von Rad argued seven decades ago, that the writing becomes properly historical, liberated from the heavy dependence on legend and sheer authorial invention. The Book of Kings, in more miscellaneous fashion, and with more conspicuous interventions of the Deuteronomist, continues the historical narrative, tapping the royal annals of both kingdoms but also liberally introducing folktales and legends, especially visible in the cycle of stories about Elijah and Elisha.

What results from this amalgam is a richly overflowing miscellany. It incorporates folk memories or fantasies about ideal and magically powerful figures; historical accounts of deadly court intrigues; representations of the intricate and dangerous complexities of life in the political realm; and reports of the great powers surrounding the small kingdoms of Israel and Judah and of their military campaigns in the land of Canaan. Over it all hovers the somber awareness of the Deuteronomist that these two nation-states, located at the crossroads of aggressive empires to the east and to the south, lived under constant threat and in the end might not endure. What did endure, embodied in the stories themselves, was the people's memories, their vision of God and history and national purpose. All these, preserved in their Hebrew texts, they would one day bring back from exile as the potent instrument of an unprecedented national revival.

THE PROPHETS

Prophecy in the sense of soothsaying and the prediction of future events was of course widespread in the ancient Near East, as it is in many early cultures. Figures who practice prophecy of this sort appear in some of the narratives in the Former Prophets. But in the middle decades of the eighth century B.C.E. a new phenomenon emerged—prophets who, while retaining a good deal of the predictive function of their earlier counterparts, assumed the role of the conscience of the people, carrying out missions of moral castigation directed not just at rulers—as, say, in the case of Elijah in the Book of Kings—but at the general populace. They delivered their message in a form of elevated speech that was often, though not always, framed as poetry, a procedure encouraged by the fact that they typically claimed to be quoting God's very words ("Thus said the Lord" is the recurrent introductory formula for their prophecies). Some of the prophets were poets of the first rank—this is manifestly the case for Isaiah son of Amoz and for the anonymous poet of the Babylonian exile whose prophecies are included in the Book of Isaiah beginning in chapter 40, and there is remarkable poetry in Jeremiah, Amos, Micah, and in others of these figures. Elsewhere in the Bible, with the exception of Ezra–Nehemiah, the authors remain cloaked in anonymity, but the work of the prophets is, one might say, signed. We know who most of these writers were (even if the production of different prophets is often editorially inserted in the books that bear their name), and we are even given a certain amount of biographical information, some of it quite arresting, about a few of them.

This untypical highlighting of authors reflects a shared sense on the part of the prophets themselves that the vocation of mediating the word of God is a challenging and even anguishing undertaking—Jeremiah is the prime example—in which the imperative of a divine mission in an individual life draws simultaneous attention to the content of God's message and to the particular human bearer of the message. The scathing critique that the prophets focus on their society oscillates between outrage against the perversion of justice, the exploitation of the poor and helpless, debauchery, and misrule, on the one hand, and cultic betrayal, the worship of pagan deities, on the other. Although both emphases appear in most of the Prophets, some favor one (Isaiah is above all a moral critic) and some the other (the slide into paganism is what especially provokes Ezekiel).

Given the immense historical distance that separates us from the prophets, it is hard to evaluate their reiterated claim that they are speaking God's words. That claim is certainly much more than a pious fraud. There are indications that the prophets, or at least many of them, may have delivered their words in some sort of ecstatic state. It is quite conceivable that they felt they had heard God speaking to them in the precise words of Hebrew poetry—sometimes sublime poetry—or visionary prose that they conveyed to their audiences. But perhaps what they heard from God was the content of the message about Israel's abominations, the destiny of disaster that awaited the people if it did not change its ways, as well as the luminous hope of national restoration after the disaster had fallen; they then proceeded to fashion this content in language, exercising their own human mastery of poetry and rhetoric. This is a complicated issue that may not be the same from one prophet to the next. It will be explored as we consider the interaction between the personality of the prophet and his message in the introductions later in this volume to the individual prophets.

Acknowledgments

The first step of this large project, the draft of my translation of Genesis, was scrupulously read by my dear friend Amos Funkenstein in what proved to be, alas, the last year of his life. His acute understanding of Hebrew philology and his rare gift for coming up with unexpected solutions to familiar problems were a model that I have striven to internalize in the subsequent volumes. My amiable friend and colleague Ron Hendel read many of the books in draft, and I have palpably benefited from his good sense and his commanding knowledge of biblical scholarship. Because I write by hand and am dependent on transcribers to convert my scrawl into an electronic text, I am grateful to Janet Livingstone, who did a large part of the whole and then had to withdraw for reasons of health, and to Jenna Scarpelli and Stefan Gutermuth, who in turn took over for the last two phases of the project. I am grateful to my copyeditor, Trent Duffy, who patiently and scrupulously went through these many pages, detecting inconsistencies, spotting typos, correcting inaccurate cross-references, and much more. Over the years, support for this assistance and for other research expenses was provided by funds from the Class of 1937 Chair at the University of California, Berkeley. After my retirement, I benefited from a research grant for emeriti professors from the Mellon Foundation and then from a generous three-year grant provided by Howard and Roberta Ahmanson.

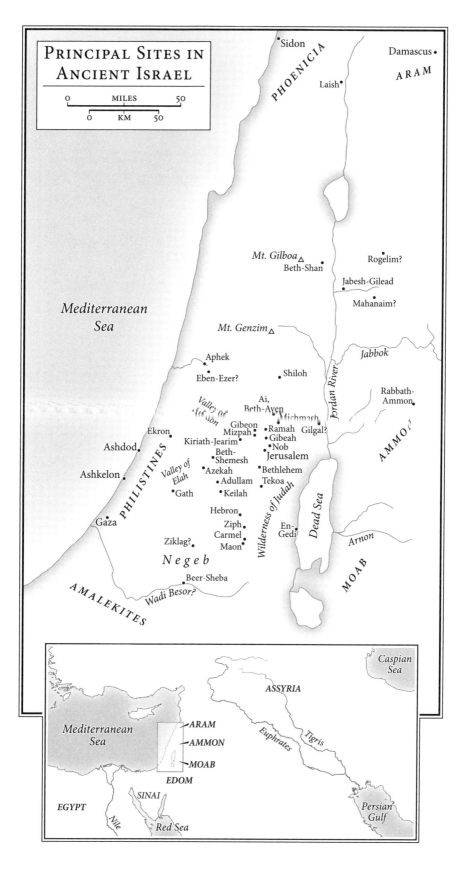

PRINCIPAL SITES IN ANCIENT ISRAEL

MILES
0   50

0   KM   50

Mediterranean
Sea

PHOENICIA

Sidon

Damascus

ARAM

Laish

Mt. Gilboa
Beth-Shan

Rogelim?

Jabesh-Gilead

Mahanaim?

Mt. Genzim

Jabbok

Jordan River

Aphek

Eben-Ezer?

Shiloh

Rabbath-
Ammon

Valley of Aijalon

Ai,
Beth-Aven

AMMON

Michmash

Ekron

Gibeon
Mizpah

Ramah
Gibeah

Gilgal?

Ashdod

Kiriath-Jearim

Nob

Beth-
Shemesh

Jerusalem

Ashkelon

Valley of
Elah

Azekah

Bethlehem

Gath

Adullam

Tekoa

Keilah

Wilderness of Judah

Dead Sea

Hebron

Gaza

Ziph

PHILISTINES

Ziklag?

Carmel
Maon

En-
Gedi

Arnon

Negeb

MOAB

Beer-Sheba

AMALEKITES

Wadi Besor?

Caspian
Sea

ASSYRIA

Mediterranean
Sea

ARAM

AMMON

Euphrates

Tigris

MOAB

EDOM

EGYPT

SINAI

Nile

Red Sea

Persian
Gulf

JOSHUA

Introduction

The Book of Joshua, sandwiched in between the grand oratory of Deuteronomy and the vivid accounts of guerilla warfare and civil war in Judges, is a text that many modern readers may find off-putting. Its early chapters do include two memorable episodes—the expedition of the two spies to Jericho and the miraculous destruction of the walls of Jericho that enables its conquest. The prevailing sense, however, of the first half of the book is ruthlessness, and the general effect of the second half is tedium. Nowhere in the Bible is there a more palpable discrepancy between the values and expectations of the ancient Near Eastern era in which the book was written and those of twenty-first-century readers.

Joshua is really two books, symmetrically divided into twelve chapters each. The first of these we may call the Book of Conquests. It appears to be predominantly the work of the school of Deuteronomy, though it is not altogether uniform, and there is evidence that other sources have been drawn on, some of them probably older than Deuteronomy. The second half of Joshua can be given the rubric the Book of Apportionments. Its provenance is largely Priestly, although it ends with an emphatic Deuteronomistic flourish. There is some narrative material in the last three chapters, but the bulk of it is devoted to mapping out the sundry tribal territories in elaborate detail.

This book as a whole is offered as a historical account of the conquest of the land and the division of its territories, but the connection with history of both its large components is tenuous. Archaeologists in the earlier twentieth century were often bent on confirming the biblical record through their discoveries, but that project has not stood the test of time. What the last several decades of archaeological investigation have established is that there was no sweeping conquest of Canaan by invaders from the east in the late thirteenth century B.C.E.—which would have been the time of Joshua— and that many of the towns listed as objects of Israelite conquest were either uninhabited at this time or did not come under Israelite rule until considerably later. Jericho, the gateway town in the Jordan Valley and the one whose conquest has become etched in collective memory, was an important forti-

fied city in the Middle Bronze Age (two or three centuries before the putative time of Joshua), but in the late thirteenth century it was an abandoned
site or at most not much more than a large village without walls. Lachish,
another important town said to have been taken by Joshua's forces, fell
under Israelite domination only during the period of the monarchy.

The fact that this narrative does not correspond to what we can reconstruct of the actual history of Canaan offers one great consolation: the
bloodcurdling report of the massacre of the entire population of Canaanite towns—men, women, children, and in some cases livestock as well—
never happened. Some reflection on why these imagined mass murders
are included in the book may provide a sense of the aim of the pseudo-
historiographical project of the Book of Joshua. The *ḥerem*, the practice
of total destruction that scholars call "the ban" (a usage adopted in the
present translation), was not unique to ancient Israel, and there is some
evidence that it was occasionally carried out in warfare by other peoples
of the region. The question is why the Hebrew writers, largely under the
ideological influence of Deuteronomy, felt impelled to invent a narrative of
the conquest of the land in which a genocidal onslaught on its indigenous
population is repeatedly stressed.

Deuteronomy, which crystallized as a canonical book during and after
the sweeping religious reforms of King Josiah—the purported discovery
of the book took place in 621 B.C.E.—articulates an agenda of uncompromising monotheism that insists on two principal points: the exclusive
centralization of the cult in Jerusalem and the absolute separation of the
Israelites from the Canaanite population. There is an underlying connection between these two emphases: the worship of YHWH in sundry local
sanctuaries and on rural hillside altars was liable to be more susceptible to
the influences of Canaanite paganism, or so the Deuteronomist seems to
have feared, than a central cult in Jerusalem overseen by a priestly bureaucracy and under the shadow of the monarchy. One strong expression of the
program to separate the population is the injunction to carry out the ban
in the conquest of the land, an undertaking that at the fictional time of the
writing of Deuteronomy (the thirteenth century B.C.E.) had not yet begun.
The Book of Joshua, then, which is offered as a report of the subsequent conquest, presents as a historical account the implementation of that wholesale
slaughter of the indigenous population in town after town.

This gruesome story is intended as an explanation of a circumstance
observed by audiences of the book in the seventh century and later—that
by then a non-Israelite Canaanite population was only vestigially in evi-

dence. Where, one might wonder, did all these peoples—seven in the traditional enumeration repeatedly invoked here—go? Joshua's answer is that
they were wiped out in the conquest, as Deuteronomy had enjoined. But
the narrative of the *ḥerem* is a cover-up as well as an explanation. If the
Canaanites seem to have disappeared, it was not because they were extirpated but because they had been assimilated by the Israelites, who had
come to exercise political dominion over large portions of the land. There is
good reason to assume that the Canaanites intermarried with the Israelites
(a taboo for the Deuteronomist), had all kinds of social and economic intercourse with them, and shared with them many of their religious practices
as well as many elements of their theology.

This story, then, of the annihilation of the indigenous population of
Canaan belongs not to historical memory but rather to cultural memory,
a concept that Ronald Handel has aptly applied to biblical literature in his
book *Remembering Abraham*. That is to say, what is reported as the national
past is grounded not in the factual historical experience of the nation but
in the image of the nation that the guardians of the national literary legacy
seek to fix for their audiences and for future generations. Thus, Israel is
represented in this narrative as "a people that dwells apart" (Numbers 23:9),
though in historical actuality its life was intricately entangled not only with
the sundry peoples of Canaan but also with the cultures of Egypt to the
south and of Mesopotamia to the east.

The story of the Gibeonites recounted in chapter 9 is in this regard an
instructive case in point. The audience of the story, we may safely infer,
would have been aware of the Gibeonites as a group of different ethnic
stock from the Israelites yet "dwelling in their midst"—that is, having close
social and economic relations with them, perhaps of the subservient order
indicated in the biblical account. But what were they doing there if the
systematic plan of the conquest was to wipe out all traces of the indigenous
inhabitants of the land? This difficulty is resolved by the account here of the
subterfuge of the Gibeonites: disguising themselves as representatives of a
people living in a distant country and hence not subject to the ban, they
trick the Israelites into making a binding pact of peaceful coexistence with
them, and hence for all future times they must be spared. The ostensible
exception to the programmatic rule of total destruction is thus given a narrative explanation or etiology.

What should also be observed about the story of the conquest in Joshua
is that it is a vision of overwhelming military triumph. It is a triumph
that is repeatedly attributed to God's power, not to Israel's martial prowess

(although a couple of the reported episodes do show cunning tactical moves on the part of the Israelites). That notion is perfectly in keeping with the Deuteronomistic view of historical causation, in which God causes Israel to prevail when it is loyal to the covenant and brings defeat on the people when Israel betrays its commitment to God. The message, however, of an irresistible sweep of the Israelite forces through the land of Canaan addresses a geopolitical situation of the Israelite nation that was quite the opposite. It was the historical fate of Israel to sit at the bloody crossroads between powerful empires to the east and the south with some dire threats from the north as well. This chronic predicament came to seem much graver in the span of years from the destruction by Assyria of the northern kingdom of Israel in 721 B.C.E. to the conquest of the southern kingdom of Judah by Babylonia in 589 B.C.E.—the very period in which the early nucleus of Deuteronomy was formulated and when the book as a whole achieved its first general recension. What must have been in the minds of a good many Judahites after 721 B.C.E. was that national existence itself was a highly contingent affair, that the people which had come to think of itself as chosen by God for a grand destiny, as the Patriarchal narratives in Genesis repeatedly asserted, could easily suffer disastrous defeat, bitter exile, perhaps even extinction. Whatever the rousing promises and consolations of theology, it would have been difficult to dismiss the awareness of imperial powers that could bring to bear overwhelming force on the tiny Israelite nation. The story of the conquest, then, served as a countermove in the work of cultural memory: Israel had entered its land in a stirring triumphal drive as a power before which no man could stand. The theological warrant for this vision, antithetical as it was to the historical facts, was that as long as Israel remained faithful to all that its God had enjoined upon it, the people would be invincible.

Against this general background of theological explanation of historical events, the story of Achan in chapter 7 is meant to play an exemplary role. Achan violates the ban, which is represented as an obligation imposed by God. The direct consequence is military defeat, and Israel cannot continue on its triumphal progress until the transgressor is singled out and punished by death. That punishment grimly extends to his entire family, as if the guilt were a kind of contagion that infected everyone in immediate contact with him and thus had to be ruthlessly expunged. If the transgression of a single person can have such dire widespread effects, how much more so when large numbers of the people backslide. This is the prospect raised by Joshua in his two valedictory addresses (chapters 23 and 24). The emphasis of both these speeches is heavily Deuteronomistic: Joshua fears that the Israelites will intermarry with the surrounding peoples and worship their gods; he expresses doubt as to whether Israel will be up to the challenge of faithfulness to this demanding God—"You will not be able to serve the LORD, for He is a holy God. He is a jealous God, He will not put up with your crimes and your offenses" (24:19). Although his audience responds with a solemn pledge of fealty, the somber prospect has been evoked that Israel will betray its God and therefore suffer cataclysmic defeat and exile. In this fashion, there is a tension between the first twelve chapters of Joshua and the conclusion of the book, a contradiction between the vision of a grand conquest and the threat of national disaster.

Some of that tension is also detectable in the discrepancy between the Book of Conquests and the Book of Apportionments. The function of the elaborate drawing of tribal borders in the second of these two texts is to convey a sense of a systematic and orderly division of the land. Because the determination of the tribal territories is made by lot (*goral*), which is a divinely inspired oracular device, the clear implication is that God dictates the boundaries within which the sundry tribes are to live. The aim is to provide theological authentication and solidity to the existing tribal territories. In fact, there were likely to have been ad hoc arrangements marked by a good deal of fluidity, with tribes encroaching on one another's territories, migrating in pursuit of better pastureland and tillable soil, and, at least in the case of Dan, being completely displaced by political circumstances. The mapping of boundaries, however, also incorporates several indications that the conquest of the land was not as comprehensive as the first twelve chapters of Joshua might lead one to conclude. This chronicle concedes that there were instances in which the Israelites were unable "to dispossess"— which is to say, conquer and destroy—the local Canaanites, an uncomfortable circumstance that the writer seeks to mitigate by noting that these unsubdued populations were reduced to the status of forced laborers as they continued to live alongside the Israelites.

The Book of Joshua thus registers a double awareness of Israel's historical predicament. The people had been promised the land by God, and its success in establishing an autonomous state, which very quickly became two states, over a large portion of Canaan was testimony to the fulfillment of that promise. The fulfillment is inscribed in the first half of the book. The conquest, however, was not total, and its permanency was menaced by a series of foreign powers. The book translates this contradiction into theological terms: Israel in the flush of its military triumph is imagined as staunchly loyal to its God, with the single exception of Achan; Israel, having taken possession of the land and drawn its boundaries, is seen as teetering on the brink of future disloyalties that will entail disastrous consequences. Though the tension between the two halves of the book is arguably an artifact of the redactional process that joined two different sources, the effect is to produce a dialectical perspective on the history of the nation. The Book of Judges follows logically from this because there it is vividly clear that Israel's tenure in the land before the monarchic period is unstable, that much of the Israelite population is either subject to foreign domination or exposed to the attacks of marauders. Accounting for the incompleteness of the conquest, which is already adumbrated in the latter part of Joshua, will become the task of the book that follows.

CHAPTER 1

And it happened after the death of Moses servant ₁ of the LORD, that the LORD said to Joshua son of Nun, Moses's attendant, saying: "Moses My servant is dead. And now, arise, cross this Jordan, you, ₂ and all this people, to the land I am about to give to them, to the Israelites. Every place where the sole of your foot treads, to you I have given it, as I ₃ spoke to Moses, from the wilderness and this Lebanon to the Great River, ₄ the River Euphrates, the whole land of the Hittites, and to the Great Sea, where the sun sets, will be your territory. No man will stand up against you ₅ all the days of your life. As I was with Moses, I shall be with you. I shall not let go of you and I shall not forsake you. Be strong and stalwart, for you will ₆

CHAPTER 1   1. *And it happened after the death of Moses.* These opening words are an explicit device to create a direct link with the end of Deuteronomy, which reports the death of Moses (Deuteronomy 34:5ff.), and the beginning of this book, in which Joshua takes up Moses's task.

servant of the LORD. This identifying phrase, reiterated in this initial passage, is a formal epithet for Moses, also used in Deuteronomy. Joshua is called his "attendant," as he is in Numbers 11:28; the implication is that the attendant of the LORD's servant will now assume the role of his master.

2. *this Jordan . . . this people.* The repeated use of the deictic *zeh,* "this" (and again in verse 4, "this Lebanon") is positional. God is addressing Joshua across the Jordan from Canaan. First, He points to "this Jordan," across which Joshua will have to take the people, then to "this people," whom Joshua must lead, and then to "this Lebanon," marking the northern limits of the land.

4. *from the wilderness and this Lebanon to the Great River, the River Euphrates.* These are utopian—or perhaps one should say fantastic—borders never occupied by Israel and never within its military capacity to occupy.

the whole land of the Hittites. This can scarcely be the region in Asia Minor that was once the center of a Hittite empire. There were Hittite immigrants scattered through Canaan from an early period. Shmuel Ahituv proposes that the phrase reflects a usage in Neo-Assyrian texts where it indicates everything west of the Euphrates, including the Land of Israel.

to the Great Sea. The "Great Sea" is, as elsewhere, the Mediterranean.

6. *Be strong and stalwart.* This reiterated exhortation clearly reflects the military setting of this initial charge by God to Joshua, who is commander in chief of the army about to invade the land.

make this people inherit the land that I vowed to their fathers to give to
7   them. But you must be very strong and stalwart to keep and do according
to all the teaching that Moses My servant charged you. You shall not swerve
8   from it to the right or the left, so that you may prosper wherever you go. This
book of teaching shall not depart from your mouth, and you shall murmur
it day and night, so that you may keep to do according to all that is written
9   in it; then you will make your ways succeed and then you will prosper. Have
I not charged you, 'Be strong and stalwart'? Do not be terror-stricken and
do not cower, for the LORD your God is with you wherever you go."

10,11   And Joshua charged the people's overseers, saying: "Pass through the midst
of the camp and charge the people, saying, 'Prepare yourselves provisions,
for in three days you are to cross this Jordan to come to take hold of the
12   land that the LORD your God is about to give you to take hold of it.'" And
to the Reubenites and to the Gadites, and to the half-tribe of Manasseh,
13   Joshua said: "Recall the word that Moses servant of the LORD charged you,
saying, 'The LORD your God is about to grant you rest and will give you
14   this land. Your wives, your little ones, and your herds shall dwell in this
land that Moses has given you across the Jordan, but you shall cross over
arrayed for combat before your brothers, all the mighty warriors, and you
15   shall help them, until the LORD grants rest to your brothers like you and
they too take hold of the land that the LORD their God is about to give to
them, and you shall return to the land of your holding and take hold of it,
which Moses servant of the LORD has given to you across the Jordan where

---

8. *This book of teaching shall not depart from your mouth.* The book in question is almost
certainly Deuteronomy, and the phrasing of the entire verse is strongly Deuteronomistic.

10. *the people's overseers.* This is the same term used in the Exodus story (5:6ff.). It derives
from a verb meaning to document or record, and so it is not necessarily a specialized
military term.

11. *three days.* This is a conventional time span in biblical narrative for an interval of relatively short duration.

13. *Recall the word that Moses . . . charged you.* The episode of the two and a half tribes that
chose to settle on land east of the Jordan is initially reported in Numbers 32.
    grant you rest. The verb here has the obvious technical sense of granting respite from
previously hostile neighboring peoples.

14. *arrayed for combat.* The Hebrew *ḥamushim* appears to derive from the word for "five,"
and it has been plausibly explained as referring to a battle formation, with troops on all four
sides and a unit of fighting men inside the rectangle. In modern Hebrew, it means "armed."

the sun rises.'" And they answered Joshua, saying, "All that you charged us 16
we will do, and wherever you send us we will go. As in all that we heeded 17
Moses, so we will heed you. Only may the LORD your God be with you as
He was with Moses. Every man who flouts your command and does not 18
heed your word in all that you charge him shall be put to death. Only be
strong and stalwart."

CHAPTER 2   And Joshua son of Nun sent out in secret two 1
men as spies from Shittim, saying, "Go, see the land, and Jericho." And
they went and they came to the house of a whore-woman whose name was
Rahab, and they slept there. And it was said to the king of Jericho, saying, 2
"Look, men of the Israelites have come here tonight to search out the land."
And the king of Jericho sent to Rahab, saying, "Bring out the men who have 3

---

17. *As in all that we heeded Moses, so we will heed you.* The Israelites in fact were repeatedly
rebellious against Moses, but it is best to view this declaration of unswerving loyalty as an
idealized representation of the people, not as an intended irony.

18. *Every man who flouts your command . . . shall be put to death.* What appears to be
reflected in these stern words is the strictness of military justice: Israel is about to enter into
battle, and whosoever does not obey the commander's orders will be summarily executed.
    Only be strong and stalwart. The opening section of Joshua comprises four speeches:
God to Joshua, Joshua to the people's overseers, Joshua to the trans-Jordanian tribes, and
the response of the trans-Jordanian tribes to Joshua. These interlocked speeches are meant
to convey a sense of perfect solidarity on the eve of the conquest of the land. Thus, the
concluding words of the tribal spokesman exactly echo God's twice-asserted exhortation
to Joshua, with the addition of the emphatic *raq,* "only."

CHAPTER 2   1. *two men as spies.* The two spies evoke the two spies in the story in
Numbers 13–14, Joshua and Caleb son of Jephunneh, who did not come back with a fearful
report like their ten companions. This story, then, on the eve of the conquest, is framed as
a pointed reversal of the failed spy mission in Numbers: there the Israelites quail before
the gigantic inhabitants of the land; here a Canaanite woman reports that the inhabitants
of the land quail before the Israelites.
    Shittim. This place-name means "the Acacias."
    the house of a whore-woman . . . and they slept there. Sometimes biblical usage adds
"woman" in this fashion to the designation of profession. "Whore," in turn, seems to be used
neutrally, not as a term of opprobrium. Though she may merely be providing the two men
lodging, the narrative coyly plays with the sexual meaning of the verb *shakhav,* which also
means simply to lie down, to sleep, or spend the night. Similarly, the verb "come to," used
in verses 3 and 4, also has a sexual meaning when the object of the preposition is a woman.
In fact, Rahab in answering the king's inquiry may be saying that the two men were merely
her customers, and hence she had no idea that they might be spies.

come to you, who came to your house, for they have come to search out the
4   whole land." And the woman had taken the two men and hidden them, and
she said, "The men indeed came to me and I did not know from where they
5   were. And as the gate was about to close at dark, the men went out. I know
not where the men went. Pursue them quickly, for you can overtake them."
6   And she had taken them up to the roof and had hidden them in the stalks
7   of flax laid out for her on the roof. And the men pursued them along the
Jordan by the fords, and they closed the gate when the pursuers had gone
8   out after them. They had not yet bedded down when she went up to them on
9   the roof. And she said to the men, "I know that the LORD has given you the
land, and that your terror has fallen upon us and that all the dwellers of the
10 land quail before you. For we have heard how the LORD dried up the waters
of the Sea of Reeds before you when you came out of Egypt, and what you
did to the two Amorite kings across the Jordan, to Sihon and to Og, whom
11 you put to the ban. And we heard, and our heart failed, and no spirit arose in
any man before you, for the LORD your God, He is God in the heavens above

---

3. *the whole land.* The king adds "whole" to the report that has been brought to him: these
spies have come on an extensive reconnaissance mission. Jericho is a city-state, the prevalent political form in Canaan in this era, and would have governed surrounding territory.

4. *the woman had taken the two men and hidden them.* The sense of the verb is evidently
pluperfect: she had hidden the spies before the arrival of the king's emissaries.
     as the gate was about to close at dark. The gates of the walled city were locked at nightfall.

5. *Pursue them quickly, for you can overtake them.* In this shrewd maneuver, Rahab simultaneously makes herself sound like a loyal subject of Jericho and encourages the king's
men to leave her house immediately, heading in what she correctly calculates will be the
wrong direction.

6. *stalks of flax laid out for her on the roof.* The flax would have been laid out on the roof to
dry in the sun. Hiding in the flax stalks may be a reminiscence of baby Moses hidden (the
same Hebrew verb) in the ark among the bulrushes.

7. *along the Jordan by the fords.* This, as Rahab has rightly surmised, would be the most
plausible route of pursuit because the men from Jericho are aware that the Israelites are
encamped east of the Jordan and assume that the spies will try to reach a ford over which
they can cross to return to their people.

9. *your terror has fallen upon us and . . . all the dwellers of the land quail before you.* Rahab
is directly quoting the Song of the Sea (Exodus 15:15–16), merely reversing the order of terms
in the poem: "all the dwellers of Canaan quailed. / Terror and fear did fall upon them." Her
words are a verbatim confirmation of the assertion in the Song that the great news of the
event at the Sea of Reeds reached the Canaanites and dismayed them.

10. *what you did to the two Amorite kings.* This triumph, reported in Numbers 21, at the other
end of the story of Wilderness wanderings from the victory at the Sea of Reeds, is a recent
event, perhaps having occurred in the last few months before the present narrative moment.

and on the earth below: And now, pray, vow to me by the Lord, for I have   12
done kindness with you, that you, too, shall do kindness with my father's
house and give me a faithful sign, and let my father and mother live, and my   13
brothers and my sisters, and all that is theirs, and save our lives from death."
And the men said to her, "Our own lives in your stead to die! So long as you   14
do not tell of this mission of ours. And so, when the Lord gives us this land,
we shall do faithful kindness with you." And she lowered them with a rope   15
through the window, for her house was in the outer wall, and in the wall she
dwelled. And she had said to them, "Go to the high country, lest the pursu-   16
ers encounter you, and hide there three days until the pursuers come back.
Then you may go on your way." And the men had said to her, "We will be   17
clear of this vow that you made us vow. Except, when we come into the land,   18
this scarlet cord you must tie in the window through which you lowered
us, and your father and your mother and all your father's house you must
gather to you within the house. And so, whosoever comes out of the doors   19
of your house to the street, his blood shall be on his head, and we will be

---

11. *for the Lord your God, He is God in the heavens above and on the earth below.* Rahab is
cast as a good monotheist, persuaded of the Lord's supreme sovereignty, as the Israelites
are expected to be, by His dramatic intervention in history.

14. *Our . . . lives in your stead to die.* This drastic offer expresses their recognition of the
awesome solemnity of the vow they are taking.

15. *for her house was in the outer wall.* Many fortified cities in the region had a double
wall, and most interpreters understand the seemingly redundant *qir haḥomah* ("wall of
the wall") as an indication of the outer wall. In this way, being lowered by a rope from her
window enables them to get out of the city even though the gate is locked.

16. *And she had said to them.* The context requires construing the verbs here and at the
beginning of the next verse as pluperfects. Otherwise, one is left with the absurd situation
of this dialogue taking place at a distance, both parties shouting, after she has lowered
them with the rope.
   Go to the high country. This is the mountainous area to the west of the Jordan Valley
and in the opposite direction from the one taken by the pursuers. The terrain would also
have afforded hiding places.
   three days. As in chapter 1, the time span is formulaic, but it is also a plausible interval
to wait until the pursuers have given up the chase.

17. *We will be clear of this vow.* Having stated that they are prepared to die in her stead should
they violate the terms of the vow, they now stress that they will have no obligation to carry
it out unless she strictly adheres to her own terms that they stipulate.

18. *this scarlet cord you must tie in the window.* This is a purely practical stipulation: the
attackers need a sign to know which house they are to spare. The scarlet cord recalls the
scarlet thread attached to the hand of the newborn twin Zerah in Genesis 38:28–30 and
probably also the blood smeared on the lintel to ward off the Destroyer in Exodus 12:7–13.

clear. But whoever will be with you in the house, his blood is on our head if
20 any hand should touch him. And should you tell of this mission of ours, we
21 will be clear of your vow that you made us vow." And she said, "According
to your words, so shall it be." And she sent them off and they went, and she
22 tied the scarlet cord in the window. And they went and came to the high
country and stayed there three days, until the pursuers went back. And the
23 pursuers searched all along the way and did not find them. And the two
men went back and came down from the high country and crossed over to
24 Joshua son of Nun and recounted to him all that had befallen them. And
they said to Joshua, "Yes, the LORD has given all the land into our hands,
and what's more, all the dwellers of the land quail before us."

1 CHAPTER 3   And Joshua rose early in the morning, and they
journeyed on from Shittim and came to the Jordan, he and all the Israelites,
2 and they spent the night there before they crossed over. And it happened
at the end of three days that the overseers passed through the midst of the
3 camp. And they charged the people, saying, "When you see the Ark of

---

20. *And should you tell of this mission of ours, we will be clear of your vow.* The concluding
statement regarding a release from the vow concerns the vital interest of the two spies rather
than the practical provision for the safety of Rahab and her family.

21. *she tied the scarlet cord in the window.* Though it is possible to understand this as an act
she performs later, it may be that, mindful of the grave warning of the two men, she hastens
to affix the agreed-on sign as soon as they leave, even though she knows the attack will not
come for at least several days.

22. *all along the way.* This would be the road parallel to the Jordan.

23. *crossed over.* Now they take a ford across the Jordan back to the Israelite camp.

24. *all the dwellers of the land quail before us.* They are directly quoting one of those inhabitants, Rahab, who in turn is quoting the Song of the Sea. Thus the line from the poem
becomes a kind of refrain that punctuates the middle and the end of this episode.

CHAPTER 3   1. *crossed over.* The verb 'avar, which means either to cross over or,
as in verses 2 and 4, to pass through or over, is repeated eight times in this chapter, thus
marking the episode as a portentous liminal moment when the people of Israel cross over
from their long Wilderness wanderings into the land they have been promised.

2. *at the end of three days.* The recurrence of this formulaic interval suggests a certain symmetry with the experience of the spies, who hide out in the high country for three days.

3. *the Ark of the Covenant.* The Ark contains the stone tablets of the Law. It is imagined as
both a sacred and a magical object, and as such is also a numinous vessel carried into battle,
as one sees in the early chapters of Samuel.

the Covenant of the LORD your God, with the levitical priests carrying it,
then you shall journey from your place and go after it. But keep a distance ₄
between you and it, about two thousand cubits in measure. Do not come
close to it. So that you may know the way in which you should go, for you
have not passed over this way in time past." And Joshua said, "Consecrate ₅
yourselves, for tomorrow the LORD will do wonders in your midst." And ₆
Joshua said to the priests, saying, "Carry the Ark of the Covenant, and
cross over before the people." And they carried the Ark of the Covenant
and went before the people. And the LORD said to Joshua, "This day I shall ₇
begin to make you great in the eyes of all Israel, so they may know that as
I was with Moses, I shall be with you. And you, charge the priests, bear- ₈
ers of the Ark of the Covenant, saying, 'When you come to the edge of the
waters of the Jordan, you shall stand still in the Jordan.'" And Joshua said ₉
to the Israelites, "Draw near and hear the words of the LORD your God."
And Joshua said, "By this you shall know that a living God is in your midst, ₁₀
and He will utterly dispossess before you the Canaanite and the Hittite
and the Hivvite and the Perizzite and the Girgashite and the Amorite and
the Jebusite. Look, the Ark of the Covenant of the Master of all the earth ₁₁

---

4. *But keep a distance.* The Ark, saturated with divine aura, is also a dangerous object. In
2 Samuel 6, when Uzza puts his hand on the Ark to prevent it from slipping from the cart
in which it is carried, he is struck dead.
  about two thousand cubits. This would be a little over half a mile.

7. *as I was with Moses, I shall be with you.* The "wonder" that God is about to perform will
in fact replicate a miracle done for Moses.

9–10. *And Joshua said . . . And Joshua said.* As a rule, when the formula for the introduction of dialogue is repeated without an intervening response from the second party, the
repetition indicates some difficulty in response—puzzlement, amazement, embarrass-
ment, and so forth. Here the repetition has a purely dramatic function. Joshua invites the
people to draw close; they do so, scarcely having an opening to say anything to him; then,
when his audience is gathered around him, Joshua goes on to give detailed instructions.

10. *the Canaanite and the Hittite.* In all, seven peoples are mentioned, filling out the formulaic number. The list itself is heterogeneous: Canaanite and Amorite are general designations for the inhabitants of this territory; the Hittites are immigrants from Asia Minor
who were probably not a distinctive Canaanite people in any political sense; little is known
about the Perizzites and the Girgashites, though the latter may have come from Asia Minor.
In any case, the enumeration of seven peoples does reflect a historical memory of Canaan
divided up among small city-states.

11. *Master of all the earth.* This is not an epithet that occurs in the Torah, and since designations of the deity are important indicators of sources, its use may point to a literary source
distinct from those of the Pentateuch.

12 is about to cross over the Jordan before you. And now, take for yourselves
13 twelve men from the tribes of Israel, one man from each tribe. And so
when the footsoles of the priests, bearers of the Ark of the LORD, Master
of all the earth, rest in the waters of the Jordan, the waters of the Jordan
coming down from above will be cut off and stand up as a single mound."
14 And it happened, when the people journeyed forth from its tents to cross
the Jordan, with the priests, bearers of the Ark of the Covenant before the
15 people, and when the bearers of the Ark reached the Jordan and the feet
of the priests, bearers of the Ark, were immersed in the water's edge—the
16 Jordan being full to all its banks throughout the harvest days—the water
coming down from above stood still, rose up in a single mound, very far off
from the town of Adam which is by Zanethan, and the water going down
to the Arabah Sea, the Salt Sea, was completely cut off, and the people

---

12. *take for yourselves twelve men from the tribes of Israel.* These men play no role in what
immediately follows, though in the next chapter they are assigned the task of placing twelve
stones in the riverbed. While this verse could be construed as a prolepsis, it is more likely
that it was erroneously transposed in copying from the next section of the story, where it
is duplicated in 4:2.

13. *the waters of the Jordan coming down.* This formulation harbors an etymological pun.
The Jordan, *Yarden,* is called that because it "comes down" (verbal stem *y-r-d*) from mountain heights in the north to the Dead Sea, the lowest point on the face of the earth.

14–16. *And it happened.* The syntax of these three verses, constituting one long run-on
sentence, is quite untypical of biblical prose, and its use here builds a sense of climactic
fulfillment as the miracle is enacted.

15. *the Jordan being full to all its banks throughout the harvest days.* This rather awkward parenthetical clause, still further complicating the syntax, appears to be an effort
to explain a difficulty. As we learned in chapter 2, there are numerous fords across the
Jordan, and the two spies obviously used one of those to cross back and forth. But the
story needs an impassable Jordan to enable the miracle of immobilizing its waters, and
so we are reminded that in this moment at the beginning of the spring (in the month of
Nissan), the river would have been overflowing after the winter rains. The reference to
harvest days is a little puzzling because early April is too soon for a harvest. Perhaps the
phrase means to say that this high level of the Jordan continues until the end of the first
harvest in late May-early June.

16. *rose up in a single mound.* These words are the clearest indication that this incident
is a repetition of the drying up of the Sea of Reeds because the rare term *ned,* "mound,"
is used, as it is in the Song of the Sea (Exodus 15:8). History for the biblical writers moves
forward but also repeats itself in significant patterns. This notion prepared the way for later
typological conceptions of history.

   very far off from the town of Adam which is by Zanethan. This odd and seemingly gratuitous specification of a place at some distance from the reported event is a strategy of
"documenting" the miracle by locating it along geographical coordinates.

   the Arabah Sea. The Arabah is the geological rift through which the Jordan runs.

crossed over opposite Jericho. And the priests, bearers of the Ark of the 17
Lord's Covenant, stood firm on dry ground in the middle of the Jordan,
with all Israel crossing over on dry ground until the whole nation finished
crossing the Jordan.

CHAPTER 4   And it happened, when the whole nation had 1
finished crossing over the Jordan, that the Lord said to Joshua, saying,
"Take for yourselves from the people twelve men, one man from each tribe, 2
and charge them, saying, 'Carry from here, from the Jordan, from the place 3
where the feet of the priests stand firm, twelve stones and bring them across
with you and set them down at the encampment where tonight you will
spend the night.'" And Joshua called to twelve men whom he had readied 4
from the Israelites, one man from each tribe. And Joshua said to them, 5
"Cross over before the Ark of the Lord your God into the middle of the
Jordan and each of you lift up one stone on his shoulder according to the
number of the tribes of Israel, so this may be a sign in your midst: Should 6
your children ask you tomorrow, saying, 'What are these stones to you?,'
you shall say, 'That the waters of the Jordan were cut off before the Ark of 7
the Lord's Covenant, when it was crossing over the Jordan, the waters of
the Jordan were cut off, and these stones became a memorial for the Israelites forever.'" And thus did the Israelites do, as Joshua had charged them, 8
and they carried twelve stones from the Jordan as the Lord had spoken to
Joshua, according to the number of the tribes of Israel, and they brought
them across with them to the encampment and set them down there. And 9
Joshua set up twelve stones in the middle of the Jordan in the place where
the feet of the priests, bearers of the Ark of the Covenant, had stood, and

---

17. *dry ground.* The Hebrew here, *ḥaravah*, is a different word from *yabashah*, "dry land,"
the term used in Exodus 14–15 and also in Genesis.

CHAPTER 4   6. *Should your children ask you tomorrow.* This is a liturgical or, as
some put it, catechistic formula, which has fairly close parallels in Exodus 12:26–27, Exodus
13:14–15, and Deuteronomy 6:20. "Tomorrow" is, of course, a homey idiom for "in future
times." The commemorative stones become a didactic occasion for recounting the ancient
miracle to future generations.

9. *And Joshua set up twelve stones in the middle of the Jordan.* This second set of twelve stones
looks redundant. There may have been a competing account of the event in which the convey-
ers of the traditional material felt that the more appropriate memorial was on the very spot
where the feet of the priests had stood, and the redactor decided to include both versions.
This would, however, be an underwater memorial scarcely visible except when the Jordan
was nearly dry. But see the next comment on the question of the stones' visibility.

10 they have been there to this day. And the priests, bearers of the Ark of
the Covenant, were standing in the Jordan until all the mission that the
Lord had charged Joshua to speak to the people was finished, as all that
11 Moses had charged Joshua. And the people hurried and crossed over. And
it happened, when all the people had finished crossing over, that the Ark of
12 the Lord, and the priests with it, crossed over before the people. And the
Reubenites and the Gadites and the half-tribe of Manasseh crossed over
13 in battle array before the Israelites as Moses had spoken to them, about
forty thousand, vanguard of the army, crossed over before the Lord for
14 battle to the plains of Jericho. On that day the Lord made Joshua great in
the eyes of all Israel, and they feared him as they had feared Moses all the
15,16 days of his life. And the Lord said to Joshua, saying, "Charge the priests,
bearers of the Ark of the Covenant, that they come up from the Jordan."
17,18 And Joshua charged the priests, saying, "Come up from the Jordan." And
it happened when the priests, bearers of the Ark of the Lord's Covenant,
came up from within the Jordan, that the priests' footsoles pulled up onto
dry ground and the waters of the Jordan went back to their place and
19 flowed as in time past over all its banks. And the people had come up from
the Jordan on the tenth of the first month, and they camped at Gilgal at
20 the eastern edge of Jericho. And these twelve stones that they had taken
21 from the Jordan, Joshua set up at Gilgal. And he said to the Israelites,

---

and they have been there to this day. This is an explicitly etiological tag absent in the
report about the other set of twelve stones. It leads one to wonder whether there in fact
might have been a pattern of stones in the riverbed detectable from the surface around
which this story was woven.

10. *as all that Moses had charged Joshua.* This clause is puzzling because Moses clearly had
no role in instructing Joshua about the procedure for crossing the Jordan. The clause does
not appear in the Septuagint, and one suspects a scribe inadvertently added it here because
it was a set formula, and akin to the concluding clause of verse 12, where the reference to
Moses is appropriate.

14. *feared him.* The context makes clear that the force of the verb is not an experience of
fright but reverence or, perhaps more specifically, acceptance of his authority. After the
enactment of a miracle that closely corresponds to the great miracle performed for Moses
at the Sea of Reeds, Joshua's position as legitimate leader is fully confirmed.

16. *Ark of the Covenant.* Here a different term *'edut* ("witnessing") is used, but it appears
to be a synonym for *brit,* "covenant."

19. *on the tenth of the first month.* This is the month of Nissan, approximately corresponding
to April. The tenth of Nissan is four days before the Passover festival.
    the eastern edge of Jericho. This would mean the edge opposite Jericho's territory.

20. *And these twelve stones . . . Joshua set up at Gilgal.* The name Gilgal means "circle"
(although it is given a secondary etymology in the next episode), and so we may assume

saying, "When your children ask their fathers tomorrow, saying, 'What are these stones?,' you shall inform your children, saying, 'On dry land Israel   22 crossed over this Jordan. For the LORD your God dried up the waters of   23 the Jordan before them until they crossed over, as the LORD your God had done to the Sea of Reeds, which He dried up before us until we crossed over, so that all the peoples of the earth might know the hand of the LORD,   24 for it is strong, so that you might fear the LORD your God at all times.'"

CHAPTER 5   And it happened, when the Amorite kings who   1 were across the Jordan to the west, and all the Canaanite kings who were by the sea, heard that the LORD had dried up the waters of the Jordan before the Israelites until they crossed over, their heart failed and there was no longer any spirit within them before the Israelites.

At that time the LORD said to Joshua, "Make you flint knives and again cir-   2 cumcise the Israelites a second time." And Joshua made flint knives and he   3

---

that the stones were set up in a circle. Gilgal was an important cultic site in the first two centuries of the monarchy and figures significantly in the stories of Samuel, Elijah, and Elisha. As with other sacred places in ancient Israel, it may well have been a locus of pagan worship before it was taken over by the Israelites. There is some likelihood, then, that the stones arrayed in a circle were originally *matseivot*, cultic steles, and that the story is framed to make them integral to the monotheistic narrative.

22. *dry land.* Here *yabashah* is used, the term that occurs in Exodus 14–15.

23. *which He dried up before us.* The switch from third person ("dried up the waters of the Jordan before them") to first-person plural reflects the operation of the commemorative ritual: it was the Israelites of Joshua's generation who experienced the miracle at the Jordan, but all Israel of every generation—beginning with everyone over twenty who was with Moses, the generation that has purportedly died out—participates in the defining moment of the parting of the Sea of Reeds, replicated at the Jordan.

24. *so that all the peoples of the earth might know the hand of the LORD.* This theme is similar to the one reiterated in the narrative of the Ten Plagues in Exodus. Its validity will then be confirmed in the first verse of chapter 5, which in all likelihood is the actual conclusion of this narrative unit.

so that you might fear the LORD your God at all times. The repetition of "so that," *lema'an,* inscribes a causal chain: the other nations recognize the power of the God of Israel through this great miracle, and Israel fears, or reveres, its God both through the direct experience of the miracle and through its confirmation in the eyes of the surrounding peoples.

CHAPTER 5   2. *flint knives.* The story takes place in the Late Bronze Age and was composed sometime in the Iron Age, but flint knives are introduced precisely because they are archaic, and hence the appropriate implements for this ritual act. In the enigmatic story of the Bridegroom of Blood, Exodus 4:24–26, Moses's wife takes a flint knife to circumcise

4 circumcised the Israelites at the Hill of Foreskins. And this is the reason
that Joshua circumcised them: all the people who had come out of Egypt,
all the males, the men of war, had died out on the way in the wilderness
5 when they came out of Egypt. For all the people who came out were circumcised, but all the people who were born in the wilderness on the way
6 when they came out of Egypt were not circumcised. For forty years did the
Israelites go in the wilderness until the whole generation was finished, the
men of war coming out of Egypt, who had not heeded the LORD's voice, as
the LORD had vowed to them not to show them the land that the LORD had
vowed to their fathers to give to us, a land flowing with milk and honey.
7 And their sons He put up in their stead, them did Joshua circumcise, for
they were uncircumcised, as they had not been circumcised on the way.
8 And it happened when the whole nation had finished being circumcised,
9 they remained in their place until they revived. And the LORD said to
Joshua, "I have rolled away from you the shame of Egypt," and the name
10 of the place has been called Gilgal to this day. And the Israelites encamped

---

their son, and the phrase "on the way" that is used in this story appears three times here in
relation to the lack of circumcision

4. *Joshua circumcised them.* The object of the verb in this clause, "them," is merely implied.
    the males, the men of war. This is an indication of age, twenty years old being the begin-
ning point for military service. This generation, now died out, is about to be replaced by a
new generation of adult males who will carry out the campaign of invasion.

6. *the whole generation.* The Masoretic Text reads "the whole nation," which is surely too
sweeping, but several Hebrew manuscripts as well as the Targum show "generation" instead
of "nation."
    who had not heeded the LORD's voice. The specific reference is to the pusillanimous
report of the ten spies, an episode already invoked in the story of the two spies who go to
Jericho. The ten spies in fact use the formula of a land flowing with milk and honey.

7. *they had not been circumcised.* Literally, "they had not circumcised them."

8. *they remained in their place until they revived.* It must be said that, in realistic terms,
circumcision of all the fighting men just three days before battle is joined would be a rather
imprudent measure. But the writer is focusing on the state of ritual purity necessary for
the celebration of Passover and for the conduct of warfare, and so he is prepared to have us
assume that all the men are fully recovered and ready for action after three days.

9. *I have rolled away from you the shame of Egypt.* The verb here, *galoti*, is an etymological
pun on Gilgal, a word that can mean either "circle" or, as in this instance, "wheel." The
"shame of Egypt" may have a double sense, referring to slavery—now, as free men entered
into the covenant of Abraham, the Israelites are ready to conquer their own land—and to
their uncircumcised condition, which was not the case while they were in Egypt but was
entailed by their flight from Egypt and their wanderings, during which it was not feasible
to circumcise the male infants.

at Gilgal and performed the Passover rite on the fourteenth day of the month, in the evening, on the plains of Jericho. And they ate from the 11 yield of the land from the day after the Passover sacrifice, flatbread and parched grain on that very day. And the manna ceased on the day after, 12 when they ate from the yield of the land, and the Israelites no longer had manna, and they ate from the produce of the land of Canaan in that year.

And it happened when Joshua was at Jericho that he raised his eyes and 13 saw, and look, a man was standing before him, his sword unsheathed in his hand. And Joshua went toward him and said to him, "Are you ours or our foes'?" And he said, "No. For I am the commander of the LORD's 14 army. Now have I come." And Joshua fell on his face to the ground and did obeisance, and he said to him, "What does my master say to his servant?" And the commander of the LORD's army said to Joshua, "Take off your 15

---

10. *performed the Passover rite.* Of all the stipulated festival sacrifices, it was the Passover that confirmed a person's full participation in the community of Israel. For a male, being circumcised was a necessary condition for taking part in the rite, as is made clear in Exodus 12:44. The celebration of the first Passover took place on the eve of the departure from Egypt, and so this second Passover marks the liminal moment of leaving the wilderness for the land as the first Passover marks the leaving of Egypt for the wilderness.

11. *they ate from the yield of the land.* Evidently, the Israelite troops have been foraging in the territory adjacent to Jericho. The substitution of the produce of the land for the manna is another marker of the end of the Wilderness experience.

13. *at Jericho.* The Hebrew particle b^e, which usually means "in," here must refer to the vicinity of Jericho, which Joshua may be reconnoitering.
   and look, a man was standing before him. This is a crystal-clear instance of the use of the presentative *hineh*, "look," as a shifter to the character's visual perspective. The as yet unidentified figure is thus called "a man" because that is how he appears to Joshua.
   Are you ours or our foes'? The translation seeks to emulate the compactness of the Hebrew, *halanu 'atah 'im-letsareinu*. This brisk wording is beautifully appropriate to the military context, as a sentry might urgently challenge an unknown figure, wasting no words.

14. *I am the commander of the LORD's army.* This is a bit of fleshed-out mythology not attested to elsewhere. God, who is not infrequently a warrior god, is often referred to as the LORD of Armies, but elsewhere there are no indications that He has an officer staff. This piece of imagining is perfectly apt in a dedication scene for Joshua because the LORD's emissary can address him as (superior) commander to commander.
   Now have I come. This pronouncement, just two words in the Hebrew, is meant to sound portentous: now is the beginning of my great mission of conquest in which you will serve as my human deputy.

15. *Take off your sandal from your foot, for the place on which you stand is holy.* This is a direct quotation of God's words to Moses at the burning bush, Exodus 3:5, with the mar-

sandal from your foot, for the place on which you stand is holy." And so
Joshua did.

1 CHAPTER 6   And Jericho was shut tight before the Israelites—
2 no one came out and no one went in. And the LORD said to Joshua, "See,
I have given into your hand Jericho and its king and the mighty warriors.
3 And you shall go round the town, all the men of war, encircling the town
4 once. Thus you shall do six days. And seven priests shall bear seven ram's
horns before the Ark, and on the seventh day you shall go round the town
5 seven times and the priests shall blow the ram's horns. And so, when the
horn of the ram sounds a long blast, when you hear the sound of the ram's
horn, all the people shall let out a great shout, and the wall of the town shall
fall where it stands, and the people shall go up, every man straight before
6 him." And Joshua son of Nun called to the priests and said to them, "Bear
the Ark of the Covenant, and seven priests shall bear seven ram's horns
7 before the Ark of the Covenant." And he said to the people, "Cross over
and go round the town, and the vanguard will cross over before the Ark of
8 the LORD." And it happened as Joshua spoke to the people that the seven

---

ginal difference that both "sandal" and "foot" are plurals in the Exodus story (here the
singular usage implies the plural and might be thought of as a kind of synecdoche). The
alignment of the present episode with the one of Moses at Mount Horeb points to differences as well as similarities. Both stories are dedication episodes as a leader is about to
embark on his mission. But Moses is addressed by God Himself, as is appropriate for the
greatest of prophets and the lawgiver, and at the site is a miraculously burning bush, proleptic of the moment when this very mountain will be enveloped in lightning during the
great epiphany. Joshua is the legitimate heir of Moses but a lesser figure and no prophet,
so he is addressed by the commander of the LORD's army, not by God Himself, and there
is no pyrotechnic display on this holy ground.

CHAPTER 6   2. *and the mighty warriors.* The Masoretic Text lacks "and," which has
been added in the translation.

3. *town.* At most, Jericho would have had a scant few thousand inhabitants. So "city" would
be an exaggeration.

4. *seven priests . . . seven ram's horns . . . on the seventh day . . . seven times.* The rite devised
to bring down the walls of the town involves a quadrupling of the sacred number seven. But
the destruction of the town is also an anti-Creation story: six days they go round the wall,
and on the climactic seventh day, it collapses and the town is reduced to rubble.
    ram's horns. These were primitive trumpets that produced a shrill and piercing sound.
They were used to assemble troops in battle and at coronations.

5. *the people.* Given the military context, 'am may have its secondary sense of "troops."

priests bearing the seven ram's horns before the LORD crossed over and blew
on the ram's horns, with the Ark of the LORD's Covenant going after them.
And the vanguard was going before the priests who were blowing the ram's   9
horns, and the rear guard was going behind the Ark as they went and blew
the ram's horns. And Joshua had charged the people, saying, "You shall not   10
shout and you shall not let your voice be heard, and no word shall come out
of your mouths until the moment I say to you, 'Shout,' and then you shall
shout." And the Ark of the LORD went round the town encircling it once,   11
and they came to the camp and spent the night in the camp. And Joshua   12
rose early in the morning, and the priests bore the Ark of the LORD. And   13
the seven priests bearing seven ram's horns before the Ark of the LORD
went along blowing the ram's horns, with the vanguard going before them
and the rear guard going behind the Ark of the LORD, along they went
blowing the ram's horns. And they went round the town once on the second   14
day, and they returned to camp—so did they do six days. And it happened   15
on the seventh day that they rose early as dawn broke and went round the
town in this fashion seven times. Only on that day did they go round the
city seven times. And it happened when the priests blew the ram's horns for 16
the seventh time that Joshua said to the people "Shout! For the LORD has
given the town to you. And the town and all that is within it shall be under 17
the ban to the LORD, except that Rahab the whore shall live and whoever is

---

9. *blowing.* The consonantal text seems to read "they blew," but the Masoretic marginal
correction properly has this as *toq'ey*, "blowing."

10. *until the moment.* The literal sense of the Hebrew is "until the day," but the word for
"day," *yom*, is often a fluid indicator of time.

17. *the ban.* This total prescription of destruction, *ḥerem*, of the conquered city, which
means annihilating its population and its animals and, at least in this instance, dedicating all objects of value to the LORD's treasury, is the grimmest aspect of this triumphalist
story. The enactment of the *ḥerem* is in keeping with the reiterated injunction in Deuteronomy to exterminate the native population of Canaan. That project is what Moshe Wein-
feld has called a "utopian" plan because it is highly unlikely that it was ever acted upon.
For the Deuteronomist, it is a brutal way of expressing the absolute separation from the
pagan population—a separation that never really occurred—called for in his program of
uncompromising monotheism, and the hallmark of the Deuteronomist is often detectable
in Joshua. The *ḥerem* was not an Israelite invention, as there is archaeological evidence that
it was sometimes practiced by various Canaanite peoples.
    except that Rahab the whore shall live and whoever is with her in the house. There is, of
course, a contradiction here with the story of the collapse of the wall. If the wall around
the town collapsed, how could Rahab, whose house was in the wall, have been saved, and
what good would the scarlet cord, which implied protection against conscious human
destroyers, have done? The medieval Hebrew commentator David Kimchi tried to save
the consistency of the text by proposing that only one part of the wall fell, through which

18 with her in the house, for she hid the messengers whom we sent. Only you, you must keep from the ban, lest you covet and take of the ban and put the 19 camp of Israel under the ban and stir up trouble for it. And all the silver and gold and vessels of bronze and iron shall be holy to the LORD, they shall 20 enter into the LORD's treasury." And the people shouted and blew the ram's horns, and it happened when the people had heard the sound of the ram's horn, the people let out a great shout, and the wall fell where it stood, and the people went up into the town, every man straight before him, and they 21 took the town. And they put under the ban everything that was in the town, from man to woman, from lad to elder, and to ox and sheep and donkey, 22 by the edge of the sword. And to the two men who had spied out the land Joshua had said, "Go into the house of the whore-woman, and bring the

---

breach the Israelites entered the town, though all the encircling with ram's horns certainly leads one to imagine that the entire wall came down. One suspects that the story of the two spies and the story of the ram's horns reflect two different traditions about the conquest of Jericho. Indeed, if the plan was to bring down the walls miraculously, there would scarcely have been any need to reconnoiter the town and the surrounding terrain, and the tale of the spies appears to assume a scenario in which the Israelite warriors will break into the city using conventional means of warfare.

18. *lest you covet.* The received text reads, "lest you put under the ban," *pen taharimu*, which doesn't make much sense. The translation follows the Septuagint, which appears to have used a Hebrew text that showed *pen tahmedu* (a reversal of consonants and a *dalet* for the similar-looking *resh*), "lest you covet."

20. *the people let out a great shout, and the wall fell where it stood.* Attempts have been made to recover a historical kernel for this fabulous event by proposing that it records the memory of an earthquake that leveled Jericho. (In fact, Jericho was built on a seismic fault and has been subject to earthquakes over the ages.) But nothing in the telling of the tale remotely suggests an earthquake. The ground is not said to move, and the destruction occurs through the deployment of sevens and the ram's horns' blasts and the shouting. One can also dismiss the idea of shock waves of sound splitting the walls as a scientific non-starter. The whole point of the story is its miraculous character. Almost everywhere in biblical narrative, Israel triumphs not through any martial powers, which get scant representation, but because God battles for Israel (compare the Song of the Sea, the Song of Deborah, and Moses' upraised arms in the defeat of the Amalekites). This story, then, is framed to vividly illustrate how the Israelite conquest of the first principal Canaanite town in the Jordan Valley is entirely due to the spectacular intervention of the LORD, Who gives Joshua the detailed instructions for the procedures of circumambulating the town with the Ark and the ram's horns. It should also be noted that the extensive archaeological exploration of Jericho indicates that its conquest by Joshua could not have taken place. There was a very old town on this site, but it was destroyed by the Middle Bronze Age, and at the putative time of Joshua's conquest in the Late Bronze Age, toward the end of the thirteenth century B.C.E., there had been no walled town on this site at least for a couple of centuries. The writer no doubt had in mind Jericho's antiquity—it is one of the oldest cities in the world—and its role as eastern gateway to Canaan, but historically it could not have been an object of Joshua's conquest.

woman out from there and all that is hers, as you vowed to her." And the 23
young spies came and brought out Rahab and her father and her mother
and her brothers and all that was hers, and all her clan they brought out,
and they put them outside the camp of Israel. And the town they burned 24
in fire and everything in it. Only the silver and the gold and the vessels
of bronze and iron they placed in the treasury of the LORD's house. And 25
Rahab the whore and her father's house and all that was hers Joshua kept
alive, and she has dwelled in the midst of Israel to this day, for she hid the
messengers that Joshua had sent to spy out Jericho. And Joshua imposed 26
a vow at that time, saying, "Cursed be the man before the LORD who will
arise and rebuild this town, Jericho.

> With his firstborn shall he found it,
>   and with his youngest set up its portals."

And the LORD was with Joshua, and his fame was throughout the land. 27

---

23. *the young spies.* Only here are they identified as *neʿarim,* "lads" or young men, although
it is possible that the term has its secondary sense of "elite soldiers."

24. *the LORD's house.* This phrase is an anachronism—in general, it refers to the Temple—
because at the time of the conquest there would have been only a portable sanctuary, not
referred to as a "house."

25. *she has dwelled in the midst of Israel to this day.* This clause must mean that Rahab's
descendants have dwelled in the midst of Israel to this day. It is thus an etiological note,
explaining how a particular Canaanite clan came to be naturalized Israelites.

26. *Cursed be the man . . . who will . . . rebuild this town.* The reason for the implacability
toward Jericho is not entirely clear since there is no indication that its inhabitants perpetrated war crimes, as did the Amalekites in Exodus. Perhaps this should be understood in
the context of the miraculous destruction of the walls: that event is a token for the laying
low of the inhabitants of the land before the invading Israelites (something that never
happened historically), and so as a sign and symbol of the whole conquest, the town razed
through divine intervention should never be rebuilt.
   With his firstborn shall he found it, / and with his youngest set up its portals. The solemnity of the vow is reinforced by casting this dire prediction in a line of poetry. Rashi nicely
catches the narrative progression from the first verset to the second: "At the beginning of
the foundation when he rebuilds it, his firstborn son will die, whom he will bury and go on
until the youngest dies at the completion of the work, which is setting up the portals." In 1
Kings 16:34, it is recorded that at the time of Ahab, "Hiel the Bethelite built up Jericho. At
the cost of Abiram his firstborn he laid its foundation and at the cost of Segib his youngest
he put up its gates, according to the word of the LORD that He spoke through Joshua son of
Nun." Joshua's curse may have been formulated to explain a calamitous event that occurred
three and a half centuries later.

1 CHAPTER 7   And the Israelites violated the ban, and Achan
son of Carmi, son of Zabdi, son of Zerah from the tribe of Judah took from
the ban, and the LORD's wrath flared against the Israelites.

2 And Joshua sent men from Jericho to Ai, which is by Beth-Aven to the east
of Bethel, and he said to them, saying, "Go up and spy out the land," and
3 the men went up and spied out Ai. And they came back to Joshua and said
to him, "Let not the whole people go up. Let about two thousand men or
three thousand men go up and strike Ai. Do not weary the whole people
4 there, for they are few." And about three thousand men from the people
5 went up there, and they fled before the men of Ai. And the men of Ai struck
down about thirty-six of them and pursued them from before the gate as
far as Shebarim and struck them down on the slope. And the people's heart
6 failed and turned to water. And Joshua tore his robes and flung himself on
his face to the ground before the Ark of the LORD till evening—he and the
7 elders of Israel—and they put dust on their heads. And Joshua said, "Alas,
O Master LORD, why did You insist on bringing this people across the
Jordan to give us into the hand of the Amorite and to destroy us? Would
8 that we had been content to dwell across the Jordan. I beseech you, my
Master, what should I say after Israel has turned tail before its enemies?

CHAPTER 7   1. *the Israelites violated the ban . . . Achan . . . took from the ban.* This
conjunction of subjects intimates why, in the harsh retribution of this episode, Achan must
be extirpated: his violation of the ban imparts guilt, as though by contagion, to the whole
people, as the defeat at Ai will immediately demonstrate.

3. *about two thousand men or three thousand men.* Boling's contention that *'elef* here is not
a number but means a "contingent," perhaps no more than twenty or thirty men, may be
supported by the fact that thirty-six deaths in the defeat are regarded as a catastrophic loss.
This is not, however, conclusive evidence because the Israelites are supposed to carry out
the conquest virtually unscathed, as at Jericho. Boling's claim that the particle k^e before
the number means "precisely" and not, as it usually does, "about," is dubious because the
alternative of "two or three," whether thousand or contingents, suggests approximation,
not exactitude.

5. *pursued them from before the gate.* The evident strategy is a sudden sortie from the gate
of the town, taking the besiegers, who are too few in number, by surprise.

7. *why did You insist on bringing this people across the Jordan to give us into the hand of the
Amorite and to destroy us?* Joshua's complaint is distinctly reminiscent of the complaints of
the Israelites in the wilderness to Moses, asking him why he brought them into the wilderness to perish instead of leaving them in peace in Egypt. The echo may suggest that Joshua
is not quite as fit a leader as Moses.

And the Canaanites and all the dwellers in the land will hear and draw 9
round us and cut off our name from the earth. And what will You do for
Your great name?" And the LORD said to Joshua, "Rise up. Why have you 10
fallen on your face? Israel has offended and also has broken My covenant 11
that I charged them and also has taken from the ban and also stolen and
also denied it and also put it in their bags. And the Israelites have not been 12
able to stand up against their enemies. They have turned tail before their
enemies, for they themselves have come under the ban. I will not continue
to be with you if you do not destroy the banned things from your midst.
Rise, consecrate the people, and say 'Consecrate yourselves for the morrow, 13
for thus the LORD God of Israel has said, There are banned things in your
midst, O Israel! You will not be able to stand up against your enemies until
you remove the banned things from your midst. And you shall draw near 14
in the morning according to your tribes. And it shall be, that the tribe on
which the LORD lets the lot fall shall draw near according to its clans, and
the clan on which the LORD lets the lot fall shall draw near according to
its households, and the household on which the LORD lets the lot fall shall
draw near according to its men. And it shall be, that he on whom the lot 15
falls for taking the banned things shall be burned in fire, he and all that is
his, because he broke the LORD's covenant and because he has done a scurrilous thing in Israel.'" And Joshua rose early in the morning and brought 16
Israel near according to its tribes, and the lot fell on the tribe of Judah. And 17
he brought near the clans of Judah, and the lot fell on the clan of Zerah, and

---

9. *the Canaanites.* There is a loose interchange of reference between "Amorites" and
"Canaanites."

And what will You do for Your great name? God's reputation as all-powerful deity is
contingent on the success of His chosen people. Moses uses the same argument when God
in His anger threatens to wipe out Israel.

11. *also . . . also . . . also . . . also.* These repetitions of *gam*—which equally has the sense of
"even" or "actually"—vividly express God's wrathful indignation.

12. *they themselves have come under the ban.* Through the contamination of having taken
objects devoted to destruction, they have become subject to destruction. The word "themselves" has been added in the translation for the sake of clarity.

14. *draw near.* This is a technical term for approaching the Ark of the Covenant.

lets the lot fall. The verb repeatedly used in this section also means "to catch" or "to
trap." What is involved in this process is an oracular device—most likely the Urim and
Thummim—that yields a binary yes/no answer, thus serving to select one from many.

17. *the clans of Judah.* The received text has "the clan of Judah," but a tribe is not a clan.
Several Hebrew manuscripts show the more plausible plural form.

18 he brought near the clan of Zerah, and the lot fell on Zabdi. And he brought
   near his household according to the men, and the lot fell on Achan son of
19 Carmi son of Zerah of the tribe of Judah. And Joshua said to Achan, "My
   son, show honor, pray, to the LORD God of Israel, and make confession to
   Him, and tell me, pray, what you have done. Do not conceal it from me."
20 And Achan answered Joshua and said, "Indeed, it is I who offended against
21 the LORD God of Israel, and thus and so I have done. I saw in the booty a
   fine fur mantle and two hundred shekels of silver and an ingot of gold fifty
   shekels in weight, and I coveted them and took them, and there they are,
   buried in the ground within my tent, and the silver is underneath them."
22 And Joshua sent messengers and they ran to the tent, and there it was
23 buried in his tent, with the silver underneath it. And they took these from
   within the tent and brought them to Joshua and to all the Israelites, and
24 he presented them before the LORD. And Joshua took Achan son of Zerah

---

19. *My son, show honor, pray, to the LORD God of Israel, and make confession to Him.* Joshua's language in addressing Achan is cunningly gentle, suggesting he intends to draw in his interlocutor and then lead him to divulge his crime. He begins by calling Achan "my son," elsewhere an affectionate form of address in the Bible; he uses the polite particle of entreaty, *na'*, "pray," and at first does not mention guilt but rather honoring God. The idiom for "make confession," *ten todah*, more frequently means "to give thanks," so it sounds almost as though Joshua were about to say something quite positive to the man who will be made to confess his guilt and then undergo horrendous punishment.

20. *Indeed, it is I who offended.* Achan's immediate and full confession is probably best explained by his awareness that the oracle has singled him out, the lot falling on him alone of all the multitude of Israel, and so he feels he has no choice but to admit his guilt. Joshua's ostensibly fatherly approach to him may also make him sense that he is a member of this community now gravely endangered by his act, and hence he must make restitution, whatever the price.

   thus and so I have done. Although this is an idiom that can be used in place of a detailed account, here it is proleptic: the precise content of "thus and so" is laid out in the next verse.

21. *a fine fur mantle.* The Masoretic Text reads "a fine Shinar mantle," neatly rendered in the King James Version as "a goodly Babylonish garment" because Shinar is another name for Babylon. There is no evidence that Shinar specialized in exporting fine apparel, and this translation reads instead of *shin'ar*, deleting the middle consonant, *sei'ar*, "hair" or "fur."

24. *And Joshua took Achan . . . and the silver and the mantle . . . and his sons and his daughters.* The lining up in a single syntactic string of human beings, material treasure, and animal possessions is disturbing. The evident assumption about the family members is that they have been contaminated by Achan's violation of the ban, and hence they must perish with him. One notes that Achan has considerable possessions (the donkey and ox may well be collective nouns), which makes his crime all the more heinous. The collective punishment is nevertheless troubling.

and the silver and the mantle and the ingot of gold and his sons and his
daughters and his ox and his donkey and his flock and his tent and all that
was his, and all Israel was with him, and he brought them up to the Valley
of Achor. And Joshua said, "Even as you have stirred up trouble for us, the 25
LORD shall stir up trouble for you on this day." And all Israel pelted them
with stones and burned them in fire and pelted them with stones. And they 26
piled up over him a great heap of stones to this day, and the LORD turned
back from His blazing wrath. Therefore is the name of that place called the
Valley of Achor to this day.

CHAPTER 8   And God said to Joshua, "Do not be afraid and 1
do not cower. Take with you all the combat troops and rise, go up to Ai. See,
I have given in your hand the king of Ai and his people and his town and his
land. And you shall do to Ai as you did to Jericho and to its king. Only its 2
booty and its cattle you may plunder. Set up for yourself an ambush against
the town behind it." And Joshua arose, and all the combat troops with him, 3
to go up to Ai. And Joshua chose thirty thousand men, sturdy warriors, and
sent them out at night. And Joshua charged them, saying, "See, you are to lie 4

---

the Valley of Achor. This means the Valley of Trouble, making the end of this story
an etiological tale about the origin of the place-name. It may have been originally called
the Valley of Trouble for entirely different reasons—for example, because its terrain was
treacherous or bleak and barren.

25. burned them in fire and pelted them with stones. The burning may refer only to the
material objects because it was not customary to burn bodies after stoning. The repeated
clause about pelting with stones seems redundant.

26. Therefore is the name of that place called. This is an explicit etiological formula.

CHAPTER 8   2. Only its booty and its cattle you may plunder. Ai, like Jericho, is to
be put to the ban, its structures burned and all its inhabitants massacred, but an exception
is made for booty, which the conquering Israelites are allowed to take.

3. the combat troops. Throughout this episode, 'am, elsewhere "people," clearly has this
military sense.
    thirty thousand men. The very large number here for men in an ambush is cited by
proponents of the idea that 'elef must refer to a small contingent and does not mean a thousand. But highly exaggerated numbers are often used in ancient narrative, and the sense of
"contingent" in the count of the deaths of the town's inhabitants in verse 25 is problematic.

4–8. Although God had said he would deliver Ai to Joshua, it is Joshua's shrewdness as a
strategist that brings about the fall of the town. The elaboration of the details of military
strategy is untypical of biblical narrative. Scholars have pointed out a similarity not only

in ambush against the town behind the town. Do not keep very far away from
5   the town, and all of you must be on the ready. And I and the troops that are
with me, we shall draw near the town, and so, when they come out toward
6   us as before, we shall flee from them, and they will come out after us till we
draw them away from the town, for they will think, 'They are fleeing from us
7   as before,' and we shall flee from them. And you will rise from the ambush
and take hold of the town, and the LORD your God will give it into your hand.
8   And so, when you seize the town, you will set fire to the town, according to
9   the word of the LORD you will do. See, I have charged you." And Joshua sent
them off, and they went to the ambush, and they stayed between Bethel and
10   Ai to the west of Ai. And Joshua spent that night among the troops. And
Joshua rose early in the morning and marshaled the troops, he and the elders
11   of Israel, before the troops, to Ai. And all the combat troops who were with
him went up and approached and came opposite the town, and they camped
12   to the north, with the ravine between them and Ai. And he took about five
thousand men and set them as an ambush between Bethel and Ai to the west
13   of the town. And they put the troops, the whole camp, to the north of the
town, and its covert contingent, to the west of the town. And Joshua spent

---

in strategy but also in wording between this story and the account of the siege of Gibeah in
the civil war reported in Judges 20, and it is generally thought that this story draws on the
one in Judges. Joshua shrewdly capitalizes on the previous defeat of the Israelites at Ai by
seeming to repeat the same tactical error, positioning his troops in front of the town gate
and then retreating. This time, however, he hides an attack unit behind the town that will
move forward against it once the armed men of the town have been drawn out in pursuit
of the main body of Israelites.

4. *behind the town.* This would be west of the town. The main gates of the town are evidently
on the eastern side, and the main Israelite camp is northeast of the city.

10. *before the troops.* This phrase looks odd and may reflect a scribal error.

12. *And he took about five thousand men.* This verse seems to replicate verses 3–4 using a different (somewhat more plausible) number—5,000 instead of 30,000. It also puts the sending
out of the ambush troops after the general encampment, not before it. Two different versions
may have been awkwardly spliced together.

13. *And they put the troops, the whole camp.* Like the translation, the wording of the Hebrew
is a bit clumsy and the syntax ambiguous.
   its covert contingent. The Hebrew 'aqev usually means "heel." There is no evidence
that it means "rear guard," as some claim, and an ambush is not a rear guard. It is equally
questionable that it could mean "far edge," again an inappropriate term for ambush. The
translation follows the Targum of Jonathan, Rashi, and Kimchi, in relating 'aqev to 'oqbah,
a term that suggests deviousness and that might apply to an ambush.

that night in the valley. And it happened, when the king of Ai saw it, that the   14
men of the town hurried in the early morning and came out toward Israel to
do battle, he and all his troops, at the set place opposite the Arabah. He did
not know there was an ambush against him behind the town. And Joshua   15
and all Israel were routed before them and fled on the road to the wilderness.
And all the troops who were in the town were mustered to pursue Joshua,   16
and were drawn away from the town. And not a man remained in the town,   17
in Ai, who did not go out after Israel, and they left the town open and pursued
Israel. And the LORD said to Joshua, "Reach out with the javelin that is in   18
your hand toward Ai, for into your hand I shall give it," and Joshua reached
out with the javelin that was in his hand toward the town. And the ambush-   19
ers rose quickly from their place and ran as his hand reached out, and they
entered the town and took it, and they hurried and set the town on fire. And   20
the men of Ai turned behind them and saw and, look, smoke was rising from
the town toward the heavens, and they had no place in any direction to flee,
while the troops who had fled to the wilderness became the pursuers. And   21
Joshua and all Israel saw that the ambushers had taken the town and that the
smoke from the town was rising, and they struck down the men of Ai. And   22
these had come out of the town toward them so that they were in the midst

---

Joshua spent that night. The Masoretic Text reads *wayelekh*, "walked," but a few manuscripts show *wayalen*, "spent the night," which seems more plausible.

14. *the Arabah.* This is the north-south rift of the Jordan Valley and is equivalent to the
wilderness several times mentioned in this episode.

15. *were routed.* The obvious implication in context is: pretended to be routed. The verb used
wayinagʿu (literally, "were smitten/plagued") comes instead of the expected *wayinagfu*,
and may be influenced by the parallel passage in Judges 20, where the same verbal stem is
employed in a different sense.

18. *Reach out with the javelin that is in your hand.* The exact nature of the weapon, *kidon*, is
in dispute. (Modern Hebrew has adopted it as the term for bayonet.) Some scholars think
it is a kind of scimitar. In any case, the outstretched *kidon* is both a signal for the men in
the ambush to move against the town and a magical act pointedly reminiscent of Moses's
upraised staff in the battle against Amalek reported in Exodus 17.

21. *the ambushers.* The Hebrew term *ha'orev* can refer either to the ambush or, as a collective
noun, to the combatants carrying out the ambush.

22. *And these had come out of the town toward them.* These are the ambushers, who, having
put the town to the torch, now attack its troops outside, who are caught in a pincer movement between the main Israelite force and the ambushers (whether 5,000 or 30,000). The
reference to no place to flee in verse 20 may be out of chronological order because it makes
good sense here, when the men of Ai are attacked from both sides.

of Israel, who were on both sides, and they struck them down till they left
23 among them no remnant or survivor. And the king of Ai they caught alive
24 and brought him forth to Joshua. And it happened, when Israel had finished
killing all the inhabitants of Ai in the field, in the wilderness where they
had pursued them, all of them by the edge of the sword to the last of them,
25 all Israel turned back to Ai and struck it with the edge of the sword. And
all who fell on that day, men and women, came to twelve thousand, all the
26 people of Ai. And Joshua did not pull back his hand that he had reached
out with the javelin until he had put all the inhabitants of Ai under the
27 ban. Only the cattle and the booty of that town did the Israelites plunder,
28 according to the word of the LORD that He charged to Joshua. And Joshua
burned Ai and turned it into an everlasting heap, a devastation to this day.
29 And the king of Ai he impaled on a pole till eventide, and when the sun was
setting, Joshua gave orders, and they took his corpse down from the pole
and flung it by the entrance of the town gate and put over it a pile of stones
30 to this day. Then did Joshua build an altar to the LORD God of Israel on
31 Mount Ebal, as Moses the servant of the LORD had charged the Israelites,
as it is written in the book of the teaching of Moses, "an altar of whole
stones, over which no iron has been brandished," and they offered up on

---

24. *turned back to Ai and struck it with the edge of the sword.* The gruesome reality of this
report is as follows: the ambushing force, after setting fire to the town and then coming
out to join in the attack on the troops of Ai, now comes back with the main Israelite camp
to the town to slaughter the women and elders and children left there.

29. *impaled on a pole.* This is the form of execution that many modern scholars think likely.
But the traditional rendering of "hanged on a tree" remains a distinct possibility.
 they took his corpse down from the pole and flung it by the entrance of the town gate. The
use of the verb "flung" is a clear indication that this is not an honorable burial, though the
biblical prohibition against leaving a body hanging overnight is preserved. The place of
burial may point toward the area in front of the gates of the town where the Israelites were
killed in their earlier attack.

30. *Then did Joshua build an altar.* This textual unit invokes the two mountains of blessing and curse mentioned in Deuteronomy 11:26–32, and is a direct implementation of the
command in Deuteronomy 27:2–3, "on the day that you cross the Jordan into the land that
the LORD your God is about to give you, you shall set up for yourself great stones and coat
them with plaster. And you shall write on them the words of this teaching. . . ." But the
placement of the episode has puzzled both ancient and modern commentators. Temporally,
it does not happen right after the crossing of the Jordan as it should, and geographically,
the Israelites at Ai are not opposite Mount Ebal and Mount Gerizim.

31. *an altar of whole stones, over which no iron has been brandished.* This is an approximate
quotation of Exodus 20:25.

it burnt offerings to the LORD, and they sacrificed well-being sacrifices. And he wrote there on the stones the repetition of the teaching of Moses, 32 which he had written in the presence of the Israelites. And all Israel and 33 its elders and its overseers and its judges were standing on both sides of the Ark opposite the levitical priests, bearers of the Ark of the Covenant of the LORD, sojourner and native alike, over against Mount Gerizim, and its other half over against Mount Ebal, as Moses, servant of the LORD, had formerly charged to bless Israel. And afterward he read out all the words of 34 the teaching, the blessing and the curse, according to all that is written in the book of the teaching. There was no word of all that Moses had charged 35 that Joshua did not read out before the whole assembly of Israel and the women and the little ones and the sojourners who went in their midst.

CHAPTER 9   And it happened when all the kings heard who 1 were beyond the Jordan, in the high country and in the lowland and along the whole shore of the Great Sea opposite Lebanon, the Hittite and the Amorite, the Canaanite, the Perizzite, the Hivvite and the Jebusite, that they 2 gathered together to do battle with Joshua and with Israel in united resolve. And the inhabitants of Gibeon had heard what Joshua did to Jericho and to 3 Ai. And they on their part acted with cunning and provisioned themselves 4

---

32. *the repetition of the teaching of Moses.* The Hebrew *mishneh torat mosheh* refers to Deuteronomy (that Greek name itself being a rendering of the Hebrew *mishneh torah*). The Deuteronomist behind this story is clearly promoting the interests of his own privileged text.

CHAPTER 9   1. *beyond the Jordan.* Since all the peoples enumerated here are Canaanites living on the western side of the Jordan, this phrase would have to mean beyond the Jordan from the viewpoint of the Israelites coming from the eastern side, even though elsewhere it almost always refers to trans-Jordanian territory.

2. *in united resolve.* The literal sense of the Hebrew is "with one mouth." It is historically quite unlikely that the divided city-kingdoms of Canaan could have constituted themselves as a single united force.

4. *they on their part acted with cunning.* In context, the "on their part" (or "too") must refer to the immediately preceding story of the conquest of Ai. There the Israelites used the cunning of the ambush strategy to destroy the town; here, by contrast, cunning is used by the Gibeonites to save themselves.
    provisioned themselves. The Masoretic Text reads *wayitstayru*, which might mean "they painted themselves"—that is (perhaps), "they disguised themselves." An emendation yields *wayitsdaydu* (the letters *resh* and *dalet* look quite similar), which seems more plausible, especially given the prominence of the cognate noun *tsayid*, "provisions," in this episode.

and took worn-out sacks for their donkeys and worn-out and cracked and
5 trussed-up wineskins, and worn-out and patched sandals on their feet and
worn-out cloaks upon them, and all the bread of their provision was dry
6 and moldy. And they went to Joshua at the Gilgal camp and said to him
and to the men of Israel, "We have come from a faraway land, and now seal
7 a pact with us." And the men of Israel said to the Hivvites, "Perhaps you
8 dwell in our midst, so how can we seal a pact with you?" And they said to
Joshua, "We are your servants." And Joshua said to them, "From where are
9 you and from where do you come?" And they said to them, "From a very
faraway land, your servants have come through the fame of the LORD your
God, for we have heard the report of Him and all that He did in Egypt,
10 and all that He did to the two Amorite kings who were across the Jordan,
to Sihon king of Heshbon and to Og king of Bashan which is in Ashtaroth.
11 And our elders and all the inhabitants of our land said to us, saying, 'Take
in your hand provisions for the way and go to them and say to them, We
12 are your servants, and now seal a pact with us.' This bread of ours we took
still warm as provisions from our homes on the day we went out toward
13 you, and now, look, it is dry and has turned moldy. And these wineskins
that we filled were new, and now they are cracked, and these cloaks of ours
14 and our sandals have worn out from the very long way." And the men took

---

trussed-up. The wineskins are held together with cords or strips of leather because they are falling apart.

6. *We have come from a faraway land.* With the evidence of the just consummated destruction of Jericho and Ai, the Gibeonites seem aware that the Israelites are embarked on a campaign to annihilate the indigenous population of Canaan, and so they adopt the subterfuge of pretending to be from a land far from Canaan. This entire story is in fact an elaborate etiological tale that betrays the shaky historical basis of this canonical account of the conquest. Deuteronomy, with its call for a radical separation from the pagan peoples of the land, enunciated a program of genocide. Such a program was never actually carried out, and the situation of Israel among the Canaanites was by and large the opposite: the two populations frequently mingled, and the Israelites were often open to cultural and religious influences from the Canaanite peoples. The author of this episode was trying to resolve a contradiction: a particular group of Canaanites—the Gibeonites—not only were living cheek by jowl with the Israelites but were performing subservient duties at an Israelite sanctuary at Gibeon. The story comes to explain how the Gibeonites were not wiped out, as the program of total destruction dictated, and how they came to play a role in an Israelite cultic place.

9. *a very faraway land.* Pushed by Joshua, they add "very" to their previous words.

14. *And the men took from their provisions.* It may seem puzzling that Israelites should want to eat the dry and moldy bread of the Gibeonites, but Kimchi is probably right in surmising that breaking bread—even virtually inedible bread—with the strangers was a way of ritually confirming a treaty of peace with them.

from their provisions, and they did not inquire of the LORD. And Joshua 15
made peace with them, and sealed a pact with them to preserve their lives,
and the chieftains of the community made a vow to them. And it happened 16
at the end of three days after they had sealed the pact with them, that they
heard that they were neighbors and were dwelling in their midst. And the 17
Israelites journeyed forth and came to their towns on the third day, and
their towns were Gibeon and Chephirah and Beeroth and Kiriath-Jearim.
But the Israelites did not strike them down, for the chieftains of the com- 18
munity had made a vow to them in the name of the LORD God of Israel, and
all the community complained against the chieftains. And all the chief- 19
tains said to the whole community, "We have made a vow to them in the
name of the LORD God of Israel, and now we cannot touch them. This let 20
us do to them, letting them live, that there be no fury against us for the vow
we made to them." And the chieftains said of them, "Let them live, and they 21
will be hewers of wood and drawers of water for the whole community, as
the chieftains have said of them." And Joshua called to them and spoke to 22
them, saying, "Why did you deceive us, saying, 'We are very far away from
you,' when you dwell in our midst? And now, you are cursed, and no slave 23
or hewer of wood or drawer of water for the house of my God will cease to
be among you." And they answered Joshua and said, "For it was indeed told 24

---

they did not inquire of the LORD. This is the technical idiom for inquiring of an oracle.
Without such guidance, Joshua and the Israelites are taken in by the deception.

17. *on the third day.* Though this is the formulaic number for relatively short journeys, it is
also an implication that the Gibeonite towns are well within the borders of Canaan.

19. *We have made a vow to them . . . and now we cannot touch them.* Vows made in the name
of the deity—compare the story of Jephthah's daughter in Judges 11—are irrevocable and
cannot be renegotiated.

20. *fury.* The Hebrew *qetsef* means divine rage, characteristically manifested in a plague.

21. *hewers of wood and drawers of water.* These are menial workers at the lowest point in
the social hierarchy, as is clear in Deuteronomy 29:9–10: "You are stationed here today all
of you before the LORD your God, your heads, your tribes, your elders, and your overseers,
every man of Israel. Your little ones, your wives, and your sojourner who is in the midst of
your camps, from the hewer of your wood to the drawer of your water."

23. *for the house of my God.* In verse 21, it was "for the whole community." In historical
fact, the Gibeonites could conceivably have performed these functions in both the sacred
and the profane realm.
    will cease to be among you. Literally, "will not be cut off from you."

24. *For it was indeed told to your servants.* In this fiction, the Gibeonites somehow have
been given a full report of the promise of the land and the program of genocide articulated
in Deuteronomy.

to your servants that the LORD your God had charged Moses to give all the
land to you and to destroy the inhabitants of the land before you. And we
25 were very afraid for our lives because of you, and so we did this thing. And
now, here we are in your hand. What is good and what is right in your eyes
26 to do to us, do." And he did thus to them and saved them from the hand
27 of the Israelites, and they did not kill them. And on that day Joshua made
them hewers of wood and drawers of water for the community and for the
LORD's altar to this day, at the place He was to choose.

1 CHAPTER 10   And it happened when Adoni-Zedek king of
Jerusalem heard that Joshua had taken Ai and put it under the ban, as he
had done to Jericho and its king, so had he done to Ai and its king, and
that the inhabitants of Gibeon had made peace with Israel and were in
2 their midst, that he was very afraid, for Gibeon was a big town, like one
of the royal towns, and it was bigger than Ai, and all its men were war-
3 riors. And Adoni-Zedek king of Jerusalem sent to Hoham king of Hebron
and to Piram king of Jarmuth, Japhia king of Lachish, and Debir king of
4 Eglon, saying, "Come up to me and help me, and let us strike Gibeon,
5 for it has made peace with Joshua and with the Israelites." And the five
Amorite kings, the king of Jerusalem, the king of Hebron, the king of
Jarmuth, the king of Lachish, the king of Eglon, gathered together, they
and all their camps, and they encamped against Gibeon and did battle

---

26. *saved them from the hand of the Israelites.* This formulation may suggest that, despite
the solemn vow, there was some popular sentiment among the Israelites, outraged by this
deception, to destroy the Gibeonites. The quick maneuver of the chieftains implemented
by Joshua to make them menial servants would be devised to fend off such an assault.

27. *to this day.* This is the formal marker of the etiological tale: if you wonder why the
Gibeonites are hewers of wood and drawers of water for the Israelites, this story explains it.
   at the place He was to choose. This phrase in Deuteronomistic texts invariably refers
to Jerusalem, but it is a misplaced editorial tic here because the sanctuary in question is
located at Gibeon.

CHAPTER 10   1. *Adoni-Zedek.* The name means "master of justice" or "master of
victory," and as several medieval Hebrew commentators note, it is probably a hereditary
title rather than a proper name. Melchizedek king of Salem (probably a variant of "Jerusalem"), mentioned in Genesis 14:18, has a similar titular name, which means "king of
justice" or "king of victory."

2. *like one of the royal towns.* Even though there is no monarchy in Gibeon, its size and
importance make it the equivalent of a royal town.

against it. And the men of Gibeon sent messengers to Joshua at the Gilgal 6
camp, saying, "Do not let go of your servants. Come up quickly to us
and rescue us and help us, for all the Amorite kings who live in the high
country have gathered against us." And Joshua came up from Gilgal, he 7
and all the combat troops with him, and all the valiant warriors. And 8
the LORD said to Joshua, "Do not fear them, for I have given them into
your hand. No man of them will stand up before you." And Joshua came 9
against them suddenly—all night long he had come up from Gilgal. And 10
the LORD panicked them before Israel, and they struck them a great blow
at Gilgal, and they pursued them on the road of the ascent to Beth-Horon,
and they struck them down as far as Azekah and as far as Makkedah. And 11
it happened when they fled before Israel, that they were on the descent
from Beth-Horon when the LORD flung down on them great stones from
the heavens as far as Azekah, and those who died from the hailstones were
many more than the Israelites killed by the sword. Then did Joshua speak 12
to the LORD on the day the LORD gave the Amorites over to the Israelites,
and he said in the sight of Israel:

> "O sun in Gibeon halt,
>   and the moon in Aialon Valley."

---

6. *Do not let go of your servants.* That is, hang on to us; do not leave us in the lurch.

   help us. The simple verb "to help" also has technical sense, exhibited in many psalms and in narrative contexts such as this, which is to render military support.

7. *the combat troops . . . all the valiant warriors.* These terms probably indicate that Joshua led elite troops, the ancient Near Eastern equivalent of commandos, on this mission.

9. *Joshua came against them suddenly.* By marching all night long the considerable distance from Gilgal to Gibeon, he is able to carry out a surprise attack, perhaps just at daybreak.

10. *and the LORD panicked them.* This is a vivid illustration of the system of dual causation sometimes adopted by the biblical writers. The soldiers of the alliance of five kings are of course in the first instance panicked by Joshua's surprise attack, a shrewd tactical maneuver, but now the panic is explained as God's direct intervention.

11. *the descent from Beth-Horon.* This is the same steep road that is called "ascent" in the previous verse, now imagined from Beth-Horon looking down rather than the other way around.

   great stones from the heavens. This wording gives the initial impression of an entirely supernatural event, but then it is explained naturalistically as a reference to hailstones. Even so, the hailstones would have had to be improbably big in order to be lethal.

12. *O sun in Gibeon halt.* The reason for the prayer is explained in the next verse: the sun is to halt its movement across the sky and the moon not to appear in its place in order to give Joshua a long extension of daylight in which to hunt down and destroy his enemies.

13   And the sun halted
                     and the moon stood still
                          till the nation wreaked vengeance on its foes.

Is it not written in the Book of Jashar?—"And the sun stood still in the
14 middle of the heavens and did not hasten to set for a whole day. And there
    was nothing like that day before it or after it, in the LORD's heeding the
15 voice of a man, for the LORD did battle for Israel." And Joshua went back,
16 and all Israel with him, to the Gilgal camp. And those five kings fled and
17 hid in a cave at Makkedah. And it was told to Joshua, saying, "The five kings
18 have been found hiding in the cave at Makkedah. And Joshua said, "Roll
    great stones over the mouth of the cave, and set men over it to guard them.
19 As for you, do not stand still. Pursue your enemies and cut them down from
    behind. Do not let them enter their towns, for the LORD your God has given
20 them into your hand." And it happened when Joshua and the Israelites had
    finished striking them a very great blow, to the last of them, that a remnant
21 of them survived and entered the fortified towns. And the troops came back
    safely to the camp to Joshua, no man so much as snarled at the Israelites.
22 And Joshua said, "Open the mouth of the cave, and bring these five kings
23 out to me from the cave." And so they did, and they brought those five kings
    out to him from the cave—the king of Jerusalem, the king of Hebron, the

---

13. *the Book of Jashar.* This lost text is also mentioned in 2 Samuel 1:18 as the literary source
in which David's elegy for Saul and Jonathon appears. It is safe to assume that it is a very old
book, largely poetic or even epic, in which martial themes are prominent. The name *jashar*
would appear to mean "the upright," though Shmuel Ahituv, mindful of the practice of
calling books by their opening words, interestingly proposes that it could mean "he sang"
(revocalizing *jashar* as *jashir*).

And the sun stood still. This translation construes the remainder of this verse as a continuation of the quotation from the Book of Jashar. It does not scan as poetry, but the
language is elevated, with epic flourishes.

did not hasten to set. Psalm 19 imagines the sun racing across the sky like a warrior running on his path, and that mythological imagery is probably behind the verb "hasten" here.

19. *cut them down from behind.* The verb *zanev*, derived from *zanav*, "tail," means etymologically "to cut off the tail." It is used in Deuteronomy 25:18.

20. *to the last of them.* More literally, "until they came to an end." But as the next clause
makes clear, this actually means that they were almost entirely wiped out but some escaped.

21. *no man.* The Hebrew says "to no man," but the prefix *l^e* is probably a dittography triggered by *le yisra'el*, "at [or to] Israel."

king of Jarmuth, the king of Lachish, the king of Eglon. And it happened 24
when they brought out those kings to Joshua, that Joshua called out to all
the men of Israel and said to the captains of the men of war who had gone
with him: "Put your feet on the necks of these kings." And they drew near
and put their feet on their necks. And Joshua said to them, "Do not fear 25
and do not cower. Be strong and stalwart, for thus shall the LORD do to all
your enemies with whom you do battle." And afterward Joshua struck them 26
down and put them to death, and he impaled them on five poles, and they
remained impaled on the poles till evening. And it happened as the sun 27
was setting that Joshua gave the command and they took them down from
the poles and flung them into the cave in which they had hidden, and they
put great stones over the mouth of the cave, to this very day. And Joshua 28
took Makkedah on that day and struck it and its king with the edge of the
sword and every living thing within it. He left no survivor, and he did to
the king of Makkedah as he had done to the king of Jericho. And Joshua 29
moved on, and all Israel with him, from Makkedah to Libnah, and he did
battle with Libnah. And the LORD gave it as well into the hand of Israel 30
with its king, and he struck it with the edge of the sword and every living
thing within it. He left no survivor, and he did to its king as he had done
to the king of Jericho. And Joshua moved on, and all Israel with him, from 31
Libnah to Lachish, and he camped against it and did battle against it. And 32
the LORD gave Lachish into the hand of Israel, and he took it on the second

---

24. *Put your feet on the necks of these kings.* As both Egyptian and Assyrian art abundantly demonstrate, this was a symbolic gesture by the victors for subjugating the defeated
enemies.

26. *he impaled them on five poles.* Since it would be somewhat odd to hang a dead body by
the neck, this particular verse offers credibility to the view that the Hebrew verb in question
when applied to an execution means to impale, not to hang. Impaling the body for public
display would be an act of shaming.

27. *to this very day.* This is again the etiological tag—the story explains why one finds great
stones piled over the mouth of the cave at Makkedah.

28. *and Joshua took Makkedah on that day and struck it and its king.* Here begins a catalogue
of Joshua's conquests, conveyed in more or less identical formulas, and probably from a
different literary source.

32. *And the LORD gave Lachish into the hand of Israel.* This notation is still another indication of the tenuous relation to history of this account of the conquest because extrabiblical
evidence shows that in the thirteenth century B.C.E. (the time of Joshua) and well beyond it,
Lachish was not in Israelite hands. Altogether, this report of a lightning campaign in which
a large swath of the land was conquered does not accord with the archaeological record for

day and struck it by the edge of the sword and every living thing within it,
33 as all that he had done to Libnah. Then did Horam king of Gezer come up to
help Lachish, and Joshua struck him down, and all his troops with him, till
34 he left no survivor of him. And Joshua moved on, and all Israel with him,
from Lachish to Eglon, and they camped against it and did battle against
35 it. And they took it on that day and struck it with the edge of the sword and
every living thing within it. On that day he passed it under the ban as all
36 he had done to Lachish. And Joshua went up, and all Israel with him, from
37 Eglon to Hebron, and they did battle against it. And they took it and struck
it with the edge of the sword, and its king and all its towns and every living
thing within it. He left no survivor, as all he had done to Eglon, and he put
38 it under the ban and every living thing within it. And Joshua, and all Israel
39 with him, turned back to Debir and did battle against it. And he took it, and
its king and all its towns, and he struck them with the edge of the sword,
and he put under the ban every living thing within it. He left no survivor.
As he had done to Hebron, so he did to Debir and its king and as he had
40 done to Libnah and to its king. And Joshua struck the whole land, the high
country and the Negeb and the lowland and the slopes and all their kings.
And he left no survivor of it. And every breathing thing he put under the
41 ban as the LORD God of Israel had charged. And Joshua struck them from
42 Kadesh-Barnea to Gaza, and the whole land of Goshen to Gibeon. And all
these kings and their land Joshua took in one fell swoop, for the LORD God

---

the history of this period. One might also observe an internal contradiction between the catalogue of conquests and the episode that precedes it. One of the five kings put to death at the Makkedah cave is the king of Jerusalem, the very man who organized the anti-Israelite alliance. One would expect that the conquest of Jerusalem should then logically figure in this account, but it was of course general knowledge that Jerusalem remained in Jebusite hands until over two centuries later, when it was taken by David. One suspects that the source from which the catalogue of conquests was drawn knew nothing of an Adoni-Zedek king of Jerusalem who played a central role in these battles, and that the redactor did not reconcile the two accounts.

40. *the Negeb and the lowland.* In David's time, much of the Negeb was dominated by the Amalekites, and the lowland was Philistine territory.

41. *from Kadesh-Barnea.* This would be extravagantly far to the south, in the northern part of the Sinai peninsula.

42. *in one fell swoop.* Literally, "one time" or "at once." This hyperbolic flourish again raises the problem of historicity.

of Israel did battle for Israel. And Joshua, and all Israel with him, turned 43
back to the Gilgal camp.

CHAPTER 11   And it happened when Jabin king of Hazor 1
heard, that he sent to Jobab king of Madon and to the king of Shimron and
the king of Achshaph, and to the kings who were in the north, in the high 2
country and in the Arabah, south of Chinneroth, and in the lowland and in
Naphoth-Dor on the west, the Canaanite from the east, and to the west, and 3
the Amorite and the Hittite and the Perizzite and the Jebusite in the high
country, and the Hivvite below Hermon in Mizpah land. And they sallied 4
forth, they and all their camps with them, troops more numerous than the
sand that is on the shore of the sea in number, and very many horses and
chariots. And all these kings joined forces and came and camped together 5
by the waters of Merom to do battle with Israel. And the LORD said to 6
Joshua, "Do not fear them, for tomorrow at this time I shall cause all of
them to be slain before Israel. Their horses you will hamstring and their
chariots you will burn in fire." And Joshua, and all the combat troops with 7

CHAPTER 11   1. when Jabin king of Hazor heard. Though no grammatical object
for the verb appears, the obvious sense is that he heard of Joshua's initial conquests. The
pointed parallel with 10:1 makes this clear. Altogether, this whole chapter appears to have
been composed to create a symmetrical complement to the account of the defeat of the
southern alliance in the previous chapter. Here, the alliance is one of northern kings.
The reach of this new conquest, going all the way to Sidon in Lebanon and, to the south
on the Mediterranean coast, to Misrephoth-Mayim, is scarcely historical, and it seems
devised to convey the idea of the completeness of the conquest of the land.

   Hazor. This was an important city in northeastern Canaan in the Middle Bronze Age,
a memory perhaps reflected in making its king the leader of the alliance, but by Joshua's
time it had become a relatively small town.

2. *Chinneroth.* This is the same place as Kinneret, the Sea of Galilee.

3. *Hermon.* This is a mountain to the northeast, on the border between present-day Israel
and Syria.

5. *the waters of Merom.* The location is in the high country of north-central Canaan.

6. *Their horses you will hamstring and their chariots you will burn in fire.* The chariot, a formidable instrument of warfare, was not generally adopted by the Israelites, who were essentially guerilla fighters from the high country, for another two centuries. These Canaanite
chariots in all likelihood were made out of wood, hence the burning. As to hamstringing
of the horses, Boling and others think this was a cunning strategy to disable the horses at
the onset of the battle, although it is not entirely clear how easy it would have been for the

him, came against them suddenly at the waters of Merom, and fell upon
8 them. And the LORD gave them into the hand of Israel, and they struck
them down and pursued them to Greater Sidon and to Misrephoth-Mayim
and to Mizpeh Valley to the east, and they struck them down until no
9 survivor was left of them. And Joshua did to them as the LORD had said
to him, their horses he hamstrung and their chariots he burned in fire.
10 And Joshua came back at that time and took Hazor, and its king he struck
down with the sword. For Hazor in those days was chief of these kingdoms.
11 And he struck down every living person who was in it with the edge of
the sword, putting it under the ban. No breathing person was left, and he
12 burned Hazor in fire. And all the towns of these kings and all their kings
Joshua took and struck them down with the edge of the sword, he put them
13 under ban as Moses servant of the LORD had charged. Only all the towns
standing on their mounds Israel did not burn, except for Hazor alone that
14 Joshua burned. And all the booty of these towns and the cattle the Israelites
plundered. Only the human beings they struck down with the edge of the
15 sword until they had destroyed them—they left no breathing person. As
the LORD had charged Moses His servant, so Moses charged Joshua, who
16 neglected nothing of all that the LORD had charged Moses. And Joshua

---

Israelite warriors to get close enough to the chariots in order to maim the horses. Alternately, they might have hamstrung the horses after the victory in order to make sure they
would not be used again to draw chariots, a possibility encouraged by the previous verse
in which the enemy troops appear to be defeated before the hamstringing.

7. *came against them suddenly at the waters of Merom.* This is the same strategy of surprise
attack used against the southern alliance, with the enemy caught unawares at its own
encampment.

11. *living person . . . breathing person.* The two Hebrew terms, *nefesh* and *neshamah*, are
phonetically and semantically related. *Nefesh* is the life-breath and, by extension, the living
person; *neshamah* explicitly means breath or anything that breathes.

13. *the towns standing on their mounds.* The "mound," *tell,* is the heaped-up layers of earlier habitation on which old cities stand. (It has become a technical archaeological term.)
What the expression may mean in context is towns of notable antiquity, though that is not
entirely certain.

15. *As the LORD had charged Moses.* The genocidal imperative is spelled out several times
in Deuteronomy.

16. *the high country of Israel.* This rather odd phrase, matched in verse 21 with "the high
country of Judah," probably reflects an awareness of the division into a southern and northern kingdom after the death of Solomon.

took all this land, the high country and all the Negeb and all the land of
Goshen and the lowland and the Arabah and the high country of Israel
and its lowland, from Mount Halak going up to Seir as far as Baal-Gad in   17
the Lebanon valley beneath Mount Hermon. And their kings he captured
and struck them down and put them to death. Many days Joshua did battle   18
with these kings. There was no town that made peace with the Israelites   19
except the Hivvites dwelling in Gibeon. Everything they took in battle. For   20
it was from the LORD to harden their heart for battle against Israel, so that
they would be put under the ban with no mercy shown them in order that
they be destroyed, as the LORD had charged Moses. And Joshua came at   21
that time and cut down the Anakites from the high country, from Hebron,
from Debir, from Anab, and from the high country of Judah and from all
the high country of Israel, with their towns, Joshua put them under the ban.
No Anakites were left in the land of the Israelites. Only in Gaza, in Gath,   22
and in Ashdod did they remain. And Joshua took the whole land accord-   23
ing to all that the LORD had spoken to Moses. And Joshua gave it in estate
to Israel according to their divisions by their tribes. And the land was at
rest from war.

---

17. *Mount Halak.* Boling wittily and accurately observes that this could be translated as
Bald Mountain.

18. *Many days.* The Hebrew *yamim* is an elastic indicator of time, and so it could mean here
months or even years.

20. *For it was from the LORD to harden their heart for battle against Israel.* This is one of two
verbs used in the Exodus story for the hardening or toughening of the heart of Pharaoh.
There, the divinely instigated obduracy was in order to enable the display of God's overwhelming power. Here it is to provide grounds for wiping out the indigenous population.

21. *the Anakites.* Although in the present context this looks like a gentilic designation, in
other biblical texts the word refers to giants.

22. *Only in Gaza, in Gath, and in Ashdod did they remain.* These are three of the five
Philistine towns on the southern part of the Mediterranean coast. Goliath the Philistine
was, of course, a giant, though the Hebrew *'anaq* is not attached to him in the story in
1 Samuel 17. It is conceivable that the association of huge physical proportions with the
Anakites derives from a perception that the Philistines, of original Aegean stock, were
bigger than the indigenous population of Canaan though archaeological evidence suggests the Canaanites were also big. The Philistines invaded the coastal areas around
1200 B.C.E., but later writers (as in Genesis) imagined them as longtime residents of the
coastal strip.

₁ CHAPTER 12   And these are the kings of the land whom
the Israelites struck down and whose land they took hold of, across the
Jordan where the sun rises, from Wadi Arnon to Mount Hermon and all the
₂ Arabah to the east: Sihon king of the Amorites who dwelled in Heshbon,
who ruled from Aroer on the banks of Wadi Arnon and within the wadi,
₃ and half of Gilead as far as Wadi Jabbok, border of the Ammonites, and
the Arabah as far as Lake Chinneroth to the east and as far as the Arabah
Sea, the Salt Sea, to the east, by way of Beth-Jeshimoth, and to the south
₄ below the slopes of Pisgah. And the region of Og king of Bashan, from the
₅ remnant of the Rephaim, who dwelt in Ashtaroth and in Edrei, and ruled
over Mount Hermon and Salkah and all of the Bashan as far as the border
of the Geshurite and the Maacathite and half of Gilead, the border of Sihon
₆ king of the Amorites. Moses servant of the LORD and the Israelites struck
them down, and Moses servant of the LORD gave it as an inheritance to the
₇ Reubenites and to the Gadites and to the half-tribe of Manasseh. And these
are the kings of the land whom Joshua and the Israelites struck down on the
other side of the Jordan to the west, from Baal-Gad in the Lebanon valley
as far as Mount Halak, which goes up toward Seir. And Joshua gave it to the
₈ tribes of Israel as an inheritance according to their divisions. In the high
country and in the lowland and in the Arabah and on the slopes and in the
wilderness and in the Negeb of the Hittite, the Amorite, the Canaanite, the
Perizzite, the Hivvite, and the Jebusite:

CHAPTER 12   1. *And these are the kings of the land whom the Israelites struck down
. . . across the Jordan where the sun rises.* The second half of the Book of Joshua, which
begins in the next chapter, essentially abandons narrative to offer, after this catalogue
of conquests, a tabulation of the apportioning of the land according to tribal divisions.
Only in the three concluding chapters do we return to narrative. The first six verses of
this chapter report the victories of Moses over the sundry trans-Jordanian kings that are
narrated in Numbers. The remainder of the chapter gives us a list of Joshua's victories west
of the Jordan.

3. *Lake Chinneroth.* As before, this is a variant form of Lake Kinneret, or the Sea of
Galilee.

4. *the remnant of the Rephaim.* Some scholars think this term originally referred to
elite warriors. In biblical usage it can mean either "shades," which is scarcely a relevant
sense here, or "giants." In Deuteronomy 3:11, Og is reported to have possessed gigantic
proportions.

6. *Moses servant of the* LORD *gave it as an inheritance.* By the time this material was edited,
late in the seventh century B.C.E. or in the sixth century, the Israelites no longer had possession of this trans-Jordanian region. The list thus serves as a kind of ideal map of sovereignty
in times past.

the king of Jericho—one,   9
the king of Ai which is alongside Bethel—one,
the king of Jerusalem—one,   10
the king of Hebron—one,
the king of Jarmuth—one,   11
the king of Lachish—one,
the king of Eglon—one,   12
the king of Gezer—one,
the king of Debir—one,   13
the king of Geder—one,
the king of Hormah—one,   14
the king of Arad—one,
the king of Libnah—one,   15
the king of Adullam—one,
the king of Makkedah—one,   16
the king of Bethel—one,
the king of Tapuah—one,   17
the king of Hepher—one,
the king of Aphek—one,   18
the king of Sharon—one,
the king of Madon—one,   19
the king of Hazor—one,
the king of Shimron-Merom—one,   20
the king of Achshaph—one,
the king of Taanach—one,   21
the king of Megiddo—one,
the king of Kedesh—one,   22
the king of Jokneam in Carmel—one,
the king of Dor in Naphoth-Dor—one,   23
the king of Goiim in Gilgal—one,
the king of Tirzah—one,   24
all the kings were thirty-one.

---

9. *the king of Jericho—one.* This system of tallying is unusual. The evident aim is to arrive at a complete sum of all the conquests. Though, as we have seen, the historical reality of much of this account is in doubt, the numbering of thirty-one kings does accurately reflect a historical situation in which Canaan was splintered into a large number of city-kingdoms controlling quite small territories. Even if these rulers actually bore the title of king, they probably were closer to what today would be thought of as tribal warlords. This list obviously picks up names from the preceding narrative report, although it also includes several kings not mentioned earlier.

1 CHAPTER 13   And Joshua was old, advanced in years. And
the LORD said to him, "You are old, advanced in years, and very much of the
2 land remains to take hold of. This is the land remaining: all the provinces
3 of the Philistines and all of the Geshurites, from the Shihor, which faces
Egypt, to the region of Ekron to the north, it is reckoned Canaanite. The five
Philistine overlords, the Gazite, and the Ashdodite, the Ascolonite, the Git-
4 tite, and the Ekronite. And the Avvites on the south, all the Canaanite land
5 from Arah of the Sidonians to Aphek, which is on the Amorite border, and
the land of the Giblite, and all of Lebanon to the east, from Baal-Gad below
6 Mount Hermon to the approach to Hamath. All the inhabitants of the high
country from Lebanon to Misrephoth-Mayim, all the Sidonians, I Myself
will dispossess them before the Israelites, only to make it fall in estate to
7 Israel as I have charged you. And now, divide this land in estate among
8 the nine tribes and the half-tribe of Manasseh, with whom the Reubenites
and the Gadites took their estate that Moses gave them across the Jordan
9 to the east, as Moses servant of the LORD gave them, from Aroer, which

---

CHAPTER 13   1. *very much of the land remains to take hold of.* There is a tension
between the section that begins here and the previous account of Joshua's conquest. In
the preceding chapters, one gets the impression of a grand sweep of victories in which the
Israelite forces led by Joshua took town after town, virtually the whole land. But the audience of this narrative was well aware that there were substantial regions of the land that
for long periods were not controlled by the Israelites, and this awareness is registered here.

2. *all the provinces of the Philistines.* In fact, the Philistines did not establish their pentapolis
along the Mediterranean shore, having arrived perhaps from the Aegean, until a generation
or more after the putative time of Joshua.

3. *overlords.* The Hebrew *seren* is in all likelihood a loanword from the Philistine language.
Some scholars think it is cognate with the Greek *tyrranos.*
      the Avvites. These are an indigenous Canaanite people bordering on Philistine territory
who remained unconquered by the Philistines.

4. *from Arah.* The received text reads "and from Arah." Arah is not a known place-name,
and some emend it to Acco, which was a Sidonian town. Strenuous scholarly efforts have
been made, and will not be recapitulated here, to identify all the towns and regions. Some
names in the list nevertheless defy identification, and there are elements in the geographical indications that seem scrambled.

7. *the nine tribes and the half-tribe of Manasseh.* These are the tribes that settled west of the
Jordan, the other two and a half tribes remaining on the east side of the Jordan.

8. *with whom the Reubenites and the Gadites took their estate.* That is, these two tribes
plus the other half of the tribe of Manasseh. The more likely historical scenario is not that
Israelites settled east of the Jordan in the original conquest but that they migrated there by
stages later in search of land.

is on the banks of Wadi Arnon, and the town that is in the wadi, and the
plain from Medeba to Dibon, and all the towns of Sihon king of the Amori- 10
tes, who reigned in Heshbon, to the border of the Ammonites, and Gilead 11
and the territory of the Geshurites and the Maacathites, and all of Mount
Hermon and all Bashan to Saleah, and all the kingdoms of Og in Bashan, 12
who reigned in Ashtaroth and in Edrei—he remained from the remnant
of the Rephaim, and Moses struck them down and dispossessed them. But 13
the Israelites did not dispossess the Geshurites and the Maacathites, and
Geshur and Maacath have dwelled in the midst of Israel to this day. Only 14
to the tribe of Levi he gave no estate. The fire offerings of the LORD God
of Israel, they are its estate, as He had spoken to it. And Moses gave to the 15
tribe of the Reubenites according to its clans, and it became their territory 16
from Aroer, which is on the banks of Wadi Arnon, and the town that is in
the wadi and the whole plain to Medeba. Heshbon and all its towns that are 17
on the plain, Dibon and Bamoth-Baal and Beth-Baal-Meon, and Jaza and 18
Kedemoth and Mephaath, and Kiriathaim and Sibma and Zereth-Shahar 19
on the Mountain of the Valley, and Beth-Peor and the slopes of Pisgah 20
and Beth-Jeshimoth, and all the towns of the plain and all the kingdom of 21
Sihon king of the Amorites, who reigned in Heshbon, whom Moses struck
down—and the princes of Midian, Evi and Rekem and Zur and Hur and
Reba, princes of Sihon who dwelled in the land. And Balaam son of Beor, 22
the soothsayer, the Israelites killed by the sword with the rest of their slain.
And the border of the Reubenites was the Jordan. This was the estate of 23

---

10. *border.* The Hebrew *gevul* sometimes means "border" and sometimes "territory" or "region," the meaning shifting in this chapter.

12. *he remained from the remnant of the Rephaim.* See the comment on 12:4.

13. *Maacath.* This is either a variant, archaic form of Maachah or a scribal error.
    dwelled in the midst of Israel. As elsewhere, this phrase does not mean that they were geographically integrated with Israel but that they had peaceful relations with the Israelites.

14. *the fire offerings of the LORD God of Israel, they are its estate.* A substantial part of these sacrifices was not burned and thus was available to the Levites as food. This verse, reiterated at the end of the chapter, probably reflects a Deuteronomistic background in which the cult has been centralized in Jerusalem.

22. *Balaam son of Beor.* The killing off of Balaam, who in Numbers 22–24 delivered, against his own intention, a grand prophecy of blessing about Israel, may reflect a nationalist nervousness over the prominence of this Aramean soothsayer. Lest one think he lived happily ever after once he had returned to his native land, here he is included among the victims of the conquest.

24 the Reubenites by their clans, the towns and their hamlets. And Moses
25 had given it to the tribe of Gad and to the Gadites by their clans, and it
became their territory: Jazer and all the towns of Gilead and half of the land
26 of the Ammonites as far as Aroer, which is just before Rabbah, and from
Heshbon as far as Ramoth-Mizpeh, and Betonim, and from Mahanaim to
27 the border of Lidber, and in the Valley, Beth-Haran and Beth-Nimrah and
Succoth and Zaphon, the rest of the kingdoms of Sihon king of Heshbon,
from the Jordan and its border to the edge of the Sea of Chinnereth across
28 the Jordan to the east. This is the estate of the Gadites according to their
29 clans, the towns and their hamlets. And Moses gave it to the half-tribe
of Manasseh and it went to the half-tribe of the Manassites according to
30 their clans, and their territory was from Mahanaim, all of Bashan, all the
kingdom of Og king of Bashan, and all of Havvoth-Jair, which is in Bashan,
31 sixty towns, and half of Gilead and Ashtaroth and Edrei, the royal towns
of Og in Bashan, to the sons of Machir son of Manasseh, to half of the sons
32 of Machir according to their clans. These were what Moses apportioned in
33 estate in the plains of Moab across the Jordan to the east of Jericho. But to
the tribe of Levi Moses gave no estate—the LORD God of Israel, He is their
estate, as He had spoken to them."

1 CHAPTER 14   And these are what the Israelites took in estate
in the land of Canaan, which Eleazar the priest and Joshua son of Nun
2 and the patriarchal heads of the Israelite tribes gave them in estate, in the
portion of their estate, as the LORD had charged through Moses for the
3 nine and a half tribes. For Moses had given an estate to the two and a half
tribes across the Jordan, but to the Levites he gave no estate in their midst.
4 For the sons of Joseph were two tribes, Ephraim and Manasseh. And they
gave no share in the land to the Levites except for towns to dwell in and
5 their pastures for their livestock and their possessions. As the LORD had
6 charged Moses, so did the Israelites do, and they divided up the land. And
the Judahites came forward to Joshua in Gilgal, and Caleb son of Jephun-

---

CHAPTER 14   1. *in the land of Canaan.* As the next two verses make clear, this
phrase indicates the land west of the Jordan.

4. *except for towns to dwell in.* These towns were a practical concession to the Levites from
the other tribes and not inalienable territory.

6. *And the Judahites came forward.* Although what is in question is the inheritance of
Caleb, head of one of the clans of Judah, it is also regarded as a tribal issue because he is
part of the tribe.

neh the Kenizzite said to him, "You yourself know the word that the LORD spoke to Moses man of God about me and about you in Kadesh-Barnea. I 7 was forty years old when Moses servant of the LORD sent me from Kadesh-Barnea to spy out the land, and I brought him back word just as I thought. But my brothers who came up with me made the people's heart faint, yet 8 I followed after the LORD my God. And Moses vowed on that day, saying, 9 'The land on which your foot trod shall surely be yours in estate, and your sons', for all time, for you have followed after the LORD my God.' And now, 10 look, the LORD has kept me alive, as He had spoken, forty-five years since the LORD spoke this word to Moses while Israel went in the wilderness. And now, look, I am eighty-five years old. I am still today as strong as the 11 day Moses sent me. As my vigor then is my vigor now, for battle and for command. And now, give me this mountain, as the LORD spoke on that 12 day, for you yourself heard on that day that there were giants there and great fortified towns. Perhaps the LORD will be with me and I shall dispossess them as the LORD has spoken." And Joshua blessed him and gave 13 Hebron to Caleb son of Jephunneh in estate. Therefore has Hebron been 14 in estate to Caleb son of Jephunneh the Kenizzite to this day because he

---

You yourself know. Caleb uses the emphatic form in which the personal pronoun is added before the conjugated verb, because Joshua was there with him, joining him in the positive minority report against the fearful assessment of the other ten spies.

7. *brought him back word.* This phrase is used in the spy narrative in Numbers 13:26.
 just as I thought. That is, honestly. The literal sense is "as it was with my heart."

8. *made the people's heart faint.* The literal sense of the Hebrew is "made the people's heart melt," but in English that phrase unfortunately suggests gushing sentiment. The same idiom is used in the recapitulation of the story of the spies in Deuteronomy 1:28.
 I followed after the LORD my God. The literal sense of the idiom is "I filled after." The clear meaning is to carry out implicitly the will or command of someone. The same expression is used in the original story of the spies in Numbers 14:24.

10. *I am eighty-five years old.* The Talmudic sages, calculating that the incident of the spies took place two years into the forty years of Wilderness wandering, conclude from this that the conquest of the land took seven years.

11. *As my vigor then is my vigor now, for battle and for command.* The region around Hebron still requires conquering, as Caleb's words in verse 12 show. The idiom rendered as "command" is literally "to go out and to come back," and it means to lead troops in battle.

12. *you yourself heard on that day that there were giants there.* The narrative context makes clear that the Hebrew *'anaqim* is not in this instance a gentilic ("Anakites") but means "giants," the adversaries of daunting proportions before whom the ten fearful spies felt themselves to be like grasshoppers.

14. *Therefore.* As often elsewhere the Hebrew *'al-ken* introduces an etiological explanation.

15 followed after the LORD God of Israel. And the name of Hebron formerly was Kiriath-Arba—he was the biggest person among the giants. And the land was at rest from war.

1 **CHAPTER 15**   And the portion for the Judahites according to their clans was southward to the border of Edom, the Wilderness of Zin on 2 the far south. And their southern boundary was from the edge of the Salt 3 Sea, from the tongue that turns southward. And it extended to the south, to the ascent of Akrabbim, and passed on to Zin and went up from the south to Kadesh-Barnea, and passed on to Hezron and went up to Addar 4 and swung round to Karka. And it passed on to Azmon and extended to the Wadi of Egypt, and the far reaches of the border came to the sea. This 5 shall be for you the southern boundary. And the boundary to the east is the Salt Sea south of the Jordan, and the boundary on the northern side 6 from the tongue of the Sea to the mouth of the Jordan. And the boundary went up to Beth-Hoglah and passed on north of Beth-Arabah, and the 7 boundary went up to the Stone of Bohan son of Reuben. And the boundary went up to Debir from the Valley of Achor and turned north to Gilgal, which is opposite the Ascent of Adummim, which is south of the wadi, and the boundary passed on to the waters of Ein-Shemesh, and its far reaches 8 were to Ein-Rogel. And the boundary went up to the Vale of Ben-Hinnom to the flank of the Jebusite on the south, which is Jerusalem, and it went up to the mountaintop which overlooks the Vale of Ben-Hinnom to the

---

15. *Kiriath-Arba.* The Hebrew name means "city of four"—perhaps, as many scholars have inferred, because it was divided into four neighborhoods. But here "Arba" is construed as a man's name—the largest of the indigenous giants.

CHAPTER 15   1. *the portion.* The Hebrew *goral* means "lot"—evidently, an aleatory device used to portion out the various territories—and through metonymy, it also means what is indicated by the lot, the portion or share.
    southward to the border of Edom. What begins here and runs through the chapter is an elaborate geographical tracing of Judah's tribal territory. The general reader can scarcely be expected to follow all these details, and any reader would need a complicated map to do it. What is noteworthy is the inordinate amount of space devoted to Judah's possessions, which appear to cover most of central and southern Israel from the Jordan to the Mediterranean. As many scholars have inferred, this account probably reflects a later period—seventh century?—when a centralized monarchy coming from the tribe of Judah governed the entire southern kingdom, with Jerusalem as its capital. The towns in this list are so numerous that many of them were probably not much bigger than substantial villages. Some of the names are well-known, can be confidently located, and are sites of important biblical events. Others remain elusive.

west, which is at the end of the Valley of Rephaim to the north. And the ₉
border swung round from the mountaintop to the spring of the waters of
Nephtoah and extended to the towns of the high country of Ephron, and
the boundary swung round to Baalah, which is Kiriath-Jearim. And the ₁₀
boundary turned from Baalah westward to Mount Seir and passed on
northward to the flank of Mount Jearim, which is Kesalon, and went down
to Beth-Shemesh and passed on to Timnah. And the boundary extended ₁₁
to the flank of Ekron to the north, and the boundary swung round to
Shikkron and passed on to Mount Baalah and extended to Jabneel, and
the far reaches of the boundary were to the sea. And the western bound- ₁₂
ary—the Great Sea. And this boundary is the boundary of the Judahites
all around, according to their clans. And Caleb the son of Jephunneh ₁₃
was given a share in the midst of the Judahites at the behest of the LORD
through Joshua—Kiriath-Arba, father of the giant, which is Hebron. And ₁₄
Caleb dispossessed from there the three sons of the giant, Sheshai and
Ahiman and Talmai, offspring of the giant. And he went up from there ₁₅
to the inhabitants of Debir, and the name of Debir formerly was Kiriath-
Sepher. And Caleb said, "Whoever strikes Kiriath-Sepher and takes it, to ₁₆
him I shall give Achsah my daughter as wife." And Othniel son of Kenaz, ₁₇
Caleb's brother, took it, and he gave him Achsah his daughter as wife. And ₁₈
it happened when she came, that she enticed him to ask a field of her father,
and she alighted from the donkey, and Caleb said to her, "What troubles
you?" And she said, "Give me a present, for you have given me desert- ₁₉
land, and you should give me springs of water." And he gave her the upper
springs and the lower springs. This is the estate of the tribe of the Judahites ₂₀
according to their clans. And the towns at the edge of the Judahites by the ₂₁

---

9. *Baalah, which is Kiriath-Jearim.* This, like at least one other item on the list, cites first an
old pagan name and then its replacement (which means "Forest City").

13. *Caleb.* He was the other one of the twelve spies, besides Joshua, who brought back an
encouraging report about the land, and Hebron with the surrounding territory was to be
his reward.

17. *Othniel.* He is to become the first of the Judges.

18. *she enticed him to ask a field of her father.* The Septuagint reads "he enticed her," which
makes the sequence of events easier to follow, but perhaps one should hew to the philological principle of adopting the more difficult reading. In that case, Achsah enticed her
husband but then did the asking herself, perhaps because Othniel's request was rebuffed.

19. *present.* More literally, "blessing."
　　desert-land. In the Hebrew "Negeb-land," the Negeb serving as the model for arid country. The term is associated by etymology with dryness.

22 boundary of Edom to the south were Kabzeel and Eder and Yagur. And
23 Kinah and Dimonah and Adadah. And Kedesh and Hazor and Ithnan.
24,25 Ziph and Telem and Bealoth. And Hazor-Hadattah and Kerioth-Hezron,
26,27 which is Hazor. Amam and Shema and Moladah. And Hazar-Gaddah and
28 Heshmon and Beth-Pelet. And Hazar-Shual and Beersheba and Bezio-
29,30,31 thiah. Baalah and Iim and Ezem. And Eltolad and Kesil and Hormah. And
32 Ziklag and Madmenah and Sansanah. And Lebaoth and Shilhin and Ain
    and Rimmon. All the towns with their pasturelands came to twenty-nine.
33,34 In the lowland: Eshtaol and Zorah and Ashnah. And Zanoah and Ein-
35 Gannim, Tapuah and Einan. Jarmuth and Adullam, Socoh and Azekah.
36 And Shaaraim and Aditaim and Gederah and Gederothaim—fourteen
37 towns with their pastureland. Zenan and Hadashah and Migdal-Gad.
38,39 And Dilan and Mizpeh and Joktheel. Lachish and Bozkath and Eglon.
40,41 And Cabbon and Lahmas and Kithlish. And Gederoth, Beth-Dagon, and
42 Naamah and Makkedah—sixteen towns with their pasturelands. Libnah
43,44 and Ether and Ashan. And Iphtah and Ashmah and Nezib. And Keilah
45 and Achzib and Mareshah—nine towns with their pasturelands. Ekron
46 with its hamlets and its pasturelands. From Ekron westward, all that is
47 by Ashdod, with their pasturelands. Ashdod, its hamlets and its pasture-
    lands, Gaza, its hamlets and its pasturelands, to the Wadi of Egypt, and
48 the Great Sea is the boundary. And in the high country, Shamir and Jattir
49,50 and Socoh. And Dannah and Kiriath-Sannah, which is Debir. And Anab
51 and Eshtamoa and Anim. And Goshen and Holon and Giloh—eleven
52,53 towns with their pasturelands. Arab and Dumah and Eshan. And Janim
54 and Beth-Tapuah and Aphekah. And Humtah and Kiriath-Arba, which
55 is Hebron, and Zior—nine towns with their pasturelands. Maon, Carmel,
56,57 Ziph, and Juttah. And Jezreel and Jokneam and Zanoah. Kain, Gibeah,
58 and Timnah—ten towns with their pasturelands. Halhul, Beth-Zur and
59 Gedor. And Maaroth and Beth-Anot and Eltekon—six towns with their
60 pasturelands. Kiriath-Baal, which is Kiriath-Jearim, and Rabbah—two
61 towns with their pasturelands. In the wilderness, Beth-Arabah, Middin,
62 and Secacah. And Nishban and Salt Town and Ein-Gedi—six towns with
63 their pasturelands. But the Jebusites, the inhabitants of Jerusalem, the

---

46. *Ekron . . . Ashdod.* These towns, like Gaza in the next verse, are Philistine cities. They
could scarcely have been allotted to Judah in the thirteenth century, though by the time
this list was compiled the Philistines had long been vanquished.

63. *But the Jebusites, the inhabitants of Jerusalem, the Judahites were not able to dispossess.*
The writer is obliged to make this notation because it was well-known that Jerusalem

Judahites were not able to dispossess, and the Jebusites have dwelled alongside the Judahites to this day.

CHAPTER 16   And the portion for the sons of Joseph came 1 out—from the Jordan at Jericho to the waters of Jericho to the east of the wilderness that goes up from Jericho through the high country of Beth-el. And 2 it went out to Beth-el, Luz, and passed on to the boundary of the Ataroth Archite. And it went down westward to the boundary of the Japhletite as far 3 as the boundary of lower Beth-Horon and as far as Gezer, and its far reaches were to the Sea. And the sons of Joseph, Manasseh and Ephraim, took their 4 estates. And the boundary of the Ephraimites according to their clans—the 5 boundary of their estate on the east was Ataroth Addar as far as Upper Beth-Horon. And the boundary went out to the Sea, to Michmethath on the 6 north, and the boundary swung round to the east of Taanath-Shiloh, and passed through it to the east of Janoah. And it went down from Janoah to 7 Ataroth and to Naarath and touched on Jericho and came out at the Jordan. From Tapuah the boundary goes westward to Wadi Kanah, and its far 8 reaches are to the Sea. This is the estate of the Ephraimite tribe according to its clans. And the towns set apart for the Ephraimites within the estate of the 9 Manassite—all the towns and their pasturelands. And they did not dispos- 10

---

remained in Jebusite hands until David conquered it, more than two centuries after the time of Joshua.

and the Jebusites have dwelled alongside the Judahites to this day. This second clause is somewhat misleading after the first clause. It could not mean, as it may appear, that the Jebusites were never conquered but rather that after having been conquered by David, many of them remained as landholding residents of the city. See the account of David's purchase of the threshing floor of Araunah the Jebusite for use as a cultic site in 2 Samuel 24:18–25)—he buys it and does not take it by right of conquest.

CHAPTER 16   1. *And the portion for the sons of Joseph came out.* As above, the Hebrew *goral*, "portion," refers both to the aleatory device used to indicate the portion of territory and to the result of using the device—that is, the portion itself. In this instance, the verb "came out" refers to the toss of the oracular stone rather than to the boundary.

2. *Beth-el, Luz.* The received text brackets these two names together, but in Genesis 28:19 we are informed that Luz was the older name that was replaced by Beth-el.

9. *the towns set apart for the Ephraimites within the estate of the Manassite.* This indication suggests that not all the tribal boundaries were hard and fast, and that there were sometimes enclaves of one tribe within the territory of another tribe.

sess the Canaanites dwelling in Gezer, and the Canaanites have dwelled in the midst of Ephraim to this day, and they became forced laborers.

1 CHAPTER 17   And the portion for the tribe of Manasseh, for he was Joseph's firstborn, to Machir Manasseh's firstborn, father of
2 Gilead, for he was a man of war—Gilead and Bashan were his. And to the remaining sons of Manasseh according to their clans, to the sons of Abiezer and to the sons of Helek and to the sons of Asriel and to the sons of Shechem and to the sons of Hepher and to the sons of Shemida— these are the male offspring of Manasseh son of Joseph according to their
3 clans. And Zelophehad son of Hepher son of Gilead son of Machir son of Manesseh did not have sons but daughters, and these are the names of
4 his daughters: Mahlah and Noa, Hoglah, Milkah, and Tirzah. And they approached Eleazar the priest and Joshua son of Nun and the chieftains, saying, "The LORD charged Moses to give us an estate in the midst of our kinsmen." And he gave them at the LORD's behest an estate in the midst of
5 their father's kinsmen. And the shares of Manasseh fell out as ten, besides
6 the land of Gilead and Bashan that is across the Jordan. For the daugh- ters of Manasseh took an estate in the midst of his sons, and the land of
7 Gilead went to the remaining sons of Manasseh. And the boundary of Manasseh was from Asher to Michmethath, which is by Shechem, and the
8 boundary went southward to the inhabitants of Ein-Tapuah. The land of Tapuah was Manasseh's, but Tapuah to the boundary of Manasseh was the

---

10. *they became forced laborers.* In keeping with the historiographical agenda of the writers, whatever Canaanite population that is not destroyed or driven out becomes subjugated to the Israelites. It is questionable whether this corresponds to historical reality.

CHAPTER 17   1. *for he was Joseph's firstborn.* Hence the clan of Machir is alotted the choice region of Gilead and Bashan. But the further notation about Machir as "a man of war" suggests that it was the military prowess of the clan that enabled it to take hold of this territory.

3. *And Zelophehad . . . did not have sons but daughters.* This report of the inheritance of the daughters of Zelophehad picks up the story that appears in Numbers 27:1–11, echoing some of its language.

4. *kinsmen.* The Hebrew *aḥim* here has to have its extended sense and cannot mean "broth- ers" because these five women have no brothers.

5. *the shares . . . fell out.* The verb here reflects the use of a lottery or some kind of aleatory device, but the term for "shares," *ḥavalim*, also means "ropes" and has the sense of share or portion of land because ropes were used to measure out the land.

Ephraimites'. And the boundary went down to Wadi Kanah south of the   9
wadi. These towns were Ephraim's in the midst of the towns of Manasseh,
and the boundary of Manasseh was north of the wadi, and its far reaches
were to the Sea, south of Ephraim and north of Manasseh, and the Sea was   10
its boundary, and they touched Asher from the north and Issachar from
the east. And within Issachar and Asher, Manasseh had Beth-She'an and   11
its hamlets and Ibleam and its hamlets and the inhabitants of Dor and its
hamlets and the inhabitants of Taanach and its hamlets and the inhabitants of Megiddo and its hamlets—the three regions. And the Manas-   12
sites were unable to take hold of these towns, and the Canaanites went on
dwelling in this land. And it happened when the Israelites grew strong,   13
that they subjected the Canaanites to forced labor, but they did not absolutely dispossess them. And the sons of Joseph spoke to Joshua, saying,   14
"Why did you give me in estate one portion and one share when I am a
numerous people, and until now the LORD has blessed me?" And Joshua   15
said to them, "If you are a numerous people, go up to the forest and clear
it for yourself there in the land of the Perizzite and the Rephaim, for the
high country of Ephraim is too cramped for you." And the sons of Joseph   16
said, "The high country is not enough for us, and there are iron chariots
among all the Canaanites who dwell in the valley land, those in Beth-She'an

---

10. *south of Ephraim*. This phrase is confusing because the text is describing the boundaries of Ephraim.

12. *take hold of these towns*. The Hebrew verb means "dispossess." Either a logical object
such as "inhabitants" has dropped out of the text, or the verb is used here in the sense it has
in a different conjugation (*yarash* instead of *horish*), "to take hold of."

14. *Why did you give me*. It is fairly common in biblical dialogue assigned to collective
speakers to use the first-person singular.
     and until now. The Hebrew wording is obscure and the text may be corrupt.

15. *go up to the forest and clear it*. There is archaeological evidence that a good deal of
deforestation took place in this period in the high country, with the trees replaced by ter-
raced agriculture.
     the land of the Perizzite and the Rephaim. This geographical designation is obscure and
may reflect a scribal error.

16. *there are iron chariots among all the Canaanites*. These armored vehicles, readily
deployed in the valleys but not in mountainous regions, give a military advantage to the
Canaanites over the Israelites, who, by and large, conducted warfare in guerilla style. (The
characterization of "iron," however, may be an exaggeration because the archaeological
evidence indicates that Canaanite chariots were primarily built of wood.) Thus the members of the Joseph tribes fear that they will not be able to overcome the Canaanites in the
flatlands.

17 and its hamlets and those in the Valley of Jezreel." And Joshua said to the
house of Joseph, to Ephraim and to Manasseh, saying, "You are a numerous
18 people and you have great power. You shall not have just one portion. But
the high country shall be yours, for it is forest and you shall clear it, and its
far reaches will be yours, for you shall dispossess the Canaanites, though
they have iron chariots and though they are strong."

1 CHAPTER 18   And the whole community of Israelites assembled at Shiloh and they set up the Tent of Meeting there, and the land was
2 conquered before them. And there remained seven tribes among the Isra-
3 elites that had not taken the share of their estate. And Joshua said to the
Israelites, "How long will you be idle about coming to take hold of the land
4 that the LORD God of your fathers has given to you? Set out for yourselves
three men to a tribe, that I may send them and they may rise up and go
about the land and write it out according to their estate, and come to me.
5 And they shall share it out in seven parts. Judah will stay by its territory in
6 the south, and the house of Joseph will stay by its territory in the north. As
for you, you shall write out the land in seven parts and bring them back to
7 me here, and I shall cast a lot for you here before the LORD our God. But

---

17. *You are a numerous people and you have great power.* Joshua seizes on the very phrase
the Josephites have used to claim more territory and employs it in a double sense: as a
numerous people, you deserve more than a single portion, and as a numerous people, you
have the power to conquer the Canaanites.

CHAPTER 18   1. *And the whole community of Israelites assembled at Shiloh.* This
marks a shift from the role of the encampment at Gilgal as the national assembly place.
Shiloh, as its representation in the early chapters of 1 Samuel indicates, was a central sanctuary, until its destruction by the Philistines sometime in the eleventh century B.C.E. Placing
the Tent of Meeting there would have confirmed its centrality. In subsequent narratives, the
Tent of Meeting is not mentioned but rather the Ark of the Covenant, which would have been
within the Tent of Meeting.

2. *And there remained seven tribes.* If one subtracts Judah, Reuben, Ephraim, Manasseh,
and Levi, all of which have already been accounted for, seven tribes are left to be given
their tribal territories.

6. *write out the land.* Still more literally, this would be "write the land." The obvious sense is
to draw up a set of notations of the boundaries of the tribal territories.
  I shall cast a lot for you here before the LORD. The drawing up of tribal boundaries by
the representatives of the seven tribes is then to be confirmed by divine lot. As Shmuel
Ahituv has shown, the use of such a lottery for the division of land was widespread in the
ancient Near East.

the Levites have no share in your midst, for the LORD's priesthood is their estate." And Gad and Reuben and the half-tribes of Manasseh had taken their estate across the Jordan to the east, which Moses servant of the LORD had given them. And the men rose up and went off, and Joshua charged 8 those who went to write out the land, saying, "Up, go about in the land and write it out and come back to me, and here I shall cast the lot for you before the LORD in Shiloh. And the men went off and passed through the land 9 and wrote it out by towns into seven parts in a scroll, and they came back to Joshua, to the camp at Shiloh. And Joshua cast the lot for them in Shiloh 10 before the LORD, and Joshua shared out the land to the Israelites according to their portions. And the lot of the tribe of the Benjaminites fell out, and 11 the territory by their lot came out between the Judahites and the Josephites. And they had the boundary on the northern edge from the Jordan, and the 12 boundary went up to the flank of Jericho on the north and went up to the high country westward, and its far reaches were the Wilderness of Beth-Aven. And the boundary passed on from there to the flank of Luz, which 13 is Bethel, to the south, and the boundary went down to Atroth Addar in the high country that is south of Lower Beth-Horon. And the boundary 14 swung round south toward the sea of the high country which is opposite Beth-Horon to the south, and its far reaches were at Kiriath-Baal, which is Kiriath-Jearim, town of the Judahites. This was the western edge. And 15 the southern edge was from the border of Kiriath-Jearim, and the boundary went out westward, and went out to the spring of the waters of Naphtoah. And the boundary went down to the edge of the high country which 16 is opposite the Vale of Ben-Hinnom, which is in the Valley of Rephaim to the north, and it went down the Vale of Hinnom to the flank of the Jebusites on the south and down to Ein-Rogel. And it swung round from 17 the north and went out to Ein-Shemesh and went out to Geliloth, which is over against the Ascent of Adummim, and it went down to the Stone of Bohan son of Reuben. And it passed on northward to the flank opposite 18 the Arabah and went down to the Arabah. And the boundary passed on 19

---

10. *cast the lot.* The Hebrew text here uses a different verb from the one in verse 6, but both mean to cast or fling, suggesting that the mechanism for the lot involved dicelike objects.

11. *fell out.* Literally, "went up."

16. *Vale of Ben-Hinnom . . . the Valley of Rephaim.* The Hebrew uses two different words for "valley," *gei'* and *'emeq*. It is possible that the former designates a smaller topographical entity. Both valleys are within the perimeters of modern-day Jerusalem, though they would have been outside the city to the west in ancient times.

northward to the flank of Beth-Hoglah to the edge of the Jordan, and the
far reaches of the boundary northward were at the tongue of the Salt Sea at
20 the southern end of the Jordan. This was the southern boundary. And the
Jordan marked its boundary at the eastern edge. This was the estate of the
21 Benjaminites by its boundaries all around, according to their clans. And
the towns that were the Benjaminite tribe's were Jericho and Beth-Hoglah
22,23 and Emek-Keziz, and Beth-Arabah and Zemaraim and Bethel, and Avvim
24 and Parah and Ophrah, and Chephar-Ammonah and Ophni and Geba—
25,26 twelve towns and their pasturelands. Gibeon and Ramah and Beeroth, and
27 Mizpeh and Chephirah and Mozah, and Rekem and Irpeel and Taralah,
28 and Zela-Eleph, and the Jebusite, which is Jerusalem, Gibeath, Kiriath-
Jearim. Fourteen towns and their pasturelands—this was the estate of the
Benjaminites according to their clans.

1 CHAPTER 19   And the second lot fell out for Simeon, for the
tribe of the Simeonites according to their clans, and their estate was within
2 the estate of the Judahites. And they had in their estate Beersheba and
3,4 Sheba and Moladah, and Hazar-Shual and Belah and Ezem, and Eltolad and
5 Bethul and Hormah, and Ziklag and Beth-Marcaboth and Hazar-Susah,
6 and Beth-Lebaoth and Sharuhen—thirteen towns and their pasturelands.
7,8 Ayin, Rimmon, Ether and Ashan—four towns and their pasturelands, and
all the pasturelands that are around these towns as far as Baalath-Beer,
Ramath-Negeb—this is the estate of the tribe of the Simeonites according

---

28. *Jerusalem*. It is a little surprising that Jerusalem, conquered from the Jebusites by David,
who was a Judahite, is here assigned to the tribe of Benjamin. It has been suggested that
this apportionment reflects a later period, when the unity of Benjamin and Judah, the two
southern tribes, was firmly established and the old rivalry between the two, registered in
the Book of Samuel, had long since vanished.

Kiriath-Jearim. The Masoretic Text reads *qiryat 'arim*, "Kiriath towns" (or "city of
towns"). This translation adopts a proposal, in part based on the Septuagint, that a haplography occurred, with the original text reading *qiryat ye'arim 'arim*, "Kiriath-Jearim,
[fourteen] towns."

CHAPTER 19   1. *their estate was within the estate of the Judahites*. Unlike the other
tribes, Simeon did not have a territory with clear-cut boundaries but rather enclaves within
the territory of Judah. This situation is reflected in the curse Jacob pronounces on Simeon
and Levi: "I will divide them in Jacob, / disperse them in Israel" (Genesis 49:7). (Levi's dispersal was manifested in its having no tribal territory, only levitical towns.) The anomaly
of the portion assigned to Simeon is explained in verse 9.

to their clans. The estate of the Simeonites was from the territory of the   9
Judahites, for the share of the Judahites was too large for them, and the
Simeonites took an estate within their estate. And the third lot fell out for   10
the Zebulunites according to their clans, and the boundary of their estate
was as far as Sarid. And their boundary went up westward to Maralah and   11
touched Dabbesheth and touched the wadi which is opposite Jokneam.
And it turned back from Sarid eastward where the sun rises to the bound-   12
ary of Cisloth-Tabor, and it went out to Dabereth and went up to Japhia.
And from there it passed on eastward, toward the sunrise, to Gath-Hepher,   13
Ittah, Kazin, and it went out and swung round to Neah. And the bound-   14
ary on the north turned round to Hannathon, and its far reaches were the
Vale of Iphtah-El, and Kattath and Nahalal and Shimron and Idalah and   15
Bethlehem—twelve towns and their pasturelands. This is the estate of the   16
Zebulunites according to their clans, these towns and their pasturelands.
The fourth lot fell out for Issachar, for the Issacharites according to their   17
clans. And their boundary was to Jezreel and Chesulloth and Shunem, and   18,19
Hapharaim and Shion and Anaharath, and Rabbith and Kishon and Ebez,   20
and Remeth and Ein-Gannim and Ein-Haddah and Beth-Pazzez. And the   21,22
boundary touched Tabor and Shahazimah and Beth-Shemesh, and the far
reaches of their boundary were at the Jordan—sixteen towns and their
pasturelands. This is the estate of the Issacharites according to their clans,   23
and the towns and their enclosures. And the fifth lot fell out to the tribe of   24
the Asherites according to their clans. And their boundary was Helkath   25
and Hali and Beten and Akshaph, and Alammelech and Amad and Mishal.   26
And it touched Carmel on the west and Shihor-Libnath. And it turned back   27
to Beth-Dagon where the sun rises and touched Zebulun and the Vale of
Iphtah-El on the north, Beth-Emek and Neiel, and the boundary came out
to Cabul on the north, and Ebron and Rehob and Hammon and Kanah, as   28
far as Greater Sidon. And the boundary turned back to Ramah and as far   29
as the fortress city of Tyre, and its far reaches, and the boundary turned
back to Hosah, and its far reaches were the Sea, Mehebel, to Achzib, and   30
Ummah and Aphek and Rehob—twenty-two towns and their pasturelands.

---

27. *the Vale of Iphtah-El.* The Masoretic Text here reads "the sons of Iphtah-El," a noun that doesn't make sense as the object of the verb "touched." This translation reflects the reading of the Septuagint.

28. *as far as Greater Sidon.* The territory of Asher could not have included Sidon, a Phoenician city, but perhaps the qualifier "greater" is meant to suggest something like the far southern reach of the region controlled by Sidon.

31 This is the estate of the tribe of Asherites according to their clans—these
32 towns and their pasturelands. For the Naphtalites the sixth lot came out,
33 for the Naphtalites according to their clans. And their boundary was from
Heleph, from Elon-in-Zaananim and Adami-Nekeb and Jabneel as far as
34 Kum, and its far reaches were at the Jordan. And the boundary turned back
westward to Aznoth-Tabor and went from there to Hukok and touched
Zebulun from the south and touched Asher from the west and Judah at
35 the Jordan where the sun rises. And the fortress towns were Ziddim, Zer,
36 Hamath, Rakkath, and Chinnereth, and Adamah and Ramah and Hazor,
37,38 and Kedesh and Edrei and Ein-Hazor, and Iron and Migdal-El, Horam,
Beth-Anath and Beth-Shemesh—nineteen towns and their pasturelands.
39 This is the estate of the tribe of the Naphtalites according to their clans,
40 the towns and their pasturelands. For the tribe of the Danites according to
41 their clans the seventh lot came out. And the territory of their estate was
42 Zorah and Eshtaol and Ir-Shemesh, and Shaalbim and Ajalon and Ithlah,
43,44 and Elon and Timnathah and Ekron, and Eltekeh and Gibthon and Baal-
45,46 ath, and Jehud and Benei Brak and Gath-Rimmon, and the Jarkon Waters
47 and Rakkon by the boundary over against Joppa. And the territory of the
Danites fell from their hands. And the Danites went up and did battle with
Leshem and took it. And they struck it with the edge of the sword and took
hold of it and dwelled in it. And they called Leshem Dan, like the name of
48 Dan their forefather. This is the estate of the tribe of the Danites according
to their clans—these towns and their pasturelands.

49 And they finished taking possession of the land according to its boundaries, and the Israelites gave Joshua son of Nun an estate in their midst.

---

47. *And the territory of the Danites fell from their hands.* More literally: "went out from
them." Their original territory was in the southwestern region bordering on Philistine
country—a location reflected in the stories about Samson, who was a Danite. At some
relatively early point, perhaps as early as the twelfth century B.C.E., the Danites were forced
out of their original tribal territory and migrated to the far north of the country, where
they conquered a new area for settlement. This northern location is reflected in the story
of Micah's idol in Judges 18. The reading of this verse in the Septuagint shows a report
that might be the original version or might be an explanatory gloss: "The Danites did not
dispossess the Amorites, who forced them into the high country. The Amorites did not let
them come down into the plain, and their territory was too confining for them."
    Leshem. Elsewhere, this town is called Layish.

49. *the Israelites gave Joshua son of Nun an estate in their midst.* One infers that Joshua
waited until all the tribes had been allocated their territories before he took his own estate.
As Shmuel Ahituv notes, his portion was a special assignment of territory to the commander in chief.

At the behest of the LORD they gave him the town that he had asked for, 50
Timnath-Serah in the high country of Ephraim, and he rebuilt the town
and dwelled in it. These are the estates that Eleazar the priest and Joshua 51
son of Nun and the heads of the Israelite tribes conferred by lot in Shiloh
before the LORD at the entrance to the Tent of Meeting. And they finished
sharing out the land.

CHAPTER 20   And the LORD spoke to Joshua, saying: "Speak 1,2
to the Israelites, saying, Set aside for yourselves the towns of asylum about
which I spoke to you through Moses where a murderer, one who strikes 3
down a person in errance, without intending, may flee, and they will be an
asylum for you from the blood avenger. And he may flee to one of these 4
towns and stand at the gateway to the town and speak his words in the
hearing of the elders of that town, and they will take him to them into that
town and give him a place and he will dwell with them. And should the 5
blood avenger pursue him, they will not hand the murderer over to him, for
he struck down his fellow man without intending, and he had not been his
enemy in times past. And he shall dwell in that town until he stands before 6

---

50. *rebuilt.* The Hebrew verb ordinarily means "to build," but in contexts where the object
is in ruins, as may be the case here because of conquest, it can mean "rebuild."

CHAPTER 20   1. *the towns of asylum about which I spoke to you through Moses.* The
laws for the town of asylum are laid out in Numbers 35 and restated, in somewhat different
terms, in Deuteronomy 19. Although the literary formulation of the laws here was probably
done two or three centuries after the founding of the monarchy, the laws themselves reflect
the tribal period when there was no centralized judicial authority, and vendetta justice
prevailed in cases of murder or manslaughter.

3. *a murderer.* The Hebrew *rotseah*, which generally means "murderer," also encompasses
"manslayer," as in the present context. Perhaps it is used to stress the gravity of destroying
a life, even unintentionally.
    in errance, without intending. This duplication of language brings together the term
used in Numbers with the one used in Deuteronomy.
    blood avenger. The literal sense of this designation is "blood redeemer." That idiom
reflects an archaic notion that when the blood of one's kin is shed, it has been lost to—or
perhaps drained away from—the family, and it must be "redeemed" by shedding the blood
of the killer.

6. *until he stands before the community in judgment, until the death of the high priest.* These
look suspiciously like contradictory terms. The fugitive has already received what amounts
to a verdict of innocent when the elders accept his plea in the gateway of the town (the place
of judgment). If a general amnesty obtains after the death of the high priest, why does the
fugitive have to stand trial a second time? It is possible that the writer responsible for this
passage was uneasy with the idea of a blanket exculpation at the time of the death of the

the community in judgment, until the death of the high priest who will be
in those days. Then the murderer shall return and come to his town and
7 to his home and to the town from which he had fled." And they dedicated
Kedesh in the Galilee in the high country of Naphtali and Shechem in the
high country of Ephraim and Kiriath-Arba, which is Hebron, in the high
8 country of Judah, and across the Jordan from Jericho, to the east, Bezer in
the wilderness on the plain, from the tribe of Reuben and Ramoth in Gilead
from the tribe of Gad and Golan in Bashan from the tribe of Manasseh.
9 These were the towns marked out for all the Israelites and for the sojourners sojourning in their midst to flee there, anyone striking down a person
in errance, that he not die by the hand of the blood avenger, until he stand
before the community.

1 CHAPTER 21   And the heads of the patriarchal houses of the
Levites approached Eleazar the priest and Joshua son of Nun and the heads
2 of the patriarchal houses of the Israelite tribes, and they spoke to them in
Shiloh in the land of Canaan, saying, "The LORD charged through Moses
3 to give us towns in which to dwell and their fields for our cattle." And the
Israelites gave these towns and fields to the Levites from their estate at the
4 behest of the LORD. And the lot came out for the Kohathite clans, and by
lot the sons of Aaron the priest from the Levites had thirteen towns from

---

high priest and wanted to emphasize that the fugitive's innocence had to be determined
by judicial proceedings.

   and to the town from which he had fled. This phrase seems redundant after "to his town."
Perhaps one should drop the "and" and read it as an explanatory apposition, "to his town.
. . . to the town from which he has fled."

9. *to flee there, anyone striking down a person in errance, that he not die by the hand of the
blood avenger*. This phraseology repeats the language of the beginning of this section in
an envelope structure.

   until he stand before the community. He stands before the community to be judged, as
verse 6 makes explicit. Here at the end, no mention is made of the death of the high priest,
perhaps because the writer wanted to emphasize judicial proceedings, not amnesty.

CHAPTER 21   2. *The LORD charged . . . to give us towns*. It is difficult to assess to
what extent the list of levitical towns reflects historical reality. It is improbable that the
Levites actually had forty-eight of their own settlements, or that the other tribes would have
ceded that much real estate to them. Ahituv plausibly suggests that what they were given
was quarters within the towns, which continued to be part of the domain of the host tribe.

4. *the sons of Aaron the priest*. Through verse 19, we have the apportionment of towns to
the priests (*kohanim*). What follows is the apportionment to the Levites, who make up the
rest of the tribe of Levi.

the tribe of Judah and from the tribe of Simeon and from the tribe of Benjamin. And the remaining Kohathites had by lot ten towns from the tribe 5
of Ephraim and from the tribe of Dan and from the half-tribe of Manasseh.
And the sons of Gershon according to their clans had by lot thirteen towns 6
from the tribe of Issachar and from the tribe of Asher and from the tribe
of Naphtali and from the half-tribe of Manasseh in Bashan. The sons of 7
Merari according to their clans had twelve towns from the tribe of Reuben
and from the tribe of Gad and from the tribe of Zebulun. And the Israelites 8
gave to the Levites by lot these towns and their fields as the LORD had charged
through Moses. And they gave from the tribe of the Judahites and from the 9
tribe of the Simeonites these towns which will here be called by name.
And it came to the sons of Aaron for the Kohathite clans from the sons of 10
Levi, for theirs was the first lot, and they gave them Kiriath-Arba father of 11
Anak, which is Hebron, in the high country of Judah, and its fields around
it. And the town's open land and its pastureland they gave to Caleb son of 12
Jephunneh in his holding. And to the sons of Aaron the priest they gave the 13
town of asylum for the murderer, Hebron and its fields, and Libnah and its
fields, and Jattir and its fields and Eshtamoa and its fields, and Holon and 14,15
its fields and Debir and its fields, and Ain and its fields and Juttah and its 16
fields, and Beth-Shemesh and its fields—nine towns from these tribes. And 17
from the tribe of Benjamin, Gibeon and its fields and Geba and its fields,
Anathoth and its fields and Almon and its fields—four towns. All the towns 18,19
of the sons of Aaron, the priest, were thirteen towns and their fields. And 20
for the clans of the Kohathites, the remaining Levites of the Kohathites,
the towns of their lot were from the tribe of Ephraim. And they gave 21
the towns of asylum for the murderer, Shechem and its fields in the high
country of Ephraim and Gezer and its fields, and Kibzaim and its fields 22
and Beth-Horon and its fields—four towns. And from the tribe of Dan, 23
Elteta and its fields, Gibthon and its fields, Ajalon and its fields, Gath- 24
Rimmon and its fields—four towns. And from the half-tribe of Manasseh, 25
Taanach and its fields and Gath-Rimmon and its fields—two towns. All 26
the towns and their fields were ten for the remaining Kohathites. And 27

8. *these towns and their fields.* In an agricultural economy, the houses within the town
would have been places of residence but not sites from which income could be generated.
Hence the need to have a share in the fields outside the town where crops could be grown
or flocks pastured. For these areas outside the town, three terms are used: *migrash*, "field,"
as here; *hatseir*, "pastureland," evidently an enclosed field; and (verse 12) *sadeh*, "open land,"
probably extending beyond the *migrashim*.

21. *towns of asylum.* As this list makes clear, all the towns of asylum are levitical towns, but
many others assigned to the Levites are not towns of asylum.

to the Gershonites from the clans of the Levites, from the half-tribe of
Manasseh the asylum town for the murderer, Golan in Bashan and its fields
28 and Beeshterah and its fields—two towns. And from the tribe of Issachar,
29 Keshion and its fields, Dobrath and its fields, Jarmuth and its fields, Ein-
30 Gannim and its fields—four towns. And from the tribe of Asher, Mishal
31 and its fields, Abdon and its fields. Helkath and its fields and Rehob and
32 its fields—four towns. And from the tribe of Naphtali, the town of asylum
for the murderer, Kedesh in the Galilee and its fields and Hamath-Dor
33 and its fields and Kartan and its fields—three towns. All the towns of the
Gershonites according to their clans were thirteen towns and their fields.
34 And for the clans of the remaining Merarites, from the tribe of Zebulun,
35 Jokneam and its fields, Kartah and its fields, Dimnah and its fields, Nahalal
36 and its fields—four towns. And from the tribe of Gad, the town of asylum
for the murderer, Ramoth in Gilead and its fields, and Mahanaim and its
37 fields, Heshbon and its fields and Jazer and its fields—all the towns were
38 four. All the towns for the remaining Merarites according to their clans
39 that were their lot came to twelve towns. All the towns of the Levites within
40 the holdings of the Israelites were forty-eight towns and their fields. These
41 towns, each town and its fields all around, thus these towns were. And
the LORD gave to Israel the whole land that He had vowed to give to their
42 fathers, and they took hold of it and dwelled in it. And the LORD granted
them rest round about, as all that He had vowed to their fathers, and no
man of all their enemies could stand against them—the LORD delivered all
43 their enemies into their hand. Nothing failed of all the good things that the
LORD had spoken to the House of Israel—everything came about.

---

36. *And from the tribe of Gad.* In between the end of the preceding verse and these words, some Hebrew manuscripts insert the following: "and from the tribe of Reuben Bezer and its fields and Johzah and its fields, Kedemoth and its fields, and Mephath and its fields—four towns."

40. *These towns, each town and its fields all around, thus these towns were.* The syntax of the Hebrew is rather crabbed, but this seems to be the sense of the verse.

43. *Nothing failed.* The literal sense of the Hebrew is "nothing fell."
    the good things. The Hebrew uses a singular noun and it could also be understood to mean "the good word."

CHAPTER 22   Then did Joshua call to the Reubenites and the ₁
Gadites and to the half-tribe of Manesseh, and he said to them, "You have ₂
kept all that Moses, servant of the LORD, charged you, and you have heeded
my voice in all that I have charged you. You have not forsaken your broth- ₃
ers for many days until this day, and you have kept the watch of the LORD
your God. And now the LORD your God has granted rest to your brothers, ₄
as He had spoken to them, so now turn and go off to your tents, to the land
of your holding that Moses, servant of the LORD, gave to you across the
Jordan. Only watch carefully to do the command and the teaching that ₅
Moses, servant of the LORD, charged you, to love the LORD your God and
to walk in all His ways, to keep His commands and to cling to Him and to
serve Him with all your heart and with all your being." And Joshua blessed ₆
them and sent them off, and they went to their tents. And to the half-tribe ₇
of Manasseh Moses had given land in Bashan, and to the other half Joshua
gave land with their brothers west of the Jordan. And what's more, when
Joshua sent them off to their tents and blessed them, he said to them, saying, ₈
"With many possessions return to your tents and with very abundant livestock, with silver and with gold and with bronze and with iron and with a
great many cloaks. Share the booty of your enemies with your brothers."
And the Reubenites and the Gadites and the half-tribe of Manasseh turned ₉
back and went from Shiloh, which is in the land of Canaan, to go to the land
of Gilead, to the land of their holding in which they had taken hold at the

---

CHAPTER 22   1. *Then did Joshua call.* Boling aptly describes the Hebrew phrasing *'az yiqra' yehoshu'a* as "an expansive opening to a climactic unit." The small stylistic
flourish in the translation seeks to mirror this effect.

the Reubenites and the Gadites and to the half-tribe of Manasseh. The book began with
the necessity for the trans-Jordanian tribes to join their brothers in the conquest of the land
west of the Jordan. Now that the conquest is complete, we come back to these tribes, in an
envelope structure, as they are sent back to their own territory.

3. *for many days.* These are the days, or period, of the conquest.

4. *granted rest.* As elsewhere, this idiom indicates subduing all enemies.

5. *to do the command and the teaching . . . to keep His commands and to cling to Him and to
serve Him with all your heart and with all your being.* This string of phrases is a hallmark
of Deuteronomistic prose.

8. *Share the booty of your enemies.* The source of the great abundance of possessions just
listed is here spelled out.

10   behest of the Lord through Moses. And they came to the Jordan districts
      that are in the land of Canaan, and the Reubenites and the Gadites and the
11   half-tribe of Manasseh built there a great altar to be seen by all. And the
      Israelites heard, saying, "Look, the Reubenites and the Gadites and the half-
      tribe of Manasseh have built an altar over against the land of Canaan in the
12   Jordan districts across from the Israelites." And the Israelites heard, and all
      the community of the Israelites assembled at Shiloh to go up against them
13   as an army. And the Israelites sent Phineas son of Eleazar the priest to the
14   Reubenites and to the Gadites and to the half-tribe of Manasseh, and ten
      chieftains were with him, one chieftain for a patriarchal house for each of
      the tribes of Israel, each the head of a patriarchal house for the clan-groups
15   of Israel. And they came to the Reubenites and to the Gadites and to the
16   half-tribe of Manasseh and spoke with them, saying: "Thus said the whole
      community of the Lord: 'What is this violation that you have committed
      against the God of Israel, to turn back today from the Lord by building
17   for yourselves an altar to rebel today against the Lord? Is the crime of
      Peor, from which we have not been cleansed to this day, too little for us, as
18   the scourge came upon the community of the Lord? As for you, you turn
      back today from the Lord, and it will happen that should you rebel today
      against the Lord, tomorrow His fury will be against the whole community

---

10. *the Jordan districts.* These lie evidently alongside the Jordan, though one cannot determine a precise location.

   to be seen by all. The words "by all" have been added in the translation because of the
requirements of English usage. The literal sense is "a great altar for sight."

16. *Thus said.* This is the so-called messenger-formula, regularly used to introduce the text
of a message, whether oral or written.

   to turn back today from the Lord by building for yourselves an altar. The idiom "to
turn back" is repeated five times in this single episode, always in the sense of "to fall away
from," "to abandon." The objection to building an altar east of the Jordan is a little odd
because regional altars were permissible in this period, and the trans-Jordanian territory,
allotted by God through Moses to the two and a half tribes, could not plausibly be defined
as "unclean" land. There was, however, an officially authorized altar in front of the sanctuary at Shiloh, and this new altar was thought to set up illegitimate competition to the
cis-Jordanian one. Many scholars have detected a Priestly agenda in this story.

17. *the crime of Peor, from which we have not been cleansed to this day.* This episode, which
involves an orgiastic sexual rite in which Israelite men are lured by Midianite women, is
recounted in Numbers 25. The punishment for the transgression is a plague that sweeps
through the ranks of Israel. The Israelites' claim here that they still have not been cleansed
of the crime of Peor may reflect some present-day epidemic, which is construed theologically as continuing punishment for that initial crime. Perhaps, then, the Israelites understand the erection of an altar east of the Jordan, where the hinterland is pagan, as the top
of a slippery slope leading to corruption by pagan practices.

of Israel. And if indeed the land of your holding is unclean, cross over to 19
the land of the LORD's holding where the LORD's sanctuary dwells and take
a holding within it, but do not rebel against the LORD, and against us do
not rebel, in your building yourselves an altar other than the altar of the
LORD our God. Did not Achan son of Zerah violate the ban, and the fury 20
was against the whole community of Israel while he, a single man, did not
perish through his crime?'" And the Reubenites and the Gadites and the 21
half-tribe of Manasseh answered and spoke to the heads of the clan-groups
of Israel: "God of gods is the LORD. God of gods is the LORD! He knows, 22
and Israel shall know. If in rebellion and in violation against the LORD, to 23
build us an altar to turn back from the LORD, do not rescue us this day. And
if to offer up on it burnt offering and grain offering, and if to prepare on it
well-being offerings—let the LORD seek it out. Or if not from concern for 24
one thing we have done this, saying, 'Tomorrow your sons will say to our
sons, saying, What do you have to do with the LORD God of Israel, when the 25
LORD has fixed a boundary, the Jordan, between you and us, O Reubenites
and Gadites? You have no share in the LORD.' And your children will prevent our children from fearing the LORD. And so we thought, 'Let us act, 26
pray, to build an altar not for burnt offerings and not for sacrifices, but let it 27
be a witness between you and us and for our generations after us to do the
service of the LORD before Him with our burnt offerings and our sacrifices

---

19. *an altar other than the altar of the LORD our God.* Although the first part of this verse
introduces the notion of trans-Jordan as an "unclean" land, the emphasis here is on the idea
that there should be no alternative to the nationally recognized shrine at Shiloh.

20. *Achan.* Achan's transgression in violating the ban (chapter 7) is comparable to the putative transgression of the tribes east of the Jordan only in regard to its consequences—it is
not the transgressor but the whole people that suffers because of the violation.

22. *God of gods is the LORD.* This solemn, repeated pronouncement marks the beginning
of a sacred vow in which the two and a half tribes declare the innocence of their intentions
before God and Israel.
    He knows, and Israel shall know. The difference in tense is significant: God knows that
we did not intend to betray Him in building this grand altar, and when we have finished
making our declaration, Israel will know as well.

23. *do not rescue us this day.* If in fact the building of the altar was meant as an act of rebellion against God, let your assembled army destroy us.

25. *your children will prevent our children from fearing the LORD.* The phrase "fearing the
LORD" does not indicate an inner state of piety but rather participation in the national
cult: the cis-Jordanian tribes, seeing that the two and a half tribes live beyond the Jordan
in territory that the Israelite majority may not regard as an intrinsic part of the land, will
exclude them from nation and cult.

and our well-being offerings, that your children say not tomorrow to our
28 children, You have no share in the LORD.' And we thought, when it happens
that our generations tomorrow say to us, we shall say, 'See the image of the
LORD's altar that your forefathers made, not for burnt offerings and not for
29 sacrifices but as a witness between you and us. Far be it from us to rebel
against the LORD and to turn back today from the LORD to build an altar
for burnt offerings and for grain offerings and for sacrifice other than the
30 altar of the LORD our God which is before His sanctuary.'" And Phineas
the priest, and the chieftains of the community and the heads of the clan-
groups of Israel with him, heard what the Reubenites and the Gadites and
31 the Manassites had spoken, and it was good in their eyes. And Phineas son
of Eleazar the priest said to the Reubenites and to the Gadites and to the
Manassites, "Today we know that the LORD is in our midst, for you have
not committed this violation against the LORD, and so you have saved the
32 Israelites from the LORD's hand." And Phineas son of Eleazar the priest,
and the chieftains with him, turned back from the Reubenites and from
the Gadites, from the land of Gilead to the land of Canaan, to the Israelites,
33 and they brought back word to them. And the thing was good in the eyes
of the Israelites, and the Israelites blessed God, and they did not think to
go up as an army to lay ruin to the land in which the Reubenites and the
34 Gadites were dwelling. And the Reubenites and the Gadites called the altar
Witness, "for it is a witness among us that the LORD is God."

---

28. *See the image of the LORD's altar.* The altar we have built is a symbolic altar, the image
or simulacrum (*tavnit*) of the LORD's altar that we, like you, recognize as the authorized
site of public worship.

31. *and so you have saved the Israelites from the LORD's hand.* That is, you have saved us
from attacking you without warrant, an act that would then have brought down retribution on us.

33. *the Israelites blessed God, and they did not think to go up as an army to lay ruin to
the land.* This concluding narrative episode of the Book of Joshua is a story of civil war
averted and national reconciliation, whereas the Book of Judges concludes with the story
of a bloody civil war.

34. *called the altar Witness.* The received text says only "called the altar," but some Hebrew
manuscripts as well as the Targum Yonatan show the more coherent text with the additional word as it is translated here. Rashi arrives at the same conclusion by inferring an
ellipsis: "This is one of the abbreviated biblical texts, and it is necessary to add to it one
word: 'and the Reubenites and the Gadites and the Manassites called the altar Witness.'"

CHAPTER 23   And it happened many years after the LORD 1
had granted rest to Israel from all their enemies round about that Joshua
grew old, advanced in years. And Joshua called to all Israel, to its elders 2
and to its chieftains and to its judges and to its overseers. And he said to
them, "I have grown old, advanced in years. As for you, you have seen all 3
that the LORD your God has done to all these nations before you, for the
LORD your God, it is He who did battle for you. See, I have made all these 4
remaining nations fall to you in estate according to your tribes, and all the
nations that I cut off, from the Jordan to the Great Sea where the sun goes
down. And the LORD your God, it is He Who will drive them back before 5
you and dispossess them before you, and you will take hold of their land
as the LORD your God has spoken to you. And you must be very strong to 6
keep and to do all that is written in the book of Moses's teaching, not to
swerve from it to the right or to the left, not to come among these nations 7
that remain alongside you, nor to invoke the name of their gods nor swear
by them nor worship them and bow to them. But to the LORD your God you 8
shall cling as you have done till this day. And the LORD has dispossessed 9
before you great and mighty nations, and you—no man has stood before
you till this day. One man of you pursues a thousand, for the LORD your 10
God, it is He Who does battle for you as He spoke to you. And you must be 11
very careful for your own sake to love the LORD your God. For should you 12
indeed turn back and cling to the rest of these remaining nations alongside

---

CHAPTER 23   1. *after the LORD had granted rest to Israel from all their enemies.*
This ringing declaration is subverted by the threat of exile that hovers over the end of
the chapter. This is a tension that runs through both Joshua and Judges: God has enabled
Israel to conquer all its enemies, yet the land is not completely conquered, and enemies
threaten both within it and from surrounding nations. Even in this passage, the conquest
of the Canaanite peoples alternates between being a completed process, as here, or a future
activity, as in verse 5.

2. *I have grown old, advanced in years.* As several commentators have noted, Joshua's valedictory address stands in a line with those of Moses, Samuel, and David.

4. *all the nations that I cut off.* The Hebrew of this verse seems a little scrambled, with this
clause appearing after "from the Jordan." In addition, "the Great Sea" lacks "to" in the
Hebrew, and the preposition has been supplied in the translation.

6. *you must be very strong to keep and to do all that is written in the book of Moses's teaching.*
Here, as in much of the speech, the phraseology is strongly reminiscent of Deuteronomy.
In the book as a whole, the presence of the Deuteronomist is palpable but intermittent. As
editor, he appears to have wanted to put his strong imprint on the conclusion.

you and intermarry with them and come among them, and they among
13 you, you must surely know that the LORD your God will no longer dispossess these nations before you, and they will become a trap and a snare for
you and a whip against your side and thorns in your eyes, until you perish
14 from this good country that the LORD your God has given you. And, look,
I am about to go today on the way of all the earth, and you know with all
your heart and with all your being that not a single thing has failed of all
the good things that the LORD your God has spoken about you. Everything
15 has befallen you, not a single thing of it has failed. And it shall be, just as
every good thing that the LORD your God has spoken of you has befallen
you, so shall the LORD bring upon you every evil thing until He destroys
16 you from this good country that the LORD your God has given you. When
you overturn the pact of the LORD your God that He charged you and you
go and worship other gods and bow to them, the wrath of the LORD will
flare against you, and you will perish swiftly from the good land that He
has given you.

1 CHAPTER 24   And Joshua gathered all the tribes of Israel at
Shechem, and he called to the elders of Israel and to its chieftains and to its
2 judges and to its overseers, and they stood forth before God. And Joshua

---

13. *a whip against your side.* The Masoretic Text reads *leshotet,* which would mean, implausibly, "to roam." The assumption of this translation is that the second *tet* is a dittography
and hence the Hebrew originally read *leshot,* "as a whip."

14. *I am about to go . . . on the way of all the earth.* David on his deathbed, 1 Kings 2:2, uses
the same language.
    not a single thing. This could also be construed as "not a single word."

15. *until He destroys you from this good country.* The term for "country," *'adamah,* often
means "soil," and its use here might reflect a desire to introduce a connotation of the land's
fruitfulness. The notion that Israel will be driven from its land if it betrays its pact with God
is preeminently Deuteronomistic. The years after 621 B.C.E., with the Assyrian and then the
Babylonian threat uppermost in the minds of the Judahites as well as the memory of the
uprooting of the northern kingdom of Israel a century earlier, were a time when, with good
reason, national existence in the Land of Israel had come to seem painfully precarious.

CHAPTER 24   1. *And Joshua gathered all the tribes.* The book appropriately ends
with a renewal of the covenant between Israel and its God, followed by the obituary notices
for Joshua and Eleazar.

2. *Your forefathers dwelled across the Euphrates . . . and they served other gods.* Joshua's
recapitulation of national history begins all the way back with Abraham's ancestral

said to all the people: "Thus said the LORD God of Israel: 'Your forefathers
dwelled across the Euphrates long ago—Terah father of Abraham and father
of Nahor, and they served other gods. And I took your father Abraham from 3
across the Euphrates and led him to the land of Canaan, and I multiplied
his seed and gave him Isaac. And I gave to Isaac Jacob and Esau, and I gave 4
to Esau the high country of Seir to take hold of, but Jacob and his sons went
down to Egypt. And I sent Moses and Aaron, and I struck Egypt with plagues 5
that I wrought in its midst, and afterward I brought you out. And I brought 6
your forefathers out of Egypt, and you came to the sea, and the Egyptians
pursued your forefathers with chariots and horsemen in the Sea of Reeds.
And they cried out to the LORD, and He put a veil of darkness between 7
you and the Egyptians and brought the sea against them, and it covered
them, and your own eyes saw that which I wrought against Egypt, and you
dwelled in the wilderness many years. And I brought you to the land of the 8
Amorites dwelling across the Jordan, and they did battle against you, and I
gave them into your hand, and you took hold of their land, and I destroyed
them before you. And Balak son of Zippor king of Moab rose up and did 9
battle against Israel, and he sent out and called Balaam son of Beor to curse
you. And I was unwilling to listen to Balaam, and in fact he blessed you, 10
and I saved you from his hand. And you crossed the Jordan and came to 11

---

family in Mesopotamia. ("Euphrates" in the Hebrew, as elsewhere in biblical usage, is "the
River"). But he immediately reminds his audience that before Abraham these people were
idolators, for the danger of backsliding into idolatry is uppermost in his mind throughout
the speech.

4. *Jacob and Esau.* It is noteworthy that Esau, together with his territorial inheritance, is
mentioned with Jacob. There may be a gesture of restitution here for Jacob's stealing the
paternal blessing.

5. *I struck Egypt with plagues that I wrought in its midst.* The Hebrew text shows what looks
like a small glitch: "I struck Egypt with plagues as [or when, *ka'asher*] I wrought in its
midst." The Septuagint has a smoother reading: "I struck Egypt with plagues as I wrought
signs in its midst."

7. *a veil of darkness.* The Hebrew *ma'afel,* cognate to the more common *'apheilah,* "darkness," is unique to this verse. The clear reference is to the pillar of cloud in Exodus.

8. *the land of the Amorites dwelling across the Jordan.* These are the trans-Jordanian kings
vanquished by Israel under Moses, as reported in Numbers and in Deuteronomy.

9. *Balak . . . did battle against Israel.* Because no actual battle is reported in Numbers 22:36–
41, some commentators have claimed that a variant tradition is reflected here, but this is an
unnecessary inference. Balak clearly saw Israel as his enemy and sought to destroy it using
the curses of a professional hexer as his weapon of choice.

Jericho, and the lords of Jericho did battle against you—the Amorite and the Perizzite and the Canaanite and the Hittite and the Girgashite, the

12 Hivvite and the Jebusite. And I gave them into your hand. And I sent the hornet before you, and it drove them from before you—the two Amorite

13 kings—not by your sword and not by your bow. And I gave you a land in which you had not toiled and towns that you had not built, and you dwelled in them; from vineyards and olive groves that you did not plant

14 you are eating the fruit.' And now, fear the Lord and serve Him in wholeness and truth, and put away the gods that your forefathers served across

15 the Euphrates and in Egypt, and serve the Lord. And if it be evil in your eyes to serve the Lord, choose today whom you would serve, whether the gods that your forefathers served across the Euphrates or whether the gods of the Amorites in whose land you dwell, but I and my household

16 will serve the Lord." And the people answered and said, "Far be it from

17 us to forsake the Lord to serve other gods. For the Lord our God, it is He Who brings our forefathers and us up from the land of Egypt, from the house of slaves, and Who has wrought before our eyes these great signs and guarded us on all the way that we have gone and among all the peoples

18 through whose midst we have passed. And the Lord drove out before us all the peoples, the Amorites, inhabitants of the land. We, too, will serve

---

11. *the Amorite and the Perizzite and the Canaanite and the Hittite and the Girgashite, the Hivvite and the Jebusite.* It is odd that all the seven peoples of Canaan are introduced here as though they had fought at Jericho, whereas no mention of a Canaanite alliance appears in the Jericho story. Perhaps Jericho, as the gateway town of Canaan and the first conquered, triggered the invocation of all these peoples, in a kind of synecdoche.

12. *the hornet.* This is the traditional understanding of *tsir'ah*, leading some scholars to claim that noxious insects were actually used as weapons. But, on etymological grounds, as I proposed in comments on Exodus 23:28 and Deuteronomy 7:20, the term could mean "the Smasher," a mythological rather than a zoological entity.

13. *you are eating the fruit.* "Fruit" is implied by ellipsis. Pointedly, the verb for enjoying the fruit of vineyard and olive grove switches from past to a present participle, emphasizing to the audience that they themselves are benefiting from the conquest.

14. *in wholeness and truth.* Many construe these two Hebrew nouns as a hendiadys, having the sense of "in absolute truth."

15. *whether the gods that your forefathers served . . . or . . . the gods of the Amorites.* There is surely a note of sarcasm here: if you really want to serve foreign gods, just take your pick between Mesopotamian and Canaanite deities.

18. *all the peoples, the Amorites.* "Amorites" is sometimes a particular people and sometimes a general rubric for the sundry peoples of Canaan.

the LORD, for He is our God." And Joshua said to the people, "You will 19
not be able to serve the LORD, for He is a holy God. He is a jealous God,
He will not put up with your crimes and your offenses. For should you 20
forsake the LORD and serve alien gods, He shall turn back and do harm to
you and put an end to you after having been good to you." And the people 21
said to Joshua, "No! For we will serve the LORD." And Joshua said to the 22
people, "You are witnesses for yourselves that you have chosen the LORD
to serve Him." And they said, "We are witnesses." "And now, put away the 23
alien gods that are in your midst, and bend your hearts to the LORD God
of Israel." And the people said to Joshua, "The LORD we will serve and His 24
voice we will heed." And Joshua sealed a pact for the people on that day 25
and set it for them as statute and law at Shechem. And Joshua wrote these 26
things in the book of God's teaching, and he took a great stone and set it
under the terebinth that is in God's sanctuary. And Joshua said to all the 27
people, "Look, this stone shall be witness for us because it has heard all
the LORD's sayings that He spoke to us, and it shall be witness to you lest
you deny your God." And Joshua sent the people each man to his estate. 28

And it happened after these things that Joshua son of Nun servant of the 29
LORD died, a hundred ten years old. And they buried him in the territory of 30
his estate in Timnath-Serah, which is in the high country of Ephraim north
of Mount Gaash. And Israel served the LORD all the days of Joshua and all 31
the days of the elders who outlived Joshua and who had known all the acts
of the LORD that He wrought for Israel. And the bones of Joseph, which the 32

---

19. *You will not be able to serve the LORD, for He is a holy God.* In the face of the people's
solemn declaration to remain faithful to the God of Israel, Joshua expresses grave doubt:
YHWH is a holy God, making severe demands of exclusive loyalty, and I don't believe you
will be able to meet these demands. This view sets the stage for the series of idolatrous
backslidings in Judges.

25. *set it for them as statute and law.* The same phrase is used in Exodus 15:25.

26. *the book of God's teaching.* This is a new designation, on the model of "the book of
Moses's teaching" and so can refer either to Deuteronomy or to the Five Books of Moses,
unless what Joshua writes is an appendix to them.

27. *this stone shall be witness.* Commemorative stone markers confirming treaties appear a
number of times in the Hebrew Bible and were common in much of the ancient Near East.

29. *servant of the LORD.* Here at the end Joshua is given the same epithet as Moses.
   a hundred ten years old. The narrative pointedly allots Joshua ten years fewer than
Moses, using instead the Egyptian number for a very full life span.

Israelites had brought up from Egypt, they buried in Shechem in the plot of
land that Jacob had bought from the sons of Hamor for a hundred *kesitahs*,
33 so that it became an estate for the sons of Joseph. And Eleazar the son of
Aaron died, and they buried him on the hill of Phineas his son, which had
been given to him in the high country of Ephraim.

---

33. The received text of Joshua ends on a relatively harmonious note of renewal of the
covenant and the death in ripe old age of the military leader Joshua and the priestly
leader Eleazar. But the ancient Greek translator used a Hebrew text that concludes more
discordantly with the following verse, which confirms Joshua's doubts and looks forward
to Judges: "And the Israelites went each man to his place and to the town, and the Israelites served Ashtoreth and the Ashtaroth and the gods of the peoples round about them,
and the LORD gave them into the hand of Eglon king of Moab, and he ruled over them
eighteen years." Though a variant manuscript might have added this report in order to
create a bridge with the beginning of Judges, it seems more likely that a scribe or an editor
deleted it out of motives of national piety, so as not to conclude the book with an image
of Israel's shame.

JUDGES

Introduction

Like so many biblical books, Judges reflects an editorial splicing together of disparate narrative materials. Some of these materials, at least in their oral origins, could conceivably go back to the last century of the second millennium B.C.E., incorporating memories, or rather legendary elaborations, of actual historical figures. In any case, the redaction and final literary formulation of these stories are much later—perhaps, as some scholars have inferred, toward the end of the eighth century B.C.E., some years after the destruction of the northern kingdom in 721 B.C.E. and before the reforms of King Josiah a century later.

The word *shofet*, traditionally translated as "judge," has two different meanings—"judge" in the judicial sense and "leader" or "chieftain." The latter sense is obviously the relevant one for this book, though the sole female judge, Deborah, in fact also acts as a judicial authority, sitting under the palm tree named after her. The narrative contexts make perfectly clear that these judges are ad hoc military leaders—in several instances, guerilla commanders—but it would have been a gratuitous confusion to readers to call this text the Book of Chieftains or even to designate these figures in the text proper as chieftains or leaders rather than judges.

The first two chapters are both a prologue to what follows and a bridge from the end of the Book of Joshua. They incorporate a report of Joshua's death and an account of the incompletion of the conquest of the land, for which at least two rather different explanations are offered. The unconsummated conquest sets the stage for the sequence of stories in which Israel is sorely oppressed by enemies on all sides—the Philistines based on the coastal plain, the Midianites and the Moabites to the east, and the Canaanites in the heartland of the country. From the latter part of chapter 3 to the end of chapter 12, there is a formulaic rhythm of events: Israel's disloyalty to its God, its oppression by enemies as punishment for the dereliction, the crying out to God by the Israelites, God's raising up a judge to rescue them. This process of "raising up" leaders is what led Max Weber to borrow a term from the Greek and call a political system of this sort charismatic leadership. That is, the authority of the leader derives neither from a hereditary

line nor from election by peers but comes about suddenly when the spirit
of the LORD descends upon him: through this investiture, he is filled with
a sense of power and urgency that is recognized by those around him, who
thus become his followers.

The pattern remains the same, but for some of the Judges we have no
more than a bare notice of their name and their rescuing Israel (see, for
example, the very first judge, Othniel son of Kenaz, 3:9–10) whereas for
others we are given a detailed report of an act of military prowess (Ehud)
or a whole series of narrative episodes (Gideon, Jephthah). The story of the
fratricidal Abimelech breaks the sequence of Judge narratives but provides
foreshadowing of the bloody civil war at the end of the book.

The last in the series of Judges is Samson, who is in several ways quite
unlike those who precede him. Only Samson is a figure announced by
prenatal prophecy, with the full panoply of an annunciation type-scene.
Only in the case of Samson is the first advent of the spirit of the LORD indicated not by a verb of descent (*tsalaḥ*) or investment (*labash*) but of violent
pounding (*paʿam*). Unlike the other judges, Samson acts entirely alone,
and his motive for devastating the Philistines is personal vengeance, not
an effort of national liberation. Most strikingly, only Samson among all the
Judges exercises supernatural power. It seems likely, as many scholars have
concluded, that the sequence of episodes about Samson reflects folkloric
traditions concerning a Herculean, quasimythological hero, though the
narrative as it has been formulated shows evidence of subtle literary craft.
In any case, the Samson stories, editorially placed as the last in the series
of Judge narratives, exemplify the breakdown of the whole system of charismatic leadership. Samson, battling alone with unconventional weapons
or with his bare hands, more drawn to the sexual arena than to national
struggle, hostilely confronted by fellow Israelites, sowing destruction all
around him to the very end, like the fire with which he is associated from
before his conception, is a figure of anarchic impulse: the man in whom the
spirit of the LORD pounds down enemies but offers no leadership at all for
his people, which may be a final verdict on the whole system of governance
by charismatic warriors represented in the preceding episodes of the book.

The Samson narrative suggests that the shape given to Judges by its
editors may be more purposeful than is often assumed. What follows the
Samson cycle is the bizarre story of Micah's idol (chapters 17–18) and then
the grisly tale of the concubine at Gibeah who is gang-raped to death by
the local Benjaminites, leading to a costly civil war between Benjamin
and the other tribes (chapters 19–21). These two blocks of material are

often described as an appendix to the Book of Judges, and although it is true that they differ strikingly in subject matter and to some extent in style from the stories about the Judges, they also show significant connections as well both with the immediately preceding Samson narrative and with the book as a whole. Divisiveness in the Israelite community, adumbrated in Samson's confrontation with the men of Judah, is vividly manifested both in the story of Micah and that of the concubine. Micah's narrative begins with his stealing eleven hundred shekels (the exact amount that the Philistines offer to Delilah) from his mother. Part of this purloined fortune, returned to his mother, is used to create a molten image of dubious monotheistic provenance, which will then become an object of contention. The displaced Danites, arriving on the scene as a military contingent, have no compunction about confiscating a whole set of cultic objects and buying off the young Levite whom Micah has hired to minister in his private sanctuary. The Danites then go on to conquer a new northern town in which to settle their southern tribe, but this is hardly a story that ends with the land quiet for forty years: tensions, verging on a clash of arms, between Micah and the Danites; dishonesty and deception, venality and the ruthless pursuit of personal and tribal self-interest—such far-from-edifying behavior dominates the story from beginning to end.

The morality exhibited in the book's concluding narrative is even worse. Another Levite, considerably more egregious than the one engaged by Micah, ends up reenacting the story of Sodom with a bitter reversal. In this tale devoid of divine intervention, there are no supernatural beings to blind the brutal sexual assailants; the Levite pushes his concubine out the door to be raped all night long; and when he finds her prostrate on the threshold in the morning, he brusquely orders her to get up so that they can continue their journey, not realizing at first that she has expired. His remedy for this atrocity is as bad as the violation itself: he butchers her body into twelve parts that he sends out to the sundry tribes to rouse their indignation against Benjamin, and the ensuing civil war, in which the other tribes suffer extensive casualties, comes close to wiping out the tribe of Benjamin. Unbridled lust, implacable hostility, and mutual mayhem provide ample warrant for the implicitly monarchist refrain of these chapters: "In those days there was no king in Israel. Every man did what was right in his own eyes."

Anarchy and lust link these stories directly with the Samson narrative. But the theme of violence, threatened in Micah's story, shockingly realized in the narrative that follows, ties in the concluding chapters of Judges with everything that precedes them in the book. Judges represents, one might say, the Wild West era of the biblical story. Men are a law unto themselves— "Every man did what was right in his eyes." There are warriors who can toss a stone from a slingshot at a hair and not miss; a bold left-handed assassin who deftly pulls out a short sword strapped to his right thigh to stab the Moabite king in the soft underbelly; another warrior-chieftain who panics the enemy camp in the middle of the night with the shock and awe of piercing ram's horn blasts and smashed pitchers.

All this is certainly exciting in a way that is analogous to the gunslinger justice of the Wild West, but there is an implicit sense, which becomes explicit at the end of the book, that survival through violence, without a coherent and stable political framework, cannot be sustained and runs the danger of turning into sheer destruction. In the first chapter of the book, before any of the Judges are introduced, we are presented with the image of the conquered Canaanite king, Adoni-Bezek, whose thumbs and big toes are chopped off by his Judahite captors. This barbaric act of dismemberment, presumably intended to disable the king from any capacity for combat, presages a whole series of episodes in which body parts are hacked, mutilated, crushed. King Eglon's death by Ehud's hidden short sword is particularly grisly: his killer thrusts the weapon into his belly all the way up to the top of the hilt, and his death spasm grotesquely triggers the malodorous release of the anal sphincter. Women are also adept at this bloody work: there is a vividly concrete report of how Jael drives the tent peg through the temple of Sisera the Canaanite general and into the ground; another woman, this one anonymous, smashes the head of the nefarious Abimelech with a millstone she drops on him from her perch in a besieged tower. Samson's slaughter of a thousand Philistines with a donkey's jawbone is surely a messy business of smashing and mashing—no neat spear's thrust here—though descriptive details are not offered. The grand finale of Samson's story, in which thousands of Philistine men and women, together with the Israelite hero, are crushed by the toppling temple, is an even more extensive crushing and mangling of bodies.

Against this background, one can see a line of imagistic and thematic continuity from the maiming of Adoni-Bezek at the very beginning of the book to the dismembering of the concubine at the end. That act of chopping a body into pieces, of course, is intended as a means to unite the tribes against Benjamin and its murderous rapists, but there is a paradoxical tension between the project of unity—unity, however, for a violent purpose—

and the butchering of the body, the violation of its integrity, which in the biblical world as in ours was supposed to be respected through burial. The famous lines that Yeats wrote at a moment of violent upheaval in European and Irish history precisely capture the thematic thrust of Judges:

> Things fall apart; the centre cannot hold;
> Mere anarchy is loosed upon the world,
> The blood-dimmed tide is loosed. . . .

After this dark impasse to which the Book of Judges comes, it will be the task of the next great narrative sequence, which is the Book of Samuel, concluding in the second chapter of 1 Kings, to imagine a political means to create a center and leash the anarchy. That goal is in part realized, but the undertaking itself is an arduous one; and because these stories turn increasingly from legend and lore to a tough engagement in history, even as a center begins to hold, the blood-dimmed tide is never stemmed.

CHAPTER 1   And it happened after the death of Joshua that 1
the Israelites inquired of the LORD, saying, "Who will go up for us first
against the Canaanite to do battle with him?" And the LORD said, "Judah 2
shall go up. Look, I have given the land into his hand." And Judah said to 3
Simeon his brother, "Go up with me in my portion, and let us do battle with
the Canaanite, and I, too, shall go with you in your portion." And Simeon
went with him. And Judah went up, and the LORD gave the Canaanite and 4
the Perizzite into their hand, and they struck them down in Bezek—ten
thousand men. And they found Adoni-Bezek in Bezek and did battle with 5
him, and they struck down the Canaanite and the Perizzite. And Adoni- 6
Bezek fled, and they pursued him and seized him, and they chopped off

---

CHAPTER 1   1. *And it happened after the death of Joshua.* These words are a pointed
repetition of the formula that begins the Book of Joshua, "And it happened after the death
of Moses."

the Israelites inquired of the LORD. This idiom indicates inquiry of an oracle in all likelihood, the Urim and Thummim, which could be used to yield a yes-no answer or to select
an individual from a group. Some commentators have suggested that after Joshua's death,
there was no longer a central leader with access to God and hence the oracular device was
necessary.

2. *Judah shall go up.* The prominence of Judah in the vanguard of the conquest patently
reflects a later period when Judah was the seat of the Davidic monarchy and the chief
remaining tribe. The report here moves from Judah's military success in the south to the
failures of the other tribes in the north.

3. *Simeon his brother.* This indication of fraternity and military cooperation probably
derives from a moment in later history when Simeon was closely allied with or assimilated
in Judah.

4. *ten thousand men.* Like almost all numbers in biblical narrative, this is formulaic, meant
to indicate a large group. The reference to "seventy kings" in verse 7 is similarly formulaic, although it does register the fact that Canaan was divided among many small city-
kingdoms, which were often at war with one another.

5. *Adoni-Bezek.* This name, which means "master of Bezek," appears to be a hereditary title
rather than a proper noun.

6. *they chopped off his thumbs and his big toes.* The mutilation, which on the evidence of
Adoni-Bezek's own words in the next verse was evidently a common practice, is both a

7 his thumbs and his big toes. And Adoni-Bezek said: "Seventy kings, their thumbs and their big toes chopped off, used to gather scraps under my table. As I have done, so has God paid me back." And they brought him to
8 Jerusalem, and he died there. And the Judahites did battle against Jerusalem, and they took it and struck it down with the edge of the sword,
9 and the town they set on fire. And afterward the Judahites went down to do battle with the Canaanite dwelling in the high country and the
10 Negeb and the lowland. And Judah went against the Canaanite dwelling in Hebron—and the name of Hebron was formerly Kiriath-Arba—and
11 they struck down Sheshai and Achiman and Talmai. And they went from there against the inhabitants of Debir—and the name of Debir was for-
12 merly Kiriath-Sepher. And Caleb said, "Whoever strikes Kiriath-Sepher
13 and takes it, to him I shall give Achsah my daughter as wife." And Othniel son of Kenaz, Caleb's younger brother, took it, and he gave him Achsah
14 as wife. And it happened when she came, that she enticed him to ask a field of her father, and she alighted from the donkey, and Caleb said to
15 her, "What troubles you?" And she said to him, "Give me a present, for

---

humiliation and a means of permanently preventing the captured leader from becoming a combatant again because he would be unable to wield a bow or sword or run on the battlefield. It should be observed, moreover, that this grisly detail is an apt thematic and imagistic introduction to Judges, the most violent of all the books of the Bible. In the stories that follow, swords will be thrust into bellies, tent pegs into heads; people will be variously mashed and crushed; and toward the end of the book, the dismembered parts of a murdered woman's body will be sent out to the sundry tribes in order to ignite a civil war. The mutilation of the king, then, introduces us to a realm of political instability in which both people and groups are violently torn asunder.

7. *And they brought him to Jerusalem, and he died there.* This notation and the one in the next verse about the total destruction of Jerusalem by Judah are a puzzlement. It is contradicted here by verse 21, in which it is said that Judah was unable to drive out the Jebusites but continued to coexist with them. 2 Samuel 5 reports, with some historical plausibility, that it was David who conquered Jerusalem from the Jebusites (almost two centuries after the putative time of the events in Judges). One suspects that the Judahite writer was swept up by the momentum of his own historical moment: Jerusalem had long been the capital city of the Davidic monarchy, and so it was difficult for the writer to imagine that it had not been part of the initial conquest of his tribe.

12. *Whoever strikes Kiriath-Sepher and takes it, to him I shall give Achsah my daughter as wife.* The story here, including the two previous verses, repeats in virtually identical language the story told in Joshua 15:13–19. The offer of the hand of the daughter to the victorious hero is an obvious folkloric motif and recurs in the episode of David and Goliath.

13. *Othniel.* He is to become the first judge.

you have given me desert-land, and you should have given me springs of
water." And Caleb gave her the upper springs and the lower springs. And 16
the sons of the Kenite, the father-in-law of Moses, came up from the Town
of Palms with the Judahites from the Wilderness of Judah which is in the
Negeb of Arad, and they went and dwelled with the people. And Judah 17
went with Simeon his brother and they struck down the Canaanite dwelling in Zephath and put it under the ban, and they called the name of the
town Hormah.

And Judah took Gaza and its territory and Ashkelon and its territory and 18
Ekron and its territory. And the LORD was with Judah, and he took posses- 19
sion of the high country, but he was not able to dispossess the inhabitants
of the valley, for they had iron chariots. And they gave Hebron to Caleb 20
as Moses had spoken, and he dispossessed from there the three sons of
the giant. But the Jebusite dwelling in Jerusalem, the Benjaminites did not 21
dispossess, and the Jebusite has been dwelling with the Benjaminites in
Jerusalem to this day. And the sons of Joseph, too, went up to Bethel, and 22

---

15. *desert-land.* The term *negev* (rendered elsewhere in this translation as the place-name
"Negeb") means terrain that supports little or no vegetation, probably deriving from a
verbal stem that means "dry" or "desolate." The region in the southern part of the Land of
Israel is that sort of terrain and hence is given the geographical name Negeb. Another term,
midbar, is represented in this version, as it is in most English translations, as "wilderness"
because it includes land in which animals can graze.

16. *the Town of Palms.* On the basis of other biblical occurrences, this is Jericho.

17. *Hormah.* The name puns on *ḥerem*, "ban."

18. *And Judah took Gaza and its territory.* This verse is another instance in which the
writer's location in a time when the Philistine coastal enclave had long been subdued is
retrojected to the period of the Judges. Here three of the five towns of the Philistine pen-
topolis are said to be conquered by Judah. But in the subsequent narrative, down to the time
of David, the Philistines remain autonomous and a potent military threat; and in Judges
itself, in the Samson story, Gaza is very much in the hands of the Philistines.

19. *was not able.* The Hebrew of the received text sounds odd at this point: "was not able"
occurs in Onkelos's Aramaic version.

20. *the three sons of the giant.* Though many interpreters prefer to understand the last term
here, *ʿanaq*, as a proper noun, it does mean "giant," and there is a clear tradition reflected
in Numbers, Deuteronomy, Joshua, and Judges that some of the indigenous inhabitants of
the land were giants.

22. *Bethel.* The report now moves to the north. Bethel was to become a central cultic location in the northern kingdom of Israel after the split in the monarchy.

23 the LORD was with them. And the House of Joseph scouted out Bethel—
24 and the name of the town was formerly Luz. And the lookout saw a man
coming out of the town and said to him, "Show us, pray, the way into the
25 town, and we shall deal kindly with you." And he showed them the way
into the town, and they struck the town by the edge of the sword, but the
26 man and his clan they sent off. And the man went to the land of the Hittites and built a town and called its name Luz—that is its name to this day.
27 And Manasseh did not take possession of Beth-She'an and its hamlets nor
Taanach and its hamlets nor the inhabitants of Dor and its hamlets nor
the inhabitants of Ibleam and its hamlets nor the inhabitants of Megiddo
28 and its hamlets, but the Canaanite went on dwelling in this land. And it
happened, when Israel grew strong, that it put the Canaanite to forced
29 labor, but it did not dispossess him. And Ephraim did not dispossess the
Canaanite dwelling in Gezer, and the Canaanite dwelled in his midst in
30 Gezer. Zebulun did not dispossess the inhabitants of Kitron, nor the inhabitants of Nahalal, and the Canaanite dwelled in his midst and did forced
31 labor. Asher did not dispossess the inhabitants of Acco, nor the inhabitants
32 of Sidon, Ahiab, Ach zib, Helbah, Aphek, and Rehob. And the Asherite
dwelled in the midst of the Canaanites, inhabitants of the land, for he did
33 not dispossess them. Naphtali did not dispossess the inhabitants of Beth-
Shemesh and the inhabitants of Baal-Anath, and he dwelled amidst the
Canaanites inhabitants of the land, and the inhabitants of Beth-Shemesh
34 and of Beth-Anath did forced labor for them. And the Amorites drove the
Danites into the high country, for they did not let them come down into
35 the valley. And the Amorite continued to dwell in Mount Heres, in Ajalon,

---

24. *the way into the town.* Yigal Yadin has cited archaeological evidence that some Canaanite towns had tunnels that provided secret access to them. That sounds plausible here
because the lookouts are surely not asking directions to the main gate of the town.

28. *Israel . . . put the Canaanite to forced labor, but it did not dispossess him.* Whether this
subjugation of the Canaanite population to the Israelites was a historical fact or is merely
a face-saving formula for the failure of the conquest is uncertain. In any case, the chapter
from this point on spells out a theme of incompletion that had fluctuated through the Book
of Joshua. In the first half of Joshua, the conquest of the land appears to be comprehensive;
in the second half, there are some indications that much remains to be conquered. Now we
have a whole catalogue of failed conquests, all attributed to the northern tribes that would
constitute the breakaway kingdom of Israel.

31. *Acco . . . Sidon, Ahiab, Achzib.* These coastal towns bring us far to the north, near present-
day Haifa and beyond, with Sidon actually being a Phoenician city.

and in Shaalbim, but the hand of the house of Joseph lay heavy upon them, and they did forced labor. And the territory of the Amorites was from the 36 Ascent of Akrabbim, from Sela on up.

CHAPTER 2   And a messenger of the LORD came up from 1 Gilgal to Bochim, and he said: "I have taken you up from Egypt and brought you to the land that I swore to your fathers, and I said, I will never break My covenant with you. As for you, you shall not seal a covenant 2 with the inhabitants of this land—their altars you shall smash. And you did not heed My voice. What is this you have done? And I also said, 'I will 3 not drive them out before you, and they shall become thorns to you, and their gods shall become a snare for you." And it happened, when the LORD's 4 messenger spoke these words to the Israelites, that the people raised their voices and wept. And they called the name of the place Bochim, and they 5 sacrificed there to the LORD. And Joshua sent off the people, and the Isra- 6 elites went every man to his estate to take hold of the land. And the people 7 served the LORD all the days of Joshua and all the days of the elders who

---

35. *upon them.* These words are merely implied in the Hebrew.

CHAPTER 2   1. *Bochim.* The name, which means "weepers," is proleptic, and its origin will be explained in verses 5–6.

I have taken you up from Egypt. The LORD's messenger is not speaking in his own person but is serving as God's mouthpiece, quoting His words.

I said. This verb in Hebrew can also mean "I thought" (perhaps an ellipsis for "I said in my heart"), and it is not clear whether God actually addresses these words to Israel or merely thinks them. The same ambiguity hovers over "I also said" in verse 3.

2. *their altars you shall smash.* This is in keeping with the vehement antipagan agenda of Deuteronomy.

3. *thorns.* The Hebrew *tsidim* would appear to mean "sides." A common expression in contexts like this one is "thorns [*tsinim*] in your side." This might be an ellipsis here, or, more likely, the similarity of the two words might have led a scribe to inadvertently replace *tsinim* with *tsidim.*

6. *And Joshua sent off the people.* The appearance of Joshua makes it clear that this entire passage loops back chronologically to the end of the Book of Joshua (chapter 24), when Joshua addresses the people, perhaps not long before his death.

7. *And the people served the LORD all the days of Joshua.* This entire verse approximately repeats Joshua 24:31.

outlived Joshua, who had seen the great acts of the LORD that He did for
8   Israel. And Joshua son of Nun servant of the LORD died, a hundred ten years
9   old. And they buried him in the territory of his estate, in Timnath-Heres
10 in the high country of Ephraim north of Mount Gaash. And that whole
    generation as well was gathered to its fathers, and another generation arose
    after them that did not know the LORD or the acts He had done for Israel.
11 And the Israelites did evil in the eyes of the LORD, and they served the
12 Baalim. And they forsook the LORD God of their fathers Who had brought
    them out of the land of Egypt, and they went after other gods, of the gods of
    the peoples that were all around them, and they bowed to them and vexed
13 the LORD. And they forsook the LORD and served Baal and the Ashtoroth.
14 And the LORD's wrath flared up against Israel, and He gave them into the
    hand of plunderers who plundered them, and He handed them over to their
    enemies all around, and they were no longer able to stand up against their
15 enemies. Whenever they sallied forth, the LORD's hand was against them
    for harm, as the LORD had spoken and as the LORD had vowed to them, and
16 they were in sore straits. And the LORD raised up judges and rescued them
17 from their plunderers. And their judges, too, they did not heed, for they

---

the great acts. The Hebrew uses a singular noun with collective force. The same usage
occurs in verse 10.

11. they served the Baalim. This is the plural form of Baal, the Canaanite weather god and
probably the most widely worshipped deity in the Canaanite pantheon. Many interpreters
infer that the plural form indicates Baal and other pagan gods.

13. Baal and the Ashtoroth. Here "Baal" is singular and "Ashtoroth" shows a feminine plural
ending (the singular in this traditional transliteration would be "Ashtoreth"). Ashtoreth
is the Canaanite fertility goddess, though in some Ugaritic texts she appears also as a
warrior-goddess. The plural form, as with Baalim in verse 11, may suggest that a variety of
pagan goddesses is meant.

15. Whenever they sallied forth, the LORD's hand was against them for harm. This whole
passage articulates a clear-cut theological explanation for Israel's failure to conquer the
entire land: its swerve into idolatry enrages God and causes Him to bring about Israel's
defeat by its enemies.

16. judges. The Hebrew verbal noun shofet means both one who judges and one who rules,
and the latter sense is more prominent here and in all that follows in this book. As a result,
some modern translations opt for "chieftain" or an equivalent term. The shofet was an ad
hoc military leader (in this regard, "chieftain," suggesting a fixed and perhaps hereditary
political institution, is misleading). From the subsequent narratives in this book, the Judge
was seen by his followers—or, at any rate, by the writer—as a figure suddenly invested with
a divine spirit that impelled him to action and enabled his success. It is precisely on the

went whoring after other gods and bowed to them, they swerved quickly
from the way in which their fathers had gone to heed the LORD's command. They did not do so. And when the LORD raised up judges for them,   18
the LORD was with the judge and rescued them from the hand of their
enemies all the days of the judge, for the LORD felt regret for their groaning
because of their oppressors and their harassers. And it happened, when the   19
judge died, they went back and acted more ruinously than their fathers,
to go after other gods, to serve them, to bow to them. They left off nothing
of their actions and their stubborn way. And the LORD's wrath flared up   20
against Israel, and He said, "Because this nation has violated My covenant
that I charged to their fathers and has not heeded My voice, I on my part   21
will not continue to dispossess before them any of the nations that Joshua
left when he died in order to test Israel through them, whether or not they   22
will keep the LORD's way to go in it." And the LORD had left aside these   23
nations, not dispossessing them quickly, and He had not given them into
the hand of Joshua.

---

model of the biblical judges that Max Weber borrowed the term "charisma" from the Greek
to indicate a purely personal political power.

18. *the LORD was with the judge and rescued them from the hand of their enemies all the
days of the judge.* A theological reason is offered here for a continuing unstable military
situation. The Judges were basically guerilla commanders. A judge, exercising personal
magnetism and military prowess, could for a certain amount of time harass and drive back
enemy forces that were probably superior in numbers and weaponry, but such successes
were bound to be temporary. This fluctuating pattern is explained in terms of cultic loyalty
and backsliding: under the charismatic influence of the Judge, the Israelites were faithful
to their God; when the Judge died, they reverted to their pagan practices. Verse 17 suggests
that they did not heed their judges, or only temporarily.

19. *their actions.* The implication in context is "evil actions," though the Hebrew noun used
is not intrinsically negative.

21–22. *the nations that Joshua left when he died in order to test Israel through them.* Here a
new theological explanation of the incompleteness of the conquest is introduced. Joshua,
given his sweeping military successes reported in Joshua 1–12, might well have conquered
the entire land, but he left some of it in Canaanite hands in order to see whether future
generations of Israel would be faithful to their God and thus be worthy of taking hold of
the rest of the land. God's words in these two verses affirm that the people has failed the
test and so will not be able to complete the conquest. The next verse then makes clear that
Joshua's leaving part of the land unconquered was actually God's devising.

1 CHAPTER 3   And these are the nations that the LORD left aside
2 to test Israel through them—all who knew not the wars of Canaan, only
so that the generations of Israel might know, to teach them warfare, which
3 before they did not know: the five overlords of the Philistines and all the
Canaanites and the Sidonites and the Hivvites dwelling in the high country
4 of Lebanon from Mount Baal Hermon to Lebo-Hamath. And they came to
test Israel through them, to know whether they would heed the command
5 of the LORD with which He charged their fathers by Moses. And the Israelites dwelled in the midst of the Canaanites, the Hittites and the Amor-
6 ites and the Perizzites and the Jebusites. And they took their daughters for
themselves as wives, and their own daughters they gave to their sons, and
7 they served their gods. And the Israelites did evil in the eyes of the LORD,
and they forgot the LORD their God, and they served the Baalim and the
8 Asheroth. And the LORD's wrath flared up against Israel, and He handed
them over to Cushan Rishathaim king of Aram Naharaim, and the Isra-
9 elites served Cushan Rishathaim eight years. And the Israelites cried out
to the LORD, and the LORD raised up a rescuer for the Israelites, Othniel

---

CHAPTER 3   1. *all who knew not the wars of Canaan.* The translation mirrors the
looseness of the Hebrew syntax, although this clause clearly modifies "Israel."

2. *to teach them warfare, which before they did not know.* Here an entirely different reason
for the incompleteness of the conquest is introduced: Israel had to learn the skills of war in
gradual stages through conflict with the Canaanites before it was prepared to conquer them.

4. *to test Israel . . . to know whether they would heed the command of the LORD.* Now the
writer reverts to the theological explanation for the incompleteness of the conquest put
forth in 2:21–23.

7. *the Asheroth.* In the plural feminine form, a different Canaanite goddess is evoked, not
Ashtoreth but Asherah, the consort of the sky god El.

8. *Cushan Rishathaim king of Aram Naharaim.* There are two oddities in this name and
title. Rishathaim, which means "double-evil," sounds more like a symbolic epithet than an
actual name. Aram Naharaim is Mesopotamian Aram (there were Arameans closer to the
eastern border of Israel), which would be a long distance from which to exert temporary
dominance over any population west of the Jordan.

9. *Othniel son of Kenaz, Caleb's young brother.* He has already figured in the narrative
both in this book and in Joshua as the conqueror of Hebron. In that instance, however, his
military prowess was not enabled by the descent of the spirit upon him, according to the
pattern of the Judges. His appearance now as the first judge is no doubt intended to establish a bridge between the period of Joshua and the period of the Judges. All the elements
of the Judge paradigm are evident: Israel's defection, its subjugation, its crying out, God's
response in raising up a rescuer, the descent of the spirit, the ensuing victory. But only the
outline of the pattern appears—no details are offered of Othniel's exploits.

son of Kenaz, Caleb's young brother, who rescued them. And the spirit of   10
the LORD was upon him, and he led Israel and went out to battle, and the
LORD gave into his hand Cushan Rishathaim king of Aram, and his hand
was strong against Cushan Rishathaim. And the land was quiet forty years,   11
and Othniel son of Kenaz died.

And the Israelites continued to do evil in the eyes of the LORD, and the   12
LORD strengthened Eglon king of Moab over Israel because they had done
evil in the eyes of the LORD. And he gathered round him the Ammonites   13
and the Amalekites, and he struck Israel and they took hold of the Town
of Palms. And the Israelites served Eglon king of Moab eighteen years.   14
And the Israelites cried out to the LORD, and the LORD raised up a rescuer   15
for them, Ehud son of Gera the Benjaminite, a left-handed man. And the
Israelites sent tribute in his hand to Eglon king of Moab. And Ehud made   16
himself a double-edged sword, a *gomed* in length, and strapped it under
his garments on his right thigh. And he presented the tribute to Eglon   17
king of Moab, and Eglon was a very fat man. And it happened when he   18
had finished presenting the tribute that he sent away the people bearing
the tribute. And he had come back from Pesilim, which is by Gilgal. And   19
he said, "A secret word I have for you, king." And he said, "Silence!" And

---

15. *the Benjaminite.* The tribe of Benjamin, as the subsequent narrative will affirm, was
noted for its skill in battle.

a left-handed man. The literal sense of the Hebrew idiom is "a man impaired [or bound up]
in his right hand." Ehud's left-handedness plays a crucial part in his assassination of Eglon.

in his hand. Though the idiom means "through his agency," with verse 18 making clear
that there are at least several people physically bearing the considerable tribute, the use
of "hand" picks up the appearance of the ominous left hand in the previous verse and its
lethal deployment in verse 21.

16. *a gomed.* This measure of length occurs only here, but it has an evident cognate, *gar-
mida*, in rabbinic Aramaic, which is a cubit, about seventeen inches. This would be short
enough to conceal the weapon strapped to the thigh. The double edge of the straight sword
makes it a thrusting weapon. Typical swords of this period were single-edged and sickle-
shaped and were wielded by slashing.

17. *Eglon was a very fat man.* The name Eglon strongly suggests *'egel,* "calf." In this satiric
view of the enemy, he is a gross fatted calf, ready for slaughter.

19. *Pesilim.* This appears to be a place-name, but it means "the idols" (there is a definite
article), and so it is probably a cultic site.

Silence! The Hebrew *hass* is onomatopoeic, something like shhh! When Ehud tells Eglon
that he has a secret to convey, these words elicit exactly the response intended by the assassin: the king doesn't want anyone else to hear, so he tells Ehud to keep quiet and orders

20 all those standing in attendance on him went out from his presence. When
Ehud had come to him, he was sitting alone in the cool upper chamber that
he had. And Ehud said, "A word of God I have for you." And he rose from
21 the seat. And Ehud reached with his left hand and took the sword from his
22 right thigh and thrust it into his belly. And the hilt, too, went in after the
blade and the fat closed over the blade, for he did not withdraw the sword
23 from his belly, and the filth came out. And Ehud went out to the vestibule
24 and closed the doors of the upper chamber and locked them. He had just

---

everyone else out of the chamber. It should be noted that Ehud's words to the king are
abrupt, lacking the language of deference ("my lord the king") required when addressing a
royal personage. Eglon, in his eagerness to hear the secret, takes no note of this.

20. *A word of God.* At first, Eglon might have thought that the secret word was some piece of
military intelligence that this supposed collaborator was offering him. Now Ehud presents
it as an oracle, something that would be especially likely if Eglon is aware that he has arrived
by way of Pesilim. (In this second bit of dialogue, Ehud is even more abrupt, now omitting
the title "king.") Eglon rises either because this is the proper posture in which to receive
an oracle or because of his eagerness to hear the "word of God" up close. By standing, of
course, he makes himself a perfect target for the sword thrust.

21. *Ehud reached with his left hand.* Because Eglon does not see this as the weapon hand,
Ehud gains a decisive moment as he whips out the sword before Eglon can make a move
to evade it.

22. *the hilt, too, went in after the blade.* The image of the weapon entirely encased in Eglon's
corpulence is deliberately grotesque.
    the filth. The Hebrew *parshedonah* clearly shows the element *peresh*, excrement. The
anomalous ending of the word may be a scribal duplication of the ending of *misderonah*,
"to the vestibule," which is the third word after this one in the Hebrew text. The release
of the anal sphincter in the death spasm adds a scatological note to the representation of
the killing of Eglon.

23. *Ehud went out to the vestibule.* The exact meaning of the Hebrew noun is uncertain,
and our knowledge of the floor plan of Moabite palaces remains imperfect in this regard,
though one scholar, Baruch Halperin, has made a heroic effort to reconstruct the architectural scene. But this would have to be some sort of courtyard or rear chamber on the other
side of the king's special chamber from the anteroom in which his attendants await him.
The closing and locking of the doors, then, would be pluperfect: Ehud locks them from
within and goes out through another, unspecified, exit.

24. *and, look, the doors of the upper chamber were locked.* The use of the presentative *hineh,*
"look," to mark a shift to the characters' point of view is tactically effective here and in what
follows: the courtiers are confronted by locked doors, and perplexed.
    He must be relieving himself. The scatological detail is comic here: they can clearly smell
the consequences of the released sphincter, and they use their inference to explain both the
locked doors and the long delay.

gone out, when Eglon's courtiers came and saw, and, look, the doors of
the upper chamber were locked. And they said, "He must be relieving
himself in the cool chamber." And they waited a long while, and, look, 25
no one was opening the doors of the upper chamber. And they took the
key and opened them, and, look, their master was fallen to the ground,
dead. And Ehud had escaped while they tarried, and he passed Pesilim 26
and escaped to Seirah. And it happened when he came, that he blasted 27
the ram's horn in the high country of Ephraim, and the Israelites came
down with him from the high country, and he was before them. And he 28
said to them, "Come down after me, for the LORD has given your enemies,
Moab, in your hand." And they came down after him and took the fords of
the Jordan from Moab, and they did not let anyone cross over. And at that 29
time they struck down Moab, about ten thousand men, every stout fellow
and every valiant man, and not a man escaped. And on that day Moab 30
was laid low under the hand of Israel. And the land was quiet eighty years.

---

25. *they took the key and opened them.* These doors evidently can be locked or unlocked
from either side.

    and, look, their master was fallen to the ground, dead. The management of narrative
point of view is both eloquent and dramatic. They look and first make out "their master"
(which is how they would have silently referred to him), take in the fact that he is sprawled
on the floor, and then realize, at the very end of the syntactic chain, that he is dead. (With
the short sword entirely buried in his belly, it is possible that no blood would be visible.)

26. *And Ehud had escaped while they tarried.* The courtiers' long wait while they supposed
their king was relieving himself gives the assassin ample time to get away.

27. *he blasted the ram's horn.* It often happens in biblical narrative that two juxtaposed
scenes are linked by the repetition of a term, in a different sense. The verb *taqaʻ* means "to
stab" or "to thrust" and is used for Ehud's killing of Eglon. But it also means "to blast" (on a
ram's horn or trumpet), which is what he does now as a signal to rally fighters around him.

28. *Come down after me.* The received text says *ridfu ʼaharay*, which means "pursue me,"
an idiom that always suggests hostile intent. The Septuagint reads *redu,* "come down," and
it is very likely that the extra consonant, generating a wrong meaning, was inadvertently
introduced through scribal copying in the Masoretic Text.

29. *every stout fellow.* The Hebrew adjective *shamen* usually means "fat" but here has the
sense of "stalwart" or "strong," a double meaning also exhibited by the English term "stout."
Its use here, however, clearly plays back ironically against the corpulence of Eglon.

30. *eighty years.* In this case, it is twice the formulaic forty.

31 And after him there was Shamgar son of Anath. And he struck down the
Philistines, six hundred men, with an ox-goad, and he, too, rescued Israel.

1 CHAPTER 4   And the Israelites continued to do evil in the
2 eyes of the LORD—and Ehud had died. And the LORD handed them over
to Jabin, king of Canaan, who reigned in Hazor, and the commander of
3 his army was Sisera, and he lived in Harosheth-Goiim. And the Israelites
cried out to the LORD—for he had nine hundred iron chariots and he
4 had oppressed the Israelites mightily for twenty years. And Deborah, a
prophet-woman, wife of Lappidoth, she it was who judged Israel at that
5 time. And she would sit under the Palm of Deborah between Ramah and

---

31. *Shamgar son of Anath.* Anath is the Canaanite warrior-goddess. Some scholars think
Shamgar may incorporate the name of the Hurrian sun god. It is a puzzle that this judge
should sport two eminently pagan names. It is possible that the folk-traditions on which the
tales of the Judges draw might actually reflect a fluid and syncretic situation in this early
period in which on occasion a warrior of Canaanite lineage might have fought alongside
some Israelite group.

with an ox-goad. This unconventional weapon anticipates Samson's slaying Philistines with the jawbone of a donkey. The very oddness of this detail—the sole detail we are
given about Shamgar's exploits—might suggest an actual memory of a fighter who used an
improvised destructive implement, though the number of six hundred killed (six hundred
is a set figure for military contingents) is unlikely.

CHAPTER 4   1. *and Ehud had died.* The Hebrew indicates a pluperfect by placing
the subject before the verb and using the suffix conjugation (*qatal*) of the verb: Ehud's death
leaves a hiatus, and Israel reverts to its wayward behavior.

2. *Jabin, king of Canaan.* This designation is a kind of hyperbole because there was no
single king of Canaan. Hazor, however, was an important city, and so its king would have
exercised considerable power among the city-states of Canaan. Later in the chapter, Jabin
is called "king of Hazor."

3. *iron chariots.* As elsewhere, this characterization is an exaggeration, perhaps meant
to emphasize the fearsome power of the chariots, because in this era the chariots were
wooden, with at most iron reinforcing elements.

4. *a prophet-woman.* The translation mirrors the structure of the Hebrew, which does not
say *nevi'ah* ("prophetess") but *'ishah nevi'ah.* The introduction of the "woman" component,
which is not strictly required by idiomatic usage, highlights the prominence of woman
vis-à-vis man that is evident both in Deborah's relation to Barak and in the story of Jael
and Sisera.

she it was who judged Israel at that time. The figure of Deborah manifests the ambiguity
of the role of "judge," *shofet.* She is called a prophet because she evidently has a direct line of
intelligence about God's strategic plans for Israel. In this, she resembles the martial judges,
who are invested with the spirit of God. She is not called a judge, perhaps because she her-

Bethel in the high country of Ephraim, and the Israelites would come up
to her for judgment. And she sent and called to Barak son of Abinoam 6
from Kedesh-Naphtali and said to him, "Has not the LORD God of Israel
charged you: 'Go, and draw around you on Mount Tabor and take with
you ten thousand men from the Naphtalites and the Zebulunites. And 7
I shall draw down to you at the Kishon Wadi Sisera, the commander of
Jabin's army, and his chariots and his force, and I shall give him into your
hand.'" And Barak said to her, "If you go with me, I will go, and if you 8
do not go with me, I will not go." And she said, "I will certainly go with 9
you, but it will not be your glory on the way that you are going, for in the
hand of a woman the LORD will deliver Sisera." And Deborah rose and
went with Barak to Kedesh. And Barak mustered Zebulun and Naphtali 10
at Kedesh, and he brought up at his heels ten thousand men, and Deborah went up with him. And Heber the Kenite had separated from Kayin, 11
from the sons of Hobeb father-in-law of Moses, and he pitched his tent at
Elon-in-Zaananim, which is by Kedesh. And they told Sisera that Barak 12
son of Abinoam had gone up to Mount Tabor. And Sisera mustered all 13
his chariots, nine hundred iron chariots, and all the troops that were with

---

self, as a woman, does not go out to the battlefield, but she is the subject of the verb "judge,"
a capacity she exercises in the judicial sense, as becomes entirely clear in the next verse.

6. *Has not the LORD God of Israel charged you*. Deborah would know what God commands
Barak because she is a prophet.

draw around you. The Hebrew verb says merely "draw," although the evident meaning
in context is to muster or rally. This verb is pointedly repeated in God's speech in the next
verse: Barak is to draw fighters around him, and God will then draw the enemy into a place
where he will be defeated.

8. *If you go with me, I will go*. Barak's hesitancy makes it evident that the male commander
needs this woman behind him in order to go out to battle. Thus he becomes a kind of proxy
for Deborah, who is to all intents and purposes also a "judge" in the military sense.

9. *for in the hand of a woman the LORD will deliver Sisera*. The sentence has a double meaning. The woman in the first instance is the "prophet-woman" Deborah, who can rightly
take credit for the victory. It also turns out to be Jael, whose actual hand, driving in the
tent peg, will finish off Sisera.

10. *Zebulun and Naphtali*. In this prose version, which is almost certainly later than the
poetic version in chapter 5, there are only two tribes involved and not an alliance of several
tribes.

at his heels. The literal sense of the Hebrew is "at his feet."

11. *Kayin*. This name is conventionally represented as "Cain" but is here spelled as it is to
indicate that the ethnic group is the same as Heber's identifying ethnic tag, "the Kenite."

14 him, from Harosheth-Goiim to the Kishon Wadi. And Deborah said to
Barak, "Arise, for this is the day that the LORD has given Sisera into your
hand. Has not the LORD sallied forth before you?" And Barak came down
15 from Mount Tabor, and ten thousand men after him. And the LORD panicked Sisera and all the chariots and all the camp by the edge of the sword
16 before Barak, and Sisera got down from the chariot and fled on foot. And
Barak had pursued the chariots and the camp as far as Harosheth-Goiim,
and all the camp of Sisera fell by the edge of the sword, not one remained.
17 And Sisera had fled on foot to the tent of Jael, wife of Heber the Kenite,
for there was peace between Jabin king of Hazor and the house of Heber
18 the Kenite. And Jael came out to meet Sisera and said to him, "Turn aside,
my lord, turn aside to me, do not fear." And he turned aside to her, to the
19 tent, and she covered him with a blanket. And he said to her, "Give me,
pray, a bit of water to drink, for I am thirsty." And she opened the skin of
20 milk and gave him to drink and covered him. And he said to her, "Stand
at the opening of the tent, and then, should a man come and ask you, 'Is
21 there a man here?,' you shall say there is not." And Jael wife of Heber took
the tent peg and put a mallet in her hand and came to him stealthily and
drove the peg through his temple and it sunk into the ground—as for him,
22 he had been asleep, exhausted—and he died. And, look, Barak was pursu-

14. *Has not the LORD sallied forth before you?* In almost all the reports of battle in the Deuteronomistic History, YHWH figures as the warrior-god who defeats the enemy, and there
is little representation of human acts of martial prowess or strategic cunning. The next verse
invokes a characteristic locution: the LORD "panics" the enemy, thus causing his defeat.

15. *Sisera got down from the chariot.* The same Hebrew verb is used here as when Barak
"came down" from Mount Tabor: the first coming down is a rapid descent in an attack, and
the second is a flight on foot from an encumbered or perhaps damaged chariot.

18. *Turn aside, my lord, turn aside to me.* Her words, with an alliteration of sibilants in the
Hebrew (*surah, 'adoni, surah 'elay*), are soothingly reassuring, almost seductive.

19. *she opened the skin of milk and gave him to drink.* Sisera has asked for water; Jael in a
gesture of hospitality offers him milk. The detail picks up a line from the poem (5:25), but
whereas the poem, in an epic flourish, has her offering the milk in a "princely bowl," the
prose narrative turns this into the homey realistic receptacle of a skin bag. It also highlights,
as the poem does not, the ironic suggestion of Jael's playing a maternal role toward the man
she is about to kill: first she covers him with a blanket, then she gives him milk to drink
and readjusts the blanket.

20. *should a man come and ask you, 'Is there a man here?'* The repetition of "man" (*'ish*) plays
against the previous repetitions of "woman" as the man speaking is about to be undone
by a woman.

21. *and it sunk into the ground.* This grisly detail indicates that Jael has driven in the sharpened tent peg with terrific power.

ing Sisera, and Jael went out to meet him and said to him, "Come, that I may show you the man you seek." And he went inside, and, look, Sisera was fallen, dead, the peg in his temple.

And on that day God laid low Jabin king of Canaan before the Israelites. 23
And the hand of the Israelites came down ever harder upon Jabin king of 24
Canaan till they cut off Jabin king of Canaan.

CHAPTER 5   And Deborah sang, and Barak son of Abinoam 1
with her on that day, saying:

> "When bonds were loosed in Israel,   2
>   when the people answered the call, bless the LORD!

---

22. *Come, that I may show you the man you seek.* She was instructed to answer the question "Is there a man here?" by saying "there is not." Meeting Barak in front of her tent, she volunteers the information that there is a man within before being asked, but she withholds the fact that it is a dead man.

    and, look, Sisera was fallen, dead, the peg in his temple. As with the report of the courtiers seeing the dead Eglon in chapter 3, the character's visual point of view is marked by the presentative *hineh*, "look," and the sequence of details follows his visual intake: the identity of the man, Sisera; the fact that he is lying on the ground; the fact that he is dead; the instrument of death thrust through his temple.

23. *God laid low Jabin king of Canaan.* Jabin had not taken part in the battle. Now, after the defeat of his principal force and his armored corps under the command of Sisera, he and his kingdom are laid low by the Israelites.

24. *the hand of the Israelites came down ever harder.* The literal sense of the Hebrew is "the hand of the Israelites went ever harder."

CHAPTER 5   1. *And Deborah sang, and Barak son of Abinoam with her.* The use of a singular verb (feminine) followed by a compound subject is an indication in biblical grammar that the first of the subjects named is the primary actor and the second one ancillary to the action. Deborah is introduced as singer of the victory song, but that is not a claim of authorship, and elsewhere in the poem she is addressed in the second person. In any case, the scholarly consensus is that this is one of the oldest texts in the Bible, perhaps composed not long after the battle it reports, around 1100 B.C.E. Its language abounds in archaisms, many of them uncertain in meaning and probably some of them scrambled in scribal transmission.

2. *When bonds were loosed in Israel.* The Hebrew verb can mean undoing hair or casting off restraints. In the context here, it might refer to a time of wildness in military crisis when the ordinary social and political order was in abeyance.

    when the people answered the call. The noun here (*'am*) and the verbal stem *n-d-b* often occur as joined terms. The verb suggests volunteering or answering the call, but is also

3   Hear, O kings, give ear, O chiefs—
          I to the LORD, I shall sing.
             I shall hymn to the LORD, God of Israel.
4   O LORD, when You came forth from Seir,
          when You strode from the fields of Edom,
       the earth heaved, the very heavens dripped rain,
          the clouds, O they dripped water.
5   Mountains melted before the LORD—
          He of Sinai—
             before the LORD, God of Israel.
6   In the days of Shamgar son of Anath,
          in the days of Jael, the caravans ceased,
             and wayfarers walked on roundabout paths.
7   Unwalled cities ceased,
          in Israel, they ceased,
       till you arose, Deborah,
          till you arose, O mother in Israel.
8   They chose new gods,

---

particularly associated with noblemen, who would be the ones to fling themselves into the
fray as leaders with the rest of the people following them.

4. *Seir . . . Edom.* These places mark the route of conquest from the southeast toward
Canaan reported in Numbers and Deuteronomy. YHWH as warrior god marches ahead
of the people.
   dripped rain. "Rain" is merely implied in the Hebrew.

6. *In the days of Shamgar . . . in the days of Jael, the caravans ceased.* Shamgar, the first
of the Judges, is represented as chronologically overlapping with Jael, the heroine of the
poem. Israelite caravans, according to the poem, were unable to journey safely because of
the danger from Canaanite warriors.

7. *Unwalled cities.* There are wildly different interpretations of the obscure Hebrew noun
perazon. This translation links it to the verbal stem *p-r-ts,* "to breach," and understands it
to indicate a town without walls. At a moment of grave military instability, Israelites could
no longer live in such unprotected places.
   ceased, / in Israel, they ceased. This pattern of incremental repetition (the increment here
is "in Israel") strongly marks this poem and is a hallmark of its archaic character. Incremental repetition is the most explicit form of development or intensification from the first half of
the line to the second, a pattern in which something is literally added in the second verset.
   till you arose, Deborah, / till you arose, O mother in Israel. This is another line built on
incremental repetition. Although the ending of the verbs looks, according to later norma-
tive grammar, like a first-person singular, it is almost certainly an archaic second-person
feminine ending.

8. *They chose new gods.* As in the prose narratives, cultic disloyalty leads to military catastrophe—"then was there war at the gates."

then was there war at the gates.
No shield nor lance was seen
    amidst forty thousand of Israel.
My heart to the leaders of Israel,   9
    who answered the call for the people, bless the LORD!
Riders on pure-white she-asses,   10
    sitting on regal cloths.
        O wayfarers, speak out,
louder than the sound of archers,   11
    by the watering places.
There let them retell the LORD's bounties,
    His bounties for unwalled cities in Israel.
    Then the LORD's people went down to the gates.
Awake, awake, O Deborah,   12
    awake, awake, O speak the song.
Arise, Barak,
    take your captives, Abinoam's son!
Then the remnant of the mighty came down,   13
    the LORD's people came down from amidst the warriors.
From Ephraim, their roots in Amalek.   14

---

9. *who answered the call for the people.* Here the association of the verbal stem *n-d-b* with nobility is made explicit because these are "the leaders of Israel." The martial ethos of noble warriors prepared to risk all has a certain affinity with the Homeric poems.

10. *Riders on pure-white she-asses.* In this early period, these would be the mounts of noblemen or princes.

11. *archers.* Although this is a common understanding of *meḥatsetsim*, linking it to *ḥets*, "arrow," widely different interpretations have been proposed. If in fact the word refers to archers, the sound would be the twanging of many bows and the whizzing of arrows as volleys are shot.
    unwalled cities. This is the same word that is used in verse 7. God's "bounties" would be in reestablishing a safe order for the tribes of Israel in which they could once more live in unfortified towns.
    went down to the gates. Battle is often engaged before the gates of the city.

12. *speak the song.* Yairah Amit proposes that the choice of the verb "speak," *dabri*, is motivated by a pun on the name Deborah. The phrase here is the increment in still another incremental repetition.

13. *came down.* The Masoretic vocalization *yerad* is anomalous and has led many interpreters to see an entirely different verb here. The most plausible construction, however, is to understand it as an archaic variant of *yarad*, "came down." Since battle is joined at a wadi and the Israelite forces assemble in the hills, "came down" seems appropriate.

> After you, O Benjamin, with your forces!
> From Machir the leaders came down,
>   and from Zebulun, wielders of the baton.
15 And the commanders of Issachar with Deborah,
>   and Issachar like Barak, in the valley ran free.
> In the clans of Reuben,
>   great were the heart's probings.
16 Why did you stay among the sheepfolds,
>   listening to the piping for the flocks?
> In the clans of Reuben,
>   great were the heart's probings.
17 Gilead across the Jordan dwelled,
>   and Dan, why did he linger by the ships?
> Asher stayed by the shore of the sea,
>   and by its inlets he dwelled.
18 Zebulun, a people that challenged death,
>   and Naphtali on the heights of the field.
19 Kings came, did battle,
>   then Canaan's kings did battle,
> in Taanach, by the waters of Megiddo,
>   no spoil of silver did they take.

---

14. *After you, O Benjamin, with your forces.* The tribe of Benjamin, known for its military prowess, would be a likely candidate to lead the allied tribes into the fray.

15. *great were the heart's probings.* The translation follows several variant manuscripts that show *ḥiqrey,* "probings," as in the next verse, instead of *ḥiqeqey,* "rulings" (?). Given that Reuben is denounced in the next line for not joining the assembled tribes in battle, this phrase is probably sarcastic: the Reubenites give themselves to indecisive thought and speculation instead of marshaling their forces for battle. This entire verse and the next one reflect a real situation a century before the monarchy in which there is no central governing force and not all the tribes can be counted on to "answer the call" in a time of crisis.

17. *Dan, why did he linger by the ships?* The reference is puzzling because Dan did not occupy coastal territory either in its early phase east of the Philistines or in its later migration to the north.

18. *challenged death.* Literally, "exposed its life to death."

19. *Kings came, did battle, / then Canaan's kings did battle.* This is another fine flourish of incremental repetition. "Then" is repeated through the poem, marking its narrative momentum. Unlike the narrative version of this story in chapter 4, which has only one enemy king, Jabin, the Canaanite forces here are led more plausibly by an alliance of kings.

no spoil of silver did they take. This is the first clear indication that they are defeated. It also anticipates the self-deluding notion of the Canaanite noblewomen at the end of the poem that their men are about to bring home an abundance of spoils.

From the heavens the stars did battle,   20
    from their course they did battle with Sisera.
The Kishon Wadi swept them off,   21
    an ancient wadi the Kishon Wadi.
        March on, my being, in valor!
The hooves of the horses hammered,   22
    from the gallop, the gallop of his steeds.
'Curse Meroz,' said the LORD's messenger,   23
    'Curse, O curse its dwellers,
for they did not come to the aid of the LORD,
    to the aid of the LORD midst the warriors.'
Blessed above women Jael,   24
    wife of Heber the Kenite,
        above women in tents be she blessed.
Water he asked for, milk did she give,   25
    in a princely bowl she served him curds.

---

20. *From the heavens the stars did battle.* This is a characteristic move of Israelite war poetry: no feats of valor on the battlefield are reported, for the victory comes from divine intervention. The fact that in Hebrew idiom the clustered stars are referred to as the "army" or "host" (*tzava'*) of the heavens encourages this representation of the stars battling on behalf of Israel.

21. *The Kishon Wadi swept them off.* Although the poem's narrative report here is highly elliptical, it looks as though there is an evocation of the victory at the Sea of Reeds: perhaps here, too, the chariots are disabled in the muck of the wadi, which might be the concrete manifestation of the stars' battling for Israel.

22. *The hooves of the horses hammered.* This pounding of hoofbeats steps up the "march" or "tread," of the preceding line. The entire line in Hebrew is strongly alliterative and onomatopoeic, an effect the translation seeks to emulate.

23. *Curse Meroz.* Nothing is known about this particular town other than its representation in the poem as a place of egregious failure to join the general effort of battle.
    the aid of the LORD midst the warriors. In this incremental repetition, it is evident that YHWH needs His human warriors in order to be victorious. The poem wavers in this fashion between understanding victory as a miraculous event and as the accomplishment of heroic deeds by brave warriors. Jael at the end certainly needs no divine assistance.

24. *above women in tents be she blessed.* This incremental repetition, by introducing an ostensibly automatic epithet for women with their domestic sphere, "in tents," sets the scene for the killing with the tent peg.

25. *Water he asked for, milk did she give.* Unlike the prose narrative, there is no dialogue, with its delineation of interaction of characters, only a series of gestures and acts.
    in a princely bowl she served him curds. This is an eloquent flourish and heightening of the giving of milk in the first verset. At the same time, the offering of the bowl to Sisera

26   Her hand for the tent peg reached out
            and her right hand for the workman's hammer.
        And she hammered Sisera, cracked his head.
            She smashed and pierced his temple.
27   Between her legs he kneeled, fell, lay,
            between her legs he kneeled, he fell,
                where he kneeled he fell, destroyed.
28   Through the window she looked out, moaned,
            Sisera's mother, through the lattice:
        'Why is his chariot so long in coming,
            why so late the clatter of his cars?'
29   The wisest of her ladies answer her,
            she, too, replies on her own:
30   'Why, they will find and share out the spoils—

(who has not yet been named) focuses visual attention on the hands of the woman bearing the bowl, and in the next line those hands will be murderous.

26. *Her hand for the tent peg reached out.* This would have to be her left hand. In the elliptical narrative report of the poem, we are not told that Sisera has fallen asleep, although the understanding of the prose story that this is the case sounds plausible. Alternatively, as he was drinking, his face deep in the bowl, she might have attacked him from behind, though he appears to be facing her when he falls.

　　she hammered Sisera, cracked his head. / She smashed and pierced his temple. The noun "hammer" at the end of the previous line now becomes a verb. In a related way, the entire report of the killing uses sequences of overlapping verbs, like cinematic frames one after the other—here: hammered, cracked, smashed, pierced. The verb "hammered" was previously applied to hoofbeats.

27. *Between her legs he kneeled, fell, lay.* His death agony is a kind of grotesque parody and reversal of sexual assault, a common practice in warfare, as we are reminded at the beginning of verse 30. This triadic line is one of the most brilliant deployments of incremental repetition in the poem, culminating in the climactic increment "destroyed" at the end.

28. *Through the window she looked out.* In a maneuver akin to cinematic *faux raccord*, we do not yet know that the "she" is Sisera's mother, and for a moment we might even imagine that the poem is referring to Jael, though the window could not belong in a tent.

　　moaned. The Hebrew verbal stem *y-b-b* appears only here in the biblical corpus, and so one must surmise from context that it is some sort of lament, moan, or complaint.

　　window . . . lattice. It then becomes apparent that the scene has switched from the simple setting of a tent to a luxurious palace.

　　the clatter of his cars. The term "clatter" is more literally "pounding" and thus picks up the hammering hoofbeats of verse 22.

30. *they will find and share out the spoils.* The reason for the delayed return, they imagine, is that the victorious warriors are taking time to gather booty.

a damsel or two for every man.
Spoil of dyed stuff for Sisera,
   spoil of dyed stuff,
dyed needlework,
   needlework pairs for every neck.'
Thus perish all Your enemies, O Lord!   31
   And be His friends like the sun coming out in its might."

And the land was quiet forty years.

CHAPTER 6   And the Israelites did evil in the eyes of the 1
Lord, and He gave them into the hand of Midian seven years. And the 2
hand of Midian was strong over Israel. Because of Midian the Israelites
made themselves the dugouts that are in the mountains and the caves and
the strongholds. And it happened when Israel planted, that Midian and 3
Amalek and the Easterners came up against them. And they encamped 4
against them and destroyed the yield of the land all the way to Gaza,
and they would not leave a source of livelihood in Israel, nor sheep nor

---

a damsel or two. The Hebrew *raḥam* is an archaic term, with a cognate that figures in
Ugaritic texts, hence the choice of "damsel." But it is transparently linked with *reḥem*,
"womb," and so might conceivably be a coarser term for a captive woman. In this warrior culture, the women unquestionably assume that it is the prerogative of the men to
bring back fresh bedmates for themselves—even two to a customer—from the conquered
enemy.

   spoil of dyed stuff. But the women can anticipate their own special share in the
spoils—gorgeous embroidered cloth taken from the women of the enemy. If this is the
raiment of the captive women, they will have no need of such finery as sex slaves of
their captors.

CHAPTER 6   1. *Midian*. The Midianites, unlike the indigenous peoples of Canaan
confronted by Deborah and Barak, are nomads whose chief territory is east of the Jordan.

2. *the dugouts*. On the basis of an Arab cognate, the term probably refers to some sort of
man-made trench. In modern Hebrew, this word, *minharah*, is used for "tunnel."

   strongholds. These would not be architectural structures but the tops of crags that are
adapted as fortifications.

4. *destroyed the yield of the land*. The Midianites are not an invading army but ruthless
marauders, and so they pillage the fields or use them for grazing and confiscate the Israelites' livestock.

5   ox nor donkey. For they with their flocks and tents would come up, like
    locusts in multitude, and they and their camels were beyond numbering,
6   and they came into the land to destroy it. And Israel was sorely impover-
7   ished because of Midian, and the Israelites cried out to the LORD. And it
8   happened, when the Israelites cried out to the LORD about Midian, that
    the LORD sent a prophet-man to the Israelites, and he said to them, "Thus
    said the LORD God of Israel, 'It is I Who brought you up from Egypt and
9   brought you out from the house of slaves. And I saved you from the hand
    of Egypt and from the hand of all your oppressors, and I drove them out
10 before you and I gave you their land. And I said to you—I am the LORD
    your God. You shall not revere the gods of the Amorite in whose land you
11 dwell. And you did not heed My voice.'" And the LORD's messenger came
    and sat under the terebinth that is in Ophrah, which belongs to Joash the
    Abiezerite, and Gideon his son was threshing wheat in the winepress to
12 conceal it from Midian. And the LORD's messenger appeared to him and
13 said, "The LORD is with you, valiant warrior." And Gideon said to him,
    "Please, my lord, if the LORD is with us, why has all this overtaken us, and
    where are all His wonders of which our fathers told us, saying, 'Did not
    the LORD bring us up from Egypt?' And now the LORD has abandoned us
14 and given us into the grip of Midian." And the LORD's messenger turned
    to him and said, "Go in this power of yours and rescue Israel from the
15 grip of Midian. Have I not sent you?" And he said to him, "Please, my

---

5. *camels.* These beasts, only recently domesticated toward the end of the second millennium B.C.E., were the distinctive mounts of the desert-dwelling Midianites. The Israelites
for the most part used donkeys.

11. *Gideon.* The name transparently derives from the verbal stem *g-d-ʿ*, which means "to
hack down." Since the name appears to be a consequence of his first act in the story, one
might guess that his original name was actually the pagan name Jerubaal, which would
mean, "Baal contends [for his loyal worshippers]," and not, as verse 32 suggests, "Let Baal
contend for himself," or perhaps, referring to Gideon, "he contends with Baal."

12. *the LORD's messenger.* The Masoretic Text reads "the LORD," but some Hebrew manuscripts have "the LORD's messenger." The same problem occurs in verse 16. There are scholars who think "messenger" was piously added earlier and later in the passage in order to
avoid excessive anthropomorphism, but, on the other hand, the image of God Himself
poking at something with the tip of a walking stick (verse 21) would be anomalous, and so it
seems wiser to assume that the interlocutor throughout is a divine emissary, not the divinity.
    valiant warrior. He has not yet earned this epithet, which is thus predictive, and in fact
he seems, as Yairah Amit has observed, a rather fearful man.

14. *Go in this power of yours.* This phrase probably suggests that the LORD's messenger is
conferring power on Gideon.

lord, how shall I rescue Israel? Look, my clan is poor in Manasseh, and
I am the youngest in my father's house." And the LORD's messenger said 16
to him, "For I shall be with you, and you will strike down Midian as a
single man." And he said to him, "If, pray, I have found favor in your 17
eyes, give me a sign that you are speaking with me. Pray, do not move 18
from here until I come to you and bring out my offering and set it before
you." And he said, "I shall sit here until you return." And Gideon had 19
gone and prepared a kid and an *ephah* worth of flour of flatbread. He put
the meat in a basket and the broth in a pot, and he brought it out to him
under the terebinth and brought it forward. And God's messenger said to 20
him, "Take the meat and the flatbread, and set them on yonder crag, and
pour out the broth." And so he did. And the LORD's messenger reached 21
out with the tip of the walking stick that was in his hand and touched the
meat and the flatbread, and fire went up from the rock and consumed the
meat and the flatbread. And the LORD's messenger went from his sight.
And Gideon saw that he was a messenger of the LORD. And Gideon said, 22
"Alas, LORD my Master, for I indeed have seen a messenger of the LORD
face-to-face." And the LORD said to him, "It is well with you. Do not fear. 23
You shall not die." And Gideon built there an altar to the LORD, and called 24
it YHWH Shalom. To this day it is still in Ophrah of the Abiezerites. And 25
it happened on that night that the LORD said to him, "Take the bull which
is your father's and the second bull, seven years old, and you shall destroy
the altar of Baal which is your father's, and the cultic pole that is on it

---

15. *my clan is poor . . . I am the youngest.* Such professions of inadequacy regularly occur
in the call narratives of the prophets, and they are evident in Moses's call narrative—that
is, the call to prophecy. In fact, the possession of numerous servants (or, perhaps, slaves)
indicates that Gideon's family is well off.

20. *pour out the broth.* Though the liquid in question is not conventional in the cult, this
looks like a libation.

21. *And the LORD's messenger went from his sight.* Given the fact that he has just miraculously ignited a fire on the rock, it is likely that his going away is equally miraculous—a
sudden vanishing.

22. *Alas, LORD my Master.* Here the direct reference to God is appropriate because one
would pray to God, not to a divine emissary. But Gideon fears that beholding even a messenger of God could mean death for him.

24. *YHWH Shalom.* That is, "the LORD—it is well," the words God spoke to Gideon.

25. *the second bull.* This second bull is a puzzle because nothing afterward is done in the
story with what appears to be a first bull. Some scholars solve the problem by emending
sheini, "second," to *shamen,* "fat," thus eliminating the multiplicity of bulls.

26 you shall cut down. And you shall build an altar to the LORD your God
on top of this stronghold on the surface, and you shall take the second
bull and offer it up as a burnt offering on the wood of the cultic pole that
27 you cut down." And Gideon took ten men of his servants and did as the
LORD had spoken to him. And it happened as his father's household and
28 the men of the town feared to do it by day, that he did it at night. And the
men of the town rose early in the morning, and, look, the altar of Baal was
shattered and the cultic pole that was on it was cut down, and the second
29 bull was offered up on the altar that had been built. And every man said
to his fellow, "Who has done this thing?" And they inquired and sought
30 out, and they said, "Gideon son of Joash has done this thing." And the
men of the town said to Joash, "Bring out your son that he may die, for
he has shattered the altar of Baal and cut down the cultic pole that was
31 on it." And Joash said to all who stood round him, "Will you contend for
Baal, will you rescue him? Let he who would contend for him be put to
death by morning. If he is a god, he will contend for himself, for his altar
32 has been shattered." And he was called on that day Jerubaal, which is to
say, "Let him contend for himself, for his altar has been shattered."

33 And all of Midian and Amalek and the Easterners gathered together, and
34 they crossed over and camped in the Valley of Jezreel. And the spirit of the
LORD invested Gideon, and he blasted the ram's horn, and Abiezer was
35 mustered behind him. And he sent messengers throughout Manasseh,
and it, too, was mustered behind him. And he sent messengers in Asher

---

26. *this stronghold.* See the comment on verse 2.

on the surface. The Hebrew *ma'arakhah* is a little odd. It usually refers to anything
arrayed in a set order, like the items in a sacrifice or troops in an army. Perhaps here it is
a kind of metonymy, as David Kimchi surmised, indicating the flat surface of the rock on
which the sacrifice is to be laid out.

27. *the men of the town feared to do it by day.* Here the fearful ones are Gideon's subordi-
nates, not Gideon himself. This nocturnal act is of a piece with the clandestine threshing
of wheat in a winepress. However, the people feared here are not Midianite marauders but
the Israelite inhabitants of the town, who have made Baal worship the official cult there, as
we see vividly in their resolution to execute Gideon for having desecrated the altar of Baal.

31. *Let he who would contend for him be put to death.* Joash shrewdly argues that if Baal has
real power as a god, he will fight his own battles and exact punishment from the person
who violated his altar. If he does not do that, he is not worthy of worship.

33. *crossed over.* The term indicates crossing the Jordan from their habitual territory to
the east.

34. *blasted the ram's horn.* As in the Ehud story, this is a call to arms.

and in Zebulun and in Naphtali, and they went up to meet them. And 36
Gideon said to God, "If You are going to rescue Israel by my hand as You
have spoken, look, I am about to place a fleece of wool on the threshing 37
floor. If there is dew on the fleece alone but on the ground it is dry, I shall
know that You will rescue Israel by my hand as You have spoken." And 38
so it was: he rose early the next day and squeezed the fleece and wrung
out dew from the fleece, a bowlful of water. And Gideon said to God, "Let 39
Your wrath not flare up against me. I would speak just this one time more
and I would make a trial, pray, just this one time more with the fleece. Let
it be dry on the fleece alone, and on the ground let there be dew." And, so 40
God did on that night, and it was dry on the fleece alone and on all the
ground there was dew.

CHAPTER 7   And Jerubaal, that is, Gideon, rose early, and 1
all the troops that were with him, and they camped by Ein Harod. And
the camp of Midian was north of Gibeath Hamoreh in the valley. And the 2
LORD said to Gideon, "The troops that are with you are too many for Me to
give Midian into their hand, lest Israel boast to Me saying, 'My own hand
made me victorious.' And, now, call out, pray, in the hearing of the troops, 3
saying: 'Whoever is fearful and trembling, let him turn round from Mount
Gilead.'" And twenty-two thousand turned back from the troops, and ten
thousand remained. And the LORD said to Gideon, "The troops are still 4
too many. Bring them down to the water and I shall sift them out for you
there. And so, of whom I say to you, 'This one shall go with you,' he shall

---

37. *I am about to place a fleece of wool.* Moses, too, was given signs before the beginning
of his mission, but the apprehensive Gideon sets up an elaborate test for a sign and then
reverses its terms for a second test.

39. *Let Your wrath not flare up.* Gideon obviously feels he is pushing matters with God, but
he nevertheless requires an additional proof that God will be with him when he leads the
insurrection against the powerful Midianites.
    Let it be dry on the fleece alone, and on the ground let there be dew. This is a more miracu-
lous outcome than the first test because fleece would naturally absorb moisture that might
well evaporate from the ground.

CHAPTER 7   2. *The troops that are with you are too many.* One suspects that behind
this tale of a test that eliminates the vast majority of the fighting men there may lie a historical memory of a small group of guerillas that defeated numerically superior Midianite
forces in a surprise attack.

3. *turn round.* The verb *ts-p-r* is unusual and the meaning uncertain, but there is a noun
derived from this root that suggests going around.

go with you, and all of whom I say, 'This one shall not go with you,' he shall
5 not go." And he brought the troops down to the water. And the LORD said
to Gideon, "Whoever laps the water with his tongue, as a dog laps, set him
6 apart, and whoever kneels on his knees to drink, set him apart." And the
number of those lapping from their hand to their mouth came to three
hundred men. And all the rest of the troops kneeled on their knees to drink
7 water. And the LORD said to Gideon, "With the three hundred men who
lapped I shall make you victorious and give Midian into your hand, and
8 let all the other troops go each to his place. And they took the provisions
of the troops in their hand as well as their ram's horns, and he sent off all
the men of Israel each to his tent, and he held onto the three hundred men.
9 And the camp of Midian was below him in the valley. And it happened on
that night that the LORD said to him, "Arise. Go down into the camp, for
10 I have given it into your hand. And if you are afraid to go down, go down
11 both you and Purah your lad. And you shall listen to what they say, and
then your hands will be strengthened and you shall go down into the camp."
And he went down, and Purah his lad with him, to the edge of the armed
12 men who were in the camp. And Midian and Amalek and all the Easterners lay along the valley, like locusts in multitude, and their camels were
beyond numbering, like the sand that is on the shore of the sea in multitude.
13 And Gideon came, and, look, a man was recounting a dream to his fellow,

---

5. *Whoever laps the water with his tongue, as a dog laps.* The point of the first of the two
winnowing procedures—sending home whoever is afraid—is self-evident. This second
elimination procedure is at first blush peculiar because similarity to a dog—in general a
reviled animal in the biblical world—might not appear to be a recommendation for a good
soldier. The lapping of the water, as the next verse clarifies, is not done by putting face to
water source but rather by scooping up water in one's palm and then lapping it. The fighters
who drink in this way remain alert and ready for combat even as they drink, unlike those
who kneel to drink. Perhaps the feral and dangerous connotations of "dog" in Hebrew
usage are also invoked here.

8. *of the troops.* The troops in question would have to be those who were sent back, leaving their provisions and ram's horns (which in this context serve as battle horns) behind.

10. *if you are afraid to go down.* God has already experienced Gideon's hesitancy in the two
miraculous signs Gideon asked of Him.
     your lad. The all-purpose noun *na'ar* in this context clearly indicates a function like
"attendant" or even "armor bearer."

12. *like locusts in multitude . . . beyond numbering, like the sand that is on the shore of the
sea.* This repetition of the vastness of the Midianite forces is an obvious counterpoint
to the bare three hundred men whom Gideon now leads. The Hebrew writer evinces a
special fascination with the numerous camels, the unfamiliar mounts of the Midianite
marauders.

and he said, "Look, I dreamed a dream, and, look, a loaf of barley bread
was rolling over through the camp of Midian and came up to the tent and
struck it and overturned it and the tent fell." And his fellow answered and 14
said, "That could only be the sword of Gideon son of Joash man of Israel.
God has given into his hand Midian and all its camp." And it happened, 15
when Gideon heard the recounting of the dream and its explanation, that
he bowed down and went back to the camp of Israel and said, "Arise, for
the LORD has given into your hand the camp of Midian." And he split the 16
three hundred men into three columns and put ram's horns in everyone's
hand and empty pitchers with torches inside the pitchers. And he said to 17
them, "Look to me and do the same, and just when I come to the edge of the
camp, so as I do, do the same. And when I blast on the ram's horn, and all 18
those by me, you too shall blast on the ram's horns all round the camp and
say, 'For the LORD and for Gideon!'" And Gideon came, and the hundred 19
men who were with him, to the edge of the camp, at the beginning of the
middle watch—they had just then posted the watchmen—and they blasted

---

13. *loaf.* The meaning of the Hebrew *tselil* is disputed. Some interpreters link it to the root
ts-l-l, which means to make a ringing noise and thus understand it to have a sense like "com-
motion" or "noise." Rolling noise, however, is a problematic notion. Many medieval Hebrew
commentators derive it, plausibly, from *tseli*, "roast," construing it as a term for a round flat
loaf baked over coals, which in fact is how Bedouins to this day make their *pittah*. It remains
a puzzle as to why bread, and specifically barley bread, is the instrument of destruction in the
dream, other than its being totally unexpected in this function, like Gideon's strategy with
the horns and the torches. It might be linked with the first image of Gideon threshing grain.

15. *he bowed down.* This may be a gesture of obeisance to God, Who, as he now confidently
knows, is about to make him triumph.

16. *he split the three hundred men into three columns.* This move makes it possible for Gideon's men to come down on the Midianite from three sides. Perhaps four sides would have
been even more strategically effective, but that consideration is trumped by the numerical
neatness of three hundred divided by three.

17. *Look to me and do the same.* In the Hebrew, the force of this command is underscored
by a rhyme: *mimeni tir'u wekhein ta'asu.*

18. *and all those by me.* These would be the one hundred men in the column headed by
Gideon, as we see in the next verse.
    For the LORD and for Gideon. Some Hebrew manuscripts and two ancient versions show
"sword for the LORD," as in verse 20.

19. *at the beginning of the middle watch.* The night was divided into three watches (which
here neatly correspond to the tripartite division of Gideon's fighters), so this would be
sometime approaching midnight, when the Midianite troops were deep in slumber.
    they had just then posted the watchmen. Either they have not yet settled into their posi-
tions of observation or they are not yet fully alert because they have just been wakened to
take up their watch.

20 on the ram's horns and smashed the pitchers that were in their hands. And
    the three columns blasted on the ram's horns and broke the pitchers and
    held the torches with their left hand, and their right hand the ram's horns
21 to blast on, and called out: "Sword for the LORD and for Gideon!" And each
    one stood in his place all round the camp. And all the camp ran off and
22 shouted and fled. And they blasted on the three hundred ram's horns and
    the LORD set every man's sword against his fellow throughout the camp,
    and the camp fled to Beth-Shittah, toward Sererah, to the banks of the
23 Meholah brook by Tabbath. And the men of Israel rallied, from Naphtali
24 and from Asher and from all Manasseh, and they pursued Midian. And
    Gideon sent messengers throughout the high country of Ephraim, saying,
    "Come down to meet Midian and take from them the water sources, as far
    as Beth-Barah, and the Jordan." And all the men of Ephraim rallied and
25 took the water sources as far as Beth-Barah, and the Jordan. And they took
    the two Midianite commanders, Oreb and Zeeb, and they killed Oreb at
    the Rock of Oreb, and Zeeb they killed in the Winepress of Zeeb, and they

---

20. *held the torches with their left hand, and their right hand the ram's horns.* Presumably, their swords remained strapped to their sides as they rely entirely on the effect of panic caused by the sudden blaring sound and the torchlight.

21. *each one stood in his place.* These are the horn-blowing, torch-wielding Israelites.

22. *the LORD set every man's sword against his fellow.* In other accounts of Israelite victories, we are told that the LORD "panicked" the enemy. Only here do we get the mechanism of the panic, which in fact is a stratagem devised by Gideon to terrorize the sleeping army.

   brook. Though most translations treat *'avel* as a proper noun ("Abel"), it means "brook," being an alternate form of the more common *yuval*. Representing it as "brook" clarifies the meaning of "banks" (the Hebrew *sefat* is a singular noun).

24. *Gideon sent messengers.* Having routed the large Midianite army with only three hundred men, he now rallies behind him a much larger force to pursue the fleeing enemy.

   took the water sources. In the first instance, they take hold of brooks to the west of the Jordan, where they can readily cut down the Midianites seeking to ford the streams, and then they take hold of the fords of the Jordan itself. The prominence of bodies of water in the destruction of the Midianites loops back to the test of how the Israelite fighters drink water from a stream.

25. *Oreb and Zeeb.* The two names mean, respectively, "raven" and "wolf." Animal names were common among the Northwest Semites, including the Israelites.

   they brought to Gideon from across the Jordan. The fleeing Midianite commanders are overtaken and killed east of the Jordan, having eluded the Israelite forces holding the fords. Gideon himself is still on the west side of the Jordan. He will cross it in the next episode in pursuit of the enemy.

pursued Midian. And the heads of Oreb and Zeeb they brought to Gideon from across the Jordan.

CHAPTER 8   And the men of Ephraim said to him, "What 1 is this thing you have done to us, not to call us when you went to do battle with Midian?" And they contended vehemently with him. And he said to 2 them, "What have I done now to you? Are not the gleanings of Ephraim's grapes better than the vintage of Abiezer? Into your hand God gave the com- 3 manders of Midian, Oreb and Zeeb, and what could I have done like you?" Then their anger against him abated when he spoke this thing. And Gideon 4 came to the Jordan, about to cross over, he and the three hundred men who were with him, famished and in pursuit. And he said to the men of Suc- 5 coth, "Give, pray, some loaves of bread to the troops that are at my heels, for they are famished, and I am pursuing Zebah and Zalmunna, the Midianite kings." And the notables of Succoth said, "Is the palm of Zebah and 6 Zalmunna already in your hand that we should give bread to your army?" And Gideon said, "Then when the LORD gives Zebah and Zalmunna into 7 my hand, I will harrow your flesh with the thorns and thistles of the wilderness!" And he went up from there to Penuel, and he spoke to them in the 8

CHAPTER 8   2. *What have I done now to you?* The received text says "like you," but many manuscripts show "to" (literally, "in" or "against"). An error in copying may have been triggered by "what could I have done like you" in verse 3.

Are not the gleanings of Ephraim's grapes better than the vintage of Abiezer? Gideon now exhibits a new skill as a leader—the shrewd use of persuasive rhetoric. The Ephraimites had been resentful because Gideon did not summon them to fight in the first stage of the conflict with Midian. He responds with a pointed aphorism that would have spoken to any viticulturist: Ephraim, having been responsible for the capture and execution of Oreb and Zeeb, is so much superior to Gideon's clan, Abiezer, that the stray grapes it leaves behind in the harvest are better than what Abiezer actually harvests in the vineyard.

5. *the Midianite kings.* It is improbable that Midian would have more than one king, so the term appears to be used loosely here to mean "leader."

6. *Is the palm of Zebah and Zalmunna already in your hand.* Given the extended period during which the Israelites were painfully vulnerable to the Midianites, the town elders don't really believe that Gideon will subdue this enemy, and so, in fear of Midianite retribution, they do not want to offer him aid. Amit proposes that the palm is mentioned because of a practice, attested among the Egyptians, of slicing off the palms of a defeated enemy.

7. *I will harrow your flesh with the thorns.* This fierce declaration—the literal sense of the Hebrew verb used is "thresh"—and of the matching one to the elders of Penuel is less a matter of personal vengeance than of military justice: the failure to give provisions to an army that is in desperate need is an act of treason and will be punished as such.

same fashion, and the men of Penuel answered him as the men of Succoth
9 had answered. And he said as well to the men of Penuel, saying, "When I
10 come back safe and sound, I will smash this tower!" And Zebah and Zalmunna were in Karkor and their camps with them, about fifteen thousand,
   all who remained from all the Easterners, and their fallen were a hundred
11 fifty thousand sword-wielding men. And Gideon went up on the road of the
   tent dwellers east of Nobah and Jogbahah, and he struck the camp when the
12 camp thought itself secure. And Zebah and Zalmunna fled, and he pursued
   them and took the two Midianite kings, Zebah and Zalmunna, and he
13 made all the camp tremble. And Gideon son of Joash came back from the
14 battle at Heres Ascent. And he caught a lad from the men of Succoth, and
   questioned him and the lad wrote down for him the notables and the elders
15 of Succoth, seventy-seven men. And he came to the men of Succoth and
   said, "Here are Zebah and Zalmunna about whom you insulted me saying,
   'Is the palm of Zebah and Zalmunna already in your hand that we should
16 give bread to your famished men?'" And he took the elders of the town and
   the thorns and the thistles of the wilderness and harrowed with them the
17 men of Succoth. And the tower of Penuel he smashed, and he killed the men
18 of the town. And he said to Zebah and Zalmunna, "Who are the men whom
   you killed in Tabor?" And they said, "They were just like you, like princes

---

11. *the road of the tent dwellers.* These would be encampments of nomads (still evident in
the Jordan Valley)—Gideon is heading into desert country.
   thought itself secure. "Thought itself" is merely implied in the Hebrew.

14. *the lad wrote down for him the notables and the elders of Succoth.* The captive boy is constrained to be an informer. Though it is likely that literacy at this moment in the history of
Israel was limited to a privileged elite, the writer evidently assumed that it was sufficiently
widespread that he could attribute the skill of writing to a random lad seized by Gideon.

15. *give bread to your famished men.* Gideon, in his verbatim repetition of the words of the
notables, adds a single telling word, "famished," which was used by the narrator but not
by them, and changes "army" to "men." That is to say: to famished fighting men you were
brazen enough to deny food.

16. *harrowed with them the men of Succoth.* Given that he goes on to kill the elders of
Penuel, we may infer that the same fatal result is achieved at Succoth by the harrowing—a
slow and painful death. In the Masoretic Text, the verb used appears to mean "cause to
know" (hence the bizarre King James Version, in which Gideon "taught" the elders with
thorns and thistle). The Septuagint shows "harrowed" (a difference of one consonant in
the Hebrew), which is the likely reading.

18. *They were just like you, like princes in their features.* The Midianite kings imagine
that they are flattering Gideon, but in divulging the family resemblance, they pronounce
their own death sentence. By the ethic of family blood vengeance, he now feels obliged
to kill them.

in their features." And he said, "They were my brothers, my mother's sons. 19
By the LORD, had you let them live, I would not kill you." And he said to 20
Jether his firstborn, "Rise, kill them!" And the lad did not draw his sword,
for he was afraid, for he was still a lad. And Zebah and Zalmunna said, 21
"You rise and stab us, for as the man, so is his valor." And Gideon rose and
killed Zebah and Zalmunna, and he took the crescent ornaments that were
on the necks of their camels. And the men of Israel said, "Rule over us, you 22
and also your son and also your son's son, for you have rescued us from the
hand of Midian." And Gideon said to them, "I will not rule over you nor 23
will my son rule over you. The LORD will rule over you." And Gideon said 24
to them, "Let me ask something of you—give me, every man of you, his ring
taken as booty," for they had golden rings, as they were Ishmaelites. And 25
they said, "We will certainly give." And they spread out a cloak, and each
man flung there his ring taken as booty. And the weight of the golden rings 26
for which he had asked came to seventeen hundred shekels of gold, besides
the pendants and the garments of purple that had been on the Midianite

---

19. *my mother's sons.* And not the sons of any other of my father's wives. The connection,
then, with Gideon is a strong one because these were not merely half brothers.

20. *Jether his firstborn.* Blood vengeance is a family affair, and so Gideon wants his firstborn
to carry out the sentence. He may also want to toughen him to killing, which is, in a sense,
the family business.

   he was afraid. He was afraid, of course, not of the captive (and probably fettered) kings
but of the act of stabbing them.

21. *You rise and stab us, for as the man, so is his valor.* Killing is a grown man's business for
both sides in the martial code of this story. They also may assume that a proven warrior
like Gideon will finish them off with one swift blow.

   the crescent ornaments. This detail is proleptic of the agreement to which he comes
with his men.

23. *I will not rule over you nor will my son rule over you. The LORD will rule over you.* This
emphatic repetition of their proposal that he establish a dynasty reflects an ideology cir-
culating in premonarchic Israel, and which will still be maintained by the prophet Samuel.
The vehicle of the LORD's rule is the spirit, or charisma, with which He invests the ad hoc
leaders of Israel.

24. *And Gideon said to them.* This repetition of the formula for introducing dialogue without an intervening response from the second party in the dialogue indicates that they are
baffled, or perhaps even angered, by his refusal to accept their offer of kingship. Gideon
realizes that he now has to propose something to placate or reassure them, but what he
proposes proves to be disastrous.

   rings. These are earrings or nose-rings, not rings worn on the finger.

   as they were Ishmaelites. Ishmaelite and Midianite are often interchangeable terms.
These semi-nomadic folk were evidently known for wearing golden ornaments.

27 kings and besides the collars that were on the necks of their camels. And
Gideon made them into an ephod and set it out in his town, in Ophrah,
and all Israel went whoring after it there, and it became a snare for Gideon
28 and for his household. And Midian was laid low before Israel, and they no
29 longer lifted their heads, and the land was quiet forty years. And Jerubaal
30 son of Joash went and returned to his house. And Gideon had seventy sons,
31 issue of his loins, for he had many wives. And his concubine who was in
32 Shechem also bore him a son, and he named him Abimelech. And Gideon
son of Joash died in ripe old age and was buried in the grave of Joash his
33 father the Abiezerite in Ophrah. And it happened when Gideon died that
the Israelites again went whoring after the Baalim, and they made Baal-
34 Berith their god. And the Israelites did not recall the LORD their God Who
35 had saved them from the hand of all their enemies round about. And they
did not do kindness with the house of Jerubaal-Gideon as all the good he
had done for Israel.

1 CHAPTER 9   And Abimelech son of Jerubaal went to his
mother's brothers and to all the clan of his mother's patriarchal house,
2 saying, "Speak, pray, in the hearing of all the notables of Shechem: 'What
is better for you, that seventy men should rule over you, all the sons of
Jerubaal, or that one man should rule over you? And you should remember
3 that I am your bone and your flesh.'" And his mother's brothers spoke

---

27. *Gideon made them into an ephod.* The clear allusion in this episode is to Aaron's fashioning the Golden Calf from the golden ornaments that he collects from the Israelites. In other
contexts, the ephod is a priestly breastplate or an oracular device. The latter function may
come into play here. In any case, the declaration that Israel "went whoring after it" clearly
indicates it was treated as a sacred icon to be worshipped instead of God.

31. *Abimelech.* This name, which had some general currency (see Genesis 20), incorporates
the element *melekh*, "king," the very role that Gideon rejected when it was offered but that
this reprobate son will try to arrogate for himself. Although Gideon himself dies in ripe
old age, retribution, perhaps for making the ephod, overtakes his offspring through the
malefic agency of Abimelech.

CHAPTER 9   1. *to his mother's brothers and to all the clan of his mother's patriarchal
house.* The initial base of support that he enlists is his relatives—first his uncles and then
the larger clan.

2. *that one man should rule over you.* His language takes us back to the proposal of Gideon's
warriors that he rule over them, with the scoundrel Abimelech obviously assuming the
opposite view from Gideon's about the advisability of monarchic rule.

about him all these words in the hearing of the notables of Shechem and
their heart was swayed to follow Abimelech, for they said, "He is our kinsman." And they gave him seventy shekels of silver from the house of Baal- 4
Berith, and Abimelech hired with them no-account reckless men, and they
followed him. And he came to his father's house in Ophrah and killed his 5
brothers, the sons of Jerubaal, seventy men on one stone, and Jotham the
youngest son of Jerubaal was left, for he had hidden. And all the notables 6
of Shechem and all Beth-Millo gathered and proclaimed Abimelech king
by the standing terebinth which is in Shechem. And they told Jotham, and 7
he went and stood on the top of Mount Gerizim, and he raised his voice
and called out and said to them: "Listen to me, O notables of Shechem, that
God may listen to you. Once upon a time the trees went to anoint a king 8
over them. And they said to the olive tree, 'Reign over us.' And the olive 9
tree said, 'Have I left off my rich oil, for which God and men honor me, that
I should go sway over the trees?' And the trees said to the fig tree, 'Go, you, 10
reign over us.' And the fig tree said to them, 'Have I left off my sweetness 11
and my goodly yield that I should go sway over the trees?' And the trees 12
said to the vine, 'Go, you, reign over us.' And the vine said to them, 'Have 13
I left off my new wine, that gladdens God and men, that I should go sway
over the trees?' And all the trees said to the thornbush, 'Go, you, reign over 14
us.' And the thornbush said to the trees, 'If you are really about to anoint 15
me king over you, come shelter in my shade. And if not, a fire shall come

4. *the house of Baal-Berith.* This is the local pagan temple. One should keep in mind
throughout this story that the principal actors are Canaanites, not Israelites, and that
Abimelech, though his father was an Israelite, shows no allegiance to the people or the
God of Israel.

5. *on one stone.* This detail, which is repeated in the story, suggests an execution-style
killing: first he captures and fetters his brothers, then murders them one by one, probably
either by stabbing or beheading.

6. *the standing terebinth.* Though this is a reasonable construction of the two Hebrew
words, they look odd syntactically.

8. *Once upon a time.* The Hebrew formula *hayoh hayah* signals the beginning of a parable.
The attempts of some scholars to scan it as formal verse are unconvincing, but its rhythmic
character and its use of stylized repetition, with the three-plus-one folktale structure, set
it apart formally from the surrounding narrative.

13. *gladdens God and men.* This might also justifiably be construed as "gladdens gods and men,"
reflecting a mythological background in which the gods, as in Greek tradition, quaff wine.

15. *come shelter in my shade.* This is, of course, sarcastic—the lowly thornbush gives no
shade. The argument of the parable works both against Abimelech—a low and prickly

16 out from the thornbush and consume the cedars of Lebanon.' And now, if
you have acted truly and honestly in making Abimelech king over you and
if you have acted well toward Jerubaal and his house and have acted toward
17 him as he deserves, for my father fought for you and risked his life and
18 saved you from the hand of Midian, yet you rose up against my father's
house today and killed seventy men on one stone and made Abimelech
the son of his slavegirl king over the notables of Shechem, for he was your
19 kinsman. And if you have acted truly and honestly toward Jerubaal and
toward his house on this day, rejoice in Abimelech and let him, too, rejoice
20 in you. And if not, let a fire come out from Abimelech and consume the
notables of Shechem and Beth-Millo, and let a fire come out from the nota-
21 bles of Shechem and from Beth-Millo and consume Abimelech." And
Jotham fled and ran off and went to Beer and stayed there because of Abi-
22,23 melech his brother. And Abimelech lorded it over Israel three years. And
God sent an evil spirit between Abimelech and the notables of Shechem, and
24 the notables of Shechem betrayed Abimelech, that the outage of the seventy
sons of Jerubaal and their blood should come upon Abimelech their
brother, who killed them, and upon the notables of Shechem, who abetted
25 him in killing his brothers. And the notables of Shechem laid ambushes
for him on the mountaintops, and they robbed whoever passed over them
26 on the way. And it was told to Abimelech. And Gaal son of Ebed came with
his kinsmen and passed through Shechem, and the notables of Shechem
27 trusted him. And they went out to the field and harvested their vineyards

---

character—and against the institution of kingship: only a nasty and unproductive type
would aspire to the power of a king.

    a fire shall come out. It is in the nature of kings to broadcast destruction, as Abi-
melech has already done in murdering his seventy brothers and as he will do much
more extensively. In the last moments of his lethal career, he will in fact use fire as a
weapon.

18. *the son of his slavegirl.* Jotham chooses a term of opprobrium for the concubine, just as
Sarah does for Hagar in Genesis 21:10.

24. *abetted him.* Literally, "strengthened his hands."

25. *they robbed whoever passed.* Despoiling wayfarers is hardly required to combat Abimelech, and so it is a sign that the notables of Shechem are as scurrilous as he, and both parties
will come to a bad end. In fact, these depredations may be what gives away to Abimelech
their location on the heights.

26. *Gaal son of Ebed.* The patronymic means either "son of a slave" or Ebed is a shortened
form for "Obadiah," which means "slave/servant of God."

27. *held a celebration.* The vintage celebration involves drinking, and it is in a state of
drunkenness that Gaal can confidently incite the celebrants to rebel against Abime-

and trod the vintage and held a celebration and came to the house of their god and ate and drank and reviled Abimelech. And Gaal son of Ebed said, 28 "Who is Abimelech and who the men of Shechem that we should be subject to them? Were not the son of Jerubaal and Zebul his officer subject to the men of Hamor father of Shechem? So why should we be subject to him? Would that this people were in my hands. I would remove Abimelech, and 29 I would say to Abimelech, 'Muster the full strength of your army and sally forth.'" And Zebul, the commander of the town, heard the words of Gaal 30 son of Ebed, and his wrath flared. And he sent messengers to Abimelech in 31 Arumah, saying, "Look, Gaal son of Ebed and his kinsmen are coming to Shechem, and they are about to turn the town against you. And now rise 32 in the night, you and the troops who are with you, and lie in ambush in the field. And so, in the morning, as the sun comes up, rise early and attack the 33 town, and, look, he and the troops who are with him will be coming out toward you, and you shall do whatever you are able." And Abimelech rose, 34 and all the troops who were with him, in the night, and they lay in ambush against Shechem in four columns. And Gaal son of Ebed came out and 35 stood at the entrance of the gate of the town, and Abimelech and the troops who were with him rose up from the ambush. And Gaal saw the troops and 36 said to Zebul, "Look, troops are coming down from the mountaintops." And Zebul said to him, "You are seeing the shadows of the mountains as though they were men." And Gaal spoke again and said, "Look, troops are 37 coming down from the heartland and one column is coming from Elon

---

lech, who is, after all, a ruthless killer and also, as will become clear, a savvy military commander.

28. *Were not the son of Jerubaal and Zebul his officer subject to . . . Hamor father of Shechem?* Abimelech is the son of an Israelite father who was not a native of Shechem. As such, he has no legitimate claim to dominate the Shechemites.

29. *Muster the full strength of your army.* Literally, "multiply your army," the idea being: show me all you have—I can handle it.

31. *Arumah.* The received text says Tormah, but Abimelech is in Arumah.

36. *the shadows of the mountains.* The Hebrew has a singular "shadow." Zebul's canny strategem is to make Gaal think there is no army swooping down on him until it is too late. Given that it is very early in the morning, mountains to the east would cast long shadows.

37. *troops are coming down from the heartland.* Some time has elapsed, and Gaal now can clearly see that these are troops, and that one column is headed toward him from a particular place, Elon Meonenim (which means "Soothsayers' Terebinth"). The exact meaning of *tabur ha'arets*, translated here as "heartland," is uncertain because *tabur* appears only here and in Ezekiel 38:12. The Septuagint renders it as "navel of the land," and in later Hebrew this was taken up as the word for "navel."

38 Meonenim." And Zebul said to him, "Where then is your big mouth that
   you should have said, 'Who is Abimelech that we should be subject to him?'
   Are not these the troops whom you scorned? Sally forth now, pray, and do
39 battle with them." And Gaal sallied forth before the notables of Shechem
40 and did battle with Abimelech. And Abimelech pursued him, and he fled
41 from him, and many slain fell as far as the entrance of the gate. And Abimelech stayed in Arumah, and Zebul drove out Gaal and his kinsmen from
42 dwelling in Shechem. And it happened the next day that the troops sallied
43 forth to the field, and they told Abimelech. And he took his troops and split
   them into three columns and lay in ambush in the field. And he saw and,
   look, the troops were sallying forth from the town, and he rose against
44 them and struck them. And Abimelech and the column that was with him
   attacked and took a stance at the entrance of the town's gate, and the two
45 columns attacked whoever was in the field. And Abimelech did battle with
   the town all that day, and he took the town and killed the people who were
46 in it and smashed the town and sowed it with salt. And all the notables of
   Shechem Tower heard, and they went into the redoubt of the house of El-
47 Berith. And it was told to Abimelech that all the notables of Shechem Tower
48 had gathered together. And Abimelech went up Mount Zalmon, he and all
   the troops who were with him, and he took one of the axes in his hand and
   cut down a bough and lifted it up and put it on his shoulder. And he said
   to the troops who were with him, "What you saw me doing, quick, do as I
49 do." And all the troops cut down each one his bough and followed Abime-

---

38. *your big mouth.* The Hebrew says only "your mouth," but a sarcastic sense of this sort
is strongly implied.

42. *the troops.* These troops are the armed men of Shechem.

44. *the column.* The Masoretic Text shows a plural, but Abimelech would have to be leading
only one of the three columns, and the singular is reflected in one version of the Septuagint.

45. *sowed it with salt.* Although there is some dispute about the meaning of this gesture,
sowing a field with salt would make it infertile, so the likely intention is to mark the site as
a place of eternal desolation.

46. *Shechem Tower.* In all likelihood this name indicates a place close to Shechem but not
part of it.
   the redoubt. The Hebrew *tsariaḥ* is a rare term, and its exact meaning is uncertain. Its
occurrence in 1 Samuel 13:6 suggests it was some sort of fortified underground structure.
   the house of El-Berith. The god to which this temple is dedicated is probably the same
as Baal-Berith, mentioned in verse 4.

48. *one of the axes.* The received text reads "the axes," but the Septuagint appears to have
used a Hebrew text that showed "one of the axes."

lech and put them against the redoubt and set fire with them to the redoubt. And all the people of Shechem Tower died, about a thousand men and women. And Abimelech went to Thebez and camped against Thebez and 50 took it. And there was a tower stronghold within the town, and all the men 51 and women and all the notables of the town fled there and shut themselves in and went up on the roof of the tower. And Abimelech came up to the 52 tower and did battle against it. And he approached the entrance of the tower to burn it in fire. And a certain woman flung down an upper millstone on 53 Abimelech's head and shattered his skull. And he called quickly to the lad 54 who was his armor bearer and said to him, "Draw your sword and put me to death lest they say, 'A woman killed him.'" And his lad ran him through and he died. And the men of Israel saw that Abimelech had died and each 55 man went back to his place. And God turned back the evil of Abimelech 56 that he had done to his father to kill his seventy brothers. And all the evil 57 of the men of Shechem God turned back on their heads, and the curse of Jotham son of Jerubaal came down upon them.

CHAPTER 10   And after Abimelech Tola son of Pua, son of 1 Dodo, a man of Issachar, arose to rescue Israel, and he dwelled in Shamir in the high country of Ephraim. And he led Israel twenty-three years, 2 and he died and was buried in Shamir. And after him Jair the Gileadite 3 arose and led Israel twenty-two years. And he had thirty sons who rode on 4

---

53. *a certain woman.* It is noteworthy that in this book based on a male warrior culture, first Jael and now this anonymous woman of Thebez deliver deathblows to an enemy. In a more seductive feminine mode, Delilah will bring down the Israelite hero Samson.

an upper millstone. This is the lighter of the two millstones and therefore feasible for a woman to lift up and drop from the tower.

54. *lest they say, "A woman killed him."* In 2 Samuel 11:21, we learn from Joab's words to the messenger that in fact Abimelech's death by the hand of a woman had become proverbial. His last wish, then, is frustrated.

CHAPTER 10   1. *after Abimelech.* This is merely an indication of chronology since Abimelech was no rescuer of Israel.

Tola son of Pua, son of Dodo. The first five verses of this chapter are devoted to bare notices of two judges, Tola and Jair, with no accompanying narrative material. The number of years of their leadership, respectively, twenty-three and twenty-two, are not formulaic, which could conceivably mean that they record actual historical memory.

4. *he had thirty sons who rode on thirty donkeys.* In this period, donkeys, not horses, were the usual mounts for nobility. The number of sons, donkeys, and towns looks

thirty donkeys, and they had thirty towns. They call them Jair's Hamlets
5 to this day, which are in the land of Gilead. And Jair died and was buried
in Camon.

6 And the Israelites once again did evil in the eyes of the LORD and served
the Baalim and the Ashtaroth and the gods of Aram and the gods of Sidon
and the gods of Moab and the gods of the Ammonites and the gods of the
7 Philistines. And they forsook the LORD and did not serve Him. And the
LORD's wrath flared against Israel, and He handed them over to the Philis-
8 tines and to the Ammonites. And they smashed and shattered the Israelites
in that year—eighteen years, all the Israelites who were across the Jordan in
9 the land of the Amorites which is in Gilead. And the Ammonites crossed
the Jordan to do battle as well with Judah and Benjamin and the house of
10 Ephraim, and Israel was sorely distressed. And the Israelites cried out to
the LORD, saying, "We have offended against you and we have forsaken our
11 God and served the Baalim." And the LORD said to the Israelites, "Was it
not from Egypt and from the Amorites and from the Ammonites and from
12 the Philistines, and the Sidonites and Amalek and Maon—they oppressed
13 you and you cried out to me and I rescued you from their hand? But you
forsook Me and served other gods. Therefore I will no longer rescue you.
14 Go, cry out to the gods you have chosen. Let them rescue you in the hour
15 of your distress." And the Israelites said to the LORD, "We have offended.

formulaic, but the detail about riding is odd enough that it might reflect a remembered historical fact.

6. *served the Baalim and the Ashtaroth and the gods of Aram.* The first two items are generic terms for pagan gods and goddesses, respectively; adding the gods of the five surrounding peoples mentioned here, one comes to the formulaic number seven.

7. *to the Philistines and to the Ammonites.* These are enemies to the southwest and to the northeast of the major concentration of Israelite population.

8. *in that year—eighteen years.* If the received text is correct (some manuscripts of the Septuagint do not show "in that year"), this would mean that the Philistines and the Ammonites battered Israel in direct assaults for a year and continued to dominate them for eighteen years.

11. *Was it not from Egypt.* The syntax is a little odd, but this is probably best construed as a periodic sentence continuing to the end of verse 12 with the verb "rescued" referring back to the chain of nations, most of which are preceded by "from." Rashi neatly observes, "Seven rescues appear here corresponding to the seven idolatries that they practiced."

15. *We have offended.* God's sarcastic invitation to Israel to turn for help to the gods it has worshipped drives home to them the point that only He can save them from their enemies.

Do to us whatever is good in Your eyes, but save us, pray, this day." And 16
they removed the alien gods from their midst and served the LORD, and He
could not bear the misery of Israel.

And the Ammonites were mustered and camped in Gilead, and the Israel- 17
ites gathered and camped at Mizpah. And the troops, the commanders of 18
Gilead, said to each other, "Whoever the man who begins to do battle with
the Ammonites, he shall become chief of all the inhabitants of Gilead."

CHAPTER 11   And Jephthah the Gileadite was a valiant 1
warrior, and he was the son of a whore-woman, and Gilead had begotten
Jephthah. And Gilead's wife bore him sons, and the wife's sons grew up 2
and they drove Jephthah out and said to him, "You shall not inherit in our
father's house, for you are the son of another woman." And Jephthah fled 3
from his brothers and dwelled in the land of Tob, and no-account men drew

---

Do to us whatever is good in Your eyes. The Hebrew uses an emphatic form, literally,
"You, do to us." What they are saying is that they are ready to submit to punishment for
their defection, but they nevertheless implore God to rescue them from oppression, which
is too unbearable a punishment.

17. *And the Ammonites were mustered.* A new unit begins here: the circumstances for the
impending battle with the Ammonites are established, and the need for a military leader
sets the stage for the appearance of Jephthah.

18. *the troops, the commanders of Gilead.* Perhaps 'am here means "people." The apposi-
tional phrase "the commanders of Gilead" is awkward and might be a scribal gloss.
    the man who begins to do battle. They scarcely permit themselves to imagine victory but
are prepared to proclaim as chief whoever will dare to fight the Ammonites.

CHAPTER 11   2. *Gilead's wife bore him sons.* The probable, though not inevitable,
inference is that the legitimate sons were born after Jephthah, he belonging to his father's
wild-oats phase.
    You shall not inherit in our father's house. This declaration, accompanied by the banish-
ment, appears to be a performative speech-act with legal force.
    for you are the son of another woman. They don't dare call his mother a whore to his
face, and so they use a euphemism. Their behavior toward him, however, is brutal (in this
regard, see the next comment).

3. *And Jephthah fled from his brothers.* The fact that he has to flee suggests that their driving
him out was implemented with a threat of doing him bodily harm.
    the land of Tob. This is a remote region in the northeastern sector of Gilead.
    no-account men. The same term, *reiqim* (literally, "empty") is also used for the merce-
naries hired by Abimelech. It probably refers to men without property, on the margins of

4 round Jephthah and sallied forth with him. And it happened after a time
5 that the Ammonites did battle with Israel. And it happened when the
   Ammonites did battle with Israel, that the elders of Gilead went to take
6 Jephthah from the land of Tob. And they said to Jephthah, "Come, be our
7 captain, that we may do battle with the Ammonites." And Jephthah said
   to the elders of Gilead, "Did you not hate me and drive me out from my
   father's house, and why do you come to me now when you are in distress?"
8 And the elders of Gilead said to Jephthah, "Therefore now we have come
   back to you, and you shall go with us and do battle with the Ammonites,
9 and you shall become chief for us, for all the inhabitants of Gilead." And
   Jephthah said to the elders of Gilead, "If you bring me back to do battle
   with the Ammonites and the LORD gives them to me, it is I who will be
10 your chief." And the elders of Gilead said to Jephthah, "May the LORD be
11 witness between us that we will surely do according to your word." And
   Jephthah went with the elders of Gilead, and the people set him over them

---

society, who have nothing to lose and readily join a band of guerillas or bandits. The young
David also puts together a private militia of this sort when he flees from Saul.

5. *the elders of Gilead went to take Jephthah from the land of Tob.* Their going to seek him
out in the badlands where he has located with his fighters obviously reflects the dire straits
in which they find themselves.

6. *Come, be our captain.* Their initial speech to him is brusque, devoid of deference or
diplomatic gesture. The position they offer him is military commander, *qatsin*.

7. *Did you not hate me and drive me out from my father's house.* We now learn something
new about the banishment: the brothers' harsh act either had the tacit endorsement of the
elders or was actively abetted by them.

8. *Therefore now we have come back to you.* The "therefore" amounts to a concession on
their part: precisely because we were complicit in your banishment, we now come to you to
make amends. "Come back" or "bring back" is a thematic key word in this story.
    chief. Now they up the political ante: he will not be merely a captain but chief, or head,
ro'sh, of the whole community.

9. *If you bring me back.* The man who was driven out now contemplates being brought back,
as the elders have "come back" to him. Instead of accepting the immediate offer to be chief,
he stipulates that he will assume that position only if he is victorious in battle, but he would
have to become captain in order to undertake the battle.
    it is I. The Hebrew puts the pronoun "I," usually not needed, before the conjugated verb
in a structure of emphasis.

10. *May the LORD be witness.* Literally, "May the LORD listen."

11. *the people set him over them as chief and captain.* In the event, both positions are conferred on him before the battle.
    Jephthah spoke all his words before the LORD. This is a prayer before the battle or perhaps
an inquiry of an oracle.

as chief and captain, and Jephthah spoke all his words before the LORD at Mizpah.

And Jephthah sent messengers to the king of the Ammonites, saying, "What 12 is between you and me that you have come to do battle in my land?" And 13 the king of the Ammonites said to Jephthah's messengers, "For Israel took my land when it came up from Egypt, from the Arnon to the Jabbok and to the Jordan. And now, give them back in peace." And Jephthah again sent 14 messengers to the king of the Ammonites, and he said to him, "Thus says 15 Jephthah: Israel did not take the land of Moab and the land of the Ammonites, but when it came up from Egypt, Israel went in the wilderness as far 16 as the Sea of Reeds and came to Kadesh. And Israel sent messengers to the 17 king of Edom, saying, 'Let me pass, pray, through your land,' and the king of Edom did not listen. And to the king of Moab, too, they sent and he would not agree. And Israel stayed in Kadesh. And they went through the wilder- 18 ness and swung round the land of Edom and the land of Moab and came from the east of the land of Moab and camped across the Arnon and did not come into the territory of Moab because the Arnon is the border of Moab. And Israel sent messengers to Sihon king of the Amorites, king of Heshbon, 19 and said to him, 'Let us pass, pray, through your land to our place.' And 20 Sihon did not trust Israel to pass through his territory, and Sihon gathered all his troops, and they camped at Jahaz and did battle with Israel. And the 21 LORD God of Israel gave Sihon and all his troops into the hand of Israel, and they struck them down, and Israel took hold of all the land of the Amorites, the inhabitants of that land. And they took hold of all the territory of the 22 Amorites from the Arnon to the Jabbok and from the wilderness to the Jordan. And so, the LORD God of Israel dispossessed the Amorites before His 23 people Israel, and would you possess it? Do you not take possession of what 24

---

12. *And Jephthah sent messengers to the king of the Ammonites.* The scholarly consensus is that this entire passage of attempted diplomatic negotiation has been spliced in from another source. According to the account in Numbers 20 and 33, it is Moab, not Ammon, that refuses right of transit to Israel and, in fact, Moab is mentioned first here (verse 15) and more often, together with Edom and the Amorites. "The land of the Ammonites" may well be an editorial addition intended to link this passage with the surrounding narrative. Chemosh, the deity mentioned in verse 24, is the national god of the Moabites, whereas the Ammonite god would be Milcom.

24. *Do you not take possession of what Chemosh your god gives you to possess?* The theological assumption of this statement is perfectly characteristic of this early period of Israelite history. Israel has its own God, YHWH ("the LORD"), believed to be more powerful than other gods, but each nation has its guiding deity, assumed to look after the national destiny.

Chemosh your god gives you to possess? And all that the LORD our God has
25 given us to possess, of that we shall take possession. And now, are you really
better than Balak son of Zippor king of Moab? Did he strive with Israel, did
26 he do battle with them? When Israel dwelled in Heshbon and in its hamlets
and in Aroer and in its hamlets and in all the towns that are along the Arnon
27 three hundred years, why did you not recover them in all that time? I on my
part have committed no offense against you, yet you are doing evil to battle
with me. Let the LORD, Who is judge, judge today between the Israelites and
28 the Moabites." But the king of the Ammonites did not listen to Jephthah's
words that he had sent him.

29 And the spirit of the LORD was upon Jephthah, and he passed through
Gilead and Manasseh and passed through Mizpeh Gilead, and from Mizpeh
30 Gilead he passed on to the Ammonites. And Jephthah made a vow to the
31 LORD and said, "If You indeed give the Ammonites into my hand, it shall be
that whatever comes out of the door of my house to meet me when I return
safe and sound from the Ammonites shall be the LORD's, and I shall offer
32 it up as a burnt offering." And Jephthah crossed over to the Ammonites to
33 do battle with them, and the LORD gave them into his hand. And he struck
them from Aroer to where you come to Minnith, twenty towns, and to
Abel Ceramim, a very great blow, and the Ammonites were laid low before
34 Israel. And Jephthah came to his house at Mizpah, and, look, his daughter

---

25. *Did he strive with Israel, did he do battle with them?* In fact, he fought against Israel, as
is reported in Numbers 22, but to no avail, for YHWH caused him to be defeated.

29. *And the spirit of the LORD was upon Jephthah.* Only now, when Jephthah actually leads his
troops into battle, do we have the formula of the investment by the divine spirit, the leader's
charisma, that is used for most of the other judges.

31. *whatever comes out of the door of the house to meet me.* The Hebrew is ambiguous: it could
mean "whatever" or "whoever." Some scholars have argued for the latter because "to meet"
seems to imply a person, but the Hebrew, which is in fact a preposition and not a verb, has
the sense of "toward," and it seems unlikely that Jephthah would have deliberately envisaged
human sacrifice from the start. In any case, it is a rash vow: the Midrash Tanhuma shrewdly
notes that the first creature out of the house could have been a dog or a pig, animals unfit for
sacrifice. The vow focuses on the act of return to the house, but the killing of Jephthah's only
child will mean the destruction of his house in the extended sense of the term.

32. *the LORD gave them into his hand.* This is all we are provided by way of a description
of the battle.

34. *and, look.* As repeatedly used elsewhere, the presentative term marks the switch to the
visual point of view of the character.

was coming out to meet him with timbrels and with dances, and she was
an only child—besides her, he had neither son nor daughter. And it hap- 35
pened when he saw her, that he rent his garments, and he said, "Alas, my
daughter, you have indeed laid me low and you have joined ranks with my
troublers, for I myself have opened my mouth to the LORD, and I cannot
turn back." And she said to him, "My father, you have opened your mouth 36
to the LORD. Do to me as it came out from your mouth, after the LORD
has wreaked vengeance for you from your enemies, from the Ammonites."
And she said to her father, "Let this thing be done for me: let me be for 37
two months, that I may go and weep on the mountains and keen for my
maidenhood, I and my companions." And he said, "Go." And he sent her 38
off for two months, her and her companions, and she keened for her maid-

---

with timbrels and with dances. It was the role of young women to celebrate the victory
in this fashion. The dance of joy will immediately turn into lamentation.

35. *my daughter.* This is an affectionate form of address, like "child."

for I myself have opened my mouth to the LORD. The Hebrew incorporates a crucial pun.
Jephthah's name, *yiftah,* means "he opens." The verb used here, *patsah,* is slightly different
from the verb *patah* on which the name is based, but it is a close phonetic and semantic
cousin. The belief shared by father and daughter is that vows to God are irrevocable and
nonnegotiable: what comes out of the mouth cannot be brought back ("I cannot turn back,"
a locution heavy with ironic resonances in light of Jephthah's attempt to come back to the
house from which he was driven).

36. *Do to me as it came out from your mouth.* Neither she nor her father can bring themselves to mention explicitly the horrific content of the vow. She speaks almost as though
the vow were an autonomous agent that came out of her father's mouth and cannot be
called back.

37. *And she said to her father.* This is one of the most arresting instances of the convention of repeating the formula for the introduction of speech with no intervening answer
in order to indicate a difficulty in responding on the part of the interlocutor in the dialogue. Jephthah, hearing his daughter's declaration that she is willing to become a burnt
offering in fulfillment of the vow, is dumbfounded and doesn't know what to say. His
daughter then goes on to add her special request to the affirmation of compliance she
has just uttered.

weep. The Hebrew verb *weyaradti* in the form in which it appears would normally mean
"and I shall go down," but going down upon mountains doesn't make much sense. The
least strained solution is to assume it is a scrambling of *'arid,* which in Psalm 55:3 is a verb
associated with weeping or complaint. Another possibility is to link the term here with the
rare verbal stem *r-w-d,* which probably means something like "wander."

38. *And he said, "Go."* Jephthah's extreme brevity of response suggests a man choked with
emotion, barely able to speak.

her and her companions. Here and in the previous verse, it is unambiguous in the
Hebrew that the companions are female—nubile young women like Jephthah's daughter.

39 enhood on the mountains. And it happened at the end of the two months,
that she came back to her father, and he did to her as he had vowed, and
40 she had known no man. And it became a fixed practice in Israel that each
year the daughters of Israel would go to lament the daughter of Jephthah
the Gileadite four days in the year.

1 CHAPTER 12   And the men of Ephraim were mustered and
they crossed over northward and said to Jephthah, "Why did you cross over
to do battle with the Ammonites, but us you did not call to go with you?
2 We will burn down your house upon you." And Jephthah said to them, "I
and my people were in strife and the Ammonites sorely afflicted me, and I
3 summoned you, but you did not rescue me from their hand. And I saw that
you were not about to rescue me, and I put my life at risk and crossed over

---

39. *he did to her as he had vowed.* The narrator, like father and daughter in the dialogue,
avoids spelling out the terrible act of child sacrifice. This whole story has parallels elsewhere in the ancient Mediterranean world, the most obvious being Agamemnon's sacrifice
of his daughter Iphigenia in order to obtain favorable winds to sail to the Trojan war. The
parallel episode within the Bible is the Binding of Isaac, but here, in contrast to Genesis
22, the ending is tragic.

and she had known no man. This concluding note about her virginity underscores the
point of keening for her maidenhood: she is cut off from the living without ever having had
the opportunity to enjoy the fulfillment that life has in store for a woman.

40. *each year the daughters of Israel would go to lament the daughter of Jephthah.* The long-
standing scholarly hypothesis that this is an etiological tale to explain an annual ritual
still seems valid: one suspects a pagan practice in which young women go off to mourn the
descent into the underworld each year of a vegetation goddess, a virgin like themselves,
roughly analogous to the Greek Persephone and to the Mesopotamian male vegetation
god, Tammuz.

CHAPTER 12   1. *they crossed over.* This verb—Hebrew ʿavar—is a key word in the
episode. In their challenge to Jephthah, they will say, "Why did you cross over?" These
occurrences prepare the way for the testing of the Ephraimite fugitives who seek to cross
over the Jordan at the fords (the Hebrew noun for "ford" derives from this same verb, ʿavar).

We will burn down your house. Jephthah, who was driven from his father's house and
whose familial house has been destroyed in the sacrifice of his daughter, is now threatened
with the destruction of his physical house.

2. *I and my people were in strife and the Ammonites sorely afflicted me.* The received text is
syntactically distorted here, reading: "I and my people were in strife with the Ammonites
very." The translation adopts a reading attested in several versions of the Septuagint, which
appear to have used a Hebrew text that had one additional word, ʿinuni, "they afflicted me"
before "very" (or "very much").

to the Ammonites, and the LORD gave them into my hand. And why have
you come up to me this day to do battle with me?" And Jephthah gathered 4
all the men of Gilead and did battle with Ephraim, and the men of Gilead
struck down Ephraim, for Ephraim's fugitives had said, "You, Gilead, are in
the midst of Ephraim, in the midst of Manasseh." And Gilead took the fords 5
of the Jordan from Ephraim, and it happened when a fugitive of Ephraim
would say, "Let me cross over," the men of Gilead would say to him, "Are
you an Ephraimite?" and he would say "No." And they would say to him, 6
"Say, pray, shibboleth," and he would say "sibboleth," and he would not
manage to pronounce it right, and they would seize him and slaughter him
at the fords of the Jordan. And at that time forty-two thousand of Ephraim
fell. And Jephthah led Israel six years, and Jephthah the Gileadite died and 7
was buried in his town, in Gilead.

And after him Ibzan from Bethlehem led Israel. And he had thirty sons, and 8,9
thirty daughters he sent outside, and thirty girls he brought for his sons from
outside. And he led Israel seven years. And Ibzan died and was buried in 10
Bethlehem. And after him Elon the Zebulunite led Israel ten years. And Elon 11,12
the Zebulunite died and was buried in Ajalon in the land of Zebulun. And 13
after him Abdon son of Hillel the Pirathonite led Israel. And he had forty 14
sons and thirty grandsons who rode on seventy donkeys. And he led Israel
eight years. And Abdon son of Hillel the Pirathonite died and was buried
in Pirathon in the land of Ephraim in the high country of the Amalekite.

---

4. *Ephraim's fugitives had said, "You, Gilead, are in the midst of Ephraim, in the midst of
Manasseh."* The obscure wording here has given rise to conflicting interpretations. The
one followed in this translation is Rashi's proposal: even the least important, the fugitives,
of Ephraim tell the Gileadites that they are no more than a tolerated presence in the midst
of Ephraim and its brother tribe, Manasseh. In the denouement of the civil war, all the
Ephraimite warriors will become fugitives to be slaughtered at the fords of the Jordan.

6. *shibboleth . . . sibboleth.* In contrast to the English use of "shibboleth," here it is a pass-
word. The necessary inference is that in the dialect of Hebrew spoken by the Ephraimites,
sh was pronounced as *s*. The Hebrew word can mean either "stream" or "stalk of grain," but,
given the proximity to the Jordan, the former sense is more likely. One might note that what
comes out of the mouth of the fugitives leads to death, as was the case with Jephthah's vow.
    forty-two thousand. As with numbers elsewhere, this is hardly realistic.

7. *in his town, in Gilead.* The Masoretic Text reads "in the towns of Gilead," but the Septuagint shows the reading adopted here.

9. *outside.* The probable meaning is "outside the clan."

14. *who rode on seventy donkeys.* See the comment on 10:4.

1 CHAPTER 13   And the Israelites once more did evil in the eyes of the LORD, and He gave them into the hand of the Philistines for forty years.

2 And there was a man from Zorah from the clan of the Danite, and his name
3 was Manoah. And his woman was barren, she had born no child. And a messenger of the LORD appeared to the woman and said to her, "Look, pray, you are barren and have born no child. But you shall conceive and bear a
4 son. And now, guard yourself, pray, and drink no wine or strong drink and
5 eat no unclean thing. For you are about to conceive and bear a son, and no razor shall touch his head, for the lad shall be a nazirite of God from the womb. And he shall begin to rescue Israel from the hand of the Philistines."
6 And the woman came and said to her husband, saying, "A man of God came to me, and his appearance was like the appearance of a messenger of God, very fearsome. And I did not ask him from where he was, and his name he
7 did not tell me. And he said to me, 'You are about to conceive and bear a son. And now, drink no wine or strong drink and eat no unclean thing, for

---

CHAPTER 13   2. *his woman was barren.* The Hebrew noun *'ishah*, like *femme* in French, can mean either "woman" or "wife." This translation renders it as "woman" throughout the chapter because it is a thematic key word that sets the stage for the story of Samson and his involvement with women. Indeed, the reason that she is not given a name, in contrast to her husband, may be to enable the narrator to repeat the word "woman" again and again in this episode.

his woman was barren, she had born no child. These words signal the inception of the annunciation type-scene. Of all the Judges, only Samson is accorded this scene, which, as we shall see, has several features that distinguish it from the other annunciations.

4. *strong drink.* The indication in verse 14 that specifically products of the vine are prohibited is evidence that this is liquor, *sheikhar*, derived from grapes, a form of grappa.

5. *touch his head.* Literally, "go up on his head."

nazirite. The nazirite (see Numbers 6) is a person who takes on himself special vows of abstinence. The noun derives from a verbal stem that means to be separated or set apart.

he shall begin to rescue Israel. The divine messenger chooses his words carefully: any victory Samson achieves over the Philistines will be incomplete.

6. *A man of God.* Since he appears to her in human form, however "fearsome," she has no reason to assume that he is a divine being, though he might seem to resemble one.

7. *drink no wine or strong drink.* Since the fetus feeds from the mother, the clear implication is that this prohibition, which begins in her pregnancy, will also be obligatory for the future nazirite. Nazirites in general refrain from alcoholic beverages. It is noteworthy that she says nothing about the ban on cutting the hair, which is another general practice for nazirites.

the lad shall be a nazirite of God from the womb till his dying day.'" And 8
Manoah entreated the LORD and said, "Please, my Master, the man of God
whom you sent, let him, pray, come again to us and teach us what we should
do for the lad who is to be born." And God heeded Manoah's voice, and the 9
messenger of God came again to the woman, when she was sitting in the
field and Manoah her husband was not with her. And the woman hurried 10
and ran and told her husband and said to him, "Look, the man that came to
me during the day has appeared to me." And Manoah arose and went after 11
his wife and came to the man and said to him, "Are you the man who spoke
to the woman?" And he said, "I am." And Manoah said, "Now, may your 12
word come true! What shall be the conduct of the lad and his acts?" And 13
the LORD's messenger said to Manoah, "From all that I said to the woman
she must guard herself. From all that comes from the vine she shall not 14
eat, and wine and strong drink she shall not drink, and no unclean thing
shall she eat. All that I charged her she must keep." And Manoah said to 15
the LORD's messenger, "Let us detain you, pray, and we shall prepare a kid
for you." And the LORD's messenger said to Manoah, "If you detain me, I 16
cannot eat of your food, and if you prepare a burnt offering, to the LORD

---

till his dying day. For the divine messenger's "will begin to rescue Israel," she substitutes
this phrase, ominously introducing the idea of Samson's death into the story before he is
even conceived.

9. *And God heeded Manoah's voice, and the messenger of God came again to the woman.*
In fact, God does not send a response to the two of them ("come again to us") as Manoah
asked but only to the woman who is alone in the field. This version of the annunciation
type-scene systematically sidelines the man, who really doesn't grasp what is going on.

10. *during the day.* This slightly obscure phrase evidently refers to the day before.

12. *his acts.* The Hebrew uses a singular.

13. *From all that I said to the woman she must guard herself.* There is a little note of annoy-
ance in these words: after all, I already explained to your wife what should be done about
the child, and so why are you being so obtuse as to ask me to repeat myself? As a matter of
fact, the celestial messenger does not directly answer Manoah's question about what will
be the conduct of the child because everything he says pertains to the restrictions that the
future mother must observe. It is probably implied that all these restrictions must be followed by the son as well. The most striking aspect of this response to Manoah is a crucial
omission: no word is said about not cutting the hair, as though this were a secret shared
between the divine messenger and the woman that neither will entrust to Manoah. In the
ensuing story, it is the secret of Samson's indomitable strength that, when revealed to a
woman, brings about his downfall.

16. *I cannot eat of your food.* The word for "food" here is literally "bread," but because the
proffered meal is kid's meat, the literal translation could be confusing. The alimentary

you shall offer it up." For Manoah did not know that he was a messenger of
17 the LORD. And Manoah said to the LORD's messenger, "What is your name?
18 When your word comes true, we shall honor you." And the LORD's mes-
19 senger said to him, "Why do you ask my name when it is a mystery?" And
    Manoah took the kid and the grain offering and offered them up on a rock
    to the LORD, and the other was performing a wonder, with Manoah and his
20 woman watching. And it happened when the flame went up from the altar
    to the heavens, that the LORD's messenger went up in the flame of the altar,
    with Manoah and his woman watching, and they fell on their faces to the
21 ground. And the LORD's messenger appeared no more to Manoah and to
22 his woman. Then Manoah knew that he was a messenger of the LORD. And
    Manoah said to his woman, "We are doomed to die, for we have seen God."
23 And his woman said to him, "Had the LORD desired to put us to death, He
    would not have taken from our hand burnt offering and grain offering, nor
    would He have shown us all these things and at this time instructed us in

---

ground rules, one should note, for divine beings have changed: in Genesis 18, God and
His two supernatural companions partake of the feast that Abraham prepares for them.

For Manoah did not know. Even at this late point in the story, he still doesn't get it. And
thus he goes on to ask for the name of the mysterious stranger, so that after the birth of the
child he can find a way to pay honor to the bearer of the good tidings.

18. *a mystery.* The Hebrew root of this term is the same as the verb for performing a wonder
in the next verse.

19. *the other.* The Hebrew simply says "he." This translation is meant to avoid the erroneous
notion that it is Manoah who is performing the wonder.

20. *the LORD's messenger went up in the flame of the altar.* Of all the annunciation scenes,
only here does the bringer of the annunciation disappear into the heavens in a column of
flame. That pyrotechnic exit of course points to the supernatural character of the child
to be born, but, even more strategically, it announces the motif of fire that will recur in
Samson's story. At the end, even when fire is not present either literally or in the figurative
language of the story, it remains as a powerful analogue for Samson, the hero who blindly
sows destruction, like fire.

21. *And the LORD's messenger appeared no more.* This clause could equally mean that he
disappeared from their sight and that he did not again come to them.

Then Manoah knew. It takes all this to get him finally to recognize the real identity of
the bearer of the tidings.

23. *Had the LORD desired to put us to death, He would not have taken from our hand burnt
offering and grain offering, nor would He have shown us all these things.* As her husband
quails in terror, she calmly points out to him with impeccable logic that God could scarcely
have intended to kill them (for beholding a divine creature) if He went to all the trouble of
conveying to them instructions about their promised son. The annunciation type-scene is
fundamentally matriarchal, the revelations being vouchsafed to the future mother, but here
we are given a virtually satiric version of the annunciation, highlighting male obtuseness

this manner." And the woman bore a son, and she called his name Samson, 24
and the lad grew up, and the LORD blessed him. And the spirit of the LORD 25
began to drive him in the camp of Dan between Zorah and Eshtaol.

CHAPTER 14   And Samson went down to Timnah and saw a 1
woman in Timnah of the daughters of the Philistines. And he went up and 2
told his father and his mother and said, "A woman I have seen in Timnah
of the daughters of the Philistines, and now, take her for me as a wife."
And his father and his mother said to him, "Is there no woman among 3
your kinsmen's daughters or in all my people that you should go to take a
wife from the uncircumcised Philistines?" And Samson said to his father,
"Her take for me because she pleases me." But his father and his mother 4
did not know that it was from the LORD, for He sought a pretext from the

---

and the good sense of the woman. This scene thus becomes a perfect prelude to the story of
a brawny male hero whose lapses of judgment in regard to women entangle him in repeated
difficulties and ultimately destroy him.

24. *Samson.* Although the *-on* suffix of the Hebrew *Shimshon* is used for quite a few biblical
names, it could also be related to *'on,* "potency," making the name suggest "sun of potency."
Some scholars have conjectured that behind this figure there might be traditions about a
solar deity. In any case, the link with the sun is another warrant for the fire motif. In terms
of mythological patterns, this figure also bears some resemblance to Hercules, a muscular
hero who performs arduous labors.

25. *drive him.* Now, at last, we get the descent of the spirit on the Judge. But the carefully
chosen verb is unique to Samson: it means, more literally, "to pound/pulsate [within]" him,
and neatly adumbrates his career of intermittent violent action.

CHAPTER 14   1. *Samson went down to Timnah and saw a woman.* The first common
noun that appears in the Samson narrative is "woman," a word that will be reiterated and
that picks up the repeated use of "woman" in the annunciation scene. "Woman" is also the
very first word of dialogue assigned to Samson (and for that reason, this translation follows
the syntactic order of the Hebrew).

3. *my people.* Some scholars emend this to "your people."
    the uncircumcised Philistines. This is a recurrent epithet for the Philistines, a people
of Hellenic origin, and is not used for the Canaanites, who in some instances may have
possibly practiced circumcision. The foreskin is an obvious mark of difference but it also
focuses a sense of sexual recoil: the Philistine woman, whom Samson would have as a sexual
partner, belongs to an uncircumcised people and was begotten by an uncircumcised male.
    because she pleases me. The literal sense is "because she is right in my eyes." Since there
is no indication that Samson has exchanged a single word with the woman, we may infer
that his only reason for wanting her as wife is physical attraction—what he has seen.

4. *it was from the LORD.* The theological explanation is a little shaky: God knows that the
only way to get this particular hero to act against the Philistines is to involve him with a

5 Philistines, and at that time the Philistines were ruling over Israel. And
Samson went down, and his father and his mother with him, to Timnah,
and they came as far as the vineyards of Timnah, and, look, a young
6 lion came roaring at him. And the spirit of the LORD seized him, and he
ripped it apart as one would rip apart a kid, with nothing in his hand, and
7 he did not tell his father and his mother what he had done. And he went
8 down and spoke to the woman, and she pleased Samson. And he came
back after a time to marry her and turned aside to see the place where the
lion had fallen, and, look, there was a swarm of bees in the lion's carcass,
9 and honey. And he scooped it up into his palms and went off eating as he
went, and he went to his father and to his mother and gave them, and they
ate. And he did not tell them that he had scooped up the honey from the
10 lion's carcass. And his father went down to the woman, and Samson made
11 a feast there, for thus did the young men do. And it happened when they
12 saw him, that they took thirty companions to be with him. And Samson
said to them, "Let me pose you a riddle. If you actually explain it to me
during the seven days of the feast and find the solution, I shall give you
13 thirty fine cloths and thirty changes of garment. And if you are not able

---

woman, which will lead to his being tricked by her countrymen, which then will provoke
him to vengeance.

5. *and, look, a young lion came roaring at him.* The shift of perspective marked by "look" is
of course to Samson's viewpoint. At this moment, though he has been accompanied by his
parents, he is clearly separated from them, and they do not witness the killing of the lion.
Arnold Ehrlich proposes that Samson, as an energetic young man, has bounded far ahead
of his parents, who are walking slowly on the path to Timnah.

6. *And the spirit of the LORD seized him.* In Samson's case, the divine afflatus enables violent
action by the hero and is not the charisma of an ad hoc military leader. All his heroic acts
are performed by him alone.
    he did not tell his father and his mother. Samson has a penchant for secrets, but he gets
himself in trouble when he reveals his secrets to women.

7. *he went down and spoke to the woman.* The verb "spoke" here, as in some other contexts,
is probably a technical term for a proposal of marriage.

9. *And he scooped it up into his palms.* It should be noted that carcasses are considered to
be ritually unclean, so that by taking food from the lion's bones Samson is violating one of
the terms of the nazirite vow. The setting, moreover, is a vineyard, although he does not
touch the grapes.

11. *companions.* They are, in effect, designated companions for the bridegroom during the
seven days of the feast, though Samson has no personal relationship with them.

12. *find the solution.* The Hebrew uses an ellipsis, merely the verb "find."
    I shall give you thirty fine cloths and thirty changes of garment. The confident Samson
takes on himself an indemnity in the bet thirty times that of each of the Philistine men.

to explain it to me, you shall give me thirty fine cloths and thirty changes of garment." And they said to him, "Pose your riddle, that we may hear it." And he said to them: 14

> "From the eater food came forth,
>   and from the strong sweet came forth."

And they could not explain the riddle for three days. And it happened on   15 the fourth day that they said to Samson's wife, "Entice your husband that he explain the riddle or we will burn you and your father's house in fire. Did the two of you call us here to beggar us?" And Samson's wife wept   16 before him and said, "You only hate me and don't love me. You posed a riddle to my countrymen, but to me you did not explain it." And he said to her, "Look, to my father and my mother I did not explain it, and shall I explain it to you?" And she wept before him the seven days that they had   17 the feast, and it happened on the seventh day, that he explained it to her, for she had badgered him. And she explained the riddle to her country-

---

14. *From the eater food came forth.* The Hebrew uses cognate terms: from the eater what-is-eaten came forth. The riddle, as is appropriate for riddles, is cast in a line of verse. It is, of course, an unfair riddle (hence Samson's confidence) because it depends on unique circumstances known only to the riddler, and nothing in its formulation provides a clue to the solution.

15. *on the fourth day.* The translation follows the Septuagint; the Masoretic Text reads "on the seventh day," but it is not credible that they would have waited until the very last moment, and this would also contradict the report that she pestered him for the solution day after day. There remains some problem about the number of days because in verse 17 she is said to have been weeping before Samson seven days, not four.

Entice. The Hebrew verb in context means something like "cajole" or "coax," but it also has a sexual connotation, "entice" or "seduce," and the Philistine men are clearly suggesting that she use her feminine wiles on her husband.

or we will burn you and your father's house in fire. Here the fire motif introduced in the annunciation scene enters the story proper. This is, of course, an offer that the woman cannot refuse.

Did the two of you call us here to beggar us? The Hebrew conjugates the verb "call" (in the sense of "invite") in the plural, and the translation uses "the two of you" to make that clear: in effect, they are angrily accusing the woman of conspiring against them with her Israelite husband.

here. Reading *halom*, with the Septuagint, for the Masoretic *halo'*.

16. *You only hate me and don't love me.* Here the dialogue has a sharp edge of realism: if you really loved me, you wouldn't keep secrets from me. And her speech, moreover, is accompanied by tears. Samson tries to resist and hold on to the secret, as we see in his immediate response, but in the end he succumbs to her persistent tears and imploring.

18   men. And the townsmen said to him on the seventh day before the sun
      went down:

>   "What is sweeter than honey,
>   and what is stronger than a lion?"

And he said to them:

>   "Had you not plowed with my heifer,
>   you would not have solved my riddle."

19   And the spirit of the LORD seized him, and he went down to Ashkelon and
      struck down from among them thirty men and took their armor, and he
      gave the changes of garment to the explainers of the riddle. And his wrath
20   flared, and he went up to his father's house. And Samson's wife was given
      to one of his companions who had been in his company.

---

18. *before the sun went down.* They wait until the last possible moment to spring the answer
on him, an effect perhaps highlighted here by the use of a quasi-epic flourish *beterem yavo'*
haharsah in which the word for sun, *harsah*, is archaic and poetic instead of the standard
shemesh.

   Had you not plowed with my heifer, / you would not have solved my riddle. Their statement
of the solution to the riddle, like the riddle itself, is cast in a line of verse with three accents
in each verset. Samson's response is equally a 3/3 line, although he also uses rhyme (an occasional occurrence in biblical poetry): *'eglati / hidati.* The plowing image is obviously sexual:
if you had not played around with my wife, she would not have revealed the secret to you.
Thus, Samson has no notion that his wife acted under a death threat but instead imagines
that she has been unfaithful to him—perhaps, with thirty different men! He therefore departs
enraged not only against the thirty "companions" but also against his wife.

19. *he went down to Ashkelon.* Timnah is a small Philistine town in the lowlands (Shephelah),
whereas Ashkelon is one of the five principal Philistine towns on the Mediterranean coast.

   their armor. From the one other biblical occurrence of this term, *halitsah,* in 2 Samuel
2:21, it is clear that it refers to armor, not clothing in general. Samson, then, chooses to
confront and kill armed warriors. It is probably the armor that he sends as "changes of
garment" to the thirty men who were at his wedding: this would be an act of defiance,
demonstrating to them the bold and deadly thing he has done. No mention is made of
the fine cloths, perhaps because the armor is far more than the equivalent in value of fine
cloth and garment.

20. *Samson's wife was given to one of his companions.* The marriage is in effect annulled,
and the plowing with Samson's heifer takes place after the fact of his mentioning it to the
companions.

   one of his companions who had been in his company. The Hebrew uses a cognate noun
and verb and literally says, "his companion." The subject and object of the verb are ambigu-

CHAPTER 15   And after a time, in the days of the wheat har- 1
vest, Samson visited his wife with a kid, and he said, "Let me come to my
wife in the chamber," and her father would not let him come in. And her 2
father said, "I surely thought that you altogether hated her, and I gave her
to your companion. Is not her younger sister better than she? Let her be
yours instead of her." And Samson said to them, "This time I am clear of 3
the Philistines, for I am about to do harm to them." And Samson went and 4
caught three hundred foxes and took torches and turned tail to tail and put
one torch between each two tails. And he set fire to the torches and sent 5
them into the Philistines' standing grain and set fire to the stacked grain
and the standing grain and the vineyards and the olive trees. And the Phi- 6
listines said, "Who did this?" And they said, "Samson, the son-in-law of the
Timnite, for he took his wife and gave her to his companion." And the Philistines came up and burned her and her father in fire. And Samson said to 7
them, "If this is what you do, I will be avenged of you, and then I will stop."

---

ous: it could be read either as "he [the companion] befriended/was companion to him
[Samson]" or "he [Samson] befriended/was companion to him [the companion]."

CHAPTER 15   1. *Let me come to my wife in the chamber.* What he has in mind is
obviously sex, and, in fact, the initial verb could also be construed as "let me come to bed
with my wife."

2. *I surely thought that you altogether hated her.* He has two good reasons for thinking
this: Samson's angry declaration that his wife has been unfaithful to him with the thirty
companions (14:18) and his abrupt return to his own father's house.

3. *to them.* Evidently, he is addressing not only his father-in-law but other Philistines he
views as complicit in wronging him.
    This time I am clear of the Philistines. I am clear of guilt for what I will do to them,
seeing as how they have behaved toward me. The emphasis on "this time" returns later
in the story.

4. *caught three hundred foxes.* Most of the numbers in the story are multiples of three.
Samson, himself a feral hero, is repeatedly involved with animals: the lion, the foxes, and
then the jawbone of a donkey. The foxes, running wild through the fields with fire at their
tails, are an effective delivery system for spreading incendiary destruction.

5. *the stacked grain and the standing grain and the vineyards and the olive trees.* These items
cover most of the principal products of agriculture in this region, and, moreover, the wheat
harvest is just taking place, so the overall destruction is devastating.

6. *burned her and her father in fire.* Many manuscripts and two ancient translations read
"her and her father's house." Fire answers fire now, and it is in the nature of fire uncontrolled to destroy everything in its path, much like Samson.

7. *If this is what you do, I will be avenged of you.* The Philistine retaliation leads to a second
round of vengeance for Samson.

8   And he struck them a great blow, hip on thigh, and went down and stayed in
9   the crevice of the rock of Eitam. And the Philistines came up and camped
10   in Judah and deployed at Lehi. And the men of Judah said, "Why have you
     come up against us?" And they said, "We have come up to bind Samson,
11   to do to him as he has done to us." And three thousand men of Judah went
     down to the crevice of the rock of Eitam and said to Samson, "Do you not
     know that the Philistines rule over us? And what have you done to us?" And
12   he said to them, "As they did to me, so I have done to them." And they said
     to him, "We have come down to bind you, to give you into the hand of the
     Philistines." And Samson said to them, "Vow to me that you yourselves will
13   not harm me." And they said to him, "No, for we will certainly bind you
     and give you into their hand, but we will not put you to death." And they
14   bound him with two new ropes and brought him up from the rock. He was
     coming up to Lehi when the Philistines shouted to greet him, and the spirit
     of the LORD seized him, and the ropes that were on his arms became like
15   flax burning in fire, and his bonds fell apart from upon his hands. And he

---

8. *he struck them a great blow, hip on thigh.* The implication is that he battered down a large
throng of Philistines, though the number in this case is not specified. The word for "hip"
actually means "leg" or "calf of the leg," but "hip on thigh" is a fine old locution coined
by the King James translators that effectively conveys the intended sense of a murderous
thrashing.

9. *Lehi.* As elsewhere, the name, which means "jawbone," is proleptic, and is explained in
verse 17.

10. *to bind Samson.* He is such a lethally powerful adversary that before they can think of
killing him, they have to imagine immobilizing him by trussing him up. The notion of
binding Samson will return in Delilah's dealings with him.

11. *three thousand men.* This is still another multiple of three.
    As they did to me, so I have done to them. This unbending code of vengeful retaliation
is fully shared by Samson and the Philistines. Compare verse 10.

12. *Vow to me that you yourselves will not harm me.* He uses the emphatic pronoun before
the conjugated verb to make sure that they are not the ones who intend to harm him. If they
were, he would have to exert his power and wreak havoc among his countrymen, which he
wants to avoid. On this condition, he allows himself to be bound.

14. *the ropes that were on his arms became like flax burning in fire.* The fire motif is continued here in a simile, as it will be in Delilah's failed attempts to have him bound. New
ropes also occur in the Delilah episode, the idea being that new ropes are in no way worn
or frayed and so are very hard to break.
    fell apart. Literally, "melted."

found the fresh jawbone of a donkey and reached out his hand and took it, and he struck down a thousand men with it. And Samson said: 16

> "With a donkey's jawbone,
> mound upon mound,
> With a donkey's jawbone,
> I struck down a thousand men."

And it happened when he finished speaking, that he flung the jawbone 17
from his hand, and he called that place Ramath Lehi. And he was very 18
thirsty, and he called out to the LORD: "You Yourself gave a great victory
in the hand of your servant, and now should I die from thirst and fall into
the hand of the uncircumcised?" And God split open the hollow that was 19
in Lehi, and water came out of it, and he drank and his spirit returned
and he revived. Therefore has its name been called Ein Hakkore to this
day. And he led Israel in the days of the Philistines twenty years.   20

---

15. *the fresh jawbone of a donkey.* The skeletal remains of the beast are relatively new, and so the jawbone would not be dry and brittle. As before, Samson fights with an improvised and unconventional weapon. This is the second time he comes in contact with what is left of an animal carcass—an unclean object: the first time, he draws out something sweet; now, antithetically, he finds a weapon.

16. *With a donkey's jawbone, / mound upon mound.* Samson seals his conquest, like Lamech in Genesis 4, with an exulting poem of triumph. The meaning of the second verset of this line is not certain. A long tradition of interpretation understands it as "mounds"—perhaps, the mounds of bodies of the slain. In that case, the two Hebrew words *hamor hamoratayim* would be a pun on *hamor,* "donkey." But the word for "mound" requires different vowels, so it is possible that the phrase is actually an incremental repetition of "donkey" in the first verset and means "a donkey, a pair."

17. *Ramath Lehi.* The name means "casting of the jawbone."

19. *hollow.* The Hebrew *makhteish* means "mortar" (as in mortar and pestle) and by extension a concave formation in rock.

   Ein Hakkore. In this etiology of the name, it is understood to mean "the spring of the one who calls out." But the Hebrew *qorei',* one who calls out, has a homonym that means "partridge," and it is likely that a place originally called Partridge Spring, because partridges frequented the area, was given this new narrative explanation for its name.

20. *And he led Israel . . . twenty years.* This notice of the length of Samson's career seems out of place because further episodes of his story follow. The statement is repeated at the very end of his story, where we would expect it, with the verb "led" (or "judged") in the pluperfect.

1 **CHAPTER 16**   And Samson went to Gaza, and he saw there
2 a whore-woman and came to bed with her. And it was told to the Gazites
   saying, "Samson has come here." And they lay in ambush for him all night
   long at the town gate, and they plotted together all night long, saying,
3 "At morning's light, we shall kill him." And Samson lay till midnight,
   and he arose at midnight and seized the doors of the town's gate and the
   two doorposts and pulled them free with the bolt and put them on his
   shoulders and took them up to the top of the mountain that faces Hebron.

4 And it happened afterward that he loved a woman in Nahal Sorek, and her
5 name was Delilah. And the Philistine overlords went up to her and said
   to her, "Entice him and see in what his great power lies and with what we
   can prevail against him and bind him to torture him. As for us, each of us
6 will give you eleven hundred silver shekels." And Delilah said to Samson,
   "Tell me, pray, in what your great power lies, and with what could you be
7 bound to be tortured?" And Samson said, "If they were to bind me with

---

CHAPTER 16   1. *he saw there a whore-woman.* This is a precise verbal echo of his
first encounter with a Philistine woman, only the professional designation "whore" being
added. There is a certain parallel with the story of the two spies who came to Jericho
to Rahab the whore, but Samson comes only for his own pleasure, avails himself of the
woman's services, and does not have to hide or flee because he can rely on his strength.

2. *And it was told.* Those words are added from the Septuagint.

3. *seized the doors of the town's gate.* In this provocative act, he not only asserts his invulnerability but also leaves the town exposed.

4. *he loved a woman in Nahal Sorek.* In this climactic episode in the series of three women
with whom Samson is involved, we are told that he actually loves the woman, and of the
three, only Delilah is given a name. Nahal Sorek (Wadi of the Vine) is in Israelite territory,
and Delilah may well be an Israelite woman.

5. *the Philistine overlords.* The term *seranim* always appears in the plural and is the title of
the rulers of the five towns that make up the Philistine pentapolis. Many scholars think
it is cognate with the Greek *tyrranos.* The fact that the overlords themselves should come
to make the appeal to Delilah reflects the importance they attach to the capture of this
deadly Israelite adversary.
    bind him to torture him. They are frank about their brutal intentions toward Samson:
instead of killing him on the spot, they want him rendered helpless so that they can torment
and abuse this despised enemy who has wreaked such havoc among them.
    eleven hundred silver shekels. This is a vast sum—5500 shekels all told—and so more
than enough to appeal to her mercenary impulses.

6. *with what could you be bound to be tortured.* In repeating the words of the overlords,
Delilah does not hesitate to speak openly of torture. Presumably, she is putting this to
Samson as a merely hypothetical condition, although the talk of binding and torture also
makes this sound like a perverse sex game they are playing.

seven moist thongs that had not been dried out, I would be weakened and become like any man." And the Philistine overlords brought up to her seven 8 moist thongs that had not been dried out, and she bound him with them. And the ambush was laid in her chamber. And she said to him, "Philistines 9 are upon you, Samson!" And he snapped the cords as the wick of tow snaps when it touches fire, and the secret of his power was not known. And Delilah 10 said to Samson, "Look, you have mocked me and spoken lies to me. Now, tell me, pray, with what could you be bound?" And he said to her, "If they 11 make sure to bind me with new ropes with which no task has been done, I would be weakened and become like any man." And Delilah took new ropes 12 and bound him with them, and she said to him, "Philistines are upon you, Samson!" And the ambush was laid in the chamber. And he snapped them from his arms like a thread. And Delilah said, "Until now you have mocked 13 me and spoken lies to me. Tell me, with what could you be bound?" And he said to her, "If you weave my head's seven tresses together with the web and drive them with a peg into the wall, I would be weakened and become like any man." And she drove them with a peg into the wall, and she said 14 to him, "Philistines are upon you, Samson!" And he awoke from his sleep and pulled free the peg and the loom and the web. And she said to him, 15 "You only say 'I love you,' but your heart is not with me. Three times now

---

7. *moist thongs.* These are either animal tendons or cords plaited from leather—in either case, still moist so that they are very hard to tear apart.

9. *when it touches fire.* The fire motif returns in the simile.

12. *Delilah took new ropes.* Here the aid of the Philistine overlords is not mentioned, though it may be implied.

13. *If you weave my head's seven tresses together with the web.* Only now do we learn how Samson wears his uncut hair (and one should note the magical number seven). In the third of his three false explanations, he edges toward the real secret because his hair is involved. This version also comes close to his actual predicament because it conjures up entanglement in a woman's instrument, the loom.

 and drive them with a peg into the wall, I would be weakened and become like any man. Both these clauses are absent in the Masoretic Text, which is manifestly incomplete here, but they appear in the Septuagint, in the Targum Yonatan, and in the Peshitta.

14. *And she drove them with a peg into the wall.* "Into the wall" is supplied from the Septuagint. The driving of the peg recalls Jael and Sisera, but in this instance the woman's deadly intent is not realized.

15. *You only say "I love you."* She uses the same feminine argument as Samson's first wife.

 Three times now. The folktale pattern of three times—in this case, three times with a fourth time that swerves to a new outcome—is made an object of deliberate attention. The story as a whole is organized around threes—three women, and the multiples of three killed by Samson.

you have mocked me and have not told me in what lies your great power."
16 And it happened when she badgered him with her words day after day and
17 beleaguered him, that he was vexed unto the death. And he told her all that
was in his heart, and he said, "No razor has touched my head, for I have
been a nazirite of God from my mother's womb. Were I shaven, my power
would turn away from me and I would be weakened and become like any
18 man." And Delilah saw that he had told her all that was in his heart, and
she sent and called the Philistine overlords, saying, "Come up, for he has
told me all that is in his heart." And the Philistine overlords came up to her
19 and brought the silver in their hand. And she put him to sleep on her knees
and called the man and shaved his head's seven tresses, and she began to
20 torture him, and his power turned away from him. And she said, "Philistines are upon you, Samson!" And he awoke from his sleep, and said, "I will
go out as all the other times and shake myself loose," but he did not know
21 that the LORD had turned away from him. And the Philistines seized him
and gouged out his eyes. And they brought him down to Gaza and bound
22 him in fetters, and he was put to grinding in the prison. And the hair of his
23 head began to grow as soon as it was shaven. And the Philistine overlords
had gathered to offer a great sacrifice to Dagon their god and to celebrate,
24 and they said, "Our god has given into our hand Samson our enemy." And
the people saw him and praised their god, for they said, "Our god has given

---

17. *all that was in his heart.* Literally, "all his heart."

19. *she put him to sleep on her knees.* This is, of course, necessary so that his hair can be
cut, but it is also a powerful image of the seductive woman lulling the mighty hero and
reducing him to a baby in her lap.
   called the man and shaved his head's seven tresses. The verb "shaved" is conjugated in the
feminine. Some emend it to a masculine form; others claim, with little philological warrant,
that it means "caused him to be shaved." It makes more sense to assume that Delilah, who
can't very well move with Samson asleep on her knees, calls the man to bring her a razor so
that she can then shave Samson's head. Her performance of the act herself is thematically
and psychologically apt: the seductress cuts away the source of Samson's potency.
   she began to torture him. She is the very first to torment him in an appropriately sadistic
move.

20. *as all the other times.* The times motif recurs here (the Hebrew, *kefaʿam befaʿam*, doubles
the word "time").

21. *gouged out his eyes.* A Freudian would see an upward displacement of castration in this
act, but it should be noted that these were the eyes that saw the women who led to all the
trouble. Gouging out the eyes was also a punishment for a rebellious vassal (compare the
blinding of Zedekiah by the Babylonians, 2 Kings 25:7).

into our hand our enemy, the destroyer of our land, him who brought down
many victims among us." And it happened when they were merry that they   25
said, "Call Samson, that he may play for us." And they called Samson from
the prison, and he played before them, and they set him between the pillars.
And Samson said to the lad who was holding his hand, "Let me rest and   26
feel the pillars on which the temple stands, that I may lean on them." And   27
the temple was filled with men and women, and all the Philistine overlords
were there, and on the roof about three thousand men and women watching
as Samson played. And Samson called to the LORD and said "My Master,   28
LORD, recall me, pray, and strengthen me just this time, O God, that I may
avenge myself in one act of vengeance from the Philistines for my two eyes."
And Samson grasped the two central pillars on which the temple stood and   29
pushed against them, one with his right hand and one with his left hand.
And Samson said, "Let me die with the Philistines!," and he pushed power-   30
fully, and the temple fell on the overlords and on all the people who were
in it. And the dead that he killed in his death were more than he had killed
in his life. And his kinsmen and all his father's household came down and   31
bore him off and buried him between Zorah and Eshtaol in the grave of
Manoah his father. And he had led Israel twenty years.

---

25. *that he may play for us.* The playing might be dancing or, more likely, blindly stumbling
about, while the audience laughs (the same Hebrew verb as "play").

26. *Let me rest.* This might also be construed to mean "lead me."

27. *all the Philistine overlords were there.* So that Samson's vengeance may be complete, the
rulers of the five Philistine towns, the very men who plotted his blinding and captivity,
are present.
     on the roof about three thousand men and women. Again, we have a multiple of three. It
is clearly implied that there are many more people in the main space of the temple.

28. *just this time.* At the penultimate moment of the story, the thematically fraught word
pa'am, "time," appears again. It shows, pointedly, the same root as the verb "drive" or
"pound" in 13:25 that marks the beginning of Samson's narrative.
     that I may avenge myself in one act of vengeance from the Philistines. It is true that
Samson in his last moment turns in prayer to God—perhaps feeling that his great strength
has returned but not being quite sure and in any case recognizing that its ultimate source
is God. But even now, his motive is personal vengeance: one sees why the messenger of
the LORD prophesied that Samson would no more than "begin" to rescue Israel from the
Philistines.

30. *And the dead that he killed in his death were more than he had killed in his life.* Samson's
career as an Israelite champion ends in an act of wholesale destruction in which he, too,
dies, like fire that consumes everything in its path and eventually itself as well.

1 CHAPTER 17   There was a man from the high country of
2 Ephraim, and his name was Micayhu. And he said to his mother, "The
eleven hundred silver shekels that were taken from you, and you yourself
uttered a curse and even said it in my hearing—look, the silver is with me,
it is I who took it." And his mother said, "Blessed are you, my son, to the
3 Lord." And he gave back the eleven hundred silver shekels to his mother,
and his mother said, "I had solemnly dedicated the silver to the Lord from
my hand to my son, to make a statue and molten image, and now I give it
4 back to you." And he gave the silver to his mother, and his mother took two
hundred silver shekels and gave them to the silversmith, and he made out
of it a statue and molten image. And they were in the house of Micayhu.
5 And the man Micah had a house God, and he made an ephod and teraphim

---

CHAPTER 17   1. *There was a man from the high country of Ephraim.* This formula
signals the beginning of a story that does not involve a judge. The two narratives that
unfold respectively in chapters 17–18 and 19–21 constitute a kind of epilogue to the Book
of Judges, illustrating the general condition of moral and political anarchy in the period
before the monarchy.

   Micayhu. Later in the story, the name appears without the theophoric ending as "Micah."

2. *the eleven hundred silver shekels.* Rashi shrewdly observes that this is the precise
amount that each of the Philistine overlords paid Delilah: "The episodes are linked
through the evil silver equal in amount, and in both cases it is a kind of silver that leads
to disaster."

   you yourself uttered a curse. She pronounced a curse on whoever stole the silver.

   look, the silver is with me. He evidently is frightened by the curse and so is ready to admit
he has "taken" (he avoids saying "stolen") the silver and will now give it back.

   Blessed are you. Ehrlich suggests that by these words she seeks to reverse the curse.

3. *to make a statue and molten image.* Amit argues that this is a hendiadys—a statue that is
a molten image, though in 18:20 they are separated syntactically by ephod and teraphim.
In any case, although the mother dedicates the silver to the Lord, this expression has a
strong association with idolatry.

   and now I give it back to you. If the received text is correct, the silver passes back and
forth: he takes it from her, gives it back to her; she gives it to him; he gives it back to her.
This rapid exchange may be intentional: it is "hot" treasure, first stolen by the son from his
mother, then earmarked for a questionable end.

4. *two hundred silver shekels.* Either this is the payment for the silversmith's work and the
remaining nine hundred shekels are used to fashion the statue, or she has quietly pocketed
nine hundred, despite her pious vow.

5. *an ephod and teraphim.* These are both divinatory devices, the latter term used elsewhere to designate household idols. Micah is clearly setting up shop in his little house of
God, probably with the intention of exacting payment for rendering sundry cultic services.

and installed one of his sons, and he became a priest for him. In those days 6
there was no king in Israel, every man did what was right in his eyes. And 7
there was a lad from the town of Bethlehem in Judah from the clan of Judah,
and he was a Levite, and he sojourned there. And the man went from the 8
town, from Bethlehem in Judah, to sojourn wherever he chanced, and he
came to the high country of Ephraim to the house of Micah, wending his
way. And Micah said to him, "From where do you come?" And the Levite 9
said to him, "I am from Bethlehem in Judah, and I go to sojourn wherever
I chance." And Micah said to him, "Stay with me, and be father and priest 10
for me, and I on my part will give you ten silver shekels a year and a set of
clothing and your board." And the Levite went, and the Levite agreed to 11
stay with the man, and the lad became for him like one of his sons. And 12
Micah installed the Levite, and the lad became a priest for him, and he was
in Micah's house. And Micah said, "Now I know that the LORD will deal 13
well with me, for the Levite has become my priest."

---

6. *every man did what was right in his eyes.* The last phrase here is the same one used in 14:3
by Samson in relation to the Philistine woman he sees in Timnah, but there it is translated
as "pleases me" because the character is referring to a woman he finds attractive.

7. *Bethlehem in Judah.* There was another Bethlehem ("house of bread") in Zebulun.

    from the clan of Judah. This looks like a contradiction because he is a Levite. It has
been proposed that the story harks back to an early moment in Israelite history when the
Levites' tribal identity may not have crystallized and "Levite" might be the designation of
a cultic officiant.

    sojourned. This is a term of temporary residence, and as the story unfolds, it is evident
that the Levite is an itinerant.

10. *father and priest.* "Father" here means someone in a position of authority. In fact, the
Levite is a "lad," a generation younger than Micah, as one may infer from verse 12. Micah
had already installed one of his sons to act as priest, but he prefers to have the Levite because
he is a cultic professional (whether hereditary or not is unclear).

    ten silver shekels a year. If this is a reasonable annual income, the amount of eleven
hundred shekels would have been enormous.

    And the Levite went. This brief clause (two Hebrew words) seems extraneous, and some
textual critics propose deleting it.

12. *and he was in Micah's house.* The blandness of the verb "to be" here—not "he dwelled/
stayed" or "he sojourned"—introduces a hint of ambiguity about his relation to Micah's
house. In the event, he will betray Micah and move on.

1 CHAPTER 18   In those days there was no king in Israel. And
in those days the tribe of the Danites was seeking an estate for itself in
which to dwell, for till that day no estate had fallen to it in the midst of the
2 tribes of Israel. And the Danites sent out from their clans, from the pick of
them, five men who were valiant warriors from Zorah and from Eshtaol
to spy out the land and to search it, and they said to them, "Go, search the
land." And they came to the high country of Ephraim to Micah's house,
3 and they spent the night there. They were at Micah's house, and they recognized the voice of the Levite lad and turned aside there and said to him,
"Who brought you here, and what are you doing in this place, and what
4 do you have here?" And he said to them, "Thus and so has Micah done
5 for me, and he has hired me, and I have become a priest for him." And
they said to him, "Inquire, pray, of God, that we may know whether our
6 way on which we go will prosper." And the priest said to them, "Go in
7 peace—before the LORD is your way on which you go." And the five men
went and came to Laish, and they saw the people within it dwelling secure
in the manner of the Sidonians, quiet and secure, and no one in the land
troubled them, and there was no heir to the throne, and they were far off
8 from the Sidonians, nor did they have any dealings with other people. And

---

CHAPTER 18   1. *till that day no estate had fallen to it in the midst of the tribes of
Israel.* This formulation gives the impression that no tribal territory was assigned to the
Danites. The actual case was that they were not able to hold their own against their Philistine neighbors and the local Canaanites and so were driven to migrate. The Philistine
pressure on Dan is evident in the Samson narrative, which immediately precedes this story.

3. *they recognized the voice of the Levite lad.* Given his itinerancy, they may have actually run
across him somewhere else in the south. Others conjecture that they detect a Judahite accent.

4. *Thus and so has Micah done for me.* This summarizing formula, which one would not
find in novelistic dialogue, is occasionally introduced into biblical dialogue. "Thus and so"
obviously refers to the Levite's appointment as priest with the annual stipend.

5. *Inquire, pray, of God.* This idiom indicates inquiry of an oracle; the probable instrument
would have been the ephod.

6. *before the LORD is your way on which you go.* Though the burden of this clause is that God
will favor their endeavor, the formulation is a bit vague and even ambiguous: like oracles
everywhere, the Levite is hedging his bets.

7. *dwelling secure in the manner of the Sidonians.* The inhabitants of the Phoenician city of
Sidon, to the north on the Mediterranean coast, were evidently thought to live relatively
free of fear from foreign attacks.
    they were far off from the Sidonians, nor did they have any dealings with other people.
Although the gist of these two clauses is that Laish was isolated and had no allies on which
to rely, the wording—especially of the second clause—is somewhat obscure.

they came back to their kinsmen in Zorah and Eshtaol, and their kinsmen
said to them, "How is it with you?" And they said, "Arise, and let us go   9
up against them, for we have seen the land, and, look, it is very good, and
you remain silent! Do not be idle about going to come and take hold of
the land. When you come, you will come to a people that dwells secure,   10
and the land is spacious—why, God has given it into your hand!—a place
in which nothing on earth is lacking." And the six hundred men from   11
the tribe of the Danites, from Zorah and Eshtaol, girded in battle gear,
journeyed from there. And they went up and camped at Kiriath-Jearim   12
in Judah. Therefore have they called that place the Camp of Dan to this
day—there it is, west of Kiriath-Jearim. And they passed on from there   13
to the high country of Ephraim and came to Micah's house. And the   14
five men who had gone to spy out the land of Laish spoke up and said to
their kinsmen, "Did you know that in these houses there are an ephod
and teraphim and a statue and molten image? And now, know what you
should do." And they turned aside there and came to the house of the   15
Levite lad, at Micah's house, and asked him how he fared. And the six   16
hundred men girded in their battle gear, who were from the Danites, stationed themselves at the entrance of the gate. And the five men who had   17
gone to spy out the land came in there, took the statue and the ephod and
the teraphim and the molten image, and the priest was stationed at the
entrance to the gate, and the six hundred men girded in battle gear. And   18
the former group had come into Micah's house and taken the statue and
the ephod and the teraphim and the molten image. And the priest said to

---

10. *a people that dwells secure.* As the use of this phrase in verse 7 makes clear, the gist is that
this people lives in a sense of security, not suspecting that they will be attacked.

11. *six hundred men.* As the recurrence of this number in military contexts in the Book of
Samuel suggests, this is the fixed size of a combat unit, something like a battalion.

14. *these houses.* From the plural, one infers that Micah's house was part of a small
compound.
    And now, know what you should do. Anticipating the conquest of Laish, they want to
acquire the paraphernalia to set up a cult there after they take the town.

16. *the six hundred men . . . stationed themselves at the entrance of the gate.* The five spies,
whom the Levite already knows, are sent in to parlay with him, while the armed enforcers
wait at the gate.

17. *took the statue and the ephod and the teraphim and the molten image.* They immediately
seize the cultic objects, not asking the Levite, who is in no position to resist.

18. *And the former group.* The Hebrew says merely "and these," but it has to refer to the five
spies in contradistinction to the six hundred men.

19 them, "What are you doing?" And they said to him, "Be quiet! Put your
hand over your mouth and go with us and be father and priest for us. Is it
better for you to be priest for the house of one man or to be priest for a tribe
20 and clan in Israel?" And the priest was pleased, and he took the ephod and
21 the teraphim and the statue, and joined the troops. And they turned and
went, and they put before them the little ones and the cattle and the heavy
22 goods. They had gone a distance from Micah's house when the people in
the houses that were by Micah's house were mustered, and they overtook
23 the Danites. And they called out to the Danites, and they turned round
and said to Micah, "What's the matter with you that you have mustered?"
24 And he said, "My god that I made you have taken and the priest, and you
have gone off. And what else do I have, and how is this you say to me,
25 'What's the matter with you'?" And the Danites said to him, "Don't raise
your voice to us, lest embittered men assault you and you lose your life and
26 the lives of your household." And the Danites went on their way, and Micah
saw that they were stronger than he, and he turned and went back to his

---

19. *Put your hand over your mouth and go with us and be father and priest for us.* They follow
an implied threat—shut up, if you know what is good for you—with the inducement of an
offered position.

20. *And the priest was pleased.* Nobody in this story, beginning with Micah and his mother,
has noble motives. The Levite immediately recognizes that this new position, priest for a
tribe, is a considerable advancement, no doubt with a larger salary, and so he happily col-
ludes in the theft of the cultic articles.

21. *they put before them the little ones and the cattle and the heavy goods.* Only now do we
learn that the six hundred warriors are not just a raiding party but the first wave of a tribal
migration, having brought with them their children (and presumably their wives) and their
possessions. They put all these in front of them because the attack they anticipate would
come from the rear, from a pursuing party of Micah and his men.

24. *My god that I made.* His language here, in keeping with "statue" and "molten image,"
is frankly pagan. No one in this story appears to be a serious monotheist. Even though the
narrative was composed late (see the comment on verse 30), the whole bizarre story appears
to be an authentic reflection of an early moment in premonotheistic Israelite history when
the exclusive worship of YHWH was not generally established.

25. *embittered men.* This is their condition because they have been displaced from their
tribal territory and are for the moment homeless.

26. *Micah saw that they were stronger than he.* The story plays out through force. Micah
can scarcely contend with six hundred heavily armed ruthless men who have just threatened to kill him and his whole household, and so he has to let them keep the precious

house. And they had taken what Micah made and the priest that he had. 27
And they came against Laish, against a quiet and secure people, and they
struck them down with the sword, and the town they burned in fire. And 28
there was none to save it, for it was far off from Sidon, nor did they have any
dealings with other people. And it was in the Valley of Beth-Rehob. And
they rebuilt the town and dwelled in it. And they called the town Dan, like 29
the name of Dan their forefather who was born to Israel, but Laish was the
name of the town at first. And the Danites set up the statue for themselves, 30
and Jonathan son of Gershom son of Moses, he and his sons were priests
for the tribe of the Danites till the day the land went into exile. And they 31
set out for themselves Micah's statue that he had made all the days that the
house of God was in Shiloh.

---

objects they have stolen from him, which he had fashioned with silver he originally stole
from his mother.

27. *they struck them down with the sword.* No moral considerations are involved. These
people have attractive land; Dan needs land; the Danites slaughter the inhabitants of Laish
and build their own town there.

29. *like the name.* The Masoretic Text reads "in the name," but many Hebrew manuscripts
show the standard idiom "like the name."
   who was born to Israel. The reference is to Jacob, not to the nation.

30. *Jonathan son of Gershom son of Moses.* At the very end, we are given the name and
genealogy of the Levite. The Masoretic Text inserts a superscript *nun* in *Moshe*, Moses,
turning it into *Menashe*, Manasseh, but this can't be right because Gershom was the son of
Moses and Manasseh is not a priestly tribe. Rashi aptly explains the orthographic oddity:
"Out of respect for Moses, a *nun* is inscribed in order to change the name." The genealogy
marks a steep decline: Moses's own grandson is a base sacerdotal mercenary, officiating in
a cult that is at the very least semipagan. Placing the Levite just two generations after Moses
would mean that the whole story is supposed to take place very early, at the beginning of
the twelfth century B.C.E., a temporal location that has the inconvenient consequence of
putting the Danite migration before the time of Samson, a Danite living in the south near
the Philistines.
   till the day the land went into exile. The reference is to the exile of the northern kingdom
of Israel by the Assyrians in 721 B.C.E., which means that the story, at least in its final formulation, had to be composed after that date, unless this final notation is a later editorial
addition.

31. *all the days that the house of God was in Shiloh.* The anomalous introduction of this
reference to the Shiloh sanctuary at the very end of the story is in all likelihood, as Yair
Zakovitch has argued, an editorial move to link the material here with the beginning of
the Book of Samuel, where Shiloh plays a central role.

1 CHAPTER 19   And it happened in those days, when there was no king in Israel, that a Levite man was sojourning in the far reaches of the high country of Ephraim, and he took for himself a concubine-

2 woman from Bethlehem in Judah. And his concubine played the whore against him and went away from him to her father's house in Bethlehem

3 in Judah, and she was there for a while, four months. And her husband arose and went after her to speak to her heart to bring her back, and his lad was with him and a pair of donkeys. And she brought him into her father's house, and the young woman's father saw him and rejoiced to greet

4 him. And his father-in-law, the young woman's father, entreated him, and he stayed with him three days, and they ate and drank and lodged there.

5 And it happened on the fourth day that they rose early in the morning, and he got up to go, and the young woman's father said to his son-in-law, "Refresh yourself with a morsel of bread, and afterward you may both go."

6 And the two of them sat and ate together, and the young woman's father said to the man, "Consent, pray, to spend the night, that you may enjoy

7 good cheer." And the man got up to go, and his father-in-law pressed him

8 and he stayed and spent the night there. And he rose early in the morning on the fifth day to go, and the young woman's father said, "Refresh

---

CHAPTER 19   1. *a Levite*. Though nothing further is made in the story of his status as Levite, and no reference is made to any sacerdotal function performed by him, there is an obvious link with the morally dubious Levite lad in the immediately preceding story. Hereditary connection with the cult is clearly no guarantee of character.

2. *played the whore against him*. Given that a man and his concubine are involved, this could refer to sexual infidelity, but the fact that she goes off to her father's house and that he wants her back argues for the metaphorical sense of this idiom: she pulled away from him, no longer wanted to remain with him.

3. *his lad was with him and a pair of donkeys*. Both servant and donkey will have a role to play as the story darkens.
     the young woman's. The fact that she is young, a *na'arah*, will make what ensues all the more painful.
     rejoiced to greet him. The rejoicing may be from the father's perception that his daughter and the Levite will now be reconciled, but there is an odd emphasis in the story that the father is somehow smitten with the Levite, to the exclusion of concern for his daughter.

5. *a morsel of bread*. This is a polite understatement for a full meal.

6. *enjoy good cheer*. This mood idiom usually implies feasting and drinking.

7. *his father-in-law pressed him and he stayed*. In this story that turns on the refusal and then violation of hospitality, the father-in-law's importuning of his guest looks in its exaggeration like a grotesque parody of hospitality.

yourself, pray." And they lingered till the day was waning, and the two
of them ate. And the man got up to go, he and his concubine and his lad. 9
And his father-in-law, the young woman's father, said to him, "Look, the
day is declining toward evening. Spend the night, pray. Look, the day is
gone. Spend the night here, that you may enjoy good cheer, and tomorrow
you both will rise early on your way, and you will go to your tent." But the 10
man did not want to spend the night, and he arose and went and came
opposite Jebus, which is to say, Jerusalem, and with him were the pair of
saddled donkeys and his concubine with him. They were by Jebus, and the 11
day was very far spent, and his lad said to his master, "Come, pray, and
let us turn aside to this town of the Jebusites that we may spend the night
there." And his master said to him, "We shall not turn aside to a town of 12
strangers who are not of the Israelites. Let us pass on as far as Gibeah."
And he said to his lad, "Come and let us approach one of the places, and 13
we shall spend the night in Gibeah or in Ramah." And they passed on and 14
went, and the sun set on them by Gibeah, which is Benjamin's. And they 15
turned aside to come to spend the night, and he came and sat in the town
square, but there was no man to take them in to spend the night. And, look, 16
an old man was coming from his work in the field in the evening. And
the man was from the high country of Ephraim and he was sojourning

---

8–9. *the day was waning . . . the day is declining toward evening.* This proliferation of expressions for the approach of night underscores the zone of danger into which the Levite and
his concubine will enter as night falls.

8. *the two of them ate.* The Levite and his father-in-law. The concubine is not part of the
feast.

10. *the pair of saddled donkeys.* At the end of the story, one of them will carry a grisly load
on its back.

12. *We shall not turn aside to a town of strangers.* In the event, this consideration proves
to be a bitter delusion because Israelites will behave more barbarically to them than any
strangers.

13. *And he said to his lad.* The repetition of the formula for introducing speech indicates that
the servant is perplexed or disturbed by what his master says but has no way of answering
him: why, he must be thinking, does he insist that we move on when the only reasonable
thing to do would be to seek refuge in this nearby Jebusite town?

15. *but there was no man to take them in.* This is the first signal of the network of allusions
to the story of the visit of the two divine messengers to Sodom in Genesis 19.

16. *the man was from the high country of Ephraim.* Pointedly, the sole person in Gibeah
prepared to honor the civilized obligation of hospitality is not a Benjaminite.

17 in Gibeah, but the people of the place were Benjaminites. And he raised
his eyes and saw the wayfaring man in the town square, and the old man
18 said, "Where are you going and from where do you come?" And he said
to him, "We are passing from Bethlehem in Judah to the far reaches of the
high country of Ephraim—I am from there, and I have gone to Bethlehem
in Judah—and I am going to the house of the Lᴏʀᴅ, but no man is taking
19 me in. And there is even straw and provender for our donkeys, and there
is even bread and wine for me and for your slavegirl and for the lad who
20 is with your servant. Nothing is lacking." And the old man said to him.
"It is well with you. Only all your lack is upon me. Only do not spend the
21 night in the square." And he brought him into his house and mixed fodder
22 for the donkeys, and they washed their feet and ate and drank. They were
making good cheer when, look, the men of the town, worthless men, drew
round the house, pounding on the door, and they said to the old man who
was master of the house, saying, "Bring out the man that has come to your
house that we may know him." And the man who was master of the house
23 went out to them and said, "No, my brothers, no, pray, do no harm. Seeing
that this man has come into my house, do not do this scurrilous thing.
24 Here are my virgin daughter and his concubine. Let me, pray, bring them

---

18. *to the house of the* Lᴏʀᴅ. This is a little odd because there is no indication that he lives
in a sanctuary back in the far reaches of the high country of Ephraim. Also, instead of the
preposition *'el,* "to," the text shows an accusative particle, *'et.* Many, following the Septuagint, emend the two Hebrew words here to read, "to my house."

20. *Only all your lack is upon me.* The old man refuses the Levite's offer to bring his own
provisions into the house.
    Only do not spend the night in the square. The old man knows how dangerous it would
be to spend the night outside exposed to the lubricious townsmen. The parallel with the
story of Lot and his two daughters begins to become explicit.

22. *They were making good cheer.* As before, this is a mood idiom associated with eating
and drinking.
    worthless men. This judgmental phrase is added to the near verbatim quotation from
Genesis 19:4.
    Bring out the man . . . that we may know him. This is a direct quotation of Genesis 19:5,
except that there the plural "men" appears because there are two of them. The gang-rapists'
initial preference is homosexual, but they clearly would also have been aware that the
stranger was traveling with a young woman.

23. *No, my brothers, no, pray, do no harm.* These words are quoted from Genesis 19.8.
    scurrilous thing. The Hebrew *nevalah* is a term generally used for shameful sexual acts.

24. *Here are my virgin daughter and his concubine.* This replicates Lot's offer of his two
virgin daughters to the rapists (Genesis 19:8). One does not know which is the more outrageous proposal, offering his daughter to be gang-raped or his guest's concubine, over whom
he surely does not have jurisdiction.

out, and rape them and do to them whatever you want. But to this man
do not do this scurrilous act." But the men did not want to listen to him,   25
and the man seized his concubine and brought her out to them. And they
knew her and abused her all night long till morning, and they let her go at
daybreak. And the woman came toward morning and fell at the entrance   26
to the house of the man where her master was as the light was coming up.
And her master arose in the morning and opened the doors of the house   27
and went out to go on his way. And, look, the woman, his concubine, was
fallen at the entrance of the house, her hands on the threshold. And he   28
said to her, "Get up, and let us go." And there was no answer. And he took
her on his donkey, and the man arose and went to his place. And he came   29
into his house and took a cleaver and held his concubine and cut her up

---

rape them and do to them whatever you want. The parallel text in Genesis 19:8 lacks the
brutally direct "rape" (or "abuse"). Its insertion makes us wonder all the more what kind
of father the old man is and what kind of host he is to the young woman, whom he appears
to regard as a piece of disposable property.

25. *the man seized his concubine and brought her out to them.* In the event, it is the Levite,
prepared to do anything to save his own skin, who thrusts his concubine into the clutches of
the rapists. No action follows on the old man's offer of his daughter to the rapists. Perhaps,
seeing the Levite thrust his concubine outside, he concludes that one victim will suffice.

   And they knew her and abused her all night long till morning. The source story in Genesis takes place in legendary times when there was supernatural intervention in human
affairs. The two strangers, because they are divine beings, blind the would-be rapists and
secure the safety of those within the house. In the latter-day era of the present story, there
is no miraculous intervention—the female victim is gang-raped all night long and dies at
daybreak from the prolonged violent abuse.

26. *fell at the entrance to the house.* She expires in this liminal space, her arms stretching
out across the threshold of the house where she might have been safe, her body sprawled
on the ground before the house, which is the outside zone of anarchic and destructive lust.

27. *her master.* Only at the end of the story is he called, repeatedly and almost ironically,
"her master."

   arose . . . and opened the doors of the house and went out to go on his way. He is all brisk
business and seems unconcerned about the fate of his concubine.

   And, look, the woman, his concubine. Only now does he look down and see her brutal-
ized body, identifying her first as a woman and then as his concubine.

28. *Get up, and let us go.* He at first does not realize that she is dead. This brusque command
reveals his utter moral callousness: he expects the woman, after having been gang-raped
hour after hour, to pick herself up quickly and join him on the journey back.

   he took her on his donkey. At first, we may think he means to give her a decent burial
near his home.

29. *took a cleaver and held his concubine and cut her up limb by limb into twelve pieces.*
Although the intention is to trigger outrage in all the tribes—the number twelve is automatic, but it would actually be eleven, because Benjamin is excluded—over the atrocity that

limb by limb into twelve pieces, and he sent her through all the territory
30 of Israel. And so whoever saw her would say, "There has not been nor has
there been seen such a thing from the day the Israelites came up from the
land of Egypt to this day. Pay heed about her, take counsel, and speak."

1 CHAPTER 20   And all the Israelites went out, and the community assembled as one man from Dan to Beersheba in the land of
2 Gilead before the LORD at Mizpah. And all the leaders of the people, all
the tribes of Israel in the assembly of God's people, took their stance, four
3 hundred thousand sword-wielding foot soldiers. And the Benjaminites
heard that the Israelites had gone up to Mizpah. And the Israelites said,
4 "Speak! How did this evil come about?" And the Levite man, husband of
the murdered woman, answered and said, "I came with my concubine to
5 Gibeah to spend the night. And the notables of Gibeah rose against me and
surrounded the house upon me at night. Me they thought to kill, and my
6 concubine they raped, and she died. And I seized my concubine and cut
her up and sent her through all the lands of Israel's estate, for they did a

---

has been perpetrated, the act itself is barbaric, and in biblical terms, it is a desecration of
the human body. It should be said, moreover, that the Levite until this point has himself
been singularly lacking in outrage over the gang-rape of his concubine. In any case, the
butchering of her body completes the set of images of mutilation and other violence done to
the body that begins in the opening chapter of Judges with the chopping off of the thumbs
and big toes of the captured king Adoni-Bezek.

CHAPTER 20   1. *as one man*. This phrase recurs in the story, emphasizing the
solidarity of the eleven tribes in their opposition to Benjamin.

2. *four hundred thousand sword-wielding foot soldiers*. Although military numbers in all
these stories are exaggerated, this figure is especially fantastic. At no time in the history of
ancient Israel could the nation have deployed this large an army.

4. *husband of the murdered woman*. Only now does the narrative spell out that the night-
long gang-rape is tantamount to murder.
    I came with my concubine. The Hebrew uses "I came" in the singular, followed by a
second grammatical subject of the verb "my concubine," a form that indicates that the first
subject of the verb is primary. The Levite remains true to character, making the woman
ancillary to himself.

5. *Me they thought to kill*. In fact, the men of Gibeah sought to have sex with him, a detail
the Levite prefers not to mention, substituting for it a purported direct threat to his life.
    and my concubine they raped. He says nothing about the fact that he himself thrust her
out the door into the hands of the rapists.

6. *I seized my concubine and cut her up*. He has already said that she died, but this way
of putting it creates the macabre impression of his cutting up the person, not the corpse.

foul and scurrilous thing in Israel. Look, you are all Israelites. Offer a word 7
of counsel here." And the whole people rose as one man, saying, "We will 8
not go each to his tent and we will not turn aside each to his home! And 9
now, this is the thing we shall do to Gibeah: we shall go up against it by lot.
And we shall take ten men out of a hundred from all the tribes of Israel and 10
a hundred out of a thousand and a thousand out of ten thousand to take
provisions for the troops, to do for those coming to Benjamin's Gibeah,
according to all the scurrilous thing they did in Israel." And all the men 11
of Israel gathered at the town, joined as one man. And the tribes of Israel 12
sent throughout the tribe of Benjamin, saying, "What is this evil that has
come about among you? And now, give over the worthless men who are in 13
Gibeah that we may put them to death and root out the evil from Israel."
But the Benjaminites did not want to heed the voice of their Israelite brothers. And the Benjaminites gathered from the towns at Gibeah to go out to 14
battle with the Israelites. And the Benjaminites from the towns mustered 15
on that day twenty-six thousand sword-wielding men, besides the inhabitants of Gibeah who mustered seven hundred picked men. From all these 16
troops there were seven hundred picked men, left-handers; every one of

---

7. *Offer a word of counsel here.* Obviously, the word he assumes his tale will elicit is a resolution of vengeance.

10. *ten men out of a hundred.* Though it seems evident that 10 percent of the assembled
troops are to provide logistical support to the warriors, the wording—ten out of a hundred,
a hundred out of a thousand, a thousand out of ten thousand—is a bit confusing.
   for those coming to Benjamin's Gibeah. The translation follows the reading in the Septuagint. The Masoretic Text looks garbled here: "for their coming."

12. *the tribe of Benjamin.* The received text shows, illogically, a plural, "tribes," but both the
Septuagint and the Vulgate have a singular noun.

13. *But the Benjaminites did not want to heed the voice of their Israelite brothers.* The Israelites at first sought to punish only the perpetrators of the murderous sex crime. The refusal
of the Benjaminites to hand them over then sets the stage for the bloody civil war.

14. *gathered from the towns.* These would have to be the sundry towns besides Gibeah that
were in the tribal territory of Benjamin.

15. *twenty-six thousand sword-wielding men.* There is an unresolved discrepancy between this
number and verse 35, where the total number of Benjaminite fighting men is given as 25,100.

16. *left-handers.* This might have been a genetic trait common among the Benjaminites, or
they might have trained themselves to use their left hand in combat, like the great tennis
player Rafael Nadal. One recalls that the Benjaminite Ehud used his left-handed prowess
to take Eglon by surprise.
   every one of them could sling a stone at a hair and not miss. Thus the Benjaminites,
although vastly outnumbered, are formidable warriors. The large casualties they inflict on
the first two days of battle may be because they can accurately strike their enemies from

17 them could sling a stone at a hair and not miss. And the men of Israel,
except for Benjamin, mustered four hundred thousand sword-wielding
18 men, every one of them a man of war. And they arose and went up to
Bethel and inquired of God, and the Israelites said, "Who shall go up first
for us in battle with the Benjaminites?" and the LORD said, "Judah first."
19 And the Israelites arose in the morning and encamped against Gibeah.
20 And the men of Israel went out to battle with Benjamin, and the men of
21 Israel were arrayed for battle with them at Gibeah. And the Benjaminites
sallied forth from Gibeah, and they laid waste among Israel on that day
22 twenty-two thousand men. And the troops of the men of Israel summoned their strength and once again were arrayed for battle in the place
23 where they had been arrayed on the first day. And the Israelites went up
and wept before the LORD till evening, and they inquired of the LORD,
saying, "Shall I once again join battle with my Benjaminite brother?" And
24 the LORD said, "Go up against him." And the Israelites drew near to the
25 Benjaminites on the second day. And Benjamin sallied forth to meet them
from Gibeah on the second day, and they laid waste among the Israelites
26 another eighteen thousand men, all of them sword-wielding. And the
Israelites and all the troops went up and came to Bethel and wept, and
they sat there before the LORD and fasted on that day till evening, and
they offered up burnt offerings and well-being sacrifices before the LORD.
27 And the Israelites inquired of the LORD—and in those days the Ark of
28 God's Covenant was there, and Phineas son of Eleazar son of Aaron was
in attendance before Him in those days—saying, "Shall I once again sally

---

a distance, with a weapon that has a greater range than a spear and can be deployed more
mobily than a bow.

18. *inquired of God.* It was standard procedure throughout the ancient Near East to inquire
of an oracle before battle.

    Judah first. The oracle is extremely terse, and it offers no guidance as to how to conduct
the battle.

21. *laid waste.* This is an unusual idiom for killing enemies in battle (the literal sense is:
"waste to the ground"). It is possible that the usage, repeated several times in the story, is
intended to evoke an association of cutting off progeny because it is precisely the idiom
used to describe Onan's practice of coitus interruptus (Genesis 38:9). The question of progeny and the survival of Benjamin becomes urgent in the next chapter.

23. *Go up against him.* Again, the oracle offers no counsel or prediction about the battle.

27. *in those days the Ark of God's Covenant was there.* This clause and the next, which runs
through the first half of verse 28, are an editorial interpolation intended to explain to a later
audience why the Israelites had come to Bethel to inquire of the oracle.

forth in battle with my Benjaminite brother or shall I leave off?" And the LORD said, "Go up, for tomorrow I shall give him into your hand." And Israel placed ambushers round about Gibeah. And the Israelites went up against the Benjaminites on the third day and were arrayed against Gibeah as on the times before. And the Benjaminites sallied forth to meet the troops, they were drawn away from the town, and they began to strike down from the troops, as on the times before, on the highways, one going up to Bethel and one to Gibeah, about thirty men of Israel. And the Benjaminites thought, "They are routed before us as before." But the Israelites had said, "Let us flee and draw them away from the town to the highways." And all the men of Israel had arisen from their place and were arrayed in Baal-Tamar, and the Israelite ambush was emerging from its place west of Gibeah. And ten thousand picked men from all Israel came opposite Gibeah, and the battle was fierce, but the Benjaminites did not know that harm was about to touch them. And the LORD routed Benjamin before Israel, and the Israelites laid waste among Benjamin on that day twenty-five thousand one hundred men, all of them sword-wielding. And the Benjaminites saw that they were routed. And the men of Israel gave ground before Benjamin, for they trusted the ambush that they had set for Gibeah. And the ambushers rushed out and assaulted Gibeah, and the ambushers drew together and struck the whole town with the edge of the sword. And the time that had been set for the men of Israel

29
30
31
32
33
34
35
36
37
38

---

28. *Go up, for tomorrow I shall give him into your hand.* Following the familiar folktale pattern of three repetitions with a reversal the third time, God now assures the Israelites that this time they will be victorious. Some interpreters see a contradiction between God's granting the victory and its achievement through a military stratagem—the ambush and the false retreat—but this account is actually in keeping with the system of dual causation one often finds in biblical narrative: events are attributed to divine intervention but are implemented by human initiative.

31. *the highways.* Unlike *derekh*, which is any kind of road or way, these *mesilot* are paved roads.

  about thirty men. In this third battle, the casualties they inflict before they are trapped and overwhelmed are insignificant.

37. *the ambushers drew together and struck the whole town with the edge of the sword.* The stratagem used here to capture and destroy the town is identical with the one deployed by the Israelite forces against Ai in Joshua 8. Many scholars think that the writer in Joshua drew on this story.

38. *the time that had been set for the men of Israel with the ambushers was when they sent up a column of smoke.* In the parallel episode in Joshua, it is Joshua who gives the signal by

with the ambushers was when they sent up a column of smoke from the
39   town, the men of Israel were to turn round in the battle. And Benjamin
had begun to strike down among the men of Israel about thirty men, for
they thought, "Why, he is surely routed before us as in the first battle."
40   And the column began to go up from the town, a pillar of smoke, and
Benjamin turned around to its rear and, look, the entire town had gone
41   up in smoke to the heavens. And the men of Israel turned round, and the
men of Benjamin panicked, for they saw that harm had touched them.
42   And they turned from before the men of Israel to the wilderness road,
but the battle overtook both them and the ones from the town. They were
43   laying waste to them within it. They had encircled Benjamin, pursued
him to Menuhah, led him to a point over against Gibeah from the east.
44   And eighteen thousand men of Benjamin fell, all of them valiant men.
45   And they turned and fled to the wilderness to the Rock of Rimmon, but
they picked off five thousand men of them on the highways, and they
overtook them at Gidom and struck down two thousand men of them.
46   And all those who fell of Benjamin on that day came to twenty-five thou-
47   sand sword-wielding men, all of them valiant men. And six hundred men
turned and fled to the wilderness to the Rock of Rimmon and stayed at
48   the Rock of Rimmon four months. And the men of Israel had turned back
against the Benjaminites, and they struck them by the edge of the sword
from the town, from man to beast, whatever was there. All the towns, too,
that were there they set on fire.

---

raising his javelin, as Moses raised his staff against Amalek. Here we have the more likely
military device of a signal fire. The Masoretic Text has an anomalous word *herev* ("much"?)
after "the ambushers," but this is in all likelihood a dittography for *ha'orev*, "the ambushers," and so it has been deleted in the translation.

39. *And Benjamin had begun to strike down among the men of Israel about thirty men.* This
duplicates verse 31 and may reflect an editorial glitch.

41. *they saw that harm had touched them.* They now realize that they are caught in a pincer
move between the ambushers and the main Israelite force.

42. *They were laying waste to them within it.* The wording of the Hebrew is somewhat
crabbed, and this trait is reflected in the translation.

47. *six hundred men . . . stayed at the Rock of Rimmon.* It seems unlikely that this wilderness
crag was either impregnable or invisible to the pursuing army, so the Israelites may have
made a decision to spare some remnant of the Benjaminite fighting men.

48. *they struck them by the edge of the sword from the town, from man to beast.* This formulation would seem to suggest that Gibeah and the other Benjaminite towns were put under
the ban, the *herem.* For the phrase "from man to beast," the translation, following some

CHAPTER 21   And the men of Israel had vowed at Mizpah, 1
saying, "No man of us will give his daughter as wife to Benjamin." And 2
the people came to Bethel and stayed there till evening before God, and
they raised their voice and wept bitterly. And they said, "Why, O LORD 3
God of Israel, has this come about in Israel, that today one tribe should
be missing from Israel?" And it happened on the next day that the people 4
rose early and built an altar there and offered up burnt offerings and
well-being offerings. And the Israelites said, "Who has not come up in 5
the assembly to the LORD from all the tribes of Israel?"—for great was
the vow concerning whoever had not gone up to the LORD at Mizpah,
saying, "He is doomed to die." And the Israelites were regretful about 6
Benjamin their brother, and they said, "Today one tribe has been cut off
from Israel. What shall we do for wives for those who remain, as we have 7
vowed to the LORD not to give our daughters to them as wives?" And they 8
said, "Which is the one of the tribes of Israel that did not come up to
the LORD at Mizpah?" And, look, not a man had come to the camp from
Jabesh-Gilead to the assembly. And the troops were mustered, and, look, 9
there was no man there from the inhabitants of Jabesh-Gilead. And the 10
community sent there twelve thousand of the valiant men and charged
them, saying, "Go and strike down the inhabitants of Jabesh-Gilead by

---

manuscripts and two ancient versions, reads *mimetim* (literally, "from people") rather than
the Masoretic *metom* ("unwounded spot").

CHAPTER 21   1. *the men of Israel had vowed at Mizpah.* The Hebrew indicates a pluperfect because this solemn vow was taken before the beginning of the war with Benjamin.

3. *Why . . . has this come about in Israel.* Now, after the victory, the people are confronted
with a dilemma because of their binding vow, for its consequence will be the elimination
of one of the twelve tribes of Israel.

5. *for great was the vow.* This second vow, to destroy whoever held back from joining in the
war against Benjamin, will be used to find a way out of the first vow.

6. *cut off.* The Hebrew uses a rather violent verb, *nigda'* (literally, "hacked off"), instead of
the usual *nikhrat.* Some scholars prefer to read *nigra',* "is taken away," which would be in
keeping with "missing" in verse 3.

8. *Jabesh-Gilead.* This northern territory to the east of the Jordan was allied with Benjamin,
as will be clear in the story of Saul in 1 Samuel. Many have inferred that the whole story
of the civil war and of the place of Jabesh-Gilead in its aftermath is meant to discredit
Benjamin, Saul's tribe.

10. *Go and strike down the inhabitants of Jabesh-Gilead.* Jabesh-Gilead is to be put under the
ban, all its population except for female virgins to be massacred. It is historically unlikely
that the *herem* was practiced by one set of Israelites on another, and as Amit points out, it

11   the edge of the sword, and the women and the little ones. And this is
     the thing that you shall do: every male and every woman who has lain
12   with a male you shall put under the ban." And they found among the
     inhabitants of Jabesh-Gilead four hundred young virgin women who
     had not lain with a male, and they brought them to the camp at Shiloh,
13   which is in the land of Canaan. And all the community sent and spoke
     to the Benjaminites who were at the Rock of Rimmon, and they declared
14   peace with them. And Benjamin came back at that time, and they gave
     them the women that they had kept alive from the women of Jabesh-Gilead,
15   but they did not find enough for them. And the people had become regret-
     ful concerning Benjamin, for the LORD had made a breach in the tribes of
16   Israel. And the elders of the community said, "What shall we do for wives
17   for those left, for the women of Benjamin have been destroyed?" And they
     said, "How will a remnant be left for Benjamin, that a tribe not be wiped
18   out from Israel, and we cannot give them wives from our daughters, for the
19   Israelites vowed, saying, 'Cursed be he who gives a wife to Benjamin'?" And
     they said, "Look, there is a festival to the LORD every year in Shiloh, which
     is north of Bethel, east of the highway that goes up from Bethel to Shechem
20   and south of Lebonah." And they charged the Benjaminites, saying, "Go
21   and lie in wait in the vineyards. And when you see that, look, the daughters
     of Shiloh come out to dance, you shall snatch each of you his wife from the

---

would have been a singularly bad solution to the dilemma of Benjamin's survival to achieve
it by wiping out a whole group of Israelites, men, women, and children.

12. *they brought them to the camp at Shiloh.* The setting now shifts from Bethel to Shiloh,
laying the ground for the opening chapters of the Book of Samuel, which are centered in
Shiloh.

14. *but they did not find enough for them.* There are six hundred Benjaminites at the Rock
of Rimmon, so the shortfall in brides is two hundred. But in all likelihood, the story of the
delivery of the four hundred young women from Jabesh-Gilead and the story of the snatching of the dancing girls in the vineyards are two different versions of how the surviving
Benjaminites got their brides that have been edited together, with the numerical deficiency
introduced in the first story so that it can be made up in the second.

19. *there is a festival to the LORD every year in Shiloh.* The name and nature of the festival
are unspecified. The fact that it is said to be in Shiloh might encourage the inference that
it was a special local celebration at Shiloh. On the other hand, the Mishnah (Ta'anit 4:8)
reports a practice on the fifteenth of Av and on Yom Kippur in which the nubile young
women went out dancing in the vineyards in borrowed white garments to be chosen as
wives by the young men of the community.

21. *you shall snatch each of you his wife from the daughters of Shiloh.* What is involved is
a kind of abduction, not rape, or, if the report in the Mishnah is historically grounded, a

daughters of Shiloh, and you shall go to the land of Benjamin. And should 22
their fathers or their brothers come in dispute to us, we shall say to them,
'We showed mercy to them, for no man of them took his wife in battle, for
it was not you who gave to them. Now should you bear guilt?'" And thus 23
the Benjaminites did, and they took wives according to their number from
the dancing girls whom they stole away, and they returned to their estate
and rebuilt the towns and dwelled within them. And the Israelites went off 24
from there at that time each man to his tribe and to his clan, and they went
out from there each man to his estate.

In those days there was no king in Israel. Every man did what was right 25
in his own eyes.

---

collective mating ceremony. This odd tale of snatching brides during the celebration of a
festival has parallels in Herodotus (where it is a festival honoring Artemis) and in Livy's
well-known story of the abduction of the Sabine women (where the festival is dedicated to
Neptune). In any case, the Book of Judges, which begins in violence and is dominated by
violence, ends here on an upbeat note with dancing girls and the taking of brides.

22. *We showed mercy to them, for no man of them took his wife in battle.* This whole speech
is somewhat garbled (and the verb that means "show mercy" is conjugated in an untenable
way in the Masoretic Text). The received text has "we took," but three ancient versions
read "they took." The sense one can extract, without entirely rewriting the verse, is: The
Benjaminites did not take these young women as war captives; we showed mercy to them
and arranged for the taking of brides; you yourselves did not give the girls as brides, for
the vow against doing that was incumbent on you. Now why should you oppose our proper
procedure and incur guilt?

23. *stole away.* The Hebrew verb *gazal*, it should be said, generally indicates the illicit appro-
priation of someone else's possessions.

25. *In those days there was no king in Israel. Every man did what was right in his own eyes.*
This refrain is now inserted at the end as a kind of epilogue to the Book of Judges. The state
of political anarchy has been especially manifest in the story of the concubine at Gibeah
and the civil war it triggers, and perhaps in the war's aftermath as well. The refrain sets
the stage for the Book of Samuel, which will move in swift steps to the founding of the
monarchy.

SAMUEL

Introduction

The major sequence that runs, according to the conventional book and chapter divisions of later editorial traditions, from 1 Samuel 1 to 1 Kings 2 is one of the most astounding pieces of narrative that has come down to us from the ancient world. The story of David is probably the greatest single narrative representation in Antiquity of a human life evolving by slow stages through time, shaped and altered by the pressures of political life, public institutions, family, the impulses of body and spirit, the eventual sad decay of the flesh. It also provides the most unflinching insight into the cruel processes of history and into human behavior warped by the pursuit of power. And nowhere is the Bible's astringent narrative economy, its ability to define characters and etch revelatory dialogue in a few telling strokes, more brilliantly deployed.

It must also be said, after nearly two centuries of excavative scholarship, that the precise literary history and authorship of this great narrative remain beyond recovery. To specialists who have exercised painstaking analysis in order to expose an intricate patchwork of sources and historical layers in the book as a whole and in most of its episodes, it may seem a provocation or an expression of ignorance to speak at all of the story of Samuel, Saul, and David. Even a reader looking for unity must concede that certain passages are not of a piece with the rest. The most salient of these is the coda placed just before the end of the David story (2 Samuel 21–24), which comprises material from four different sources, none of them reflecting the style or perspective of the David story proper. It may be unwise to think of these disparate passages as intrusions because creating a purposeful collage of sources was demonstrably a standard literary procedure in ancient Israel. In any case, the architectonic cohesion of the narrative from the birth of Samuel to the death of David has been made increasingly clear by the innovative literary commentary of the past four decades, and much of the richness and complexity of the story is lost by those who imagine this book as a stringing together of virtually independent sources: a prophetic Samuel narrative, a cycle of Saul stories, a History of the Rise of David, a Succession Narrative, and so forth.

Readers should not be confused by the conventional division into books. The entities 1 and 2 Samuel are purely an artifact of ancient manuscript production. Scrolls used by scribes were roughly the same length, and when the Hebrew Bible was translated into Greek in the third century B.C.E., a single scroll was not long enough to encompass the whole book, so it was divided into two parts in no way intrinsic to the original composition. (The Talmud speaks of a single Book of Samuel.) It is also demonstrable that the first two chapters of 1 Kings, as I shall try to show in my commentary, are the real conclusion of the book, subtly echoing earlier moments in the story and evincing the same distinctive literary mastery. Later redactors placed these two episodes at the beginning of Kings so that they could serve as a preface to the story of Solomon.

But if the ancient editors passed this material down to posterity as a book, what are we to make of its composite nature? Two fundamental issues are involved: the presence of the so-called Deuteronomist in the book, and the introduction of purportedly independent narratives. In regard to the second of these two considerations, the baseline for modern scholarly discussion was set in a 1926 monograph by the German scholar Leonhard Rost. He concentrated on what he saw as two independent narratives—an Ark Narrative (1 Samuel 4–7:1, plus 2 Samuel 6) and a Succession Narrative (2 Samuel 9–20 and 1 Kings 1–2). The argument for an originally independent Ark Narrative has a good deal of plausibility: there are some stylistic differences in this segment; human agents, at the center of the surrounding narrative, are marginal; miraculous intervention by God, not in evidence elsewhere, is decisive; and the figure of Samuel with which the story began temporarily disappears. The Ark Narrative is often thought to be the oldest component of the Book of Samuel, perhaps actually pre-Davidic, because it does not envisage a royal cult in Jerusalem and has no interest in the more political concerns of the larger story. Even in this case, however, the narrative in question has to be read in the context of the comprehensive literary structure into which it has been integrated, whether by editorial ingenuity or by the allusive artistry of the author of the David story. Thus, the old priest Eli, sitting at the gate awaiting the news of disaster from the battlefield (news that will include the death of his sons), generates a haunting avatar in the aging David at Mahanaim, sitting between the two gates of the walled city, anxiously awaiting the messenger from the battlefield who will tell him of the death of his son. A second scene of receiving catastrophic tidings is tied in with Eli: the old priest hears an uproar in the town, asks what it means, and then a messenger arrives to give him a breathless report of the terrible defeat, just as the usurper Adonijah, at the end of the David story, will hear an uproar in the town and then a breathless report from an eyewitness of the developments that have destroyed his hopes for the throne.

The argument for an independent Succession Narrative, long embraced by scholarly consensus, is shakier. Rost's contention that it is stylistically distinct from the preceding text is unconvincing, and his notions of style are extremely vague. One may question whether the succession to the throne is actually the central concern of this sequence of episodes, which are more powerfully focused on David's sin and the consequent theme of the unfolding of the prophet's curse on the house of David. (This theme has a certain affinity with Greek tragedy, as Faulkner, ultimately a better reader of the David story than Rost, keenly understood in *Absalom, Absalom!*) The powerful imaginative continuities in the representation of David from agile youth to decrepit old age speak for themselves. To read, for example, David's grim response to the death of his infant son by Bathsheba (2 Samuel 12) as part of an independent Succession Narrative, unrelated to his previous public utterances and acts in a purported History of the Rise of David, is to do palpable violence to the beautiful integrity of the story as the probing representation of a human life. Over the past four decades, admirable work has been done by scholars from different points on the geographical and methodological map to illuminate the fine and complex interconnections among the various phases of the story of David, Saul, and Samuel. The most notable contributions are those of the Dutch scholar J. P. Fokkelman, the North American Robert Polzin, and the Israeli Shimon Bar-Efrat, and I shall frequently follow their precedent or build on their insights in my comments on the text.

The other pervasive question about the stratification of this book involves its Deuteronomistic editing. No one knows with certainty when the main part of the original narrative was written, though there is good reason to place it, as a recurrent scholarly view does, quite close to David's own time, in the first half of the tenth century B.C.E. (Gerhard von Rad proposed the court of Solomon as the setting for the composition of the story.) Samuel is set into the larger history that runs from Joshua to the end of 2 Kings and that scholarly usage designates as the Deuteronomistic History. The book was probably edited at the time of King Josiah's cultic and theological reforms in the late seventh century B.C.E., although it may well have undergone a secondary Deuteronomistic redaction in the Babylonian exile, during the sixth century B.C.E. But to what extent is Samuel a product of the work of the Deuteronomist? The bulk of the story shows no traces of the peculiar brand of nationalist pietism that marks the Deuteronomistic movement—its emphasis on the purity and the centralization of the cult, its insistence on a direct causal link between Israelite defection from its covenant with God and national catastrophe, and its distinctive and strikingly formulaic vocabulary for expressing this outlook. The compelling conclusion is that the Deuteronomistic editors did no more with the inherited narrative than to provide some minimal editorial framing and transition (far less than in the Book of Judges) and to interpolate a few brief passages. Thus I strenuously disagree with Robert Polzin, one of the most finely perceptive readers of this book (in his two volumes *Samuel and the Deuteronomist* and *David and the Deuteronomist*). Exercising great ingenuity, Polzin sees the historical perspective of the Deuteronomist manifested in all the minute details of the story.

Let me recall a signal instance I mentioned in my introduction to the Former Prophets (pages xlv–lvi), where the Deuteronomist has patently inserted a bit of dialogue of his own contrivance into the story that probably antedates his editing by more than three centuries, for the contrast with what immediately follows vividly illustrates the kind of world that defines David, Joab, Saul, Abner, and all these memorable figures steeped in the bitter juices of politics and history. Here, full quotation with commentary may be helpful. On his deathbed, David summons Solomon in order to convey to him an oral last will and testament (1 Kings 2: 2–6):

> I am going on the way of all the earth. And you must be strong, and be a man. *And keep what the LORD your God enjoins, to walk in His ways, to keep His statutes, His commands, and His dictates and His admonitions, as it is written in the Teaching of Moses, so that you may prosper in everything you do and in everything to which you turn. So that the LORD may fulfill His word that He spoke unto me, saying, "If your sons keep their way to walk before Me in truth with their whole heart and with their whole being, no man of yours will be cut off from the throne of Israel."* And, what's more, you yourself know what Joab son of Zeruiah did to me, what he did to the two commanders of the armies of Israel, Abner son of Ner and Amasa son of Jether—he killed them, and shed the blood of war in peace, and put the blood of war on his belt that was round his waist and on his sandals that were on his feet. And you must act in your wisdom, and do not let his gray head go down in peace to Sheol.

Every word in the italicized section of the passage shows the fingerprints of the Deuteronomist. The phraseology is almost identical with recurrent phraseology in the Book of Deuteronomy: the heavy stress on "keeping" and "commands," whole strings of terms such as "walk in His ways," "His statutes, His commands, and His dictates and His admonitions," "so that you may prosper in everything you do," "to walk before Me in truth with their whole heart and with their whole being." The very mention of the "Teaching [*torah*] of Moses" is a Deuteronomistic rallying point that would scarcely have been invoked in the tenth century. Stylistically, moreover, these long-winded sentences loaded with didactically insistent synonyms are nothing like the sentences spoken by characters in the David story.

Why did the Deuteronomist interpolate these lines of dialogue? The most plausible inference is that, given his brand of pious monotheism, he was uncomfortable with the vengeful way the founding king of the divinely elected dynasty speaks on his deathbed. David and Joab go back together half a century. David has been repeatedly dependent on Joab's resourcefulness and ruthlessness as his principal strongman, but he also feels himself to have been terribly wronged by his henchman—above all, in Joab's self-interested and treacherous murders of two army commanders whom David had embraced (and also in his killing of Absalom, against the king's explicit orders, which David refrains from mentioning). The image of Joab splashed in blood from waist to feet strongly recalls the narrative report of his butchering Amasa with a stealthy sword thrust to the belly, and invokes the recurrence of spilled blood as material substance and moral symbol throughout the story. When David enjoins the proverbially wise Solomon to act in his wisdom, the quality in question is not the wisdom of the Torah of Moses but rather the wisdom of a Talleyrand. Soon after David's death, Solomon will show how adept he is in exercising that faculty of wary calculation. The Deuteronomistic editor could not delete this material, but he sought to provide a counterweight to its unblinking realism by first having David on his deathbed speak in a high moral tone. In fact, nobody in the David story talks like this. The dialogues show nothing of this hortatory style, nothing of this unalloyed didacticism. It is not that the writer is devoid of any ideological viewpoint: he believes in a morally imperative covenantal relationship between God and Israel; he believes in the authority of prophecy; and he believes in the divine election of the Davidic line. But one must hasten to say that he believes in all these things only with enormous dialectic complication, an order of complication so probing that at times it borders on subversion.

The dialectic complication of national ideology is a phenomenon worth explaining, for it brings us to the heart of the greatness of the David story. Biblical scholarship by and large has badly underread this book by imagining that ideological strands can be identified like so many varieties of potatoes and understood as simple expressions of advocacy. In this fashion, it is repeatedly claimed in the critical literature that one component of the book is prophetic, promoting the interests of prophetic circles; that another is "Saulide"; that a third is basically a narrative apologetic for the Davidic dynasty; and so forth. All of this strikes me as badly misconceived, and it is blind to the complexity of vision of this extraordinary writer.

The representation of the prophet Samuel is instructive in this connection. It has been conjectured that a "prophetic" writer, active perhaps a century or two after the reported events, is responsible for this portion of the book as well as for the ones in which Nathan the prophet figures. But there is scant evidence in the text for the construction of this hypothetical entity. It is rather like assuming that Shakespeare must have been a "royalist," or perhaps even royal, writer in order to have written *Henry IV.* What, in fact, is the writer's attitude toward Samuel? There is no question that he is shown to be a prophet confirmed in his vocation by God Himself, as the dedication scene, in which God calls to him in the night at the Shiloh sanctuary (1 Samuel 3), makes clear. It is concomitantly stressed that Samuel has been chosen to exercise a spiritual authority that will displace the priestly authority of the house of Eli, on which an irrevocable curse is pronounced soon after the report of Samuel's birth. The entire people becomes subservient to Samuel, and they feel that only through the initiative of the prophet (however grudging) can they get the king they want. In all this, one could claim that the story is confirming a prophetic ideology by reinforcing the notion of the indispensability of prophetic authority to Israelite national life.

Yet as in the case of Saul, David, and all the principal figures around them, Samuel is a densely imagined character, and, it must be said, in many respects a rather unattractive one. The Israeli poet Yehuda Amichai neatly catches the dubiety of the mature Samuel in a wry little poem: "When Samuel was born, she said words of Torah, / 'For this lad I prayed.' / When he grew up and did the deeds of his life, / she asked, 'For this lad I prayed?'" The prophet Samuel may have God on his side, but he is also an implacable, irascible man, and often a palpably self-interested one as well. His resistance to the establishment of the monarchy may express a commitment to the noble ideal of the direct kingship of God over Israel, but it is also motivated by resentment that he must surrender authority, and the second of his two antimonarchic speeches is informed by belligerent self-defensiveness about his own career as national leader. When he chooses Saul, he wants to play him as his puppet, dictating elaborate scenarios to the neophyte king, even setting him up for failure by arriving at an arranged rendezvous at the last possible moment. He is proud, imperious, histrionic—until the very end, when he is conjured up by Saul as a ghost on the eve of the fatal battle at Mount Gilboa.

It would be misleading, I think, to imagine that any of this is intended to discredit the idea of prophetic authority. Samuel is invested with prophetic power by an act of God. But the writer understands that he is also a man, all too human, and that any kind of power, including spiritual power, can lead to abuse. Samuel toys with the idea of creating a kind of prophetic dynasty through his two sons, even though they are just as corrupt as the two sons of Eli, whose immoral behavior seals the doom of their father's priestly line. Is Samuel's choice of Saul really dictated by God, or rather by his own human preconceptions? (He is on the point of making the same mistake twice when he is ready to anoint David's eldest brother, Eliab, another strapping young man who seems to stand out from the crowd.) When he insists it is God's will that the entire population and all the livestock of Amalek should be slaughtered, and then offers King Agag as a kind of human sacrifice to the Lord, does he act with divinely authorized prophetic rightness, or, as Martin Buber thought, is he confusing his own human impulses with God's will? The story of Samuel, then, far from being a simple promotion of prophetic ideology, enormously complicates the notion of prophecy by concretely imagining what may become of the imperfect stuff of humanity when the mantle of prophecy is cast over it.

The representation of David is another instance, far more complex and compelling, of the complication of ideology through the imaginative reconstruction of historical figures and events. Before I try to explain how that process is played out in the David story, a few words are in order about the relation of this entire narrative to history.

As with almost every major issue of biblical studies, there have been sharp differences among scholars on this particular question. On the one hand, Gerhard von Rad in the 1940s and others after him have seen the David story as the beginning of history writing in the Western tradition. On the other hand, one group of contemporary scholars, sometimes known as minimalists, is skeptical about whether there ever was a King David and likes to say that this narrative has about the same relation to historical events as do the British legends about King Arthur. The gritty historical realism of the story—what Hans Frei shrewdly identified as its "history-like" character—surely argues against the notion that it is simply legendary. Were David an invention of much later national tradition, he would be the most peculiar of legendary founding kings: a figure who early on is shown as a collaborator with the archenemies of Israel, the Philistines; who compounds adultery with murder; who more than once exposes himself to humiliation, is repeatedly seen in his weakness, and oscillates from nobility of sentiment and act to harsh vindictiveness on his very deathbed. (On this last point, the editorial intervention of the Deuteronomist that we observed suggests that he had inherited not a legendary account but a historical report that made him squirm.) If, moreover, the bulk of the story was actually composed within a generation or two, or perhaps three, after the reported actions, it is hard to imagine how such encompassing national events as a civil war between the house of Saul and the house of David, the Davidic campaigns of conquest east of the Jordan, and the usurpation of the throne by Absalom with the consequent military struggle, could have been invented out of whole cloth.

This narrative nevertheless has many signs of what we would call fictional shaping—interior monologues, dialogues between the historical personages in circumstances where there could have been no witness to what was said, pointed allusions in the turns of the dialogue as well as in the narrative details to Genesis, Joshua, and Judges. What we have in this great story, as I have proposed elsewhere, is not merely a report of history but an imagining of history that is analogous to what Shakespeare did with historical figures and events in his history plays. That is, the known general contours of the historical events and of the principal players are not tampered with, but the writer brings to bear the resources of his literary art in order to imagine deeply, and critically, the concrete moral and emotional predicaments of living in history, in the political realm. To this end, the writer feels free to invent an inner language for the characters, to give their dialogues revelatory shape, to weave together episodes and characters with a fine mesh of recurrent motifs and phrases and analogies of incident, and to define the meaning of the events through allusion, metaphor, and symbol. The writer does all this not to fabricate history but in order to understand it.

In this elaborately wrought literary vehicle, David turns out to be one of the most unfathomable figures of ancient literature. He begins as the fair-haired boy of Israel—if the term "red" or "ruddy" in his initial description refers to hair color, it might be something like auburn. Everyone seems to love him. He is beautiful, he is musical, and he is brave and brilliantly resourceful on the battlefield. He is also, from the start, quite calculating, and it can scarcely be an accident that until the midpoint of his story every one of his utterances, without exception, is made on a public occasion and arguably is contrived to serve his political interests. The narrative repeatedly reveals to us the churning fears and confusions within Saul while blocking access to David's inner world. Beset by mortal dangers, David is constantly prepared to do almost anything in order to survive: with the help of his devoted wife, Michal, wordlessly fleeing Saul's assassins; playing the drooling madman before the Philistine king Achish; serving as vassal to the Philistines, massacring whole towns in order to keep his real actions unknown to his overlords; profiting politically from the chain of violent deaths in the house of Saul while vehemently dissociating himself from each of the killings. He is, in sum, the first full-length portrait of a Machiavellian prince in Western literature. The Book of Samuel is one of those rare masterworks that, like Stendhal's *Charterhouse of Parma,* evinces an unblinking and abidingly instructive knowingness about man as a political animal in all his contradictions and venality and in all his susceptibility to the brutalization and the seductions of exercising power.

And yet, David is more than a probing representation of the ambiguities of political power. He is also an affecting and troubling image of human destiny as husband and father and as a man moving from youth to prime to the decrepitude of old age. The great pivotal moment of the whole story in this regard is when he turns to his perplexed courtiers, after putting aside the trappings of mourning he had assumed for his ailing infant son, now dead, and says, "I am going to him. He will not come back to me." These are the very first words David pronounces that have no conceivable political motive, that give us a glimpse into his inwardness, revealing his sense of naked vulnerability to the inexorable mortality that is the fate of all humankind. For the rest of the story, we shall see David's weakness and his bonds of intimate attachment in fluctuating conflict with the imperatives of power that drive him as a king surrounded by potential enemies and betrayers.

The story of David, in turn, cannot be separated from the story of the man he displaces, Saul. (The moral and psychological complication with which both men are imagined argues powerfully against the simplification of sorting out the book into "Davidic" and "Saulide" narratives.) As a number of observers have proposed—perhaps most vividly, in a series of ballads, the early-twentieth-century Hebrew poet Saul Tchernikhovsky—Saul is the closest approximation of a tragic hero in the Hebrew Bible. A farm boy from Benjamin seeking his father's lost donkeys, he is overtaken by a destiny of kingship of which he had not dreamed and that at first he tries to escape. Ambivalence and oscillation are the hallmarks of the story of Saul, and the writer may have been led to mirror this condition in his abundant use of paired or even tripled episodes: three different coronation scenes are required for the reluctant Saul; two tales of Saul among the prophets, the first elevating him at the beginning of his career and the second devastating him at the end; two incidents of Saul's hurling his spear at David; two encounters with the fugitive David, who spares his life and receives a pledge of love and a kind of endorsement from Saul, still not to be trusted by David as the older man veers wildly between opposed feelings.

The stories of Saul and David interlock antithetically on the theme of knowledge. Saul, from first to last, is a man deprived of the knowledge he desperately seeks. At the outset, he has to turn to the seer Samuel in order to find his father's asses. In subsequent episodes, he has no luck with oracles and divination in guiding him on his military way, and he tries to coerce fate by imposing a rash vow of fasting on his troops in the midst of battle. He seizes on the report of informers in his pursuit of David, but David continues to elude him. At the very end, on the eve of his last battle, he tries oracle and prophecy and dreams in order to find out what the impending future will be, but all fail, and he is compelled to resort to the very art of necromancy that he himself had made a capital crime. The knowledge he then receives from the implacable ghost of Samuel is nothing but the news of his own imminent doom.

David, on the other hand, at first seems peculiarly favored with knowledge. The position that he is brought to the court to fill is for a man "skilled in playing" (the literal meaning of the Hebrew is "*knowing* to play") and "prudent in speech." In what follows, David demonstrates impressive prudence and agile resourcefulness. It also emerges that once he has become a fugitive, he is rapidly equipped with an oracular ephod and a priest to use it and so, in contrast to Saul, has a direct line of communication with God in making his key decisions. Much later in the story, when things have begun to fall apart, the wise woman from Tekoa will tell David, "My lord is wise as with the wisdom of a messenger of God, to know everything in the land" (2 Samuel 14:20). By this point, however, it has become painfully evident that her words are a gesture of deference to the king that is ironically contradicted by fact. The knowing David of the earlier part of the narrative has become the king isolated in his palace. He must even send intermediaries to discover the identity of the naked beauty bathing on the rooftop in view of his palace, though she seems to be the daughter of one of the members of his own elite guard. He is singularly unaware of his son Amnon's lust for his half sister Tamar, then of Absalom's plot to murder Amnon in revenge, then of Absalom's scheme to usurp the throne. The pitiful image of the shivering, bedridden David, ignorant of the grand feast of self-coronation arranged by his son Adonijah, then reminded or perhaps rather persuaded by Bathsheba and Nathan that he has promised the throne to Solomon, is the ultimate representation of the painful decline of knowledge in this once perspicacious figure, the brilliant successor to the purblind Saul.

Who could have written a story like this, and what could his motives have been? The way this question is typically posed in biblical studies is to ask what interests the writer could have been serving, but it seems to me that framing the issue in those terms involves a certain reductionism that harks back to the historical positivism of the nineteenth century. Although it is safe to assume that no biblical author wrote merely to entertain his audiences, and although there is no evidence of a class of professional storytellers in ancient Israel analogous to the bards of Greece, the social location and political aims of the biblical writer remain unclear. (The Prophets, who sometimes incorporated autobiographical passages in their writing, and who stand out sharply as critics of society and often of the royal establishment, are the one clear exception to this rule.) Scholars of the Bible often speak of "schools" or "circles" of biblical writing (Prophetic, Priestly, Wisdom, Davidic, and so forth), but in fact we have no direct knowledge of such groups as cultural institutions. The one school or movement for which a very strong case can be made is the Deuteronomistic movement. In this instance, a comprehensive, uncompromising reform of cultic practice, theology, and law was instituted during the reign of Josiah, around 621 B.C.E. The Book of Deuteronomy was composed, with abundant satellite literature to come after it, as a forceful literary instrument of the reform. In the great speeches of Deuteronomy, literature has patently been marshaled to inculcate an ideological program. Yet the very contrast we observed in 1 Kings 2 between the didacticism of the Deuteronomist and the worldly realism of the author of the David story argues for the idea that the latter had very different aims in mind from the simple promotion of a political program.

My guess is that the author of the David story thought of himself as a historian. But even if he frequented the court in Jerusalem, a plausible but not at all necessary supposition, he was by no means a writer of court annals or chronicles of the kings of Judah, and, as I have argued, he was far from being an apologist for the Davidic dynasty. I would imagine that he was impelled to write out of a desire to convey to his contemporaries and to posterity a true account of the significant events involved in the founding of the monarchy that governed the nation. It is conceivable that he had some written reports of these events at his disposal or at any rate drew on oral accounts of the events. Perhaps he had spoken with old-timers who were actual participants, or, if one places him very early, he himself might have been an observer of some of what he reports. He also did not hesitate to exploit etiological tales (Saul among the prophets) and folktales (David slaying the giant Goliath) in order to flesh out his historical account and dramatize its meanings. Although committed to telling the truth about history, his notion of historical factuality was decidedly different from modern ones. His conception of history writing involved not merely registering what had happened and who had been the principal actors but also reflecting on the shifting interplay between character and historical act, on the way social and political institutions shape and distort individual lives, on the human costs of particular political choices.

The author of the David story was in all likelihood firmly committed to the legitimacy of the Davidic line. In the book he wrote, after all, God explicitly elects David once Saul has been rejected and later promises that the throne of David will remain unshaken for all time. But the author approaches the David story as an imaginative writer, giving play to that dialectic fullness of conception that leads the greatest writers (Shakespeare, Stendhal, Balzac, Tolstoy, Proust, to name a few apposite instances) to transcend the limitations of their own ideological points of departure. Even though the vocational identity of "imaginative writer" was not socially defined in ancient Israel as it would be in later cultures, the accomplished facts of literary art in many cultures, ancient and modern, suggest that the impulse of literary creation, with the breadth of vision that at its best it encourages, is universal.

The person who wrote this story is not only a formidably shrewd observer of politics and human nature but also someone who manifestly delights in the writerly pleasures of his craft and is sometimes led to surprising insights by his exploration of those pleasures. He has an ear for dialogue, and for the contrastive treatment of the two interlocutors in particular dialogues, that Joyce might have envied. Though both narrator and characters are sparing in figurative language, the metaphors he gives them are telling, and sometimes set up electrically charged links between one moment of the story and another. This writer has a keen sense of the thematic uses of analogy between one episode and another, as when he gives

us Amnon lying in a pretended sickbed so that he can summon his sister
Tamar to serve his violent lust, right after the story of David's rising from
his siesta bed to see the bathing Bathsheba and then summon her to the
palace for his illicit pleasure. (Both prohibited sexual acts lead to murder
and political disarray.) Like most of the great masters of narrative art, the
author of the David story is constantly asking himself what it must be like
concretely—emotionally, psychologically, morally, even physically—to be
one or another of these characters in a particular predicament, and it is this
salutary imaginative habit that generates many of the dialectic complications of the historical account. Saul on the last night of his life is represented
as not merely fearful of the Philistine foe but driven by desperation into
the necromancer's den. This last gesture of grasping for knowledge denied
makes the fate of the defeated king seem wrenching, indeed, tragic. David's
flight from Absalom is not merely a story of political intrigue and opposing
interests but also a tale of anguished conflict between father and king in the
same man, culminating in David's horrendous stutter of grief over Absalom's death and followed by Joab's harsh rebuke to him for his behavior.

One of the hallmarks of this whole writerly relation to the historical
material is the freighted imagining of the detail not strictly necessary to
the historical account. Let me offer one brief instance that may stand for
all the others. David's first wife, Michal, it will be recalled, is married off
by her father, Saul, to a man named Paltiel son of Laish after David's flight
from his father-in-law's assassins. We know nothing about Paltiel except
his name, and nothing about Michal's feelings concerning the union with
him imposed by her father. When Abner, the commander of the forces
of the house of Saul, comes to transfer his fealty to David and end the
civil war, David stipulates that Michal daughter of Saul must first be sent
back to him. (Presumably, his motive is strictly political.) Michal is duly
removed by Abner's decree from Paltiel, with no word or emotion of hers
reported by the writer. What he does give us are these few, indelible words:
"And her husband went with her, weeping as he went after her, as far as
Bahurim. And Abner said to him, 'Go back!' And he went back" (2 Samuel
3:16). To a sober historian, this moment might well seem superfluous. To
a great imaginative writer like the author of this story, such moments are
the heart of the matter. Paltiel never even speaks in the story, but his weeping speaks volumes. He is a loving husband caught between the hard and
unyielding men who wield power in the world—Abner, Saul's tough field
commander, and his adversary turned ally, David, who insists on the return
of the woman he has acquired with a bloody bride-price because he calcu-

lates that as Saul's daughter she will bolster his claim to be Saul's legitimate successor. The tearful Paltiel walking after the wife who is being taken from him, then driven back by the peremptory word of the strongman with whom he cannot hope to contend, is a poignant image of the human price of political power. If history, in the hackneyed aphorism, is the story told by the victors, this narrative achieves something closer to the aim that Walter Benjamin defined as the task of the historical materialist, "to brush history against the grain." Lacking all but the scantiest extrahistorical evidence, we shall probably never know precisely what happened in Jerusalem and Judah and the high country of Benjamin around the turn of the first millennium B.C.E., when the Davidic dynasty was established. What matters is that the anonymous Hebrew writer, drawing on what he knew or thought he knew of the portentous historical events, has created this most searching story of men and women in the rapid and dangerous current of history that still speaks to us, floundering in history and the dilemmas of political life, three thousand years later.

1 Samuel

CHAPTER 1   And there was a man from Ramathaim-Zophim, 1
from the high country of Ephraim, and his name was Elkanah son of Jero-
ham son of Elihu son of Tohu son of Zuph, an Ephraimite. And he had two 2
wives; the name of the one was Hannah and the name of the other, Peninnah. And Peninnah had children but Hannah had no children. And this 3
man would go up from his town year after year to worship and to sacrifice
to the LORD of Armies at Shiloh, and there the two sons of Eli, Hophni and

---

CHAPTER 1   The story of Hannah provides an instructive illustration of the conventions of narrative exposition that govern a large number of biblical stories. First the main
character or characters are identified by name, pedigree, and geographical location. The only
verb used is "to be" (verses 1–2). In this instance the standard biblical story beginning, "there
was a man," is in part a false lead because the real protagonist of the story is Elkanah's wife
Hannah. Then there is a series of reported actions in the iterative tense—that is, an indication of habitually repeated actions (verses 3–7). (In all this, compare Job 1.) The narrative
then zooms in to a particular moment, one of those annually repeated events of Hannah's
frustration at Shiloh, by way of Elkanah's dialogue (verse 8), which could not plausibly be an
iterative event. At this point, we have moved from prelude to story proper. The writer himself
seems quite conscious of this play between recurring units of time and specific moments in
time: the word *yamim*—"days," but often as in verse 3 with the sense of "annual cycle"—is
used five times, together with the singular *yom*, in an iterative sense, at the beginning of verse
4. (These recurrences are complemented by "year after year," *shanah beshanah*, in verse 7.)

2. *And he had two wives.* The reference to two wives, one childbearing, the other childless,
immediately alerts the audience to the unfolding of the familiar annunciation type-scene.
The expected sequence of narrative motifs of the annunciation scene is the report of the wife's
barrenness (amplified by the optional motif of the fertile co-wife less loved by the husband
than is the childless wife); the promise, through oracle or divine messenger or man of God, of
the birth of a son; cohabitation resulting in conception and birth. As we shall see, the middle
motif is articulated in a way that is distinctive to the concerns of the Samuel story.

3. *the two sons of Eli.* The reference is initially puzzling but points forward to the focus on
proper and improper heirs to the priesthood in Samuel's story.

4 Phineas, were priests to the LORD. And when the day came round, Elkanah
   would sacrifice and give portions to Peninnah his wife and to all her sons
5 and her daughters. And to Hannah he would give one double portion, for
6 Hannah he loved, and the LORD had closed her womb. And her rival would
   torment her sorely so as to provoke her because the LORD had closed up
7 her womb. And thus was it done year after year—when she would go up to
   the house of the LORD, the other would torment her and she would weep
   and would not eat.

8 And Elkanah her husband said to her, "Hannah, why do you weep and
   why do you not eat and why is your heart afflicted? Am I not better to you
9 than ten sons?" And Hannah arose after the eating in Shiloh and after the
   drinking, while Eli the priest was sitting in a chair by the doorpost of the
10 LORD's temple. And she was deeply embittered, and she prayed to the LORD,
11 weeping all the while. And she vowed a vow and said, "LORD of Armies, if
   You really will look on Your servant's woe and remember me, and forget not
   Your servant and give Your servant male seed, I will give him to the LORD

---

5. *And to Hannah he would give one double portion.* The Hebrew phrase, which occurs
only here, means literally "one portion [for the?] face," and has perplexed commentators.
The conclusion of several modern translators that the phrase means "only a single portion" makes nonsense out of the following words that the allotment was an expression of
Elkanah's special love. It seems wisest to follow a long tradition of commentators who take
a cue from the doublative ending of *'apayim*, the word for "face" (perhaps even a textual
corruption for another word meaning "double") and to construe this as a double portion
to Hannah who, alas, unlike Peninnah, has no children.

7. *And thus was it done.* The Hebrew is literally "thus did he do," but the impersonal masculine active singular is often used in this kind of passive sense.
     the other. The Hebrew simply says "she," but the antecedent is clearly Peninnah.

8. *Am I not better to you than ten sons?* The double-edged poignancy of these words is that
they at once express Elkanah's deep and solicitous love for Hannah and his inability to
understand how inconsolable she feels about her affliction of barrenness. All the annunciation stories must be understood in light of the prevalent ancient Near Eastern view that a
woman's one great avenue to fulfillment in life was through the bearing of sons. It is noteworthy that Hannah does not respond to Elkanah. When she does at last speak, it is to God.

11. *I will give him to the LORD.* Hannah's prayer exhibits a directness of style, without ornament or conventional liturgical phrasing, and an almost naïve simplicity: if you give him
to me, I will give him to you. This canceling out of the two givings is reconciled by the
introduction of another verb at the end of the story: Hannah "lends" to God the child He
has given her.

all the days of his life, no razor shall touch his head." And it happened as   12
she went on with her prayer before the Lord, with Eli watching her mouth,
as Hannah was speaking in her heart, her lips alone moving and her voice   13
not heard, Eli thought she was drunk. And Eli said to her,   14

> "How long will you go on drunk?
> Rid yourself of your wine!"

And Hannah answered and said, "No, my lord! A bleak-spirited woman am   15
I. Neither wine nor strong drink have I drunk, but I have poured out my
heart to the Lord. Think not your servant a worthless girl, for out of my   16
great trouble and torment I have spoken till now." And Eli answered and   17
said, "Go in peace, and may the God of Israel grant your petition which
you asked of Him." And she said, "May your servant but find favor in your   18
eyes." And the woman went on her way, and she ate, and her face was no
longer downcast. And they rose early in the morning and bowed before the   19
Lord and returned and came to their home in Ramah. And Elkanah knew
Hannah his wife and the Lord remembered her. And it happened at the   20

---

no razor shall touch his head. As an expression of her dedication of the prayed-for child, Hannah vows that he will be a nazirite (like Samson), a person specially dedicated to God who took a vow of abstinence from certain activities. (The literal meaning of the Hebrew is "no razor will go up on his head.") The nazirites also refrained from wine, which throws an ironic backlight on Eli's subsequent accusation that Hannah is drunk. A few biblical texts link nazirite and prophet.

14. *How long will you go on drunk?* The central annunciation motif of the type-scene is purposefully distorted. Since Hannah receives no direct response from God—she prays rather than inquires of an oracle—Eli the priest should be playing the role of man of God or divine intermediary. But at first he gets it all wrong, mistaking her silent prayer for drunken mumbling, and denouncing her in a poetic line (marked by semantic and rhythmic parallelism) of quasiprophetic verse. When in verse 17 he accepts her protestation of innocent suffering, he piously prays or predicts—the Hebrew verb could be construed either way—that her petition will be granted, but he doesn't have a clue about the content of the petition. The uncomprehending Eli is thus virtually a parody of the annunciating figure of the conventional type-scene—an apt introduction to a story in which the claim to authority of the house of Eli will be rejected, and ultimately, sacerdotal guidance will be displaced by prophetic guidance in the person of Samuel, who begins as a temple acolyte but then exercises a very different kind of leadership.

15. *bleak-spirited.* The Hebrew, which occurs only here as a collocation, is literally "hard-spirited."

turn of the year that Hannah conceived and bore a son, and she called his name Samuel, "For from the LORD I asked for him."

21 And the man Elkanah with all his household went up to offer to the LORD
22 the yearly sacrifice and his votive pledge. But Hannah did not go up, for she had said to her husband, "Till the lad is weaned! Then I will bring him
23 and we will see the LORD's presence, and he shall stay there always." And Elkanah her husband said to her, "Do what is right in your eyes. Stay till you wean him, only may the LORD fulfill what your mouth has uttered." And the

---

20. *she called his name Samuel.* There is a small puzzlement in the Hebrew because it is the name Saul, *Sha'ul,* not Samuel, *Shmu'el,* that means "asked" (or "lent"). This has led some modern scholars to speculate that a story originally composed to explain the birth of Saul was transferred to Samuel—perhaps because Saul's eventual unworthiness to reign made it questionable that he should merit a proper annunciation scene. But it must be said that the only evidence for this speculation is the seeming slippage of names here. That could easily be explained, as by the thirteenth-century Hebrew commentator David Kimchi, if we assume Hannah is playing on two Hebrew words, *sha'ul me'el,* "asked of God." In any case, biblical writers allowed themselves considerable license in etymologizing names.

21. *the yearly sacrifice.* The annual cycle of iterative actions invoked at the beginning is seemingly resumed, but everything is different now that Hannah has born a son, and she herself introduces a change in the repeated pattern.

   votive pledge. Although this is the same Hebrew term, *neder,* that is used for Hannah's vow at the beginning of verse 11, its most likely referent here is a vowed thanksgiving offering on the part of the husband for his wife's safe delivery of a son.

22. *Till the lad is weaned.* The word for "lad," *na'ar,* is quite often a tender designation of a young son. Though it typically refers to an adolescent, or even to a young man at the height of his powers (David uses it for the usurper Absalom), it evidently can also be used for an infant. Nursing and weaning (compare the end of this verse and the beginning of the next verse) are insisted on here with a peculiar weight of repetition and literalness. This usage surely intimates the powerful biological bond between Hannah and the longed-for baby and thus points to the pain of separation she must accept, whatever the postponement, according to the terms of her own vow. In the Ark Narrative that follows, there will be a surprising recurrence of this image of nursing mothers yearning for their young. At this point, the only other indication of her feelings about the child is the term "lad" that she uses for him.

   we will see the LORD's presence. Or, even more concretely, "the LORD's face." The anthropomorphism of this ancient idiom troubled the later transmitters of tradition sufficiently so that when vowel-points were added to the consonantal text, roughly a millennium after the biblical period, the verb "we will see" (*nir'eh*) was revocalized as *nir'ah* ("he will be seen"), yielding a more chastely monotheistic "he will appear in the LORD's presence."

23. *what your mouth has uttered.* The Masoretic Text has "His word." But a fragment of Samuel found in Cave 4 at Qumran reads "what your mouth has uttered," which, refer-

woman stayed and nursed her son till she weaned him. And she took him up   24
with her when she weaned him, with a three-year-old bull and one *ephah* of
flour and a jar of wine, and she brought him to the house of the LORD, and
the lad was but a lad. And they slaughtered the bull and they brought the lad   25
to Eli. And she said, "Please, my lord, by your life, my lord, I am the woman   26
who was poised by you here praying to the LORD. For this lad I prayed, and   27
the LORD granted me my petition that I asked of Him. And I on my part   28
granted him for the asking to the LORD; all his days he is lent to the LORD."
And she bowed there to the LORD.

---

ring directly to Hannah's vow at Shiloh, makes much better sense since God, after all, has
made no promises.

24. *a three-year-old bull.* This is again the reading of the Qumran Samuel text. The Masoretic Text has "three bulls," but only one bull is sacrificed in the next verse, and three-year-
old beasts were often designated for sacrifice.

25. *they slaughtered the bull . . . they brought the lad.* The plural subject of these verbs is
evidently Elkanah and Hannah. The simple parallelism of the brief clauses is eloquent: both
the bull and the child are offerings to the LORD, and Samuel's dedication to the sanctuary
is, surely for the parents, a kind of sacrifice. It may be relevant that the term "lad," *na'ar*, is
precisely the one used for Isaac when he is on the point of being sacrificed and for Ishmael
when he is on the brink of perishing in the wilderness. Perhaps that background of usage
also explains the odd insistence on "the lad was but a lad" at the end of the preceding verse.
Given the late weaning time in the ancient world, and given Hannah's likely impulse to
postpone that difficult moment, one might imagine the child Samuel to be around the age
of four or five.

26. *Please, my lord.* As in their previous encounter, Hannah's speech is full of deference
and diffidence in addressing the priest—a reverence, we may already suspect, that he does
not entirely deserve.

27. *For this lad I prayed.* She spells out the act of petition and its precise fulfillment, insisting
twice on the root *sh-'-l*, "to ask." The Hebrew is literally: "my asking that I asked of Him."

28. *granted him for the asking to the LORD; all his days he is lent to the LORD.* The English
here is forced to walk around an elegant pun in the Hebrew: in the *qal* conjugation, *sh-'-l*
means to ask or petition; in the *hiph'il* conjugation the same root means to lend; and the
passive form of the verb, *sha'ul*, can mean either "lent" or "asked."
    And she bowed. The translation again follows the reading of the Samuel fragment dis-
covered at Qumran. The Masoretic Text reads "and he bowed" (a difference of one initial
consonant in the Hebrew), but it is Hannah, not Elkanah, who has been speaking for the
last two verses.

CHAPTER 2

1   And Hannah prayed and she said:
             "My heart rejoiced through the LORD,
                 my horn is raised high through the LORD.
             My mouth is wide to bolt down my foes;
                 for I was gladdened by Your rescue.
2   There is no one holy like the LORD,
             for there is no one beside You,
                 and there is no bastion like our God.
3   Do not go on talking high and mighty—
             arrogance slips from your mouth—
           for a God all-knowing is the LORD,
             and His is the measure of actions.

CHAPTER 2   According to the standard collagelike convention of biblical narrative composition, Hannah's psalm has been set into the story at a later stage in the editorial process than the original tale, and it gives evidence of having been taken from a familiar repertory of thanksgiving or victory psalms. The reference to the anointed king at the end of the poem assumes the institution of the monarchy, not established until two generations after the moment when Hannah is said to have pronounced this prayer. It is clearly the invocation in verse 5 of the barren woman who bears seven that encouraged the introduction here of this particular text. But the larger thematic assertion in the poem of God's power to reverse fortunes, plunging the high to the depths and exalting the lowly, is a fitting introduction to the whole Saul-David history. This psalm (verses 1–10) and David's victory psalm (2 Samuel 22) echo each other and act as formal "bookends" to the extended narrative sequence that includes the stories of Samuel, Saul, and David.

1. *my horn is raised high.* This archaic Hebrew animal imagery is worth preserving literally in English, as did Tyndale and the King James Version. The idea seems to be that the animal's horn is its glory and power, held high, perhaps in triumph after goring an enemy into submission. There is a sequence of body parts at the beginning of the first three versets of the poem, two literal and the middle one metaphorical: "my heart," "my horn," "my mouth." The raising high of the horn is crucial to the thematic unfolding of the poem, which reiterates a pattern of vertical movement, elevation and descent, that manifests God's power to reverse the fortunes of humankind. The upraised horn at the beginning returns in the envelope structure of the last line, a prayer that the LORD "raise high His anointed's horn." That final image, in turn, involves a hidden pun, because the Hebrew "horn" (*qeren*, actually one of the rare Semitic terms cognate with Indo-European—*cornu/horn*) is also the receptacle containing the oil with which the king is anointed.

My mouth is wide to bolt down my foes. The Hebrew does not express but implies "bolt down." The conventional rendering of this idiom as "gloated" is an evasion of its intimation of predatory violence.

The warriors' bow is shattered   4
    and stumblers gird up strength.
The sated are hired for bread   5
    and the hungry cease evermore.
The barren woman bears seven
    and the many-sonned woman is bleak.
The LORD deals death and grants life,   6
    brings down to Sheol and lifts up.
The LORD impoverishes and bestows wealth,   7
    plunges down and also exalts.
He raises the poor from the dust,   8
    from the dung-heaps the wretched He lifts
to seat among princes,
    a throne of honor He bequeaths them.
For the LORD's are the pillars of earth,
    upon them He founded the world.
The steps of His faithful he watches,   9
    and the wicked in darkness turn dumb,
        for not by might will a man prevail.
The LORD shatters His adversaries,   10

---

4. *shattered.* The verb used is restricted to poetry; a noun derived from it means "rubble" or "tiny broken fragments," hence the sense seems to be more extreme than the standard term "to break."

5. *the hungry cease evermore.* The Masoretic Text is rather cryptic. This translation revocalizes the last Hebrew word of the line *'ad* ("until," or, by a long conjectural stretch, "prey") as *'od*, an adverb indicating persistence through time. The Masoretes attached the word to the beginning of the next clause, where, however, its semantic function is equally unclear.

8. *to seat among princes.* The language here might anticipate the monarchic flourish at the end of the poem. "Throne" *(kis'ei)* in the next line can mean either throne or chair. Robert Polzin has made an elaborate argument for seeing not only Hannah's prayer but all the early chapters of 1 Samuel as a grand foreshadowing of the fate of the monarchy with the old and failing Eli, who will die falling off his chair or throne, as a stand-in for the Davidic kings.

9. *the wicked in darkness turn dumb.* The verb obviously refers to death—the underworld in other psalms is sometimes called *dumah*, the realm of silence or speechlessness, a noun cognate with the verb *yidamu* used here. Those who talked high and mighty, their mouths spewing arrogance (verse 3), are now forever silenced.

10. *The LORD shatters His adversaries.* The Masoretic Text reads, "LORD, Your adversaries are shattered." But the Samuel fragment from Qumran has God as the subject of a verb in the singular (a difference of only one letter) with the adversaries as the object. This makes better syntactic sense, especially since it is God who is thundering against the enemies in

against them in the heavens He thunders.
The Lord judges the ends of the earth:
may He grant strength to His king
and raise high His anointed's horn."

11 And Elkanah went to Ramah to his home while the lad was ministering to
12 the Lord in the presence of Eli the priest. And the sons of Eli were worthless
13 fellows; they did not know the Lord. And this was the priest's practice with
    the people: each man would offer his sacrifice, and the priest's lad would
14 come when the meat was boiling, a three-pronged fork in his hand. And
    he would thrust into the cauldron or the pot or the vat or the kettle, what-
    ever the fork would pick up, the priest would take away with it. Thus they
15 would do to all the Israelites who came there, to Shiloh. Even before they
    had burned off the fat, the priest's lad would come and say to the man who
    was sacrificing, "Hand over meat to roast for the priest, for he won't take
16 boiled meat from you, only raw." And the man would say, "Let them burn
    off the fat now and then take for yourself whatever you want," and he would
    say, "No! For you shall hand it over now, and if not, I will take it by force."
17 And the lads' offense was very great before the Lord, for they scorned the
18 Lord's offering. And Samuel was ministering in the presence of the Lord,
19 a lad girt in linen ephod. And a little cloak would his mother make him and

---

the second half of the line. The verb "shatter" is the same one used for the warriors' bow
in verse 4.

14. *the cauldron or the pot or the vat or the kettle.* This catalogue of implements is quite
untypical of biblical narrative (and in fact the precise identification of the sundry cooking
receptacles is unsure). The unusual specification serves a satiric purpose: Eli's sons are
represented in a kind of frenzy of gluttony poking their three-pronged forks into every
imaginable sort of pot and pan. This sense is then heightened in the aggressiveness of the
dialogue that follows, in which Eli's sons insist on snatching the meat uncooked from the
worshippers, not allowing them, as was customary, first to burn away the fat.

18. *ephod.* A short garment, chiefly of linen, worn by priests. The Hebrew term has a second
meaning, a device for divination manipulated by the officiating priests, and that is the
evident sense of ephod when it recurs in verse 28.

19. *And a little cloak would his mother make him.* This is a poignant instance of the expressive reticence of biblical narrative. We have been told nothing about Hannah's feelings as a
mother after her separation from the child for whom she so fervently prayed. This minimal
notation of Hannah's annual gesture of making a little cloak for the son she has "lent" to
the Lord beautifully intimates the love she preserves for him. The garment, fashioned as a
gift of maternal love, stands in contrast to the ephod, the acolyte's official garb for his cultic
office. Moreover, the robe (*me'il*) will continue to figure importantly in Samuel's life, and
even in his afterlife, as we shall have occasion to see.

would bring up to him year after year when she came up with her husband
to offer the yearly sacrifice. And Eli would bless Elkanah and his wife and   20
would say, "May the Lord bestow on you seed from this woman in place of
the loan she has lent to the Lord," and they would go back to their place.
For the Lord singled out Hannah and she conceived and bore three sons   21
and two daughters. And the lad Samuel grew up with the Lord.

And Eli was very old. And he heard of all that his sons did to all the Isra-   22
elites, and that they lay with the women who flocked to the entrance of the
Tent of Assembly. And he said to them, "Why do you do such things of   23
which I hear—evil things about you from all these people? No, my sons!   24
For it is not good, what I hear that the Lord's people are spreading about.
If a man offends against man, God may intercede for him, but if against the   25
Lord a man should offend, who can intercede for him?" And they did not
heed their father's voice, for the Lord wanted to put them to death. And   26
the lad Samuel was growing in goodness with both the Lord and with men.

And a man of God came to Eli and said to him, "Thus says the Lord! Did   27
I not reveal myself to your father's house when they were in Egypt, slaves
to Pharaoh's house? And did I not choose him from all the tribes of Israel   28
as a priest for me, to go up to My altar, to burn incense, to carry an ephod
before Me? And I gave to your father's house all the Israelites' burnt offerings. Why do you trample on My sacrifice and My offering which I have   29

---

year after year. The phrase takes us back to the iterative tense of the beginning of the story.

22. *and that they lay with the women.* This whole clause is missing in the Qumran scroll
and in one version of the Septuagint; in fact, sexual exploitation was not mentioned in the
initial narrative report of the sons' misdeeds. There is, however, a consonance between
their appetitive impulse in snatching the meat and grabbing the women, perhaps reinforced
by the satiric, and phallic, image of thrusting forks into bubbling pots.

   flocked. The Hebrew verb might also mean "ministered."

27. *a man of God came to Eli.* This enunciation of a curse on the house of Eli, at the very
beginning of the Samuel story, is introduced at precisely the corresponding place in the
narrative as the denunciation and admonition of the divine messenger at the beginning of
Judges (chapter 2). An analogous curse will be pronounced by Nathan the prophet on the
house of David (2 Samuel 12) and will be enacted in the subsequent narrative.

   slaves to Pharaoh's house. The Masoretic Text lacks "slaves to" but it is attested in the
Qumran Samuel scroll, in the Septuagint, and in the Targum of Yonatan ben Uziel.

29. *My sacrifice and My offering which I have commanded.* The Masoretic Text reads "which
I commanded [as a?] habitation [*ma'on*]." Since that makes no sense, and all attempts to
rescue a meaning seem forced, I have assumed that *ma'on* is an excrescence, perhaps inad-

commanded, and you honor your sons more than Me, to batten upon the
30 first portions of each offering of Israel My people? Therefore, says the LORD
God of Israel, I indeed said, 'Your house and your father's house will walk
before Me forever,' but now, says the LORD, God forbid I should do it! For
those who honor Me will I honor, and my spurners shall be dishonored.
31 Look, a time is coming when I will cut down your seed and the seed of your
32 father's house, and there shall be no elder in your house. And you shall look
with a jaundiced eye at all the bounty bestowed upon Israel, and there will be
33 no elder in your house for all time. Yet no man of you will I cut off from My
altar, to make your eyes waste away and your spirit ache, and the increase of
34 your house shall fall by the sword of men. And this is the sign for you—that
which comes upon your two sons, Hophni and Phineas, on a single day the
35 two of them shall die! And I will set up for Myself a stalwart priest, according
to my heart and my spirit he shall act, and I will build him a stalwart house
36 and he shall walk before My anointed for all time. And it will happen that
whoever remains from your house shall come to bow before him for a bit

---

vertently transposed by a scribe from verse 32, where it also occurs rather enigmatically.
Several points in the curse pronounced by the man of God look textually defective.

30. *will walk before Me.* The biblical idiom suggests dedicated service of a deity.
    honor . . . dishonored. The Hebrew terms mean, etymologically, "heavy" and "light"
(that is, "weighty" and "worthless"). These antonyms will recur at strategic moments in
the Ark Narrative and in the story of David.

32. *look with a jaundiced eye.* The received text at this point is very doubtful, yielding,
literally, a nonsense chain: "you will look narrow habitation." This translation adopts an
emendation that has considerable scholarly currency: *'ayin* instead of *ma'on* (a difference of
one consonant in the Hebrew). That yields the idiom *tsar-'ayin,* "jealously" or "with a jaundiced eye." But the Qumran text and one version of the Septuagint lack the entire clause.

33. *no man of you will I cut off.* The usual understanding of these words is that God will
leave them alive to witness in pain the destruction of the family. This interpretation seems
a bit strained because in the next verse God promises to destroy both of Eli's sons on a
single day. Perhaps the clause originally read, "every man of you will I cut off," though this
phrasing is not reflected in any of the ancient versions.
    fall by the sword of men. Again, both the Qumran fragment and Version B of the Sep-
tuagint confirm this reading, which seems much likelier than the Masoretic Text's cryptic
"shall die [as?] men."

35. *a stalwart priest . . . a stalwart house.* The Hebrew *ne'eman* in the first instance means
"faithful" or "trustworthy," in the second instance, "well-founded," "enduring." The present translation draws on an older sense of "stalwart," which can be applied to structures and
inanimate objects as well as to people. The probable referent of the prophecy is the house
of Zadok, which was to become the priestly line in the Davidic monarchy.
    before My anointed. Like Hannah's psalm, this whole passage of prophecy appears to
presuppose a historical context in which the monarchy was an established fact.

of silver and a loaf of bread, and he shall say, 'Add me on, pray, to one of the priestly details for a crust of bread to eat.'"

CHAPTER 3   And the lad Samuel was ministering to the LORD 1 in Eli's presence, and the word of the LORD was rare in those days, vision was not spread about. And it happened on that day that Eli was lying in his 2 place, his eyes had begun to grow bleary, he could not see. The lamp of God 3 had not yet gone out, and Samuel was lying in the temple of the LORD, in which was the Ark of God. And the LORD called to Samuel, and he said, 4 "Here I am." And he ran to Eli and he said, "Here I am, for you called me," 5 and he said, "I did not call. Go back, lie down." And he went and lay down. And the LORD called once again, "Samuel!" And Samuel rose and went to 6 Eli and said, "Here I am, for you called me." And he said, "I did not call,

---

CHAPTER 3   1. *the word of the* LORD *was rare . . . vision was not spread about.* The "word of the LORD" is often a technical term referring to oracular message. Inquiring of the oracle would have been a priestly function, and so there is an intimation here of some sort of breakdown in the professional performance of the house of Eli. But the same phrase also is used to announce prophecy, and "vision" is a prophetic term: the whole episode concerns the transition from priestly to prophetic authority.

2. *he could not see.* Eli's blindness reflects not only his decrepitude but his incapacity for vision in the sense of the previous verse. He is immersed in permanent darkness while the lad Samuel has God's lamp burning by his bedside.

3. *The lamp of God had not yet gone out.* Since the sanctuary lamp would have burned through most of the night, this may be an indication, as Kyle McCarter Jr. has proposed, that the scene occurs close to dawn. But the symbolic overtones of the image should not be neglected: though vision has become rare, God's lamp has not yet gone out, and the young ministrant will be the one to make it burn bright again (see verses 19–21, plus 4:1a). The actual lamp would have been a concave earthenware vessel filled with oil.

5. *he ran to Eli and he said, "Here I am."* These words make clear that the previous "Here I am" is not a direct response to God but rather the boy's calling-out from the inner chamber of the sanctuary to Eli in the outer room, thinking that it is Eli who called him. Samuel's thrice-repeated error in this regard reflects not only his youthful inexperience but, as the sixteenth-century Hebrew exegete Yosef Karo has proposed, the general fact that "the word of the LORD was rare," revelation an unfamiliar phenomenon.

6. *"Samuel!"* In an intensifying pattern, as the folktale structure of three repetitions with a final reversal unfolds, God's address is now represented more immediately in dialogue instead of indirectly as in verse 4. The third time, God will say, "Samuel, Samuel!"

I did not call, my son. Until this point, we have been told nothing about Eli's relationship with Samuel. The introduction of this single term of affection, "my son," reveals the fondness of the blind and doomed Eli for his young assistant. His own biological sons have of course utterly betrayed his trust.

7 my son. Go back, lie down." And Samuel did not yet know the LORD, and
8 the word of the LORD had not yet been revealed to him. And the LORD
   called still again to Samuel, a third time, and he rose and went to Eli and
   said, "Here I am, for you called me." And Eli understood that the LORD was
9 calling the lad. And Eli said to Samuel, "Go lie down, and should someone
   call to you, say, 'Speak, LORD, for Your servant is listening.'" And Samuel
10 went and lay down in his place. And the LORD came and stood poised and
   called as on each time before, "Samuel, Samuel!" And Samuel said, "Speak,
11 for Your servant is listening." And the LORD said to Samuel, "I am about to
12 do such a thing in Israel that whoever hears of it, both his ears will ring. On
   that day I will fulfill against Eli all that I have spoken concerning his house,
13 from beginning to end. And I have told him that I was passing judgment on
   his house for all time because of the sin of which he knew, for his sons have
14 been scorning God and he did not restrain them. Therefore I have sworn
   against the house of Eli, that the sin of the house of Eli will not be atoned
15 by sacrifice and offering for all time." And Samuel lay until morning, and

---

9. *Speak, LORD, for Your servant is listening.* This is virtually a formula of deferential
response to superior authority. When Samuel repeats these words in verse 10, he omits
"Lord," perhaps, as Shimon Bar-Efrat has suggested, in diffidence about addressing God.

12. *all that I have spoken concerning his house.* This clause, and the one beginning "I have
told him" in the next verse, refer back to the prophecy of doom pronounced by the man
of God in chapter 2.

13. *his sons have been scorning God.* The Masoretic Text reads, "his sons have been scorning for themselves [*lahem*]," but the last Hebrew word has long been recognized as a *tiqun
sofrim*, a scribal euphemism for *'elohim*, God—that is, the scribes were loath to write out so
sacrilegious a phrase as scorning, or cursing, God. The verb here is commonly used in the
sense of "to damn" or "to express contempt." In this case, the sons' contempt would have
been expressed by their snatching of choice portions from the sacrificial meat.
    he did not restrain them. The Hebrew *kihah* occurs only here as a transitive verb in the
pi'el conjugation, although it is fairly common as an intransitive verb in the *qal* conjugation, meaning "to grow weak," "to become dark," or, as with the eyes of Eli in verse 2,
"bleary." The transitive sense of the verb would then be something like "to incapacitate,"
to prevent someone from doing something. Its unusual usage in this sentence is obviously
meant to align Eli's failing in parental authority with the failing of his sight.

11–13. It is noteworthy that God's first message to Samuel is a prophecy of doom. Its content not only indicates the overthrow of the priestly authority of the house of Eli and the
implicit move to a different sort of authority to be embodied by the prophet Samuel, but
also adumbrates the rather dour and dire role Samuel will play as leader, in relation to both
Israel and to Saul.

15. *And Samuel lay until morning.* The verb does not necessarily imply that he fell asleep
again after this riveting revelation, and if in fact the whole scene takes place close to dawn,
there would be little time before the first light roused him.

he opened the doors of the house of the LORD, and Samuel was afraid to
tell the vision to Eli. And Eli called to Samuel and said, "Samuel, my son," 16
and he said, "Here I am." And he said, "What is the thing He spoke to you? 17
Pray, do not conceal it from me. Thus and more may God do to you if you
conceal from me anything of all the things He spoke to you." And Samuel 18
told him all the things and he did not conceal from him, and he said, "He
is the LORD. What is good in His eyes let Him do."

And Samuel grew up and the LORD was with him, and He let not fall to the 19
ground any of his words. And all Israel, from Dan to Beersheba, knew that 20
Samuel was stalwart as a prophet to the LORD. And the LORD continued to 21
appear in Shiloh, for the LORD was revealed to Samuel in Shiloh through
the word of the LORD, and Samuel's word was upon all Israel.   4:1a

---

he opened the doors of the house of the LORD. He resumes his usual business as faithful temple ministrant, almost as though he wanted to shrug off the divine revelation that
implied a more portentous role for him than that of priestly acolyte.

Samuel was afraid to tell the vision. The divine message is called a vision though it was
conveyed through words rather than images. The term used here, *mar'eh*, is different from
ḥazon, the word that occurs in verse 1, though both refer to sight, the faculty Eli lacks.

17. *Thus and more may God do to you.* This is a set idiom for abjuration: may terrible things
befall you if you fail to perform what I require of you.

18. *What is good in His eyes let Him do.* Old Eli's response is pious resignation to the prophecy of doom. He of course is aware of his sons' misdeeds and of his own failure to intervene
successfully.

19. *He let not fall to the ground any of his words.* The antecedent of "his" is ambiguous, but
since the point of the narrative report is to confirm Samuel's prophetic authority, the more
likely reading is that God did not allow any of Samuel's words to go awry but fulfilled all
of His prophet's predictions.

20. *from Dan to Beersheba.* That is, from the far north, near Phoenician territory, to the
Negeb in the south.

stalwart. Or, "faithful." That is, Samuel's authority as prophet was recognized by all Israel.

21. *And the LORD continued to appear . . . the LORD was revealed.* This emphatic indication
is an obvious counterpoint to the first verse of the chapter: instead of being withheld, divine
communication is now regular and repeated through the person of Samuel.

4:1a. Although the conventional chapter division attaches this brief clause to the next episode, it is clear that it is actually a final summary of Samuel's new authority at the end of his
dedication story. The next words of the text (chapter 4:1b) in fact refer to a military initiative
undertaken by the Israelites without Samuel's authorization.

1b CHAPTER 4   And Israel sallied forth in battle against the
Philistines, and they encamped by Eben-Ezer, while the Philistines were
2 encamped at Aphek. And the Philistines drew up their lines against Israel,
and the battle forces were deployed, and Israel was routed by the Philistines, and they struck down in the lines in the field about four thousand
3 men. And the troops came into the camp, and the elders of Israel said,
"Why has the LORD routed us today before the Philistines? Let us take to
us from Shiloh the Ark of the Covenant of the LORD, that it may come into
4 our midst and rescue us from the hands of our enemies." And the troops
sent to Shiloh and they bore from there the Ark of the Covenant of the
LORD of Armies enthroned on the cherubim, and there the two sons of

---

CHAPTER 4   1b. *the Philistines*. The Philistines were part of the general incursion
of the so-called Sea Peoples from the Aegean—the prophet Amos names Crete as their land
of origin—into the eastern Mediterranean region perhaps less than a century before the
early-eleventh-century setting of our story. (There is some evidence that they first migrated
to Anatolia, then moved southward.) They established a powerful presence in Canaan on
the coastal plain, concentrated in the region a little south of present-day Tel Aviv. They were
intrepid warriors (note the martial exhortation of verse 9) and also exercised a mastery of
military science and military technology. In the coastal plain, they were able to deploy iron
chariots (which seem to have been lacking among the Israelites) as well as infantry. Perhaps
their failure to extend their mini-kingdom of five allied cities more than a dozen or so miles
eastward from the coast was related to a loss of the strategic advantage of chariots as they
went up into the high country.

2. *the Philistines drew up their lines . . . and the battle forces were deployed*. Interestingly,
the language of strategic deployment is attached only to the Philistines. "Battle forces" is,
literally, "battle." Although the precise indications of these terms are unclear, their use
elsewhere in the Bible makes it evident that they had a technical military application.

the lines. The Hebrew, *ma'arakhah,* is a singular, with the sense of "battle formation"
or "front line."

3. *Let us take to us*. The addition of this seemingly superfluous personal pronoun suggests
how the elders arrogate to themselves a sacred object for their own purposes, conceiving
the Ark magically or fetishistically as a vehicle of power that they can manipulate for
military ends.

the Ark of the Covenant of the LORD. This would have been a large case made of acacia
wood, with carved cherubim on its top, containing the stone tablets of the Law given at
Sinai. As the material residue of the defining encounter between God and Israel, these
tablets were viewed as the most sacrosanct possession of the nation. Hence the horror at
the end of this episode over the news that the Ark has been captured by the Philistines.

4. *troops*. The Hebrew has a collective noun, *'am,* "people," which in military contexts refers
to the ordinary soldiers.

the Ark of the Covenant of the LORD of Armies enthroned on the cherubim. This extravagantly full title is a kind of epic flourish reflecting the power that the elders of Israel attri-

Eli were with the Ark of the Covenant of God—Hophni and Phineas. And 5
when the Ark of the Covenant of the LORD came into the camp, all Israel
let out a great shout, and the earth resounded. And the Philistines heard 6
the sound of the shouting and said, "What is the sound of this great shouting in the camp of the Hebrews?" And they knew that the Ark of the LORD
had come into the camp. And the Philistines were afraid, for they thought, 7
"God has come into the camp." And they said, "Woe to us! For it was never
so in times gone by. Woe to us! Who will save us from the hands of these 8
mighty gods? They are the very gods who struck Egypt with every blow in
the wilderness. Muster strength and be men, O Philistines, lest you become 9
slaves to the Hebrews as they were slaves to you. Be men and do battle!"
And the Philistines did battle and Israel was routed, and every man fled to 10
his tent and the blow was very great, thirty thousand foot soldiers of Israel
fell. And the Ark of the LORD was taken, and the two sons of Eli died— 11
Hophni and Phineas. And a man of Benjamin ran from the lines and came 12
to Shiloh that day, his garments torn and earth on his head. He came, and, 13

---

bute to the Ark. "Armies" ("hosts" in older translations) underscores the LORD's martial
nature. The cherubim are fierce winged beasts imagined as God's celestial steeds, and so
the carved cherubim on the Ark are conceived as the earthly "throne" of the invisible deity.

   Hophni and Phineas. In an odd stylistic tie, each time the two sons are mentioned in this
chapter, their proper names are stuck on at the very end of the sentence, as though their
precise identity were being isolated for opprobrium.

6. *the camp of the Hebrews.* "Hebrews" is generally the designation of the Israelites when
they are named by other peoples.

7. *God has come into the camp.* Here *'elohim* is the subject of a verb in the singular, but in
verse 8, in proper polytheistic fashion, the Philistines use the same term but construe it
grammatically as a plural, "gods."

8. *every blow.* The Hebrew *makah* also means "plague," an obviously appropriate sense here,
but it is important that the writer uses the same word in verse 10, though with a military
meaning, for a theological irony is intended in the pun: they feared the might of the LORD
Who struck such terrible blows against Egypt, and then they themselves strike a blow
against Israel, which actually does not have God in its midst, only His sacred paraphernalia. Here as elsewhere in the Bible, the national fiction is maintained that all the peoples of
Canaan were intimately familiar with the Exodus story and deeply impressed by it.

9. *Muster strength and be men.* There may be a pointed antithesis in their speech between
"gods" and "men." In any case, they summon stirring rhetoric to rouse themselves from
their fear of a supernatural adversary and to go out to do battle.

12. *his garments torn and earth on his head.* This disheveled appearance is not because of
the fighting but reflects the customary signs of mourning.

look, Eli was seated in a chair by the road on the lookout, for his heart was
trembling over the Ark of God, and the man had come to tell in the town
14   and the whole town cried out, and Eli heard the sound of the outcry and said,
"What is this sound of uproar?" The man had hurried, and he came and told
15   Eli. And Eli was ninety-eight years old, his eyes were rigid and he could not
16   see. And the man said to Eli, "I am the one who has come from the lines, I
17   from the lines fled today." And he said, "What happened, my son?" And the
bearer of tidings answered and said, "Israel fled before the Philistines, and
what's more, there was a great rout among the troops, and what's more, your
18   two sons died—Hophni and Phineas—and the Ark of God was taken." And
the moment he mentioned the Ark of God, Eli fell backward from his chair
through the gate and his neckbone was broken and he died, for the man was
19   old and heavy. And he had judged Israel forty years. And his daughter-in-

---

13. *Eli was seated in a chair by the road.* Similarly, in chapter 1, he was seated in a chair in
the temple—in both instances a token of his infirmity, his passivity or incapacity as leader.
The Hebrew phrase behind "by the road" is textually problematic, as is the related phrase
attached to the word "gate" in verse 18. Scholarly opinion differs as to whether Eli is sitting by the road, by the gate, or, like David in 2 Samuel 18, above the gate. The last of these
possibilities would best explain his breaking his neck when he falls, but it is by no means
the inevitable meaning of the Hebrew, and the Hebrew preposition in verse 18 actually
indicates *through* the gate.

   his heart was trembling over the Ark of God. Apprehension over the fate of his scurrilous
sons is not mentioned.

14. *What is this sound of uproar?* Eli's question pointedly, and ironically, parallels the question asked by the Philistines in verse 6 about the jubilant uproar from the Israelite camp.
At the very end of the David story (1 Kings 1), the usurper Adonijah will ask virtually the
same question about an uproar that spells disaster for him and his followers.

15. *his eyes were rigid.* The idiom for Eli's blindness has a stark finality here that it does not
have in 3:2. Presumably a good deal of time has elapsed since that moment of the young
Samuel's dedication as prophet, and the process of blindness is now complete. It is because Eli
can see nothing that he must ask with particular urgency about the reason for all the shouting.

16. *I am the one who has come from the lines, I from the lines fled today.* This odd repetition
may reflect a stammer of nervousness or confusion, as Shimon Bar-Efrat has proposed.

17. The report of the battle moves from a general indication of the defeat, to the admission
of a rout, to the death of Eli's two sons, and, finally, to what is assumed to be the worst
catastrophe, the capture of the Ark. It should be noted that 1 and 2 Samuel are in part
organized around a series of interechoing scenes in which a messenger brings ill tidings.
The bearer of ill tidings to Adonijah at the very end of this long narrative also nervously
repeats *wegam*, "what's more" as he recounts the catastrophe.

18. *And he had judged Israel forty years.* This notice, with its use of the formulaic forty years,
is odd because Eli certainly has not been a judge, either in the military-charismatic or the

law, Phineas's wife, was big with child, and when she heard the report about the taking of the Ark, and that her father-in-law and her husband were dead, she crouched down and gave birth, for her birth pangs overwhelmed her. And as she was on the point of death, her attendant women spoke up, "Fear 20 not, for you have born a son." And she did not answer or pay heed. And she 21 called the boy Ichabod, which is to say, "Glory is exiled from Israel"—for the taking of the Ark and for her father-in-law and her husband. And she said, 22 "Glory is exiled from Israel, for the Ark of God is taken."

CHAPTER 5   And the Philistines had taken the Ark of God 1 and brought it from Eben-Ezer to Ashdod. And the Philistines took the Ark 2

---

juridical sense. This sentence could be an attempt to establish a carryover from the Book of Judges, or it could be an inadvertent editorial repetition of the Judges formula.

19. *big with child.* The Hebrew says literally "was pregnant to give birth."
    she crouched down. In the ancient Near East, women generally gave birth in a kneeling position, leaning on a special birthing stone—examples have been uncovered by archaeologists called in Hebrew a *mashber*.

21. *Ichabod ... Glory is exiled.* The Hebrew name is conventionally construed to mean "Inglorious," though Kyle McCarter Jr. has argued that the more probable meaning is "Where is glory?" or "Alas for glory!" In any case, it is a most peculiar name—the dying mother, overcome by the loss of the Ark (which affects her much more than her husband's demise), inscribing the national catastrophe in her son's name. Where one must agree unhesitatingly with McCarter is that the verb in this verse and the next should be rendered as "exiled" and not, as it is customarily translated, as "departed." Exile is what it clearly denotes, and it is surely significant that this whole large sequence of stories that will provide an account of the founding of Israel's dynasty and the crystallization of its national power begins with a refrain of glory exiled from Israel. It is also noteworthy that the term for "glory," *kavod,* is transparently cognate with *kaved,* "heavy," the adjective used to explain Eli's lethal tumble from his chair—the leader who might be supposed to represent Israel's glory exhibits only deadly heaviness.

CHAPTER 5   The Ark Narrative at this point leaves behind the house of Eli, Samuel, and the paramount question of Israel's leadership in order to tell a bizarre satiric story of a battle between cult objects—the potent Ark of the Covenant, which is conceived as the conduit for the cosmic power of the God of Israel, and the idol of Dagon, vainly believed to be a real deity by the Philistines. The dominant tone of the story is a kind of monotheistic triumphalism; accordingly, themes from the story of the plagues of Egypt are replayed, though in a virtually scatological key.

1. *from Eben-Ezer to Ashdod.* The Ark is carried down from Eben-Ezer, in the western part of the territory of Ephraim (roughly ten miles from the coast and just a little to the north of present-day Tel Aviv) to Ashdod, on the Mediterranean, in the heart of Philistine territory.

of God and brought it to the house of Dagon and set it up alongside Dagon.
3 And the Ashdodites arose on the next day and, look, Dagon was fallen forward to the ground before the Ark of the LORD. And they took Dagon and
4 set him back in his place. And they arose the next morning and, look, Dagon
was fallen forward to the ground before the Ark of the LORD, and Dagon's
head and both his hands were chopped off upon the threshold—his trunk
5 alone remained on him. Therefore the priests of Dagon, and all who enter
the house of Dagon, do not tread on the threshold of the house of Dagon
6 to this day. And the hand of the LORD was heavy upon the Ashdodites and

---

2. *Dagon*. This god is now generally thought to be a vegetation or fertility god, its name
cognate with the Hebrew *dagan*, "grain" (and not, as was once widely imagined, with the
Hebrew *dag*, "fish").

  set it up alongside Dagon. Either to amplify the power of their own deity or to express
the subservience of the God of Israel to Dagon.

3. *and, look, Dagon was fallen forward to the ground*. This clause and the parallel one in the
next verse reflect the visual perspective of the Ashdodites when they come into the temple
early in the morning and make their shocking discovery. Tyndale's translation gets into
the spirit of the scene, although with a certain creative license, by rendering this as "lay
grovelling upon the ground."

4. *his trunk alone remained on him*. The Masoretic Text has, cryptically, "Dagon alone
remained on him," but several of the ancient translations appear to have used a version
which read *geivo*, "his trunk," instead of *Dagon*. Dagon's first downfall might be attributed
to a natural, accidental cause—the idol's somehow slipping from its pedestal. This second
incident, in which the hands and head of the idol have been chopped off, offers to the Philistines clear proof of divine intervention. Hacking the hands and feet off war prisoners
was a well-known barbaric practice in the ancient Near East, and similar acts of mutilation
are attested in the Book of Judges.

5. *Therefore*. This is the introductory formula for etiological explanations. An observed
Philistine practice of skipping over the sanctuary threshold, as a special measure for enter-
ing sacred space, is reinterpreted as a reminiscence of the victory of Israel's God over
Dagon.

6. *the hand of the LORD was heavy upon the Ashdodites*. The word *kaved*, previously associated with Eli's corpulence and linked by root with *kavod*, "glory," recurs here in a clause
that introduces the first of several echoes of the plagues against Egypt.

  tumors. Many translations render this as "hemorrhoids," and there is a little confusion
in the Masoretic Text: the consonantal written version (*ketiv*) has "tumors," but the tradition for reciting the text (*qeri*) indicates "hemorrhoids." This confusion is compounded
because the Septuagint, seconded by Josephus, includes a plague of mice not in evidence
in the Masoretic version, and the golden mice of the next chapter look very much like a
response to just such a plague. The fact, moreover, that hemorrhoids are a humiliating but
not lethal disorder and are not spread by epidemic, whereas the Philistines protest that they
are dying, gives support to an interpretation at least as old as Rashi: the plague in question

He devastated them, and He struck them with tumors, Ashdod and all its
territories. And the people of Ashdod saw that it was so, and they said, "Let 7
not the Ark of the God of Israel stay among us, for His hand is hard upon
us and upon Dagon our god." And they sent and gathered to them all the 8
Philistine overlords and they said, "What shall we do with the Ark of the
God of Israel?" And they said, "To Gath let the Ark of the God of Israel be
brought round." And they brought round the Ark of the God of Israel. And 9
it happened after they had brought it round that the hand of the LORD was
against the town—a great panic. And He struck the people of the town,
young and old, and they had tumors in their secret parts. And they sent 10
the Ark of God on to Ekron, and it happened when the Ark of God came
to Ekron that the Ekronites cried out, saying, "They have brought round to
me the Ark of the God of Israel to bring death to me and my people." And 11
they sent and gathered all the Philistine overlords and they said, "Send the
Ark of the God of Israel back to its place, and let it not bring death to me
and my people." For there was death panic throughout the city, the hand
of God was very heavy there. And the people who did not die were struck 12
with tumors, and the town's outcry rose to the heavens.

---

is bubonic plague, carried by rats (metamorphosed in this story into mice, and associated
with the epidemic but perhaps not clearly understood as the bearers of the disease); the
tumors are the *buboes* of bubonic plague, which might especially afflict the lower body,
including the rectal area.

8. *overlords.* The Hebrew term *seranim* is a Philistine loanword and is applied only to Philistines as a touch of local color (like calling Spanish aristocrats "grandees"). Some scholars
have linked the word with the Greek *tyrranos.* Since there is only one *seren* for each Philistine
city, they are clearly more than just "lords."

   Gath. The Ark is carried around to three of the five Philistine cities. The other two are
Gaza and Ashkelon.

9. *the hand of the LORD was against the town—a great panic.* This apposition reflects the
Hebrew syntax, which sounds a little peculiar, but there is not convincing evidence of a
defective text here.

   they had tumors in their secret parts. The verb *yisatru* is peculiar. This translation follows Rashi, Kimchi, and the King James Version in linking it with *seter,* "secret place."

12. *the town's outcry rose to the heavens.* This clause balances on the edge of an ambiguity.
"The heavens" (*hashamayim*) can be simply the sky or the abode of God. Is God, Who has
been present in the story through His acts, His heavy hand—but not, as it were, in person—
listening to the anguished cries of the Philistines, or is this merely an image of the shrieks
of the afflicted Philistines echoing under the silent vault of the heavens?

1 **CHAPTER 6**   And the Ark of the LORD was in Philistine coun-
2 try seven months. And the Philistines called to the priests and the soothsayers, saying, "What shall we do with the Ark of the LORD? Tell us, how
3 shall we send it back to its place." And they said, "If you are about to send
back the Ark of the God of Israel, do not send it back empty-handed, for
you must give back to Him a guilt offering. Then you will be healed and
there will be atonement for you. Why should His hand not relent from
4 you?" And they said, "What guilt offering should we give back to Him?"
And they said, "The number of the Philistine overlords is five. Five golden
tumors and five golden mice. For a single plague is upon all of you and upon
5 your overlords. And you shall make images of your tumors and images
of your mice that are ravaging the land, and you shall give glory to the
God of Israel—perhaps He will lighten His hand from upon you and from
6 upon your god and your land. And why should you harden your hearts as
Egypt and Pharaoh hardened their hearts? After He made sport of them,

---

CHAPTER 6   This chapter—the episode actually ends in the first verse of chapter
7—which concludes the Ark Narrative, also brings to a climax the traits that set it off from
the larger narrative of Samuel, Saul, and David in which it is placed. Instead of the sharply
etched individual characters of the surrounding narrative, we have only collective speakers and agents. Instead of the political perspective with its human system of causation, the
perspective is theological and the culminating events of the story are frankly miraculous.
God, Who does not speak in this narrative, manifests His power over Philistines and Israelites alike through supernatural acts in the material realm, as the strange tale of the cart
and the golden images vividly demonstrates.

3. *send it back.* The Hebrew *meshalḥim* is the same verb repeatedly used for Pharaoh's sending Israel out of Egypt and thus sustains the network of allusions to the Exodus story. In
Exodus, the Israelites, too, were told that they would not leave Egypt "empty-handed" but
would take with them golden ornaments despoiled from the Egyptians.

   there will be atonement for you. The Masoretic Text has "it will become known to you"
(*wenod'a lakhem*), but the reading of both the Qumran Samuel scroll and the Septuagint,
wenikaper lakhem, "and it will be atoned for you," makes far better sense.

5. *you shall give glory to the God of Israel—perhaps He will lighten His hand.* Once again,
the writer harks back to the play of antonyms, *kavod/kaved* (glory/heavy) and *qal* (light,
and in other contexts, worthless). Glory has been exiled from Israel with the capture of the
Ark: now, with the restitution of the Ark together with an indemnity payment of golden
images, glory will be restored. This process helps explain the insistence on the term "give
back" associated with the guilt offering.

6. *harden your hearts.* This phrase is not only an explicit link with the Exodus story, but
also continues the play on glory/heaviness because the literal Hebrew idiom is "make your
heart heavy" (the verb *kabed*).

did they not let the Hebrews go, and off they went? And so, fetch and make 7
one new cart, and two milch cows that no yoke has touched, and harness
the cows to the cart, but bring their calves back inside. And you shall fetch 8
the Ark of the LORD and set it on the cart, and the golden objects that
you give back to Him as a guilt offering you shall place in a chest at its
side, and you shall send it away and off it will go. And you will see—if 9
on the road to its own territory, to Beth-Shemesh, it will go up, He it was
Who did this great evil to us, and if not, we shall know that it was not
His hand that afflicted us but chance that came upon us." And so the men 10
did: they took two milch cows and harnessed them to the cart, but their
calves they shut up inside. And they placed the Ark of the LORD on the 11
cart and the chest and the golden mice and the images of their tumors.
And the cows went straight on the way, on the way to Beth-Shemesh, on a 12
single road they went, lowing as they went, and they veered neither right
nor left, with the Philistine overlords walking after them to the border of

---

let the Hebrews go. The Hebrew says "let them go," but the lack of antecedent for the
pronoun would be confusing in English.

7. *one new cart.* It is to be an undefiled instrument made specifically for this ritual purpose.
   that no yoke has touched. The cows, too, are uncompromised by use in ordinary labor,
though the more important point is that they are entirely devoid of experience as draft
animals, so that their ability to pull the cart straight to Beth-Shemesh would have to be a
manifestation of God's intervention, or of the intrinsic power of the Ark.
   their calves back inside. This, of course, is the crux of the test: the milking cows will have
to go against nature in plodding forward into Israelite territory with their calves behind
them, shut up in the manger and waiting to be fed.

8. *chest.* The Hebrew *'argaz* appears only here. Postbiblical Hebrew consistently understood
it as "chest," though some scholars, on the basis of Semitic cognates, have argued for the
meaning of "pouch." It may be more plausible that precious objects would be placed in
orderly fashion in a chest rather than piled up in a pouch.

11. *the Ark of the LORD . . . and the chest and the golden mice and the images of their tumors.*
This whole scene has a certain grotesquely comic and incongruous effect: Israel's most
sacred cult object drawn in a cart by two cows with swollen udders, and alongside the Ark
golden images of vermin and tumors.

12. *straight on the way, on the way to Beth-Shemesh, on a single road they went . . . and they veered
neither right nor left.* Against the spareness and swift efficiency of normal Hebrew narrative
style, the writer here lavishes synonyms and repetitions in order to highlight the perfect geom-
etry of the miracle: against all conceivable distractions of biology or sheer animal unknowing-
ness, the cows pursue an arrow-straight southeast trajectory from Ekron to Beth-Shemesh.
   lowing as they went. This small but vivid descriptive detail is an even more striking

13 Beth-Shemesh. And the men of Beth-Shemesh were harvesting the wheat
    harvest in the valley, and they raised their eyes and saw the Ark, and they
14 rejoiced at the sight. And the cart had come to the field of Joshua the Beth-
    Shemeshite and it came to rest there, and a great stone was there, and they
    split the wood of the cart, and the cows they offered up as a burnt offer-
15 ing to the LORD. And the Levites had brought down the Ark of the LORD
    and the chest that was with it, in which were the golden objects, and they
    placed them on the great stone, and the men of Beth-Shemesh offered up
16 burnt offerings and sacrificed sacrifices on that day to the LORD. The five
17 Philistine overlords saw, and they returned to Ekron on that day. And these
    are the golden tumors that the Philistines gave back as guilt offering to the
    LORD: for Ashdod, one; for Gaza, one; for Ashkelon, one; for Gath, one;
18 for Ekron, one. And the golden mice were the number of all the Philistine

---

exception to the stringent economy that governs biblical narrative. The last thing one
would expect in a biblical story, where there is scant report of the gestures of the human
actors, is a specification of sounds made by draft animals. The point, however, is that
the milch cows—more driven by the Ark than hauling it—are going strenuously against
nature: their udders full of milk for the calves they have been forced to leave behind, they
mark with maternal lowing their distress over the journey they cannot resist. There is a
peculiar resonance between this episode and Hannah's story in chapter 1. There, too, a
nursing mother does not want to be separated from her young, and, as we noted, special
emphasis is placed on the physical acts of nursing and weaning. (The connection between
the two episodes is underscored in the Hebrew, which literally calls the cows' young their
"sons," not their calves.) In both stories, sacrifice is offered after mother and young are
separated. Here, of course, the mothers become the objects of the sacrifice; in Hannah's
story, it is a bull, and, in symbolic rather than literal fashion, the son as well. Though all
these correspondences seem too pointed to be coincidental, it is unclear whether they
represent the literary artifact of the redactor, or an allusion by the author of the Samuel
story to the Ark Narrative.

13. *the men of Beth-Shemesh were harvesting.* The Hebrew uses an ellipsis: "Beth-Shemesh
were harvesting."

14. *the cows they offered up.* One connection between the Ark Narrative, with its concern for
sanctity, and the Samuel–Saul–David cycle, with its preoccupation with politics, is a kind
of brooding sense of the cruel price exacted for dedication to the higher cause. The milch
cows are burned on the improvised altar; Hannah and her son, Samuel, must be separated
in *his* dedication to the sanctuary; and later both Saul and David will pay terrible costs in
their personal lives for their adhesion to power.

17. *And these are the golden tumors.* The introductory formula suggests a kind of ritual or
epic catalogue, so that we know there is in fact one golden image corresponding to each of
the five Philistine towns, just as the soothsayers had stipulated.

18. *the golden mice were the number of all the Philistine towns.* This appears to contradict
the explicit directions in verse 4, that there should be exactly five golden mice. Kimchi

towns, from the fortified cities to the unwalled villages. And the great stone on which they set the Ark of the LORD is to this day in the field of Joshua the Beth-Shemeshite. And He struck down men of Beth-Shemesh, 19 for they had looked into the Ark of the LORD, and he struck down from the people seventy men [fifty thousand men], and the people mourned, for the LORD had struck down the people with a great blow. And the people 20 of Beth-Shemesh said, "Who can stand before this holy LORD God, and to whom will He go up away from us?" And they sent messengers to the 21 inhabitants of Kiriath-Jearim, saying, "The Philistines have brought back the Ark of the LORD. Come down and carry it up to you." And the men of 7:1 Kiriath-Jearim came and carried up the Ark of the LORD and brought it to the house of Abinadab on the hill, and Eleazar his son they consecrated to watch over the Ark of the LORD.

---

resolves the discrepancy by proposing that, in the event, as added insurance for all the villages (since the mice had overrun the fields), the Philistines went beyond their instructions and fashioned multiple images of the mice.

And the great stone. The Masoretic Text reads 'avel (brook or meadow) instead of 'even (stone), but both the Septuagint and the Qumran scroll have the latter reading. The Masoretic Text also has "and to" (we'ad) preceding this word, but that is probably an inadvertent scribal duplication of the preposition that occurs twice before in the verse.

19. fifty thousand men. This figure makes no sense because Beth-Shemesh was a small agricultural village. It appears in all the ancient versions, but Josephus seems to have possessed a text in which only the much more plausible number seventy appeared. The fact that the Hebrew has no indication of "and" between "seventy" and "fifty thousand" is further evidence that the latter number is an intrusion in the text.

a great blow. As in 4:8, the Hebrew for "blow" can also mean "plague." If there is a historical kernel to this whole story, an epidemic ravaging the Philistines could have easily spread to the bordering Israelites, perhaps even through the agency of the cart and the Ark.

20. Who can stand before this holy LORD God. Throughout the Ark Narrative, including what may be its epilogue in 2 Samuel 7, runs an archaic sense of God's sacred objects as material precipitates of an awesome and dangerous power. This notion led Leonhard Rost, one of the earliest scholars to argue for an entirely distinct Ark Narrative, to assume that the author must have been a priest, although that is hardly an inevitable inference, as these attitudes were widely held in ancient Near Eastern cultures. The phrase "stand before" means idiomatically "to serve."

will He go up. The Hebrew could equally be construed as "will it go up," referring to the Ark. From the point of view of the terrified speakers, it may amount to the same thing.

21. And they sent messengers to the inhabitants of Kiriath-Jearim. There seems to be no question of sending the Ark back to Shiloh, which has led to the scholarly inference that the Shiloh sanctuary was destroyed in the wake of the defeat at Aphek. The destruction of Shiloh is in fact attested in other sources.

2   CHAPTER 7   And it happened from the day the Ark dwelled
in Kiriath-Jearim that the days grew many and became twenty years, and
3   the whole house of Israel was drawn after the LORD. And Samuel said to
the whole house of Israel, saying, "If with your whole heart you now return
to the LORD, put away the alien gods from your midst and the Ashtaroth,
and set your heart firm for the LORD and serve Him alone, that He may
4   rescue you from the hand of the Philistines." And the Israelites put away
the Baalim and the Ashtaroth and they served the LORD alone.

5   And Samuel said, "Assemble all Israel at Mizpah that I may intercede for
6   you before the LORD. And they assembled at Mizpah and they drew water
and spilled it before the LORD and they fasted on that day and there they

---

CHAPTER 7   This chapter, which offers a summary account of Israel's religious
reformation and military ascendancy under Samuel's rule, serves as a bridge between the
Ark Narrative and the great narrative of the founding of the monarchy that will occupy
the rest of 1 and 2 Samuel and the first two chapters of 1 Kings.

2. *twenty years.* This is half the formulaic figure of forty years that recurs so frequently in
the Book of Judges. The period of twenty years could refer to the time until David brings
the Ark up to Jerusalem, though given the immediate narrative context, the more likely
reference is the time until Samuel assembles the tribes at Mizpah. During this period, the
presence of the Ark at Kiriath-Jearim inspires the people to cultic loyalty to God.

   was drawn after. The Hebrew *yinahu* is anomalous. The usual meaning of this verbal
root, "to weep," makes little sense here (though it was followed by the King James translators). The present translation adopts the proposal of Rashi, who may simply have been
interpreting from context. The Hebrew could also be a scribal error for *yinharu*, which
clearly means "to be drawn after."

3. *with your whole heart.* This phrase, and Samuel's language here in general, is notably
Deuteronomistic, and the narrative line in this chapter follows the Deuteronomistic theological assumption that cultic faithfulness leads to military success. Neither this language
nor this assumption is much in evidence in the main body of the Samuel–Saul–David
narrative.

   Ashtaroth. The form is a feminine plural of Ashtoreth (Astarte), the Canaanite fertility
goddess. The plural indicates either a plurality of goddesses or—more likely—the multiple
icons of Astarte.

4. *Baalim.* This is the masculine plural of Baal, the principal Canaanite male deity.

5. *Mizpah.* Mizpah appears as a point of tribal assembly at two significant junctures in
the Book of Judges. The name means "lookout" and in the Hebrew has a definite article.

6. *they drew water and spilled it before the LORD.* This act is a small puzzle because a water-
drawing ritual is otherwise known only from the late Second Temple period (through
Mishnaic sources), and there it is associated with fertility and the fall Festival of Succoth.
The context makes clear that in this instance it must be a rite of penitence or purification.

said, "We have offended the Lord." And Samuel judged Israel at Mizpah.
And the Philistines heard that the Israelites had assembled at Mizpah, and 7
the Philistine overlords came up against Israel, and the Israelites heard
and were afraid of the Philistines. And the Israelites said to Samuel, "Do 8
not hold still from crying out for us to the Lord our God, that He rescue
us from the hand of the Philistines." And Samuel took one suckling lamb 9
and offered it up whole as a burnt offering to the Lord, and Samuel cried
out to the Lord on behalf of Israel, and the Lord answered him. And 10
just as Samuel was offering up the offering, the Philistines drew near to
do battle with Israel, and the Lord thundered with a great sound on that
day upon the Philistines and panicked them, and they were routed before
Israel. And the men of Israel sallied forth from Mizpah and pursued the 11
Philistines and struck them down as far as below Beth-Car. And Samuel 12
took a single stone and set it up between Mizpah and Shen, and he called
its name Eben-Ezer and he said, "As far as here has the Lord helped us."
And the Philistines were brought low and they no longer came into Israelite 13

Rashi puts it succinctly: "It can only be a symbol of abnegation, that is, 'Behold we are in
your presence like this water spilled forth.'"

7. *the Philistines heard that the Israelites had assembled.* Either the Philistines assumed
that the assembly was a mustering of the tribes for war, which might not have been far
off the mark (compare the assembly at Mizpah at the end of Judges 10), or they decided to
seize this opportunity of the gathering of Israel for cultic purposes in order to attack the
assembled tribes.

9. *one suckling lamb.* The Hebrew is literally "milk lamb" (*teleh halav*). The choice of the
sacrificial animal strikes an odd little echo with the two milch cows sacrificed at the end of
the Ark Narrative and with the emphasis on nursing and weaning in Samuel's own infancy.

10. *the Lord thundered . . . and panicked them.* The key terms restate a recurrent pattern
in 1 Samuel: God's hand, or God's voice (the thunder), comes down on the enemy, and the
enemy is smitten with "panic" (*mehumah*). Compare, also, the end of Hannah's poem: "the
Lord shatters His adversaries, / against them in the heavens He thunders." Essentially, it is
God Who does battle, with the Israelite foot soldiers merely mopping up after His celestial
bombardment. This Deuteronomistic view will fade from the Saul and David narratives.

12. *Shen.* If the Masoretic Text is correct (the Septuagint reflects a different place-name),
this name means "cliff" and, like Mizpah, it is preceded by a definite article.
    Eben-Ezer. The name means "stone of help," with "help" bearing a particularly martial
implication. This place may not be the same as the one where the Ark was captured. In any
case, the recurring name is meant to signify the righting of old wrongs.
    As far as here. The Hebrew phrase could be either temporal ("up until now") or spatial,
but the placing of a stone as a marker makes the latter more likely: as far as this point the
Lord granted us victory.

country, and the hand of the LORD was against the Philistines all the days
14 of Samuel. And the towns that the Philistines had taken from Israel were
returned to Israel, from Ekron as far as Gath, and their territories Israel
retrieved from the hand of the Philistines. And there was peace between
15 Israel and the Amorite. And Samuel judged Israel all the days of his life.
16 And he would go about from year to year and come round Bethel and Gilgal
17 and Mizpah and would judge Israel in all these places. And his point of
return was Ramah, for there his home was, and there he judged Israel. And
he built there an altar to the LORD.

1 CHAPTER 8   And it happened when Samuel grew old that he
2 set his sons up as judges for Israel. And the name of his firstborn son was

---

13. *the hand of the LORD was against the Philistines all the days of Samuel.* Since under Saul's
kingship the Philistines remained a dominant military power, "all the days of Samuel"
could refer only to the period of Samuel's actual leadership. In any case, there are later
indications that even under Samuel the Philistines remained powerful.

14. *peace between Israel and the Amorite.* This seemingly incongruous notice actually
throws light, as Shmuel Avramsky has proposed, on Israel's military-political situation.
The Amorites—a designation often used loosely by the biblical writers for the indigenous
Canaanite peoples—had also been dominated by the Philistine invaders, and Israel's success against the Philistines may have been facilitated by an alliance, or at least a non-
aggression pact, with the Amorites.

15. *And Samuel judged Israel.* The precise nature of his leadership is left ambiguous, as befits
this transitional figure in Israel's political evolution. Some of the "judging" may actually
be performance of a judicial function, as the next verse indicates that Samuel operated as a
kind of circuit judge, although he may well have carried out cultic or priestly duties as well
(the towns at which he stopped are all cultic sites). He is also judge in the sense of "chieftain"
or political leader, though he plays this role not as a warrior, according to the model of the
Book of Judges, but as exhorter and intercessor. He is also, as we shall see in the Saul story,
a seer and a reprover-prophet.

16. *from year to year.* This locution for iterative annual peregrination takes us back to
Hannah and Elkanah at the very beginning of the Samuel story.

17. *his point of return was Ramah.* The Hebrew says literally "his return was Ramah." This
is evidently the same place as Ramathaim Zofim, where his parents lived. Samuel's circuit
is an uneven ellipsis roughly twenty miles across in the northern part of the territory of
Benjamin (Saul's tribe) and the southern part of the territory of Ephraim, in north-central
Israel. It is far from encompassing all the tribal territories.

CHAPTER 8   1. *he set his sons up as judges for Israel.* It is a signal expression of the
ambiguity of Samuel's role as leader that he oversteps his mandate as judge (*shofet*—both
judicial authority and ad hoc political leader) by attempting to inaugurate a kind of dynas-

Joel and the name of his secondborn was Abijah—judges in Beersheba. But 3
his sons did not go in his ways and they were bent on gain and took bribes
and twisted justice.

And all the elders of Israel assembled and came to Samuel at Ramah. And 4,5
they said to him, "Look, you yourself have grown old and your sons have not
gone in your ways. So now, set over us a king to rule us, like all the nations."
And the thing was evil in Samuel's eyes when they said, "Give us a king to 6
rule us." And Samuel prayed to the LORD. And the LORD said to Samuel, 7
"Heed the voice of the people in all that they say to you, for it is not you they
have cast aside but Me they have cast aside from reigning over them. Like 8
all the deeds they have done from the day I brought them up from Egypt
to this day, forsaking Me and serving other gods, even so they do as well to
you. So now, heed their voice, though you must solemnly warn them and 9
tell them the practice of the king that will reign over them." And Samuel 10
said all the words of the LORD to the people who were asking of him a king.

---

tic arrangement. The two sons who betray their trust of office are a nice parallel to Eli's
two corrupt sons, who essentially were displaced by Samuel.

2. *judges in Beersheba.* It is a little puzzling that Samuel should send both his sons from
north-central Israel to this city in the south. Josephus evidently was familiar with a tradition in which one son was sent to Bethel in the north and the other to Beersheba, a more
plausible deployment.

3. *bent on gain . . . twisted justice.* The two verbs are different conjugations of the same root,
n-t-h, which means to bend off from the straight and narrow.

6. *the thing was evil in Samuel's eyes.* Samuel is ideologically opposed to the monarchy
because he is committed to the old idea of the ad hoc inspired leader, *shofet*, who is a kind
of direct implementation of God's rule through the divine spirit over the unique nation
of Israel. God appears to agree with him but yields to political necessity. It is noteworthy
that when the elders' words are replayed in this verse from Samuel's point of view, the very
phrase rejecting covenantal status that must especially gall him, "like all the nations," is
suppressed.

8. *forsaking Me and serving other gods.* Both the locutions used and the preoccupation
with cultic loyalty are notably Deuteronomistic, and the coupling of the shift in style with
this theme leads one to suspect a seventh-century B.C.E. interpolation here, since there has
been no question of idolatry in the immediate context. The elders' expressed concern has
been rather with the breakdown of the institution of the judge in Samuel's corrupt sons.
The grounds for the argument for and against monarchy will shift once again in Samuel's
speech (verses 11–18).

10. *asking of him a king.* The Hebrew participle *sho'alim* takes us back to the verb of asking
used in Samuel's naming and points forward to *Sha'ul*, Saul.

11 And he said, "This will be the practice of the king who will reign over you:
    Your sons he will take and set for himself in his chariots and in his cavalry,
12 and some will run before his chariots. He will set for himself captains of
    thousands and captains of fifties, to plow his ground and reap his harvest
    and to make his implements of war and the implements of his chariots.
13 And your daughters he will take as confectioners and cooks and bakers.
14 And your best fields and your vineyards and your olive trees he will take

---

11. *the practice of the king.* This whole episode turns repeatedly on an untranslatable pun.
Mishpat means "justice," the very thing that Samuel's sons have twisted by taking payoffs.
Mishpat also means "habitual behavior," "mode of operation," or "practice." As a verb the
same root means either "to judge" or "to rule": it is used (in a verbal noun) in the former
sense in verses 1 and 2, in the latter sense in verses 5 and 6. The recurrent scholarly assumption that this whole attack on the encroachments of the monarchy reflects a knowledge of
Solomon's reign or of later Davidic kings is by no means inevitable: all the practices enumerated—military conscription, the corvée, expropriation of lands, taxation of the agricultural
output—could easily have been familiar to an early writer from observing the Canaanite
city-states or the larger imperial regimes to the east and the south.

who will reign over you. The people had spoken of the king ruling/judging them (the
verb *shafat*); Samuel unambiguously speaks of reigning (*malakh*, the cognate verb of
melekh, king).

Your sons he will take. Samuel's speech is solidly constructed as a hammering piece
of antimonarchic rhetoric. All the cherished possessions to be expropriated by the king
are placed emphatically at the beginning of each clause, followed by the verb of which
they are objects. "He will take" (one word in the Hebrew, *yiqaḥ*) is insisted on with anaphoric force. The speech moves systematically from the expropriation of sons and daughters to land and produce to slaves and beasts of burden, ending with the climactic "you
will become his slaves." A modern American reader might easily be reminded of the
rhetoric of a radical libertarian inveighing against the evils of big government and the
encroachments of its bureaucracies and taxation. In no part of his pragmatic argument
does Samuel mention the Deuteronomistic themes of abandoning the LORD or betraying
His direct kingship.

11–12. *chariots . . . cavalry . . . captains.* The first item in the indictment of monarchy is
military conscription. As is clear in the response of the people (verse 20), the consolidation
of national military power under the king is precisely what attracts them to monarchy.
All this leads one to suspect that the domination over the Philistines was by no means so
comprehensive as claimed by the narrator in chapter 7.

12. *to plow his ground and reap his harvest.* The Hebrew is literally "to plow his plowing
and harvest his harvest."

to make his implements. After conscripting men to fight and men to perform agricultural service, the king will also draft the artisan class for his purpose—ironsmiths,
carpenters, wheelwrights, and so forth.

his chariots. Samuel's emphasis from the start on chariots signals the political shift
he envisions, for chariots were the instruments of the monarchies with which Israel contended, whereas the Israelites in this early stage did not have this sort of military technology at their disposal, at least according to the Book of Judges.

and give to his servants. And your seed crops and your vineyards he will 15
tithe and give to his eunuchs and to his servants. And your best male and 16
female slaves and your cattle and your donkeys he will take and use for his
tasks. Your flocks he will tithe, and as for you, you will become his slaves. 17
And you will cry out on that day before your king whom you chose for 18
yourselves and the LORD will not answer you on that day." And the people 19
refused to heed Samuel's voice and they said, "No! A king there shall be
over us! And we, too, will be like all the nations and our king shall rule 20
us and sally forth before us and fight our battles." And Samuel listened to 21
all the words of the people and he spoke them in the LORD's hearing. And 22
the LORD said to Samuel, "Heed their voice and make them a king." And
Samuel said to the men of Israel, "Go every man to his town."

CHAPTER 9   And there was a man of Benjamin whose name 1
was Kish son of Abiel son of Zeror son of Bechorath son of Aphiah, a Ben-

---

14. *give to his servants.* "Servants" in a royal context would be the functionaries of the royal bureaucracy, whose service to the king was in fact often rewarded by land grants.

16. *your cattle.* The Masoretic Text has "your young men" (*bahureikhem*), but the reading of the Septuagint, *beqarkhem*, "your cattle," is much more likely, given the fact that the sons and daughters have already been mentioned and that the next term is "your donkeys."

18. *you will cry out . . . and he will not answer you.* The language used here in relation to the king is precisely the language used elsewhere in relation to God (compare 7:9, where the people implore Samuel to "cry out" on their behalf to God). Cries to *this* power will not be answered by God.

19. *A king there shall be over us.* They do not say, "We will have a king" but "A king shall be over us."

20. *rule us.* Again, the people use the ambiguous key verb, *shafat*, "to rule/judge."
     sally forth before us. This phrase reflects a specific military idiom—the full version of it is, literally, "to go out and come in before us," that is, to lead in battle, to execute maneuvers. The military power that can accrue to the nation through the king is what is uppermost in the minds of the people.

22. *Go every man to his town.* Though God has just instructed Samuel to comply with the people's demand for a monarchy, Samuel's immediate response instead is to send them back to their homes. His acquiescence remains grudging: he appears to be buying time, perhaps with the claim that he needs to find a suitable candidate. The reluctance will persist, and grow, after he has encountered Saul and anointed him.

CHAPTER 9   1. *And there was a man of Benjamin whose name was Kish.* The formulaic phrasing—"there was a man," followed by name, home region, and genealogy—signals to the audience that we are beginning a discrete new story within the larger narrative. (Compare the beginning of Hannah's story in 1:1–2.)

2 jaminite, a man of great means. And he had a son whose name was Saul,
a fine and goodly young fellow, and no man of the Israelites was goodlier
3 than he, head and shoulders taller than all the people. And some asses
belonging to Kish, Saul's father, were lost, and Kish said to Saul his son,
4 "Take, pray, with you one of the lads, and rise, go seek the asses." And
he passed through the high country of Ephraim and he passed through
the region of Shalishah, but they did not find them. And they passed
through the region of Shaalim, and there was nothing there, and they
5 passed through the region of Benjamin, but they did not find them. They
were just coming into the region of Zuf when Saul said to his lad who was
with him, "Come, let us turn back, lest my father cease worrying about
6 the asses and worry about us." And he said to him, "Look, pray, there is a
man of God in this town, and the man is esteemed—whatever he says will
surely come to pass. Now then, let us go there. Perhaps he will tell us of

---

2. *head and shoulders taller than all the people.* The Hebrew says literally "from his shoulders
taller than all the people." Saul's looming size, together with his good looks, seems to be an
outward token of his capacity for leadership, but as the story unfolds with David displacing
Saul, his physical stature becomes associated with a basic human misperception of what
constitutes fitness to command.

5. *They were just coming . . . when.* This relatively infrequent indication of simultaneous
actions occurs four times in this single episode. The writer seems to want to highlight a
crucial series of temporal intersections and concatenations as Saul moves unwitting toward
his destiny as king.

   Zuf. This is, of course, Samuel's home region.

   Come, let us turn back. According to the general principle of biblical narrative that the
first reported speech of a character is a defining moment of characterization, Saul's first
utterance reveals him as a young man uncertain about pursuing his way, and quite concerned about his father. This concern, especially in light of the attention devoted to tense
relations between fathers and sons in the ensuing narrative, is touching, and suggests that
the young Saul is a sensitive person—an attribute that will be woefully submerged by his
experience of political power. But as this first dialogue unfolds, it is Saul's uncertainty that
comes to the fore because at every step he has to be prodded and directed by his own servant.

6. *there is a man of God in this town . . . whatever he says will surely come to pass.* The fact
that neither Saul nor his servant seems to have heard of Samuel by name (and the town, too,
is left unnamed) has led many scholars to conclude that this story comes from a different
source. But, as Robert Polzin has vigorously argued, the palpable shift between chapter 8
and chapter 9 may rather reflect "the varying play of perspectives (between narrator and
reader, between reader and character, and between character and character) that forms the
stuff of sophisticated narrative." Saul's entire story, until the night before his death on the
battlefield, is a story about the futile quest for knowledge of an inveterately ignorant man.
Samuel may have been presented before as the spiritual leader of all the tribes, but this particular Benjaminite farm boy knows nothing of him, and Saul's servant, who presumably

our way on which we have gone." And Saul said to his lad, "But look, if we   7
are to go, what shall we bring to the man? For the bread is gone from our
kits and there is no gift to bring to the man of God. What do we have?"
And the lad answered Saul once again and he said, "Look, I happen to have   8
at hand a quarter of a shekel of silver that I can give to the man of God,
that he may tell us our way." In former times in Israel, thus would a man   9
say when he went to inquire of God, "Come, let us go to the seer." For the
prophet today was called in former times the seer. And Saul said to his lad,   10
"What you say is good. Come, let us go." And they went on to the town
in which the man of God was. They were just coming up the ascent to the   11
town when they met some young women going out to draw water, and
they said to them, "Is there a seer hereabouts?" And they answered them   12

---

has also spent all his time on the farm, has picked up merely a local rumor of his activity but
not his name. From the rural-popular perspective of both, and in keeping with the themes
of knowledge and prediction of this story, Samuel is not a judge and political leader but a
"man of God" and a "seer" (compare verse 9) who can predict the future.

he will tell us of our way on which we have gone. The Hebrew verb clearly indicates some
sort of past action and not, as one might expect, "on which we should go." Perhaps they feel
so lost that they need the seer to tell them where they have been heading. In the event, it is
toward a kingdom, not toward lost asses.

7. *But look, if we are to go, what shall we bring.* The diffident Saul is on the point of quitting
before the encounter. He needs the counsel, and the provident quarter-shekel, of his servant
in order to move forward and make the portentous connection with Samuel.

bread. As in general biblical usage, this is a synecdoche for food.

9. *In former times in Israel.* This terminological notice simultaneously alerts the audience
to the gap between the time of the story (the eleventh century B.C.E.) and the audience's
own time (at the very least, two or three generations later) and underscores the ambiguity
of Samuel's transitional role as leader: he is variously called judge, man of God, seer, and
prophet, and he also performs priestly functions.

to inquire of God. The idiom means to inquire of an oracle.

10. *What you say is good.* Saul the future leader follows someone else's lead—here, a slave's.

11. *they met some young women going out to draw water.* The wells would have typically
been outside the walls of the city. The encounter between a young man in foreign territory
with young women (*ne'arot*) drawing water seems to signal the beginning of a betrothal
type-scene (compare Rebekah, Rachel, and Zipporah at their respective wells). But the
betrothal scene is aborted. Instead of a betrothal feast, there will be a sacrificial feast that
adumbrates a rite of coronation. The destiny of kingship to which Saul proceeds will lead
to grimmer consequences than those that follow in the repeated story of a hero who finds
this future bride at a well.

12–13. The reply of the young women is notable for its garrulousness. One talmudic sage
sought to explain this trait with a simple misogynistic formula: "women are talkative"

and said, "There is. Look, he is straight ahead of you. Hurry now, for today
he has come to town, for the people have a sacrifice today on the high
13   place. As soon as you come into town, you will find him before he goes up
on the high place to eat. For the people will not eat till he comes, as he will
bless the sacrifice and then the guests will eat. So go up, for today you will
14   find him." And they went up to the town. They were just coming into the
15   town when Samuel came out toward them to go up to the high place. And
16   the LORD had disclosed to Samuel the day before Saul's arrival, saying, "At
this time tomorrow I will send to you a man from the region of Benjamin
and you shall anoint him prince over My people Israel and he shall rescue
My people from the hand of the Philistines. For I have seen the plight of My
17   people, yes, their outcry has reached Me." And Samuel saw Saul, and the
LORD answered him, "Here is that man of whom I said to you, 'This one will
18   govern My people.'" And Saul approached Samuel in the gateway and said,

---

(*Berakhot* 48b), whereas, more amusingly, the Midrash proposes that the young women
kept repeating themselves because they were so smitten by Saul's beauty. The clues in the
immediately preceding narrative context suggest a less fanciful explanation: seeing the
evident signs of confusion and incomprehension in Saul's face, the women take elaborate
measures to spell out where Samuel is to be found and what Saul should do in order to
be sure not to miss him. In all this, it is noteworthy, as Polzin has observed, that Samuel,
having agreed to find a king for Israel, has made no move whatever toward that purpose.
Instead, the future king "finds" him.

the high place. The *bamah* was an elevated place, a kind of open-air natural altar, perhaps sometimes with a structure erected alongside it (see the "hall" in verse 22), where
sacrifices were generally offered in the period before the centralization of the cult in Jerusalem. The kind of sacrifice involved here is one in which parts of the animal would be
burned on the altar and the rest eaten in a ceremonial feast.

16. prince. The Hebrew *nagid* is not used to refer to leaders before this moment in Israelite
history and is used only rarely after the very early years of the monarchy. It is a term that
suggests the exercise of political power in a designated role of leadership rather than in the
manner of the ad hoc charismatic leadership of the *shofet*, or Judge. But God, in keeping
with this transitional moment and perhaps even in deference to Samuel's keen resentment
of the monarchy, pointedly does not use the word "king."

he shall rescue My people. Again, the previously reported ascendancy over the Philistines seems to have vanished, and God endorses military effectiveness as the rationale for
the monarchy.

the plight of My people. The Masoretic Text lacks "the plight of," though the phrase
appears to have been in the version used by the Septuagint translators. It is conceivable that
what we have here is not an inadvertent scribal omission but an ellipsis.

17. And Samuel saw Saul. The seer sees the divinely designated object of his sight, and God
immediately confirms that this is the man. Or, in the light of subsequent developments,
Samuel is persuaded that he has received direct instruction from God. All the knowledge
is on Samuel's side rather than on Saul's.

"Tell me, pray, where is the house of the seer?" And Samuel answered Saul 19
and said, "I am the seer. Go up before me to the high place, and you will
eat with me today, and I shall send you off in the morning, and whatever is
in your heart I shall tell you. And as to the asses that have been lost to you 20
now three days, pay them no heed, for they have been found. And whose is
all the treasure of Israel? Is it not for you and all your father's house?" And 21
Saul answered and said, "Am I not a Benjaminite, from the smallest of the
tribes of Israel, and my clan is the least of all the tribe of Benjamin? So why
have you spoken to me in this fashion?" And Samuel took Saul and his lad 22
and brought them into the hall, and he gave them a place at the head of the
guests, about thirty men. And Samuel said to the cook, "Bring the portion 23
that I gave to you, about which I said, 'Set it aside.'" And the cook lifted up 24
the thigh and put it before Saul. And Samuel said, "Here is what is left. Put
it before you and eat, for it has been kept for you for the appointed time as

---

18. *where is the house of the seer?* Addressing the very seer himself, Saul picks up no clues
that Samuel is anything but an ordinary passerby. He also assumes that the seer has a house
in the town, although the young women have said that the seer has come to town for the
sacrifice. (The scholarly assumption that the unnamed town must be Samuel's hometown,
Ramah, is not entirely compelling.)

20. *as to the asses.* It is at this point that Samuel reveals his access to supernatural knowledge: no one has told him that Saul was looking for asses, but Samuel knows both of the
lost animals and where to find them.
   whose is all the treasure of Israel? This is a deliberately oblique reference to kingship: if
all the choice possessions of Israel are to be yours, why worry about a few asses? Although
the Hebrew term ḥemdah can mean "desire," it more often has the sense of "desired, or
valued, thing," as in the common idiom, *kley ḥemdah,* "precious objects."

21. *a Benjaminite, from the smallest of the tribes of Israel.* The young Saul is no doubt overcome by Samuel's hint of a throne, but the language is also part of an etiquette of deference.
In fact, Benjamin was one of the most powerful tribes, and given Kish's affluence, his clan
would scarcely have been so humble.
   all the tribe of Benjamin. The Masoretic Text has "tribes" but the Septuagint reflects the
more logical singular. The plural form is in all likelihood a scribal replication of the plural
in "tribes of Israel" at the beginning of the verse.

22. *a place at the head of the guests.* Samuel offers no explanation to the assembled company
as to why this signal honor is accorded to the strangers.

23. *Set it aside.* The Hebrew reads literally "Put it by you."

24. The text here seems clearly defective at two different points. The phrase "lifted up the
thigh" is followed by an anomalously ungrammatical form of "and that which is on it"
(*weheʻaleyha*). It seems best to delete this word, as does the Septuagint. The phrase "as I
said to the people" is no more than an interpretive guess about an asyntactic chain of three
words in the Hebrew, which literally are "saying the-people I-invited."

25 I said to the people I invited." And Saul ate with Samuel on that day. And
they came down from the high place into the town, and they made a bed
26 for Saul on the roof, and he slept. And as dawn was breaking, Samuel called
out to Saul on the roof, saying, "Arise and I shall send you off." And Saul
27 arose, and the two of them, he and Samuel, went outside. They were just
going down past the edge of the town when Samuel said to Saul, "Tell the
lad to pass on before us." And he passed on. "As for you, stand now, that I
may let you hear the word of God."

1 CHAPTER 10   And Samuel took the cruse of oil and poured
it over his head and kissed him, and he said, "Has not the LORD anointed
2 you over His inheritance as prince? When you go away from me today

---

25. *they made a bed for Saul on the roof, and he slept.* The Masoretic Text has "he spoke
with Saul on the roof and they rose early." The present translation follows the far more
plausible reading of the Septuagint: the report of speech on the roof is odd because no
content or explanation for it is given, and the rising early is contradicted by the fact that
in the next phrase Samuel calls up to Saul on the roof in order to rouse him. Evidently, a
scribe substituted the common word *wayidaber*, "he spoke," for the more unusual word
wayirbedu, "they made a bed" (the same consonants with the order reversed). *Wayishkav*,
"and he slept," differs from *wayashkimu*, "and they rose early," by one consonant in the
unvocalized text.

    the roof. Presumably, the encounter takes place during the warm season, and the roof
would be a cool sleeping place.

27. *Tell the lad to pass on before us.* Every step that Samuel takes here in conferring the
kingship on Saul is clandestine. He speaks to him only after they have reached the outskirts of the town, and he is sure first to get Saul's servant out of earshot. This course of
action is rather puzzling because the people, after all, have already publicly declared to the
prophet that they want him to choose a king for them. Samuel's need to proceed in secrecy
may reflect his persistent sense that the monarchy is the wrong path for the people, or it
might be an expression of doubt as to whether this strapping young Benjaminite is really
the right man for the job, despite the unambiguous indication that the prophet has just
received from God.

CHAPTER 10   1. Anointment is the biblical ritual of conferring kingship, like coronation in the later European tradition. Samuel carries out this act secretly, on the outskirts
of the town, conferring on Saul, in keeping with the term God has used, the title *nagid*,
"prince," rather than "king."

2. *When you go away from me today.* This elaborate set of instructions and predictions is, as
Robert Polzin has argued, a strategy for asserting continued control over the man Samuel
has just anointed. Every predictive step manifests Samuel's superior knowledge as prophet,
and all the instructions reduce the new king to Samuel's puppet.

you shall find two men by Rachel's Tomb in the region of Benjamin at Zelzah, and they will say to you, 'The asses that you went off to seek have been found, and, look, your father has put aside the matter of the asses and is worrying about you, saying, What shall I do about my son?' And you shall slip onward from there and you shall come to the Terebinth 3 of Tabor, and there three men will find you who are going up to God at Bethel, one bearing three kids and one bearing three loaves of bread and one bearing a jug of wine. And they will greet you and give you two loaves 4 of bread, and you shall take from their hand. Afterward you shall come 5 to Gibeath-Elohim, where the Philistine prefect is. And as you come into town there, you shall encounter a band of prophets coming down from the

---

Rachel's Tomb. The burial site of the mother of Benjamin, the eponymous founder of the tribe, underscores Saul's own tribal affiliation.

at Zelzah. This otherwise unattested name may not be a place-name but an error in transcription in the Masoretic Text.

your father has put aside the matter of the asses and is worrying about you. According to the fixed procedure of verbal recycling in biblical narrative, the predicted words of the two men are nearly identical with Saul's first words to his servant. One should note that in the scenario Samuel lays out for him, Saul has no opportunity to respond to his father's concern for his absence: on the contrary, his new regal obligations rush him onward toward a daunting rite of initiation.

3. *slip onward.* The Hebrew verb *halaf* suggests passing through a medium and may well indicate the clandestine nature of Saul's movements.

the Terebinth of Tabor. Evidently, a cultic site.

three men . . . three kids . . . three loaves of bread. The triple three is a folktale pattern. It also manifests a mysterious design clearly grasped by Samuel, who annunciates this whole prediction, and into which Saul is thrust unwittingly. The three men bear meat (or animals that can be turned into meat), bread, and wine—the three symbolic staffs of life. They will offer Saul the primary of the three, bread (in counterpoint to the "worthless fellows" at the end of the episode who give the new king no tribute).

5. *Gibeath-Elohim.* The name means Hill of God, but it would seem to be the same as the Gibeah of Judges 19, in which the Benjaminites perpetrate a lethal gang-rape, and is also known as Gibeath-Benjamin and Gibeath-Saul.

the Philistine prefect. This glancing reference to a Philistine garrison deep within Benjaminite territory is still another indication of the Philistines' military ascendancy. That might be another reason for keeping the anointment secret, at least until the new king can consolidate military force around him. The Masoretic Text has a plural "prefects," but three different ancient translations reflect a singular.

a band of prophets. These are professional ecstatics who would whip themselves into a frenzy with the insistent rhythms of the musical instruments mentioned—a phenomenon familiar in enthusiastic religious sects worldwide—and then would "prophesy," become caught up in ecstatic behavior, which could involve glossolalia ("speaking in tongues"), dancing, writhing, and the like. The chief connection between these figures and the later

high place, preceded by lute and drum and flute and lyre, and they will be
6 speaking in ecstasy. And the spirit of the LORD shall seize you, and you
7 shall go into ecstasy with them and you shall turn into another man. And
when these signs come upon you, do what your hand finds to do, for God
8 is with you. And you shall go down before me to Gilgal, and, look, I shall
be coming down to you to offer burnt offerings and to sacrifice well-being
sacrifices. Seven days shall you wait until I come to you, and I shall inform
9 you what you must do." And it happened as he turned his back to go off
from Samuel, that God gave him another heart and all these signs came to
pass on that day.

---

literary prophets is the idea that both are involuntarily inhabited by an overpowering
divine spirit.

lute. The Hebrew word for this instrument, *nevel*, is identical with the word for "jug"
used at the end of verse 3 (the homonymity may be explained by a perceived lyre shape in
the jug). It is a fairly common procedure in biblical narrative to link segments in immediate sequence by using this sort of pun as a linchpin. Here it has the effect of intimating
an uncanny link between the first and second stages of the script Samuel is designing
for Saul.

6. *you shall turn into another man.* The drastic nature of this process is surely meant by
Samuel to be startling: nothing less will do in order to transform this diffident farmer's son
into a king than to be devastated by the divine spirit, violently compelled to radical metamorphosis. This whole story of Saul among the prophets is repeated, with very significant
changes, in chapter 19, near the end of his tortuous career. As we shall have occasion to
see, the seeming repetition, far from being a regrettable "doublet" produced in redaction,
is entirely purposeful: the same etiological tale is rotated 180 degrees to show us first Saul
being invested with the spirit, and with the monarchy, and then divested of the monarchy
by the spirit.

7. *do what your hand finds.* The biblical idiom means do whatever is within your power.

8. *you shall go down before me to Gilgal . . . Seven days shall you wait.* The third stage in the
set of predictions/instructions that Samuel announces to Saul is in fact not carried out until
much later. Saul's divergence from the prophet's script adumbrates his future failures of
obedience in relation to Samuel. Polzin has made the shrewd argument that the unfulfilled
prediction also reflects Samuel's failure as a prophet, and that he has actually placed Saul
in a double bind by telling him that he may do whatever he wants because God is with him
and yet "has paradoxically commanded strict royal dependence upon prophetic direction."
Samuel, in other words, seems to want both a king and a puppet.

9. *as he turned his back.* The Hebrew *shekhem* is also the word for "shoulder," and so reminds
us of Saul's regal stature, head and shoulders above all the people.

God gave him another heart and all these signs came to pass. These words are a kind
of proleptic headnote for the narrative report that follows, and it is not implied that the
transformation and the signs occurred the very moment Saul turned to go.

And they came there to Gibeah, and look, a band of prophets was coming 10
toward him, and the spirit of the LORD seized him and he went into ecstasy
in their midst. And so, whoever knew him from times gone by, saw, and, 11
look, with the prophets he spoke in ecstasy, and each would say to his fellow,

> "What has befallen the son of Kish?
> Is Saul, too, among the prophets?"

And one man from there would answer and say, "And who is their father?" 12
Therefore it became a proverb, "Is Saul, too, among the prophets?" And he 13
ceased from his ecstasy and came to the high place. And Saul's uncle said 14

---

10. *And they came there to Gibeah.* There is no report of the first of Samuel's predicted
encounters, with the three men bearing kids, bread, and wine. It is unclear whether this
reflects merely a narrative ellipsis or whether this, too, is an unfulfilled prophecy. The
report of the meeting with the two men who announce that the asses have been found is
also omitted. In any case, the transformative meeting with the band of ecstatics is obviously
the chief focus of the writer's attention.

the spirit of the LORD seized him. This same phrase, or a slight variant of it, is repeatedly
used in the Book of Judges to indicate the inception of the judge's enterprise as charismatic military leader. There is some overlap with Saul's taking on the kingship, which will
also involve military leadership, but the report of ecstasy or "prophesying" is a new element, with its more radical implication that the new leader must become "another man."

11. *Is Saul, too, among the prophets?* This evidently proverbial question, its full origins
scarcely remembered, is the perplexity that generates the etiological tale. The question
seems to be proverbial of a case of extreme incongruity (like the English "bull in a china
shop")—what on earth is a man like Saul doing among the prophets? The tale then comes
to explain how the saying arose. But the etiological tale, together with its antithetical
counterpart in chapter 19, figures significantly in the literary design of the Saul story.
Even the characterizing theme of Saul's repeated exclusion from predictive knowledge is
inscribed in the question "Is Saul, too, among the prophets?" The people ask their question
about Saul in a line of poetry (consisting of two parallel versets). The verse form explains
why Saul is first referred to as "son of Kish" because in poetry based on parallelism, it is
the fixed procedure for treating proper names to use the given name in one verset and, in
lieu of a synonym, the patronymic in the other. Thus, the claim made by some scholars
that "son of Kish" is derogatory has no basis.

12. *who is their father?* The reference is obscure. The least convoluted explanation makes the
prophets the antecedent of "their." The meaning then would be that unlike Saul, whose father
is Kish, a landholder and a man of substance, the ecstatics are a breed apart, with no father
anyone can name (the leader of a band of prophets was called idiomatically their father). The
prevalent attitude toward such prophets was ambivalent: they were at once viewed as vehicles
of a powerful and dangerous divine spirit, and as crazies (compare Hosea 9:7).

14. *Saul's uncle.* The appearance, without introduction, of an uncle (and not Saul's father,
who after his brief initial appearance is never brought into the narrative proper) is puz-

to him and to his lad, "Where did you go?" And he said, "To seek the asses.
15 And we saw that they were nowhere and we came to Samuel." And Saul's
16 uncle said, "Tell me, pray, what did Samuel say to you?" And Saul said to his
uncle, "He indeed told us that the asses had been found." But the matter of
the kingship of which Samuel had spoken he told him not.

17,18 And Samuel mustered the people to the LORD at Mizpah. And he said to
the Israelites, "Thus said the LORD God of Israel: 'I brought Israel up out
of Egypt and I rescued you from the hand of Egypt and from the hand of
19 all the kingdoms that have oppressed you.' And you on your part have cast
aside your God Who rescues you from all your ills and troubles, and you
have said, 'No! A king you shall put over us!' And so, stand forth before
20 the LORD by your tribes and your clans." And Samuel brought forward all
21 the tribes of Israel and the lot fell to the tribe of Benjamin. And he brought
forward the tribe of Benjamin by its clans and the lot fell to the Matrite
clan, and the lot fell to Saul son of Kish, and they sought him but he was
22 not to be found. And they inquired again of the LORD: "Has a man come

---

zling. It has been proposed that this uncle is Ner the father of Abner, who will become Saul's commander in chief, but if that is the case, why is he left unnamed here?

16. *But the matter of the kingship . . . he told him not.* Saul's studied reticence confirms the clandestine character of his anointment.

17. *And Samuel mustered the people.* This national assembly is the second of three episodes that inaugurate Saul's kingship. One should not leap too quickly to the conclusion that these are merely a stitching together of variant sources. From the writer's viewpoint, the institution of the monarchy, with Saul as first king, is both a difficult and a dubious process, and it cannot happen all at once. First there is the clandestine anointment, followed by an initiatory experience, under the nose of the Philistine prefect. Then there is a public proclamation of the king, at which time sufficient forces can be marshaled to bolster him against the Philistines.

18. *Thus said the LORD God of Israel.* Samuel begins his speech with the so-called messenger-formula, which is used to initiate prophetic messages. His speech is in fact a kind of prophetic denunciation of the people for having "cast aside" God in demanding a king and so is a reprise of his antimonarchic harangue in chapter 8, even as he implements the choice of a king.

20. *the lot fell.* The Hebrew verb *lakad* that is used for the drawing of lots means to be caught or trapped. As both Polzin and McCarter note, the only other biblical instances of such drawing of lots among the tribes are in order to discover a culprit, and so Samuel has chosen a mechanism associated with incrimination and punishment.

22. *Has a man come here?* This translation reads *'ad halom* instead of the Masoretic *'od halom*, which would mean "again here."

here?" And the LORD said, "Look, he is hidden among the gear." And they   23
ran and fetched him from there, and he stood forth amidst the people, and
he was head and shoulders taller than all the people. And Samuel said to all   24
the people, "Have you seen whom the LORD has chosen? For there is none
like him in all the people." And all the people shouted and said, "Long live
the king!" And Samuel spoke out to the people the practice of kingship and   25
wrote it on a scroll and placed it before the LORD. And Samuel sent all the
people away to their homes. And Saul, too, had gone to his home in Gibeah,   26
and the stalwart fellows whose hearts God had touched went with him. And   27
worthless fellows had said, "How will this one rescue us?" And they spurned
him and brought him no tribute, but he pretended to keep his peace.

Look, he is hidden among the gear. This detail is virtually a parody of the recurring
motif of the prophet-leader's unwillingness to accept his mission. Saul the diffident farm
boy had expressed a sense of unworthiness for the high office Samuel conferred on him.
Now, confronted by the assembled tribes and "trapped" by the process of lot drawing, he
tries to flee the onus of kingship, farcically hiding in the baggage.

24. *there is none like him in all the people.* Perhaps especially because Saul has been hauled
out from the midst of saddle packs and sundry impediments, Samuel now executes a gesture of public relations: look at this strapping, handsome fellow—there is none in Israel
who can match him. In the event, he proves wrong about Saul's fitness for the throne, and
one may even wonder whether Samuel's proclamation that this is the one God has chosen
(confirmed by the narrator's previous report) is not a misperception to justify his own
(erring) choice.
    Long live the king. The people's proclamation does not use *nagid* (prince) but the unam-
biguous *melekh* (king).

25. *the practice of kingship.* The phrase here, *mishpat hamelukhah*, is close enough to *mishpat hamelekh*, the term used in chapter 8, and so the reasonable inference is that the content
of the speech is a reiteration of the dangers of encroachment of individual rights by the king
that Samuel warned of in the assembly at Ramah.

26. *stalwart fellows.* The translation follows the Qumran Samuel text and the Septuagint
in reading *giborey hahayil* instead of the Masoretic *hahayil*, "the troop." The phrase, as
many commentators have noted, is an obvious antithesis to "worthless fellows" in the next
sentence.

27. *How will this one rescue us?* "This one" (*zeh*) is contemptuous.
    but he pretended to keep his peace. The Masoretic Text has two Hebrew words here,
wayehi kemaharish, which bear this meaning and have the attraction of indicating the
inception of court intrigues and calculations at the very beginning of Saul's reign—he
is aware of political dissidence but chooses for the moment not to react. It must be said,
however, that the Qumran Samuel fragment, supported by allied readings in the Septuagint
and Josephus, has *wayehi kemehodesh* (the graphemes for *r* and *d* are quite similar), "And
it happened after about a month," affixing these two words at the beginning of the next
episode rather than at the end of this one.

1 CHAPTER 11   And Nahash the Ammonite came up and encamped against Jabesh-Gilead. And all the men of Jabesh said to Nahash, 2 "Make a pact with us, and we shall be subject to you." And Nahash the Ammonite said to them, "This is how I shall make a pact with you—with the gouging out of the right eye of every one of you, and I shall make it a 3 disgrace for all Israel." And the elders of Jabesh said to him, "Leave us alone for seven days, that we may send messengers through all the territory of 4 Israel, and if there is none to rescue us, we shall come out to you." And the messengers came to Gibeath-Saul and spoke the words in the hearing of 5 the people, and all the people raised their voices and wept. And, look, Saul

---

CHAPTER 11   1. *Nahash the Ammonite.* During this period, the Ammonite kingdom, in the region to the east of the Jordan, was the second great military threat to the Israelites, after the Philistines to the west. David would later besiege the Ammonite capital, Rabbath-Ammon (near the site of present-day Amman). This episode, marking the inception of Saul's military activity, has several details that will be echoed later in the David story.

Jabesh-Gilead. This Israelite settlement, in the tribal territory of Manasseh, was located several miles east of the Jordan and hence was exposed to Ammonite attack. In the story of the concubine at Gibeah—Saul's hometown—the men of Jabesh-Gilead refuse to fight in the civil war against Benjamin, and so some special kinship between them and Saul's tribe is inferable. The Samuel scroll found in Cave 4 at Qumran reports a general campaign by Nahash against the trans-Jordanian Israelites. Here are the verses from the Qumran version (brackets indicate reconstructed letters or words, where there are gaps in the scroll): "[and Na]hash king of the Ammonites oppressed the Gadites and the Reubenites mightily and gouged out the right eye of e[very] one of them and imposed fe[ar and terror] on [I]srael, and there remained not a man of the Israelites be[yond] the Jordan [who]se right eye Nah[ash king of] the Ammonites did n[ot] [gou]ge out. Only seven thousand men [fled from] the Ammonites and came to [J]abesh-Gilead. And after about a month"—the words that follow are identical with verse 1 in the Masoretic Text.

2. *the gouging out of the right eye.* Mutilation of captives was a fairly common practice. Josephus explains that the blinding of the right eye would have impaired the ability to fight because the left eye was largely covered by the shield in battle. In any case, submitting to this ghastly mutilation was a mark of great humiliation, or "disgrace" (*ḥerpah*).

3. *Leave us alone for seven days.* Nahash's seemingly surprising agreement to this condition is by no means a sign of generosity but must be understood from his viewpoint as an additional opportunity to humiliate the Israelites: he scarcely imagines that the disunited tribes will produce a "rescuer," and thus the impotent tribes will all be forced to witness helplessly the mutilation of their trans-Jordanian kinsmen.

4. *the messengers came to Gibeath-Saul.* The men of Jabesh-Gilead have told Nahash they would search through "all the territory of Israel." But perhaps they know something he does not—that Israel already has a tribally acclaimed ruler and military leader who resides in Gibeah, but who has not yet begun to act. The scholarly assumption that this entire story blatantly contradicts the previous account of Saul's election as king and hence must derive from an independent source is by no means necessary.

was coming in behind the oxen from the field, and Saul said, "What is the matter with the people that they are weeping?" And they recounted to him the words of the men of Jabesh. And the spirit of God seized Saul when he heard these words, and he was greatly incensed. And he took a yoke of oxen and hacked them to pieces and sent them through all the territory of Israel by the hand of messengers, saying, "Whoever does not come out after Saul and after Samuel, thus will be done to his oxen!" And the fear of the LORD fell on the people, and they came out as one man. And Saul marshaled them in Bazek, and there were three hundred thousand Israelites and thirty thousand men of Judah. And he said to the messengers who had come, 6 7 8 9

---

6. *the spirit of God seized Saul.* As many commentators have noted, the story here explicitly follows the model of the inception of the charismatic leader's career in Judges, when a kind of berserker spirit enters him and ignites him with eagerness to do battle. Saul's coming in from the field behind the oxen is also reminiscent of the pattern in Judges in which an agriculturalist (compare Gideon) is transformed by an access of the spirit into a warrior. Given the uncertainty about the new monarchic dispensation, it is quite possible that Saul, after having been proclaimed king at Mizpah, might have returned to his work in the field, awaiting the occasion when he would begin to act on his new royal authority. The archetypal tale of the farmer who steps forward to save the nation in time of crisis will recur in Roman tradition in the story of Cincinnatus at the plow.

7. *he took a yoke of oxen and hacked them to pieces.* This violent symbolism doubly distinguishes Saul from the model of the ad hoc warrior-leader in Judges. The dismemberment of the oxen is an explicit repetition of the dismemberment of the concubine at the end of Judges 19 after she has been gang-raped to death by the men of Gibeah (later the home of Saul). In Judges, too, the bloody members were used to assemble all the tribes of Israel to war, though the person who hacked the body to pieces was not a judge but rather a morally dubious Levite, the husband of the dead woman. The allusion here is exquisitely ambiguous. Is this an act of restitution, a setting right of the ghastly civil war caused by the atrocity at Gibeah, or does it inaugurate the narrative of Saul's public actions under the shadow of an earlier act of turpitude? Saul also differs from the judges in behaving like a king, for he prepares for war by instituting a kind of military conscription binding on all the tribes (the judges depended on volunteers and worked locally). Kings, like mafia capos, operate through coercion: Saul, in sending the hacked-up oxen parts to his fellow Israelites with the threat "Whoever does not come out . . . thus will be done to his oxen," is presenting them with an offer they cannot refuse.

after Saul and after Samuel. The medieval Hebrew commentator Kimchi offers a shrewd explanation for Saul's adding Samuel to his exhortation. "Since not all of them had accepted him as king, he said 'after Samuel.'"

the fear of the LORD. This seemingly pious phrase might also mean "a terrible fear," and it is, after all, Saul's frightening threat conveyed by the bloody oxen parts that moves the people.

8. *three hundred thousand.* As usual, the inflated figure does not reflect historical reality. The ten-to-one ratio between Israel and Judah does mirror the ratio of ten tribes to one.

"Thus shall you say to the men of Jabesh-Gilead: 'Tomorrow victory will be
yours as the sun grows hot.'" And the messengers came and told the men of
10 Jabesh and they rejoiced. And the men of Jabesh said [to the Ammonites],
"Tomorrow we shall come out to you and you may do to us whatever is good
11 in your eyes." And it happened on the next day that Saul set the troops in
three columns. And they came into the camp in the morning watch and
struck down Ammon till the heat of the day, and so those who remained
12 were scattered and not two of them remained together. And the people said
to Samuel, "Whoever said, 'Saul shall not be king over us,' give us these men
13 and we shall put them to death." And Saul said, "No man shall be put to
death this day, for today the LORD has wrought victory in Israel."

14 And Samuel said to the people, "Come, let us go to Gilgal and we shall
15 renew there the kingship." And all the people went to Gilgal and they made
Saul king there before the LORD at Gilgal, and they sacrificed their well-
being sacrifices before the LORD, and Saul rejoiced there, and all the men
of Israel with him, very greatly.

---

10. *[to the Ammonites]*. The bracketed words, not in the Hebrew, are added to make clear
that it is no longer the messengers who are being addressed.

    Tomorrow we shall come out to you. These words are intended to lull the Ammonites
into a false sense of security before Saul's surprise attack in the last hours before dawn
("the morning watch").

12. *Saul shall not be king over us.* The "not" appears in some variant manuscripts. The
Masoretic Text as it stands is usually construed as a question: "Saul will be king over us?"
Robert Polzin tries to save the simple declarative sense of the Masoretic Text by proposing
that after Saul has just powerfully acted like one of the old-time judges, the people, with
the implicit endorsement of Saul, are inclined to retract their own insistence on monarchy
and return to the institution of judgeship. This reading is ingenious, but may create more
problems than it solves. The report of continuing dissidence about Saul's claim to the
throne, as at the end of the previous chapter, in fact sets the stage for much that will follow.

13. *No man shall be put to death this day.* Saul's magnaminity, after his demonstration of
coercion and military effectiveness, strikes a positive note at the beginning of his reign,
though he will later prove to be utterly ruthless against subjects he suspects of disloyalty.

14. *we shall renew there the kingship.* This clause helps make sense of the triple story of Saul's
dedication as king. First there was the clandestine anointment, with no publicly visible
consequences. Then there was the tribal assembly at Mizpah in which a reluctant Saul was
chosen by lot and proclaimed king. After that event, however, he appears to have returned
for the time being to private life. Now, following his signal success in mustering the tribes
and defeating Ammon, Samuel calls for a new assembly to reconfirm Saul's standing as
king, which will then be seen in subsequent episodes manifested in the institutions and
power of a regular court.

CHAPTER 12   And Samuel said to all Israel, "Look, I have ₁
heeded your voice in all that you said to me and have set a king over
you. And so now the king walks before you and I have grown old and ₂
gray, and my sons, they are here with you, and I have walked before you
from my youth till this day. Here I am! Witness against me before the ₃
LORD and before His anointed. Whose ox have I taken and whose donkey
have I taken, whom have I wronged and whom have I abused, and from
whose hand have I taken a bribe to avert my eyes from him? I shall return
it to you!" And they said, "You have not wronged us and you have not ₄
abused us, and you have not taken a thing from any man." And he said ₅
to them, "The LORD is witness against you, and His anointed is witness
this day, that you have found not a thing in my hand." And they said, "He
is witness." And Samuel said to the people, "Witness is the LORD, Who ₆
appointed Moses and Aaron and Who brought up your fathers from the

---

CHAPTER 12   1. *And Samuel said to all Israel.* It is not clear whether Samuel's
farewell speech takes place at Gilgal on the ceremony of "renewing the kingship" mentioned at the end of the preceding chapter, or whether this is a separate occasion. It does
seem in character for Samuel that he would end up converting the coronation assembly
into still another diatribe against the monarchy and an apologia for his own authority as
prophet-judge.

    I have heeded your voice. The phrase takes us back to the tribal convocation in chapter
8, when the grudging Samuel was enjoined by God to heed the people's voice and make
them a king.

2. *the king walks before you.* As we have had occasion to note earlier, this idiom means to
serve or act as a functionary.

    my sons, they are here with you. This slightly odd reference to Samuel's sons is in all like-
lihood a final verbal gesture toward the dynasty he has failed to create: Samuel's crooked
sons have already disqualified themselves from assuming his mantle, but here he appears
to take a last wistful look at that prospect—my sons are here among you, but you insist
instead on a king.

3. *Whose ox have I taken and whose donkey have I taken.* Samuel's profession of innocence,
as Kyle McCarter Jr. has aptly noted, picks up antithetically his admonition against the
"practice of the king" in chapter 8. There he warned repeatedly that the king would "take"
all the people's cherished possessions. Here he proclaims that he, the prophet-judge, has
taken nothing. In both instances, he shows himself a master of rhetoric.

    abused. The Hebrew verb means etymologically to crush or smash.

6. *Witness is the LORD.* The Masoretic Text lacks "witness" (*'ed*), which is supplied by the
Septuagint. (The next clause also looks textually problematic because the verb rendered
here as "appointed," *'asah,* actually means "made" and is not idiomatic.) It is noteworthy
that Samuel sets up his entire speech as a legal disputation between him and the people in
which all the evidence, as they are compelled to admit, stands in his favor.

7 land of Egypt! And now, stand forth, that I may seek judgment with you
   before the Lord, and I shall tell you all the Lord's bounties that He did
8 for you and for your fathers. When Jacob came into Egypt, and your
   fathers cried out to the Lord, the Lord sent Moses and Aaron, and they
9 brought your fathers out of Egypt and settled them in this place. And they
   forgot the Lord your God, and He delivered them into the hand of Sisera
   commander of Hazor, and into the hand of the Philistines, and into the
10 hand of the king of Moab, and they fought against them. And they cried
   out to the Lord and said, 'We have offended, for we have abandoned the
   Lord and served the Baalim and the Ashtaroth. And now, rescue us from
11 the hand of our enemies, and we shall serve You.' And the Lord sent
   Jerubaal and Bedan and Jephthah and Samuel, and He rescued you from
12 the hand of your enemies all around, and you dwelled in safety. And you

---

7. *and I shall tell you.* The Masoretic Text lacks these words, but the next phrase, "all the
Lord's bounties," preceded by the accusative particle *'et*, clearly requires a verb, and the
appropriate verb is reflected in the Septuagint.

8. *When Jacob came into Egypt, and your fathers cried out.* The Septuagint inserts between
these two clauses the words "the Egyptians oppressed them." But the Greek translators may
have simply filled out a narrative ellipsis in the original Hebrew text.

10. *we have abandoned the Lord and served the Baalim and the Ashtaroth.* Samuel's speech
seems to be an intertwining of an early story with a Deuteronomistic (seventh-century or
sixth-century) editorial recasting. The vehement opposition to the monarchy would be
original, perhaps even going back to the historical figure of Samuel. The Deuteronomistic
school on its part was by no means antimonarchic, though it wanted to limit the monarch
with the rules of the Book of God's Teaching (the Torah). On the other hand, the sin of
idolatry is not an issue in the Samuel story, but it is a Deuteronomistic preoccupation. It is
at this point in the speech that we encounter clusters of Deuteronomistic verbal formulas:
"abandoned the Lord and served the Baalim," "delivered [literally, sold] into the hand of,"
"fear the Lord and serve Him and heed His voice," "serve Him truly with all your heart."

11. *Bedan.* The name of this judge is otherwise unknown, but since there is no reason to
assume that the list in the Book of Judges is exhaustive, it seems prudent not to emend this
into a familiar name.
   and Samuel. It makes sense that Samuel would refer to himself by name rather than
with the first-person pronoun because he wants to set himself as a matter of official record
in the great roll call of Judges.

12. *Nahash king of the Ammonites.* Since there had been no question of Nahash in the original demand for a king in chapter 8, many scholars have inferred that the present episode
reflects a different tradition, in which the call for monarchy is specifically linked with
the Ammonite incursion reported in chapter 11. But Moshe Garsiel proposes an interesting political reading that preserves the unity of the text. The original request for a king
stresses the need for a military leader but mentions no particular enemy, perhaps because

saw that Nahash king of the Ammonites had come against you and you
said to me, 'No! A king shall reign over us,' though the LORD your God
was your king. And now, here is the king you have chosen, for whom you 13
have asked, and here the LORD has put over you a king. If you fear the 14
LORD and serve Him and heed His voice and rebel not against the LORD's
words, and if both you and the king who reigns over you will follow the
LORD your God, He will rescue you. But if you heed not the voice of the 15
LORD and you rebel against the LORD's words, the hand of the LORD will
be against you and against your king to destroy you. Even now, take your 16
stance and see this great thing that the LORD is about to do before your
eyes. Is it not wheat harvest today? I shall call unto the LORD and He will 17
send thunder and rain, and mark and see, that the evil you have done is
great in the eyes of the LORD, to ask for yourselves a king." And Samuel 18
called unto the LORD, and the LORD sent thunder and rain on that day,

---

the people fear to name the dominant Philistines. Saul would have initially been installed
in the ceremony at Mizpah as a sort of vassal king (or, alternatively, leader of an underground movement), for the Philistines had garrisons in the territory of Benjamin. Now,
after Saul's military success against the Ammonites, Samuel explicitly associates the call for
a monarchy with Nahash's assault on Israel. This meeting at Gilgal would also have been
an occasion to enlist the allegiance to Saul of the trans-Jordanian tribes.

13. *the king you have chosen, for whom you have asked.* Several times Samuel plays sardonically on "asked" (*sha'al*) and "Saul" (*Sha'ul*). Garsiel also suggests a pun as well in "chosen"
(*baḥar*) and the introductory designation of Saul as a "fine fellow" (*baḥur*, literally "chosen
one"). Although the story of the institution of the monarchy indicates that God does the
choosing, there is no real contradiction—Samuel, in his acute discomfort with the monarchy that has displaced his own authority, readily imputes the choosing to the people, despite
his awareness that God has supposedly chosen. God on His part no more than acquiesces
in the people's stubborn insistence on a king. The ambiguity of Saul's divine election will
continue to be manifested in the narrative.

14. *rebel not against the LORD's words.* The Hebrew says literally "against the LORD's mouth,"
but the same verb (root *m-r-h*) appears elsewhere with "words" as object, and the two formulations are variants of the same idiom.

   He will rescue you. The Masoretic Text lacks a clause stating what will happen if Israel
remains faithful to God. These words (which would reflect a single verb with its suffix in
the Hebrew) are supplied from the Septuagint.

15. *against your king to destroy you.* The Masoretic Text reads "against your fathers" (without "to destroy you"). This makes no sense because it is a prediction of future catastrophe.
Some ancient and medieval interpreters construe the word "as against your fathers," but the
Septuagint's reading, reflected in this translation, is more likely because Samuel repeatedly
brackets "you and your king" sarcastically in this speech.

17. *wheat harvest.* That is, early summer, when no rain falls in Israel.

and all the people feared the Lord greatly, and they feared Samuel as well.
19 And all the people said to Samuel, "Intercede on behalf of your servants
with the Lord your God, that we may not die, for we have added to our
20 offenses an evil thing to ask for ourselves a king." And Samuel said to
the people, "Fear not. You have done all this evil, but swerve not from
21 following the Lord and serve the Lord with all your heart. And swerve
not after mere emptiness that will not avail or rescue, for they are mere
22 emptiness. For the Lord will not desert His people for the sake of His
23 great name, as the Lord has undertaken to make you His people. I on my
part, too, far be it from me to offend the Lord by ceasing to intercede on
24 your behalf. I shall instruct you in the good and straight way. Only fear
the Lord and serve Him truly with all your heart, for see the great things
25 He has done for you. And if indeed you do evil, both you and your king
will be swept away."

1 CHAPTER 13   Saul was [ ] years old when he became king, and
[-] two years he reigned over Israel.

---

19. *an evil thing to ask for ourselves a king.* Through the pressure of Samuel's oration, this "renewal of the kingship" most peculiarly turns into a collective confession of the sin of having wanted a king.

21. *swerve not after mere emptiness.* "Swerve" is once again Deuteronomistic terminology—to veer off from the straight and narrow path of the Lord. The Masoretic Text inserts "that" (*ki*) after this verb, creating a small problem of syntax, but the Septuagint deletes the word. The present translation adds the adjective "mere" to "emptiness" (*tohu*) in order to convey the full pejorative sense of the noun, which in many contexts suggests futility and is associated with the emptiness of the desert (compare the *tohu wabohu*, "welter and waste," of the beginning of Genesis).

23. *far be it from me to offend the Lord by ceasing to intercede on your behalf.* One should note how deftly Samuel upstages the king whom he has just helped the people to confirm in office. It is true, his argument runs, that you have made the sinful error of choosing yourself a king. (Samuel of course makes no allowance for God's role in the choice, which might express grudging divine recognition of a new political necessity.) That cannot be reversed, but never fear—I will still be here to act as the intercessor you will desperately continue to need.

CHAPTER 13   1. *Saul was [] years old . . . and [-] two years he reigned.* The Masoretic Text, notoriously defective at this point, says "Saul was a year old . . . and two years he reigned." This whole sentence is absent from the Septuagint, leading one to suspect that the redactor here stitched into the narrative a textual fragment in which there were lacunae in the numbers that he did not presume to fill in.

And Saul chose for himself three thousand from Israel, and two thousand 2
were with Saul at Michmash and in the Bethel high country, and a thousand were with Jonathan at Gibeath-Benjamin, and the rest of the people
he sent away each man to his tent.

And Jonathan struck down the Philistine prefect who was in Gibeah and 3
the Philistines heard of it. And Saul blew the ram's horn throughout the
land, saying, "Let the Hebrews hear!" And all Israel heard, saying, "Saul has 4
struck down the Philistine prefect, and, indeed, Israel has become repugnant to the Philistines." And the people rallied round Saul at Gilgal. And 5
the Philistines had assembled to do battle against Israel—thirty thousand
chariots and six thousand horsemen and troops multitudinous as the sand
on the shore of the sea. And they came up and encamped at Michmash, east
of Beth-Aven. And the men of Israel saw that they were in straits, for the 6
troops were hard-pressed, and the troops hid in caves and among thorns
and among rocks and in dugouts and in pits. And Hebrews had crossed the 7

---

3. *Jonathan struck down the Philistine prefect.* Though the Hebrew uses the standard idiom
for killing someone in battle, the context of Israel's subservience to the Philistines suggests
that this was an act of assassination, intended to trigger general rebellion. Jonathan enters
the narrative without introduction. The neophyte king had himself seemed a rather young
man, but with the casualness about chronology characteristic of the biblical storyteller,
Saul now has a grown son.

in Gibeah. The text reads "Geba," but the two names, which continue to alternate,
appear to be variants of the same name.

Saul blew the ram's horn . . . saying, "Let the Hebrews hear!" The ram's horn, which
produces shrill, piercing sounds, was often used for a call to arms. The "hearing" of the
Israelites is counterpointed to the just reported "hearing" of the Philistines. "Hebrews" is
usually the term used by foreigners for the Israelites. As J. P. Fokkelman has observed, Saul
invokes "a name used in contempt by enemies such as Pharaoh and the Philistines . . . in
order to arouse his people's pride and fortify their will to resist."

4. *Saul has struck down.* Though Jonathan was the assassin, Saul, as political leader of the
rebel forces, is credited with responsibility for the act.

Israel has become repugnant. The literal meaning of the Hebrew idiom is very much
like "to be in bad odor with," but that antiquated English idiom has a certain Victorian
fussiness not suitable to this narrator.

5. *thirty thousand chariots.* This inflated figure is reduced to three thousand in the
Septuagint.

6. *in dugouts.* The Hebrew term *tsariah* appears only here and in Judges 9:46. Although the
context in Judges has led some interpreters to construe it as a tower, extrabiblical evidence
from Late Antiquity argues for a chamber, or sepulcher, hewn out of rock.

7. *And Hebrews had crossed.* Here the narrator's use of "Hebrews" may have been encouraged by the attraction of a folk-etymological pun: *'ivrim* (Hebrews) *'avru* (had crossed).

Jordan into the territory of Gad and Gilead, while Saul was still at Gilgal,
8   and all the troops were trembling behind him. And he waited seven days
for the fixed time Samuel had set, and Samuel did not come, and the troops
9   began to slip away from him. And Saul said, "Bring forth to me the burnt
offering and the well-being sacrifice," and he offered up the burnt offering.
10 And it happened as he finished offering the burnt offering that, look, Samuel
11 was coming, and Saul went out toward him to greet him. And Samuel said,
"What have you done?" And Saul said, "For I saw that the troops were slipping away from me, and you on your part had not come at the fixed time,
12 and the Philistines were assembling at Michmash. And I thought, 'Now the
Philistines will come down on me at Gilgal, without my having entreated
the LORD's favor.' And I took hold of myself and offered up the burnt offer-
13 ing." And Samuel said to Saul, "You have played the fool! Had you but kept
the command of the LORD your God that He commanded you, now the

---

Saul was still at Gilgal. This cultic site is, according to a common identification, near
Jericho in the Jordan Valley. The "Hebrews"—perhaps the general population and not the
army—who cross the Jordan appear to be fleeing the Philistines to the relative safety of the
territory of Gad and Gilead to the northeast.

8. the fixed time Samuel had set. The words "had set" (one word in the Hebrew) are lacking in the Masoretic Text but are supplied by two of the ancient versions. The fact that
the Hebrew word in question, sam, has the same consonants as the first two consonants
of Samuel's name may have led to the scribal error. The entire story of Samuel's fixing a
period of seven days for Saul to await him at Gilgal before the offering of sacrifices goes
back to 10:8. The fulfillment of that initial instruction to the new king has been interrupted by the election of Saul by lottery, his campaign against the Ammonites, and the
renewal of the kingship at Gilgal. One must assume either that the order to await Samuel at
Gilgal was for an eventual meeting at an unspecified future time or that one literary strand
of the Saul story has been interrupted by the splicing in of other strands (chapters 11–12).
    the troops began to slip away from him. Battle could not be engaged without first entreat-
ing the favorable disposition of the deity through sacrifice (compare Saul's words of explanation in verse 12). Saul's men are beginning to give up hope and to desert; so he feels, with
good reason, that he can afford to wait no longer.

10. as he finished offering the burnt offering that, look, Samuel was coming. The timing gives
the distinct appearance of a cat-and-mouse game played by Samuel. He is not absolutely
late, but he has waited until the last possible moment—sometime well into the seventh day
(or it might even be the eighth day), by which time Saul has been obliged to take matters
into his own hands.

12. I took hold of myself. The Hebrew verb hit'apeq means to force yourself to do, or to refrain
from doing, something. The same verb is used when the tearful Joseph "could no longer
hold himself in check" in the presence of his brothers (Genesis 45:1).

13. Had you but kept the command of the LORD. The Masoretic Text has a declarative, "you
have not kept," but the structure of the whole sentence argues strongly for emending lo'

LORD would have made your kingdom over Israel unshaken forever. But 14
now, your kingdom shall not stand. The LORD has already sought out for
Himself a man after His own heart, and the LORD has appointed him prince
to His people, for you have not kept what the LORD commanded you." And 15
Samuel arose and went up from Gilgal to Gibeath-Benjamin. And Saul
mustered the troops remaining with him, about six hundred men. And Saul 16
and Jonathan his son and the troops remaining with them were staying at
Gibeath-Benjamin, and the Philistines had encamped at Michmash. And a 17
raiding party sallied forth from the Philistine camp in three columns—one
column turned toward the road to Ophrah, to the Shual region, and one 18
column turned toward the road to Beth-Horon, and one column turned
toward the border road that looks out over the Zeboim Valley, toward the

---

("not") to *lu* ("if" introducing a clause contrary to fact). Samuel flatly assumes that his own commands and the commandments of the LORD are entirely equivalent. In fact, it is he, not God, who has given Saul the elaborate instructions about waiting seven days at Gilgal. In a kind of prophet's tantrum, Samuel insists again and again in this speech on the words "commanded" and "command." (In verse 14, "appointed him prince" is literally "commanded him prince.")

made your kingdom . . . unshaken forever. The Hebrew verb *hekhin* means both to establish and to keep on a firm foundation (*makhon*), and so it is misleading to translate it only as the initiating "to establish."

14. *your kingdom shall not stand.* Samuel's rage over the fact that Saul has offered the sacrifice derives from his construing that act as a usurpation of his own prerogatives as master of the cult (though there are other biblical instances of kings who offer sacrifices). One suspects that Samuel has set up Saul for this "failure," and that he would have been content only with a puppet king.

The LORD has already sought out for Himself a man after His own heart. Although this would have to be a veiled prediction of the advent of David, in naturalistic terms, the incensed Samuel is in a way bluffing: fed up with Saul, he announces to the king that God has already chosen a successor—about whom Samuel himself as yet knows nothing whatever, nor has he even had time for a communication from God that there will be a successor.

appointed him prince to His people. As Polzin shrewdly notes, David will later use these very words (2 Samuel 6:21) when he angrily tells Saul's daughter Michal that it is he who has been divinely elected to replace her father.

15. *to Gibeath-Benjamin.* It looks improbable that Samuel would now go off after this confrontation to Gibeah, which is Saul's hometown. The text at this point in the Septuagint has him going "on the way," leaving the more likely outcome that he abandons Saul and his small handful of men at Gibeah to tackle the Philistines.

about six hundred men. By this point, 1400 have "slipped away."

17. *the Shual region.* The name literally means "Foxland."

18. *Zeboim Valley.* Or, Jackal Valley.

19 desert. And no smith could be found in all the land of Israel, for the Philis-
20 tines had said, "Lest the Hebrews make sword or spear!" And all Israel would
    go down to the Philistines for every man to put an edge on his plowshare and
21 his mattock and his ax and his sickle. And the price of the sharpening was
    a *pim* for the plowshares and the mattocks and the three-pronged forks and
22 the axes, and for setting the goads. And so it was, on the day of battle, that
    no sword nor spear was found in the hands of all the troops who were with
23 Saul and Jonathan, but in the hands of Saul and Jonathan his son. And the
    Philistine garrison sallied forth to the pass of Michmash.

1   CHAPTER 14   And when the day came round, Jonathan son
    of Saul said to the lad bearing his armor, "Come, let us cross over to the Phi-
    listine garrison which is on the other side there," but his father he did not
2   tell. And Saul was sitting at the outskirts of Gibeah under the pomegran-
    ate tree which is at Migron, and the troops that were with him were about
3   six hundred men. And Ahijah son of Ahitub brother of Ichabod son of

---

19. *no smith could be found in all the land of Israel.* This bit of background notation vividly reflects the abject status of the Israelites under Philistine domination. Ironsmiths are
banned among them to prevent their developing the weaponry needed for rebellion.

20. *his sickle.* The reading used here is, as in the Septuagint, *ḥermesho*, instead of the Masoretic *maḥareshato*, "his plowshare," which repeats the first term in the list.

21. *the price of the sharpening was a* pim. The italicized term occurs only here in the Bible,
but the archaeologists have found stone weights marked *pim*, which is two-thirds of a shekel
(here, evidently, a silver shekel). The Philistines, then, not only deprive the Israelites of the
technology for making weapons but also reap a profit from their smithless vassals for the
maintenance of the agricultural tools they need for their livelihood.
      the three-pronged forks. A commonly proposed emendation yields "a third of a shekel
for the forks and the axes and for the setting of the goads." This change would make sense
if in fact the sharpening of these implements were half the work of sharpening plowshares
and mattocks, but that is not entirely clear.

CHAPTER 14   1. *but his father he did not tell.* One assumes that his father would
have forbidden him to go out on so dangerous a mission, but there is also an implicit contrast between Saul, sitting under the pomegranate tree, hesitant to act in the face of the
superior forces of the enemy, and Jonathan, prepared to execute a daring commando raid.

3. *Ahijah son of Ahitub brother of Ichabod.* The genealogy here casts a certain suspect light
on Saul: the priest who accompanies him to the battlefield, and on whose prognostication
he relies, belongs to the blighted—and rejected—house of Eli.

Phineas son of Eli priest of the LORD at Shiloh was bearer of the ephod, and the troops did not know that Jonathan had gone. And in the pass through 4 which Jonathan sought to cross over to the Philistine garrison there was a rocky crag on one side and on the other side, and the name of the one was Bozez and the name of the other Seneh. The one crag loomed to the north 5 facing Michmash and the other to the south facing Gibeah. And Jonathan 6 said to the lad bearing his armor, "Come, let us cross over to the garrison of these uncircumcised! Perhaps the LORD will act for us, for nothing holds the LORD back from rescue, whether by many or by few." And his armor 7 bearer said to him, "Do you whatever your heart inclines—here I am with you, my heart as yours." And Jonathan said, "Look, we are about to cross 8 over to the men and we shall be exposed to them. If thus they say, 'Stand 9 still until we get to you,' we shall stand where we are and not go up to them. And if thus they say, 'Come up to us,' we shall go up, for the LORD will 10 have given them in our hand, and that will be the sign for us." And the two 11 of them were exposed to the Philistine garrison, and the Philistines said,

---

bearer of the ephod. The title, *nose' ephod,* is formally parallel to "armor bearer," *nose' kelim,* and so suggests a contrast between Saul, who relies on divination, and Jonathan, who relies on his weapons.

4. *the pass through which Jonathan sought to cross over.* The Philistines and the Israelites are encamped on the tops of two steep hills facing each other, with a deep gully, or wadi, running between them. Jonathan and his armor bearer are able to make their way down the slope unseen by taking cover among the crags and under overhangs. But Jonathan realizes that there will be a moment of truth in this tactic, for when they reach the floor of the gully, they will be "exposed" (verse 8) to the Philistine outpost.

5. *loomed.* The Hebrew *mutsaq* means literally "column." It might conceivably be a scrambled scribal repetition of the next Hebrew word in the text, *mitsafon,* "from the north."

6. *these uncircumcised.* This designation for the Philistines is of course contemptuous. Its spirit is precisely reflected, from the other side of the ethnic barrier, in Othello's reference to a Turk he killed in battle as a "circumcised dog."

7. *Do whatever your heart inclines—here I am with you, my heart as yours.* The translation follows the reading of the Septuagint. The Masoretic Text conveys the same general idea, though a bit less coherently: "Do whatever is in your heart, incline you—here I am with you as your heart."

10. *that will be the sign for us.* Readers from the Talmud to our own times have construed this as a kind of divination. It is far more likely that a further contrast is implied between Saul, who depends on divination, and Jonathan, who is thinking in pragmatic military terms: if they invite us to come up to them, that will be our great opportunity; if they order us to await their descent, we may have no recourse (except, perhaps, flight at the last moment).

"Look, Hebrews are coming out of the holes where they've been hiding."
12 And the men of the garrison spoke out to Jonathan and his armor bearer
and said, "Come up to us, and we'll teach you something!" And Jonathan
said to his armor bearer, "Come up behind me, for the LORD has given them
13 into the hand of Israel." And Jonathan climbed up on his hands and knees
with his armor bearer behind him, and they fell before Jonathan with his
14 armor bearer finishing them off behind him. And the first toll of dead that
Jonathan with his armor bearer struck down was about twenty men, with
15 arrows and rocks of the field. And terror shook the camp in the field and
all the troops. The garrison and the raiding party were also shaken, and
16 the earth trembled, and it became dire terror. And the lookouts attached to
Saul at Gibeath-Benjamin saw and, look, the multitude was melting away
17 and going off yonder. And Saul said to the troops who were with him, "Call
the roll, pray, and see who has gone from us," and they called the roll and,
18 look, Jonathan and his armor bearer were absent. And Saul said to Ahijah,
"Bring forth the ephod." For on that day he was bearing the ephod before

---

11. *Look, Hebrews are coming out of the holes where they've been hiding.* These words accord
perfectly with the report in 13:6 of the Israelites hiding in every nook and cranny, and also
vividly express the contempt of the Philistines for the Hebrews, whom they depict as so
many vermin. The contempt is extended in the taunting challenge to Jonathan and his lad
in the next verse.

13. *Jonathan climbed up on his hands and knees.* Although it is not easy to reconstruct the
exact tactic of surprise, this notation makes clear that instead of walking up the slope
directly to the Philistine outpost, Jonathan and his armor bearer manage to slip off to one
side and make their way up the slope by a circuitous route, crouching and crawling in order
to take shelter among the rocks, and thus come upon the outpost undetected.

14. *the first toll of dead.* The literal meaning of the Hebrew is "the first blow."
    with arrows and rocks of the field. The translation adopts the reading of the Septuagint.
The Masoretic Text has here "within about half a furrow long, an acre [?] of field," but that
sequence of Hebrew words looks scrambled.

15. *terror shook.* The Hebrew *ḥaradah* means both terror and shaking.
    dire terror. The Hebrew is literally "terror of God," but the latter word, *'elohim*, serves
as an intensifier. In any case, the idiom functions as a kind of pun—dire terror is terror
caused by God.

16. *going off yonder.* The translation presupposes *halom* ("yonder"), a repeated word in this
episode, instead of the Masoretic *wahalom*, which could mean either, asyntactically, "and
yonder" or "and hitting" (that is, the Philistines were going on, hitting each other).

18. *Bring forth the ephod.* The Masoretic Text, both in this clause and the next, has "Ark of
God" instead of "ephod," but the reading of the Septuagint, *ephod*, is compelling on several
grounds. We have been informed earlier that the Ark of God was left, not to be moved for

the Israelites. And it happened that as Saul was speaking to the priest, the 19
tumult in the Philistine camp was growing greater and greater. And Saul
said to the priest, "Pull back your hand." And Saul and all the troops who 20
were with him rallied and entered into the fighting, and, look, every man's
sword was against his fellow—a very great panic. And there were Hebrews 21
who were previously with the Philistines, who had come up with them into
the camp, and they, too, turned round to be with Israel under Saul and
Jonathan. And all the men of Israel who were hiding out in the high country 22
of Ephraim had heard that the Philistines were fleeing, and they, too, gave
chase after them in the fighting. And the LORD delivered Israel on that day. 23a

And the fighting moved on past Beth-Aven. And the men of Israel were 23b,24
hard-pressed on that day. And Saul made the troops take an oath, saying,
"Cursed be the man who eats food until evening, until I take vengeance

---

the foreseeable future, at Kiriath-Jearim. The Ark was not an instrument of divination, like
the ephod, and what Saul wants Ahijah to do here is to divine. It is possible that Ahijah's
lineal connection with the keepers of the Ark at Shiloh led some early transmitter of the
text to align this episode with the earlier story in which the Ark—quite misguidedly was
brought out from Shiloh to the battlefield. The Masoretic Text also reads, asyntactically,
"for the Ark of God on that day was, and the Israelites," whereas the Septuagint, far more
coherently, has "for on that day he was bearing the ephod before the Israelites."

19. *Pull back your hand.* That is, desist from the act of divination you have begun—it is
no longer necessary, for the auditory evidence of the Philistine rout has reached our ears.

20. *and, look, every man's sword was against his fellow.* This spectacle of total, self-mutilat-
ing panic (*mehumah*) in the camp of the enemy is a recurrent motif that goes back to Judges
(compare the effect of Gideon's surprise attack on the Midianite camp), and is a kind of
narrative realization of God's direct intervention in battle to grant victory to Israel. The
foundational instance of this motif is the victory at the Sea of Reeds in Exodus.

21. *Hebrews who were previously with the Philistines.* Given the subject status of the Israelites, it is not surprising that some of them would have been conscripted by the Philistines,
either as soldiers or to perform menial tasks for the troops. They are referred to here as
"Hebrews" because that is how their Philistine masters would have referred to them.

24. *And the men of Israel were hard-pressed.* The explanation for being hard-pressed is not
certain. The Hebrew term, *nigas*, most naturally refers to being at a military disadvantage,
but here the Israelites appear to have the upper hand. The other possibility is that the men
are weak from hunger, not having had the opportunity to eat in their hot pursuit of the
Philistines. The oath Saul exacts would then compound this predicament. It should be said
that the Septuagint reflects a different text for this entire clause: "And Saul committed a
great blunder on that day."
    Cursed be the man who eats food. As we shall have occasion to see later in the David
narrative, it was a fairly common practice (though by no means an automatic one) for fight-

25 upon my enemies!" And all the troops tasted no food. And the whole coun-
26 try came into the forest, and there was honey on the ground. And the
   troops entered the forest and, look, there was a flow of honey, but none
27 touched his hand to his mouth, for the troops feared the vow. But Jonathan
   had not heard when his father made the troops swear, and he reached with
   the tip of the staff that was in his hand and dipped it into the honeycomb
28 and brought his hand back to his mouth, and his eyes lit up. And a man
   from the troops spoke up and said, "Your father made the troops solemnly
   swear, saying, 'Cursed be the man who eats food today.' And so the troops
29 were famished." And Jonathan said, "My father has stirred up trouble for
   the land. See, pray, that my eyes have lit up because I tasted a bit of this
30 honey. How much better still if the troops had really eaten today from the
   booty of their enemies that they found, for then the toll of Philistines would
31 have been all the greater." And they struck down the Philistines on that
32 day from Michmash to Ajalon, and the troops were very famished. And

---

ing men to take on themselves a vow of abstinence from food, in order to enter the battle
in what amounted to a state of dedicated ritual purity. But Saul in this instance makes a
miscalculation, imposing a fast on hungry men, in an effort to force the hand of divinity.
(Thus the Septuagint's version of the first clause of this verse might be regarded as an
interpretive gloss on the lapidary formulation of the received text.)

25. *And the whole country came into the forest.* This sounds as odd in the Hebrew as in
translation because "country" (*ha'arets*) is not an idiomatic term for "people." Extensive
textual surgery yields this conjectural reconstruction of an original clause: "and there was
honeycomb on the ground." An additional difficulty in this passage is that the common
Hebrew term *ya'ar*, "forest," has a rare homonym that means honeycomb. (In verse 27, the
term that occurs is *ya'arah*, which is unambiguous both because with the feminine suffix
it can refer only to honeycomb and because it is joined with *devash*, "honey.") But the
received text in our verse has the preposition "into" (*b^e*), which presumes that *ya'ar* means
"forest" and not "honeycomb."

27. *his eyes lit up.* The idiom used for the refreshing effect of a taste of food is a pointed one
because, as Shimon Bar-Efrat has noted, the verb "to light up" (the Hebrew verb *'or*) plays
antithetically on Saul's "cursed (*'arur*) be the man."

29. *My father has stirred up trouble.* The verb *'akhar* that is used here is doubly important.
Etymologically, it means "to muddy," as in stirring up muck in a pond. Thus, it is an antithesis to the lighting up of the eyes Jonathan has just experienced through partaking of food.
It is also the verb Jephthah invokes when he sees it is his daughter who has come out to
greet him: "and you have joined ranks with my troublers" (Judges 11:35). The echo sets up a
network of intertextual links with the Jephthah story: here, too, a father who is a military
leader seeks to influence the outcome of the battle by a rash vow that is an unwitting death
sentence on his own child.

31. *And they struck down the Philistines.* Although the form of the two verbs does not indicate it, the narrative logic of the scene compels us to construe this sentence as a pluperfect

the troops pounced on the booty and took sheep and cattle and calves and
slaughtered them on the ground, and the troops ate them together with the
blood. And they told Saul, saying, "Look, the troops are offending the LORD   33
by eating together with the blood!" And he said, "You have acted treacherously. Roll a big stone over to me now." And Saul said, "Spread out among   34
the troops, and say to them, 'Every man bring forth to me his ox and his
sheep and slaughter them here and eat, and you shall not offend the LORD
by eating together with the blood.'" And all the troops brought forth each
man what he had in hand that night and they slaughtered it there. And Saul   35
built an altar to the LORD, it was the first altar he built to the LORD.

And Saul said, "Let us go down after the Philistines by night and despoil   36
them till daybreak, and we shall not leave a man among them." And they
said, "Whatever is good in your eyes, do." And the priest said, "Let us
approach God yonder." And Saul inquired of God, "Shall I go down after   37
the Philistines? Will You give them in the hand of Israel?" And He did not
answer him on that day. And Saul said, "Draw near, all you chiefs of the   38
troops, mark and see, wherein is this offense today? For as the LORD lives   39

---

summary of the day's action, responding to Jonathan's reference to the "toll" (literally,
"blow") exacted from the Philistines.

32. *the troops pounced on the booty . . . ate them together with the blood.* The first verb here
has pejorative force, being generally used for birds of prey descending on their victims.
Biblical law repeatedly prohibits the consumption of meat together with the blood because
the blood is regarded as the sacred stuff of life. The slaughtering on the ground here would
make it more difficult to allow the blood to drain off, as would have been done in slaughtering on a stone platform or altar. (Note Saul's correction of the practice in verses 33–34.)
Jonathan's tasting a bit of honey thus leads to an orgy of gluttonous consumption of meat
with blood. This consequence attaches an association of violation of sacred law to Jonathan's act, but the ultimate fault lies with Saul, who by imposing a fast on already famished
men has set them up to abandon all restraint the moment the taboo against eating is broken.

34. *what he had in hand.* This accords with the Septuagint, *'asher beyado*, against the
Masoretic, "his bull in his hand," *shoro beyado*.

37. *And Saul inquired of God . . . And He did not answer him.* Although it was extremely
common for military leaders everywhere in the ancient Near East to consult an oracle
before going into battle, Saul's failed inquiry here participates in a larger pattern in his
story: he is constantly seeking knowledge of what is about to happen (as in his quest for a
seer to help him locate the asses at the very beginning), but this knowledge is repeatedly
withheld from him.

38. *wherein is this offense.* Saul assumes that the oracle did not respond because someone
among his troops committed some "offense." The narrator does not necessarily endorse
this assumption.

Who delivers Israel, were it in Jonathan my son, he would be doomed to
40 die!" And none answered him from all the troops. And he said to all Israel,
"You will be on one side and I and Jonathan my son on the other side."
41 And the troops said to Saul, "What is good in your eyes, do." And Saul
said, "LORD, God of Israel! Why did You not answer Your servant today?
If there is guilt in me or in Jonathan my son, O LORD God of Israel, show
Urim, and if it is in Your people Israel, show Thummim." And the lot fell
42 on Jonathan and Saul, and the troops came out clear. And Saul said, "Cast
43 between me and Jonathan my son." And the lot fell on Jonathan. And Saul
said, "Tell me, what have you done?" And Jonathan told him and said, "I
indeed tasted from the tip of the staff that was in my hand a bit of honey.
44 Here I am, ready to die!" And Saul said, "So may God do to me, and even

---

39. *were it in Jonathan my son.* "It" refers to the just mentioned "offense." Is this a flourish
of rhetorical emphasis, or, as J. P. Fokkelman has suggested, does it open the possibility
that Saul has Jonathan in mind? In the immediately preceding episode, after all, Jonathan
has gone out on a military operation without permission. Jonathan now is brought forth
as the possible perpetrator of some further, not yet specified offense, which will prove to
be the tasting of the honey. In any case, there seems to be some deep ambivalence between
father and son well before the appearance of David at court.

41. *LORD, God of Israel! Why did You not answer Your servant today? If there is guilt in me
or in Jonathan my son ... show Urim, and if it is in Your people Israel, show Thummim.*
This version comes from the Septuagint. The Masoretic Text here has the short and cryptic "Show Thammim [sic]." Saul's frustrated reference to his failure to receive an answer
from the oracle makes a great deal of narrative sense (see the comment on verse 37). The
Septuagint version also makes intelligible the process of oracular lottery. The Urim and
Thummim were two divinatory objects attached to the ephod, probably in a special com-
partment. They may have been in the form of stones or tokens with lettering on them. They
provided indication of binary oppositions: thus the question addressed to the oracle had
to take the form of yes or no, *x* or *y*. The opposition may have been underscored by the fact
that Urim and Thummim begin, respectively, with the first and last letter of the Hebrew
alphabet. More speculatively, Urim might be linked with *'aror,* "to curse," and Thummim
with the root *t-m-m,* whole or innocent.
    the lot fell on Jonathan and Saul. The same idiom of being "caught" by the lot that was
used for Saul's election recurs here in the devolution of the curse on Jonathan.

42. *Cast between me and Jonathan.* Since the Urim and Thummim can provide only binary
responses, it is necessary to divide again into two alternatives in order to get an answer.

43. *indeed tasted ... a bit of honey.* Jonathan begins by clearly and emphatically admitting
responsibility, using the infinitive absolute followed by the verb (literally, "taste I have
tasted"). But he chooses, with precision, the minimal verb "taste" rather than "eat" and
holds back its minimal object, "a bit of honey," for the very end of the sentence.

more, for Jonathan is doomed to die!" And the troops said to Saul, "Will 45
Jonathan die, who has performed this great rescue in Israel? Heaven forbid,
as the Lord lives, that a single hair of his head should fall to the ground!
For with God has he wrought this day." And the troops saved Jonathan, and
he did not die. And Saul went away from pursuing the Philistines and the 46
Philistines went back to their place.

And Saul had taken hold of the kingship over Israel, and he did battle 47
round about with all his enemies, with Moab and with the Ammonites
and with Edom and with the kings of Zobah and with the Philistines, and
wherever he turned he would inflict punishment. And he triumphed and 48
struck down Amalek and rescued Israel from the hand of its plunderers.

And Saul's sons were Jonathan and Ishvi and Malkishua, and the names of 49
his two daughters were Merab the firstborn and Michal the younger. And 50
the name of Saul's wife was Ahinoam daughter of Ahimaaz. And the name
of his commander was Abiner son of Ner, Saul's uncle. And Kish, Saul's 51

---

45. *And the troops said to Saul, "Will Jonathan die."* As several commentators have observed,
this is a precise reversal of the incident after Saul's victory over Nahash, in which the troops
sought to kill dissidents and Saul saved their lives. Now he has become the severe autocrat,
and his son's well-earned popularity with the troops saves the prince.

47. *Saul had taken hold of the kingship.* The verb used, *lakad*, is the same one just invoked
for the process of being caught, trapped, taken hold of, in the divine lottery. Saul himself
was "caught" for kingship. Now, through conquest, he catches, or secures, the kingship.
There is thus surely an undertone of ambiguity in this report of his success as monarch.

    he would inflict punishment. The Hebrew *yarshiʿa* usually means to condemn someone
as guilty in a court of justice. But a related idiom, "to do justice," *ʿasot shephatim*, also
means to carry out punitive acts against an enemy. The Masoretic version is to be preferred
to the Septuagint's *yoshiʿa*, "he would rescue," because in this narrative, God, not Saul, is
represented as the rescuer. Apparently, the implication is that he carried out punishing
expeditions against Israel's enemies to the east of the Jordan without actually conquering
them, as David was to do.

49. *And Saul's sons.* This entire notice of Saul's family and of his conquests is placed as a
formal marker of conclusion to the body of the Saul story. What follows is the episode that
will definitively disqualify him for the throne in Samuel's eyes, and then David will enter the
scene. The episode in which Saul pronounces a death sentence on his son and heir heralds
the climactic encounter with Samuel over Amalek in which the prophet will pronounce the
end of Saul's incipient dynasty. Eventually, Saul and Jonathan, the parties jointly indicated
by the first cast of the Urim, will perish in battle on the same day.

50. *Abiner.* A variant vocalization of Abner.

52 father, and Ner, Abner's father, were sons of Abiel. And the fighting against the Philistines was fierce all the days of Saul, and when Saul saw any warrior or valiant fellow, he would gather him to himself.

1   CHAPTER 15   And Samuel said to Saul, "Me has the LORD sent to anoint you as king over His people Israel. And now, heed the voice
2   of the words of the LORD. Thus says the LORD of Armies, 'I have made reckoning of what Amalek did to Israel, that he set against him on the
3   way as he was coming up from Egypt. Now, go and strike down Amalek, and put under the ban everything that he has, you shall not spare him, and you shall put to death man and woman, infant and suckling, ox and sheep, camel and donkey.' "

---

52. *And the fighting against the Philistines.* Saul has greater success on the eastern front, but he is unable to subdue the Philistines. In the end, they will destroy him in their victory at Gilboa.

when Saul saw any warrior . . . he would gather him to himself. This report of constant military conscription indicates the institutionalization of the monarchy and also accords with Samuel's warning about the burden of conscription that the king would impose.

CHAPTER 15   1. *Me has the LORD sent.* Samuel, by placing the accusative first-person pronoun at the beginning of his speech (normal Hebrew usage would simply attach an accusative suffix to the verb), once again highlights his own centrality to this whole process: it is only because he, as God's unique delegate, has anointed Saul that Saul can claim to be king. In this way, Samuel sets the stage rhetorically for the prerogative of canceling Saul's kingship that he will exercise later in this episode.

heed the voice of the words of the LORD. This redundant phrasing is a little odd, but it is dictated by the pressure of the thematically fraught key phrase, "heed [or listen to] the voice," that defines the entire episode. Saul fails to listen as he fails to see.

2. *reckoning of what Amalek did to Israel.* After Amalek massacred the Israelite stragglers (see Deuteronomy 25:18), Israel was commanded to destroy all remnants of the Amalekites.

set against him. This phrase may be an ellipsis for "set ambushes against him."

3. *put under the ban everything that he has.* The verb here is in the plural, evidently including the troops together with Saul, though the subsequent verbs in this verse are in the singular. The "ban" (*ḥerem*), one of the cruelest practices of ancient Near Eastern warfare, is an injunction of total destruction—of all living things—of the enemy. Amalek is, of course, the archetypal implacable enemy of Israel, but it should be said that here, as throughout the Samuel story, there is at least some margin of ambiguity as to whether the real source of this ferocious imperative is God or the prophet who claims to speak on His behalf.

you shall not spare him. The Hebrew verb *ḥamal* straddles two senses, to feel mercy for and to allow to survive, and the ambiguity between the emotional and the pragmatic sense is exploited throughout the story.

And Saul summoned the troops and assembled them at Telaim, two hun- 4
dred thousand foot soldiers and ten thousand men of Judah. And Saul came 5
up to the city of Amalek and lay in wait in the ravine. And Saul said to the 6
Kenite, "Go, turn away, come down from amidst the Amalekite, lest I sweep
you away together with him, for you did kindness to all the Israelites when
they came up from Egypt." And the Kenite turned away from the midst
of Amalek. And Saul struck down Amalek from Havilah till you come to 7
Shur, which is before Egypt. And he caught Agag king of Amalek alive, and 8
all the people he put under the ban with the edge of the sword. And Saul, 9
and the troops with him, spared Agag and the best of the sheep and the
cattle, the fat ones and the young ones, everything good, and they did not
want to put them under the ban. But all the vile and worthless possessions,
these they put under the ban.

And the word of the LORD came to Samuel, saying, "I repent that I made 10,11
Saul king, for he has turned back from Me, and My words he has not fulfilled." And Samuel was incensed and he cried out to the LORD all night

---

4. *summoned the troops.* The word for "summoned" (there are several more common terms
for mustering troops in the Bible) is quite rare, and literally means "made them listen."
The same verb as "to listen" in a different conjugation, it continues to call attention to this
thematically weighted activity.

   two hundred thousand foot soldiers and ten thousand men of Judah. The troops from
Judah are presumably also foot soldiers, and so an ellipsis is probable: "and another ten
thousand foot soldiers from the men of Judah."

6. *Go, turn away, come down from amidst.* These overlapping imperative verbs are obviously
meant to underscore the urgency of the command. The Kenites appear to have been a tribe
of migratory metalsmiths (the meaning of their name) somehow allied with Israel (compare
Judges 4–5), although the nature of the "kindness" they did for Israel is not known.

9. *And Saul, and the troops with him, spared Agag.* The Hebrew says simply "Saul and the
troops spared Agag," but because a singular verb is used with the plural subject, it signals
to the audience that Saul is the principal actor and the troops only accessories. (This highlighting of the first-mentioned agent through a singular verb for a plural subject is a general
feature of biblical usage.) When confronted by Samuel, Saul will turn the responsibility for
the action on its head. "Spared" momentarily sounds as though it could mean "had mercy
on," but then it is also attached to cattle and sheep. There is a morally scandalous pairing
in the selective massacre Saul and his troops perpetrate: they kill all the defective animals
and every man, woman, child, and infant, while sparing the good, edible animals and the
king (perhaps with the idea that some further profit can be extracted from him).

   the fat ones. The Masoretic Text has *mishnim* (two-year-olds?), but, in a reversal of
consonants, the Syriac and the Targum reflect *shmenim*, fat ones.

11. *Samuel was incensed.* The reasons for his rage are wonderfully unspecified, or perhaps
overdetermined. He may well be incensed with Saul, or with the people who coerced him

12 long. And Samuel rose early in the morning to meet Saul, and it was told to
Samuel, saying, "Saul has gone to Carmel and, look, he has put up a monument for himself, and has turned about and passed onward, and gone down
13 to Gilgal." And Samuel came to Saul, and Saul said to him, "Blessed be
14 you to the LORD! I have fulfilled the word of the LORD." And Samuel said,
"And what is this sound of sheep in my ears, and the sound of cattle that
15 I hear?" And Saul said, "From the Amalekite they have brought them, for
the troops spared the best of the sheep and the cattle in order to sacrifice to
16 the LORD your God, and the rest we put under the ban." And Samuel said,
"Hold off, that I may tell you what the LORD spoke to me this night." And
17 he said, "Speak." And Samuel said, "Though you may be small in your own
eyes, you are the head of the tribes of Israel, and the LORD has anointed
18 you king over Israel. And the LORD sent you on a mission and said to you,
'You shall put under the ban the offenders, Amalek, and do battle against
them till you destroy them all.'

---

into this whole distasteful monarchic business in the first place, or even with God for
making him heed the people.

12. *Carmel.* This is not the Carmel near Haifa but a town in the tribal territory of Judah, in
the general vicinity of Hebron.

   he has put up a monument for himself. This would be a victory marker, probably in the
form of a stele.

14. *this sound of sheep . . . and the sound of cattle.* "Sound" and "voice" are the same word
in Hebrew (*qol*), and so the thematic key word of the episode comes to the fore: Saul had
been enjoined to listen to the voice of the LORD; now Samuel tells him that all that can be
heard (the same verb as "listen" in Hebrew) is the bleating and mooing "voice" of the very
flocks which, according to God's word, should have been destroyed.

15. *they have brought them.* Saul first uses a vague third-person plural, entirely shifting the
responsibility to unnamed others who have done the bringing.

   the troops spared the best of the sheep and the cattle. In verse 9, of course, it was expressly
reported that Saul, with the troops as accessories, spared the flocks.

   in order to sacrifice to the LORD your God. This pious justification for the act was
nowhere in evidence in the narrator's initial account of it (verses 8–9). Although it is
common enough in biblical usage when addressing a holy man to say "the LORD your
God," that locution, invoked twice in this story by Saul, stresses the distance between him
and God and his sense that it is Samuel who has proprietary claims on the divinity.

17. *Though you may be small in your own eyes.* Samuel is obviously harking back to Saul's
initial expression of unworthiness for the throne ("from the smallest of the tribes of Israel,"
9:21), as if to say, Well, you may not really amount to much, as you yourself said at the outset,
but you nevertheless have taken upon yourself the solemn responsibility of king.

18. *mission.* Literally, "a way."

   till you destroy them all. The Masoretic Text, illogically, has "till they destroy them all,"
but the second-person suffix is supplied in some of the ancient versions.

And why did you not heed the voice of the LORD, for you pounced on the 19
booty and did evil in the eyes of the LORD?" And Saul said to Samuel, 20
"But I heeded the voice of the LORD and went on the way the LORD sent
me, and I brought back Agag king of Amalek, but Amalek I put under
the ban. And the troops took from the booty sheep and cattle, the pick 21
of the banned things, to sacrifice to the LORD your God at Gilgal." And 22
Samuel said,

> "Does the LORD take delight in burnt offerings and sacrifices
>   as in heeding the voice of the LORD?
> For heeding is better than sacrifice,
>   hearkening, than the fat of rams.
> For the diviner's offense is rebellion,   23
>   the transgression of idols—defiance.
> Since you have cast off the word of the LORD,
>   He has cast you aside as king."

---

19. *why did you not heed the voice of the LORD.* Samuel hammers home the thematic point
of the whole confrontation: Saul, actually the initiator, proclaims he has listened to the
voice of the people (verse 24)—as, ironically, Samuel himself was enjoined by God to do in
chapter 8—instead of to the voice of God. This antithesis is more pointed in the Hebrew
because the more general meaning of the word for "troops," *'am*, is "people."

you pounced on the booty. Samuel uses the same verb for greedy predation that was used
to describe the orgy of meat eating after the breaking of the vow of fasting in chapter 14.

21. *the troops took.* Once again, Saul shifts the responsibility for the act from himself to
his troops.

22. *Does the LORD take delight in burnt offerings.* Samuel caps his prophetic denunciation
with the declamation of a prophetic poem. The theme that God requires obedience, not
rote performance of the cult, is a common one among the later "literary" prophets, though
in their poetry obedience to God means refraining from acts of exploitation rather than
carrying out a program of extermination.

heeding the voice of the LORD. The thematic phrase is now placed in the foreground
of the prophetic poem, reinforced by "heeding [or listening] is better than sacrifice" and
"hearkening" in the next lines.

23. *the diviner's offense is rebellion.* That is, rebellion is as great a sin as divination or sorcery.
The choice of the comparison is not accidental, considering Saul's repeated futile attempts
to divine the future.

the transgression of idols—defiance. The first phrase in the Hebrew is literally "transgression and idols," but is readily construed as a hendiadys (two words for a single concept)
without emending the text. The gist of this parallel verset: defiance is as great a sin as the
worship of idols (*teraphim*).

24 And Saul said to Samuel, "I have offended, for I have transgressed the utterance of the LORD, and your word, for I feared the troops and listened
25 to their voice. Now then, forgive, pray, my offense, and turn back with me,
26 that I may bow down before the LORD." And Samuel said to Saul, "I will not turn back with you, for you have cast aside the word of the LORD and He
27 has cast you aside from being king over Israel." And Samuel turned round
28 to go, and Saul grasped the skirt of his cloak, and it tore. And Samuel said to him, "The LORD has torn away the kingship of Israel from you this day
29 and given it to your fellow man who is better than you. And, what's more, Israel's Eternal does not deceive and does not repent, for He is no human to
30 repent." And Saul said, "I have offended. Now show me honor, pray, before the elders of my people and before Israel, and turn back with me, that I
31 may bow to the LORD your God. And Samuel turned back from Saul, and

---

24. *I have transgressed the utterance of the LORD, and your word.* The Hebrew is literally "the mouth of the LORD." There is a kind of hesitation in Saul's words: I have violated God's command, and yours as well. Is there a difference between the two? Though there may well be, Saul is in no position to argue that Samuel's words are not God's.

25. *turn back with me, that I may bow down.* It would have been Samuel's function to offer the sacrifice. For Samuel not to accompany Saul to the altar would be a manifest public humiliation, a gesture of abandonment.

27. *Saul grasped the skirt of his cloak, and it tore.* The "little cloak" that Hannah would bring each year for the child Samuel has now become the prophet's flowing robe. Samuel, who never misses a cue to express his implacability toward Saul, immediately converts the tearing of the cloak into a dramatic symbol of Saul's lost kingdom. The Saul story, as we shall see, will return to cloaks and to their torn or cut skirts.

29. *Israel's Eternal does not deceive and does not repent.* Samuel's use of the verb "repent" strikes a peculiar dissonance. We in fact have been told that God repented that He made Saul king. What Samuel says here is that God will not change His mind about changing His mind. But might not this verbal contradiction cast some doubt on Samuel's reliability as a source for what God does and doesn't want? There even remains a shadow of a doubt as to whether the election of Saul in the first place was God's, or whether it was merely Samuel's all-too-human mistake.

30. *show me honor.* Saul reverts to the recurrent term *kabed*—"honor" or "glory" (as in "glory is exiled from Israel"). Knowing that Samuel has rejected him, he implores the prophet at least to help him save face in offering the sacrifice.

31. *Samuel turned back from Saul.* All English versions render this, erroneously, to indicate that Samuel nevertheless accompanied Saul to the sacrifice. But the expression "turn back with" (*shuv 'im*), as in verse 30, and "turn back from [literally, after]" (*shuv 'aharei*) are antonyms, the latter meaning unambiguously "to abandon." (It is precisely the latter idiom that we see in God's condemnation of Saul in verse 11.) Samuel is completing his rejection of Saul here by refusing to accompany him in the cult, shaming him by forcing him to offer the sacrifice without the officiating of the man of God.

Saul bowed to the Lord. And Samuel said, "Bring forth to me Agag king 32
of Amalek!" And Agag went to him with mincing steps, and he thought,
"Ah, death's bitterness is turned away!" And Samuel said,   33

> "As your sword has bereaved women,
>   more bereaved than all women your mother!"

And Samuel cut him apart before the Lord at Gilgal. And Samuel went to 34
Ramah, while Saul went up to his home in Gibeath-Saul.

And Samuel saw Saul no more till his dying day, for Samuel was grieved 35
about Saul, and the Lord had repented making Saul king over Israel.

CHAPTER 16   And the Lord said to Samuel, "How long are 1
you going to grieve about Saul when I have cast him aside from reigning

---

32. *with mincing steps.* The Hebrew adverbial term *ma'adanot* is much disputed. Some
interpret it as "stumbling," others, by a reversal of consonants, read it as "in fetters." But the
root of the word seems to point with the least strain to '-*d-n*—"pleasure," "delicate thing."
That makes sense if one construes Agag's words (the meaning of which is also in dispute)
as the expression of a last illusion: I have been spared in the general massacre, and now I
am brought to parlay with the chief holy man of the Hebrews for some important purpose;
so surely they will not kill me.

33. *Samuel cut him apart before the Lord.* There is a long-standing consensus that the
unique verb used here means something to this effect. The ghastly idea seems to be a kind
of ritual butchering.

34. *Ramah . . . Gibeath-Saul.* Each returns to his hometown. Their relationship is to all
intents and purposes finished.

35. *Samuel was grieved about Saul.* Or is it over the fact that he made the mistake of first
choosing Saul? As J. P. Fokkelman notes, this sentence includes both death (*mot*) and grieving or mourning (*'abel*), even though Saul is still alive: "we realize that Saul as king is dead;
no stronger expression of the termination of his monarchy can be imagined."

CHAPTER 16   1. *And the Lord said to Samuel.* In the preceding episodes, the typical form of divine communication was Samuel's report of what God had said, although
at Samuel's first sighting of Saul, a brief direct message from God is offered. As we have
observed, these reports open up a certain margin of doubt as to whether the purported
divine injunctions are really God's or Samuel's. The present episode unfolds systematically
through repeated dialogue between God and Samuel, and so God's judgments are rendered
with perfect, authoritative transparency. Evidently, the writer (or redactor) felt that the
initial election of David had to be entirely unambiguous. As the story continues, God will
no longer play this role of direct intervention.

over Israel? Fill your horn with oil and go. I am sending you to Jesse the
2 Bethlehemite, for I have seen Me among his sons a king." And Samuel
said, "How can I go? For should Saul hear, he will kill me." And the LORD
said, "Take a heifer with you, and you will say, 'To sacrifice to the LORD I
3 have come.' And you will invite Jesse to the sacrifice. And I Myself shall
let you know what you must do, and you will anoint for Me the one that I
4 say to you." And Samuel did what the LORD had spoken, and he came to
Bethlehem, and the elders of the town came trembling to meet him and
5 they said, "Do you come in peace?" And he said, "In peace! To sacrifice
to the LORD I have come. Sanctify yourselves and come with me to the
sacrifice." And Jesse sanctiified his sons and invited them to the sacri-
6 fice. And it happened when they came that he saw Eliab and he said, "Ah

---

I have seen Me among his sons a king. The verb "to see" (*ra'ah*) followed by the preposition *l* has the idiomatic sense of "to provide," but it is essential to preserve the literal
meaning because this entire episode is built on the repetition of the thematically weighted
word "to see," just as the previous episode turned on "to listen."

2. *For should Saul hear, he will kill me.* Suddenly, a whole new political perspective is thrown
on the estrangement between Samuel and Saul. The prophet may claim the higher ground
of divine authority, but it is the king who has the armed divisions, and who might be ready
to use them if Samuel should take any active steps to replace him. At this point, Samuel's
"grieving" over Saul begins to look like grieving over the mistake he made in first choosing
him. God, understanding Samuel's political predicament, suggests to him a cover story for
his trip from Ramah to Bethlehem, in the tribal territory of Judah.

3. *invite Jesse to the sacrifice.* The kind of sacrifice in question, *zevah*, involves both the
ritual act and a feast made of the substantial parts of the animal not burned on the altar.

4. *came trembling.* Their reaction is another reflection of the dangerous political situation: the estrangement between Samuel and Saul appears to be generally known, and
the elders are terrified at the idea that Samuel may have come to designate a new king,
or otherwise subvert the reigning monarch, which could bring royal retribution down
on Bethlehem.
    and they said, "Do you come in peace?" The Masoretic Text has "he said," but both the
Septuagint and the Qumran Samuel scroll show the plural. Both also add "O seer" to the
question of the elders.

6. *he saw Eliab.* Nothing could illustrate more vividly Samuel's persistent unreliability as
seer (*ro'eh*). Having made a fatal mistake by electing Saul, "head and shoulders taller than
all the people," convinced he was directed by God, Samuel is poised to repeat his error in
being impressed by the "appearance" and "lofty stature" of Jesse's firstborn. This whole
story is also a heightened and stylized playing out of the theme of the reversal of primogeni-
ture that dominates Genesis. Instead of an elder and a younger son, Jesse has the formulaic
seven sons, plus an eighth, the youngest of all, who will be chosen.

yes! Before the LORD stands His anointed." And the LORD said to Samuel, 7
"Look not to his appearance and to his lofty stature, for I have cast him
aside. For not as man sees does God see. For man sees with the eyes and
the LORD sees with the heart." And Jesse called Abinadab and made him 8
pass before Samuel, and he said, "This one, too, the LORD has not chosen."
And Jesse made Shammah pass by, and he said, "This one, too, the LORD 9
has not chosen." And Jesse made his seven sons pass before Samuel, and 10
Samuel said to Jesse, "The LORD has not chosen these." And Samuel said 11
to Jesse, "Are there no more lads?" And he said, "The youngest still is left,
and, look, he is tending the flock." And Samuel said to Jesse, "Send and
fetch him, for we shall not sit to eat until he comes here." And he sent and 12
brought him. And he was ruddy, with fine eyes and goodly to look on.
And the LORD said, "Arise, anoint him, for this is the one." And Samuel 13
took the horn of oil and anointed him in the midst of his brothers. And
the spirit of the LORD gripped David from that day onward. And Samuel
rose and went to Ramah.

---

7. *for I have cast him aside.* The language of rejection links the strapping Eliab with the lofty
Saul.

    does God see. These words, absent from the Masoretic Text, are supplied by the
Septuagint.

    the LORD sees with the heart. Some construe this as "into the heart." In any case, the
heart is the seat of understanding, or insight, in biblical physiology.

8–9. The verbatim repetition reflects the stylization of the episode, which is set off from
the surrounding narrative by its formal symmetries. After the first three named sons,
the rest pass by in summary by invocation of a narrative "et cetera" principle, with the
formulaic wrap-up at the end of verse 10, "the LORD has not chosen these."

11. *he is tending the flock.* By his sheer youth, he has been excluded from consideration,
as a kind of male Cinderella left to his domestic chores instead of being invited to the
party. But the tending of flocks will have a symbolic implication for the future leader of
Israel, and, in the Goliath story, it will also prove to have provided him with skills useful
in combat.

12. *he was ruddy, with fine eyes and goodly to look on.* David's good looks will play a crucial role in the magnetic effect he is to have on women and men. But he is not big, like his
brother Eliab, and Samuel has no opportunity to make a judgment on his appearance, for
David is brought from the flock sight unseen, and then God immediately informs Samuel,
"this is the one."

13. *anointed him in the midst of his brothers.* The anointment takes place within the family
circle and is a clandestine act.

14 And the spirit of the LORD had turned away from Saul, and an evil spirit
15 from the LORD had struck terror in him. And Saul's servants said to him,
16 "Look, pray, an evil spirit from God has stricken terror in you. Let our
lord, pray, speak. Your servants are before you—we shall seek out a man
skilled in playing the lyre, and so, when the evil spirit of God is upon you,
17 he will play and it will be well with you." And Saul said to his servants, "See
18 for me, pray, a man who plays well, and bring him to me." And one of the
lads answered and said, "Look, I have seen a son of Jesse the Bethlehemite,
skilled in playing, a valiant fellow, a warrior, prudent in speech, a good-
19 looking man, and the LORD is with him." And Saul sent messengers to Jesse
20 and said, "Send me David your son, who is with the flock." And Jesse took
a donkey laden with bread and a skin of wine, and a kid, and he sent them

---

14. *And the spirit of the* LORD *had turned away from Saul.* In the transfer of election of
monarchs, one gets the picture of a kind of spiritual seesaw. As the spirit of the LORD
descends on and seizes David, it departs from Saul. That vacuum is promptly filled by "an
evil spirit from the LORD." In the theopsychology of ancient Israel, extraordinary states
were explained as investments by a divine spirit. The charisma of leadership, now passed
to David, was a descent of the spirit. Saul's psychosis—evidently, fits of depression later
manifested as paranoia—is possession by another kind of spirit from the LORD.

15. *Saul's servants.* These would be his court officials or attendants.

16. *we shall seek out a man.* The Hebrew is literally "they will seek out a man."
    a man skilled in playing the lyre. In modern terms, what they have in mind is a kind of
music therapist. But David's mastery of the lyre evinces both his power over the realm of
the spirit (or of spirits) and his future association with song and poetry.

17–18. *See for me...I have seen.* The insistence on this verb picks up the key word of the preceding episode. Saul first uses it in the sense God did in verse 1, "provide."

18. *Look, I have seen a son of Jesse.* This volunteered information is a bit peculiar because,
before any real search is undertaken, one of the young men in court already has a candidate,
and from a different tribal region. Is it possible that word of David's clandestine anointment has circulated among limited groups, and that the anonymous "lad" may be a kind
of pro-David mole in the court of Saul? It is also noteworthy that, just as at the beginning
of his story, in his quest for the lost asses, Saul did not know what to do and was dependent
on the counsel of his "lad" (*na'ar*); here one of his lads (*ne'arim*) offers the needed advice
for dealing with his melancholia.
    a valiant fellow, a warrior. These details of the characterization are surprising, for all
that should be known about David is that he is a handsome shepherd boy with musical
skills. The influence of the subsequent narrative has clearly made itself felt here, and these
epithets may even be an editorial maneuver to harmonize this episode with the next one,
in which David makes his debut before Saul not as a lyre player but as a military hero.

20. *a donkey laden with bread.* The Hebrew uses what appears to be an ellipsis "a donkey
of bread."
    bread . . . a skin of wine . . . a kid. As Robert Polzin has shrewdly observed, these items

by the hand of David his son to Saul. And David came to Saul and stood in 21
his presence, and Saul loved him greatly, and he became his armor bearer.
And Saul sent to Jesse, saying, "Let him stand, pray, in my presence, for 22
he has found favor in my eyes." And so, when the spirit of God was upon 23
Saul, David would take up the lyre and play, and Saul would find relief, and
it would be well with him, and the evil spirit would turn away from him.

CHAPTER 17   And the Philistines gathered their camps for 1
battle, and they gathered at Socoh, which is in Judah, and they encamped
between Socoh and Azekah, at Ephes-Dammim. And Saul and the men 2
of Israel had gathered and encamped in the Valley of the Terebinth and
they deployed to do battle against the Philistines. The Philistines took their 3
stand on the hill on one side and Israel took its stand on the hill on the
other side, with the ravine between them. And the champion sallied forth 4

---

replicate the items that Samuel told Saul would be carried by the three men he was to
encounter (10:3). David, then, is beginning anew the process on which Saul launched.

21 *and Saul loved him greatly.* As Fokkelman has noted, Saul is the first of many people in
this narrative reported to love David—the very man he will come to think of as his bitter
enemy.

   he became his armor bearer. This is not the position proposed by Saul's courtiers. Perhaps there was no set position of court lyre player, and so Saul gives David an appointment
that will ensure his constant proximity.

22. *Let him stand . . . in my presence.* The Hebrew idiom means to be in someone's service,
though it also can suggest being presented to a dignitary, its evident meaning in verse 21.

23. *would find relief.* The Hebrew employs an untranslatable pun: the verb "would find
relief," *rawaḥ,* is a transparent cognate of *ruaḥ,* "spirit."

   the evil spirit would turn away from him. In an elegant verbal symmetry the episode that
began with the (good) spirit of the LORD turning away from Saul concludes with the evil
spirit turning away from him, thanks to David's musical mastery over the domain of spirits.

CHAPTER 17   3. *the hill on one side . . . the hill on the other . . . the ravine between
them.* As we have seen before, this positioning of the opposing armies on opposite hilltops
was a characteristic procedure of warfare in the hilly terrain of central Israel. But the
opening verses also set up the strong spatial perspective through which this episode is
organized. The perspective of the previous story was implicitly vertical: from God above to
Samuel below, in the household of Jesse in Bethlehem. Here, by contrast, is a richly elaborated horizontal deployment of troops and individuals. God is out of the picture, except
for the invocation through David's words.

4. *the champion.* The literal meaning of the Hebrew is "the man between"—that is, the
man who goes out between the opposed battle lines to fight a counterpart. That particular
Hebrew term thus reinforces the spatial definition of the story.

from the Philistine camps, Goliath was his name, from Gath, his height
5   was six cubits and a span. A bronze helmet he had on his head, and in
    armor of mail he was dressed, and the weight of the armor was five thou-
6   sand bronze shekels. And greaves of bronze were on his legs and a spear of
7   bronze between his shoulder blades. The shaft of his spear like a weaver's
    beam, and the blade of his spear six hundred iron shekels. And his shield
8   bearer went before him. And he stood and called out to the Israelite lines
    and said to them, "Why should you come forth to deploy for battle? Am I
    not the Philistine, and you are slaves to Saul? Choose you a man and let him
9   come down to me! If he prevail in battle against me and strike me down, we
    shall be slaves to you, but if I prevail and strike him down, you will be slaves
10 to us and serve us." And the Philistine said, "I am the one who has insulted
    the Israelite lines this day! Give me a man and let us do battle together!"
11 And Saul heard, and all Israel with him, these words of the Philistine, and
    they were dismayed and very frightened.

---

six cubits and a span. This would make him over eight feet tall.

5–6. *A bronze helmet . . . armor of mail . . . greaves of bronze . . . a spear of bronze.* This
"Homeric" enumeration of armor and weapons is quite untypical of the Hebrew Bible.
The thematic effect is clear: Goliath is represented as a hulking man of material military
impedimenta—everything is given gargantuan size or weight, again with untypical specification. All this will be counterposed to David's declaration on the battlefield that "not by
sword nor spear does the LORD deliver."

five thousand bronze shekels. The armor alone is about 125 pounds.

7. *his shield bearer went before him.* For this reason the shield is not included in the catalogue of Goliath's armor. The gargantuan proportions of his dependence on the material
implements of warfare are reinforced by the fact that he enters the battlefield with a man
walking before him carrying his (presumably massive) shield.

8. *Am I not the Philistine.* Most often in the body of the story he is referred to as "the Philistine" and not by the name Goliath. This has led many scholars to infer that a tradition
about Goliath was superimposed on an original story featuring an archetypal "Philistine."

9. *we shall be slaves to you.* In the event, this condition is not fulfilled: the Philistines retreat
in disarray, but will later regroup to continue their war against the Israelites.

10. *I am the one who has insulted the Israelite lines.* Nearly all the English versions render
the verb here as "defied," which is one end of the semantic range of the Hebrew *ḥeref.* But
the verb is transparently linked with the noun *ḥerpah*—insult, disgrace, shame. By his
taunting words, Goliath has laid an insult on Israel that only a victorious champion can
"take away" (see verse 26).

11. *And Saul heard . . . and they were dismayed.* Saul, as the man head and shoulders taller
than all the people, might be thought to be the one Israelite fighter who stands a chance

And David was the son of this Ephrathite man from Bethlehem in Judah 12
named Jesse, and he had eight sons, and the man in the days of Saul was
old, advanced in years. And the three oldest sons of Jesse went after Saul to 13
the war. And the names of his three sons who went to the war were Eliab
the firstborn and the second-born Abinadab and the third Shammah. As 14
for David, he was the youngest, and the three oldest had gone after Saul.
And David would go back and forth from Saul's side to tend his father's 15
flock in Bethlehem. And the Philistine came forward morning and eve- 16
ning and took his stand, forty days. And Jesse said to David his son, "Take, 17
pray, to your brothers this *ephah* of parched grain and these ten loaves of
bread and rush them to the camp to your brothers. And these ten wedges 18
of cheese you shall bring to the captain of the thousand and you shall see
if your brothers are well, and you shall take their token. And Saul and they 19
and all the men of Israel are in the Valley of the Terebinth fighting with
the Philistines." And David rose early in the morning and left the flock 20
with a keeper and bore [the provisions] and went off as Jesse had charged
him. And when he came to the staging ground, the army going out to the

---

against Goliath. Instead, he leads his own troops in fearfulness: the stage is set for his
deplacement by David.

12. *David was the son of this Ephrathite man.* The use of the demonstrative pronoun "this"
is peculiar. It seems to be the first of several attempts (presumably, by the redactor) to
harmonize this account of David's debut in Saul's court with the previous one, by referring
to Jesse as someone already mentioned. Polzin has noted that demonstrative pronouns
are unusually prominent in this whole episode: in many instances, they express contempt
("this Philistine"), but they are also sometimes necessary pointers in the emphatically
spatial organization of the story.

15. *And David would go back and forth from Saul's side.* The last phrase has a sense close
to "from Saul's presence" and is another stratagem for harmonizing the two episodes. It
invites us to suppose that David divided his time between playing the lyre for Saul and
tending his father's flocks. The implicit assumption, however, of the story that unfolds is
that David is unknown in the court of Saul, and that any to-and-fro movement between
Bethlehem and the front would be to bring provisions to his older brothers.

17. *Take, pray, to your brothers.* If Saul has organized a standing army, it seems that his quar-
termaster corps still leaves something to be desired, and whatever rations may be provided
for the troops need to be supplemented. In the same connection of skimpy provisions, Jesse
sends a gift of ten wedges of cheese to his sons' commander.

18. *take their token.* Jesse expects his sons to send back some object with David as assurance
that they are alive and well.

20. *the staging ground.* The Hebrew is literally "the circle," but the context (and a few allied
ones elsewhere in the Bible) suggests a technical military sense.

21 lines was shouting the battle cry. And Israel and the Philistines deployed
22 line against line. And David left the gear that was on him with the keeper
of the gear and he ran to the lines and came and asked his brothers if they
23 were well. As he was speaking to them, look, the champion was coming up
from the Philistine lines, Goliath the Philistine from Gath was his name,
24 and he spoke words to the same effect, and David heard. And all the men
of Israel, when they saw the man, fled from him and were very frightened.
25 And a man of Israel said, "Have you seen this man coming up? Why, to
insult Israel he comes up! And the man who strikes him down the king
will enrich with a great fortune, and his daughter he will give him, and
26 his father's household he will make free of levies in Israel." And David said
to the men who were standing with him, "What will be done for the man
who strikes down yonder Philistine and takes away insult from Israel? For

---

22. *David left the gear that was on him with the keeper.* The phrase used precisely echoes his
leaving the flock with a keeper. The narrative invokes a series of divestments by David of
impediments for which he has been made responsible—flock, provisions, and then Saul's
armor.

25. *the man who strikes him down the king will enrich . . . and his daughter he will give him.*
It is at this point that the folkloric background of the second story of David's debut becomes
particularly clear. The folktale pattern is one that is very familiar from later European
tradition: a community is threatened by a giant, ogre, or dragon that nobody can face. The
king offers great wealth, and the hand of his daughter, to the man who can slay the giant.
A young man from the provinces then appears on the scene, who in his youth and slight
stature seems quite unfit for the daunting challenge, but by wit and resourcefulness, using
unexpected means, he conquers the ogre. The appeal of this archetypal folktale no doubt
made it attractive for inclusion in the David narrative. What must be emphasized, however,
is that the folkloric materials have been historicized and even to an extent psychologized.
The slaying of the giant becomes an emblem for Israel's prevailing over the numerically
superior forces all around it as well as for the resourcefulness of its first dynastic king in
securing power. The dialogue between David and his oldest brother vividly evokes a thick
background of sibling jealousies. And David appears here—in the first scene in which he
is assigned speech in the narrative—as a poised master of rhetoric, who knows how to use
publicly enunciated words to achieve political ends.

26. *And David said . . . , "What will be done for the man."* These are David's first recorded
words in the narrative—usually, in biblical narrative convention, a defining moment of
characterization. His first words express his wanting to know what will be gained—implicitly, in political terms—by the man who defeats Goliath. The inquiry about personal profit
is then immediately balanced (or covered up) by the patriotic pronouncement "who is this
uncircumcised Philistine that he should insult the battle lines of the living God?" David has,
of course, just heard one of the troops stipulate the reward for vanquishing the Philistine,
but he wants to be perfectly sure before he makes his move, and so he asks for the details to
be repeated. One sees how the folktale has been artfully historicized, subtly drawn into the
realm of politics and individualized character.

who is this uncircumcised Philistine that he should insult the battle lines of the living God?" And the troops said to him to the same effect, "Thus 27 will be done for the man who strikes him down." And Eliab his oldest 28 brother heard when he spoke with the men, and Eliab was incensed with David and he said, "Why is it you have come down, and with whom have you left that bit of flock in the wilderness? I'm the one who knows your impudence and your wicked impulses, for it's to see the battle that you've come." And David said, "What now have I done? It was only talk." And 29,30 he turned away from him toward someone else, and he spoke to the same effect, and the troops answered him with words like the ones before. And 31 the words David had spoken were heard, and they told them to Saul, and he fetched him. And David said to Saul, "Let no man's heart fail him! Your 32 servant will go and do battle with this Philistine." And Saul said to David, 33 "You cannot go against this Philistine to do battle with him, for you are a lad and he is a man of war from his youth." And David said to Saul, "A 34 shepherd has your servant been for his father with the flock. When the lion

---

28. *that bit of flock.* Eliab prefixes a term of diminution, *meʿat,* to "flock" to express his contempt for David. The demonstrative pronoun, as elsewhere in the chapter, is also contemptuous, even as it points to the spatial distance between the battlefield and the pastureland around Bethlehem.

I'm the one who knows. The relative clause here reflects the special emphasis of the Hebrew first-person pronoun *'ani,* which ordinarily would not be used because the verb that follows it, *yadʿati,* has a first-person ending. The same structure occurs in Goliath's boasting speech in verse 10.

your wicked impulses. The literal meaning of the Hebrew is "the wickedness of your heart," the heart being in biblical language the seat of understanding and the place where plans or desires are shaped.

29. *It was only talk.* The translation follows an interpretation that goes back to the Aramaic Targum of Late Antiquity and to Rashi in the Middle Ages. But the Hebrew—literally, "Is it not a word?"—is gnomic. The ambiguity is compounded because *davar* can mean "word," "message," "matter," "thing," "mission," and more.

30. *And he turned away from him toward someone else.* Ignoring his brother's rebuke, David wants to hear the details of the reward a third time.

32. *Let no man's heart fail him.* The Septuagint has "Let not my lord's heart fail him," but this could easily be an explanatory gloss. David uses a generalizing phrase because he doesn't want to come out and say directly what all can see, that the king's heart is failing him (literally, "falling").

34. *A shepherd has your servant been.* David's carefully contrived speech proclaims his tested courage and strength but, interestingly, is silent about the shepherd's weapon—the slingshot—that he intends to use against Goliath.

35 or the bear would come and carry off a sheep from the herd, I would go out
    after him and strike him down and rescue it from his clutches. And if he
    would rise against me, I would seize his beard and strike him and kill him.
36 Both lion and bear your servant has struck down, and this uncircumcised
    Philistine will be like one of them, for he has insulted the battle lines of
37 the living God." And David said, "The LORD Who has rescued me from
    the lion and the bear will rescue me from the hand of this Philistine."
38 And Saul said to David, "Go, and may the LORD be with you." And Saul
    clothed David in his own battle garb and put a bronze helmet on his head
39 and clothed him in armor. And David girded his sword over his garments,
    but he was unable to walk, for he was unused to it, and David said to
    Saul, "I cannot walk in these, for I am unused to it." And David removed
40 them. And he took his stick in his hand and chose five smooth stones from
    the creek and put them in the shepherd's pouch he had, in the satchel, and

---

35. *from his clutches.* The Hebrew says literally, "from his mouth."

    I would seize his beard. This of course refers only to the lion, not to the bear, but this sort of focusing of the narrative report on one of its two instances is perfectly natural in biblical usage, and no emendation of the word for "beard" is called for.

37. *And David said.* This is a particularly striking instance of the biblical convention that can be schematized as: And X said to Y; (no response from Y); and X said to Y, with the intervening silence being dramatically significant. Saul is nonplussed by these extravagant claims on the part of the young shepherd from Bethlehem, and he doesn't know what to say. David, observing the skepticism of his interlocutor, now invokes God by way of explanation ("The LORD who has rescued me from the lion and the bear"). This theological argument persuades Saul. For another instance of the X said to Y, X said to Y convention, compare Goliath's boast and Israel's silence in verses 8–10.

38. *his own battle garb.* The Hebrew *madim* is not the ordinary term for "garment" but is most often used for the special garments worn either by men in battle or by priests in the cult (hence the present translation adds "battle"). The fact that this word is related etymologically to *midah*, proportion or measure, is relevant to the incident as it unfolds, since David is clothed in battle gear too big for him.

39. *he was unable to walk.* The translation, with the Septuagint, reads *wayil'e*, instead of the Masoretic *wayo'el* (a simple reversal of letters in the consonantal text), which would yield "he undertook to walk."

    I cannot walk in these, for I am unused to it. David states the obvious fact that, as a shepherd boy, he is not used to marching about in heavy armor, with a big sword. What he chooses not to mention is that since this is the armor of the hulking Saul, it is in any case far too big for him. Thematically, heroic fitness will be seen to reside in something other than being head and shoulders taller than all the people, or six cubits tall, like Goliath.

40. *he took his stick.* That is, his shepherd's staff, which he is used to carrying. David evidently does this as a decoy, encouraging Goliath to imagine he will use cudgel against sword (compare verse 43) and thus camouflaging the lethal slingshot.

his slingshot was in his hand, and he came forward toward the Philistine. And the Philistine was drawing near to David, the man bearing the shield 41 before him. And the Philistine looked and saw David, and he despised 42 him, for he was a lad, and ruddy, with good looks. And the Philistine said 43 to David, "Am I a dog that you should come to me with sticks?" And the Philistine cursed David by his gods. And the Philistine said, "Come to me, 44 that I may give your flesh to the fowl of the heavens and the beasts of the field!" And David said to the Philistine, "You come to me with sword and 45 spear and javelin, and I come to you with the name of the LORD of Armies, God of the battle lines of Israel that you have insulted. This day shall the 46 LORD give you over into my hand and I will strike you down and take off your head, and I will give your corpse and the corpses of the Philistine camp this day to the fowl of the heavens and the beasts of the earth, and all the earth shall know that Israel has a God! And all this assembly shall 47 know that not by sword nor by spear does the LORD rescue, for the LORD's is the battle and he shall give you into our hand!" And it happened as the 48 Philistine arose and was drawing near David that David hastened and ran out from the lines toward the Philistine. And he reached his hand into the 49 pouch and took from there a stone and slung it and struck the Philistine

---

40–41. *he came forward toward the Philistine . . . the Philistine was drawing near.* The spatial realization of the whole episode is nearing its climax: on the two hilltops, the opposing camps; in front of them, the battle lines; between the hostile lines, David and the Philistine "man between" approaching each other. In a moment, they will be close enough to exchange insults. Goliath will invite David to take the last few steps forward so that they can engage in hand-to-hand combat—"Come to me, that I may give your flesh to the fowl of the heavens" (verse 44). Instead of traversing this final interval of space, David will surprise his adversary by taking him down with a slung stone, accurately aimed at the exposed forehead beneath his huge bronze helmet.

45. *You come to me with sword and spear and javelin.* This short list of weapons harks back to the epic catalogue of weapons and armor that introduced Goliath to the story. David's rejoinder to the Philistine is couched in impeccable terms of standard Israelite belief: as in the Psalms, it is not sword or might that gives victory but the LORD. David speaks almost as though he expects to prevail through a miracle of divine intervention ("all the earth shall know that Israel has a God!"), but in fact his victory depends on his resourcefulness in exploiting an unconventional weapon, one which he would have learned to use skillfully as a shepherd.

46. *Your corpse and the corpses.* This is the reading of the Septuagint. The Masoretic Text lacks "your corpse."

48. *David hastened and ran out from the lines toward the Philistine.* This last gesture would encourage the Philistine to think David was rushing up for the awaited hand-to-hand combat. In fact, David is darting in close enough to get a good shot with his sling. To do this (verse 49), he will break his charge, stop, and let fly with the sling.

in his forehead, and the stone sank into his forehead and he fell on his face
50 to the ground. And David bested the Philistine with sling and stone, and
he struck down the Philistine and killed him, and no sword was in David's
51 hand. And David ran up and stood over the Philistine and took the sword
from him and pulled it out of its sheath and finished him off and cut off his
head with it. And the Philistines saw that their warrior was dead, and they
52 fled. And the men of Israel and Judah rose and shouted and gave chase to
the Philistines until you come to the ravine and until the gates of Ekron, and
the Philistine dead fell on the way to Shaaraim and as far as Gath and Ekron.
53 And the Israelites came back from pursuing the Philistines and looted their
54 camps. And David took the Philistine's head and brought it to Jerusalem,
but his weapons he put in his tent.

55 And when Saul saw David sallying forth toward the Philistine, he said to
Abner the commander, "Whose son is the lad, Abner?" And Abner said, "By

---

51. *took the sword . . . and finished him off.* The gigantic Philistine is stunned but perhaps not
dead, and so David completes his kill with the sword he takes from the prostrate Goliath.

52. *to the ravine.* The Septuagint corrects *gay'* to *Gath,* with the end of this verse in mind.
But there is a ravine between the two hills on which the armies are encamped, and what
the narrator may be saying is that the Philistines fled westward by way of the ravine to
their own territory.

54. *brought it to Jerusalem.* This notation is problematic because Jerusalem at this point
is still a Jebusite city. The report is either proleptic or simply out of place chronologically.
David's bringing the sword into his tent may also be questionable because, as someone who
has not been a member of the army, he would have no tent. Some scholars, influenced by
the fact that Goliath's sword later appears in the sanctuary at Nob, have proposed reading
here "in the tent of the LORD."

55. *Whose son is the lad, Abner?* It is at this point that the evident contradiction between
the two stories of David's debut is most striking. If David had been attending Saul in
court as his personal music therapist, with Saul having explicitly sent a communication
to Jesse regarding David's entering his service, how could he, and Abner as well, now be
ignorant of David's identity? Efforts to harmonize the two stories in terms of the logic of
later conventions of realism seem unconvincing (for example, amnesia has been proposed
as a symptom of Saul's mental illness, and Abner pretends not to recognize David in deference to the ailing king). The prevalent scholarly view that chapters 16 and 17 represent two
different traditions about David's beginnings is persuasive. (To complicate matters, most
scholars detect two different strands in chapter 17.) What we need to ask, however, is why
the redactor set these two stories in immediate sequence, despite the contradictions that
must have been as evident to him as to us. A reasonable conclusion is that for the ancient
audience, and for the redactor, these contradictions would have been inconsequential in
comparison with the advantage gained in providing a double perspective on David. In the
Greek tradition, there were competing versions of the same myths, but never in a single
text. Modern Western narrative generally insists on verisimilar consistency. In the Bible,

your life, king, I do not know." And the king said, "Ask you, pray, whose son   56
is the youth?" And when David returned from striking down the Philistine,   57
Abner took him and brought him before Saul, the Philistine's head in his
hand. And Saul said, "Whose son are you, lad?" And David said, "The son   58
of your servant Jesse the Bethlehemite."

CHAPTER 18   And it happened as he finished speaking with   1
Saul, that Jonathan's very self became bound up with David's, and Jonathan
loved him as himself. And Saul took him on that day and did not let him go   2
back to his father's house. And Jonathan, and David with him, sealed a pact   3
because he loved him like himself. And Jonathan took off the cloak that   4

---

however, the variants of a single story are sometimes placed in a kind of implicit dialogue
with one another (compare the two accounts of creation at the beginning of Genesis).
Here, in the first, vertically oriented story, with its explicit instructions from God to man,
David is emphatically elected by God, is associated with the spirit and with song, and gains
entrée in the court of Saul by using song to master the spirit. In the second story, with its
horizontal deployment in space, David makes his way into Saul's presence through martial
prowess, exhibiting shrewdness, calculation, and rhetorical skill. Interestingly, it is this
folktale version of David's debut rather than the theological one that will lead directly into
the historical (or at least, historylike) narrative of David's rise and David's reign. But the
redactor must surely have felt that both the "spiritual" and the political-military sides of
the figure of David had to be represented in the account of his origins. It is also noteworthy
that this whole episode, which launches David on his trajectory to the throne, ends with
Saul once more in a state of ignorance, compelled to ask twice about David's identity, and
getting no answer until David himself speaks out.

CHAPTER 18   1. *as he finished speaking with Saul.* The speech referred to is the
exchange between David and Saul after the vanquishing of Goliath. This is a clear instance
in which the (late medieval) chapter division actually interrupts a narrative unit.
    Jonathan loved him as himself. No reason is given, so one may infer that Jonathan was
smitten by David's personal charm and perhaps by the sheer glamour of his victory, which
exceeded even Jonathan's own military exploits. It is noteworthy that throughout this narrative David is repeatedly the object but never the subject of the verb "to love"—in this
chapter, Jonathan, the people, and Michal are all said to love David.

3. *And Jonathan, and David with him, sealed a pact.* This is one of the most significant
instances of the expressive grammatical pattern in which there is a plural subject with a
singular verb, making the first member of the plural subject the principal agent: the initiative for the pact of friendship is Jonathan's, and David goes along with it.

4. *Jonathan took off the cloak.* This gesture strongly invites comparison with Saul's failed
effort to dress David in his battle gear in the previous episode. This time David accepts
the proffered garments and weapons: practically, they are presumably his own size, but he
also is now ready to assume a regular role in the army. The first item Jonathan offers is his
cloak, *me'il*, the very piece of clothing Samuel associated symbolically with kingship. Bear-

was on him and gave it to David, and his battle garb, and even his sword
5 and his bow and his belt. And David would sally forth, wherever Saul sent
him he would succeed. And Saul set him over the men of war, and it was
6 good in the eyes of the troops and also in the eyes of Saul's servants. And it
happened when they came, when David returned from striking down the
Philistine, that the women came out from all the towns of Israel in song
and dance, to greet Saul the king with timbrels and jubilation and lutes.
7 And the celebrant women called out and said,

"Saul has struck down his thousands
and David his tens of thousands!"

8 And Saul was very incensed, and this thing was evil in his eyes, and he
said, "To David they have given tens of thousands and to me they have
9 given the thousands. The next thing he'll have is the kingship." And Saul
10 kept a suspicious eye on David from that day hence. And on the next day,
an evil spirit of God seized Saul and he went into a frenzy within the
house when David was playing as he was wont to, and the spear was in

---

ing that in mind, J. P. Fokkelman has proposed that "with his cloak Jonathan is conveying
to David the crown prince's rights and claims to the throne." Perhaps one should say that
he is conveying these subliminally or proleptically rather than as a fully conscious act.

5. *Saul set him over the men of war.* The designation for fighting men is also the one Saul uses
for Goliath. Moshe Garsiel has suggested that this may be a term for elite troops, and that
later, when Saul appoints David captain of a thousand (verse 13), he is in effect transferring
him to the position of an ordinary officer.

6. *lutes.* As is often the case with ancient musical instruments, the precise identification of
the term is in doubt. The Hebrew *shalishim* derives from *sheloshah*, "three," but it could
refer either to a three-stringed lute, which was fairly common in the ancient Near East, or
perhaps to a triangle.

8. *To David . . . tens of thousands and to me . . . the thousands.* It is a fixed rule in biblical
poetry that when a number occurs in the first verset, it must be increased in the parallel
verset, often, as here, by going up one decimal place. Saul shows himself a good reader of
biblical poetry: he understands perfectly well that the convention is a vehicle of meaning,
and that the intensification or magnification characteristic of the second verset is used to
set David's triumphs above his own. Saul, who earlier had made the mistake of listening to
the voice of the people, now is enraged by the people's words.

10. *went into a frenzy.* The verb here is the same one that refers to "speaking in ecstasy" or
"prophesying" in the episode of Saul among the prophets, but in the present context only
the connotation of raving and not that of revelation is relevant.
    when David was playing as he was wont to. The present version of the story at this point
seeks to integrate the account of David as victor over Goliath with the preceding report of

Saul's hand. And Saul cast the spear, thinking, "Let me strike through 11
David into the wall." And David eluded him twice. And Saul was afraid 12
of David, for the LORD was with him, but from Saul He had turned away.
And Saul removed him from his presence and set him as captain of a 13
thousand, and he led the troops into the fray. And David succeeded in 14
all his ways, and the LORD was with him. And Saul saw that he was very 15
successful, and he dreaded him. But all Israel and Judah loved David, for 16
he led them into the fray.

And Saul said to David, "Here is my eldest daughter, Merab. Her shall I 17
give you as wife, only be a valiant fellow for me and fight the battles of the
LORD." And Saul had thought, "Let not my hand be against him but let the

---

David as Saul's personal lyre player. Evidently, when he is not playing the lyre, he is sent out
intermittently at the head of the elite troops. After this incident, Saul removes him entirely
from the court by making him a regular commander. The one thing Saul cannot afford to
do is to dispense with David's brilliant services as a military leader. In the Hebrew, "was
playing" is literally "was playing with his hand," which sets up a neat antithesis to the spear
in Saul's hand ("with" and "in" are represented by the same particle, *b^e* in Hebrew).

11. *Let me strike through David.* Saul picks up the verb of striking from the song of the
celebrant women that so galled him.

12. *for the LORD was with him.* This emphatic refrainlike phrase recalls the Joseph story
(see especially Genesis 39), another tale of a handsome shepherd boy who ascends to regal
grandeur. Like Joseph, David is repeatedly said to "succeed" (though different verbs are
used in the two stories.) Allusions to the Joseph story will turn from this initial consonance
to ironic dissonance.

15. *Saul saw . . . and he dreaded him.* Throughout this pivotal episode, Saul's feelings and
motives remain perfectly transparent—here, through the narrator's report of his emotions,
and in the next scene, through interior monologue. At the same time, David is pointedly
left opaque. No word of his is reported when Jonathan gives him his cloak and battle gear.
We know that Saul is afraid of David but not whether David is afraid of Saul, who, after
all, has tried to kill him. And when David speaks in the next scene, it will be manifestly a
speech framed for a public occasion, which leaves his real motives uncertain.

16. *led them into the fray.* The Hebrew says literally, "was going out and coming in before
them," an idiom that means to lead in battle.

17. *Here is my eldest daughter, Merab.* Only now is the promise of the hand of the king's
daughter for the vanquisher of Goliath implemented. But the fulfillment of that promise,
as it turns out, is part of a plan to destroy David.
   Let not my hand be against him. The interior monologue leaves no doubt about Saul's
intentions. Could it be that his very transparency as a political schemer, manifested in the
means of narrative presentation, is a reflection of his incapacity in the harsh realm of politics? David, by contrast, knows how to veil his motives and intentions—a veiling replicated
in the narrative strategies used to present him.

18 hand of the Philistines be against him." And David said to Saul, "Who am
I and who are my kin, my father's clan in Israel, that I should be the king's
19 son-in-law?" And it happened at the time for giving Merab the daughter
20 of Saul to David, that she was given to Adriel the Meholathite as wife. And
Michal the daughter of Saul loved David, and they told Saul, and the thing
21 was pleasing in his eyes. And Saul thought, "I shall give her to him, that
she may be a snare to him, and that the hand of the Philistines may be
against him." And Saul said to David, "Through the second one you can
22 be my son-in-law now." And Saul charged his servants: "Speak to David
discreetly, saying, 'Look, the king desires you, and all his servants love
23 you, and now, then, become son-in-law to the king.'" And Saul's servants
spoke these words in David's hearing and David said, "Is it a light thing
in your eyes to become son-in-law to the king, and I am a poor man, and
24 lightly esteemed?" And Saul's servants told him, saying, "Words of this sort
25 David has spoken." And Saul said, "Thus shall you say to David: 'The king

---

18. *Who am I and who are my kin.* The translation adopts a scholarly proposal of considerable currency to revocalize the Masoretic *ḥayai*, "my life" as *ḥayi*, "my kin," a conjectured
term based on the Arabic. David's protestation of unworthiness recalls Saul's when Samuel
hinted he was going to confer the kingship on him. Perhaps these words are dictated by
court etiquette, the commoner obliged to profess unworthiness when offered the honor of
a royal connection. Perhaps the young David may actually feel unworthy of the honor. But
it is also clearly in his interest to conceal from the jealous king any desire he may harbor to
marry the king's daughter, for such an alliance could be converted into an implicit claim
to be successor to the throne.

20. *And Michal the daughter of Saul loved David.* Not only is she the third party in this
chapter said to love David, but she is also the only woman in the entire Hebrew Bible explicitly reported to love a man. Nothing is said, by contrast, about what David feels toward
Michal, and as the story of their relationship sinuously unfolds, his feelings toward her will
continue to be left in question.

21. *Through the second one.* The Hebrew is quite cryptic, and the text might be defective
here. Literally, it says, "through two" (*bishtayim*). This has variously been interpreted to
mean: through two daughters (if not one, then the other); through two conditions (vanquishing the Philistines and bringing back their foreskins?); for two reasons (perhaps, "the
king desires you" and "all his servants love you").

22. *discreetly.* The root of the Hebrew adverb refers to covering up, but the usual translation of "secretly" is misleading. This is not a clandestine communication but one in which
the servants—that is, Saul's court attendants—must be careful to cover up their master's
real intentions.

24. *Words of this sort David has spoken.* Saul may well have counted on the fact that David
would initially demur, perhaps because he was the youngest son of eight and thus lacked a
suitable bride-price for a princess. This refusal would then set the stage for Saul's extravagant proposal, which he assumed would be a fatal one, of a hundred dead Philistines.

has no desire for any bride-price except a hundred Philistine foreskins, to take vengeance against the king's enemies.'" And Saul had devised to make David fall by the hand of the Philistines. And Saul's servants told these 26 words to David, and the thing was pleasing in David's eyes, to become son-in-law to the king. And the time was not done, when David arose and went, 27 he and his men, and he struck down among the Philistines two hundred men, and David brought their foreskins and made a full count to the king, to become son-in-law to the king, and Saul gave him Michal his daughter as wife. And Saul saw and marked that the LORD was with David, and 28 Michal the daughter of Saul loved him. And Saul was all the more afraid 29 of David, and Saul became David's constant enemy. And the Philistine 30 captains sallied forth, and whenever they sallied forth, David succeeded more than all Saul's servants, and his name became greatly esteemed.

---

25. *The king has no desire for any bride-price except a hundred Philistine foreskins.* The language Saul directs to David through his attendants—note that he now has begun to communicate with David only through intermediaries—makes it sound as though this were a small thing instead of an enormous thing. Beyond this story, there is no indication that the Israelites had a custom of collecting the foreskins of the uncircumcised Philistines like scalps. Fokkelman shrewdly notes that the foreskins are associated with (impure) sexuality and conjectures that "by this condition Saul really wants to contaminate David"—just as Saul is using his own daughter's sexuality as a lure to destroy David. "He thinks," Fokkelman goes on to observe, "that this rival has outdone him amongst the women and now uses woman as a trap."

Saul had devised to make David fall. The narrator continues his systematic effort to make Saul's intentions transparent.

26. *And the time was not done.* Literally, "the days were not filled." The presumable reference is to a period fixed by Saul during which David was to go out and bring back the grisly trophies. Garsiel has interestingly proposed that the idiom here deliberately echoes a phrase used in the Jacob story (Genesis 29:21) and signals a whole network of allusions to the Jacob narrative: in both stories the young man is a candidate to marry two sisters and gets the one not at first intended; in both stories he must provide a bride-price he cannot pay for from material resources; in both stories he must "count out" (literally "fill") payment to a devious father-in-law; eventually each man flees his father-in-law, aided and abetted by his wife; and in each instance, as we shall see, household idols (*teraphim*) are involved. Later in the David story, other kinds of parallels with Jacob will be invoked.

28–30. These verses constitute a formal concluding frame to the whole episode, much like the concluding verses in Genesis 39, which mirror the opening ones. Once again, in a pointed repetition of phrases, the following is brought to our attention: David's success, the fact that the LORD is with him, Saul's fear of David, Michal's love of David, and David's great reputation. The concluding words of the chapter, "his name became greatly esteemed," are a pointed antithesis to his protestation of unworthiness, "I am a poor man, and lightly esteemed."

1 CHAPTER 19   And Saul spoke to Jonathan his son and to all his servants to put David to death, but Jonathan the son of Saul was very
2 fond of David, and Jonathan told David, saying, "Saul my father seeks to put you to death, and so now, be on the watch, pray, in the morning, and
3 stay in a secret place and hide. And I on my part shall come out and stand by my father in the field where you are, and I shall speak of you to my
4 father. And if I see something, I shall tell you." And Jonathan spoke well of David to Saul his father and said to him, "Let not the king offend against his servant David, for he has not offended you, and his deeds have been
5 very good toward you. He took his life in his hands and struck down the Philistine, and the LORD made a great victory for all Israel. You saw and rejoiced, and why should you offend with innocent blood to put David to
6 death for no cause?" And Saul heeded Jonathan's voice, and Saul swore, "As
7 the LORD lives, he shall not be put to death." And Jonathan called to David, and Jonathan told him all these things. And Jonathan brought David to Saul, and he served him as in times gone by.

8 And there was still more fighting, and David sallied forth and did battle with the Philistines and struck a great blow against them, and they fled
9 before him. And an evil spirit of the LORD came upon Saul as he was sit-
10 ting in his house, his spear in his hand and David playing. And Saul sought

---

CHAPTER 19   1–2. *Jonathan his son . . . Jonathan the son of Saul.* In keeping with the biblical practice of using relational epithets to underscore a thematic point, Jonathan is identified as Saul's son at the very moment when he takes David's part against his father.

4. *Let not the king offend.* Saul's royal power is palpable in the dialogue, for his own son is careful to address him by title in the deferential third person.

6. *Saul heeded Jonathan's voice, and . . . swore.* Saul's paranoia and uncontrolled outbursts manifest themselves in an intermittent cycle. He is amenable to the voice of reason and conscience, and vows in presumably good faith not to harm David, but further evidence of David's military brilliance will unleash another round of violent impulses. In consequence, through this sequence of the narrative David oscillates between being a proscribed person and someone Saul expects to be a faithful member of his court.

9. *his spear in his hand and David playing.* As in the previous incident of the spear cast at David, the Hebrew exhibits the pointed antithesis of "his spear in his hand [*beyado*]" and David "playing by hand [*beyad*]." Conventional biblical scholarship explains the repetition of incident, and the other doublets in this narrative, as an inclusion of two versions of the same event from different sources. It is at least as plausible to assume that the author of the Saul and David narrative had a fondness for paired incidents that could be used to good literary effect. Saul's mental disturbance involves compulsive repetition. He does his best to be reconciled with David, his soothing lyre player and indispensable military leader, but the recurrent flashes of jealousy drive him again to the same lethal action. After the

to strike the spear through David into the wall, but he slipped away from Saul, and Saul struck the spear into the wall. Then David fled and escaped on that night. And Saul sent messengers to David's house to keep watch 11 over him and to put him to death in the morning. And Michal his wife told David, saying, "If you do not get yourself away tonight, tomorrow you'll be dead." And Michal let David down from the window, and he went off and 12 fled and got away. And Michal took the household gods and put them in the 13 bed, and the twist of goat's hair she put at its head, and covered them with a cloth. And Saul sent messengers to take David, and she said, "He is ill." 14 And Saul sent messengers to see David, saying, "Bring him up to me in the 15 bed, that he may be put to death." And the messengers came, and, look, the 16 household gods were in the bed and the twist of goat's hair at its head! And 17

---

second occurrence of spear throwing, David realizes he must flee the court, but he does not imagine that Saul will send assassins to surround his house.

10. *Saul struck ... David fled.* As several interpreters have noted, these are the very two verbs used in verse 8 to report David's military triumph over the Philistines: as David battles Israel's enemies, the distraught king battles David.

11. *Michal his wife.* This is another pointed familial identification. Previously, she was referred to as Saul's daughter.

If you do not get yourself away tonight, tomorrow you'll be dead. It is striking that we are given Michal's urgent dialogue here but not a word of response from David, only the chain of his rapid actions after she lets him down (by an improvised rope?) from the window— "he went off and fled and got away." Perhaps this asymmetrical presentation of the two characters is meant to suggest David's breathless flight, with no time for conversation. In any case, it continues the pattern of occluding David's inner responses that we observed in chapter 18. Michal is risking a great deal in order to save David. We have no idea about his feelings toward her as she does this.

13. *Michal took the household gods ... and the twist of goat's hair ... and covered them with a cloth.* She adopts the familiar trick used by prisoners round the world of concocting a dummy to mask an escape. But the means she chooses introduce another elaborate allusion to the Jacob story. The household gods (*teraphim*) are what Rachel stole and hid from her father when Jacob fled from him. Like Rachel, who pleads her period and does not get up from the cushions under which the *teraphim* are hidden, Michal also invokes illness (verse 14) to put off the searchers. Both stories feature a daughter loyal to her husband and rebel-ling against a hostile father. Michal puts goat's hair at the head of the bed because, being black or dark brown, it would look like a man's hair, but goats (and the color of their hair) are also prominent in the Jacob story. Finally, the cloth or garment (*beged*) used to cover the dummy recalls the repeated association of garments with deception in the Jacob story. Laban, of course, never finds his *teraphim*, whereas Saul's emissaries, to their chagrin, find the *teraphim* instead of the man they are looking for.

15. *Bring him up to me in the bed.* If Michal claims David is ill, Saul will have him brought up bed and all.

Saul said to Michal, "Why have you thus deceived me, and let my enemy go, and he got away?" And Michal said to Saul, "He said to me: 'Let me go. Why should I kill you?'"

18 And David had fled and gotten away and had come to Samuel at Ramah and told him all that Saul had done to him. And he, and Samuel with him,
19 went and stayed at Naioth. And it was told to Saul, saying, "Look, David
20 is at Naioth in Ramah." And Saul sent messengers to take David, and they saw a band of prophets in ecstasy with Samuel standing poised over them, and the spirit of God came upon Saul's messengers and they, too, went into
21 ecstasy. And they told Saul, and he sent other messengers, and they, too, went into ecstasy. And Saul still again sent a third set of messengers, and
22 they, too, went into ecstasy. And he himself went to Ramah, and he came as far as the great cistern which is in Secu, and he asked and said, "Where are
23 Samuel and David?" And someone said, "Here, at Naioth in Ramah." And he went there, to Naioth in Ramah, and the spirit of God came upon him, too, and he walked along speaking in ecstasy until he came to Naioth in
24 Ramah. And he, too, stripped off his clothes, and he, too, went into ecstasy

---

17. *Why have you thus deceived me.* These words are close to the ones spoken by the outraged Laban to Jacob (Genesis 31:26).

Why should I kill you? This purported death threat by David is of course pure invention by Michal in order to make it seem that she was forced to help David flee.

18. *David had fled and gotten away and had come to Samuel.* The twice-repeated verbs of safe flight are reiterated once more. David takes refuge with the man who anointed him, although it is not entirely clear whether the prophet's authority will really protect him, or the prophet.

Naioth. Some have claimed this is not a place-name but a common noun, *nawot*, "oases" (according to one suggestion, a collection of huts where the prophets resided). But then one would expect a definite article, which does not occur. Naioth is most plausibly construed as a little village or place of temporary residence in the vicinity of the town of Ramah.

20. *Samuel standing poised over them.* The image is implicitly military: the term for "poised" (*nitsav*) is cognate with the terms for garrison and prefect. Samuel, like the pope, commands no divisions, but the band of ecstatics are his troops, and the infectious spirit of God that inhabits them and devastates Saul's emissaries acts as a defensive perimeter.

22. *And he himself went.* Again, we have the folktale symmetry of three identical repetitions, then a fourth repetition with a crucial change.

Where are Samuel and David? Once more, Saul (*Sha'ul*) has to ask (*sha'al*). This particular question recalls his initial question in chapter 9 about where the seer was.

24. *he . . . stripped off his clothes . . . and lay naked.* In the clash between Saul and Samuel that marked their final estrangement, Samuel had explicitly associated garment with

before Samuel and lay naked all that day and all that night. Therefore do they say, "Is Saul, too, among the prophets?"

CHAPTER 20   And David fled from Naioth in Ramah and   1
came and said before Jonathan: "What have I done? What is my crime
and what my offense before your father that he should seek my life?" And   2
he said to him, "Heaven forbid! You shall not die! Look, my father will do
nothing, whether great or small, without revealing it to me, and why should

---

kingship. Now the frenzy that seizes Saul drives him to strip off his garments—implicitly, to divest himself of the kingship, just as the first episode of Saul among the prophets was an investment with kingship. Robert Polzin brilliantly links this moment with Michal's use of a garment and the contrasting narrative presentations of David and Saul: "Whereas Michal covers David's bed with his clothes (verse 13) Saul strips off his clothes and lies naked all day and night (verse 24)—a graphic picture of how the narrator hides David and bares Saul throughout the last two chapters."

Therefore do they say, "Is Saul, too, among the prophets?" This is the same etiological tag as at the end of the first story of Saul among the prophets in chapter 10. The doublet, far from being a stammer of transmission or inept or automatically inclusive redaction, is vividly purposeful, providing a strong frame for Saul's painful story. Fokkelman states the effect nicely: "The same faculty for the numinous and the same sensitivity for suddenly being lifted into a higher state of consciousness which occurred there [in chapter 10] under the positive sign of election, appear here under the negative sign of being rejected, and now bring Saul into a lower state of consciousness, a kind of delirium." The conventions of verisimilitude of a later literary tradition would lead one to conclude that this encounter would have to have occurred either at the beginning of Saul's career or at the end, but not twice. To the ancient audience, however, the recurrence would not have seemed a contradiction, and the conflicting valences given to the explanation of the proverbial saying add to the richness of the portrait of Saul, formally framing it at beginning and end.

CHAPTER 20   1. *David . . . said before Jonathan.* The seeming awkwardness of the preposition is actually strategically calculated. The normal usage would be "said *to*" (*'el*). "Before" (*lifney*) is a preposition that commonly designates approach to the presence of regal or seigniorial authority. (Compare its occurrence in David's words, "what my offense *before* your father.") This speech is a remarkable instance of the pattern of occluding the personal side of David that we have been following. Quite strikingly, these are David's first reported words to Jonathan, though Jonathan's devotion to David and one speech to David (19:2–3) have been duly recorded. It is noteworthy that this is not a personal communication to Jonathan but a kind of political statement—a protestation of innocence cast in patently rhetorical language ("What have I done? What is my crime . . . ?"). David speaks to Jonathan less as an intimate friend than as a courtier, later in the dialogue even invoking the deferential self-reference of "your servant."

2. *why should my father hide this thing from me?* If one considers Saul's previous behavior and his relationship with Jonathan, this faith in his father's openness with him seems

3 my father hide this thing from me? It cannot be!" And David swore again
and said, "Your father surely knows that I have found favor in your eyes,
and he will think, 'Let not Jonathan know this, lest he be pained.' And
indeed, as the LORD lives and as you live, there is but a step between me
4 and death." And Jonathan said, "Whatever you desire, I shall do for you."
5 And David said to Jonathan, "Look, it is the new moon tomorrow, and I
am supposed to sit with the king to eat. Let me go and I shall hide in the
6 field till the evening of the day after tomorrow. Should your father in fact
mark my absence, you shall say, 'David has urgently asked of me that he
run to Bethlehem his town, for the seasonal sacrifice is to take place there
7 for the whole clan.' If thus he says, 'Good!,' it is well with your servant.
But if in fact he is incensed, know that the evil has been resolved by him.
8 And you shall keep faith with your servant, for into a pact of the LORD you
have brought your servant with you. And if there be any crime in me, put
9 me to death yourself, for why should you bring me to your father?" And

---

singularly misplaced. Throughout, Jonathan remains well meaning and naïve, against the
wary, calculating David.

3. *David swore again.* It is ill advised to emend the verb here, as some scholars have proposed. In fact, David's first speech ("before" Jonathan) was a kind of oath of innocence,
and now he continues to swear, rather than simply speaking.

    there is but a step between me and death. This vivid image surely is meant to recall the
quick dodging step that twice enabled David to elude Saul's hurled spear.

5. *the new moon.* In early biblical times, this was an important festival. Sacrifices were
offered, ceremonial feasts were held, and ordinary business was not transacted.

    the day after tomorrow. The Masoretic Text has "the third evening," treating *hashelishit*
as an adjective modifying "evening," although it has the wrong gender suffix. It is more
likely a noun meaning the day after tomorrow (the day on which one speaks being day one
in the sequence of three). One should then read *'erev hashelishit* instead of the Masoretic
ha 'erev hashelishit. In any case, the number three will play an important role as the episode develops.

7. *If thus he says, "Good!," it is well with your servant.* After Saul's attempts on David's life by
the "hand of the Philistines," by the spear in his own hand, and by a team of assassins, can
David really believe that any statement by the king of favorable disposition means it will
be well with him? Polzin has shrewdly suggested that David's real intention is "to provoke
Saul to an angry outburst that would remove Jonathan's misconceptions, not his own."

8. *faith.* The two parties to a pact, contract, or other binding agreement owe each other
hesed, faithful performance of their covenantal obligations.

    into a pact of the LORD you have brought your servant with you. David's formulation of
the arrangement is pointed and quite accurate: it was Jonathan who initiated the pledge of
mutual fealty out of his love for David, and who drew David into the commitment.

Jonathan said, "Heaven forbid you say it! If in fact I learn that the evil has
been resolved by my father, would I not tell it to you?" And David said to 10
Jonathan, "Who will tell me if your father answers you harshly?" And Jona- 11
than said, "Come, let us go out to the field." And the two of them went out
to the field. And Jonathan said to David, "Witness the LORD God of Israel, 12
that I will sound out my father at this hour tomorrow, [or] the day after, and
whether he is well disposed to David or not, I will send to you and reveal to
you. Thus may the LORD do to Jonathan, and even more, if it seems good to 13
my father [to bring] the evil upon you, I will reveal it to you and I will send
you off and you shall go safely and the LORD shall be with you as He was
with my father. Would that while I am still alive you may keep the LORD's 14
faith with me, that I not die, and that you do not cut off your faithfulness 15
from my house for all time, not even when the LORD cuts off all David's
enemies from the face of the earth. For Jonathan has sealed a pact with the 16
house of David and the LORD shall requite it from the hand of David." And 17

---

9. *Heaven forbid you say it.* The Hebrew has, elliptically, "Heaven forbid you."

10. *Who will tell me.* David is not questioning Jonathan's good faith but registering a practical difficulty: if Saul is in fact determined to kill him, how will Jonathan be able to get
word to him?

12. *Witness the LORD.* The word "witness" (*'ed*) is absent in the Masoretic Text but is
reflected in Josephus and the Peshitta.
   tomorrow, [or] the day after. Again, the time reference in the Hebrew is somewhat confusing. The text reads literally "tomorrow the third day" or even "the morrow of the third day."

13. *if it seems good to my father [to bring] the evil.* The ironic antithesis of good and evil is
patent. All ancient versions lack "to bring," which seems required by the context. The word
may have been inadvertently deleted by a scribe because it closely resembles the preceding
word in the text—*'avi* (my father), *lehavi'* (to bring).
   the LORD shall be with you as He was with my father. Here Jonathan explicitly recognizes
that the persecuted David is to displace Saul, his father.

14. *Would that.* This translation treats the Hebrew consonants as *welu* instead of the Masoretic *welo'* ("and not").

16. *Jonathan has sealed a pact.* The Hebrew idiom is literally "cut" (with "pact" implied)
and so picks up the play of the two different occurrences of "cut off" in the previous sentence (the same verb in a different conjugation). Jonathan's insistence that David not cut
off Jonathan's descendants once he gains power will have prominent ramifications later
in the story.
   requite it from the hand of David. The Masoretic Text has "from the hand of the enemies
of David," but the substitution of a person's "enemies" for the person himself is a common
Hebrew scribal euphemism (here, so as not to say something negative about David), as both
Rashi and David Kimchi recognized in the Middle Ages.

Jonathan once again swore to David in his love for him, for he loved him as
18 he loved himself. And Jonathan said to him, "Tomorrow is the new moon,
19 and your absence will be marked because your place will be vacant. The day
after tomorrow you will go all the way down and come to the place where
20 you hid on the day of the deed and stay by the Ezel stone. As for me, I shall
shoot three arrows to the side of it, as though I were aiming at a target.
21 And look, I shall send the lad, 'Go, find the arrows!' If I expressly say to the
lad, 'Look, the arrows are on this side of you, fetch them,' come, for it will
22 be well with you, and nothing will be the matter, as the LORD lives. But if
thus I say to the youth, 'Look, the arrows are on the far side of you,' go, for
23 the LORD will have sent you away. And as for the matter of which you and
I have spoken, look, the LORD is witness between you and me for all time."

24 And David hid in the field, and it was the new moon, and the king sat down
25 to table to eat. And the king sat in his place as he was wont to do, in the
seat by the wall, and Jonathan preceded him, and Abner sat by Saul's side,
26 and David's place was vacant. And Saul spoke no word on that day, for he
27 thought, "It is a mischance. He is unclean and has not been cleansed." And
it happened on the day after the new moon, the second day, that David's
place was still vacant. And Saul said to Jonathan his son, "Why has not the
28 son of Jesse come to the feast either yesterday or today?" And Jonathan

---

19. *The day after tomorrow.* The Masoretic vocalization *weshilashta* treats this as a verb (to do something a third time or in a third instance), but it is more plausible to vocalize it as a noun, *ushelishit,* "and on the third day." (See the second comment on verse 5.)

    you will go all the way down. The Hebrew, literally "you will go down very much" (or, "you will wander very much"), is problematic.

    the place where you hid on the day of the deed. The meaning has been disputed, but the most likely reference is to David's hiding, and Jonathan's speaking in his defense, in 19:1–7.

23. *the LORD is witness.* Again, "witness" is absent from the Masoretic Text but supplied by the Septuagint.

24. *to table.* The Hebrew is literally "to the bread."

25. *Jonathan preceded him.* This translation reads *weyiqdam* instead of the Masoretic *way-aqom* ("and he rose"). The seating arrangement remains a little obscure, but the verb *qadam* cannot mean "to sit opposite," as some scholars have claimed.

26. *He is unclean.* Since on the new moon celebrants partook of a sacrificial feast, they would have to be in a state of ritual purity. (A seminal emission, for example, which might be hinted at in the Hebrew term for "mischance," would render a person impure until the evening of the day on which he cleansed himself by ablution.)

27. *the son of Jesse.* At the end of the Goliath episode, Saul wanted to know whose son David was. Now he refers to him repeatedly only by patronymic, which is dismissive, rather like

said to Saul, "David has urgently asked of me to go to Bethlehem. And he 29
said to me, 'Let me go, pray, for we have a clan sacrifice in the town, and
my brother has summoned me to it. And so, if I have found favor in your
eyes, let me, pray, get away that I may see my brothers.' Therefore has he
not come to the king's table." And Saul was incensed with Jonathan and 30
he said to him, "O, son of a perverse wayward woman! Don't I know you
have chosen the son of Jesse to your own shame and the shame of your
mother's nakedness? For as long as the son of Jesse lives on the earth, you 31
and your kingship will not be unshaken! And now, send and fetch him
to me, for he is a dead man!" And Jonathan answered Saul his father and 32
said to him, "Why should he be put to death? What has he done?" And 33
Saul cast the spear at him to strike him down, and Jonathan knew that it

---

our using a person's last name only. David's status in Saul's eyes is a constant reflex of
Saul's acute ambivalence: the king wants him at court as a royal intimate, or, alternately, as
someone under surveillance; yet he makes him flee the court as persona non grata.

29. *my brother has summoned me.* Jonathan, in playing out the scenario David has dictated to him, improvises one element—that David has gone off to his hometown at the
express urging of his brother, and in order to be with his brothers. His evident intention
is to provide a palliative to David's absence: he had to go to Bethlehem because of family
pressure. But Saul's outraged response suggests that Jonathan's invention has the opposite
effect. Saul concludes that David's loyalty to his clan takes precedence over his loyalty
to his king, and he may even suspect that David means to use his clan as a power base to
challenge the throne.

    let me . . . get away. Jonathan inadvertently substitutes for "run" in David's instructions
the very verb of escape repeatedly used when David fled Saul's assassins.

30. *O, son of a perverse wayward woman.* All English translations have treated the last
Hebrew term here, *mardut*, as "rebellion," deriving it from the root *m-r-d*, "to rebel." But
this form (with the *ut* suffix of abstraction) would be anomalous in the Hebrew, whereas the
vocalization in the received text yields a Hebrew word well known in rabbinic Hebrew and
meaning "discipline." (The verbal root is *r-d-h*, "to rule sternly.") She is "perverse against
discipline"—hence "wayward" in this translation.

    the shame of your mother's nakedness. This is quite violent. "Nakedness" refers to the
sexual part (as in the idiom for taboo intercourse, "uncovering the nakedness of"), and
so, it has virtually the force of "your mother's cunt," though the language is not obscene.

31. *he is a dead man.* The Hebrew is literally "son of death," thus playing back on "son of
Jesse."

32. *Why should he be put to death? What has he done?* These two questions are four compact
words in the Hebrew.

33. *Saul cast the spear at him to strike him down.* Saul's madness is vividly reflected in his
attempt to kill his own son in the same way that he tried to kill David—just after he has been
urging Jonathan to protect the security of his own future kingship. The act thus expresses
his blind destructive impulse toward his own dynasty.

34 was resolved by his father to put David to death. And Jonathan rose from
    the table in burning anger, and he ate no food on the second day of the
    new moon because he was pained for David and because his father had
    humiliated him.

35 And it happened in the morning that Jonathan went out to the field for the
36 fixed meeting with David, and a young lad was with him. And he said to
    his lad, "Run, find, pray, the arrows that I shoot." The lad ran, and he shot
37 the arrow beyond him. And the lad came to the place of the arrow that
    Jonathan had shot, and Jonathan called after the lad and said, "Look, the
38 arrow is on the far side of you." And Jonathan called after the lad, "Quick,
    hurry, don't stand still!" And Jonathan's lad gathered up the arrows and
39 came to his master. And the lad knew nothing, but Jonathan and David
40 knew the matter. And Jonathan gave his gear to his lad and said to him, "Go,
41 bring them to town." Just as the lad came, David arose from by the mound
    and fell on his face to the ground and bowed three times, and each man
    kissed the other and each wept for the other, though David the longer.

---

34. *because he was pained for David and because his father had humiliated him.* The Hebrew
text does not have "and" but it is clearly implied.

35. *And it happened in the morning.* On the third day there are three figures in the field and
three arrows will be shot. The triangle of two knowing persons and one ignorant one is an
ironic replication of the David–Jonathan–Saul triangle. The lad's running after the arrows
may also pick up David's (fictitious) "running" to Bethlehem.

36. *the arrow.* Some scholars, bothered by the switch from three arrows to one, have
emended the text to reduce all plurals of arrow to a singular. The maneuver is misconceived because, as we have seen before, Hebrew narrative readily switches from multiple
instances to a particular case.

37. *Jonathan called after the lad.* Again, the use of the preposition is quite precise because
the lad has run on ahead of Jonathan.

38. *gathered up the arrows.* The Masoretic Text has "arrow" in the singular at this point,
but the verb "to gather up" (*laqet*) accords much better with collecting several objects, and
Jonathan's having shot all three of the arrows earlier mentioned would require more time
on the part of the lad and hence would give Jonathan and David more of an opportunity
to talk in confidence.

40. *Jonathan gave his gear to his lad.* Fokkelman reminds us that Jonathan earlier gave his
armor and weapons to David, and now "the successor to the throne indicated by Saul . . .
devotes himself defenselessly to the intimate contact with the man who, according to his
father, is his rival."

41. *arose from by the mound.* This follows the Septuagint. The Masoretic Text has "arose
from the south."

And Jonathan said to David, "Go in peace, for the two of us have sworn in   42
the name of the LORD, saying, 'The LORD is witness between me and you,
and between my seed and your seed, for all time.'" And Jonathan arose   21:1
and came to the town.

CHAPTER 21   And David came to Nob, to Ahimelech the   2
priest, and Ahimelech trembled to meet David and said to him, "Why are
you alone and no one is with you?" And David said to Ahimelech the priest,   3
"The king has charged me with a mission, and said to me, 'Let no one know
a thing of the mission on which I send you and with which I charge you.'
And the lads I have directed to such-and-such a place. And now, what do   4
you have at hand, five loaves of bread? Give them to me, or whatever there
is." And the priest answered David and said, "I have no common bread at   5
hand, solely consecrated bread, if only the lads have kept themselves from
women." And David answered the priest and said to him, "Why, women   6
were taboo to us as in times gone by when I sallied forth, and the lads'

---

42. *The LORD is witness.* As in the previous occurrences in Samuel of this formula of vow
taking, the Masoretic Text lacks "witness," but that word is reflected in the Septuagint.
It may well be an idiomatic ellipsis in the original Hebrew version, but the problem with
leaving it that way in the English is that it could sound as though Jonathan were saying that
the LORD will intervene between him and David ("the LORD will be between me and you").
Polzin contends that the double meaning is intended, but that reading seems a little strained.

CHAPTER 21   2. *Nob.* This is the very beginning of David's flight after the exchange
with Jonathan in the field, and Nob is less than three miles south of Gibeah, his approximate point of departure.
    Why are you alone and no one is with you? The doubling of the question (in a pat-
tern that is reminiscent of the parallelism of verse) reflects Ahimelech's astonishment: a
prominent commander in Saul's army would not ordinarily go about without his retinue.
From his first sight of David, Ahimelech suspects that he may be a fugitive, which is why
he "trembles" to meet him—fear of the powerful king's retribution stalks the land.

4. *five loaves of bread.* The number five is sometimes used idiomatically in biblical Hebrew
to mean "a few."

5. *if only the lads have kept themselves from women.* Ordinarily, consecrated bread would
be eaten only by the priests. Ahimelech is willing to stretch the point if David's "lads"—his
fighting men—are not in a state of ritual impurity through sexual intercourse.

6. *women were taboo to us.* This is the second reference in this narrative to a general practice
of refraining from sexual activity during periods of combat.
    the lads' gear was consecrated. The term for "gear," the all-purpose *kelim*, could equally
refer to weapons, clothing, and vessels for containing food. There are no grounds for
restricting the meaning here to the last of these three items, as some interpreters have done.

gear was consecrated, even if it was a common journey, and how much
7 more so now the gear should be consecrated." And the priest gave him
what was consecrated, for there was no bread there except the Bread of
the Presence that had been removed from before the LORD to be replaced
8 with warm bread when it was taken away. And there a man of Saul's
servants that day was detained before the LORD, and his name was Doeg
9 the Edomite, chief of the herdsmen who were Saul's. And David said to
Ahimelech, "Don't you have here at hand a spear or a sword? For neither
my sword nor my gear have I taken with me, for the king's mission was
10 urgent." And the priest said, "The sword of Goliath the Philistine whom
you struck down in the Valley of the Terebinth, here it is, wrapped in a
cloak behind the ephod. If this you would take for yourself, take it, for
there is none other but it hereabouts." And David said, "There's none like
it. Give it to me."

---

7. *the Bread of the Presence.* This would be twelve loaves laid out in display on a table in
the sanctuary. When they were replaced with fresh loaves, the old loaves could be eaten
by the priests. Robert Polzin proposes a link between the eating of forbidden food here
and in the story of Jonathan and the honey. Death will ensue, although not for the eater.

8. *And there a man of Saul's servants.* This seemingly intrusive notation is a piece of ominous foreshadowing. For the moment, all we can pick up is a certain dissonance in the
presence of a foreigner in the sanctuary and the nearness of a high official of Saul's to the
fugitive David. The ghastly consequences of David's visit to Nob (chapter 22) will pivot on
Doeg's fatal presence. His identity as Edomite reflects the enlistment of foreign mercenaries in the new royal bureaucracy. It also marks him as a man who will have no inhibitions
in what he does to Israelites, even Israelite priests.
     detained before the LORD. The verb is derived from the same root ('-ts-r) as the one used
for "taboo" in verse 6, but it is unclear whether the reference is to being detained at the
sanctuary for some unspecified reason or being detained from participation in the cult.

9. *For neither my sword nor my gear have I taken.* David, of course, has fled weaponless from
his encounter with Jonathan in the field. Now he uses the supposed urgency of his royal
mission to explain his lack of arms and to ask for a weapon.

10. *If this you would take for yourself, take it, for there is none other but it hereabouts.* The last
exchange between Ahimelech and David is a vivid instance of the biblical use of contrastive
dialogue. The priest's language is a wordy hesitation dance of repetitions and synonymous
expressions. David responds with the most imperative succinctness (just four words in the
Hebrew): "There's none like it. Give it to me." The fact that this huge sword might be too
big for David is submerged by the symbolic notion that it is the weapon of the Philistine
champion he vanquished which he now takes up. In any case, David is no longer a raw
shepherd lad but a battle-hardened warrior.

And David rose on that day and fled from Saul and he came to Achish king   11
of Gath. And the servants of Achish said to him, "Is not this David king of   12
the land? Is it not he for whom they call out in dance, saying,

> 'Saul has struck down his thousands
> and David his tens of thousands.' "

And David took these words to heart, and he was very afraid of Achish   13
king of Gath. And he altered his good sense in their eyes and played   14
the lunatic before them, and he scrabbled on the doors of the gate and
drooled onto his beard. And Achish said to his servants, "Look, do you   15
see this man is raving mad! Why would you bring him to me? Do I lack   16
madmen that you should bring this one to rave for me? Should this one
come into my house?"

---

11. *he came to Achish king of Gath.* David flees to the southwest to the one place where he
imagines he will be safe from Saul's pursuit—enemy territory. Such a crossing over to the
enemy is a familiar enough move on the part of political refugees. Gath was the hometown
of Goliath, and so one must assume that David planned to enter the city incognito, as an
anonymous Hebrew fugitive. He would clearly have had to hide the telltale sword before
coming into town.

12. *David king of the land.* The Philistine courtiers, unfortunately, immediately identify
David and can even quote the song sung by the Israelite women after his victories. Their
characterization of him as "king of the land" is no doubt a tribute to his preeminence on
the battlefield but also is an inadvertent confirmation of his clandestine election, of his
displacing Saul. Appropriately, though, as J. P. Fokkelman notes, they use a somewhat
vague designation instead of the more official "king of Israel."

13. *he was very afraid of Achish.* He has come unarmed and, evidently, alone, and now he
realizes he has been recognized.

16. *Do I lack madmen that you should bring this one to rave for me?* Achish's words are a
mirror of outrage and disgust. As Shimon Bar-Efrat has nicely observed, Achish three
times uses the root for raving mad (*meshuga‘*), three times the first-person pronoun, and
three times the root *b-w-'* ("to bring" or "to come"). Thus David has succeeded in making
himself so revolting that he arouses in Achish a primitive revulsion from the spectacle of
the insane, so that the king simply wants to get David out of sight rather than have him
killed. This is an extraordinary moment in the story of the founding king of Israel: David,
the glamorous young hero of the preceding episodes, is prepared to do whatever is necessary in order to survive, even if it means making himself appear to be the most repulsive
of humankind. It is an even lowlier disguise than Odysseus's as beggar, and it is also not
the last experience of humiliation into which David in adversity will willingly plunge. It
is noteworthy that David feigns madness in order to survive and eventually become king,
in contrast to Saul, whose genuine madness reflects his loss of control over the kingdom.

1 CHAPTER 22   And David went from there and got away to
the Cave of Adullam, and his brothers heard, as well as all his father's
2 household, and they came down to him there. And every man in straits
and every man in debt and every man who was embittered gathered round
him, and he became their captain, and there were about four hundred men
3 with him. And David went from there to Mizpeh of Moab. And he said to
the king of Moab, "Pray, let my father and my mother come out with you
4 until I know what God will do with me." And he led them into the presence
of the king of Moab and they stayed with him all the time that David was
5 in the stronghold. And Gad the prophet said to David, "You must not stay
in the stronghold. Go, and come you to the territory of Judah." And David
went and came to the forest of Hereth.

_____

CHAPTER 22   1. *Adullam.* The location is in the hilly terrain at the western edge
of the tribal territory of Judah, near the Philistine region.

   his brothers . . . all his father's household. Saul's rage over the notion that David would
have neglected the new moon festivity at the palace to join his brothers in Bethlehem is
given an after-the-fact political confirmation here: David's brothers and clansmen rally
round him, forming a kind of family militia. But there is a push as well as a pull in their
going out to David in the badlands: if they remained in Bethlehem, they would be subject
to retribution by Saul's soldiery. David's decision to move his parents across the border to
Moab (verse 3) is another reflection of fear of royal vengeance against the family. Jesse,
earlier characterized as very aged, would have been too old to join the fighting men.

   2. *every man in straits . . . in debt . . . embittered.* David's guerilla band has a core drawn
from his clan and a rank and file of the dispossessed and malcontent—men with nothing
to lose who have been oppressed by the established order. David's social base as guerilla
chieftain is strongly reminiscent of Jephthah's (Judges 11).

   3. *Mizpeh of Moab.* The word *mizpeh* (or in some places, *mizpah*) means "outlook" or
"vista," and so this particular Mizpeh must be identified as the one in Moab, east of the
Jordan. If the Book of Ruth provides reliable genealogy, David's great-grandmother Ruth
was a Moabite, and so David here may be calling on a family connection in requesting
asylum for his parents.

   4. *all the time that David was in the stronghold.* The identity of the stronghold has puzzled
interpreters, especially because David is said to have set up headquarters in a cave. Some
have argued that the two terms refer to the same place, but the Hebrew for "stronghold,"
metsudah, usually refers to a height. Others read "cave," *meʿarah,* for *metsudah.* That proposal is problematic because Adullam is in the territory of Judah, and in verse 5 David is
enjoined to leave the stronghold and head for the territory of Judah. The most reasonable
inference is that after the parlay with the king of Moab, David moves his fighting men
from Adullam at the western border of the territory of Judah to an unspecified stronghold,
probably in the craggy border region between Moab and Israel.

   5. *Gad the prophet.* This figure appears in the story without introduction or explanation.
What is important is that we see David with an open line of communication with the divinity, in sharp contrast to Saul.

And Saul heard that David was discovered, and the men who were with him, 6
and Saul was sitting in Gibeah under the tamarisk on the height, his spear
in his hand and all his servants poised in attendance upon him. And Saul 7
said to his servants poised in attendance upon him, "Listen, pray, you Benjaminites: will the son of Jesse give every one of you fields and vineyards,
will he make every one of you captains of thousands and captains of hundreds, that all of you should have conspired against me and none revealed 8
to me when my son made a pact with the son of Jesse, and none of you was
troubled for my sake to reveal to me that my son has set up my servant to
lie in wait against me as on this very day?" And Doeg the Edomite, who was 9
poised in attendance with Saul's servants, spoke out and said, "I saw the son
of Jesse coming to Nob to Ahimelech the son of Ahitub. And he inquired 10
of the LORD, and provisions he gave him, and the sword of Goliath the Philistine he gave him." And the king sent to summon Ahimelech the son of 11
Ahitub and all his father's household, the priests who were in Nob, and they
all came to the king. And Saul said, "Listen, pray, son of Ahitub." And he 12

---

6. *Saul heard that David was discovered.* From this point onward, the narrative will switch
back and forth deftly between David and Saul. It now turns to an ominous piece of unfin-
ished business—Saul's response to the priest of Nob who helped David in his flight. The
specific reference of Saul's hearing "that David was discovered" could well be intelligence
that places David's hideout at the stronghold. That would explain why Gad urges David to
move on from the stronghold to a forest in Judahite territory.

his spear in his hand. The same spear in hand with which he sought to kill David, and
then Jonathan. This small detail thus foreshadows the massacre of an entire town that
Saul will order.

7. *you Benjaminites.* Evidently, the inner circle at the court is enlisted from his own tribe.
The tribal affiliation helps explain the sarcasm of his rhetorical questions: could they really
expect someone from the tribe of Judah to bestow all these bounties on them?

fields . . . vineyards . . . captains. As Moshe Garsiel has aptly noted, Saul's paranoid outburst picks up key terms from Samuel's warning about the "practice of the king" in chapter
8. It is also noteworthy that Saul's distraught speech takes the form of one lone onrushing
sentence (all the way to the end of verse 8). Once again, Saul refers to David contemptuously
solely by patronymic, as "the son of Jesse."

8. *none revealed to me.* Once again, Saul's problem, which is also the symptom of his paranoia, is that he feels essential knowledge is denied him.

10. *he inquired of the LORD.* There was no report in chapter 21 of Ahimelech's inquiring of
the oracle for David, and it seems unlikely that so essential a fact would have been simply
elided by the narrator. The first item, then, in Doeg's denunciation of Ahimelech looks like
a fabrication—and one that would especially enrage Saul, who has repeatedly had access
to divine knowledge blocked.

12. *son of Ahitub.* It is a shocking piece of rudeness for Saul to address someone invested
with the authority of priesthood merely by patronymic.

13 said, "Here I am, my lord." And Saul said, "Why did you conspire against
    me, you and the son of Jesse, giving him bread and sword and inquiring of
    God for him, so that he set up to lie in wait against me on this very day?"
14 And Ahimelech answered the king and said, "And who of all your servants is
    like David, loyal and the king's son-in-law and captain of your palace guard
15 and honored in your house? Did I this day for the first time inquire for him
    of God? Far be it from me! Let not the king impute anything to his servant
    or to all my father's house, for your servant knew nothing of all this, neither
16 great nor small." And the king said, "You are doomed to die, Ahimelech,
17 you and all your father's house!" And the king said to the sentries poised in
    attendance on him, "Turn round and put to death the priests of the LORD,
    for their hand, too, is with David, for they knew he was fleeing and did not
    reveal it to me!" And the king's servants did not want to reach out their hand
18 to stab the priests of the LORD. And the king said to Doeg, "You, then, turn

---

14. *who of all your servants is like David.* Ahimelech may still be laboring under the delusion
that the fugitive David was embarked on a special secret mission for Saul. His testimony to
David's loyalty and eminence will of course stoke Saul's already blazing anger.

15. *Did I this day for the first time inquire for him of God?* Some interpreters read this as a
declarative sentence, but the context compels one to construe it as a question: I never previously consulted the oracle for David, and why on earth would I do it now? (Perhaps he is
suggesting that consultation of the oracle is a service to be offered only to the king.) He is
silent, however, about providing bread and sword, which in fact he has done.

16. *you and all your father's house.* Ahimelech is the great-grandson of Eli. The slaughter of
the entire clan of priests here is the grim fulfillment of the curse on the house of Eli first
enunciated by the man of God in 2:27–36.

17. *for their hand, too, is with David.* The Hebrew adverb *gam*, often a general term of
emphasis, surely has the force of "too" here: the paranoid Saul sees conspirators on all
sides—his son, his Benjaminite court attendants, and now the priests of Nob.
    the king's servants did not want to reach out. Beyond any moral considerations and any
concern for the king's sanity, it would be a violation of a taboo to murder the priests of the
LORD.
    to stab. The core meaning of the Hebrew verb *pagaʿ* is the meeting or intersection
of two material bodies or human agencies. It can mean "to encounter," "to accost," and,
by extension, "to entreat," but in contexts of violent action, it refers to the "encounter"
between forged blade and flesh. The verb "to strike down" (*hikah*, as in verse 19) indicates
the consummated act of killing. In verse 21, the narrator uses *harag*, the unadorned verb
that means "to kill."

18. *You, then.* Saul emphatically adds the second-person pronoun *'atah* to the imperative
verb: if none of my Israelite subjects will kill the priests, you, then, as an Edomite, may
carry out my orders.

round and stab the priests," and Doeg the Edomite turned round and he it was who stabbed the priests and he put to death on that day eighty-five men who wore the linen ephod. And he struck down Nob the priests' town 19 with the edge of the sword, man and woman, infant and suckling, ox and donkey and sheep, all by the edge of the sword.

And one son of Ahimelech the son of Ahitub got away, and his name was 20 Abiathar, and he fled after David. And Abiathar told David that Saul had 21 killed the priests of the LORD. And David said to Abiathar, "I knew on that 22 day that Doeg the Edomite was there, that he would surely tell Saul. I am the one who caused the loss of all the lives of your father's house. Stay with 23 me. Do not fear, for whoever seeks my life seeks your life, so you are under my guard."

CHAPTER 23   And they told David, saying, "Look, the Philis- 1 tines are fighting against Keilah and they are looting the threshing floors."

---

who wore the linen ephod. This is a kind of epic epithet for priests.

19. *man and woman, infant and suckling.* Saul, with the Edomite Doeg as his cat's-paw, flings himself into an orgy of mass murder, killing not only the adult priests but every living creature in Nob. Now he is carrying out the ban he executed only imperfectly against Amalek (the terms used are virtually identical), but the massacre is directed at his own innocent people. Saul's madness has become sinister and lethal, like that of Macbeth, who also becomes a murderer of children—the well-meaning farmer's son who became king has turned into a bloody tyrant.

all by the edge of the sword. "All" catches the force of the Hebrew preposition *'ad* ("even" or "as far as") reiterated before each term in the catalogue of the massacre.

20. *And one son of Ahimelech . . . got away.* This sole survivor (his name means "my father remains") will then be able to provide David with priestly services, including access to the oracle.

22. *I am the one who caused the loss of all the lives.* The Hebrew uses an ellipsis, "caused all the lives," but the sense is clearly loss of life.

CHAPTER 23   1. *Keilah.* Keilah is a town on the western perimeter of the territory of Judah, facing the Philistine border. Its vulnerability to Philistine incursions is thus understandable. David's men (verse 3) speak as though Keilah were not part of Judah because as a border town it seems to them much more dangerous than their location deep within their own tribal territory. Some scholars have speculated that Keilah was an independent town without tribal affiliation.

2 And David inquired of the LORD, saying, "Shall I go and strike down these Philistines?" And the LORD said to David, "Go and strike down the
3 Philistines and rescue Keilah." And David's men said to him, "Look, we're afraid here in Judah, and how much more so if we go to Keilah against the
4 Philistine lines!" And David again inquired of the LORD, and the LORD answered him and said, "Rise, go down to Keilah, for I am about to give
5 the Philistines into your hand." And David, and his men with him, went to Keilah and did battle with the Philistines, and he drove off their cattle and struck them a great blow, and David rescued the inhabitants of Keilah.
6 And it happened when Abiathar the son of Ahimelech fled to David at Keilah, that the ephod came down in his hand.

7 And it was told to Saul that David had come to Keilah, and Saul said, "God has given him in my hand, for he is closed inside a town with double gate
8 and bolt." And Saul summoned all the troops for battle to go down to
9 Keilah to lay seige against David and his men. And David knew that Saul was scheming evil against him and he said to Abiathar the priest, "Bring
10 forth the ephod." And David said, "LORD, God of Israel, Your servant has indeed heard that Saul seeks to come to Keilah to destroy the town on my
11 count. Will the notables of Keilah hand me over to him? Will Saul come down, as Your servant has heard? LORD, God of Israel, tell, pray, Your ser-

---

2. *David inquired of the LORD.* The means of inquiry are not specified, but since his questions invite the usual yes-or-no response, it seems likely he is using the ephod and not, as some interpreters have claimed, a more immediate mode of communication with God. The information, then, in verse 6 that the fugitive priest Abiathar has arrived from Nob with the ephod is probably retrospective. The phrase "at Keilah" (one word in Hebrew) in that verse perhaps should be deleted as an inadvertent scribal duplication of "Keilah" at the end of the preceding verse—by the testimony of chapter 22, Abiathar fled to David when David was in the forest of Hereth in Judah, before he undertook the rescue mission to Keilah.

6. *the ephod came down in his hand.* From the viewpoint of the ancient audience, the ephod would have been indispensable as an instrument of what we would call military intelligence. An ephod, we should recall, is also a priestly garment. At Nob, Saul slaughtered eighty-five priests "who wore the linen ephod." Fokkelman perceptively describes the appearance of the oracular ephod in David's camp as a "countermove by God"—"Saul may bloody the 85 linen priestly garments called the ephod, but the one ephod which acts as a medium for the decisive word of God turns up at the place of the alternative anointed one."

7. *given him in my hand.* The Masoretic Text has *nikar,* "made a stranger," but the Septuagint reflects a verb meaning "sold" or "handed over."

11. *Will the notables . . . hand me over . . . ? Will Saul come down.* Since the binary device of the ephod can give only one answer of yes or no, David receives an answer only to the second question and then is obliged to repeat the first question (verse 12) in order to get a response to it.

vant." And the LORD said, "He will come down." And David said, "Will 12
the notables of Keilah hand me over, and my men, to Saul?" And the LORD
said, "They will hand you over." And David arose, and his men with him, 13
about six hundred men, and they came out from Keilah and moved about
wherever they could, and to Saul it was told that David had gotten away
from Keilah, and he ceased going out.

And David stayed in the wilderness in strongholds, and he stayed in the 14
high country in the wilderness of Ziph. And Saul sought him all the while
but God did not give him into his hand. And David saw that Saul had come 15
out to seek his life, and David was in the wilderness of Ziph in the forest.
And Jonathan the son of Saul arose and went to David in the forest and 16
bade him take heart in the LORD. And he said to him, "Do not fear, for the 17
hand of Saul my father shall not find you, and it is you who shall be king
over Israel, and I on my part will be your viceroy, and even Saul my father

---

12. *They will hand you over.* It may seem base ingratitude on the part of the Keilah notables
to betray the man who has just rescued their town from the Philistines. But they must
fear Saul's retribution should they collaborate with David at least as much as they fear the
Philistines. The political paradox of the situation that has evolved is evident: David has
achieved a victory against Israel's principal enemy; Saul now moves to destroy that victor,
enlisting the aid of the people David saved.

14. *in the wilderness in strongholds.* Since the Hebrew term for strongholds (*metsadah* or
metsudah—attempts to distinguish the two being questionable) generally occurs in wilderness settings, it seems likely that these are not built-up structures but rather natural
formations that afforded effective defensive positions, such as promontories surrounded
by outcroppings of rock.
   in the wilderness of Ziph. The location is in the tribal territory of Judah, about five miles
southeast of Hebron and about ten miles southeast of Keilah, where David has just fought
the Philistines.

16. *bade him take heart in the LORD.* The literal meaning of the Hebrew idiom used is
"strengthened his hand in the LORD." The Hebrew thus is able to pick up the word "hand"
at the beginning of Jonathan's speech, "the hand of my father Saul shall not find you."

17. *I on my part will be your viceroy.* For the second time, Jonathan makes a pact with
David in which he concedes that it is David who will inherit the throne. There is a pattern
of incremental repetition here: only now does Jonathan specify that he will be David's
viceroy (literally "second," *mishneh*, but this is an ellipses for *mishneh lamelekh*, "second
to the king"). The faithful Jonathan persists in his naïveté, imagining that he will be able
to serve as viceroy to his dear friend, who is also the man destined to displace the dynasty
Saul would have established. As an alleged doublet, this episode has narrative plausibility:
Jonathan first confirmed a pact with David when he told him he must flee from Saul; now,
no doubt at some risk to himself, he is impelled to seek out the fugitive and beleaguered
David in order to assure him of his continuing loyalty and encourage him in his adversity.
Once again, characteristically, David's response to Jonathan is not reported.

18 knows it." And the two of them sealed a pact before the LORD, and David
    stayed in the forest but Jonathan went to his house.

19 And Ziphites came up to Saul at Gibeah, saying, "Is not David hiding out
    among us in the strongholds in the forest on the hill of Hachilah to the
20 south of the wasteland? And so whenever you may desire, O king, to come
    down, come down, and ours is the part to deliver him into the hand of the
21 king." And Saul said, "Blessed are you to the LORD, for you have shown pity
22 on me. Go, pray, make certain, and mark and see the place where his foot
    treads, and who has seen him there, for it has been said to me that he is
23 very cunning. See and mark all the hideouts where he may take cover there
    and come back to me when you are certain and I shall go with you. And if
    indeed he is in the land, I shall search for him among all the clans of Judah."
24 And they arose and went to Ziph ahead of Saul, and David and his men
25 were in the wilderness of Maon in the desert south of the wasteland. And

---

19. *Ziphites*. Since no definite article is used, this appears to be one group of Ziphites and
not a delegation representing the entire clan. The motive for betraying David could equally
be desire for a reward and fear of retribution should Saul discover that they had allowed
David to hide out in their territory: the ruthless massacre at Nob would have been a grim
object lesson duly noted throughout the Israelite populace.

   in the strongholds in the forest on the hill of Hachilah to the south of the wasteland. The
Ziphite informers want to make their identification of David's whereabouts as precise as
possible, hence the unusual string of geographical indications. As it emerges, the intelligence they provide is still not precise enough for the frustrated Saul, as his response ("make
certain . . . when you are certain") clearly shows. It should be said that most translators have
treated the last geographical term used by the Ziphites, "the wasteland," as a proper noun
(*yeshimon*), but because it bears a definite article, and because *yeshimon* is a well-attested
common noun, it is preferable not to construe it as a place-name. This episode uses three
different terms for uninhabited terrain—wilderness, wasteland, and desert (or four, if one
adds forest)—which has the cumulative effect of emphasizing how David is constrained to
take refuge beyond the populated areas of Israel.

21. *you have shown pity on me*. Saul uses the same verb for pity or "sparing" that was
prominently deployed in the Amalek story. The idea that the poor king, thwarted by a
cunning and malicious David, needs to be shown pity is surely another manifestation of
his paranoia—we might say, of its maudlin side.

22. *where his foot treads*. The Hebrew says literally "where his foot is." The focus on David's
foot reflects the eye of the pursuer on the track of his elusive prey.

   for it has been said to me. The Hebrew reads literally, "for he has said to me," but there
is no need to emend the text because biblical Hebrew sometimes uses a third-person masculine singular verb with no specified grammatical subject to perform the function of the
passive. Notice that Saul claims someone has told him David is very cunning—not, which
is the case, that Saul himself has decided that his "enemy" is cunning.

24. *Maon*. This would be roughly three miles due south of the wilderness of Ziph.

Saul went, and his men with him, to seek David. And it was told to David, and he went down to the crag and stayed in the wilderness of Maon, and Saul heard, and pursued David into the wilderness of Maon. And Saul went 26 on one side of the mountain and David and his men on the other side of the mountain, and David made haste to go off from before Saul, while Saul and his men were circling the mountain after David and his men to catch them. Just then a messenger came to Saul, saying, "Hurry, and go, for the 27 Philistines have invaded the land!" And Saul turned back from pursuing 28 David and went to meet the Philistines. Therefore do they call that place the Crag of the Divide.

And David went up from there and stayed in the strongholds of Ein-Gedi. 24:1

CHAPTER 24   And it happened when Saul turned back from 2 the Philistines that they told him, saying, "Look, David is in the wilderness of Ein-Gedi." And Saul took three thousand picked men from all Israel and 3

---

26. *Saul and his men were circling the mountain.* Kyle McCarter Jr. has made the plausible suggestion that what is indicated in this language is a pincer movement: Saul's forces are moving around the circumference of the mountain on two sides in order to trap David between them, who is on the far side of the mountain. He, evidently realizing the nature of Saul's maneuver, scrambles to flee—"David made haste to go off from before Saul"—before the pincer snaps shut.

27. *Hurry, and go, for the Philistines have invaded the land.* This last-minute diversion of course has the effect of rescuing David from Saul, but it also points up the madness of his obsessive pursuit of David: at a time when Israel's major national enemy is repeatedly sending troops against the territory Saul is supposed to be governing and protecting, he is devoting his attention, and his troops, to the pursuit of David.

28. *the Crag of the Divide.* This etiological notice explains the place-name, *sela' hamahleqot*, as deriving from the "divide" between Saul's forces, which went one way, and David's, which went another. Several commentators have proposed that the name derived not from *mahloqet*, "division," but from *halaq*, "smooth," and so the original meaning would have been Slippery Crag, or Unforested Crag.

24:1. *the strongholds of Ein-Gedi.* David now flees eastward from the forest area of Ziph, south of Hebron in the central region of Judah's territory, to Ein-Gedi, in the rocky heights overlooking the Dead Sea. He would have felt safer in this remote region with its forbidding terrain. But Ein-Gedi is an oasis, which would have provided a water supply and vegetation for him and his troops

CHAPTER 24   3. *three thousand picked men.* David, it should be recalled, commands a guerilla band of about six hundred men; so he is outnumbered five to one and is facing elite troops.

4 he went to seek David over the rocks of the wild goats. And he came to the
   sheepfolds along the way, and there was a cave there, and Saul went in to
   relieve himself, while David and his men were sitting in the far end of the
5 cave. And David's men said to him, "Here is the day that the LORD said to
   you, 'Look, I am about to give your enemy into your hands, and you may do
   to him whatever seems good in your eyes.'" And David rose and stealth-
6 ily cut off the skirt of the cloak that was Saul's. And it happened then that
   David was smitten with remorse because he had cut off the skirt of the cloak
7 that was Saul's. And he said to his men, "The LORD forbid me, that I should
   have done this thing to my master, the LORD's anointed, to reach out my
8 hand against him, for he is the LORD's anointed." And David held back his

---

4. *Saul went in to relieve himself . . . David and his men . . . in the far end of the cave.* The
topography is quite realistic, for the cliffs overlooking the Dead Sea in the region of Ein-
Gedi are honeycombed with caves. Power and powerlessness are precariously balanced in
this episode. David and his men are in all likelihood hiding in the far end of the cave from
Saul's search party. Had a contingent of soldiers entered the cave, they would have been
trapped. Instead, Saul comes in alone, and he is in a double sense exposed to David and
his men.

5. *Here is the day that the LORD said to you.* David's eager men exhibit a certain theological
presumptuousness. They surely know that their leader has been secretly anointed to be
king, but nothing in the preceding narrative indicates a divine promise that God would
deliver Saul into David's hands.

   do to him whatever seems good in your eyes. They carefully avoid the plain word
"kill."

6. *David was smitten with remorse.* The Hebrew is literally "David's heart smote him."

   he had cut off the skirt of the cloak that was Saul's. Clearly, what David feels is that he
has perpetrated a kind of symbolic mutilation of the king by cutting off the corner of his
garment—not with anything like a scissors, of course, but surely with his sword, his instrument for killing his enemies. The cloak (*me'il*) has already been linked emblematically with
kingship in the final estrangement between Samuel and Saul, and so David is in symbolic
effect "cutting away" Saul's kingship. For all the remorse he feels, he will continue to make
double use of the corner of the cloak, as we shall see.

7. *that I should have done this thing to my master, the LORD's anointed.* Some interpreters
have read this whole episode as an apology for David's innocence and piety in relation to
Saul. But the very gesture of piety is also self-interested—David, after all, is conscious that
he, too, is the LORD's anointed, and it is surely in his long-term interest that the reigning
king's person should be held sacred by all his subjects.

8. *David held back his men.* The meaning of the verb *shisa'* is disputed, but it is most plausibly linked with the noun *shesa'*, a split or cleft. The sense here would then be: he "split
off" his men from Saul, using his words to interpose a kind of barrier between them and

men with words and did not let them rise against Saul, and Saul rose from
the cave and went on the way. And David then rose and came out of the 9
cave and called after Saul, saying, "My lord the king!" And Saul looked
behind him, and David knelt, his face to the ground, and bowed down.
And David said to Saul, "Why should you listen to people's words, saying, 10
'Look, David seeks to harm you'? Look, this day your eyes have seen that 11
the LORD has given you into my hand in the cave, and they meant to kill
you, and I had pity for you and said, 'I will not reach out my hand against
my master, for he is the LORD's anointed.' And, my father, see, yes, see the 12
skirt of your cloak in my hand, for when I cut off the skirt of your cloak
and did not kill you, mark and see that there was no evil or crime in my
hand and I did not offend you, yet you stalk me to take my life. Let the 13
LORD judge between me and you, and the LORD will avenge me of you,

---

the king. In any case, the first clause of this verse appears to respond to the men's initial
inclination to kill Saul (verse 5) rather than following from David's remorse over the cutting
of the garment—a chronological displacement noted as early as Rashi.

9. *David . . . came out of the cave and called after Saul.* David is taking a calculated risk.
Saul could, after all, order his troops to attack David and the men behind him in the cave.
David first throws Saul off his guard by paying obeisance to him as king and prostrat-
ing himself—hardly what one would expect of a fugitive or rebel. He then counts on the
persuasive power of his own rhetoric, and on the telltale scrap of the king's cloak that he
clutches, to deflect Saul from his lethal intentions. David is cannily self-protective but he
is also a gambler.

10–11. *Why should you listen to people's words . . . this day your eyes have seen.* Instead of
rumor heard about David's harmful intentions, here is ocular evidence of his innocence—
and of God's having devised to give David the upper hand over Saul.

11. *and they meant to kill you.* The Masoretic Text has "he meant," which may be either
corrected to a plural, as some of the ancient versions do, or construed as "someone said."

12. *my father see, yes, see the skirt of your cloak in my hand.* It is, appropriately, ambiguous whether "my father" is a form of respectful address to an authority or an attempt to
reach back to the moment of affectionate intimacy in their relationship. We may note
that David, for all the remorse he felt over having cut off the skirt of Saul's garment,
makes great display of it now as evidence of having had Saul entirely at his mercy. The
proof of his innocence is thus inseparable from the reminder of the power he had over
his rival.

13. *Let the LORD judge between me and you . . . the LORD will avenge me of you.* David's
great protestation of innocence and his purported gesture of reconciliation move toward a
barely veiled threat: you are the one who has wronged me, and vengeance will be exacted,
but by God, not by me.

14 but my hand will not be against you. As the proverb of the ancients says,
    'From wicked men does wickedness come forth,' but my hand will not be
15 against you. After whom has the king of Israel come forth, after whom are
16 you chasing? After a dead dog, after a single flea? The LORD will be arbiter
    and judge between me and you, that He may see and plead my case and judge
17 me against you." And it happened when David had finished speaking these
    words to Saul, that Saul said, "Is this your voice, my son, David?" And Saul
18 raised his voice and wept. And he said to David, "You are more in the right

---

14. *the proverb of the ancients.* The Masoretic Text has "ancient," in the singular, but the
Qumran Samuel scroll, more plausibly, shows the plural form.

From wicked men does wickedness come forth. The gnomic saying—only three words
in the Hebrew!—that David chooses to cite is archly double-edged: Wicked acts are perpetrated only by the wicked, so I won't be the one to touch you. But there is also the distinct
hint that the wicked person in question could be Saul himself. Though David cannot know
this, Saul will die by his own hand.

but my hand will not be against you. The words that the writer attributes to David
ironically echo the words of Saul's first murderous plot against David, conveyed in interior monologue, when Saul said, "Let not my hand be against him but let the hand of the
Philistines be against him" (18:17).

15. *has the king of Israel come forth.* The very verb attached to the wicked in the proverb!

After a dead dog, after a single flea? In his peroration, David outdoes himself in professing his humble station. A dead dog was proverbial in ancient Israel as a contemptible,
worthless thing, but David goes the idiom one better by saying he is scarcely more important than a single flea on the dead dog's carcass, a brilliant adaptation to prose of the logic
of intensification of biblical poetry, in which a term introduced in the first part of the line
is raised to the second power semantically in the parallel second half.

16. *judge me against you.* The Hebrew is literally "judge me from your hand," that is, judge
me favorably and rescue me from your hand. The term thus picks up the insistence on
"hand" throughout David's speech.

17. *Is this your voice, my son, David?* These first words of Saul's response to David are
one of the most breathtaking instances of the biblical technique of contrastive dialogue.
David's speech had been, by biblical standards, quite lengthy, and very much a speech—a
beautifully crafted piece of rhetoric, with complex political aims in mind. Saul responds
with four choked Hebrew words, *haqolkha zeh beni Dawid?* His designation of David as
"my son" is free of the ambiguity attached to David's calling him "my father." This is one
of those extraordinary reversals that make biblical narrative such a probing representation
of the oscillations and the unpredictability of human nature: David's words have cut to the
quick of the king's conscience, and suddenly the obsessive pursuer feels an access of paternal affection, intertwined with remorse, for his imagined enemy. Saul asks his question
because he has to shake himself to believe his enemy is his friend, because he stands at a
certain distance from David (who has called out "after" Saul), and also because his eyes are
blinded with tears. He is thus reminiscent of the blind father Isaac, who was able to make
out the voice, but not the identity, of his son Jacob, and from whom a blessing was wrested.

18. *You are more in the right than I.* These words echo the ones pronounced by Judah, referring
to his vindicated daughter-in-law Tamar, who will become the progenitrix of David's line.

than I, for it is you who requited me good whereas I requited you evil. And 19 you told today how you wrought good with me, when the LORD delivered me into your hand and you did not kill me. For if a man finds his enemy, does he 20 send him off on a good way? The LORD will repay you with good for what you have done for me this day. And so, look, I know that you will surely be king 21 and that the kingship of Israel will stay in your hands. And now, swear to me 22 by the LORD that you shall not cut off my seed after me and that you shall not blot out my name from my father's house." And David swore to Saul, and 23 Saul went home while David and his men went up to the stronghold.

CHAPTER 25   And Samuel died, and all Israel gathered and 1 mourned him, and they buried him at his home in Ramah. And David arose and went down to the wilderness of Paran.

And there was a man in Maon, whose stock was in Carmel, and the man 2 was very great; he had three thousand sheep and a thousand goats. And it happened when he was shearing his sheep in Carmel—and the man's 3 name was Nabal and his wife's name was Abigail, and the woman had a good mind and lovely looks, but the man was hard and evil in deeds, and a

---

you who requited me good . . . I requited you evil. The antithesis of good and evil is played on through the next three verses and should not be sacrificed in the English for the sake of imagined idiomatic fluency.

21. *I know that you will surely be king.* This marks Saul's first open admission that David is the "fellow man who is better than you" of whom Samuel spoke (15:28). He has been doubly convinced—by God's having put him at David's mercy and by David's refusal to harm him, a kingly act and not the act of a rebel and usurper.

CHAPTER 25   1. *the wilderness of Paran.* This geographical indication is puzzling because, unless there is some other place called Paran, it would refer to the Sinai desert, where it would make no sense for David to go and where he could scarcely be if he and his men are engaged with Nabal's shepherds in Judah. The Septuagint reads "wilderness of Maon."

2. *Maon . . . Carmel.* Both places are in the tribal territory of Judah, in the vicinity of Hebron, and just a few miles apart.

3. *the man's name was Nabal.* On the face of it, this is an improbable name because *nabal* in Hebrew plainly means "base fellow," "churl," or "fool," as Abigail (verse 25) will point out. It is at least conceivable that the name is not originally Hebrew, and various meanings drawn from other ancient Near Eastern languages have been proposed for it, such as "archer" and "chosen one of the god."
    a good mind and lovely looks. As yet, we do not know why this characterization will be important. Her shrewd intelligence will be vividly demonstrated in her brilliant speech to David, and her physical attractiveness will stir his matrimonial interest in her.

4   Calebite—David heard in the wilderness that Nabal was shearing his sheep.
5   And David sent ten lads, and David said to the lads, "Go up to Carmel, and
6   come to Nabal and ask him in my name how he fares. And say, 'Thus may
    it be this time next year, that you fare well, and your house fare well, and
7   all that is yours fare well. And so, I have heard that they are doing your
    shearing. Now, the shepherds who belong to you were with us—we did not
    humiliate them and nothing of theirs was missing the whole time they were
8   at Carmel. Ask your lads and they will tell you! And may our lads find favor
    in your eyes, for we have come on a festive day. Give, pray, whatever you
9   can to your servants and to your son, to David.' " And David's lads came
    and spoke to Nabal all these words in David's name, and they paused.
10 And Nabal answered David's servants and said, "Who is David and who

---

and a Calebite. The Calebites were non-Israelites who in effect joined the tribe of
Judah. Several medieval Hebrew commentators detected a double meaning because *kalibi*
could also be construed as "doglike."

6. *Thus may it be this time next year*. The compact Hebrew phrase *koh leḥay* occurs only here,
and its meaning has been disputed. This translation adopts an interpretation that goes back
to Rashi, which is based on the similarity to a well-known idiom, *ka'et ḥayah*. That would
make sense in terms of the narrative situation: the prosperous Nabal is obviously "faring
well" at the moment, and David's greeting of peace (to fare well in the Hebrew idiom is to
possess *shalom*) contains a veiled threat—let us hope that you continue to fare well a year
from now.

7. *we did not humiliate them*. This is the same verb used for Jonathan's sense of his father's
treatment of him (20:34), although here it has the meaning of "molest."
    nothing of theirs was missing. The message is that David's men did not permit themselves
to take any of Nabal's flock, and perhaps also that as armed men they defended Nabal's
people against marauders (compare verse 16, "They were a wall around us both night and
day"). But there is a certain ambiguity as to whether David was providing protection out
of sheer goodwill or conducting a protection racket in order to get the necessary provisions
for his guerilla band.

8. *our lads*. The Hebrew says "the lads"—"our" is added for the sake of clarity, to distinguish
David's retainers from Nabal's.
    for we have come on a festive day. The time of sheepshearing was a sort of holiday, with
feasting and drinking. Nabal's own feast back home at Maon (verse 36) may have been
encouraged by the festivities in which he joined with his shearers out in the field.
    Give, pray, whatever you can to your servants. The request for a payoff is politely worded,
and no quantities are specified.
    to your son, to David. This is an expression of deference or humility to the powerful and
presumably older Nabal. It also strikes an ironic note of correspondence with the language
of David's encounter with Saul at the cave near Ein-Gedi in the previous episode. There,
David addressed Saul as "my father," and the king, in an access of feeling, called David
"my son."

10. *Who is David and who is the son of Jesse?* This sarcastic question, in verse-like paral-

is the son of Jesse? These days many are the slaves breaking away from
their masters. And shall I take my bread and my water and my meat that I   11
slaughtered for my shearers and give it to men who come from I know not
where?" And David's lads whirled round on their way and went back and   12
told him all these words. And David said to his men, "Every man, gird his   13
sword!" And every man girded his sword, and David, too, girded his sword.
And about four hundred men went up after David, while two hundred
stayed with the gear.

And to Abigail the wife of Nabal one of the lads told, saying, "Look, David   14
sent messengers from the wilderness to greet our master, and he pounced
on them. And the men have been very good to us and we were not humili-   15
ated and we missed nothing the whole time we went about with them when
we were out in the field. They were a wall around us both night and day the   16
whole time we were with them tending the sheep. And now, mark and see   17
what you must do, for the evil is resolved against our master and against

---

lelism, picks up another ironic correspondence with Saul, who after the vanquishing of
Goliath asked whose son this was. In Nabal's case, of course, the question expresses the
contempt of a rich landowner for David and his ragtag band of dispossessed men and
malcontents ("men who come from I know not where").

many are the slaves breaking away from their masters. On the surface, these words
reflect the disdain of a propertied man (who would also be a slaveholder) for all landless
rebels who threaten the established social hierarchy. But there is also a barbed hint that
David himself is a slave or subject (the same word in Hebrew) who has rebelled against
his master, Saul.

11. *shall I take my bread and my water.* The Septuagint has "wine" instead of "water." In
any case, Nabal's harsh and contemptuous response to David's men vividly illustrates
that he is a "hard" man, and a churlish one. His outrage over the notion of parting with
any of his possessions is nicely indicated, as Shimon Bar-Efrat has noted, by the fact
that there are eight grammatical expressions of the first-person singular in this one
sentence.

12. *Every man, gird his sword.* The angry David wastes no words: he merely gives the urgent
command to take up weapons and move out for the kill.

15. *And the men have been very good to us.* In keeping with the general practice of biblical
dialogue, the servant recycles the language of David's message to Nabal—"we were not
humiliated and we missed nothing the whole time"—but amplifies it by adding this clause
as well as the image in the next verse, "They were a wall around us both night and day."
He thus makes emphatically clear that David's men really provided protection faithfully,
whether in the simple sense or in the racketeering sense.

17. *And now, mark and see what you must do.* Unlike the "lads" who address Saul, this one
offers no specific advice to Abigail, for she is more than clever enough to figure out what
steps she must immediately take.

18 all his house, and he is such a scoundrel no one can speak to him." And
Abigail hurried and fetched two hundred loaves of bread and two jugs of
wine and five dressed sheep and five seahs of parched grain and a hundred
raisin cakes and two hundred fig cakes, and she put them on the donkeys.
19 And she said to her lads, "Pass on ahead of me and I'll be coming right
20 after you." But her husband she did not tell. And so she was riding on the
donkey coming down under the cover of the mountain and, look, David
21 and his men were coming down toward her, and she met them. And David
had said, "All in vain did I guard everything that belonged to this fellow
in the wilderness, and nothing was missing from all that was his, and he
22 paid me back evil for good! Thus may God do to David and even more, if
I leave from all that is his until morning a single pisser against the wall!"
23 And Abigail saw David and hurried and got down from the donkey and
24 flung herself on her face before David and bowed to the ground. And she
flung herself at his feet and said, "Mine, my lord, is the blame! But let your
25 servant speak in your ears, and hear the words of your servant. Pray, let
not my lord pay mind to this scoundrel of a man, to Nabal, for just like his
name he is, his name means Base and baseness is with him. And as for me,

---

20. *And so she was riding on the donkey coming down under the cover of the mountain and,
look, David and his men were coming.* The two parties moving toward each other introduce
a moment of suspense, for David, after all, as the next verse (with a pluperfect verb) makes
utterly clear, is armed and angry. The "look" (*hineh*) is used in characteristic fashion to indicate
Abigail's visual perspective: he at first doesn't see her because she is coming down the sheltered
slope of the mountain, but she sees him and his men with their swords girded ready for battle.

22. *a single pisser against the wall.* The literal meaning of the Hebrew is properly followed
in the King James Version, as it is in this translation. The phrase, of course, is a rough and
vivid epithet for "male," and one that occurs only in curses. Its edge of vulgarity seems
perfectly right for David's anger.

23–24. *flung herself on her face . . . bowed to the ground . . . flung herself at his feet.* In a world
where an angry king could massacre every man, woman, and child in Nob, Abigail has no
way of knowing whether David will have an impulse to kill her on the spot. (She has not
heard the words that limit the threat of slaughter to the males.) Thus, her first move in
this highly dangerous situation, before she speaks a word, is to demonstrate her absolute
submission to David through these extravagant gestures of obeisance.

24. *Mine.* The shrewdness of her extraordinary speech begins with the very first syllable she
utters. She immediately takes all the blame on herself, though in the next breath she will
be sure to transfer it heartily to her contemptible husband. At the same time, she exploits a
momentary pun, for the word *bi* ("mine," "in me") in other contexts can mean "I beseech
you," so she initiates her address to David with what sounds like a term of imploring.

25. *this scoundrel of a man . . . his name means Base . . . And as for me.* It is hard to think of
another instance in literature in which a wife so quickly and so devastatingly interposes

your servant, I never saw my lord's lads whom you sent. And now, my lord, 26
as the LORD lives and as you live—the LORD Who kept you from coming
into bloodguilt with your own hand rescuing you—and now, like Nabal may
your enemies be who seek evil against my lord. And now, this blessing that 27
your servant has brought to my lord, let it be given to the lads who go about
in the footsteps of my lord. Forgive, pray, the crime of your servant, for the 28
LORD will surely make for my lord a stalwart house, for my lord fights the
battles of the LORD and no evil will be found in you all your days. And when 29
a person rises to pursue you, to seek your life, my lord's life will be bound
in the bundle of the living with the LORD your God, and the lives of your

---

distance between herself and her husband. She rapidly denounces her spouse and then
counterposes herself ("And as for me," *wa'ani*) as a person who had no part in the rude
rejection of David's emissaries. Abigail of course wants to save her own neck, but she clearly
has been chafing over her marriage with a boorish, unpleasant, and probably older man,
and she sees an opportunity here.

26. *Who kept you from coming into bloodguilt.* Abigail is no doubt speaking in general, but
the reader can scarcely forget the immediately preceding episode, in which David refused
to harm Saul when he had him in his power.

27. *this blessing that your servant has brought.* The obvious sense of "blessing" (*berakhah*) in
context is "gift," but the primary meaning of the word is worth preserving for two reasons.
First, it is clearly intended to answer to David's reiterated use of "blessed" in his response to
Abigail. Then, as Moshe Garsiel has aptly observed, it is a key term in a network of allusions to
the moment in Genesis 33 when Jacob is reunited with his brother Esau: Esau, too, approaches
dauntingly with four hundred armed men; Jacob, like Abigail, prostrates himself before the
figure he fears; and he, too, has brought with him generous tribute to be offered in concili-
ation, which he refers to not as a "gift" (*minhah*) but as a "blessing." And in Genesis 33, that
term plays back against the fraught meanings of "blessing" in the larger Jacob–Esau narrative.

28. *Forgive, pray, the crime of your servant.* "Servant" is in the feminine, but the conventional
"handmaiden" sounds too fussy. By way of deference, Abigail once again speaks as though
the fault were hers, though she has made it quite clear that her husband alone is the guilty one.
   a stalwart house. A stalwart, or enduring, house is precisely what was promised the
priestly line that was to replace the house of Eli (2:35).
   no evil will be found in you all your days. Abigail exploits the temporal ambiguity of the
Hebrew imperfective verb to make a statement that is both descriptive of the way David has
conducted himself and predictive of the way he will, or should, conduct himself.

29. *when a person rises to pursue you.* The generality of "a person" (*'adam*) picks up David's
use of the same word in the preceding episode when he addresses Saul ("Why should you
listen to people's words" [*divrey 'adam*]), and, even more pointedly, recalls his very first
speech to Saul in 17:32, "Let no man's heart [*lev' adam*] fail him," where the term seems to
refer to Saul himself, who may be the hidden referent here.
   bound in the bundle of the living. Although Kyle McCarter Jr., following Tur-Sinai, has
claimed that "bundle" (*tsror*) actually means document or book, a more plausible identification is the pouch in which little stones keeping a tally of live sheep were placed. Thus

30   enemies He will sling from the hollow of the sling. And so, when the LORD
     does for my lord all the good that He has spoken about you and He appoints
31   you prince over Israel, this will not be a stumbling and a trepidation of the
     heart to my lord, to have shed blood for no cause and for my lord to have
     carried out his own rescue, then will the LORD do well with my lord, and
32   you will remember your servant." And David said to Abigail, "Blessed is the
33   LORD, God of Israel, Who has sent you this day to meet me. And blessed
     is your good sense and blessed are you, for this day you held me back from
34   coming into bloodguilt with my own hand rescuing me. And yet, as the
     LORD, God of Israel, lives, Who kept me from harming you, had you not
     hurried and come to meet me, there would not have been left to Nabal by
35   morning's light a single pisser against the wall!" And David took from her
     hand what she had brought him, and to her he said, "Go up in peace to your
     house. See, I have heeded your voice and granted your petition."

---

both this positive image and the negative one of the slingshot would be associated with
sheepherding. And as Shimon Bar-Efrat had nicely observed, *tsror* in biblical Hebrew also
means "stone," the object that would normally be placed in the hollow of the sling; so there
is a punning cross-link between the two images.

   will sling from the hollow of the sling. Instead of being bound up and safely kept, their
lives will be flung out into the void of extinction. (The literal sense of the preposition
attached to "hollow" in the Hebrew is "in.") Abigail has chosen her metaphor shrewdly
because it would be general knowledge that David used his sling to destroy a formidable
enemy.

30–31. *when the LORD . . . appoints you prince over Israel, this will not be a stumbling and a
trepidation of the heart to my lord.* Abigail deftly pitches her argument to David's political
self-interest. Once he makes the move from guerilla chieftain to monarch, he will not want
his record stained by blood he has spilled. It is therefore more prudent to let God take care
of his enemies—"the LORD" in biblical parlance being the piously proper way to talk about
the course of events, but its pragmatic equivalent being "other people" or "circumstances."

31. *and you will remember your servant.* These final words of Abigail's lengthy and carefully calculated speech are strategically chosen, and discreet. What, in fact, does she have
in mind? The Israeli novelist Meir Shalev, in a perceptive and lively essay on this story,
makes a bold and, to my mind, persuasive proposal. Abigail has matrimony in view, once
her cantankerous old husband is out of the way, but why does she think she will deserve so
signal an honor, or reward, from David? Shalev argues that when Abigail dissuades David
from killing Nabal, repeatedly assuring him that the LORD will pay off David's scores
against him, she is really suggesting herself as the agency for "the LORD." She is, in other
words, proposing to David that she carry out a kind of contract killing of her husband, with
the payoff that she will become the wife of the handsome young warrior and future king.

32–34. David, though persuaded by Abigail's prudent advice, cannot resist one last reminder
that he was indeed about to cut down every pisser against the wall in the house of Nabal.

And Abigail came to Nabal, and, look, he was having himself a feast in his 36
house like a king's feast, and Nabal's heart was of good cheer, and he was
exceedingly drunk. And she told him nothing, neither great nor small. And 37
it happened in the morning when the wine was gone out of Nabal that his
wife told him these things and his heart died within him and he became
like a stone. And it happened after about ten days that the LORD smote 38
Nabal and he died.

And David heard that Nabal had died, and he said, "Blessed is the LORD 39
Who has taken up my cause of insult against Nabal, and His servant He
has withheld from evil, and Nabal's evil the LORD has brought down on his
own head." And David sent and spoke out for Abigail to take her as wife.
And David's servants came to Abigail at Carmel and spoke to her, saying, 40
"David sent us to you to take you to him as wife." And she arose and bowed, 41
her face to the ground, and said, "Look, your servant is but a slavegirl to
wash the feet of my lord's servants." And Abigail hurried and rose and rode 42
on the donkey, her five young women walking behind her, and she went
after David's messengers, and she became his wife. And Ahinoam David 43

---

36. *And she told him nothing.* Abigail again makes a careful calculation: she does not want to
convey the scary news to him while he is enveloped in an alcoholic haze.

37. *in the morning when the wine was gone out of Nabal.* She catches him cold sober, and
perhaps even with a painful hangover.
    his heart died within him and he became like a stone. The terrifying information that
David had been on his way—or did she say, was still on his way?—with four hundred armed
men intent on mayhem triggers a paralyzing heart attack or, perhaps, a stroke (the biblical understanding of physiology not being ours). Abigail gives the distinct appearance of
counting on her husband's cowardice and on a bad heart she might have been aware of from
previous manifestations of ill health. If this assumption is correct, she would be using her
knowledge of his physical frailty to carry out the tacit contract on his life—bloodlessly, with
God Himself left to do the deed (compare the end of verse 38). Robert Polzin perceptively
notes that the figurative use of the stone for paralysis cinches a circle of images: the enemies
flung from the hollow of the sling and the smooth stone with which David killed Goliath.

39. *David . . . spoke out for Abigail.* In biblical idiom, the verb "to speak" followed by
the preposition b^e instead of the usual *'el* ("to") means to enter into discussion about a
betrothal. David, losing no time, has certainly grasped the veiled implication of Abigail's
last words to him.

41. *your servant is but a slavegirl to wash the feet of my lord's servants.* In one last flourish of the etiquette of humility, she professes herself unworthy of so great an honor as to
become David's wife. But perhaps this is just what she has been aiming to become, and so,
once again "hurrying," she sets off to join her new husband. She then vanishes from the
subsequent narrative.

44 had taken from Jezreel, and both of them became his wives. And Saul had given Michal his daughter, David's wife, to Palti son of Laish, who was from Gallim.

1 **CHAPTER 26**   And the Ziphites came to Saul at Gibeah, saying, "Is not David hiding out at the hill of Hachilah facing the waste-
2 land?" And Saul arose and went down to the wilderness of Ziph, and with him three thousand picked men of Israel, to seek David in the wilderness
3 of Ziph. And Saul camped at the hill of Hachilah which is facing the waste-land, along the way; and David was staying in the wilderness, and he saw
4 that Saul had come after him into the wilderness. And David sent spies and

---

44. *And Saul had given Michal his daughter, David's wife, to Palti.* The legality of this act is questionable. David's having taken two wives—of Ahinoam all we know is her place of origin—while hiding out from Saul is no justification because, given the practice of polygamy, he could have done that even if he were living under the same roof with Michal. Saul's motive is political, to deprive David of one claim to the throne by removing the connection through marriage with the royal family. But that connection has already been established, as the narrator's identification of Michal as "David's wife" is meant to remind us. We can only guess what Michal, who we know loved David, feels about being passed around in this fashion, or what she feels about the man her father has imposed on her. Later, we will be accorded a brief but unforgettable glimpse into Palti's feelings for Michal.

CHAPTER 26   1. *And the Ziphites came to Saul at Gibeah.* This verse, echoing much of the language of 23:19, announces the beginning of the last of the elaborately paired episodes that structure the story of David and Saul. Scholarly consensus assumes that these doublets reflect different sources or traditions bearing on the same events, although the possibility cannot be rejected out of hand that the original writer may have deliberately composed his story with paired incidents. In any case, the pairings need to be read as part of the purposeful compositional design of the redacted version of the narrative that we have. As the Russian formalist critic Viktor Shklovsky observed long ago, every parallelism in a literary text serves to point up a certain semantic difference. Here, we note at the outset that the elaborately detailed intelligence about David's whereabouts provided by the Ziphites in 23:19 is largely absent from this briefer account: this story will prove to be an *inversion* of the earlier one, David discovering Saul instead of the other way around. Another indication that the doublet is manipulated as an element of purposeful design is the fact that this episode simultaneously repeats *two different* previous episodes—not only the earlier story of Saul's pursuit of David into the wilderness of Ziph but also the encounter between David and Saul at the cave near Ein-Gedi (chapter 24). There, just as here, David refused to kill Saul when he, or one of his men, could have done so, and there he professed his innocence to a remorseful Saul who called him as he does here, "my son, David."

3. *he saw that Saul had come after him.* The placement of this second account of pursuit in the wilderness of Ziph after Saul's solemn pledge in chapter 24 not to harm David underlines the compulsive character of his obsession with David. Whatever his avowed

he knew with certainty that Saul had come. And David arose and came to 5
the place where Saul had camped. And David saw the place where Saul lay,
and Abner son of Ner and Saul were lying within the staging ground, and
the troops were encamped around him. And David spoke up and said to 6
Ahimelech the Hittite and to Abishai son of Zeruiah, saying, "Who will come
down with me to Saul, to the camp?" And Abishai said, "I on my part shall
go down with you." And David came, and Abishai, to the troops by night, 7
and, look, Saul was lying asleep within the staging ground, his spear thrust
into the ground at his head, and Abner and the troops were lying around
him. And Abishai said to David, "God has this day delivered your enemy 8
into your hand, and now, let me, pray, strike him through with the spear
into the ground just once, I will need no second blow." And David said to 9

---

good intentions, Saul cannot restrain his impulse to destroy his rival. There is thus strong
narrative logic in the recurrence: after this last encounter with Saul, David will sensibly
conclude that he can no longer trust the king's professions of good faith, and he will take
flight beyond the borders of Israel.

4. *David sent spies and he knew with certainty.* In contrast to the episode in chapter 23, it
is David here who commands military intelligence. The writer makes this point neatly by
using the same (relatively unusual) phrase, *'el nakhon*, "with certainty," which in chapter
23 was spoken by Saul, referring to the information about David he expected to get from
the Ziphites.

6. *Ahimelech the Hittite.* In biblical usage, "Hittite" is a loose designation for Canaanite
peoples and does not necessarily refer to the Indo-European group that originated in Anatolia. The presence of a foreigner in David's inner circle of warriors suggests an openness
of his band of disaffected men to adventure seekers, freebooters, and other mobile types
in the Canaanite population. Ahimelech is nowhere else mentioned in the biblical record,
which has led some scholars to infer that the mention of this foreigner may be an authentic
early notice of a historical personage. The name itself is Hebrew.
  Abishai son of Zeruiah. If the report in Chronicles is reliable, Zeruiah was David's
sister—hence the unusual matronymic instead of a patronymic. David the warrior-
chieftain is surrounded by his three nephews, the three bloody-minded sons of Zeruiah:
two of them impetuous (Abishai and Asahel), the third, who is David's commander, ruthlessly calculating (Joab).

8. *God has this day delivered your enemy into your hand.* These words explicitly echo the
words of David's men when they discover Saul unawares in the cave.
  strike him through with the spear . . . just once, I will need no second blow. This bit of
warrior's bravado helps us make an important connection, as J. P. Fokkelman has nicely
observed: twice Saul hurled this same spear at David, who eluded him. Abishai on his part
vows he will deliver one swift, lethal blow.

9. *And David said.* Abishai, dumbfounded, offers no response to David's forbidding him
to harm this archenemy, and so David has to explain that God will settle accounts with
Saul in His own good time.

Abishai, "Do no violence to him! For who can reach out his hand against
10   the LORD's anointed and be guiltless?" And David said, "As the LORD
lives, the LORD will smite him, or his day will come and he will die, or in
11   battle he will go down and perish. The LORD forbid that I should reach out
my hand against the LORD's anointed! And so now, take, pray, the spear
12   which is at his head and the water jug and let us go off." And David took
the spear and the water jug at Saul's head, and they went off, with no one
seeing and no one knowing and no one waking, for they were all asleep, for
13   the LORD's deep slumber had fallen upon them. And David crossed over to
the opposite slope and stood on the mountaintop from afar, great was the
14   distance between them. And David called out to the troops and to Abner
son of Ner, saying, "Will you not answer, Abner?" And Abner answered and
15   said, "Who are you, that you have called out to the king?" And David said
to Abner, "Are you not a man, and who is like you in Israel, and why have
you not guarded your lord the king? For one of the troops has come to do

---

Do no violence to him. Instead of one of three expected verbs, "to strike down," "to kill,"
"to put to death," David uses the verb *hishḥit*, which basically means "to destroy," but which
can carry the association, as Kyle McCarter Jr. rightly observes, of mutilation or deface-
ment, the taboo acts that should not be perpetrated on the person of the king.

11. *take . . . the spear*. In the episode at the cave, David carried away the cut-off corner of
Saul's garment, which had been symbolically linked with kingship. The spear is an alternative image of kingship, obviously more directly associated with martial potency, and so this
version conveys a greater sense that David is depriving Saul of something essential in the
token of kingship he bears off. Again, the placement of this version of the paired episodes
is telling, for the next time we see Saul in the narrative he will be undone on the battlefield
by the Philistines and will turn his own weapon against himself.
     and the water jug. The spear protects life by destroying; the water jug sustains life for
the warrior in battle under the hot sun.

12. *And David took the spear and the water jug*. David takes them himself, after having
ordered Abishai to do it. The medieval Hebrew exegete David Kimchi offers a shrewd
explanation: "He changed his mind and didn't want Abishai to approach the king, lest he
prove unable to restrain himself and kill Saul."

14. *Who are you, that you have called out to the king?* Some ancient versions omit "to
the king" because David has called out to Abner, not to Saul. David's shouting from the
prominence, however, occurs in the middle of the night, and it clearly has awakened Saul,
which seems to be what is bothering Abner. David has chosen Saul's commander as his
first interlocutor in order to stress the sacred responsibility of those around the king to
protect his person. His noble words are not devoid of self-interest because David is clearly
conscious of the fact that he is the future king.

violence to the king your lord. It is not good, this thing that you have done,   16
as the LORD lives, for you all deserve death, because you did not guard your
master, the LORD's anointed. And now, see, where are the king's spear and
the water jug that were at his head?" And Saul recognized David's voice   17
and he said, "Is this your voice, my son, David?" And David said, "It is my
voice, my lord the king." And he said, "Why is it that my lord chases after   18
his servant, for what have I done, and what evil is in my hand? And now,   19
let my lord the king hear, pray, the words of his servant. If the LORD has
incited you against me, let Him be appeased by an offering, and if it be men,
cursed are they before the LORD, for they have banished me today from
joining the LORD's inheritance, saying, 'Go, serve other gods.' And now, let   20
not my blood fall to the ground away from the LORD's presence, for the king
of Israel has come forth to seek a single flea, as he would chase a partridge
in the mountains." And Saul said, "I have offended. Come back, my son,   21

---

15. *one of the troops has come to do violence to the king.* Although this could refer to Abishai, the essential referent is David himself—something he does not want to say in so many
words.

16 *you all deserve death.* "All" is supplied in the translation in order to convey the fact that
here the pronoun "you" is a plural in the Hebrew. This death sentence pronounced on Saul's
entire entourage is extravagant, but Abner at least will die a violent death.

17. *Is this your voice, my son, David?* These are the identical words he pronounces outside
the cave near Ein-Gedi. Here, he "recognizes" the voice—as, symbolically, in this remission
of his madness, he recognizes his paternal bond with David—but he is not entirely sure
because of the darkness, and so he asks.

18. *what evil is in my hand?* As elsewhere, "hand" and "in my hand" have multiple valences.
What David literally has in his hand as he speaks is the king's spear!

19. *If the LORD has incited . . . if it be men.* These two alternatives are a kind of diplomatic
maneuver. David doesn't want to put the blame squarely on Saul, so he proposes that the
king was "incited" either by God for some mysterious reason or by malicious people.
    let Him be appeased by an offering. The Hebrew says literally, "let Him smell [the fra-
grant odor of] an offering."
    banished me . . . from . . . the LORD's inheritance. The LORD's inheritance clearly refers
to the Land of Israel. Since every national region had its own cult, David is saying that to
be excluded from his own national borders is tantamount to being obliged to worship other
gods. In fact, his flight from Saul has been mostly within Israelite territory, but he seems to
be anticipating that his next move, for his own safety, will have to be into Philistine country.

20. *to seek a single flea, as he would chase a partridge in the mountains.* The language of the
entire clause recycles the words David used to conclude his speech outside the cave. But the
dead dog has been deleted and a partridge has been introduced instead. This image is less

David, for I will not harm you again inasmuch as my life was precious in
22 your eyes this day. I have played the fool and have erred gravely." And David
answered and said, "Here is the king's spear. Let one of the lads cross over
23 and take it. And the LORD will pay back to a man his right actions and his
loyalty, for the LORD gave you today into my hand and I did not want to
24 reach out my hand against the LORD's anointed. And, look, just as I valued
your life highly today, may the LORD value my life highly and may He save
25 me from every strait." And Saul said to David, "Blessed are you, my son,
David. You shall surely do much and you shall surely win out." And David
went on his way, but Saul returned to his place.

1 CHAPTER 27   And David said in his heart, "Now, I shall
perish one day by the hand of Saul. There is nothing better for me than
to make certain I get away to Philistine country. Then Saul will despair

---

forceful, but its attraction in the Hebrew, as several commentators have noted, is a witty
pun: partridge (*qore'*) is a homonym for "he who calls out." David (verse 14) was identified
by Abner as the one who called out to the king—a caller out on the mountain, a partridge
pursued on the mountains.

22. *And David answered and said, "Here is the king's spear."* It is noteworthy that David
does not immediately respond to Saul's renewed profession of regret and good faith. (The
Masoretic consonantal text, the *ketiv*, tries to rescue this lapse by representing these words
as a vocative, "Here is the spear, king," but the *qeri*, or pronounced Masoretic version,
properly renders it as *ḥanit hamelekh*, "the king's spear.") In the encounter at the cave,
David vowed he would not harm Saul's descendants, though his actual words were not
reported. Here, he first gives an impersonal order to have the spear brought back to Saul. It
is only when he goes on to recapitulate his profession of innocence that he again addresses
Saul. By this point, he no longer trusts any promises Saul may make not to harm him but
hopes that God will note his own proper conduct and therefore protect him (verse 24).

24. *I valued your life highly.* The literal Hebrew idiom is "your life was great in my eyes."

25. *Blessed are you, my son, David.* These words of fatherly blessing are the last ones Saul
speaks to David: the two never meet again. It is notable that in their previous encounter,
Saul explicitly conceded that David would replace him as king, whereas here he merely says
in general language, "You shall surely do much and you shall surely win out."
     David went on his way, but Saul returned to his place. This is a biblical formula for mark-
ing the end of a narrative unit, but it also nicely distinguishes between the two men: David
continues on the move while Saul goes back to his set place of residence.

CHAPTER 27   1. *And David said in his heart.* This is the first actual interior monologue given for David. The decision to "cross over" (verse 2) to the enemy is a momentous
one, and the writer wants to make it perfectly clear that David had definitively realized Saul
was bound to kill him sooner or later ("I shall perish one day by the hand of Saul") unless
he moved to the safety of enemy territory.

of seeking me anymore through all the territory of Israel, and I shall get away from him." And David arose, and he crossed over, he and the six 2 hundred men who were with him, to Achish son of Maoch, king of Gath. And David stayed with Achish in Gath, he and his men, each man with his 3 household, David with his two wives, Ahinoam the Jezreelite and Abigail wife of Nabal the Carmelite. And it was told to Saul that David had fled to 4 Gath, and he no longer sought after him. And David said to Achish, "If, 5 pray, I have found favor in your eyes, let them give me a place in one of the outlying towns that I may dwell there. For why should your servant dwell in the royal town with you?" And Achish gave him Ziklag on that 6 day. Therefore has Ziklag belonged to the kings of Judah until this day. And the span of time that David dwelled in Philistine country was a year 7 and four months. And David went up, and his men with him, and they 8 raided the Geshurite and the Gerizite and the Amalekite, for they were the inhabitants of the land of old, till you come to Shur and to the land

---

2. *he crossed over . . . to Achish . . . king of Gath.* For those scholars who have argued that David is no more a historical figure than King Arthur, this whole episode constitutes a problem: why would a much later, legendary, and supposedly glorifying tradition attribute this act of national treachery to David? (It would be rather like the invention of a story that Winston Churchill spent 1914–1918 in Berlin, currying the favor of the kaiser.) The compelling inference is that the writer had authentic knowledge of a period when David collaborated with the Philistines; he was unwilling to omit this uncomfortable information, though he did try to mitigate it.

3. *David stayed with Achish in Gath . . . each man with his household.* The circumstances have changed drastically since David arrived in Gath alone and was obliged to play the madman. Now he comes with six hundred men under his command, a fighting unit that could be of great use to Achish, and essentially offers to become Achish's vassal. The notice about the households sets the stage for the Amalekite raid on Ziklag in chapter 29, for we now become aware that David's guerilla band carries in its train a sizable group of wives and children.

5. *For why should your servant dwell in the royal town with you?* On his part, David would like to establish his own headquarters and enjoy much greater freedom of movement. But given that his six hundred men with multiple wives and children could easily have made up a group of two or three thousand people, they would have in fact been a rather burdensome presence in a modest-sized Philistine city.

6. *Ziklag.* The best archaeological guess is that this is a site a few miles to the northwest of Beersheba, in an area under Philistine jurisdiction but facing the border with Israel.
   Therefore has Ziklag belonged to the kings of Judah. This seemingly technical geopolitical notice serves a function of historical foreshadowing, as Fokkelman observes: David, the Philistine vassal and fugitive from Saul, is destined to found a lasting dynasty, "the kings of Judah."

8. *for they were the inhabitants of the land of old, till you come to Shur.* There might be a textual distortion here: several versions of the Septuagint read "the inhabited land from Telem to Shur." But the Masoretic version has a certain logic: what David sets out to do is

9 of Egypt. And David struck the land, and he left not a man or woman
alive, and he took sheep and cattle and donkeys and camels and clothes,
10 and he returned and came to Achish. And Achish said, "Where were you
raiding now?" And David said, "The Negeb of Judah and the Negeb of the
11 Jerahmeelite and the Negeb of the Kenite." And neither man nor woman
did David leave alive to bring to Gath, thinking, "Lest they tell about us,
saying, 'Thus did David.' " And such was his practice all the time he
12 dwelled in Philistine country. And Achish trusted David, saying, "He has
surely become repugnant to Israel and he will be my perpetual vassal."

28:1 And it happened at that time that the Philistines had gathered their ranks
for the army to do battle with Israel, and Achish said to David, "You surely
know that with me you must sally forth in the ranks, both you and your

---

to attack the age-old inhabitants of the land, who are Israel's staunch enemies, throughout
this southern region. In doing this, he is also serving Achish's purposes, for these peoples
are equally hostile to the Philistines (like the Israelites, latecomer interlopers in Canaan).

9. *he left not a man or woman alive.* The narrator offers no indication of whether he thinks
these massacres are morally objectionable or merely what Israel's traditional enemies
deserve. A pragmatic reason for the butchery will be given in verse 11. It should be noted that
David is not carrying out a total "ban" (*ḥerem*) against these groups because he keeps all the
livestock as booty, thus palpably building up a base of wealth for himself and his followers.

10. *Where were you raiding now?* Achish of course wants to know about the military activities of his vassal. David answers with a flat lie, claiming he has been conducting raids
against his own tribe, Judah, and against two ethnic groups more or less attached to Judah.
In fact, he has been attacking only non-Israelite groups.

The Negeb. The term Negeb means "dry land" and refers to the desert stretching across
southern Israel from near the Dead Sea to near the coastal plain. Its subregions are then
identified by the tribe or ethnic group that inhabits each.

11. *Lest they tell about us, saying, "Thus did David do."* David wipes out all these populations because he wants no one surviving to bring word back to Gath that he has restricted
his attacks entirely to Canaanite and related peoples, and also that he has been enriching
himself with more booty than he has been sharing with Achish his overlord by way of
tribute. David is clearly a man who will do anything to survive. His words here will come
back in a surprising new context in his elegy for Saul and Jonathan, when he says, "Tell it
not in Gath."

12. *Achish trusted David.* He believes the lie, or so it seems.

my perpetual vassal. The Hebrew *'eved* has the general meaning of "slave" or "servant,"
but the present episode makes the sense of "vassal" compelling.

28:1. *You surely know that with me you must sally forth.* Despite the just reported "trust" in
David, Achish appears to harbor a lingering doubt (hence the coercive edge of "you surely
know") as to whether David will actually fight against his fellow Israelites, something that,
to Achish's knowledge, David has only claimed to do (27:10).

men." And David said, "Then you yourself know what your servant will do." 2
And Achish said to David, "Then I shall make you my bodyguard for life."

CHAPTER 28   And Samuel had died, and all Israel mourned 3
him, and they buried him in Ramah, in his town. And Saul had taken away
the ghosts and the familiar spirits from the land.

And the Philistines gathered and came and camped at Shunem. And Saul 4
gathered all Israel and they camped at Gilboa. And Saul saw the Philistine 5
camp, and he was afraid, and his heart trembled greatly. And Saul inquired 6
of the LORD, and the LORD did not answer him, neither by dreams nor by
the Urim nor by prophets. And Saul said to his servants, "Seek me out a 7
ghostwife, that I may go to her and inquire through her." And his servants

---

2. *you yourself know what your servant will do.* This is an artful dodge: it could be construed,
as David means it to be construed, as "yes, of course, I'll do it," but the language evasively
does not repeat Achish's words about sallying forth (against Israel).

    I shall make you my bodyguard for life. As befits a ruler addressing a former enemy with
whom he is in uneasy alliance, Achish's gesture is a studied ambiguity—either he is rewarding David for his loyalty by making him a permanent bodyguard, or he is seeking to main-
tain surveillance over David by an appointment that would keep him close to the court.

CHAPTER 28   3. *And Samuel had died.* This second obituary notice for Samuel,
with a pluperfect verb, is introduced in order to set the stage for the conjuration of Samuel's
ghost.

    Saul had taken away the ghosts and the familiar spirits from the land. The two Hebrew
terms, *'ovot* and *yid'onim*, are generally paired, and both refer to the spirits of the dead.
(The latter is derived from the verbal root *y-d-'* "to know," and so prepares the way for the
reappearance of the theme of [withheld] knowledge that has been stalking Saul from the
beginning of his story.) The ghosts and familiar spirits are linked metonymically with
the necromancers who call them up—it is the latter who of course would have been the
actual object of Saul's purge—but the terms themselves primarily designate the spirits.
Biblical views about postmortem existence tend to fluctuate. Often, the dead are thought
to be swallowed up in "the Pit" (*she'ol*) where they are simply silenced, extinguished forever. Sometimes, the dead are imagined as continuing a kind of shadowy afterlife in the
underworld, rather like the spirits of the dead in Book 11 of the *Odyssey*. Following on this
latter view, necromancy in the ancient Hebrew world is conceived not as mere hocus-pocus
but as a potentially efficacious technology of the realm of spirits, which, however, has been
prohibited by God, Who wants no human experts interfering in this realm. Saul, then, has
been properly upholding monotheistic law—reflected in Leviticus—in proscribing necromancy, but in his desperation, he is now about to violate his own prohibition.

6. *the LORD did not answer.* One last time, Saul is excluded from divine knowledge, all
the accepted channels for its conveyance, being enumerated here—dream interpretation,
oracular device, prophecy.

8 said to him, "There is a ghostwife at Ein-Dor." And Saul disguised himself
and put on different clothes, and he went—he together with two men—and
they came to the woman by night, and he said, "Conjure me, pray, a ghost,
9 and summon up the one I say to you." And the woman said to him, "Look,
you yourself know what Saul did, that he cut off the ghosts and the familiar
spirits from the land, and why do you entrap me to have me put to death?"
10 And Saul swore to her by the LORD, saying, "As the LORD lives, no blame
11 will befall you through this thing." And the woman said, "Whom shall I
12 summon up for you?" And he said, "Samuel summon up for me." And the
woman saw Samuel and she screamed in a loud voice, and the woman said

---

8. *Saul disguised himself and put on different clothes.* The narrative motivation is obvious:
as the very ruler who has made necromancy a capital crime (see verse 9), Saul can scarcely
come to engage the services of a necromancer unless he is disguised as a commoner. But
his disguise also is the penultimate instance of the motif of royal divestment. As we have
seen, clothing is associated with Saul's kingship—the torn or cut garment is the tearing of
his kingship, and among the ecstatics surrounding Samuel, Saul stripped himself naked.
Now, in an unwitting symbolic gesture, he divests himself of his royal garments before
going to learn of his own impending death.

9. *you yourself know.* An ironically emphatic use of "to know" to the man who never knows
what he needs to.

    he cut off the ghosts. In place of the more abstract term, "to take away," used by the nar-
rator in verse 3, she, from her perspective as a threatened practitioner, chooses the violent
verb "to cut off."

    why do you entrap me. She uses the verb of entrapment with neat precision, for she fears
that the stranger who has come to her may be an undercover agent for Saul's necromancy
enforcement authority.

10. *Saul swore to her by the LORD.* The irony of Saul's doing this in a negotiation with a
conjurer of spirits is vividly caught by the Midrash: "Whom did Saul resemble at that
moment? A woman who is with her lover and swears by the life of her husband" (Yalkut
Shimoni 2:247:139).

12. *the woman saw Samuel and she screamed in a loud voice.* What terrifies her is not
the apparition of Samuel but the sudden realization of the identity of her nocturnal
visitor. How does she know it is Saul? The most persuasive explanation has been offered
by Moshe Garsiel. As other biblical references to conjuration of the dead suggest, the
usual method would be for the necromancer to listen to and interpret the supposed
"chirping" (*tsiftsuf*) or murmuring sounds made by shadows or wispy wraiths believed
to be the presences of the dead. (There is scant biblical evidence for the claim that the
necromancer was a medium from whose throat the ghost spoke.) In this case, however,
the spirit appears not as a murmuring wisp or shadow but as the distinctly defined image
of Samuel, in his prophet's cloak (see verses 13–14), and the woman of Ein-Dor immediately realizes that it is only for the king that the prophet Samuel would have thus risen
from the underworld in full-body image. It is noteworthy that the narrator is discreetly
silent about the actual mechanics of the conjuration procedure, perhaps out of a kind of
monotheistic reticence.

to Saul, "Why did you deceive me, when you are Saul?" And the king said 13
to her, "Do not fear. But what do you see?" And the woman said to Saul,
"A god do I see rising up from the earth." And he said to her, "What does 14
he look like?" And she said, "An old man rises up, and he is wrapped in a
cloak." And Saul knew that it was Samuel, and he bowed to the ground and
did obeisance. And Samuel said, "Why have you troubled me to summon 15
me up?" And Saul said, "I am in dire straits, and the Philistines are fighting
against me and God has turned away from me and no longer answers me,
neither through prophets nor dreams, and I called to you to let me know
what I should do." And Samuel said, "And why do you ask me, when the 16

---

13. *Do not fear. But what do you see?* Saul assures her that even though he is the very king
who prohibited necromancy, he will stand by his vow that no blame will be attached to her.
What he urgently wants to know is the identity of the conjured presences—she can see the
spirit, but he cannot, so once more Saul needs some mediation for the knowledge he seeks.

A god do I see rising up from the earth. The Hebrew balances precariously on a linguistic
ambiguity that has no happy English equivalent. The word for "god" here is *'elohim*, which
when treated grammatically as a singular (it has a plural ending) usually means God. In the
plural, it often refers to "gods" in the polytheistic sense. It also occasionally means "angel"
or "divine being," and some have argued, unconvincingly, that it sometimes means "judge."
A further complication here is that the ghostwife uses *'elohim* with a plural participle (and
hence the King James Version renders it as "gods"). It seems likely that the grammatical
crossover we have just reviewed encouraged a fluidity of usage in which the plural might
sometimes be employed with a singular sense, even when the referent was not the one
God. In the immediately following question and response between Saul and the woman,
it is presupposed that she has seen only one male figure, and the narrator has already told
us she has seen Samuel. When she says she sees *'elohim* rising up, she probably means an
imposing figure like unto a god or an angel, or perhaps she is using it as a term for "spirit."

14. *wrapped in a cloak.* It is the cloak, *me'il*, that clinches the identification for Saul—the
same prophet's cloak that he clung to and tore. From childhood, when Samuel's mother
would make him a new *me'il* each year, to the grave, Samuel is associated with this garment.

15. *Why have you troubled me.* In perfect character, Samuel begins by addressing an angry
question to Saul, using a verb that refers to disturbing a person from sleep, or from the sleep
of death. In divergence from the usual necromantic procedure, the ghost of Samuel speaks
directly to Saul, who in turn questions Samuel himself. In fact, the ghostwife appears to have
absented herself at this point, for the indication in verse 21, "And the woman came to Saul
and saw that he was very distraught," is that she is returning to the room after having left it.

*I am in dire straits, and the Philistines are fighting . . . and God has turned away . . . and I
called to you.* The desperate Saul spills out all the causes for his desperation in one breathless run-on sentence, which this translation tries to reproduce.

neither through prophets nor dreams. Addressing a prophet, Saul makes prophecy the
first item. He deletes the Urim—perhaps, it has been suggested, because of his guilty recollection of his massacre of the priests at Nob.

16. *why do you ask me.* Once again, in this case sardonically, there is a play on Saul's name
(*Sha'ul*) and the verb "to ask" (*sha'al*).

17 Lord has turned away from you and become your foe? And the Lord has
    done to you as He spoke through me, and the Lord has torn the kingship
18 from your hand and given it to your fellow man, to David. In as much as you
    did not heed the voice of the Lord and you did not carry out His burning
    wrath against Amalek, therefore has the Lord done this thing to you this
19 day! And the Lord shall give Israel, too, together with you, into the hands
    of the Philistines. And tomorrow—you and your sons are with me. The
    camp of Israel, too, shall the Lord give into the hand of the Philistines."
20 And Saul hastened and flung himself full length on the ground and was
    very frightened by Samuel's words. Neither did he have strength, for he had
21 eaten no food all day and all night. And the woman came to Saul and saw

---

17. *the Lord has torn the kingship from your hand.* As this particular clause highlights,
Samuel's entire speech is a recapitulation of the denunciatory speech he made to Saul at
the end of the Amalek episode (chapter 15). The tearing of the kingship "from your hand"
visually recalls Saul's hand grasping the torn skirt of Samuel's cloak. There, Samuel had
said God would give the throne to "your fellow man who is better than you." Now, of course,
he can spell out the name David.

18. *you did not heed the voice of the Lord.* The phrasal motif of "heeding the voice" from
chapter 15 is again invoked. After Samuel's return to the underworld, the woman of Ein-
Dor, on a purely mundane plane, will speak twice about heeding voices (verses 21–22).

19. *And tomorrow—you and your sons are with me.* Saul, having come to seek advice on
the eve of a great battle, is given a denunciation concluding with a death sentence, conveyed in these words with spooky immediacy, as the ghost of Samuel beckons Saul and his
sons down into the underworld. This entire scene is conceivably one of the inspirations
for Macbeth's encounter with the three witches, though the biblical writer, in contrast to
Shakespeare, places it at the penultimate moment of his doomed king's story.

The camp of Israel, too. There is no need to perform textual surgery on this sentence
simply because it repeats the burden of the first sentence of the verse. It would be perfectly
in character for Samuel to rub in the news of the imminent catastrophe: not only will you
and your sons perish, but, as I have said, all your forces will be defeated by the Philistines,
your kingship ending in wholesale failure.

20. *Saul hastened and flung himself full length on the ground.* Most translators have interpreted the second verb here as an involuntary one ("fell"). But the verb "to hasten" (*miher*)
is generally part of a sequence of voluntary actions, as its use in verse 24 ("and she hastened
and butchered it and took") neatly illustrates. Saul, in his terror and despair, flings himself
to the ground, and then scarcely has the strength to get up. The Hebrew for "full length"
includes the component *qomah*, "stature," and so is a reminder that the man of majestic
stature is now cast to the ground in final defeat.

for he had eaten no food. There is no convincing evidence to support the claim of some
scholars that a person had to fast before seeing a necromancer. Perhaps Saul's fasting is a
reflex of his distraught condition, but he may well be fasting because he is about to enter into
battle. (It appears that his two bodyguards have also not eaten.) This would invite a con-

that he was very distraught, and she said to him, "Look, your servant has
heeded your voice, and I took my life in my hands and heeded your words
that you spoke to me. And now, you on your part, pray heed the voice of   22
your servant, and I shall put before you a morsel of bread, and eat, that you
may have strength when you go on the way." And he refused and said, "I   23
will not eat." And his servants pressed him, and the woman as well, and
he heeded their voice and arose from the ground and sat upon the couch.
And the woman had a stall-fed calf in the house. And she hastened and   24
butchered it and took flour and kneaded it and baked it into flatbread,
and set it before Saul and before his servants, and they ate, and they arose   25
and went off on that night.

CHAPTER 29   And the Philistines gathered all their camps   1
at Aphek, while Israel was encamped by the spring in Jezreel. And the Phi-   2
listine overlords were advancing with hundreds and with thousands, and
David and his men were advancing at the rear with Achish. And the Phi-   3

---

nection, which has been made by both Fokkelman and Garsiel, with the vow of abstinence
from food that Saul earlier imposed on his troops (chapter 15). There, he was ready to put
Jonathan to death for having tasted a bit of honey; here, he will end by partaking of a feast.

22. *a morsel of bread.* She says this to play down what she will serve him, which is a hearty
dinner, with a main course of veal.

24. *the woman had a stall-fed calf.* It would have taken several hours to accomplish this
slaughtering and cooking and baking. One must imagine Saul sitting in the house at Ein-
Dor, brooding or darkly baffled or perhaps a little catatonic. It is an odd and eerie juncture
of the story. David has already twice been saved, from death and then from bloodguilt, by
women. Saul is now given sustaining nurture by a woman—but only to regain the strength
needed to go out to the battlefield where he will die.

CHAPTER 29   1. *the Philistines gathered all their camps at Aphek.* The "all" stresses
that this is a massing of the entire Philistine army, not merely a division or two, for a
decisive confrontation with the Israelites. As Robert Polzin notes, the first major clash
with the Philistines in 1 Samuel began with the Philistines' camping at Aphek (4:1b), so the
mention of their encampment here at the same site creates a kind of symmetrical frame for
the book. Aphek is roughly forty miles south of Jezreel, not far from Philistine territory,
and would have served as a general staging ground. The Philistine army then advances
northward to camp at Shunem (28:4), just opposite Saul's forces at the spring of Jezreel and
near Mount Gilboa.

2. *David and his men were advancing at the rear with Achish.* Given David's double role as
Achish's vassal and as his special bodyguard, his position in battle should have been alongside Achish. Until this mention of David, we might have imagined that the report of the

listine captains said, "Who are these Hebrews?" And Achish said to the
Philistine captains, "Is this not David, servant of Saul king of Israel, who
has been with me these many days or years, and I have found nothing amiss
4   in him from the day he fell in with me until this day?" And the Philistine
captains were furious with him, and the Philistine captains said to him,
"Send the man back and let him go back to his place that you set aside for
him there, and let him not come down with us into battle, so that he become
not our adversary in battle. For how would this fellow be reconciled with
5   his master—would it not be with the heads of our men? Is this not David
for whom they sing out in the dances, saying,

> 'Saul has struck down his thousands
> and David his tens of thousands'?"

---

deployment of forces was a direct continuation of the account of Saul's seance at Ein-Dor
on the night before the battle. Now it rapidly becomes clear that the narrative has again
switched tracks from Saul to David, suspending the fulfillment of Saul's dire fate in order
to follow the movement of his successor, who approaches the very same battlefield as part
of the enemy forces, only to be turned away. The switch in narrative focus also involves
backtracking in time: we left Saul in the dark of the night (also a symbolic darkness for
him); the deployment of armies and the Philistine dialogues take place on the previous day;
David's early departure, "just when it is brightening" (an antithesis to Saul in the dark, as
J. P. Fokkelman notes), will be on the morning of the battle.

3. *the Philistine captains*. These are the military commanders, *sarim*, and they should not
be thought of as synonymous with the overlords (*seranim*) of the five Philistine cities. It
is the military men who, understandably, fear a serious security risk in the presence of a
Hebrew contingent in their ranks.

Who are these Hebrews? The Hebrew is literally "What are these Hebrews?," which many
translations interpret as "What are these Hebrews doing here?" Again, "Hebrews" is the
term used by foreigners for the Israelites.

David, servant of Saul king of Israel. Achish means to stress that Saul's former courtier
and commander has defected to the Philistine side, but his choice of words inadvertently
reminds the Philistine captains that David may still be loyal to Saul.

these many days or years. Some scholars suspect that these two terms reflect a conflated
text, and that one should simply read "these many days." It could, however, make sense for
Achish to be a little vague about the time and to exaggerate it in order to emphasize David's
loyalty—in fact, David has been with him one year and two months.

fell in with me. Kyle McCarter Jr. proposes that the verb has the sense of "to defect."

4. *would it not be with the heads of our men?* They actually use a euphemism, "the heads of
these men," in order to avoid pronouncing a terrible fate on themselves. Perhaps another
euphemism is involved, through upward displacement, since in chapter 18 it was a different
part of the anatomy of the slain Philistines that David brought back to Saul.

And Achish called to David and said to him, "As the LORD lives, you are 6
upright, and your going into the fray with the camp has been good in my
eyes, for I have found no evil in you from the day you came to me until
this day. But in the eyes of the Philistine overlords you are not good. And 7
so now, return, and go in peace, and you shall do no evil in the eyes of the
Philistine overlords." And David said to Achish, "But what have I done, and 8
what have you found in your servant from the day I appeared in your presence until this day, that I should not come and do battle with the enemies
of my lord the king?" And Achish answered and said to David, "I know 9
that you are as good in my eyes as a messenger of God. But the Philistine
captains have said, 'He shall not go up with us to battle.' And so now, rise 10
early in the morning, you and the servants of your lord who have come with
you, and rise early in the morning when it is just brightening for you, and

---

6. *As the LORD lives.* It is curious that a Philistine should be swearing by the LORD, unless,
as has been argued, he is leaning over backward to adopt David's perspective.

you are upright. In fact, David has been lying to Achish about the object of his raids
(27:8–11).

good in my eyes . . . I have found no evil in you. This entire exchange turns on the neat
antithesis between good and evil, rather like the exchange between Saul and David outside
the cave near Ein-Gedi. Achish will go on to say, quite extravagantly, that David is "as good
in my eyes as a messenger of God" (verse 9). The reader, however, may well wonder whether
David is in fact so unambiguously good.

in the eyes of the Philistine overlords you are not good. Some scholars, following the
Septuagint, read here "you are good," contending that Achish claims a difference of opinion
between the overlords and the captains. It makes better sense simply to assume that he is
referring the negative view of David to the highest echelon of authority, though in fact the
complaint came from the field commanders.

8. *what have I done . . . that I should not . . . do battle with the enemies of my lord the king?*
Continuing to play the role of the perfect Philistine vassal, David protests his eagerness
to fight the Israelites, although in point of fact he must be immensely relieved to escape
from the intolerable position of battling against his own people. As several interpreters
have noticed, the words he archly chooses have a double edge because "my lord the king"
could be a covert reference to Saul, in which case the "enemies" would be the armies of
Achish and his confederates. Whether David, lacking this providential way out, would
really have pitted himself against his own people is another imponderable in the character
of this elusive figure.

from the day I appeared in your presence. The idiomatic force of the phrase is "from
the day I entered your service." Achish had simply said, "from the day you came to me."

10. *you and the servants of your lord.* The translation follows the reading in the Septuagint.
The Masoretic Text, a little less coherently, lacks "you."

11 go." And David rose early, he and his men, to go in the morning to return
to Philistine country, while the Philistines went up to Jezreel.

1 CHAPTER 30   And it happened when David and his men
came to Ziklag on the third day that the Amalekites had raided the Negeb,
2 and Ziklag, and they had struck Ziklag and burned it in fire. And they had
taken the women captive, from the youngest to the oldest, they put no one
3 to death. And they drove them off and went on their way. And David, and his
men with him, came to the town, and, look, it was burned in fire, and their
4 wives and their sons and their daughters were taken captive. And David, and
the troops who were with him, raised their voices and wept until there was
5 no strength left in them to weep. And David's two wives were taken captive,
6 Ahinoam the Jezreelite and Abigail wife of Nabal the Carmelite. And David

---

11. *to Philistine country.* They are in fact headed to the place Achish has "set aside" for them
at the eastern border of Philistine country—the town of Ziklag. Disaster awaits them there.

CHAPTER 30   1. *on the third day.* If, as seems plausible, David and his men were
sent away from the Philistine ranks just before the engagement with the Israelites, the
battle, ending in the catastrophic defeat of Saul's forces, took place while David was traveling southward. The writer, it seems, wants to get David as far away as he can from the
battlefield in the Valley of Jezreel, perhaps to remove him from any possible implication in
Saul's death. But an indirect question lurks in the margin of the narrative, for we are left
to wonder what would have been the outcome of the battle had David turned against his
Philistine allies, as their field commanders feared he would.

the *Amalekites had raided the Negeb, and Ziklag.* David must initially confront a military disaster on his own home front that mirrors the disaster which, unknown to him, has
unfolded in the north. His habitual enemies, the Amalekites, have of course exploited the
absence of the fighting men at Ziklag.

burned it in fire. It is possible, although not entirely certain, that the idiomatic force of
this seemingly redundant idiom, which occurs frequently, is "utterly consumed," "burned
to the ground."

2. *they put no one to death.* At first blush this notice casts a favorable light on the Amalekites in comparison to David, whose practice as a raider has been general massacre of the
conquered population. What becomes clear, however, is that the Amalekites (who do not
have David's motive of secrecy) consider the women and children to be part of the booty
and have carried them off in order to exploit them as slaves. The appearance of the Egyptian man (verse 11) serves as a reminder of the Amalekites' role as slaveholders, and of how
inhumanely they treat their slaves.

they drove them off. This rather brutal verb is typically used for driving animals as in
verse 20, and so highlights the rapaciousness of the Amalekites.

6. *And David was in dire straits, for the troops thought to stone him.* The initial phrase might
momentarily be construed as referring to David's feelings ("and he felt very distressed"),
but it is immediately made clear that the reference is to the practical predicament in which

was in dire straits, for the troops thought to stone him, for all the troops
were embittered, every man over his sons and his daughters. And David took
strength in the LORD his God. And David said to Abiathar the priest, son of 7
Ahimelech, "Bring forth, pray, the ephod." And Abiathar brought forth the
ephod to David. And David inquired of the LORD, saying, "Shall I pursue 8
this raiding party? Shall I overtake it?" And He said, "Pursue, for you will
surely overtake it, and you will surely rescue." And David went, he and the 9
six hundred men who were with him, and they came to the Wadi Besor,
and those to be left stayed behind. And David continued the pursuit, he 10
and four hundred men, and the two hundred men who were too exhausted
to cross the Wadi Besor stayed behind. And they found an Egyptian man 11

---

he suddenly finds himself in relation to his men. As before, David's real emotions remain
opaque—we know only of his participation in the public orgy of weeping. This moment
is also a vivid reminder, as are others in the Saul–David story, of how precarious political
power is: David, the charismatic and brilliant commander who has led his men through a
host of dangers, suddenly discovers that these hard-bitten warriors are ready to kill him
because of the disastrous turn of events. It was he, after all, who drew them to the north
with the Philistine army, leaving Ziklag exposed.

   David took strength in the Lord his God. He finds encouragement in the face of mortal
despair—specifically, as the next verse explains, by calling for the oracle. In this fashion,
he staves off the assault his men are contemplating by dramatically showing that they still
have means of redress against the Amalekites, and that he has a special channel of communication with God.

7. *Bring forth, pray, the ephod.* As several interpreters have observed, there is an antithetical
contrast here between David, who has priest and ephod to convey to him God's oracular
counsel, and Saul, who, frustrated in all his attempts to discover God's intentions, resorts
to forbidden necromancy.

8. *you will surely rescue.* The ephod, as we have noted before, can yield only a binary yes-
or-no answer, so the gist of the oracle is that David should pursue the raiding party. But
rescuing the captives, which is surely paramount in the minds of the embittered guerilla
fighters, was not an explicit part of David's inquiry of the oracle—perhaps because he was
afraid to presume so much. The "yes" from the oracle is now taken to imply that David and
his men will both overtake the raiders and rescue their dear ones.

9. *those to be left stayed behind.* The first phrase (literally, "the ones being left") has bothered some commentators, but it is in keeping with occasional biblical usage to introduce
this sort of proleptic reference, creating what from a modern point of view is a redundancy
between the first and second phrases.

10. *were . . . exhausted.* The verb *piger* may be related to the noun *peger,* "corpse," and so
would have the sense of "dead tired." It should be kept in mind that David and his men had
been traveling three days from the Philistine camp, and now they have had to continue on
into the desert at top speed in order to overtake the raiding party.

11. *they found an Egyptian man in the field.* This is the first of three memorable instances
in the David story in which a foreigner brings intelligence of a dire event, although in

in the field and took him to David, and they gave him bread and he ate,

12 and they gave him water. And they gave him a slice of pressed figs and two raisin cakes. And he ate, and his spirits revived, for he had eaten no

13 bread and drunk no water three days and three nights. And David said to him, "To whom do you belong, and where are you from?" And he said, "I am an Egyptian lad, the slave of an Amalekite man, and my master aban-

14 doned me, for I have been sick now three days. We on our part had raided the Negeb of the Cherithites and that of Judah and the Negeb of Caleb,

15 and Ziklag we burned in fire." And David said to him, "Will you lead me down to this raiding party?" And he said, "Swear to me by God that you will not put me to death and that you will not hand me over to my master.

16 Then I shall lead you down to this raiding party." And he led him down, and, look, they were sprawled out all over the ground eating and drinking and reveling with all the vast booty they had taken from the land of the

17 Philistines and the land of Judah. And David struck them from daybreak till the evening of the next day, and not a man of them got away except for

18 four hundred lads who rode off on camels and fled. And David rescued all

19 that the Amalekites had taken, and his own two wives David rescued. And

---

this case the subject of the intelligence is not the event itself but the whereabouts of the perpetrators.

12. *for he had eaten no bread and drunk no water.* The act of abandoning a sick slave in the desert to perish of thirst and hunger dispels any illusions we may have harbored about the humanity of the Amalekites. Fokkelman has proposed a correspondence (in his calculation, also a synchronicity) between the starving Egyptian and the fasting Saul at Ein-Dor.

13. *I am an Egyptian lad.* The term "lad" (na'ar) does not necessarily indicate chronological age here but rather subservient status, a decorous synonym for "slave," which the Egyptian proceeds to use.

16. *and, look, they were sprawled out.* The presentative "look" (hineh) as an indicator of transition from the narrator's overview to the character's point of view has particular tactical importance here. The Amalekites, as we can infer from the fact that four hundred escape the general slaughter, must number well over a thousand. David arrives with only four hundred men. But he finds the raiders entirely vulnerable to a surprise attack—drunk, sated, and sleeping (rather like the Hessian mercenaries whom Washington caught unawares by the Delaware after their Christmas feast). The term rendered as "sprawled out" (netushim) derives from a verbal root that means to abandon or cast away, and so in this context suggests some kind of dissipation. The people who left the Egyptian to starve to death in the desert are now exposed to destruction through their unrestrained indulgence in food and drink.

17. *four hundred lads.* Again, the versatile na'ar is not an indication of chronological age but is used in its military sense, which appears to be something like "elite troops," or perhaps simply "fighting men."

nothing of theirs was missing, from the youngest to the oldest, from sons to
daughters to booty, all that they had taken for themselves, David restored
it all. And David took all the sheep and the cattle. They drove before them   20
that livestock and said, "This is David's booty."

And David came to the two hundred men who had been too exhausted   21
to go with David, so he had them stay at the Wadi Besor. And they came
out to greet David and to greet the troops who were with him, and David
approached with the troops and asked how they fared. And every wicked   22
and worthless man of the men who had gone with David spoke up and
said, "Inasmuch as they did not go with us, we will give them nothing
from the booty that we rescued, only each man his wife and his children,
that they may drive them off and go." And David said, "You must not do   23
so, my brothers, with what the LORD has given us. For He has guarded us
and has given into our hands the raiding party that came against us. And   24
who would listen to you in this matter? Rather, as the share of him who
goes down into battle is the share of him who stays with the gear, together

---

20. *They drove before them that livestock.* The Masoretic Text has the syntactically problematic "before that livestock" (*lifney hamiqneh hahu'*). This translation is based on a small
emendation, *lifneyhem* ("before them"), assuming a haplography—an inadvertent scribal
deletion of repeated letters, since the last two letters of *lifneyhem* (*heh* and *mem*) are also
the first two letters of *hamiqneh*.

This is David's booty. Since the Amalekites had been raiding throughout the Negeb,
both in Judahite and Philistine territory, they would have assembled a very large collection
of plundered flocks. Thus David has abundant livestock to distribute as "gifts"—the word
also means "blessing" or "greeting"—to the sundry elders of Judah.

21. *he had them stay.* The Masoretic Text has "they had them stay" (a difference of one
vowel). The Septuagint has the singular subject.

22. *that they may drive them off.* The coarseness of the ill-spirited men is reflected in the
verb they use for taking away the wives and children, *nahag*, which, as we have noted, usually means to drive cattle. (Compare the irate Laban's use of the same verb in reference to
Jacob's treatment of Rachel and Leah, Genesis 31:26.)

23. *with what the LORD has given us.* The syntactical link of this clause with what precedes
is not entirely clear. Given the ideology of victory that David assumes—all triumph and
all spoils of war come from God—it is best to construe the particle *'et* that introduces the
clause not as a sign of the accusative but as "with."

24. *who stays with the gear.* There is an implicit rationale for giving an equal share to those
who remain behind—beyond the consideration of exhaustion, they have played a role in
guarding the gear, thus enabling the other fighting men to proceed to battle with a light-
ened load. It is for this reason that David "had them stay" (or "posted them") at the ford of
the wadi. In all respects, this episode is meant to demonstrate David's attributes as leader:

25 shall they share." And so from that day hence it became a set practice
26 in Israel until this day. And David came to Ziklag and he sent from the
   booty to the elders of Judah, to his friends, saying, "Here is a gift for you
27 from the booty of the LORD's enemies," to those in Bethel, and to those
28 in Ramoth-Negeb, and to those in Jattir, and to those in Aroer, and to
29 those in Siphmoth, and to those in Eshtamoa, and to those in Racal, and
   to those in the towns of the Jerahmeelite, and to those in the towns of the
30 Kenite, and to those in Hormah, and to those in Bor-Ashan, and to those
31 in Athach, and to those in Hebron and in all the places where David, with
   his men, had moved about.

1 **CHAPTER 31**   And meanwhile the Philistines were battling
   against Israel, and the men of Israel fled before the Philistines, and they fell
2 slain on Mount Gilboa. And the Philistines followed hard upon Saul and
   his sons, and the Philistines struck down Jonathan and Abinadab and Mal-
3 kishua, the sons of Saul. And the battle went heavy against Saul, and the
   archers, the bowmen, found him, and he quaked with fear of the archers.

---

he finds strength in the face of disaster, consults God's oracle, intrepidly leads his troops in
a counterattack, and now makes the most equitable arrangement for the division of spoils.

26. *he sent from the booty to the elders of Judah, to his friends.* This act shows David the
consummate political man, shoring up support among the sundry leaders of his home tribe
of Judah (hence the catalogue of place-names), and preparing for himself a base in Hebron
(at the end of the catalogue), the principal town of Judah, where he will soon be proclaimed
king. Some scholars have been troubled by "to his friends" (*lerei'eihu*, which would normally
mean "to his friend") and have sought to emend it. David Kimchi, however, persuasively
argues that the ostensibly singular noun can be legitimately read as a plural on the basis of
other biblical precedents, and that the reference to "friends" makes good political sense:
these are the same elders of Judah who provided cover for David during the period when he
was hiding out from Saul in his own tribal territory. The verb "move about" (*hithalekh*) in the
wrap-up verse of this section is an allusion to precisely this period, for it recalls David's flight
with his men from Saul at Keilah in 23:13—"and [they] moved about wherever they could."

CHAPTER 31   1. *And meanwhile the Philistines were battling.* The Hebrew does not
explicitly say "meanwhile," but it is implied by the unusual use of the participial form of
the verb (literally, "are battling") to begin the narrative unit. Rashi neatly catches the effect:
"As when a person says, 'Let us return to the previous subject.'"

3. *the archers, the bowmen.* It has been argued that the duplication reflects a conflation
of two textual variants, but it may be that the writer intended to highlight the use of
the bow, in contrast to other weapons. In characteristic biblical fashion, the narrative
offers no details of the battle, but the following broad outline can be reconstructed: The
major engagement of forces takes place in the Jezreel Valley, to the northwest of Mount
Gilboa. The level ground of the valley would have given the Philistines the opportunity
to deploy their iron chariots, one of their great strategic advantages over the Israelites.

And Saul said to his armor bearer, "Draw your sword and run me through 4
with it, lest these uncircumcised come and run me through and abuse me."
But the armor bearer did not want to do it because he was very frightened,
and Saul took the sword and fell upon it. And the armor bearer saw that 5
Saul was dead, and he, too, fell upon his sword, and he died with him. And 6
Saul died, and his three sons and his armor bearer, and all his men as well,
together on that day. And the men of Israel who were on the other side of the 7
valley and on the other side of the Jordan saw that the men of Israel had fled
and that Saul and his sons were dead, and they abandoned the towns and
fled, and the Philistines came and occupied them.

And it happened the next day that the Philistines came to strip the slain, 8
and they found Saul and his three sons fallen on Mount Gilboa. And they 9
cut off his head and stripped him of his armor, and they sent throughout

---

In the rout of the Israelites that ensues, Saul's forces retreat to the high ground of Mount
Gilboa, where the Philistine chariots would have greater difficulty maneuvering. But the
Philistines send contingents of archers—the bow being the ideal weapon to use against
an army in flight—who exact heavy casualties from the Israelite forces.

he quaked with fear. A revocalization of the verb favored by many scholars yields "he
was badly wounded." But there is much to be said for the Masoretic vocalization: Saul's fear
has been a recurring theme in the narrative; here it would be matched by the armor bearer's
great fear of violating the king; and it is far from clear that Saul is seriously wounded when
he decides to commit suicide (if he were, would he have the strength to fling himself on
his sword?).

4. *and abuse me.* Like the urgent request of the dying Abimelech in Judges 9, with whom the
dying Saul has sometimes been compared, Saul's last wish will be denied him—the Philistines, though deprived of the opportunity to kill him, will decapitate his body and defile it
by hammering it up on the wall of Beth-Shan.

6. *and all his men as well.* The parallel texts in both 1 Chronicles 10 and in the Septuagint
lack this phrase. The argument for it is that it reinforces the image of martial solidarity in
defeat: Saul, his sons, his armor bearer, his men, all perish "together" (*yaḥdaw*).

7. *they abandoned the towns . . . and the Philistines came and occupied them.* After this
major victory, the Philistines manage to cut the Israelite settlement in two by establishing a
sedentary presence across the lower Galilee from the coastal plain to the Jordan, separating
the tribes in the far north from Benjamin and Judah to the south.

9. *they cut off his head and stripped him of his armor.* Saul's successor, David, had marked
his entry on the scene by cutting off the head of a Philistine; now they cut off Saul's head.
The stripping of the armor—and the all-purpose Hebrew *kelim* could also include his
clothing—is the final divestment of Saul, who is stripped before the prophets, stripped of
his royal garments at Ein-Dor, and now lies naked on the battlefield in ultimate defeat.

they sent throughout the Philistine country. There is some grammatical ambiguity as to
whether they simply sent tidings, or Saul's armor as visible token of the victory. The parallel
verse in Chronicles lacks "temples of."

the Philistine country to bring the tidings to the temples of their idols
10 and to the people. And they put his armor in the temple of Ashtaroth,
11 and his body they impaled on the wall of Beth-Shan. And the inhabitants
12 of Jabesh-Gilead heard what the Philistines had done to Saul. And every
valiant fellow arose, and they went all night long, and they took Saul's
corpse, and the corpses of his sons from the wall of Beth-Shan, and they
13 came back to Jabesh and burned them there. And they took their bones
and buried them under the tamarisk in Jabesh, and they fasted seven days.

---

10. *his body they impaled on the wall of Beth-Shan.* Throughout the ancient Mediterranean
world, there was a horror about leaving a corpse unburied (compare, for example, the
potency of this question in Sophocles's *Antigone*). Saul's corpse, moreover, is disfigured
through decapitation. Beth-Shan (or, Beth-She'an) is a town about eleven miles to the
southwest of Mount Gilboa, near the Jordan.

11. *the inhabitants of Jabesh-Gilead.* This settlement is roughly another twelve miles to
the southeast of Beth-Shan, on the eastern side of the Jordan, and hence just beyond the
perimeter of the new Philistine occupation. It was Jabesh-Gilead that Saul rescued from
Nahash the Ammonite (chapter 11) to inaugurate his career as king and general, and there
are kinship bonds between Jabesh-Gilead and Saul's tribe of Benjamin.

12. *every valiant fellow arose.* It would have been a very dangerous exploit to sneak into
the territory now controlled by the Philistines and, under the cover of night, to make off
with the corpses.
   the corpses of his sons. This is an amplification of the Philistine atrocity, since we were
not previously informed that the bodies of the sons were impaled along with Saul's.
   and burned them there. Cremation was not the usual Israelite practice, but it may be,
as Kimchi has proposed, that in this case the bodies were burned because the flesh had
already begun to rot.

13. *and they fasted seven days.* This, too, is an unusual practice as a mourning rite. Perhaps it
merely reflects the grievousness of the loss that the men of Jabesh-Gilead have experienced,
though Fokkelman makes the interesting proposal that the seven days of fasting are a
counterpart to the seven days Nahash the Ammonite allowed Jabesh-Gilead for a deliverer
(who turned out to be Saul) to appear.

2 Samuel

CHAPTER 1   And it happened after the death of Saul, when 1
David had returned from striking down Amalek, that David stayed in
Ziklag two days. And it happened on the third day that, look, a man was 2
coming from the camp, from Saul, his garments torn and earth on his
head. And it happened when he came to David, that he fell to the ground
and did obeisance. And David said to him, "From where do you come?" 3
And he said, "From the camp of Israel I have gotten away." And David said 4
to him "What has happened? Pray, tell me." And he said, "The troops fled
from the battle, and also many of the troops have fallen and died, and also
Saul and Jonathan his son died." And David said to the lad who was telling 5
him, "How do you know that Saul died, and Jonathan his son?" And the 6

CHAPTER 1   1. *after the death of Saul . . . David had returned from striking down Amalek.* As the story unfolds, an odd symmetry emerges: David has just struck down Amalek; an Amalekite says he has struck down Saul; David has this Amalekite put to death.

2. *look, a man was coming . . . his garments torn and earth on his head.* The "look" signals the visual perspective of David and his entourage: what they see is a man who has adopted the most visible signs of conventional mourning. The Amalekite wants to make it clear that he regards Saul's death, and the defeat, as a catastrophe, though, as we shall see, he really has another purpose in mind.

4. *What has happened?* The words he uses, *meh hayah hadavar,* are identical with those spoken to the messenger who brings the news of the disastrous defeat to Eli in 1 Samuel 4:16. There are several other echoes here of that earlier scene.

5. *the lad who was telling him.* The repetition of this phrase (see next verse), as J. P. Fokkelman has noted, calls attention to the act of telling and by underlining that act may make us wonder whether this is an authentic report or a fabrication.

lad who was telling him said, "I just chanced to be on Mount Gilboa, and, look, Saul was leaning on his spear, and, look, chariots and horsemen had
7 overtaken him. And he turned round behind him and saw me and called
8 to me, and I said, 'Here I am.' And he said to me, 'Who are you?' And I
9 said to him, 'I am an Amalekite.' And he said to me, 'Pray, stand over me and finish me off, for the fainting spell has seized me, for while life is still
10 within me. . . .' And I stood over him and finished him off, for I knew that he could not live after having fallen. And I took the diadem that was on his

---

6. *I just chanced to be on Mount Gilboa.* Does one accidentally stumble onto a battlefield while the killing is still going on? A more likely scenario is that the Amalekite came onto the battlefield immediately after the fighting as a scavenger, found Saul's corpse before the Philistines did, and removed the regalia.

Saul was leaning on his spear. From Saul's words in verse 9, what this means is not that he was resting but that he was entirely spent, barely able to stand.

8. *I am an Amalekite.* Only now, in the middle of the story, is the national identity of the messenger revealed. The fact that he was an Amalekite means he would have felt no recoil of taboo about doing violence to the king of Israel—something Saul appears to grasp at once. (Compare Doeg the Edomite's slaughter of the priests of Nob in 1 Samuel 22.) But there is also dramatic irony here: Saul lost his hold on the kingship when he failed to kill the Amalekite king; now he begs an Amalekite to kill him, the king of Israel.

9. *Pray, stand over me and finish me off.* "Stand over" suggests that Saul himself is barely standing, that he is collapsed against the support of his spear—the very spear that has been associated with his kingship and with his outbursts of rage. "Finish me off" is somewhat inelegant as English diction, but the nuance of the Hebrew (the *polel* conjugation of the verbal stem that means "to die") is essential to the story: Saul feels he is dying, and he asks the Amalekite lad not to kill him but to finish him off before the Philistines can get to him. The Amalekite and David concur in this indication of what the Amalekite does to Saul.

the fainting spell. The Hebrew noun appears only here. It may be related to a root that suggests "confusion," or, alternately, "weakness."

for while life is still within me. This clause, which has vexed some critics and has led to emendations, is most simply construed as a broken-off sentence that the failing Saul does not have the strength to complete.

10. *I stood over him and finished him off.* This whole story obviously contradicts the account of Saul's death by his own hand in 1 Samuel 31. Predictably, this has led many critics to imagine two conflicting "sources." It is reassuring that more recent scholarly consensus has come to the sensible conclusion that the Amalekite lad is lying. Having come upon Saul's body, he sees a great opportunity for himself: he will bring Saul's regalia to David, claim personally to have finished off the man known to be David's archenemy and rival, and thereby overcome his marginality as resident alien ("sojourner," *ger*) by receiving a benefaction from the new king—perhaps a portion of land at David's disposal. Fokkelman shrewdly notes that the Amalekite, instead of removing the diadem and armband from Saul's body, might better have buried the body or dragged it off and so saved it from desecration by the Philistines.

for I knew that he could not live after having fallen. The Amalekite sees Saul's condition "leaning" on his spear to be equivalent to having fallen ("for the fainting spell has seized

head and the band that was on his arm, and I have brought them here to
my lord." And David took hold of his garments and tore them, and all the 11
men who were with him did so, too. And they keened and they wept and 12
they fasted till evening for Saul and for Jonathan his son and for the LORD's
people and for the house of Israel because they had fallen by the sword. And 13
David said to the lad who had told him, "From where are you?" And he said,
"The son of an Amalekite sojourner am I." And David said to him, "How 14
were you not afraid to reach out your hand to do violence to the LORD's
anointed?" And David called to one of the lads and said, "Come forward, 15
stab him." And he struck him down, and he died. And David said to him, 16
"Your blood is on your own head, for your mouth bore witness against you,
saying, 'I was the one who finished off the LORD's anointed.'" And David 17
sang this lament for Saul and for Jonathan, and he said to teach hard things 18
to the sons of Judah—look, it is written down in the Book of Jashar:

---

me") and assumes, as does Saul himself in this account, that in any case the king will not
survive.

14. *How were you not afraid . . . to do violence to the LORD's anointed?* Although the Israelite
piety of David's statement is noteworthy, his words, as in the previous episodes in which
he warned against harming Saul, are also politically self-interested because he, too, is the
LORD's anointed. In fact, now with Saul's death, he alone is the LORD's anointed.

16. *your mouth bore witness against you.* There is no way of knowing whether David actually
believes the Amalekite's story, but it is certainly convenient for him to be able to point an
accusing finger at someone with whom he has had nothing to do as the person responsible
for Saul's death, and then to order immediate punishment.

   the LORD's anointed. At the end of the episode, David makes a point of using the epithet
of divinely grounded royal status instead of simply calling his predecessor "Saul," as the
Amalekite (who never even refers to him as "king") had done.

17. *And David sang this lament.* We have been aware since 1 Samuel 16 of David's gift as a
lyre player and (presumably) as a singer. Only now do we hear him in action as a singer-
poet. This grandly resonant lament, cast in archaic epic diction, marks a great moment
of transition in the larger narrative, as the David–Saul story becomes the David story. It
is also another public utterance of David's that beautifully serves his political purposes,
celebrating his dead rival as it mourns his loss and thus testifying that David could never
have desired Saul's death.

18. *to teach hard things.* The Masoretic Text has "to teach the bow"—a problematic reading because the lament scarcely provides instruction in the arts of war. Some critics delete
"bow" (*qeshet*), following the Septuagint. The present translation revocalizes *qeshet* as
qashot, with Fokkelman.

   look, it is written down in the Book of Jashar. This lost work, mentioned elsewhere in
the Bible, was obviously familiar to the ancient audience. The title probably means "Book
of the Upright," though another reading of *yashar*, as a verb rather than as a noun, yields
"Book of Songs." (This, however, requires revocalizing the word.) It might have been an
anthology of archaic Hebrew poems.

19   "The splendor, O Israel, on your heights lies slain,
                 how have the warriors fallen!
20   Tell it not in Gath,
                 proclaim not in Ashkelon's streets.
            Lest the Philistine daughters rejoice,
                 lest the daughters of the uncircumcised gloat.
21   O hills of Gilboa—no dew!
                 and no rain upon you, O lofty fields.
            For there the warriors' shield was besmirched,
                 the shield of Saul unburnished with oil.
22   From the blood of the slain,
                 from the warriors' fat—
            Jonathan's bow did not retreat,
                 and the sword of Saul never turned away empty.
23   Saul and Jonathan, beloved and dear,

---

20. *Tell it not in Gath.* There is an ironic echo here of the account of David's activities as vassal to the king of Gath, activities that he did not want told in Gath (see 1 Samuel 27:11).

Lest the Philistine daughters rejoice. In this martial culture, the young women had the role of celebrating the victors ("Saul has struck down his thousands. . . ."), gloating over the defeated enemy, and enjoying the spoils the men brought back from their conquest (compare verse 24).

21. *O hills of Gilboa.* As Shimon Bar-Efrat has observed, apostrophe is the dominant form of address throughout the elegy. David first turns, in a plural verb, to Israel at large ("Tell it not in Gath"), then to the hills of Gilboa, then to Saul and Jonathan, then to the daughters of Israel, then to Jonathan alone. The apostrophe is a form of address that underscores the actual absence of the person or object addressed and so is especially apt for an elegy.

lofty fields. The Hebrew *usedeh terumot* is a little obscure. The simplest solution is to treat the initial particle *u* as an excrescence and to read the phrase as a poetic inversion of the similar *meromey sadeh* in Judges 5:18. In the parallelism here, "lofty fields" would be an epithet for "hills of Gilboa."

unburnished with oil. The shields were made of leather, often studded with metal plates. Rubbing them with oil before battle would have made their outer surface slippery and thus would have enhanced their effectiveness in deflecting weapons. But the Hebrew for "unburnished," *beli mashiah*, is a pun—it means "unanointed" or "messiah-less," a haunting intimation that the LORD's anointed is no more. Clearly, the image of the royal shield lying befouled in the dust is a powerful metonymy for Saul himself.

22. *Jonathan's bow . . . the sword of Saul.* After the image of the implement of defense, the shield, lying cast aside, we get a retrospective picture of these two offensive weapons destroying the enemy. The idea of the sword or the bow consuming flesh and blood is conventional in ancient Near Eastern martial poetry.

in their life and their death they were not parted.
They were swifter than eagles,
   and stronger than lions.
O daughters of Israel, weep over Saul,   24
   who clothed you in scarlet and bangles,
      who studded your garments with jewelry of gold.
How have the warriors fallen   25
   in the midst of the battle.
Jonathan, upon your heights slain!
   I grieve for you, my brother, Jonathan.   26
   Very dear you were to me.
More wondrous your love to me
   than the love of women.
How have the warriors fallen,   27
   and the gear of battle is lost."

---

23. *in their life and their death they were not parted.* This is, of course, an extravagant ide-alization on the part of the elegist since father and son were almost estranged and twice Saul was on the point of killing Jonathan.

24. *O daughters of Israel, weep.* The invocation of the daughters of Israel to weep over the king who brought them precious booty is a symmetrical antithesis to the initial warning to keep the news away from the daughters of the Philistines, who would rejoice.

26. *I grieve for you, my brother, Jonathan.* Jonathan several times proclaimed his love for David. It is only in Jonathan's death, and at the distance of apostrophe, that David calls him "my brother" and says that Jonathan was dear to him.
   More wondrous . . . than the love of women. Repeated, unconvincing attempts have been made to read a homoerotic implication into these words. The reported details of the David story suggest that his various attachments to women are motivated by pragmatic rather than emotional concerns—and in one instance, by lust. This disposition, however, tells us little about David's sexual orientation. The bond between men in this warrior culture could easily be stronger than the bond between men and women.

27. *How have the warriors fallen, / and the gear of battle is lost.* The first clause here echoes the second verset of the opening line of the poem and so closes the elegy in a ringing envelope structure. The second clause beautifully picks up the image of the cast-off shield lying in the dust, and of the relentless bow and sword that will never more be borne into battle. It is misguided to render the verb at the end as "perished" (King James Version, New Jewish Publication Society) because that presupposes that "gear of battle" is actually an epithet for Saul and Jonathan. Far more effectively, the lament concludes with a concrete image of shield and sword and bow abandoned, and by a simple process of metonymy we vividly understand the fate of the two men who once wielded them.

1 CHAPTER 2   And it happened afterward that David inquired
of the LORD, saying, "Shall I go up into one of the towns of Judah?" And the
LORD said to him, "Go up." And David said, "Where shall I go up?" And
2 He said, "To Hebron." And David went up there, and his two wives as well,
3 Ahinoam the Jezreelite and Abigail wife of Nabal the Carmelite. And his
men who were with him David brought up, each man and his household,
4a and they settled in Hebron. And the men of Judah came and anointed
David there as king over the house of Judah.

4b And they told David, saying, "It was the men of Jabesh-Gilead who buried
5 Saul." And David sent messengers to the men of Jabesh-Gilead and said
to them, "Blessed are you to the LORD, that you have done this kindness
6 with your lord, with Saul, and have buried him. And now, may the LORD
show faithful kindness to you, and I on my part as well shall do this bounty
7 for you because you have done this thing. And now, may your hands be
strengthened and be you men of valor, for your lord Saul is dead, and it is
I whom the house of Judah has anointed as king over them."

CHAPTER 2   1. *David inquired of the LORD.* In keeping with the repeated emphasis
of the preceding narrative, David, at each crucial juncture, solicits guidance from God's
oracle before he makes his move.

   go up into one of the towns of Judah. The preposition is used with precision: David does
not want to "go up to one of the towns" but "into one of the towns"—that is, to set up headquarters in the town, leaving Ziklag at the edge of Philistine territory.

   Where shall I go up? Given the binary character of the oracle's response, the actual form
of the question would have been "Shall I go up to Hebron?" But the question is recast in its
present form to emphasize that God has picked out Hebron from all the towns of Judah.

4a. *king over the house of Judah.* It is a little odd for a single tribe to have a "king," but the
act is deliberately presumptive on David's part—first the king of Judah, eventually of all the
tribes. Saul's son Ish-Bosheth, by contrast, becomes king of an alliance of northern tribes.
The text is silent on the Philistines' view of David's move to kingship in Hebron, but one
can assume they countenanced it as a reasonable act on the part of their vassal opposing
the house of Saul.

5. *David sent messengers to the men of Jabesh-Gilead.* This is another shrewd political
maneuver. The men of Jabesh-Gilead had been closely allied with Saul. David, seizing the
occasion of their act of bravery, summons them, praises their burying of Saul, and offers
them an unspecified "bounty" (or "benefice"—literally, "good thing").

7. *for your lord Saul is dead, and it is I whom the house of Judah has anointed as king over*
them. David finesses Saul's hostility toward him and presents himself as the legitimate successor: just as the men of Jabesh-Gilead have been valorous in burying Saul, they should
now show valor in following the newly anointed David.

And Abner son of Ner commander of Saul's army had taken Ish-Bosheth 8
son of Saul and brought him over to Mahanaim and made him king over 9
Gilead and over the Asherite and over Jezreel and over Ephraim and over
Benjamin and over Israel altogether. Forty years old was Ish-Bosheth when 10
he became king over Israel, and two years did he reign. But the house of
Judah followed David. And the span of time that David was king in Hebron 11
over the house of Judah was seven years and six months.

And Abner son of Ner with the servants of Ish-Bosheth sallied forth from 12
Mahanaim to Gibeon. And Joab son of Zeruiah and the servants of David 13
had sallied forth, and they met each other by the pool of Gibeon, and they
took up their positions on either side of the pool. And Abner said to Joab, 14
"Pray, let the lads arise and play before us." And Joab said, "Let them arise."

---

8. *Abner . . . had taken Ish-Bosheth.* Abner the commander in chief is clearly the real power
here, and this surviving son of Saul is little more than a puppet king. The original name
(reflected in Chronicles) was Ish-Baal, with the "baal" component being a general epithet
for God (or god), not necessarily referring to the Canaanite deity. But because of its pagan
associations, the sternly monotheistic later editors systematically substituted *boshet* for
ba'al, *boshet* meaning "shame."

Mahanaim. The location is to the east of the Jordan and hence outside the new area of
Philistine conquest.

9. *Asherite.* The Masoretic Text reads "Ashurite," which would be, implausibly, a non-
Israelite people. Some critics emend to "Geshurite," but that is a Canaanite group, and so
the emendation perpetuates the problem. It is simplest to read this word as a reference to
the northern tribe of Asher.

and over Israel altogether. Shimon Bar-Efrat has made the plausible proposal that this
final phrase is not a summary of the preceding list but the last stage in a chronological
process: Ish-Bosheth extended his rule gradually, beginning with Gilead in trans-Jordan
and moving westward into the territory the Philistines had conquered. It was only after a
time that he actually ruled "over Israel altogether."

10. *two years did he reign.* At first thought, his reign should have been nearly as long as
David's seven and a half years in Hebron. But if it took him five years to consolidate his
control over the northern tribes, the reign of two years would make perfect sense.

12. *Abner . . . sallied forth from Mahanaim to Gibeon.* The reason for this expedition may
have been David's attaching the men of Jabesh-Gilead, who had clearly been in Saul's camp,
to himself. Gibeon is in the territory of Benjamin, just a few miles northwest of Jerusalem.

14. *let the lads arise and play before us.* The "lads" (*ne'arim*) are elite warriors. The verb
"play" clearly indicates gladiatorial, or representative, combat. (Goliath calling for an Israelite champion to fight him is another instance of combat through designated representative.) It is, however, deadly combat and not just a form of jousting, as the details of the
fighting make clear.

15 And they arose and crossed over—twelve in number for Benjamin and for
16 Ish-Bosheth son of Saul and twelve from the servants of David. And each
man grasped the head of the other with his sword at the side of the other,
and they fell together. And they called that place the Field of Flints, which
17 is in Gibeon. And the fighting was very fierce on that day, and Abner with
18 the men of Israel were routed by the servants of David. And the three
sons of Zeruiah were there, Joab and Abishai and Asahel. And Asahel was
19 as swift-footed as one of the gazelles of the open field. And Asahel chased
20 after Abner, and he swerved not to the right or left in going after Abner. And
21 Abner turned round and said, "Are you Asahel?" And he said, "I am." And
Abner said to him, "Swerve you to your right or your left and seize for
yourself one of the lads, and take you his armor." But Asahel did not want to

---

15. *twelve in number.* Throughout this strange episode, as Robert Polzin has aptly observed,
there is an "extended ritualization of action as it is described through extensive stylization
of language." The ritual combat is virtually an allegory of the civil war that it inaugurates.
(Polzin reads it as an allegory of Israelite monarchy.) The twelve champions on each side
recall the twelve tribes of Israel—an image of a nation destructively divided against itself.
(The number of fallen soldiers on Abner's side will be 360—30 times 12—and on Joab's side
20, an eighteenth part of the other side's casualties.) The implausibility of the account of
combat, then, would have been overridden for the writer by the neatness of its symbolic
function.

16. *each man grasped the head of the other with his sword at the side of the other.* The evidence of artifacts from the ancient world suggests that precisely this mode of ritualized
combat was quite widespread. A bas-relief found in Syria, roughly contemporaneous with
our story, an Egyptian carving, archaic Greek vase paintings, and a Roman sculpture all
show warriors in precisely this posture.
    they fell together. All twenty-four warriors were killed—hardly a surprising outcome if
each man was free to wield a sword against his adversary's side. Because there can be no
decisive outcome in this encompassing mutual slaughter, general fighting then breaks out.
    the Field of Flints. It is not clear whether they were fighting with flint weapons (perhaps
because these were archaic and part of the ritualized combat), or whether the old term had
become a general designation for knives or swords.

17. *Abner with the men of Israel were routed.* Given the relatively low number of casualties, it seems likely that fewer than a thousand on each side were engaged. In such limited
combat, the veterans of David's battle-hardened guerilla band of six hundred might have
had a distinct advantage.

20. *Are you Asahel?* Abner, who surely would not have had any compunction about killing
some other Judahite, realizes, quite accurately, that it will mean trouble for him to kill one
of the sons of Zeruiah. Asahel, the ace sprinter, sounds very much like the youngest of the
three, although we are not told specifically about the order of their birth.

21. *his armor.* This noun, *ḥalitsah*, appears only here and in the Samson story. It is rendered
in modern translations, erroneously, as "tunic," "garment," or even "belt," but as we know
from the *Iliad*, it is rather armor that a warrior takes from a slain foe on the battlefield.

turn away from him. And Abner once more said to Asahel, "Turn you away 22
from me. Why should I strike you to the ground, and how would I show
my face to Joab your brother?" And he refused to turn aside, and Abner 23
struck him in the belly with the butt of the spear and the spear came out
behind him, and he fell there and died on the spot. And it happened that
whoever came to the place where Asahel fell and died, stood still. And Joab 24
and Abishai chased after Abner, and as the sun was setting, they had come
to the hill of Ammah, which faces Giah on the way to the wilderness of
Gibeon. And the Benjaminites gathered behind Abner and formed a single 25
band, and they took a stance on the top of a certain hill. And Abner called 26
out to Joab and said, "Must the sword devour forever? You surely know that
it will be bitterness in the end. And how long will you not say to the troops
to turn back from their brothers?" And Joab said, "As God lives, had you 27
but spoken, from this morning the troops would have given up pursuit of

---

(The King James Version actually gets it right here but not in the Samson story.) The word
is related to *haluts*, "vanguard," and the vanguard fighters would surely have worn armor.

22. *Why should I strike you to the ground.* Abner, the seasoned warrior, is coolly confident
that if necessary he has the skill and the combat experience to kill this impetuous young
man.

   how would I show my face to Joab your brother? The literal wording of the Hebrew is
"lift up my face." What is at stake here is not merely a question of diplomatic relations with
the opposing commander but vendetta justice (Hebrew, *ge'ulat hadam*, "redemption of the
blood"): if Abner sheds the blood of Joab's brother, Joab will feel honor-bound to shed the
blood of the killer in return.

23. *struck him in the belly with the butt of the spear.* Asahel is pursuing Abner at top speed.
Abner, to save his own life, uses an old soldier's trick: he suddenly stops short and thrusts
his spear backward, under his pursuer's shield (if Asahel is carrying one) and into the soft
belly. The momentum of Asahel's rapid running would have contributed to the penetrating
force of the spear's butt.

24. *Ammah . . . Giah.* The first name means "conduit," the second "gushing," and so both
may be related to an aqueduct system linked to the pool at Gibeon.

26. *You surely know that it will be bitterness in the end.* This grim prognostication hovers
over not only the continuing civil war but the entire David story. In the previous verse,
Abner's forces were reported regrouping and taking up a defensive position on the hilltop,
so they are now, after the rout, in a state to inflict serious casualties on their adversaries if
Joab persists. Therefore he agrees to the truce, though he surely has vendetta on his mind.

27. *had you but spoken.* The Masoretic Text has "had you not spoken." This has led some
interpreters to construe "morning" as "tomorrow morning" (that is, the troops would have
gone on pursuing you all night long had you not spoken up now). But this is strained because
the Hebrew *'az mehaboker* (literally, "then from the morning") idiomatically refers to the
morning of the day on which one is speaking. One should either emend "had not" (*lulei'*)
to "had" (*lu*) or, as Rashi proposed long ago, construe the former in the sense of the latter.

28 their brothers." And Joab sounded the ram's horn, and all the troops halted,
29 and they no longer chased after Israel, and they fought no more. And Abner
and his men went all that night through the Arabah, and they crossed the
Jordan and went all the way through the ravine and came to Mahanaim.
30 And Joab had turned back from pursuing Abner, and he gathered together
all the troops, and nineteen of David's servants were missing, and Asahel.
31 And David's servants had struck down from Benjamin and from Abner's
32 men three hundred and sixty men. And they bore off Asahel and buried
him in his father's grave, which is in Bethlehem, and Joab and his men went
all night long, and day brightened for them in Hebron.

1 **CHAPTER 3**   And the fighting between the house of Saul and
the house of David went on a long time, and David grew stronger and the
house of Saul weaker and weaker.

2 And sons were born to David in Hebron. And his firstborn was Amnon,
3 by Ahinoam the Jezreelite. And the second was Chileab, by Abigail wife of

---

29. *the Arabah.* This is a north-south depression running from the Sea of Galilee all the
way to the Gulf of Aqabah.

   the ravine. The Hebrew term *bitron* might conceivably be a place-name. The root means
to cleave or split and occurs in the Song of Songs collocated with "mountains," yielding
something like "mountains of the divide." The scholarly proposal that this word means
"middle of the morning" has no warrant in ancient Hebrew usage.

32. *all night long.* Perhaps the reason for this forced march through the night is that Joab's
troops want to get safely out of Benjaminite territory, not entirely trusting the truce.

CHAPTER 3   1. *And the fighting.* This summary notice at the head of the chapter
follows directly from the story of the battle at Gibeon that precedes it: the truce on that day
is only temporary, and a drawn-out civil war ensues.

2. *And sons were born to David.* The insertion of this genealogical list here may be motivated
by the fact that the northern tribes, brought round by Abner, are about to cast their lot with
David, making him monarch of the entire nation and thus a properly dynastic king. But
succession to the throne is not simple, and the list bristles with future disasters: Amnon,
who will rape his half sister and will be murdered by her brother; Absalom, who will usurp
the throne; Adonijah, who will proclaim himself king while the infirm, aged David lies in
bed unawares.

3. *Chileab.* The Septuagint and the Qumran Samuel fragment have a different name, Dalu-
iah. In any case, this son plays no role in the ensuing narrative, nor do Shephatiah and
Ithream.

Nabal the Carmelite. And the third was Absalom son of Maachah daughter
of Talmai king of Geshur. And the fourth was Adonijah son of Haggith. 4
And the fifth was Shephatiah son of Abital. And the sixth was Ithream, by 5
Eglah wife of David. These were born to David in Hebron.   6

And it happened during the fighting between the house of Saul and the
house of David that Abner kept growing in strength in the house of Saul.
And Saul had a concubine named Rizpah daughter of Aiah. And Ish- 7
Bosheth said to Abner, "Why did you come to bed with my father's concubine?" And Abner was very incensed over the words of Ish-Bosheth, and 8
he said, "Am I a dog's head attached to Judah? Today I have kept faith with
the house of Saul your father, with his kinsmen and his companions, in not

---

Maachah daughter of Talmai king of Geshur. Geshur is a small trans-Jordanian kingdom at the foot of the Golan. The marriage is clearly a political act through which David
establishes an alliance in the north, outflanking the house of Saul. It is conceivable that
Absalom's later aspiration to the throne may be influenced by his awareness that, alone
of David's sons, he is grandson of a king. After the killing of Amnon, he will take refuge
in Geshur.

5. *Eglah wife of David.* It is a little odd that only she is so designated. This might be because
she stands at the end of the list, or because there was knowledge of another Eglah who was
not David's wife. In all this, one notes that David the guerilla leader with his two wives has
now become David the king with a whole royal harem.

6. *Abner kept growing in strength.* This is the same verb, in a different conjugation, as
in the opening verse of the chapter, which reported David's growing strength and the
weakening of the house of Saul. As the Saulide forces are progressively harder pressed in
the continuing war, the nominal king becomes more and more dependent on his military
commander; and Abner, while not actually pretending to the throne, arrogates more and
more power to himself.

7. *Why did you come to bed with my father's concubine?* This crucial act is elided in the
narrative report and revealed only in Ish-Bosheth's indignant question. To take sexual
possession of a king's consort was to make an implicit claim to the power he exercised,
as we shall see again when Absalom publicly cohabits with David's concubines. "To come
to bed with"—literally, "to come into"—is an idiom for sexual intercourse that generally
indicates sexual possession of a woman with whom a man has not been previously intimate.
(I explain the semantic logic of the idiom in the second comment on Genesis 6:14.)

8. *Am I a dog's head attached to Judah?* The dog in biblical idiom regularly figures as a contemptible beast—the antonym of the fierce and regal lion. The phrase "attached to Judah" is
lacking in the Septuagint, and some critics have inferred that it is a scribal interpolation. It
might make sense, however, as a compounding of the insult because Judah is the despised
enemy of Benjamin, the tribe of Saul.

handing you over to David, and you dare reproach me with guilt over the
9 woman today? Thus may God do to Abner, and even more, for as the LORD
10 has sworn to David, just so will I do for him—to transfer the kingship from
the house of Saul and to set up the throne of David over Israel and over
11 Judah from Dan to Beersheba!" And he could say back not a word more to
Abner in his fear of him.

12 And Abner sent messengers to David in his stead, saying, "To whom should
the land belong? Make a pact with me and, look, my hand will be with you
13 to bring round to you all Israel." And he said, "Good. I shall make a pact
with you. But one thing do I ask of you, namely, you shall not see my face
until you bring Michal daughter of Saul when you come to see my face."
14 And David sent messengers to Ish-Bosheth son of Saul, saying, "Give back
my wife Michal, whom I betrothed with a hundred Philistine foreskins."

---

you dare reproach me with guilt over the woman. Abner's angry protest has a nice double
edge. You are entirely dependent on my loyal support, he tells Ish-Bosheth, so how could
you dare object to so trivial a thing as my taking a particular woman as sexual partner?
Alternately, the implication could be: you are entirely dependent on me, so how could you
object to my taking possession of this sexual symbol of political power? You should have
been content that I left you nominally on the throne.

9. *for as the LORD has sworn to David.* Ish-Bosheth's protest about Rizpah drives Abner,
David's military adversary, to embrace the notion that God has promised the throne to
David. Rather than continue to serve a carping, pusillanimous man like Ish-Bosheth, who
neither fully accepts Abner's power nor knows how to exercise power on his own, Abner now
is ready to throw his weight with a truly kingly leader and to help him become king over all
the nation's tribes (verse 10).

11. *he could say back not a word.* The contrast between the angry Abner and the quaking
Ish-Bosheth is all the stronger because the puppet king's fearful silence is set against what
is by biblical standards a rather long speech—one continuous outburst.

13. *see my face.* An idiom used for coming into the presence of royalty.
   Michal daughter of Saul. The first marriage buttresses David's claim to reign over all
Israel, including the tribe of Benjamin. That is why he identifies Michal to Abner as Saul's
daughter. There is no indication that he has a personal motive of affection as well as a
political one in wanting Michal back.

14. *sent messengers to Ish-Bosheth.* It is to be inferred that Abner has made clear to Ish-
Bosheth that he must accede to this demand.
   my wife Michal, whom I betrothed with a hundred Philistine foreskins. In turning to the
man who has jurisdiction over Michal (and her second husband), David makes clear now
that she is his wife, whom he legitimately acquired by providing the bride-price of a hundred
Philistine foreskins stipulated by her father, Saul.

And Ish-Bosheth sent and took her from her husband, from Paltiel son of 15
Laish. And her husband went with her, weeping as he went after her, as far 16
as Bahurim. And Abner said to him, "Go back!" And he went back.

And Abner parlayed with the elders of Israel, saying, "Time and again in the 17
past you sought to have David become king over you. And now, act, for the 18
LORD has said, 'By the hand of David My servant will I rescue My people
Israel from the hand of the Philistines and from the hand of all their enemies.'" And Abner spoke as well in the hearing of Benjamin, and Abner went 19
as well to speak in David's hearing in Hebron all that was good in the eyes
of Israel and in the eyes of Benjamin. And Abner came to David in Hebron, 20
and with him were twenty men. And David made a feast for Abner and for
the men who were with him. And Abner said to David, "Let me rise and go 21
and gather to my lord the king all Israel, that they may make a pact with you,
and you shall reign over all your heart desires." And David sent Abner off,

---

15. *from her husband.* The Masoretic Text has "a husband" (or, "a man"), but the possessive
pronoun is supplied in the Septuagint and the Vulgate as well as in at least two Hebrew
manuscripts.

16. *weeping as he went.* There is scarcely a more striking instance of the evocative compactness of biblical narrative. We know almost nothing about Paltiel. He speaks not a word of
dialogue. Yet his walking after Michal, weeping all the while, intimates a devoted love that
stands in contrast to David's relationship with her. Paltiel is a man whose fate is imposed
on him. Michal was given to him by Saul, evidently without his initiative. He came to love
her. Now he must give her up, and confronted by Saul's strongman with the peremptory
order to go back, he has no choice but to go back.

17. *Time and again in the past.* The idiom for "times gone by," *temol shilshom* (literally,
"yesterday and the day before"), is reinforced by the emphatic adverb *gam*, repeated before
each of the two components of the idiom, probably as an indication of repeated acts in times
past. Most commentators refer the idea of Israel's wanting David as king to his immense
popularity during his early military successes (1 Samuel 18). But there was no intimation
then that the people wanted to replace Saul with David on the throne. The suggestion of
repeated popular support for David's claims might well point to an otherwise unreported
undercurrent of dissatisfaction with the house of Saul and an interest in going over to David
as a result of the losing civil war, if it is not Abner's own diplomatic invention.

21. *And David sent Abner off, and he went in peace.* The going in peace befits the feast of
reconciliation and the agreed-on pact. The writer contrives to repeat this sentence verbatim three times (here, verse 22, verse 23). But when Joab refers to this very same departure
of Abner from Hebron in verse 24, he substitutes for "in peace" (*beshalom*) the emphatic
infinitive *halokh* ("going off"). This ominous substitution, as I put it in *The Art of Biblical
Narrative,* "falls like the clatter of a dagger after the ringing of bells"—especially because
"to go" sometimes occurs in the Bible as a euphemism for dying (see Job 27:21 and Jeremiah

22 and he went in peace. And look, David's servants and Joab had come from a
   raid, and abundant booty they brought with them, and Abner was not with
23 David in Hebron, for he had sent him off, and he went in peace. And Joab
   and all the force that was with him had come, and they told Joab, saying,
   "Abner son of Ner has come to the king, and he sent him off, and he went in
24 peace." And Joab came to the king and said, "What have you done? Look,
   Abner has come to you! Why did you send him off, and he went, going off?
25 You know that Abner son of Ner to dupe you has come and to learn your
26 comings and goings and to learn all that you do." And Joab went out from
   David's presence and sent messengers after Abner, and they brought him
27 back from the cistern of Sirah, and David did not know. And Abner came
   back to Hebron, and Joab drew him aside into the gate to speak with him
   deceptively, and he struck him there in the belly, and he died for the blood
28 of Asahel, Joab's brother. And David heard afterward and said, "Innocent am

---

22:10). Polzin has noted that this entire episode is a crowded juncture of comings and
goings. The least complicated inference to be drawn from that fact is that this is a crucial
moment of transition in the David story: the house of Saul comes to treat with the house of
David; the long conflict with Saul, culminating in civil war, comes to an end; David is about
to become king of the whole Israelite nation; a new line of division now emerges between
David and his chief henchman, Joab. All this flurry of transition and realignment is nicely
caught in the multiple comings and goings of Abner and Joab and the troops.

24. *Look, Abner has come to you.* The simple idiom for arrival (*ba' 'el*) ironically echoes Ish-
Bosheth's use of the very same idiom in its sexual sense ("come into," "come to bed with")
in his complaint to Abner. The sexual undertone is sustained in the next verse because the
prominent verb "to dupe" (*pitah*) has the primary meaning of "seduce."

26. *the cistern of Sirah.* The actual location has not been identified, but it would have to be
in the general vicinity of Hebron.
   and David did not know. The narrator takes pains to underscore David's innocence of
involvement in Joab's scheme of murder. David on his part will take extravagant steps to
declare his innocence.

27. *deceptively.* The Hebrew adverb *basheli* occurs only here. It derives either from the root
sh-l-h, "to delude," or from the root *sh-l-w*, "to be quiet." Those who favor the latter root
render it, with a small leap of semantic inference, as "privately."
   he struck him there in the belly. Although this is the same part of the body in which the
now avenged Asahel received his fatal wound from Abner, there is a world of difference
between the two killings. Abner struck down Asahel in a deft maneuver as Asahel was
pursuing him on the battlefield with intent to kill. Joab draws Abner aside into the gate
under the pretence of speaking confidentially with him, and, catching him unawares, stabs
him in the belly.
   for the blood of Asahel. Joab's vendetta is accomplished. But it has not escaped notice that
he is also eliminating a rival for the position of commander in the new united monarchy.

I, and my kingship, before the LORD for all time of the blood of Abner son of
Ner! May the bloodguilt come down on the head of Joab and all his father's   29
house, and may there never lack in the house of Joab a sufferer of discharge
from his member and running sores on his skin and a man clutching the
woman's spindle, and one falling by the sword and one wanting for bread!"
And Joab and Abishai his brother had lain in wait for Abner because he put   30
to death Asahel their brother in Gibeon in the fighting. And David said   31
to Joab and to all the troops who were with him, "Tear your garments
and gird on sackcloth and keen for Abner." And King David was walking
behind the bier. And they buried Abner in Hebron. And the king raised   32
his voice and wept over the grave of Abner, and all the people wept. And   33
the king lamented over Abner and said,

---

28. *Innocent am I.* David's first eminently political reflex is to dissociate himself categorically from the killing.

of the blood of Abner son of Ner. The Qumran Samuel text puts a full stop after "before
the LORD for all time," then makes this phrase the subject of the next clause: "May the blood
of Abner son of Ner come down on the head of Joab." The Masoretic Text has simply "May
it come down on the head of Joab," and this translation supplies "blood guilt" (plural of
dam, "blood") for the sake of clarity.

29. *discharge from his member.* The single Hebrew word *zav* refers to a man suffering from
diseased discharge from the male organ.

running sores on his skin. This is again one word in the Hebrew, *metsor'a,* rendered
as "leper" in the older translations but now generally thought to indicate a different skin
disease.

a man clutching the woman's spindle. Some prefer to interpret the Hebrew term as
"crutch," thus linking it with the two preceding images of disease. This noun, *pelekh,*
occurs quite infrequently, but there is scant indication in the biblical corpus that as a
wooden implement it meant anything but "spindle." The word "woman's" is added in the
translation to catch the nuance of scorn in a man's being reduced to woman's work. All
in all, David puts together a first-class curse to emphasize the distance between him and
Abner's killer. This bloodguilt, many times compounded, will indeed come down on Joab's
head, but not until the end of David's life.

30. *had lain in wait for Abner.* The Masoretic Text reads "had killed Abner" *(hargu le'avner).*
There are two problems with that reading. It is a flat repetition of what has already been
reported more vividly (only adding the information that Abishai was complicit in the act),
and the use of the particle *le* (as a preposition, it means "to" or "for") to indicate the direct
object of a verb is an Aramaicism generally restricted to Late Biblical Hebrew. The Qumran
Samuel scroll has a different verb, evidently (the first consonant is not visible on the parchment) *tsafnu,* "to lie in wait," "to hide."

33. *lamented.* This is David's second poetic lament *(qinah)* in quick sequence in the text.
It is much briefer than the lament over Jonathan and Saul and derives its power from the
lapidary character of its language.

> "Like the death of the base
> should Abner have died?
34   Your hands—never bound,
> your feet never placed in fetters!
> As one falls before scoundrels you fell."

35   And all the people continued to weep over him. And all the people came
to give David bread to eat while it was still day, and David swore, saying,
"Thus and more may God do to me, if before the sun sets I taste bread or
36   anything at all." And all the people took note and it was good in their eyes,
37   all that the king had done was good in the eyes of the people. And all the
people and all Israel knew on that day that it had not been from the king
38   to put to death Abner son of Ner. And the king said to his servants, "You
must know that a commander and a great man has fallen this day in Israel.
39   And I am gentle, and just anointed king, and these sons of Zeruiah are too
hard for me. May the LORD pay back the evildoer according to his evil!"

---

the death of the base. The term for "base fellow," *naval*, is the one encountered in 1
Samuel 25 as an explanation for the name of Nabal, Abigail's husband. A *naval* is someone
who, as Kyle McCarter Jr. rightly observes, perpetrates *nevalah*, a contemptible or scandalous act. It is an outrage, David says, that a noble figure such as Abner should have been cut
down in stealth as some scoundrel might perish at the hands of hired assassins.

34. *Your hands—never bound, / your feet never placed in fetters.* The elliptical nature of the
language has led to some dispute over interpretation. It is most plausibly understood as a
brief retrospection on Abner's glory days as a martial hero: no one ever succeeded in taking
him captive, in putting him in a prisoner's humiliating fetters.

As one falls before scoundrels you fell. But now the noble Abner has been undone by
treachery. In all the grandeur of the poetry, the sharp rebuke to the sons of Zeruiah, who
figure as vulgar cutthroats, is clear.

37–38. The vehemence with which David here is repeatedly dissociated from the killing of
Abner leads one to suspect that, beyond his desire to exculpate himself on the spot, there
may have been a lingering shadow of suspicion that he ordered the killing, a suspicion that
the writer takes pains to dispel.

39. *I am gentle, and just anointed king.* David's plight as a self-proclaimed "gentle" or
"tender" man (*rakh*) vis-à-vis the "hard" sons of Zeruiah will continue to play a crucial
role in the story. But though he dissociates himself from Joab and Abishai and goes so far
as to pronounce a scathing curse on them and their descendants, he makes no move to get
rid of them, and continues to depend on their activity as strongmen. And what of Joab's
reaction to all this bitter denunciation? Is it possible that he prudently understands it is
politic for the king to dissociate himself from the killing by denouncing the killers in poetry
and prose? There is also a question here about the relation between the two phrases David
uses. Many translations explain the link as "though anointed king." That construction is
possible, although it would be an unusual use of the Hebrew particle *we* ("and"). The pres-

CHAPTER 4   And the son of Saul heard that Abner had died in 1
Hebron, and he was utterly shaken, and all Israel was dismayed. And the son 2
of Saul had two men, commanders of raiding parties, the name of the one
was Baanah and of the other Rechab, sons of Rimmon the Beerothite, who
was of the Benjaminites, for Beeroth, too, was reckoned with Benjamin. And 3
the Beerothites fled to Gittaim and have been sojourners there till this day.

And Jonathan son of Saul had a lame son, five years old he was when the 4
news of Saul and Jonathan came from Jezreel. And his nurse bore him off
and fled, and it happened in her haste to flee that he fell and was crippled.
And his name was Mephibosheth. And the sons of Rimmon the Beerothite, 5
Rechab and Baanah went and came in the heat of the day to the house
of Ish-Bosheth as he was taking his midday rest. And, look, the woman 6

---

ent translation adds "just," on the assumption that David is dramatizing his predicament as
a gentle person on whom the kingship has been newly thrust and who must contend with
these hard sons of Zeruiah. In point of fact, he was anointed in Hebron several years earlier,
but this might be either rhetorical exaggeration or a reference to his brand-new condition
of king of the nation, not just of the tribe of Judah.

CHAPTER 4   1. *the son of Saul.* The son in question is Ish-Bosheth. Both the Septuagint and the Qumran Samuel scroll read, erroneously, "Mephibosheth." It has been
surmised that scribes deleted the mistaken name without replacing it with the correct one.
    was utterly shaken. The Hebrew says literally "his hands grew weak," the hands being an
idiomatic token of strength or courage. The force of the idiom is a little like the colloquial
English "lost his grip."

2. *sons of Rimmon the Beerothite, who was of the Benjaminites.* The Beerothites are an originally non-Israelite group who have become what we might call naturalized Benjaminites.
The two brothers are considered sufficiently Benjaminite to have been entrusted with positions as the commanders of raiding parties—also making them experienced killers—and
so we are meant to understand that the pusillanimous Ish-Bosheth is betrayed by his own
tribesmen. At the same time, the foreign origin of Baanah and Rechab participates in the
recurring pattern of the foreign messenger bringing news of a disaster to David. Finally, the
treacherous killing of the king by two brothers echoes the immediately preceding episode,
in which two brothers, Joab and Abishai, are said to lie in wait for and kill Abner.

4. *Jonathan . . . had a lame son.* The notice is inserted here to make clear that after the
murder of Ish-Bosheth, there will be no fit heir left from the house of Saul, for Saul's one
surviving grandson is crippled.
    Mephibosheth. As with Ish-Bosheth/Ish-Baal, the original form of the name was
Mephibaal, a component meaning "shame" substituted for the theophoric *ba'al* with its
pagan associations.

6. *And, look, the woman who kept the gate.* The translation of this entire verse follows the
text reflected in the Septuagint, out of a sense that the received text at this point is simply

who kept the gate had been gleaning wheat, and nodded and fell asleep.
7 Andthey came into the house as he was lying in his bed in his bedchamber, and they struck him and killed him and cut off his head and took his
8 head and went off through the Arabah all night long. And they brought
Ish-Bosheth's head to David in Hebron and said to the king, "Here is the
head of Ish-Bosheth son of Saul your enemy, who sought your life. The
LORD has granted my lord the king vengeance this day against Saul and
9 his seed." And David answered Rechab and Baanah his brother, the sons
of Rimmon the Beerothite, and he said to them, "As the LORD lives, Who
10 saved my life from every strait, he who told me, saying 'Look, Saul is dead,'
and thought he was a bearer of good tidings, I seized him and killed him
11 in Ziklag instead of giving him something for his tidings. How much more
so when wicked men have killed an innocent man in his bed in his house,

---

not viable. The Masoretic Text is problematic as idiomatic Hebrew usage, includes one
entirely unintelligible phrase, and is redundant with the narrative report of the next verse.
It reads: "and they [feminine pronoun!] came into the midst of the house, taking wheat [?],
and they struck him in the belly, and Rechab and Baanah his brother got away."

gleaning wheat. This odd little domestic detail suggests that Ish-Bosheth does not
inhabit a grand palace with royal guards but lives in modest homey circumstances.

nodded and fell asleep. Both the king and the gatekeeper are asleep when the assassins
arrive, so they can slip by her and easily dispatch him.

7. *as he was lying in his bed in his bedchamber.* This twice-asserted detail underlines the
scurrilousness of the act of assassination. The next time we encounter a king taking his
siesta, it will be David before he rises to behold Bathsheba. Again, murder will ensue,
although the king himself will be the perpetrator.

8. *Ish-Bosheth son of Saul your enemy, who sought your life.* The two sons of Rimmon make
exactly the same misguided calculation as the Amalekite messenger in chapter 1, imagining
that David will be delighted to hear of the destruction of anyone associated with Saul and
will reward the bearers of the news.

11. *when wicked men have killed an innocent man in his bed in his house.* Either this detail
has been elided in the dialogue reported for Baanah and Rechab when they come before
David, or he has received advance word of the killing and its circumstances from another
source. In all this, the common scholarly view is that the narrative is framed as an apology
for David, taking pains to clear him of any complicity in the deaths, first of Saul, then of
Abner, and now of Ish-Bosheth. But it is still more plausible that the writer is continuing his representation of David as the consummately politic man: whether he really feels
moral revulsion against these assassins we have no way of knowing, but he surely is aware,
as he was after the murder of Abner, that it is in his political interest to put the greatest
possible distance between himself and the killers of Saul's son, and what better way to
do this than to have them executed on the spot? David is nevertheless a beneficiary of
the murder, for now there is no claimant to the throne whom the northern tribes might
follow instead of him.

and so, will I not requite his blood from you and rid the land of you?" And 12
David commanded the lads, and they killed them and chopped off their
hands and feet and hung them by the pool in Hebron. And Ish-Bosheth's
head they took and buried in the grave of Abner in Hebron.

CHAPTER 5   And all the tribes of Israel came to David in 1
Hebron, and they said, "Here we are, your bone and your flesh are we. Time 2
and again in the past when Saul was king over us you were the one who led
Israel into the fray, and the LORD said to you,

> 'It is you who will shepherd My people Israel
>   and it is you who will be prince over Israel.'"

And all the elders of Israel came to the king in Hebron, and King David 3
made a pact with them in Hebron before the LORD and they anointed David

---

12. *chopped off their hands and feet.* The dismembering of malefactors or prisoners was
a common ancient Near Eastern practice, as we have seen before (and compare the first
chapter of Judges). Here the corpses are defiled by cutting off the hands that did the killing
and the feet that carried the killers into the victim's bedchamber. The whole episode ends
in a strange image cluster of detached body parts: the hands and feet of the two executed
assassins and the head of their victim. Even as David is about to assume control of a united
monarchy, we have an intimation of mayhem and dismemberment that is an apt thematic
prelude to the story of David's reign.

CHAPTER 5   1. *all the tribes of Israel came to David.* "The tribes of Israel," in keeping
with the consistent usage of the preceding narrative, refers to the northern tribes that had
been loyal to the house of Saul. With the assassination of Abner and then of Ish-Bosheth,
they understandably now turn to David.

2. *you were the one . . . It is you.* The language of the tribal representatives puts considerable
emphasis on the second-person pronoun: you are the one that we, and God, have chosen.
The divine declaration of David's legitimacy as ruler, quoted by the tribal spokesmen, is
appropriately given the elevated status of poetry.

3. *all the elders of Israel came to the king.* This is not a duplication of the report in verse 1
from another source, as is often claimed. The convention used here is the well-attested one
of "resumptive repetition": when an interrupted narrative strand is resumed, a phrase from
the point of interruption is repeated verbatim to mark the return to the main line. Here, the
move to confirm David as king of Israel, with which the episode began, after the insertion
of the tribes' dialogue (verses 1–2), is carried forward. It is the role of the tribal rank and
file to proclaim fealty, but of the elders to sign a pact and anoint David, and so "elders" is
now strategically substituted for "tribes" of the first verse. One should note that the tribes

4 as king over Israel. Thirty years old was David when he became king, forty
5 years he was king. In Hebron he was king over Judah seven years and six
   months, and in Jerusalem he was king thirty-three years over all Israel and
   Judah.

6 And the king went, and his men with him, to Jerusalem, to the Jebusite, the
   inhabitant of the land, and he said to David, saying, "You shall not enter
   here unless you can remove the blind and the lame," which is to say, "David
7 shall not enter here!" And David captured the stronghold of Zion, which
8 is the City of David. And David said on that day, "Whoever strikes down
   the Jebusite and reaches the conduit and the lame and the blind utterly

---

come "to David" whereas the elders come "to the king," for they are about to consummate
the official business of kingmaking.

4. *forty years he was king*. In biblical usage, this is a formulaic number—in Judges often used
to indicate a full term of governing. But the specificity of "seven years and six months" in
Hebron has the look of a real number, whether or not it is historically precise.

6. *the king went . . . to Jerusalem*. The chronological link between this action and what
precedes, as well as the chronology of the subsequent events in the chapter, is not clear.
The principle of organization appears to be thematic or ideological rather than temporal.
What we have here is a catalogue of salient actions by which David consolidates his new
monarchy: the conquest of a capital city in the center of the north-south axis of the country that does not belong to any tribal territory (the same logic that led to the creation of
Washington as capital in the District of Columbia, not part of any state); the construction
of a palace with the assistance of a Phoenician alliance; the begetting of many offspring,
including the future heir to the throne, Solomon; the defeat of the Philistines. The birth of
Solomon is the clearest indication that these notices do not follow the chronology of the
preceding narrative.
    the blind and the lame. This puzzling phrase, together with its even more enigmatic
occurrence in verse 8, is a notorious crux. The most disparate theories have been proposed
for how to read the words of the text and how to reconstruct what is said to go on in the
conquest of the city. The Qumran Samuel scroll for this verse reads: "You shall not enter
here, for the blind and the lame have incited [*hesitu* for Masoretic *hesirkha*], saying, 'David
shall not enter here.'" This variant has the advantage of fluency, but one suspects it may
have been invented to make a difficult traditional text more intelligible. The explanation
proposed by Yigal Yadin is probably the most plausible: he points to a Hittite text for the
swearing in of troops in which a blind woman and a lame man are set before the men
with the monitory imprecation that their fate will be like that of those wretches if they
fail in their duty. The Jebusites, then, might have displayed the lame and the blind on the
ramparts with an analogous curse against those who would presume to attack the city.
This taunting curse would explain why these maimed figures are "despised by David."

8. *Whoever strikes down the Jebusite and reaches the conduit*. These words are the other
salient element of the crux, with debate still raging over the meaning of "conduit" (*tsinor*).

despised by David . . ." Therefore do they say, "No blind man nor lame shall enter the House." And David stayed in the stronghold and called it the City 9 of David, and David built round the rampart and within. And David grew 10 greater and greater, and the LORD God of Armies was with him.

And Hiram king of Tyre sent messengers to David with cedarwood and 11 carpenters and stonemasons, and they built a house for David. And David 12 knew that the LORD had set him up unshaken as king over Israel and had exalted his kingship for the sake of His people Israel.

And David took other concubines and wives from Jerusalem after coming 13 from Hebron, and other sons and daughters were born to David. And these 14 are the names of those born to him in Jerusalem: Shammua and Shobab and Nathan and Solomon, and Ibhar and Elishua and Nepheg and Japhia, 15 and Elishama and Eliada and Eliphelet. 16

Some scholars have claimed it refers here to the windpipe, or a lower part of the anatomy, of the Jebusites who are to be struck down, but there is no Hebrew evidence for *tsinor* as anything but a water channel or tube, and the argument from the analogy of shape is a weak one. Moreover, the verb used here, *naga'*, means primarily "to touch," and in some biblical contexts, "to reach" or "take charge of" but not "to strike." The most likely reference, then, is to a daring route of surprise access into the city. A frequently proposed candidate is Warren's Shaft, discovered in 1867, an underground tunnel feeding in from the Gihon Spring on a slope outside the wall to the east. Though everything about this report remains uncertain, David may be saying that whoever manages to crawl through the tunnel, make his way up the vertical shaft that transects it, and cut down the Jebusites within the town together with their loathsome display of lame and blind will be given a great reward. (The reward clause is missing; one is supplied in the parallel verse in Chronicles—"will become a chief and commander.")

No blind man nor lame shall enter the House. The story is thus given an etiological turn as an explanation for a known taboo, evidently pertaining to the temple but perhaps to David's "house" (that is, the palace). One wonders whether there is an invitation here to think of Jonathan's lame son—which would be another gesture for denying the Saulides all future claim to the throne.

11. *Hiram king of Tyre.* Hiram as a provider of timber and artisans points forward to Solomon's construction of the Temple. If this is the Hiram with whom Solomon had dealings, David's palace building would have been undertaken rather late in his own reign in order to coincide with Hiram's regnal span.

13. *from Jerusalem.* Some Septuagint versions read "in Jerusalem."

17 And the Philistines heard that David had been anointed as king over Israel,
    and all the Philistines came up to seek David. And David heard and went
18 down to the stronghold. The Philistines had come and deployed in the
19 Valley of Rephaim. And David inquired of the LORD, saying, "Shall I go up
    against the Philistines? Will You give them into my hand?" And the LORD
20 said, "Go up, for I will surely give the Philistines into your hand." And
    David came into Baal-Perazim, and David struck them down there, and
    he said, "The LORD has burst through my enemies before me like a burst-
    ing of water!" Therefore did he call the name of that place Baal-Perazim.
21 And they abandoned their idols there, and David with his men bore them
22 off. And once more the Philistines came up and deployed in the Valley of
23 Rephaim. And David inquired of the LORD, and He said, "You shall not go
    up. Turn around behind them and come at them from opposite the willows.
24 And as soon as you hear the sound of marching in the tops of the willows,
    then you must move boldly, for then shall the LORD go out before you to
25 strike down the camp of the Philistines." And David did just as the LORD

---

17. *the Philistines heard.* David's assumption of the throne of all the tribes of Israel means
that he has decisively cast aside his vassal status, and so the Philistines, who all along have
been warring with the northern tribes, assemble their united forces ("all the Philistines")
to suppress the new monarchy.

   the stronghold. The claim often made that this refers to the stronghold at Adullam
(compare 1 Samuel 22) is unlikely because the battle here is entirely in the immediate vicinity of Jerusalem. This would have to be the stronghold within the city, referred to in verse
9. David can "go down" to it because his residence in Jerusalem could be topographically
above the stronghold.

18. *the Valley of Rephaim.* The location is outside the walls of the Jebusite city, a couple of
miles to the west.

20. *burst through my enemies . . . like a bursting of water.* The existing place-name is etiolog-
ically reinscribed to fit the military victory. Baal-Perazim may mean "god of earthquakes."
The image of bursting through—the Hebrew term means "breach"—could suggest that
David's forces have succeeded in punching a hole in the Philistine lines rather than in
producing a general rout.

23. *opposite the willows.* The Hebrew *bekha'im* resists botanic identification—mulberry
tree, pear tree, mastic bush, and others have been proposed. Some think it is a place-name,
but the next verse makes that unlikely.

24. *the sound of marching in the tops of the willows.* Presumably, this is the wind. But it
gives a sense that mysterious unseen agents of the LORD are advancing against the Philistines. More practically, some interpreters have proposed that the sound of the wind in the
branches provided a cover for the sound of David's troops stealthily advancing for their
surprise attack from the rear.

had commanded him, and he struck down the Philistines from Geba till you come to Gezer.

CHAPTER 6

And David gathered again all the picked men of 1 Israel, thirty thousand. And David arose and went, and all the troops who 2 were with him, to Baalah in Judah to bring up from there the Ark of God, over which the name of the LORD of Armies enthroned on the cherubim is called. And they mounted the Ark of God on a new cart and carried it 3 off from the house of Abinadab, which is on the Hill, and Uzza and Ahio, the sons of Abinadab, were driving the cart, and Ahio was walking before 4 the Ark. And David and the whole house of Israel were playing before the 5 LORD with all their might in song on lyres and tambourines and castanets and cymbals. And they came to the threshing floor of Nacon, and Uzza 6

---

25. *from Geba till you come to Gezer.* Unlike the first victory, David now inflicts a general defeat on the Philistine forces, driving them back from the territory in central Canaan that they had occupied after triumphing over Saul at Gilboa. David has now completed the consolidation of his rule over all the land, and his real troubles are about to begin.

CHAPTER 6   1. *thirty thousand.* Some modern commentators understand *'alafim*, "thousands," as "military contingents," and thus reduce the number of troops to a few hundred elite soldiers. But *'alafim* in a non-numerical sense refers to clans, not military units; and as we have abundantly seen, exaggerated numbers are common in these stories. Polzin, moreover, has aptly observed that thirty thousand is precisely the number of Israelites slain when the Ark was captured by the Philistines (1 Samuel 4).

2. *to Baalah in Judah.* This place-name is a synonym for the Kiriath-Jearim of 1 Samuel 7:1—see, for example, Joshua 15:9. The Qumran Samuel scroll in fact reads here: "Baalah, which is Kiriath-Jearim in Judah." The Masoretic Text reads *ba'aley yehudah*. Because this erroneous phrase was construed to mean "the notables of Judah," a *mem* prefix ("from") was added to it to yield "from the notables of Judah." But David is clearly going *to* the place Baalah.

3. *a new cart.* The new cart is a vehicle unpolluted by any previous secular use.

4. The Masoretic Text begins this verse with a whole clause that is a scribal duplication (dittography) of the first half of verse 3: "And they carried it off from the house of Abinadab which is on the Hill." This clause is not present in the Qumran Samuel, in the Septuagint, or in the parallel verse in 1 Chronicles 13:7. The Masoretic Text also repeats the adjective "new" (*hadashah*) at the end of verse 3, a repetition not reflected in the other ancient versions.

5. *with all their might in song.* The translation reads here *bekhol 'oz uveshirim* with 1 Chronicles 13:8. The Masoretic Text has *bekhol 'atsey beroshim*, "with all cypress woods," which only by a long interpretive stretch has been made to refer to percussion instruments.

6. *the threshing floor of Nacon.* The proper name here is in question. The Qumran Samuel reads "Nadon."

reached out to the Ark of God and took hold of it, for the oxen had slipped.
7 And the LORD's wrath flared up against Uzza, and God struck him down
there for reaching out his hand to the Ark, and he died there by the Ark
8 of God. And David was incensed because the LORD had burst out against
9 Uzza. And that place has been called Perez-Uzza to this day. And David was
afraid of the LORD on that day and he said, "How can the Ark of the LORD
10 come to me?" And David did not want to remove the Ark of the LORD to
himself in the City of David, and David had it turned aside to the house of
11 Obed-Edom the Gittite. And the Ark of the LORD remained in the house
of Obed-Edom three months and the LORD blessed Obed-Edom and all his
12 house. And it was told to King David, saying, "The LORD has blessed the
house of Obed-Edom and all that he has on account of the Ark of God."
And David went and brought up the Ark of God from the house of Obed-
Edom to the City of David with rejoicing.

13 And it happened when the bearers of the Ark of the LORD had taken six
14 steps that he sacrificed a fatted bull. And David was whirling with all his

---

7. *the LORD's wrath flared up . . . and God struck him down*. This is an archaic story that
defies later ethical categories: the Ark, as God's terrestrial throne, is invested with awesome
divine power (compare 1 Samuel 6). To touch it, even in an effort to keep it from slipping off
the cart, is to risk being consumed by its indwelling mana, as when one comes in contact
with a high-voltage electric core. God's wrath against Uzza triggers an answering wrath
(the same verb in the Hebrew) on the part of David, frustrated in his purposes and now
wondering whether he will ever manage to bring this symbol and earthly focus of God's
power to his newly conquered capital.

for reaching out his hand to the Ark. The translation follows the parallel version in
1 Chronicles 13:10. The Masoretic Text here has a single incomprehensible word, *shal*,
which might be simply two consonants from the initial words of the lost clause recorded
in Chronicles.

8. *Perez-Uzza*. The Hebrew is construed to mean "bursting out against Uzza." The naming
story forms an antithetical symmetry with the story in 2 Samuel 5 of Baal-Perazim, there
associated with God's "bursting through" the Philistine ranks.

11. *Obed-Edom the Gittite*. He is a foreigner, perhaps (though this is not certain) from Philistine Gath—conceivably someone who had attached himself to David during his sojourn
there.

13. *when the bearers of the Ark of the LORD had taken six steps*. Some construe this as an
imperfect verb: with every six steps David would sacrifice a bull. Apart from the difficulty
that these constant sacrifices would make the procession interminable and require scores
of thousands of bulls, the imperfect would require the verb "to be" at the beginning of the
sentence to appear in the suffix conjugation *wehayah*, instead of the way it is, in the prefix
conjugation, *wayehi*, which implies a singulative, not an iterative, tense for the verb.

might before the LORD, girt in a linen ephod. And David and the whole 15
house of Israel were bringing up the Ark of the LORD in shouts and with
the sound of the ram's horn. And as the Ark of the LORD came into the City 16
of David, Michal daughter of Saul looked out through the window and saw
King David leaping and whirling before the LORD, and she scorned him in
her heart. And they brought the Ark of the LORD and set it up in its place 17
within the tent that David had pitched for it, and David offered up burnt
offerings before the LORD and well-being sacrifices. And David finished 18
offering up the burnt offerings and the well-being sacrifices, and he blessed
the people in the name of the LORD of Hosts. And he shared out to all the 19
people, to all the multitude of Israel, every man and woman, one loaf of
bread and one date cake and one raisin cake, and every one of the people
went to his home.

And David turned back to bless his house. And Michal daughter of Saul 20
came out to meet David, and she said, "How honored today is the king

---

15. *girt in a linen ephod.* The wearing of the ephod surely underscores the fact that in the
procession of the Ark into Jerusalem, David is playing the roles of both priest and king—a
double service not unknown in the ancient Near East (compare Melchizedek in Genesis
14:18). The ephod was probably a short garment tied around the hips or waist, and so David
whirling and leaping might easily have exposed himself, as Michal will bitterly observe.

16. *Michal daughter of Saul looked out through the window and saw King David.* The preceding verse reports the shouts of jubilation and the shrill blasts of the ram's horn: first
she hears the procession approaching from the distance, then she looks out and sees David
dancing. Strategically, her repeated epithet in this episode of final estrangement is "daughter of Saul," not "wife of David," and the figure she sees is not "David her husband" but
"King David." Shimon Bar-Efrat neatly observes that at the beginning of their story a loving
Michal helped David escape "through the window" from her father's henchmen while now
she looks at him from a distance "through the window," in seething contempt.

17–20. Instead of proceeding directly to the confrontation between Michal and David, as
we might expect, the narrative lingers for a long moment over David's cultic ministrations
and royal benefactions to the people. One can imagine that Michal continues to watch
David from the window, performing his role as the people's darling, and that she continues
to simmer.

19. *date cake.* The Hebrew *'eshpar* appears nowhere else and so it is only a guess as to what
sort of delicacy it might be. Some traditional commentators construe it as a portion of meat.

20. *How honored today is the king of Israel.* Astoundingly, until this climactic moment,
there has been no dialogue between Michal and David—only her urgent instructions for
him to flee in 1 Samuel 19 and his silent flight. We can only guess what she may have felt
all those years he was away from her, acquiring power and wives, or during the civil war

of Israel who has exposed himself today to the eyes of his servants' slave-
21 girls as some scurrilous fellow would expose himself!" And David said to
Michal, "Before the LORD, Who chose me instead of your father and instead
of all his house, to appoint me prince over the LORD's people, over Israel,
22 I will play before the LORD! And I will be dishonored still more than this
and will be debased in my own eyes! But with the slavegirls about whom
23 you spoke, with them let me be honored!" And Michal daughter of Saul had
no child till her dying day.

---

with her father's family. We are equally ignorant of her feelings toward her devoted second
husband, Paltiel son of Laish. Now the royal couple are finally represented meeting, and
when Michal speaks out, it is in an explosion of angry sarcasm. Her first significant word
"honored" (balanced in David's rejoinder by two antonyms, "dishonored" and "debased")
is a complex satellite to the story of the grand entry of the Ark with which it is linked.
When the Ark was lost to the Philistines (1 Samuel 4), the great cry was that "glory [or
honor, kavod—the same verbal root Michal uses here] is exiled from Israel." Now glory/
honor splendidly returns to Israel, but the actual invocation of the term is a sarcastic one,
bitterly directed at David, who will then hurl back two antonyms and try to redefine both
honor and dishonor to his wife. The logic of the larger story's moral and historical realism
requires that no triumph should be simple and unambiguous, that strife and accusation
pursue even the fulfillment of national destiny. One should also note here that Michal
speaks to her husband in the third person, not deferentially but angrily, and refers to him
by public title, not in any personal relation to her.

   who has exposed himself today to the eyes of his servants' slavegirls. The verb "to expose"
is clearly used in the sexual sense. The proud Michal's reference to the lowly slavegirls'
enjoying the sight of David's nakedness probably suggests an edge of sexual jealousy as well
as political resentment in her rage against him. He has, after all, assembled a harem during
their years apart, and there is no indication that he has resumed sexual relations with her
after having her brought back to him forcibly for obviously political motives.

   as some scurrilous fellow would expose himself. The social thrust of the comparison
is evident: she is a king's daughter, whereas he has now demonstrated that he is no more
than riffraff.

21. Before the LORD. Isaac Abravanel, the Hebrew commentator who was also Ferdinand
and Isabella's financial advisor until the expulsion of 1492, aptly explains this: "Had he
danced before some person to honor him, it would have been a contemptible act, for his
status was higher than any other person's. But in his leaping before the LORD there is no
cause for contempt." Thus David can go on to say that he will perform ostensibly debasing
acts, even debasing in my own eyes (emending this to "His eyes" only clouds matters), acts
that in paradoxical fact are the opposite of debasement.

22. with the slavegirls . . . with them let me be honored. David flings back Michal's sarcastic
"how honored," suggesting that, unlike Michal, the simple slavegirls will understand that
his gyrations before the Ark are an act of reverence and will honor him for it. And there
may also be a sexual edge in his rejoinder: I will display myself to whomever I please, and
it is I who will decide whether it is honorable or not.

23. And Michal daughter of Saul had no child till her dying day. The whole story of David
and Michal concludes on a poised ambiguity through the suppression of causal explana-

CHAPTER 7   And it happened when the king was dwelling 1
in his house and the LORD had granted him respite all around from his
enemies, that the king said to Nathan the prophet, "See, pray, I dwell in 2
a cedarwood house while the Ark of God dwells within curtains." And 3
Nathan said to the king, "Whatever is in your heart, go, do, for the LORD is
with you." And it happened on that night, that the word of the LORD came 4
to Nathan, saying, "Go, say to My servant, to David, 'Thus says the LORD: 5
Is it you who would build Me a house for Me to dwell in? For I have dwelled 6
in no house from the day I brought up the Israelites out of Egypt until this

---

tion: Is this a punishment from God, or simply a refusal by David to share her bed, or is
the latter to be understood as the agency for the former?

CHAPTER 7   1. *And it happened when the king was dwelling in his house.* This transitional note establishes a link with the previous episode, in which David brought the
Ark into Jerusalem and had his final confrontation with Michal, which in a sense was
the final blow to the house of Saul. What follows is a major caesura in the David story—a
long pause marked by ideological reflections on the future, before David must deal once
again with external enemies and then be engulfed by internecine strife in his court. The
language of both Nathan's night-vision and David's prayer is strikingly different from that
of the surrounding narrative—more hortatory, more formulaic, more reminiscent of the
Deuteronomistic school that would come to dominate Israel's national literature nearly
four centuries after the reign of David. The literary archaeology that has been performed
on these two long passages remains in contention, some scholars claiming these are late
compositions of a Deuteronomistic writer, others arguing that two or more authentically
old literary strata have been joined together and framed by a later editor. These are not
issues that it will be useful to attempt to resolve here. What is worth noting is the deliberate
structural separation effected by these two passages between everything that precedes the
ensconcing of throne and Ark in Jerusalem and everything that follows.
   respite . . . from his enemies. The respite is partial, and temporary, because the subsequent chapters report further military campaigns.

2. *Nathan the prophet.* Not previously mentioned, and of unspecified background, he will
play an important role in what follows.
   a cedarwood house. The palace would have been a stone structure with cedar paneling
within. Cedar was an expensive import item brought from Lebanon (see 5:11).
   curtains. The term is an obvious synecdoche for tent (compare 6:17).

3. *Whatever is in your heart, go, do.* Nathan's response to the brilliantly successful king,
who has demonstrated through his triumphs that God is with him, is perfectly reasonable.
But in the night-vision God will give different directions.

5. *Thus says the LORD.* The "messenger-formula" signals the beginning of explicit prophetic
discourse. God's address to Nathan as a whole emphasizes the act of speech, being constructed as an elaborate nesting of quoted speech within quoted speech.

6. *I have dwelled in no house.* This is not, as some interpreters have claimed, the expression of a pre-Solomonic anti-temple ideology. The author of this episode is faced with the
difficulty of explaining a historical fact, that David did not build the Temple, as we might

7 day, but I have gone about in tent and tabernacle. Wherever I went about
   among all the Israelites, did I speak a word with any of the tribal chiefs
   of Israel whom I charged to shepherd My people Israel, saying, Why did
8 you not build me a cedarwood house? And now, thus shall you say to My
   servant, to David, Thus says the LORD of Hosts: I Myself took you from
   the pasture, from following the flocks, to be prince over My people, over
9 Israel. And I have been with you wherever you have gone, and I have cut
   down your enemies before you. And I will make you a great name, like the
10 name of the great of the earth. And I will set aside a place for My people,
   for Israel, and plant them, and they shall abide there and no longer quake,
11 and the wicked shall no more afflict them as before, from the day that I
   appointed judges over My people Israel. And I will grant you respite from
   all your enemies, and the LORD declares that it is He Who will make you
12 a house. When your days are full and you lie with your fathers, I will raise
   up your seed after you, who will issue from your loins, and I will make
13 his kingship unshaken. He it is who will build a house for My name, and
14 I will make the throne of his kingship unshaken forever. I will be a father

---

have expected, but rather it was his son Solomon who carried out the construction. The
probable historical reason was that David was too preoccupied with the struggles within his
own court and family. In Chronicles, the reason given is that he had shed blood. Here, the
argument God makes is that it is an act of presumption for a mere mortal to build a temple
for the unhoused God of Israelite history. But this line of reasoning actually enhances the
theological importance of Solomon's temple, for it suggests that God Himself will build a
house when He is good and ready, using the human agency He chooses. Thus the Temple
that is to be raised up by David's seed will have a more than human importance, being at
once a token of God's indwelling among His people Israel and a divine underwriting of
the Davidic dynasty.

   in tent and tabernacle. The latter was a portable shrine made of boards and curtains.
Presumably, local sanctuaries such as the one at Shiloh are assimilated into the archetype
of tabernacle, being neither cultic centers for the entire nation nor grand edifices like the
Solomonic temple.

10–11. *no more afflict them as before, from the day that I appointed judges.* Although the
Judges succeeded in temporarily driving off Israel's sundry oppressors, the period as a
whole was one of instability and recurrent harassment by enemy peoples.

11. *it is He Who will make you a house.* Both in this prophecy and in David's prayer the
double meaning of "house" is repeatedly exploited. God will grant David a house—that
is, a continuing dynasty, and then will have David's son build Him a house—that is, a
temple. The house in which David dwells in the opening verse of this chapter is of course
his palace in Jerusalem.

to him and he will be a son to Me, so should he do wrong, I will chastise him with the rod men use and with the afflictions of humankind. But My 15 loyalty shall not swerve from him as I made it swerve from Saul whom I removed from before you. And your house and your kingship shall be 16 steadfast forever, your throne unshaken forever.'" In accordance with all 17 these words and in accordance with all this vision, so did Nathan speak to David.

And King David came and sat before the LORD and said, "Who am I, LORD 18 God, and what is my house, that you have brought me this far? And even 19 this is too little in Your eyes, LORD God, for You have also spoken of Your servant's house in distant time, and this is a man's instruction, LORD God. And how can David speak more to You, when You know Your servant, 20 LORD God? For the sake of Your word, and according to Your heart You 21 have done all these great things, to make known to Your servant. There- 22 fore are You great, O LORD God, for there is none like You and there is no

---

14. *the rod men use . . . the afflictions of humankind.* God will discipline the future king as a father disciplines his son, and with familiar human tribulations, not with supernatural bolts from the heavens.

15. *My loyalty.* The Hebrew *ḥesed* is the faithfulness and goodwill that one party of a pact owes to the other.

 whom I removed. The Hebrew uses the same verb that is rendered here in the immediately preceding phrase as "made it swerve."

18. *David came and sat before the LORD.* David comes into the tent in which the Ark has been placed. The verb "sat," *yashav,* is identical with the verb at the beginning of the chapter that also means "dwell," and thus establishes a structural parallel between the passage on the postponed building of the Temple and David's prayer.

19. *You have also spoken of Your servant's house in distant time.* These words refer directly to the prophecy conveyed to Nathan in verses 12–16, and thus undermine the claim of some scholars that David's prayer was originally part of the story of the introduction of the Ark to Jerusalem (chapter 6), from which it was supposedly separated by the insertion of Nathan's prophecy.

 this is a man's instruction. That is, he would scarcely think himself worthy of all this divine bounty about which God has just instructed him. But this is no more than an interpretive guess, because the meaning of the Hebrew—*zo't torat ha'adam*—is obscure.

22. *Therefore are You great, O LORD God.* Although the thread of piety in David's complex and contradictory character could be perfectly authentic, he does not elsewhere speak in this elevated, liturgical, celebratory style, and so the inference of the presence of another

23 god beside You, in all we have heard with our own ears. And who is like
Your people Israel, a unique nation upon earth, whom a god has gone out
to redeem as a people to make Him a name and to do great and awesome
things for them, to drive out from before Your people whom You redeemed
24 from Egypt nations with their gods? And You made Your own people
25 Israel unshaken forever, and You, O LORD, became their God. And now
LORD God, the word that You have spoken to Your servant concerning
26 his house—make it stand forever and do as You have spoken. And may
Your name be great forever, so it be said, 'The LORD of Armies is God over
Israel, and the house of David Your servant shall be unshaken before You.'
27 For You, O LORD of Armies, God of Israel, have revealed to Your servant,
saying, 'A house will I build you.' Therefore has Your servant found the
28 heart to pray to you this prayer. And now, O LORD God, You are God and
Your words must be truth, You have spoken of this bounty to Your servant.
29 And now, have the goodness to bless the house of Your servant to be before
You forever, for it is You, LORD God, Who have spoken, and with Your
blessings may Your servant's house be blessed forever."

---

writer in this passage is plausible. Yet it is at least conceivable that the original writer has
introduced this celebratory rhetoric to punctuate David's moment of respite in the story.

23. *for them.* The Masoretic Text, at several points in these verses problematic, has "for you"
(plural). The Qumran Samuel and the Septuagint have no pronoun.

   to drive out. The Masoretic Text is syntactically odd and semantically obscure. The
parallel verse in Chronicles omits "for your land" and adds "to drive out," as does this
translation.

25. *the word that You have spoken to Your servant concerning his house.* This word has just
been conveyed to David through Nathan as God's intermediary. It is humanly understandable that David should now fervently pray to God that the grand promise of the night-vision
be fulfilled in time to come.

29. *it is You, LORD God, Who have spoken, and with Your blessings may Your servant's
house be blessed forever.* The fondness of biblical prose for thematic key words is especially prominent in the grand theological performance that is David's prayer, in which
the key words function as formal rhetorical motifs. The salient repeated terms are
"speak" (the act of God's promise and continuing revelation), "house" (dynasty and
palace but, in this speech, not temple), "blessing" (in the final sentence it occurs three
times in three different forms), and "forever" (the adverbial index of the permanence
of God's promise).

CHAPTER 8   And it happened thereafter that David struck 1
down the Philistines and subjugated them, and David took Metheg-Ammah
from the hand of the Philistines. And he struck down Moab, and measured 2
them out with a line, making them lie on the ground, and he measured
two lengths of a line to put to death and one full length to keep alive. And
Moab became tribute-bearing vassals to David. And David struck down 3
Hadadezer son of Rehob, king of Zobah as he went to restore his monument by the Euphrates River. And David captured from him one thousand 4
seven hundred horsemen and twenty thousand foot soldiers, and David

---

CHAPTER 8   1. *And it happened thereafter.* This characteristically vague temporal
reference actually reflects the achronological arrangement of the narrative material at this
point. Chapter 7 was a long pause in the progress of the larger story that was devoted to
the theological grounds for the postponement of building a temple and to the promise of
a perpetual Davidic dynasty. Chapter 8 offers a summary of David's conquests (which in
historical fact would have spanned at least several years) resulting in the establishment of
a small empire. We then revert to the intimate story of David.

David struck down the Philistines and subjugated them. Neither the Hebrew terms of
the text nor the scant extrabiblical evidence allows one to conclude whether David actually
occupied the Philistine cities on the coastal plain or merely reduced them to vassal status.
In any case, he put an end to the Philistine military threat and was free to turn his attention
to adversaries east of the Jordan.

Metheg-Ammah. There are differences of opinion as to whether this is an otherwise
unknown place-name or the designation of some precious trophy (*meteg* is an equestrian
bit, *'amah* is a watercourse) taken from the Philistines.

2. *Moab.* It should be recalled that Moab, with whom David is linked by ancestry, provided
refuge for his parents from Saul. Perhaps now that David has consolidated an Israelite
monarchy, each side views the other as a threat. Or perhaps Moab has been compelled by
proximity to join forces with the anti-Israelite kingdoms east of the Jordan.

and measured them out with a line. This procedure is not otherwise known.

3. *Zobah.* Aram Zobah was at this point the large dominant kingdom of Mesopotamia, to
the north and east of biblical Israel.

as he went to restore his monument. Presumably, the absence of the king from the
Aramean heartland exposed it to David's attack. The term *yad* here (usually "hand") is construed in its occasional sense of "monument" or "stele," though the idiom *heshiv yad* (literally, "to bring back the hand") also has the sense of "strike." Were that the case here, however,
one would probably expect an object to the striking ("brought his hand back against X.").

4. *one thousand seven hundred horsemen.* The numbers reflected in Chronicles and in the
Septuagint as well as in the Qumran Samuel scroll are "one thousand chariots and seven
thousand horsemen."

David hamstrung all the chariot horses. The most likely explanation for this cruel act is
that the Israelites, who initially fought on mountainous terrain, as yet made no significant
use of cavalry, and so David's only concern would be to disable the horses in order that

5 hamstrung all the chariot horses, leaving aside a hundred of them. And
   the Arameans of Damascus came to aid Hadadezer, king of Zobah, and
   David struck down twenty-two thousand men from among the Arameans.
6 And David set up prefects in Aram-Damascus, and the Arameans became
   tribute-bearing vassals to David, and the LORD made David victorious
7 wherever he went. And David took the golden quivers that had belonged
8 to the servants of Hadadezer and brought them to Jerusalem. And from
   Betah and from Berothai, the towns of Hadadezer, King David took a great
   abundance of bronze.

9 And Toi king of Hamath heard that David had struck down all the forces
10 of Hadadezer. And Toi sent Joram his son to King David to ask after his
   well-being and to salute him for having done battle with Hadadezer and for
   striking him down, as Hadadezer was Toi's adversary. And in Joram's hand
11 there were vessels of silver and vessels of gold and vessels of bronze. These,
   too, did King David consecrate to the LORD, together with the silver and
12 the gold that he consecrated from all the nations he had conquered: from
   Edom and from Moab and from the Ammonites and from the Philistines
   and from Amalek and from the plunder of Hadadezer son of Rehob, king

---

they could not be used against him in the future. The hundred horses left unmaimed might
perhaps be for use as a small experiment with cavalry, or as draft animals.

7. *the golden quivers.* The relatively rare Hebrew term *shelatim* has often been understood
as "shields," but most of the other biblical occurrences encourage the notion of something
that contains arrows, as Rashi observed, and this sense is supported by cognates in Babylonian and Aramaic.

9. *Toi king of Hamath.* Hamath lay to the northwest of the kingdom of Aram Zobah, in
present-day Syria. It was a neo-Hittite state.

10. *And Toi sent Joram his son to King David.* Sending the prince as emissary is a token of
the importance that the king attaches to the mission. The vessels of precious metals are a
peace offering to David or, from another perspective, an advance payment of tribute. Toi,
as a king who has been threatened by the Arameans, has good reason to pledge fealty to
David, but he surely also wants to ward off any possible military thrust of the expansionist
Israelites against his own kingdom.

12. *from Edom.* The Masoretic Text has "from Aram," but Chronicles, the Septuagint, and
the Peshitta all have Edom, a kingdom contiguous with Moab, which immediately follows.
Aram (Zobah) is mentioned at the end of the verse.

of Zobah. And David made a name when he came back from striking down ₁₃
the Edomites in the Valley of Salt—eighteen thousand of them. And he set ₁₄
up prefects in Edom, throughout Edom he set up prefects, and all Edom
became vassals to David, and the LORD made David victorious wherever
he went.

And David was king over all Israel, and it was David's practice to mete out ₁₅
true justice to all his people. And Joab son of Zeruiah was over the army, ₁₆
and Jehoshaphat son of Ahilud was recorder. And Zadok son of Ahitub ₁₇
and Abiathar son of Ahimelech were priests, and Seraiah was scribe. And ₁₈
Benaiah son of Jehoida was over the Cherithites and the Pelethites, and
David's sons served as priests.

---

13. *from striking down the Edomites.* Again, the Masoretic Text has "Aram" in contradiction
to several other ancient versions. Since the Valley of Salt was most probably in the vicinity
of the Dead Sea, it would have been Edomite, not Aramean, territory.

15. *And David was king over all Israel.* The chronicle of David's conquests is followed by a
kind of epilogue—a notice of the royal bureaucracy.

16. *recorder.* The Hebrew term *mazkir* could also be represented as "remembrancer." It is
not entirely clear what his duties were, although they obviously went far beyond being a
mere clerk. He may have been in control of the royal archives. It has been proposed that he
was also chief of protocol in the palace.

17. *Abiathar son of Ahimelech.* The Masoretic Text makes Ahimelech the son and Abiathar
the father, in flat contradiction to the occurrences of these two figures both earlier and
later in the narrative.

scribe. As with "recorder," the responsibilities were more than those of an amanuensis.
They might have included diplomatic translation and even counseling in affairs of state.

18. *the Cherithites and the Pelethites.* There is debate over the national identity of the
latter, but the consensus is that the former are people of Cretan origins, part of the wave
of so-called Sea Peoples who immigrated to Canaan from the Aegean toward the beginning of the eleventh century B.C.E. David has taken care to set up a special palace guard
of foreign mercenaries on whose loyalty he can rely, in contrast to Israelites who might
have motives of tribal allegiance or support for some pretender to the throne in an attempt
to displace him.

and David's sons served as priests. This curious detail is probably parallel to the report
of a palace guard of foreign origins: just as David creates an elite military contingent outside the framework of the Israelite troops, he invests his own sons with sacerdotal duties
within the circle of the court, outside the framework of the hereditary priesthood that
controlled the public cult.

1 CHAPTER 9   And David said "Is there anyone who is still left from the house of Saul, that I may keep faith with him for the sake of 2 Jonathan?" And there was a servant of the house of Saul named Ziba, and they called him to David, and the king said to him, "Are you Ziba?" And 3 he said, "Your servant." And the king said, "Is there anyone at all left from the house of Saul, that I might keep God's faith with him?" And Ziba said 4 to the king, "There is yet a son of Jonathan's, who is crippled." And the king said, "Where is he?" And Ziba said, "Why, he is in the house of Machir 5 son of Amiel from Lo-Debar." And King David sent and fetched him from 6 the house of Machir son of Amiel from Lo-Debar. And Mephibosheth son

---

CHAPTER 9   1. *And David said.* We are immediately alerted to the fact that we are returning from the chronicle summary of chapter 8 (where there is no dialogue) and from the long set speeches of chapter 7 to the main body of the David story because once again the narrative is carried forward to a large extent by dialogue. We are again plunged into a world of personal and political transactions engaged through exchanges of spoken language.

Is there anyone who is still left from the house of Saul. The added emphasis of "still," '*od* (compare the analogous emphatic phrase in verse 3), reflects David's genuine uncertainty as to whether, after all the deaths of the Saulides previously reported, there are in fact any surviving descendants of Saul. The courtiers who are queried evidently don't know, so they propose summoning a retainer of Saul's in order to put the question to him. The fact that David is later complicit in the execution of seven men of the house of Saul (chapter 21) has led many analysts to conclude that the original place of that episode was before the present chapter. Robert Polzin, on the other hand, argues that the postponement of the report in chapter 21 is deliberately delayed exposition, meant to reveal another troubling facet of David near the end of his story.

3. *keep God's faith.* The "faith" in question (*ḥesed*) is not credal but faithful performance of one's obligation in a covenant, a term that also has the connotation of "kindness." "God" here has the force of an intensifier. The covenant that is explicitly alluded to is the one between Jonathan and David (1 Samuel 20:42). That tight link is one of several arguments against the view widely held ever since the 1926 study of Leonhard Rost that this episode marks the beginning of a wholly independent Succession Narrative, which continues until 1 Kings 2.

who is crippled. Ziba's mention of the surviving Saulide's handicap is probably intended to assure David that Mephibosheth will not pose any challenge to the throne.

4. *Lo-Debar.* Mephibosheth was evidently taken to this northern trans-Jordanian town because it was a place of refuge. It is in the general vicinity of Jabesh-Gilead, the town inhabited by Saul's allies and perhaps kinsmen. Mephibosheth, it will be recalled, was five years old when he was dropped by his nurse and crippled in the flight after the defeat at Gilboa. Since it seems implausible that more than fifteen or so years would have passed since that moment, one may surmise that he is now a man in his twenties.

6. *Mephibosheth ... flung himself on his face and prostrated himself.* These gestures of abasement may have been standard etiquette in approaching a monarch, but Ziba is not

of Jonathan son of Saul came to David and flung himself on his face and prostrated himself. And David said, "Mephibosheth!" And he said, "Your servant here." And David said to him, "Fear not, for I will surely keep faith 7 with you for the sake of Jonathan your father, and I will give back to you all the land of Saul your grandfather, and as for you, you shall eat bread at my table always." And he prostrated himself and said, "What is your servant 8 that you should have turned to a dead dog like me?" And the king called to 9 Ziba, Saul's lad, and said to him, "All that was Saul's and his whole household's I give to your master's son. And you shall work the soil for him, you 10 and your sons and your slaves, and you shall bring food to your master's house and they will eat. But Mephibosheth will always eat bread at my table." And Ziba had fifteen sons and twenty slaves. And Ziba said to the 11 king, "Whatever my lord the king commands his servant, thus will his servant do." And Mephibosheth ate at David's table like one of the king's sons. And Mephibosheth had a little son named Micah, and all who dwelled in 12

---

reported making them. Mephibosheth is clearly terrified that the king may have summoned him in order to have him put to death David's possible complicity in the deaths of other figures associated with the house of Saul might well have been a matter of continuing speculation in Benjaminite circles. As Fokkelman aptly notes, it would have been a particularly painful business for a man crippled in both legs to fling himself down in this fashion.

7. *I will give back to you all the land of Saul.* With the descendants of Saul fled or dead, the king had expropriated Saul's ancestral land around Gibeah.

9. *Saul's lad.* The Hebrew *na'ar* denotes subservience, but it is unclear whether, as some have claimed, it indicates Ziba's role as majordomo (the philological grounds for that construction are shaky) or rather his subaltern status in the house of Saul.

10. *your slaves.* The Hebrew term *'eved* straddles the sense of freeborn underling and slave. Ziba evidently belongs to the former category, and so the designation *'eved* is rendered as "servant" when it is attached to him. It seems likely that the underlings of a prosperous servant would be slaves. Polzin has noted that different forms of this verbal stem occur ten times in the chapter, which is all about establishing lines of dominance and subservience.

and you shall bring food for your master's house and they will eat. The translation here follows the text of the Septuagint. The Masoretic Text reads: "and you shall bring and it will be food for your master's son and he will eat it." That version can be maintained only with strain, for the very next clause informs us that Mephibosheth was not dependent on the yield of his own land but resided in Jerusalem, sustained at the royal table.

11. *And Mephibosheth ate at David's table.* Again, the translation follows the Septuagint. The Masoretic Text has "And Mephibosheth is eating at my table," but the Bible never gives reported speech without an explicit introduction ("and David said").

13 Ziba's house were servants to Mephibosheth. And Mephibosheth dwelled in Jerusalem, for at the king's table he would always eat. And he was lame in both his feet.

1 CHAPTER 10   And it happened thereafter that the king of the
2 Ammonites died and Hanun his son was king in his stead. And David said, "Let me keep faith with Hanun son of Nahash as his father kept faith with me." And David sent his servants in order to console him for his father, and
3 David's servants came to the land of the Ammonites. And the Ammonite

---

13. *for at the king's table he would always eat.* The refrainlike repetition of this clause should give us pause. David is indeed treating Jonathan's crippled son like one of his own sons, "keeping faith" or "showing kindness" to the offspring of his dead comrade, as he had pledged. He surely means his benefaction to be publicly perceived. At the same time, it is clearly in David's interest to keep the only conceivable Saulide pretender to the throne close at hand, under easy scrutiny. Mephibosheth's condition is ostensibly that of an unofficially adopted son, but with an uneasy suspicion that it is really a kind of luxurious house arrest.

   And he was lame in both his feet. This emphatic concluding reiteration of his physical impairment might be intended, as some commentators have proposed, to explain why he could not travel back and forth between his estate and Jerusalem. But it surely also strikes a plaintive note at the end, underscoring the vulnerability of Mephibosheth, whether cosseted or held under surveillance in the Jerusalem court. As the court becomes more and more the arena of plots and murderous conflict, Mephibosheth will be victimized by someone close to him. This notice at the end about Mephibosheth's lameness also underscores the continuing antithesis between the fates of the house of Saul and the house of David: King David came into Jerusalem whirling and dancing before the LORD; the surviving Saulide limps into Jerusalem, crippled in both legs

CHAPTER 10   1. *And it happened thereafter.* Once again this vague temporal formula reflects the achronological ordering of the text. Since the Aramean king Hadadezer is reported in 8:3–7 to have been decisively defeated by David and to have become David's vassal, the campaign that is represented here, in which Hadadezer musters Aramean forces east of the Euphrates in order to confront David, must have taken place as part of David's victorious struggle with Aram Zobah registered in the summary of chapter 8. This whole account of military operations—given its rather dry technical style, it may well have been drawn from Davidic annals—is meant to establish the facts of continuing armed conflict with the Ammonites, which is the crucial background for the story of David and Bathsheba in the next chapter.

2. *Let me keep faith with Hanun son of Nahash as his father kept faith with me.* This chapter, like the preceding one, opens with a declaration of David's desire to keep faith with, or do kindness to, the son of a father toward whom he feels some prior obligation. There is no notice in the previous narrative of Nahash's having done favors for David, but several scholars have surmised that Nahash's enmity toward Saul (see 1 Samuel 11) might have led

commanders said to Hanun their lord, "Do you imagine David is honoring your father in sending you consolers? Is it not in order to search out the city and to spy on it and to overthrow it that David has sent his servants to you?" And Hanun took David's servants and shaved off half the beard of 4 each and cut off half their diplomat's garb down to their buttocks, and sent them off. And they told David, and he sent to meet them, for the men were 5 very humiliated, and the king said, "Stay here in Jericho until your beards grow back and you can return."

And the Ammonites saw that they had become repugnant to David, and 6 the Ammonites sent and hired Arameans from Beth-Rehob and Arameans from Zobah, twenty thousand foot soldiers, and King Maacah with a thousand men, and the men of Tob, twelve thousand men. And David heard and 7

---

him to provide refuge or logistical support to David and his men when they were being hunted down by Saul.

3. *to search out the city.* As Moshe Garsiel notes, the walled cities of the ancient Near East often had tunnels, underground conduits, or other points of vulnerability that could provide access to the enemy in a siege. David's forces may have broken into Jerusalem in this fashion. (See the first comment on 5:8.)

4. *shaved off half the beard of each and cut off half their diplomats' garb.* Shaving the beard is an insult to the masculinity of the ambassadors, all the more so because it is done in a disfiguring way, with half the beard left uncut. The exposure of one buttock, by cutting away half the garment vertically, is similarly shaming, perhaps sexually shaming. The garments in question, moreover, are not ordinary clothes, *begadim*, but *madim*, garb worn in the performance of an official function (compare the "battle garb," *madim*, that Saul gives to David in 1 Samuel 17:38). The Ammonites thus are not merely insulting the ambassadors personally but provocatively violating their diplomatic privilege. In all this, we observe an extravagant reflection of the symbolic violation of Saul by David when he cut off a corner of the king's robe.

5. *Stay here in Jericho.* The town of Jericho is in the Jordan Valley just west of the Jordan, and is plausibly the first place of habitation that the ambassadors would come to on crossing back from Ammonite territory.

6. *And the Ammonites saw.* Shimon Bar-Efrat observes that this narrative sequence is formally structured by the "seeing" of David's trans-Jordanian adversaries (here, verse 14, verse 15, verse 19), in counterpoint to David's "hearing." The latter implies receiving word at a distance, as does the associated locution, "it was told to David," whereas the former signifies immediate observation. Thus Joab, making out the deployment of hostile forces on the battlefield, is also said to see.

7. *David heard and sent out Joab.* Throughout this chapter and the next, the verb "to send" is repeatedly linked with David: for the first time, he plays the role not of martial leader but of

8 sent out Joab together with the whole army of warriors. And the Ammonites
   sallied forth and drew up for battle at the entrance to the gate, and Aram
9 Zobah and Rehob and the men of Tob were apart in the field. And Joab saw
   that there was a battle line against him in front and behind, and he chose
   from all the picked men of Israel and drew them up to meet the Arameans.
10 And the rest of the troops he gave into the hand of Abishai his brother, and
11 he drew them up to meet the Ammonites. And he said, "If the Arameans
   prove too strong for me, you will rescue me, and if the Ammonites prove
12 too strong for you, I shall come to rescue you. Be strong, and let us find
   strength for the sake of our people and for the sake of the towns of our God,
13 and the LORD will do what is good in His eyes!" And Joab advanced, and
   the troops who were with him, to battle against the Arameans, and they
14 fled before him. And the Ammonites saw that the Arameans had fled, and
   they fled from Abishai and went into the town, and Joab turned back from
   the Ammonites and came to Jerusalem.

---

sedentary king, delegating the military task to his commander. This new state of affairs will
have major implications in the Bathsheba story.

   the whole army of warriors. This is a slight variant, supported by three ancient versions,
of the Masoretic Text, which reads "the whole army, the warriors."

9. *there was a battle line against him in front and behind.* The Israelite forces are in danger
of being caught in the pincer movement between the Aramean mercenaries advancing
on them from the northeast and the Ammonites, presumably to the south. Joab rapidly
improvises a counterstrategy, selecting a corp of elite troops to assault the larger force
of Arameans and sending his brother Abishai with the rest of the troops against the
Ammonites. Such attention to military detail is quite untypical of biblical narrative, as
is the rousing battlefield exhortation (verse 12) with which Joab concludes his instructions. The point of such detail is surely to show Joab as a superbly competent and resolute
field commander, just before the great pivotal episode in the next chapter in which Joab
maintains the siege against Rabbath-Ammon while his commander in chief slumbers,
and lusts, in Jerusalem.

10. *the rest of the troops he gave.* Polzin observes, with puzzlement, that this story proceeds
by dividing things in half: beards, clothing, anti-Israelite forces, Israelite troops. One wonders whether this narrative dynamic of mitosis, even though it is a saving strategy in Joab's
case, might be a thematic introduction to all the inner divisions in court and nation, the
fractures in the house of David, that take up the rest of the narrative.

14. *and went into the town.* The town into which they withdraw under pressure from
Abishai's troops is not named. It could be the capital, Rabbath-Ammon (present-day
Amman), though some analysts have wondered whether Hanun would be so unwise as
to wait until the Israelites were at the gates of his own city before taking a decisive stand.
Another candidate that has been proposed is Medbah, an Ammonite town considerably
farther to the south.

And the Arameans saw that they had been routed by Israel, and they 15
reassembled. And Hadadezer sent and brought out the Arameans who 16
were beyond the Euphrates, and their forces came with Shobach the commander of Hadadezer's army at their head. And it was told to David, and 17
he gathered all Israel and crossed the Jordan, and they came to Helam.
And the Arameans drew up their lines against David and did battle with 18
him. And the Arameans fled before Israel, and David killed seven hundred
charioteers of the Arameans and forty thousand horsemen, and Shobach,
the commander of their army, he struck down, and he died there. And all 19
the kings who were vassals to Hadadezer saw that they had been routed
by Israel, and they made peace with Israel and became its vassals, and the
Arameans were afraid to rescue the Ammonites again.

CHAPTER 11   And it happened at the turn of the year, at the 1
time the kings sally forth, that David sent out Joab and his servants with

---

15. *they reassembled.* This major regrouping for a second campaign against the Israelites
involves the enlisting of greater numbers of troops from the Arameans east of the Euphrates, ethnic kin and in all likelihood political vassals to the people of Aram Zobah.

17. *he gathered all Israel.* Alerted to the augmented size of the trans-Jordanian forces, David
musters his entire national army and this time elects to command it himself.

19. *And all the kings who were vassals . . . made peace with Israel.* Seeing who has the military
upper hand, they take a small and logical step in exchanging vassal status under Hadadezer
for vassal status under David. It should be noted that this whole annalistic prelude to the
story of David and Bathsheba concludes with an invocation of "all the kings." The immediately following episode begins by mentioning "the time the kings sally forth"—although,
as we shall see, the noun itself there is pointedly ambiguous—and the tale that unfolds will
powerfully raise the question of what constitutes kingly behavior.

CHAPTER 11   Chapters 11 and 12, the story of David and Bathsheba and its immediate aftermath, are the great turning point of the whole David story, as both Meir Sternberg
and Robert Polzin have duly observed; and it seems as though the writer has pulled out
all the stops of his remarkable narrative art in order to achieve a brilliant realization of
this crucially pivotal episode. The deployment of thematic key words, the shifting play of
dialogue, the intricate relation between instructions and their execution, the cultivated
ambiguities of motive, are orchestrated with a richness that scarcely has an equal in ancient
narrative. Although the analytic scholars have variously sought to break up these chapters into editorial frame and Succession Narrative, Prophetic composition and old source,
emending patches of the text as they proceed, such efforts are best passed over in silence,
for the powerful literary integrity of the text speaks for itself.

1. *at the turn of the year.* The most plausible meaning is the beginning of the spring, when
the end of the heavy winter rains makes military action feasible.
    at the time the kings sally forth. There is a cunning ambiguity here in the Hebrew text. The

him and all Israel, and they ravaged the Ammonites and besieged Rabbah.
And David was sitting in Jerusalem.

2   And it happened at eventide that David arose from his bed and walked
    about on the roof of the king's house, and he saw from the roof a woman
3   bathing, and the woman was very beautiful. And David sent and inquired
    after the woman, and the one he sent said, "Why, this is Bathsheba daughter

---

received consonantal text reads *mal'akhim*, "messengers," though many manuscripts show
melakhim, "kings." As Polzin observes, the verb "to sally forth" (or, in nonmilitary contexts,
"to go forth") is often attached to kings and never to messengers, so "kings" is definitely the
more likely reading, though the ghost of "messengers" shows through in the letters of the
text. Polzin beautifully describes this double take: "the verse clearly doubles back on itself
in a marvelous display of narrative virtuosity: at a time when kings go forth, David did not,
making it a time, therefore, when messengers must go forth; at a time when messengers
go forth, David, remaining in Jerusalem, sent Joab, his servants and all Israel to ravage
Ammon." What some see here as a scribal error may well be a deliberate orthographic pun

David sent out Joab. The verb "to send"—the right verb for "messengers"—occurs eleven
times in this chapter, framing the beginning and the end. This episode is not a moral
parable but a story anchored in the realities of political history. It is concerned with the
institutionalization of the monarchy. David, now a sedentary king removed from the field
of action and endowed with a dangerous amount of leisure, is seen constantly operating
through the agency of others, sending messengers within Jerusalem and out to Ammonite
territory. Working through intermediaries, as the story will abundantly show, creates a
whole new order of complications and unanticipated consequences.

And David was sitting in Jerusalem. The verb for "sitting" also means "to stay" (compare
verse 12), but it is best to preserve the literal sense here because of the pointed sequence—
sitting, lying, rising—and because in biblical usage "to sit" is also an antonym of "to go
out" (or sally forth).

2. *at eventide.* The Hebrew term *'et'erev* echoes ironically with the phrase *'et tse't*, "at the
time of sallying forth" in the previous verse. A siesta on a hot spring day would begin not
long after noon, so this recumbent king has been in bed an inordinately long time.

he saw from the roof. The palace is situated on a height, so David can look down on the
naked Bathsheba bathing, presumably on her own rooftop. This situation of the palace
also explains why David tells Uriah to "go down" to his house. Later in the story, archers
deal destruction from the heights of the city wall, the Hebrew using the same preposition,
me'al, to convey the sense of "from above."

3. *the one he sent said.* The Hebrew uses an unspecified "he said."

Bathsheba daughter of Eliam wife of Uriah the Hittite. It is unusual to identify a woman
by both father and husband. The reason may be, as Bar-Efrat suggests, that both men are
members of David's elite corps of warriors. Although Uriah's designation as Hittite has
led some interpreters to think of him as a foreign mercenary, the fact that he has a pious
Israelite name ("the LORD is my light") suggests that he is rather a native or at least a naturalized Israelite of Hittite extraction. In any case, there is obvious irony in the fact that
the man of foreign origins is the perfect Good Soldier of Israel, whereas the Israelite king
betrays and murders him.

of Eliam wife of Uriah the Hittite." And David sent messengers and fetched 4
her and she came to him and he lay with her, she having just cleansed herself
of her impurity, and she returned to her house. And the woman became 5
pregnant and sent and told David and said, "I am pregnant." And David 6
sent to Joab: "Send me Uriah the Hittite." And Joab sent Uriah the Hittite
to David.

And Uriah came to him, and David asked how Joab fared and how the 7
troops fared and how the fighting fared. And David said to Uriah, "Go 8
down to your house and bathe your feet." And Uriah went out from the
king's house and the king's provisions came out after him. And Uriah lay 9
at the entrance to the king's house with all the servants of his master, and

---

4. *David sent . . . and fetched her and she came to him and he lay with her.* It is not uncommon for biblical narrative to use a chain of verbs in this fashion to indicate rapid, single-
minded action. What is unusual is that one verb in the middle of this sequence switches
grammatical subject—from David to Bathsheba. When the verb "come to" or "come into"
has a masculine subject and "into" is followed by a feminine object, it designates a first act
of sexual intercourse. One wonders whether the writer is boldly toying with this double
meaning, intimating an element of active participation by Bathsheba in David's sexual
summons. The text is otherwise entirely silent on her feelings, giving the impression that
she is passive as others act on her. But her later behavior in the matter of her son's succession
to the throne (1 Kings 1–2) suggests a woman who has her eye on the main chance, and it
is possible that opportunism, not merely passive submission, explains her behavior here as
well. In all of this, David's sending messengers first to ask about Bathsheba and then to call
her to his bed means that the adultery can scarcely be a secret within the court.
    cleansed herself of her impurity. The reference is to the ritually required bath after the
end of menstruation. This explains Bathsheba's bathing on the roof and also makes it clear
that she could not be pregnant by her husband.

5. *I am pregnant.* Astonishingly, these are the only words Bathsheba speaks in this story.
In keeping with the stringent efficiency of biblical narrative, the story leaps forward from
the sexual act to the discovery of pregnancy.

8. *Go down to your house and bathe your feet.* Some interpreters have made this more heavy-
handed than it is by construing the final phrase as a euphemism for sex (because "feet"
in the Bible is occasionally a euphemism for the male genitals). But in the biblical world,
bathing the feet is something travelers regularly do when they come from the dusty road.
This bathing of the feet stands in a kind of synecdochic relation to Bathsheba's bathing of
her whole body, discreetly suggesting that after the bathing of the feet, other refreshments
of the body will ensue.
    the king's provisions. David has not explicitly mentioned food or wine, but he sends a
kind of catered dinner after Uriah, hoping that the feast with Bathsheba will get husband
and wife into the desired amorous mood.

9. *And Uriah lay at the entrance of the king's house.* The verb "to lie," according to David's
expectations, should have been followed by "with his wife." Instead, we have not sex but a

10   he went not down to his house. And they told David, saying, "Uriah did
     not go down to his house." And David said to Uriah, "Look, you have come
11   from a journey. Why have you not gone down to your house?" And Uriah
     said to David, "The Ark and Israel and Judah are sitting in huts, and my
     master Joab and my master's servants are encamped in the open field, and
     shall I then come to my house to eat and to drink and to lie with my wife?
12   By your life, by your very life, I will not do this thing." And David said to
     Uriah, "Stay here today as well, and tomorrow I shall send you off." And
13   Uriah stayed in Jerusalem that day and the next. And David called him, and
     he ate before him and drank, and David made him drunk. And he went out
     in the evening to lie in the place where he lay with the servants of his master,

---

soldier's sleeping with his comrades, who are guarding the king. It should be remembered
(compare 1 Samuel 21) that soldiers in combat generally practiced sexual abstinence.

11. *sitting in huts.* Some construe *sukot,* "huts," as a place-name, the city of Succoth a
little east of the Jordan. But if the Ark is sent out of Jerusalem to the front, it would
make no sense to detain it at a logistics center only halfway to the battlefield, and Uriah's
point is that neither the Ark nor the troops enjoy proper shelter (while David is "sitting
in Jerusalem").

   shall I then come to my house to eat and to drink and to lie with my wife? Uriah now spells
out all that David left unsaid when he urged him to go down to his house. The crucial detail
of sleeping with Bathsheba comes at the very end. Menakhem Perry and Meir Sternberg,
in a pioneering Hebrew article in 1968 (revised by Sternberg for his English book of 1985),
raised the provocative issue of deliberate ambiguity (comparing the strategy of this story
with the two mutually exclusive readings possible for Henry James's short story "The Turn
of the Screw"). In their view, there are two equally viable readings. If Uriah does *not* know
that David has cuckolded him, he is the instrument of dramatic irony—the perfect soldier
vis-à-vis the treacherous king who is desperately trying to manipulate him so that the
husband will unwittingly cover the traces of his wife's sexual betrayal. If Uriah *does* know
of the adultery, he is a rather different character—not naïve but shrewdly aware, playing a
dangerous game of hints in which he deliberately pricks the conscience of the king, cogni-
zant, and perhaps not caring, that his own life may soon be forfeit. More recently, Moshe
Garsiel has proposed a reconciliation of these two readings: when Uriah first arrives from
the front, he is unaware of what has occurred; after the first night with his comrades at the
palace gate, he has been duly informed of the sexual betrayal, so that in his second dialogue
with the king, he cultivates a rhetoric of implicit accusation. Garsiel observes that when
Uriah swears emphatically by David's life (verse 11), he does not add the deferential "my
lord the king."

13. *David called him.* The verb here has the idiomatic sense of "invite."

   he ate before him. The preposition is an indication of hierarchical distance between
subject and king.

   David made him drunk. "David" has been added for clarity. The Hebrew says only "he
made him drunk." Plying Uriah with wine is a last desperate attempt, and a rather crude
one, to get him to have sex with his wife.

but to his house he did not go down. And it happened in the morning that 14
David wrote a letter to Joab and sent it by the hand of Uriah. And he wrote 15
in the letter, saying, "Put Uriah in the face of the fiercest battling and draw
back, so that he will be struck down and die." And it happened, as Joab 16
was keeping watch on the town, that he placed Uriah in the place where he
knew there were valiant men. And the men of the town sallied forth and did 17
battle with Joab, and some of the troops, some of David's servants, fell, and
Uriah the Hittite also died. And Joab sent and told David all the details 18
of the battle. And Joab charged the messenger, saying, "When you finish 19
reporting all the details of the battle to the king, if it should happen that 20
the king's wrath is roused and he says to you, 'Why did you approach the
town to fight? Did you not know they would shoot from the wall? Who 21
struck down Abimelech son of Jerubbesheth? Did not a woman fling down
on him an upper millstone from the wall, and he died in Thebez? Why did

---

14. *sent it by the hand of Uriah.* The letter would be in the form of a small scroll with either
a seal or threads around it. David is counting on the fact that Uriah as a loyal soldier will
not dream of opening the letter. If he does not know of the adultery, he has in any case no
personal motive to look at the letter. If he does know, he is accepting his fate with grim
resignation, bitterly conscious that his wife has betrayed him and that the king is too powerful for him to contend with.

15. *so that he will be struck down and die.* With no possibility of making Uriah seem
responsible for Bathsheba's pregnancy, David now gravely compounds the original crime
of adultery by plotting to get Uriah out of the way entirely by having him killed. What
follows in the story makes it clear that bloodshed, far more than adultery, is David's indelible transgression.

17. *some of the troops . . . fell, and Uriah the Hittite also died.* As Perry and Sternberg have
keenly observed, one of the salient features of this story is the repeated alteration of instructions by those who carry them out. It is, indeed, a vivid demonstration of the ambiguous
effecting of ends through the agency of others, which is one of the great political themes of
the story. The canny Joab immediately sees that David's orders are impossibly clumsy (perhaps an indication that the Machiavellian David has suddenly lost his manipulative cool-
ness): if the men around Uriah were to draw back all at once, leaving him alone exposed,
it would be entirely transparent that there was a plot to get him killed. Joab, then, coldly
recognizes that in order to give David's plan some credibility, it will be necessary to send
a whole contingent into a dangerous place and for many others beside Uriah to die. In this
fashion, the circle of lethal consequences of David's initial act spreads wider and wider.

21. *Did not a woman fling down on him an upper millstone.* The specificity of the prospec-
tive dialogue that Joab invents for a wrathful David may at first seem surprising. The
story of the ignominious death of Abimelech at the hand of a woman (Judges 9:52–54)
may have become a kind of object lesson in siege strategy for professional soldiers—when
you are laying siege against a city, above all beware of coming too close to the wall. One
suspects also that Joab's emphasis on a woman's dealing death to the warrior—Abimelech

you approach the wall?' Then shall you say, 'Your servant Uriah the Hittite
22 also died.'" And the messenger went and came and told David all that Joab
23 had sent him for. And the messenger said to David, "The men overpowered
us and sallied forth against us into the field, and then we were upon them
24 back to the entrance of the gate. And they shot at your servants from the
wall, and some of the king's servants died, and your servant Uriah the
25 Hittite also died." And the king said to the messenger, "Thus shall you say
to Joab, 'Let this thing not seem evil in your eyes, for the sword devours
sometimes one way and sometimes another. Battle all the more fiercely
against the city and destroy it. And so rouse his spirits.'"

---

had asked his armor bearer to run him through so that it would *not* be said he was killed
by a woman!—points back to Bathsheba as the ultimate source of this chain of disasters.
(This would be Joab's soldierly judgment, not necessarily the author's.)

Your servant Uriah the Hittite also died. Joab obviously knows that this is the message
for which David is waiting. By placing it in the anticipatory "script" that he dictates to the
messenger, he is of course giving away the secret, more or less, to the messenger. Might
this, too, be calculated, as an oblique dissemination of David's complicity in Uriah's death,
perhaps to be used at some future point by Joab against the king? In any case, given David's
track record in killing messengers who bear tidings not to his liking, Joab may want to be
sure that this messenger has the means to fend off any violent reaction from the king, who
would not have been expecting a report of multiple casualties.

23. *and then we were upon them back to the entrance of the gate.* The astute messenger offers
a circumstantial account that justifies the mistake of approaching too close to the wall: the
Ammonites came out after the Israelites in hot pursuit; then the Israelites, turning the tide
of battle, were drawn after the fleeing Ammonites and so were tricked into coming right
up to the gates of the city.

24. *and your servant Uriah the Hittite also died.* The messenger has divined the real point
of Joab's instructions all too well. He realizes that what David above all wants to hear is the
news of Uriah's death, and rather than risk the whole outburst, indicated by the prospec-
tive dialogue invented by Joab with the reference to the woman who killed Abimelech,
the messenger hastens to conclude his report, before the king can react, by mentioning
Uriah's death. Thus the narrative makes palpable the inexorable public knowledge of
David's crime.

25. *the sword devours sometimes one way and sometimes another.* The king responds by
directing to Joab what sounds like an old soldier's cliché (on the order of "every bullet has
its billet"). These vapid words of consolation to the field commander are an implicit admission that Joab's revision of David's orders was necessary: David concedes that many a good
man had to die in order to cover up his murder by proxy of Uriah.

Battle all the more fiercely. The Hebrew is literally "make fierce [or strengthen] your
battle." The phrase is an emphatic formal echo of "the fiercest battling" in verse 15.

And so rouse his spirits. Literally, "and strengthen him"—that is, Joab.

And Uriah's wife heard that Uriah her man was dead, and she keened over 26
her husband. And when the mourning was over, David sent and gathered 27
her into his house and she became his wife. And she bore him a son, and
the thing that David had done was evil in the eyes of the LORD.

CHAPTER 12   And the LORD sent Nathan to David, and he 1
came to him and said to him: "Two men there were in a single town, one

---

27. *when the mourning was over.* Normally, the mourning period would be seven days.
Bathsheba, then, is even more precipitous than Gertrude after the death of Hamlet the elder
in hastening to the bed of a new husband. She does, of course, want to become David's wife
before her big belly shows.

David sent and gathered her into his house and she became his wife. Throughout this
story, David is never seen anywhere but in his house. This sentence at the end strongly
echoes verse 4: "David sent . . . and fetched her and she came to him and he lay with her."

the thing that David had done was evil in the eyes of the LORD. Only now, after the
adultery, the murder, the remarriage, and the birth of the son, does the narrator make an
explicit moral judgment of David's actions. The invocation of God's judgment is the introduction to the appearance of Nathan the prophet, delivering first a moral parable "wherein
to catch the conscience of the king" and then God's grim curse on David and his house.

CHAPTER 12   1. *And the LORD sent.* The second stage of the story of David and
Bathsheba—the phase of accusation and retribution—begins with a virtual pun on a prominent thematic word of the first half of the story. David was seen repeatedly "sending" messengers, arranging for the satisfaction of his lust and the murder of his mistress's husband
through the agency of others. By contrast, God here "sends" his prophet to David—not an
act of bureaucratic manipulation but the use of a human vehicle to convey a divine message of conscience.

Two men there were. Nathan's parable, from its very first syllables, makes clear its own
status as a traditional tale and a poetic construction. The way one begins a storyteller's
tale in the Bible is with the formula "there was a man"—compare the beginning of Job,
or the beginning of the story of Hannah and Elkanah in 1 Samuel 1. The Hebrew prose of
the parable also is set off strongly from the language of the surrounding narrative by its
emphatically rhythmic character, with a fondness for parallel pairs of terms—an effect this
translation tries to reproduce. The vocabulary, moreover, includes several terms that are
relatively rare in biblical prose narrative: *kivsah* (ewe), *ra'sh* (poor), *helekh* (wayfarer), *'oreah*
(traveler). Finally the two "men" of the opening formula are at the end separated out into
"rich man," "poor man," and "the man who had come" (in each of these cases, Hebrew *'ish*
is used). This formal repetition prepares the way, almost musically, for Nathan's two-word
accusatory explosion, *'atah ha'ish*, "You are the man!" Given the patently literary character
of Nathan's tale, which would have been transparent to anyone native to ancient Hebrew
culture, it is a little puzzling that David should so precipitously take the tale as a report of
fact requiring judicial action. Nathan may be counting on the possibility that the obverse
side of guilty conscience in a man like David is the anxious desire to do the right thing. As
king, his first obligation is to protect his subjects and to dispense justice, especially to the

2 was rich and the other poor. The rich man had sheep and cattle, in great
3 abundance. And the poor man had nothing save one little ewe that he had
   bought. And he nurtured her and raised her with him together with his
   sons. From his crust she would eat and from his cup she would drink and
4 in his lap she would lie, and she was to him like a daughter. And a wayfarer
   came to the rich man, and it seemed a pity to him to take from his own sheep
   and cattle to prepare for the traveler who had come to him, and he took the
5 poor man's ewe and prepared it for the man who had come to him." And
   David's anger flared hot against the man, and he said to Nathan, "As the
6 LORD lives, doomed is the man who has done this! And the poor man's ewe
   he shall pay back fourfold, inasmuch as he has done this thing, and because
7 he had no pity!" And Nathan said to David, "You are the man! Thus says

---

disadvantaged. In the affair of Bathsheba and Uriah, he has done precisely the opposite.
Now, as he listens to Nathan's tale, David's compensatory zeal to be a champion of justice
overrides any awareness he might have of the evident artifice of the story.

3. *eat . . . drink . . . lie.* As Polzin observes, these terms effect full contact with the story of
David and Bathsheba, being the three activities David sought to engage Uriah in with his
wife (compare Uriah's words in 11:11). The parable begins to become a little fantastic here
in the interest of drawing close to the relationships of conjugal intimacy and adultery to
which it refers: the little lamb eats from her master's crust, drinks from his cup, and lies in
his lap ("lap" as a biblical idiom has connotations not merely of parental sheltering but also
of sexual intimacy: compare verse 8, "I gave . . . your master's wives in your lap").

4. *it seemed a pity to him.* The Hebrew uses an active verb, "he pitied," preparing for a literal
ironic reversal in verse 6, "he had no pity"—or, "he did not pity."
    to prepare. The Hebrew is literally "to do" or "to make." When the verb has as its direct
object a live edible animal, it means to slaughter and cook.

5. *David's anger flared hot against the man.* Nathan's rhetorical trap has now snapped shut.
David, by his access of anger, condemns himself, and he becomes the helpless target of the
denunciation that Nathan will unleash.
    doomed is the man. Actually, according to biblical law someone who has illegally taken
another's property would be subject to fourfold restitution (verse 6), not to the death penalty. (The Hebrew phrase is literally "son of death"—that is, deserving death, just as in 1
Samuel 26:16.) David pronounces this death sentence in his outburst of moral indignation,
but it also reflects the way that the parable conflates the sexual "taking" of Bathsheba
with the murder of Uriah: the addition of Bathsheba to the royal harem could have been
intimated simply by the rich man's placing the ewe in his flock, but as the parable is told,
the ewe must be slaughtered, blood must be shed. David himself will not be condemned to
die, but death will hang over his house. As the Talmud (Yoma 22B) notes, the fourfold retribution for Uriah's death will be worked out in the death or violent fate of four of David's
children: the unnamed infant son of Bathsheba, Tamar, Amnon, and Absalom.

7. *Thus says the LORD God of Israel.* After the direct knife thrust of "You are the man!,"
Nathan hastens to produce the prophetic messenger-formula in its extended form, in this

the LORD God of Israel. 'It is I who anointed you king over Israel, and it is I
Who saved you from the hand of Saul. And I gave you your master's house 8
and your master's wives in your lap, and I gave you the house of Israel and
of Judah. And if that be too little, I would give you even as much again.
Why did you despise the word of the LORD, to do what is evil in His eyes? 9
Uriah the Hittite you struck down with the sword, and his wife you took for
yourself as wife, and him you have killed by the sword of the Ammonites!
And so now, the sword shall not swerve from your house evermore, seeing 10
as you have despised Me and have taken the wife of Uriah the Hittite to be
your wife.' Thus says the LORD, 'I am about to raise up evil against you from 11

way proclaiming divine authorization for the dire imprecation he pronounces against
David and his house.

7–8. *It is I who anointed you. . . . And if that be too little, I would give you even as much
again.* In the first part of this speech, there are several ironic echoes of David's prayer
in chapter 7, in which David thanks God for all His benefactions and professes himself
unworthy of them.

8. *and your master's wives in your lap.* At least in the account passed down to us, there is no
mention elsewhere of David's having taken sexual possession of his predecessor's consorts,
though this was a practice useful for its symbolic force in a transfer of power, as Absalom
will later realize.

9. *Uriah the Hittite you struck down with the sword.* The obliquity of working through
agents at a distance, as David did in contriving the murder of Uriah, is exploded by the
brutal directness of the language: it is as though David himself had wielded the sword.
Only at the end of the sentence are we given the explanatory qualification "by the sword
of the Ammonites."

10. *the sword shall not swerve from your house evermore.* As Bar-Efrat notes, David's
rather callous message to Joab, "the sword sometimes consumes one way and sometimes
another," is now thrown back in his face. The story of David's sons, not to speak of his
descendants in later generations, will in fact turn out to be a long tale of conspiracy, internecine struggle, and murder. One of the most extraordinary features of the whole David
narrative is that this story of the founding of the great dynasty of Judah is, paradoxically,
already a tale of the fall of the house of David. Once again, no one has grasped this tragic
paradox more profoundly than William Faulkner in his recasting of the story in *Absalom, Absalom!* The author of the David story continually exercises an unblinking vision
of David and the institution of the monarchy that exposes their terrible flaws even as he
accepts their divinely authorized legitimacy.

11. *I am about to raise up evil against you from your own house.* As befits a predictive curse,
the agents of the evil are left unnamed. The disaster announced is clearly the rebellion of
Absalom—as the reference to public cohabitation with David's wives makes clear—and
the rape of Tamar and the murder of Amnon that lead up to it. But further "evil" from the
house of David will persist to his deathbed, as Absalom's rebellion is followed by Adonijah's
usurpation.

your own house, and I will take your wives before your eyes and give them
to your fellow man, and he shall lie with your wives in the sight of this sun.
12 For you did it in secret but I will do this thing before all Israel and before
13 the sun.'" And David said to Nathan, "I have offended against the LORD."
And Nathan said to David, "The LORD has also remitted your offense—you
14 shall not die. But since you surely spurned the LORD in this thing, the son
born to you is doomed to die."

15 And Nathan went to his house, and the LORD afflicted the child whom
Bathsheba wife of Uriah the Hittite had borne David, and he fell gravely
16 ill. And David implored God for the sake of the lad, and David fasted, and
17 he came and spent the night lying on the ground. And the elders of his
house rose over him to rouse him up from the ground, but he would not,
18 nor did he partake of food with them. And it happened on the seventh day
that the child died, and David's servants were afraid to tell him that the
child was dead, for they said, "Look, while the child was alive, we spoke to
him and he did not heed our voice, and how can we say to him, the child is
19 dead? He will do some harm." And David saw that his servants were whis-
pering to each other and David understood that the child was dead. And
David said to his servants, "Is the child dead?" And they said, "He is dead."

---

12. *For you did it in secret but I will do this thing before all Israel.* The calamitous misjudgments that defined David's dealings with Bathsheba and Uriah were a chain of bungled
efforts at concealment. Now, in the retribution, all his crimes are to be revealed.

14. *spurned the LORD.* The Masoretic Text has "spurned the enemies of the LORD," a scribal
euphemism to avoid making God the object of a harsh negative verb.

15. *Bathsheba wife of Uriah the Hittite.* At this point, she is still identified as wife of the
husband she betrayed in conceiving this child.

16. *fasted . . . and spent the night lying on the ground.* David's acts pointedly replicate those
of the man he murdered, who refused to go home and eat but instead spent the night lying
on the ground with the palace guard.

18. *on the seventh day.* Seven days were the customary period of mourning. In this instance,
David enacts a regimen of mourning, in an effort to placate God, before the fact of death.
    He will do some harm. Presumably, the courtiers fear that David will do harm to himself
in a frenzy of grief.

19. *He is dead.* In Hebrew, this is a single syllable, *met*, "dead"—a response corresponding
to idiomatic usage because there is no word for "yes" in biblical Hebrew, and so the person
questioned must respond by affirming the key term of the question. It should be noted,
however, that the writer has contrived to repeat "dead" five times, together with one use of
the verb "died," in these two verses: the ineluctable bleak fact of death is hammered home
to us, just before David's grim acceptance of it.

And David rose from the ground and bathed and rubbed himself with 20
oil and changed his garments and came into the house of the LORD and
worshipped and came back to his house and asked that food be set out for
him, and he ate. And his servants said to him, "What is this thing that 21
you have done? For the sake of the living child you fasted and wept, and
when the child was dead, you arose and ate food?" And he said, "While 22
the child was still alive I fasted and wept, for I thought, 'Who knows, the
LORD may favor me and the child will live.' And now that he is dead, why 23
should I fast? Can I bring him back again? I am going to him and he will
not come back to me."

And David consoled Bathsheba his wife, and he came to her and lay with 24
her, and she bore a son and called his name Solomon, and the LORD loved

---

20. *David rose . . . bathed . . . rubbed himself with oil . . . changed his garments . . . worshipped . . . ate.* This uninterrupted chain of verbs signifies David's brisk resumption of the
activities of normal life, evidently without speech and certainly without explanation, as the
courtiers' puzzlement makes clear. The entire episode powerfully manifests that human
capacity for surprise, and for paradoxical behavior, that is one of the hallmarks of the great
biblical characters. David here acts in a way that neither his courtiers nor the audience of
the story could have anticipated.

23. *Can I bring him back again? I am going to him and he will not come back to me.* If the
episode of Bathsheba and Uriah is the great turning point of the David story, these haunting words are the pivotal moment in the turning point. As we have repeatedly seen, every
instance of David's speech in the preceding narrative has been crafted to serve political
ends, much of it evincing elaborately artful rhetoric. Now, after the dire curse pronounced
by Nathan, the first stage of which is fulfilled in the death of the child, David speaks for
the first time not out of political need but in his existential nakedness. The words he utters
have a stark simplicity—there are no elegies now—and his recognition of the irreversibility
of his son's death also makes him think of his own mortality. In place of David the seeker
and wielder of power, we now see a vulnerable David, and this is how he will chiefly appear
through the last half of his story.

24. *David consoled Bathsheba his wife.* Now, after the terrible price of the child's life has
been paid for the murder of her husband, the narrator refers to her as David's wife, not
Uriah's. A specific lapse of time is not mentioned, but one must assume that at least two or
three months have passed, during which she recovers from the first childbirth.
    she . . . called his name Solomon, and the LORD loved him. As a rule, it was the mother
who exercised the privilege of naming the child. Despite some scholarly efforts to construe
the name differently, its most plausible etymology remains the one that links it with the
word for "peace" (the Hebrew term *Shelomoh* might simply mean "His peace"). The LORD's
loving Solomon, who will disappear from the narrative until the struggle for the throne
in 1 Kings 1, foreshadows his eventual destiny, and also harmonizes this name giving with
the child's second name, Jedidiah, which means "God's friend."

25 him. And He sent by the hand of Nathan the prophet and called his name
Jedidiah, by the grace of the LORD.

26 And Joab battled against Rabbah of the Ammonites and he captured the
27 royal town. And Joab sent messengers to David and said,

> "I have battled against Rabbah.
> Yes, I captured the Citadel of Waters.

28 And so now, assemble the rest of the troops and encamp against the city
and capture it, lest it be I who capture the city and my name be called upon
29 it." And David assembled all the troops and went to Rabbah and battled
30 against it and captured it. And he took the crown of their king from his
head, and its weight was a talent of gold, with precious stones, and it was
set on David's head. And the booty of the city he brought out in great
31 abundance. And the people who were in it he brought out and set them to
work with saws and iron threshing boards and iron axes and he put them

---

25. *Jedidiah, by the grace of the LORD.* For the last phrase, this translation adopts a proposal
by Kyle McCarter Jr. The usual meaning of the preposition used, *ba'avur,* is "for the sake
of." It remains something of a puzzlement that the child should be given two names, one
by his mother and the other by God through His prophet. One common suggestion is that
Jedidiah was Solomon's official throne name. But perhaps the second name, indicating
special access to divine favor, reflects a political calculation on the part of Nathan: he is
already aligning himself with Solomon (and with Bathsheba), figuring that in the long
run it will be best to have a successor to David under some obligation to him. In the event,
Nathan's intervention will prove crucial in securing the throne for Solomon.

26. *Joab battled against Rabbah.* It is possible, as many scholars have claimed, that the conquest of Rabbah, in the siege of which Uriah had perished, in fact occurs before the birth of
Solomon, though sieges lasting two or more years were not unknown in the ancient world.

27. *I have battled against Rabbah.* Joab is actually sending David a double message. As duti-
ful field commander, he urges David (verse 28) to hasten to the front so that the conquest
of the Ammonite capital will be attributed to him. And yet, he proclaims the conquest in
the triumphal formality of a little victory poem (one line, two parallel versets) in which it
is he who figures unambiguously as conqueror. This coy and dangerous game Joab plays
with David about who has the real power will persist in the story.
    the Citadel of Waters. The reference is not entirely clear, but the narrative context indi-
cates that Joab has occupied one vital part of the town—evidently, where the water supply
is—while the rest of the town has not yet been taken.

30. *the crown of their king.* The Septuagint reads "Milcom" (the Ammonite deity) instead
of *malkam,* "their king."

31. *set them to work with saws and iron threshing boards and iron axes.* The meaning of this
entire sentence is a little uncertain, but the most plausible reading is that David impressed

to the brick mold. Thus did he do to all the Ammonite towns. And David, and all the troops with him, returned to Jerusalem.

CHAPTER 13   And it happened thereafter—Absalom, David's 1 son, had a beautiful sister named Tamar, and Amnon, David's son, loved her. And Amnon was so distressed that he fell sick over Tamar his sister, 2 for she was a virgin and it seemed beyond Amnon to do anything to her. And Amnon had a companion named Jonadab son of Shimeah brother of 3 David, and Jonadab was a very wise man. And he said to him, "Why are 4 you so poorly, prince, morning after morning? Will you not tell me?" And Amnon said to him, "Tamar the sister of Absalom my brother I do love."

---

the male Ammonites into corvée labor. Some have suggested that the Ammonites were forced to tear down the walls of their own cities with the cutting tools listed in the catalogue here, although the reference to the brick mold at the end indicates some sort of construction, not just demolition.

CHAPTER 13   1. *a beautiful sister.* The catastrophic turn in David's fortune began when he saw a beautiful woman and lusted after her. Now, the curse pronounced by Nathan on the house of David begins to unfold through the very same mechanism: a sexual transgression within the royal quarters resulting in an act of murder elsewhere. Several important terms and gestures here reinforce this link with the story of David and Bathsheba.
    Amnon . . . loved her. The love in question will be revealed by the ensuing events as an erotic obsession—what the early rabbis aptly characterized as "love dependent upon a [material] thing."

2. *she was a virgin and it seemed beyond Amnon to do anything to her.* The last phrase here has a definite negative connotation (rather like the British "to interfere with her") and makes clear the narrow carnal nature of Amnon's "love" for Tamar. Sexual tampering with a virgin had particularly stringent consequences in biblical law.

3. *companion.* The Hebrew *rea'* could simply indicate a friend, though in royal contexts it is also the title of someone who played an official role as the king's, or the prince's, companion and councillor. The emphasis on Jonadab's "wisdom"—in biblical usage, often a morally neutral term suggesting mastery of know-how in a particular activity—makes the technical sense of councillor more likely, though one role does not exclude the other.

4. *And he said to him.* Shimon Bar-Efrat has aptly observed that the whole story of the rape of Tamar is constructed out of seven interlocking scenes with two characters in each, one of whom appears in the next scene. (The story of the stealing of Isaac's blessing in Genesis 27 has the same structure.) The sequence is: (1) Jonadab–Amnon, (2) Amnon–David, (3) David–Tamar, (4) Tamar–Amnon, (5) Amnon–attendant, (6) attendant–Tamar, (7) Tamar–Absalom. J. P. Fokkelman adds to this observation that the spatial and structural center of this design is the bed in Amnon's inner chamber (4), where the rape is perpetrated.
    Tamar the sister of Absalom my brother. Kyle McCarter Jr. vividly notes that Amnon's speech with its alliterated initial aspirants in the Hebrew "is a series of gasping sighs" (*'et-tamar' ahot 'avshalom 'ahi 'ani 'ohev*).

5 And Jonadab said to him, "Lie in your bed and play sick, and when your
father comes to see you, say to him, 'Let Tamar my sister, pray, come and
nourish me with food and prepare the nourishment before my eyes, so that
6 I may see and eat from her hand.'" And Amnon lay down and played sick,
and the king came to see him, and Amnon said to the king, "Let Tamar
my sister, pray, come, and shape a couple of heart-shaped dumplings before
7 my eyes, that I may take nourishment from her hand." And David sent to
Tamar at home, saying, "Go, pray, to the house of Amnon your brother, and
8 prepare nourishment for him." And Tamar went to the house of Amnon
her brother—he lying down—and she took the dough and kneaded it and
9 shaped it into hearts before his eyes and cooked the dumplings. And she
took the pan and set it before him, but he refused to eat. And Amnon said,
"Clear out everyone around me!" and everyone around him cleared out.

---

5. *Lie in your bed and play sick.* David at the beginning of the Bathsheba story was first seen
lying in bed, and then he arranged to have the desired woman brought to his chamber. Jonadab on his part observes that Amnon already looks ill (verse 2) and so suggests that he play
up this condition by pretending to be dangerously ill and in need of special ministrations.

nourish me. The Hebrew verbal root *b-r-h* and the cognate noun *biryah* ("nourishment") denote not eating in general but the kind of eating that is sustaining or restoring
to a person who is weak or fasting. When you eat a *biryah* you become *bar'i*, healthy or fat,
the opposite of "poorly," *dal*. The distinction is crucial to this story.

so that I may see and eat from her hand. Perhaps Amnon is encouraged to say this
because, as a person supposed to be gravely ill, he would want to see with his own eyes that
the vital nourishment is prepared exactly as it should be. The writer is clearly playing with
the equivalence between eating and sex, but it remains ambiguous whether Jonadab has
in mind the facilitating of a rape, or merely creating the possibility of an intimate meeting
between Amnon and Tamar.

6. *the king came to see him.* As the events work out, David, who sinned through lust, inadvertently acts as Amnon's pimp for his own daughter.

shape a couple of heart-shaped dumplings. The verb and its object are both transparently
cognate with *lev* (or *levav*), "heart." The term could refer to the shape of the dumplings, or
to their function of "strengthening the heart" (idiomatic in biblical Hebrew for sustaining or
encouraging). In the Song of Songs, this same verb is associated with the idea of sexual arousal.

9. *Clear out everyone around me.* The identical words are pronounced by another princelike
figure, Joseph, just before he reveals his true identity to his brothers (Genesis 45:1). In Genesis,
these words preface the great moment of reconciliation between long-estranged brothers.
Here they are a prelude to a tale of fraternal rape that leads to fratricide. The story of the rape
of Tamar continues to allude to the Joseph story, in reverse chronological order and with
pointed thematic reversal. The moment before the rape echoes the encounter between Joseph
and Potiphar's wife (Genesis 39) in the middle of the Joseph story, and the attention drawn
to the ornamented tunic that the violated Tamar tears takes us back to Joseph's ornamented
tunic at the beginning of his story (Genesis 37). From such purposeful deployment of allusion,
the inference is inevitable that the author of the David story was familiar at least with the J
strand of the Joseph story in a textual version very like the one that has come down to us.

And Amnon said to Tamar, "Bring the nourishment into the inner cham- 10
ber, that I may take nourishment from your hand." And Tamar took the
dumplings that she had made and brought them to Amnon her brother
within the chamber. And she offered them to him to eat, and he seized her 11
and said to her, "Come lie with me, my sister." And she said to him, "Don't, 12
my brother, don't abuse me, for it should not be done thus in Israel, don't
do this scurrilous thing. And I, where would I carry my shame? And you, 13
you would be like one of the scurrilous fellows in Israel. And so, speak, pray,
to the king, for he will not withhold me from you." And Amnon did not 14
want to heed her voice, and he overpowered her and abused her and bedded

---

11. *Come lie with me, my sister.* The core of this abrupt command is a citation of the words
of Potiphar's wife to Joseph, "Lie with me." Perhaps, as some have suggested, "Come" has
a slight softening effect. The addition of "my sister" of course highlights the fact that this
sexual assault is also incestuous.

12. *Don't, my brother.* Tamar's response constitutes a structural allusion to Joseph and
Potiphar's wife, for he, when confronted by the sexual brusqueness of her terse "lie with
me," also responds, in contrastive dialogue, with a nervous volubility in a relatively lengthy
series of breathless objections.
　　it should not be done thus in Israel . . . this scurrilous thing. The language here echoes that
of another sexual episode in Genesis, the rape of Dinah (Genesis 34). Again, the divergence
in the parallel is significant, for Dinah's rapist comes to love her after violating her and
wants to make things good by marriage, whereas Amnon despises Tamar after he possesses
her, and drives her away. The rape in both stories leads to murderous fraternal vengeance.
But our writer's brilliant game of literary allusion does not end here, for, as Robert Polzin has
pointed out, Tamar's words are also a precise echo of the plea of the Ephraimite in Gibeah
to the mob of rapists: "No, my brothers . . . do not do this scurrilous thing" (Judges 19:23).
That story ended in the woman's being gang-raped to death, an act that in turn led to bloody
civil war—as Tamar's rape will lead to fratricide and, eventually, rebellion and civil war.

13. *speak, pray, to the king, for he will not withhold me from you.* Marriage between a half
brother and a half sister is explicitly banned by biblical law. Perhaps, it has been suggested,
this prohibition was not yet held to be binding in the early tenth century, or in the royal
circle in Jerusalem. But it is at least as plausible that the desperate Tamar is grasping at any
possibility to buy time and deflect her sexual assailant: why do this vile thing and take me
by force when you can enjoy me legitimately?

14. *he overpowered her and abused her and bedded her.* The three transitive verbs in quick
sequence reflect the single-minded assertion of male physical force. In the analogous story
of Joseph and the Egyptian woman, because the gender roles are reversed, the sexually
assaulted male is strong enough to break free from the woman's grasp and flee. Here, the
assaulted woman cannot break her assailant's grip (verse 11), and so she now succumbs to
brute force. The verb represented as "bedded" (*shakhav*) is the same one used by Jonadab
in verse 5 ("Lie in your bed," *shekhav 'al-mishkavkha*) and in Amnon's "lie with me." But
when it has a direct feminine object (instead of "lie *with*"), it suggests sexual violation, and
a transitive verb is called for in the English.

15 her. And Amnon hated her with a very great hatred, for greater was the
    hatred with which he hated her than the love with which he had loved her.
16 And Amnon said, "Get up, go!" And she said to him, "Don't!—this wrong is
    greater than the other you did me, to send me away now." And he did not
17 want to heed her. And he called his lad, his attendant, and said, "Send this
18 creature, pray, away from me and bolt the door behind her!" And she had
    on an ornamented tunic, for the virgin princesses did wear such robes. And

---

15. *greater was the hatred with which he hated her than the love with which he had loved her.*
The psychological insight of this writer is remarkable throughout the story. Amnon has
fulfilled his desire for this beautiful young woman—or, given the fact that she is a bitterly
resistant virgin, perhaps it has hardly been the fulfillment he dreamed of. In any case, he
now has to face the possibly dire consequences to himself from her brother Absalom, or
from David. The result is an access of revulsion against Tamar, a blaming of the victim for
luring him with her charms into all this trouble.

Get up, go! The brutality of these imperative verbs is evident. They are also, as Bar-Efrat
neatly observes, exact antonyms, in reverse order, of the two imperative verbs of sexual
invitation he used before, "Come, lie."

16. *Don't!—this wrong is greater.* There is a textual problem here in the Hebrew, which seems
to say, "Don't—about this wrong . . ." (*'al-'odot hara'ah*). Some versions of the Septuagint
read here, "Don't, my brother" (*'al 'aḥi*), as in verse 12, but this could reflect an attempt to
straighten out a difficult text rather than a better Hebrew version used by the ancient Greek
translators.

to send me away now. "Now" is added in the translation in order to remove an ambiguity
as to when the sending away is done. "Sending away" is an idiom that also has the sense of
"divorce"—precisely what the rapist of a virgin is not allowed to do in biblical law. If some
modern readers may wonder why being banished seems to Tamar worse than being raped,
one must say that for biblical women the social consequence of pariah status, when the law
offered the remedy of marriage to the rapist, might well seem even more horrible than the
physical violation. Rape was a dire fate, but one that could be compensated for by marriage,
whereas the violated virgin rejected and abandoned by her violator was an unmarriageable
outcast, condemned to a lifetime of "desolation" (verse 20).

17. *Send this creature, pray, away from me.* "This creature" reflects the stingingly contemptuous monosyllabic feminine demonstrative pronoun, *zo't* ("this one"). Note that at
the same time that Amnon speaks brutally to Tamar, he is polite to his servant, using the
particle of entreaty *na'* ("pray").

and bolt the door behind her. Having devised such an elaborate strategy for drawing
Tamar into the inner chamber where he can have his way with her, he now has her thrust
out into the open square, with the door bolted against her as though she were some insatiable, clinging thing against which he had to set up a barricade.

18. *ornamented tunic.* The translation for this term follows a suggestion of E. A. Speiser.
(The famous King James Version rendering in Genesis is "coat of many colors.") Others
interpret this as a garment reaching the ankles. In any case, Tamar and Joseph are the only
two figures in the Bible said to wear this particular garment. Joseph's, too, will be torn, by
his brothers, after they strip him of it and toss him into the pit, and they will then soak it

his attendant took her outside and bolted the door behind her. And Tamar   19
put ashes on her head, and the ornamented tunic that she had on she tore,
and she put her hand on her head and walked away screaming as she went.
And Absalom her brother said to her, "Has Amnon your brother been with   20
you? For now, my sister, hold your peace. He is your brother. Do not take
this matter to heart." And Tamar stayed, desolate, in the house of Absalom
her brother. And King David had heard all these things, and he was greatly   21
incensed. And Absalom did not speak with Amnon either evil or good, for   22
Absalom hated Amnon for having abused Tamar his sister.

And it happened after two years that Absalom had a sheepshearing at Baal-   23
Hazor, which is near Ephraim, and Absalom invited all the king's sons.

---

in kid's blood. Tamar's ornamented tunic may well be bloodstained, too, if one considers
what has just been done to her as a virgin.

19. *put her hand on her head.* This is a conventional gesture of mourning, like the rending
of the garment and the sprinkling of ashes on the head.

20. *Has Amnon your brother been with you?* Absalom, addressing his screaming, tearstained,
disheveled sister, exercises a kind of delicacy of feeling in using this oblique euphemism
for rape.
   He is your brother. This identification, which plays back against the heavily fraught,
often ironic uses of "brother" and "sister" throughout the story, would hardly be a consolation. What Absalom may be suggesting is that, were it any other man, I would avenge your
honor at once, but since he is your brother, and mine, I must bide my time ("*For now,* my
sister, hold your peace.")
   Do not take this matter to heart. The idiom he uses echoes ironically against the making
of heart-shaped dumplings to which Amnon enjoined her.

21. *King David had heard all these things, and he was greatly incensed.* The Qumran Samuel
and the Septuagint add here: "but he did not vex the spirit of Amnon his son, for he loved
him, since he was his firstborn." But this looks suspiciously like an explanatory gloss, an
effort to make sense of David's silence. That imponderable silence is the key to the mount-
ing avalanche of disaster in the house of David. Where we might expect some after-the-fact
defense of his violated daughter, some rebuke or punishment of his rapist son, he hears, is
angry, but says nothing and does nothing, leaving the field open for Absalom's murder of
his brother. In all this, the rape of Tamar plays exactly the same pivotal role in the story of
David as does the rape of Dinah in the story of Jacob. Jacob, too, "hears" of the violation
and does nothing, setting the stage for the bloody act of vengeance carried out by his sons
Simeon and Levi. By the end of the episode, Jacob is seen at the mercy of his intransigent
sons, and that is how this once powerful figure will appear through the rest of his story. An
analogous fate, as we shall abundantly see, awaits David from this moment on.

23. *a sheepshearing.* The sheepshearing is a grand occasion for feasting and drinking (compare 1 Samuel 25:2–8), and so it is proper to speak of "having" a sheepshearing as one would
have a celebration.

24 And Absalom came to the king and said, "Look, pray, your servant has a
     sheepshearing. Let the king, pray, go, and his servants, with your servant."
25 And the king said to Absalom, "No, my son, we shall not all of us go, and
     we shall not burden you." And he pressed him but he did not want to go,
26 and he bade him farewell. And Absalom said to him, "If not, pray, let
     Amnon my brother go with us." And the king said to him, "Why should
27 he go with you?" And Absalom pressed him, and he sent Amnon with
28 him, together with all the king's sons. And Absalom charged his lads,
     saying, "See, pray, when Amnon's heart is merry with wine and I say to
     you, 'Strike down Amnon,' you shall put him to death, fear not, for is it not
29 I who charge you? Be strong, and act as valiant men." And Absalom's lads
     did to Amnon as Absalom had charged them, and all the king's sons arose
30 and rode away each on his mule and fled. And as they were on the way,
     the rumor reached David, saying, "Absalom has struck down all the king's
31 sons, and not one of them remains." And the king arose and tore his gar-
     ments and lay on the ground, with all his servants standing in attendance
32 in torn garments. And Jonadab son of Shimeah brother of David spoke up

---

24. *Let the king, pray, go.* Given David's increasingly sedentary habits, Absalom appears to
count on the fact that his father will refuse the invitation, and this refusal will then give
greater urgency to his invitation of Amnon. Had Absalom begun by asking David to help
him persuade Amnon to go the festivities, David might have been suspicious about Absalom's motives, since the grudge he bore his half brother would scarcely have been a secret.
In any case, Absalom is making David his go-between to lure Amnon to his death, just as
Amnon made David his go-between to lure Tamar to her violation.

27. *with all the king's sons.* This phrase recurs like a refrain from this point on: David is
haunted by the specter of the ultimate catastrophe, that "all the king's sons" have perished,
a specter that will cast a shadow over the subsequent events of the story as well. The man
promised an everlasting house is threatened with the prospect (like his avatar, Faulkner's
Sutpen, in *Absalom, Absalom!*) of being cut off without surviving progeny.

28. *when Amnon's heart is merry with wine.* The heart that lusted after Tamar and asked her
to make heart-shaped dumplings will now be befuddled with wine to set up the murder.

29. *each on his mule.* In this period in ancient Israel, the mule was the customary mount
for royal personages.

31. *the king arose and tore his garments and lay on the ground.* These acts of mourning are
reminiscent of Tamar's and of David's own when his infant son by Bathsheba was deathly
ill. Again there is a resemblance to Jacob, who flings himself into extravagant mourning
over a son supposed to be dead who is actually alive (Genesis 37).

32. *they have put to death.* Jonadab, exercising his "wisdom," is careful not to condemn
Absalom immediately, but instead first uses a plural verb with an unspecified agent. Then
he introduces Absalom as the source of the determination to kill Amnon, choosing a verb,
"abused," that concedes the crime of rape. Whether or not this was a possibility he had

and said, "Let not my lord think, 'All the lads, the king's sons, they have put to death,' for Amnon alone is dead, for it was fixed upon by Absalom from the day he abused Tamar his sister. And now, let not my lord the king 33 take the matter to heart, saying, 'All the king's sons have died,' but Amnon alone is dead."

And Absalom fled. And the lookout lad raised his eyes and saw and, look, a 34 great crowd was going round the side of the mountain from the road behind it. And Jonadab said to the king, "Look, the king's sons have come, as your 35 servant has spoken, so it has come about." And just as he finished speaking, 36 look, the king's sons came, and they raised their voices and wept, and the king, too, and all his servants wept very grievously. And Absalom had fled, 37 and he went to Talmai son of Amihur king of Geshur. And David mourned 38 for his son all the while. And Absalom had fled and gone to Geshur, and he was there three years. And David's urge to sally forth against Absalom was 39 spent, for he was consoled over Amnon, who was dead.

---

in mind when he offered counsel to Amnon, he now implicity distances himself from Amnon's act.

33. *let not my lord the king take the matter to heart.* This is virtually the same idiom Absalom used to Tamar in consoling her after the rape.

34. *going round the side of the mountain from the road behind it.* The Hebrew has "the road behind it" before "the side of the mountain," such proleptic use of pronominal reference sometimes occurring in biblical Hebrew. The Septuagint reads "from the Horonim road" (*miderekh horonim*) instead of "from the road behind it" (*miderekh aharaw*).

36. *wept very grievously.* The literal Hebrew phrasing is "wept a very great weeping."

37. *Talmai son of Amihur king of Geshur.* Absalom takes refuge in the court of his maternal grandfather in Geshur, to the north and east of the Jordan, outside David's jurisdiction.
    David mourned for his son all the while. As verse 39, which will mark the beginning of a new narrative episode, makes clear, the son he is mourning is the dead Amnon, not the absent Absalom.

39. *David's urge to sally forth against Absalom was spent.* The received text is either defective or elliptical at this point. The verb *watekhal* is feminine, though there is no feminine noun in the clause. Many have construed it as the predicate of an omitted noun, *nefesh*, which coupled with this verb would yield idiomatically "David pined after Absalom." Such paternal longings scarcely accord with David's refusal to see his son once he has returned to Jerusalem, or with the very necessity of elaborate manipulation in order to get him to agree to rescind Absalom's banishment. The Qumran Samuel scroll, though incomplete at this point, appears to have the feminine noun—*ruah*—"spirit," "impulse," "urge"—as the subject of the verb. An abatement of hostility against Absalom rather than a longing for him makes much more sense in terms of what follows.

1   CHAPTER 14   And Joab son of Zeruiah knew that the king's
2   mind was on Absalom. And Joab sent to Tekoa and fetched a wise woman
    from there and said to her, "Take up mourning, pray, and, pray, don
    mourning garments, and do not rub yourself with oil, and you shall be
3   like a woman a long while mourning over a dead one. And you shall come
    to the king and speak to him in this manner—" and Joab put the words in
4   her mouth. And the Tekoite woman said to the king, and she flung herself
    on her face to the ground and bowed down, and she said, "Rescue, O king!"
5   And the king said to her, "What troubles you?" And she said, "Alas, I am
6   a widow-woman, my husband died. And your servant had two sons, and
    they quarreled in the field, and there was no one to part them, and one
7   struck down the other and caused his death. And, look, the whole clan
    rose against your servant and said, 'Give over the one who struck down his

---

CHAPTER 14   1. *the king's mind was on Absalom.* The preposition *'al* is ambiguous,
and it could also mean "against."

2. *Joab sent to Tekoa.* Tekoa is a village about ten miles north of Jerusalem. Why does Joab
contrive to make David agree to Absalom's return? Given his relentlessly political character, it seems likely that Joab perceives Absalom's continuing banishment as a potential
source of rebellion against the throne, and concludes that the safest course is to reconcile
the king with his son. This calculation will prove to be gravely misguided because Joab
does not reckon with David's ambivalence toward his fratricidal son (see verse 24) or with
the impulse to usurpation that the ambivalence will encourage in Absalom.

   a wise woman. It should be noted that the whole David story, seemingly dominated by
powerful martial men, pivots at several crucial junctures on the intervention of enterprising "wise women." The first of these is Abigail, though, unlike two of the others, she is
not assigned the epithet "wise woman" as a kind of professional title. Later, a resourceful
woman hides the two spies who are bringing intelligence of Absalom to David in trans-
Jordan. In the subsequent rebellion of Sheba son of Bichri, another wise woman prevents
Joab's massacre of the besieged town of Abel Beth-Maacah.

   like a woman a long while mourning over a dead one. The phrasing here pointedly echoes
"David mourned for his son all the while" in 13:37.

3. *Joab put the words in her mouth.* As Robert Polzin observes, the entire episode turns on
manipulation of people through language, with abundant repetition of the verb "speak."
In contrast to the common practice elsewhere in biblical narrative, we are not given the
actual script that Joab dictates to the woman, which she will then repeat to David. This
omission heightens the sense that, using a general outline provided by Joab, the woman is
in fact brilliantly improvising—which in some ways she would have to do, given the fact
that she is not reciting an uninterrupted speech but responding to David's declarations,
picking up clues from the way he reacts.

4. *Rescue, O king!* This is a formulaic plea used by petitioners for royal justice.

6. *they quarreled in the field . . . and one struck down the other.* As several commentators
have noted, her formulation aligns the story with the archetypal tale of Cain and Abel. The
fratricidal Cain is banished, but also given a sign to protect him from blood vengeance.

brother, that we may put him to death for the life of his brother whom he killed, and let us destroy the heir as well. And they would have quenched my last remaining ember, leaving my husband no name or remnant on the face of the earth." And the king said to the woman, "Go to your house and I 8 myself shall issue a charge concerning you. And the Tekoite woman said to 9 the king, "Upon me, my lord the king, and upon my father's house, let the guilt be, and the king and his throne shall be blameless." And the king said, 10 "The man who dares speak to you I will have brought to me, and he will not touch you anymore." And she said, "May the king, pray, keep in mind the 11 LORD your God, that the blood avenger should not savage this much and let them not destroy my son." And he said, "As the LORD lives, not a single hair of your son's shall fall to the ground!" And the woman said, "Let your 12 servant, pray, speak a word to my lord the king." And he said, "Speak." And 13

---

7. *and let us destroy the heir as well.* Although it is unlikely that the clansmen would have actually said these words, there is no need to tamper with the text. The wise woman, in reporting the dialogue, insinuates her own anxious maternal perspective into this last clause. The implication is that the members of the clan would like to kill the remaining son not only to execute justice but in order to get his inheritance.

8. *I myself shall issue a charge concerning you.* Although David emphatically announces (by adding the first-person pronoun *'ani*) that he himself will take up the case, his language remains vague ("issue a charge"), and the Tekoite woman's response in the next verse clearly indicates that she requires something further of him.

9. *Upon me . . . the guilt . . . and the king and his throne shall be blameless.* The legal issue involved is bloodguilt. From David's vagueness, she infers that he is loath to intervene on behalf of the fratricide because by so doing he, and his throne, would take on the guilt of allowing the killing to go unavenged.

10. *The man who dares speak to you I will have brought to me.* Her declaration that she and her father's house will bear the guilt for allowing the killer to live—evidently construed by David as a performative speech-act, efficacious once uttered—encourages the king to declare that he will absolutely protect her against the vengeful kinsmen who are seeking out her son.

11. *let them not destroy my son.* The woman is still not satisfied, for David's pledge to safeguard her did not mention her son: she wants to extract an explicit declaration from David that he will protect the life of her son.

    not a single hair of your son's shall fall to the ground. Now she has what she has been after, with David's hyperbolic declaration about guarding the well-being of the fratricidal son, she is prepared to snap shut the trap of the fiction, linking it to David's life, just as Nathan did with the parable of the poor man's ewe. We should note that not a single hair of the fictitious son is to fall to the ground, whereas the extravagantly abundant hair of his real-life referent, Absalom, will be cut annually in a kind of public ceremony.

12. *Let your servant, pray, speak.* She uses these words of entreaty to preface the transition to the real subject, David and Absalom.

the woman said, "Why did you devise in this fashion against God's people? And in speaking this thing, the king is as though guilty for the king's not
14 having brought back his own banished one. For we surely will die, like water spilled to the ground, which cannot be gathered again. And God will not bear off the life of him who devises that no one of his be banished.
15 And so now, the reason I have come to speak this thing to the king my lord is that the people have made me afraid, and your servant thought, 'Let me but speak to the king. Perhaps the king will do what his servant
16 asks. For the king would pay heed to save his servant from the hand of the person bent on destroying me and my son together from God's heritage.'
17 And your servant thought, 'May the word of my lord the king, pray, be a respite, for like a messenger of God, so is my lord the king, understanding
18 good and evil.' And may the LORD your God be with you." And the king

---

13. *against God's people.* The implicit key concept here is "inheritance," which links her fiction to the national political situation. She may be hinting that Absalom is the appropriate heir to the throne. In any case, his banishment is potentially divisive to the kingdom.

in speaking this thing, the king is as though guilty. The Hebrew of this whole sentence is rather crabbed, an effect reproduced in the translation. Rather than reflecting difficulties in textual transmission, her language probably expresses her sense of awkwardness in virtually indicting the king: he is "as though guilty," for "in speaking this thing," in declaring his resolution to protect the fratricidal son, he has condemned his own antithetical behavior in the case of Absalom. But the woman is careful not to mention Absalom explicitly by name—she struggles verbally in the crossover from fiction to life, knowing she is treading on dangerous ground.

14. *we surely will die, like water spilled to the ground.* Moving beyond Absalom to a wise woman's pronouncement on human fate, she breaks free of her verbal stumbling and becomes eloquent. The spilled water as an image of irreversible mortality is an obvious and effective counterpoint to her previous image of the ember that should not be quenched. It also picks up thematically David's own bleak reflection on the irreversibility of death after his infant son expires (chapter 12).

God will not bear off the life of him who devises that no one of his be banished. As the wise woman switches back from philosophic statement to the juridical issue confronting David, her language again becomes knotty and oblique. What she is saying is that God will scarcely want to punish the father who brings back his banished son, even though bloodguilt remains unavenged.

15. *the reason I have come to speak this thing to the king.* The Tekoite woman, having nervously broached the issue of David and Absalom, now hastily retreats to the relative safety of her invented story about two sons, as though that were the real reason for her appearance before the king. The dramatic and psychological logic of this entire speech argues against scholarly attempts to make it more "coherent" by moving around whole swatches of it.

17. *respite.* The king's word will give her respite from her persecutors, the would-be killers of her son. The Hebrew term *menuḥah* also points to a bound locution, *menuḥah wenaḥalah*, "respite and inheritance," the very thing the kinsmen would take from her.

said to the woman, "Pray, do not conceal from me the thing that I ask you."
And the woman said, "Let my lord the king speak, pray." And the king 19
said, "Is the hand of Joab with you in all this?" And the woman answered
and said, "By your life, my lord the king, there is no turning right or left
from all that my lord the king has spoken! For your servant Joab, he it was
who charged me, and he it was who put in your servant's mouth all these
words. In order to turn the thing round your servant Joab has done this 20
thing. And my lord is wise, as with the wisdom of a messenger of God, to
know everything in the land." And the king said to Joab, "Look, pray, I have 21
done this thing. Go and bring back the lad Absalom." And Joab flung him- 22
self on his face to the ground and bowed down. And he blessed the king,
and Joab said, "Your servant knows that I have found favor in the eyes of
my lord the king, for the king has done what his servant asked." And Joab 23
rose and went to Geshur and he brought Absalom to Jerusalem. And the 24
king said, "Let him turn round to his house, and my face he shall not see."
And Absalom turned round to his house, and the king's face he did not see.

And there was no man so highly praised for beauty as Absalom in all 25
Israel—from the sole of his foot to the crown of his head, there was no

---

19. *Is the hand of Joab with you in all this?* David rightly infers that a village wise woman
would have no motive of her own for undertaking this elaborate stratagem, and so someone in court with political aims must be behind her. Polzin shrewdly proposes that Joab
may actually have wanted David to detect him at the bottom of the scheme: "The woman's
eventual admission that she has been sent by Joab (verses 19–20) may itself be part of Joab's
indirect message to David—something like, 'Bring Absalom back or I may side with him
against you.'"

   there is no turning right or left from all that my lord the king has spoken. She is saying
two things at once—that the king has hit the target in saying that Joab is behind her, and
that, having committed himself by his own speech to protect the fratricidal son, he cannot
now permit himself to continue Absalom's banishment.

20. *my lord is wise, as with the wisdom of a messenger of God.* It is of course she who has
been demonstrably wise. David will soon show unwisdom by bringing Absalom back while
resisting real reconciliation, and his subsequent blindness to Absalom's demagogic activities within a stone's throw of the court indicates that there is much in the land about which
he knows nothing.

21. *bring back the lad Absalom.* Momentarily, David refers to Absalom by a term (*na'ar*)
that is generally an expression of paternal affection. He will use the same word repeatedly
during Absalom's rebellion to stress his concern for Absalom's safety.

25. *there was no man so highly praised for beauty.* Both Absalom and his sister Tamar are
remarkable for their beauty (as was the young David). For Absalom, this will become an
asset he trades on in his appeal for popular support.

26 blemish in him. And when he cut his hair, for from one year's end till the next he would cut it, as it grew heavy upon him, he would weigh the hair
27 of his head, two hundred shekels by the royal weight. And three sons were born to Absalom and a daughter named Tamar, she was a beautiful woman.
28 And Absalom lived in Jerusalem two years, but the king's face he did not
29 see. And Absalom sent to Joab in order to send him to the king, but he did not want to come to him, and he sent still a second time, but he did not want
30 to come. And he said to his servants, "See Joab's field next to mine, in which he has barley—go set it on fire!" And Absalom's servants set fire to the field.
31 And Joab rose and came to Absalom's house and said to him, "Why did
32 your servants set fire to the field that belongs to me?" And Absalom said to Joab, "Look, I sent to you, saying, 'Come here that I may send you to the king, saying, Why did I come from Geshur? It would be better for me were I still there. And now, let me see the face of the king, and if there be guilt

---

26. *when he cut his hair . . . he would weigh the hair of his head.* There is clearly something narcissistic about this preoccupation with his luxuriant hair. It is of course a foreshadowing of the bizarre circumstances of Absalom's death (chapter 18:9–15). Beyond that, the spectacular growth of hair invokes a comparison with Samson, who never cut his hair until the cutting of the hair against his will led to his undoing. The parallel with Samson is extended in the burning of Joab's field, which recalls the foxes with torches tied to their tails used by Samson to set fire to the fields of the Philistines. Perhaps the parallel with Samson is meant to foreshadow Absalom's fate as a powerful leader whose imprudence brings him to an early death.

27. *And three sons were born to Absalom and a daughter named Tamar, she was a beautiful woman.* Later, we are informed (18:18) that Absalom was childless. The two reports can be harmonized only with considerable strain, and it is best to view them as contradictory traditions incorporated in the final text. But it is noteworthy that, against patriarchal practice, the sons are left unnamed here, and only the daughter, named after Absalom's raped sister, is not anonymous. It is unnecessary to assume that this second beautiful Tamar was born after the violation of her aunt by Amnon: here she is represented as a woman, and it seems unlikely that so many years would have passed from the time of Tamar's rape until Absalom's resumption of residence in Jerusalem.

29. *he did not want to come.* Throughout this story, there is a precarious game of power going on. Joab has manipulated David to effect Absalom's return, but seeing that the king remains estranged from Absalom, Joab does not want to push his luck by interceding at court on Absalom's behalf. The power of the king may be qualified, but he remains the king.

30. *set it on fire.* Absalom's Samson-like burning of the field is a strong indication that he is a man prepared to use violence to achieve his ends: mafia style, he presents Joab with an offer he can't refuse.

32. *if there be guilt in me, let him put me to death.* Absalom of course knows he is responsible for the killing of Amnon, but he construes that act as something other than "guilt" because it was done to avenge the violation of Tamar—a crime David left unpunished.

in me, let him put me to death.'" And Joab came to the king and told him. 33
And he called to Absalom and he came to the king and bowed down to
him, his face to the ground before the king, and the king kissed Absalom.

CHAPTER 15   And it happened thereafter that Absalom made 1
himself a chariot with horses and fifty men running before him. And Absa- 2
lom would rise early and stand by the gate road, and so, to every man
who had a suit to appear in judgment before the king, Absalom would call
and say, "From what town are you?" And he would say, "From one of the
tribes of Israel is your servant." And Absalom would say to him, "See, your 3
words are good and right, but you have no one to listen to you from the
king." And Absalom would say, "Would that I were made judge in the land, 4
and to me every man would come who had a suit in justice, and I would
declare in his favor." And so, when a man would draw near to bow down 5
to him, he would reach out his hand and take hold of him and kiss him.

---

33. *he . . . bowed down to him, his face to the ground.* Fokkelman notes that there is a series
of three acts of prostration before the king—first the Tekoite woman, then Joab, and now
Absalom, the third bowing-down ostensibly consummating the reconciliation of father
and son toward which all three acts are directed.

   and the king kissed Absalom. The noun used (rather than "David") may suggest that this
is more a royal, or official, kiss than a paternal one. It clearly gives Absalom no satisfaction,
as his initiative of usurpation in the next episode strongly argues.

CHAPTER 15   1. *a chariot with horses and fifty men running before him.* All this
vehicular pomp and circumstance, as other biblical references to chariots, horses, and runners in conjunction with kings suggest, is a claim to royal status. The gestures of usurpation
are undertaken in Jerusalem, under David's nose, yet the king, who has been described by
the Tekoite woman as "knowing everything in the land," does nothing.

2–5. This whole tableau of Absalom standing at the gate to the city, accosting each new-
comer, professing sympathy for his cause, and announcing that were he the supreme judicial authority, he would rule in the man's favor, is a stylized representation of the operation
of a demagogue. It is hard to imagine realistically that Absalom would tell each person
so flatly that, whatever the legal case, he would declare in his favor, but the point of the
stylization is clear: the demagogue enlists support by flattering people's special interests,
leading them to believe that he will champion their cause, cut their taxes, increase their
social security benefits, and so forth.

3. *you have no one to listen to you from the king.* The heart of Absalom's demagogic pitch
is his exploiting what must have been widespread dissatisfaction over the new centralized
monarchic bureaucracy with its imposition of taxes and corvées and military conscription:
there is no one in this impersonal palace to listen to you with a sympathetic ear, as I do.

5. *he would reach out his hand and take hold of him and kiss him.* The odd "rhyming" of
Absalom's kiss to each man he seduces and David's kiss to Absalom at the end of the imme-

6   And Absalom would act in this fashion to all the Israelites who appeared
in judgment before the king, and Absalom stole the hearts of the men of
Israel.

7   And it happened at the end of four years that Absalom said to the king, "Let
8   me go, pray, and pay my vow that I pledged to the LORD in Hebron. For your
servant made a vow when I was staying in Geshur in Aram, saying, "If the
9   LORD indeed brings me back to Jerusalem, I shall worship the LORD." And
10 the king said to him, "Go in peace to Hebron." And he arose and went to
Hebron. And Absalom sent agents through all the tribes of Israel, saying,
"When you hear the sound of the ram's horn, you shall say, 'Absalom has
11 become king in Hebron.'" And with Absalom two hundred men went from
Jerusalem, invited guests going in all innocence, and they knew nothing.
12 And Absalom sent Ahitophel the Gilonite, David's councillor, from his
town, from Giloh, while he was offering the sacrifices, and the plot was
13 strong, and the people with Absalom were growing in number. And the
informant came to David, saying, "The hearts of the men of Israel are fol-
14 lowing Absalom." And David said to all his servants who were with him

---

diately preceding chapter is obvious. Could it suggest, retrospectively, that David's kiss has
an element of falseness that recurs, grossly magnified, in Absalom's kiss? It should also be
noted that Absalom's gesture of "taking hold" of each of his political victims is verbally
identical with Amnon's "taking hold" of Tamar before the rape.

7. *at the end of four years.* The Masoretic Text has "forty years," an untenable number in
this narrative context, but four different ancient versions show "four years."

pay my vow that I pledged to the LORD in Hebron. Haim Gevaryahu proposes that the
vow is to offer an exculpatory sacrifice for the crime of manslaughter. With three years in
Geshur and another four in Jerusalem, Absalom would have come to the end of the period
of seven years of penance that, according to some ancient parallels, might have applied to
such crimes. Absalom of course wants to go off to Hebron—David's first capital city—in
order to proclaim himself king at a certain distance from his father's palace. It also appears
that he feels he can call on a base of support from Judah, his father's tribe. But why is
David not suspicious when his son proposes to pay his cultic vow in Hebron rather than
in Jerusalem? Gevaryahu, citing Greek analogues, makes the interesting suggestion that a
fratricide who had not yet atoned for his crime was not permitted to worship in the same
sanctuary as his father and brothers.

11. *invited guests going in all innocence.* In a shrewd maneuver, Absalom takes with him a
large contingent of people not known to be his partisans, and not willing participants in the
conspiracy, and in this way he wards off suspicion about the aim of his expedition. Once in
Hebron, the two hundred men would presumably be caught up in the tide of insurrection.

14. *Rise and let us flee.* Suddenly, under the pressure of crisis, with intelligence that Absalom
has overwhelming support, David shakes himself from his slumber of passivity, realizing

in Jerusalem, "Rise and let us flee or none of us will escape from Absalom. Hurry and go, lest he hurry and overtake us and bring down harm upon us and strike the town with the edge of the sword." And the king's servants   15 said to the king, "Whatever my lord the king chooses, look, we are your servants." And the king went out, and all his household with him, on foot,   16 and the king left his ten concubines to watch over the house. And the king,   17 and all the people with him, went out on foot, and they stopped by the outlying house. And all his servants were crossing over alongside him,   18 and all the Cherithites and the Pelethites and all the Gittites, six hundred men who had come at his heels from Gath, were crossing over before

---

he must move at once if he is to have any chance of surviving. Against superior forces, the walled city of Jerusalem would be a death trap. As Fokkelman aptly puts it, "Once again he is in contact with his old self. . . . Once again men seek his death and he enters the wilderness both figuratively and literally."

15. *Whatever my lord the king chooses, look, we are your servants.* As the episode unfolds, there is a constant counterpoint between those who reveal their unswerving loyalty to David no matter how grim the outlook and the betrayal of David by his son and all those who have rallied to the usurper.

16. *the king left his ten concubines to watch over the house.* This gesture sounds as though it might be an expression of hope that David will return to Jerusalem. In the event, it produces a disastrous consequence that fulfills one of the dire terms of Nathan's curse in chapter 12.

17. *the king, and all the people with him, went out on foot.* This restatement of the first clause of the previous verse reflects the device that biblical scholars call "resumptive repetition": after an interruption of the narrative line—here, the introduction of the information about the concubines—the words just before the interruption are repeated as the main line of the narrative resumes. Moreover, the emphasis through repetition on going by foot suggests how David and his entourage have been reduced from royal dignity in this abrupt flight.

the outlying house. The literal meaning of the Hebrew is "the house of distance." It clearly means the last house in the settled area beyond the walls of the city.

18. *all his servants were crossing over.* The verb "to cross over" (*'avar*), abundantly repeated, is a thematic focus of the episode. David and his followers are crossing over eastward from Jerusalem, headed first up the Mount of Olives and then down the long declivity to the Jordan, which they will cross (the verb *'avar* is often used for Jordan crossing) in their flight. The entire episode is unusual in the leisurely panoramic view it provides of the eastward march from the city. Instead of the preterite verb form ordinarily used for narration, participial forms ("were crossing over") predominate, imparting a sense of something like a present tense to the report of the action.

Cherithites . . . Pelethites . . . Gittites. This elite palace guard, which we have encountered before, are Philistine warriors who became David's followers, probably when he was residing in Gath. Ittai's expression of loyalty suggests that they were more than mere mercenaries.

19 the king. And the king said to Ittai the Gittite, "Why should you too go
with us? Go back, stay with the king. For you are a foreigner, and you are
20 also in exile from your own place. Just yesterday you came, and today
should I make you wander with us, when I myself am going to wherever
I may go? Turn back, and bring back your brothers. Steadfast kindness
21 to you!" And Ittai answered the king and said, "As the LORD lives, and
as my lord the king lives, whatever place that my lord the king may be,
22 whether for death or for life, there your servant will be." And David said,
"Go and cross over." And Ittai crossed over, and all his men and all the
23 children who were with him. And all the land was weeping loudly and
all the people were crossing over, and the king was crossing over the
Wadi Kidron, and all the people were crossing over along the road to
24 the wilderness. And, look, Zadok and all the Levites were also with him,
bearing the Ark of the Covenant of God, and they set down the Ark of
God, and Abiathar came up, until all the people had finished crossing
25 over from the town. And the king said to Zadok, "Bring back the Ark
of God to the town. Should I find favor in the eyes of the LORD, He will
26 bring me back and let me see it and its abode. And should He say thus, 'I

---

19. *Ittai.* His name is close to the preposition *'iti,* "with me." Both Moshe Garsiel and Robert
Polzin have proposed that the name has a symbolic function: Ittai is the loyalist who insists
on remaining with David. Polzin notes that this preposition is constantly reiterated in the
episode, rather than its synonym *'im*: David, for example, says to Ittai, "Why should you
too go with us [*'itanu*]?"

stay with the king. This designation of the usurping son would be especially painful for
David to pronounce. He does it in order to try to persuade Ittai that he should cast his fate
with the person exercising the power of king.

20. *Steadfast kindness to you.* The translation reproduces the elliptical character of the
Masoretic Text at this point. The Septuagint has an easier reading: "May the LORD show
steadfast kindness to you."

21. *whether for death or for life.* Given the grim circumstances, this loyal soldier unflinchingly puts death before life in the two alternatives he contemplates.

23. *and the king was crossing over the Wadi Kidron.* In the slow-motion report of the flight,
reinforced by the participial verbs, David is now crossing the Kidron brook at the foot
of the slope descending eastward from the walled city. He will then make his way up the
Mount of Olives.

25. *Bring back the Ark of God to the town.* Given the difficulties David encountered in
bringing the Ark to Jerusalem in the first place, and given the disastrous consequences
at the time of Eli in carrying it out to the battlefield, it is understandable that he should
want the Ark left in Jerusalem. He makes this act a token of his reiterated fatalism about
his predicament.

want no part of you,' let Him do to me what is good in His eyes." And the 27
king said to Zadok the priest, "Do you see? Go back to the town in peace,
and Ahimaaz your son and Jonathan son of Abiathar—your two sons
with you. See, I shall be tarrying in the steppes of the wilderness until 28
word from you reaches me to inform me." And Zadok, and Abiathar with 29
him, brought back the Ark of God to Jerusalem, and they stayed there.
And David was going up the Slope of Olives, going up weeping, his head 30
uncovered, and he walking barefoot, and all the people who were with
him, everyone with his head uncovered, went on up weeping the while.
And to David it was told, saying, "Ahitophel is among the plotters with 31
Absalom." And David said, "Thwart, pray, the counsel of Ahitophel, O
Lord." And David had come to the summit, where one would bow down 32
to God, and, look, coming toward him was Hushai the Archite, his tunic

---

27. *and the king said to Zadok the priest.* Again we see the distinctive biblical convention
in the deployment of dialogue: when the first party speaks and the second party does not
respond, and a second speech of the first party is introduced, there is an intimation of
some sort of failure of response. Zadok is nonplussed by David's instructions to return the
Ark and also by David's fatalism. Now, in his second speech, David provides a practical,
strategic rationale for Zadok's going back to the city with the Ark—he and his two acolytes
will then be able to act as spies for David (see the end of his speech in verse 28).

30. *his head uncovered.* There is a difference of philological opinion as to whether the verb
here means covered or uncovered. The usual meaning of the root is "to cover," but an uncovered head is more likely as a gesture of mourning—which is clearly intended—and this
could be an instance of the same term denoting antonyms, like the English verb "cleave."

31. *And to David it was told.* The Masoretic Text reads, "And David told," but both the
Qumran Samuel and the Septuagint reflect the more likely idea—a difference of one
Hebrew letter—that someone told David.

32. *the summit, where one would bow down to God, and, look, coming toward him was
Hushai.* This crucial moment in the story is an especially deft manifestation of the system
of double causation that Gerhard von Rad and others after him have attributed to the
David narrative: everything in the story is determined by its human actors, according to
the stringent dictates of political realism; yet, simultaneously, everything is determined by
God, according to a divine plan in history. David, informed that his own shrewd political
advisor Ahitophel is part of Absalom's conspiracy, urgently and breathlessly invokes God,
"Thwart, pray, the counsel of Ahitophel, O Lord." Then he reaches a holy site, an altar
on the crest of the Mount of Olives ("where one would bow down to God"), and here he
sees Hushai, his loyalty betokened by the trappings of mourning he has assumed, coming
toward him. Theologically, Hushai is the immediate answer to David's prayer. Politically,
David seizes upon Hushai as the perfect instrument to thwart Ahitophel's counsel, so from
a certain point of view David is really answering his own prayer through his human initiative. Yet the encounter with Hushai at a place of worship leaves the lingering intimation
that Hushai has been sent by God to David.

33 torn and earth on his head. And David said, "If you cross over with me,
34 you will be a burden to me. But if you go back to the town and say to
Absalom, 'Your servant, O king, I will be. Your father's servant I always
was, and now I am your servant,' you shall overturn Ahitophel's counsel
35 for me. And are not Zadok and Abiathar the priests there with you? And
so, whatever you hear from the king's house you shall tell to Zadok and to
36 Abiathar the priests. Look, there with them are their two sons, Ahimaaz,
who is Zadok's, and Jonathan, who is Abiathar's, and you shall send to
37 me by their hand whatever you hear." And Hushai, David's friend, came
to the city, as Absalom was coming into Jerusalem.

1 CHAPTER 16   And when David had crossed over a little
beyond the summit, look, Ziba, Mephibosheth's lad, was there to meet
him, with a yoke of saddled donkeys and on them two hundred loaves of
bread and a hundred raisin cakes and a hundred of summer fruit and a jug

---

34. *say to Absalom, "Your servant, O king, I will be."* David, passive to a fault in the preceding
episodes, now improvises in the moment of crisis a detailed plan for subverting Absalom,
even dictating to Hushai the exact script he is to use when he comes before the usurper.

35. *are not Zadok and Abiathar the priests there with you?* David is both offering encouragement to Hushai, assuring him that he will not be the sole, isolated undercover agent in
Jerusalem, and indicating to him what every spy needs to know, that there will be a reliable
network for transmitting intelligence to the command center for which the spy is working.

CHAPTER 16   1. *David had crossed over.* The verbal motif of "crossing over," which
virtually defines David's flight eastward from Jerusalem to trans-Jordan, is continued here.
It will be given another odd turn in verse 17 when the bloody-minded Abishai volunteers
to "cross over" and lop off Shimei's head.
    a little beyond the summit. The summit in question is of course the top of the Mount
of Olives, where David has just encountered Hushai and sent him off to Jerusalem as an
undercover agent. Polzin acutely observes that the two low points of David's abasement—
his humiliation by Shimei and the sexual possession of his concubines by his son—both
take place on an elevation: near the summit and on the palace roof. The Hebrew term for
summit used here is *ro'sh,* which is the ordinary word for "head," and as Polzin goes on to
note, "head" is an organizing image of the entire episode: David goes up the mountainside
with his head uncovered in a sign of mourning, as do the people with him. Hushai puts dirt
on his head as a related expression of mourning. Both Hushai and Ziba are encountered
on or near the head of the mountain. Abishai is prepared to cut off Shimei's head. And, as
in other languages, head also designates political leader—an ironic verbal background to
his moment when the head of all Israel has been displaced. Finally, Absalom's usurpation
will come to a violent end when his head—the narrator does not say hair—is caught in the
branches of a tree.

of wine. And the king said to Ziba, "What would you with these things?" 2
And Ziba said, "The donkeys are for the king's household to ride upon,
and the bread and the summer fruit for the lads to eat, and the wine for
the exhausted to drink in the wilderness." And the king said, "And where 3
is your master's son?" And Ziba said to the king, "Why, he is staying in
Jerusalem, for he has said, 'Today the house of Israel will give back to me
my father's kingdom.'" And the king said to Ziba, "Look, everything of 4
Mephibosheth's is yours!" And Ziba said, "I am prostrate! May I find favor
in your eyes, my lord the king."

And King David came as far as Bahurim, and, look, from there out came a 5
man from the clan of the house of Saul, Shimei son of Gera was his name,
and he came cursing. And he hurled stones at David and at all King David's 6
servants, and all the troops and all the warriors were at his right and at his

---

2. *for the king's household.* That is, for a couple of members of the king's immediate family.
David, it should be recalled, has set off on foot.

  the exhausted. The Hebrew term *ya 'ef*—also, by metathesis, *'ayef,* as in verse 14—
straddles the two meanings of exhausted and famished.

3. *And where is your master's son?* Mephibosheth, who is crippled in both legs, would scarcely
have been up to joining the flight from Jerusalem. But David, overwhelmed by betrayals
from within his own court, is suspicious of Mephibosheth's absence, and it is clear that Ziba
has been counting on this suspicion in his scheme to discredit Mephibosheth and take over
his property. It is noteworthy that, at this late date, David still refers to Mephibosheth as
"your master's son," still thinks of the long-dead Jonathan as Ziba's real master.

  Today the house of Israel will give back to me my father's kingdom. There is no corrobo-
rating evidence in the story that Mephibosheth actually said these words. What in fact
seems to be happening is that Ziba is flatly lying about his master in order to make himself
appear to be the only loyal subject worthy of David's benefactions, and of title to Saul's
property. The notion Ziba puts forth that Absalom would have turned over the throne to
the surviving Saulide is highly improbable, but what he proposes to David is that the purportedly treacherous Mephibosheth sees in the general political upheaval of the rebellion
an opportunity to reinstate the house of Saul.

5. *as far as Bahurim.* This is a village in the vicinity of Jerusalem on the eastern slope of
the Mount of Olives.

6. *and all the troops and all the warriors were at his right and at his left.* Perhaps Shimei
is counting on the abject mood of David and his men to guarantee his safety in this act
of extreme provocation. Yet he is clearly playing a very dangerous game—the history of
David's warriors and of the sons of Zeruiah in particular as ruthless and implacable enemies is well-known to him, as the very language of his words of revilement attest. Only a
great, pent-up rage against David, joined now with gloating over David's being thrust from
power, could explain Shimei's act.

7 left. And thus said Shimei as he cursed, "Get out, get out, you man of blood,
8 you worthless fellow! The LORD has brought back upon you all the blood of
the house of Saul, in whose place you became king, and the LORD has given
the kingship into the hand of Absalom your son, and here you are, because
9 of your evil, for you are a man of blood." And Abishai son of Zeruiah said to
the king, "Why should this dead dog curse my lord the king? Let me, pray,
10 cross over and take off his head." And the king said, "What do I have to do
with you, O sons of Zeruiah? If he curses, it is because the LORD has said to
11 him, 'Curse David,' and who can say, 'Why have you done this?'" And David

---

7. *Get out, get out, you man of blood, you worthless fellow.* The blood that, according to the
narrative itself, David has on his hands is that of Uriah the Hittite, and of the fighting men
of Israel who perished at Rabbath-Ammon with Uriah. But the Benjaminite Shimei clearly
believes what David himself, and the narrative with him, has taken pains to refute—that
the blood of the house of Saul is on David's hands: Abner, Ish-Bosheth, and perhaps even
Saul and Jonathan (for David was collaborating with the Philistine Achish when they fell
at Gilboa). Hence the phrase Shimei hurls at David in his next sentence, "all the blood of
the house of Saul, in whose place you became king," suggesting a conjunction of murder
and usurpation.

8. *and here you are, because of your evil.* Most translations understand the last phrase (a
single word in the Hebrew) to mean "You are in evil circumstances," but the prefix *bet*,
which can mean "in," also has a *causal* meaning, and that makes more sense here: David
has come into dire straits, losing the throne, displaced by his own son, because of his own
evil actions.

9. *Why should this dead dog curse my lord the king?* We have seen previously the idiomatic
use of "dead dog" to mean the lowest of the low, David applying this designation to himself
in his speech to Saul at Ein-Gedi. Here the polar contrast between "dead dog" and "my
lord the king" is striking. But Abishai is also reviving the literal force of the idiom, since he
proposes to deal swift death to the snarling Shimei. This is not the first time that Abishai
has been prepared to kill someone on the spot: when he accompanied David into Saul's
camp (1 Samuel 26:8), he had to be restrained from his impulse to dispatch Saul with a
single thrust of the spear.

10. *If he curses, it is because the LORD has said to him, "Curse David."* This is one of the
most astonishing turning points in this story that abounds in human surprises. The proud,
canny, often implacable David here resigns himself to accepting the most stinging humiliation from a person he could easily have his men kill. David's abasement is not a disguise,
like Odysseus's when he takes on the appearance of a beggar, but a real change in condition—from which, however, he will emerge in more than one surprising way. The acceptance of humiliation is a kind of fatalism: if someone commits such a sacrilegious act
against the man who is God's anointed king, it must be because God has decreed it. Behind
that fatalism may be a sense of guilt: I am suffering all this because of what I have done, for
taking Bathsheba and murdering her husband, for my inaction in Amnon's rape of Tamar
and Absalom's murder of Amnon. The guilt is coupled with despair: as David goes on to
say, When my own son is trying to kill me, what difference could it make if this man of
a rival tribe, who at least has political grounds for hostility toward me, should revile me?

said to Abishai and to all his servants, "Look—my son, the issue of my loins, seeks my life. How much more so, then, this Benjaminite. Leave him be and let him curse, for the LORD has told him. Perhaps the LORD will see my afflic- 12 tion and the LORD may requite me good for his cursing this day." And David, 13 and his men with him, went off on the way, and Shimei was walking round the side of the mountain alongside him, cursing and hurling stones at him and flinging dirt. And the king came, and all the troops who were with him, 14 exhausted, and took a breathing stop there. And Absalom and all the troops, 15 the men of Israel, had come to Jerusalem, and Ahitophel was with him.

And it happened when Hushai the Archite, David's friend, came to Absa- 16 lom, that Hushai said, "Long live the king, long live the king!" And Absa- 17 lom said to Hushai, "Is this your loyalty to your friend? Why did you not go with your friend?" And Hushai said to Absalom, "On the contrary! Whom 18 the LORD has chosen, and this people and every man of Israel—his I will be and with him I will stay. And, besides, whom should I serve? Should it 19 not be his son? As I served your father, so will I be in your service." And 20 Absalom said to Ahitophel, "Give you counsel: what shall we do?" And 21

---

13. *cursing and hurling stones at him and flinging dirt.* It is with this image that the episode concludes—Shimei walking along, angrily persisting in his insults, the dirt flung a material equivalent of the words uttered.

14. *came.* Some indication of where he came seems to be required. One version of the Septuagint supplies "to the Jordan" as the answer. That would be a plausible stopping place.

15. *And Absalom . . . had come to Jerusalem, and Ahitophel was with him.* This brief switch of narrative tracks, in a pluperfect verbal form, lays the ground for the fateful clash of counsels between Ahitophel and Hushai and also provides the necessary indication that David and his people have succeeded in fleeing a good many miles to the east by the time Absalom's forces enter the city.

16. *David's friend.* As we have noted, *rea'*, "friend" or "companion," is a court title, but when Absalom uses it, he leans on the ordinary sense of friendship.

   Long live the king. Fokkelman nicely observes that "what he particularly does not say is 'long live King Absalom.'" Thus, in a dramatic irony evident to the audience of the story and of course concealed from Absalom, Hushai is really wishing long life to *his* king— David. And again in his response to Absalom's question about his disloyalty to David, he avoids the use of Absalom's name in a sentence that he secretly applies to David: "Whom the LORD has chosen . . . his I will be and with him I will stay."

19. *And, besides, whom should I serve? Should it not be his son?* Only now does Hushai invoke the line of explanation that David instructed him to use when he came before Absalom.

20. *Give you counsel.* Both the verb and the ethical dative "you" are in the plural, though Absalom is said to be speaking to Ahitophel. Shimon Bar-Efrat proposes that the language implies Absalom is addressing both Ahitophel and Hushai, although it is from Ahitophel

Ahitophel said to Absalom, "Come to bed with your father's concubines whom he left to watch over the house, and let all Israel hear that you have become repugnant to your father, and the hand of all who are with you will
22 be strengthened." And they pitched a tent for Absalom on the roof, and he
23 came to bed with his father's concubines before the eyes of all Israel. And the counsel of Ahitophel that he would give in those days was as one would inquire of an oracle of God, even so was every counsel of Ahitophel, for David and for Absalom as well.

1 CHAPTER 17   And Ahitophel said to Absalom, "Let me pick,
2 pray, twelve thousand men, and let me rise and pursue David tonight. And

---

as his official advisor that he expects to receive counsel. The plural forms, then, suggest that Absalom has been persuaded by Hushai and has accepted him into his circle of court councillors. That inference helps make sense of the immediately following encounter in which both men appear as members of Absalom's national security council.

21. *Come to bed with your father's concubines.* Cohabiting with the sexual consorts of a ruler is an assertion of having taken over all his prerogatives of dominion. Ahitophel's shrewd counsel especially addresses the effect on public opinion of the action proposed: after it, no one will be able to imagine a reconciliation between Absalom and his father ("let all Israel hear that you have become repugnant to your father"), and so the hand of Absalom's supporters will be strengthened, for no one will hedge his support, thinking that David and Absalom will somehow come to terms.

22. *he came to bed with his father's concubines before the eyes of all Israel.* The tent on the roof ensures sexual privacy, but Absalom's entering into it with each of the women is a public display of the act of cohabitation. Either this is to be accepted as an unrealistic event, given that there are ten concubines, or Absalom is supposed to be not only beautiful and hirsute but also a sexual athlete. His act, of course, is a fulfillment of Nathan's dire curse in chapter 12. As several commentators have noted, the usurper's sexual transgression of David's women takes place on the very palace roof from which his father first looked lustfully at Bathsheba.

23. *the counsel of Ahitophel . . . was as one would inquire of an oracle of God.* This quasireligious trust in Ahitophel's counsel is obviously from the point of view of those who seek it, there being a sour irony in likening the sordid, if pragmatic, counsel to have sex with the king's concubines to a divine oracle. In any event, this observation throws a retrospective light on David's disturbance over the news that Ahitophel was among the conspirators and his prayer to God to confound Ahitophel's counsel (15:31). Ahitophel, it seems, is a kind of Israelite Metternich or Bismarck, and David fears that in losing him he has lost a vital strategic resource. The canniness of Ahitophel's military advice will be evident in his clash with Hushai.

CHAPTER 17   1. *Let me pick . . . twelve thousand men . . . and pursue David tonight.* Ahitophel not only offers counsel but proposes to undertake the command of the expedition himself, in striking contrast to Hushai, who begins with a lengthy descriptive statement and then uses a third-person verbal form (verse 11, "let all Israel gather round you")

let me come upon him when he is tired and slack-handed, and I shall panic him, and all the troops who are with him will flee, and I shall strike down the king alone. And let me turn back all the troops to you, for it is one man ₃ you seek, and all the troops will be at peace." And the thing seemed right in ₄ the eyes of Absalom and in the eyes of all the elders of Israel. And Absalom ₅ said, "Call, pray, to Hushai the Archite, too, and let us hear what he, too, has to say." And Hushai came to Absalom, and Absalom said to him, saying, "In ₆ the following manner Ahitophel has spoken. Shall we act on his word? If not, you must speak." And Hushai said to Absalom, "The counsel that Ahitophel ₇ has given is not good this time." And Hushai said, "You yourself know of ₈

---

to express his recommended course of action. It seems as though the urgent Ahitophel has taken on the attribute of his rival's name, which carries the verb *ḥush*, "hurry."

2. *let me come upon him when he is tired and slack-handed.* This is, of course, very sound advice: David and his men are in fact fatigued from their flight to the banks of the Jordan (16:14), and are likely to be vulnerable to a surprise attack.

I shall strike down the king alone. Ahitophel seeks to avoid a protracted civil war: if he can panic David's forces into a general retreat, the death of David will then put an end to the opposition, and his troops are likely to transfer their loyalty to Absalom. The image of one man struck down as the troops flee may ironically echo David's plan for doing away with Uriah.

3. *for it is one man you seek.* The Masoretic Text has three simple Hebrew words here that make no sense as a syntactic sequence: *keshuv hakol ha'ish* ("as-return all the-man"). Many modern interpreters follow the Septuagint, which rearranges the Hebrew letters to read *keshuv kalah le'ishah*, "as a bride returns to her husband." But, as Bar-Efrat contends, this would be a strange image for the movement of troops to the opposite side and it would violate the pointedly unmetaphoric, businesslike character of Ahitophel's language, which stands in sharp contrast to Hushai's elaborately figurative rhetoric of persuasion. This translation therefore adopts Bar-Efrat's proposal that *keshuv hakol* is an inadvertent scribal repetition of *we'ashiva kol* ("let me turn back all") at the beginning of the verse; that phrase is omitted here, and *'ish 'eḥad*, "one man," is presumed instead of *ha'ish 'asher*, "the man who."

4. *the elders of Israel.* This term clearly designates an official group, a kind of royal council. Ahitophel, addressing this group, acts as national security advisor.

5. *Hushai the Archite, too.* Although Hushai does not have Ahitophel's official standing, he has sufficiently won Absalom's trust that the usurper is at least curious to see whether Hushai will concur with Ahitophel. This will prove to be a fatal error.

7. *not good this time.* Shrewdly, Hushai begins by implicity conceding that as a rule Ahitophel's counsel is good—but in this specific instance, the trusty advisor has exhibited a lapse in judgment.

8. *And Hushai said.* Absalom is silent, astounded that anyone should deny the self-evident rightness of Ahitophel's counsel. So the formula for introducing direct discourse, according to the biblical convention, must be repeated, and now Hushai launches upon his cunningly devised argument.

You yourself know. Hushai's opening rhetorical move is to flatter his interlocutor: I hardly have to tell you what you yourself well know, that your father is a very dangerous adversary who cannot be attacked impulsively, without proper preparation.

your father and his men that they are warriors and that they are bitter men,
like a bear in the field bereaved of its young. And your father is a seasoned
9 fighter and he will not spend the night with the troops. Look, he will now
be hiding in some hollow or some other place, and it will happen when they
fall from the very first that he who hears of it will say, 'There's a rout among
10 the troops who follow Absalom.' And though he be a valiant fellow whose
heart is like the heart of a lion, he will surely quail, for all Israel knows that
11 your father is a warrior, and valiant men are those who are with him. And
so I counsel you—let all Israel gather round you, from Dan to Beersheba,
multitudinous as the sand that is on the seashore, and you in person will go
12 forward into battle. And we shall come upon him in whatever place that he
may be, and we shall light upon him as the dew falls upon the ground, and
13 not a single one will be left of all the men who are with him. And should he

---

warriors . . . bitter men . . . like a bear in the field . . . a seasoned fighter. Hushai uses language that, as Bar-Efrat and others have noted, recapitulates a series of moments from the
earlier story of David. What he is doing in effect is invoking the legend of the heroic David,
who as a boy slew bear and lion (compare the lion simile in verse 10), and who gathered
round him bitter men, warriors, seasoned fighters.

he will not spend the night with the troops. This image of David as the constantly wake-
ful, elusive guerilla leader scarcely accords with the figure David has cut in the last several
years of reported narrative—sleeping through the long afternoon while his army fights
in Ammon, sedentary in his palace while internecine struggle goes on between his own
children.

9. *he will now be hiding in some hollow or some other place.* Hushai's rather vague language
once again evokes the time when David was a fugitive from Saul, hiding in caves and
wildernesses.

when they fall from the very first. The unspecified subject of the verb—actually emended
by some as "the troops"—clearly refers to Absalom's forces: ambushed by the wily David,
they will quickly panic.

10. *he will surely quail.* The literal meaning of the Hebrew is "he will surely melt."

11. *multitudinous as the sand . . . on the seashore.* This traditional simile is used to convey
the idea that only overwhelmingly superior numbers, achieved through a general (and
time-consuming!) conscription, can prevail against so formidable a foe as David.

12. *we shall light upon him as the dew falls upon the ground.* Hushai, as Fokkleman has
observed, pairs the traditional simile of the sands of the seashore with a more innovative,
yet related simile of dew on the field. The dew falls silently, effortlessly, and this is how this
huge army will "light upon" David's forces. Dew, elsewhere an image of peacetime blessing,
is here associated with destruction.

not a single one will be left of all the men who are with him. Ahitophel proposed a strategy
through which it might be possible to kill David alone and then to enlist the support of
his followers. Hushai's counsel is to annihilate David's forces, a much more violent means
of preventing civil war. The bloodthirsty alternative evidently appeals to something in

withdraw into a town, all Israel will bear ropes to the town and haul it away
to the wadi until not a stone remains there." And Absalom said, and every 14
man of Israel with him, "The counsel of Hushai the Archite is better than the
counsel of Ahitophel." And the LORD had ordained to overturn Ahitophel's
good counsel in order for the LORD to bring evil upon Absalom.

And Hushai said to Zadok and to Abiathar the priests, "Such-and-such did 15
Ahitophel counsel Absalom and the elders of Israel, and such-and-such I
on my part counseled. And now, send quickly and inform David, saying, 16
'Spend not the night in the steppes of the wilderness, but rather cross over
onward, lest disaster engulf the king and all the troops who are with him.' "
And Jonathan and Ahimaaz were stationed at Ein-Rogel, and the slavegirl 17
would go and inform them and they would go and inform King David,
for they could not be seen coming into the town. And a lad saw them and 18
informed Absalom, and the two of them went quickly and came to the house
of a man in Bahurim who had a well in his courtyard, and they went down

---

Absalom, who is unwilling to trust the future loyalty of the troops who have remained
with David.

13. *should he withdraw into a town.* This little addendum to Hushai's scenario is intended to
anticipate an obvious objection to it: the recommended course of action would give David
time to pull back his forces to a strong defensive position in a fortified town. Hushai's
counterargument is that with so huge an army, Absalom's people could easily take down
the walls of the town stone by stone.

14. *The counsel of Hushai . . . is better than the counsel of Ahitophel.* This entire episode
turns on an ingenious reversal of values. The straight-talking, clear-seeing advisor is
defeated by the lying secret agent who musters the resources of a figurative, psychologically manipulative rhetoric to achieve his ends. Yet it is the master of deception who serves
the forces of legitimacy while the plain dealer looks out for the interests of a usurper and
would-be parricide.
    the LORD had ordained to overturn Ahitophel's good counsel. This theological explana-
tion can be viewed as adding an overarching perspective, or as merely secondary, to the
thoroughly human machinations of Hushai, instigated by David.

16. *And now, send quickly and inform David.* Although Zadok and Abiathar presumably
know that Absalom has chosen to follow Hushai's counsel, they appear to be nervous that
he may change his mind and implement Ahitophel's strategy, for they urge David not to
waste a moment but to flee eastward across the Jordan.

17. *Ein-Rogel.* The site of this village has not been confidently identified, but it would have
to be near Jerusalem to the east.

18. *the house of a man in Bahurim.* This village on the eastern slope of the Mount of Olives
is the hometown of Shimei, who cursed David. What appears to be reflected is a political
reality in which the populace is divided between loyalists and supporters of the usurper.

19 into it. And the woman took a cloth and stretched it over the mouth of the
20 well and spread groats on top of it, so that nothing could be noticed. And
    Absalom's servants came to the woman in the house and said, "Where are
    Ahimaaz and Jonathan?" And she said to them, "They've crossed over past
    the water reservoir." And they searched and they found nothing and they
21 went back to Jerusalem. And it happened after they had gone that Ahimaaz
    and Jonathan came up from the well and went and informed King David,
    and they said to David, "Rise and cross over the water quickly, for thus has
22 Ahitophel counseled against you." And David rose, and all the troops with
    him, and they crossed over the Jordan. By the light of morning not a single
    one was missing who had not crossed over the Jordan.

23 And Ahitophel saw that his counsel was not acted on, and he saddled his
    donkey and arose and went to his home to his town, and he left a charge

---

19. *And the woman took a cloth.* The woman is evidently the wife of the man from Bahurim
(the same Hebrew word means both "woman" and "wife," like *femme* in French and *Frau* in
German). This is still another instance in the David story in which the enterprising intervention of a shrewd woman saves the day. As has often been noted, this moment alludes to
the story told in Joshua 2 of Rahab the harlot, who hides the two spies sent out to Jericho by
Joshua. In Joshua, the spies are hidden up above, in the roof thatch; here they hide below in
the well. There may be a certain agricultural affinity between the covering of thatch and the
cloth covered with groats (if that is what the anomalous Hebrew *rifot* means) under which
the pairs of spies hide. In any case, the destruction of all the men of Jericho who sought
Joshua's spies foreshadows the destruction of Absalom's army.

20. *They've crossed over past the water reservoir.* Rahab, too, gives the pursuers false directions about where the spies have gone. Here, the thematically crucial "cross over" is again
invoked. The meaning of *mikhal*, the word rendered here as "reservoir," is a little doubtful,
though it could be derived from a verbal root that means "to contain."

21. *cross over the water quickly, for thus has Ahitophel counseled against you.* The two couriers now assume the worst-case scenario, that Ahitophel's counsel will after all be followed.
The reference to crossing over the water is a clear indication that David is encamped on
the west bank of the Jordan.

23. *he saddled his donkey and arose and went to his home to his town, and he left a charge
for his household, and he hanged himself.* This haunting notice of Ahitophel's suicide shows
him a deliberate, practical man to the very end, making all the necessary arrangements for
his family and being sure to do away with himself in his hometown, where he knows he
will be readily buried in the ancestral tomb. Ahitophel kills himself not only because, in
quasi-Japanese fashion, he has lost face, but also out of sober calculation: he realizes that
Hushai's counsel will enable David to defeat Absalom, and with the old king returned to
the throne, an archtraitor like Ahitophel will surely face death. Thus, in tying the noose
around his own neck, he anticipates the executioner's sword.

for his household, and he hanged himself and died. And he was buried
in the tomb of his father. And David had come to Mahanaim when Absa- 24
lom crossed over the Jordan, he and every man of Israel with him. And 25
Absalom had placed Amasa instead of Joab over the army, and Amasa
was the son of a man named Ithra the Ishmaelite, who had come to bed
with Abigail daughter of Jesse, sister of Zeruiah, Joab's mother. And Israel 26
and Absalom camped in the land of Gilead. And it happened when David 27
came to Mahanaim that Shobi son of Nahash from Rabbath-Ammon and
Machir son of Amiel from Lo-Debar and Barzillai the Gileadite from
Rogelim brought couches and basins and earthenware, and wheat and 28
barley and flour and parched grain and beans and lentils and honey and 29
curds from the flock and cheese from the herd. These they offered to
David and the troops with him to eat, for they thought, "The troops are
hungry and exhausted and thirsty in the wilderness."

CHAPTER 18   And David marshaled the troops that were 1
with him and set over them commanders of thousands and commanders

---

24. *Mahanaim.* This is an Israelite walled city in trans-Jordan.

25. *Ithra the Ishmaelite.* There are two different problems with the identification of Amasa's
progenitors in the Masoretic Text. The Masoretic version has "Israelite," but this national
label (rather than identification by tribe) would be strange here, and the same Ithra in 1
Chronicles 2:17—called there, in a variant of the name, Jether— is said, more plausibly, to
be the son of an Ishmaelite. The fact that the father is a member of another national-ethnic
group accords with the report that he "had come to bed with Abigail," for that sexual term by
no means necessarily implies marriage. The Masoretic Text makes Nahash, an Ammonite,
Abigail's father, but it looks as though that name may have drifted into this verse in scribal
transcription from verse 27. 1 Chronicles 2 more plausibly reports that Jesse was Abigail's
father. She would then be the sister of David and of Zeruiah, Joab's mother; and so Amasa
and Joab, the two army commanders, are first cousins, and both of them David's nephews.

28. *beans and lentils.* The received text adds "and parched grain" at the end of the list, an
apparent scribal duplication of the word that occurs just before "beans and lentils." This
detailed catalogue of vitally needed victuals, preceded by the utensils required to serve
them and something like bedrolls, is a vivid expression of loyalty to David's beleaguered
forces on the part of the trans-Jordanian Israelites and their Ammonite vassals. Barzillai's
faithfulness will be singled out when David returns.

29. *curds from the flock.* This reflects a very minor emendation of the Masoretic Text, which
says "curds and flock." In the next phrase, the Hebrew word for "cheese" (*shefot*) has no
precedent but is usually understood as cheese because of the alimentary context and the
likely root of the word.

2 of hundreds. And David sent out the troops—a third under Joab and a
   third under Abishai son of Zeruiah, Joab's brother, and a third under Ittai
   the Gittite. And the king said to the troops, "I, too, will surely sally forth
3 with you." And the troops said, "You shall not sally forth. For if we must
   flee, they will pay us no mind, and should half of us die, they will pay us
   no mind, for you are like ten thousand of us, and so it is better that you
4 be a help for us from the town." And the king said to them, "Whatever
   is good in your eyes I shall do." And the king stood by the gate and all
5 the troops sallied forth by their hundreds and their thousands. And the
   king charged Joab and Abishai and Ittai, saying, "Deal gently for me with
   the lad Absalom." And all the troops heard when the king charged the
6 commanders concerning Absalom. And the troops sallied forth to the
   field to meet Israel, and the battle took place in the forest of Ephraim.
7 And the troops of Israel were routed there by David's servants, and great

---

CHAPTER 18   2. *I, too, will surely sally forth with you.* The aging David, as we have
had occasion to note (see the second comment on 11:1), has long been a sedentary monarch
rather than a field commander. In the present crisis, he imagines he can rise again to his
old role, but the troops, who diplomatically make no reference to age or infirmity, clearly
recognize he is not up to it.

3. *should half of us die, they will pay us no mind.* Like Ahitophel, the troops assume that the
real object of Absalom's attack is David. But they essentially propose an opposite scenario
to Absalom's: David will remain safe inside the fortified town, well behind the lines, while
the troops—not panicked, as Ahitophel would have had it, but strategically deployed—will
do battle against Absalom's army.
   for you are like ten thousand of us. This is the reading of numerous Hebrew manuscripts and the Septuagint and Vulgate. The Masoretic Text reads "for now we are like ten
thousand."

4. *the king stood by the gate.* J. P. Fokkelman has noted a wry correspondence here with
the beginning of Absalom's usurpation, when he took a stance by the gate of the city and
accosted each man who came by in order to enlist him to his cause.

5. *Deal gently.* This is the time-honored and eloquent rendering of the King James Version.
But some philologists derive the rare verb here from a root that means "to cover" and hence
construe it in context as "protect." This construction would make it a closer synonym of
the verb used in the soldier's repetition of David's injunction in verse 12, "watch over."

7. *the troops of Israel were routed there.* The elision of the precise details of the battle is
entirely consistent with the narrative treatment of battles elsewhere in the Bible. One may
assume that the three divisions of seasoned fighters, led by their experienced commanders,
attacked the Israelite army from three different sides, panicking it into disorderly flight—
an outcome indicated in the "devouring" forest, where presumably the fleeing soldiers
lost their way, stumbled, became entangled in the undergrowth, perhaps even slashed at

was the slaughter there, twenty thousand. And the battle spread out over 8
all the countryside, and the forest devoured more of the troops than
the sword devoured on that day. And Absalom chanced to be in front 9
of David's servants, Absalom riding on his mule, and the mule came
under the tangled branches of a great terebinth, and his head caught in
the terebinth, and he dangled between heaven and earth, while the mule
which was beneath him passed on. And a certain man saw and informed 10
Joab and said, "Look, I saw Absalom dangling from the terebinth." And 11
Joab said to the man informing him, "And look, you saw, and why did

---

each other in the dark of the wood. Throughout this episode, Absalom's forces are "Israel"
and David's are his "servants." The former are numerically superior, but they behave like
a poorly organized conscript army facing professional soldiers.

9. *his head caught in the terebinth, and he dangled between heaven and earth, while the mule
which was beneath him passed on.* This striking and bizarre image of Absalom's penultimate moment provides a brilliant symbolic summation of his story. Most obviously, the
head of hair that was his narcissistic glory is now the instrument of his fatal entrapment,
Absalom the commander microcosmically enacting the fate of his army "devoured" by the
forest. There is nothing supernatural here—David's forces have shrewdly taken advantage
of the irregular terrain—yet there is a sense that nature is conspiring against Absalom and
his men. The mule is in this period the usual mount for princes and kings (one should
recall that all the king's sons ride away on their mules after Absalom has Amnon killed), so
Absalom's losing his mule from under him is an image of his losing his royal seat. Having
climbed from exile and rejection to the throne, he now dangles helplessly between sky and
earth. The mule's "passing on" (*'avar*), as Polzin notes, picks up the key verb ("cross over")
that has characterized David's flight from the royal city. Fokkelman brilliantly shows that
there is also a whole series of contrastive parallels between Absalom's fate and that of his
councillor Ahitophel: "The councillor rides calmly on his ass to his home while the prince
is abandoned by his mule, a fatal loss. He is thrown into an unknown, nameless and ignominious grave while Ahitophel is 'buried in his father's grave'. . . . With all these contrasts,
they have one detail in common: both finally hang."

   he dangled. The Masoretic Text has "he was given," but ancient translations into Aramaic, Syriac, Greek, and Latin, now confirmed by the Qumran Samuel scroll, read "dangled," a difference of a single consonant in the Hebrew.

11. *And look, you saw.* The contemptuous Joab throws the soldier's own words back into
his face: if that's what you really saw, why didn't you have the brains to finish him off on
the spot and get the reward I would have given you? Joab, in his unflinching resolution to
kill Absalom in defiance of David's explicit orders to the contrary, remains the consummately calculating political man—something David once was but no longer is. When Joab
thought it was politically prudent to reconcile David with Absalom, he took elaborate steps
to achieve that end. Now he realizes that an Absalom allowed to survive is likely to be a
source of future political dissension and that the only sure way to eliminate this threat is
Absalom's death.

you not strike him to the ground there, and I would have had to give you
12 ten pieces of silver and a belt?" And the man said to Joab, "Even were I
to heft in my palms a thousand pieces of silver, I would not reach out
my hand against the king's son, for within our hearing the king charged
you and Abishai and Ittai, saying, 'Watch for me over the lad Absalom.'
13 Otherwise, I would have wrought falsely with my own life, and nothing
14 can be concealed from the king, while you would have stood aloof." And
Joab said, "Not so will I wait for you!" And he took three sticks in his
palm and he thrust them into Absalom's heart, still alive in the heart of
15 the terebinth. And ten lads, Joab's armor bearers, pulled round and struck
16 down Absalom and put him to death. And Joab sounded the ram's horn,
and the troops came back from pursuing Israel, for Joab held back the
17 troops. And they took Absalom and flung him into the big hollow in the
forest, and they heaped up over it a very big mound of stones. And all
Israel had fled, each to his tent.

---

12. *were I to heft in my palms a thousand pieces of silver.* The soldier responds to Joab's
contempt with righteous indignation, multiplying the hypothetical reward a hundredfold
and turning the general act of giving silver into a concrete hefting of its weight in order
to express how sacred he holds the king's injunction, which, we now see, has in fact been
heard by "all the troops" (verse 5).

14. *he took three sticks in his palm.* Over against the soldier's palms hyperbolically hefting
a thousand pieces of silver, Joab's palm grasps a blunt instrument of violence. The Hebrew
shevatim means "sticks," not "darts," as it is often translated, and had they been darts, the
blow would surely have been fatal. On the contrary, it seems probable that Joab's intention
is not to kill the prince—after all, this military man is an experienced killer—but rather to
stun him and hurt him badly, and then to spread the responsibility for the death by ordering the warriors to finish him off. Fokkelman proposes that the three sticks jibe with the
three divisions of the army, so that Joab performs a deliberately symbolic act, "executing
the rebellious prince on behalf of the whole army."
      into Absalom's heart, still alive in the heart of the terebinth. The two hearts, one a vul-
nerable human organ, the other the dense of center of the tangle of branches, produce an
unsettling effect.

15. *lads.* The Hebrew *ne'arim,* "lads," in its sense of elite fighting men, rings dissonantly
against David's repeated paternal designation of Absalom as *na'ar,* "lad."

16. *sounded.* The Hebrew reflects an untranslatable pun because the verb *taqa',* "to make
a piercing sound with a horn," also means to thrust or stab, and is the word just used to
report Joab's blow to the heart.

17. *the big hollow.* An alternative rendering is "pit," but "hollow" is used here to preserve the
verbal identity in the Hebrew between this moment and Hushai's imaginary description
in chapter 17 of David's hiding in "one of the hollows." To be flung into a hole in the field
and covered with a heap of stones is a shameful burial.

And Absalom had taken and heaped up a cairn for himself in his lifetime, 18
which is in the Valley of the King, for he said, "I have no son to make my
name remembered." And he called the cairn after his name, and it is called
Absalom's Monument to this day.

And Ahimaaz son of Zadok had said, "Let me run, pray, and bear tidings 19
to the king that the LORD has done him justice against his enemies." And 20
Joab said to him, "You are no man of tidings this day. You may bear tidings on another day, but this day you shall bear no tidings, for the king's
son is dead." And Joab said to the Cushite "Go, inform the king of what 21
you have seen," and the Cushite bowed down before Joab and ran off. And 22
Ahimaaz son of Zadok once again said to Joab, "Whatever may be, let me,
too, pray, run after the Cushite." And Joab said, "Why should you run, my
son, when yours are not welcome tidings?" "Whatever may be, I will run!" 23
And he said to him, "Run." And Ahimaaz ran by the way of the Plain, and
he overtook the Cushite.

---

18. *Absalom had . . . heaped up a cairn.* This brief notice, in the pluperfect tense, draws a
pointed contrast with Absalom's ignominious grave. The same verb, "to heap up," is used
for both, and the cairn, or commemorative pile of stones (*not* a "pillar") is the grandiose
image that is transformed into the pile of stones over Absalom's body.

　　I have no son to make my name remembered. Faulkner's *Absalom, Absalom!*, with reference to both its David figure and its Absalom figure, beautifully catches the pathos of these
words. Those who have sought to harmonize this verse with 14:27, where Absalom is said
to have fathered three sons, propose that the sons died, their early death explaining why
they are left unnamed.

21. *the Cushite.* This Nubian is the third foreign messenger introduced into the story (the
other two are the Egyptian slave who informs David of the whereabouts of the Amalekite
raiding party and the Amalekite who reports Saul's death to David). Joab appears to exhibit
a certain paternal concern for Ahimaaz, a priest and a faithful agent of David's during the
insurrection—in the next verse he addresses him as "my son." Joab is keenly aware that
David has in the past shown himself capable of killing the bearer of ill tidings in a fit of
rage, and so the commander prefers to let a foreigner take the risk.

22. *yours are not welcome tidings.* The Hebrew—literally, "finding tidings"—is anomalous,
and has inspired both emendation and excessively ingenious interpretation. The immediate
context suggests "welcome" as the most plausible meaning, and this could easily be an idiom
for which there are no other occurrences in the biblical corpus, which, after all, provides only
a small sampling of ancient Hebrew usage. In fact, these two words, *besorah motsei't*, could
well be an idiomatic ellipsis for *besorah motsei't hen*, "tidings finding favor (in his eyes)."

23. *by the way of the Plain.* The Plain in question is the Jordan Valley on the east side of
the river. Some have suggested that Ahimaaz overtakes the Cushite not by speed but by
running along a flatter, if less direct, route in the Jordan Valley riverbed, but verses 25–27
indicate that Ahimaaz outruns the Cushite.

24 And David was sitting between the gates, and the lookout went up on the
   roof of the gate on the wall, and he raised his eyes and saw and, look, a
25 man was running alone. And the lookout called and told the king, and
26 the king said, "If he's alone, there are tidings in his mouth." And he came
   on, drawing nearer. And the lookout saw another man running, and the
   lookout called to the gatekeeper and said, "Look, a man is running alone."
27 And the king said, "This one, too, bears tidings." And the lookout said, "I
   see the running of the first one as the running of Ahimaaz son of Zadok,"
   and the king said, "He is a good man and with good tidings he must come."
28 And Ahimaaz called out and said to the king, "All is well." And he bowed
   down to the king, his face to the ground, and he said, "Blessed is the LORD
   your God Who has delivered over the men who raised their hand against
29 my lord the king." And the king said, "Is it well with the lad Absalom?"

---

24. *David was sitting between the gates.* Walled cities in ancient Israel and environs often had double walls, with an inner and outer gate and a small plaza between them. Moshe Garsiel neatly observes that David's ambivalence about the armed struggle is spatially figured by his physical location: he wanted to sally forth with the army; the troops wanted him within the town; he stations himself in between. Before the battle he stood by the gate; now he is seated by the gate, awaiting the news from the front—as Polzin notes, exactly like Eli, who is told of the death of his two sons.

   the lookout went up on the roof of the gate . . . and he raised his eyes and saw. This moment is quite exceptional, and striking, in representing the arrival of the two messengers visually, from the perspective of the lookout on the wall reporting to David down below in the gate plaza. David's troubles with all his sons, it should be remembered, began when he himself looked down from a roof and saw a woman bathing.

25. *If he's alone, there are tidings in his mouth.* A solitary runner is likely to be a courier. Soldiers, whether in retreat or maneuvering, would travel in groups.

27. *He is a good man and with good tidings he must come.* This obvious non sequitur suggests that the desperately anxious David is grasping at straws. In fact, as revelatory dialogue, it shows us just how desperate he feels.

28. *All is well.* This is one word in the Hebrew, *shalom*. That word is the last two syllables of Absalom's name in Hebrew, *'Avshalom*, a link David will reinforce when he nervously asks, "Is it well [*shalom*] with the lad Absalom ['*Avshalom*]?"

   Who has delivered over the men who raised their hands against my LORD *the king.* Ahimaaz hastens to report, in terms that express both his Israelite piety and his loyalty to the king, the general defeat of the usurper's army. He of course says nothing of Absalom's fate.

29. *Is it well with the lad Absalom?* This seems to be David's overriding concern, not the military victory. Again and again, he insists on the term of affection, "lad," for the rebel son who would have killed him. The tension between his political role, which, as Joab understood, requires Absalom's destruction, and his paternal role is painfully palpable. In this connection, it is noteworthy that David, so much the emotionally vulnerable father here, is consistently referred to as "the king," not as "David."

And Ahimaaz said, "I saw a great crowd to send the king's servant Joab, and your servant, and I know not what . . ." And the king said, "Turn aside, stand by!" And he turned aside and took his place. And, look, the 30,31
Cushite had come and the Cushite said, "Let my lord the king receive the tidings that the LORD has done you justice against all who rose against you." And the king said to the Cushite, "Is it well with the lad Absalom?" And 32
the Cushite said, "May the enemies of my lord the king be like the lad, and all who have risen against you for evil!"

CHAPTER 19   And the king was shaken. And he went up to 1
the upper room over the gate and he wept, and thus he said as he went, "My son, Absalom! My son, my son, Absalom! Would that I had died in your

---

I saw a great crowd to send the king's servant. This is nearly gibberish but not because of any corruption of the text. Ahimaaz has been posed a question he does not dare answer, and so he begins to talk nervously and incoherently ("and I know not what . . .").

30. *Turn aside, stand by.* David, realizing he is unlikely to extract anything from the babbling Ahimaaz, decides to wait and interrogate the second messenger, whose arrival is imminent.

31. *Let my lord the king receive the tidings.* The Cushite is considerably more brusque than his predecessor. He does not begin with a reassuring "All is well." There is no indication of his bowing down before the king. He proceeds quickly to the report of the victory, and though the language of that report approximately parallels Ahimaaz's language, it is briefer, and ends with "against you" instead of the more deferential "against my lord the king."

32. *May the enemies of my LORD the king be like the lad.* The Cushite promptly and clearly responds by reporting Absalom's death, although even he has enough sense to phrase it indirectly, neither mentioning Absalom by name nor using the word "died." In referring to the usurper as "the lad," he is quoting David, but without having picked up the crucial cue of David's paternal feelings reflected in the word. He blithely assumes that because Absalom was at the head of "all who have risen against" the king, the news of his death will be welcome. It strikes exactly the right note that the Cushite's very last word is "evil" (or, "harm").

CHAPTER 19   1. *My son, my son, Absalom!* Much of the way experience transforms David in the course of his story can be seen through his changing responses to the deaths of those close to him. When Jonathan and Saul died, he intoned an eloquent elegy. When Abner was murdered, he declaimed a much briefer elegy, coupled with a speech dissociating himself from the killing. When his infant son by Bathsheba died, he spoke somber words about his own mortality and the irreversibility of death. Now, the eloquent David is reduced to a sheer stammer of grief, repeating over and over the two Hebrew words, *beni 'Avshalom,* "my son, Absalom." Although the narrator continues to refer to David only as "the king," in the shifting conflict between his public and private roles the latter here takes over entirely: Absalom is not the usurper who drove him from the throne but only "my son," and David is the anguished father who would rather have died, that his son might have lived.

2 stead! Absalom, my son, my son!" And it was told to Joab, "Look, the king
3 is weeping and he is grieving over Absalom." And the victory on that day
turned into mourning for all the troops, for the troops had heard on that
4 day, saying, "The king is pained over his son." And the troops stole away
on that day to come to the town as troops disgraced in their flight from the
5 battle would steal away. And the king covered his face, and the king cried
6 out with a loud voice, "My son, Absalom! Absalom, my son, my son!" And
Joab came to the king within the house and said, "You have today shamed
all your servants who have saved your life today and the lives of your sons
and daughters and the lives of your wives and the lives of your concubines,
7 to love those who hate you and to hate those who love you. For you have
said today that you have no commanders or servants. For I know today

---

3. *for the troops had heard on that day.* Before the battle they had all heard David's admonition to his commanders to do no harm to Absalom. Now they hear of his grief and are smitten with shame and apprehension—whether out of empathy for their beloved leader, or guilt over the complicity some of their number share in Absalom's death, or fear of potential violence between David and Joab.

4. *the troops stole away . . . as troops disgraced in their flight from the battle.* This striking image of victory transformed into the bitterness of defeat picks up verbal threads, as Moshe Garsiel has perceptively noted, from the beginning of Absalom's insurrection (chapter 15). There, the usurper stood at the gate, as David is here made to go out and sit in the gate. Absalom was said to "steal the heart" of the men of Israel as here the men steal away, and in order to recover dominion David is enjoined to speak to their heart (verse 8). The disheartened slipping away of the troops suggests that Joab is addressing an imminent danger of the disintegration of the army.

5. *the king covered his face.* The gesture makes perfect psychological sense, while the verb used, *la'at,* is the same one David chose when he said "Deal gently [*le'at*] with the lad Absalom."

6. *within the house.* The implication is that Joab speaks with David in private. The thematic opposition to this term is "in the gate," where Joab will send David.
   You have today shamed all your servants who have saved your life today. Again and again here Joab insists on the word "today." It is this very moment, he suggests, this crucial turning point, that you must seize in order to reestablish your reign. You cannot allow yourself to think of the past, of your history as Absalom's father: as king, you must confront *today,* with its challenge and its political responsibilities.

7. *to love those who hate you and to hate those who love you.* Joab uses rhetorical exaggeration in order to elevate David's paternal attachment to Absalom into a generalized, perverse political principle: if you show such extravagant fondness for the usurper who sought your life, then you are behaving as though all your enemies were your friends and your friends your enemies.
   For you have said today that you have no commanders or servants. That is, by exhibiting such love for your archenemy, you are showing flagrant disregard for the loyal officers and followers to whose devotion you owe your life.

that were Absalom alive and all of us today dead, then would it have been
right in your eyes! And now, rise, go out, and speak to the heart of your   8
servants. For by the LORD I have sworn, if you go not out, that not a man
shall spend the night with you, and this will be a greater evil for you than   ·
any evil that has befallen you from your youth until now." And the king   9
arose and sat in the gate, and to all the troops they told, saying, "Look, the
king is sitting in the gate." And all the troops came before the king, while
Israel had fled each man to his tent.

And all the people were deliberating throughout the tribes of Israel, saying,   10
"The king rescued us from the clutches of our enemies and he saved us from
the clutches of the Philistines, but now he has fled the land before Absalom,
and Absalom, whom we anointed over us, has died in battle. And now why   11
do you not speak up to bring back the king?" And King David had sent to   12
Zadok and to Abiathar the priests, saying, "Speak to the elders of Judah,
saying, 'Why should you be the last to bring back the king to his house

---

8. *speak to the heart of your servants.* This personal act of rallying the men is deemed
urgently necessary by Joab because the army has already begun to disperse ("steal away").

   if you go not out . . . not a man shall spend the night with you. These words are a naked
threat: if David does not follow Joab's order, the commander will encourage the army to
abandon the king, and he will be alone, without power or troops, engulfed in "a greater
evil" than any that has befallen him in his long and arduous career. In all this, Joab's verbal
assault on David, however motivated by pressing considerations of practical politics, is
also a defense of his own flouting of David's injunction to protect Absalom. David at this
point knows only the bare fact of his son's death, not who was responsible for it. This is
something that he will inevitably soon learn, and that bitter knowledge is surely registered
in his decision to replace Joab with Amasa (verse 14).

9. *the king arose and sat in the gate.* Fokkelman brilliantly observes the disparity between
Joab's exhortation and the report of David's action. Joab had said, "go out, and speak to the
heart of your servants." Instead of these active gestures, we see David passively sitting in the
gate while the troops come to him, and we are given no reported speech for him. In Fokkelman's reading, this gap between command and act "call[s] up the image of a man beaten to
a pulp, who can barely stand, and does only the minimum requested or expected of him."

10. *deliberating.* The verb *nadon* in this verse is conventionally related to the noun *madon,*
"quarrel" or "contention." But in fact what the people say is not contentious, and it is preferable to derive the passive (perhaps implicitly reflexive) verbal form here from *dun,* to judge,
consider, or deliberate.

12. *Why should you be the last to bring back the king.* Throughout this episode, there is
a central focus on who will be first and who will be last to show support for the Davidic
restoration. The northern tribes, Israel, have already evinced support (verse 10), and David
is concerned to enlist the backing of his own tribe, Judah, which had largely swung to
Absalom during the insurrection.

13 when the word of all Israel has come to the king regarding his house? You
are my brothers. You are my bone and my flesh, and why should you be the
14 last to bring back the king?' And to Amasa you shall say, 'Are you not my
bone and my flesh? So may the LORD do to me, and even more, if you will
15 not be commander of the army before me for all time instead of Joab,'" And
he inclined the heart of all the men of Judah as a single man, and they sent
to the king: "Come back, you and all your servants."

16 And the king turned back, and he came to the Jordan, and Judah had come
17 to Gilgal to go to meet the king to bring the king across the Jordan. And
Shimei son of Gera the Benjaminite from Bahurim hastened and went
18 down with the men of Judah to meet King David. And a thousand men
were with him from Benjamin, and Ziba, the lad of the house of Saul and
his fifteen sons and his twenty slaves with him, and they rushed down to

---

regarding his house. Or simply, "to his house." Many textual critics regard this phrase
as a mistaken scribal duplication of the same phrase earlier in this verse.

13. *You are my bone and my flesh.* That is, you are Judahites, just as I am, and so there is
actual kinship between us.

14. *to Amasa . . . "Are you not my bone and my flesh?"* Now the phrase is no longer hyperbolic, for Amasa is David's nephew. The extraordinary offer of the post of commander of
the army to Absalom's general in the rebellion reflects David's knack for combining personal and political motives. It is a slap in the face to Joab, the killer of David's son, against
whom David evidently does not dare to take any more direct steps of vengeance. At the
same time, the hesitation of the Judahites in rallying behind the restored king suggests that
an act such as the appointment of Amasa as commander may be required to enlist their
support. Joab, not surprisingly, will not quietly acquiesce in his abrupt dismissal from the
office he has held since the beginning of David's career.

15. *he inclined the heart.* It is not clear whether the Hebrew, characteristically overgenerous
in its use of pronouns, intends the "he" to refer to David or to Amasa. In either case, David's
overture succeeds in bringing the tribe of Judah into his camp.

16. *to bring the king across the Jordan.* The verb ʿ*avar,* "cross over," and its causative form,
haʿavir, "to bring across," which thematically defined David's exodus from Jerusalem in
chapter 15, dominates this episode, too, as the crossing over in flight to the east is reversed
by the crossing over westward back to Jerusalem.

17. *Shimei son of Gera.* There is an approximate symmetry between David's encounters in
his exodus from Jerusalem and those that now occur in his return. Then he met a hostile
Shimei, now he meets a contrite Shimei. Then he met Ziba, who denounced his master
Mephibosheth; now he meets Mephibosheth himself, who defends his own loyalty. Then he
spoke with Ittai, the loyalist who insisted on accompanying him; now he speaks with Barzillai, the proven loyalist who refuses to accompany him back to the capital. The encounter
with Hushai, who becomes David's secret agent, has no counterpart here.

the Jordan before the king. And as the crossing over was going on, to bring 19
across the king's household and to do what was good in his eyes, Shimei son
of Gera flung himself before the king as he was crossing the Jordan and he 20
said to the king, "Let not my lord reckon it a crime, and do not remember
the perverse thing your servant did on the day my lord the king went out
from Jerusalem, that the king should pay it mind. For your servant knows 21
that it was I who offended, and, look, I have come today first of all the
house of Joseph to go down to meet my lord the king." And Abishai son of 22
Zeruiah spoke out and said, "For this should not Shimei be put to death?
For he cursed the LORD's anointed." And David said, "What do I have to 23
do with you, sons of Zeruiah, that you should become my adversary today?
Should today a man of Israel be put to death? For I surely know that today I
am king over Israel." And the king said to Shimei, "You shall not die." And 24
the king swore to him.

And Mephibosheth son of Saul had come down to meet the king, and he 25
had not dressed his feet or trimmed his moustache, and his garments he
had not laundered from the day the king had gone until the day he came

---

21. *first of all the house of Joseph to go down to meet my lord the king.* Shimei, who has
rushed down to the Jordan in order to demonstrate his newfound loyalty to David, uses
"the house of Joseph" loosely to refer to the northern tribes. He is, of course, actually from
the tribe of Benjamin. He "goes down" because his hometown of Bahurim is in the high
country near Jerusalem.

22. *For this should not Shimei be put to death?* Abishai remains true to character, for the
third time prepared to kill someone on the impulse of the moment.

23. *What do I have to do with you, sons of Zeruiah.* These words by now are a kind of refrain,
as David seeks to dissociate himself from the murderous sons of Zeruiah. It is noteworthy
that though Abishai alone has just spoken, David, mindful of the killing of Absalom,
includes Joab as well in his protest by using the plural "sons of Zeruiah."
  Should today a man of Israel be put to death? David's "today" is an implicit rejoinder
to Joab's "today" in the confrontation over his mourning Absalom. This day of victorious
return is a moment for national reconciliation and hence for a general amnesty for both the
Saulides and the supporters of Absalom. In the course of time, it will appear that David in
effect restricts his pledge not to harm Shimei to an extended "today."

25. *he had not dressed his feet or trimmed his moustache, and his garments he had not laundered.* These acts of mourning, reported to us by the authoritative narrator, are an indication that in fact Mephibosheth remained loyal to David throughout the insurrection, and
that Ziba's denunciation was a self-interested calumny. (Some interpret "dressing"—literally "doing"—the feet as cutting the toenails, though the parallel usage often cited from
Deuteronomy has "toenails," not "feet," as the object of the verb "to do.")

26 back safe and sound. And it happened when he came from Jerusalem to meet the king, that the king said to him, "Why did you not go with me,

27 Mephibosheth?" And he said, "My lord the king! My servant deceived me. For your servant thought, 'I'll saddle me the donkey and ride on it and go

28 with the king,' for your servant is lame. And he slandered your servant to my lord the king, and my lord the king is like a messenger of God, and do

29 what is good in your eyes. For all my father's house are but men marked for death to my lord the king, yet you set your servant among those who eat at your table. And what right still do I have to cry out still in appeal to the

30 king?" And the king said to him, "Why should you still speak your words?

31 I say—you and Ziba shall divide the field." And Mephibosheth said to the king, "Let him even take all, seeing that my lord the king has come safe and sound to his house."

---

26. *when he came from Jerusalem.* The Masoretic Text simply says "Jerusalem" but this encounter presumably takes place down by the Jordan. One version of the Septuagint removes the word from this verse and places it at the end of verse 25.

27. *I'll saddle me the donkey . . . for your servant is lame.* The evident implication is that it would have taken the crippled Mephibosheth some time to get ready to go after the fleeing king. Meanwhile, his servant headed out before him in order to denounce him, perhaps actually leaving his master awaiting his help to saddle the donkey.

29. *For all my father's house are but men marked for death to my lord the king.* Mephibosheth's choice of words—the literal phrasing of the Hebrew is "men of death"—is an oblique, perhaps inadvertent, concession that he shares what must have been the general suspicion among the Saulides that David was responsible for the chain of violent deaths in the house of Saul.

30. *Why should you still speak your words?* David cuts off Mephibosheth impatiently, picking up the "still" that the anxious supplicant has just twice used.

you and Ziba shall divide the field. This "Solomonic" judgment may actually be another sign that David has lost his ruler's grip. For if Ziba has told the truth about his master, Mephibosheth as a traitor would deserve nothing, except perhaps capital punishment. And if Ziba was lying, then the servant would deserve nothing except a harsh legal penalty for defamation. Perhaps Mephibosheth is paying a price for having betrayed that he thought David was responsible for the Saulide deaths: in this reading, David knows Mephibosheth is telling the truth, but he punishes him for assuming David was involved in the killings by decreeing Mephibosheth will lose half his property.

31. *Let him even take all.* By this verbal gesture, Mephibosheth shows himself loyal to David to the end, regardless of personal benefit. These words could well be an implicit judgment on the unwisdom of David's decree.

And Barzillai the Gileadite had come down from Rogelim, and he crossed 32
over the Jordan with the king to send him off from the Jordan. And Barzil- 33
lai was very aged, eighty years old, and he had provided for the king during
his stay in Mahanaim, for he was a very wealthy man. And the king said 34
to Barzillai, "You, cross over with me, and I shall provide for you by me
in Jerusalem." And Barzillai said to the king, "How many are the days of 35
the years of my life that I should go up with the king to Jerusalem? Eighty 36
years old I am today. Do I know between good and evil? Does your servant taste what I eat and what I drink? Do I still hear the voice of men and
women singing? And why should your servant still be a burden on my lord
the king? Your servant can barely cross over the Jordan, and why should 37
the king give me this recompense? Let your servant, pray, turn back, that 38
I may die in my own town by the tomb of my father and my mother, and,
look, let your servant Chimham cross over with my lord the king, and
do for him what is good in your eyes." And the king said, "With me shall 39
Chimham cross over, and I will do for him what is good in your eyes, and
whatever you choose for me, I will do for you." And all the troops crossed 40
over the Jordan, and the king crossed over, and the king kissed Barzillai
and blessed him, and he went back to his place. And the king crossed over 41

---

32. *Barzillai the Gileadite.* David's three encounters at the ford of the Jordan from a pro-
gressive series on the scale of loyalty: first Shimei, who has heaped insults on him and now
pleads for forgiveness; then Mephibosheth, whose loyalty, although probably genuine, has
been called into question by Ziba; and then the unswervingly devoted old man, Barzillai.

35. *How many are the days of the years of my life.* Though this rhetorical question literally
echoes the question that Pharaoh asks the aged Jacob, the meaning is the opposite—not
"How long have I lived?" but "How long could I possibly have left to live?"

38. *your servant Chimham.* This is presumably Barzillai's son.

40. *the king kissed Barzillai.* This entire catastrophic sequence in the David story began
with David's cold kiss to the son from whom he had been estranged, followed by Absalom's
calculated kiss for every man he enlisted to his cause at the gate of the city. Now the king
bestows a kiss of true affection upon the loyal old man who provided for him and his troops
in their moment of need.

41. *the king crossed over . . . and Chimham crossed over with him, and . . . they brought the
king across.* The crossing over eastward of the banished king, which never should have
occurred, is now decisively reversed, as David and all his people come across the Jordan and
head for Jerusalem. But, as the immediately following dialogue intimates, David's political
troubles are far from over.

to Gilgal, and Chimham crossed over with him, and all the people of Judah,
42 they brought the king across, and half of the people of Israel as well. And,
look, all the men of Israel were coming toward the king, and they said to the
king, "Why have our brothers, the men of Judah, stolen you away, bringing
the king across the Jordan with his household, and all David's men with
43 him?" And all the men of Judah answered the men of Israel, "For the king is
kin to us. And why should you be incensed over this thing? Have we eaten
44 anything of the king's? Have we been given any gift?" And the men of Israel
answered the men of Judah and they said, "We have ten parts in the king,
even in David, more than you, and why have you treated us with contempt?
Was not our word first to bring back the king?" And the word of the men
of Judah was harsher than the word of the men of Israel.

---

to Gilgal. This is the gathering place where Saul was consecrated as king and later severed by Samuel from his role as God's anointed.

half of the people of Israel as well. In all likelihood, "half" is used loosely to indicate
simply that some members of the northern tribes took part in bringing David to Gilgal.

42. *and they said to the king.* Although their complaint is addressed to the king, he never
answers them. Instead, as Fokkelman notes, the scene breaks down into a squabble between
Israelite and Judahite. Once again, David appears to be losing his regal grip.

43. *the king is kin to us.* That is, David is actually a member of the tribe of Judah.

44. *We have ten parts in the king, even in David, more than you.* Though ten to one might
merely be idiomatic for great preponderance, it seems likely that they allude to the fact that
they are ten tribes to Judah's one—if David is king of the entire nation, this gives them ten
times the claim to the king that Judah has. The phrase "even in David" (or, "also in David")
is a little odd, and the Septuagint reads instead, "also I am firstborn more than you." It
should be noted that all the pronouns in this dialogue in the Hebrew are cast in the first-
person singular, referring to a singular, collective "man of Israel" and "man of Judah," but
that usage doesn't quite work in English.

the word of the men of Judah was harsher than the word of the men of Israel. The episode
concludes in a clash of words, to be followed by a clash of swords. The implication of the
greater "harshness" (or, "hardness") of the Judahite words is aptly caught by the medieval
Hebrew commentator David Kimchi: "Their word was harsher and stronger than the word
of the men of Israel, and the men of Judah spoke harshly to the men of Israel, with the king
saying nothing to them. Therefore the men of Israel were incensed and they followed after
[the rebel] Sheba son of Bichri."

CHAPTER 20   And there chanced to be there a worthless 1
fellow named Sheba son of Bichri, a Benjaminite. And he blew the ram's
horn and said,

> "We have no share in David,
>   no portion have we in Jesse's son—
>   every man to his tent, O Israel!"

And all the men of Israel turned away from David to follow Sheba son 2
of Bichri, but the men of Judah clung to their king from the Jordan to
Jerusalem.

And David came to his house in Jerusalem, and the king took his ten con- 3
cubine women whom he had left to watch over the house, and he placed
them in a house under watch, but he did not come to bed with them, and
they were shut up till their dying day in living widowhood.

CHAPTER 20   1. *there chanced to be there.* The narrative is a direct continuation of
the end of the previous chapter, and so "there" is the national assembly grounds at Gilgal
where the northern tribes, Israel, and the tribe of Judah have just quarreled. The northern-
ers, resentful of the harshness of the Judahites' words, in which the members of David's
own tribe claimed a special proprietary relationship with the king, are ripe for the appeal
of a demagogue such as Sheba, who is at once identified as "a worthless fellow."
    We have no share in David. This is a defiant reversal of the claim just made by the Isra-
elites that they had "ten parts" in the king. Later, in 1 Kings, when the monarchy actually
splits in two, the same rallying cry will be used by the secessionists.

2. *the men of Judah clung to their king.* David is, of course, "their" king because he is from the
tribe of Judah. The reach of the tribe stretches west to east, from the Jordan to Jerusalem,
and also to the south of Jerusalem, while the rebel forces are to the north.

3. *David came to his house in Jerusalem, and . . . took his ten concubine women.* The
concubines have become taboo to David because they cohabited with Absalom his son.
But this whole sad notice suggests that David now cannot fully "come back to his house."
The women he left, perhaps foolishly and surely futilely, "to watch over the house" are
now sequestered "in a house under watch." There is a wry echo in all this of that early
moment of David's investment of Jerusalem when he was confronted by another wife
he had left behind who had slept with another man—Michal. She had no child "till her
dying day"—an image of interrupted conjugality that is multiplied tenfold here with
the concubines.

4 And the king said to Amasa, "Muster me the men of Judah, in three days,
5 and you take your stand here." And Amasa went to muster Judah, and he
6 missed the appointed time that was set for him. And David said to Abishai,
"Now Sheba son of Bichri will do us more harm than Absalom. You, take
your master's servants and pursue him, lest he find him fortified towns,
7 and elude our gaze." And Joab's men sallied forth after him, and the Cherithites and the Pelethites and all the warriors. And they sallied forth from
8 Jerusalem to pursue Sheba son of Bichri. They were just by the great stone
which is in Gibeon when Amasa came before them, and Joab was girt in

---

4. *the king said to Amasa.* Amasa, Absalom's commander in the rebellion, has been designated by David to replace Joab. At the margins of the narrative report lurks the question,
Where is Joab? The answer forthcoming will be savage.

take your stand. That is, report to me.

6. *Now Sheba son of Bichri will do us more harm than Absalom.* Although it is not clear why
Amasa is late for his appointed meeting with David (perhaps his appearance at Gibeon in
verse 8 suggests that he decided, out of military considerations, to pursue Sheba at once
without reporting back to the king), David's unjustified panic is another indication that
he has lost his political composure. By sending out Abishai, Joab's brother, to give chase
after Sheba, he sets up the circumstances for Joab's murder of Amasa and his subsequent
return to power.

You, take your master's servants. The obtrusively imperative "you" is very brusque, at
the same time expressing David's intention to designate Abishai, and not his brother, to
command the pursuit.

and elude our gaze. The two Hebrew words here, *wehitsil 'eynenu*, are problematic. They
might mean "and save [himself] [from] our eyes" (the bracketed words would be implied
via ellipsis by the Hebrew); or, if the verb here is vocalized differently, the words might
mean "and cast a shadow over our eyes." Needless to say, many emendations have been
proposed. In any case, the idea strongly suggested by the context is that Sheba would place
himself beyond the reach of pursuit by withdrawing into fortified towns. In the event, he
is trapped inside just such a town.

7. *Joab's men sallied forth.* J. P. Fokkelman must be credited with seeing what an extraordinary designation this is. David has dismissed Joab. The elite warriors are in any case
David's men (note how David has just referred to them in addressing Abishai as "your
master's servants"). The fact that they are here called "Joab's men" suggests where the real
power is, and where Joab's brother Abishai assumes it must be. The clear implication is that
the supposedly dismissed Joab is actually leading his men in the pursuit.

8. *They were just by the great stone which is in Gibeon.* Gibeon, it should be recalled, is the
very place where the civil war between the house of Saul (Israel) and the house of David
(Judah) began. That first battle (2 Samuel 2) began with a choreographed duel between
twelve champions from each side, each warrior clasping the head of his adversary and
stabbing him in the side. Joab's posture in the killing of Amasa strikingly recalls those
lethal gestures.

his battle garb, and he had on a belt for a sword strapped to his waist in its sheath, and as he came forward, it slipped out.And Joab said to Amasa, 9 "Is it well with you, my brother?" And Joab's right hand grasped Amasa's beard so as to kiss him. And Amasa did not watch out for the sword which 10 was in Joab's hand, and he struck him with it in the belly and spilled his innards to the ground—no second blow did he need—and he died. And Joab with Abishai his brother pursued Sheba son of Bichri. And a man 11 stood over him, one of Joab's lads, and said, "Whoever favors Joab and whoever is for David—after Joab!" And Amasa was wallowing in blood 12

---

he had on a belt for a sword strapped to his waist . . . and as he came forward, it slipped out. The sword—often, as here, a weapon closer to a long dagger—was customarily strapped against the left thigh, for easy unsheathing across the lower belly by a right-handed fighter. Joab may have deliberately fastened the sword to his waist so that it would slip out of the scabbard as he leaned forward to embrace Amasa. The last two verbs here are rather cryptic in the Hebrew: literally "he/it went out and she/it fell/slipped." Since "sword" is feminine in Hebrew, that is the only likely subject for "slipped," and "he" (Joab) is the plausible masculine subject for "went out" (or, "came forward"), though it could also be the scabbard. Josephus's reading of this verse remains the most persuasive one: the wily Joab, deliberately allowing his dagger to slip to the ground as he bends forward, then snatches it up with his left hand while his right hand grasps Amasa's beard.

9. *so as to kiss him.* We remember David's cool kiss to Absalom, then Absalom's demagogic kiss, as we witness this kiss, which is a prelude to murder.

10. *Amasa did not watch out for the sword which was in Joab's hand.* His attention caught by Joab's gesture of affection, Amasa does not think to look at Joab's left hand, which one would not normally expect to hold a weapon. (Has Joab learned the lesson of Ehud, Judges 3, who takes the Moabite king Eglon by surprise with a dagger thrust to the belly delivered by the left hand?) Joab's manual proficiency as a killer reinforces the perception that he struck at Absalom in the heart with sticks, not "darts," in order to hurt him badly but deliberately not to finish him off. The phrase "did not watch out" rhymes ironically with the plight of the ten concubines left to watch over the house and condemned to a house under watch.

he struck him with it in the belly and spilled his innards to the ground. It is by a blow to the belly (*homesh*) that Abner's brother Asahel died at this same place, Gibeon, and by a thrust to the belly that Joab killed Abner in revenge. The spilling of the innards implies a horrendous welter of blood, and that gruesome image of violent death will then pursue Joab through the story to his own bloody end.

11. *Whoever favors Joab and whoever is for David.* In dismissing Joab, David had severed himself from his longtime commander. This henchman of Joab's smoothly sutures the rift by bracketing Joab and David in these parallel clauses, publicly assuming that Joab is once more David's commander.

12. *Amasa was wallowing in blood . . . and . . . all the troops had come to a halt.* The soldiers come to a halt because they are confounded by seeing their commander reduced to a bloody

in the midst of the road, and the man saw that all the troops had come to
a halt, and he moved Amasa aside from the road to the field and flung a
cloak over him when he saw that all who came upon him had come to a
13 halt. When he had been removed from the road, every man passed on after
14 Joab to pursue Sheba son of Bichri. And he passed through all the tribes of
Israel to Abel of Beth-Maacah, and all the Bichrites assembled and they,
15 too, came in after him. And all the troops who were with Joab came and
besieged him in Abel of Beth-Maacah, and they heaped up a siege mound
against the town and it stood up against the rampart, and they were savag-
16 ing the wall to bring it down. And a wise woman called out from the town,

> "Listen, listen—speak, pray, to Joab,
>   approach here, that I may speak to you."

17 And he approached her, and the woman said, "Are you Joab?" And he said,
18 "I am." And she said to him, "Listen to the words of your servant." And he
said, "I am listening," And she said, saying,

---

corpse, and they also recoil from the idea of treading on the blood of the murdered man,
who lies in the midst of the roadway.

14. *And he passed through.* The switch in scene is effected, in accordance with an established
technique of biblical narrative, by a repetition of the verb in a slightly different meaning:
the Judahite soldiers "pass on" beyond the corpse at Gibeon; the object of their pursuit
"passes through" the territories of the northern tribes.
    Abel of Beth-Maacah. "Abel" means "brook." Thus "Beth-Maacah" is required in order
to distinguish it from other place-names that have a brook component. This fortified town
is located near the northern border of ancient Israel.
    they, too, came in after him. That is, they withdraw with him into the shelter of the
fortified town.

15. *savaging the wall.* This is the first of several verbal clues intended to establish a link
between this episode involving a "wise woman" and the episode of the wise woman of
Tekoa that prepared the way for Absalom's return to Jerusalem, which then eventuated
in the rebellion. Both women seek to deflect an impulse of vengeful violence. The Tekoite
implores the king to take steps "that the blood avenger not savage this much" (2 Samuel
14:11). She fears those bent on "destroying me and my son together from God's heritage"
(14:16), just as the wise woman of Abel of Beth-Maacah asks Joab, "Why should you engulf
the LORD's heritage?" He responds by saying "Far be it from me . . . that I should engulf
and that I should destroy", "destroy" uses the same root as the verb rendered as "savage."

16. *Listen, listen—speak, pray, to Joab.* As befits a professional wise woman in a place evidently famous for its oracle (see verse 18), she speaks in poetry, in a style that is elevated,
ceremonially repetitive, hieratic, and at least a little obscure.

"Surely would they speak in days of old, saying:
   'Surely will they ask counsel of Abel, and thus conclude.'
I am of the peaceable steadfast of Israel.   19
   You seek to put to death a mother city in Israel.
      Why should you engulf the LORD's heritage?"

And Joab answered and said, "Far be it from me, far be it, that I should   20
engulf and that I should destroy. It isn't so. But a man from the high coun- 21
try of Ephraim named Sheba son of Bichri has raised his hand against the
king, against David. Give over him alone, that I may turn away from the
town." And the woman said to Joab, "Look, his head is about to be flung to

---

18. *Surely would they speak . . . Surely will they ask counsel.* The Hebrew expresses this
emphasis by repeating the verbal root, first as infinitive, then in conjugated form: *daber
yedaberu, sha'ol yesha'alu.* Since the woman extravagantly uses this sort of initial reiteration three times in four clauses, the effect is incantatory. The burden of what she says here
is that Abel has long been a revered city, so why would Joab think of destroying it?

   and thus conclude. This might mean, come to a conclusion regarding the question posed
to the oracle at Abel, but the Hebrew is rather enigmatic, perhaps because the wise woman
herself is quoting an ancient proverb, in archaic language, about the town.

19. *I am of the peaceable steadfast of Israel.* She at once affirms her loyalty to the national
cause ("I am no rebel," she implies) and her commitment to peace rather than violence.
Some interpreters understand the first term of this construct chain, *shelumey 'emuney
yisra'el,* as "whole" (from *shalem*), but the context argues for a reference to peace.

   to put to death a mother city in Israel. The literal Hebrew is "town and mother," a hendiadys that clearly means something like "principal town." (The phrase would remain idiomatic in later Hebrew.) Since in biblical Hebrew the suburbs or outlying villages around a
town are called "daughters," the logic of the idiom is evident. It is, however, an idiom that
appears only here in the entire biblical corpus, and there is thematic point in its use. In
this narrative reflecting a male warrior culture and acts of terrible violence, from decapitation to evisceration, a series of female figures—Abigail, the Tekoite, the wise woman of
Abel—intervene to avert violence. The city itself is figured as a mother; its destruction
would be a kind of matricide, and the wise woman speaks on behalf of the childbearers
and nurturers of life in Israelite society to turn aside Joab's terrible swift sword.

21. *But a man from the high country of Ephraim.* This region is part of the territory of
Benjamin, Saul's tribe. By providing this identification, Joab distinguishes the rebel who
is the object of his pursuit from the non-Benjaminite inhabitants of Abel of Beth-Maacah.

   against the king, against David. By using this apposition (instead of the usual "King
David") Joab implicitly responds to some doubt as to whether in fact it is David who is the
king. Recent political events might well have triggered general questioning about David's
grip on the monarchy.

   Look, his head is about to be flung to you. This decisive woman, instead of using a simple
future form, employs a participial form introduced by the presentative *hineh,* as if to say:
it's already on the way to being done.

22 you from the wall." And the woman came in her wisdom to all the people, and they cut off the head of Sheba son of Bichri and flung it to Joab. And he blew the ram's horn and they dispersed from the town, every man to his tent, but Joab came back to Jerusalem.

23 And Joab was over all the army of Israel and Benaiah son of Johoiada was
24 over the Cherithites and the Pelethites. And Adoram was over the corvée,
25 and Jehoshaphat son of Ahilud was recorder. And Sheva was scribe, and
26 Zadok and Abiathar, priests. And Ira the Jairite was also a priest to David.

---

22. *in her wisdom.* The wisdom is her shrewdness in finding a way to avert a general massacre (as the wise Abigail had done in mollifying David, bent on vengeance) and perhaps also in the aptness of rhetoric she no doubt employs to persuade the people.

he blew the ram's horn and they dispersed . . . every man to his tent. These phrases echo the ones used in verse 1 to report the beginning of Sheba's rebellion, and thus conclude the episode in a symmetric envelope structure.

but Joab came back to Jerusalem. He comes back to Jerusalem, not to his house ("tent") in nearby Bethlehem. The implication, as Bar-Efrat notes, is that he now resumes his post as David's commander. David evidently has little say in the matter, being confronted with a fait accompli of military power. This clause then provides a motivation for the introduction of the notice of David's governing council in the next three verses.

23. *Joab was over all the army of Israel.* This list of David's royal bureaucracy parallels the one in 8:16–18, with a couple of instructive differences. The two serve as bookends to David's reign in Jerusalem. The first is introduced after he has consolidated his mini-empire, and this one after the suppression of two successive rebellions and just before the account of David's last days in 1 Kings 1–2. (As we shall see, the remaining four chapters of 2 Samuel are actually a series of appendices to the story proper and not a direct continuation of it.) In chapter 8, Joab was simply "over the army." Here, after the defeat of the secessionist northern tribes, he is said to be "over all the army of Israel." Adoram as supervisor of the corvée does not appear in the earlier list but is inserted here to anticipate the role he will play in Solomon's grand building projects, and he may in fact have been a much later appointment by David. The name of the royal scribe, Sheva, is anomalous in the Hebrew, and may be the same person identified in chapter 8 as Seraiah.

26. *And Ira the Jairite was also a priest to David.* In addition to the hereditary priests of the public cult just mentioned, David has a kind of special royal chaplain. In chapter 8, it is David's sons who are said to perform this service. Either later editors were uneasy with this intimation of priestly dynasty in the royal family, or David, after all the tribulations he has suffered because of two of his sons, decided to designate someone else as his chaplain.

CHAPTER 21   And there was a famine in the days of David 1
three years, year after year. And David sought out the presence of the LORD.
And the LORD said, "On account of Saul and on account of the house of
bloodguilt, because he put the Gibeonites to death." And the king called to 2
the Gibeonites and said to them—and the Gibeonites were not of Israelite
stock but from the remnant of the Amorites, and the Israelites had vowed
to them, but Saul sought to strike them down in his zeal for the Israelites

---

CHAPTER 21   Chapters 21–24 appear to be a series of appendices to the David story
proper, manifestly written by different writers in styles that exhibit notable differences
from that of the main narrative, and also certain differences in ideological assumptions
and even in what are presumed to be the narrative data of David's history. It should, however, be kept in mind that creating a collage of disparate sources was an established literary technique used by the ancient Hebrew editors and sometimes by the original writers
themselves. Recent critics have abundantly demonstrated the compositional coherence of
chapters 21–24 and have argued for some significant links with the preceding narrative. For
that reason, it may be preferable to think of this whole unit as a coda to the story rather than
as a series of appendices. The structure of the chapters is neatly chiastic, as follows: a story
of a national calamity in which David intercedes; a list (chapter 21); a poem (chapter 22); a
poem; a list (chapter 23); a story of a national calamity in which David interceded (chapter
24). The temporal setting of these materials is unclear but they seem to belong somewhere
in the middle of David's career, and do not follow from the late point in his reign reported
in the immediately preceding account of the rebellion of Sheba son of Bichri. The editors
placed these chapters here, rather than after David's death, and then set the account of
his last days, which they interrupt, at the beginning of 1 Kings in order to underline the
dynastic continuity between David's story and Solomon's, which then immediately follows
as the first large unit of the Book of Kings.

1. *David sought out the presence of the LORD.* The idiom means to seek an audience (with a
ruler), though what is referred to in practical terms is inquiry of an oracle. The rest of the
verse gives God's response to the question put to the oracle. At the very outset, a difference in idiom from the main narrative, where people consistently "inquire of the LORD,"
is detectable. The idiom preferred by this new author emphasizes hierarchical relationship
rather than the practical business of putting a question to the oracle.

2. *and the Gibeonites were not of Israelite stock.* The syntactic looseness of this long parenthetical sentence (compare the similar syntax in verse 5) is uncharacteristic of the David
story proper.
    the Israelites had vowed to them. The story of the vow to do no harm to this group of
resident aliens is reported in Joshua 9:15.
    but Saul sought to strike them down. There is no way of knowing whether this massacre of
Gibeonites by Saul reflects historical fact, but there is not the slightest hint of it in the story
of Saul recounted in 1 Samuel. As with the differences of style, one sees here the presence of
a distinctly different literary source.

3 and for Judah. And David said to the Gibeonites, "What shall I do for you
4 and how shall I atone, that you may bless the LORD's heritage?" And the
   Gibeonites said to him, "We have no claim of silver and gold against Saul
   and his house, and we have no man in Israel to put to death." And he said,
5 "Whatever you say, I shall do for you." And they said to the king, "The
   man who massacred us and who devastated us—we were destroyed from
6 having a stand in all the territory of Israel—let seven men of his sons be
   given to us, that we may impale them before the LORD at Gibeah of Saul,
7 the LORD's chosen." And the king said, "I will give them." And the king
   spared Mephibosheth son of Jonathan son of Saul because of the LORD's
8 vow that was between them, between David and Jonathan son of Saul. And
   the king took the two sons of Rizpah daughter of Aiah, whom she had born
   to Saul, Armoni and Mephibosheth, and the five sons of Merab daughter of
9 Saul, whom she had born to Adriel son of Barzillai the Meholathite. And
   he gave them into the hands of the Gibeonites, and they impaled them on

---

3. *What shall I do for you and how shall I atone.* The speech and acts of David in this story
show nothing of the psychological complexity of the experience-torn David whose story we
have been following. He speaks in flat terms, almost ritualistically, fulfilling his public and
cultic functions as king. And after this brief initial exchange with the Gibeonites, the writer
entirely abandons dialogue, which had been the chief instrument for expressing emotional
nuance and complication of motive and theme in the David story.

4. *We have no claim of silver and gold . . . we have no man in Israel to put to death.* The second
clause is really an opening ploy in negotiation: they say they have no claim to execute any
Israelite ("claim" in the first clause is merely implied by ellipsis in the Hebrew), suggesting that they are waiting for David to agree to hand Israelites over to them in expiation of
Saul's crime.

   Whatever you say, I shall do for you. David's submissiveness to the Gibeonites reflects a
notion of causation and the role of human action scarcely evident in the main narrative. A
famine grips the land because its former ruler violated a national vow. Collective disaster
can be averted only by the expiatory—indeed, sacrificial—offering of human lives. This
archaic world of divine retribution and ritual response is very far from the historical realm
of realpolitik in which the story of David has been played out.

6. *impale.* There is no scholarly consensus on the exact form of execution, except that it
obviously involves exhibiting the corpses. Some understand it as a kind of crucifixion.

   before the LORD at Gibeah of Saul, the LORD's chosen. "Before the LORD" is an explicit
indication of the sacrificial nature of the killings. Many scholars have doubted that the
Saulides would be executed in Saul's own town and emend this to read "at Gibeon, on the
mount of the LORD." If the phrase "the LORD's chosen" is authentic, it would be spoken
sarcastically by the Gibeonites.

8. *Merab.* This is the reading of one version of the Septuagint and of many Hebrew manuscripts. The Masoretic Text has "Michal," who had no children and who, unlike her sister
Merab, was not married to Adriel son of Barzillai.

the hill before the LORD, and the seven of them fell together. And they were put to death in the first days of the harvest, the beginning of the barley harvest. And Rizpah daughter of Aiah took sackcloth and stretched it out 10 over herself on the rock from the beginning of the harvest till the waters poured down on them from the heavens, and she did not allow the fowl of the heavens to settle on them by day nor the beasts of the field by night. And David was told what Rizpah daughter of Aiah, Saul's concubine, had 11 done. And David went and took the bones of Saul and the bones of Jonathan 12 his son from the notables of Jabesh-Gilead who had stolen them from the square of Beth-Shan, where the Philistines had hanged them on the day the Philistines struck down Saul at Gilboa. And he brought up from there 13 the bones of Saul and the bones of Jonathan his son, and they collected the bones of the impaled men. And they buried the bones of Saul and of Jona- 14 than his son in the territory of Benjamin in Zela, in the tomb of Kish his father, and they did all that the king had charged. And God then granted the plea for the land.

---

9. *the seven of them fell together.* Robert Polzin neatly observes that this phrase precisely echoes "they fell together" of 2:16—the account of the beginning of the civil war at this very same place, Gibeon. He also notes how this whole episode is organized around recurring units of three and seven, the latter number *shiv'ah* punning on the reiterated *shevu'ah*, vow.

the beginning of the barley harvest. This would be in April. The bereaved Rizpah then watches over the corpses throughout the hot months of the summer, until the rains return— heralding the end of the long famine—in the fall.

10. *Rizpah . . . took sackcloth and stretched it out over herself.* The verb here is the one gener- ally used for pitching tents, so the translations that have Rizpah spreading the cloth over the rock are misleading. What she does is to make a little lean-to with the sackcloth to shield herself from the summer sun.

she did not allow the fowl of the heavens to settle on them. The antecedent of "them" is of course the corpses. As in the ancient Greek world, leaving a corpse unburied is a primal sacrilege, a final desecration of the sacredness of the human person. Rizpah, watching over the unburied corpses, is a kind of Hebrew Antigone. David had delivered the seven descen- dants of Saul to the Gibeonites with the single-minded intention of expiating the crime that had caused the famine. Evidently, he gave no thought to the possibility that the Gibeonites would desecrate the bodies of the Saulides after killing them by denying them burial.

11. *And David was told what Rizpah . . . had done.* Rizpah's sustained act of maternal hero- ism finally achieves its end: the king is shaken out of his acquiescence in the Gibeonite inhumanity.

12. *David went and took the bones of Saul and the bones of Jonathan.* According to the account in 1 Samuel 31, they were cremated. Either this report reflects a conflicting tradi- tion or "bones" here has to be understood as "ashes."

14. *they buried the bones of Saul and of Jonathan his son. . . . And God then granted the plea for the land.* It should be noted that the end of the famine does not come with the sacrifi-

15 And once again there was fighting between the Philistines and Israel, and
   David went down, and his servants with him, and they did battle with
16 the Philistines, and David grew weary. And Ishbi-Benob, who was of the
   offspring of the titan, the weight of his weapon three hundred weights
   of bronze, and he was girded with new gear—he meant to strike down
17 David. And Abishai son of Zeruiah came to his aid and struck down the
   Philistine and put him to death. Then David's men swore to him, saying,
   "You shall not sally forth with us again to battle, lest you snuff out the
   lamp of Israel."

18 And it happened thereafter that once again there was fighting with the
   Philistines, at Gob. Then did Sibbecai the Hushathite strike down Saph,
19 who was of the offspring of the titan. And once again there was fighting

---

cial killing of the seven Saulides but only after all of them, together with Saul himself and
Jonathan, are given fitting burial in their own place (a biblical desideratum). In this strange
story, David is seen handing over the surviving offspring of Saul to be killed, but only for
the urgent good of the nation, after which he pays posthumous respect to the line of Saul.
It is conceivable that this story reflects an alternative narrative tradition to the more politically complex one of the David story proper through which David is exonerated from what
may well have been a widespread accusation that he deliberately liquidated all of Saul's
heirs, with the exception of Mephibosheth.

15. *David grew weary.* This phrase probably indicates an aging David, though not yet the
vulnerable sedentary monarch of the conflict with Absalom.

16. *Ishbi-Benob.* This name looks as bizarre in the Hebrew as in transliteration and probably
betrays a corrupt text. (The textual obscurities that abound in this section in all likelihood
reflect the fact that this is an old literary document imperfectly transmitted.) There have
been attempts to revocalize the name as a verb, but those in turn necessitate extensive
tinkering with other parts of the verse.
   of the offspring of the titan. The Hebrew *rafah* (with a definite article here) elsewhere
means "giant." The ending is feminine and it is not clear whether the reference is to a
progenitrix or a progenitor.
   the weight of his weapon. The Hebrew for "weapon," *qayin*, appears only here, and so
the translation is merely inference from context. It might be related to a word that means
"metalsmith." The invocation of the titanic weight of the weapon (spear?) is of course
reminiscent of the earlier description of Goliath.
   girded with new gear. The Hebrew says simply "girded with new [feminine ending]."
Some assume the reference is to sword, which is feminine in Hebrew.

17. *You shall not sally forth with us again.* This fragmentary episode is obviously remembered because it marks a turning point in David's career. It is at least consonant with
the image of David at Mahanaim asked by his men to stay behind as they go out to the
battlefield.

with the Philistines at Nob, and Elhanan son of Jair the Bethlehemite struck down Goliath the Gittite, and the shaft of his spear was like a weaver's beam.

And once again there was fighting, at Gath. And there was a man of huge 20 measure, who had six fingers on each hand and six toes on each foot, twenty-four in all, and he, too, was sprung from the titan. And he insulted 21 Israel, and Jonathan son of Shimei, David's kinsman, struck him down. These four were sprung from the titan, and they fell at the hand of David 22 and at the hand of his servants.

CHAPTER 22   And David spoke to the LORD the words of this 1 song on the day the LORD rescued him from the clutches of all his enemies and from the clutches of Saul, and he said: 2

---

19. *Elhanan son of Jair.* So he is identified in the parallel report in Chronicles. The Masoretic Text here reads "Elhanan son of Ja'arey 'Orgim," but the last word, *'orgim,* means "weavers," and seems clearly a scribal duplication of *'orgim* at the very end of the verse.

Elhanan. . . struck down Goliath the Gittite. This is one of the most famous contradictions in the Book of Samuel. Various attempts, both ancient and modern, have been made to harmonize the contradiction—such as the contention that "Goliath" is not a name but a Philistine title—but none of these efforts is convincing. Of the two reports, this one may well be the more plausible. In the literary shaping of the story of David, a triumph originally attributed, perhaps with good reason, to Elhanan was transferred to David and grafted onto the folktale pattern of the killing of a giant or an ogre by a resourceful young man. The writer used this material, as we have seen, to shape a vivid and arresting portrait of David's debut.

22. *These four were sprung from the titan, and they fell at the hand of David.* Stylistically, the entire unit from verse 15 to the end of the chapter has the feel of a deliberately formulaic epic catalogue (rather than an actual epic narrative, which the earlier Goliath story in 1 Samuel 17 more closely approximates). Formally, the predominant number three of the famine story is succeeded by four here—just as in biblical poetic parallelism three is conventionally followed by four (for example, Amos 1:3, "For three trespasses of Damascus / and for four, I will not turn it back").

CHAPTER 22   1. *And David spoke to the LORD the words of this song.* It was a common literary practice in ancient Israel to place a long poem or "song" (*shirah*) at or near the end of a narrative book—compare Jacob's Testament, Genesis 49, and the Song of Moses, Deuteronomy 32. In the case of the Book of Samuel, David's victory psalm and Hannah's psalm, respectively a song of the male warrior's triumph and a song contextualized as an expression of maternal triumph, enclose the large narrative like bookends, and there is even some interechoing of language between the two poems. These long

"The Lord is my crag and my fortress
  and my own deliverer.
3   God, my rock where I shelter,
       my shield and the horn of my rescue,
     My bulwark and refuge,
       my rescuer, saves me from havoc.
4   Praised! did I call the LORD,
       and from my enemies I was rescued.
5   For the breakers of death beset me,
       the underworld's torrents dismayed me.
6   The snares of Sheol coiled round me,
       the traps of death sprang against me.
7   In my strait I called to the LORD,
       to my God I called,
     And from His palace He heard my voice,
       My cry in His ears.

---

concluding poems were presumably selected by the editor or composer of the book from a variety of texts available in the literary tradition and then ascribed to a principal character of the story. There is, of course, a persistent biblical notion of David the poet as well as of David the warrior-king, and the idea that he actually composed this poem, though unlikely, cannot be categorically dismissed. In any case, most scholars (Albright, Cross and Friedman, Robertson) detect relatively archaic language in the poem and date it to the tenth century, David's time. The archaic character of the language makes the meaning of many terms conjectural. Even in the ancient period, some of the older locutions may already have been obscure to the scribes, who seem to have scrambled many phrases in transmission; but in contrast to the confident practice of many biblical scholars, caution in presuming to reconstruct the "primitive" text is prudent. It should be noted that this same poem occurs in the Book of Psalms as Psalm 18, with a good many minor textual variants. In several instances, the reading in Psalm 18 seems preferable, but here, too, methodological caution is necessary: Psalm 18 appears to be a secondary version of the poem, and its editor at least in some cases may have clarified obscurities through revision.

2. *my crag and my fortress.* Albright notes that many of the northwest Semitic gods were deified mountains. Thus the imagery of the god as a lofty rock or crag abounds in the poetic tradition upon which the biblical poet drew. It also makes particular sense for a poem of military triumph, since a warrior battling in the mountainous terrain of the land of Israel would keenly appreciate the image of protection of a towering cliff or a fortress situated on a height.

3. *horn.* The idiom is drawn from the goring horn of a charging ram or bull. In keeping with the precedent of the King James Version, it is worth preserving in English in order to suggest the concreteness and the archaic coloration of the poem.

5. *For the breakers of death beset me.* The condition of being mortally threatened is regularly figured in the poetry of Psalms as a descent, or virtual descent, into the terrifying shadows of the underworld.

The earth heaved and quaked,   8
   the heavens' foundations shuddered,
      they heaved, for He was incensed.
Smoke went up from His nostrils,   9
   consuming fire from His mouth,
      coals before Him blazed.
He tilted the heavens, came down,   10
   dense mist beneath His feet.
He mounted a cherub and flew,   11
   He soared on the wings of the wind.
He set darkness as shelters around Him,   12
   a massing of waters, the clouds of the skies.
From the radiance before Him,   13
   fiery coals blazed.
The LORD from the heavens thundered,   14
   the Most High sent forth His voice.
He let loose arrows and routed them,   15
   lightning, and struck them with panic.
The channels of the sea were exposed,   16
   the world's foundations laid bare,
by the LORD's roaring,
   the blast of His nostrils' breath.
He reached from on high and He took me,   17
   He drew me out of vast waters,
saved me from enemies fierce,   18

---

8. *The earth heaved and quaked.* God's descent from His celestial palace to do battle on behalf of his faithful servant is imagined as a seismic upheaval of the whole earth.

9. *Smoke went up from His nostrils.* The poetic representation of God, drawing on premonotheistic literary traditions such as the Ugaritic Baal epic, is unabashedly anthropomorphic. One must be cautious, however, in drawing theological inferences from this fact. Modes of literary expression exert a powerful momentum beyond their original cultural contexts, as Milton's embrace of the apparatus of pagan epic in *Paradise Lost* vividly demonstrates. The LORD figures as a fierce warrior, like Baal, because that works evocatively as poetry. This God of earthquakes and battles breathes fire: in an intensifying narrative progression from one verset to the next and then from line to line, smoke comes out of His nostrils, His mouth spews fire, in His awesome incandescence coals ignite before Him, and then He begins his actual descent from on high.

11. *He mounted a cherub and flew.* The cherub is a fierce winged beast, the traditional mount of the deity.
   He soared on the wings of the wind. The translation reads with Psalm 18 *wayeda'*, instead of the weaker *wayera'*, "He was seen" (the Hebrew graphemes for *d* and *r* being very close).

<blockquote>

from my foes who had overwhelmed me.

19   They sprang against me on my most dire day,
        but the LORD was a stay then for me.

20   He led me out to an open place.
        He freed me for He took up my cause.

21   The LORD dealt with me by my merit,
        by the cleanness of my hands, requited me.

22   For I kept the ways of the LORD,
        I did no evil before my God.

23   For all His statutes are before me,
        from His laws I have not swerved.

24   I have been blameless before Him,
        I kept myself from sin.

25   The LORD requited me by my merit,
        by the cleanness of my hands before His eyes.

26   With the loyal You act in loyalty,
        with the blameless warrior You are without blame.

27   With the pure You show Your pureness,

</blockquote>

---

19. *They sprang against me.* The verb here—its basic meaning is to meet or greet, sometimes before the person is ready—repeats "the traps of death sprang against me" in verse 6: first that act of being taken by surprise occurs metaphorically, and now again in the literal experience of the speaker on the battlefield.

21. *The LORD dealt with me by my merit.* It is often claimed that verses 21–25 are a Deuteronomistic interpolation in the poem—that is, seventh century B.C.E. or later. The evidence is not entirely persuasive because the theological notion of God's rewarding the innocence of the individual by rescuing him from grave danger is by no means a Deuteronomistic innovation, and adherence to "statutes" and "laws" (verse 23), though encouraged in the Deuteronomistic literary environment, is neither its unprecedented invention nor its unique linguistic marker.

25. *by the cleanness of my hands.* The Masoretic Text has merely "by my cleanness" (*kevori*), but the parallel version in Psalm 18 shows *kevor yadai* "by my cleanness of hands," as do the Septuagint and other ancient translations of this line. The concrete juxtaposition of idioms anchored in body parts—"cleanness of hands" for "innocence" and "before Your eyes" for "in Your sight"—is characteristic of biblical usage.

26. *with the blameless warrior You are without blame.* Many textual critics consider "warrior" to be an interpolation and either delete it or substitute for *gibor*, "warrior," *gever*, "man." The parallelism of these four versets, in each of which God, in a verb, answers in kind to the adjectivally defined human agent, is better preserved without "warrior." The profession of blamelessness scarcely accords with David's behavior in the body of the story.

with the perverse You twist and turn.
A lowly people You rescue,   28
   You cast Your eyes down on the haughty.
For You are my lamp, O LORD!   29
   The LORD has lit up my darkness.
For through You I rush a barrier,   30
   through my God I vault a wall.
The God Whose way is blameless,   31
   the LORD's speech is without taint,
     a shield He is to those who shelter in him.
For who is god but the LORD,   32
   who is a rock but our God?
The God, my mighty stronghold,   33
   He frees my way to be blameless,
makes my legs like a gazelle's,   34
   and stands me on the heights,

---

27. *twist and turn.* This English phrase represents a single reflexive verb in the Hebrew. It is the sole instance in this series of four versets in which the verb describing God's action has a root different from the adjective characterizing the kind of person to whom God responds, although there is still a manifest semantic connection between the two terms here, and this works quite nicely as a small variation on the pattern to conclude the series.

28. *A lowly people You rescue, / You cast Your eyes down on the haughty.* The opposition between low and high is conventional in the poetry of Psalms—it also figures in Hannah's Song—but is nonetheless effective. The speaker's people is "lowly" in the sense that it is miserable, afflicted, endangered by superior forces. God on high looks down on the lofty who seem to have the upper hand and, as the triumphant images from verse 39 onward make clear, brings them low.

30. *I rush a barrier . . . vault a wall.* The speaker who has just been seen among "a lowly people" and then vouchsafed a beam from God's lantern as he gropes in the dark now suddenly takes the offensive, charging the enemies' ramparts.

33. *The God, my mighty stronghold.* Although this phrase, *ma'uzi ḥayil,* is intelligible as it stands, the variant in Psalm 18, supported by the Qumran Samuel scroll, is more fluent and sustains a parallelism of verbs between the two halves of the line. That reading is *hame'azreni ḥayil,* "Who girds me with might."
  He frees my way to be blameless. The verb here, *wayater,* is problematic. The most obvious construction would be as a term that generally means "to loosen," though the syntactic link with "blameless" (there is no explicit "to be" in the Hebrew) is obscure. The version in Psalm 18 substitutes *wayiten,* "he kept" (or "set"), but the use of that all-purpose verb may simply reflect the scribe's bafflement with the original verb.

34. *makes my legs like a gazelle's, / and stands me on the heights.* The swiftness of the gazelle accords nicely with the image in verse 30 of the warrior sprinting in assault against the

35   trains my hands for combat,
               makes my arms bend a bow of bronze.
36   You gave me Your shield of rescue,
               Your battle cry made me many.
37   You lengthened my stride beneath me,
               and my ankles did not trip.
38   I pursued my foes and destroyed them,
               never turned back till I cut them down.
39   I cut them down, smashed them, they did not rise,
               they fell beneath my feet.
40   You girt me with might for combat,
               those against me You brought down beneath me,

---

ramparts of the foe. Standing secure on the heights, then, would mark the successful conclusion of his trajectory of attack: the victorious warrior now stands on the walls, or within
the conquered bastion, of the enemy. The *ai* suffix of *bamotai*, "heights," normally a sign
of the first-person possessive, is an archaic, or poetic, plural ending. The sense proposed
by some scholars of "my back [or, thighs?]" is very strained, and destroys the narrative
momentum between versets that is a hallmark of biblical poetry.

35. *makes my arms bend a bow of bronze.* The verb *niḥat* has not been satisfactorily
explained, nor is its syntactic role in the clause clear. This translation, like everyone else's,
is no more than a guess, based on the possibility that the verb reflects a root meaning "to
come down," and so perhaps refers to the bending down of a bow.

36. *Your battle cry.* This noun, *'anotkha*, is still another crux. The least farfetched deriva-
tion is from the verbal steam *'-n-h*, which means either "to answer," thus yielding a sense
here of "answering power," or "to call out," "speak up." Given the sequence of concrete
warfare images in these lines, from bronze bow to saving shield, this translation proposes,
conjecturally, "battle cry," with the established verbal noun *'anot*, "noise" or "calling-out"
in mind. Compare Exodus 32:18: "the sound of crying out in triumph" (*qol 'anot gevurah*).
The battle cry would use God's name (perhaps something like "sword of the Lord and of
David") with the idea that it had a potency that would infuse the warrior with strength
and resolution and strike fear in the enemy. Thus the battle cry makes the solitary fighter,
or the handful he leads, "many" against seemingly superior forces.

37. *You lengthened my stride beneath me, / and my ankles did not trip.* This focus on the long,
firm stride jibes with the previous images of rapid running against the enemy and anticipates the evocation in the lines that follow of the victorious warrior's feet trampling the foe.

38. *till I cut them down.* The English phrase, chosen to reflect the rhythmic compactness of
the original, represents a Hebrew verb that means "to destroy them utterly," or, "to finish
them off," but the former phrase is too much of a mouthful and the latter is the wrong level
of diction. In any event, the narrative sequence of being provided with armor and weapons
and charging against a fleeing enemy is now completed as the victor overtakes his adversaries and tramples them to death.

You showed me my enemies' nape,   41
  my foes, I demolished them.
They cried out—there was none to rescue,   42
  to the LORD, He answered them not.
I crushed them like dust of the earth,   43
  like street mud, I pounded them, stomped them.
You delivered me from the strife of peoples,   44
  kept me at the head of nations
    a people I knew not did serve me.
Foreigners cowered before me,   45
  by what the ear heard they obeyed me.
Foreigners did wither,   46
  filed out from their forts.
The LORD lives and blessed is my Rock,   47
  exalted the God, Rock of my rescue!
The God Who grants vengeance to me   48
  and brings down peoples beneath me,
frees me from my enemies,   49
  from those against me You raise me up,

---

42. *there was none to rescue, / to the LORD, He answered them not.* The frustration of the enemy's desperate prayers is meant to be a pointed contrast to the situation of the speaker of the poem, who calls out to the LORD and is saved (verse 4).

44. *the strife of peoples.* The translation follows the minor variation of the parallel reading in Psalm 18, *merivey ʿam,* literally, "the strife of people." The Masoretic Text here reads *merivey ʿami,* "the strife of my people," which may simply mean the battles in which my people is embroiled, but it also inadvertently suggests internal strife. Despite the presence of Saul in the poem's superscription, the immediately following lines here indicate external enemies.
   kept me at the head of nations. This phrase and the language of the next verset are perfectly consonant with David's creation of an imperial presence among the peoples of the trans-Jordan region.

45. *Foreigners cowered before me.* All that can be said in confidence about the Hebrew verb is that it indicates something negative. The common meaning of the root is "to deny" or "to lie." Perhaps that sense is linked in this instance with the foreigners' fawning on their conqueror.

46. *filed out from their forts.* The meanings of both the verb and the noun are in dispute. The verb *ḥagar* usually means "to gird," but the text in Psalm 18, more plausibly, inverts the second and third consonants, yielding *ḥarag,* which is generally taken to mean "emerge from," or "pop out from," a restrictive framework. The noun *misgerotam* is clearly derived from the root *s-g-r,* "to close," and "fort" (an enclosure) seems fairly plausible. (The proposal of "collar" has little biblical warrant and makes rather bad sense in context.)

from a man of violence You save me.

50   Therefore I acclaim You among nations, O Lᴏʀᴅ,
and to Your name I would hymn.

51   Tower of rescue to His king,
keeping faith with His anointed,
for David and his seed, forever."

1 CHAPTER 23   And these are the last words of David:

"Thus spoke David son of Jesse,
thus spoke the man raised on high,
anointed of the God of Jacob,
and sweet singer of Israel.

---

50. *Therefore I acclaim You . . . O Lᴏʀᴅ.* In keeping with a formal convention of the thanksgiving psalm, or *todah*, the poem concludes by explicitly stating that the speaker has acclaimed or given thanks (the verb cognate with the noun *todah*) to God.

and to your name I would hymn. The pairing in poetic parallelism of the two verbs, *hodah*, "acclaim," and *zimer*, "hymn," is common in the conclusion of thanksgiving psalms.

51. *Tower of rescue.* The variant reading in Psalm 18, supported by the consonantal text here but not by its Masoretic vocalization, is "making great the rescues [or victories] of" (instead of the noun, *migdol*, "tower," the verb *magdil*, "to make big"). The one attraction of the Masoretic reading here of this word is that it closes the poem with an image that picks up the multiple metaphors of a lofty stronghold at the beginning.

keeping faith with His anointed, / for David and his seed, forever. Many critics have seen the entire concluding verse as an editorial addition, both because of the switch to a third-person reference to the king and because of the invocation of dynasty, beyond the temporal frame of the warrior-king's own victories. The inference, however, is not inevitable. Switches in grammatical person, even in a single clause, occur much more easily in biblical Hebrew than in modern Western languages, and if the triumphant speaker of the poem is actually David or in any event is imagined to be David, it is quite possible that he would conclude his account of attaining imperial greatness by a prayer that the dynasty he has founded will continue to enjoy God's steadfast support for all time.

CHAPTER 23   1. *these are the last words of David.* David's victory psalm in the preceding chapter is now followed by a second archaic poetic text, quite different in style, unrelated to the psalm tradition, and a good deal obscurer in many of its formulations. Although there is scholarly debate about the dating of this poem, the consensus puts it in or close to David's own time in the tenth century ʙ.ᴄ.ᴇ. The mystifying features of the language certainly suggest great antiquity, and it is just possible that the poem was really by David. The exact application of "the last words of David" is unclear. In terms of the narrative, they are not literally his last words because he will convey a deathbed testament

> The LORD's spirit has spoken in me,   2
>   his utterance on my tongue.
> The God of Israel has said,   3
>   to me the Rock of Israel has spoken:
> He who rules men, just,
>   who rules in the fear of God.
> Like morning's light when the sun comes up,   4
>   morning without clouds,
>   from radiance, from showers—grass from earth.
> For is not thus my house with God?   5

to Solomon (1 Kings 2). The phrase might be intended to designate the last pronouncement in poetry of David the royal poet.

Thus spoke David. This introductory formula is a mark of prophetic or oracular language—compare the beginning of Balaam's third oracle in Numbers 24:3.

raised on high. The two Hebrew words reflected in this translation, *huqam 'al*, have a gorgeous strangeness as compacted idiom—so strange that both the Septuagint and the Qumran Samuel prefer a more common Hebrew locution, *heqim 'el*, "God has raised up." In either case, the phrase refers to David's elevation to the throne.

sweet singer of Israel. The eloquent and famous wording of the King James Version (KJV) seems worth emulating (though the KJV uses "psalmist"), because the divergent proposals for understanding the phrase are scarcely more certain than that of the KJV. The literal meaning of *ne'im zemirot yisra'el* is "sweet one [or favorite] of the chants of Israel." The root *z-m-r* has a homonymous meaning—strength—which has encouraged some interpreters to construe this as "preferred of the Strong One [or Stronghold] of Israel" in parallel to "anointed of the God of Israel." It must be said, however, that there are no instances in which the root *z-m-r* in the sense of strength serves as an epithet for the deity.

2. *The LORD's spirit has spoken in me.* This does not mean, as some have understood, that David is claiming actual status as a prophet but rather that he is attesting to an access of oracular elevation as he proclaims his lofty (and enigmatic!) verse.

3. *He who rules men, just.* The translation reproduces the cryptic (elliptic?) syntax of the Hebrew, adding a clarifying comma (the Hebrew of course has no punctuation).

who rules in the fear of God. The compacted syntax of the Hebrew has no "in," but most interpreters assume it is implied.

4. *from radiance, from showers—grass from earth.* The meaning of these images is much disputed, and some critics move "from radiance" altogether back to the preceding clause. The tentative reading presumed by the translation is as follows: The anointed king has been compared to the brilliant rising sun on a cloudless morning (solar imagery for kings being fairly common in ancient Near Eastern literature). The poet now adds that from the sun's radiance, coupled with rainfall, grass springs forth from the earth. Thus the rule of the just king is a source of blessed fruitfulness to his subjects.

5. *For is not thus my house with God?* The Hebrew grammar here is a little confusing. It is most plausible to construe both this clause and the one at the end of the verse not as

An eternal covenant He gave me,
>   drawn up in full and guaranteed.
For all my triumph and all my desire
>   will He not bring to bloom?

6   And the worthless man is like a thorn—
>   uprooted every one,
>   they cannot be picked up by hand.

7   Should a man touch them,
>   he must get himself iron
>   or the shaft of a spear.
And in fire they'll be utterly burned where they are."

8 These are the names of the warriors of David: Josheb-Basshebeth, a Tahchemonite, head of the Three, he is Adino the Eznite. He brandished his

---

negative statements but as affirmative questions. The image of bringing to bloom in the
concluding clause suggests that David's dynasty in relation to God is to be imagined like
the earth in relation to sun and showers and like the people in relation to the king: because
of the everlasting covenant with David, God will make his house blossom.

6. *the worthless man is like a thorn— / uprooted every one.* The antithesis between flourishing soft grass and the prickly thorn torn from its roots is manifest (though it must be said
that "uprooted" for the obscure *munad* is conjectural, if widely accepted).

7. *he must get himself iron.* The translation adopts the common proposal that the verb
yimale' (literally, "he will fill") is an ellipsis for *yimale' yado,* "he will fill his hand," "equip
himself with"). Others emend it to read *'im lo',* "except [with]."
   or the shaft of a spear. The Hebrew is usually construed as "and the shaft," but the particle *waw* does occasionally have the force of "or," which is more plausible here.
   in fire they'll be utterly burned. The only suitable disposition of these nasty thorns is to
rake them up with an iron tool or a spear shaft and make a bonfire of them, in order to get
entirely rid of the threat they pose. The fact that weapons are used for the raking suggests
the political referent of the metaphor. Such will be the fate of mischief makers ("the worthless")—evidently all who would presume to oppose the legitimate monarchy.
   where they are. This phrase reflects a single, highly dubious word in the Masoretic Text,
bashavet. That word may well be an inadvertent repetition by a baffled scribe of the seventh
Hebrew word in the following verse. The whole phrase in which that term occurs is itself
textually problematic.

8. *These are the names of the warriors of David.* This list of military heroes and their exploits
is perhaps the strongest candidate of any passage in the Book of Samuel to be considered
a text actually written in David's lifetime. The language is crabbed, and the very abundance of textual difficulties, uncharacteristic for prose, reflects the great antiquity of the
list. These fragmentary recollections of particular heroic exploits do not sound like the
invention of any later writer but, on the contrary, like memories of remarkable martial
acts familiar to the audience (for example, "he . . . killed the lion in the pit on the day of
the snow" [verse 20]) and requiring only the act of epic listing, not of narrative elabora-

spear over eight hundred slain at a single time. And after him Eleazar son 9
of Dodo son of Ahohi, of the three warriors with David when they insulted
the Philistines gathered there for battle and the Israelites decamped. He 10
arose and struck down Philistines until his hand tired and his hand stuck
to the sword. And the LORD wrought a great victory on that day, and the
troops came back after him only to strip the slain. And after him Shammah 11
son of Agei the Ararite. And the Philistines gathered at Lehi, and there was
a plot of land there full of lentils, and the troops had fled before the Philistines. And he took a stand in the plot and saved it and struck down the 12
Philistines. And the LORD wrought a great victory. And three of the Thirty, 13
at the head, went down in the harvest to David at the cave of Adullam, with
the Philistine force camped in the Valley of Rephaim. And David was then 14
in the stronghold and the Philistine garrison then at Bethlehem. And David 15
had a craving and said, "Who will give me water to drink from the well of
Bethlehem, which is by the gate?" And the three warriors broke through 16

---

tion. It should also be noted that the list invokes the early phase of David's career—when
the Philistines were the dominant military force in the land, when David was at Adullam
and in "the stronghold," and when Asahel, destined to perish at the hands of Abner at the
beginning of the civil war, was an active member of David's corp of elite fighters.

Josheb-Basshebeth a Tahchemonite. So reads the Masoretic Text. But this looks quite
dubious as a Hebrew name. One version of the Septuagint has Ish-Baal (alternately, Jeshbaal),
which by scribal euphemism also appears as Ish-Bosheth and hence may have produced
the confusion in the Masoretic Text. Many authorities prefer the gentilic "Hachmoni," in
accordance with the parallel verse in Chronicles.

the Three. Throughout the list, there are confusions between three, third, and thirty.
The received text at this point seems to read *shalishim,* "commanders of units of thirty,"
but "three" makes far better sense.

He brandished his spear. This whole phrase, which seems strictly necessary to make
the sentence intelligible, is lacking in the Masoretic Text but appears in the parallel verse
in Chronicles.

10. *to strip the slain.* No object of the verb "to strip" appears in the Hebrew, but this may be
a simple ellipses for a common military idiom rather than a scribal omission.

11. *at Lehi.* The translation presupposes a minor emendation of the Masoretic *lahayah*
(meaning obscure, though some understand it as "in a force") to *lehi,* a place-name, which
the rest of the clause seems to require.

there was a plot of land there full of lentils. The homey specificity of the detail is another
manifestation of the feeling of remembered anecdote in this catalogue of exploits.

13. *at the head.* The Hebrew says only "head," but the word seems to have an adverbial function, and so "at the head" is not unlikely.

15. *Who will give me water to drink from the well of Bethlehem.* Or "Would that I might
drink water . . ." Bethlehem, of course, is David's hometown, at this juncture a headquarters
of the occupying Philistine forces. David expresses a sudden yen to taste the sweet water

the Philistine camp and drew water from the well of Bethlehem, which is
by the gate, and they bore it off and brought it to David. But he would not
17 drink it, and he poured it out in libation to the LORD. And he said, "Far be
it from me that I should do such a thing. Shall I drink the blood of men who
have gone at the risk of their lives?" And he would not drink it. These things
18 did the three warriors do. And Abishai brother of Joab son of Zeruiah—he
was chief of the Thirty. And he brandished his spear over three hundred
19 slain, and he had a name with the Three. Of the Thirty he was most honored and so he became their captain, but he did not attain to the Three.
20 And Benaiah son of Jehoida from Kabzeel, son of a valiant man, great in
deeds—he struck down the two sons of Ariel of Moab and he went down
21 and killed the lion in the pit on the day of the snow. And he struck down
an Egyptian man, a man of daunting appearance, a spear was in the hand
of the Egyptian. And he went down to him with a staff and stole the spear
22 from the hand of the Egyptian and he killed him with his own spear. These
things did Benaiah son of Jehoida do, and he had a name with the Three

---

he remembers from that well by the gate of his native town, although he scarcely intends
this as a serious invitation to his men to undertake anything so foolhardy as to attempt
breaking through the Philistine lines in order to get it. Presumably, the three warriors—it
is unclear as to whether they are identical with the Three just named, for they are said to
be part of the Thirty—do not misunderstand David's intentions. Rather, as daring fighters,
they decide to take him at his word and risk their necks in raiding the Philistine garrison
at Bethlehem in order to prove they can execute a seemingly impossible mission. It is easy
to understand how such an exploit would be vividly recalled and registered in the epic list.

17. *Shall I drink the blood of men.* The verb (one word in the Hebrew) "shall I drink" is missing from the Masoretic Text, though present in both the parallel verse in Chronicles and
in the Septuagint. It is possible that some ancient scribe recoiled from an expression that
had David drinking human blood, even in a hyperbolic verbal gesture.

18. *he was chief of the Thirty.* The received text here and in verse 19 reads "Three," but this
makes no sense, as we are told that Abishai "did not attain to the Three."
     with the Three. Or, "in the three." Since Abishai is not a member of the Three, this
would have to mean that his prowess won him a reputation even among the legendary
Three. Another solution is to emend the initial *ba* ("in," "among") to *ka* ("like"), yielding
"he had a name like the Three."

20. *son of a valiant man.* Many textual critics conclude that "son of" (*ben*) is an erroneous
scribal addition.
     he struck down the two sons of Ariel of Moab. These words are among the most enigmatic
in the report of the exploits of David's heroes. The words "two sons of" (*sheney beney*) are
supplied from the Septuagint in an effort to make this clause at least a little intelligible.
"Ariel" is probably a cultic site or object in Moab.

22. *he had a name with the Three Warriors.* See the comment on verse 18. The same problem
is reflected here.

Warriors. Of the Thirty he was honored but he did not attain to the Three. 23
And David put him over his royal guard. Asahel brother of Joab was in the 24
Thirty, and Elhanan son of Dodo of Bethlehem. Shammah the Harodite, 25
Elika the Harodite, Helez the Paltite, Ira son of Ikkesh the Tekoite, Abiezer 26,27
the Anathothite, Mebunnai the Hushathite. Zalmon the Ahohite, Maha- 28
rai the Netophathite, Heleb son of Baanah the Netophathite, Ittai son of 29
Ribai from Gibeah of the Benjaminites, Benaiah the Pirathonite, Hiddai 30
from Nahalei-Gaash, Abi-Albon the Anbathite, Azmaveth the Barhumite, 31
Eliahba the Shaalbonite, sons of Jashen Jonathan, Shammah the Hararite, 32,33
Ahiam son of Sharar the Ararite, Eliphelet son of Ahasbai son of the Maa- 34
cathite, Eliam son of Ahitophel the Gilonite, Hezrai the Carmelite, Paarai 35
the Arbite, Igal son of Nathan from Zobah, Bani the Gadite, Zelek the 36,37
Ammonite, Naharai the Beerothite, armor bearer to Joab son of Zeruiah,
Ira the Ithrite, Gareb the Ithrite, Uriah the Hittite—thirty-seven in all. 38,39

CHAPTER 24   And once more the wrath of the LORD was 1
kindled against Israel, and He incited David against them, saying, "Go,

---

25. *the Harodite.* All these identifying terms in the list designate the villages from which the warriors come. A likely location of the biblical Harod would be not far from Bethlehem. The earlier names in the list cluster geographically in the territory of Judah, David's tribe. Some of the later names indicate places in the territories of tribes to the north—perhaps reflecting new recruits to the elite unit after the conclusion of the civil war. Toward the end of the list there are also non-Israelites: these could have been mercenaries, or perhaps rather naturalized subjects of the new monarchy.

32. *sons of Jashen Jonathan.* This identification definitely looks scrambled. "Sons of" appears not to belong, and many textual critics omit it. "Jonathan," as a second proper name immediately after "Jashen," is also problematic, and one wonders whether Jashen (Hebrew *yashen* means "sleeping") was ever a name.

34. *Eliam son of Ahitophel.* One notes that the son of the state councillor who betrayed David for Absalom was a member of David's elite corps. He might also be the same Eliam who is Bathsheba's father.

39. *Uriah the Hittite.* Is it an intended irony that the list of David's picked warriors concludes with the man he murdered? The irony may be an artifact of the editor, if this list was composed after the events recorded in the Bathsheba story.
    thirty-seven in all. As elsewhere in biblical tabulations, it is hard to make this figure compute. One system of counting yields a total of thirty-six, and the addition of Joab—rather surprisingly, omitted from the list—would produce thirty-seven.

CHAPTER 24   1. *And once more the wrath of the LORD was kindled against Israel.* The reason for God's wrath is entirely unspecified, and attempts to link it to events in the preceding narrative are quite unconvincing. In fact, this entire narrative unit (which some

2 count Israel and Judah." And the king said to Joab, commander of the force
that was with him, "Go round, pray, among all the tribes of Israel, from Dan
to Beersheba, and take a census of the people, that I may know the number
3 of the people." And Joab said to the king, "May the LORD your God add to
the people a hundred times over with the eyes of my lord the king behold-
4 ing. But why should my lord the king desire this thing?" And the king's
word prevailed over Joab and over the commanders of the force, and Joab,
and the commanders of the force with him, went out from the king's
5 presence to take a census of the people, of Israel. And they crossed the
Jordan and camped in Aroer south of the town, which is in the middle of

---

scholars claim is itself composite) is strikingly different in theological assumptions, in
its imagination of narrative situation and character, and even in its style from the David
story proper as well as from the tale of David and the Gibeonites in chapter 21 with which
it is symmetrically paired. Perhaps, indeed, there is no discernible reason for God's fury
against Israel. The God of this story has the look of acting arbitrarily, exacting terrible
human costs in order to be placated. Unlike the deity of 1 Samuel 1–2 Samuel 20, He is
decidedly an interventionist God, pulling the human actors by strings, and He may well
be a capricious God, here "inciting" David to carry out a census that will only bring grief
to the people.

2. *Joab, commander of the force.* A different vocabulary is another indication that a different writer is at work here. Throughout the David narrative, Joab is designated *sar hatsava'*,
"commander of the army," but here the terminology changes to the unusual *sar hahayil*,
"commander of the force." Similarly, the verb for "go round," *sh-w-t*—it is attached to the
Adversary in the frame story of Job—is distinctive of this narrative.

3. *But why should my LORD the king desire this thing?* Underlying the story is both a cultic
and a superstitious fear of the census, reflected in Joab's objection to it. Several commentators have noted that according to Exodus 30:12 every Israelite counted in a census was
required to pay a half shekel as "ransom" (*kofer*) for his life. Since such payment could not
be realistically expected in a total census of the nation, masses of people would be put in
a condition of violation of ritual. But there is also a folkloric horror of being counted as
a condition of vulnerability to malignant forces. In Rashi's words: "For the evil eye holds
sway over counting." Beyond these considerations, Joab the commander may have a political concern in mind: the census served as the basis for conscription (compare the notation
in verse 9 of those counted as "sword-wielding men"), and thus imposing the census might
conceivably have provoked opposition to the threatened conscription and to the king who
was behind it. It is noteworthy that the census is carried out by army officers.

5. *they crossed the Jordan and camped in Aroer.* Aroer is roughly fifteen miles east of the
Dead Sea. The trajectory of the census takers describes a large ellipsis: first to the southeast
from Jerusalem, then north through trans-Jordan to Gilead and beyond, then west through
the northernmost Israelite territory to the sea, then all the way south to Beersheba, and
back to Jerusalem. All this, which will lead to wholesale death, is accomplished in nine
months and twenty days—the human gestation period.

the Wadi of Gad and by Jazer. And they came to Gilead and to the region 6
of Tahtim-Hodshi, and they came to Dan-Jaan and round toward Sidon.
And they came to the fortress of Tyre and to all the towns of the Hivvite 7
and the Canaanite, and they went out to the Negeb of Judah, to Beersheba.
And they went round through all the land and returned at the end of 8
nine months and twenty days to Jerusalem. And Joab gave the number 9
of the census of the people to the king, and Israel made up eight hundred
thousand sword-wielding men, and Judah five hundred thousand men.
And David was smitten with remorse afterward for having counted the 10
people. And David said to the LORD, "I have offended greatly in what I
have done. And now, LORD, remit the guilt of your servant, for I have
been very foolish." And David arose in the morning, and the word of the 11
LORD had come to Gad the prophet, David's seer, saying, "Go and speak 12
to David—'Thus says the LORD: Three things I have taken against you.
Choose you one of them, and I shall do it to you. Seven years of famine 13
in your land, or three months when you flee before your foes as they
pursue you, or let there be three days of plague in your land.' Now, mark
and see, what reply shall I bring back to Him Who sent me?" And David 14
said to God, "I am in great straits. Let us, pray, fall into the LORD's hand,
for great is His mercy, and into the hand of man let me not fall." And the 15

---

6. *Tahtim-Hodshi.* The name is suspect, but efforts to recover an original name behind it
remain uncertain.

7. *the fortress of Tyre.* Evidently a mainland outpost to the south of Tyre proper, which was
on an island.

9. *sword-wielding.* The Hebrew says literally "sword-drawing."

10. *I have offended greatly in what I have done.* In contrast to the cogent sense of moral
agency and moral responsibility in the David story proper, there is a peculiar contradiction here: David confesses deep contrition, yet he has, after all, been manipulated by God
("incited") to do what he has done.

11. *Gad the prophet, David's seer.* Gad was mentioned earlier (1 Samuel 22:5). His appearance here by no means warrants the claim of Kyle McCarter Jr. and others that this story
is the work of a "prophetic" writer. Visionary intermediaries between king and God were
a common assumption in the ancient world. Gad is called "seer" (*hozeh*), not the way prophetic writers would ordinarily think of prophets (and also not the term used for Samuel
in 1 Samuel 9). Above all, the prophetic current in biblical literature does not presuppose
either this kind of arbitrarily punitive God or the accompanying hocus-pocus with choices
of punishment and divine messengers of destruction visible to the human characters.

14. *Let us . . . fall into the LORD's hand . . . and into the hand of man let me not fall.* There
is a puzzle in David's choice because only one of the three punishments—the flight from

Lord sent a plague against Israel from morning until the fixed time, and
from Dan to Beersheba seventy-seven thousand men of the people died.

16   And the messenger reached out his hand against Jerusalem to destroy it,
and the Lord regretted the evil and said to the messenger who was sowing
destruction among the people, "Enough! Now stay your hand." And the
17   Lord's messenger was at the threshing floor of Araunah the Jebusite. And

---

enemies—clearly involves human agency. Perhaps David has in mind that an extended
famine would lead to absolute dependence on those foreign nations unaffected by the
famine, as in the story of Joseph's brothers going down to Egypt. In all this, it should
be noted that David is scarcely the same character we have seen in the body of his story.
Instead of that figure of conflicting feelings and emotions so remarkable in psychological
depth, we have a flat character instigated to act by God, then expressing remorse, then
speaking in rather official tones in his role as political ruler and cultic chief responsible
for all the people.

15. *the fixed time.* There is some question about what this refers to, though the grounds for
emending the text to solve the problem are shaky. The phrase ought logically to refer to the
end of the ordained three days of the plague. Yet David's intercession to stop the plague short
before it engulfs Jerusalem suggests that the plague does not go on for the full three days.
The difficulty might be resolved simply by assuming that the initial verb—"and the Lord
sent a plague against Israel"—refers to the initiating of the process according to the promised time limitations: God sends a plague against Israel intended to rage for the stipulated
time of three days, but after it has devastated the people on a terrible scale for a certain time
(perhaps two days?), David, aghast that these horrors should visit his own city as well, takes
steps to induce God to cut the plague short.

16. *And the messenger reached out his hand against Jerusalem to destroy it.* Once again, the
apparatus and the theology of this story reflect a different imaginative world from that
of the main narrative about David, in which there are no divine emissaries of destruction brandishing celestial swords. The text of the Qumran Samuel scroll, paralleled in
1 Chronicles 21, makes the mythological character of this story even clearer: "and David
raised his eyes and saw a messenger of the Lord standing between earth and heaven, his
sword unsheathed in his hand reaching out against Jerusalem, and David and the elders
fell on their faces, covered with sackcloth."
    stay your hand. Literally, "let your hand go slack, unclench it."
    the Lord's messenger was at the threshing floor of Araunah the Jebusite. In this fashion,
the last-minute averting of the destruction of Jerusalem is linked with the etiological tale
explaining how the site of the future temple was acquired. (Although the Temple is not
explicitly mentioned, this acquisition of an altar site in Jerusalem is clearly placed here to
prepare the way for the story of Solomon the temple builder that is to follow.) Thus, the first
sacrifice offered on this spot is associated with a legendary turning away of wrath from
Jerusalem—a token of the future function of the Temple. The name Araunah is not Semitic
and is generally thought to be Hittite or Hurrian. Some scholars claim it is a title, not a name.
In any event, Araunah's presence indicates that the conquered Jebusites were not massacred
or entirely banished but continued to live in Jerusalem under David as his subjects.

David said to the LORD when he saw the messenger who was striking down the people, thus he said, "It is I who offended, I who did wrong. And these sheep, what have they done? Let your hand be against me and my father's house." And Gad came to David on that day and said to him, "Go up, raise 18 to the LORD an altar on the threshing floor of Araunah the Jebusite." And 19 David went up according to the word of Gad, as the LORD had charged. And Araunah looked out and saw the king and his servants crossing over 20 toward him, and Araunah went out and bowed down to the king, his face to the ground. And Araunah said, "Why has my lord the king come to his 21 servant?" And David said, "To buy the threshing floor from you to build an altar to the LORD, that the scourge may be held back from the people. And Araunah said to David, "Let my lord the king take and offer up what 22 is good in his eyes. See the oxen for the burnt offering and the threshing boards and the oxen's gear for wood. All of it Araunah has, O king, given 23 to the king." And Araunah said to the king, "May the LORD your God show you favor." And the king said to Araunah, "Not so! I will surely buy it from 24

---

17. *It is I who offended.* The Qumran text reads here, "It is I, the shepherd, who did evil." That, of course, neatly complements "these sheep" in the next clause, but it is hard to know whether "shepherd" was original or added by a later scribe to clarify the sheep metaphor.

21. *Why has my LORD the king come to his servant?* Isaac Abravanel aptly notes that it would not have been customary for the king to come to his subject: "You should have sent for me, for the lesser man goes to the greater and the greater does not go to the lesser." Abravanel, a councillor to Ferdinand and Isabella who was in the end exiled by them, would have been keenly familiar with such protocol.

to build an altar to the LORD, that the scourge may be held back. According to the ritualistic assumptions of this narrative, it requires not merely contrition but a special sacrifice to placate the deity. This leads one to suspect that the story, far from being prophetic literature, may have originated in some sort of priestly circle.

22. *Let my lord . . . take . . . what is good in his eyes.* In this whole exchange, there is a distinct parallel to Abraham's bargaining with Ephron the Hittite for the purchase of a gravesite at Hebron in Genesis 23. Ephron, too, first offers to make a gift to Abraham of what he requires, but the patriarch, like David here, insists on paying full price in order to have undisputed possession of the property.

the oxen for the burnt offering and the threshing boards and the oxen's gear. What Araunah does not offer David is the land itself, which he clearly wants. Both the threshing board and the "gear" (presumably, the yoke) would have been wooden. Since the sacrifice needs to be performed at once in order to avert the plague, Araunah is quick to offer not only the sacrificial beasts but firewood on the spot.

23. *All of it Araunah has, O king, given to the king.* The Hebrew, with the repeated "king," looks peculiar, though it is intelligible if the first "king" is construed as a vocative. Some emend the verse to read "all of it has Araunah your servant given to my lord the king."

you for a price, and I will not offer up burnt offerings to the LORD my God
at no cost." And David bought the threshing floor and the oxen for fifty
25 shekels of silver. And David built there an altar to the LORD and offered up
burnt offerings and well-being sacrifices, and the LORD granted the plea
for the land and the scourge was pulled back from Israel.

---

25. *the LORD granted the plea for the land.* This is, of course, a near verbatim repetition of the
words that conclude the story of David and the Gibeonites' execution of the descendants of
Saul (21:14). The repetition may well be an editorial intervention intended to underscore the
symmetry between the tale of a scourge averted by David's intercession at the beginning
and at the end of this large composite coda to 1 and 2 Samuel. Although neither of these
stories is especially continuous with the David story proper, both reflect a connection with
it in the emphasis on guilt that the king incurs, which brings disaster on the nation and
which requires expiation. But the writer of genius responsible for the larger David narrative
imagines guilt in far more probing moral terms and does not assume that the consequences
of moral offenses and grave political misjudgments can be reversed by some ritual act.

KINGS

∎ ∎ ∎

Introduction

The Book of Kings, like the Book of Samuel, as Josephus and early rabbinic sources indicate, was originally one book, not two. Its first two chapters, moreover, are clearly a completion of the story of David, showing the masterly hand of the great writer who fashioned the long narrative of Israel's founding king. The ancient editors set this material at the beginning of the Book of Kings because it reports Solomon's accession to the throne, though that story is intertwined with the wrenching portrait of the aging and failing David and his troubled relationship with his henchman Joab and his actual and potential enemies within and without the court. Once this story is completed, the Book of Kings proper exhibits an approach to politics, character, and historical causation that is quite different from the one that informs the David story.

Kings proves to be the most miscellaneous of the books assembled as the Former Prophets, although all of them are composite at least to some degree. The encompassing redactional framework is patently Deuteronomistic. The measure of every king is whether he did evil in the eyes of the LORD, and doing evil, with only a few limited exceptions, is conceived in cultic terms. The Deuteronomistic compiler repeatedly invokes the stipulation that there can be only one legitimate place of worship, which is the temple in Jerusalem—an idea that became firmly entrenched only with King Josiah's reforms around 621 B.C.E., scant decades before the Babylonian exile. Through most of these stories, the editor holds clearly in view the destruction of the northern kingdom of Israel in 721 B.C.E. and evidently also the destruction of the southern kingdom of Judah in 586 B.C.E. Since there is no hint, even at the end of the narrative, of any return to Zion after the exile, scholars have plausibly inferred that the book as a whole was put together in the early decades after the destruction of Judah.

It was put together, however, from a variety of widely disparate sources, which is why it is best to think of the person or persons responsible for its final form as a compiler or compilers. The large unit at the very beginning (1 Kings 1–11) in itself illustrates the composite character of the book as a whole. The first two chapters, as I have noted, belong to the end of the David story, exhibiting its brilliant deployment of dialogue and of techniques of narrative repetition and its shrewd sense of realpolitik. Chapter 3 begins with an emphatically theological story of God's appearance to Solomon in a dream and the king's request for the gift of wisdom. This encounter with the divine is followed in the second half of the chapter by the often recalled Judgment of Solomon, a fable obviously meant to illustrate his wisdom and clearly reflecting a different narrative genre, the folktale. Chapter 4 is a roster of Solomon's royal bureaucracy, quite different from anything that precedes it.

The first half of chapter 5 is taken up with a report of the material grandeur of Solomon's court and of his unsurpassed wisdom, manifested in his composition of proverbs and poems. The next two and a half chapters focus on Solomon's great building projects, the Temple and the palace, undertaken with the collaboration of Hiram king of Tyre. Chapter 8 recounts the dedication of the Temple, most of it being the grand speech delivered by Solomon on that occasion (and deemed by many scholars to be a later composition). Chapter 9 begins with God's theologically freighted response to Solomon, then moves on to more of his royal projects. In chapter 10 we get the enchanting folktale of the visit to Solomon's court of the Queen of Sheba. The following chapter, the last in Solomon's story, switches gears to show us the hitherto exemplary king led into the encouraging of pagan practices by his sundry foreign wives.

At the very end of the Solomon narrative, the editor informs us that "the rest of the acts of Solomon and all that he did, and his wisdom, are they not written in the Book of the Acts of Solomon?" (1 Kings 11:42). We may infer that at least some of the material in chapters 3–11 was drawn from this source, which seems to have been some sort of court annal. The reports of the royal bureaucracy and of Solomon's building projects, including a great abundance of architectural details and catalogues of furnishings, and of his marriage to Pharaoh's daughter, are likely candidates for this annalistic source. Other sources appear to have been tapped for the two folktales and probably also for the account at the end of Solomon's backsliding into pagan ways.

The sundry stories of the kings that come after the Solomon narrative approximately follow this pattern of drawing together disparate documents. More than any other narrative book of the Bible, the stories in Kings are repeatedly and insistently framed by formulaic declarations. Wayward monarchs being preponderant, one king after another is said to swerve from the ways of the LORD, and in the case of the northern kingdom, to follow the dire path of its founder, Jeroboam son of Nebat, who offended and led Israel to offend. Again and again, the compiler, with his overriding concern for the exclusivity of the cult in the Jerusalem temple, inveighs against both northern and southern kings in formulaic language for allowing the people to burn incense and offer sacrifice on "the high places," that is, local rural altars. And the story of each king is concluded, like Solomon's, by a notation that the rest of the acts of this monarch are recorded in the Book of the Acts of the Kings of Judah or the Book of the Acts of the Kings of Israel, depending on whether the king is southern or northern.

The reasonable inference from this editorial procedure is that much of the factual material of the Book of Kings was drawn from these two annalistic sources, one for the Kingdom of Judah and the other for the Kingdom of Israel. There is no way of knowing how much of the two lost annals was left out of the canonical text, though it seems likely that a good deal of circumstantial detail about the various kings was deemed irrelevant to this narrative, encompassing four centuries of Israelite history, that is meant to expound the cumulative chain of actions that led to two nationally traumatic events, the destruction of the northern kingdom in 721 B.C.E. and, 135 years later, the destruction of its southern counterpart.

But we should not think of the Book of Kings merely as a series of extracts from two sets of royal annals. The Deuteronomistic editor provides a good deal of interpretation of the events, especially in his repeated insistence that cultic disloyalty to YHWH brought about the national catastrophes, and in all likelihood he also introduces some of his own narrative invention in order to support his interpretation of the history he conveys. Beyond these interventions, he incorporates materials from sources that are clearly not annalistic. In the later chapters of 2 Kings, there are a few extended passages perhaps taken directly from a narrative section of Isaiah, and, at the very end, a short section is drawn from Jeremiah (although it could well be the other way around—that the two Prophetic books drew from Kings). Elsewhere, there are numerous stories about prophets—not "writing prophets" but men of God who roam the countryside and are active players in the political realm—that have a strong folkloric stamp. Scholars have conjectured that there were collections of tales about prophets, probably produced in Prophetic circles, which the later compiler decided to include in the large narrative. However, the fact that these stories are about prophets does not necessarily mean that they were the product of a Prophetic milieu, and I would propose that what is most salient about them is their generic character as folktales—stories spun out by the people awestruck by the remembered or imagined powers of these men of God.

There is, in fact, a palpable tension between the narrative of the kings and the tales of the prophets, however they intersect. The royal narrative appears to be historical, at least in its broad outlines. The kingdom did split in two after the death of Solomon around 930 B.C.E. There is no reason to doubt the reports of chronic political instability, especially in the northern kingdom where there was no authorized dynasty, involving a long and bloody sequence of court conspiracies, assassinations of kings, and usurpations. Israel's and Judah's struggles with the Arameans, the Assyrians, and finally the Babylonians were actual historical events, many of them attested in the Assyrian and Babylonian annals that have been uncovered by modern archaeology. The compiler of Kings, then, registers the course of historical events in the two kingdoms, making efforts to synchronize their chronology with reference to regnal spans, though his commitment to theological historical causation leads him occasionally to introduce a supernatural event into the historical account. Thus, the Assyrian emperor Sennacherib did in fact conduct a campaign against Judah and neighboring regions toward the end of the seventh century B.C.E. and laid siege against Jerusalem in 601 B.C.E., then withdrew for reasons that remain uncertain. The author of Kings, however, chooses to represent the lifting of the siege as the result of an act of divine intervention in which the Assyrian army is suddenly stricken with a mysterious plague. This retreat of the Assyrian forces confirms his view that Jerusalem is a divinely protected city, the exclusive place that God has chosen to set his name upon. In this view, it is only the pagan outrages and the murderous practices of King Manasseh that later tip the balance and determine the destruction of Jerusalem.

If the accounts of the kings are by and large historical, the tales of the prophets—preeminently, the cycle of stories about Elijah and Elisha—abound in displays of supernatural powers that set them off not only from the royal history but also from virtually everything that precedes them in the Book of Samuel. Fire is brought down from the heavens to consume a sacrifice in a confrontation with the prophets of Baal; a dead child is revived; a cruse of oil becomes bottomless to provide for a destitute widow; a precious borrowed axehead, sunk in the Jordan, floats to the surface; Elijah does not die but ascends in a chariot of fire to the heavens. In the actual miracle-count, Elisha somewhat surpasses his master Elijah, but it is

Elijah who is embraced by later tradition, singled out at the end of Malachi as the man who will announce the coming of the redeemer; serving as a model for the Gospel writers in their stories of the miraculous acts performed by Jesus; and becoming a cherished folk hero in later Jewish tradition. It is Elijah rather than Elisha who enjoys this vivid afterlife because he is the master, not the disciple, and perhaps also because he is finally the more sympathetic figure of the two—it is hard to forget Elisha's initial act of sending bears to devour the boys who mock him, an event that already caused discomfort among the early rabbis.

The Elijah stories, it should be said, are not only a chronicle of signs and wonders but the representation of a rather arresting character. First we see him in flight, hiding out from Ahab's wrath. Then he shows himself as the iron-willed spokesman of God, denouncing Ahab to his face as "the troubler of Israel." After his triumph over the Baal prophets on Mount Carmel, finding himself nevertheless again mortally threatened by Ahab and Jezebel, he flees to the wilderness where he despairs, asking God, "Enough, now, LORD. Take my life, for I am no better than my fathers" (1 Kings 19:4). But the despair is countered by the epiphany vouchsafed him in the wilderness, and he climbs back from his nadir again to confront Ahab after the judicial murder of Naboth contrived by Jezebel—"Have you murdered and also taken hold?" (1 Kings 21:19).

In all this, as in the Samson stories and elsewhere in the Bible, the folktale fondness for wondrous acts is interfused with a subtle narrative art in which dialogue, cunning patterns of repetition, and intimations of the character's inwardness are impressively deployed. Among all the narratives of monarchs, southern and northern, in the Book of Kings, pride of place is accorded to two characters—King Solomon and Elijah the prophet. Solomon is the embodiment of the regal grandeur of Israel's divinely elected monarchy, and as such great attention is lavished on his wealth, his grand royal enterprises, and his wisdom. He, like Elijah, will survive in later tradition as a figure both unmatched and revered. At the end of his story, he is seen falling away from his high calling, thus providing a rationale for the dividing of the kingdom and, ultimately, for its destruction. Elijah's story ends in a fiery ascent, assuring his future standing as the harbinger of the messiah and the folk hero who will come to the wretched of his people in their hour of distress.

The compiler who put Kings together for posterity above all sought to provide an account of the nation's history and an explanation of why that history took the course it finally did. The artful crafting of narrative was not one of his conscious aims. The deep-seated storytelling impulse, however, that drives so much biblical narrative manifests itself in this book as well, in some degree in the luminous tales about King Solomon and even more in the cycle of stories marked by confrontation, triumph, and dejection about Elijah the Tishbite.

1 Kings

CHAPTER 1   And King David had grown old, advanced in 1
years, and they covered him with bedclothes, but he was not warm. And 2
his servants said to him, "Let them seek out for my lord the king a young
virgin, that she may wait upon the king and become his familiar, and lie
in your lap, and my lord the king will be warm." And they sought out a 3
beautiful young woman through all the territory of Israel, and they found

---

CHAPTER 1   1. *And King David had grown old.* Although an editor, several centuries after the composition of the story, placed this episode and the next one at the beginning
of the Book of Kings, and after the coda of 2 Samuel 21–24, because of the centrality in them
of Solomon's succession, they are clearly the conclusion to the David story and bear all the
hallmarks of its author's distinctive literary genius. There are strong stylistic links with
the previous David narrative; the artful deployment of dialogue and of spatial shifts is very
similar; and there are significant connections of phrasing, motif, and theme.

   they covered him with bedclothes, but he was not warm. This extraordinary portrait of
a human life working itself out in the gradual passage of time, which began with an agile,
daring, and charismatic young David, now shows him in the extreme infirmity of old age,
shivering in bed beneath his covers.

2. *Let them seek out for my lord the king a young virgin.* The language used by the courtiers
recalls that of the mentally troubled Saul's courtiers, "We shall seek out a man skilled
in playing the lyre" (1 Samuel 16:16)—the very words that were the prelude to the young
David's entrance into the court.

   become his familiar. The exact meaning of the Hebrew noun *sokhenet* is uncertain. Some
translate it as "attendant" on the basis of the context. The verbal stem from which the word
is derived generally has the meaning of "to become accustomed," hence the choice here
of "familiar"—of course, in the social sense and not in the secondary sense linked with
witchcraft. The only other occurrence of this term in the biblical corpus, Isaiah 22:15, seems
to designate a (male) court official.

   and lie in your lap. Nathan in his denunciatory parable addressed to David represented
the ewe, symbolic of Bathsheba, lying in the poor man's lap (2 Samuel 12:3).

4 Abishag the Shunamite and brought her to the king. And the young woman
was very beautiful, and she became a familiar to the king and ministered
to him, but the king knew her not.

5 And Adonijah son of Haggith was giving himself airs, saying, "I shall be
king!" And he made himself a chariot and horsemen with fifty men run-
6 ning before him. And his father never caused him pain, saying, "Why have
you done thus?" And he, too, was very goodly of appearance, and him
7 she had born after Absalom. And he parlayed with Joab son of Zeruiah
8 and with Abiathar the priest, and they lent their support to Adonijah. But
Zadok the priest and Benaiah son of Jehoiada and Nathan the prophet and
9 Shimei and Rei and David's warriors were not with Adonijah. And Adonijah made a sacrificial feast of sheep and oxen and fatlings by the Zoheleth
stone which is near Ein-Rogel, and he invited all his brothers, the king's

---

4. *the young woman was very beautiful . . . but the king knew her not.* David, lying in bed
with this desirable virgin, but now beyond any thought or capacity of sexual consummation, is of course a sad image of infirm old age. At the same time, this vignette of geriatric
impotence is a pointed reversal of the Bathsheba story that brought down God's curse on
the house of David, triggering all the subsequent troubles of dynastic succession. There,
too, David was lying in his bed or couch (*mishkav,* as in verse 47 here), and there, too, he
sent out emissaries to bring back a beautiful young woman to lie with him, though to
antithetical purposes.

5. *was giving himself airs.* The reflexive verb has a root that means to raise up (hence the
King James Version, "exalted himself"). Since a common noun derived from that verb,
nasi', means "prince," the reflexive verb might even have the sense of "acting the part of
a prince."

    he made himself a chariot and horsemen with fifty men running before him. These acts
of regal presumption are the same ones carried out by the usurper Absalom, Adonijah's
older brother.

6. *his father never caused him pain.* The obvious sense of the verb in context is "reprimand."
The Septuagint reads "restrained him" (*'atsaro* instead of *'atsavo*), either because the Greek
translators had a better Hebrew version here or were smoothing out the Hebrew.

    And he, too, was very goodly of appearance. As the second clause of this sentence makes
clear, the "too" refers to Absalom, the son Haggith bore David before Adonijah.

8. *Shimei and Rei.* The Septuagint reads "Shimei and his companions" (*re'aw* instead of *re'i*).

9. *made a sacrificial feast.* The Hebrew verb *z-b-ḥ* refers both to the sacrifice of the animals,
the greater part of which was kept to be eaten, and to the feast. This is clearly a ceremonial
feast at which the monarchy is to be conferred on Adonijah.

    the Zoheleth stone which is near Ein-Rogel. The spring (Hebrew *'ayin*) of Rogel is within
a couple of miles of Jerusalem. The spatial proximity becomes important later in the story
because Adonijah's supporters, after they finish their feast, are able to hear the shouting

sons, and all the men of Judah, the king's servants. But Nathan the prophet 10
and Benaiah and the warriors and Solomon his brother he did not invite.

And Nathan said to Bathsheba, Solomon's mother, saying, "Have you not 11
heard that Adonijah son of Haggith has become king, and our lord David
knows it not? And now, come let me give you counsel that you may save 12
your own life and the life of your son Solomon. Go and get you to King 13
David and say to him, 'Has not my lord the king sworn to your servant,
saying: Solomon your son shall be king after me, and he shall sit on my

---

from the city. Zoheleth means "creeping thing," which has led some scholars to conjecture
that this location was a sacred site dedicated to the worship of a snake deity.

and all the men of Judah, the king's servants. Like his brother Absalom, Adonijah draws
on a base of support from his own tribe, Judah. In political and royal contexts, the phrase
"the king's servants" usually refers to courtiers, members of the king's inner circle.

10. *But Nathan the prophet and Benaiah.* In keeping with the established convention of
biblical narrative, this list of the uninvited and the report of Adonijah's self-coronation
feast will be repeated more or less verbatim, with subtle and significant changes reflecting
who the speaker is.

and the warriors. One should remember that Joab, commander of the army, was not listed
in 2 Samuel 23 as a member of "the Three Warriors," David's elite fighting corps. Although
few in number, they would have been a formidable counterforce in a struggle for the throne.

11. *Bathsheba, Solomon's mother.* After her fatal affair with David, she disappears from the
narrative. Now, after some two decades or perhaps more of elapsed time, she resurfaces.
Whereas the beautiful young wife was accorded no dialogue except for her report to David
of her pregnancy, the mature Bathsheba will show herself a mistress of language—shrewd,
energetic, politically astute.

Adonijah . . . has become king, and our lord David knows it not. J. P. Fokkelman notes
the play on words in the Hebrew between *'Adoniyah* ("my lord is Yah") and *'adoneinu* ("our
lord"). Playing also on the double sense of the Hebrew verb "to know," the writer represents
David in a state of both sexual and cognitive impotence: he knows not Abishag and he
knows not Adonijah's initiative to assume the throne.

13. *Has not my lord the king sworn to your servant.* The script that Nathan dictates to Bathsheba invokes a central ambiguity, which the writer surely intends to exploit. Perhaps David
actually made a private vow to Bathsheba promising that Solomon would succeed him.
There is, however, no mention of such a vow anywhere in the preceding narrative, including the report of Solomon's God-favored birth, where one might expect it. This opens up
a large, though by no means certain, possibility that Nathan the man of God has invented
the vow and enlists Bathsheba's help in persuading the doddering David that he actually
made this commitment.

Solomon your son shall be king after me, and he shall sit on my throne. The verselike parallelism of David's purported vow has the effect of impressing it on memory. It is repeated
three times: here by Nathan, then by Bathsheba as she carries out Nathan's orders, then by
David, who will make one small but crucial change in the wording of the formula.

14 throne. And why has Adonijah become king?' Look, while you are still
15 speaking there, I shall come after you and fill in your words."And Bath-
    sheba came to the king in the inner chamber, and the king was very old,
16 with Abishag the Shunamite ministering to the king. And Bathsheba did
    obeisance and bowed down to the king, and the king said, "What troubles
17 you?" And she said to him, "My lord, you yourself swore by the LORD your
    God to your servant, 'Solomon your son shall be king after me, and he
18 shall sit on my throne.' And now, look, Adonijah has become king and
19 my lord the king knows it not. And he has made a sacrificial feast of oxen
    and fatlings and sheep in abundance and has invited all the king's sons
    and Abiathar the priest and Joab commander of the army, but Solomon
20 your servant he did not invite. And you, my lord the king, the eyes of all
    Israel are upon you to tell them who will sit on the throne of my lord the king
21 after him. And it will come about when my lord king lies with his fathers,

---

14. *fill in your words.* Many translate the Hebrew verb that means "to fill" as "confirm." But
in fact what Nathan will do is to complement Bathsheba's speech, adding certain elements
and not repeating certain others.

15. *the inner chamber.* At an earlier moment, a figure from David's house, Amnon, was
seen lying ill (or pretending) while a beautiful woman came to him in the inner chamber.

16. *Bathsheba did obeisance and bowed down to the king.* Whatever the actual relationship between Bathsheba and David at this very late point in his life, it seems reduced to a
punctilious observance of palace protocol. In the background, silent, stands the beautiful
young Abishag, now the king's bedmate but not really his consort.

17. *My lord, you yourself swore by the LORD your God.* Bathsheba edits the script Nathan
has given her in two ways: the third-person address to the king is switched to the second
person, allowing her to introduce an emphatic, "you yourself" (in the Hebrew the addition
of the pronoun *'atah* before the conjugated verb); and the vow is said to have been made
solemnly "by the LORD your God." If in fact the vow is a fabrication, perhaps Nathan the
prophet was leery of invoking God's name in connection with it.

19. *oxen and fatlings and sheep in abundance.* The last term, "in abundance," is added to
the verbal chain from the narrator's initial report of the feast, a small magnification of
the scale of the event that Adonijah has staged.
    but Solomon your servant he did not invite. Nathan had not incorporated a list of the
excluded in his instructions to her. Bathsheba singles out only her own son among the uninvited, but she is careful to identify him to David not as "my son" but as "your servant,"
emphasizing Solomon's status as loyal subject.

20. *the eyes of all Israel are upon you to tell them who will sit on the throne.* Now improvising,
Bathsheba uses words that strongly evoke David's authority, though in fact he has been out
of the picture, failing and bedridden.

21. *when my lord the king lies with his fathers . . . I and my son Solomon will be held offenders.* With admirable tact, she uses a decorous euphemism for dying, and then expresses

that I and my son Solomon will be held offenders." And, look, she was 22
still speaking with the king when Nathan the prophet came in. And they 23
told the king, saying, "Here is Nathan the prophet." And he came before
the king and bowed to the king, his face to the ground. And Nathan said, 24
"My lord the king, have you yourself said, 'Adonijah shall be king after me
and he shall sit on my throne'? For he has gone down today and made a 25
sacrificial feast of oxen and fatlings and sheep in abundance, and he has
invited all the king's sons and the commanders of the army and Abiathar
the priest, and there they are eating and drinking before him, and they
have said, 'Long live King Adonijah!' But me—your servant—and Zadok 26
the priest and Benaiah son of Jehoiada and Solomon your servant he did
not invite. Has this thing been done by my lord the king without inform- 27
ing your servant who will sit on the throne of my lord the king after him?"
And King David answered and said, "Call me Bathsheba." And she came 28
before the king and stood before the king. And the king swore and said,
"As the LORD lives Who rescued me from every strait, as I swore to you by 29,30
the LORD God of Israel, saying, 'Solomon your son shall be king after me,

---

her perfectly plausible fear that as king, Adonijah would take prompt steps to eliminate
both her and Solomon. (Compare Nathan's "save your own life and the life of your son.")

23. *Here is Nathan the prophet.* Nathan in his role as prophet is formally announced to
David by the courtiers. According to biblical convention, there are no three-sided dialogues. Bathsheba presumably withdraws as soon as she sees Nathan enter. In verse 28, after
the conversation with Nathan, David has to summon her back. All this takes place not in
the throne room but in the "inner chamber," where David lies in bed.

24. *have you yourself said, "Adonijah shall be king."* Unlike Bathsheba, Nathan makes no
reference to a vow regarding Solomon, presumably because it would have been a private
vow to her. Instead, he refers to observable public events: have you authorized the succession of Adonijah? He uses the identical formula for succession that has already twice been
attached to Solomon ("shall be king after me . . . shall sit on my throne").

25. *he has invited all the king's sons and the commanders of the army.* Nathan's more political version of the unfolding usurpation adds to the list of Adonijah's supporters the whole
officer corps of the army.

  Long live King Adonijah. This vivid acclamation of Adonijah's kingship, not reported by
the narrator, is calculated to rouse David's ire. The evocation of the coronation feast ("they
are eating and drinking before him") is similarly more vivid than Bathsheba' s account.

26. *But me—your servant.* Nathan takes pains, in righteous indignation as prophet to the
throne, to highlight his own exclusion, at the very beginning of the list.

30. *as I swore to you by the LORD God of Israel.* Whether or not David actually made this
vow to Bathsheba, by now he is thoroughly persuaded that he did. Note that he raises Bathsheba's language to still another level of politically efficacious resonance: Nathan had made
no mention of God in invoking the vow; Bathsheba had said "you . . . swore by the LORD

31 and he shall sit on my throne in my stead,' even so will I do this day." And
Bathsheba did obeisance, her face to the ground, and bowed to the king
32 and said, "May my lord King David live forever." And David said, "Call to
me Zadok the priest and Nathan the prophet and Benaiah son of Jehoiada."
33 And they came before the king. And the king said to them, "Take with
you your lord's servants and mount Solomon my son on my special mule
34 and bring him down to the Gihon. And Zadok the priest shall anoint him
there, with Nathan the prophet, as king over Israel, and sound the ram's
35 horn and say, 'Long live King Solomon.' And you shall come up after him,
and he shall come and sit on my throne, and he shall be king after me,
36 him have I charged to be prince over Israel and over Judah." And Benaiah
son of Jehoiada answered the king and said, "Amen! May thus, too, say
37 the LORD, my lord the king's God. As the LORD has been with my lord the
king, thus may He be with Solomon and make his throne even greater than
the throne of my lord King David."

---

your God"; David now encompasses the whole national realm in declaring, "as I swore to
you by the LORD God of Israel."

he shall sit on my throne in my stead. David introduces a crucial change into the formula
for the promise of succession, as Fokkelman shrewdly observes: to the understandable
"after me" of the first clause he adds "in my stead," implying not merely that Solomon will
succeed him but that Solomon will replace him on the throne while he is still alive. Accordingly, David then proceeds to give instructions for an immediate ceremony of anointment.
In the face of Adonijah's virtual coup d'état, David appears to realize that he is no longer
physically capable of acting as monarch and protecting himself against usurpation, and
that the wisest course is to put his chosen successor on the throne without a moment's delay.

31. May my lord King David live forever. Bathsheba's tact remains flawless. Now that she has
extracted from David exactly the commitment she wanted, she wishes him, hyperbolically,
eternal life, even as he teeters on the edge of the grave.

33. your lord's servants. That is, David's courtiers.

my special mule. Literally, "the mule that is mine." Seating Solomon on the royal mule
is the first public expression of the conferral of the kingship on him.

the Gihon. This is a brook just outside the city walls. David enjoins his officials to act
rapidly in anointing Solomon while Adonijah's coronation feast is still under way a couple
of miles off.

35. he shall come and sit on my throne. This reiterated symbolic statement is now literal-
ized: after the anointment at the Gihon brook, Solomon is to be brought to the palace and
publicly seated on the throne.

him have I charged to be prince. The term nagid, "prince," previously attached to Saul
and now to David, appears for the last time to designate the monarch. He is to be prince
over Judah, where Adonijah has gathered support, as well as over Israel.

And Zadok the priest, with Nathan the prophet and Benaiah son of 38
Jehoiada and the Cherithites and the Pelethites, went down and mounted
Solomon on King David's mule and led him to the Gihon. And Zadok the 39
priest took the horn of oil from the Tent and anointed Solomon, and they
blew the ram's horn and all the people said, "Long live King Solomon!"
And all the people went up after him, and the people were playing flutes 40
and making such revelry that the very earth split apart with their noise.
And Adonijah heard, and all the invited guests who were with him, and 41
they had finished eating, and Joab heard the sound of the ram's horn and
said, "Why this sound of the town in an uproar?" He was still speaking 42
when, look, Jonathan son of Abiathar the priest came. And Adonijah said,
"Come! For you are a valiant fellow and you must bear good tidings." And 43
Jonathan answered and said to Adonijah, "Alas, our lord King David has
made Solomon king. And the king has sent with him Zadok the priest and 44
Nathan the prophet and Benaiah son of Jehoiada and the Cherithites and
the Pelethites, and they have mounted him on the king's mule. And Zadok 45
the priest and Nathan the prophet have anointed him king at the Gihon,

---

38. *the Cherithites and the Pelethites.* These members of the palace guard of Philistine origin
provide a show of arms for the act of anointing Solomon.

39. *took the horn of oil from the Tent.* The Tent in question is obviously the cultic site where
the Ark of the Covenant is kept—the emphasis is that the oil of anointment is sanctified oil.

40. *the people were playing flutes and making such revelry that the very earth split apart
with their noise.* This hyperbolic report of the public rejoicing over Solomon's succession
to the throne serves two purposes: the tremendous clamor is so loud that the sound reaches
Adonijah and his supporters at Ein-Rogel (verse 41), and it is a vocal demonstration that
the choice of Solomon immediately enjoys extravagant popular support. This latter consideration is crucial for the politics of the story because it makes clear that Adonijah has
no hope of mustering opposition to Solomon.

41. *Adonijah heard, and all the invited guests . . . and Joab heard the sound of the ram's horn.*
As a couple of commentators have noted, Adonijah and his followers hear only the hubbub
from the town, whereas Joab, the military man, picks up the sound of the *shofar*, the ram's
horn. This would be either a call to arms or the proclamation of a king.

42. *For you are a valiant fellow and you must bear good tidings.* This obvious non sequitur
ominously echoes David's anxious words about Ahimaaz (2 Samuel 18), "He is a good
man and with good tidings he must come." Jonathan's very first word, "alas," shows how
mistaken Adonijah is.

43. *our lord King David has made Solomon king.* Jonathan flatly begins with the brunt of
the bad news, then fleshes out the circumstances to make it all the worse. He at once identifies David as "our lord," conceding that, after all, David retains a monarch's authority to
determine his successor.

and they have gone up from there reveling, and the town is in an uproar.
46 This is the sound you heard. And what's more, Solomon is seated on the
47 royal throne. And what's more, the king's servants have come to bless our
lord King David, saying, 'May your God make Solomon's name even better
than your name and make his throne even greater than your throne.' And
48 the king bowed down on his couch. And what's more, thus has the king
said, 'Blessed is the LORD God of Israel Who has granted today someone
49 sitting on my throne with my own eyes beholding it.' " And all of Adonijah's
50 invited guests trembled and rose up and each man went on his way. And
Adonijah was afraid of Solomon, and he rose up and went off and caught
51 hold of the horns of the altar. And it was told to Solomon, saying, "Look,
Adonijah is afraid of King Solomon and, look, he has caught hold of the
horns of the altar, saying, 'Let King Solomon swear to me today that he will
52 not put his servant to death by the sword.' " And Solomon said, "If he prove

---

46–48. *And what's more, Solomon is seated. . . . And what's more, the king's servants have
come. . . . And what's more, thus has the king said.* Jonathan's long, breathless account of
the installation of Solomon as king, with its reiterated "what's more" (*wegam*), conveys an
excited cumulative sense of the chain of disasters that have destroyed all of Adonijah's
hopes. He goes beyond what the narrator has reported to depict Solomon actually seated
on the throne, receiving his father's blessing.

48. *someone sitting on my throne.* Some textual critics propose instead the Masoretic reading "a son sitting on my throne."

49. *each man went on his way.* Terrified, the supporters of Adonijah's claim to the throne
disperse. This moment is reminiscent of the dispersal and flight of "all the king's sons"
from Amnon's feast after Absalom's men murder Amnon.

50. *caught hold of the horns of the altar.* The typical construction of ancient Israelite altars,
as archaeology has confirmed, featured a curving protuberance at each of the four corners,
roughly like the curve of a ram's horn. The association of horn with strength may explain
this design. Gripping the horns—actually, probably one horn—of the altar was a plea for
sanctuary: at least in principle, although not always in practice, a person in this posture
and in this place should be held inviolable by his pursuers.

51. *Let King Solomon swear . . . that he will not put his servant to death.* Adonijah, compelled
by force majeure, fully acknowledges Solomon's kingship and his own status as subject in
his plea for mercy.

52. *And Solomon said.* Until this point, Solomon has been acted upon by others, and no
dialogue has been assigned to him. Now that he is king, he speaks with firm authority.
    If he prove a valiant fellow. In immediate context, the force of the idiom *ben ḥayil* is obvi-
ously something like "a decent fellow." But its usual meaning is worth preserving because
it precisely echoes the term Adonijah addressed to Jonathan (verse 42), and it also points
up ironically that Adonijah now is trembling with fear.

a valiant fellow, not a hair of his will fall to the ground, but if evil be found
in him, he shall die." And King Solomon sent, and they took him down 53
from the altar, and he came and bowed to King Solomon, and Solomon
said to him, "Go to your house."

CHAPTER 2   And David's time to die grew near, and he 1
charged Solomon his son, saying: "I am going on the way of all the earth. 2
And you must be strong, and be a man. And keep what the LORD your 3
God enjoins, to walk in His ways, to keep His statutes, His commands,

---

if evil be found in him, he shall die. The evil Solomon has in mind would be further
political machinations. He thus does not agree to swear unconditionally, as Adonijah had
pleaded, not to harm his half brother, and he will make due use of the loophole he leaves
himself.

53. *Go to your house.* This injunction concludes the episode on a note of ambiguity. Solomon
is distancing Adonijah from the palace. He sends him to the presumed safety of his own
home, or is it to a condition of virtual house arrest? In any case, Adonijah is surely meant
to be kept under surveillance, and Solomon has already put him on warning.

CHAPTER 2   3–4. These two relatively long verses are an unusual instance of the
intervention of a Deuteronomistic editor in the dialogue of the original David story that
was composed perhaps nearly four centuries before him. The language here is an uninterrupted chain of verbal formulas distinctive of the Book of Deuteronomy and its satellite
literature: *keep what the LORD your God enjoins, walk in His ways, keep His statutes, His
commands, and His dictates and admonitions, so that you may prosper in everything you do
and in everything to which you turn, walk before Me in truth with their whole heart and with
their whole being.* The very mention of the Teaching [*torah*] of Moses is a hallmark of the
Deuteronomist, and as phrase and concept did not yet have currency in the tenth century.
The long sentences loaded with synonyms are also uncharacteristic of the author of the
David story, and there is no one in that story—least of all, David himself—who speaks in
this high-minded, long-winded, didactic vein. Why did the Deuteronomistic editor choose
to intervene at this penultimate point of the David story? It seems very likely that he was
uneasy with David's pronouncing to Solomon a last will and testament worthy of a dying
mafia capo: be strong and be a man, and use your savvy to pay off all my old scores with
my enemies. In fact, David's deathbed implacability, which the later editor tries to mitigate by first placing noble sentiments in his mouth, is powerfully consistent with both the
characterization and the imagination of politics in the preceding narrative. The all-too-
human David on the brink of the grave is still smarting from the grief and humiliation
that Joab's violent acts caused him and from the public shame Shimei heaped on him, and
he wants Solomon to do what he himself was prevented from doing by fear in the one case
and by an inhibiting vow in the other. In practical political terms, moreover, either Joab,
just recently a supporter of the usurper Adonijah, or Shimei, the disaffected Benjaminite,
might threaten Solomon's hold on power, and so both should be eliminated.

and His dictates and His admonitions, as it is written in the Teaching of
Moses, so that you may prosper in everything you do and in everything

4 to which you turn. So that the LORD may fulfill His word that He spoke
unto me, saying, 'If your sons keep their way to walk before Me in truth
with their whole heart and with their whole being, no man of yours will

5 be cut off from the throne of Israel.' And, what's more, you yourself know
what Joab son of Zeruiah did to me, what he did to the two commanders of
the armies of Israel, Abner son of Ner and Amasa son of Jether—he killed
them, and shed the blood of war in peace, and put the blood of war on his

6 belt that was round his waist and on his sandals that were on his feet. And
you must act in your wisdom, and do not let his gray head go down in peace

7 to Sheol. And with the sons of Barzillai the Gileadite keep faith, and let
them be among those who eat at your table, for did they not draw near me

8 when I fled from Absalom your brother? And, look, with you is Shimei son
of Gera the Benjaminite from Bahurim, and he cursed me with a scathing
curse on the day I went to Mahanaim. And he came down to meet me at

---

5. *what he did to the two commanders of the armies of Israel.* David is silent about the third
murder perpetrated by Joab, and the one that caused him the greatest grief—the killing of
Absalom. Perhaps he does not mention it because it was a murder, unlike the other two,
that served a reason of state. But it was surely the one act he could not forgive.

   shed the blood of war in peace, and put the blood of war on his belt . . . and on his sandals.
Both killings were done on the roadway, Joab approaching his victim with gestures of
peace. In the case of Abner, his rival had come to make peace with David, and the phrase
"went in peace [*shalom*]" was attached to Abner in a triple repetition (2 Samuel 3). In the
case of Amasa, Joab's last words to him before stabbing him in the belly were "Is it well
[*shalom*] with you, my brother?" (2 Samuel 20:9). The virtually visual emphasis of blood
on belt and sandals recalls in particular the murder of Amasa, who lay in the middle of
the road wallowing in blood, while the mention of Joab's belt looks back to his stratagem
of belting his sword to his waist so that it would fall out when he bent over, to be picked up
by his left hand. The reference to Joab's waist and feet conveys an image of a man splashed
all over with blood. Beyond this integration of details from the preceding narrative in the
words David chooses, the concentration on blood reflects a general belief that blood shed
in murder lingers not only over the murderer but also over those associated with the victim
like a contaminating miasma until it is "redeemed" or "taken away" by vengeance.

6. *you must act in your wisdom.* The wisdom of Solomon in the subsequent narrative is
proverbial, but what David already has in mind here is political shrewdness: Joab is, after
all, a formidable adversary, and Solomon will have to choose the right time and place, when
Joab is without allies or protection, to dispatch him.

   do not let his gray head go down in peace to Sheol. This proverbial phrase is actualized
here because we realize that Joab, after half a century as David's commander—forty regnal
years plus several years before that in David's guerilla band—is now an old man. He who
shed the blood of war in peace will not be allowed to go down in peace to the underworld.

the Jordan, and I swore to him by the LORD, saying, 'I will not put you to death by the sword.' And now, do not hold him guiltless, for you are a wise ₉ man, and you will know what you should do to him, and bring his gray head down in blood to Sheol!" And David lay with his fathers and he was ₁₀ buried in the City of David. And the time that David was king over Israel ₁₁ was forty years—in Hebron he was king seven years and in Jerusalem he was king thirty-three years. And Solomon sat on the throne of David like ₁₂ his father, and his kingdom was wholly unshaken.

And Adonijah son of Haggith came to Bathsheba, Solomon's mother, and ₁₃ she said, "Do you come in peace?" And he said, "In peace." And he said, ₁₄ "There is something I have to say to you." And she said, "Speak." And he ₁₅ said, "You yourself know that mine was the kingship, and to me did all Israel turn their faces to be king, yet the kingship was brought round and became my brother's, for from the LORD was it his. And now, there is one ₁₆

---

9. *for you are a wise man, and you will know what you should do to him.* In regard to Shimei, the "wisdom" Solomon must exercise is to find some legal loophole to obviate his father's vow not to harm the Benjaminite. In the event, Solomon does this with considerable cleverness. David's vow to Shimei was made at a moment when it seemed politically prudent to include the man who had cursed him in what was probably a general amnesty after the suppression of the rebellion. It is understandable that later on David would regret this binding act of forgiveness to a vile-spirited enemy.

bring his gray head down in blood to Sheol. Shimei had screamed at the fleeing David, "man of blood." Now David enjoins Solomon to send him to the netherworld in blood. In his long career, David has had noble moments as well as affectingly human ones, but it is a remarkable token of the writer's gritty realism about men in the vindictive currents of violent politics that the very last words he assigns to David are *bedam She'ol*, "in blood to Sheol."

11. *forty years.* One may assume this is no more than an approximation of David's regnal span since forty years, as the Book of Judges repeatedly shows, is a formulaic number for a full reign.

13. *Adonijah son of Haggith.* The reappearance of Solomon's rival follows hard upon the report that his kingdom was unshaken, introducing a potential dissonance. Adonijah was not included in David's list of enemies to be eliminated because he is Solomon's problem, not David's.

Do you come in peace? After Adonijah's attempt to seize the throne that was then given to her son, Bathsheba is understandably uncertain about Adonijah's intentions in coming to see her.

15. *You yourself know that mine was the kingship . . . yet the kingship was brought round and became my brother's, for from the LORD was it his.* Adonijah tries to have it both ways in his overture to Bathsheba: on the one hand, the kingship really was his, and he enjoyed

17 petition I ask of you, do not refuse me." And she said, "Speak." And he said,
   "Pray, say to Solomon the king, for he would not refuse you, that he give me
18 Abishag the Shunamite as wife." And Bathsheba said, "Good, I myself shall
19 speak for you to the king." And Bathsheba came to King Solomon to speak
   to him about Adonijah. And the king arose to greet her and bowed to her
   and sat down on his throne and set out a throne for the queen mother, and
20 she sat down to his right. And she said, "There is one small petition that I
   ask of you, do not refuse me." And the king said to her, "Ask, Mother, for I

---

popular support; on the other hand, he is prepared to be reconciled with the idea that it was God's determination that the crown should pass on from him to his brother. There may be a note of petulance here: Adonijah speaks of his situation as though he deserved some sort of consolation prize. It will prove a fatal imprudence that he should have addressed this complaint to the mother of the man he sought to anticipate in seizing the throne.

17. *that he give me Abishag the Shunamite as wife.* The promotion of fruitful ambiguity through narrative reticence so characteristic of the author of the David story is never more brilliantly deployed. What is Adonijah really up to? He approaches Solomon's mother because he thinks she will have special influence over the king and because he is afraid to go to Solomon himself. Perhaps, Adonijah imagines, as a mother she will have pity for him and do him this favor. But in taking this course, Adonijah betrays the most extraordinary political naïveté. Why does he want Abishag? The political motive would be that by uniting with a woman who had shared the king's bed, though merely as a bedwarmer, he was preparing the ground for a future claim to the throne. (The act of his brother Absalom in cohabiting with David's concubines stands in the background.) If this motive were transparent, as it turns out to be in Solomon's reading of the request, it would be idiotic for Adonijah to ask for Abishag. Perhaps he feels safe because Abishag was not technically David's consort. Perhaps the political consideration is only at the back of his mind, and he really is seeking consolation in the idea of marrying a beautiful young woman who has, so to speak, a kind of association by contiguity with the throne. In any case, he will pay the ultimate price for his miscalculation.

18. *I myself shall speak for you to the king.* As with Adonijah, there is no explanation of her motive. But given the shrewdness with which Bathsheba has acted in the previous episode, it is entirely plausible that she immediately agrees to do this favor for Adonijah because she quickly realizes what escapes him—that it will prove to be his death sentence, and thus a threat to her son's throne will be permanently eliminated.

19. *and bowed to her.* The Septuagint has "and kissed her" because of the anomaly of a king's bowing to his subject.

20. *There is one small petition that I ask of you.* In accordance with the established convention of biblical narrative, she uses the very same words Adonijah has spoken to her, adding only the adjective "small." This is just a tiny request, she appears to say, full knowing that Solomon is likely to see it, on the contrary, as a huge thing—a device that could be turned into a ladder to the throne on which Solomon sits. One should note that this whole large narrative begins when a woman who is to become a mother (Hannah) puts forth a petition (*she'eilah,* the same word used here).

shall not refuse you." And she said, "Let Abishag the Shunamite be given ₂₁ to Adonijah your brother as wife." And King Solomon answered and said ₂₂ to his mother, "And why do you ask Abishag the Shunamite for Adonijah? Ask the kingship for him, as he is my older brother, and Abiathar the priest and Joab son of Zeruiah are for him." And King Solomon swore by the ₂₃ LORD, saying, "Thus may God do to me and even more, for at the cost of his life has Adonijah spoken this thing! And now, as the LORD lives, Who ₂₄ seated me unshaken on the throne of David my father, and Who made me a house just as He had spoken, today shall Adonijah be put to death." And King Solomon sent by the hand of Benaiah son of Jehoiada, and he ₂₅ stabbed him and he died. And to Abiathar the priest did the king say, "Go ₂₆ to Anathoth to your own fields, for you are a doomed man, but on this day I shall not put you to death, for you bore the Ark of the LORD God before David my father and you suffered through all that my father suffered." And ₂₇ Solomon banished Abiathar from being priest to the LORD, so as to fulfill the word of the LORD that He spoke concerning the house of Eli at Shiloh.

---

22. *as he is my older brother, and Abiathar . . . and Joab . . . are for him.* If he makes the dead king's consort his wife, that, together with the fact that he is my elder and has powerful supporters in the court, will give him a dangerously strong claim to the throne. In the Hebrew, the second clause appears to say "and for him and for Abiathar . . . and for Joab," which makes little sense, and so the small emendation, deleting the second and third occurrence of "for" (a single-letter prefix in the Hebrew), is presumed in the translation.

26. *to Abiathar the priest.* Throughout this episode centering on Adonijah, Solomon shows himself to be decisive, emphatic, and ruthless—a worthy son of his father. The moment he hears of Adonijah's pretensions to the late king's nurse-bedmate, he orders him to be killed immediately. He then proceeds to remove from office and banish the key priestly supporter of Adonijah, and he will go on to deal with Joab as well.

on this day I shall not put you to death. There is a veiled threat in this formulation: right now I shall not kill you, and in any case you had better stay away from Jerusalem on the farm at Anathoth.

for you bore the Ark of the LORD . . . and you suffered through all that my father suffered. Solomon is circumspect in not ordering the execution of a priest—in sharp contrast to Saul, who thought he might protect his kingship from a perceived threat by massacring a whole town of priests who he imagined were allied with his rival. Solomon also honors the fact that Abiathar has shared many years of danger and hardship with David, and during that time never betrayed David, as Joab did.

27. *so as to fulfill the word of the LORD . . . concerning the house of Eli.* One sees how this chapter concludes a grand narrative that begins in 1 Samuel 1, and is not merely the end of a supposedly independent Succession Narrative.

28 And the news reached Joab, for Joab had sided with Adonijah, though with
    Absalom he had not sided, and Joab fled to the Tent of the LORD, and he
29 grasped the horns of the altar. And it was told to the king that Joab had fled
    to the Tent of the LORD, and there he was by the altar, and Solomon sent
30 Benaiah son of Johoiada, saying, "Go, stab him." And Benaiah came to the
    Tent of the LORD and said to him, "Thus says the king, 'Come out.'" And he
    said, "No, for here I shall die." And Benaiah brought back word to the king,
31 saying, "Thus did Joab speak and thus did he answer me." And the king
    said, "Do as he has spoken, and stab him and bury him, and you shall take
    away the blood that Joab shed for no cause, from me and from my father's
32 house. And the LORD will bring back his bloodguilt on his own head, for
    he stabbed two men more righteous and better than himself and he killed
    them by the sword, unbeknownst to my father David—Abner son of Ner,
    commander of the army of Israel, and Amasa son of Jether, commander of
33 the army of Judah. And their blood will come back on the head of Joab and
    on the head of his seed forever, but for David and his seed and his house

---

28. *And the news reached Joab . . . and Joab fled to the Tent of the LORD.* With Adonijah dead
and Abiathar banished, Joab realizes that all who remain from the recent anti-Solomon
alliance have been isolated and cut off. This relentlessly political general recognizes that
he has no power base left to protect him against the resolute young king. He has only the
desperate last remedy of seeking sanctuary at the altar.

30. *Thus says the king, "Come out."* Solomon's blunt order was simply to stab Joab, but
Benaiah, steely executioner though he has shown himself, is loath to kill a man clinging to
the altar, and so he directs Joab to come down out of the Tent of the LORD.

31. *stab him and bury him.* Solomon's command is to take Joab's life in the very place of
sanctuary ("for here shall I die"), a decision that is in accordance with biblical law: "And
should a man scheme against his fellow man to kill him by cunning, from My altar you
shall take him to die" (Exodus 21:14). But Solomon also enjoins Benaiah to see to it that
Joab, who was after all a stalwart soldier and once David's boon companion, should have a
proper burial and not be thrown to the scavengers of sky and earth—the ultimate indignity
in ancient Mediterranean cultures.

32. *for he stabbed two men more righteous and better than himself . . . unbeknownst to my
father David.* Solomon in his "wisdom" has thus used the purported renewal of the Adonijah conspiracy to carry out the will of vengeance his father conveyed to him, and for the
precise reasons David stipulated.

33. *their blood will come back on the head of Joab and on the head of his seed.* The miasma of
blood guilt settles on the house of Joab for all time: a curse on the house of Joab was not part
of David's injunction, but perhaps Solomon means to ward off any prospect that resentful
descendants of Joab will seek to marshal forces against the Davidic line.

   but for David and his seed and his house there will be peace evermore. There is an
emphatic contrast between permanent blessing on the line of David and an everlasting
curse on the line of Joab, with "peace" counterpointed to "blood," as in verse 5.

and his throne there will be peace evermore from the LORD." And Benaiah 34
son of Jehoiada went up and stabbed him and put him to death, and he
was buried at his home in the wilderness. And the king put Benaiah son of 35
Jehoiada in his stead over the army, and Zadok the priest did the king put
instead of Abiathar.

And the king sent and called to Shimei and said to him, "Build yourself a 36
house in Jerusalem and dwell in it, and do not go out from there hither and
yon. For should you cross the Wadi Kidron, on the very day you go out, 37
you must surely know that you are doomed to die, your blood will be on
your own head." And Shimei said to the king, "The thing is good. Even as 38
my lord the king has spoken, so will his servant do." And Shimei dwelled
in Jerusalem a long while. And it happened at the end of three years that 39
two of Shimei's slaves ran away to Achish son of Maacah, king of Gath, and
they told Shimei, saying, "Look, your slaves are in Gath." And Shimei arose 40
and saddled his donkey and went to Gath, to Achish, to seek his slaves, and
Shimei went and brought his slaves from Gath. And it was told to Solomon 41

---

34. *he was buried at his home in the wilderness.* This notation has puzzled commentators
because one would assume that Joab's home (like David's original home) was in the town
of Bethlehem. The Hebrew for "wilderness," *midbar,* has the basic meaning of uninhabited
terrain, and it is not improbable that Joab would have had a kind of hacienda removed from
the town. Nevertheless, the report of Joab's burial in the wilderness concludes his story on a
haunting note. That resonance has been nicely caught by the medieval Hebrew commentator Gersonides: "he was buried in the wilderness, which was the home fitting for him, for
it would not be meet for a man like him to be part of civil society [*lihyot medini*] because
he had killed men by devious means and by deception."

37. *should you cross the Wadi Kidron.* This brook runs at the foot of Jerusalem to the east,
and Shimei would have to cross it to go back to his native village of Bahurim.
    your blood will be on your own head. Again, behind these words lies the spectacle of
Shimei reviling David with the epithet "man of blood" and asking that the blood of the
house of Saul come down on his head.

38. *The thing is good.* Shimei has no alternative but to agree—better virtual confinement
in the capital city than death.

40. *Shimei arose and saddled his donkey and went to Gath . . . to seek his slaves.* According
to several ancient Near Eastern codes (though not Israelite law), authorities were obliged to
return a runaway slave. Evidently, by this point peaceful relations obtained between Israel
and the Philistine cities. Lulled into a false sense of security by the passage of three years ("a
long while"), Shimei may be allowing his cupidity for recovering lost property to override
the concern he should have preserved about Solomon's injunction not to leave Jerusalem.
Or he may be a bad reader of Solomon's oral text, construing the ban on crossing the Wadi
Kidron as implicit permission to leave the city temporarily in the opposite direction, so
long as he does not try to return to his hometown.

42 that Shimei had gone from Jerusalem and had come back. And the king
sent and called Shimei and said to him, "Did I not make you swear by the
LORD and warn you, saying, 'The day you go out and move about hither
and yon, you must surely know that you are doomed to die,' and you said
43 to me, 'The thing is good. I do hear it.' And why have you not kept the
44 LORD's oath and the command with which I charged you?" And the king
said to Shimei, "You yourself know all the evil, which your own heart
knows, that you did to David my father, and the LORD has brought back
45 your evil on your own head. But King Solomon shall be blessed and the
46 throne of David shall be unshaken before the LORD forevermore." And
the king charged Benaiah son of Jeohaiada, and he went out and stabbed
him, and he died.

And the kingdom was unshaken in Solomon's hand.

---

42. *Did I not make you swear by the LORD.* In the actual report, only Solomon swore (the
Septuagint supplies an oath for Shimei), though perhaps Shimei's taking a solemn oath is
implied in verse 38.

　The thing is good. I do hear it. Solomon adds "I do hear it" (*shama'ti*) to the actual
report in verse 38 of Shimei's words, in order to emphasize that Shimei gave full and
knowing assent to Solomon's terms. Fokkelman notes that there is a pun on Shimei's own
name—*Shim'i/shama'ti.*

43. *And why have you not kept the LORD's oath.* Here, then, is Solomon's wisdom in carrying out his father's will: he has set Shimei up, waiting patiently until he violates the oath,
which then frees Solomon of any obligation lingering from David's earlier oath to do no
harm to Shimei.

45. *But King Solomon shall be blessed.* As in the killing of Joab, the imprecation pronounced
over the doomed man is balanced by the invocation of the LORD's perpetual blessing on
the house of David.

46. *And the kingdom was unshaken in Solomon's hand.* This seemingly formulaic notice at
the very end of the story is a last touch of genius by that unblinking observer of the savage
realm of politics who is the author of the David story: Solomon's power is now firmly
established, blessed by the God Who has promised an everlasting covenant with David
and his descendants; but the immediately preceding actions undertaken so decisively and
so shrewdly by the young king involve the ruthless elimination of all potential enemies.
The solid foundations of the throne have been hewn by the sharp daggers of the king's
henchmen.

CHAPTER 3   And Solomon became son-in-law to Pharaoh 1
king of Egypt, and he took Pharaoh's daughter and brought her to the City
of David till he could finish building his house and the house of the LORD
and the wall of Jerusalem all around. But the people were sacrificing on the 2
high places, for a house had not been built for the LORD as yet in those days.
And Solomon loved the LORD, going by the statutes of David his father, but 3
on the high places he was sacrificing and burning incense. And the king 4
went to Gibeon to sacrifice there, for it was a great high place—a thousand
burnt offerings would Solomon offer up on that altar. In Gibeon did the 5
LORD appear to Solomon in a night-dream, and God said, "Ask. What shall
I give you?" And Solomon said, "You Yourself did great kindness with Your 6
servant David my father, as he walked in Your presence in truth and in justice and in the heart's rightness with You. And You kept for him this great

---

CHAPTER 3   1. *And Solomon became son-in-law to Pharaoh.* The Hebrew verb,
although it involves marriage, indicates an establishment of relationship between the
groom and the father of the bride. The marriage is thus politically motivated and will be
the first of many such unions for Solomon in his effort to consolidate the mini-empire
created by his father.

   took. This ordinary verb often has the force of "marry," as here.

2. *But the people were sacrificing on the high places.* Since the Temple was not yet built, there
was no alternative to these local altars on hilltops. But the notation reveals the unease of the
Deuteronomist with a moment when both the people and Solomon himself offered sacrifices
at sites other than the center of the cult in Jerusalem. The strong presence of the Deuteronomist and the shift that reveals itself in the subsequent passages to a different kind of
narrative suggest that the book has now moved on from the David story to the work of very
different writers.

3. *Solomon loved the LORD.* This is not said of David. There may be a play on Solomon's
other name, Jedidiah, which means friend, or lover (though different from the verb used
here), of the LORD.

4. *for it was a great high place.* Evidently, the altar at Gibeon was much larger than the one
Solomon had available in Jerusalem, hence his move to Gibeon to offer a huge sacrifice.

5. *a night-dream.* This is a lesser form of divine revelation, one even vouchsafed the pagan
king Abimelech (Genesis 20). In the David story, God calls upon Nathan the prophet in
a night-vision, but it is Nathan as intermediary who then goes to deliver the message to
David (2 Samuel 7).

6. *David my father . . . walked in Your presence in truth and in justice.* The words assigned
here to Solomon adopt the Deuteronomist's revisionist portrait of David (see the comment
on 2:3–4) as an exemplary servant of God. The actual representation of David gives us a
much more mixed picture of the man with all his calculations of power and his weaknesses
and moral failings.

7 kindness and gave him a son sitting on his throne to this day. And now, O
LORD my God, You Yourself made Your servant king in place of my father
8 when I was a young lad, not knowing how to lead into the fray. And Your
servant was in the midst of Your people that You chose, a multitudinous
people that could not be numbered and could not be counted for all its
9 multitude. May You give Your servant an understanding heart to discern
10 between good and evil. For who can judge this vast people of Yours?" And
the thing was good in the eyes of the LORD that Solomon had asked for this
11 thing. And God said to him, "Inasmuch as you have asked for this thing
and you did not ask long life for yourself and did not ask wealth for yourself and did not ask for the life of your enemies, but you asked to discern
12 and understand justice, look, I am doing according to your words. Look, I
give you a wise and discerning heart, so that your like there will not have
13 been before you, and after you none like you shall arise. And even what
you did not ask I give to you—both wealth and honor, so that there will
14 not have been any man like you among kings all your days. And if you go
in My ways, to keep My statutes and My commands, as David your father
15 went, I shall grant you length of days." And Solomon awoke and, look, it
was a dream. And he came to Jerusalem and stood before the Ark of the
LORD's Covenant and offered up burnt offerings and prepared well-being
16 sacrifices and made a feast for all his servants. Then two whore-women did
17 come to the king and stood in his presence. And the one woman said, "I

---

7. *not knowing how to lead into the fray.* The account of Solomon's reign does not represent
him as a military leader combating surrounding nations, but in assuming the throne he
does have dangerous enemies in the court who could have contested the succession.

9. *May You give Your servant an understanding heart.* Solomon's legendary wisdom is here
given a divine etiology: it is the one gift he asks of God, and it is granted.
　　vast. Elsewhere this term usually means "heavy."

13. *wealth and honor, so that there will not have been any man like you among kings.* This
statement, of course, is a fantastic exaggeration because the head of a small kingdom like
Israel could scarcely compare with the monarchs who commanded the great empires to
the east and the south. Solomon, quite unlike David, is manifestly woven out of the stuff
of legend in this literary account.

16. *Then two whore-woman.* The introduction of the story with "then," *'az,* is unusual in
Hebrew narrative. It clearly serves to mark a direct link with the preceding episode: the gift
of wisdom that God has granted Solomon will now be exemplified in this tale.
　　stood in his presence. A primary function of the monarch, in the Bible and in the Ugaritic
texts before it, is to administer justice, and so the two whores come before him to make
their case against each other.

beseech you, my lord. I and this woman live in a single house, and I gave
birth alongside her in the house. And it happened on the third day after 18
I gave birth that this woman, too, gave birth, and we were together, no
stranger was with us in the house, just the two of us in the house. And this 19
woman's son died during the night, as she had lain upon him. And she 20
rose in the middle of the night and took my son from by me, your servant
being asleep, and she laid him in her lap, and her dead son she laid in my
lap. And I rose in the morning to nurse my son, and, look, he was dead, 21
and when I examined him in the morning, look, he was not my son whom
I had born." And the other woman said, "No, for my son is the living one 22
and your son is dead." And the other said, "No, for your son is dead and
my son is the living one." And they spoke before the king. And the king 23
said, "This one says, 'This is my live son and your son is dead,' and this
one says, 'No, for your son is dead and my son is the living one.'" And the 24
king said, "Fetch me a sword." And they brought a sword before the king.
And the king said, "Cut the living child in two, and give half to one and 25
half to the other." And the woman whose son was alive said to the king, 26
for her compassion welled up for her son, and she said, "I beseech you, my
lord, give her the living newborn but absolutely do not put him to death."

---

17. *a single house . . . gave birth alongside her in the house.* The repetition of "house" (which
recurs still again twice in the next verse) both underlines the idea of their sharing quarters
and reflects the style of this story, which abounds in symmetrical repetitions. It may not
be coincidental that the larger narrative of Solomon begins (verse 1) by twice using the
same word, "house."

18. *no stranger was with us.* There are therefore no witnesses.

19. *as she had lain upon him.* There is thus a suggestion that the mother of the dead child
may have been negligent, and at any rate she was inadvertently responsible for her infant's
death.

22. *"No, for my son" . . . And the other said, "No, for your son."* This interechoing dialogue,
heightened by the fact that neither woman is given a name, underscores the seeming unde-
cidability of the case: each is saying exactly the same thing, so how can anyone know which
one is lying? Solomon's repetition of their words in the next verse amplifies this effect.

25. *Cut the living child in two.* This momentarily shocking decree, which then will be seen
to be a manifestation of Solomon's wisdom, is a clear expression of the fabulous or folktale
character of the whole story. There is an approximate equivalent of the Judgment of Solomon in Indian literature that some scholars think may even have been its ultimate source,
reaching ancient Israel through oral transmission. In any case, it sounds very much like
a tale of surprising wisdom told among the people, or perhaps among many peoples, that
was eventually attributed to Solomon.

And the other was saying, "Neither mine nor yours shall he be. Cut him
27 apart!" And the king spoke up and said, "Give her the living newborn, and
28 absolutely do not put him to death. She is his mother." And all Israel heard
of the judgment that the king had judged, and they held the king in awe,
for they saw that God's wisdom was within him to do justice.

1 **CHAPTER 4**   And Solomon was king over all Israel.
2   And these are the names of the officials he had:
       Azariah son of Zadok the priest.
3   Elihoreph and Ahijah sons of Shisha, scribes.
       Jehoshaphat son of Ehilud, recorder.
4   And Benaiah son of Jehoiada, over the army.
       And Zadok and Abiathar, priests.
5   And Azariah son of Nathan, over the prefects.
       And Zabud son of Nathan the priest, the king's companion.

---

26. *Neither mine nor yours shall he be.* Finally, the bewildering symmetry between the two
women is shattered, and the false mother reveals herself.

    Cut him apart. This plural imperative is a single word in the Hebrew, *gezoru* ("cut"),
exposing the brutal lack of maternal feeling of the lying woman.

28. *for they saw that God's wisdom was within him.* This concluding flourish confirms that
God's promise to Solomon of a discerning heart has been amply realized.

CHAPTER 4   1. *And Solomon was king over all Israel.* This declaration of his sovereignty over the entire nation prefaces the catalogue of his royal bureaucracy.

2. *And these are the names of the officials he had.* Everything that follows in this chapter
is another indication of the composite character of the Solomon narrative. First we have
the story of his ascent to the throne, which is actually the last episode of the David story
and manifestly written by its brilliant author. Then we are given the report of Solomon's
dream-vision in which he asks for the gift of wisdom, which is followed by the folktale of
Solomon's Judgment, illustrating the exercise of that wisdom. Now we are presented with
two documents listing the royal bureaucracy. The first lists the members of his cabinet
in the Jerusalem court, and the second the prefects overseeing the sundry regions of the
country and making sure each supplies its due provision—a form of taxation—to the royal
court. Both these sections may be old documents, though there are at least a few seemingly
scrambled entries and probably some later additions.

    son of Zadok. Zadok is the priest who sided with Solomon in his struggle for the throne.
Not surprisingly, several of the members of the king's inner circle listed here are either his
supporters, or the sons of his supporters, in that struggle.

4. *Benaiah.* He is the man Solomon sent to kill Joab.

And Ahishar, over the house,   6
and Adoniram son of Abda, over the forced labor.

And Solomon had twelve prefects over all Israel, and they provisioned the   7
king and his household—one month in a year each one had to provision.
And these were their names: Ben-Hur, in the high country of Ephraim.   8
Ben-Deker, in Makaz and in Shaalbim and Beth-Shemesh and Elon-   9
Beth-Hanan. Ben-Hesed, in Arubboth, his was Socho and all the land   10
of Hepher. Ben-Abinadab, all Naphath-Dor. Taphath daughter of Solo-   11
mon became his wife. Baana son of Ahilud, Taanach and Megiddo and   12
all Beth-She'an, which is by Zarethon below Jezreel, from Beth-She'an as
far as Abel-Meholah, as far as the other side of Jokneam. Ben-Geber, in   13
Ramoth-Gilead. His were the hamlets of Jair son of Manasseh that were in
Bashan. His was the region of Argob which is in Bashan, sixty great towns
with walls and bronze bolts. Ahinadab son of Iddo, at Mahanaim. Ahi-   14,15
maaz in Naphtali. He, too, took a daughter of Solomon, Bosmath, as wife.
Baanah son of Hushi, in Asher and Bealoth. Jehoshaphat son of Paruah,   16,17
in Issachar. Shimei son of Ela in Benjamin. Geber son of Uri, in the land   18,19
of Gilead, the land of Shihor king of the Amorites and Og king of Bashan.
And one prefect who was in the land of Judah. And Israel was multitudi-   20
nous as the sand of the sea in multitude, eating and drinking and rejoicing.

---

6. *forced labor.* Conscripted labor on behalf of the king was another instrument of taxation.

8. *Ben-Hur.* An oddity of the list of prefects is that many names are given with patronymic only and no first name.

19. *And one prefect who was in the land of Judah.* The Masoretic Text reads "And one prefect who was in the land." The next verse then begins "Judah and Israel were multitudinous." That division of the text is problematic for two reasons: it is unclear what a prefect "in the land," with no specified territory to supervise, would be doing; beginning a new sentence without an introductory "and" (simply, "Judah") diverges from the norm of biblical narrative style. The assumption of this translation is that in addition to the twelve prefects named, there was to be a thirteenth prefect, perhaps designated ad hoc by the king, over the king's own tribal territory, which would also be obliged to make an annual contribution to the court.

20. *eating and drinking and rejoicing.* The last term of this series could also mean "making merry." Although all the regions of the country have to make annual contributions to the court, the implication of this verse is that the prosperity—contrary to Samuel's dire warnings about the monarchy in 1 Samuel 8—was shared by the entire country as its population swelled.

1 CHAPTER 5   And Solomon ruled over all the kingdoms from
the River to the land of the Philistines and as far as the border of Egypt.
2 They offered tribute and served Solomon all the days of his life. And
Solomon's fare for a single day was thirty *kors* of fine flour and sixty *kors*
3 of plain flour, ten fatted oxen and twenty pasture-fed oxen and a hundred
4 sheep, besides deer and gazelle and roebuck and fatted geese. For he held
sway over all that was west of the River from Tiphsah as far as Gaza, over
all the kings west of the River. And he had peace on all sides round about.
5 And Judah and Israel dwelled secure, each man under his vine and under
6 his fig tree, from Dan to Beersheba, all the days of Solomon. And Solomon had forty thousand horse stalls for his chariots and twelve thousand
7 horsemen. And those prefects provisioned King Solomon and all who
were adjoined to King Solomon's table, each one for his month, they let
8 nothing lack. And they would bring the barley and the straw for the horses
and for the chargers to the place where each was, each man according to his
9 regimen. And God gave very great wisdom and discernment to Solomon
and breadth of understanding like the sand that is on the shore of the sea.
10 And Solomon's wisdom was greater than the wisdom of all the Easterners
11 and all the wisdom of Egypt. And he was wiser than all men, than Ethan
the Ezrahite and Heman and Calcol and Darda, the sons of Mahol, and
12 his fame was in all the nations round about. And he spoke three thousand

---

CHAPTER 5   1. *ruled . . . offered.* The Hebrew uses a participial form of the verb,
suggesting sustained activity over an extended time-span.
    the River. As throughout the Bible, this means the Euphrates. It is highly unlikely that
all the kingdoms to the east as far as the Euphrates could have been subject to Solomon.

2. *fare.* The literal sense is "bread," a synecdoche for all kinds of food, and the list that follows includes meat and fowl.
    kors. The *kor* is a large measure, so 30 *kors* would have been hundreds of pounds.

3. *geese.* In modern Hebrew, *barbur* means "swan," but swans were rare in ancient Israel,
and the likely fowl is the goose.

10. *greater than the wisdom of all the Easterners and all the wisdom of Egypt.* Wisdom was a
known international activity, and both Mesopotamia and Egypt were renowned for their
wisdom schools, their achievements in astronomy, mathematics, and much else. Here the
celebration of Solomon's unmatched wisdom is properly referred to the broad Near Eastern
context.

11. *Ethan . . . and Heman and Calcol and Darda.* The first two are temple poets to whom,
respectively, Psalm 88 and Psalm 89 are attributed, and the last two are mentioned in 1
Chronicles 2:6 as temple choristers, although in Chronicles the last name is spelled Dara.
The link between wisdom and the fashioning of poetry or song is a commonly shared
assumption in the ancient Near East.

proverbs, and his poems came to five thousand. And he spoke of the trees, 13
from the cedar that is in Lebanon to the moss that springs from the wall,
and he spoke of beasts and birds and creeping things and fish. And from 14
all peoples they came to listen to Solomon's wisdom, from all the kings of
the earth who had heard of his wisdom.

And Hiram king of Tyre sent his servants to Solomon, for he had heard 15
that they had anointed him king in his father's stead, for Hiram was
friendly toward David always. And Solomon sent to Hiram, saying, "You 16,17
yourself knew of David my father that he could not build a house for the
LORD his God because of the fighting that was all round him, until the
LORD should set them under his footsoles. And now, the LORD my God 18
has granted me rest all around. There is no adversary nor evil chancing.
And I am about to build a house for the name of the LORD my God as the 19
LORD spoke to David my father, saying, 'Your son whom I put in your
stead on your throne, he shall build the house for My name.' And now, 20
charge that they cut down cedars from Lebanon, and my servants will
be with your servants, and the wages of your servants I shall give you,
whatever you say, for you yourself know that there is no man among us
who knows how to cut down trees like the Sidonians." And it happened 21

---

12. *proverbs.* The proverb was thought of as a quintessential expression of wisdom, a notion
evident in the Book of Proverbs, attributed by tradition to Solomon, in part because of this
passage. The proverb was formulated in verse, and other kinds of poetry as well are supposed
to have been composed by Solomon.

13. *trees . . . beasts . . . birds . . . creeping things . . . fish.* Solomon's wisdom includes a mastery
of the whole realm of nature. The words here gave rise to later legends that Solomon was
able to speak the language of animals.

15. *Hiram king of Tyre.* Tyre is the principal city on the Phoenician coast.
    Hiram was friendly toward David always. These words may reflect an actual historical
alliance. It was David who subdued the Philistines, the great enemies of the Phoenicians on
the Mediterranean coast, and that victory might conceivably have enabled the commercial
and colonial impetus enjoyed by Phoenicia in the tenth century B.C.E.

17. *should set them under his footsoles.* This posture of subjugation appears in quite a few
ancient Near Eastern bas-reliefs celebrating the victory of a king.

20. *my servants will be with your servants.* This proposal of joint labor may have been motivated by a desire to expedite the costly work. Hiram doesn't mention it in his response,
perhaps because he is not enthusiastic about the idea, but verse 27 reports that ten thousand
Israelite workers were sent each month to Lebanon.
    no man among us . . . knows how to cut down trees like the Sidonians. Sidon is another
Phoenician city, and "Sidonians" is often used as a general term for Phoenicians. It is in

when Hiram heard Solomon's words that he greatly rejoiced, and he said,
"Blessed is the LORD today, that He has given David a wise son over this
22 large people." And Hiram sent to Solomon, saying, "I have heard what
you sent to me. I will meet all you desire in cedarwood and in cypress-
23 wood. My servants will come down from Lebanon to the sea, and I will
turn the wood into rafts in the sea, to the place that you will tell me, and
I will break it up there and you will bear it off. And you on your part will
24 meet my desire to provide the bread of my house." And so Hiram gave to
25 Solomon cedar trees and cypress trees, all he desired. And Solomon gave
to Hiram twenty thousand *kors* of wheat as provision for his house and
twenty thousand *kors* of fine-pressed oil. Thus would Solomon give to
26 Hiram year after year. And the LORD had given wisdom to Solomon as He
had spoken to him. And there was peace between Hiram and Solomon,
27 and the two sealed a pact. And King Solomon exacted forced labor from
28 all Israel, and the forced labor came to thirty thousand men. And he sent
them to Lebanon—ten thousand a month, by turns they were a month in

---

their territory that there are large stands of timber, which they used to build ships and as
a valuable export, and so they were experienced lumberjacks.

21. *when Hiram heard Solomon's words.* A possible though not necessary inference from
this formulation is that Solomon's message was oral, but the emissary or a courtier might
have read out a written message to the king.

   he greatly rejoiced. He has good reason to rejoice because he sees here the opportunity
for a lucrative agreement. The words that immediately follow are his exclamation and not
part of his message in response to Solomon.

23. *My servants will come down from Lebanon to the sea.* They will take charge of transporting the timber from the mountainsides to the seashore.

   the wood. This word is added in the translation for clarity. The Hebrew says "them," a
plural accusative suffix referring to "the trees."

   turn the wood into rafts. Binding the cut logs together into improvised rafts is a widespread device for transporting timber by water.

   meet my desire to provide the bread of my house. Solomon had offered to pay the wages of
Hiram's workers. Hiram now counters this proposal by stipulating a much higher price—
the cost of provisions for the Phoenician court with all its entourage for the entire period
in which the labor is done. In this whole exchange, there is an element of canny bargaining
reminiscent of the negotiations over a gravesite between Abraham and Ephron the Hittite
in Genesis 23.

25. *twenty thousand* kors *of wheat . . . twenty thousand* kors *of fine-pressed oil.* The price
exacted, one notes, is very high. Solomon provides wheat and olive oil, which the Land of
Israel had in abundance. The mountainous terrain of Lebanon did not favor the cultivation
of these crops but was ideally suited for timber, which Israel lacked.

Lebanon and two months at his house. And Adoniram was over the forced labor. And Solomon had seventy thousand porters and eighty thousand 29 quarriers in the mountains, besides Solomon's prefect officers who were 30 over the labor, three thousand three hundred, who held sway over the people doing the labor. And the king gave the order, and they moved great 31 stones, costly stones, for the foundation of the house, hewn stones. And 32 Solomon's builders and Hiram's builders and the Gebalites carved and readied the timber and the stones to build the house.

CHAPTER 6　　　　And it happened in the four hundred and 1 eightieth year after the Israelites came out of Egypt, in King Solomon's fourth year in the month of Ziv, which is the second month, that he set out to build a house to the LORD. And the house that King Solomon built 2 was sixty cubits in length and twenty in width and thirty cubits in height. And the outer court that was in front of the great hall of the house was 3 twenty cubits in length along the width of the house, ten cubits in width

---

31. *they moved great stones.* The stones, of course, would have been a much bigger challenge to transport than the wood, which was floated most of the way, but there were quarries in the mountains of Judah not far from Jerusalem.

32. *And Solomon's builders and Hiram's builders and the Gebalites.* It emerges that there was a blended labor force of Phoenicians and Israelites both in Lebanon and in Jerusalem. The Gebalites are residents of the Phoenician town of Gebal. One may infer from the separate reference to them here that they constituted a kind of guild with special building skills, perhaps as stonemasons.

CHAPTER 6　　　　1. *the four hundred and eightieth year.* This is a manifestly schematic figure, produced by multiplying two formulaic numbers, forty and twelve. In fact, the number of years from the Exodus to the building of the Temple would be not much more than half of 480.

　　　in the month of Ziv. This name for the second month, which would roughly correspond to May, is borrowed from the Phoenician, and that may be why an explanatory gloss is added, "which is the second month." The term for month is also not the standard term, *ḥodesh*, but rather *yareaḥ* (literally, "moon"). *Ziv* means "brilliance," "bright light."

2. *sixty cubits.* This would be less than 120 feet, perhaps as little as 100 feet, which makes Solomon's temple a relatively intimate structure—the Chartres cathedral is three times as long, and the great mosque at Cordova, before its conversion into a church, still larger. These dimensions may be historically accurate.

4 along the house. And he made inset and latticed windows for the house.
5 And he built on the wall of the house a balcony all around the walls of
the house in the great hall and in the sanctuary, and he made supports
6 all around. And the lowest balcony was five cubits in width and the
middle one six cubits in width and the third one seven cubits in width,
for he set recesses in the house all around on the outside so as to fasten
7 nothing to the walls of the house. And the house when it was built, of
whole stones brought from the quarry it was built, and no hammers nor
8 axes nor any iron tools were heard in the house when it was built. The
entrance at the middle support was on the right side of the house, and
on spiral stairs they would go up to the middle chamber and from the
9 middle to the third. And he built the house and finished it, and he pan-
10 eled the house with cedar beams and boards. And he built the balcony
over all the house, five cubits in height, and it held the house fast in
11,12 cedarwood. And the word of the LORD came to Solomon, saying: "This
house that you build—if you walk by My statutes and do My laws and
keep all My commands to walk by them, I shall fulfill My word with
13 you that I spoke to David your father, and I shall dwell in the midst of

---

4. *he made inset and latticed windows for the house.* The reader should be warned that the precise meaning of these and other architectural terms here is uncertain. Because of the perennial fascination with Solomon's temple, many elaborate attempts to reconstruct its exact configuration have been made, in analytic descriptions, drawings, and scale models, but all of these remain highly conjectural. What is clear is that, like the sanctuary in Exodus, it had a tripartite structure: an outer court (*'ulam*), a great hall (*heikhal*), and an inner sanctuary (*devir*) in which the Ark of the Covenant was placed.

5. *balcony . . . supports.* The meaning of both these Hebrew terms, *yatsia'* and *tsela'ot*, is much disputed.

7. *of whole stones . . . it was built, and no hammers nor axes nor any iron tools were heard in the house.* The stones were dressed at the site of the quarry and then set in place in Jerusalem. This procedure in part picks up the instructions for building the altar in Exodus 20:25: "you shall not build them of hewn stones, for your sword you would brandish over it and profane it."

9. *And he built the house and finished it.* This report of completion marks the finishing of the stone structure. What follows is an account of the paneling, carving, and finishing of the structure.

12. *if you walk by My statutes and do My laws.* The language in God's speech is preeminently Deuteronomistic.

the Israelites, and I shall not forsake My people Israel." And Solomon 14
built the house and finished it. And he built the walls of the house from 15
within with cedar supports from the floor of the house to the ceiling,
overlaid it with wood within, and he overlaid the floor of the house with
cypress supports. And he built the twenty cubits from the corners of the 16
house with cedar supports from the floor to the walls, and he built it from
within the sanctuary, the Holy of Holies. And the house was forty cubits, 17
which was the great hall. And cedar was the house inside, a weave of birds 18
and blossoms. Everything was cedar, no stone was seen. And the sanctu- 19
ary in the innermost part of the house he readied to place there the Ark
of the Covenant of the LORD. And before the sanctuary twenty cubits in 20
length and twenty cubits in width and twenty cubits in height he overlaid
with pure gold, and he overlaid the altar with cedar. And Solomon over- 21
laid the house from within with pure gold, and he fastened gold chains in
front of the sanctuary and overlaid it with gold. And the house he overlaid 22
with gold till the whole house was finished, and the whole altar which
was in the inner sanctum he overlaid with gold. And in the sanctuary he 23
made two cherubim of olivewood, one cherub with a five-cubit wing and 24
the other wing five cubits, ten cubits from one edge of its wings to the
other. And the second cherub was ten cubits, a single measure and shape 25
for both cherubim. The height of the one cherub was ten cubits, and the 26
same for the second cherub. And he placed the cherubim within the inner 27

---

14. *And Solomon built the house and finished it.* These words are what scholars call a "resumptive repetition" of verse 9. That is, when the continuity of a narrative is interrupted—here,
by God's address to Solomon—phrases or sentences from just before the break are repeated
as the narrative resumes its forward momentum.

16. *and he built it from within the sanctuary, the Holy of Holies.* This is the first of several
places in this chapter where the Hebrew syntax seems a little doubtful.

18. *a weave.* The "weave" of course is a carving of interlaced ornamental figures.
    Everything was cedar, no stone was seen. The cedarwood paneling entirely covered the
stone surfaces. The pervasive use of wooden elements made the stone structure thoroughly
flammable, as the Babylonian army would demonstrate when it destroyed the temple in
586 B.C.E.

23. *two cherubim.* In a borrowing from Canaanite mythology, the cherubim were imagined,
at least in poetry, as God's mounts. (The word *keruv* means either "mount" or "hybrid.")
They were fierce-looking winged beasts, probably with leonine bodies and heads, perhaps
resembling the Egyptian sphinx and other bas-relief figures that have been found across
the Near East.

chamber. And the wings of the cherubim were spread, and the wing of the one touched the wall and that of the second cherub touched the other
28 wall, and their inner wings touched wing to wing. And he overlaid the
29 cherubim with gold. And all the walls of the house all round he wove in carvings of intertwined cherubim and palms and birds, within and with-
30 out. And the floor of the house he overlaid with gold, within and without.
31 And the entrance of the sanctuary he made of olivewood doors, five-sided
32 capitals and doorposts, and two olivewood doors. And he wove on them a weave of cherubim and buds and overlaid them with gold, and he worked
33 the gold down over the cherubim and the palms. And the same he did for
34 the entrance of the great hall, four-sided olivewood doorposts. And the two doors were cypresswood, the two supports of the one door cylindrical
35 and the two supports of the other door cylindrical. And he wove cherubim and palms and buds and overlaid them with gold directly over the incising.
36 And he built the inner court in three rows of hewn stone and a row of cut
37 cedars. In the fourth year did he lay the foundations of the LORD's house,
38 in the month of Ziv. And in the eleventh year, in the month of Bul, which is the eighth month, he finished the house in all its details and in all its designs, and he was seven years building it.

---

30. *the floor of the house he overlaid with gold.* From what can be made out from the preceding description, the gold would have been overlaid on the cedar paneling.

31. *five-sided capitals and doorposts.* The translation of the three Hebrew words here is conjectural, and the text looks suspect. It may well be that the ancient scribes were as confused as we moderns by the architectural details and thus scrambled words at some points.

33. *four-sided.* The Hebrew term is problematic in the same way that "five-sided" is in verse 31.

35. *directly over the incising.* This is still another architectural indication of uncertain meaning.

38. *in the eleventh year.* Thus the years of the building of the Temple are reported to conform to the sacred number seven, as the end of this verse confirms with a flourish.
    in the month of Bul. This is still another Phoenician month name, accompanied by an explanatory gloss, as is Ziv in verse 1, and again the unusual term *yareaḥ* is used for "month." As the eighth month, it would come in the late fall, and the name Bul may derive from a word that means "harvest."

CHAPTER 7   And his own house Solomon was building for ₁
thirteen years, and he finished his house. And he built the Lebanon Forest ₂
House, a hundred cubits in length and fifty cubits in width and thirty cubits
in height with four rows of cedar columns and cedar beams on the columns.
And it was paneled in cedarwood from above on the supports, which were ₃
on the columns, forty-five, fifteen in each row. And there were windows in ₄
three rows, three tiers face-to-face. And all the entrances and the doorposts ₅
were square-windowed, three tiers face-to-face. And the Court of Columns ₆
he made fifty cubits in length and thirty cubits in width, and the court was
in front of the columns, and the columns with a beam over them. And the ₇
Court of the Throne, where he meted out justice, the Court of Justice, did
he make, and it was paneled in cedarwood from floor to roof-beams. And ₈
in his house in which he would dwell, there was another court besides the
outer court made in the same fashion, and he made a house for Pharaoh's
daughter whom Solomon had married, like this court. All these were of ₉
costly stones, hewn in measure, smoothed with an adze inside and out, and
from the foundation up to the coping and on the outside up to the great
court, and founded with costly stones, great stones, stones of ten cubits and ₁₀
stones of eight cubits. And above were costly stones hewn in measure, and ₁₁
cedarwood. And the great court all around had three rows of hewn stone ₁₂

CHAPTER 7   1. *his own house.* Solomon's two main building projects were the
Temple and the palace. No date is given for the inception of the palace, but the notation in
9:7 that the building of the two structures together took twenty years would indicate that
the palace was begun after the Temple was completed. The palace, the bigger of the two
structures, took almost twice as long to build.

2. *the Lebanon Forest House.* This structure is evidently so called because of the rows of
Lebanon cedar it contained. Some think it may have served as an armory.

4. *three tiers face-to-face.* This is the first of many places in this chapter where the architectural indications are quite obscure in the Hebrew, whether because of scribal scrambling or
because we have lost the precise applications of this technical vocabulary. In much of what
follows, then, any translation, including this one, is no more than educated guesswork.

6. *beam.* The Hebrew *'av* usually means "cloud," leading some to speculate that here it
might refer to some sort of canopy or cover.

7. *from floor to roof-beams.* The Masoretic Text reads "from floor to floor," but the Septuagint, more plausibly, has "from floor to roof-beams."

8. *he made a house for Pharaoh's daughter.* Although the ground plan of the palace is hard to
reconstruct, the fact that a separate residence was built for one of Solomon's wives reflects
the grandeur of the overall construction.

and a row of cedar planks, as for the inner court of the house of the LORD
and for the outer court of the house.

13,14 And King Solomon sent and fetched Hiram from Tyre. He was the son of
a widow-woman from the tribe of Naphtali, and his father was a Tyrean
man who was a coppersmith, and he was filled with wisdom and discerning and knowledge to do every task in bronze. And he came to King
15 Solomon and did all his task. And he fashioned the two pillars of bronze,
eighteen cubits the height of each column, and a twelve-cubit line went
16 round the second pillar. And he made two capitals to put on the tops of
the pillars, cast in bronze, five cubits the height of the one capital and
17 five cubits the height of the other capital. Nets of meshwork, chainwork
wreaths for the capitals that were on the top of the pillars, seven for the
18 one capital and seven for the other. And he made the pillars, with two
rows around over the one net to cover the capitals that were on top of the
19 pomegranates, and so he did for the other capital. And the capitals that
were on top of the pillars in the outer court were a lily design, four cubits
20 high. And the capitals on the two pillars above as well, opposite the curve
that was over against the net, and the pomegranates were in two hundred
21 rows around on the second capital. And he set up the pillars for the great
hall and set up the right pillar and called its name Jachin and set up the
22 left pillar and called its name Boaz. And on the top of the pillars was a

---

13. *And King Solomon sent and fetched Hiram from Tyre.* The legendary and schematic
character of the narrative at this point is manifest: it is highly unlikely that the Phoenician
king himself would come to Jerusalem to perform or even supervise the building work.
What this refers to is that Hiram may have sent master artisans from Tyre to participate
in the project.

14. *He was the son of a widow-woman from the tribe of Naphtali.* It is even more unlikely
that a Phoenician king would have had an Israelite mother, and a woman previously married, besides. The narrative here may be reaching to establish a genetic connection between
Israel and the foreign king who helped to build both the Temple and the palace.

 his father was a Tyrean man who was a coppersmith. The notion of an artisan king (both
Hiram's father and Hiram are represented as that) sounds odd, but the idea is that the king
is imagined to embody the distinctive skills and expertise of his people.

20. *the curve.* The Hebrew is literally "belly," and its architectural meaning is uncertain.

21. *Jachin . . . Boaz.* The naming of pillars and altars was not uncommon in the ancient
Near East. These two names mean "he will firmly found" (*yakhin*) and "strength in him"
(the latter is an attested personal name). Both names appear to refer to the stability of the
royal dynasty.

lily design. And the task of the pillars was finished. And he made the 23
cast-metal sea ten cubits from edge to edge, circular all around, and five
cubits in height, and a line of thirty cubits going all around. And birds 24
beneath its edge going all around it, ten cubits, encompassing the sea all
around, two rows cast in its casting. It stood on twelve oxen, three facing 25
north and three facing west and three facing south and three facing east.
And the sea was on top of them, and their hind parts were inward. And 26
its thickness was a hand-span, and its rim like the design of a cup's rim,
blossom and lily, two thousand *bats* did it hold. And he made ten stands 27
of bronze, four cubits in length each stand and four cubits in width and
three cubits in height. And this was the design of the stands: they had 28
frames, and there were frames between the rungs. And on the frames 29
between the rungs were lions, oxen, and cherubim on the bevels, so it was
above and below the lions and the oxen, hammered metal spirals. And 30
each stand had four bronze wheels and bronze axletrees. And its four legs
had brackets beneath the laver. The brackets were cast in spirals opposite
each. And its spout was within the capital a cubit above it, and its spout 31
was round in the design of a stand, a cubit and a half. And on its spout,
too, there was woven-work. And their frames were square, not round
And the four wheels were beneath the frames, and the axletrees of the 32
wheels inserted in the stand. And the height of each wheel was a cubit
and a half. And the design of the wheels was like the design of a chariot's 33
wheels. Their axletrees and rims and their spokes and their hubs were
all of cast metal. And the four brackets at the four corners of each stand, 34
of a piece with the stand were its brackets. And on top of the stand was 35

---

23. *the cast-metal sea.* This is essentially a metal pool, to be used by the priests to bathe
hands and feet before they perform their ritual duties. The Hebrew uses the rather grand
term "sea" (*yam*) perhaps to suggest a cosmic correspondence between the structure of the
Temple and of creation at large.

   a line. The translation reads, with many Hebrew manuscripts, *qaw* for the incomprehensible Masoretic *qawoh.*

26. *two thousand* bats. The *bat* is a relatively large unit of liquid measure, but the precise
quantity is uncertain.

28. *rungs.* The meaning of the Hebrew *shelabim* is conjectural, but a laddered structure
may be involved.

30. *four bronze wheels.* Wheeled ritual vessels have been uncovered across the Near East.
   in spirals opposite each. The Hebrew here is particularly obscure.

31. *woven-work.* As elsewhere, the term refers to carved interlaced figures.

a circular form all around, and on top of the stand its brackets and its
36 frames were of a piece with it. And he carved on the panels of its brackets
and on its frames cherubim, lions, and palms, each laid bare, and a spiral
37 all around. Thus did he make the ten stands, each cast the same, a single
38 measure and a single shape they all had. And he made ten lavers of bronze,
each laver would hold forty *bats*, four cubits each laver on each stand, for
39 the ten stands. And he placed the stands, five on the right side of the house
and five on the left side of the house. And the sea he placed on the right
40 side of the house to the east, facing south. And Hiram made the lavers
and the shovels and the basins. And Hiram completed doing the task that
41 he had done for King Solomon in the house of the LORD: two pillars and
two globes of the capitals that were on top of the pillars and two nets to
42 cover the two globes of the capitals that were on top of the pillars, and
four hundred pomegranates for the nets, two rows of pomegranates for
43 every net to cover the globes of the capitals that were on the pillars, and the
44 ten stands and the ten lavers on the stands, and the one sea and the twelve
45 oxen beneath the sea. And the bowls and the shovels and the basins and
those vessels that Hiram made for King Solomon in the house of the LORD,
46 burnished bronze. In the plain of the Jordan did the king cast them, in the
47 thick of the ground, between Succoth and Zarethan. And Solomon left
all the vessels unweighed on account of their very great abundance; the
48 measure of the bronze was not taken. And Solomon made all the vessels
that were in the house of the LORD, the gold altar and the gold table on
49 which was the bread of display, and the pure gold lampstands, five on the
right and five on the left in front of the sanctuary, and the gold blossoms

---

36. *each laid bare.* The Hebrew *kema'ar 'ish* is not intelligible. The translation is based on a tentative guess that the first of these words is a verbal noun derived from the root '-r-h, "lay bare."

40. *And Hiram completed doing the task that he had done.* This is an explicit echoing of Genesis 2:2, suggesting that the work of building the Temple is analogous to the work of building the world.

41. *two pillars and two globes.* What begins here is a summarizing catalogue of all the sacred furniture fashioned for the Temple.

45. *those.* The translation reads, with many Hebrew manuscripts, *ha'eleh* for the incomprehensible Masoretic *ha'ehel* (a simple reversal of consonants, which is a common scribal error).

46. *in the thick of the ground.* The casting was done in earthen molds.

47. *unweighed.* This term is merely implied in the Hebrew.

and lamps and tongs, and the pure gold bowls and the snuffers and the 50
basins and the ladles and fire-pans, and the gold sockets for the doors of
the inner house, for the Holy of Holies, for the doors of the great hall of
the house. And the task that King Solomon had done was finished in the 51
house of the LORD, and Solomon brought the dedicated things of David
his father, the silver and the gold, and he placed the vessels in the treasury
of the house of the LORD.

CHAPTER 8

CHAPTER 8   Then did Solomon assemble the elders of Israel, 1
all the heads of the tribes, the patriarchal chieftains of the Israelites, round
King Solomon in Jerusalem, to bring up the Ark of the Covenant of the
LORD from the City of David, which is Zion. And every man of Israel 2
assembled round Solomon in the month of Ethanim, which is the seventh
month, at the festival. And all the elders of Israel came, and the priests 3
carried the Ark. And they brought up the Ark of the LORD and the Tent of 4
Meeting and all the sacred vessels that were in the Tent, and the priests and
the Levites brought them up. And King Solomon and all the community 5
of Israel who had gathered round him were with him before the Ark, sacrificing sheep and oxen that could not be numbered for their abundance.
And the priests brought the Ark of the Covenant of the LORD to its place, 6
to the sanctuary of the house, to the Holy of Holies, beneath the wings of

---

50. *snuffers.* Others, including many Jewish commentators from Late Antiquity on, construe this to mean "musical instruments."

51. *And the task that King Solomon had done was finished.* Through both this long chapter
and the preceding one, it should be observed that Solomon virtually disappears as an
individualized character: the king here functions as an impersonal royal "he" who directs
these elaborate building projects.

CHAPTER 8   1. *the City of David, which is Zion.* Though part of Jerusalem, this
area is distinct from the Temple mount, to its west. The Ark was kept here in a temporary
structure (probably the Tent of Meeting) after David brought it up to Jerusalem (see 2
Samuel 6:12),

2. *the month of Ethanim, which is the seventh month.* Again, a nonstandard nomenclature
for the months is used, necessitating the explanatory gloss. The seventh month would correspond approximately to October, and the festival celebrated on this occasion (see verse
65) is Succoth, which, because it was a seven-day festival at the end of the fall harvest, was
of the three pilgrim festivals the one for which the greatest number of celebrants came to
Jerusalem from all over the country. Solomon thus chooses wisely the time for dedicating
the Temple.

7 the cherubim. For the cherubim spread wings over the place of the Ark,
8 and the cherubim sheltered the Ark and its poles from above. And the poles
   extended, and the ends of the poles could be seen from the Holy Place in
   the front of the sanctuary, but they could not be seen from without, and
9 they have been there to this day. There was nothing in the Ark except the
   two stone tablets that Moses had put there on Horeb, which the LORD had
   sealed as a covenant with the Israelites when they came out of the land of
10 Egypt. And it happened when the priests came out of the Holy Place, that
11 a cloud filled the house of the LORD. And the priests could not stand up to
   minister because of the cloud, for the LORD's glory filled the house of the
12 LORD. Then did Solomon say:

> "The LORD meant to abide in thick fog.
13 > I indeed have built You a lofty house,
>   a firm place for Your dwelling forever."

14 And the king turned his face and blessed all the assembly of Israel with
15 all the assembly of Israel standing. And he said: "Blessed is the LORD God
   of Israel Who spoke with His own mouth to David my father, and with
16 His own hand has fulfilled it, saying, 'From the day that I brought out My
   people Israel from Egypt, I have not chosen a town from all the tribes of

---

7. *its poles.* The Ark was a portable structure, carried on poles.

9. *as a covenant.* These words are merely implied by the verb "sealed."

11. *the LORD's glory filled the house.* The manifestation of God's glory, as is clear from a number of biblical texts, is a dense cloud. The ultimate source of this idea may be the poetic image of God, drawn from the Canaanite representation of Baal, as a dweller or rider of the clouds.

12. *Then did Solomon say.* This solemn declaration about where God abides is cast in a triadic line of poetry.
   The LORD meant to abide in thick fog. What tradition—especially, poetic tradition—tells us of Him is that He abides in the clouds above.

13. *I indeed have built You a lofty house.* But with the erection of the Temple, a new era is inaugurated in which the God of Israel has an earthly abode.
   a firm place for Your dwelling. This phrase, which will be repeated in Solomon's lengthy address, occurs at the end of the Song of the Sea, Exodus 15:17.

15. *to David my father.* This weighted designation is reiterated throughout the speech: Solomon, consolidating his own rule through the construction of the Temple, repeatedly emphasizes that he is David's son and sole heir and that God's promises to his father are now fulfilled in him.

Israel to build a house for My name to be there, but I chose David to be over My people Israel.' And it was in the heart of David my father to build 17 a house for the name of the LORD God of Israel. And the LORD said to 18 David my father, 'Inasmuch as it was in your heart to build a house for My name, you have done well, for it was in your heart. Only you will not build 19 the house, but your son, who issues from your loins, he will build the house for My name.' And the LORD has fulfilled His word that He spoke, 20 and I arose in place of David my father and sat on the throne of Israel as the LORD spoke and I have built the house for the name of the LORD God of Israel. And I have set there a place for the Ark in which is the covenant 21 of the LORD that He sealed with our fathers when He brought them out of the land of Egypt." And Solomon stood before the LORD's altar over against 22 all the assembly of Israel and spread his palms toward the heavens. And 23 he said, "LORD God of Israel! There is no god like You in the heavens above and on the earth below, keeping the covenant and the kindness for Your servants who walk before You with all their heart, which You kept for 24 David my father, what You spoke to him, and You spoke with Your own mouth, and with Your own hand You fulfilled it, as on this day. And now, 25 LORD God of Israel, keep for Your servant David my father what You spoke to him, saying, 'No man of yours will be cut off from before Me, sitting on the throne of Israel, if only your sons will keep their way to walk before Me as you have walked before Me.' And now, God of Israel, may Your 26

---

20. *I arose in place of David my father.* It should be recalled, as Solomon's phrasing here invites us to recall, that he was designated by his father to assume the throne while his father was still alive.

for the name of the LORD. The Temple is understood to enhance the glory or reputation ("the name") of the LORD.

21. *in which is the covenant.* The two stone tablets are conceived as the material equivalent of the covenant between God and Israel (see verse 9).

22. *spread his palms toward the heavens.* This conventional gesture of prayer is visible in many ancient Near Eastern statues and bas-reliefs.

23. *LORD God of Israel.* The first part of Solomon's speech is an address to Israel in which he reminds the people that God's promise to David is now fulfilled through his acts. At this point, he proceeds to voice a prayer to God.

There is no god like You in the heavens above and on the earth below. This wording may, like the Song of the Sea, reflects an older concept in which there are gods besides YHWH, but they are insubstantial and cannot compete with Him.

walk before You with all their heart. The language here is Deuteronomistic. The idiom "walk before" suggests entering into a relationship of devoted servitude.

27 words, pray, be shown true that You spoke to David my father. But can
God really dwell on earth? Look, the heavens and the heavens beyond the
heavens cannot contain You. How much less this house that I have built.
28 Yet turn to the prayer of Your servant and to his plea, LORD God of Israel,
to hearken to the glad song and to the prayer that Your servant prays
29 before You today, so that Your eyes be open to this house night and day,
to this place of which You have said, 'My name is there,' to hearken to the
30 prayer that Your servant prays in this place. And may You hearken to the
plea of Your servant and of Your people Israel, which they will pray in this
place, and may You hearken in Your dwelling place in the heavens, and
31 hearken and forgive what a man offends against his fellow and bears an
oath against him to bring a curse on him, and the oath comes before Your
32 altar in this house. But You will hearken in the heavens and judge Your
servant to condemn the guilty, to bring down his way on his head, and to
vindicate him who is right, to mete out to him according to his righteous-
33 ness. When Your people Israel are routed by an enemy, for they will offend
You, and they come back to You and acclaim Your name and pray and
34 plead to You in this house, You will hearken in the heavens and forgive the
offense of Your people Israel, and bring them back to the land that You
35 gave to their fathers. When the heavens are shut up and there is no rain,
for the Israelites will have offended against You, and they pray in this place
and acclaim Your name, You shall forgive the offense of Your servants and
36 turn back from their offense, for You will answer them. You will hearken
in the heavens and forgive the offense of Your servants, Your people Israel,

---

27. *can God really dwell on earth?* Solomon now touches on a theological problem raised
by the building of the Temple: it is figuratively and symbolically God's dwelling place, but
Solomon wants to deflect any literal notion that God actually abides in a human structure.

30. *hearken to the plea of Your servant and of Your people.* Throughout Solomon's prayer,
the emphasis is on the Temple as a place of prayer and supplication, a kind of terrestrial
communications center for speaking with God. Sacrifice is not mentioned. It is possible,
though not demonstrable, that the stress on prayer rather than sacrifice reflects some influence of the prophets, beginning with Isaiah in the late seventh century B.C.E. There are
other features of Solomon's speech that look late.

34. *bring them back to the land.* It is unlikely that the historical Solomon in the mid-tenth
century B.C.E., at the very moment of his royal grandeur, with peace all around, should have
introduced into his prayer, in the hearing of all Israel, this stark intimation of a future exile.
The plausible inference is that the speech, or at the very least this part of it, was composed
after the exile of the northern kingdom in 721 B.C.E. and perhaps even after the destruction
of the southern kingdom in 586 B.C.E.

35. *the Israelites.* The Hebrew says simply "they," but this implied antecedent is introduced
in the translation to avoid the impression that it is the heavens that have offended.

for You will teach them the good way in which they should walk, and You
will give rain upon Your land that You have given to Your people in estate.
Should there be famine in the land, should there be plague, blight, mildew,   37
locusts, caterpillars, should his enemy besiege him in the gates of his land,
any affliction, any disease, any prayer, any plea that any man have in all   38
Your people Israel, that every man know his heart's affliction, he shall
spread out his palms in this house. And You shall hearken in the heavens,   39
the firm place of Your dwelling, and You shall forgive and act and give to
a man according to his ways, as You know his heart, for You alone know
the heart of all men. So that they may fear You all the days that they live   40
on the land that You gave to their fathers. And the foreigner, too, who is   41
not from Your people Israel and has come from a distant land for the sake
of Your name, if he hearkens to Your great name and Your strong hand   42
and Your outstretched arm and comes and prays in this house, You will   43
hearken in the heavens, the firm place of Your dwelling and do as all that
the foreigner will call out to You, so that all the peoples of the earth may
know Your name to fear You as does Your people Israel, to know that Your
name has been called on this house that I have built. Should your people   44
go out to battle against its enemy on the way that You send them, they shall
pray to the LORD through the city that You have chosen and the house that
I have built for Your name. And You shall hearken in the heavens to their   45
prayer and to their plea, and You shall do justice for them. Should they   46
offend against You, for there is no man who does not offend, and You are
furious with them and give them to the enemy, and their captors take them
off to a distant or nearby land, and they turn their heart back to You in the   47

37. *Should there be famine in the land.* This long run-on sentence—and there are more
like it as the speech continues—is not typical of biblical prose style, although the Book
of Deuteronomy exhibits a fondness for lengthy, periodic sentences, most of them more
syntactically controlled that this one.

39. *And You shall hearken in the heavens, the firm place of Your dwelling.* This refrainlike
clause picks up the previous notion that God does not actually dwell in the Temple but in
the heavens above, from which He is disposed to listen to the prayers enunciated in the
Temple because He regards it as a favored focal point for prayer.

41. *And the foreigner, too.* This sympathetic attitude toward the devoutness of foreigners
who join the community of Israel sounds rather like a theme in Deutero-Isaiah, though
one might argue that Solomon's cordial relations, political, commercial, and marital, with
surrounding nations might be reflected here.

44. *through the city.* Others understand the preposition as "in the direction of."

46. *their captors take them off.* At this point, the prospect of exile becomes more explicit
and emphatic.

land in which they are captive, and turn back to You and plead with You in the land of their captors, saying, 'We have offended and have done
48 wrong, we have been evil,' and they turn back to You with all their heart and all their being in the land of their enemies who took them in captivity, and they pray to you through their land that You gave to their fathers, the
49 city that You chose and the house that I have built for Your name, You shall hearken from the heavens, the firm place of Your dwelling, to their prayer
50 and to their plea, and do justice for them. And You shall forgive Your people who have offended against you for all their crimes that they committed, and You shall grant them mercy before their captors, who will have
51 mercy upon them. For they are Your people and Your estate that You
52 brought out of the land of Egypt from the forge of iron. So that Your eyes be open to the plea of Your servant and the pleas of Your people Israel, to
53 listen to them whenever they call to You. For You set them apart for You as an estate from all the peoples of the earth as You spoke through Moses Your servant when You brought out our fathers from Egypt, O Master
54 LORD." And it happened when Solomon finished praying to the LORD all this prayer and plea, that he rose from before the LORD's altar from kneel-
55 ing on his knees with his palms stretched out to the heavens. And he stood
56 and blessed all the assembly of Israel in a loud voice, saying: "Blessed is the LORD Who has granted to his people Israel as all that He spoke. Not a single thing has failed of all His good word that He spoke through Moses His
57 servant. May the LORD our God be with us as He was with our Fathers.
58 May He not forsake us and not abandon us, to incline our heart to Him to walk in all His ways and to keep His commands and His statutes and His
59 laws with which He charged our fathers. And may these words that I

---

47. *We have offended and have done wrong, we have been evil.* These words were incorporated in the short confession of sins in the Yom Kippur liturgy.

48. *through their land.* Again, the translation understands this to mean that they will invoke their land, though it could mean that they will turn in the direction of the land as they pray.

50. *their captors, who will have mercy upon them.* It is noteworthy that the defeat or humiliation of Israel's enemies is not envisaged but rather the prospect that the captors will have compassion and treat them kindly. It is tempting to see in these words a reflection of Cyrus's beneficence toward the exiled Israelites, but it is hard to know whether any of the speech could have been written that late.

56. *Blessed is the LORD.* This last part of Solomon's quoted words, to the end of verse 61, is a kind of peroration that concludes his long address, appropriately invoking the divine promises to Moses and the importance of continuing loyalty to the covenant, framed once again in Deuteronomistic language.

pleaded before the LORD be near the LORD our God day and night to do justice for His servant and justice for His people Israel day after day, so 60 that all the peoples of the earth may know that the LORD is our God, there is none else. And may your heart be whole with the LORD our God to walk 61 in His statutes and to keep His commands as on this day." And the king 62 and all Israel with him were offering sacrifice before the LORD. And Solo- 63 mon offered up the well-being sacrifices that he sacrificed to the LORD, twenty-two thousand oxen and a hundred twenty thousand sheep. And the king and all the Israelites dedicated the house of the LORD. On that day 64 the king sanctified the midst of the court that was before the house of the LORD, for he did there the burnt offering and the grain offering and the fat of the well-being sacrifices. For the bronze altar that was before the LORD was too small to hold the burnt offering and the grain offering and the fat of the well-being sacrifices. And at that time Solomon performed the fes- 65 tival and all Israel his people was with him, a great assembly from Lebo-Hamath to the Wadi of Egypt, seven days and seven days—fourteen days. On the seventh day he sent off the people, and they blessed the king and 66 went to their tents, rejoicing and of good cheer over all the good that the LORD had done for David his servant and for Israel His people.

CHAPTER 9   And it happened when Solomon finished build- 1 ing the house of the LORD and the house of the king and all Solomon's desire that he was pleased to do, that the LORD appeared to Solomon a 2 second time as He had appeared to him in Gibeon. And the LORD said to 3

63. *twenty-two thousand oxen and a hundred twenty thousand sheep.* These imposing numbers are surely a fantastic embellishment of the actual ceremony.

65. *from Lebo-Hamath.* This town was at the border of Lebanon in the north.
      seven days and seven days—fourteen days. The wording is a little confusing. The designated span of the pilgrim festival of Succoth was seven days. Solomon evidently doubled the time, adding a second week of celebration. But the report in the next verse that he sent the people home on the seventh day might suggest that he continued a more private celebration, perhaps involving only the royal house and priests, for the second week. Alternately, "he sent off the people on the seventh day" might mean the seventh day of the second week

CHAPTER 9   2. *the LORD appeared to Solomon a second time.* Solomon's royal enterprise is framed by two revelations. Early in his reign, God appears to him at Gibeon and grants him the gift of wisdom (3:5–14). The wisdom is first manifested in the episode of the Judgment of Solomon and in his composing proverbs. His great building projects, now completed, may reflect another kind of wisdom because they consolidate his rule. Now God comes to him to tell him that the sanctity of the Temple is divinely ratified.

him: "I have hearkened to your prayer and to your plea that you pleaded
before Me. I have sanctified this house that you built to set My name there
4 forever, and My eyes and My heart shall be there for all time. As for you,
if you walk before Me, as David your father walked, wholeheartedly and
uprightly, to do as all that I have charged you, My statutes and My laws to
5 keep, I shall raise up the throne of your kingdom over Israel forever as I
spoke to David your father, saying, 'No man of yours shall be cut off from
6 the throne of Israel.' If you and your sons actually turn back from Me and
you do not keep My commands, My statutes that I gave you, and you go
7 and serve other gods and bow down to them, I shall cut Israel off from the
land that I gave them, and the house that I have sanctified for My name
will I send away from My presence, and Israel shall become a byword and
8 a mockery among all the peoples. And this house will turn into ruins—all
who pass by it will be dismayed and whistle in derision and say, 'Why did
9 the LORD do thus to this land and to this house?' And they will say, 'Because
they forsook the LORD their God Who brought their fathers out of the land
of Egypt and held fast to other gods and bowed down to them and served
them. Therefore has the LORD brought upon them all this harm.'"

10 And it happened at the end of the twenty years that Solomon was build-
11 ing the two houses, the house of the LORD and the house of the king, that

---

4. *if you walk before Me, as David your father walked.* The legitimacy of the dynasty neces-
sitates this idealized representation of David. In fact, the older—and probing—narrative
of David shows him to be deeply flawed—an adulterer, a murderer, and a man beset with
weaknesses.

  to do as . . . I have charged you, My statutes and My laws to keep. As in Solomon's speech
at the dedication of the temple, the language is emphatically Deuteronomistic.

7. *I shall cut Israel off from the land.* The invocation of the specter of exile, as earlier, looks
like the reflection of a later historical moment.

  I will send away from My presence. This is a slightly odd idiom to attach to the Temple.
Its usual connotation is divorce, a trope often used by the Prophets for God's disaffection
with Israel.

  a byword and a mockery. This phrase is also fairly common in the Prophets to indicate
Israel's national humiliation.

8. *this house will turn into ruins.* The received text reads, "this house will be exalted." This
translation reads instead of *'elyon,* "exalted" or "high," *'iyyim,* "ruins," along with the
Syriac and two versions of the Vulgate.

9. *Because they forsook the LORD.* In keeping with the Deuteronomistic theology, it is cultic
infidelity that will cause the catastrophe of exile.

10. *the twenty years.* That is, seven for the building of the Temple and another thirteen for
the palace.

Hiram king of Tyre had furnished Solomon with cedarwood and cypresswood and gold as all that he desired, then did Solomon give Hiram twenty
towns in the land of the Galilee. And Hiram went out from Tyre to see the 12
towns that Solomon had given him, and they were not right in his eyes.
And he said, "What are these towns that you have given me, my brother?" 13
And they have been called the Land of Cabul to this day. And Hiram had 14
sent to the king a hundred twenty talents of gold. And this is the aim of 15
the forced labor that Solomon exacted: to build the house of the LORD
and his house and the citadel, and the wall of Jerusalem and Hazor and
Megiddo and Gezer. Pharaoh king of Egypt had gone up and taken Gezer 16
and burned it in fire and killed the Canaanites who dwelled in the town,
and he gave it as a dowry to his daughter, Solomon's wife. And Solomon 17
rebuilt Gezer and Lower Beth-Horon, and Baalath and Tamor in the wil- 18
derness, in the land, and all the storehouse towns that were Solomon's, and 19

---

11. *gold.* This precious substance, which was needed for the furnishings of the Temple and
the palace, was not mentioned in the initial negotiations between Solomon and Hiram.
Though Tyre did not have its own gold mines, it would have accumulated stockpiles of gold
through its flourishing international trade.

    Solomon give Hiram twenty towns in the land of the Galilee. In the original agreement,
Solomon was to pay for the cedarwood and cypresswood with wheat and olive oil. Perhaps
Hiram's providing gold came afterward and thus required additional payment.

13. *What are these towns that you have given me, my brother?* Hiram obviously regards these
paltry towns on his southern border as poor recompense, but he maintains his diplomatic
relationship with Solomon by adding "my brother" to his objection.

    the Land of Cabul. No satisfactory explanation for the enigmatic *kabul* has been offered,
although it clearly indicates something quite negative, mirroring Hiram's disappointment.
It could mean "land of the chained one" (the one chained to a bad agreement?). It could also
mean "land like the produce" (land offered in payment, like the wheat and oil?). Perhaps
an explanatory clause in Hiram's speech has dropped out of the text.

14. *And Hiram had sent to the king a hundred twenty talents of gold.* It would make no sense
for Hiram to send Solomon gold after his dismissing the twenty towns as poor payment.
Thus, though the form of the Hebrew verb does not indicate a pluperfect, one is compelled
to understand this as a reference to his earlier shipments of gold to Solomon.

15. *And this is the aim of the forced labor.* The connection with what precedes is associative:
in the great building enterprise in which Hiram was Solomon's partner, Israelite forced
labor was used.

    the citadel. The Hebrew *milo'* derives from a root that means "to fill," perhaps suggest-
ing a raised citadel erected on landfill.

    Hazor and Megiddo and Gezer. Solomon's building projects thus extended far beyond
Jerusalem, involving fortified towns around the country.

18. *Tamor.* The Masoretic marginal note (*qeri*) reads this as "Tadmor," which is Palmyra in
Syria. That would be an improbable place for Solomon to build, so the translation adheres
to the consonantal text, indicating a town in the Negeb.

the towns for the chariots and the towns for the horsemen, and every desire
of Solomon that he desired to build in Jerusalem and in Lebanon and in all
20 the land of his dominion. All the people remaining in the land, the Amorite,
21 the Hittite, the Perizzite and the Jebusite, who were not of the Israelites, their
sons who remained after them whom the Israelites could not wholly destroy,
22 Solomon put to forced labor to this day. And of the Israelites Solomon made
no slave, for they were men of war, and his servants and his commanders
23 and his captains and the officers of his chariots and his horsemen. These
were the commander-prefects who were over the tasks of Solomon, five
24 hundred fifty holding sway over the people who performed the tasks. But
Pharaoh's daughter had gone up from the city of David to her house that he
25 built for her. Then did he build the citadel. And three times in the year Solomon offered up burnt offerings and well-being sacrifices on the altar that he
had built for the LORD, and turned it to smoke before the LORD and made
26 the house whole. And a fleet did Solomon make in Ezion-Geber, which
27 is by Eloth on the shore of the Red Sea in the land of Edom. And Hiram
sent his servants to the fleet—shipmen, adept in the sea—with Solomon's
28 servants. And they came to Ophir and took four hundred twenty talents
of gold from there and brought it to King Solomon.

---

19. *in Lebanon.* This might mean on the border of Lebanon.

21. *Solomon put to forced labor.* This notion that the indigenous inhabitants of the land
became forced laborers, subject to Israel, is put forth in the Book of Joshua.

22. *And of the Israelites Solomon made no slave.* The Israelite forced laborers paid what
amounted to a tax through their labor for a limited period of time.
     for they were men of war. Here, however, a different reason is offered for not enslaving
Israelites—their value as warriors.

25. *and turned it to smoke.* The Masoretic Text adds "with him that," which is syntactically
incoherent and looks like a scribal error.
     made the house whole. The verb *shilem*, which elsewhere means "requite," derives from
a root meaning "whole" and here may refer to an affirmation or restoration of the integrity
of the Temple through the act of sacrifice.

26. *Eloth.* This place-name is evidently identical with Elath.

27. *shipmen, adept in the sea.* The Phoenicians, of course, were a great seafaring nation, and
Solomon could well have used the expertise of his northern ally.

28. *Ophir.* This location, somewhere to the south by the shore of the Red Sea, is repeatedly
identified in the Bible as a source of gold—so much so that in poetry the name "Ophir"
alone can mean "fine gold."

CHAPTER 10

And the Queen of Sheba heard the rumor of 1 Solomon for the name of the LORD, and she came to try him with riddles. And she came to Jerusalem with a very great retinue—camels bearing a very 2 great abundance of spices and gold and precious stones, and she came to Solomon and spoke to him all that was in her heart. And Solomon told her all 3 her questions. There was no question hidden from the king that he did not tell her. And the Queen of Sheba saw all Solomon's wisdom and the house that he 4 had built, and the food on his table and the seat of his servants and the stand- 5 ing of his attendants and their garments and his cupbearers and the burnt offering he would offer up in the house of the LORD—and she was breathless. And she said to the king: "The word that I heard in my land about your doings 6

CHAPTER 10   1. *the Queen of Sheba.* The consensus is that Sheba is far to the south of ancient Israel, somewhere on the Arabian peninsula along the shore of the Red Sea. This episode is linked associatively with the immediately preceding passage in which Solomon builds fleets on the Red Sea and carries on trade in rich materials with the south.

for the name of the LORD. This phrase, repeatedly used for the building of the Temple, is a little cryptic in the present context. It might mean that Solomon's fabulous wisdom, granted to him as a special gift by God, was because of its divine source "for the name of the LORD."

2. *And she came to Jerusalem with a very great retinue.* This encounter between the queen of a southern kingdom and the great King Solomon has gripped the imagination of readers, writers, and artists over the ages. Among countless elaborations of the story in poetry and painting, an especially memorable one is "The Visit of the Queen of Sheba," a cycle of poems by the great Israeli poet Yehuda Amichai, which highlights the grand voyage over the Red Sea and teases out an erotic subtext from the biblical tale.

spoke to him all that was in her heart. The heart here is the locus of intellection, not emotion, so what she speaks are all the riddles she had carefully prepared to pose to him.

3. *And Solomon told her all her questions.* The verb "told," is regularly used for pronouncing the solution to a riddle, as in the Samson story. "Questions" here is the term that usually means "words" but has to be rendered as "questions" to make the sentence intelligible. It is something of a tease that the story does not divulge any of her riddles—of course, leaving much room for later interpreters.

4. *And the Queen of Sheba saw all Solomon's wisdom.* Scholars conventionally classify this story as a Wisdom text, a judgment that might be questioned. Wisdom is celebrated as a value, but in fact there is no Wisdom content in this story (in contrast to Proverbs or Qohelet).

and the house that he had built. She is impressed not only by Solomon's wisdom but— perhaps just as much—by the material splendor and affluence of his palace and his court. One extravagantly wealthy monarch duly recognizes the tremendous wealth of the other.

5. *the burnt offering.* Two ancient versions vocalize this word differently to yield "the ascent on which he would go up to the house of the LORD," though a grand abundance of daily sacrifices would certainly be evidence of his regal wealth.

7 and about your wisdom is true. And I did not believe these words until I came
   and my own eyes saw, and, look, the half of it was not told me. You exceed
8 in wisdom and bounty beyond the rumor that I heard. Happy are your men,
   happy your servants, those who stand in your presence perpetually, listening
9 to your wisdom. May the LORD your God be blessed, Who has desired you
   to set you on the throne of Israel through the LORD's love of Israel forever,
10 and has made you king to do judgment and justice." And she gave the king a
   hundred and twenty talents of gold and a very great abundance of spices and
   precious stones—never again did such an abundance of spice come as the
11 Queen of Sheba gave to King Solomon. And Hiram's fleet as well that bore
   gold from Ophir brought from Ophir a great abundance of sandalwood
12 and precious stones. And the king made from the sandalwood beams for
   the house of the LORD and the house of the king and lutes and lyres for the
   singers—the like of the sandalwood has not come nor been seen to this day.
13 And King Solomon gave to the Queen of Sheba all she desired, for which
   she had asked, besides what Solomon had given her in royal bounty. And
   she turned and went off to her land, she and her servants.

14 And the weight of gold that came to Solomon in a single year was six hun-
15 dred and sixty-six talents of gold, besides what he had from the merchants
   and the traffic of the traders and all the kings of Arabia and the governors

---

9. *May the* LORD *your God be blessed.* The dazzling impression that Solomon makes on the
Queen of Sheba is thus seen as a confirmation of the greatness of YHWH, the God of Israel.
At the same time, the whole story of the triumphal encounter of Israel's king with a great
queen from the distant south is a vivid illustration of Solomon's supreme regal grandeur,
which has been a repeated theme in the preceding chapters.

10. *And she gave the king a hundred and twenty talents of gold.* There is no indication that
a wager was involved in solving the riddles, as in the Samson story, although that is possible. The more likely explanation of her act is that she is moved to offer a generous gift
from her own great wealth as a gesture of appreciation to the wise and great king. In verse
13, we learn that she on her part asks for an exchange of gifts, to which Solomon readily
agrees. Some interpreters see this part of the story as an oblique reflection of trade relations
between Israel and Sheba, though it may be more plausible to read it simply as a diplomatic
exchange of regal generosity.
    a very great abundance of spices. The Arabian peninsula was in fact known in the ancient
world for its spices and perfumes, something of which Shakespeare was still aware when
he had Lady Macbeth say, "All the perfumes of Araby will not sweeten this little hand."

11. *And Hiram's fleet . . . that bore gold from Ophir.* The obvious associative connection is
the bringing of precious materials from southern regions. Ophir probably was also in the
Arabian peninsula.

of the land. And King Solomon made two hundred shields of hammered 16
gold, six hundred measures of gold he put on each shield, and three hundred 17
bucklers of hammered gold, three hundred measures of gold on each buckler.
And the king put them in the Lebanon Forest House. And the king made a 18
great ivory throne and overlaid it with choicest gold. Six steps the throne 19
had, and a round top behind it the throne had, and arms on each side at
the seat and two lions standing by the arms. And twelve lions stood there 20
on the six steps on each side. Its like was not made in all the kingdoms.
And all King Solomon's drinking vessels were gold, and all the vessels of 21
the Lebanon Forest House pure gold. There was no silver—in Solomon's
days it was counted as naught. For the king had a Tarshish fleet in the sea 22
together with Hiram's fleet bearing gold and silver, ivory, apes, and parrots.
And King Solomon was greater than all the kings of the earth in wealth 23
and in wisdom. And the whole earth sought Solomon's presence to hear 24
his wisdom that God had put in his heart. And they would bring each his 25
tribute, vessels of silver and vessels of gold and cloaks and arms and spices,
horses and mules, the set amount year by year. And Solomon gathered 26
chariots and horsemen, and he had a thousand four hundred chariots and

---

16. *two hundred shields of . . . gold.* These shields and bucklers (the precise distinction
between the two Hebrew terms cannot be determined) made of gold are obviously not fashioned to be used in combat but as ornamental objects, evoking by their form the king's
military power and by their substance his great wealth.

17. *three hundred.* The received text reads "three," too little if six hundred are used for the
shields, but two ancient versions show "three hundred."
  the Lebanon Forest House. If this evidently impressive hall in the palace was, as some
claim, an armory, it might have been a symbolic armory because the shields displayed in it
were not actually for military use. Verse 21 notes that *everything* in the House of Lebanon
was made of pure gold, so it could even have been a kind of treasury.

22. *a Tarshish fleet.* Tarshish is generally thought to be a Mediterranean port far to the
west, though scholars differ about its precise location. The allied fleets of Solomon and
Hiram, however, were plying the Red Sea, so it is more likely that the term refers to a kind
of ship—the sort built in Tarshish or outfitted to reach far-off Tarshish. It has also been
proposed that the term derives from the Greek *tarsos,* "oar," and so designates a sailing ship
that is also equipped with oars.
  parrots. Others understand the term to mean "peacocks," although parrots are a better
pairing with apes.

23. *And King Solomon was greater than all the kings of the earth in wealth and in wisdom.*
This stature has just been demonstrated in the story of the Queen of Sheba.

26. *And Solomon gathered chariots and horsemen.* The reiterated emphasis on Solomon's
chariots and horses might reflect historical reality, but it also echoes, perhaps a little ominously, the warning in Deuteronomy 17:16 for the future king, "Only let him not get himself

twelve thousand horsemen, and he led them to the chariot towns, and with
27 the king in Jerusalem. And the king made silver in Jerusalem as abundant
28 as stones, and cedar as the sycamores in the lowlands. And the source of
Solomon's horses was from Muzri and from Kue. The king's merchants
29 would take them from Kue for a set price. And a chariot coming up out
of Muzri cost six hundred silver shekels and a horse a hundred fifty. And
thus by the sea to all the kings of the Hittites and to the kings of Aram they
would bring them out.

1 **CHAPTER 11**   And King Solomon loved many foreign
women—Pharaoh's daughter and Moabites, Ammonites, Edomites, Sido-

---

many horses." The text in Deuteronomy, of course, might be a response to Solomon's royal
extravagances.

twelve thousand horsemen. The fact that the number of horsemen is so much greater
than the number of chariots suggests that the term *parashim* refers both to charioteers
and to cavalrymen.

28. *And the source of Solomon's horses was from Muzri and from Kue.* Both the geography
and the terminology for Solomon's international horse trading in these last two verses of
the chapter are rather obscure. The received text reads Mitsrayim, "Egypt," which was not
known for the export of horses, but many scholars emend this to Mutsri, a town in northern
Syria (Kue is in Asia Minor). The substitution of a familiar term for an unfamiliar word is
one of the most common causes of scribal error.

29. *coming up.* Literally, "would come up and go out." Some interpreters take this as an
idiom for "export," but that is not entirely clear.

by the sea. The Masoretic Text reads *beyadam*, "in their hand," which is obscure because
there is no clear antecedent for "their." This translation follows the Septuagint, which
appears to have used a Hebrew text that read *bayam*, a difference of a single consonant.
The transportation of horses from the north by ship along the Mediterranean coast seems
plausible.

to all the kings of the Hittites and to the kings of Aram. This would mean that Solomon
not only purchased horses for his own use but engaged in an international trade of horses.
It is also possible that the preposition "to" (a single-consonant particle) is a scribal error
for "from."

CHAPTER 11   1. *And King Solomon loved many foreign women.* These words mark a
strong shift in the perception of Solomon. Up to this point, he had been portrayed as an ideally wise and fabulously wealthy king to whom God gave rousing promises and who built
God's house in Jerusalem. The previous mentions of his marriage to Pharaoh's daughter
do not put that alliance in any negative light. (Later prohibitions on intermarriage were not
operative in the early centuries of Israelite national existence.) Here, however, the legendary profusion of Solomon's foreign wives—a full thousand—leads to the sin of idolatry.
The Deuteronomistic editor, for all the inherited stories of Solomon's grandeur, needed an

nians, Hittites, from the nations of which the LORD had said to the Isra- 2
elites, "You shall not come among them and they shall not come among
you, for they will surely lead your heart astray after their gods." To these
did Solomon cling in love. And he had seven hundred princess wives and 3
three hundred concubines, and his wives led his heart astray. And it hap- 4
pened in Solomon's old age that his wives led his heart astray after other
gods, and his heart was not whole with the LORD his God like the heart
of David his father. And Solomon went after Ashtoreth goddess of the 5
Sidonians and after Milcom abomination of the Ammonites. And Solo- 6
mon did evil in the eyes of the LORD, and he did not obey the LORD like
David his father. Then did Solomon build a high place for Chemosh the 7
abomination of Moab on the mountain facing Jerusalem and for Molech
the abomination of the Ammonites. And, thus did he do for all his foreign 8
wives who would burn incense and would sacrifice to their gods. And the 9
LORD was furious with Solomon, for his heart had gone astray from the
LORD God of Israel, Who had appeared to him twice, and had charged 10
him about this thing not to go after other gods, and he had not kept what
the LORD had charged. And the LORD said to Solomon: "Inasmuch as 11
this was with you and you did not keep My covenant and my statutes
that I charged to you, I will surely tear away the kingdom from you and
give it to your servant. But in your days I will not do it, for the sake of 12
David your father. From the hand of your son I will tear it away. Only the 13

---

explanation for the splitting of the kingdom after Solomon's death, and he now provides it
in a manner in keeping with Deuteronomy's conception of historical causation, in which
idolatry leads to national disaster.

2. *from the nations of which the LORD had said . . . , "You shall not come among them."* The
Moabites and the Ammonites in particular were singled out for this ban.

To these did Solomon cling in love. This expression suggests that the wise Solomon was
besotted with his foreign wives and hence ready to follow their lead in cultic practice.

3. *his wives led his heart astray.* One may infer that he initially allowed them freedom of
worship and then was drawn into their pagan ways.

7. *Then did Solomon build a high place for Chemosh.* The building of "high places"—typically, rural hilltop altars—is a bête noire of the Deuteronomist both because he insists on
the exclusivity of the Jerusalem temple and because such altars were vulnerable to pagan
influences. Here Solomon is seen taking an active role in the pagan cult, actually promul-
gating it.

11. *give it to your servant.* In royal contexts, "servant," *'eved*, usually means "courtier."
Jeroboam, who will appear later in the story, is a member of the royal bureaucracy and
hence Solomon's "servant."

entire kingdom I will not tear away. One tribe I will give to your son, for
the sake of David my servant and for the sake of Jerusalem, which I have
14 chosen." And the LORD raised up an adversary against Solomon, Hadad the
15 Edomite, who was of the royal seed in Edom. And it had happened when
David was in Edom, when Joab commander of the army went up to bury the
16 fallen, that he struck down every male in Edom. For six months Joab had
stayed there, and all Israel with him, until he cut off every male in Edom.
17 And Hadad fled, and Edomite men of his father's servants with him, and
18 went to Egypt, and Hadad was a young lad. And they arose from Midian
and came to Paran, and they took men with them from Paran and came to
Egypt to Pharaoh king of Egypt, and he gave him a house, and he decreed
19 food for him, and he gave him land. And Hadad found great favor in the
eyes of Pharaoh, and he gave him a wife, the sister of his own wife Tahpanes
20 the royal consort. And Tahpanes's sister bore him his son Genubath, and
Tahpanes weaned him in Pharaoh's house, and Genubath was in Pharaoh's
21 house in the midst of Pharaoh's sons. And Hadad had heard in Egypt that
David lay with his fathers and that Joab the commander of the army was
dead, and Hadad said to Pharaoh, "Send me off, that I may go to my land."
22 And Pharaoh said to him, "Why, what are you lacking with me that you

---

13. *One tribe I will give to your son.* It should be two tribes because the breakaway kingdom
in the north will have ten. Either "one" is used hyperbolically, to emphasize how little
will be left to Solomon's line, or it reflects the assimilation of Benjamin into Judah, which
became to all intents and purposes the only tribe of the southern kingdom.

14. *adversary.* The Hebrew *satan* does not strictly mean "enemy" but something like "trou-
blemaker," someone who is a stumbling block.

18. *from Midian.* This kingdom to the southeast of Israel would have been a way station
between Edom, farther north, and Egypt.
    came to Paran. Paran is in the Sinai desert, south of Midian and on the way to Egypt.
    Pharaoh . . . gave him a house . . . food . . . land. The Pharaoh in David's time, unlike the
successor who gave his daughter to Solomon, was hostile to Israel. His providing refuge
and sustenance to this Edomite refugee from David's onslaught is politically motivated,
with the calculation that at some future point Hadad might prove useful in the conflict
with David.

19. *the royal consort.* Translations invariably render this as "the queen." But the Hebrew
does not call her queen, *malkah,* but rather *gevirah,* a term that elsewhere (including 15:13 in
this book) designates the queen mother. Tahpenes could not be the king's mother because
she is his wife, but *gevirah* seems to be extended to a woman intimately related to the king
though lacking the full authority and status of queen.

20. *Tahpanes weaned him.* This looks odd because as his aunt, she certainly would not have
suckled the child. The attachment of this verb to her might suggest that she had a kind of
adoptive relationship with the infant, a child fathered by a foreigner, and so in some symbolic or even legal fashion could be said to preside over his weaning.

should seek to go to your land?" And he said, "No. Send me off." And God 23
raised up against him as adversary Rezon son of Eliadu, who had fled from
Hadadezer his master, king of Zobah. And he gathered men about him and 24
became the commander of a troop after David killed them, and they went
to Damascus and dwelled there, and they reigned in Damascus. And he was 25
an adversary against Israel all the days of Solomon, together with all the
harm that Hadad had done, and he loathed Israel and reigned over Aram.

And Jeroboam son of Nebat, an Ephraimite from Zeredah, whose mother's 26
name was Zeruah, a widow-woman, was a servant to Solomon. And he
raised his hand against the king. And this is how he raised his hand against 27
the king: Solomon had built the Citadel, had closed the breaches of the City
of David his father. And the man Jeroboam was an able fellow and Solo- 28
mon saw that the lad could carry out tasks, and he appointed him over all
the heavy labor of the house of Joseph. And it happened at that time that 29
Jeroboam went out from Jerusalem, and the prophet Ahijah the Shilonite

---

22. *No. Send me off.* No continuation of the story is given, so there is no way of knowing
whether Hadad was repatriated. If he was, then he would presumably have taken up his
role as "adversary" to Solomon, son of the man who had massacred the male population of
Edom. Verse 25 suggests that in fact he played this role.

23. *who had fled from Hadadezer his master.* Rezon is not referred to as being "of the royal
seed." The implication may be that he was a plebeian who may have been part of a conspiracy against the king.

24. *they reigned in Damascus.* The use of the plural may make sense in this context: Rezon
is not of royal stock; he has gathered around him a private militia; and it is this group of
fighting men who have seized control of Damascus.

25. *together with.* The Hebrew preposition looks a little strange but could simply mean that
the harm perpetrated by Rezon was in addition to the harm done by Hadad.

26. *a servant to Solomon.* The precise nature of the service he performs in Solomon's court
is spelled out in verse 28.

28. *an able fellow.* The Hebrew *gibor hayil* in military contexts means "valiant warrior," but
it can also indicate in pacific contexts either competence or wealth.
    the lad. The Hebrew *na'ar* here might refer not to youth but to subordinate position.
    could carry out tasks. More literally, "was a carrier-out of tasks."
    the heavy labor. This activity is linked with the building and the repair of breaches in
the wall mentioned in the previous verse. The Hebrew *sevel* derives from a root that means
bearing burdens.

29. *the prophet Ahijah.* The only prophet who has appeared in this story until now is
Nathan, but from this point there will be many. Unlike the so-called literary prophets, they
do not deliver extensive poetic messages of rebuke or consolation, but they do pronounce
what the future will be.

found him on the way, he covering himself in a new cloak and the two of
30 them alone in the field. And Ahijah caught hold of the new cloak and tore
31 it into twelve pieces. And he said to Jeroboam, "Take you ten pieces, for
thus said the LORD God of Israel: 'I am about to tear away the kingdom
32 from Solomon's hand and give it to the ten tribes. And the one tribe shall
be his for the sake of My servant David and for the sake of Jerusalem, the
33 city that I have chosen from all the tribes of Israel, inasmuch as they have
forsaken Me and have bowed down to Ashtoreth goddess of the Sidonians
and to Chemosh god of Moab and to Milcom god of the Ammonites, and
they have not walked in My ways to do what is right in My eyes and My
34 statutes and My laws, like David his father. But I will not take the entire
kingdom from his hand, for I will keep him as a prince all the days of his
life for the sake of David whom I chose, who kept My commands and My
35 statutes. And I will take the kingship from the hand of his son and give it
36 to you—the ten tribes. And to his son I will give one tribe, so that there
be a lamp for David my servant for all time before Me in Jerusalem, the
37 city that I have chosen to set My name there. And you will I take, and you
38 shall reign over all that you desire, and you shall be king over Israel. And
it shall be, if you hearken to all that I charge you and walk in My ways and
do what is right in My eyes to keep My statues and My commands as did
David My servant, I shall be with you and build for you a lasting house, as
39 I built for David, and I shall give Israel to you. And I shall afflict the seed
40 of David because of this, but not for all time.' " And Solomon sought to

---

the two of them alone in the field. By its subversive nature, Ahijah's communication to
Jeroboam has to be in a clandestine setting.

30. tore it into twelve pieces. Turning the torn cloak into a sign picks up Saul's tearing of
Samuel's cloak, which Samuel immediately turns into a sign that God will tear the kingship away from Saul. The earlier tearing of the garment was inadvertent, whereas this act
is deliberately carried out as a symbol of what will happen.

34. prince. God's words, as quoted by Ahijah, avoid the authoritative title "king" and instead
use an ambiguous word that often designates a tribal chieftain. Solomon's kingship, one
sees, is already slipping away.

36. so that there be a lamp for David my servant. The language of the prophecy labors to
preserve the notion of a divinely elected Davidic dynasty even as most of the kingdom is
about to be shorn from the line of David.

38. if you hearken to all that I charge you. Once again, the language is explicitly
Deuteronomistic.

39. because of this. Presumably the reference is to the idolatrous backsliding under the rule
of Solomon.

put Jeroboam to death, and Jeroboam arose and fled to Egypt, to Shishak king of Egypt, and he stayed in Egypt until Solomon's death. And the rest 41 of the acts of Solomon and all that he did, and his wisdom, are they not written in the Book of the Acts of Solomon? And the time that Solomon 42 reigned in Jerusalem over all Israel was forty years. And Solomon lay with 43 his fathers and was buried in the City of David his father. And Rehoboam his son reigned in his stead.

CHAPTER 12   And Rehoboam came to Shechem, for all 1 Israel had come to Shechem to make him king. And it happened when 2 Jeroboam son of Nebat heard, and he was still in Egypt where he had fled from King Solomon, and Jeroboam had stayed in Egypt, that they sent and 3 called to him, and Jeroboam and all the assembly of Israel came and spoke to Rehoboam, saying, "Your father made our yoke heavy, and you, now 4 lighten the hard labor of your father and his heavy yoke that he put on us,

---

40. *And Solomon sought to put Jeroboam to death.* No report is given of the actions by Jeroboam that might have provoked the king's attempt to kill him (the Septuagint supplies details, but these are of doubtful authority), but one must assume that after the encounter with Ahijah, Jeroboam took steps—like Macbeth after the prophecy of the witches—to secure the throne for himself.

Shishak king of Egypt. This is clearly a Pharaoh who has come after the one who gave his daughter to Solomon, and who regards Solomon's kingdom with suspicion, if not hostility.

41. *the Book of the Acts of Solomon.* This text would seem to be some sort of court annals. It is quite possible that the writer or writers responsible for Solomon's story beginning with 1 Kings 3 drew materials from this book, though that remains in the realm of conjecture.

42. *forty years.* This is, of course, a formulaic number—one frequently used to designate the length of time a leader in the Book of Judges remained in power. In all likelihood, it reflects knowledge that Solomon reigned for a relatively long time, a full generation in biblical terms.

CHAPTER 12   1. *for all Israel had come to Shechem to make him king.* Shechem was a frequent assembly point in the tribal period. One might have expected, however, that the coronation would take place in Jerusalem. In this national meeting at Shechem there appears to be an intimation that Rehoboam's succession to the throne was not an automatic matter, or, to put this differently, that the Davidic rule over what had been, barely half a century earlier, a federation of tribes was not entirely assured. Thus Rehoboam comes out from Jerusalem to an assembly that he hopes will acclaim or ratify his succession. His knowledge of Jeroboam's ambitions for the throne may be a motivator.

4. *made our yoke heavy.* The literal sense of the Hebrew verb is "made hard," but in all the subsequent occurrences of "yoke" in this story, the more expected "heavy" is used.

now lighten the hard labor. The people refer, of course, to the punishing taxation through forced labor necessitated by Solomon's vast building projects. Requests for remission of

5 that we may serve you." And he said to them, "Go off another three days
6 and come back to me," and the people went off. And King Rehoboam took
counsel with the elders who stood in the service of his father while he was
7 alive, saying, "How do you counsel to respond to this people?" And, they
spoke to him, saying, "If today you will be a servant to this people and serve
them and answer them and speak good words to them, they will be servants
8 to you always." And he forsook the counsel of the elders that they had given
him and took counsel with the young men with whom he had grown up,
9 who stood in his service. And he said to them, "What do you counsel that
we should respond to this people that has spoken to me, saying, 'Lighten
10 the yoke that your father put on us'?" And the young men with whom he
had grown up spoke to him, saying, "Thus shall you say to these people
who have spoken to you, saying, 'Your father made our yoke heavy, and
you, lighten it for us.' Thus shall you say to them, 'My little finger is thicker
11 than my father's loins. And now, my father burdened you with a heavy yoke,
and I will add to your yoke. My father scourged you with whips, and I will
12 scourge you with scorpions.'" And Jeroboam, and all the people with him,
came to Rehoboam on the third day, as the king had said, "Return to me
13 on the third day." And the king answered the people harshly and forsook
14 the counsel of the elders that they had given him. And he spoke to them
according to the counsel of the young men, saying, "My father made your

---

taxes and obligations to the crown when a new king assumed the throne were common in
the ancient Near East.

6. *the elders.* These would be a group of state councillors, experienced men who are not
necessarily aged but knowledgeable.

7. *this people.* They are referred to by all parties in this story with the demonstrative pronoun, distancing them and indicating them as a refractory group with which one must
know how to deal properly.

8. *the young men with whom he had grown up.* The word for "young men," *yeladim*, usually means "child" or even "infant." Since we later learn that Rehoboam was forty when
he became king, these are actually middle-aged men. The term may have been chosen to
underscore their puerile behavior. In any case, the episode surely reflects the ancient predisposition to seek wisdom from elders, as Job's three friends repeatedly stress.

10. *My little finger is thicker than my father's loins.* This extravagant metaphor is the advice
of arrogance. In the event, Rehoboam deletes these words in his response to the people. A
few interpreters have seen a sexual allusion here, perhaps because of the proximity to loins,
with "little finger" a euphemism for the male member (in rabbinic Hebrew, "little member"
means "penis"). That would be in keeping with the macho brashness of these words.

11. *I will scourge you with scorpions.* These would be either actual scorpions, perhaps poisonous, or an iron implement with a ragged head, perhaps one carved to resemble a scorpion.

yoke heavy and I will add to your yoke. My father scourged you with whips
and I will scourge you with scorpions." And the king did not hearken to the 15
people, for it was brought about by the LORD in order to fulfill His word
that the LORD had spoken through Ahijah the Shilonite to Jeroboam son
of Nebat. And all Israel saw that the king had not hearkened to them, and 16
the people responded to the king, saying,

> "We have no share in David
>   nor an estate in the son of Jesse.
> To your tents, O Israel!
>   See to your house, O David!"

And Israel went to their tents. As to the Israelites dwelling in the towns 17
of Judah, Rehoboam was king over them. And King Rehoboam sent out 18
Adoram, who was over the forced labor, and all Israel stoned him and he
died. Then King Rehoboam hastened to mount a chariot to flee to Jerusalem. And Israel has rebelled against the house of David to this day. And 19,20
it happened when all Israel heard that Jeroboam had come back, that they
sent and called him to the community and made him king over all Israel.
There was no one following the house of David save Judah alone. And 21
Rehoboam came to Jerusalem and assembled all the house of Judah and
the tribe of Benjamin, a hundred eighty thousand picked warriors to do
battle with the house of Israel to bring back the kingship to Rehoboam

---

15. *for it was brought about by the* LORD. Rehoboam's alienating the people has been reported
in realistic—possibly historical—terms as a very unwise policy decision. Now, however, it
is given a theological explanation: this is the means through which God causes Ahijah's
prophecy to be fulfilled.

16. *See to your house, O David!* The people's response, in two lines of poetry, vividly
expresses the distance they now feel from the Davidic monarchy: Rehoboam's brutal language makes them realize that this recently founded dynasty has been a bad idea, and that
they owe no fealty to it.

18. *Adoram.* Earlier, his name was given a longer form, Adoniram.
   who was over the forced labor. It is precisely the forced labor that had been the people's
chief complaint. Rehoboam, not yet realizing that his writ no longer extends over the whole
people, sends out the chief overseer over the forced labor, unwittingly consigning him to
his death.
   Then King Rehoboam hastened to mount a chariot. Adoram's murder by the mob makes
Rehoboam realize that his own life is in danger.

21. *the tribe of Benjamin.* Part of Benjamin remained loyal to the house of David.
   the house of Israel. Henceforth, this phrase will refer to the northern tribes, in contradistinction to Judah.

22 son of Solomon. And the word of the LORD came to Shemaiah man of
23 God, saying, "Say to Rehoboam son of Solomon king of Judah and to all
24 the house of Judah and Benjamin and the rest of the people, saying, Thus
said the LORD, 'You shall not go up and you shall not do battle with your
Israelite brothers. Go back each man to his house, for from Me has this
thing come about.'" And they heeded the LORD's word and turned back
from going, according to the LORD's word.

25 And Jeroboam rebuilt Shechem in the high country of Ephraim and
26 dwelled in it. And he went out from there and rebuilt Penuel. And Jeroboam
said in his heart, "Now the kingdom will turn back to the house of David,
27 if this people go up to do sacrifices in the house of the LORD in Jerusalem, the heart of this people will turn back to their master, to Rehoboam
king of Judah, and they will kill me and turn back to Rehoboam king of
28 Judah." And the king took counsel and made two golden calves and said
to the people, "Enough for you to go up to Jerusalem! Here are your gods,
29 Israel, who brought you up from the land of Egypt." And he placed one

---

22. *Shemaiah man of God.* He is clearly a prophet, precisely like Ahijah, but here an alternate designation is used.

24. *And they heeded the LORD's word.* It is not clear that they would automatically concede the divine authority of words pronounced by a particular prophet or man of God. In
this instance, however, the prospect of a bloody civil war and of a military confrontation
between two tribes and ten may have disposed them to accept the prophecy. It is noteworthy that "they"—the people—heed the prophecy, while no explicit mention is made of
the king. It may be that the force of the prophetic injunction swayed the people, leaving
Rehoboam no choice but to acquiesce.

25. *rebuilt Shechem . . . rebuilt Penuel.* Penuel was destroyed by Gideon to revenge the failure
of its elders to give provisions to his troops (see Judges 8). In the case of Shechem, fortification may be what is indicated.

26. *Now the kingdom will turn back to the house of David.* Jeroboam clearly understands
what Josiah in the seventh century B.C.E. will understand, that possession of a cultic center
is also a claim to centralized political authority. Thus he takes steps to create cultic places
in the north.

28. *two golden calves . . . "Here are your gods, Israel, who brought you up from the land
of Egypt."* The representation of Jeroboam's act as idolatrous—underscored by the use of
"gods" in the plural—is tendentious. Calves or bulls were often conceived as a mount or a
throne of God, precisely like those winged leonine figures, the cherubim. In all historical
likelihood, Jeroboam's intention was not to displace the worship of YHWH but merely to
create alternate cultic centers to Jerusalem with an alternate temple iconography. But the

in Bethel and the other he set in Dan. And this thing became an offense; 30
and the people marched before the one in Bethel and the other in Dan.
And he made buildings for the high places and made priests from the 31
pick of the people who were not from the sons of Levi. And Jeroboam 32
made a festival in the eighth month on the fifteenth day of the month
like the festival that was in Judah, and he went up on the altar. Thus did
he do in Bethel to sacrifice to the calves that he had made, and he set up
in Bethel the priests of the high places he had made. And he went up on 33
the altar that he had made in Bethel on the fifteenth day of the eighth
month, in the month he had devised from his own heart. And he made
a festival for the Israelites and went up on the altar to burn incense.

---

narrator pointedly represents all this in precisely the terms, with an explicit quotation, of
Aaron's golden calf (Exodus 32).

29. *one in Bethel and the other . . . in Dan.* Bethel was a well-known cultic site, and archaeologists have uncovered the remnants of a substantial cultic site at Dan in the far north.
Jeroboam's decision to create two cultic centers may be a concession on his part to the
loose and disparate nature of the constellation of tribes that constituted his new kingdom.

30. *And this thing became an offense.* It is important for the Deuteronomistic writer to
establish that the first king of Israel, despite the admonition of Ahijah, initiated idolatry
in his realm, thus setting the stage for the eventual destruction of the northern kingdom.
    and the people marched before the one in Bethel and the other in Dan. The Masoretic
Text lacks "the one in Bethel," surely an inadvertent omission. One might have expected the
phrase "to go after," the preposition used for idolatry in 11:2 and 4. Here "to go" is rendered
as "to march," presupposing that the reference is to a procession before the cultic calves.

31. *he made buildings for the high places.* The literal sense of the Hebrew is "he made a
house of high places." The reference may be to the erection of sanctuaries around the
hilltop altars.
    the pick of the people. This is what this Hebrew phrase indicates elsewhere, though
others understand it in an opposite sense, "the common people." Jeroboam, however, would
have had no motivation to enlist priests from the peasantry. His waywardness is rather
reflected in bypassing the priestly caste. See Genesis 47:2, where this same expression
appears to mean "the pick" or "the best."

32. *a festival in the eighth month.* Calendric differences have often been the lever of sectarian or political divisions among Jews. The festival referred to is Succoth, the most densely
attended of the three pilgrim festivals. Its designated date is on the fifteenth of the seventh
month, so Jeroboam, by pushing it a month later, is marking a pointed difference between
his realm and the southern kingdom.
    to sacrifice to the calves that he had made. The wording again represents the cult
Jeroboam had set up as sheer idolatry.

1　CHAPTER 13　　　And, look, a man of God came from Judah through the word of the LORD to Bethel, with Jeroboam standing on the
2　altar to burn incense. And he called out against the altar by the word of the LORD and said, "Altar, altar! Thus says the LORD: 'Look, a son is to be born to the house of David, Josiah his name, and he shall sacrifice upon you the priests of the high places who burn incense upon you, and they shall burn
3　upon you human bones.'" And he gave a portent on that day, saying, "This is the portent, that the LORD has spoken: look, the altar is about to be torn
4　asunder, and the ashes that are upon it will be spilled." And it happened when the king heard the word of the man of God that he had called out against the altar in Bethel, Jeroboam reached out his hand, saying, "Seize him." And the hand he reached out against him withered, and he could
5　not pull it back. And the altar was torn asunder and the ashes were spilled from the altar according to the portent that the man of God had given by
6　the word of the LORD. And the king spoke out and said to the man of God, "Entreat, please, the LORD your God and pray for me, that my hand come back to me." And the man of God entreated the LORD, and the king's hand
7　came back to him and was as it had been before. And the king spoke to the man of God, "Come into the house with me and dine, that I may give you a
8　gift." And the man of God said to the king, "Should you give me half your house, I would not come with you and I would not eat bread and I would
9　not drink water in this place. For thus it was charged me by the word of the

---

CHAPTER 13　　　1. *a man of God.* As before, this is an alternate designation for prophet. In this story, however, the man who comes from Judah to Bethel is consistently called a man of God, whereas the old man who will go after him and bring him home to dine is called a prophet. Verse 26 is the one seeming exception, but that may reflect a textual problem.

2. *Altar, altar!* This sort of apostrophe to an inanimate object is not a usual form of prophetic address. The man of God adopts it for shock effect, to direct attention to what he understands to be an entirely illegitimate altar and cult.

　　a son is to be born to the house of David, Josiah his name. Josiah was king of Judah three centuries after the time of this story, which thus was surely composed no earlier than the late seventh century B.C.E. The continuation of this story appears in 2 Kings 23, where Josiah is reported to have undertaken a sweeping campaign to destroy idols and the apparatus of pagan worship. In the course of that campaign, he slaughters the idolatrous priests and also exhumes bones from graves and burns them on the altar of Bethel in order to make it forever ritually impure.

7. *Come into the house with me and dine.* Jeroboam, having seen the man of God's fearsome power both in the destruction of the altar and the paralyzing and restoring of his arm, seeks to make him an ally.

LORD, saying, 'No bread shall you eat nor water shall you drink nor shall
you go back on the way that you went.'" And he went off on another way, 10
and he did not return on the way that he had come to Bethel. And a certain 11
old prophet was dwelling in Bethel, and his sons came and recounted to
him the whole deed that the man of God had done that day in Bethel, the
words that he had spoken to the king, they recounted them to their father.
And their father spoke to them, "By what way did he go?" And his sons 12
showed him the way on which the man of God who had come from Judah
had gone. And he said to his sons, "Saddle the donkey for me." And they 13
saddled the donkey for him and he mounted it. And he went after the man 14
of God and found him sitting under a terebinth. And he said to him, "Are
you the man of God who came from Judah?" And he said, "I am." And he 15
said, "Come home with me and eat bread." And he said, "I cannot go back 16
with you, nor will I eat bread nor will I drink water in this place. For a word 17
came to me, by the word of the LORD, 'You shall eat no bread nor shall you
drink water nor shall you go back to go on the way that you went.'" And he 18
said to him, "I, too, am a prophet like you, and a divine messenger spoke
to me with the word of the LORD, saying, 'Bring him back with you to your
house, that he may eat bread and drink water.'" He lied to him. And he 19

---

9. *No bread shall you eat nor water shall you drink.* This prohibition is understandable as
an expression of God's absolute rejection of Jeroboam's wayward kingdom: the man of
God must shun the king, not breaking bread with him or even drinking water in his house.

nor shall you go back on the way you went. This third prohibition is less transparent.
Perhaps the fact that he must take a different route back to Judah is meant to indicate that
the dire prophecy he has pronounced is irreversible, though it looks rather like the kind
of arbitrary injunction one often encounters in folktales: if you fail to follow these precise
stipulations for your mission, disaster will ensue.

11. *a certain old prophet.* The fact that the old prophet lies to the man of God (verse 18)
may raise questions about his legitimacy as prophet, but in verse 21 he is represented as the
authentic vehicle for the word of the LORD.

his sons. The Masoretic Text has a singular here, but two Hebrew manuscripts and
three ancient versions show a plural, the form that appears in the rest of the verse and in
the next one.

14. *And he went after the man of God.* The man of God, as the sons have reported to the
old man, has just demonstrated his credentials by performing two spectacular portents. It
would appear that, as a result, the old prophet wants to associate himself with the man of
God from Judah, perhaps enhancing his own prophetic status in this fashion.

18. *He lied to him.* Although the lie has fatal consequences, it may have been impelled by
a good intention. The old man might well have imagined that the stern prohibition was
directed against the king's house but not against the house of a prophet like himself—a

20 went back with him and ate bread in his house and drank water. And it
   happened as they were sitting at the table, that the word of the LORD came
21 to the prophet who had brought him back, and he called out to the man of
   God who had come from Judah, saying, "Thus said the LORD: 'Inasmuch
   as you have flouted the word of the LORD and not kept the command that
22 the LORD your God commanded you, and you came back and ate bread and
   drank water in the place of which He spoke to you, Do not eat bread nor
23 drink water, your carcass shall not come to the grave of your fathers.' " And
   it happened after he had eaten bread and after he had drunk water that the
24 prophet who had brought him back saddled the donkey for him. And he
   went off, and a lion found him on the way and killed him, and his carcass
   was flung down on the way with the donkey standing by him and the lion
25 standing by the carcass. And, look, people were passing by, and they saw
   the carcass flung down on the way and the lion standing by the carcass,
   and they came and spoke of it in the town in which the old prophet lived.
26 And the prophet who had brought him back from the way heard and he
   said, "It is the man of God who flouted the word of the LORD, and the LORD

---

professional colleague of the man of God. Seeing how determined the man from Judah is to
observe the prohibition, he permits himself to fabricate the story about the divine messenger.

20. *the word of the LORD came to the prophet.* The old man, now made the conduit of the
prophecy of doom pronounced upon the man of God, is forced to see how drastically mistaken he was in bringing the man home with him under false pretences.

22. *your carcass.* The Hebrew *neveilah* usually refers to an animal carcass, not to a human
corpse. Its repeated use here may emphasize the abject condition of the slaughtered man
of God, his body flung down on the way.

23. *the prophet who had brought him back saddled the donkey for him.* The Masoretic Text
reads: "and he saddled the donkey for the prophet which he had brought back." This reading is problematic because throughout the story only the old man is called a prophet, and
the other is invariably referred to as the man of God. The emendation on which the translation rests involves the change of a single consonant, *hanavi'* instead of *lanavi'* with no
alteration of the Hebrew word order.

24. *a lion found him on the way.* This part of the story is not miraculous because in ancient
Israel there was an abundance of lions in the countryside, a fact reflected in the currency
of five different terms for "lion" in biblical Hebrew.
    *his carcass was flung down on the way with the donkey standing by him and the lion
standing by the carcass.* It is in this bizarre tableau that the miraculous character of the event
is manifested. As we learn in verse 28, the lion kills the man but does not eat him and does
not harm the donkey. Moreover, he remains standing by the body and the donkey instead
of going off, as one would expect.

26. *who flouted the word of the LORD.* It must be said that the old prophet plays a rather
ambiguous role in this story. After all, it was his lie about having received instructions from

has given him over to the lion, and it has torn him apart and killed him, according to the word of the LORD that He spoke to him." And he spoke to 27 his sons, saying, "Saddle the donkey for me," and they saddled it. And he 28 went and found his carcass flung down on the way. The lion had not eaten the carcass and had not torn apart the donkey. And the prophet lifted the 29 man of God's carcass and laid it on the donkey, and he brought him back to the town of the old prophet to keen for him and to bury him. And he 30 lay his carcass in his grave and keened for him, "Woe, my brother." And it 31 happened after he had buried him that he said to his sons, saying, "When I die, bury me in the grave in which the man of God is buried; by his bones lay my bones. For the word will surely come about that he called by the 32 word of the LORD concerning the altar which is in Bethel and concerning all the buildings of the high places that are in the towns of Samaria." Yet 33 after this thing Jeroboam did not turn back from his evil way, and again he made priests from the pick of the people. Whoever desired was ordained and became one of the priests of the high places. And this thing became 34 an offense for the house of Jeroboam, to wipe it out and destroy it from the face of the earth.

---

a divine messenger that led the man of God to go back with him to his house and thus flout the word of the LORD. His pronouncement here does not appear to express any remorse or any sense of guilt about the death that he has caused. Perhaps he still feels that he acted out of good intentions and that the man of God should have strictly observed the divine prohibitions, whatever the persuasive force of an argument to the contrary.

31. *bury me in the grave in which the man of God is buried.* He had wanted to have communion with this prophetic colleague through an act of hospitality. Now he wants to have solidarity with him after his death through a common grave. In the completion of this story in 2 Kings 23, this joint burial will have a positive posthumous consequence for the old prophet because Josiah will spare the bones buried in the man of God's grave from being exhumed and burned on the Bethel altar.

32. *For the word will surely come about.* The old prophet appears to have foreseen the means by which human bones will be burned on this altar in order to render it impure—the exhumation of bones from local graves—and so he may be buying himself a kind of burial insurance by having his body buried together with the man who pronounced the dire prophecy about the altar. This entire story remains bizarre to the end.

34. *to wipe it out and destroy it from the face of the earth.* The late writer, formulating his story more than a century after the total destruction of the northern kingdom, has that historical catastrophe in mind (although the immediate reference is to the house of Jeroboam) and here offers a theological explanation, in keeping with his Deuteronomistic outlook—the offense of cultic disloyalty.

1 CHAPTER 14   At that time Abijah son of Jeroboam fell ill.
2 And Jeroboam said to his wife, "Rise, pray, and disguise yourself, that
they will not know you are Jeroboam's wife, and go to Shiloh, for Ahijah
the prophet is there, who spoke to me to become king over this people.
3 And take in your hand ten loaves of bread and cakes and a jar of honey
4 and come to him. He will tell you what will happen to the lad." And so
did Jeroboam's wife do: she rose and went to Shiloh and came to Ahijah's
house, but Ahijah could not see, for his eyes had gone blind from old age.
5 And the LORD had said to Ahijah, "Look, Jeroboam's wife is about to come
to you to ask an oracle concerning her son, for he is ill, and thus and so
shall you speak to her. And when she comes she will feign to be another."
6 And it happened when Ahijah heard the sound of her footsteps coming
through the entrance, he said, "Come in, wife of Jeroboam. Why should
you feign to be another when I have been sent to you with harsh tidings?
7 Go, say to Jeroboam, 'Thus said the LORD God of Israel: Inasmuch as I
have raised you up from the people and made you prince over My people

---

CHAPTER 14   1. *At that time.* This particular temporal reference is a generalized
formulaic phrase that does not indicate that what follows happened precisely at the same
time as the preceding events in the narrative.

3. *ten loaves of bread and cakes and a jar of honey.* It was customary to bring gifts to a
prophet or seer when seeking oracular counsel from him. These in effect constituted his
professional income.

4. *but Ahijah could not see.* This is the first indication that Jeroboam's plan has gone awry.
He has instructed his wife to go in disguise, but the disguise proves to be pointless because
the prophet is blind. In any case, God will expose the disguise in speaking to the blind
prophet. The blindness, a consequence of old age, is also an indication that a good deal of
time has passed since Ahijah's fateful encounter on the road with Jeroboam.

5. *thus and so shall you speak to her.* This convention of using a phrase like this of summary
without stipulation of the actual words is not infrequent in biblical dialogue and reflects
its formal bias of stylization. In this case, it is a means of postponing the revelation of the
prophecy of doom that Ahijah will pronounce against the house of Jeroboam.

6. *when Ahijah heard the sound of her footsteps.* This detail nicely captures the perspective
of the blind man, who has to depend on his acute sense of hearing. Though sightless, he of
course knows who has come, why she has come, and the fact that she is disguised, because
God has told him all this.

7. *prince.* In God's words, the term *melekh,* "king," is avoided, and the vaguer term *nagid,*
"prince" (etymologically, he who takes the place in front of others), is used instead for
Jeroboam.

Israel, and I have torn the kingdom from the house of David and given it   8
to you, but you have not been like My servant David, who kept My commands and who walked after Me with all his heart to do only what was
right in My eyes, and you have done evil more than all who were before   9
you and have gone and made yourself other gods and molten images to
vex Me, and Me have you flung behind your back, therefore am I about   10
to bring evil on the house of Jeroboam, and I will cut off from Jeroboam
every pisser against the wall, bondsman and freeborn in Israel, and I will
burn out from the house of Jeroboam as one burns dung till it is gone.
Jeroboam's dead in the town the dogs will eat, and the dead in the field,   11
the fowl of the heavens, for the LORD has spoken.' And you, rise, go to   12
your house. As your feet come into the town, the child will die. And all   13
Israel shall keen for him and bury him, for he alone of Jeroboam shall
come to a grave inasmuch as in him alone in the house of Jeroboam a good
thing is found before the LORD God of Israel. And the LORD will raise   14
up for Himself a king over Israel who will cut off the house of Jeroboam

---

8. *My servant David, who kept My commands.* As before, this is an idealized image of David
that does not square with the narrative in 1 and 2 Samuel.

9. *and you have done evil more than all who were before you.* In light of the fact that there
is only one king between Jeroboam and David, the reference here is probably to all the bad
behavior of the people of Israel from the backslidings in the Wilderness stories onward.

10. *I will cut off from Jeroboam every pisser against the wall.* This coarse epithet for males,
which David uses in vowing to destroy Nabal and all the males of his household (1 Samuel
25:22), may well have been formulaic in pronouncing resolutions of total destruction, so
that even God uses it.
    bondsman and freeborn. The meaning of these two Hebrew terms is much in dispute.
    as one burns dung. The Hebrew verb can mean "root out," "eradicate," but since pieces
of dried dung were used as fuel, it is fairly likely that the sense of burning is activated here,
or that there is a punning relationship between rooting out the house of Jeroboam and
burning dung. The simile of dung obviously conveys a withering sense of the value of the
house of Jeroboam.

11. *Jeroboam's dead in the town the dogs will eat.* As in the Greek world, leaving a corpse to
the degradation of scavengers was conceived as a fundamental violation of the sanctity of
the human body.

12. *As your feet come into the town.* This slightly odd phrase for arrival picks up the sound
of the woman's feet that the blind prophet heard as she came into his house.

13. *a good thing is found before the LORD.* The virtue in the sick child that earns him a proper
burial is left unspecified.

15 this day and, indeed, even now. And the LORD will strike Israel as a reed
    sways in the water, and He will uproot Israel from the good land that He
    gave to their fathers and will scatter them beyond the River inasmuch as
16 they have made their sacred poles that vex the LORD. And He will give
    Israel up because of the offenses of Jeroboam that he committed and that
17 he led Israel to commit." And Jeroboam's wife rose and went off and came
    to Tirzah. She was coming over the threshold of the house when the lad
18 died. And all Israel buried him and keened for him, according to the word
    of the LORD that He had spoken through His servant Ahijah the prophet.
19 And the rest of the acts of Jeroboam, wherein he did battle and whereby
    he reigned, why they are written in the Book of the Acts of the Kings of
20 Israel. And the time that Jeroboam reigned was twenty-two years. And he
    lay with his fathers, and Nadab his son was king in his stead.

21 And Rehoboam son of Solomon king of Judah was forty-one years old when
    he became king, and seventeen years he was king in Jerusalem, the city that
    the LORD chose to set His name there from all the tribes of Israel. And his
22 mother's name was Naamah the Ammonite. And Judah did what was evil
    in the eyes of the LORD, and they provoked Him more than all that their
23 fathers had done in their offenses that they committed. And they, too, built
    high places and steles and sacred poles on every high hill and under every
24 lush tree. And male cult-harlots, too, there were in the land. They did like

---

14. *this day and, indeed, even now.* The Hebrew words—each of them perfectly ordinary—sound a little peculiar, but the gist seems to be that the end of the house of Jeroboam is very imminent.

15. *beyond the River.* The Euphrates.

19. *the Book of the Acts of the Kings of Israel.* As with the Book of the Acts of Solomon, this appears to be some sort of royal annals that was probably drawn on as a source by the author of our narrative.

20. *And he lay with his fathers.* Since, according to the terms of the curse on the house of Jeroboam, he was not supposed to come to a proper burial, this must be taken as a general idiom for dying.

21. *And Rehoboam son of Solomon king of Judah.* From this point onward, the narrative will switch back and forth between the kings of Israel and the kings of Judah.

22. *And Judah did.* In contrast to Jeroboam, Rehoboam is not said to be directly responsible, so he may have been seen as merely permissive about pagan practice.

23. *on every high hill and under every lush tree.* This is a formulaic phrase, obviously reflecting the writer's view that the only legitimate place for the cult was in the Jerusalem temple.

all the abominations of the nations that the LORD had dispossessed before
Israel. And it happened in the fifth year of Rehoboam's reign that Shishak 25
king of Egypt came up against Jerusalem. And he took the treasures of the 26
house of the LORD and the treasures of the house of the king, and everything did he take, and he took all the gold bucklers that Solomon made.
And Rehoboam made bronze bucklers in their stead and entrusted them 27
to the officers of the royal sentries who guarded the entrance of the king's
house. And it happened, when the king would come to the house of the 28
LORD, the royal sentries would carry them and bring them back to the
chamber of the royal sentries. And the rest of the acts of Rehoboam, and 29
all that he did, are they not written in the Book of the Acts of the Kings
of Judah? And there was constant war between Rehoboam and Jeroboam. 30
And Rehoboam lay with his fathers and was buried with his fathers in the 31

But the phrase also marks what is seen as a dangerous intertwining between worship and
nature: "high places" or shrines on hilltops, rituals under sacred trees, in some instances
may have been associated with a fertility cult. There is an easy segue from the lush trees of
this verse to the male cult-harlots in the next verse.

25. *Shishak king of Egypt came up against Jerusalem.* Finally, the biblical text gives us a
Pharaoh with a name. An inscription at one entrance of a sanctuary at Karnak in fact
offers a list of towns in Judah and Israel that Shishak attacked in the course of a sweeping military campaign in 926 B.C.E. Jerusalem, however, does not appear in the list. The
language of the biblical text here is a little vague: Shishak "came up against Jerusalem"
and "took the treasures." This leaves open the possibility that he besieged the city without
conquering it and that he extorted the treasures from Rehoboam in return for lifting
the siege.

27. *the royal sentries.* The Hebrew *ratsim* means "runners," but men put in charge of palace
treasures would scarcely be couriers, and it is immediately stated that they served as guards.
Perhaps the Hebrew term was used because they also had some function of running before
the king's chariots in royal processions.

29. *the Book of the Acts of the Kings of Judah.* See the comment on verse 19.

30. *And there was constant war between Rehoboam and Jeroboam.* This brief notice suggests how selective the narratives of the kings are. Nothing is reported of the course of war
between the two kingdoms. For Jeroboam, we get only his backsliding into idolatry and the
consequent prophecies of doom for his house. For the shorter narrative about Rehoboam,
again we are told of the spread of pagan worship, and of the surrender of the treasures
to Shishak—nothing more. The story of the kings, in keeping with the Deuteronomistic
perspective, is more focused on cultic dereliction, always seen as the cause of historical
disaster, than on political history.

31. *and was buried with his fathers.* Pointedly, this phrase is absent from the report of
Jeroboam's death in verse 20.

City of David. And his mother's name was Naamah the Ammonite. And Abijam his son reigned in his stead.

1 **CHAPTER 15**   And in the eighteenth year of King Jeroboam
2 son of Nebat, Abijam was king over Judah. Three years he was king in
3 Jerusalem, and his mother's name was Maachah daughter of Absalom. And
  he went in all the offenses of his father that he had done before him, and
  his heart was not whole with the LORD his God like the heart of David his
4 forefather. For the LORD his God for David's sake had given him a lamp
5 in Jerusalem to raise up his son after him and to make Jerusalem stand, as
  David had done what was right in the eyes of the LORD and had not swerved
  from all that He charged him all the days of his life, except for the matter
6 of Uriah the Hittite. And there was war between Rehoboam and Jeroboam
7 all the days of his life. And the rest of the acts of Abijam and all that he
  did, are they not written in the Book of the Acts of the Kings of Judah?
8 And there was war between Abijam and Jeroboam. And Abijam lay with
  his fathers, and they buried him in the City of David, and Asa his son was
  king in his stead.

9 And in the twentieth year of Jeroboam king of Israel, Asa king of Judah
10 became king. And forty-one years he was king in Jerusalem, and his moth-
11 er's name was Maachah daughter of Absalom. And Asa did what was right
12 in the eyes of the LORD like David his forefather. And he rid the land of

---

And his mother's name was Naamah the Ammonite. This verbatim repetition of the identification of Rehoboam's mother from verse 21 may seem a bit odd, and could be the result
of an editorial glitch, though perhaps the writer meant to underscore both at the beginning
and the end of Rehoboam's story the link of this king with the world of idolatry.

CHAPTER 15   2. *his mother's name was Maachah daughter of Absalom.* There is a
problem in this notice because Maachah is also said (verse 10) to be the mother of the next
king, Asa, who is Abijam's son, and there is no warrant for the use of "mother" to mean
"grandmother." (In 2 Chronicles 13:2 it is reported that Abijam's mother was Michaiah,
daughter of Uriel from Gibeah. It is unlikely that the Absalom mentioned here is the same
person as David's son who usurped the throne.)

5. *except for the matter of Uriah the Hittite.* The murder of Uriah is David's great crime, but
even this notation reflects a rather selective reading of his checkered history.

6. *And there was war between Rehoboam and Jeroboam.* This would have to mean the house
of Rehoboam because it is the reign of Abijam that is being discussed. The repetition of this
whole sentence at the end of the next verse looks redundant and may reflect a scribal error.

male cult-harlots and removed the vile idols that his fathers had made.
And Maachah his mother, too, he removed from being queen mother, as 13
she had made a horror for Asherah. And Asa cut down her horror, and
burned it in the Kidron Wadi. But the high places did not disappear, only 14
the heart of Asa was whole with the LORD all his days. And he brought his 15
father's consecrated things and his own consecrated things into the house
of the LORD—silver and gold and vessels. And there was war between Asa 16
and Baasha king of Israel all their days. And Baasha king of Israel came 17
up against Judah and built Ramah so as not to allow anyone to come or
go who belonged to Asa king of Judah. And Asa took all the silver and 18
the gold remaining in the treasuries of the house of the LORD and the
king's treasuries and put them in the hand of his servants, and King Asa
sent them to King Ben-Hadad son of Tabrimmon son of Hezion of Aram,
who dwelled in Damascus, saying, "There is a pact between you and me, 19
between your father and my father. Look, I have sent you a payment of
silver and gold. Go, revoke your pact with Baasha king of Israel, that he
withdraw from me." And Ben-Hadad heeded King Asa and sent the com- 20
manders of the troops that he had against the towns of Israel, and he struck
down Ijon and Dan and all Abel-Beth Maacah and all Kinroth, with all

12. *vile idols.* The vocabulary of the Deuteronomistic writers, for understandable ideological reasons, is rich in invective terms for idols, some of them perhaps original coinages.
The Hebrew *gilulim* is formed on a root that suggests "dung."

13. *he removed from being queen mother.* From this we may infer that the role of queen
mother, *gevirah*, had certain ceremonial or perhaps even legal functions attached to it. See
the comment on 11:19.

    horror. The Hebrew *mifletset* is clearly derived from a verbal root that means to suffer
spasms of horror. Its use as an epithet for "idol" is similar to *gilulim* in verse 12.

    And Asa cut down her horror. Some sort of sacred pole was employed in the cult of
Asherah—hence the verb "cut down."

14. *But the high places did not disappear.* The reason would be either that Asa regarded
them as acceptable sites for the worship of YHWH or that they were spread across the
countryside and hence resistant to royal control.

19. *I have sent you a payment.* The noun *shohad* in most other contexts means "bribe."
Either the writer put this word in Asa's mouth to convey his own judgment that the payment to turn Ben-Hadad against Baasha was a nasty business, or—perhaps more likely—
the semantic range of *shohad* extended to mean any payment offered in order to persuade
someone to serve one's purposes.

20. *he struck down Ijon and Dan . . . with all the land of Naphtali.* Ben-Hadad's attack is
to the north, whereas Baasha's troops are concentrated in the south. This would have the
effect of making them withdraw from their positions around Ramah. (See the next verse.)

21 the land of Naphtali. And it happened, when Baasha heard, that he left off
22 building Ramah, and he stayed in Tirzah. And King Asa had mustered all
Judah, none was exempt. And they bore off the stones of Ramah and its
timbers with which Baasha had built, and King Asa built with them Geba-
23 Benjamin and Mizpah. And the rest of all the acts of Asa and all his valor
and all that he did and the towns that he built, are they not written in the
Book of the Acts of the Kings of Judah? Only in his old age he was ailing in
24 his feet. And Asa lay with his fathers and was buried with his fathers in the
City of David his forefather. And Jehoshaphat his son was king in his stead.

25 And Nadab son of Jeroboam had become king over Israel in the second
26 year of Asa king of Judah, and he was king over Israel two years. And
he did evil in the eyes of the LORD and went in the way of his father and
27 his offense that he had led Israel to offend. And Baasha son of Ahijah of
the house of Issachar plotted against him, and Baasha struck him down
in Gibethon, which was the Philistines', when Nadab and all Israel were
28 besieging Gibethon. And Baasha put him to death in the third year of Asa
29 king of Judah, and he became king in his stead. And it happened when he
became king that he struck down the whole house of Jeroboam, he did not
leave Jeroboam any breathing creature, until he destroyed him, according to the words of the LORD which He had spoken through His servant
30 Ahijah the Shilonite, for the offenses of Jeroboam that he committed and
that he led Israel to commit, through the vexation through which he vexed
31 the LORD God of Israel. And the rest of the acts of Nadab and all that he
did, are they not written in the Book of the Acts of the Kings of Israel?
32,33 And there was constant war between Asa and Baasha king of Israel. In the
third year of Asa king of Judah, Baasha son of Ahijah became king over all

---

23. *Only in his old age he was ailing in his feet.* This notice of foot disease (or perhaps
paralysis in the feet) is by no means essential to the story and so appears to reflect an actual
historical memory about the later years of King Asa, perhaps made poignant by the fact
that he had previously been a valiant military commander.

25. *And Nadab son of Jeroboam had become king over Israel.* Both the form of the verb and
the content of the statement mark this as a pluperfect: the narrative now backtracks in
order to explain how it came about that Baasha supplanted Jeroboam's son Nadab as king
of Israel.

29. *he struck down the whole house of Jeroboam.* This liquidation of all the males in the
house of Jeroboam is both the fulfillment of the prophet Ahijah's curse and common
ancient Near Eastern practice when someone usurps a royal house. One recalls Macbeth's
impulse to kill Banquo and any of his offspring in order to eliminate anyone who might
lay claim to the throne.

Israel in Tirzah, for twenty-four years. And he did evil in the eyes of the 34
LORD, and he went in the way of Jeroboam and in his offense that he had
led Israel to commit.

CHAPTER 16

And the word of the LORD came to Jehu son of 1
Hanani about Baasha, saying: "Inasmuch as I have raised you from the dust 2
and have made you prince over My people Israel, yet you went in the way of
Jeroboam and led My people Israel to offend, to vex Me with their offenses.
I am about to root out Baasha and his house, and I will make your house 3
like the house of Jeroboam son of Nebat. The dogs will eat Baasha's dead in 4
the town, and his dead in the field the fowl of the heavens will eat." And the 5
rest of the acts of Baasha and that which he did and his valor, are they not
written in the Book of the Acts of the Kings of Israel? And Baasha lay with 6
his fathers, and he was buried in Tirzah, and Elah his son was king in his
stead. And indeed through the prophet Jehu son of Hanani the word of the 7
LORD had come against Baasha and against his house, because of the evil
he had done in the eyes of the LORD to vex Him by the work of his hands, to
become like the house of Jeroboam, and because he had struck him down.

CHAPTER 16   1. *about Baasha.* The Hebrew preposition could also mean "against"
and even "to." In any case, God's address in the words of the prophecy is directed to Baasha,
not to the prophet.

4. *The dogs will eat Baasha's dead in the town.* For the force of this curse, which will recur
in connection with Ahab and Jezebel, it should be kept in mind that in ancient Israel dogs
were semiferal scavengers, not pets, and thus an apt match for "the fowl of the heavens,"
which would be vultures and related aerial scavengers.

7. *and because he had struck him down.* This clause is a little cryptic. The initial "he" has
to be Baasha, and so the person he struck down is Jeroboam. Since the destruction of the
house of Jeroboam for the offense of idolatry was announced in a divinely authorized
prophecy, one might have thought that there was no sin in Baasha's killing Jeroboam and
all the males of his house. Perhaps the writer means to suggest that ruthless murder, even
if it is the enactment of deserved retribution, remains ruthless murder, especially if the
motives of the killer are far from noble, as appears to be the case with Baasha. In all these
reports, the writer manifestly struggles with putting forth a theological explanation for
political upheavals. The history of the kingdom of Judah, whatever its vulnerabilities and
cultic derelictions, reflects relative stability: Asa's reign lasts forty years, while a series of
kings in the rival kingdom of Israel are assassinated, with one regnal span as little as two
years and another only seven days. One might infer that this instability goes back to the
fact that the northern kingdom was established by a usurper, Jeroboam, in contrast to the
Davidic dynasty in the south with its claim of divine election and the heroic figure of David
as its iconic founder. The writer, however, feels constrained to explain that each murdered
monarch perished because of his idolatrous ways.

8 In the twenty-sixth year of Asa king of Judah, Elah son of Baasha became
9 king over Israel for two years. And his servant Zimri commander of half the
   chariotry plotted against him when he was in Tirzah in a drunken stupor
10 at the house of Arzah, who was appointed over the palace, in Tirzah. And
   Zimri came and struck him down and put him to death in the twenty-
11 seventh year of Asa king of Judah, and he became king in his stead. And it
   happened when he became king, when he took his seat on the throne, that
   he struck down the whole house of Baasha, he did not leave him a pisser
12 against the wall, nor a blood-redeemer or companion. And Zimri destroyed
   the whole house of Baasha according to the word of the LORD that He had
13 spoken against Baasha through Jehu the prophet, for all the offenses of
   Baasha and the offenses of Elah his son, which they committed and which
   they led Israel to commit, to vex the LORD God of Israel with their empty
14 idols. And the rest of the acts of Elah and all that he did, are they not written in the Book of the Acts of the Kings of Israel?

15 In the twenty-seventh year of Asa king of Judah, Zimri became king in
   Tirzah for seven days, while the troops encamped at Gibethon, which
16 was the Philistines'. And the encamped troops heard, saying, "Zimri has
   hatched a plot and actually struck down the king." And all Israel made
   Omri, commander of the army, king over Israel on that day in the camp.

---

9. *commander of half the chariotry.* The inevitable inference is that the royal chariotry was
divided into two units, but the "half" here anticipates the hostile division between factions
that will occur.

    when he was in . . . a drunken stupor. Zimri shrewdly waits for this moment when Elah
will be an easy target for attack.

    who was appointed over the palace. More literally, "over the house." Elah is attending a
feast at the house of his court official.

11. *blood-redeemer.* "Blood" is merely implied. The "redeemer" is a relative who in the code
of vendetta justice has the obligation to avenge a murdered kinsman. No avenger is left
alive by Zimri.

13. *for all the offenses of Baasha and the offenses of Elah his son.* As noted above, a theological
explanation is offered for what appears to be a self-interested act of assassination on the
part of a person who wants to seize power.

16. *And all Israel.* Since Israel is now clearly split into two warring factions, this formulaic
phrase must mean all the Israelites present in the military encampment at Gibethon.

    made Omri, commander of the army, king. One sees the rapidity with which people rise
to, or claim, the throne. What this amounts to in this case is a military coup: the troops,
seeing that Zimri has assassinated Elah son of Baasha, who himself assassinated the second

And Omri, and all Israel with him, came up from Gibethon and besieged 17
Tirzah. And it happened when Zimri saw that that town was taken, he came 18
into the palace, the king's house, and he burned down the king's house
upon himself and died for the offenses that he had committed to do evil in 19
the eyes of the LORD, to go in the way of Jeroboam and in his offense that
he had done to lead Israel to commit. And the rest of the acts of Zimri and 20
the plot that he had hatched, are they not written in the Book of the Acts
of the Kings of Israel? Then was the people of Israel divided in two—half 21
the people followed Tibni son of Ginath to make him king and the other
half followed Omri. And the people who followed Omri were stronger than 22
the people who followed Tibni son of Ginath, and Tibni died, and Omri
became king.

In the thirty-first year of Asa king of Judah, Omri became king over 23
Israel for twelve years. In Tirzah he was king six years. And he bought 24
the Mount of Samaria from Shemer for two talents of silver and built up
the mount and called the name of the town that he had built up after the
name of Shemer master of Mount Samaria. And Omri did evil in the 25
eyes of the LORD, and he was more evil than all who were before him.
And he went in all the way of Jeroboam son of Nebat and in his offenses 26
that he had led Israel to commit, to vex the LORD God of Israel with their
empty idols. And the rest of the acts of Omri and his valor which he did, 27
are they not written in the Book of the Acts of the Kings of Israel? And 28
Omri lay with his fathers and was buried in Samaria, and Ahab his son
was king in his stead.

---

monarch of the northern kingdom, decide to proclaim their own commander king. Omri
prevails over Zimri because he has a large part of the army behind him.

18. *the palace, the king's house.* This is the first time in a narrative book that the term
'armon, "palace," appears. The only other occurrence in a narrative text is in Chronicles,
although it is frequently used in poetry. The usual narrative designation for "palace" is "the
king's house," which here appears as an apposition or perhaps even as a gloss on *'armon*.

21. *half the people followed Tibni son of Ginath.* No information is provided about Tibni, so
it is unclear whether he is a follower of the dead Zimri or simply an opportunist who seeks
to seize the kingship in a moment of political chaos.

22. *And the people who followed Omri were stronger.* Again, it appears that Omri prevails
because he can muster more troops.

24. *Shemer . . . Samaria.* In Hebrew, the connection between the two names is more transparent because the Hebrew for Samaria is *Shomron*.

29 And Ahab son of Omri became king over Israel in the thirty-eighth
year of Asa king of Judah, and Ahab son of Omri was king over Israel
30 in Samaria twenty-two years. And Ahab son of Omri did evil in the eyes
31 of the LORD more than all who were before him. And it happened, as
though it were a light thing for him to follow in the offenses of Jeroboam
son of Nebat, that he took as wife Jezebel, daughter of Ithbaal king of the
32 Sidonians, and he went and served Baal and bowed down to him. And he
set up an altar to Baal in the house of Baal that he had built in Samaria.
33 And Ahab made a sacred pole, and Ahab continued to act so as to vex the
LORD God of Israel more than all the kings of Israel who were before him.
34 In his days Hiel the Bethelite built up Jericho. At the cost of Abiram his
firstborn he laid its foundation and at the cost of Segib his youngest he
put up its gates, according to the word of the LORD that He spoke through
Joshua son of Nun.

---

29. *Ahab . . . was king over Israel in Samaria twenty-two years.* Despite being the most
flagrantly idolatrous of all the kings of Israel, he enjoys a relatively long reign, though he
will come to an ignominious end.

31. *Jezebel, daughter of Ithbaal king of the Sidonians.* Her name and lineage proclaim her
roots in the world of idolatry. She is a Phoenician (Sidon being a principal Phoenician city);
her father's name contains the pagan theophoric element "Baal"; her name means "Where
is the prince." The Masoretic Text polemically revocalizes the name of the Phoenician god
Zebul as *zebel*, "dung."

he went and served Baal and bowed down to him. Ahab, outdoing his royal predecessors
in Judah and Israel, does not merely tolerate the idolatry of a foreign wife but becomes an
active worshipper of Baal, even establishing a temple and altar dedicated to Baal (the next
verse) in his capital city.

34. *Hiel the Bethelite.* He appears to be a royal official.

built up Jericho. Joshua, after the destruction of Jericho, had pronounced a curse (Joshua
6:26) on whoever might presume to rebuild Jericho. The violation of that solemn prohibition by one of Ahab's people is of a piece with Ahab's building a site of worship to a pagan
god.

At the cost of Abiram his firstborn he laid its foundation. The probable meaning is
that according to the terms of Joshua's curse, his firstborn died when he laid the town's
foundations and his youngest when the gates were put up, marking the completion of the
building. But the ghost of the ancient Near Eastern practice of a foundation sacrifice, in
which a ruler sacrificed his firstborn to ensure the well-being of the city, flickers through
this grim verse.

CHAPTER 17   And Elijah the Tishbite, of the inhabitants of ₁
Gilead, said to Ahab, "As the LORD God of Israel lives, Whom I have served,
there shall be no rain or dew except by my word." And the word of the LORD ₂
came to him saying, "Go from here and turn you eastward and hide in the ₃
Wadi of Cherith, which goes into the Jordan. And it shall be, that from the ₄
wadi you shall drink, and the ravens have I charged to sustain you there."
And he went and did according to the word of the LORD, and he went and ₅
stayed in the Wadi of Cherith, which goes into the Jordan. And the ravens ₆
would bring him bread and meat in the morning and bread and meat in the
evening, and from the wadi he would drink. And it happened after a time ₇
that the wadi dried up, for there was no rain in the land. And the word of ₈
the LORD came to him, saying, "Rise, go to Zarephath, which belongs to ₉
Sidon, and stay there. Look, I have charged a widow-woman there to sustain
you." And he rose and went to Zarephath and came to the entrance of the ₁₀

CHAPTER 17   1. *Elijah the Tishbite.* Elijah springs into the narrative, like several
previous prophets, with no introduction or explanation. Part of the role he will play is like
that of his predecessors; another part is quite new, as we shall see.

Whom I have served. Literally, before Whom I have stood.

there shall be no rain or dew except by my word. A persistent drought is the background
of the stories that follow. It will be broken only at the climax of Elijah's confrontation
with the priests of Baal on Mount Carmel. He tells Ahab that he has the power to bring a
drought through his own word—a posture that previous prophets have not assumed. The
implication appears to be that the drought is a punishment for Ahab's idolatry, but Elijah
does not spell that out in his brief and peremptory speech.

3. *Go from here and turn you eastward.* God's instruction to Elijah presupposes that the
prophet is in mortal danger after his harsh words to the king and so must take refuge in a
wilderness region along the Jordan.

which goes into the Jordan. The literal sense is "which is by" or "which faces." This wadi,
unidentified by scholars, is obviously a tributary of the Jordan.

4. *the ravens have I charged to sustain you.* This is the first in a series of miraculous notes
that mark the Elijah story.

7. *after a time.* This elastic indication of time might also mean "at the end of a year."

9. *Zarephath, which belongs to Sidon.* The second place of flight for Elijah is in Phoenician
territory, a little north of the Israelite border. Thus the widow for whom Elijah miraculously
intervenes is not Israelite. Her coming to recognize the God of Israel is an ironic contrast
to Ahab, Israel's king. The closeness of Phoenician to Hebrew (if the writer thought of such
things) would have made conversation between them possible.

I have charged a widow-woman. God has not actually spoken to the widow, as will
become evident, but rather has designated her to play this role.

town, and, look, a widow-woman was there gathering sticks. And he called
to her and said, "Fetch me, pray, a bit of water in a vessel that I may drink."
11 And she went to fetch and he called to her and said, "Fetch me, pray, a crust
12 of bread in your hand." And she said, "As the LORD your God lives, I have
no loaf but only a handful of flour in the jar and a bit of oil in the cruse
and I am about to gather a couple of sticks, and I shall make it for me and
13 for my son and we shall eat it and die." And Elijah said to her, "Fear not.
Come, do as you have spoken, only first make me from there a little loaf
14 and bring it out to me, and for you and for your son make afterward. For
thus the LORD God of Israel has said, 'The jar of flour will not go empty
nor will the cruse of oil be drained until the day the LORD sends rain over
15 the land.'" And she went and did according to Elijah's word, and she ate,
16 she and he and her household, many days. The jar of flour did not go empty
nor was the cruse of oil drained, according to the word of the LORD that
17 He spoke through Elijah. And it happened after these things that the son
of the woman, mistress of the house, fell ill, and his illness was very grave,

---

10. *gathering sticks.* Her intention is to make a fire over which she can bake, Bedouin-style,
the bit of flour she carries with her.

Fetch me, pray, a bit of water in a vessel that I may drink. This request is reminiscent of
the request of Abraham's servant to Rebekah in Genesis 24. In this case, however, water
would have to be scarce because of the extended drought.

12. *we shall eat it and die.* This telescoped clause is a vivid expression of the woman's desperation. The little flour that she possesses is scarcely enough to sustain two starving people;
it will provide no more than a teasing taste, a mere scrap of flatbread baked over embers.

13. *only first make me from there a little loaf.* The order of feeding he stipulates is deliberately perverse: first the prophet then the woman and last her son, instead of the other
way around when there is not enough flour even for two. It challenges the woman to place
implicit faith in the prophet.

14. *the LORD God of Israel.* This set phrase has special force in being addressed to a Phoenician woman: it is Israel's uniquely powerful God, YHWH, who has the power to perform
these wonders.

The jar of flour will not go empty nor will the cruse of oil be drained. This is the point at
which Elijah's role as a miracle worker becomes explicit. Unlike the figure cut by Nathan
or Ahijah, Elijah looks very much like the protagonist of a cycle of folktales, providing
sustenance in time of famine through supernatural means and reviving the dead. It is obviously Elijah, not Moses or Isaiah, who establishes the template for many of the stories about
Jesus in the Gospels. It was also this aspect of Elijah as a miraculous and compassionate
intervener on behalf of the wretched of the earth that was picked up by later Jewish folklore.
His other role, as implacable reprover, was not embraced by folk-tradition.

until the day the LORD sends rain over the land. The inexhaustible jar of flour and cruse
of oil thus provide continuing drought insurance for the widow and her son.

till no breath was left in him. And she said to Elijah, "What is between you 18
and me, O man of God? You have come to me to recall my crime and to put
my son to death." And he said to her, "Give me your son." And he took him 19
from her lap and brought him up to the upper chamber where he was staying and laid him in his bed. And he called out to the LORD and said, "LORD 20
my God, have You actually done harm to the widow with whom I sojourn
to put her son to death?" And he stretched out over the child three times 21
and called out to the LORD and said, "LORD my God, let the life-breath,
pray, of the child go back into him." And the LORD heeded Elijah's voice, 22
and the child's life-breath went back into him, and he revived. And Elijah 23
took the child and brought him down from the upper chamber and gave
him to his mother, and Elijah said, "See, your son is alive." And the woman 24
said to Elijah, "Now I know that you are a man of God, and the word of the
LORD in your mouth is truth."

---

17. *till no breath was left in him.* The somewhat ambiguous phrasing in which the breath,
neshamah, has gone out of the boy leaves it unclear whether he has actually died or whether
he is in a comatose state in which breathing is barely detectable. In verses 21 and 22, it is
the "life-breath," *nefesh,* that is said to return to the child. *Neshamah* and *nefesh* are close
synonyms, though the former may be more closely associated with breathing and the latter
with life itself.

18. *What is between you and me.* This idiom, rendered literally, could mean either What quarrel
is there between you and me?, or What should I have to do with you?

   You have come to me to recall my crime. One need not assume that she has actually committed any heinous crime. Ancient Near Eastern people, both Israelites and their neighbors, usually assumed that affliction came as retribution for wrongdoing. The woman
thus feels that the very presence of a man of God has exposed to God's attention some
transgression, however inadvertent or unconscious, for which she is now punished by the
death of her only son.

19. *the upper chamber where he was staying.* In a piece of delayed exposition, we are now
informed that Elijah has not only miraculously provided flour and oil for the widow but
has taken refuge—still hiding from Ahab's wrath—in the upper chamber of her house.

21. *he stretched out over the child.* Some interpreters see here, as in the parallel story about
Elisha, an act of resuscitation through artificial respiration, though the writer probably
conceived it as a miraculous intervention, the prophet imparting the supernatural vital-
ity of his own body to the boy. Elijah's prayer to God obviously supports the notion of a
divine miracle.

24. *Now I know that you are a man of God, and the word of the* LORD *in your mouth is
truth.* She had previously addressed him as "man of God," but in anger. Now the positive
force of this identity has been confirmed by his act. The two aspects of Elijah's mission—
wonder worker and prophesier-reprover—are interdependent, the former demonstrating
to skeptics the authority of the latter. This pattern, which will be picked up in the stories

1 CHAPTER 18   And it happened after a long time, that the
word of the LORD came to Elijah in the third year, saying, "Go and appear
2 before Ahab, that I may send rain over the land." And Elijah went to appear
3 before Ahab, and the famine was severe in Samaria. And Elijah called to
Obadiah, who was appointed over the palace, and Obadiah feared the
4 LORD greatly. And it had happened, when Jezebel cut off the prophets of
the LORD, that Obadiah had taken a hundred prophets, fifty men to a cave,
5 and sustained them with bread and water. And Ahab said to Obadiah, "Go
through the land to all the water-springs and to all the wadis. Perhaps we
shall find grass and we can keep horse and mule alive and will not lose all
6 our beasts." And they divided up the land for them to pass through—Ahab
7 went one way by himself and Obadiah went another way by himself. And
it happened, when Obadiah was on the way, that, look, Elijah was coming
toward him, and he recognized him and fell on his face and said, "Are you
8 my lord Elijah?" And he said to him, "I am. Go and say to your lord, 'Elijah

---

about Jesus, does not appear in the reports about the prophets before Elijah. Sometimes
one detects a belief that the prophet has the power to project a kind of spiritual force-
field as when Samuel zaps the messengers Saul sends to him (1 Samuel 19), but Samuel
does not go around the countryside performing acts of resurrection and miraculous
provision of food.

CHAPTER 18   1. *in the third year.* This is clearly the third year of the drought. Some
interpreters think the story is evenly divided in thirds—a year at the Wadi of Cherith, a
year in the house of the widow at Zarephath, and a year in which Elijah moves across the
country, finally confronting Ahab—but there is no explicit indication of such a division.

3. *Obadiah, who was appointed over the palace, and Obadiah feared the LORD greatly.* Obadiah's name means "servant of God," a role he affirms in the risky business of hiding and
sustaining the hundred prophets of the LORD. At the same time, he is a high official in
Ahab's court.

4. *a hundred prophets.* This large number suggests they are not prophets directly assigned
a specific mission by God, like Elijah, but rather members of a kind of guild of prophets,
probably figuring as ecstatics, like the prophets in the Saul story, though with the assumption that the ecstasy is inspired by YHWH. Ahab's swerving from God, then, is seen to
have taken a new deadly turn—not only does he foster the worship of Baal but also he takes
violent steps to extirpate devotion to YHWH.

6. *And they divided up the land for them to pass through.* The cause of their separation is the
pressing severity of the drought, but it is also important that they be separated—Obadiah
would normally have remained in the palace—so that Elijah can speak to him in Ahab's
absence.

7–8. *my lord Elijah . . . say to your lord.* There is an ironic interplay between this designation
of two different men—Elijah, recognized by Obadiah as his lord through the force of his
spiritual authority, and Ahab, who is Obadiah's lord in the political hierarchy as his king.

is here.' " And he said, "How have I offended, that you should place your 9
servant in Ahab's hands to put me to death? As the LORD lives, there is 10
no nation or kingdom to which my lord has not sent to seek you out, and
they said, 'He is not here,' and he made the kingdom or nation swear that
you were not found. And now you say to me, 'Go, say to your lord, Elijah 11
is here'? And so, I shall go away from you, and the LORD's spirit will bear 12
you off to I know not where, and I shall come to tell Ahab and he won't
find you, and he will kill me. And your servant has feared the LORD from
his youth. Why, it has been told to my lord what I did when Jezebel killed 13
the prophets of the LORD, that I hid a hundred men of the prophets of the
LORD, fifty men to a cave, and I sustained them with bread and water. And 14
now you say to me, 'Say to your lord, Elijah is here,' and he will kill me!"
And Elijah said, "As the LORD of Armies lives, Whom I have served, today 15
I will appear before him." And Obadiah went to meet Ahab and told him, 16
and Ahab went to meet Elijah. And it happened, when Ahab saw Elijah, 17
that he said to him, "Is it you, troubler of Israel?" And he said, "I have not 18
troubled Israel but rather you and your father's house in your forsaking the
LORD's commands and going after the Baalim. And now, send out, gather 19
for me all Israel at Mount Carmel, and the four hundred fifty prophets of

---

9. *How have I offended.* The exchange between Obadiah and Elijah is one of the most
spectacular deployments of the biblical technique of contrastive dialogue, in which the two
speakers are sharply differentiated by antithesis in tone and attitude and, often, by an opposition between brevity and prolixity (see, for example, Joseph and Potiphar's wife in Genesis
39). Elijah expresses a concise imperative, "Go and say to your lord, 'Elijah is here,' " and
then the steely resolution at the end of the dialogue, "As the LORD of Armies lives, Whom
I have served, today I will appear before him." Obadiah, on the other hand, terrified by the
prospect of conveying this message to Ahab, spouts a stream of highly nervous volubility,
anxiously repeating twice what he regards as Elijah's impossible order to him and at the
same time defending his own record as a God-fearing man. The effect is almost comical:
he is a good man and has incurred danger in his loyalty to the LORD, but he is also an
ordinary man, susceptible to fear. The contrast to the iron-willed Elijah is striking. At the
same time, Obadiah's terror vividly reflects Ahab's ruthlessness as a paganizing monarch.

12. *the LORD's spirit will bear you off to I know not where.* For nearly three years, Elijah has
proven to be a successfully elusive fugitive from Ahab's wrath, and so Obadiah feels it is
safe to assume that the prophet will continue on this path.

19. *And now, send out, gather . . . all Israel at Mount Carmel.* Ahab may be willing to accept
this challenge instead of having Elijah killed on the spot because it presents itself as the
opportunity for a grand public triumph. Nine hundred pagan prophets will surely overwhelm one prophet of the LORD in any contest, and even the place of confrontation is favorable to the pagan cause, Mount Carmel near the northern coast and close to the border of
Lebanon being in proximity to the Phoenician sphere and a place where an altar of YHWH
lies in ruins, presumably replaced by Baal worship. The king's calculation is probably first
to humiliate Elijah before the assembled people and then to kill him.

Baal and the four hundred prophets of Asherah, who eat at Jezebel's table."
20 And Ahab sent out among all the Israelites and gathered the prophets at
21 Mount Carmel. And Elijah approached all the people and said, "How long
will you keep hopping between the two crevices? If it's the LORD God, go
follow Him, and if it's Baal, go follow him." And the people answered him
22 not a word. And Elijah said to the people, "I alone remain a prophet of the
23 LORD, and the prophets of Baal are four hundred fifty men. Let them give
us two bulls, and let them choose for themselves one bull and cut it up and
put it on the wood, but let them set no fire, and I on my part will prepare
24 the other bull and put it on the wood, but I will set no fire. And you shall
call in the name of your god, and I on my part will call in the name of the
LORD, and it shall be that the god who answers with fire, he is God." And
25 all the people answered and said, "The thing is good." And Elijah said to
the prophets of Baal, "Choose one of the bulls for yourselves and go first,
26 for you are the many, and call in the name of your god, but set no fire." And
they took the bull that he had given them, and they prepared it and called
in the name of Baal from morning to noon, saying, "O Baal, answer us!"
But, there was no voice and none answering, and they hopped about on the
27 altar that he had made. And it happened at noon that Elijah mocked them
and said, "Call out in a loud voice, for he is a god. Perhaps he is chatting or
28 occupied or off on a journey. Perhaps he is sleeping and will awake." And

---

21. *How long will you keep hopping between the two crevices?* This is obviously an idiom
that means trying to have it both ways. The Hebrew noun has three different meanings:
se'if can be a "thought" (hence "opinions" in the King James Version), a "branch," or a
"crevice." This translation assumes that the idiom invokes a concrete image, and opts for
"crevices" because of the physical evocation of a person awkwardly jumping between two
cracks in a rock.

22. *I alone remain a prophet of the LORD.* The 100 prophets hidden in caves, who have no
mission and are not standing on Mount Carmel confronting the 450 prophets of Baal,
would not count.

    four hundred fifty men. The 450 prophets of the goddess Asherah appear to be out of
the picture.

25. *Choose one of the bulls for yourselves.* He creates the impression of giving them the
advantage of, one might say, serving first.

26. *the bull that he had given them.* That is, he offered two bulls and allowed them to choose.

    they hopped about on the altar. The verb here satirically picks up the "hopping between
the two crevices" in verse 21.

27. *Perhaps he is chatting.* Though both the Prophets and Psalms denounce idols as having
ears and mouth but without the capacity for hearing or speech, Elijah turns this notion
into biting sarcasm in dialogue.

they called out in a loud voice and gouged themselves with swords and spears as was their wont till blood spilled upon them. And it happened, as ₂₉ the morning passed, that they prophesied until the hour of the afternoon offering, but there was no voice and none answering and none hearing. And ₃₀ Elijah said to all the people, "Draw near me." And all the people drew near him, and he mended the wrecked altar of the LORD. And Elijah took twelve ₃₁ stones, like the number of the tribes of Jacob's sons, to whom the word of the LORD came saying, "Israel shall be your name." And he built with the ₃₂ stones an altar in the name of the LORD and made a trench wide enough for two *seahs* of seed around the altar. And he laid out the wood and cut up ₃₃ the bull and put it on the wood. And he said, "Fill four jugs with water and ₃₄ pour it on the offering and on the wood," and he said, "Do it a second time," and they did it a second time, and he said, "Do it a third time," and they did it a third time. And the water went round the altar, and the trench, too, ₃₅ was filled with water. And it happened at the hour of the afternoon offer- ₃₆ ing that Elijah the prophet approached and said, "LORD, God of Abraham, Isaac, and Israel, this day let it be known that You are God in Israel and I am Your servant, and by Your word have I done all these things. Answer ₃₇ me, LORD, answer me, that this people may know that You are the LORD God, and that it is You Who turned their heart backward." And the LORD's ₃₈ fire came down and consumed the offering and the wood and the dirt, and the water that was in the trench it licked up. And all the people saw and ₃₉

---

28. *gouged themselves.* This is an attested pagan cultic practice, prohibited in the Torah, and is either a gesture of self-immolation or an act of sympathetic magic (blood spurting to stimulate fire springing out from the wood).

29. *prophesied.* The reflexive conjugation of the verb associated with prophecy that is used here means to fling oneself into a state of ecstasy or frenzy.
    none hearing. Literally, "no hearing."

34. *Fill four jugs with water.* Pouring water over the wood and the sacrificial animal magnifies the miraculous nature of the appearance of fire that is about to occur. Elijah, together with his gift of rhetoric and satire, is a grand stage manager at this event.

36. *at the hour of the afternoon offering.* This would be late afternoon.
    approached. This is the same verb as "draw near" in verse 30 but here has the technical sense of approaching a sacred zone.

37. *it is You Who turned their heart backward.* The clause is ambiguous. It could mean, given the narrative context: it is You Who made them again realize that YHWH alone is God. But "backward," *aḥoranit*, often has a negative connotation, so the clause could mean: it was You Who allowed them to fall back into idolatry, for God causes all things.

fell on their faces and said, "The LORD, He is God; the LORD, He is God."
40 And Elijah said to them, "Seize the prophets of Baal. Let no man of them escape." And they seized them and Elijah took them down to the Wadi of
41 Kishon and slaughtered them there. And Elijah said to Ahab, "Go up, eat
42 and drink, for it is the rumbling sound of rain." And Ahab went up to eat and to drink, while Elijah had gone up to the top of Carmel and stooped to the ground and put his head between his knees. And he said to his lad,
43 "Go up, pray, look out to the sea." And he went up and looked out and said,
44 "There is nothing." And he said "Go back" seven times. And it happened on the seventh time that he said, "Look, a little cloud like a man's palm is coming up from the sea." And he said, "Go up, say to Ahab, 'Harness
45 and come down, and let not the rain hold you back.'" And it happened, meanwhile, that the heavens grew dark with clouds, and there was wind,
46 and there was heavy rain. And Ahab rode off and went to Jezreel. And the hand of the LORD had come upon Elijah, and he girded his loins and ran before Ahab till you come to Jezreel.

1 CHAPTER 19   And Ahab told Jezebel all that Elijah had done
2 and all about how he killed all the prophets by the sword. And Jezebel sent

---

39. *The LORD, He is God.* This awestruck proclamation of faith has, appropriately, been introduced into the Yom Kippur liturgy at the very end of the concluding service.

40. *Elijah . . . slaughtered them there.* The verb used is singular, so the slaughterer is Elijah. There are other verbs for killing—this particular verb is generally used for animals. Elijah is as ruthless in his zealotry for YHWH as Ahab in his pagan despotism.

41. *Go up, eat and drink.* Feasting is in order because the drought is about to come to an end.

42. *stooped.* Usually the verb *gahar* means to stretch out, but he could scarcely be stretched out if his head is between his knees.

44. *Harness and come down.* Ahab has "gone up" to eat and drink, perhaps somewhere on the slopes of Mount Carmel. Now he will descend by chariot into the Valley of Jezreel.

46. *he girded his loins and ran before Ahab till you come to Jezreel.* Some interpret Elijah's running ahead of Ahab's chariot as a gesture of alliance with the king. More probably, he is again demonstrating a power superior to the king's: filled with the divine afflatus, he sprints ahead of the king's chariot all the way to Jezreel, outstripping the galloping horses.

CHAPTER 19   1. *all.* This word is repeated three times in the report of Ahab's speech to Jezebel, probably to suggest his emphasis in speaking to her of the enormity perpetrated by Elijah—all the things he did.
     all the prophets. In this instance, the repeated phrase "the prophets of Baal" is not used. Moshe Garsiel has aptly observed that this usage reflects the viewpoint of Ahab and Jezebel, who see the prophets of Baal as prophets *tout court*, with no need of a qualifier.

a messenger to Elijah saying, "So may the gods do to me, and even more, if by this time tomorrow I do not make your life like the life of one of them." And he was afraid, and he arose and went off to save himself, and he came 3 to Beersheba, which is Judah's, and he left his lad there. And he had gone 4 a day's journey into the wilderness, and he came and sat under a certain broom-tree, and he wanted to die, and he said, "Enough now, LORD. Take my life, for I am no better than my fathers." And he lay down and slept under 5 a certain broom-tree, and look, a divine messenger was touching him, and he said to him, "Arise, eat." And he looked, and there at his head was a 6 loaf baked on hot coals and a cruse of water. And he ate and he drank and he lay down once more. And the LORD's messenger came back again and 7 touched him and said, "Arise, eat, for your way is long." And he rose and ate 8 and drank and walked in the strength of that eating forty days and forty nights as far as the mountain of God, Horeb. And he came into a cave and 9 spent the night there, and, look, the word of the LORD came to him and said to him, "What are you doing here, Elijah?" And he said, "I have been 10 very zealous for the LORD God of Armies, for the Israelites have forsaken Your covenant—Your altars they have destroyed, Your prophets they have

---

3. *And he was afraid.* The received text reads "And he saw" (a difference of a single vowel in the Hebrew), but several Hebrew manuscripts and most of the ancient translations have "And he was afraid." One suspects that the Masoretic editors balked at the notion that the iron-willed Elijah could have shown fear. In fact, this turn in the narrative is by no means implausible: Elijah has spent two years or more hiding out from Ahab's wrath. He then decides to confront him in the conviction that a show of divine force on Mount Carmel will disabuse the king of his idolatrous illusions and make him bend to Elijah's spiritual authority. But Elijah has not reckoned with Jezebel's implacability, and now, finding that she seeks his life despite the spectacular public triumph on Mount Carmel, he is afraid and flees.

4. *Enough now, LORD. Take my life.* The fear for his life inspired by Jezebel is, here, followed by despair. If, after his tremendous performance publicly demonstrating that YHWH is God, the royal couple still seek to kill him and remain unrepentant in the idolatrous ways they have fostered in Israel, his prophetic mission has been a failure, and there is no point in his going on.

6. *a loaf baked on hot coals.* This is the immemorial Bedouin method of making flatbread (modern-day *pittah*).

7. *your way is long.* As the next verse explains, his journey on foot will take forty days, recalling Moses's forty days on the mountain.

9. *What are you doing here, Elijah?* This might be a challenge to Elijah for abandoning his people to flee to the wilderness, or it might mean, in view of the attention to the details of epiphany that will follow: what are you doing following in Moses's footsteps to Mount Horeb?

killed by the sword, and I alone remain, and they have sought to take my
11 life." And He said, "Go and stand on the mountain before the LORD, and,
look, the LORD is about to pass over, with a great and strong wind tearing
apart mountains and smashing rocks before the LORD. Not in the wind is
the LORD. And after the wind an earthquake. Not in the earthquake is the
12 LORD. And after the earthquake—fire. Not in the fire is the LORD. And after
13 the fire, a sound of minute stillness." And it happened, when Elijah heard,
that he covered his face with his mantle and he went out and stood at the
entrance to the cave, and, look, a voice came to him and said, "What are
14 you doing here, Elijah?" And he said, "I have been very zealous for the LORD
God of Armies, for the Israelites have forsaken Your covenant—Your altars
they have destroyed, and your prophets they have killed by the sword, and
15 I alone remain, and they have sought to take my life." And the LORD said
to him, "Go, return on your way to the wilderness of Damascus, and you
16 shall come and anoint Hazael king over Aram. And Jehu son of Nimshi you
shall anoint king over Israel, and Elisha son of Shephat from Abel Meholah
17 you shall anoint prophet in your stead. And it shall be, that who escapes the
sword of Hazael, Jehu shall put to death, and who escapes the word of Jehu,

---

10. *and I alone remain.* As before, the hundred prophets hidden by Obadiah are not taken
into account because they are not on a prophetic mission.

11. *Go and stand on the mountain before the* LORD. Elijah is commanded to assume the
stature of Moses, but the epiphany he is vouchsafed vigorously revises the details of Moses's
epiphany: God will reveal himself not in storm or fire or the shaking of the mountain
but in a small, barely audible sound. On Mount Carmel, God spoke through fire; here at
Horeb, he speaks in a more subtle language, for the deity is by no means limited to seismic
manifestations.

13. *What are you doing here, Elijah?* These words, and Elijah's response, replicate the
exchange between "the word of the LORD" and the prophet in verse 9. Either the repetition is intended to frame Elijah's encounter with God symmetrically, before and after the
epiphany in a virtually still voice, or it reflects a duplication in scribal transmission.

15. *you shall come and anoint Hazael king over Aram.* Perhaps this act is meant to manifest
God's sovereignty over all nations, but it seems strange, and historically altogether unlikely,
that a Hebrew prophet could have taken upon himself to anoint an Aramean king.

16. *you shall anoint prophet in your stead.* The term "in your stead" is the same one used
for royal succession. Elisha, then, is designated not merely as ministrant to Elijah but as his
successor, so there is an intimation that Elijah's days are now numbered.

17. *who escapes the sword of Hazael, Jehu shall put to death.* The prophetic campaign against
Ahab and Jezebel is now to take a new path. Since they have demonstrated that no proof of

Elisha shall put to death. And I shall leave in Israel seven thousand, every 18
knee that did not bow to Baal and every mouth that did not kiss him." And 19
he went from there and found Elisha son of Shaphat while he was plowing
with twelve yokes of oxen before him, and he was with the twelfth. And
Elijah crossed over to him and flung his mantle upon him. And he aban- 20
doned the cattle and ran after Elijah. And he said, "Let me, pray, kiss my
father and my mother and I will come after you." And he said to him, "Go,
return, for what have I done to you?" And he turned back from him and 21
took the yoke of oxen and slaughtered them, and with the wood from the
gear of the oxen he cooked the meat and gave it to the people, and they ate.
And he arose and went after Elijah and ministered to him.

CHAPTER 20   And Ben-Hadad king of Aram gathered all 1
his forces, and thirty-two kings were with him, and horses and chariots,
and he came up and besieged Samaria and battled against it. And he sent 2
messengers to Ahab king of Israel in the town and said to him, "Thus says 3

God's power will deflect them from the promotion of idolatry, they must be destroyed—
first by a foreign enemy, then by an Israelite who will depose Ahab, and in the last instance
by Elisha, who will follow Elijah's prophetic precedent in slaughtering Baal worshippers.

19. *twelve yokes of oxen.* This would make him a rather prosperous farmer, even though the
number twelve is obviously symbolic of the twelve tribes of Israel.

flung his mantle upon him. This act, which would produce an English idiom, is a clear
indication that Elijah is passing on the authority of the prophet's role to Elisha. In the
Samuel story, the prophet's vocation is similarly associated with a distinctive garment.

20. *Let me, pray, kiss my father and my mother.* This gesture of filial affection is a contrast
to the idolatrous kissing of Baal icons mentioned in verse 18.

Go, return, for what have I done to you? It seems more plausible not to construe these
words as a rebuke for hesitancy on the part of Elisha but as an assent: Why shouldn't you
go back to take fond leave of your parents? I have made no unreasonable demands of you.

21. *the gear of the oxen.* That is, the plow. Elisha's turning the wooden plow into firewood
is a sign that he is definitively putting behind him his life as a farmer to assume the role
of prophet.

he cooked the meat and gave it to the people. The slaughtering of the two oxen, then, is
not a sacrificial act, or at any rate not primarily a sacrificial act, but rather Elisha's means
of providing a kind of farewell feast for his parents and kinsmen.

CHAPTER 20   1. *thirty-two kings were with him.* This large number suggests that
these "kings" may have been no more than local warlords.

Ben-Hadad: 'Your silver and your gold are mine and your wives and your

4 goodly sons are mine.'" And the king of Israel answered and said, "As you

5 have spoken, my lord the king. Yours am I and all I have." And the messengers came back and said, "Thus says Ben-Hadad, saying: 'As I sent to
you, saying, "Your silver and your gold and your wives and your sons are

6 mine," give them over. For at this time tomorrow I will send my servants
to you and they will search your house and your servants' houses, and it
shall be that whatever is precious in their eyes they will put in their hand

7 and take.'" And the king of Israel called in all the elders of Israel and said,
"Mark, pray, and see that he intends this harm, for he has sent to me for
my wives and for my sons and for my silver and for my gold, and I did

8 not withhold them from him." And the elders and all the people said to

9 him, "Do not listen, nor should you agree." And he said to the messengers
of Ben-Hadad, "Everything concerning which you sent at first to your
servant I will do, but this thing I cannot do." And the messengers went

10 off, and brought him the response. And Ben-Hadad sent to him and said,
"So may the gods do to me and even more, if the ground of Samaria will

11 be enough for the footsteps of all the troops that are at my heels." And the

---

4. *the king of Israel.* From this point on in the story, he will be referred to only by this title
and not as "Ahab." It may be that the writer made this choice because in this entire episode
of the conflict with Aram, Ahab plays a very different role from the one in which he has
been seen up to now as Elijah's adversary. It is also possible that this entire episode, editorially set in the Ahab story, was originally about a different king.

   As you have spoken, my lord the king. Ahab's absolute submission to Ben-Hadad's imperious demands is surprising. After all, the Aramaen king has asked him to hand over not
only his treasure but his sons (presumably to be slaves) and his wives, including Jezebel
(presumably to become Ben-Hadad's consorts). Perhaps he feels that the overwhelming
numerical superiority of the Aramean forces leaves him no alternative.

6. *whatever is precious in their eyes.* The received text reads "your eyes." The translation
here reflects the reading of the Septuagint. The added demand of Ben-Hadad that becomes
a deal breaker is that the prized possessions of the king's servants—that is, his courtiers—
are also to be expropriated. Ahab had been willing to sacrifice what was his own, but now
everyone around him is asked to submit to the same exorbitant demands of the Aramean
king.

9. *but this thing I cannot do.* Ahab will not agree to the confiscation of his courtiers' possessions. Surrendering what is his own would reduce him to a vassal king; surrendering the
treasures of those around him might make him the object of a palace coup.

10. *if the ground of Samaria will be enough for the footsteps of all the troops that are at
my heels.* English translations since the seventeenth century have rendered this as "if the
dust of Samaria will suffice for handfuls." But the Hebrew word that means "handfuls" is
sho'alim, whereas the word here is *she'alim*, "footsteps." This actually yields a more coherent image: the troops commanded by Ben-Hadad are so numerous that there will scarcely

king of Israel answered and said, "Let not the buckler of armor boast like the unfastener."

And it happened when he heard this thing he was drinking, he and the 12 kings, at Succoth—that he said to his servants, "Set forth," and they set forth against the town. And, look, a certain prophet approached Ahab king 13 of Israel and said, "Thus says the LORD: 'Have you seen all this great throng? I am about to give it into your hand today, and you shall know that I am the LORD.'" And Ahab said, "Through whom?" And he said, "Thus says the 14 LORD, 'Through the aides of the provincial commanders.'" And he said, "Who will join battle?" And he said, "You." And he mustered the aides of 15 the provincial commanders, and they came to two hundred and thirty. And after them he mustered all the troops, all the Israelites, seven thousand. And they sallied forth at noon while Ben-Hadad was in a drunken stupor 16 at Succoth, he and the thirty-two kings aiding him. And the aides of the 17 provincial commanders sallied forth first. And they sent to Ben-Hadad and told him, saying, "Men have sallied forth from Samaria." And he said, "If in 18 peace they have come forth, seize them alive, and if for war they have come forth, alive seize them." And these had sallied forth from the town, the 19 aides of the provincial commanders and the forces that were behind them. And each man struck down his man, and the Arameans fled and Israel 20 pursued them, and Ben-Hadad escaped on a horse with horsemen. And 21 the king of Israel sallied forth and struck down the horses and the chariots,

---

be enough space on the soil of Samaria for all of them to stand. The use of "at my heels" (literally, "at my feet") reinforces this focus on feet.

11. *Let not the buckler of armor boast like the unfastener.* The Hebrew has a terrific compactness that, alas, is impossible in English: just four weighted words, *'al-yithalel ḥoger kemefateaḥ*. A very different side of Ahab is manifested here. In the face of Ben-Hadad's intimidating threat, he responds coolly with a pithy proverb: do not arrogantly presume before the battle is joined to know who will be the victor when the fighting is done.

12. *he was drinking, he and the kings.* The fact that Ben-Hadad is drinking with his allies just before the battle is a vivid expression of his overconfidence. In verse 16, we learn that he is in fact dead drunk when the Israelite forces attack.

17. *And they sent to Ben-Hadad.* The implied referent of "they" is presumably Aramean scouts.

18. *If in peace they have come forth.* This is the same verb, "to go out," which is rendered above as "sally forth," its technical sense in military contexts. But since Ben-Hadad is unsure whether they are coming out to surrender or to fight, the unambiguous "sally forth" would not make sense here. In either case, he unquestionably assumes he can take them as prisoners.

22 and struck a great blow against Aram. And the prophet approached the
king of Israel and said, "Go, summon strength, and mark and see what you
should do, for at the turn of the year the king of Aram will be coming up
23 against you." And the servants of the king of Aram said to him, "Their god
is a mountain god. Therefore they prevailed over us. But when we do battle
24 with them on the plain, we will surely prevail over them. And this thing
do: remove the kings each from his place and set governors in their stead.
25 And as for you, assemble a force like your force that fell, and horses like the
horses and chariots like the chariots, that we may do battle against them on
the plain. We will surely prevail over them." And he heeded their voice and
26 thus he did. And it happened at the turn of the year, that Ben-Hadad mus-
27 tered Aram and went up to Aphek for battle with Israel. And the Israelites
had been mustered and had been provisioned. And they went to meet them,
and the Israelites encamped opposite them like two little flocks of goats, but
28 the Arameans filled the land. And the man of God approached and said to
the king of Israel, "Thus says the LORD: 'Inasmuch as the Arameans have
said, The LORD is a mountain god and not a valley god, I will give all this
29 great throng into your hand and you shall know that I am the LORD.'" And
they encamped each opposite the other seven days. And it happened on the
seventh day that the battle was joined, and the Israelites struck down a hun-
30 dred thousand Aramean foot soldiers in a single day. And the remaining
ones fled to Aphek to the town, and the wall fell on twenty-seven thousand

---

22. *for at the turn of the year the king of Aram will be coming up against you.* The same phrase
is used in 2 Samuel 11:1 for the time of year when kings go forth to do battle. This would
be the spring—the spring month Nissan is the first month in the biblical calendar—when
the winter rains are over.

23. *Their god is a mountain god.* Their remark reflects the pagan view that different gods
have jurisdiction over different realms of nature. But they are also making a strategic calculation: the Aramean chariots and cavalry will give them an advantage in fighting on the
plain that they would lose on mountainous terrain.

24. *remove the kings . . . and set governors in their stead.* The governors might be military
officials more directly answerable to Ben-Hadad as their commander than the kings.

26. *Aphek.* Located near the Jordan, this would be on more level land than Mount Samaria
and in keeping with the courtiers' counsel.

27. *like two little flocks of goats.* The unusual Hebrew locution is a little uncertain in meaning (at least the "little flocks" component), though it clearly expresses the small size of the
Israelite forces in relation to Aram, a theme throughout this story.

men of those remaining, and Ben-Hadad fled and came into the town, to an inner chamber. And his servants said to him, "Look, pray, we have heard 31 that the kings of Israel are merciful kings. Let us, pray, put sackcloth on our loins and ropes on our heads and go out to the king of Israel. Perhaps he will let us live." And they bound sackcloth on their loins and ropes on 32 their heads and came to the king of Israel and said, "Your servant Ben-Hadad has said, 'Let me, pray, live.'" And he said, "Is he still alive? He is my brother." And the men divined and quickly and firmly said, "Ben-Hadad is 33 your brother!" And he said, "Come, fetch him." And Ben-Hadad came out to him, and he put him up on a chariot. And he said, "The towns that my 34 father took from your father I will give back, and you may place markets for yourself in Damascus as my father placed in Samaria, and as for me, I will send you off with a pact," and he sealed a pact with him and sent him off. And a certain man among the followers of the prophets had said to his 35 companion by the word of the LORD, "Strike me, pray," but the man had refused to strike him. And he said to him, "Inasmuch as you did not heed 36 the voice of the LORD, you are now about to go away from me, and a lion will strike you." And he went away from him and a lion encountered him

---

30. *Ben-Hadad fled and came into the town, to an inner chamber.* The boastful Ben-Hadad tries to hide in an inner chamber within a town that has already fallen to the Israelites.

32. *Is he still alive? He is my brother.* This expression of concern and solidarity is surely odd after Ben-Hadad has demanded Ahab to hand over all his treasure and his wives and children, and then promised to destroy him. Ahab appears to act out of political calculation—which will prove misguided. He may think that the Arameans are too numerous for him to hold them under long-term subjugation by occupying Aram, and that therefore he is better off showing generosity to Ben-Hadad while obliging him to relinquish the towns his father had taken from Israel.

34. *you may place markets for yourself in Damascus.* These would be something like trade missions. The implication is that in such a peace agreement the superior power is allowed to conduct trade on favorable terms in the territory of the other kingdom.

35. *Strike me, pray.* This bizarre exchange between two members of a guild of prophets, *beney hanevi'im,* proposes a rather loose analogy for Ahab vis-à-vis Ben-Hadad. If the word of the LORD prompts you to strike someone, even if you are disinclined, you must do it or face dire consequences.

36. *a lion will strike you.* Although "strike" is not a verb one would expect to be attached to a lion, it is used here to convey the idea of a quid pro quo: he who failed to strike will be struck down. Though the Hebrew verb does have the primary sense of delivering a blow, it has an extended meaning of "to kill."

37 and struck him down. And he encountered another man and said, "Strike
38 me, pray," and he struck him, hitting and wounding him. And the prophet went and stood before the king on the road and disguised himself with a
39 scarf over his eyes. And as the king was passing by, he cried out to the king and said, "Your servant sallied forth in the midst of the battle, and, look, a man turned aside and brought me a man and said, 'Guard this man. If he should indeed be missing, it is your life instead of his, or you will weigh out
40 a talent of silver.' And it happened, as your servant was doing one thing and another that, look, he was not there." And the king of Israel said to him,
41 "So be your judgment. You yourself have decreed it." And he hastened to remove the scarf from over his eyes, and the king recognized him, that he
42 was of the prophets. And he said to him, "Thus says the LORD. 'Inasmuch as you set free from My hand the man I condemned, it will be your life instead
43 of his and your people instead of his people.'" And the king of Israel went off to his house sullen and morose and came to Samaria.

---

37. *he struck him, hitting and wounding him.* The second person obeys the word of the LORD, but it may go against his better instincts.

38. *a scarf.* The Hebrew noun occurs only here, but it is clearly some sort of head cloth or scarf (perhaps the sort that Bedouins use in a sandstorm) that can be pulled down over the eyes.

39. *brought me a man.* The context would indicate that this is an enemy captive, which brings the parable close to the situation of Ahab and Ben-Hadad.
   or you will weigh out a talent of silver. This is an enormous amount, far more than the value of a captive slave. The silver is "weighed out" because this is an era before coinage, when payment is made in weights of silver and gold.

40. *So be your judgment. You yourself have decreed it.* The story of the captured enemy whom the man allows to escape functions quite like Nathan's parable of the poor man's ewe in 2 Samuel 12: the king, having condemned the reported act, does not realize until the prophet tells him that the tale is about his own malfeasance.

41. *the king recognized him.* Ahab evidently has had some personal acquaintance with the members of this group of prophets. It is even possible that they are the hundred prophets whom Obadiah hid in the caves.

42. *you set free from My hand the man I condemned.* The Masoretic Text reads "from a hand," but two ancient versions and a Hebrew manuscript have "My hand," which is more plausible. It is God Who has granted the victory to Ahab, and so the defeated king is in God's hand. It must be said that there has been no direct indication in the story until now that God has condemned Ben-Hadad to death or told Ahab he must kill him, though the prophet assumes that Ahab should have known this. Behind the theological reasoning lies a political calculation: allowing Ben-Hadad to go free will lead to a new attack on Israel.

CHAPTER 21   And it happened after these things, that Naboth 1
the Jezreelite had a vineyard that was in Jezreel near the palace of Ahab king
of Samaria. And Ahab spoke to Naboth, saying, "Give me your vineyard 2
that I may have it as a garden of greens, for it is close to my house, and let
me give you in its stead a better vineyard, or should it be good in your eyes,
let me give you silver as its price." And Naboth said to Ahab, "The LORD 3
forbid that I should give away the estate of my fathers." And Ahab came to 4
his house sullen and morose over this thing that Naboth the Jezreelite had
spoken to him and said, "I will not give away the estate of my fathers." And
he lay down on his couch and turned away his face and ate no food. And 5
Jezebel his wife came to him and said, "What is this? You are sullen in spirit
and eat no food." And he spoke to her, "When I spoke to Naboth the Jezre- 6
elite and said to him, 'Give me your vineyard for silver, or if you wish, I shall
give you a vineyard in its stead,' he said, 'I will not give you my vineyard.' "
And Jezebel his wife said to him, "You, now, must act like a king over Israel! 7

CHAPTER 21   1. *And it happened after these things.* As elsewhere, this vague temporal formula introduces a new narrative unit.

2. *Give me your vineyard.* The verb "give" sometimes means "to sell," as Ahab's subsequent
words here make clear.
    a better vineyard . . . silver as its price. Ahab initially offers fair value for the vineyard.
The alternative of a better vineyard, stated first, is the more attractive because Naboth will
still possess real estate (and a favorable possession), which was a prime consideration in
Israelite society.

3. *The LORD forbid that I should give away the estate of my fathers.* Naboth is thinking in
traditional tribal terms rather than in those of a fluid economy in which property is fun-
gible for value. Hanging on to inherited land is conceived as a sacred obligation.

4. *sullen and morose.* This phrase is pointedly picked up from the last sentence of the
previous episode.

    And he lay down on his couch and turned away his face and ate no food. Ahab, who in
the preceding episode had shown martial resolution against Ben-Hadad's threats, now acts
like a petulant adolescent. He has a child's fixation on the desired object he can't have, but
it does not occur to him to wield royal power in order to seize it.

6. *Give me your vineyard for silver.* In his repetition of his own words to Jezebel, he pointedly
switches the order, representing himself as having made the lesser offer first.
    I will not give you my vineyard. This seeming repetition is a drastic recasting of Naboth's
actual words: there is no pious "The Lord forbid" and no mention of the sacred obligation to retain the estate of his fathers. In this version, for Jezebel's benefit, Naboth sounds
merely obstinate.

7. *act like a king.* The literal sense of the Hebrew is "act [or do] kingship."

Rise, eat food, and be of good cheer. I myself will give you the vineyard of
8   Naboth the Jezreelite." And she wrote letters in Ahab's name and sealed
them with his seal and sent the letters to the elders and the notables who
9   were in his town, who dwelled with Naboth. And she wrote in the letters,
10 saying, "Proclaim a fast and seat Naboth at the head of the people. And
seat two worthless fellows opposite him, that they may bear witness against
him, saying, 'You have cursed God and king.' And take him out and stone
11 him to death." And the men of his town, the elders and the notables, who
dwelled in his town, did as Jezebel had sent to them as was written in the
12 letters that she had sent them, "Proclaim a fast and seat Naboth at the head
13 of the people." And the two worthless fellows came and sat opposite him,
and the worthless fellows bore witness against Naboth before the people,
saying, "Naboth has cursed God and king." And they took him outside the
14 town and stoned him to death. And they sent to Jezebel, saying, "Naboth
15 has been stoned and he is dead." And it happened when Jezebel heard that
Naboth had been stoned to death, Jezebel said to Ahab, "Rise, take hold of
the vineyard of Naboth the Jezreelite, who refused to give it to you for silver,
16 for Naboth is not alive, for he is dead." And when Ahab heard that Naboth

---

I myself will give you the vineyard of Naboth. She is careful not to explain the means by
which she will effect this transaction.

8. *she wrote letters in Ahab's name and sealed them with his seal.* She in effect usurps his
royal power, "acting like a king" instead of him.

who were in his town, who dwelled with Naboth. The seeming redundancy underlines
the idea that his own neighbors, alongside of whom he had always lived, will be complicit
in betraying him.

9. *Proclaim a fast.* A common function of an ad hoc communal fast was to supplicate God
when some ill had befallen the community because of an offense committed within the
community. In all likelihood, the occasion of the fast, which would have been a reason for
assembling the community, sets the stage for exposing the purported crime committed
by Naboth.

10. *seat two worthless fellows opposite him.* Her written instructions, fully accepted by the
elders, are candid about using scoundrels willing to perjure themselves in a false accusation against Naboth.

13. *the worthless fellows bore witness against Naboth.* Unlike the altered repetitions in
Ahab's report of his interchange with Naboth, every item of Jezebel's murderous instructions is precisely carried out.

15. *for Naboth is not alive, for he is dead.* Her repetition at this point of what was first
her written instructions, then the narrative report of their implementation, entirely omits

was dead, Ahab rose to go down to the vineyard of Naboth the Jezreelite to take hold of it. And the word of the LORD came to Elijah the Tishbite 17 saying, "Rise, go down to meet Ahab king of Israel, who is in Samaria. 18 Look, he is in the vineyard of Naboth where he has gone down to take hold of it. And you shall speak to him, saying, 'Thus says the LORD: Have you 19 murdered and also taken hold?' And you shall speak to him saying, 'Thus says the LORD: Where the dogs licked Naboth's blood they will lick your blood, too.' " And Ahab said to Elijah, "Have you found me, O my enemy?" 20 And he said, "I have found you. Inasmuch as you have given yourself over to doing evil in the eyes of the LORD, I am about to bring evil upon you, 21 and I will root you out, and I will cut off every pisser against the wall of Ahab's, and ruler and helper in Israel. And I will make your house like the 22 house of Jeroboam son of Nebat and like the house of Baasha son of Ahijah for the vexation with which you have vexed Me, leading Israel to offend." And for Jezebel, too, the word of the LORD came, saying, "The dogs shall 23 devour Jezebel in the flatland of Jezreel. Ahab's dead in the town the dogs 24 shall devour, and the dead in the field the fowl of the heavens shall devour." Surely there was none like Ahab, who gave himself over to doing evil in the 25

---

reference to the stoning to death or to the false accusation that led to the stoning. The redundancy of her statement to Ahab is dramatically apt: she tells her fearful husband he is no longer alive, he's actually dead, so you have nothing to worry about and can seize the vineyard.

19. *Have you murdered and also taken hold?* The Hebrew evinces the power of compressed statement: *haratsaḥta wegam yarashta* is just three words. Though Ahab was unaware of Jezebel's scheme, these words of denunciation name him directly as the murderer.

Where the dogs licked Naboth's blood. We learn not only that Naboth was stoned to death on a false accusation but also that his body was left in the open to be desecrated by scavengers.

20. *Inasmuch as you have given yourself over to doing evil.* Ahab's previously condemned transgressions were all cultic. Now an act of moral turpitude is excoriated, and it will be this that dooms his royal line.

21. *I will cut off every pisser against the wall.* This coarse epithet for males is reserved for curses.

ruler and helper. The Hebrew term is somewhat obscure, but it appears to refer to political leadership. Compare Deuteronomy 32:36.

23. *flatland.* The received text reads *ḥel*, "rampart," not a likely place for the devouring of Jezebel's body, but many Hebrew manuscripts show *ḥeleq* (one additional consonant), which means something like "cultivated field."

26 eyes of the LORD, as Jezebel his wife had enticed him to do. And he acted
   most loathsomely to go after foul idols, as all that the Amorites had done,
27 whom the LORD had dispossessed before the Israelites. And it happened
   when Ahab heard these words that he rent his garments and put sackcloth
   on his flesh and fasted and lay down in the sackcloth and walked meekly.
28,29 And the word of the LORD came to Elijah the Tishbite, saying, "Have you
   seen that Ahab has humbled himself before Me? Because he has humbled
   himself before Me, I will not bring the evil in his days. In his son's days will
   I bring the evil upon his house."

1 CHAPTER 22   And they stayed three years with no war
2 between Aram and Israel. And it happened in the third year that
3 Jehoshaphat king of Judah came down to the king of Israel. And the king
   of Israel said to his servants, "Did you know that Ramoth-Gilead is ours?
4 Yet we refrain from taking it from the hand of the king of Aram." And he
   said to Jehoshaphat, "Will you go with me to battle at Ramoth-Gilead?"
   And Jehoshaphat said to the king of Israel, "I am like you, my people like
5 your people, my horses like your horses." And Jehoshaphat said to the
6 king of Israel, "Inquire, pray, now the word of the LORD." And the king

---

26. *he acted most loathsomely to go after foul idols.* Here the chief reason for the condemnation of Ahab shifts back from ethical to cultic infraction.

29. *I will not bring the evil in his days.* This postponement of retribution proves to be rather
qualified. In the event, Ahab does not die peacefully in his bed, as one might infer from
these words, but, after the passage of some time, he is killed in battle, after which the dogs
lick his blood, in keeping with the terms of the initial prophetic curse.

CHAPTER 22   2. *Jehoshaphat king of Judah came down to the king of Israel.* The verb
here is slightly odd for a movement from south to north. It could reflect the high elevation
of the Judahite capital in Jerusalem.

3. *the king of Israel.* Throughout this long episode, with just one exception, the northern
monarch is referred to as "king of Israel," not "Ahab," in a striking divergence from most
of the preceding stories about Ahab. Some scholars, citing the contradiction of this need
to retake Ramoth-Gilead when the king of Aram had agreed to return all Israelite towns in
his terms of surrender, propose that the king of Israel here is Ahab's son Ahaziah, with that
story then being attached to the Ahab narrative. The fact that it is not Elijah but a different
prophet, Micaiah, who confronts the king, may support this view.

4. *Will you go with me to battle.* The northern and southern kingdoms had long been at war
with each other, but now they become allies, perhaps because of the threat to both of Aram.

5. *Inquire, pray, now the word of the LORD.* As we have seen before, it was standard practice in
the biblical world and throughout the ancient Near East to inquire of an oracle before a battle.

of Israel gathered the prophets, about four hundred men, and he said to
them, "Shall I go against Ramoth-Gilead for battle or should I desist?"
and they said, "Go up, that the Master may give it into the king's hand."
And Jehoshaphat said, "Is there no prophet of the LORD left here, that we   7
might inquire of him?" And the king of Israel said to Jehoshaphat, "There   8
is still one man through whom to inquire of the LORD, but I hate him,
for he will not prophesy good about me but evil—Micaiah son of Imlah."
And Jehoshaphat said, "Let not the king say thus." And the king of Israel   9
called to a certain eunuch and said, "Hurry here Micaiah son of Imlah."
And the king of Israel and Jehoshaphat king of Judah were sitting each   10
on his throne dressed in royal garb on the threshing floor at the entrance
gate of Samaria, and all the prophets were prophesying before them. And   11
Zedekiah son of Chenaanah made himself iron horns and said, "Thus
says the LORD: 'With these shall you gore the Arameans until you destroy
them.'" And all the prophets were prophesying thus, saying, "Go up to   12
Ramoth-Gilead and prosper, and the LORD shall give it into the hand of
the king." And the messenger who had gone to call Micaiah spoke to him,   13
saying, "Look, pray, the words of the prophets as with one mouth are good
for the king. Let your word, pray, be like the word of one of them, and you

---

7. *Is there no prophet of the LORD left here.* The precise cultic identity of the four hundred
prophets is ambiguous. Jehoshaphat's words here suggest that he does not regard them
as prophets of the LORD. In their own words, they invoke "the Master," which could be
YHWH or another deity. Three possibilities emerge: they are actually pagan prophets;
they are syncretistic prophets, alternately turning to YHWH and to other gods; they are
purported prophets of the LORD, claiming to speak in the name of YHWH with no actual
access to Him. It is plausible that this king of Israel, whether Ahab or his son, would keep
a throng of dubious court prophets around him.

8. *Micaiah son of Imlah.* The king withholds this name until the very end of his speech, as
though he could barely bring himself to utter it.

10. *each on his throne dressed in royal garb.* This display of royal regalia, rather odd in this
threshing floor location, sets the stage for the battle scene, when one of the two will dress
as a commoner in a futile effort to protect himself from harm.

11. *made himself iron horns.* This use of symbolic props to illustrate the prophecy is occasionally taken up by the Literary Prophets. Here, however, it is made to stand in contrast
to Micaiah's mode of operation: he resorts to no symbols but simply reports his prophetic
vision.

13. *Let your word, pray, be like the word of one of them.* The messenger is perfectly aware
that the king anticipates only bad news from Micaiah, and he tries to ward off trouble by
encouraging him to deliver a positive prophecy.

14 should speak good things." And Micaiah said, "As the LORD lives, that which
15 the LORD says to me will I speak." And he came to the king and the king
    said to him, "Micaiah, shall we go up to Ramoth-Gilead to battle or shall we
    refrain?" and he said to him, "Go up and prosper, and the LORD shall give
16 it into the hand of the king." And the king said to him, "How many times
    must I make you swear that you shall speak to me only truth in the name of
17 the LORD?" And he said, "I saw all Israel scattered over the mountains like
    sheep that have no shepherd. And the LORD said, 'These have no master. Let
18 each go back home in peace.' " And the king of Israel said to Jehoshaphat,
19 "Did I not say to you, he will not prophesy good about me but evil?" And
    he said, "Therefore hear the word of the LORD: I saw the LORD sitting on
    His throne with all the army of the heavens standing in attendance by Him
20 at His right and at His left. And the LORD said, 'Who will entice Ahab, that
    he go up and fall at Ramoth-Gilead?' And one said this way and one said
21 another way. And a spirit came out and stood before the LORD and said, 'I
22 will entice him.' And the LORD said, 'How?' And it said, 'I will go out and

---

14. *that which the LORD says to me will I speak.* His words are reminiscent of the ones
spoken by the pagan seer Balaam in Numbers 22:38. Balaam was summoned to pronounce
doom on Israel but blessed them instead; Micaiah, when the king of Israel would like him
to prophesy good, will deliver a message of doom.

17. *like sheep that have no shepherd . . . "These have no master."* In the first instance, evidently following the messenger's instructions, Micaiah prophesies victory, in a vague formulation. Now, pressed by the suspicious king, he couches his true prophecy in oblique
terms, but the response of the king of Israel in the next verse indicates his clear understanding that the sheep without a shepherd is a prediction of his own death.

19. *And he said.* Jehoshaphat does not answer the rhetorical question of the king of Israel.
Instead, Micaiah picks up the moment of silence by pronouncing a second prophecy of
doom, far more explicit than the first.
    *I saw the LORD sitting on His throne with all the army of the heavens standing in atten-
dance.* There is a convergence between the visionary scene and the actual one. As armies
assemble below, the celestial army stands in attendance on God (He is LORD of Armies, or
LORD of Hosts). The two kings have been sitting on their thrones, which, as Moshe Garsiel
has aptly observed, is precisely how Micaiah sees the LORD in his vision.

20. *Who will entice Ahab.* This story puts forth a theological explanation of false prophecy. A celestial spirit answers God's call and volunteers to lure Ahab to his destruction
by putting a false message in the mouths of the four hundred prophets claiming to speak
the word of the LORD. By means of this contrivance, everything in this story is seen to be
determined by God, and the false prophecy is not merely the human initiative of prophets
seeking to curry the king's favor. It is only here that the monarch is named as Ahab, not
"king of Israel."

become a lying spirit in the mouth of all his prophets.' And He said, 'You shall entice and you shall also prevail. Go forth and thus do.' And now, look, the 23 LORD has placed a lying spirit in the mouth of all these prophets of yours, but the LORD has spoken evil against you." And Zedekiah son of Chenaanah 24 approached and struck Micaiah on the cheek and said, "How has the spirit of the LORD passed from me to speak to you?" And Micaiah said, "You are 25 about to see on that day when you will enter the innermost chamber to hide." And the king of Israel said, "Take Micaiah and bring him back to Amon com- 26 mander of the town and to Joash the king's son, and say, 'Thus said the king: 27 Put this fellow in the prison-house and feed him meager bread and meager water until I return safe and sound.'" And Micaiah said, "If you really return 28 safe and sound, the LORD has not spoken through me." And he said, "Hear, all peoples!" And the king of Israel went up, and Jehoshaphat king of Judah 29 with him, to Ramoth-Gilead. And the king of Israel said, "I will disguise 30 myself and go into battle, but you, don your royal garb." And the king of Israel disguised himself and went into the battle. And the king of Aram had 31 charged the commanders of his thirty-two chariots, saying, "You shall battle against neither small nor great but against the king of Israel alone." And it 32 happened, when the commanders of the chariots saw Jehoshaphat, that they said, "He must be the king of Israel," and they swerved against him to do battle, and Jehoshaphat cried out. And it happened, when the command- 33 ers of the chariots saw that he was not the king of Israel, they turned back from him. But a man drew the bow unwitting and struck the king of Israel 34

---

28. *And he said, "Hear, all peoples!"* The "he" is Micaiah speaking again. The repetition of the formula for introducing direct speech, with no intervening response from the king, suggests that the king is flabbergasted by the prophet's obduracy, even in the face of imprisonment. But the hortatory "Hear, all peoples!" is an odd thing for the prophet to say in this narrative context. In fact, these three words are borrowed from the beginning of Micah's prophecies (Micah 1:2) and are almost certainly an editorial interpolation intended to establish a link between Micaiah son of Imlah and the literary prophet Micah (the same name without the theophoric suffix, who lived a century later). Some versions of the Septuagint lack these three words.

30. *I will disguise myself.* The Masoretic Text reads "disguise yourself," which is flatly contradicted by the next clause, in which the king of Israel tells Jehoshaphat to wear royal garb. Three ancient versions have the king of Israel and not Jehoshaphat disguising himself, and this is surely the original reading.

34. *drew the bow unwitting.* He is simply targeting an Israelite in a chariot, unaware that the man in commoner's clothes is the king of Israel.

between the joints of the armor. And he said to his charioteer, "Turn your
35 hand back and take me out of the fray, for I am wounded." And the battle
surged on that day, and the king was propped up in the chariot facing Aram.
And he died in the evening, and the blood of the wound spilled out onto the
36 floor of the chariot. And the rumor passed through the camp as the sun was
37 setting, saying, "Each man to his town and each man to his land." And the
38 king died, and they came to Samaria and buried the king in Samaria. And
they flushed out the chariot by the pool of Samaria, and the dogs licked his
blood, and the whores had bathed, according to the word of the LORD that
39 He had spoken. And the rest of the acts of Ahab and all that he did, and the
ivory house that he built and all the towns that he built, are they not written
40 in the Book of the Acts of the Kings of Israel? And Ahab lay with his fathers,
and Ahaziah his son was king in his stead.

41 And Jehoshaphat son of Asa had become king over Judah in the fourth
42 year of Ahab king of Israel. Jehoshaphat was thirty-five years old when
he became king, and he was king in Jerusalem twenty-five years. And his

---

35. *the king was propped up in the chariot facing Aram.* His initial command to the charioteer to carry him away from the front is not carried out, either because the fighting is so
thick that the chariot cannot get away or because the charioteer decides on his own that
the removal of the king would demoralize the troops. The dying king, propped up in the
chariot, appears to be continuing to battle.

   the floor of the chariot. The Hebrew uses an anatomical term, literally "bosom." The
passage of several hours indicates that the king dies of loss of blood from the wound, so
there would have been a considerable quantity of blood on the floor of the chariot.

36. *Each man to his town and each man to his land.* This flight of the troops on the news of
the king's death is an explicit fulfillment of Micaiah's prophecy. "I saw all Israel scattered
over the mountains like sheep that had no shepherd" and "Let each go back home in peace."

38. *And they flushed out the chariot by the pool of Samaria, and the dogs licked his blood.*
This is only an approximate fulfillment of Elijah's prophecy to Naboth. Elijah had said the
dogs would lick Ahab's blood in the place they had licked Naboth's blood, which would
be in Jezreel, not Samaria. Also, the dogs evidently do not lick the blood from the corpse
or from the chariot but from the bloodied water of the pool used to clean the chariot. This
indirection was no doubt necessary because the royal attendants would not have allowed
the king's body to be desecrated or the chariot to be invaded by dogs.

   and the whores had bathed. Presumably, they used the pool to bathe and thus the king's
blood, however diluted, passed over their bodies. This added indignity was not part of
Elijah's prophecy of doom, at least not in the versions we have in the received text.

39. *ivory house.* This is a house with ivory panels or ornamentation, as ivory would have not
been a suitable material for the structural elements of the building.

mother's name was Azubah daughter of Shilhi. And he went in all the ⁴³
ways of Asa his father, he did not turn away from them, to do what was
right in the eyes of the LORD. Only the high places were not removed. The ⁴⁴
people were still sacrificing and burning incense on the high places. And ⁴⁵
Jehoshaphat made peace with the king of Israel. And the rest of the acts ⁴⁶
of Jehoshaphat and his valor that he performed and with which he fought,
are they not written in the Book of the Acts of the Kings of Judah? And ⁴⁷
the rest of the male cult-harlots who were left in the days of Asa his father
he rooted out from the land. And there was no king in Edom but a royal ⁴⁸
governor. Jehoshaphat had fashioned Tarshish ships to go to Ophir for ⁴⁹
gold, but they did not go, for the ships had broken up in Ezion-Geber. Then ⁵⁰
did Ahaziah son of Ahab say to Jehoshaphat, "Let my servants go with
your servants in ships," but Jehoshaphat did not agree. And Jehoshaphat ⁵¹
lay with his fathers and was buried with his fathers in the City of David
his father, and Jehoram his son became king in his stead. Ahaziah son of ⁵²
Ahab had become king over Israel in Samaria in the seventeenth year of
Jehoshaphat king of Judah, and he was king over Israel two years. And he ⁵³
did what was evil in the eyes of the LORD and went in the way of his father
and in the way of his mother and in the way of Jeroboam son of Nebat,
who had led Israel to offend. And he worshipped Baal and bowed down ⁵⁴
to him and vexed the LORD God of Israel as all that his father had done.

---

44. *Only the high places were not removed.* This refrain reflects the view of the Deuteronomist that the local altars were a kind of paganism, though they could well have been legitimate places for the worship of YHWH.

48. *but a royal governor.* The Hebrew lacks "but" and sounds a little crabbed.

49. *Tarshish ships.* Since the destination of the ships is on the Red Sea, it is clear at least in this instance that "Tarshish ships" refers to a particular design of ship, not to a geographical location.

50. *Let my servants go with your servants in ships.* Perhaps the northern kingdom had greater proficiency in seafaring because of its proximity to Phoenicia. In any case, Jehoshaphat rejects the proposal, probably because he doesn't want to share the gold of Ophir.

54. *And he worshipped Baal.* If this scarcely seems a proper ending for the book, that is because Kings, like Samuel, was originally one book, the division into two reflecting merely the limits of the length of a scroll.

2 Kings

CHAPTER 1   And Moab rebelled against Israel after Ahab's ₁
death. And Ahaziah fell through the lattice in his upper chamber and ₂
became ill, and he sent messengers and said, "Go, inquire of Baal-Zebub
god of Ekron whether I shall survive this illness." But the LORD had spoken ₃
to Elijah the Tishbite: "Rise, go up to meet the messengers of the king of
Samaria and speak to them: 'Is it for lack of a god in Israel that you go to
inquire of Baal-Zebub god of Ekron?' And therefore, thus said the LORD: ₄
'From the bed you mounted you shall not come down, for you are doomed
to die.'" And Elijah went off. And the messengers came back to him, and ₅
he said to them, "Why have you come back?" And they said to him, "A ₆
man came up to meet us and said to us, 'Go back to the king who sent

---

CHAPTER 1   1. *And Moab rebelled against Israel after Ahab's death.* This notation
locates the story temporally but is not otherwise linked to it, except to indicate that Israel's
dominance over vassal states was shaken in the political uncertainty after Ahab's death.

2. *inquire.* The Hebrew verb *darash* is the technical term used for inquiring of an oracle.
From the monotheistic point of view, it is of course outrageous that a king of Israel should
go out of his way to inquire of a pagan oracle.
    Baal-Zebub. This appears to mean "Lord of the flies," and in the New Testament Baal-
Zebub, or Beelzebub, is demoted from pagan deity to demon. A plausible scholarly proposal
is that the original name was Baal-Zebul, "Baal the Prince," and that the final consonant
was changed by the Hebrew writers in order to make it a term of opprobrium.

3. *But the LORD had spoken to Elijah.* The entire episode is constructed through dialogue,
with further cited speech nesting within the dialogue, and the verb "to speak" is repeated
again and again.
    the king of Samaria. This epithet diminishes the sphere of the king of Israel.
    for lack of a god. The wording also could mean "for lack of gods."

6. *Go back to the king who sent you.* In the reiterated pattern of verbatim repetition in this
story, this clause stands out as an added element that was not part of Elijah's speech to the

you and speak to him: Thus said the LORD—Is it for lack of a god in Israel
that he sent to inquire of Baal-Zebub god of Ekron? Therefore, from the
bed you mounted you shall not come down, for you are doomed to die.'"

7 And he said to them, "What is the manner of the man who came up to
8 meet you and spoke to you these words?" And they said to him, "He is a
hairy man, and a leather belt is bound round his waist." And he said, "It
9 is Elijah the Tishbite." And he sent to him a captain of fifty with his men,
and he went up to him, and, look, he was sitting on the hilltop. And he
10 spoke to him: "Man of God! The king has spoken—come down." And
Elijah answered and spoke to the captain of the fifty: "And if I am a man
of God, let fire come down from the heavens and consume you and your
men!" And fire came down from the heavens and consumed him and
11 his men. And he persisted and sent him another captain of fifty with his
men, and he spoke out and said to him, "Man of God! Thus said the king:
12 'Quick, come down.'" And Elijah answered and spoke to him: "If I am a
man of God, let fire come down from the heavens and consume you and
your men." And fire came down from the heavens and consumed him and
13 his men. And he persisted and sent a third captain of fifty with his men,
and the third captain of the fifty went up and came and kneeled before
Elijah and pleaded with him: "Man of God! May my life, pray, and the
14 lives of these fifty servants of yours be precious in your eyes. Look, fire

---

messengers. The clause has the effect of underscoring the king's responsibility for sending
the messengers to a pagan oracle.

8. *He is a hairy man, and a leather belt is bound round his waist.* This is the first indication
in the whole cycle of stories of Elijah's appearance. There is something rough-hewn and
perhaps forbidding in his distinctive look.

9. *with his men.* Literally, "with his fifty." The usage is repeated.

10. *let fire come down from the heavens.* Celestial fire is Elijah's prophetic medium. It came
down to consume the sacrifice in the contest with the prophets of Baal at Mount Carmel.
At the end of his story, he will ascend to the heavens in a fiery chariot.

11. *And he persisted.* The literal sense is "and he went back."
    Quick, come down. In the verbatim repetition, "quick" is added, suggesting a mounting
urgency after the failure of the first contingent of fifty.

12. *spoke to him.* The Masoretic Text has "to them," but Elijah's answer ("you and your
men") makes clear he is speaking to the captain, and two Hebrew manuscripts as well as
the Septuagint and the Syriac show the singular.

13. *these fifty servants of yours.* The pleading captain is careful to address Elijah in deferential terms, as would a subject to his monarch, referring to his own troops as Elijah's servants.

has come down from the heavens and consumed the two captains of the fifty and their men, and now, may my life be precious in your eyes." And the LORD's messenger spoke to Elijah: "Go down with him. Do not fear him." And he rose and went down with him to the king. And he spoke to him: "Thus said the LORD—'Inasmuch as you have sent messengers to inquire of Baal-Zebub god of Ekron—is it for lack of a god in Israel?—to inquire of his word, therefore from the bed you mounted you shall not come down, for you are doomed to die." And he died according to the word of the LORD that Elijah had spoken, and Jehoram became king in his stead in the second year of Jehoram son of Jehoshaphat king of Judah, for he had no son. And the rest of the acts of Ahaziah that he did, are they not written in the Book of the Acts of the Kings of Israel?

CHAPTER 2   And it happened, when the LORD was going to take Elijah up to the heavens in a whirlwind, that Elijah, and Elisha with him, went from Gilgal. And Elijah said to Elisha, "Stay here, pray, for the LORD has sent me to Bethel." And Elisha said, "As the LORD lives and as you

---

15. *Do not fear him.* The captain's expressed terror of Elijah confirms that the prophet has nothing to fear from him.

16. *is it for lack of a god in Israel?* In the two preceding repetitions of this clause, it appeared at the beginning of the sentence, "Is it for lack of a god in Israel that you go . . . ?" Here, instead, it appears as an outraged interjection in the middle of the sentence after the mention of Baal-Zebub.

   therefore from the bed you mounted you shall not come down. The sentence of doom is an invariable element in the three repetitions, and always occurs at the end of the prophetic statement. The three repetitions of the prophecy are joined by the three repeated reports of a captain and his fifty men going up to Elijah. The folktale pattern, often deployed in the Bible, is used in which there are two identical repetitions and then a third that diverges from the first two (as in "Goldilocks and the Three Bears"),

17. *And he died according to the word of the LORD.* In the narrative report, nothing is allowed to intervene between Elijah's pronouncement of the prophecy of doom directly to the ailing king and the king's death.

   and Jehoram became king . . . in the second year of Jehoram . . . king of Judah, for he had no son. The seeming confusion is the result of a historical coincidence: Jehoram, brother of the heirless Ahaziah, happened to have the same name as the king reigning in Judah at that time. In a culture that favored theophoric names, this one, which means "God is exalted," might have been fairly common.

CHAPTER 2   2. *Stay here, pray, for the LORD has sent me to Bethel.* Elijah seems to have foreknowledge of his own departure from the earthly realm, and his initial sense

3 live, I will not forsake you." And they went down to Bethel. And the acolyte prophets who were in Bethel came out to Elisha and said to him, "Did you know that today the LORD is about to take your master from over you?" And
4 he said, "I, too, know. Be still!" And Elijah said to him, "Elisha, stay here, pray, for the LORD has sent me to Jericho." And he said, "As the LORD lives and as you live, I will not forsake you." And they came to Jericho. And the
5 acolyte prophets who were in Jericho approached Elisha and said to him, "Do you know that today the LORD is about to take your master from over
6 you?" And he said, "I, too, know. Be still!" And Elijah said to him, "Stay here, pray, for the LORD has sent me to the Jordan." And he said, "As the LORD lives and as you live, I will not forsake you." And the two of them
7 went. And fifty men of the acolyte prophets had gone and stood opposite
8 at a distance, and the two of them stood by the Jordan. And Elijah took his mantle and rolled it up and struck the water, and it parted on both sides,
9 and the two of them crossed over on dry ground. And it happened as they crossed over that Elijah said to Elisha, "Ask, what may I do for you before I am taken from you?" And Elisha said, "Let there be, pray, a double por-

---

is that this should be a private encounter between him and God, not to be witnessed by anyone else, not even by his disciple.

I will not forsake you. By this pronouncement, to be repeated twice, Elisha affirms that he is Elijah's loyal follower and heir. In the event, his being able actually to see his master's fiery ascension will justify his request of a double portion of the spirit investing Elijah.

3. *the acolyte prophets.* Literally, "the sons of the prophets." The prefix "sons" suggests they are not full-fledged prophets, which means they are either acolytes or members of a professional guild of prophets rather than independent prophetic agents.

Did you know that . . . the LORD is about to take your master. Evidently, Elijah's imminent departure has become general news, at least in prophetic circles.

from over you. The literal sense is "from your head."

4. *stay here, pray, for the LORD has sent me.* This episode follows the folktale patterns manifested in the previous episode of three repetitions with verbatim restatements. Here, too, there is a swerve in the third repetition: in the third instance, Elijah and Elisha do not go to a town but to the Jordan, so there is no group of acolyte prophets for them to encounter, and this third iteration concludes with Elijah's ascent to the heavens in a chariot of fire.

6. *the LORD has sent me to the Jordan.* The town of Jericho is close to the Jordan, as is clear in the next verse, when the fifty acolyte prophets can see Elijah and Elisha from a distance.

8. *and it parted on both sides.* This is, of course, a small-scale reenactment of the miracle performed by Moses in parting the waters of the Sea of Reeds. Here it is executed not with an upraised staff but with the rolled-up prophet's mantle, which Elisha will then inherit from Elijah. The point of crossing the Jordan is to have Elijah pass through this liminal zone and thus to be on the other side, beyond the land of Israel proper, when he is taken up into the heavens.

9. *a double portion of your spirit.* Though this may seem to be a presumptuous wish by Elisha to surpass his master, it could just as easily reflect a sense of inadequacy: feeling

tion of your spirit upon me." And he said, "You have asked a hard thing. If ₁₀ you see me taken from you, let it be thus for you, and if not, it will not be." And it happened as they were going along speaking, that, look, there was a ₁₁ chariot of fire, and horses of fire, and they separated the two of them, and Elijah went up to the heavens in a whirlwind. And Elisha was watching and ₁₂ he was crying out, "My father, my father, Israel's chariot and its horsemen!" And he saw him not again. And he had clung to his garments and torn them in two. And he lifted up Elijah's mantle, which had fallen from him, and ₁₃ he went back and stood on the bank of the Jordan. And he took Elijah's ₁₄ mantle that had fallen from him and struck the water and said, "Where is the LORD, God of Elijah?" And he, too, struck the water, and it parted on both sides, and Elisha crossed over. And the acolyte prophets who were ₁₅ in Jericho saw him from the other side and said, "Elijah's spirit has rested

---

himself to be no more than an ordinary man, Elisha wants a supercharge of the spirit in order to be Elijah's successor.

10. *If you see me taken from you, let it be thus for you.* Elijah himself is not entirely sure that Elisha is worthy to bear a double portion of the spirit. If God unveils his eyes to witness Elijah's miraculous ascension, that will be proof of his worthiness.

11. *a chariot of fire, and horses of fire.* As noted above, fire has been an important instrument for Elijah's prophetic activities.

Elijah went up to the heavens in a whirlwind. This story takes us into new territory. Everywhere in the Hebrew Bible, death is the definitive end, Sheol, the underworld, a hole in the ground into which the once living person goes down. The single previous intimation of Elijah's ascension is the cryptic notation about Enoch's being "taken" by God in Genesis 5:24. Elijah does not die but rides up to the celestial sphere in a fiery chariot. His ascension prepares the way for the idea of Christ's resurrection in Christian Scripture, and it is significant that Elijah and Moses are represented in the New Testament as the two chief precursors of Jesus.

12. *My father, my father, Israel's chariot and its horsemen.* Elisha obviously refers to Elijah as his father because he is his master and mentor. The metaphor of the chariot and horsemen, suggested to him by the vision of the chariot of fire before his eyes, registers the idea that Elijah has been Israel's true power, as chariotry is the driving power of an army.

And he had clung to his garments and torn them in two. Since Elijah had removed his mantle, this would be the tunic worn beneath the mantle. Elisha's clinging to it reflects his impassioned desire not to part from his master. It seems that as Elijah left him for his ascent, part of the tunic tore away in Elisha's hands. This is an ironic reversal of the request for a double portion of the spirit because he now holds half a garment.

14. *Where is the LORD, God of Elijah?* If the LORD is now to be with him as He was with Elijah, He will enable Elisha to replicate the miracles that Elijah performed.

he, too. There is an evident glitch in the Hebrew syntax. These two words in the Hebrew should appear after "and he struck." The word order in the received text produces an odd bumpiness: "He too and he struck."

15. *And the acolyte prophets . . . saw him from the other side.* Elisha's parting of the waters,

upon Elisha." And they came to meet him and bowed down before him
16 to the ground. And they said to him, "Look, pray, your servants have fifty
stalwart men. Let them go, pray, and seek your master, lest the spirit of the
LORD has borne him off and flung him down on some hill or into some
17 valley." And he said, "You shall not send." And they urged him incessantly,
and he said, "Send." And they sent fifty men and sought him three days but
18 did not find him. And they came back to him while he was still staying in
Jericho, and he said to them, "Did I not say to you, do not go?"

19 And the men of the town said to Elisha, "Look, pray, it is good to live in the
20 town as my master sees, but the water is bad and the land bereaves." And he
said, "Fetch me a new bowl and put salt in it." And they fetched it for him.
21 And he went out to the water source and flung the salt there and said, "Thus
said the LORD: 'I have healed these waters. There will no longer be death
22 and bereaving.'" And the waters have been healed to this day, according
23 to the word of Elisha that he spoke. And he went up from there to Bethel,
and as he was coming up on the road, young lads came out from the town
and jeered at him and said to him, "Away with you, baldy, away with you,
24 baldy!" And he turned behind him and saw them and cursed them in the
name of the LORD, and two she-bears came out of the forest and ripped

---

in full sight of the assembled Jericho prophets, becomes a public demonstration that he is
Elijah's prophetic heir.

19. *Look, pray, it is good to live in the town.* Having recognized Elisha as Elijah's successor,
endowed with his powers, the townsmen promptly turn to him with a request for help.
   the water is bad and the land bereaves. This is cause and effect: the bad water contami-
nates the land, which then brings death to man and beast.

21. *he . . . flung the salt there.* The agency of the miracle is deliberately paradoxical. Salt
water is not drinkable, but Elisha's salt purifies the spring of its blight.
   Thus said the LORD: "I have healed these waters." Elisha pointedly attributes the purification of the spring to God's intervention, not to a magical act on his part.

23. *Away with you, baldy.* Literally, "Go up, baldy." We learn incidentally that Elisha is bald,
in contrast to Elijah, who was a hairy man.

24. *two she-bears came out of the forest and ripped apart forty-two boys.* This murderous
response to the boys' mockery is morally scandalous. Is it meant to suggest that Elisha
does not make responsible use of his prophetic powers, that after turning death to life at
the spring he now spreads death? The early rabbis were so outraged by this story that they
felt constrained to assert it never really happened. Their formulation, "neither bears nor
forest," became idiomatic in Hebrew for a cock-and-bull story.

apart forty-two boys. And he went from there to Mount Carmel and from 25
there he came back to Samaria.

CHAPTER 3   And Jehoram son of Ahab had become king over 1
Israel in Samaria in the eighteenth year of Jehoshaphat king of Judah. And
he was king twelve years. And he did what was evil in the eyes of the LORD, 2
though not like his father nor like his mother, and he removed the pillar
of Baal that his father had made. But he clung to the offenses of Jeroboam 3
son of Nebat, who had led Israel to offend, he did not swerve from them.
And Mesha king of Moab was a sheep-breeder and he would bring back to 4
the king of Israel the wool of a hundred thousand lambs and of a hundred
thousand rams. And it happened when Ahab died that the king of Moab 5
rebelled against the king of Israel. And King Jehoram sallied forth from 6
Samaria on that day, and he mustered all Israel. And he went and sent to 7
Jehoshaphat king of Judah, saying, "The king of Moab has rebelled against
me. Will you go with me against Moab to battle?" And he said, "I will go. I
am like you, my people like your people, my horses like your horses." And 8
he said, "By what way shall we go up?" And he said, "The way of the Wilderness of Edom." And the king of Israel went, and the king of Judah and the 9

CHAPTER 3   4. *he would bring back to the king of Israel.* The context suggests that
the verb here has an iterative sense: this is the tribute that Mesha, as vassal to Israel, would
give annually to the king of Israel. David had initially reduced Moab to vassal status. At
some point, perhaps during the reign of Baasha, Moab drove out the Israelite overlords,
but King Omri again subjugated it.

a hundred thousand lambs. As with the numbers given for troops and casualties in these
narratives, the figures here are hyperbolic.

5. *when Ahab died.* Mesha exploits the political disorder following upon Ahab's death to
rebel against Israel.

7. *I am like you, my people like your people.* This speech repeats almost verbatim
Jehoshaphat's words to the king of Israel in 1 Kings 22:4. Verse 11 then repeats, with small
variations, Jehoshaphat's words in 1 Kings 22:7. All this has the look of a story floating
around in the scribal archives that was first ascribed to Ahab (although, perhaps symp-
tomatically, without using his name) and then, in different circumstances with a different
enemy and a different prophet, to Jehoram (though here, again, in the body of the story, he
is not referred to by name). It is possible that the original story was actually about a third
king whose identity, however, remains conjectural.

8. *The way of the Wilderness of Edom.* The allied forces, instead of taking a direct route

king of Edom with him, and they swung round on the way seven days, and
there was no water for the camp or for the beasts that were at their heels.
10 And the king of Israel said, "Woe, for the LORD has called forth these three
11 kings to give them into the hand of Moab." And Jehoshaphat said, "Is there
no prophet of the LORD here, that we might inquire of the LORD through
him?" And one of the servants of the king of Israel answered, "Elisha son of
12 Shaphat is here, who attended Elijah." And Jehoshaphat said, "The word of
the LORD is with him." And the king of Israel and Jehoshaphat and the king
13 of Edom went down to him. And Elisha said to the king of Israel, "What
do you and I have to do with one another? Go to your father's prophets
and to your mother's prophets." And the king of Israel said to him, "Don't!
For the LORD has called forth these three kings to give them into the hand
14 of Moab." And Elisha said, "As the LORD of Armies lives, in Whose attendance I have stood, were I not showing favor to Jehoshaphat king of Judah,
15 I would not so much as look at you nor see you, but now, fetch me a lyre
player." And it happened, as the lyre player played, the hand of the LORD
16 was upon him, and he said, "Thus said the LORD: 'Dig out this wadi into
17 hollows.' For thus said the LORD: 'You will not see wind and you will not

---

by crossing the Jordan and then driving south to Moab, swing round (that verb is used in
the next verse) in a long arc through the Negeb and then the wilderness of Edom to the
east of the Dead Sea, thus approaching Moab from the south. Their likely intention would
have been to avoid Moabite troops stationed along the northern and western perimeters
of Moabite territory. But this move takes them on a seven-day march through the desert,
during which they run out of water.

11. *attended.* The literal sense of the Hebrew idiom is "poured water on the hands of."

13. *Go to your father's prophets and to your mother's prophets.* He is referring to the syco-
phantic court prophets or actually pagan prophets who surrounded Ahab and Jezebel.

14. *were I not showing favor to Jehoshaphat.* Elisha grudgingly agrees to seek a propitious
oracle only for the sake of Jehoram's Judahite ally Jehoshaphat.

15. *as the lyre player played, the hand of the LORD was upon him.* The use of stringed instruments and percussion instruments to induce a vatic trance through their hypnotic rhythm
is known in many different traditions of ecstatic religion. In the Bible, it is typically linked
with bands of professional prophets (see, for example, 1 Samuel 10:5–6). What is unusual
here is that an individual prophet feels he has to have recourse to these musical stimuli in
order to gain access to God's word.

16. *Dig out this wadi into hollows.* In the rocky gulches in this region, rainwater would
gather in the little hollows and crevices in the rock. In this miraculous instance, however,
there will be no rain.

see rain, but that wadi will fill with water, and you and your cattle and your
beasts will drink.' And this is easy in the eyes of the LORD, and he shall give 18
Moab into your hand. And you shall strike every fortified town and every 19
fine town, and every goodly tree you shall fell, and all the springs of water
you shall stop up, and every goodly field you shall spoil with stones." And it 20
happened in the morning, as the grain offering was being offered up, that,
look, water was coming from the way to Edom, and the land was filled with
water. And all Moab had heard that the kings had come up to do battle with 21
them, and every man of sword-wielding age was mustered, and they stood
at the border. And they rose early in the morning, and the sun had dawned 22
over the water, and from a distance Moab saw the water red as blood. And 23
they said, "This blood is because the kings have surely been destroyed, each
striking down his fellow, and they are now Moab's booty." And they came 24
into the camp of Israel, and Israel rose up and struck Moab, and they fled
before them, and they struck Moab again and again. And they laid waste 25
the towns, and in every goodly field each of them flung stones and filled
it, and every spring of water they stopped up, and every goodly tree they
felled, till they left only the stones of Kir-Hareseth, and the slingers swung

---

18. *this is easy in the eyes of the LORD.* Just as the LORD can easily provide water where there
is no rain, He will be able to effect the defeat of the Moabites with no difficulty.

19. *every fine town.* The word for "fine" (or "choice"), *mivḥor,* is an odd formation (it should
be *mivḥar*), and some scholars think it is an erroneous scribal duplication of the previous
phrase, "every fortified town," *kol 'ir mivtsar.*

    every goodly tree you shall fell. This is in direct contradiction to Deuteronomy 20:19,
which prohibits cutting down an enemy's fruit trees.

22. *from a distance Moab saw the water red as blood.* The red look of the water is a result of
the early light of dawn, perhaps reinforced, as many have proposed, by the reddish sand-
stone surrounding the wadi and its bed. God's miraculous providing of water, then, serves
a double purpose: first it revives the troops and their animals after the long march in the
desert, and then it sets a trap for the Moabites.

23. *each striking down his fellow.* The Moabites assume that the potentially fragile alliance
put together by the king of Israel has fallen apart violently.

    and they are now Moab's booty. They conclude that most, if not all, of the enemy are
dead, and that they have no one to fight, only corpses to despoil.

24. *and they struck Moab again and again.* The Hebrew text looks defective at this point
(with a confusing divergence between the consonantal text and the marginal correction),
but this is the likely sense.

25. *Kir-Hareseth.* This is an alternate name for Kir-Moab, the Moabite capital.

26 round and struck it. And the king of Moab saw that the battle was hard
   against him, and he took seven hundred sword-wielding men with him to
27 break through to the king of Edom, but they were not able. And he took his
   firstborn son, who would have been king after him, and offered him up as
   a burnt offering on the wall, and a great fury came against Israel, and they
   journeyed away from him and went back to the land.

1 CHAPTER 4   And a certain woman from the wives of the acolyte prophets had cried out to Elisha, saying, "Your servant, my husband,
   died. And you know that your servant was a LORD fearer. And the creditor
2 has come to take my two children to be his slaves." And Elisha said to her,
   "What shall I do for you? Tell me, what do you have in the house?" And she
   said, "Your servant has nothing at all in the house except a cruse of oil."
3 And he said, "Go, borrow vessels for yourself from outside, from all your
4 neighbors—empty vessels, and not just a few. And you shall come and close

---

26. *he took seven hundred sword-wielding men with him to break through to the king of Edom.* He musters an elite fighting unit in an attempt to break through the besieging forces, probably driving against the vassal king of Edom as the weakest element in the alliance of three kings. The attempt is foiled, and the Moabites are driven back into the town.

27. *he took his firstborn.* A king's sacrifice of his own child, in an effort to placate the gods at a moment of military emergency, was a familiar practice in the ancient Near East.

and a great fury came against Israel. This denouement is surely perplexing from a monotheistic point of view. "Fury" (*qetsef*) is usually the term for God's devastating rage against Israel when the people has transgressed. Here, however, Israel has done no wrong. And the descent of the fury explicitly reverses Elisha's favorable prophecy. This turn of events might reflect an early tradition that accords Chemosh, the Moabite god, power that must be propitiated by human sacrifice, so that he will then blight the enemies of Moab. In any case, the story means to explain why Israel and its allies, after an initial victory, were obliged to retreat. A Moabite inscription on a stele, discovered in 1868, in which Mesha speaks in the first person, triumphantly proclaims a sweeping victory over Israel, though it is not altogether clear whether this victory is over Jehoram or his predecessor.

CHAPTER 4   1. *Your sevant, my husband.* Almost everyone in these stories addresses Elisha deferentially. In this case, Elisha may have actually been the master of this group of acolyte prophets. In the story of the almost poisoned stew in verses 38–41, he appears to take upon himself the responsibility of providing food for them.

3. *Go, borrow vessels.* All these stories about Elisha's performing miracles to aid people in distress have a strong folkloric character. They would provide direct inspiration for the

the door behind you and behind your sons, and you shall pour into these
vessels, and the full ones you shall set aside." And she went from him and 5
closed the door behind her and behind her sons. They were bringing the
vessels to her and she was pouring. And it happened when the vessels were 6
full that she said to her son, "Bring me another vessel," and he said to her,
"There are no more vessels." And the oil stopped. And she came and told 7
the man of God, and he said, "Go, sell the oil and pay your debt, and you
and your sons will live off what is left."

And one day Elisha was passing through Shunem, and there was a wealthy 8
woman there. And she urged him to break bread, and so, whenever he
passed through, he would turn aside there to break bread. And she said to 9
her husband, "Look, pray, I know that he is a holy man of God who always
passes by us. Let us make, pray, a little upper chamber and put a bed there 10
for him and a table and chair and lamp, and so when he comes to us, he
will turn aside there." And one day he came there and turned aside to the 11
upper chamber and slept there. And he said to Gehazi his lad, "Call this 12
Shunammite," and he called her, and she stood before him. And he said to 13
him, "Say to her, pray: 'Look, you have gone to all this bother for us. What
can be done for you? Shall a word be said for you to the king or to the commander of the army?' " And she said, "In the midst of my people I dwell."

---

stories about Jesus's miracles in the Gospels—the cruse of oil that is constantly full, the
raising of Lazarus from the dead, the multiplication of the fish and loaves.

8. *a wealthy woman.* The usual sense of the Hebrew adjective is "great," but it also has the
meaning of "wealthy." The fact that she has the means to add a room to her house and
furnish it argues for the sense of "wealthy."

9. *a holy man of God.* Throughout these stories, Elisha is referred to as a man of God, not
prophet. That designation does not mean "clergyman," as in modern English, but rather
someone with divine powers, and those are manifested in the sundry miracles he performs.

12. *Gehazi his lad.* This is the first mention of him. Elisha's elevated status is reflected in
his having an attendant or factotum who performs sundry tasks for him and acts as his
intermediary.
    Call this Shunammite. This form of reference seems a bit condescending, and if he has
taken the trouble to learn her name, he is not disposed to use it.

13. *Say to her, pray.* Even though the woman is now standing before Elisha, he does not
address her directly but instead has Gehazi put the question to her on his behalf.
    In the midst of my people I dwell. Though some understand this to mean that she has
no need for royal favors because she has the support of people around her, the more likely

14 And he said, "What can be done for her?" And Gehazi said, "Why, she has
15 no son, and her husband is an old man." And he said, "Call her," and he
16 called her, and she stood in the doorway. And he said, "At this fixed time,
   at this very season, you will embrace a son." And she said, "Don't, my lord,
17 man of God, don't mislead your servant." And the woman conceived and
   bore a son at that fixed time, at that very season, as Elisha had spoken to
18 her. And the child grew, and one day he went out to his father, to the reap-
19 ers. And he said to his father, "My head, my head!" And he said concerning
20 the lad, "Carry him to his mother." And he was carried and brought to his
21 mother, and he stayed on her knees till noon, and he died. And she went
   up and laid him on the bed of the man of God, and closed the door on him
22 and went out. And she called to her husband and said, "Send me, pray, one
   of the lads and one of the donkeys, that I may hurry to the man of God and
23 come back. And he said, "Why are you going to him? Today is neither new

---

meaning is that she views herself as an ordinary person, dwelling among the people, and
thus wants no part of special treatment from the court.

14. *Why, she has no son.* It seems a little suspect that Elisha needs Gehazi to point out the
fact of her childlessness. One wonders how much attention he has been paying to her.
  and her husband is an old man. This might well be the source of her fertility problems.
The phrase is a reminiscence of Sarah's words in Genesis 18:12.

16. *At this fixed time, at this very season, you will embrace a son.* These formulaic words
signal the unfolding of the annunciation type-scene. This one differs from all the others in
that the word from the man of God is not dictated from above but is his own initiative as
recompense for the woman's kindness to him. This is also the only annunciation that does
not lead to the birth of someone destined to play a significant role in the national story: the
boy is never named, and he remains no more than the son of a prosperous farmer.

17. *And the woman conceived and bore a son.* In another divergence from the set pattern of
the annunciation, there is no mention of the necessary fact that the husband "knew" his
wife. Could there be further play here with the fact of his advanced age?

19. *My head, my head!* Like Isaac, another son born after an annunciation, this child is
threatened with death out in the open.

20. *and he stayed on her knees till noon, and he died.* Her anguish is magnified by his still
being alive when he is brought to her, then expiring as she desperately tries to succor him.

23. *Why are you going to him? Today is neither new moon nor sabbath.* The husband is
surely being obtuse, for it is obvious enough why she wants to hurry off to the man of
God. Sabbaths and new moons were times when special sacrifices were offered, which one
could bring to a man of God so that he might partake of the part of the animal not burned
on the altar.
  Farewell. The Hebrew is *shalom,* the same word Gehazi used when he asked whether
it is "well" with her and her family. In saying farewell, she simply ignores her husband's
obtuse question.

moon nor sabbath." And she said, "Farewell." And she saddled the donkey 24
and said to her lad, "Drive it and go. Do not hold me back in riding unless
I say to you." And she went and came to the man of God at Mount Carmel, 25
and it happened, when the man of God saw her from a distance, that he
said to Gehazi, "Here is that Shunammite. Now hurry to meet her, pray, and 26
say to her, 'Is it well with you? Is it well with your husband? Is it well with
the child?' " And she said, "It is well." And she came to the man of God on 27
the mountain and clung to his legs. And Gehazi approached to push her
back, and the man of God said, "Let her be, for she is deeply embittered,
and the LORD has hidden it from me and not told me." And she said, "Did 28
I ask of my lord for a son? Did I not say, 'You should not deceive me'?" And 29
he said to Gehazi, "Gird your loins and take my staff in your hand and go.
Should you meet a man, do not greet him, and should a man greet you, do
not answer him. And you shall put my staff on the lad's face." And the lad's 30
mother said, "As the LORD lives and as you live, I will not forsake you." And
he rose and went after her. And Gehazi had gone before them and put the 31
staff on the lad's face, but there was no voice and no sound, and he turned
back to meet him, and he told him, saying, "The lad has not awakened."
And Elisha came into the house, and, look, the lad was dead, laid out on 32
his bed. And he came in and closed the door behind the two of them and 33
prayed to the LORD. And he climbed up and lay over the child and put his 34
mouth over his mouth and his eyes over his eyes and his palms over his
palms and stretched out over him, and the child's body grew warm. And 35

---

24. *Drive it and go.* The servant's job is to run behind the donkey on which she is riding
and prod it to move quickly with a switch or goad.

26. *And she said, "It is well."* She says these words to Gehazi because she does not want to be
detained in explaining the disaster but instead means to head directly to Elisha.

27. *and the LORD has hidden it from me.* Elisha is, after all, a prophet, but he seems in many
respects out of touch with the woman's life.

29. *And you shall put my staff on the lad's face.* Elisha assumes that his staff is imbued with supernatural powers, but this effort to revive the child through an act of pure magic does not work.

30. *I will not forsake you.* She puts her trust not in magic staffs but in the person of Elisha
and so wants him to stick with her and come back to Shunem with her, to which he agrees.

32. *laid out on his bed.* That is, laid out on Elisha's bed.

34. *and lay over the child and put his mouth over his mouth.* Although this detail may look
to a modern reader like mouth-to-mouth resuscitation, the intention of the ancient writer
was more likely that the prophet imparted his own vital warmth, fueled by prophetic aura,
to the child, reviving him in this fashion.

he went back and walked in the house this way and that, and he climbed up
and stretched out over him, and the lad sneezed a full seven times, and the
36 lad opened his eyes. And he called to Gehazi and said, "Call this Shunammite," and he called her, and she came to him, and he said, "Carry away
37 your son." And she came and fell at his feet and bowed to the ground, and
she carried away her son and went out.

38 And Elisha had gone back to Gilgal. And there was famine in the land,
and the acolyte prophets were sitting before him. And he said to his lad,
39 "Put the big pot on the fire and cook a stew for the acolyte prophets." And
one of them went out to the field to gather sprouts and found a field vine
and gathered from it field gourds, as much as his garment could hold, and
40 he came and sliced them into the stew pot, for they did not know. And
they poured for the men to eat, and it happened, as they were about to
eat, they cried out, "Death is in the pot, man of God!" And they could not
41 eat. And he said, "Fetch flour." And he flung it into the pot, and he said,
"Pour for the people, that they may eat." And there was nothing harmful
in the pot.

42 And a man had come from Baal-Shalishah, and he brought the man of
God first fruits, twenty loaves of barley bread and fresh grain in his sack.
43 And he said, "Give it to the people, that they may eat." And his attendant
said, "What? Shall I set this before a hundred men?" And he said, "Give
it to the people that they may eat. For thus said the LORD, 'Eat and leave
44 over.'" And he set it before them, and they ate and left over, according to
the word of the LORD.

1 CHAPTER 5   And Naaman, commander of the army of the
king of Aram, was a great man in the presence of his master and highly

---

39. *sprouts . . . field gourds.* As with many other flora mentioned in the Bible, the exact
identification of these plants remains uncertain. What is clear is that instead of a plant
that would have been a proper ingredient for the stew, the ignorant gatherer brings back
a poisonous plant.

41. *Fetch flour.* It is highly unlikely that flour would have the property of neutralizing the
poison, so one must take this as a purely miraculous act.

42. *sack.* This is the traditional rendering of the unique Hebrew term *tsiqalon*, from whence
it has passed into general usage in the language. But some scholars, proposing a Ugaritic
cognate, argue that it refers to a kind of grain.

esteemed, for through him the LORD had granted victory to Aram, and
the man was a valiant warrior stricken with skin blanch. And Aram had 2
sallied forth in raiding parties and captured a young girl from the land of
Israel. And she said to her mistress, "Would that my master might come 3
before the prophet who is in Samaria. Then he could cure him of his skin
blanch." And he sent and told his master, "Thus and so did the girl who is 4
from the land of Israel speak." And the king of Aram said, "Go forth, and 5
I shall send a letter to the king of Israel." And he went, and he took in his
hand ten talents of silver and six thousand pieces of gold and ten changes
of garments. And he brought the letter to the king of Israel, saying, "And 6
now, when this letter comes to you, look, I have sent to you my servant
Naaman, and you shall cure him of his skin blanch." And it happened 7
when the king of Israel read the letter, he rent his garments and said, "Am
I God, to deal death and life, that this person has sent to me to cure a man
from his skin blanch? For you must surely know and mark, pray, that he
is seeking a pretext against me." And it happened when Elisha, the man 8

CHAPTER 5   1. *for through him the LORD had granted victory to Aram.* This clause
establishes the universalist perspective of the story, in which a prophet of Israel will perform a wonder for a non-Israelite. From the viewpoint of the Hebrew writer, it is the LORD,
the God worshipped by Israel, Who determines all events, though of course the Aramean
general could not be aware that he owes his victories to YHWH.

2. *the land of Israel.* This designation is actually unusual and in all likelihood reflects the
perception of the Arameans.

3. *Would that my master might come before the prophet.* The Hebrew has only the implied
verb "be." To be or stand before someone implies a relationship of deference or even subservience, and the idiom recurs in the story. One notes that the captive Israelite girl appears to be
on good terms with her Aramean mistress, evincing solicitude for her mistress's husband.

   skin blanch. The Hebrew *tsaraʿat* is traditionally translated as "leprosy," but the leading
symptom mentioned in this narrative and elsewhere is a complete loss of pigmentation,
whereas leprosy involves lesions and lumps in the skin and sometimes a slightly paler color
but not the ghastly whiteness of which the biblical texts speak. This is, then, a disfiguring
skin disease that remains unidentified, and hence the present translation, here and elsewhere, coins a name not to be found in dermatological manuals that refers to the whiteness.

5. *I shall send a letter to the king of Israel.* The king of Aram decides to intervene on behalf
of his general on the highest diplomatic level, king to king. He barely registers the advice
that came from the captive girl to turn to the prophet because his letter to the king of Israel
makes no mention of it, in consequence of which the Israelite king is panicked.

   ten talents of silver and six thousand pieces of gold. This vast treasure is meant to be a
gift or payment to the Israelite prophet.

7. *he is seeking a pretext against me.* Confronted with the bare request from the Aramean
king in his very brief missive to cure Naaman, the Israelite king construes the entire
maneuver as a trap: when he fails to cure Naaman, the king of Aram will attack him.

of God, heard that the king of Israel had rent his garments, he sent to the
king, saying, "Why did you rend your garments? Let him come, pray, to
9 me, that he may know there is a prophet in Israel." And Naaman came
with his horses and his chariot and stood at the entrance to Elisha's house.
10 And Elisha sent a messenger to him, saying, "Go and bathe seven times
11 in the Jordan, and your flesh will be restored, and you will be clean." And
Naaman was furious, and he went off and said, "Look, I thought to myself,
he will surely come out and stand and call in the name of the LORD his
God and wave his hand toward the place and cure the skin-blanched
12 person. Are not Amanah and Parpar the rivers of Damascus better than
all the waters of Israel? Could I not bathe in them and be clean?" And
13 he turned and went off incensed. And his servants approached and said,
"Father! The prophet has spoken a great thing to you. Shall you not do it?
14 How much more so as he said to you, bathe and be clean?" And he went
down and dipped in the Jordan seven times, according to the word of the
man of God, and his flesh was restored, like the flesh of a young lad, and
15 he was clean. And he went back to the man of God, he and all his camp,

---

8. *when Elisha . . . heard that the king of Israel had rent his garments.* Word of this public
gesture of mourning or grief would have quickly spread.

9. *And Naaman came with his horses and his chariot.* Now we learn that the general has
come to Samaria with a full military retinue.
      and stood at the entrance of Elisha's house. Nevertheless, the distinguished general does
not presume to march into the house of the man of God, but stands at the entrance, awaiting
word. The word comes to him only through an intermediary, a messenger (evidently not
Elisha's personal attendant Gehazi).

11. *he will surely come out and stand and call in the name of the* LORD *his God and wave his
hand.* Naaman had expected personal intervention by the prophet that involved invocation of the deity's powerful name and magical hand gestures, probably over the "place" of
the disease.

12. *Are not Amanah and Parpar the rivers of Damascus better than all the waters of Israel?*
Damascus, after all, is situated at a fertile confluence of rivers, and to the Damascene eye,
the Jordan is no more than a muddy rivulet. If simple bathing could cure the disease, he
would have been better off doing it in Aram.

13. *The prophet has spoken a great thing to you.* They intuit that the ostensibly simple
command to dip seven times in the Jordan is actually the direction for a miraculous cure.
      How much more so. It is a great thing that can be effected through an easy act.

14. *like the flesh of a young lad.* There is an interesting echo of the phrase here, *na'ar qaton*,
with the designation of the captive girl who gave the advice, *na'arah qetanah*, "a young girl."

and he came and stood before him and said "Now, pray, I know that there is no god in all the earth except in Israel, and so, take, pray, a gift from your servant." And he said, "As the LORD lives, in Whose attendance I have 16 stood, I will not take it." And he pressed him to take it but he refused. And 17 Naaman said, "If not, let your servant be given two mules' load of soil, for your servant will no longer perform burnt offering or sacrifice to other gods but to the LORD. For this thing may the LORD forgive me: when my 18 master comes to the house of Rimmon to worship there and he leans on my arm and I worship in the house of Rimmon, may the LORD forgive me in this thing for my worshipping in the house of Rimmon." And he said 19 to him, "Go in peace." And he went away from him some distance. And 20 Gehazi, lad of Elisha man of God, thought: "Look, my master has held back Naaman the Aramean, not taking from his hand what he brought. As the LORD lives, I will run after him and take something from his hand." And 21 Gehazi chased after Naaman, and Naaman saw him running after him and alighted from the chariot to meet him and said, "Is all well?" And he 22 said, "It is well. My master sent me, saying, 'Look, just now two lads from

---

15. *stood before him.* The posture, as noted above, is deferential.

there is no god in all the earth except in Israel. The miraculous cure converts the Aramean general into a monotheist.

16. *I will not take it.* Elisha does not seek payment for services. His payment is in the triumph of Naaman's conversion.

17. *let your servant be given two mules' load of soil.* Naaman assumes that proper sacrifice to YHWH can be offered only on the soil of Israel, and so he requests permission to take some of it back with him to Aram. Some scholars see in this a reflection of the quandary of the Israelites exiled after 721 B.C.E., though that is not a necessary inference.

18. *the house of Rimmon.* This is the temple of the national god of Aram, evidently a storm god.

to worship. Literally, "to bow down," this gesture being a synecdoche for worship.

and he leans on my arm. Given Naaman's position as accompanier of the king in the temple, which would be an official duty, he can scarcely avoid going through the outward motions of Rimmon worship.

21. *Is all well?* Seeing Elisha's attendant running after him, Naaman is alarmed that something may be amiss as far as the prophet is concerned.

22. *My master sent me.* Gehazi is obliged to implement his greedy act by an outright lie: that his master needs some of the proffered gift for two newly arrived acolyte prophets. He does not dare ask for the whole splendid gift, though Naaman generously gives him twice the amount of silver he requested.

the high country of Ephraim of the acolyte prophets have come to me.
23 Give them, pray, a talent of silver and two changes of garments.'" And
Naaman said, "Be so kind as to take two talents." And he pressed him, and
he wrapped the two talents of silver in two bags, and the two changes of
garments, and he gave them to his two lads, and they bore them off before
24 him. And he came to the citadel and took them from their hand and lay
25 them aside in the house and sent away the men, and they went off. And he
had come and was standing by his master, and Elisha said to him, "From
where have you come, Gehazi?" And he said, "Your servant has not gone
26 anywhere." And he said to him, "Did not my heart come along when a man
turned back from his chariot to meet you? Is this the time to take silver and
to take garments and olive trees and vineyards and sheep and cattle and
27 slaves and slavegirls? May Naaman's skin blanch cling to you and to your
seed forever!" And he went out from before him skin-blanched as snow.

1 CHAPTER 6   And the acolyte prophets said to Elisha, "Look,
2 the place where we dwell is too cramped for us. Let us, pray, go to the Jordan
and each of us take from there one beam and make us a place to dwell
3 there." And he said, "Go." And one of them said, "Be so kind, pray, as to go
4 with your servants." And he said, "I will go." And he went with them, and
5 they came to the Jordan and cut down trees. And it happened, as one of
them was felling the beam, that the iron blade dropped into the water, and

26. *Did not my heart come along.* At this juncture, for purposes necessary to the plot in
which Gehazi's base act is exposed, Elisha exercises clairvoyance.

olive trees and vineyards and sheep and cattle and slaves and slavegirls. These items,
of course, are not part of the gift Gehazi extracted from Naaman, but Elisha implies
that the talents of silver could serve to purchase these standard markers of wealth in the
agricultural-pastoral society.

27. *May Naaman's skin blanch cling to you.* In the final turn of the universalist screw in
this story, the rapacious and dishonest Israelite is stricken with the disease of which the
Aramean general, now a devout follower of the God of Israel, has been cured.

CHAPTER 6   1. *Look, the place where we dwell is too cramped for us.* From this petition, one may infer that Elisha as master prophet was responsible for decisions regarding
the living arrangements of the acolyte prophets as well as for providing them with food. It
also is evident that they constituted a sizable group.

3. *Be so kind, pray, as to go with your servants.* They feel dependent on his guidance and
his sustaining presence.

he cried out, "Woe, my master, it is borrowed!" And the man of God said,   6
"Where did it fall?," and he showed him. And he cut off a stick and flung it
there, and the iron blade floated up. And he said, "Lift it up for yourself,"   7
and he stretched out his hand and took it.

And the king of Aram had been battling against Israel, and he took counsel   8
with his servants, saying, "At such-and-such a place is my encampment."
And the man of God said to the king of Israel, saying, "Keep yourself from   9
passing through this place, for the Arameans are deployed there." And 10
the king of Israel sent to the place of which the man of God had spoken to
him and warned about it, and he kept himself from there more than once.
And the king of Aram's heart stormed over this thing, and he called to 11
his servants and said to them, ""Will you not tell me? Who of ours is for
the king of Israel?" And one of his servants said, "No, my lord the king! 12
Rather, it is Elisha, the prophet who is in Israel, who can tell the king of
Israel the very words you speak in your bedchamber." And he said, "Go, 13
see where he is, that I might send and fetch him." And it was told to him,
saying, "Look, he is in Dothan," and he sent horses there and chariots and 14
a heavy force, and they came by night and surrounded the town. And the 15
man of God's attendant woke early to rise up, and he went out, and, look,
a force was drawn round the town, and horses and chariots. And his lad
said to him, "Woe, my master, what can we do?" And he said, "Do not fear, 16
for there are more with us than with them." And Elisha prayed and said, 17

---

5. *Woe, my master, it is borrowed.* An axehead was a valuable item, and we have already
seen that the acolyte prophets were relatively poor.

6. *the iron blade floated up.* This particular intercession on behalf of a follower is, even more
transparently than the previous one, an act of pure magic.

8. *And the king of Aram had been battling against Israel.* It is not possible to determine with
any confidence which kings they are from these generalized terms. It also looks as if these
episodes in sequence were originally independent stories collected and strung together
editorially. There is no hint here that in the previous episode an Israelite prophet cured an
Aramean general, who then went off happily, converted to monotheism.

   his servants. The Hebrew term that has the general meaning of "servants" or "slaves"
refers in royal contexts to the king's courtiers, who may well be high officials.

9. *Keep yourself from passing through this place.* Elisha again exercises prophetic clairvoyance,
a power duly recognized by the Aramean king's courtiers in verse 12.

16. *Do not fear, for there are more with us than with them.* At this point, it is not yet clear
that he is referring to supernatural forces. Elisha, more than any other of the early prophets,

"LORD, open his eyes, pray, that he may see." And the LORD opened the
lad's eyes, and he saw, and look, the mountain was filled with horses and
18 chariots of fire around Elisha. And they came down to him, and Elisha
prayed to the LORD and said, "Strike this nation with blinding light." And
19 he struck them with blinding light according to the word of Elisha. And
Elisha said to them, "This is not the way, and this is not the town. Come
after me, that I may lead you to the man whom you seek." And they went
20 after him to Samaria. And it happened, when they came to Samaria, that
Elisha said, "LORD, open the eyes of these people, that they may see." And
the LORD opened their eyes and they saw, and, look, they were in the midst
21 of Samaria. And the king of Israel said to Elisha when he saw them, "Shall
22 I indeed strike them down, my father?" And he said, "You shall not strike.
Whom you have captured with your sword and your bow you may strike.
Set out bread and water before them, that they may eat and drink and go
23 to their master." And he made a great feast for them, and they ate and they
drank, and he sent them off, and they went to their master. And the raiding
parties of Aram no longer came into the land of Israel.

24 And it happened afterward that Ben-Hadad king of Aram gathered all his
25 camp and came up and laid siege against Samaria. And there was a great

---

repeatedly resorts to miraculous powers. His master Elijah was obliged to flee for his life
when Ahab sought to kill him, but Elisha when mortally threatened can immediately count
on chariots of fire and mysterious cavalry.

17. LORD, open his eyes, pray, that he may see. Elisha, with his prophet's vision, has already
seen the supernatural army on the mountains. The narrative will go on to play with a
counterpoint of opening the eyes and blinding them with dazzling light.

18. Strike this nation with blinding light. Blinding light, sanweirim, is also what the divine
messengers at Sodom (Genesis 19:11) use to disable the mob of would-be rapists, and a
connection between these two groups impelled by nefarious intention may be suggested.

19. the man whom you seek. Your targeting of a man of God is misconceived. If you are
Israel's enemy, let me show you Israel's king.

20. And the LORD opened their eyes and they saw. Unlike the opening of the servant's eyes,
which enables him to see supernatural allies, what they see is that they are in the heart of
the enemy capital, a potentially fatal place for them, as the king's words in the next verse
make clear.

23. And he made a great feast for them. The king, taking Elisha's cue that these miraculously
captured warriors are not legitimate prisoners of war, goes one better than the prophet's
instructions and lays out a generous feast for the Arameans, not merely bread and water.

25. And there was a great famine in Samaria. Starvation in besieged towns cut off from all
food supplies was one of the great terrors of ancient warfare, a fact reflected in many bibli-

famine in Samaria, and, look, they laid siege against it till a donkey's head cost eighty pieces of silver and a quarter of a *qab* of pigeon-droppings five pieces of silver. And as the king of Israel was passing on top of the wall, a 26 woman cried out to him, saying, "Rescue me, my lord the king!" And he 27 said, "Don't! Let the LORD rescue you. From where can I rescue you, from the threshing floor or from the winepress?" And he said to her, "What's the 28 matter with you?" And she said, "This woman said to me, 'Give over your son, that we may eat him today, and my son we shall eat tomorrow.' And we 29 cooked my son and ate him and I said to her the next day, 'Give over your son, that we may eat him,' but she has hidden her son." And it happened 30 when the king of Israel heard the woman's words, he rent his garments as he was passing on top of the wall, and the people saw, and, look, sackcloth was on his flesh underneath. And he said "So may God do to me and even 31

---

cal texts. The famine here is a counterpoint to the royal feast at the end of the preceding episode.

till a donkey's head cost eighty pieces of silver and a quarter of a qab *of pigeon-droppings five pieces of silver.* The besieged population is so desperate for food that even the most inedible part of an unclean animal commands a prince's ransom. Some scholars understand the term for pigeon-droppings as a reference to carob pods, but that dilutes the hyperbolic power of the statement—that even animal filth was consumed by the starving people, and at a stiff price. *Qab* is a unit of dry measure, probably a little over a liter.

26. *Rescue me.* This cry, *hoshia'*, was the set term in pleading for justice from the king.

27. *From where can I rescue you, from the threshing floor or from the winepress?* These are, of course, places where food and drink are produced, and they are inaccessible to anyone in the besieged town. Thus the king assumes she is pleading for food. The phrase has the ring of a set idiom.

28. *Give over your son, that we may eat him today.* Cannibalism in time of siege is invoked a number of times in Prophetic poetry, and it appears to have been a reality in the ancient world, but only here do we get a direct representation of the grisly act in dialogue, as part of a narrative.

30. *when the king of Israel heard . . . the woman's words, he rent his garments.* The situation of the two women, one asking for justice from the king after her child has been cannibalized, is reminiscent of the two whores with the dead child and the living child in 1 Kings 3. This king, however, has no option to exercise Solomonic wisdom after the woman's child has been eaten, and instead, despairing, he rends his garments in an act of mourning.

sackcloth was on his flesh underneath. The king is wearing some sort of royal robe, but it has now been torn open, and the sackcloth beneath is visible.

31. *So may God do to me and even more, if the head of Elisha son of Shaphat stays on him today.* The king's fury against Elisha may be triggered by his recognition of the prophet's supernatural powers. If the man of God is able to blind and capture a heavy force of Aramean warriors, his failure to intervene on behalf of the besieged town must be a deliberately hostile act.

32 more, if the head of Elisha son of Shaphat stays on him today." And Elisha
    was sitting in his house and the elders were sitting with him. And he sent
    a man ahead of him before the messenger could come to him. And he had
    said to the elders, "Do you see that this murderer's son has sent to take off
    my head? See, when the messenger comes, close the door and squeeze him
    against the door. Is that not the sound of his master's footsteps after him?"
33 He was still speaking with them when, look, the king came down to him
    and said, "This evil is from the LORD. What more can I hope for from the
    LORD?"

1   CHAPTER 7   And Elisha said, "Hear the word of the LORD.
    Thus said the LORD: 'At this time tomorrow, a *seah* of fine flour will sell for
2   a shekel, and two *seahs* of barley for a shekel in the gate of Samaria.'" And
    the official on whose arm the king was leaning answered the man of God

---

32. *the elders were sitting with him.* The elders would constitute a political group outside
the monarchy, and harking back to the premonarchic period. They may even be a center
of opposition to the king.

    And he sent a man ahead of him. Again, he sees what is about to happen through
clairvoyance.

    the messenger. The term, which designates any agent, human or divine, here refers to
an assassin, not to someone bringing a message.

    this murderer's son. This could well refer to Jehoram, the son of Ahab, whom Elijah exco-
riated as a murderer, though some scholars prefer to understand it as "murderous person."

    close the door and squeeze him against the door. Elisha reduces the would-be hit man to
an object of farce, pinned between the door and the wall.

33. *the king came down to him.* The received text says "messenger," *mal'akh*, but the king
has been following close after his messenger, his footsteps audible, and in the next moment
in this scene (7:2), we see the king, who has just been addressed by Elisha, leaning on the
arm of his official. *Mal'akh*, then, is in all likelihood a scribal error for *melekh*, "king." See
the second comment on 2 Samuel 11:1, where the orthographic closeness of these two words
is pointedly put into play.

CHAPTER 7   1. *a seah of fine flour will sell for a shekel.* The prices stipulated here
are the antithesis of the astronomic prices for virtually inedible stuff mentioned in 6:25.
This is, then, a concrete way of saying that the deadly famine will suddenly come to an end.
It should be kept in mind that in this early period, the shekel is not a coin but a weight of
silver (about 11.5 grams). A *seah* is roughly 7.3 liters.

2. *the official on whose arm the king was leaning.* Since Naaman performs the same function
for the king of Aram, one may infer that this was a set court duty for a high-ranking figure.
But Naaman in mentioning this role of his has become a convinced believer in the power
of YHWH, whereas this official is a doubter.

and said, "Look, the LORD is about to make casements in the heavens! Can this thing be?" And he said, "You are about to see with your own eyes, but you shall not eat from there." And four men stricken with skin blanch were 3 at the entrance to the gate, and they said to one another, "Why are we sitting here till we die? Should we say, 'Let us come into the town,' with famine in 4 the town, we would die there, and if we stay here, we shall die. And now, come, let us slip off to the camp of Aram. If they let us live, we shall live, and if they put us to death, we shall die." And they rose at twilight to go into the 5 camp of Aram, and they came to the edge of the camp of Aram, and, look, there was no one there. And the LORD had made the sound of chariots, the 6 sound of horses heard in the camp of Aram, the sound of a great force, and every man said to his comrade, "Look, the king of Israel has hired against us the Hittite kings and the kings of Egypt to come against us." And they 7 rose and fled at twilight, and they abandoned their tents and their horses and their donkeys in the camp just as it was, and they ran for their lives.

Look, the LORD is about to make casements in the heavens. This remark, which invokes a memorable phrase from the Flood story (Genesis 7:11), is obviously sarcastic, the idea being that Elisha imagines the LORD will somehow rain down food from the sky for the starving Israelites.

but you shall not eat from there. Elisha's words are veiled, ominously hinting at the dire fate that will befall the official.

3. *And four men stricken with skin blanch were at the entrance to the gate.* This disfiguring skin disease was thought to be contagious, requiring quarantine, according to the laws of Leviticus. (But the requirement of quarantine is ignored in the case of a high-ranking figure such as Naaman.) The diseased men are thus outside the town, in a liminal space between the besieged city and the Aramean camp. The schadenfreude in this account of the flight of the Arameans is heightened by the fact that the discovery of their precipitous retreat is made by outcasts.

4. *If they let us live, we shall live.* Given that they are bound to die of starvation either inside the town or outside the walls, they decide that they may as well throw themselves on the mercy of the Arameans, who might just feed them and let them live rather than kill them.

6. *the king of Israel has hired against us the Hittite kings and the kings of Egypt.* If this story of an Aramean army renouncing a siege has a historical kernel, it would be here—that an alliance of kings induced the Arameans to retreat. In their fearful dialogue, they make the monarchs of both Egypt and the Hittites plurals.

7. *they . . . fled at twilight.* As in many languages, the Hebrew word for twilight, *neshef*, can refer either to sunset or dawn. Here the likely scenario is that the Arameans depart as the sun sets, their flight thus unseen from the town; the diseased men enter the camp just after the besiegers have fled; they then bring the report of what they have seen to the king in the middle of the night.

8 And these men stricken with skin blanch came to the edge of the camp and
   came into one tent and ate and drank and carried away silver and gold and
   garments, and they went off and hid them, and they returned and came into
   another tent and carried things away from there and went off and hid them.
9 And they said to each other, "We are not doing right. This day is a day of
   good tidings and we remain silent. If we wait till morning's light, guilt will
10 befall us. And now, come, let us go and tell it at the king's house." And they
   came and called out to the gatekeepers of the town and told them, saying,
   "We came into the camp of Aram, and, look, there was no one there and
   no human sound, only horses tethered and donkeys tethered, and tents
11 just as they had been." And the gatekeepers called and told it at the king's
12 house within. And the king arose in the night and said to his servants, "Let
   me tell you, pray, what the Arameans have done to us: they knew we were
   starving, and they have gone out of the camp to hide in the field, saying,
   'When they come out of the town we shall catch them alive and enter the
13 town.'" And one of his servants answered and said, "Let them take, pray,
   five of the remaining horses that are left in the town—look, they are like all
   the multitude of Israel who are left in it; look, they are like all the multitude
14 of Israel who have come to an end, and let us send and see." And they took

---

9. *guilt will befall us.* The Israelites will berate them, or worse, for not having brought the
news at once of the flight of the Arameans.

10. *the gatekeepers.* The Hebrew shows a singular noun, but "to them" is unambiguously
plural. In the next verse, "gatekeepers" has the plural ending. The gates of the town were
of course bolted, and so the diseased men had to make a special plea to the gatekeepers to
be admitted within in order to bring their great news to the king. The gatekeepers do not
let them in, but carry the news to the king.

12. *Let me tell you, pray, what the Arameans have done to us.* True to the fearful character
that the king of Israel exhibited when he received the letter from the king of Aram about
curing Naaman, he now concludes that this is a trap the Arameans have set to lure the
Israelites outside the town.

13. *five of the remaining horses that are left in the town.* The implication is that most of the
horses have been eaten. Some scholars think that "five" does not indicate a precise number
but means "a few."
   look, they are like all the multitude of Israel. The repetition of this clause in immediate
sequence might be an inadvertent scribal duplication (dittography), though it could equally
be an expression of the speaker's emotional turmoil in contemplating the terrible fact that
there are so few survivors in the town.
   they are like all the multitude of Israel who have come to an end. In the first iteration of
this clause, the verb is "who are left." Now it is "who have come to an end." There is a grim
overlap between surviving and dying: if the horses are like the people, barely surviving and

two teams of horses, and the king sent after the camp of Aram, saying, "Go and see." And they went after them to the Jordan, and, look, the whole 15 road was filled with garments and gear that the Arameans had flung down in their haste, and the messengers came back and told the king. And the 16 people went out and plundered the camp of Aram, and so, a *seah* of fine flour sold for a shekel and two *seahs* of barley for a shekel, according to the word of the LORD. And the king had appointed over the gate the official on 17 whose arm he had leaned, and the people trampled him in the gate and he died, as the man of God had spoken, as he had spoken when the king came down to him. And it happened when the man of God spoke to the king, 18 saying, "Two *seahs* of barley will sell for a shekel and a *seah* of fine flour for a shekel at this time tomorrow in the gate of Samaria," the official answered 19 the man of God and said, "And look, the LORD is about to make casements in the heavens! Can such a thing be?" And he said, "You are about to see with your own eyes, but you shall not eat from there." And so it happened 20 to him, and the people trampled him and he died.

---

on the way to joining those who have already died, there is nothing lost in sending them out on this mission.

14. *two teams of horses.* This seems the likely sense of the Hebrew, which is literally "two chariots of horses."

15. *And they went after them to the Jordan.* What may be happening is that the horses are sent down the road, with the king's men driving them from behind with cries and perhaps long whips, ready to fall back if the horses are spotted by Aramean troops. They evidently bypass the empty camp, where they fear an ambush, and discover—a significant use of the presentative "look" to mark their visual point of view—evidence that the flight is real in the garments and gear strewn over the road.

17. *the people trampled him in the gate.* This is a credible detail: the people, on the point of death by starvation, stampede through the gate to get at the food and riches they have heard are available in the Aramean camp (or to get to those who have already expropriated the flour and are selling it at the prices announced in the previous verse), and so they inadvertently trample the official. Elisha's obscure prophecy is now violently fulfilled.

18. *two seahs of barley will sell for a shekel and a* seah *of fine flour for a shekel.* The story concludes with an elaborate verbatim repetition of Elisha's prophecy and the words of the official. The only variation is that here the barley is first, the fine flour second, and the particle that means "and" is added to the official's first word. In this instance, the point of the repetition with no substantive changes is to underscore how the general prophecy, and then the prophecy specifically addressed to the official in rebuke of his skepticism, are literally and completely fulfilled.

1 **CHAPTER 8**   And Elisha had spoken to the woman whose son he revived, saying, "Arise and go, you and your household, and sojourn wherever you would sojourn, for the LORD has called forth famine and it 2 actually has come to the land for seven years." And the woman arose and did according to the man of God's word, and she went, she and her household, 3 and sojourned in the land of the Philistines seven years. And it happened at the end of seven years that the woman came back from the land of the Philistines, and she went out and cried to the king for her house and for her 4 field. And the king was speaking to Gehazi, the man of God's lad, saying, 5 "Recount to me, pray, all the great things that Elisha did." And it happened as he was recounting to the king that Elisha revived the dead, that, look, the woman whose son he had revived came crying out to the king for her house and for her field. And Gehazi said, "This is the woman, and this is her son 6 whom Elisha revived." And the king asked the woman, and she recounted to him, and he gave her a certain eunuch, saying, "Return all that is hers and all the yield of the field from the day she left the land till now."

7 And Elisha came to Damascus, with Ben-Hadad king of Aram ill, and it 8 was told to him, saying, "The man of God has come here." And the king said to Hazael, "Take tribute in your hand and go to meet the man of God

---

CHAPTER 8   1. *And Elisha had spoken to the woman.* The syntax and the form of the Hebrew verb indicate a pluperfect, as reflected in the translation—a careful indication of tense because the action about to be reported unfolds seven years after Elisha's words to the woman. Oddly, in this episode she is never referred to as "the Shunammite."

4. *And the king was speaking to Gehazi.* There is no hint here that Gehazi has been stricken with a ghastly skin disease. This is one of several indications that the stories about Elisha brought together in this cycle probably originated independently. The fact that Gehazi is a presence in the court recounting the great acts of his master has led some interpreters to infer that in this particular story Elisha is assumed to have died.

5. *crying out to the king.* The Hebrew verb used here has a technical sense of making a plea for justice from the king.

for her house and for her field. These substantial possessions have obviously been seized by others during her seven years' absence.

6. *a certain eunuch.* Although this is the plain meaning of the Hebrew noun *saris*, it is possible that the term came to designate a particular kind of court official, without reference to genital mutilation.

all the yield of the field from the day she left the land till now. She is legally entitled not only to resume possession of the land but to receive all the profit made from it during her absence.

8. *Take tribute in your hand and go to meet the man of God.* If there is any continuity between this story and the story of Naaman, Elisha's powers would be well-known and respected in the Aramean court.

and inquire of the LORD through him, saying, 'Will I survive this illness?'" And Hazael went to meet him and took tribute in his hand, from 9
all the bounty of Damascus, a load of forty camels, and he came and stood
before him and said, "Your son Ben-Hadad king of Aram has sent me to
you, saying, 'Will I survive this illness?'" And Elisha said to him, "Go, say 10
to him, 'You will surely survive,' but the LORD has shown me that he is
doomed to die." And his face froze and he was dumbfounded a long time, 11
and the man of God wept. And Hazael said, "Why is my lord weeping?" 12
And he said, "Because I know the harm that you will do to the Israelites.
Their fortresses you will send up in flames, and their young men you will
slay by the sword, and their infants you will smash, and their pregnant
women you will split open." And Hazael said, "How could your servant, a 13
dog, do this great thing?" And Elisha said, "The LORD has showed you to
me as king over Aram." And he went from Elisha and came to his master, 14
and he said to him, "What did Elisha say to you?" And he said, "He said,

---

inquire of the LORD through him. Ben-Hadad does not assume that YHWH is the one
and only God, but he has reason to think that this Hebrew deity served by Elisha has great
potency.

9. *a load of forty camels.* This makes the tribute a very grand gift.

10. *Go, say to him, "You will surely survive," but the LORD has shown me that he is doomed
to die.* Elisha's response is devious: you can tell him he will survive his grave illness, which
will be technically true because he is to die from quite a different cause. Some interpreters
imagine that Elisha is encouraging Hazael to assassinate Ben-Hadad, but this is implausible
because Elisha foresees that when he becomes king, Hazael will ravage the people of Israel.
What has happened is simply that God has revealed to him both Ben-Hadad's fate and the
future course of war between Aram and Israel.

11. *And his face froze.* This is the likely sense of the somewhat obscure Hebrew, which is
literally, "and he made his face stand [still]."
   and he was dumbfounded. The received text shows *wayasem,* "and he put." But two
Hebrew manuscripts and the Vulgate have *wayishom,* to be desolate or dumbfounded, which
is much more likely. The subject of both these verbs must be Hazael, who is astounded, and
at a loss, to hear Elisha's stark prophecy.

13. *How could your servant, a dog, do this great thing?* The humble self-designation reflects
the fact that Hazael, though he is some sort of court official, is not of the royal line. In an
inscription by the Assyrian king Shalmaneser III, Hazael is in fact referred to as "son of no
one." One notes that he has no moral compunctions about the prospect of perpetrating the
most barbaric cruelties on the men, women, and infants of Israel; on the contrary, these
were common acts in military conquest and thus part of what constituted a "great thing"
that he is not sure he is worthy to do.
   The LORD has showed you to me as king over Aram. These words may not be intended
to instigate the assassination, but they certainly have the effect of giving Hazael the idea.

15 'You will surely survive.'" And it happened the next day that he took a
cloth and soaked it in water and spread it over his face, and he died. And
Hazael became king in his stead.

16 And in the fifth year of Jehoram son of Ahab king of Israel—Jehoshaphat
had been king of Judah—Jehoram son of Jehoshaphat became king, king
17 of Judah. He was thirty-two years old when he became king, and he was
18 king in Jerusalem eight years. And he went in the way of the kings of Israel,
as the house of Ahab had done, for Ahab's daughter had become his wife,
19 and he did what was evil in the eyes of the LORD. But the LORD did not
want to destroy Judah, for the sake of David His servant, as He had said to
20 him to grant a lamp for his sons perpetually. In his days did Edom rebel
21 from under the hand of Judah, and they set a king over themselves. And
Jehoram crossed over to Zair, all the chariots with him, and it happened
that as he arose in the night, the Edomites surrounding him struck him,
22 and the captains of the chariots, and the troops fled to their tents. And
Edom has rebelled from under the hand of Judah until this day. Then did
23 Libnah rebel at that time. And the rest of the acts of Jehoram and all that
he did, are they not written in the Book of the Acts of the Kings of Judah?
24 And Jehoram lay with his fathers and was buried in the City of David, and
25 Ahaziah his son became king in his stead. In the twelfth year of Jehoram
26 son of Ahab king of Israel, Ahaziah became king, king of Judah. Ahaziah
was twenty-two years old when he became king, and he was king one year
in Jerusalem. And his mother's name was Athaliah daughter of Omri king
27 of Israel. And he went in the way of the house of Ahab and did what was evil
in the eyes of the LORD like the house of Ahab, for he was kin by marriage

---

15. *he took a cloth and soaked it in water and spread it over his face.* The subject of the verb
is Hazael. He kills the king by suffocating him (there will be no blood visible and perhaps
the courtiers will conclude that Ben-Hadad died of his illness). The king, of course, in his
greatly weakened state is in no shape to resist the murderous act.

21. *as he arose in the night, the Edomites surrounding him struck him.* The Masoretic Text
reads: as he arose in the night, he struck the Edomites surrounding him. This reading may
reflect scribal wishful thinking. To begin with, it is syntactically peculiar, and the clear
indication is that the Israelites were defeated in a successful rebellion by the Edomites. Fur-
thermore, the "troops," *'am*, who flee to their tents—that is, to their homes—is a term generally referring to Israelite troops, not, as it appears here in the received text, to Edomites.

26. *his mother's name was Athaliah daughter of Omri.* In verse 18 she is identified as Ahab's
daughter, though perhaps the Hebrew *bat* could encompass granddaughter. In any case, the
familial connection through marriage with the house of Ahab leads to trouble.

to the house of Ahab. And Jehoram son of Ahab went to battle with Hazael 28
king of Aram at Ramoth-Gilead, and the Arameans struck down Jehoram.
And King Jehoram came back to heal in Jezreel from the blows that the 29
Arameans had struck him at Ramah when he did battle with Hazael king
of Aram, and Ahaziah son of Jehoram king of Judah had gone down to see
Jehoram son of Ahab in Jezreel, for he was ill.

CHAPTER 9   And Elisha the prophet had called to one of the 1
acolyte prophets and said to him, "Gird your loins and take this cruse of
oil in your hand and go to Ramoth-Gilead. And you shall come there and 2
see there Jehu son of Jehoshaphat son of Nimshi. And you shall come and
raise him up from the midst of his brothers and bring him into the inner
chamber. And you shall take the cruse of oil and pour it on his head and 3
say, 'Thus said the LORD: I have anointed you king over Israel.' And you
shall open the door and flee and you shall not wait." And the lad went, the 4
prophet lad, to Ramoth-Gilead. And he came and, look, the commanders 5
of the force were sitting there, and he said, "I have a word for you, commander." And Jehu said, "For whom among all of us?" And he said, "For
you, commander." And he rose and entered the house and poured oil on his 6
head and said to him, "Thus said the LORD God of Israel: 'I have anointed
you king over the LORD's people, over Israel. And you shall strike down 7
the house of Ahab your master, and I will be avenged for the blood of My
servants the prophets and for the blood of all the LORD's servants from the
hand of Jezebel. And all the house of Ahab shall perish, and I will cut off 8
from Ahab every pisser against the wall and ruler and helper in Israel. And 9
I will make the house of Ahab like the house of Jeroboam son of Nebat and
like the house of Baasha son of Ahijah. And Jezebel the dogs shall devour 10

CHAPTER 9   2. *you shall come there and see there Jehu son of Jehoshaphat*. All along,
prophets have been involved in power struggles around the throne, but Elisha's initiative in
this instance is the most blatant of these involvements: he sends one of his people to anoint
Jehu as king and to prompt Jehu to assassinate the reigning king, Jehoram.

bring him into the inner chamber. The actual anointment is clandestine, and the acolyte prophet is accordingly enjoined to flee once he has performed the act, lest there be an
adverse reaction on the part of the military people around Jehu when they learn what has
occurred.

8. *I will cut off from Ahab every pisser against the wall*. This pungent epithet for males,
reserved for curses, is usually pronounced by human speakers but here is used by God in
the momentum of the curse-formula.

in the field of Jezreel, with none to bury her.'" And he opened the door
11 and fled. And Jehu had gone out to his master's servants, and someone
said to him, "Is all well? Why did this madman come to you?" And he said
12 to them, "You know this man and how he talks." And they said, "It's a lie!
Tell us, pray." And he said, "Thus and so he said to me, saying, 'Thus said
13 the LORD: "I have anointed you king over Israel."'" And they hastened
and each of them took his garment and they put them beneath him on
the top of the stairs, and they blew the ram's horn and said, "Jehu is king."
14 And Jehu son of Jehoshaphat son of Nimshi plotted against Jehoram, and
Jehoram had been on watch at Ramoth-Gilead—he and all Israel—against
15 Hazael king of Aram. And King Jehoram had gone back to Jezreel to heal
from the blows that the Arameans struck him when he did battle with
Hazael king of Aram. And Jehu said, "If you agree, let no fugitive come
16 out of the town to tell in Jezreel." And Jehu mounted and went to Jezreel,

---

11. *his master's servants.* There is an ironic point in the use of this designation for Jehu's
fellow officers. "His master" would have to be the king, against whom Jehu is about to rebel,
abetted by the other commanders of the army.

Why did this madman come to you? The groups of prophets, bonded together in a kind
of guild, were known for working themselves into ecstatic states, often with the help of
musical instruments, as the two stories of Saul among the prophets in 1 Samuel illustrate.
Calling a prophet a madman, then, makes perfect sense, and that equation occurs elsewhere in biblical literature.

12. *It's a lie.* The other officers immediately see that Jehu's response to their question about
the acolyte prophet ("You know this man and how he talks") is an evasion. Jehu then
feels constrained to divulge the truth about his clandestine anointment, counting on their
support.

13. *each of them took his garment.* What they appear to be doing is constructing a kind of
improvised throne, seating him on the top of the stairs. This is a literal realization of Elisha's injunction regarding Jehu to "raise him up from the midst of his brothers."

the top of the stairs. The Hebrew *gerem hama'alot* is unique to this verse and its meaning has been inferred from the context. In modern Hebrew, *gerem* has been adopted for
"stairwell."

14. *Jehu . . . plotted against Jehoram.* As the details of the narrative make clear, the conspiracy is a military coup whereby Jehu, as one of the army officers, seizes the throne after
killing its occupant.

Jehoram. The Hebrew here and at several other points uses a shortened form, Joram, but
the translation, to avoid confusion, shows the full form of the name throughout.

15. *If you agree.* This is probably no more than a polite way of delivering an order, though
it is possible that Jehu does not fully trust his fellow officers to follow his commands in
implementing the coup, despite their gesture of support in elevating him on the improvised
throne.

for Jehoram was in bed there, and Ahaziah king of Judah had gone down
to see Jehoram. And the lookout was stationed on the tower in Jezreel, and 17
he saw Jehu's throng as it came, and he said, "I see a throng." And Jehoram
said, "Take a horseman and send out to meet them and say, 'Do you come
in peace?'" And the horseman went to meet him and said, "Thus said the 18
king: 'Do you come in peace?'" And Jehu said, "What do you have to do
with peace? Turn round behind me!" And the lookout told, saying, "The
messenger came to them and has not come back." And he sent a second 19
horseman, and he came to them and said, "Thus said the king: 'Do you
come in peace?'" And Jehu said, "What do you have to do with peace? Turn
round behind me." And the lookout told, saying, "He came to them and 20
has not come back, and the driving is like Jehu son of Nimshi's driving,
for he drives madly." And Jehoram said, "Hitch up!" And his chariot was 21
hitched up, and Jehoram king of Israel, and Ahaziah king of Judah went
out, each in his chariot, and they went out to meet Jehu and found him in
the field of Naboth the Jezreelite. And it happened when Jehoram saw Jehu 22
that he said, "Do you come in peace, Jehu?" And he said to him, "What
do the whoring of Jezebel your mother and her abundant witchcraft have

---

17. *Jehu's throng.* The word choice is realistic: from the distance, the lookout is able to identify a crowd of advancing soldiers, which he correctly assumes to be led by Jehu.

18. *What do you have to do with peace?* Jehu's implacably hostile intentions are manifest
in his dialogue.

Turn round behind me. He also makes clear that he is the stronger party, and that the
messenger had better abandon Jehoram and join the usurper.

20. *the driving is like Jehu son of Nimshi's driving, for he drives madly.* The lookout is too
far off to see Jehu's face but can recognize his wild style of driving a chariot. In this we get
a new element of characterization of Jehu: he is known, at least in royal circles, for riding
in his chariot at breakneck speed. This wild energy is of a piece with his quickness as an
assassin, about to be manifested.

21. *And Jehoram said, "Hitch up!"* In still another instance of the pattern of two repetitions
with a divergence in the third repetition, Jehoram, after the defection of the two messengers, goes out himself to parlay with Jehu, naïvely imagining they can come to terms.

and Ahaziah king of Judah went out. Exhibiting what will prove to be fatal imprudence,
Ahaziah chooses to express his solidarity with Jehoram by joining him in going to meet
Jehu.

22. *What do the whoring of Jezebel your mother and her abundant witchcraft have to do with
peace?* In this switch from the twice-repeated formula, Jehu makes himself the mouthpiece
of Elisha's prophetic wrath against the whole house of Ahab. "Whoring" may mean, as it
often does elsewhere in the Bible, going after strange gods, although an innuendo of sexual
promiscuity is distinctly possible—calling a man's mother a whore to his face is, after all,
an especially blatant insult.

23 to do with peace?" And Jehoram whipped round the reins and fled, and
24 he said to Ahaziah, "Treachery, Ahaziah!" And Jehu bent the bow in his
   hand and struck Jehoram between his shoulders, and the arrow came out
25 through his heart, and he collapsed in his chariot. And he said to Bidkar
   his officer, "Bear him off, fling him into the field of Naboth the Jezreelite.
   For remember! You and I rode side by side after Ahab his father, and the
26 LORD delivered this message about him: 'I surely saw the blood of Naboth
   and his sons last night,' says the LORD, 'and I will pay you back in this field,'
   says the LORD. And, now, bear him off, fling him into the field according to
27 the word of the LORD." And Ahaziah king of Judah had seen, and he fled
   on the road to Beth-Gan, and Jehu pursued him and said, "Him, too, strike
   down." And they struck him in the chariot on the Ascent of Gur which is
28 by Jibleam, and he fled to Megiddo and died there. And his servants took
   him by chariot to Jerusalem and buried him there in his grave with his
29 fathers in the City of David. And in the eleventh year of Jehoram son of
30 Ahab, Ahaziah had become king over Judah. And Jehu came to Jezreel,
   and Jezebel had heard, and she put kohl round her eyes and did up her
31 hair and looked out through the window. And Jehu had entered the gate,

---

23. *whipped round the reins.* The literal sense is "turned over his hands."

24. *struck Jehoram between his shoulders.* There is no chivalry in this efficient killing: Jehu shoots the fleeing Jehoram in the back.

25. *You and I rode side by side after Ahab his father.* This is a piece of delayed exposition that sharpens our sense of Jehu's animus toward Jehoram: he and Bidkar were actually present when Ahab expropriated the field of Naboth after his judicial murder.

26. *the blood of Naboth and his sons.* No sons were mentioned in the story of the killing of Naboth. Either this detail reflects a variant version of the story, or the sons, fatherless and landless, are considered as good as dead.

27. *Him, too, strike down.* Jehu shows Machiavellian ruthlessness here. Ahaziah king of Judah was in no way involved in the egregious crimes, cultic and moral, of the house of Ahab, but he became Jehoram's ally, and, as such, he might be a potential threat to Jehu, who therefore makes sure to have him killed.
    And they struck him. This phrase (a single Hebrew word) is absent from the received text but appears in three ancient versions as well as in two Hebrew manuscripts. Without it, the sentence is semantically and syntactically incoherent.

28. *buried him there in his grave with his fathers.* Unlike Jehoram, who is flung into the field his father stole, there to be devoured by scavengers, Ahaziah is granted a proper burial.

30. *she put kohl round her eyes and did up her hair.* Though some interpreters take this as an expression of her desire to show a noble appearance, it looks more like an effort at the very end to exhibit her female attractiveness, thus picking up the sexual sense of "the whoring of Jezebel."

and she said, "Is all well, you Zimri, killer of his master?" And he lifted 32
his face toward the window and said, "Who is with me, who?" And two
or three eunuchs looked down at him. And he said, "Push her out." And 33
they pushed her out, and her blood splattered against the wall and on the
horses, and they trampled her. And he came and ate and drank, and he 34
said, "Look to this cursed creature and bury her, for she is the daughter
of a king." And they went to bury her, but they found of her only the skull 35
and the legs and the palms of the hands. And they came back and told him, 36
and he said, "It is the word of the LORD that He spoke through His servant
Elijah the Tishbite, saying, 'In the field of Jezreel the dogs shall devour the
flesh of Jezebel. And Jezebel's carcass shall be like dung upon the ground 37
in the field of Jezreel, so that they cannot say, "This is Jezebel."'"

CHAPTER 10   And Ahab had seventy sons in Samaria. And 1
Jehu wrote letters and sent them to the rulers of Samaria, to the elders of

---

31. *you Zimri, killer of his master.* Confronted by the man who has killed her son and who
she must know is now determined to kill her, Jezebel remains fierce and contemptuous.
Zimri (1 Kings 16:8–18) slaughtered the whole house of Baasha and usurped the throne but
was himself killed seven days later.

32. *Who is with me, who?* As with Jehoram's two messengers, Jehu counts on the fact that the
attendants of the house of Ahab, seeing his superior force, will turn against their masters.
Pointedly, Jehu does not deign to answer Jezebel's biting words to him.

    two or three eunuchs. As before, these may simply be court officials.

34. *Look to this cursed creature.* The Hebrew uses merely the feminine indicative *ha'arurah
hazo't* ("this cursed one") to express contempt.

    bury her, for she is the daughter of a king. Although Jehu despises Jezebel, he is conscious
of the respect due to royal personages—perhaps out of self-interest since he has just become
king himself. For the moment, he puts out of his mind the explicit prophecy that has been
delivered to him (verse 10), "And Jezebel the dogs shall devour in the field of Jezreel, with
none to bury her."

36. *It is the word of the LORD.* After the fact, Jehu, though he has just appeared to be concerned that Jezebel receive a proper burial, affirms her being consumed by canine scavengers as a fitting fulfillment of God's curse on her.

37. *so that they cannot say, "This is Jezebel."* There may be a political angle to this fulfillment of the curse: nothing recognizable of Jezebel's body is left, nothing for any potential
loyalists to venerate (as the Bolsheviks reduced the murdered family of the Czar to ashes
for just this reason).

CHAPTER 10   1. *And Ahab had seventy sons.* The number is formulaic, as in the case
of the seventy sons of Gideon in the story of Abimelech (Judges 9). "Sons" in this instance
probably refers to all the descendants of Ahab, encompassing at least two generations.

2 the town and to Ahab's tutors, saying, "And now, when this letter comes to you, and the sons of your master are with you, and the chariots and the
3 horses are with you, and the fortified towns and the weapons, you shall see to the best and the most fitting of your master's sons and put him on his
4 father's throne, and battle for your master's house." And they were very, very afraid, and they thought, "Look, two kings could not stand up against
5 him, and how can we stand?" And he who was appointed over the palace and he who was appointed over the town and the elders and the tutors sent to Jehu, saying, "We are your servants, and all that you say to us we shall do.
6 We shall make no one king. Do what is good in your eyes." And he wrote them a letter again, saying, "If you are mine and heed my voice, take off the heads of the men who are your master's sons and bring them to me at this time tomorrow in Jezreel." And the king's sons, seventy men, were with
7 the town's notables who had reared them. And it happened, when the letter came to them, that they took the king's sons and slaughtered the seventy
8 men and put their heads in baskets and sent them to him in Jezreel. And the messenger came and told him, saying, "They have brought the heads of the king's sons." And he said, "Put them in two piles at the entrance of
9 the gate until morning." And it happened in the morning that he came out and stood and said to all the people, "Well, you are innocent! Look, I plotted against my master and killed him, but who struck down all these?

Ahab's tutors. These are the tutors engaged by Ahab to look after the education and well-being of his sons and grandsons.

3. *you shall see to the best and the most fitting of your master's sons.* With characteristic deviousness, Jehu does not initially present the elders and tutors with a command but with an ostensible exhortation to elect a new king who can lead the loyalists of the house of Ahab against the forces of Jehu. He of course counts on their knowledge of his just manifested lethal efficiency that will make this proposal strike terror in their hearts.

6. *take off the heads of the men who are your master's sons.* After his oblique opening move, Jehu confronts them with the brutal command to commit mass murder on his behalf.
    bring. The received text reads "come" (a different conjugation of the same verbal stem), but three ancient versions and a few Hebrew manuscripts show "bring," which is more plausible because the killers send the heads in baskets rather than coming themselves.

8. *Put them in two piles at the entrance of the gate.* This grisly detail is another stroke of Jehu's ruthless calculation: the bloody evidence of the elimination of the whole house of Ahab is set out for public exhibition. Presumably, no one will now dare to oppose Jehu.

9. *Well, you are innocent.* This declaration is of course sarcastic (and "well" has been added in the translation to intimate the tone). Jehu has managed to make the leaders of the Samaritan establishment his accomplices in murder: they can scarcely condemn him for killing the two kings when they are directly responsible for many more deaths.

Know, then, that nothing will fail of the word of the LORD that He spoke   10
against the house of Ahab, but the LORD has done what He spoke through
his servant Elijah." And Jehu struck down all who were left of the house of   11
Ahab in Jezreel, and all his notables and his intimates and his priests, till
he left him no remnant. And he rose and went and came to Samaria. When   12
he was at Beth-Eked-ha-Roim on the way, Jehu encountered the kinsmen   13
of Ahaziah king of Judah, and he said, "Who are you?" And they said, "We
are the kinsmen of Ahaziah, and we are going down to see if all is well with
the king's sons and the sons of the queen mother." And he said, "Seize them   14
alive," and they seized them alive, and they slaughtered them at the pit of
Beth-Eked, forty-two men, he did not leave a man of them. And he went   15
from there and encountered Jehonadab son of Rechab coming toward him,
and he greeted him and he said to him, "Is your heart steadfast with me as
my heart is with yours?" And he said to him, "It certainly is." "Give me your
hand." And he gave him his hand, and he took him up to him in the chariot.
And he said, "Come with me and see my zeal for the LORD." And he drove   16
him in his chariot. And he came to Samaria and struck down all who were   17
left of Ahab in Samaria till he destroyed them, according to the word of the

---

10. *the LORD has done what He spoke through His servant Elijah.* Throughout the bloody
trajectory Jehu traces, he justifies his acts as the fulfillment of the dire prophecy against
the house of Ahab. At the same time, the ruthless elimination of any conceivable claimant
to the throne from the line he has overthrown surely serves his political interests.

13. *kinsmen.* Though the Hebrew noun has the primary meaning of "brothers," the narrative context here suggests that the more extended sense of the word is being used.
   we are going down to see if all is well with the king's sons and the sons of the queen mother.
All of these sons have just been beheaded. The kinsmen of Ahaziah, perhaps because they
have been on their way to visit the royal family of their allies in Samaria, appear not to
have heard about the murder of Jehoram and Ahaziah, or they scarcely would be going to
visit Jehoram's kinfolk.

14. *he did not leave a man of them.* Jehu is absolutely consistent in this.

15. *Jehonadab son of Rechab.* The Rechabites were known for their ascetic practice (see
Jeremiah 35:6–7), so perhaps Jehu embraces Jehonadab as an ally because he feels he can
count on Jehonadab's fanatic devotion to YHWH and his concomitant animosity toward
the followers of Baal. Jehonadab is a variant form of "Jonadab"—the Hebrew sometimes
uses one spelling and sometimes the other, as does this translation (cf. Jeremiah 35:4ff.).
   Give me your hand. These words are evidently spoken by Jehu, even though there is no
formula here for the introduction of speech.

17. *he . . . struck down all who were left of Ahab.* After the murder of the seventy sons,
there evidently were still relatives of Ahab's left to eliminate, unless "of Ahab" refers more
broadly to people loyal to Ahab.

18 LORD that He spoke to Elijah. And Jehu gathered all the people and said to
19 them, "Ahab served Baal a little. Jehu will serve him abundantly. And now,
call to me all the prophets of Baal, all his servants and all his priests, let no
one be missing, for I am about to have a great sacrifice to Baal—whoever
is missing shall not live." But Jehu dealt deviously in order to destroy the
20 servants of Baal. And Jehu said, "Call a solemn assembly to Baal," and they
21 called. And Jehu sent out through all Israel, and all the servants of Baal
came, and not a man remained who did not come. And they came to the
22 house of Baal, and the house of Baal was filled from corner to corner. And
he said to the one appointed over the wardrobe, "Bring out garments for all
23 the servants of Baal," and he brought out garments for them. And he came
into the house of Baal, and Jehonadab son of Rechab with him, and he said
to the worshippers of Baal, "Search and see if there are here with you any
24 servants of the LORD besides the servants of Baal alone." And they came to
perform sacrifices and burnt offerings, and Jehu had set for himself eighty
men outside. And he said, "Any man who escapes of the men whom I have
25 brought into your hands—his life for that man's life!" And it happened
when he finished performing the burnt offering, that Jehu said to the sentries and to the captains, "Come, strike them down. Let no man get away."
And they struck them down by the sword, and the sentries and the captains
26 flung them out, and they went to the town of the house of Baal. And they
27 brought out the sacred pillars of the house of Baal and burned them. And
they smashed the sacred pillar of Baal, and they smashed the house of Baal
28 and turned it into latrines, to this very day. And Jehu destroyed Baal from

---

19. *But Jehu dealt deviously.* The narrator wants to make sure the audience immediately
understands that Jehu's proposal of a great sacrifice to Baal is mere subterfuge.

22. *Bring out garments for all the servants of Baal.* Extending the deception, Jehu presents
festive garments to the followers of Baal, as if to enhance the pomp and ceremony of the
occasion. "Servants" throughout this passage of course means "worshippers."

24. *his life for that man's life.* "That man" has been added for the sake of clarity.

25. *they went to the town of the house of Baal.* "Town" here is a little confusing because
presumably the temple of Baal is in Samaria, where they all are (unless one assumes it was
located in a nearby suburb). One proposed emendation is instead of *'ir*, town, to read *devir*,
inner sanctum.

27. *they smashed the sacred pillar.* There may be a textual confusion here, not only because
of the switch from plural to singular pillar but also because a burnt pillar does not need
to be smashed.

Israel. But Jehu did not swerve from the offenses of Jeroboam son of Nebat, 29
who had led Israel to offend—the golden calves that were in Bethel and in
Dan. And the LORD said to Jehu, "Inasmuch as you have done well what 30
is right in My eyes, according to all that was in My heart you have done to
the house of Ahab, four generations of your sons shall sit on the throne of
Israel." But Jehu did not watch out to go by the teaching of the LORD God of 31
Israel with all his heart. He did not swerve from the offenses of Jeroboam,
who had led Israel to offend. In those days the LORD began to trim away 32
Israel, and Hazael struck them down through all the borderland of Israel,
from the Jordan, where the sun rises, all the land of Gilead, the Gadites 33
and the Reubenites and the Manassites, from Aroer, which is by the Wadi
of Arnon, and Gilead and Bashan. And the rest of the acts of Jehu, and all 34
that he did, and all his valor, are they not written in the Book of the Acts of
the Kings of Israel? And Jehu lay with his fathers, and they buried him in 35
Samaria, and Jehoahaz his son became king in his stead. And the time Jehu 36
had been king over Israel in Samaria was twenty-eight years.

CHAPTER 11   And Athaliah, Ahaziah's mother, saw that her 1
son was dead, and she arose and destroyed all the royal seed. And Jehosheba, 2

---

29. *the golden calves that were in Bethel and in Dan.* From the viewpoint of the Judahite
writer, these cultic objects were pagan images, though in historical fact they were probably
only an alternative iconography (in Judahite worship cherubim were used) to represent the
sanctuary where YHWH dwelled. The failure to "swerve from the offenses of Jeroboam"
mentioned earlier in this verse probably refers to the golden calves.

32. *trim away Israel.* The verb refers, quite accurately, to chopping off fringe areas.
    through all the borderland of Israel. The noun *gevul* can mean either "border" or "terri-
tory." Since the incursions of the Aramean king were limited to the area east of the Jordan
occupied by the two and a half tribes, the word as it is used here probably is intended to
make us think of a border region.

CHAPTER 11   1. *saw.* The Masoretic Text shows, in defiance of Hebrew grammar,
"and saw," but many Hebrew manuscripts omit the "and."
    and destroyed all the royal seed. This shocking act, which makes Athaliah far more hor-
rendous than Medea, is not explained. One should keep in mind that Athaliah appears to
be the daughter of Ahab and Jezebel, and she takes after her mother in viciousness. Seeing
that her son Ahaziah has been killed, she ruthlessly grasps an opportunity for herself by
murdering her sons and grandsons so that she can seize the throne without rivals.

2. *Jehosheba.* She is both the aunt of the infant Joash whom she saves and wife of Jehoiada
the priest, who plots the overthrow of Athaliah.

Ahaziah's sister, the daughter of King Jehoram, took Joash, Ahaziah's son, and stole him away from the king's sons who had been put to death—him and his nurse—in the bedchamber, and they hid him from Athaliah, and he
3 was not put to death. And he was with her hiding in the house of the LORD
4 six years, while Athaliah was reigning over the land. And in the seventh year Jehoiada sent and took the commanders of the hundreds of the Cherithites and the sentries and brought them to him at the house of the LORD and made a pact with them and imposed a vow on them in the house of the
5 LORD. And he showed them the king's son. And he charged them, saying, "This is the thing that you must do: a third of you, who begin your weekly
6 duty, are to keep guard at the king's house, and a third in the Horse Gate and a third in the gate behind the sentries, and you shall keep watch over
7 the house. And the two contingents among you, all who have finished their
8 weekly duty, shall keep guard over the house of the LORD for the king. And you shall draw round the king, every man with his weapons in his hand. And whosoever enters the colonnades shall be put to death. And be you
9 with the king when he goes out and when he comes in." And the commanders of the hundreds did as all that Jehoiada the priest had charged, and each took his men, those beginning their weekly duty with those finishing their

---

3. *hiding in the house of the* LORD. Jehosheba's husband, as priest (evidently, high priest), would have had jurisdiction over the temple precincts and would have been able to devise a safe hiding place within the temple.

while Athaliah was reigning over the land. Given that she has violently usurped the throne, her reign is indicated only through a participial aside, and the formulaic statement ("and X was king/queen in his stead") is avoided.

4. *And in the seventh year Jehoiada sent.* Perhaps the initiative occurs in the seventh year merely because it is the formulaic number for several years, though seven years would have given Joash time to grow from infant to young boy, at which point he could be placed on the throne with a regent as political executive.

the Cherithites. The received text says "Charite," but this is in all likelihood a shortened form or error for Cherithites, Cretan warriors who served as a palace guard.

the sentries. This may be a designation for a particular group of palace guards. The literal sense of the Hebrew is "runners."

6. *the Horse Gate.* The Hebrew says the Sur Gate, but the meaning of *Sur* is obscure, and verse 16 speaks of "the Horse Entrance," *mevo' hasusim.* Thus, *sur* may well be an error for *sus,* "horse."

8. *be you with the king when he goes out and when he comes in.* Jehoida pointedly refers to Joash as "the king," even before his coronation, in order to publicly confirm his royal status. Joash, after having been kept in hiding almost seven years, must be zealously protected in this moment of transfer of power.

weekly duty, and they came to Jehoiada the priest. And the priest gave to 10
the commanders of the hundreds the spears and the shields that were King
David's, which were in the house of the LORD. And the sentries stood, each 11
with his weapons in his hand, from the south corner of the house to the
north corner of the house, by the altar and by the house, all round the king.
And he brought out the prince and put the crown on him and the regalia, 12
and he made him king and anointed him, and they clapped their hands and
said, "Long live the king!" And Athaliah heard the sound of the sentries and 13
the people, and she came to the people at the house of the LORD. And she 14
saw, and, look, the king was standing by the pillar as was the custom, and
the commanders and the trumpets were by the king, and all the people of
the land were rejoicing and blowing the trumpets. And Athaliah rent her
garments and called out, "A plot, a plot!" And Jehoiada the priest charged 15
the commanders of the hundreds, the mustered men of the force, and said
to them, "Take her out from the colonnades, and put to death by the sword
whoever comes after her," for the priest said, "Let her not be put to death
in the house of the LORD." And they locked hands on all sides of her, and 16
she came into the king's house by way of the Horse Entrance and was put
to death there. And Jehoiada made a pact between the LORD and the king 17
and the people to be a people of the LORD, between the king and the people.
And all the people of the land came to the house of Baal and smashed it, 18
its altars and its images they utterly shattered, and Mattan priest of Baal

---

10. *the shields.* Others interpret the Hebrew term as "quivers" or "lances."

12. *the regalia.* The Hebrew *'edut* usually means "covenant," but it is hard to imagine that
any form of the covenant could be placed on the new king, so it seems more likely that the
word here is a homonym, derived from *'adi,* "ornament."

14. *all the people of the land.* Some scholars contend that the Hebrew *'am ha'arets* refers to
a particular group of Davidic loyalists in Jerusalem.

15. *Let her not be put to death in the house of the* LORD. Jehoiada, conscious of a cultic taboo,
wants no blood shed within the Temple.

17. *between the king and the people.* Although this phrase sounds redundant, it may be that
the repetition is deliberate, in order to emphasize the new solidarity between king and
people that stands in contrast to Athaliah's autocratic seizure of power.

18. *the house of Baal.* This is new information: that during Athaliah's reign a functioning
temple of Baal stood in Jerusalem. We are probably meant to infer that Athaliah, in addition to her murderous lust for power, followed the pagan ways of her mother Jezebel and
encouraged a cult of Baal in Jerusalem.

    Mattan priest of Baal. He has a good Hebrew name, so the functionaries of the cult of
Baal in Jerusalem are Judahites, not foreign priests.

they killed in front of the altars. And the priest appointed guards over the
19 house of the LORD. And he took the commanders of the hundreds and the
Cherithites and the sentries and all the people of the land, and they brought
the king down from the house of the LORD, and they entered the king's
20 house through the Gate of the Sentries, and he sat on the royal throne. And
all the people of the land rejoiced, while the town was quiet. And Athaliah
they had put to death in the king's house.

1 CHAPTER 12   Seven years old was Joash when he became
2 king. In the seventh year of Jehu, Joash became king, and he was king
in Jerusalem forty years. And his mother's name was Zibiah from Beer-
3 sheba. And Joash did what was right in the eyes of the LORD all his days, as
4 Jehoiada the priest had taught him. But the high places were not removed—
the people were still sacrificing and burning incense on the high places.
5 And Joash said to the priests, "All the silver of sacred gifts that is brought

---

19. *they brought the king down from the house of the* LORD, *and they entered the king's house
through the Gate of the Sentries.* With the vicious queen dead, they can now bring Joash
from the Temple, where he was hidden, in a grand triumphal march to the palace.

20. *And Athaliah they had put to death in the king's house.* This concluding notice is not
redundant. Cast in the pluperfect, it is a recapitulative statement of Athaliah's death that
also reminds us that as Joash is brought into the palace, the usurper who occupied it for
seven years has been eliminated.

CHAPTER 12   1. *Seven years old.* In the King James Version this appears as verse
21 of chapter 11.

3. *as Jehoiada the priest had taught him.* This clause is an addition to the recurrent formula about the behavior of the virtuous kings. It surely reflects a political reality in which
Jehoiada the high priest served as regent while the child-king was growing up.

4. *But the high places were not removed.* This repeated formula registers the view of the
editor of the Book of Kings that worship on the high places constituted actual or at least
potential paganism and violated the principles of the exclusive legitimacy of the cult in the
Jerusalem temple. In point of historical fact, Jehoiada as regent could certainly have taken
steps to eliminate the local altars on the high places if he regarded them as sinful, so we
may infer that he, his priestly colleagues, and the king did not think worship on the high
places was forbidden.

5. *All the silver.* Though many translations represent *kesef* as "money" (its later sense),
in the ninth century B.C.E. there were no coins in Israelite society, and probably still not
in the period when this narrative was composed. What the writer has in mind are small
weights of silver.

to the house of the LORD, silver currency for each person the value in silver, and any silver that a man's heart prompts him to bring to the house of the LORD—let the priests take, every man from his acquaintance, and they 6 shall repair the breaches of the house wherever a breach is found there." And it happened in the twenty-third year of King Joash, that the priests 7 did not repair the breaches of the house. And King Joash called to Jehoiada 8 the priest and to the priests and said to them, "Why are you not repairing the breaches of the house? And now, do not take silver from your acquaintances but give it for repairing the breaches of the house." And the priests 9 agreed not to take silver from the people, and not to repair the breaches of the house. And Jehoiada took a certain chest and bored a hole in its door 10 and set it by the altar on the right. When a man came into the house of the LORD, the priests, guardians of the threshold, put into it all the silver brought to the house of the LORD. And so, when they saw there was abun- 11 dant silver in the chest, the king's scribe came up, and the high priest, and they wrapped it in bundles and counted the silver that was found in the house of the LORD. And they gave the silver that had been measured out to 12 those performing the tasks, who were appointed for the house of the LORD, and they brought it out to the carpenters and to the builders working in the house of the LORD, and to the masons and to the quarriers of stone to buy 13 timber and quarried stone to repair the breaches of the house of the LORD,

---

silver currency for each person the value in silver. The exact meaning of the entire formulation about silver, persons, and sacred gifts is somewhat obscure, and widely different interpretations have been proposed.

6. *let the priests take, every man from his acquaintance.* The gist of this royal order is that the gifts in silver brought to the Temple are no longer to be passed on to the priests for their personal use but are to be dedicated to repairs of the temple building. These new instructions may reflect a power struggle between the king and the priests, with the adult Joash seeking to break loose from the domination of his guardian and uncle, Jehoiada, as his direct challenge to the high priest in verse 8 seems to suggest.

9. *and not to repair the . . . house.* This is only an ostensible contradiction. The idea is that Joash doesn't trust the priests to use the funds for the repair of the Temple. Instead, he will have all the collected silver placed in a chest, to be duly counted and paid out to the workers by a committee of two, one being the king's scribe and personal representative and the other the high priest. They in turn pass the silver on to an appointed group (verse 12) that pays it out to the work crews.

11. *they wrapped it in bundles and counted the silver.* There would probably be bundles of like weights of silver. One sees that all precautions are taken that none of the donated silver be diverted for any use except the repair of the Temple.

14 whatever was laid out for repair of the house. But no silver bowls, snuffers,
    basins, trumpets, nor golden vessels nor silver vessels were made in the
15 house of the LORD from the silver brought to the house of the LORD. But
    they would give it to those performing the tasks, that with it they should
16 restore the house of the LORD. And they made no reckoning for the men to
    whom they gave the silver, to those performing the tasks, as they worked
17 in good faith. Silver for guilt offerings and silver for offense offerings would
    not be brought to the house of the LORD. It would be for the priests.

18 Then did Hazael king of Aram come up and do battle against Gath and
19 take it. And Hazael set his face to go up against Jerusalem. And Joash king
    of Judah took all the consecrated things that Jehoshaphat and Jehoram and
    Ahaziah his fathers, kings of Judah, had consecrated, all his consecrated
    things, and all the gold that was found in the treasuries of the house of the
    LORD and in the house of the king, and he sent them to Hazael king of
20 Aram, and he went away from Jerusalem. And the rest of the acts of Joash,
    and all that he did, are they not written in the Book of the Acts of the Kings
21 of Judah? And his servants rose up and hatched a plot and struck down
22 Joash in Beth-Millo going down to Silla. And Jozabad son of Shimat and
    Jehozabad son of Shomer his servants struck him down, and he died. And
    they buried him with his fathers in the City of David, and his son Amaziah
    became king in his stead.

---

17. *It would be for the priests.* This verse indicates a compromise with the priests. They no
longer have access to general donations, but silver given for guilt offerings and offense
offerings still goes to them.

19. *And Joash king of Judah took all the consecrated things.* This amounts to the payment of
a high ransom to Hazael in order that he abandon his siege of Jerusalem. The title "king
of Judah" is perhaps added here to make an ironic point, for Joash is scarcely behaving in
a kingly fashion in emptying out the royal and temple treasuries in order to persuade a
hostile king to relinquish his attack.

21. *his servants.* As elsewhere in royal contexts, these are court officials.
    hatched a plot and struck down Joash. No explanation is given here for the conspiracy
and regicide. In the parallel passage in 2 Chronicles 24:25, the killing of Joash is said to be
an act of revenge for his killing the son of the now deceased Jehoiada. It is hard to know
whether the report in Chronicles has a historical basis, but it does suggest a tradition in
which the conspiracy was motivated by a conflict between king and priests, and it is possible that the two assassins were priests. Joash's surrendering of the temple treasures and
not just the royal treasures to the king of Aram could easily have alienated priestly circles.

CHAPTER 13   In the twenty-third year of Joash son of Ahaziah 1
king of Judah, Jehoahaz son of Jehu became king over Israel in Samaria, for
seventeen years. And he did what was evil in the eyes of the LORD and went 2
after the offenses of Jeroboam son of Nebat, who had led Israel to offend. He
did not swerve from it. And the LORD's wrath flared up against Israel, and 3
He gave them continuously into the hand of Hazael king of Aram and into
the hand of Ben-Hadad son of Hazael. And Jehoahaz implored the LORD, 4
and the LORD heeded him, for He saw Israel's oppression, for the king of
Aram oppressed them. And the LORD gave Israel a rescuer, and they came 5
out from under the hand of Aram, and the Israelites dwelled in their tents
as in former days. But they did not swerve from the offenses of the house of 6
Jeroboam, who had led Israel to offend, the way in which he had gone, and
the asherah, too, stood in Samaria. For Jehoahaz was left no troops except 7
fifty horsemen and ten chariots and ten thousand foot soldiers, for the king
of Aram had destroyed them and made them like dust to be trampled. And 8
the rest of the acts of Jehoahaz and all that he did and his valor, are they
not written in the Book of the Acts of the Kings of Israel? And Jehoahaz 9
lay with his fathers, and they buried him in Samaria. And Joash his son
was king in his stead

In the thirty-seventh year of Joash king of Judah, Joash son of Jehoahaz 10
became king over Israel in Samaria for sixteen years. And he did what 11
was evil in the eyes of the LORD, he did not swerve from all the offenses of

---

CHAPTER 13   5. *the LORD gave Israel a rescuer.* The appearance of this familiar
formula recurring in the Book of Judges is a little surprising here in the Book of Kings. It
is unlikely that the formula would refer to an Israelite king. Though the "rescuer" might
conceivably be an ad hoc military leader, it is doubtful that the political arrangements of
the monarchy would have allowed the operation of such a Judge-like figure. One scholarly
proposal is that the reference is to the Assyrian king, Adad-Nirari III, who assumed the
throne in 810 B.C.E. and four years later launched a campaign against Aram. His incursions
would have had the effect of loosening Aram's grip on Israel.

7. *ten thousand foot soldiers.* Because the cavalry and the chariots of Israel, which has
become a vassal to Aram, are reduced to a symbolic number (fifty and ten, respectively),
it is unlikely that so large a number of infantry as ten thousand would have been allowed
by their conquerors. Perhaps the text originally read not *'aseret 'alafim*, "ten thousand,"
but *'alpayim*, "two thousand."

10–13. These four verses are a striking testimony to the use of formulas in the Book of Kings.
Except for the names, there is not a word in the four verses that is not part of the recurrent
formula. But there may be an editorial glitch here because after Joash receives his formulaic
burial, he becomes an active figure in the narrative (13:14–25, 14:8–14), and then a second
notice of his death is introduced (14:15–16).

Jeroboam son of Nebat, who had led Israel to offend, the way in which he
12   had gone. And the rest of the acts of Joash and all that he did, and his valor
with which he battled against Amaziah king of Judah, are they not writ-
13   ten in the Book of the Acts of the Kings of Israel? And Joash lay with his
fathers, and Jeroboam sat on his throne, and Joash was buried in Samaria
with the kings of Israel.

14   And Elisha had fallen ill with the illness of which he would die, and Joash
king of Israel went down to him and wept in his presence and said, "My
15   father, my father, the chariot of Israel and its horsemen!" And Elisha said
to him, "Fetch a bow and arrows." And he fetched him a bow and arrows.
16   And he said to the king of Israel, "Set your hand on the bow." And he
17   set his hand, and Elisha placed his hands over the king's hands. And he
said, "Open the window to the east," and he opened it. And Elisha said,
"Shoot!" And he shot. And he said, "An arrow of rescue for the LORD, and
an arrow of rescue against Aram! And you shall strike Aram in Aphek till
18   its destruction." And he said, "Take the arrows." And he took them. And
he said to the king of Israel, "Strike to the ground!" And he struck three
19   times and he stopped. And the man of God was furious with him, and he
said, "To strike five or six times—then you would have struck Aram till
20   its destruction! And now, three times you shall strike Aram." And Elisha
died and they buried him, and the raiding parties of Moab came into the

14. *My father, my father, the chariot of Israel and its horsemen.* This evidently proverbial
epithet for a leader, which Elisha himself had applied to Elijah when he was about to die (2
Kings 2:12), expresses Joash's perception that Elisha has been a source of power and guidance for his kingdom.

15. *Fetch a bow and arrows.* As the king despairs because he is about to lose Elisha, the
prophet gives him a portent that Joash will continue to triumph after the death of the man
of God.

16. *and Elisha placed his hands over the king's hands.* This looks like an act through which
the prophet—repeatedly seen as a wonder worker—imparts something of his supernatural
power to the king.

17. *An arrow of rescue for the LORD.* The shooting of the arrow thus becomes a prophetic
symbol, a metonymy for the exercise of military might. The Hebrew *teshu'ah,* usually
"rescue," can mean "victory" in military contexts, but because Israel has been subjugated
by Aram, "rescue" may be the more salient meaning here.

19. *And now, three times you shall strike Aram.* Joash will drive back Aram three times but
fail to destroy it utterly. This detail of the beating of the arrows on the ground is meant to
explain a historical difficulty: Elisha, given his unique power, could have prophesied, and
intended to prophecy, total victory over Aram. In point of historical fact, Israel's military
success against Aram was partial and temporary. This failure is explained in folktale fash-

land, they came for a year. And as they were burying a man, they saw a raid- 21
ing party and they flung the man into Elisha's grave, and the man went and
touched Elisha's bones, and he revived and rose up on his feet. And Hazael 22
king of Aram oppressed Israel all the days of Jehoahaz, and the LORD showed 23
grace to them and pitied them and turned to them for the sake of His covenant with Abraham, Isaac, and Jacob, and He did not desire to destroy them,
He did not fling them away from His presence till now. And Hazael king of 24
Aram died, and Ben-Hadad his son became king in his stead. And Joash 25
came back and took the towns from the hand of Ben-Hadad son of Hazael
which he had taken from the hand of Jehoahaz his father in battle. Three
times did Joash strike him, and he brought back Israel's towns.

CHAPTER 14   In the second year of Joash son of Joahaz king 1
of Israel, Amaziah the son of Joash had become king, king of Judah. He was 2
twenty-five years old when he became king, and twenty-nine years he was
king in Jerusalem, and his mother's name was Jehoaddan from Jerusalem.
And he did what was right in the eyes of the LORD, but not like David his 3
forefather; as all that Joash his father had done he did do. But the high 4
places were not removed—the people were sacrificing and burning incense
on the high places. And it happened, when the kingdom was firmly in his 5
hand, that he struck down his servants who had struck down the king his

---

ion as the failure of the principal agent to carry out the entire magical act expected of him
by the man of God.

21. *and the man went and touched Elisha's bones, and he revived and rose up.* The first clause
is formulated as a kind of prolepsis: instead of "the body," we have "the man"; and "he went
and touched" makes the corpse sound as though it were already a living person. It should
be noted that Elisha's miracle-working power is imagined to be invested in his body, so
that even after death he is able to work wonders. The Elisha cycle began with a (scandalous)
episode in which he summoned bears to kill forty-two boys. Now, at the end of the cycle,
his bones perform the opposite act of reviving the dead.

25. *Three times did Joash strike him.* The Elisha cycle concludes with two different manifestations of the posthumous power of the prophet. First, his bones impart life to the man who
has died; then, the explicit terms of his prophecy to Joash, marked by the triple pounding
of the arrows on the ground, are fulfilled on the battlefield.

CHAPTER 14   5. *when the kingdom was firmly in his hand.* After Amaziah's father,
Joash, was murdered, the son was installed on the throne because evidently the quarrel of
the conspirators was with Amaziah personally and not with the Davidic dynasty. (In the
northern kingdom, where there was no authorized dynasty, one royal line was repeatedly
replaced by another after a coup.) But, understandably, the new king did not feel safe to
move against his father's killers until he had fully consolidated his power.

6   father. But the sons of the killers he did not put to death, as it is written in
    the Book of the Teaching of Moses, as the LORD charged, saying, "Fathers
    shall not be put to death over sons, and sons shall not be put to death
7   over fathers, but each man shall be put to death for his own offense." He
    struck down Edom in Salt Valley, ten thousand of them, and he seized the
8   Rock in the battle and called its name Jokthel to this day. Then did Ama-
    ziah send messengers to Joash son of Jehoahaz son of Jehu king of Israel,
9   saying, "Come let us face each other down." And Joash king of Israel sent
    to Amaziah king of Judah, saying, "The thistle which is in Lebanon sent to
    the cedar which is in Lebanon, saying, 'Give your daughter to my son as
    wife,' and the beast of the field which is in Lebanon came by and trampled
10 the thistle. You indeed have struck down Edom, and you are carried away
    by your own heart. Enjoy your glory, and stay in your house. Why should
11 you provoke evil, and you will fall, you and Judah with you?" But Amaziah
    did not heed. And Joash king of Israel came up, and they faced each other
    down, he and Amaziah king of Judah, in Beth-Shemesh, which is Judah's.
12,13 And Judah was routed by Israel, and every man fled to his tent. But Joash
    king of Israel caught Amaziah son of Joash son of Ahaziah king of Judah
    in Beth-Shemesh, and he came to Jerusalem and breached the wall of Jeru-
    salem from the Gate of Ephraim as far as the Corner Gate, four hundred

---

6. *the Book of the Teaching of Moses.* This designation almost certainly refers to Deuteronomy, which is here quoted almost verbatim (Deuteronomy 24:16). Deuteronomy, or its
initial core, was not composed until around 621 B.C.E., so the comment here is an intervention in the older story of the Deuteronomistic editor. In point of political fact, Amaziah
may have refrained from killing the offspring of the conspirators in order not to alienate
the court circles from which they came.

8. *Come let us face each other down.* No reason is given for this provocative and imprudent
military challenge. It has been suggested that Amaziah's success against Edom (verse 7) may
have encouraged him to think he could right old wrongs—perhaps a territorial dispute—
with the northern kingdom. Joash's words in verse 10 lend evidence to this interpretation.

9. *The thistle . . . the cedar.* This homey parable is vaguely reminiscent of the one declaimed
by Jotham in Judges 9. As is often the case in biblical parables, the parabolic details match
the situation to which they refer somewhat loosely. The request for the hand of the daughter
does not entirely fit Amaziah's eagerness for military confrontation, and both the cedar
and the wild beast have to refer, rather awkwardly, to Joash.

13. *Joash king of Israel caught Amaziah.* From the subsequent narrative, one must infer that
he then returned Amaziah to his Judahite subjects, but it is not explained why. Perhaps
Joash thought it sufficient to humiliate the king of Judah and strip him of his treasures
but did not want to give cause for still further embitterment between the two kingdoms.

   breached the wall of Jerusalem. This huge breach in the walls of the town would of course
have left it entirely exposed to attack.

cubits. And he took all the gold and the silver and all the vessels that were 14
found in the house of the LORD and in the treasuries of the house of the
king, and all the hostages, and he went back to Samaria. And the rest of 15
the acts of Joash that he did, and his valor with which he battled against
Amaziah king of Judah, are they not written in the Book of the Acts of the
Kings of Israel? And Joash lay with his fathers and was buried in Samaria 16
with the kings of Israel. And Jeroboam his son became king in his stead.
And Amaziah son of Joash king of Judah lived fifteen years after the death 17
of Joash son of Joahaz king of Israel. And the rest of the acts of Amaziah, 18
are they not written in the Book of the Acts of the Kings of Judah? And 19
they hatched a plot against him in Jerusalem, and he fled to Lachish, and
they sent after him to Lachish, and they sent after him to Lachish and put
him to death there. And they bore him off on horses, and he was buried in 20
Jerusalem with his fathers in the City of David. And all the people of Judah 21
took Azariah, when he was sixteen years old, and they made him king in
Amaziah his father's stead. He it was who built Elath and settled it for Judah 22
after the king lay with his fathers.

In the fifteenth year of Amaziah son of Joash king of Judah, Jeroboam son 23
of Joash became king, king over Israel, in Samaria, for forty-one years.
And he did what was evil in the eyes of the LORD, he did not swerve from 24
all the offenses of Jeroboam son of Nebat, who had led Israel to offend.
He it was who brought back the territory of Israel from Lebo-Hamath to 25
the Arabah Sea, according to the word of the LORD God of Israel which He
spoke through His servant Jonah son of Amittai the prophet, who was from
Gath Hepher. For the LORD had seen the very bitter affliction of Israel, and 26

---

19. *And they hatched a plot against him.* Once again, no reason is given for the determination of the conspirators—presumably people in the royal court—to kill the king. One possibility would be simmering resentment over his rash military provocation of the northern
kingdom and its disastrous results—the breaching of the wall, the emptying of royal and
temple treasuries. As with the assassination of Amaziah's father, the hostility is directed
against the king, not the dynasty, for his son is allowed to ascend the throne.

25. *Jonah son of Amittai.* The name of this prophet, about whom nothing is known beyond
the mention of his prophecy here, is then picked up by a writer of the Second Commonwealth period for the central figure of the narrative Book of Jonah.

26. *For the LORD had seen the very bitter affliction of Israel.* The writer faces a quandary
here: this Jeroboam is said to follow all the evil ways of Jeroboam I, yet the historical record
evidently shows military triumphs in his reign. These are explained as God's compassion
for suffering Israel and His promise not to allow them to be destroyed, even under an
evil king.

27 there was no ruler or helper, and none aiding Israel. And the LORD had
   not spoken to wipe out the name of Israel from under the heavens, but He
28 rescued them by the hand of Jeroboam son of Joash. And the rest of the
   acts of Jeroboam and all that he did, and his valor with which he battled
   and brought back Damascus and Hamath to Judah in Israel, are they not
29 written in the Book of the Acts of the Kings of Israel? And Jeroboam lay
   with his fathers, with the kings of Israel, and Zachariah his son became
   king in his stead.

1 CHAPTER 15   In the twenty-seventh year of Jeroboam king of
2 Israel, Azariah son of Amaziah became king, king of Judah. Sixteen years
   old he was when he became king, and fifty-two years he was king in Jerusa-
3 lem. And his mother's name was Jecoliah from Jerusalem. And he did what
   was right in the eyes of the LORD as all that Amaziah his father had done.
4 But the high places were not removed—the people were still sacrificing
5 and burning incense on the high places. And the LORD infected the king
   and he was stricken with skin blanch till his dying day, and he dwelled in
   the quarantine house, and Jotham the king's son was appointed over the

---

27. *the LORD had not spoken to wipe out the name of Israel from under the heavens.* One
cannot be sure exactly when these words were written. In effect, with the Assyrian conquest
of the northern kingdom in 721 B.C.E. (just two decades after the end of Jeroboam's reign),
Israel was wiped out, though perhaps one could say that its name remained.

28. *brought back Damascus.* The verb here is an extravagant flourish, for Damascus had
not once been a possession of Israel. What is realistically indicated is some military success
against the kingdom of Aram.
    to Judah in Israel. This formulation of the Masoretic Text is enigmatic because only the
most forced explanation could place Judah within Israel. The Peshitta lacks "to Judah" and
reads "to Israel," and this could be what the original text had.

CHAPTER 15   5. *he was stricken with skin blanch till his dying day.* No reason is
given for this terrible affliction: Azariah is said to have done what was right in the eyes of
the LORD, apart from allowing worship on the high places to continue, as all his predecessors had done. One may conclude that we have here the report of a historical datum—that
Azariah suffered from a disfiguring skin disease, presumed to be contagious, all his life.
The fact that God is said to have done the afflicting simply reflects the general assumption
of this and other biblical writers that all things are caused by God.
    the quarantine house. The Hebrew name of this place appears to reflect a term that
means "free." It is a "free house" either because the condition of freedom is associated, as
in one Ugaritic text, with death (here, a living death), or because someone in such a place
is free of all civic obligations.
    Jotham the king's son was appointed over the palace. The Hebrew for "palace" is simply
"house," but it is clearly the king's house, and here it is rendered as "palace" in order to avoid

palace, judging the people of the land. And the rest of the acts of Azariah 6
and all that he did, are they not written in the Book of the Acts of the Kings
of Judah? And Azariah lay with his fathers, and they buried him with his 7
fathers in the City of David, and Jotham his son became king in his stead.

In the thirty-eighth year of Azariah king of Judah, Zachariah son of 8
Jeroboam became king of Israel for six months. And he did what was evil 9
in the eyes of the LORD as his forefathers had done. He did not swerve from
the offenses of Jeroboam son of Nebat, who had led Israel to offend. And 10
Shallum son of Jabesh hatched a plot against him and struck him down in
the presence of the people and put him to death, and he became king in his
stead. And the rest of the acts of Zachariah, are they not written in the Book 11
of the Acts of the Kings of Israel? This was the word of the LORD that He 12
spoke to Jehu, saying, "A fourth generation of yours shall sit on the throne
of Israel." And so it was. Shallum son of Jabesh had become king in the 13
thirty-ninth year of Uzziah king of Judah, and he was king in Samaria
for a month. And Menahem son of Gadi came up from Tirzah and came 14
to Samaria and struck down Shallum son of Jabesh and put him to death,
and he became king in his stead. And the rest of the acts of Shallum and 15
his plot that he hatched, why, they are written in the Book of the Acts of
the Kings of Israel. Then did Menahem strike Tapuah and everything in it 16
and its territories from Tirzah, for it had not yielded, and he struck it, and
its pregnant women he ripped apart. In the thirty-ninth year of Azariah 17
king of Judah, Menahem son of Gadi became king over Israel in Samaria
for ten years. And he did what was evil in the eyes of the LORD. He did not 18

---

its seeming to refer to the quarantine house. In any case, Jotham becomes a kind of regent
because of his father's illness. Upon his father's death (verse 7), he officially becomes king.

13. *he was king . . . for a month.* The northern kingdom by this point in history, in the eighth
century B.C.E., exhibits extreme political instability—monarch after monarch is assassinated as coup follows coup. The Deuteronomistic editor makes some attempt to provide a
theological explanation for these upheavals—"This was the word of the LORD that he spoke
to Jehu"—but he cannot encompass all the rapid changes in this way. Thus no reason is
given for the fact that Shallum reigns only a month before he is murdered by Menahem.

16. *Tapuah.* The received text reads "Tipsah," a city on the eastern bank of the Euphrates
that Menahem surely could not have reached. One version of the Septuagint shows, more
plausibly, Tapuah, a town in the tribal region of Ephraim and Manasseh.
    for it had not yielded. The Hebrew wording, literally, "it had not opened," is a little odd.
    and its pregnant women he ripped apart. This barbaric practice seems to have been
embraced by several nations in the ancient Near East. See 2 Kings 8:13 and Amos 1:13, where
it is vehemently denounced.

swerve all his days from the offenses of Jeroboam son of Nebat who had led
19 Israel to offend. Pul king of Assyria came against the land, and Menahem
gave Pul a thousand talents of silver so that his hand would be with him
20 to make the kingdom firm in his hand. And Menahem exacted the silver
from Israel, from all the prosperous men, to give to the king of Assyria,
fifty shekels of silver from each man. And the king of Assyria turned back
21 and did not stay there in the land. And the rest of the acts of Menahem and
all that he did, are they not written in the Book of the Acts of the Kings of
22 Israel? And Menahem lay with his fathers, and Pekahiah his son became
23 king in his stead. In the fiftieth year of Azariah, king of Judah, Pekahiah
24 son of Menahem became king over Israel in Samaria for two years. And
he did what was evil in the eyes of the LORD. He did not swerve from the
25 offenses of Jeroboam son of Nebat who led Israel to offend. And Pekah son
of Remaliah his officer hatched a plot against him and struck him down in
the king's house, with Argob and Arieh, and with him were fifty men of the
26 Gileadites. And he put him to death and became king in his stead. And the
rest of the acts of Pekahiah and all that he did, why they are written in the
Book of the Acts of the Kings of Israel.

27 In the fifty-second year of Azariah king of Judah, Pekah son of Remaliah
28 became king over Israel in Samaria, for twenty years. And he did what was
evil in the eyes of the LORD. He did not swerve from the offenses of Jeroboam
29 son of Nebat, who had led Israel to offend. In the days of Pekah king of Israel,
Tiglath-Pileser king of Assyria came and took Ijon and Abel-Beth-Maacah
and Janoah and Kedesh and Hazor and Gilead and the Galilee, the whole
30 land of the Naphtalite, and he exiled them to Assyria. And Hosea son of Elah

---

19. *Menahem gave Pul a thousand talents of silver so that his hand would be with him to make the kingdom firm in his hand.* Menahem pays a huge tribute to Pul, thus accepting vassal status. Having seized the throne by assassinating his predecessor, he could well need foreign support against opposing groups in the court.

25. *Pekah.* This actually is the same first name as Pekahiah, simply without the theophoric suffix.
    with Argob and Arieh. These mystifying names have variously been interpreted as names of architectural structures within the palace, towns from which the killers came, and personal names.

29. *and he exiled them to Assyria.* Although the Assyrians sometimes merely reduced conquered kingdoms to vassal status, they followed a general imperial policy of exiling the conquered population in order to integrate the new territory as a province of the Assyrian empire. Assyrian inscriptions indicate that the westward thrust recorded here took place in 732 B.C.E., just a decade before the final destruction of the kingdom of Israel by Assyria and the exile of a large part of its population.

hatched a plot against Pekah son of Remaliah and struck him down and
put him to death, and he became king in his stead in the twentieth year of
Jotham son of Uzziah. And the rest of the acts of Pekah and all that he did,   31
why they are written in the Book of the Acts of the Kings of Israel.

In the second year of Pekah son of Remaliah king of Israel, Jotham son of   32
Uzziah became king, king of Judah. Twenty-five years old he was when he   33
became king, and sixteen years he was king in Jerusalem. And his mother's
name was Jerusha daughter of Zadok. And he did what was right in the eyes   34
of the LORD as all that Uzziah his father had done. But the high places were   35
not removed. The people were still sacrificing and burning incense on the
high places. He did build the Upper Gate of the house of the LORD. And   36
the rest of the acts of Jotham that he did, are they not written in the Book
of the Acts of the Kings of Judah? In those days the LORD began to let loose   37
against Judah Rezin king of Aram and Pekah son of Remaliah. And Jotham   38
lay with his fathers and was buried with his fathers in the City of David his
father. And Ahaz his son became king in his stead.

CHAPTER 16   In the seventeenth year of Pekah son of Rema-   1
liah, Ahaz son of Jotham became king, king of Judah. Twenty years old was   2
Ahaz when he became king, and sixteen years he was king in Jerusalem,
and he did not do what was right in the eyes of the LORD his God like David
his forefather. And he went in the way of the kings of Israel, and even his   3
son he passed through the fire like the abominations of the nations that the
LORD had dispossessed before the Israelites. And he sacrificed and burned   4
incense on the high places and on the hills and under every lush tree. Then   5
did Rezin king of Aram and Pekah son of Remaliah king of Israel come
up to Jerusalem for battle, but they were not able to battle against it. At   6
that time Rezin king of Aram restored Elath to Aram and drove out the

---

CHAPTER 16   3. *and even his son he passed through the fire.* This expression, featuring the verb "to pass through" (or "pass over"), is used elsewhere in reference to the pagan
cult of the Molech. It is unclear whether the expression refers to actually burning the son
as an offering to the god or to a symbolic act of passing him through or over the fire. The
translation preserves the ambiguity of the Hebrew, avoiding a rendering such as "consigned
to the fire" that some modern translators favor.

4. *under every lush tree.* This phrase, which recurs in a number of different biblical texts,
evidently refers to the worship of nature deities.

6. *Rezin king of Aram restored Elath to Aram.* It is puzzling that Rezin, in the midst of laying
siege against Jerusalem, should have gone on an expedition to Elath in the far south. This

Judahites from Elath, while the Edomites came to Elath and dwelled there
7 till this day. And Ahaz sent messengers to Tiglath-Pileser king of Assyria
saying, "I am your servant and your son. Come up and rescue me from
the hand of the king of Aram and from the hand of the king of Israel, who
8 are risen against me." And Ahaz took the silver and the gold that were in
the house of the LORD and the treasuries of the king's house, and he sent
9 them to the king of Assyria as a bribe. And the king of Assyria heeded him,
and the king of Assyria went up against Damascus and seized it and exiled
10 its people to Kir, but Rezin he put to death. And King Ahaz went to meet
Tiglath-Pileser in Damascus, and he saw the altar that was in Damascus,
and Ahaz sent to Uriah the priest the image of the altar and its design in all
11 its fashioning. And Uriah the priest built an altar according to all that King
Ahaz had sent from Damascus, so did Uriah the priest do, until the return
12 of King Ahaz from Damascus. And the king came from Damascus, and the

---

difficulty is compounded by the fact that the consonantal text has Arameans settling in
Elath, but the Masoretic marginal gloss corrects this to Edomites. (The graphic difference
in Hebrew between "Aram" and "Edom" is minimal because the letters *resh* and *dalet* are
similar in appearance.) The original verse may have read: the king of Edom restored Elath
to Edom. The Edomites could easily have taken advantage of the fact that the Judahite
forces were distracted by the siege of Jerusalem.

7. *I am your servant and your son.* This is obviously an expression of subservience or
vassaldom.

8. *Ahaz took the silver and the gold that were in the house of the LORD.* The mechanics of
this act are spelled out in verses 17–18.
    as a bribe. This amounts to protection money. The Hebrew *shoḥad* always has a nega-
tive connotation and it is a mistake to translate it as "gifts." Tiglath-Pileser was in any case
engaged in a series of campaigns against Aram, Israel, Phoenicia, and the Philistines and
thus scarcely needed encouragement, but the payment of silver and gold would have been
an expression of Ahaz's fealty to Assyria.

9. *exiled its people.* The Hebrew merely says "exiled it," but since "it," although grammatically referring to the city, actually refers to its inhabitants, an expansion in translation is
called for here.

10. *Ahaz sent to Uriah the priest the image of the altar and its design in all its fashioning.*
In the present instance, this is not an attempt to adapt pagan practice, for the narrator
makes no critical comment, and the new altar erected in Jerusalem is adapted for the cult
of YHWH and is not subsequently destroyed. Instead, Ahaz, a provincial monarch, comes
to the metropolis of Damascus, where, as a kind of cultic tourist, he sees and marvels at
the large and impressive altar constructed according to the most modern design, and he
decides to adopt it for his own temple.

king saw the altar, and the king approached the altar and went up on it. And 13
he turned his burnt offering and his grain offering to smoke and poured out
his libation and cast the blood of his well-being sacrifices on the altar. And 14
the bronze altar that was before the LORD he moved forward from the front
of the house, from between the altar and the house of the LORD and set it
along with the altar to the north. And King Ahaz charged Uriah the priest, 15
saying, "On the large altar, turn to smoke the morning's burnt offering and
the evening's grain offering and the king's burnt offering and his grain offering and the burnt offering of all the people and their grain offering and their
libations, and all the blood of the burnt offering and all the blood of the
sacrifice you shall cast upon it, and the bronze altar shall be to gaze upon."
And Uriah the priest did as all that King Ahaz had charged him. And King 16,17
Ahaz cut off the frames of the laver stands and removed the lavers from
them and took down the basin from the bronze oxen that were beneath it
and set it on the stone pavement. And the covered passage for the sabbath 18
that they had built in the house and the king's outer entrance he took away
from the house of the LORD—because of the king of Assyria. And the rest of 19
the acts of Ahaz that he did, are they not written in the Book of the Acts of
the Kings of Judah? And Ahaz lay with his fathers and was buried with his 20
fathers in the City of David, and Hezekiah his son became king in his stead.

CHAPTER 17   In the twelfth year of Ahaz king of Judah, 1
Hosea son of Elah became king in Samaria over Israel, for nine years. And 2
he did what was evil in the eyes of the LORD though not like the kings of

---

13. *he turned his burnt offering and his grain offering to smoke.* There are indications
elsewhere that the king, on special ceremonial occasions such as the dedication of a new
altar, officiated at the sacrifices, which otherwise were the province of the priests.

15. *the large altar.* This is the new altar, built according to the model of the altar in Damascus.

17. *cut off the frames of the laver stands.* As in the account of the sacred furnishings of
Solomon's temple, it is difficult to reconstruct the details of the cultic vessels, but the gen-
eral idea is that Ahaz stripped the precious metals from them to send as his tribute to
Tiglath-Pileser.

CHAPTER 17   2. *not like the kings of Israel who were before him.* The destruction
of the northern kingdom, then, is not attributed to egregious behavior on the part of its
last king but rather to the cumulative transgressions of its inhabitants, which are duly set
forth in verses 7–23.

3 Israel who were before him. Against him did Shalmaneser king of Assyria
come up, and Hosea became vassal to him and rendered tribute to him.
4 And the king of Assyria discovered a plot of Hosea's, that he had sent messengers to So king of Egypt and had not brought up tribute to the king of
Assyria as every year, and the king of Assyria seized him and locked him
5 in the prison-house. And the king of Assyria went up through all the land
6 and went up to Samaria and besieged it for three years. In the ninth year
of Hosea, the king of Assyria took Samaria and exiled Israel to Assyria
and settled them in Halah and in Habor by the river of Gozan and in the
7 towns of Media. And so, because the Israelites had offended the LORD their
God Who brought them up from the land of Egypt from under the hand of
8 Pharaoh king of Egypt, and they had feared other gods and had gone by the
statutes of the nations whom the LORD had dispossessed before Israel, and
9 that the kings of Israel had made for them, and the Israelites had done acts

---

3. *Shalmaneser king of Assyria.* Though Shalmaneser in fact attacked Israel and other territories in Canaan-Phoenicia in 725 B.C.E., he died in 721 and, according to Assyrian royal
inscriptions, the actual conquest was consummated by Sargon II. Either this information
was not available to the Hebrew historian, writing perhaps a century and a half after the
events, or he chose to simplify his narrative by speaking of a single "king of Assyria"
invading Samaria.

4. *So.* No such royal name appears in Egyptian records, and this may be a distortion of an
Egyptian title or of a different Egyptian name.
    the king of Assyria seized him. If Hosea was the Assyrian emperor's prisoner, one must
assume that the court officials in Samaria remained loyal to him (no replacement is mentioned) and thus continued the battle against the Assyrians during the three years of siege.

6. *the king of Assyria . . . exiled Israel to Assyria and settled them.* This was a general imperial policy of the Assyrians. They removed the native population of a conquered territory—though it is not clear whether in fact the entire Israelite population was exiled, as
is implied here—and replaced it with people from the existing empire in order to make
the territory an Assyrian province. The sundry groups enumerated in verse 24 who are
brought to Samaria are all inhabitants of territories conquered by the Assyrians, and so the
verb "exiled" is properly applied to their displacement from their native lands to Samaria.

7. *because the Israelites had offended the LORD their God.* The catastrophic event of the
utter destruction of the kingdom of Israel calls for a grand theological explanation, cast in
Deuteronomistic terms, and so a ringing sermonic catalogue of the transgressions of the
Israelites is introduced that runs all the way to verse 23. It is notable that all the transgressions are cultic—there is no mention of ethical failings or injustice.
    feared. This is the core meaning of this reiterated Hebrew verb, although in cultic con-
texts it obviously refers to modes of worship rather than to the emotion of fear.

8. *and that the kings of Israel had made for them.* The syntactic connection of this clause
to the rest of the sentence is ambiguous in the Hebrew. "For them" has been added in the
translation as an interpretive guess, assuming that the clause refers to the two molten
images of calves.

that were not right against the LORD their God and had built themselves high places in all their towns from watchtowers to fortress towns. And they 10 had set up for themselves pillars and sacred poles on every high hill and under every lush tree. And they had burned incense there on all the high 11 places like all the nations that the LORD had exiled before them, and they did evil things to vex the LORD. And they had worshipped the foul idols 12 about which the LORD said, "You shall not do this thing." And the LORD 13 had made every prophet, every seer, warn Israel, saying, "Turn back from your evil ways and keep My commands and My statutes, according to all the teaching that I charged your fathers, and that I sent to you through My servants the prophets." But they did not heed, and they stiffened their 14 necks like the necks of their fathers, who did not trust the LORD their God. And they spurned His statutes and His covenant that He had sealed with 15 their fathers, and His precepts that He imparted to them, and they went after empty breath and did empty things, and after the nations that were all round them, of whom the LORD had charged not to do like them. And 16 they forsook the LORD their God and made themselves a molten image of two calves, and they made a sacred pole and bowed down to all the array of the heavens, and they worshipped Baal. And they passed their sons and 17 their daughters through the fire and worked sorcery and divined, and they gave themselves over to do what was evil in the eyes of the LORD to vex him. And the LORD was greatly incensed against Israel, and He removed them 18 from His presence. None remained but the tribe of Judah alone. Judah, too, 19 had not kept the commands of the LORD their God, and they went in the way of the statutes of Israel which they had done. And the LORD spurned 20 all the seed of Israel, and He abused them and gave them into the hand of plunderers, until He flung them from His presence. For He had torn Israel 21 from Judah, and they made Jeroboam son of Nebat king, and he drove Israel away from following the LORD and led them to commit a great offense. And 22 the Israelites went in all the offenses of Jeroboam that he had done, they did

---

14. *like the necks of their fathers.* The reference is in all likelihood to the stubborn and rebellious Wilderness generation.

16. *a molten image of two calves.* As before, the writer construes this as idol worship, though these were very probably icons of the throne of YHWH, like the cherubim in the southern kingdom.
    the array of the heavens. Worship of celestial deities was a prominent feature of the last phase of First Commonwealth history.

19. *Judah, too, had not kept the commands of the LORD.* Evidently, it was not destroyed—rather, not yet—because of God's promises to David. "Commands," here and below, is singular in the Hebrew but is in effect a collective noun.

23 not swerve from it, until the LORD had removed Israel from His presence,
   as He had spoken through His servants the prophets, and He exiled Israel
24 from its land to Assyria, till this day. And the king of Assyria brought
   people from Babel and from Kirthah and from Ivvah and from Hamath
   and from Sepharvaim and settled them in the towns of Samaria instead of
25 the Israelites, and they took hold of Samaria and settled in its towns. And
   it happened at the beginning of their settling there, that they did not fear
   the LORD, and the LORD sent lions against them, and they set about kill-
26 ing them. And they said to the king of Assyria, saying, "The nations that
   you exiled and resettled in the towns of Samaria do not know the rules
   of the god of the land, and he sent lions against them, and here they are
27 killing them, for they do not know the rules of the god of the land." And
   the king of Assyria charged, saying, "Bring there one of the priests whom
   you have exiled from there, and let him settle there and teach the rules of
28 the god of the land." And one of the priests whom they had exiled from
   Samaria came and settled in Bethel, and he set about teaching them how
29 they should fear the LORD. And each nation would make its own god and
   put it in one of the houses on the high places that the Samarians had made,
30 each nation in the town in which it had settled. And the people of Babel
   made Succoth-Benoth, and the people of Kith made Nergal, and the people
31 of Hamath made Ashima. And the Avvites made Nibhaz and Tirhak, and
   the Sepharvites were burning their children in fire to Adrammelech and
32 Anammelech, the gods of Sepharvaim. And they were fearing the LORD,
   and they made priests for the high places for themselves from their pick,
33 and they would officiate in the houses of the high places. The LORD they
   would fear but their gods they would serve according to the practice of the
34 nations from which they had been exiled. Till this day they do according

---

25. *the LORD sent lions against them.* Lions were abundant in ancient Israel, a fact reflected
in the five different terms for "lion" in biblical Hebrew; and so it is possible that the displacement of population, with hunting perhaps in abeyance, created the circumstances for
an incursion of lions. In any case, the lion attacks seem to be represented as a miraculous
intervention against the new inhabitants of Samaria.

32. *they were fearing the LORD, and they made priests for the high places.* That is, they added
YHWH to their cult while continuing to worship pagan gods.

34. *Till this day they do according to their first practices.* The whole account of the cultic
practices of the Samarians, as many scholars have inferred, looks suspiciously like the
work of a post-exilic Judahite writer promoting a separatist view of the Samarians. In this
representation, the population of Samaria after 721 B.C.E. was entirely a foreign implant,
and the cult performed in Samaria was not a legitimate worship of YHWH but a promis-

to their first practices. They do not truly fear the LORD and they do not act according to their statutes and their practice and the teaching and the commands that the LORD charged the sons of Jacob, whose name He set as Israel. And the LORD sealed a covenant with them and charged them, 35 saying, "You shall not fear other gods nor shall you bow down to them, nor shall you serve them nor shall you sacrifice to them. But the LORD Who 36 brought you up from the land of Egypt with great power and with an out-stretched hand, Him shall you fear and to Him shall you bow down and to Him shall you sacrifice. And the statutes and the laws and the teaching 37 and the commands that He wrote for you, you shall keep to do always, and you shall not fear other gods. And the covenant that I sealed with you, you 38 shall not forget, and you shall not fear other gods. But the LORD your God 39 shall you fear, and He will save you from the hand of all your enemies." But they did not heed; rather, they went on doing according to their first 40 practice. And these nations would fear the LORD and serve their idols. Their 41 children too, and the children of their children, as their fathers had done, they do till this day.

---

cuous mingling of pagan and Yahwistic practices. Historically, this perception may have been wrong both in regard to the composition of the Samaritan population and in regard to the nature of its cult.

They do not truly fear the LORD. The adverb "truly" has been added in the translation to spell out what the Hebrew implies because otherwise there might be a confusion—earlier the Samaritans are said to fear the LORD, that is, to perform the outward offices of the LORD's service.

they do not act according to their statutes and their practice. It would make better sense if this read "His statutes and His practice," though there is no textual warrant for this reading.

Jacob, whose name He set as Israel. This reminder of Jacob's portentous name change underscores the notion that the people of Israel have a grand divinely ordained destiny in which the paganizing Samaritans have no part.

35. *You shall not fear other gods nor shall you bow down to them.* This entire sentence is an approximate quotation of the first of the Ten Commandments.

38. *and you shall not fear other gods.* This prohibition against worshipping other gods is repeated here three times, strongly stamping the Samaritans as a showcase instance of dereliction from the God Who gave the Decalogue to Israel.

41. *fear the LORD and serve their idols.* The verbs "fear" and "serve" are clearly equivalent terms for performing acts of worship. In this instance, instead of the pejorative designation—*gilulim* ("foul idols") associated with *gelalim*, "turds," as in verse 12—the more neutral general noun, *pesilim*, "idols," is used. This may be because when Israelites worship idols (verse 12), the act is especially disgusting, whereas one would expect benighted pagans to serve idols.

1 CHAPTER 18   And it happened in the third year of Hosea
son of Elah king of Israel that Hezekiah son of Ahaz became king, king of
2 Judah. Twenty-five years old he was when he became king, and twenty-nine
years he was king in Jerusalem. And his mother's name was Avi daughter
3 of Zachariah. And he did what was right in the eyes of the LORD as all that
4 David his forefather had done. He it was who took away the high places
and smashed the pillars and cut down the sacred pole and pulverized the
bronze serpent that Moses had made, for at that time the Israelites had
5 been burning incense to it, and it was called Nehushtan. In the LORD God
of Israel he put his trust, and after him there was none like him among all
6 the kings of Judah and among those that were before him. And he clung to
the LORD, he did not swerve from Him, and he kept His commands that
7 the LORD had charged Moses. And the LORD was with him. Wherever he
sallied forth, he prospered. And he rebelled against the king of Assyria and
8 did not serve him. He it was who struck down the Philistines as far as Gaza
9 and its territories, from watchtowers to fortress towns. And it happened in
the fourth year of King Hezekiah, which was the seventh year of Hosea son
of Elah king of Israel, that Shalmaneser king of Assyria went up against
10 Samaria and laid siege against it. And he took it at the end of three years,
in the sixth year of Hezekiah, which was the ninth year of Hosea king of

---

CHAPTER 18   4. *He it was who took away the high places.* Hezekiah is the first king
to do this. As with Josiah a century later, the motive may have been political as well as religious, for an exclusive cult in Jerusalem would clearly consolidate the power of the Judahite
king. One can assume that there was some resentment against this new policy, for the high
places were popularly viewed as legitimate—and convenient—locations for the worship
of YHWH. In Rabshakeh's provocative speech, he appears to play to this resentment by
describing the removal of the high places as an offense against YHWH.

the bronze serpent that Moses had made. The fashioning of the bronze serpent to counter
the plague of serpents is reported in Numbers 21. Archaeologists have found numerous
serpents, evidently cultic objects, and it looks as if these were objects of worship in popular
religion, which were then retrojected on Moses in the story told in Numbers.

Nehushtan. The name is transparently derived from *nehoshet,* "bronze," with a probable
pun on *nahash,* "serpent."

7. *he rebelled against the king of Assyria.* After the death of Sargon II, there was widespread
rebellion against the Assyrian overlords in the northern regions of the empire, and Hezekiah evidently exploited the upheaval to reject his own vassal condition.

9. *Shalmaneser king of Assyria went up against Samaria.* The report beginning here and
concluding in verse 12 is a recapitulation of 17:6ff. Evidently, the historical context of the
Assyrian conquest of the northern kingdom needs to be recalled here as Judah is threatened
with a similar fate.

Israel—Samaria was taken. And the king of Assyria exiled Israel to Assyria 11
and led them to Halah and Habor at the River of Gozan and to the towns of
Media. Because they had not heeded the voice of the LORD their God and 12
had broken His covenant, all that Moses servant of the LORD had charged,
yet they did not heed and they did not do it. And in the fourteenth year of 13
King Hezekiah, Sennacherib king of Assyria went up against all the fortified towns of Judah and took them. And Hezekiah king of Judah sent to the 14
king of Assyria at Lachish, saying. "I have offended. Turn back from me.
Whatever you fix for me I will bear." And the king of Assyria imposed upon
Hezekiah king of Judah three hundred talents of silver and thirty talents
of gold. And Hezekiah gave all the silver that was in the house of the LORD 15
and in the treasuries of the house of the king. At that time Hezekiah cut 16
away the doors of the LORD's temple and the columns that Hezekiah king of
Judah had overlaid, and he gave them to the king of Assyria. And the king 17
of Assyria sent Tartan and Rabsaris and Rabshakeh from Lachish to King
Hezekiah in Jerusalem with a heavy force. And they went up and came to
Jerusalem, and they went up and came and took a stance at the conduit of
the Upper Pool, which is by the road to the Fuller's Field. And they called 18
out to the king, and Eliakim son of Hilkiah who was appointed over the
house came out to them, with Shebnah the scribe and Joah son of Asaph
the recorder. And Rabshakeh said to them, "Say, pray, to Hezekiah, Thus 19

---

13. *in the fourteenth year of King Hezekiah.* Sennacherib's campaign in Phoenicia, Philistia,
and Judah in 701 B.C.E. is elaborately documented in Assyrian annals and bas-reliefs.

   all the fortified towns of Judah. According to the Assyrian annals, the imperial forces
captured forty-six Judahite towns—which may be an imperial exaggeration. The principal
one was Lachish, where Sennacherib is headquartered in the next verse. The Assyrians left
a vivid bas-relief of their archers, in characteristic high-pointed caps, assaulting this town.

14. *Whatever you fix for me I will bear.* Hezekiah's act of submission, expressed in his
readiness to pay whatever tribute Sennacherib imposes, is contradicted by the narrative
episode that begins in verse 17, where Hezekiah is represented as part of an alliance with
Egypt opposing the Assyrians. It would appear that two different sources, for reasons that
are unclear, have been spliced together rather than blended.

17. *And the king of Assyria sent.* This entire episode appears, with only minor variations, in
Isaiah 36. That passage was evidently drawn from here.

   Tartan and Rabsaris and Rabshakeh. Although these three terms are presented in the
Hebrew text without definite articles, as though they were proper names, each is actually
a title: vizier, high chamberlain (literally, "head eunuch"), and head steward. In any case,
all are clearly high officials in the Assyrian court.

18. *who was appointed over the house.* That is, the palace.

says the great king, the king of Assyria: 'What is this great trust that you
20 show? You thought, mere words are counsel and valor for battle. Now, in
21 whom did you trust that you should have rebelled against me? Now, look,
you have trusted in this shattered reed, in Egypt, which when a man leans
on it, enters his palm and pierces it. So is Pharaoh king of Egypt to all who
22 trust in him. And should you say to me, In the LORD our God we trust, is
it not He Whose high places and altars Hezekiah took away, and he said
to Judah and to Jerusalem: Before this altar you shall bow down in Jerusa-
23 lem?' And now, wager, pray, with my master, with the king of Assyria, and
I shall give you two thousand horses if you can give yourself riders for them.
24 And how could you turn away the agent of one of the least of my master's
25 servants and trust Egypt for chariots and horses? Now, was it without the
LORD that I have come up against this place to destroy it? The LORD said to
26 me, Go up against this land and destroy it." And Eliakim son of Helkiah,
and Shebnah and Joah with him, said to Rabshakeh, "Speak, pray, to your
servants Aramaic, for we understand it, and do not speak Judahite in the
27 hearing of the people who are on the wall." And Rabshakeh said to them,
"Did my master send me to you and to your master to speak these words?
Did he not send to these men sitting on the wall—to eat their own turds

---

21. *this shattered reed.* Reeds, of course, grow in abundance along the Nile.
    which when a man leans on it, enters his palm and pierces it. The metaphor is quite
realistic. The reed looks as if it could provide support, but it easily breaks when you lean
on it, and the jagged edges of the break can pierce the skin.

23. *I shall give you two thousand horses if you can give yourself riders for them.* Hezekiah's
attempted rebellion is so hopelessly pathetic, Rabshakeh says, that he could not even muster
sufficient cavalrymen were he given the horses.

24. *agent.* The Hebrew aptly uses an Assyrian imperial administrative title, *pahat* (compare
the English "pasha," which has a shared linguistic background).

26. *Speak, pray, to your servants Aramaic.* Aramaic was the most widely shared language
in the lands of the Assyrian empire east of the Jordan, and so by the late eighth century
B.C.E. it had been adopted as the diplomatic lingua franca. Thus, an educated Judahite court
official would have been fluent in Aramaic.
    do not speak Judahite. "Judahite," of course, is Hebrew, but that term for the language
never appears in the Bible. It is not explained how an Assyrian court official had a command of Hebrew.

27. *Did he not send to these men sitting on the wall.* The verb "send" is merely implied in
the Hebrew. Rabshakeh makes clear that his entire speech—itself a brilliant deployment of
political rhetoric—is precisely intended for the ears of the people. His purpose is to drive a
wedge between the rebellious Hezekiah and the people, convincing them that the uprising
is hopeless, and that, in fact, the fate of deportation to Assyria will be a happy one.

and to drink their own urine—together with you?" And Rabshakeh stood 28
and called out in a loud voice in Judahite and spoke and said, "Listen to the
words of the great king, the king of Assyria. Thus said the king. 'Let not 29
Hezekiah deceive you, for he will not be able to save you from my hand.
And let not Hezekiah have you trust in the LORD, saying, the LORD will 30
surely save us, and this city will not be given into the hand of the king of
Assyria.' Do not listen to Hezekiah, for thus said the king of Assyria: 'Make 31
terms with me and come out to me, and eat each man of his vine and each
man of his fig tree, and drink each man the water of his well, until I come 32
and take you to a land like your land—a land of grain and new wine, a land
of bread and vineyards, a land of olive trees and oil and honey. And live,
and do not die, and do not listen to Hezekiah when he misleads you, saying,
the LORD will save us. Did the gods of the nations ever save each its land 33
from the hand of the king of Assyria? Where were the gods of Hamath and 34
Arpad? Where were the gods of Sepharvaim, Hena and Ivvah? And where
were the gods of Samaria? Did they save Samaria from my hand? Who is 35
there of all the gods of the lands that saved their land from my hand, that
the LORD should save Jerusalem from my hand?'" And the people were 36
silent and did not answer a word to him, for it was the king's command,
saying, "You shall not answer him." And Eliakim son of Hilkiah, who was 37

---

30. *let not Hezekiah have you trust in the* LORD. Rabshakeh appears to be shifting grounds.
First he claimed that it was YHWH Who sent the Assyrians against Judah (verse 25), which
was a way of conveying to the people the idea that their destruction was divinely ordained
and irreversible. Now he takes a different tack: no national god has ever availed against
the great king of Assyria.

31. *Make terms with me.* The literal sense is "make a gift [or blessing] with me," but in
context, as Rashi and the King James Version after him understood, the expression means
to offer terms of surrender.
   eat each man of his vine and . . . his fig tree, and drink each man the water of his well.
The vine and the fig tree appear in a repeated proverbial expression about peaceful and
prosperous life. Eating from the vine and the fig tree and drinking well-water are a vivid
antithesis to the representation of the starving besieged population eating its own excrement and drinking its own urine.

32. *a land like your land.* The catalogue of agricultural bounty that follows closely resembles
the recurrent list of all the good things of the Land of Israel. Rabshakeh in this fashion
depicts life in exile in Assyria as a new promised land.

34. *where were the gods of Samaria.* The Masoretic Text merely has "that they saved Samaria
from my hand" immediately after the question about the sundry gods of the lands in the
northern region of the empires. One version of the Septuagint and a fragment of Kings
from the Cairo Genizah show the clause here translated, which makes the verse coherent.

appointed over the house, and Shebna the scribe and Joah son of Asaph the recorder with him, came to Hezekiah, their garments rent, and they told him Rabshakeh's words.

1 CHAPTER 19   And it happened when King Hezekiah heard, that he rent his garments and covered himself in sackcloth and went into 2 the house of the LORD. And he sent Eliakim, who was appointed over the house, and Shebna the scribe and the elders of the priest, covered in sack- 3 cloth, to Isaiah the prophet son of Amoz. And they said to him, "Thus said Hezekiah: 'A day of distress and chastisement and insult is this day.

> For children have come to the birth-stool,
> and there is no strength to give birth.

4 Perhaps the LORD will have heard all the words of Rabshakeh, whom his master the king of Assyria sent, to defame the living God, and He will chastise for the words that the LORD your God heard, and you will offer 5 prayers for the remnant that still exists.' " And the servants of King Heze- 6 kiah came to Isaiah. And Isaiah said to them, "Thus shall you say to your master: 'Thus said the LORD: Do not fear the words that you have heard, 7 with which the flunkies of the king of Assyria reviled Me. I am about to

---

CHAPTER 19   3. *For children have come to the birth-stool.* The poetic style makes these words seem initially cryptic, but the obvious meaning is that the children about to be born cannot emerge because when the mothers come to the birth-stool, they do not have the strength to push the babies out. The delegation from the king may want to speak to the prophet in his own characteristic language by first addressing him in a line of verse. In any case, the line forcefully frames their message to Isaiah with an image of desperate impotence that represents the plight of the people. As in the previous chapter, this entire episode is replicated, with only minor textual variants, in the Book of Isaiah (chapter 37). Isaiah in this narrative resembles Elijah and Elisha in being seen by others as a holy man who has the power to intercede on their behalf with God. Unlike them, however, he is a "literary prophet" who delivers his prophecies in the form of poetry, as he does here in the poem that runs from verse 21 to verse 28.

5. *And the servants of King Hezekiah came to Isaiah.* Their arrival was clearly implied by the end of verse 2. Perhaps one should construe the verb as a pluperfect, although its form does not indicate that. The same seemingly redundant clause also appears in Isaiah 37:5.

6. *flunkies.* The Hebrew ne'arim, youths or people in a subservient status, is usually represented in this translation as "lads," but its use here by Isaiah, instead of the expected 'avadim, "servants," has a pejorative connotation.

send an ill spirit into him, and he shall hear a rumor and go back to his
land, and I shall make him fall by the sword in his land.'" And Rabshakeh 8
went back and found the king of Assyria battling against Libnah, for he
had heard that he had journeyed on from Lachish. And he heard about 9
Tirhakah king of Cush, saying, "Look, he has sallied forth to do battle
with you." And he turned back and sent messengers to Hezekiah, saying,
"Thus shall you say to Hezekiah king of Judah, saying, 'Let not your god in 10
whom you trust deceive you, saying, Jerusalem will not be given into the
hand of the king of Assyria.' Look, you yourself have heard what the kings 11
of Assyria did to all the lands, annihilating them—and will you be saved?
Did the gods of the nations save them, when my fathers destroyed Gozan 12
and Haran and Rezeph and the Edomites who are in Telassar? Where is the 13
king of Hamath, and the kings of Arpad and the king of Lahir, Sepharvaim,
Hena, and Ivvah?" And Hezekiah took the letters from the hand of the 14
messengers and read them, and Hezekiah went up to the house of the LORD
and spread them out before the LORD. And Hezekiah prayed before the 15
LORD God of Israel enthroned on the cherubim: "You alone are God of all
the kingdoms of the earth. You it was made heaven and earth. Incline Your 16
ear and listen; open, LORD, Your eyes and see; and listen to the words of
Sennacherib that he sent to insult the living God. Indeed, LORD, the kings 17
of Assyria destroyed nations and their lands and consigned their gods to 18
the fire—because they are not gods but the work of human hands, wood
and stone, and they destroyed them. And now, O LORD our God, rescue us, 19
pray, from his hand, that all the kingdoms of the earth may know that You

---

7. *an ill spirit.* The Hebrew says only "a spirit," but since it induces fear followed by flight,
it appears to be a troubling spirit.

   he shall hear a rumor. What this might be is never spelled out. If the prophecy is to be
consistent with what is reported at the end of the chapter, it would be the news that his
army has been stricken with a plague.

9. *king of Cush.* Cush is Nubia, just south of Egypt and politically linked with it. Egypt was
a key player in the uprising against the Assyrian imperial forces, and so it is not surprising
that the Nubian king would oppose Sennacherib. The connection of this report with the
story of the siege against Jerusalem is not entirely clear. Perhaps Sennacherib is impelled
to finish off Jerusalem quickly so that he can turn his forces to the south.

14. *spread them out.* The Hebrew reads "spread it out," but the first part of the verse speaks
of multiple letters.

15. *You alone are God of all the kingdoms of the earth.* These words are a direct rebuttal of
the arrogant words spoken by Rabshakeh in verse 12. Hezekiah will make his rejoinder to
the Assyrian boast still more explicit in verse 17.

20 alone are the LORD our God." And Isaiah son of Amoz sent to Hezekiah,
saying, "Thus said the LORD God of Israel: 'Of which you prayed to Me
21 about Sennacherib king of Assyria I have listened.' This is the word that
the LORD spoke about him:

> 'She scorns you, mocks you,
>   the maiden, Zion's daughter.
> She wags her head at you,
>   Jerusalem's daughter.
22 Whom did you insult and revile,
>   and against whom have you lifted your voice,
> and raised your eyes up high
>   against Israel's Holy One.
23 By your messengers you insulted the Master
>   and thought, "When I ride in my chariots,
> I will go up to the heights of the mountains,
>   the far reaches of Lebanon.
> I will cut down its lofty cedars,
>   its choicest cypresses
> and will come to its uttermost heights,

---

21. *She scorns you, mocks you.* The "you" is of course Sennacherib. Zion, scorned by Sennacherib's spokesman, has nothing but contempt for the presumptuous Assyrian king.
    She wags her head at you. In biblical poetry, this is a conventional gesture of scorn.

22. *raised your eyes up high / against Israel's Holy One.* Isaiah ups the ante of denunciation: Sennacherib's presumption in declaring that he will destroy the Judahite kingdom is cast as an assault on the God of heaven and earth.

23. *I will go up the heights of the mountains, / the far reaches of Lebanon.* Although Sennacherib's imperial campaign did include Phoenicia, here he is besieging Jerusalem. The mountains of Lebanon, however, are the proverbial loftiest heights in biblical poetry, and *yarketey levanon,* "the far reaches of Lebanon," contains an echo of *yarketey tsafon,* "the far reaches of Tsafon," the dwelling place of the gods. Sennacherib's declaration at this point sounds rather like that of the overweening king who is brought down to Sheol in Isaiah 14. The cutting down of lofty cedars also figures in Isaiah 14:8.
    its uttermost heights. The received text here reads *melon,* "night encampment," but the parallel phrase in Isaiah 37:24 as well as one Hebrew manuscript shows *merom,* "heights" (a singular rendered here as a plural for the sake of the English idiom).
    the woods of its undergrowth. The Hebrew *karmel* usually means "farmland," which would be anomalous on the Lebanon heights, but as Yehuda Felix has noted, it can also mean "low shrubs" (compare Isaiah 29:17). This would be the sparse vegetation on the mountaintops above the treeline.

and the woods of its undergrowth.
It is I who have dug and drunk   24
    the waters of foreigners,
and dried up with the soles of my feet
    all Egypt's rivers."
Have you not heard from afar   25
    that which I did from time of old?
I fashioned it, brought it to pass—
    and fortified towns
        have turned into heaps of ruins.
Their inhabitants, impotent,   26
    are cast down and put to shame,
become the grass of the field
    and green growth,
thatch on the roofs
    by the east wind blasted.
And your stayings and comings and goings I know   27
    and your raging against Me.
Because of your raging against Me,   28
    and your din that came up in My ears
I will put My hook in your nose
    and My bit between your lips,
and will turn you back on the way
    on which you came.'

---

24. *the waters of foreigners.* The phrase, slightly opaque, is part of Sennacherib's boast of conquest: he has seized the territories of nations and even sunk wells to exploit their water resources.

    and dried up with the soles of my feet / all Egypt's rivers. This is an antithetical act to the digging of wells—Egypt, blessed by the Nile, abounds in water. Here the Assyrian king makes himself, at least through the hyperbole, a divine figure with the power to dry up rivers as he treads upon them.

26. *thatch on the roofs / by the east wind blasted.* The speech Isaiah attributes to Sennacherib concludes with a metaphor common in biblical poetry of the nations as mere grass, blasted by the hot wind blowing from the eastern desert.

28. *I will put My hook in your nose / and My bit between your lips.* Sennacherib had imagined himself a god. Now the God of Israel describes him as a dumb helpless beast to be driven where God wants.

    turn you back. This is Isaiah's prophecy of Sennacherib's flight back to Assyria.

29 "And this is the sign for you: eat aftergrowth this year, and in the second
year stubble, and in the third year sow and harvest and plant vineyards
30 and eat their fruit. And the remnant of the house of Judah shall add root
31 beneath and put forth fruit above. For from Jerusalem shall come forth
the surviving remnant from Mount Zion. The LORD's zeal shall do this.
32 Therefore, thus said the LORD about the king of Assyria: 'He shall not enter
this city and he shall not shoot an arrow there, and no shield shall go before
33 him, nor shall he raise a siege-work against it. In the way he comes he shall
34 go back, and he shall not enter this city, said the LORD. And I will defend
this city to rescue it, for My sake and for the sake of David My servant.'"

35 And it happened on that night that the LORD's messenger went out and
struck down the Assyrian camp, a hundred eighty-five thousand. And when
36 they rose early in the morning—look, they were all dead corpses. And Sennacherib king of Assyria pulled up stakes and went off and returned to
37 Nineveh. And it happened as he was bowing down in the house of his god
Nisroch, that Adrammelech and Sarezer struck him down with the sword,
and they escaped to the land of Ararat. And Esharaddon his son became
king in his stead.

---

29. *eat aftergrowth this year.* The "you" now is Hezekiah, and the verbs will then switch to
the plural, referring to the people. Because the invading army has laid waste to the countryside, there will be no crops for two years—and yet, as a "sign," the Judahites will survive.

35. *the LORD's messenger went out and struck down in the Assyrian camp, a hundred eighty-
five thousand.* The lifting of the siege is a historical event, though the reason for it is uncertain. If the report here is authentic, it would be because a plague swept through the Assyrian
camp. But one must say that the writer has a vested interest in representing this event as a
miraculous intervention, demonstrating God's commitment to protect Jerusalem (in contrast to Samaria, destroyed by an Assyrian king twenty years earlier).

37. *Adrammelech and Sarezer struck him down with the sword.* The two figures named
are Sennacherib's sons. One gets the impression from the narrative report that the assassination took place directly after the emperor's return to Nineveh. In fact, Sennacherib
was murdered twenty years after the military campaign of 701 B.C.E. The writer, however,
wants to present this killing in the temple of a pagan god as an immediate fulfillment
of Isaiah's prophecy (verse 7) and a prompt retribution against the boasting conqueror
depicted in Isaiah's poem.
　　And Esharaddon his son became king in his stead. Esharaddon had been Sennacherib's
chosen successor. It was evidently this choice that led Adrammelech, abetted by one of his
brothers, to kill his father, hoping to seize the throne. One infers that he then discovered
no support in the court for his claim to the crown and thus was obliged to flee with his
brother to Ararat in the far north.

CHAPTER 20   In those days Hezekiah fell mortally ill, and 1
Isaiah son of Amoz the prophet came to him and said to him, "Thus
said the LORD: 'Charge your household, for you are about to die and
you will not live.' " And he turned his face to the wall and prayed to the 2
LORD, saying, "Please, O LORD, recall, pray, that I walked before You 3
truthfully and with a whole heart and did what was good in Your eyes."
And Hezekiah wept. And it happened that Isaiah had not gone out of 4
the central court, when the word of the LORD came to him, saying, "Go 5
back, and you shall say to Hezekiah prince of My people, 'Thus said the
LORD God of David your forefather: I have heard your prayer, I have
seen your tears. I am about to heal you. On the third day you shall go up
to the house of the LORD. And I will add to your days fifteen years, and 6
from the hand of the king of Assyria I will save you and this city, and I
will defend this city for My sake and for the sake of David My servant.' "
And Isaiah said, "Fetch a clump of figs." And they fetched it and put it on 7
the burning rash, and he revived. And Hezekiah said to Isaiah, "What is 8
the sign that the LORD will heal me and I will go up on the third day to
the house of the LORD?" And Isaiah said, "This is the sign for you from 9
the LORD that the LORD will do the thing which He spoke· should the

---

CHAPTER 20   1. *In those days Hezekiah fell mortally ill.* The editor of the Book of
Isaiah will continue to replicate material from 2 Kings—this passage occurs in Isaiah 38
and 39. Again, we have integral citation with only minor textual variants. The formulaic
phrase at the beginning, "In those days," is a noncommittal temporal indicator, and it is
unclear whether Hezekiah's grave illness occurred before or after the siege of Jerusalem
reported in the previous chapter.

5. *the LORD God of David your forefather.* This epithet serves as a reminder of God's commitment to preserve the Davidic dynasty, and Hezekiah is presented as a king who does
what is right in the eyes of the LORD, like David his forefather.

6. *and from the hand of the king of Assyria I will save you.* This clause could be an indication that Hezekiah's illness preceded the siege of Jerusalem, but the inference is not entirely
certain because even after the lifting of the siege, Assyria would have remained a potential
threat.

7. *Fetch a clump of figs.* Isaiah here appears not to be performing a miracle but to be prac-
ticing folk medicine. Hezekiah, however, in the next verse requests a portent that he will
be cured.
   burning rash. Only here do we learn that *sheḥin,* burning rash, which is Job's affliction,
is a potentially fatal disease.
   and he revived. Given that Hezekiah in the next verse remains uncertain that he will
recover, the sense of "revived" (literally, "lived") here is that after the application of the fig
poultice he experienced some relief from the torment of the burning rash.

10 shadow go down ten steps or should it go back ten steps?" And Hezekiah
said, "It is easy for the shadow to incline down ten steps and not for the
11 shadow to go backward ten steps." And Isaiah the prophet called out to
the LORD, and He turned back the shadow that had gone down on the
12 Steps of Ahaz, backward ten steps. At that time Berodach-Baladan son of
Baladan king of Babylonia sent letters and a gift to Hezekiah, for he heard
13 that Hezekiah had fallen ill. And Hezekiah heard of the envoys and showed
them all his house of precious things, the silver and the gold and the spices
and the goodly oil, and his armory and all his treasuries. There was nothing
14 that Hezekiah did not show them in his house and in his kingdom. And
Isaiah the prophet came to King Hezekiah and said to him, "What did these
men say to you and from where did they come to you?" And Hezekiah said,
15 "From a distant land, from Babylonia." And he said, "What did they see in
your house?" And Hezekiah said, "All that is in my house they saw. There
16 was nothing that I did not show them of my treasuries." And Isaiah said,
17 "Listen to the word of the LORD: 'Look, a time is coming when everything
that is in your house and that your fathers stored up till this day will be
18 borne off to Babylonia. Nothing will remain,' said the LORD. 'And from
your sons who will issue from you, whom you will beget, he will take and

---

9. *should the shadow go down ten steps.* What is evidently in question is a kind of sundial, but one that is not a horizontal disk but rather a series of steps set into a wall, ten on the left side to show the shadow of the ascending sun and ten on the right side for the descending sun. A device of this sort has been found in Egypt. The King James Version and modern Hebrew understand *ma'alot* as "degrees," but these were probably actual steps, which is what the word usually means.

10. *It is easy for the shadow to incline down ten steps.* This would be the natural course of the shadow, so Hezekiah chooses instead the miraculous reversal of the progress of the shadow. That also becomes a figure for the reversal of his seemingly imminent death.

11. *the Steps of Ahaz.* The sundial in question proves to be a well-known marker in Jerusalem commissioned by King Ahaz.

12. *king of Babylonia.* The Babylonians were threatened by the Assyrian empire to the north and so were eager to make common cause with the kingdom of Judah.

13. *the envoys.* The received text has only "about them," and this identification is added in the translation for clarity.

17. *a time is coming when everything that is in your house . . . will be borne off to Babylonia.* This dire prophecy is presented as punishment for Hezekiah's imprudence in exposing all his treasures to the eyes of the Babylonian visitors. Many scholars think that the episode was added over a century later in an effort to explain the despoiling of Jerusalem during the reign of Jehoiakim in 597 B.C.E. or in the final destruction of the city in 586 B.C.E.

they will become eunuchs in the palace of the king of Babylonia.'" And   19
Hezekiah said to Isaiah, "The word of the LORD that you have spoken is
good." And he thought, "Why, there will be peace and trust in my days."
And the rest of the acts of Hezekiah and all his valor, and his making the   20
pool and the conduit so that he could bring water into the town, are they
not written in the Book of the Acts of the Kings of Judah? And Hezekiah   21
lay with his fathers, and Manasseh his son was king in his stead.

CHAPTER 21   Twelve years old was Manasseh when he   1
became king, and fifty-five years he was king in Jerusalem, and his mother's
name was Hephzibah. And he did what was evil in the eyes of the LORD,   2
like the abominations of the nations that the LORD had dispossessed before
the Israelites. And he rebuilt the high places that Hezekiah his father had   3

---

18. *they will become eunuchs in the palace of the king of Babylonia.* Although *sarisim* sometimes may refer to court officials who are not necessarily castrated, one suspects that the
core meaning that involves castration is invoked here: there could be no greater curse for a
king than to have his sons turned into eunuchs, incapable of begetting offspring.

19. *The word of the LORD that you have spoken is good.* This response by Hezekiah to the
grim prophecy is astonishing. On the surface, he seems to be saying to Isaiah that he
accepts the word of the LORD, that it must be good because it is God's will. In the next
sentence, however, he thinks to himself that what is good about it is that the disaster
will not happen in his lifetime—something that in fact Isaiah has not clearly told him.
This self-centered view of national catastrophe puts the virtuous Hezekiah in a somewhat
questionable light.

20. *his making the pool and the conduit so that he could bring water into the town.* The conduit is a remarkable engineering feat that one can walk through to this day. It is a tunnel
sloping gradually down from outside to inside, devised to introduce water into the town
in time of siege. It is roughly 550 yards in length, not at all in a straight line, and showing
evidence that two teams of workers hewed the tunnel out of the underground rock from
opposite directions, somehow managing to meet each other in the middle.

CHAPTER 21   2. *like the abominations of the nations.* The formulaic language for
reporting the cultic divagations of an Israelite king is stepped up here, and it will continue
to be intensified in the verses to follow. Manasseh, the son of one of the two most virtuous
kings of Judah, is cast as the most egregious of evil kings. It is historically plausible that
he would have encouraged pagan cults—he was a vassal to Assyria, a fact not mentioned
in our text but registered in Assyrian inscriptions—but it appears that his religious and
moral turpitude is stressed in order to explain how the kingdom of Judah was destroyed
four generations later, despite Hezekiah and his virtuous grandson Josiah. This impending
destruction is the burden of the dire prophecy in verses 11–15.

destroyed, and he made a sacred pole as Ahab king of Israel had made, and he bowed down to all the array of the heavens and worshipped them. 4 And he built altars in the house of the LORD, of which the LORD had said, 5 "In Jerusalem I will set My name. And he built altars to all the array of the 6 heavens in both courts of the house of the LORD. And he passed his son through the fire and performed sorcery and divined and conjured ghosts and familiar spirits. He did abundantly what was evil in the eyes of the 7 LORD, to vex Him. And he placed the statue of Asherah that he had made in the house of which the LORD had said to David and to Solomon his son, "In this house and in Jerusalem, which I have chosen from all the tribes of 8 Israel, will I set My name forever. And I will no longer make Israel's foot go wandering from this land that I gave to their fathers—but only if they keep to do all that I have charged them and as all the teaching that My 9 servant Moses charged them." But they did not heed, and Manasseh led them astray to do what was evil more than the nations that the LORD had 10 destroyed before the Israelites. And the LORD spoke through His servants 11 the prophets, saying, "Inasmuch as Manasseh king of Judah has done these abominations, he has done more evil than all that the Amorites did before

---

3. *he made a sacred pole.* The Hebrew *'asherah* can refer either to a special pole used in the pagan cult or to the goddess Asherah, depending on the context. In verse 7, the reference is clearly to Asherah because there could not be a statue of a sacred pole.

and he bowed down to all the array of the heavens. The worship of astral deities, not especially prominent in Canaanite religion, was widespread in Assyria, and the biblical literature produced in the last century of the First Temple period abounds in objections to it.

4. *And he built altars in the house of the LORD.* Introducing pagan worship into the Jerusalem temple was an especially heinous act, far worse than reestablishing the cult of the high places.

5. *both courts of the house of the LORD.* These are the inner and outer courts of the Temple.

6. *And he passed his son through the fire.* The ambiguity of the Hebrew wording, as noted earlier, allows one to construe this either as child sacrifice or as a nonlethal magical/cultic rite.

to vex Him. The object of the verb is merely implied in the Hebrew.

7. *Jerusalem, which I have chosen from all the tribes of Israel.* The language of the election of Jerusalem is emphatically Deuteronomistic.

9. *to do what was evil more than the nations that the LORD had destroyed.* Manasseh's offenses are so great that they even outdo those of the surrounding nations. A grim *a fortiori* notion is intimated here: if the Canaanite nations were dispossessed because of their evil acts, how much more so will this be the fate of Judah, which under their king surpassed the Canaanites in culpable behavior.

him, and he has led Judah, too, to offend with his foul idols. Therefore, thus 12
said the LORD God of Israel, I am about to bring an evil upon Jerusalem
and Judah, about which any who hears of it, both his ears will ring. And I 13
will stretch over Jerusalem the line of Samaria and the weight of the house
of Ahab, and I will wipe out Jerusalem as one wipes a bowl clean, wiping
and turning it on its face. And I will abandon the remnant of My estate 14
and give them into the hand of their enemies, and they will become plunder and spoils for all their enemies. Inasmuch as they have done what is 15
evil in My eyes and have been vexing Me from the day their fathers came
out of Egypt to this day." And Manasseh also had shed innocent blood in 16
great abundance until he filled Jerusalem with it from one end to the other,
besides his offense with which he led Judah to offend, to do what was evil
in the eyes of the LORD. And the rest of the acts of Manasseh and all that 17
he did and his offense that he committed, are they not written in the Book
of the Acts of the Kings of Judah? And Manasseh lay with his fathers , and 18
he was buried in the garden of his house, in the Garden of Uzza, and his
son Amon became king in his stead.

Twenty two years old was Amon when he became king, and two years he 19
was king in Jerusalem, and his mother's name was Meshullemeth daughter
of Haraz from Jotbah. And he did what was evil in the eyes of the LORD 20

---

11. *foul idols.* As before, the writer uses an invented invective term, *gilulim*, coined from
gelalim, "turds."

13. *the line . . . and the weight.* In the construction of buildings, in order to ensure that the
walls would be vertical, walls were measured against a plumb line—a line with a weight
attached to its bottom end. The line and the weight are thus a metaphor for the rigorous
measuring of the integrity of Jerusalem. Ironically, it is not a correction in building that
will ensue but destruction, as Samaria was measured and destroyed.

   as one wipes a bowl clean, wiping and turning it on its face. This is a homey and vivid
image of total destruction: when the last remnant of food is wiped from the bowl, leaving
no drop or crumb, the bowl can be turned upside down.

15. *and have been vexing Me from the day their fathers came out of Egypt to this day.* In the
explanation put forth here for the imminent national catastrophe, the evil Manasseh is not
unique but rather the culmination of all the backsliding and rebellion of the Israelites from
the generation of the wilderness wanderings onward.

16. *Manasseh also had shed innocent blood in great abundance.* Moral offense compounds
the cultic offenses. The victims of these many murders are in all likelihood loyalists to
YHWH, perhaps the prophets of the LORD just mentioned, who were slaughtered as Jezebel slaughtered the prophets of the LORD. It may have been this that led the Israeli biblical
scholar Yehezkel Kaufmann to describe Manasseh as "the Jezebel of the South."

21 as Manasseh his father had done. And he went in all the way in which
his father had gone, and he worshipped the foul idols that his father had
22 worshipped, and he bowed down to them. And he forsook the LORD God
23 of his fathers and did not go in the way of the LORD. And Amon's servants
24 hatched a plot against him and put the king to death in his house. And the
people of the land struck down the plotters against King Amon, and the
25 people of the land made Josiah his son king in his stead. And the rest of
the acts of Amon that he did, are they not written in the Book of the Acts
26 of the Kings of Judah? And they buried him in his grave in the Garden of
Uzza, and Josiah his son became king in his stead.

1 CHAPTER 22   Eight years old was Josiah when he became
king, and thirty-one years he was king in Jerusalem, and his mother's name
2 was Jedidah daughter of Adaiah from Bozkath. And he did what was right
in the eyes of the LORD, and he went in all the way of David his forefather
3 and did not swerve to the right or to the left. And it happened in the eighteenth year of King Josiah that the king sent Shaphan son of Azaliah son of
4 Meshullam the scribe to the house of the LORD, saying, "Go up to Hilkiah
the high priest, that he melt down the silver brought to the house of the

---

23. *And Amon's servants hatched a plot against him.* Whenever the connection is with a
king, "servants" means "courtiers." The reason for the court conspiracy is not stated. Some
have interpreted the regicide as a response to Amon's paganizing ways, and the fact that
"the people of the land" (whether the phrase indicates the general populace or a particular
political group within it) kill the conspirators and promote Josiah to the throne argues for
this understanding. Josiah was only eight years old at the time, and given his later record
of unflagging loyalty to YHWH and his devotion to the centrality of the Jerusalem cult,
those who instated him and looked after his education must surely have themselves been
loyalists to YHWH.

CHAPTER 22   2. *And he did what was right in the eyes of the LORD.* Since Josiah
was a child when he became king, one must assume that his virtuous behavior at first must
have been through the dictates of the regents who would have had to manage the affairs of
state for the first eight to ten years of his reign.

3. *the scribe.* As elsewhere, this title, in court circles, designates not someone who copies
manuscripts but a high royal official with administrative responsibilities.

4. *that he melt down the silver.* The verb as it appears here in the received text, *yatem*, is of
uncertain meaning. When this same activity is reported in verse 9, a different verb is used,
meaning "to melt down," suggesting that the original text here read *yatekh*. (The differing
last consonants resemble each other in appearance in paleo-Hebrew script.) Several ancient
versions show "melt down" at this point. People would have brought contributions to the

LORD, which the guards of the threshold had gathered from the people. And let them give it to those doing the tasks appointed over the house of the 5 LORD, that they give it to those doing the tasks in the house of the LORD, to repair the breaches of the house, to the carpenters and to the builders and 6 to the masons, to buy wood and quarried stone to repair the house. But the 7 silver given them need not be accounted for, for they deal honestly." And 8 Hilkiah the high priest said to Shaphan the scribe, "I have found a book of teaching in the house of the LORD." And Hilkiah gave the book to Shaphan and he read it. And Shaphan came to the king and brought back word to the 9 king and said, "Your servants melted down the silver that was in the house and gave it to those doing the tasks appointed over the house of the LORD." And Shaphan told the king, saying, "Hilkiah the priest gave me a book," 10 and Shaphan read it to the king. And it happened when the king heard 11 the words of the book of teaching, that he rent his garments. And the king 12 charged Hilkiah the priest and Ahikam son of Shaphan and Achbor son of Michaiah and Shaphan the scribe and Asaiah the king's servant, saying, "Go, inquire of the LORD on my behalf and on behalf of the people and on 13 behalf of all Judah concerning the words of this book that has been found,

---

Temple in the form of silver ornaments, and these then had to be melted down and broken into small weights of silver that could be used for payment of labor and materials.

5. *those doing the tasks appointed over the house of the* LORD . . . *those doing the tasks.* The first group, distinguished by the term "appointed," are administrators and foremen, probably part of the permanent staff of the Temple, and the second group are the sundry skilled workmen, in all likelihood brought into the Temple to perform these specific jobs.

8. *I have found a book of teaching.* The identical designation *sefer hatorah* occurs in Deuteronomy 30:10. The term *sefer* can mean "scroll" or "book" or indeed any written document, even a letter, but its force as "book" seems especially relevant here. For two centuries, the scholarly consensus, despite some dissent, has been that the found book is Deuteronomy. Although attributed to Moses, it would have been written in the reign of Josiah, perhaps drawing on some earlier materials. The book "found" in 621 B.C.E. was also not altogether identical with Deuteronomy as we have it, which almost certainly included some later elements, and was not edited in the form that has come down to us until the Babylonian exile. The major new emphases of the book brought to Josiah were the repeated stress on the exclusivity of the cult in Jerusalem ("the place that I shall choose") and the dire warnings of imminent disaster and exile if the people fail to fulfill its covenant with God.

11. *he rent his garments.* The most likely reason would be his hearing the grim warnings of impending catastrophe if Judah did not mend its ways. This reaction would then provide the impetus for Josiah's rigorous reforms.

13. *Go, inquire of the* LORD. This is the usual idiom for inquiring of an oracle.

for great is the LORD's wrath that is kindled against us because our fathers
have not heeded the words of this book to do as all that is written in it."
14 And Hilkiah the priest went, and Ahikam and Achbor and Shaphan, and
Asaiah with him, to Huldah the prophetess, wife of Shallum son of Tikvah
son of Harhas, keeper of the wardrobe, and she was living in the Mishneh,
15 and they spoke to her. And she said to them, "Thus said the LORD God
16 of Israel: 'Say to the man who sent you to me, Thus said the LORD: I am
about to bring evil on this place and on its inhabitants, by all the words of
17 the book that the king of Judah read, in return for their forsaking Me and
burning incense to other gods so as to vex Me with all their handiwork, and
18 My wrath shall kindle against this place and will not be extinguished.' And
to the king of Judah who sends you to inquire of the LORD, thus shall you
say to him: 'Thus said the LORD God of Israel: the words that you heard,
19 inasmuch as your heart quailed and you humbled yourself before the LORD
when you heard what I said about this place and about its inhabitants, that
they will become a desolation and a curse, and you rent your garments and
20 wept before Me, I, too, have heard, said the LORD. Therefore I am about
to gather you to your fathers, and you shall be gathered to your grave in

---

for great is the LORD's wrath. This sounds very much like a direct response to the great
catalogue of hair-raising curses (see Deuteronomy 28:15–68) in the book read out to Josiah.

14. *Huldah the prophetess.* She is the only female prophet mentioned in the Book of Kings.
She performs in every respect like the male prophets, quoting God's words directly with
the introductory messenger-formula, "Thus said the LORD," and the large royal delegation
that comes to her clearly accepts her authority as fully as they would that of a male prophet.
   Mishneh. The term means "repetition" or "addition" and was a western addition in
Jerusalem.

15. *Say to the man who sent you to me.* Pointedly avoiding in her initial speech reference to
Josiah by name or title, she reduces him to a mere sender of messages. In verse 18, she refers
to him as "the king of Judah" but continues to suppress his name.

16. *by all the words of the book that the king of Judah read.* Since the contents of the book at
this point would be known only to Josiah and Shaphan and perhaps some courtiers who
heard the reading of the text, Huldah must be presumed to know the book through her
prophetic gifts.

17. *all their handiwork.* The reference is to idols, fashioned by human hands.

20. *you shall be gathered to your grave in peace.* In fact, Josiah will be killed in battle at
Megiddo at the age of thirty-nine. Some scholars cite the discrepancy between Huldah's
prophecy and what is reported in 23:29 as evidence that the terms of the prophecy are
authentic, with Huldah's actual reassurance at the time to Josiah then contradicted by
historical events.

peace, and your eyes shall not see all the evil that I am about to bring on this place.'" And they brought back word to the king.

CHAPTER 23

And the king sent out, and all the elders of ¹ Judah and Jerusalem gathered round him. And the king went up to the ² house of the LORD, and every man of Judah and all the inhabitants of Jerusalem were with him, and the priests and the prophets and all the people from the least to the greatest. And he read in their hearing all the words of the book of the covenant that was found in the house of the LORD. And ³ the king stood on a platform and sealed a covenant before the LORD to walk after the LORD and to keep His commands and His precepts and His statutes with a whole heart and with all their being, to fulfill the words of this covenant written in this book. And all the people entered into the covenant. And the king charged Hilkiah the high priest and the assis- ⁴ tant priests and the guards of the threshold to bring out from the LORD's temple the vessels made for Baal and Asherah and for all the array of the heavens, and he burned them outside Jerusalem in the Kidron fields and bore off their ashes to Bethel. And he put down the pagan priests that the ⁵

CHAPTER 23   3. *with a whole heart and with all their being.* These are signature formulas of the Book of Deuteronomy. They occur again, expanded, in verse 25.

And all the people entered into the covenant. The received text here has the verb *waya'amed*, literally "stood," but this may be a scribal error for *waya'avor*, literally "pass through."

4. *he burned them outside Jerusalem.* Because these objects of pagan worship are impure, they are taken outside Jerusalem to be destroyed in an open space where purity does not obtain.

and bore off their ashes to Bethel. Bethel was one of the two main sanctuaries of the northern kingdom. Scattering the ashes of the statues of Baal and Asherah on that site would be a way of confirming its illegitimacy or impurity. Josiah's access to Bethel and, later in this chapter, to other northern sites probably reflects the decline of Assyrian power in the latter part of the seventh century B.C.E. It would appear that the Assyrians at this point had vacated much of the northern kingdom that it conquered in 721 B.C.E. and that Josiah attached these regimes to his own kingdom. Many scholars suspect that his campaign to establish the absolute exclusivity of the Jerusalem cult was at least in part an effort to consolidate his rule over the entire country, in effect reviving the united kingdom that existed in the era of Solomon.

5. *put down.* The Hebrew verb *hishbit*, literally, "put an end to," is a little ambiguous (hence the translation choice), but the slaughter of pagan priests reported in verse 20 suggests that the verb in this context may mean "to kill."

kings of Judah had set up to burn incense on the high places in the towns of Judah and in the environs of Jerusalem, and those burning incense to Baal and to the sun and to the moon and to the constellations and to all

6 the array of the heavens. And he took out the sacred pole from the house of the LORD outside of Jerusalem to the Kidron Wadi and burned it in the Kidron Wadi and ground it to dust and flung its ashes on the graves of

7 the common people. And he smashed the houses of the male cult-harlots that were within the house of the LORD where women would weave fabrics

8 for Asherah.And he brought all the priests from the towns of Judah and defiled the high places where the priests from Geba to Beersheba had been burning incense. And he smashed the high places of the gates that were at the entrance of the gate of Joshua commander of the town, which were

9 to a man's left at the town gate. Only, the priests of the high places would not go up to the LORD's altar in Jerusalem, but they ate flatbread in the

10 midst of their kinsmen. And he defiled the Topheth that was in the Valley of Hinnom, so that no man would pass his son or his daughter through

11 the fire to Molech. And he put down the horses that the kings of Judah would dedicate to the sun, from the entrance of the house of the LORD to the chamber of Nathan-Melech the eunuch, which is in the precincts. And

12 the chariots of the sun he burned in fire. And the altars that were on the

---

to Baal and to the sun and to the moon and to the constellations. The worship of the old Canaanite god Baal is joined with the later fashionable worship of the astral deities, probably under Assyrian influence.

6. *dust . . . ashes.* Two processes of destruction are involved here, grinding down and burning. The Hebrew terms *'afar* and *'efer* exhibit a degree of interchangeability.

  the graves of the common people. The context suggests a kind of potters' field, so that the casting of the ashes of the *'asherah* here would do further dishonor to it.

7. *fabrics for Asherah.* The Hebrew reads *batim*, "houses," probably a scribal error for *badim*, "fabrics," influenced by the appearance of "houses" at the beginning of this verse.

8. *the high places of the gates that were at the entrance of the gate of Joshua.* The Hebrew wording here is a little confusing and may reflect scribal scrambling of the text.

9. *Only, the priests of the high places would not go up to the LORD's altar . . . but they ate flatbread in the midst of their kinsmen.* These priests had officiated in the worship of YHWH on the high places. Their involvement in a cult located in an unauthorized place disqualifies them from serving in the Jerusalem temple, but they are nevertheless entitled to receive sustenance—the flatbread—with other members of the priestly caste in Jerusalem.

11. *And he put down the horses that the kings of Judah would dedicate to the sun.* Horses were associated with worship of the solar deity, probably because the Hebrews, like the Greeks, imagined the sun riding across the sky in a chariot. The verb translated as "dedicate" is literally "gave," and probably indicates sacrificing the horses to the sun—an especial abomination in Israelite eyes because the horse is an impure beast, prohibited as food.

roof of the Upper Chamber of Ahaz, which the kings of Judah had made, and the altars that Manasseh had made in the two courts of the house of the LORD, the king smashed, and he hurried off their dust from there and flung it into the Kidron Wadi. And the high places facing Jerusalem 13 that were to the right of the Mount of the Destroyer, which Solomon king of Israel had built for Ashtoreth foulness of the Sidonians and Chemosh foulness of Moab and Milcom abomination of the Ammonites—the king defiled. And he shattered the steles and cut down the sacred poles and 14 filled their place with human bones. And also the altar that was in Bethel, 15 the high place that Jeroboam son of Nebat had made, who had led Israel to offend, that altar, too, and the high places he smashed and burned the high place, grinding it to dust, and he burned the sacred pole. And Josiah 16 turned and saw the graves that were there on the mountain, and he sent and fetched the bones from the graves and burned them on the altar and defiled it, according to the word of the LORD that the man of God called out, who had called out these words. And he said, "What is that marker 17 which I see?" And the townspeople said to him, "It is the grave of the man of God who came from Judah, and who called out these things that you did on the Bethel altar." And he said, "Let him be. Let no man touch his 18 bones." And they rescued his bones, with the bones of the prophet who had come from Samaria. And the structures, too, of the high places that 19 were in the mountains of Samaria which the kings of Israel had made to vex, did Josiah remove, like all the acts that he had done in Bethel. And he 20 slaughtered all the priests of the high places who were there on the altars, and he burned human bones on them. And he went back to Jerusalem. And 21 the king charged all the people, saying, "Make a Passover to the LORD your

---

13. *the Mount of the Destroyer.* Many scholars infer that this designation, *har hamashḥit*, is a polemic distortion of *har hamishḥah*, the Mount of Anointment.

16. *fetched the bones from the graves.* Burning human bones on an altar would permanently defile it.

   according to the word of the LORD. What follows is the fulfillment of the prophecy of the man of God from Judah reported in 1 Kings 13.

18. *with the bones of the prophet who had come from Samaria.* In the story in 1 Kings 13, he is a prophet who comes to Bethel from Judah, and the reference to coming from Samaria, evidently triggered by the phrase "who came from Judah," is not in keeping with the original story (which in fact occurred before the building of Samaria).

21. *Make a Passover to the LORD your God, as it is written in this book of the covenant.* Passover was the great rite that affirmed national purpose and belonging to the nation (compare Joshua 1). Josiah suggests that the exacting stipulations for observing Passover are made fully clear only in the book found in the Temple.

22 God, as it is written in this book of the covenant. For it has not been done
    like this Passover from the days of the judges who judged Israel and all the
23 days of the kings of Israel and the kings of Judah." But in the eighteenth
24 year of King Josiah this Passover to the LORD was done in Jerusalem. And
    the ghosts, too, and the familiar spirits and the household gods and the
    foul idols and all the vile things that were seen in the land of Judah and in
    Jerusalem, Josiah rooted out, in order to fulfill the words of the teaching
    written in the book that Hilkiah the priest had found in the house of the
25 LORD. And like him there was no king before him who turned back to the
    LORD with all his heart and with all his being and with all his might accord-
26 ing to all the teaching of Moses, and after him none arose like him. Yet the
    LORD did not turn back from His great smoldering wrath, His wrath that
    had kindled against Judah, for all the vexations with which Manasseh had
27 vexed Him. And the LORD said, "Judah, too, will I remove from My pres-
    ence, as I removed Israel, and I will spurn this city Jerusalem that I chose,
28 and the house of which I said, Let My name be there." And the rest of the
    acts of Josiah and all that he did, are they not written in the Book of the Acts
29 of the Kings of Judah? In his days Pharaoh Neco king of Egypt had come
    up against the king of Assyria by the Euphrates River, and King Josiah sal-
    lied forth to meet him, and he put him to death at Megiddo when he saw
30 him. And his servants took him off dead on a chariot from Megiddo and

---

26. *Yet the LORD did not turn back from His great smoldering wrath.* The writer struggles
with a dilemma: Josiah is in his view the supremely virtuous king, and yet three generations
after him Judah is destroyed. The explanation offered is that because of the cumulative
offenses of the kings of Judah, with Manasseh the most egregious, Josiah's virtue cannot
save the nation.

29. *In his days Pharaoh Neco king of Egypt had come up.* This two-verse notice of Josiah's
death on the battlefield seems out of place, coming after the formulaic concluding statement about "the rest of the acts of Josiah." Perhaps it was tacked on at the end here because
it was a historical fact that had to be reported but with which the historian was uncomfortable, contradicting as it does both Huldah's prophecy and Josiah's exemplary virtue.

   against the king of Assyria. Something is awry here in regard to historical facts. We
know from Babylonian annals that it was against Babylonia that Pharaoh Neco led his
expeditionary force in 600 B.C.E., and Babylonia was aligned against Assyria, then in serious decline. Some scholars suggest reading "to," *'el*, instead of "against," *'al*.

   and King Josiah sallied forth to meet him. Though the geopolitics of the confrontation
at Megiddo may be a little obscure, it appears that Josiah sought to associate himself with
Babylonia and block Neco's passage to the east. In the event, he proved no match for the
Egyptians and was immediately killed.

brought him to Jerusalem and buried him in his grave. And the people of
the land took Jehoahaz son of Josiah and anointed him and made him king
in his father's stead. Twenty-three years old was Jehoahaz when he became 31
king, and three months he was king in Jerusalem, and his mother's name
was Hamutal daughter of Jeremiah from Libnah. And he did what was evil 32
in the eyes of the LORD as all that his fathers had done. And Pharaoh Neco 33
put him in bonds at Riblah in the land of Hamath, removing him as king in
Jerusalem, and he imposed a levy on the land of a hundred talents of silver
and talents of gold. And Pharaoh Neco made Eliakim, son of Josiah, king in 34
Josiah his father's stead, and changed his name to Jehoiakim. And he took
Jehoahaz and brought him to Egypt, and he died there. And Jehoiakim gave 35
the silver and the gold to Pharaoh, but he assessed the land so as to give the
silver according to Pharaoh's decree—every man according to his assessment, he wrested the silver and the gold from the people of the land to give
to Pharaoh Neco. Twenty-five years old was Jehoiakim when he became 36
king, and eleven years he was king in Jerusalem. And his mother's name
was Zebudah daughter of Pedaiah from Rumah. And he did what was evil 37
in the eyes of the LORD as all that his fathers had done.

CHAPTER 24   In his days Nebuchadnezzar king of Babylo- 1
nia came up, and Jehoiakim was his vassal for three years, and he turned

---

30. *And the people of the land took Jehoahaz ... and anointed him.* The action of ʿ*am*
haʾarets, "the people of the land," in this instance does make it look like a particular political force in the Judahite populace, capable of choosing kings.

33. *And Pharaoh Neco put him in bonds.* There were political divisions in Judah between
a pro-Babylonian party (with which Josiah would have been linked) and a pro-Egyptian
group. Neco, with commanding military force, saw to it that a pro-Egyptian king would
be set on the throne.
    in the land of Hamath. The location is northern Mesopotamia, conquered by the Egyp-
tian forces.
    he imposed a levy on the land. Neco has clearly reduced Judah to a vassal state.

34. *changed his name to Jehoiakim.* Name changing when someone assumed the throne
was fairly common in the ancient Near East. The two names in this case are essentially
the same name with different theophoric designations—ʾ*el* and *yeho* (which is the same
as *yah*/*Yahweh*).

35. *he wrested the silver and the gold.* The Hebrew verb has the connotation of extracting
by main force.

2 back and rebelled against him. And the LORD sent against him the Chaldean brigades and the Aramean brigades and the Moabite brigades and the Ammonite brigades, and He sent them against Judah to destroy it, according to the word of the LORD which He had spoken through his servants the
3 prophets. Only by the LORD's decree was this in Judah, to remove it from His presence for the offense of Manasseh, according to all that he had done.
4 And also for the innocent blood that he had shed and filled Jerusalem with
5 innocent blood. And the LORD did not want to forgive. And the rest of the acts of Jehoiakim and all that he did, are they not written in the Book of
6 the Acts of the Kings of Judah? And Jehoiakim lay with his fathers, and
7 Jehoiachin his son was king in his stead. And the king of Egypt no longer went out from his land, for the king of Babylonia had taken all that was the
8 king of Egypt's, from the Wadi of Egypt to the Euphrates River. Eighteen years old was Jehoiachin when he became king, and three months he was king in Jerusalem, and his mother's name was Nehushta daughter of Elna-
9 than from Jerusalem. And he did what was evil in the eyes of the LORD, as
10 all that his father had done. At that time the servants of Nebuchadnezzar king of Babylonia went up against Jerusalem, and the city came under siege.
11 And Nebuchadnezzar king of Babylonia came against the city, and his ser-
12 vants were besieging it. And Jehoiachin king of Judah went out to the king of Babylonia—he and his mother and his servants and his commanders and his eunuchs—and the king of Babylonia took him in the eighth year of his
13 reign. And he took out from there all the treasures of the house of the LORD and the treasures of the house of the king, and he cut up all the golden vessels that Solomon king of Israel had made in the temple of the LORD, as the

CHAPTER 24   2. *And the LORD sent against him.* According to the notion of historical causation promoted by the writer, all historical events are directly dictated by God. In point of fact, the sundry peoples of the trans-Jordan region mentioned here, all vassals to Babylonia, would have dispatched their troops against Judah at the behest of Nebuchadnezzar.

3. *was this in Judah.* The Hebrew preposition could also mean "against."

7. *And the king of Egypt no longer went out from his land.* Pharaoh Neco had sent a large expeditionary force against Babylonia in 609 B.C.E. that took up a position along the Euphrates. Now, a decade later, after the defeat at the battle of Carchemish, the Egyptians were compelled to retreat and remain within their own borders.

12. *he and his mother and his servants and his commanders and his eunuchs.* This retinue of notables, including not only military men but court officials and the queen mother, suggests that the king has come out in order to submit himself and those around him to Nebuchadnezzar.

LORD had spoken. And he exiled all Jerusalem and all the commanders and 14
all the valiant warriors, ten thousand exiles, and no artisan nor metalsmith
remained, only the poor people of the land. And he exiled Jehoiachin to 15
Babylonia, and the king's mother and the king's wives and his eunuchs and
the nobles of the land he led into exile to Babylonia. And all the fighting 16
men, seven thousand, and the artisans and the metalsmiths a thousand, all
of them battle-tested warriors. And the king of Babylonia brought them in
exile to Babylonia. And the king of Babylonia made Mattaniah his uncle 17
king in his stead, and he changed his name to Zedekiah. Twenty-one years 18
old was Zedekiah when he became king, and eleven years he was king in
Jerusalem, and his mother's name was Hamutal daughter of Jeremiah from
Libnah. And he did what was evil in the eyes of the LORD as all that Jehoia- 19
kim had done. For because of the LORD's wrath, it was against Jerusalem 20
and against Judah, till He flung them from His presence. And Zedekiah
rebelled against the king of Babylonia.

CHAPTER 25   And it happened in the ninth year of his reign, 1
in the tenth month, on the tenth of the month, that Nebuchadnezzar king
of Babylonia came—he and all his forces—against Jerusalem and camped
against it and built siege-towers all around it. And the city came under 2

---

14. *And he exiled all Jerusalem.* What this means is not the entire population but a substantial part of its elite and its skilled workers.

16. *all of them battle-tested warriors.* The syntactical position of this phrase is slightly confusing because it has to refer to the fighting men at the beginning of the sentence but not
to the artisans and eunuchs who come afterward.

20. *And Zedekiah rebelled against the king of Babylonia.* As usual, the writer provides no
political explanation—in this case, for the fact that Zedekiah, having been installed by
Nebuchadnezzar as vassal king, now decides to rebel. From the Book of Jeremiah, from
Ezekiel, and from extrabiblical sources, we know that there were sharp divisions within the
kingdom of Judah between a pro-Egyptian faction and a pro-Babylonian faction. Zedekiah
at this moment, counting on Egyptian support, joined an alliance of trans-Jordanian kingdoms plotting to overthrow Babylonian rule. In the event, Egypt did not provide support,
and the rebellion failed to materialize. The consequence was Nebuchadnezzar's assault on
Jerusalem and the destruction of the kingdom of Judah.

CHAPTER 25   1. *Nebuchadnezzar king of Babylonia came.* It appears that Nebuchadnezzar was so incensed by the betrayal on the part of his vassal king Zedekiah that
he personally led the siege against Jerusalem. At some point, however, before the actual
conquest of the city, he withdrew to a Mesopotamian outpost in Riblah (verse 5), leaving
the completion of the siege to his military deputy, Nebuzaradan (verse 9ff.).

3 siege till the twelfth year of King Zedekiah. On the ninth of the month
the famine was severe in the city and there was no bread for the people of
4 the land. *In the eleventh year of Zedekiah in the fourth month on the ninth
day* the city was breached. *And all the commanders of the king of Babylonia
came and sat in the central gate, Nergal-Sarezer, Samgar-Nebo, Sarsechim,
the chief eunuch, Nergal-Sarezer the chief magus, and all the rest of the
king of Babylonia's commanders. And it happened when Zedekiah saw them*
and all the men of war, *that they fled* by night through the gate between
the double walls which is by the king's garden, and the Chaldeans were
5 upon the city all around. And they went through the Arabah. And the
Chaldean force pursued the king and overtook him on the plain of Jeri-
6 cho, and all his force scattered from around him. And they seized the king
and brought him up to the king of Babylonia at Riblah and pronounced
7 judgment against him. And Zedekiah's sons they slaughtered before his
eyes, and Zedekiah's eyes they blinded, and they bound him in fetters and
8 brought him to Babylonia. And in the fifth month on the seventh of the
month, which was the nineteenth year of King Nebuchadnezzar, king of
Babylonia, Nebuzaradan the high chamberlain, servant of the king of Bab-
9 ylonia, came to Jerusalem. And he burned the house of the LORD and the
house of the king and all the houses of Jerusalem, and every great house

---

3. *bread.* As elsewhere, this word is probably a synecdoche for food in general.

4. *In the eleventh year of Zedekiah.* The text at this point is clearly defective, exhibiting a
subject ("all the men of war") with no predicate and lacking some narrative information.
The entire passage is replicated in Jeremiah 39, and so the translation incorporates, italicized, elements from the text in Jeremiah.

   Nergal-Sarezer. This name occurs twice here (as well as in the corresponding list in
Jeremiah), which must be a scribal duplication.

6. *pronounced judgment against him.* This would scarcely have been a proper trial but summary judgment of a vassal king who had proved himself a traitor.

7. *And Zedekiah's sons they slaughtered before his eyes.* In a pointed device of ancient Near
Eastern barbarity, the last thing he is made to see before they blind him is the slaughter
of his sons. The act is political as well as sadistic: no one is left in the line of Zedekiah to
claim the throne after him.

8. *the high chamberlain.* This is the same title attached to Potiphar in Genesis 39:1. The
Hebrew *sar hatabahim* literally means "commander of the slaughter" ("slaughter" in the
culinary sense). The title might have originally designated a head steward or chef, but it
clearly came to mean someone exercising high authority in the political and military realm.

9. *every great house.* These are the houses of the nobility, as the Aramaic translation, *batey
revavaia*, properly registers.

he burned in fire. And the wall of Jerusalem all around did the Chaldean   10
force that was the high chamberlain's shatter. And the rest of the people   11
remaining in the city and the turncoats who had gone over to the king of
Babylonia and the rest of the masses, Nebuzaradan the high chamberlain
exiled. And of the poorest of the land the high chamberlain left to be vine-   12
dressers and field workers. And the bronze pillars that were in the house   13
of the LORD and the stands and the bronze sea that was in the house of the
LORD the Chaldeans smashed and bore off their bronze to Babylonia. And   14
the pails and the scrapers and the snuffers and the ladles and all the bronze
vessels with which one ministered they took. And the fire-pans and the   15
sprinkling bowls, whatever was of gold and whatever was of silver, the high
chamberlain took. The two pillars, the one sea, the stands that Solomon had   16
for the house of the LORD—all these vessels were beyond measure. Eighteen   17
cubits was the height of one pillar with a bronze capital on its top, and the
height of the capital was three cubits, and there were pomegranates on the

---

10. *And the wall of Jerusalem . . . did the Chaldean force . . . shatter.* Destroying the wall
rendered the city totally indefensible, eradicating any possibility that it could continue to
be the capital of an independent state.

11. *the turncoats.* Literally, "those who fell." One should recall that there was a strong group
among the Judahites (including Jeremiah) who thought that the rebellion against Babylonia
was greatly ill advised, and so it is not surprising that some of these should defect to the
Babylonians.
    the masses. The Hebrew *hamon*, which in biblical usage generally refers to a loud
hubbub, may be doubtful. The parallel passage in Jeremiah 52:15 shows *ha'amon*, a collective noun for artisans, and that looks like the more likely reading.

12. *And of the poorest of the land.* The impression given here that only the poor agricultural
workers were spared the fate of exile is probably misleading. Although the Babylonians
appear to have exiled a large part of the nation's elite, both Gedaliah, who is appointed
regent by the Babylonians, and the conspirators who kill him are from the nobility. The
burial center at Katef-Hinnom, in western Jerusalem, which contains epigraphic and other
evidence of having been in continuous use through the sixth century B.C.E., was clearly a
burial place for Judahite aristocracy.

13. *And the bronze pillars.* It was common procedure in conquests to cart off the temple
treasures of the conquered. At the same time, this catalogue of precious sacred vessels
seized by the Babylonians reverses everything reported in 1 Kings 6–7 about the splendid
furnishings for the Temple and the palace that Solomon caused to be fashioned. Everything
that the grand first king after David built or made is either reduced to rubble or taken off
by the enemy,
    the bronze sea. This is a large cast-metal pool, mentioned in 1 Kings 7:23 and elsewhere.

16. *beyond measure.* More literally, "beyond weighing."

capital all around of bronze, and like these was the second pillar with the
18 meshwork. And the high chamberlain took Seraiah the head priest and
19 Zephaniah the assistant priest and the three guards of the threshold. And
from the city he took one eunuch who was the official over the men of war
and five men of those who attended in the king's presence and the scribe
of the army commander who mustered the people of the land, and sixty
20 men from the people of the land who were in the town. And Nebuzaradan
the high chamberlain took them and led them to the king of Babylonia at
21 Riblah. And the king of Babylonia struck them down and put them to death
22 in Riblah in the land of Hamath. And he exiled Judah from its land. And as
to the people remaining in the land of Judah whom Nebuchadnezzar king
of Babylonia had left, he appointed over them Gedaliah son of Ahikam
23 son of Shaphan. And all the commanders of the forces, they and the men,
heard that the king of Babylonia had appointed Gedaliah, and they came
to Gedaliah at Mizpah—Ishmael son of Nethaniah and Johanan son of
Kareah and Seraiah son of Tanhumeth the Netophahthite, and Jaazaniah
24 son of the Maachite, they and their men. And Gedaliah swore to them and
to their men and said to them, "Do not be afraid to serve the Chaldeans.
Stay in the land and serve the king of Babylonia, that it may go well with
25 you." And it happened in the seventh month that Ishmael son of Nethaniah
son of Elishama of the royal seed, and ten men with him, came and struck
down Gedaliah, and he died, as well as the Judahites and the Chaldeans

18. *And the high chamberlain took Seraiah the head priest and Zephaniah the assistant priest.* The obvious intention is to prevent a renewal of the cult in Jerusalem. The usual term for high priest (in the Hebrew, "great priest") is not used but rather "head priest," *kohen haro'sh.*

21. *And the king of Babylonia struck them down and put them to death.* No Geneva convention obtains for these ancient prisoners of war, and since they constitute the nation's military and sacerdotal elite, Nebuchadnezzar wants to eliminate them entirely,

24. *Do not be afraid to serve the Chaldeans.* Gedaliah is obviously a member of the pro-Babylonian faction among the Judahites who assumed that military resistance was not feasible and that cooperation would lead to kind treatment by the Babylonians. The men who come to see him clearly belong to the opposing faction, and they regard Gedaliah as a quisling and thus proceed to kill him.

25. *of the royal seed.* He may well have hoped to claim the throne after the death of Gedaliah.
    as well as the Judahites and the Chaldeans who were with him in Mizpah. These killings are a mark of their ruthlessness and of their thoroughness as insurgents. They murder all of Gedaliah's attendants and staff as vile collaborators, and they also kill the Chaldeans stationed with him, perhaps to eliminate them as witnesses and certainly as an act of defiance against the conquerors.

who were with him in Mizpah. And all the people arose, from the least to 26
the greatest, and the commanders of the forces, and they went to Egypt, for
they feared the Chaldeans.

And it happened in the twenty-seventh year of the exile of Jehoiachin 27
king of Judah in the twelfth month, on the twenty-seventh of the month,
that Evil-Merodach king of Babylonia, in the year he became king, lifted
up the head of Jehoiachin king of Judah from the prison-house. And he 28
spoke kindly to him and gave him a throne above the thrones of the kings
who were with him in Babylonia. And he changed his prison garments, and 29
Jehoiachin ate bread perpetually in his presence all the days of his life. And 30
his provision was a perpetual provision given him by the king day after day,
all the days of his life.

---

26. *And all the people arose, from the least to the greatest.* This is again a patent exaggeration: the historical evidence argues strongly against the notion that the entire country was emptied of its Judahite population. The logic of the flight to Egypt is that the Egyptians were the adversaries of Babylonia and the allies of the anti-Babylonian faction.

27. *Evil-Merodach.* He assumed the throne of Babylonia in 562 B.C.E. Granting pardons when one becomes king was a common ancient Near Eastern practice. Jehoiachin was taken into captivity in 597. His quarter century as prisoner may actually have been a form of house arrest because a Babylonian document from 592 records the provision of food for Jehoiachin king of Judah and his five sons, suggesting that some recognition of his royal status was accorded all along.

    lifted up the head. This is the same idiom, intimating pardon, that is used for the imprisoned chief steward in the Joseph story (Genesis 40:13).

28. *gave him a throne above the thrones of the kings who were with him.* This is probably a nationalistic flourish of the writer's because it is unlikely that Jehoiachin would have been granted a higher status than other kings held in Babylonian captivity.

29. *And he changed his prison garments.* This detail is probably a deliberate reminiscence of the Joseph story: when Joseph is freed from prison, he is clothed by Pharaoh in fine garments.

    Jehoiachin. The Hebrew says merely "he," and the proper name has been added in order to avoid confusion of pronominal reference.

30. *And his provision was a perpetual provision . . . day after day.* The historical event with which the Book of Kings ends is of course a complete catastrophe—the utter destruction of Jerusalem, including Temple and palace; the massacre of the royal line and the military and priestly elite; and the exile of a large part of the population. This concluding image, however, seeks to intimate a hopeful possibility of future restoration: a Davidic king is recognized as king, even in captivity, and is given a daily provision appropriate to his royal status. As he sits on his throne elevated above the thrones of the other captive kings, the audience of the story is invited to imagine a scion of David again sitting on his throne in Jerusalem.

ISAIAH

∎ ∎ ∎

Introduction

The Book of Isaiah may well be the greatest challenge that modern readers will find in the biblical corpus to their notions of what constitutes a book. Isaiah son of Amoz, a Jerusalemite, began his career as prophet in the 730s B.C.E. He was still active and clearly regarded as an authoritative figure, as we learn from the account in 2 Kings 19, borrowed by the editor of our text, when the Assyrians besieged Jerusalem in 701 B.C.E. Like the other biblical prophets, he claimed, and very likely believed, that his pronouncements came to him on the direct authority of God. These included vehement castigations of social and economic injustices in Judahite society and of a corrupt and drunken ruling class, as well as the excoriation of paganizing practices. Isaiah also took political stances, objecting in particular to policies that favored an alliance with Egypt against Assyria.

The bewildering fact is that the prophecies of Isaiah son of Amoz have been editorially mingled with a welter of prophecies by other hands and from later periods. In an era millennia before printing and the concept of authorial claim to texts, all the books of the Bible are open-ended affairs, scrolls in which could be inserted, whether for ideological purposes or simply through editorial predilection, writings that came from other sources—as, for example, the Book of Job includes the Hymn to Wisdom (chapter 28) and the Elihu speeches (chapters 32–37), each exhibiting a different viewpoint and a different kind of poetry from the original book. But Isaiah is an extreme case of this phenomenon. One may surmise that texts of individual prophecies, or small clusters of his prophecies, circulated in scrolls during Isaiah's lifetime and afterward, whether in the hands of his followers or of private collectors of prophetic revelation. Chapters 1–39 in the book that has come down to us incorporate the prophecies of Isaiah but also include much disparate material that is clearly later, some of it reflecting the imminent or actual fall of the Babylonian empire to the Persians in 539 B.C.E. Nothing from chapter 40 to the end of the book is the work of Isaiah son of Amoz. The strong scholarly consensus is that chapters 40–55 were composed by a prophet of the Babylonian exile, whose name is beyond recovery, prophesying a triumphant return of the exiles to Zion through the agency of the Persian emperor Cyrus (mentioned by name), who was poised to overwhelm the Babylonians. Even in this unit, however, it is far from clear that all the prophecies are from the same person. The so-called Second Isaiah is followed by a Third Isaiah in what is now the last eleven chapters of the book. The situation presupposed in these chapters is the predicament of the community in the Persian province of Yehud, or Judah, after the rebuilding of the Temple, so the historical setting would have to be the fifth century B.C.E., although probably before the decisive mission of Ezra and Nehemiah in the middle of that century. Especially in the texts grouped together as Trito-Isaiah, or Third Isaiah, scholars have detected the presence of several different writers rather than a single prophet. The claim that Third Isaiah is a disciple of Second Isaiah may be questioned because they are too far removed from each other in time—perhaps by as much as three generations. What can be safely said is that the later prophet was familiar with the poetry of his predecessor and consciously alluded to it, sometimes pointedly elaborating its imagery, just as both these prophets were familiar with and sometimes built on the prophecies of Isaiah son of Amoz.

It is above all the vehicle of poetry in all these prophets that demands close attention. While there are occasional brief prose passages, the bulk of the prophecies are cast in poetry. There are two reasons for the use of poetry, one theological and the other pragmatic. In most of these texts, the prophet represents himself as the mouthpiece for God's words—"thus said the LORD" is the frequently invoked "messenger-formula" of introduction—and it is perfectly fitting that God should address Israel not in prose, which is closer to the language of everyday human intercourse, but in the elevated and impressive diction of poetry. The more pragmatic reason for the use of verse is that, as in all poetic systems, poetry is memorable in the technical sense: its formal devices facilitate committing the words to memory. In the case of biblical poetry, this mnemonic function is realized chiefly through the structuring of the line in semantically paired halves, or versets, usually reinforced by an equal number of stressed syllables in each half of the line: "Woe, offending nation, / people weighed down with crime" (1:4). Once the first half of this line has been registered in memory, the second half readily follows, with the more compact Hebrew exhibiting three strong stresses in each of the two halves. And as usually is the case in lines of biblical poetry, the idea articulated in the first verset is driven home through a concretization of it in the second verset: the "offending nation" is realized *physically* as a "people weighed down with crime" (in the Hebrew, just three words, five syllables, *'am keved 'awon*).

The poets assembled in this book are a good deal more than didactic versifiers of religious or ethical principles. To be sure, one encounters some stretches of boilerplate verse: Prophetic poetry, like other poetic genres, has its recurrent formulas and clichés. Nevertheless, this collection exhibits the work of at least three poets of the first order of originality, perhaps even more, depending on how one attributes authorship to certain individual poems.

Thus, the pounding rhythms and the powerful images of the book's opening poem (1:2–9) convey a riveting vision of Judah devastated by Assyrian incursion as divine punishment for its collective crimes. The trope of Israel as a second Sodom comes to seem through the poetry as a palpably realized historical fact. The relatively long poem in chapter 2 that runs from verse 6 to the end of the chapter evokes a scary picture of the day when God comes to exact retribution, playing on a complex series of images of verticality in which all that is high will be brought low and God alone will loom on high. In counterpoint to such dire visions stand the luminous imaginings of an ideal age to come when the land will be governed in peace and justice and the nations will come to Zion to be instructed in the ways of God (2:2–5, 4:2–6, 9:1–6, 11:11–16, to cite the most famous of such passages). Second Isaiah preserves the memory of these glowing prophecies, but his poetry recasts the vision of a grand future in more national and historical terms, conjuring up a landscape in which a highway is cleared in the wilderness for the triumphant passage of the exiles back to their land. He is the most tender of biblical poets, tracing images of nursing mothers and dandled babes (upon which Third Isaiah will elaborate) and appropriately beginning his prophecies with the words "Comfort, O comfort My people."

All three of the principal poets in the Isaian corpus exhibit a good deal of technical virtuosity, and, of course, this will often not be visible in translation. Isaiah son of Amoz is particularly adept in thematically pointed wordplay. Thus, the scathing conclusion of the Parable of the Vineyard (5:7), has "justice," *mishpat*, flipped into *mispah*, "blight," and "righteousness," *tsedaqah,* into *tseʿaqah,* "scream," to express the perversion of values by the Judahites. The approximation of this effect in the present translation reads as follows: "He hoped for justice, and, look, jaundice, / for righteousness, and, look, wretchedness." Other plays on words resist even approximation in English. More pervasively, in all of the Isaian poets, the expressive power of the line of biblical poetry, in which the second verset concretizes, intensifies, or focuses what is expressed in the first, is exploited with great resourcefulness.

Here is a line that evokes the day of divine retribution (13:9): "Look, the LORD's day comes, ruthlessly, / *anger and smoldering wrath* [emphasis added]," in which the second verset makes vividly clear what is meant by the general notion of "the LORD's day" introduced in the first verset. One sees a related but different deployment of poetic parallelism in 26:17: "As a woman with child draws near to give birth, / *she shudders, she shakes in her pangs* [emphasis added]." Here, as often happens in biblical poetry, there is narrative development as well as intensification in the move from the first verset to the second: first the woman has come to the end of pregnancy, perhaps experiencing the early signs of labor; then she writhes in the throes of the birth pangs.

Surely these prophecies continue to speak to us because of the ethical imperatives they embody, their cries for social justice, their hopeful visions of a future of harmony after all the anguish inflicted through historical violence. But they also engage us through the power and splendor of the poetry. Perhaps the Israelites who clung to the parchment records of these sundry prophecies in the seventh and sixth centuries B.C.E. cherished them not only because they saw in them the urgent word of God but also because they somehow sensed that these were great poems.

CHAPTER 1

The vision of Isaiah son of Amoz that he saw 1 concerning Judah and Jerusalem in the days of Uzziah, Jotham, Ahaz, Hezekiah, kings of Judah.

> Hear, O heavens, and give ear, O earth,   2
>   for the LORD has spoken.
> Sons I have nurtured and raised
>   but they rebelled against Me.
> The ox knows its owner   3
>   and the donkey its master's stall.
> Israel did not know,
>   my people did not pay heed.
> Woe, offending nation,   4
>   people weighed down with crime,
> seed of evildoers,
>   sons acting ruinously.
> They have forsaken the LORD,

CHAPTER 1   1. *The vision of Isaiah.* The true beginning of Isaiah's prophecies is chapter 6, the visionary scene in the Temple where he is first commissioned as a prophet. The prophecy that immediately follows here may have been set at the beginning of the book by its editors because of the invocation of heaven and earth as the formal beginning of a long poem—compare Deuteronomy 32, the Song of Moses, which begins with similar language.

3. *the donkey its master's stall.* This line is a neat illustration of the pattern of focusing or concretization in the movement from the first verset to the second in biblical poetry. The first verset puts forth the general relation of beast to owner; the second verset (with metrical room for an additional word in the parallelism because the verb "knows" does double duty for both halves of the line and need not be repeated) then focuses on the place of nurture connecting beast and master.

4. *Woe, offending nation.* The Hebrew for this verset has a pounding rhythmic insistence, three words, four syllables, three stresses, reinforced by an internal rhyme at the beginning: *hoy goy hotei'.*

scorned Israel's Holy One,
  they have fallen behind.
5 Why would you be beaten more,
  still swerving from the way?
Every head is sick
  and every heart in pain.
6 From footsole to head
  no place in him intact,
wound, bruise,
  and open sore—
not drained, not bandaged,
  nor soothed with oil.
7 Your land is desolate,
  your towns are burned in fire.
Your soil, before your eyes
  strangers devour it,
    and desolation like an upheaval by strangers.
8 And the daughter of Zion remains
  like a hut in a vineyard,
like a shed in a patch of greens,
  like a town besieged.
9 Had not the LORD of Armies
  left us a scant remnant,
we would be like Sodom.
  We would resemble Gomorrah.

10 Listen to the word of the LORD,
  O leaders of Sodom,
give ear to our God's teaching,

---

5. *beaten.* The people has been suffering blows from its enemies as punishment for its evil ways (see verses 7–9), in which, however, it stubbornly persists.

7. *upheaval.* This word, strongly associated in Genesis with the destruction of Sodom, is the first hint of the equation between Israel and Sodom.

8. *like a town besieged.* This last verset of the two-line parallelism switches from the agricultural metaphors to the referent of the metaphors—a town encircled by enemies. This verse and the two preceding ones probably refer to the devastation wreaked by the Assyrian invading forces in 701 B.C.E.

10. *O leaders of Sodom.* This appears to be the beginning of a new prophecy, with the reference to Sodom at the end of the previous passage and at the beginning of this one providing an associative link between the two.

O people of Gomorrah.
"Why need I all your sacrifices?"   11
  says the LORD.
"I am sated with the burnt offerings of rams
  and the suet of fatted beasts,
and the blood of bulls and sheep and he-goats
  I do not desire.
When you come to see My face,   12
  who asked this of you,
    to trample My courts?
You shall no longer bring false grain offering,   13
  it is incense of abomination to me.
New moon and sabbath call an assembly—
  I cannot bear crime and convocation.
Your new moons and your appointed times   14
  I utterly despise.
They have become a burden to me,
  I cannot bear them.
And when you spread your palms,   15
  I avert My eyes from you.
Though you abundantly pray,
  I do not listen.
    Your hands are full of blood.

---

11. *Why need I all your sacrifices?* This is not a pitch for the abolition of sacrifice but rather an argument against a mechanistic notion of sacrifice, against the idea that sacrifice can put man in good standing with God regardless of human behavior. The point becomes entirely clear at the end of verse 15, when the prophet says that it is hands stained with blood stretched out in payer that are utterly abhorrent to God. Thus, the grain offering is "false" (or "futile") because it is brought by people who have oppressed the poor and failed to defend widows and orphans.

12. *to see My face.* As throughout the Masoretic Text, the verb for seeing the face of God—the original conception of the pilgrimage to the Jerusalem temple—has been piously revocalized as a passive form, "to be seen."

13. *crime and convocation.* The translation emulates the approximate alliteration in the Hebrew of *'awen we'atsarah.*

14. *I utterly despise.* The Hebrew uses *nafshi* in what amounts to an intensive form of the first-person pronoun. This translation tries to suggest this intensity by adding the adverb "utterly."

15. *Your hands are full of blood.* This shocking detail is held back until the end of these two lines of poetry: the palms lifted up in prayer are covered with blood, and that is why God averts His eyes, because He can't bear looking at them. It should be noted that Isaiah's

16   Wash, become pure,
                     Remove your evil acts from My eyes.
                     Cease doing evil.

17   Learn to do good,
                     seek justice.
                  Make the oppressed happy,
                     defend the orphan,
                        argue the widow's case."

18   "Come, pray, let us come to terms,"
                     the Lord said.
                  "If your offenses be like scarlet,
                     like snow shall they turn white.
                  If they be red as dyed cloth,
                     they shall become like pure wool.

19   If you assent and listen,
                     the land's bounty you shall eat.

20   But if you refuse and rebel,
                     by the sword you shall be eaten,
                       for the Lord's mouth has spoken."

21   How has the faithful town
                     become a whore?
                  Filled with justice,

---

outrage, as it is spelled out in verse 17, is not chiefly with cultic disloyalty, as it would be for the writers in the school of Deuteronomy, but with social injustice—indifference to the plight of the poor and the helpless, exploitation of the vulnerable, acts represented here as the moral equivalent of murder.

18. *scarlet . . . white.* Although this appears to be part of a new prophecy, the scarlet picks up the image of bloodstained hands from verse 15, and that could be the reason for the editorial placement of this prophecy here.

    pure wool. "Pure" is merely implied in the Hebrew and has been added in the translation to exclude the possibility of dyed wool.

20. *by the sword you shall be eaten.* Though "devoured" might be more appropriate for the context, the translation preserves the pointed reversal in the Hebrew of eating the bounty of the land and being eaten by the sword. In biblical usage, the cutting edge of the sword is often referred to as a mouth, and thus the sword is said to devour or eat its victims.

21. *How has the faithful town / become a whore?* This prophecy begins with *'eikhah*, the word that conventionally starts lamentations or dirges. The prophet sees it as a reason to lament that the once just town has become a place where justice is perverted.

where righteousness did lodge,
and now—murderers.
Your silver has turned to dross,   22
your drink is mixed with water.
Your nobles are knaves   23
and companions to thieves.
All of them lust for bribes
and chase illicit payments.
They do not defend the orphan,
and the widow's case does not touch them.
Therefore, says the Master, Lord of Armies, Israel's Mighty One: 24
Oh, I will settle scores with my foes
and take vengeance of my enemies,
and bring My hand back upon you   25
and take away all your dross
and bring back your judges as before   26
and your councillors as long ago.
Then shall you be called town of righteousness,
faithful city.

---

and now—murderers. As with the hands full of blood in verse 15, the shocking detail is reserved for the end.

23. *Your nobles are knaves.* The alliteration in the translation seeks to be an approximate equivalent of the fuller sound-play of the Hebrew, *sarayikh sorerim.* The point of the sound-play is that something turns into its opposite in a move from one word to an antithetical one that sounds like the first.

illicit payments. The unusual word *shalmonim* clearly means "illegitimate payments." "Payoff" in English might be an equivalent, but it is too colloquial for this poem, so the translation adds "illicit."

24. *Therefore, says the Master, Lord of Armies.* As is often the case in the poetry of the prophets, the clause for introducing divine speech is extrametrical and not strictly part of the poem.

settle scores. The verb *hinahem* usually means "to change one's mind" or "to regret" and can also mean "to be consoled." It is quite close phonetically to *hinaqem,* "to be avenged," which appears in the second verset, and the poet seems to have pushed the term here to mean something close to "vengeance."

my foes . . . my enemies. These terms commonly refer to the enemies of the people of Israel, but in a sharp polemic reversal, here they are addressed to the Israelites themselves, who through their perversion of justice have made themselves God's enemies.

26. *Then shall you be called town of righteousness, / faithful city.* This line obviously loops back to the opening line of this prophecy, verse 21, where the faithful city once filled with righteousness has become a den of murderers.

27   Zion shall be redeemed through justice,
            and those who turn back in her, through righteousness.
28   But the rebels and offenders together are shattered,
            and those who forsake the Lord shall perish.

29   For they shall be shamed of the cult-trees
            after which you lusted,
                and be disgraced by the gardens that you have chosen.
30   For you shall be like an oak
            whose leaf withers
                and like a garden where there is no water.
31   And the strong shall turn into tow
            and his deeds into a spark,
        and both shall burn together,
            with none to put it out.

1 CHAPTER 2   The word that Isaiah son of Amoz saw in a vision
concerning Judah and Jerusalem.

2   And it shall happen in future days
            that the mount of the Lord's house shall be firm-founded

---

29. *the cult-trees.* The botanical genus stipulated by the Hebrew term is "terebinths." Pagan
nature worship centering around sacred trees was widespread in Canaan. This is the first
time that Isaiah inveighs against cultic rather than moral trespasses.

    the gardens. This word, though it usually refers to gardens in an innocuously horticul-
tural sense, in the present context palpably invokes the sacred gardens that were the site
of pagan cults.

30. *oak . . . garden.* The poem picks up the tree and garden from the preceding line and turns
them into metaphors of the dire end to which the miscreants will come.

31. *the strong.* Even though some interpreters understand this as "the treasure," the antithesis between strength and flimsy combustible tow makes good poetic sense, and there is
philological warrant for construing *hason* as "strong."

    his deeds into a spark. The image is a shrewd one: the reprehensible act of the paganizer
is self-destructive, providing the spark that will destroy him.

CHAPTER 2   2. *in future days.* Older translations represent this Hebrew phrase as
"in the end of days," giving it an emphatically eschatological meaning it does not have.
The Hebrew *'aharit,* derived from the word that means "after," refers to an indefinite time
after the present.

    the mount of the Lord's house. Mount Zion in Jerusalem is here imagined as a kind of
second Sinai, from which God's teaching will go out.

at the top of the mountains and lifted over the hills.
And all the nations shall flow to it
    and many peoples shall go, and say: 3
Come, let us go up to the mount of the LORD,
    to the house of Jacob's God,
that He may teach us of His ways
    and that we may walk in His paths.
For from Zion shall teaching come forth
    and the LORD's word from Jerusalem.
And He shall judge among the nations   4
    and be arbiter for many peoples.
And they shall grind their swords into plowshares
    and their spears into pruning hooks.
Nation shall not raise sword against nation
    nor shall they learn war anymore.
O house of Jacob,   5
    come, let us walk in the LORD's light.

For you have abandoned your people,   6
    O house of Jacob.
For they are full of eastern things
    and soothsayers like the Philistines,
        and they abound in children of strangers.

---

all the nations. The universalist note struck here is new. It will be elaborated and expanded in the visions of the anonymous prophet of the Babylonian exile whose writing is appended to the Book of Isaiah, beginning with chapter 40. Some interpreters detect sixth-century B.C.E. themes throughout this prophecy.

4. *Nation shall not raise sword against nation.* God's teaching from Zion, then, is to have the effect of inaugurating a reign of universal peace. There is an imaginative boldness, or perhaps rather the courage of desperation, in this vision because Isaiah articulated it at a historical moment of continual warfare among imperial powers when the land of Israel itself, as 1:7–9 shows, was threatened with destruction by invading armies.

    learn war. Fighting was a skill that required training, as noted in Psalms and elsewhere.

6. *For you have abandoned your people.* These words clearly signal the beginning of a new prophecy, one of castigation, after the utopian vision of verses 2–5. Abandoning the people means something like abandoning its own vital interests or precious values.

    For they are full of eastern things. More literally, "they are full of the east." There is no reason to emend this, as some have proposed, to "full of sorcerers [*qosmim*] from the east" because poetry can surely deploy ellipsis.

    and they abound in children of strangers. This clause is unclear, and the meaning of the verb is especially uncertain. Some notion of adopting foreign ways (the eastern things, the Philistines) would appear to be implied.

7   And his land is filled with silver and gold
                     and no end to his treasures,
              and his land is filled with houses
                     and no end to his chariots.

8   And his land is filled with idols
                     to his handiwork he bows down,
                         to what his fingers made.

9   And the human shall bow low,
                     and man shall be brought down.
                         And do not spare them!

10   Come into the crag
                     and hide in the dust
              for the fear of the LORD
                     and from His pride's glory.

11   The eyes of human haughtiness are brought down,
                     and men's righteousness is bowed low,
              and the LORD alone shall be raised high
                     on that day.

12   For it is a day of the LORD of Armies,
                     over all the proud and lofty
                         and over all on high and lifted up.

13   And over all the Lebanon cedars
                     that are lofty and raised high

---

7. *silver and gold.* From divining and magic, the poet moves on to the accumulation of wealth and luxury items, which he sees as the royal road to idolatry (verse 8).

9. *shall bow low.* Although the sense is to be humbled, the Hebrew makes a point of using the same verb that expressed idolatry in the previous verse. This relatively long poem, running to the end of the chapter, is elaborately structured through a series of images of high things brought low and God's commanding height over all the earth. The poem makes use not only of repeated images but also of refrainlike devices.

10. *Come into the crag / and hide in the dust.* The landscape envisaged is harsh and pitiless: no forests or gardens or towns but dust and rocks, which offer terrified man inhospitable and inadequate shelter against God's wrath.

12. *lifted up.* This emends the Masoretic "lowly," which doesn't seem plausible. This whole clause is repeated as a refrain in verse 17, underscoring the high-low theme of the entire poem.

13. *the Lebanon cedars.* Throughout biblical poetry, the great cedars of Lebanon are iconic images of loftiness.

> and over all the Bashan oaks,
> and over all the lofty mountains   14
>   and over all the raised-up mountains,
> and over every looming tower   15
>   and over every fortress wall,
> and over all the Tarshish ships   16
>   and over all lovely crafts.
> And human haughtiness shall bow low   17
>   and men's loftiness be brought down,
> and the LORD alone shall be exalted
>   on that day.
> And the ungods shall utterly vanish.   18
> And they shall come into caves in the crags   19
>   and into hollows in the dust
> from the fear of the LORD
>   and from His pride's glory
>   when He rises to wreak havoc on earth.
> On that day man shall fling away   20
> his silver idols and his golden idols

---

over all. The anaphora of "over all," *'al kol,* becomes a terrific drum-beat, making a crescendo that begins in verse 12 and runs on through verse 16, all a single sentence.

15. *fortress wall.* More literally, "fortified wall."

16. *Tarshish ships.* Tarshish is an undetermined port on the Mediterranean far to the west. But the mention in the Book of Kings of Tarshish ships plying the Red Sea suggests that it may also be a term for a kind of craft constructed for long voyages.

lovely crafts. The translation follows a scholarly proposal for the noun *sekhiyot,* but its meaning is obscure, and the conclusion about what it might be is dictated chiefly by the poetic parallelism.

18. *And the ungods shall utterly vanish.* This brief sentence looks like an orphan—a verset without a paired second verset, which might have somehow been dropped in scribal transmission. Nevertheless, it contains a nice poetic effect in the internal rhyme of *'elilim,* "ungods," immediately followed by *kalil,* "utterly."

19. *caves in the crags . . . hollows in the dust.* The crag/dust parallelism as places of hiding in verse 10 is further concretized here by the addition of caves and hollows, helping us imagine the pitiful plight of the people who attempt to flee, crawling into crevices in rocks and in the ground. This miserable effort at hiding somewhere down below is the culmination of the bringing-low of man that defines the entire prophecy.

to wreak havoc. The Hebrew verb used here, and again in the refrain at the end of verse 21, is strong and violent. It suggests terrorizing and it is related phonetically to a verbal stem that means "to smash."

             that he made to bow before
                to the hedgehogs and the bats.
21   And they shall come into the crevices in the crags
                and into the clefts in the rocks
             from the fear of the Lord
                and from His pride's glory
                   when He rises to wreak havoc on earth.
22   Leave off from man,
                who has breath in his nostrils.
                   For of what account is he?

CHAPTER 3

1   For, look, the Master, Lord of Armies,
                is about to take away from Jerusalem and from Judah
             staff and stay,
                every staff of bread
                  and every staff of water,
2   warrior and fighting man,
                judge and prophet and wizard and elder,
3   commander of fifty and notable
                and councillor and craftsman and caster of spells.
4   And I shall make lads their commanders
                and babes shall rule them.

---

20. *to the hedgehogs and the bats.* The idolators themselves have fled to the bleak wilderness. Now they throw away their precious idols to creatures of the wilderness, though the precise identity of the first of these is uncertain.

22. *Leave off from man, / who has breath in his nostrils.* One might have expected, given the previous emphasis of this prophecy something like: leave off from your idols, / for they are insensate things. The point, however, is that idolatry, worshipping what man makes with his own hands, is itself an expression of human arrogance, man's assuming he can lift himself high, like his towers and battlements, through his own acts and artifacts. (One wonders whether the Tower of Babel may stand in the background of this poem.) The mention of the breath in the nostrils invokes the intrinsic fragility of human life: man is a vulnerable, ephemeral creature, his life-breath easily stopped in a moment, so how could one put trust in him?

CHAPTER 3   4. *I shall make lads their commanders.* In the political chaos that God will trigger, with all the leaders taken away (verses 1–3), mere lads and babes will be left to lead the people.

And the people shall oversee each other,   5
    one man and his fellow.
The lad shall lord it over the elder,
    and the worthless over the honored.
Should a man take hold of his brother   6
    in his father's house:
"You have a cloak. You shall be our captain
    and this stumbling block under your hand."
He shall speak out on that day, saying,   7
    "I will be no dresser of wounds
        when there is no bread nor cloak in my house.
            You shall not make me the people's captain."
For Jerusalem has stumbled   8
    and Judah has fallen.
For their tongue and their acts are against the LORD
    to defy His glorious gaze.
The look of their face bears witness against them,   9
    and their offense is like Sodom.
        They have told it, they did not hide it.
Alas for them,
    for they have paid themselves back with evil.
One says: it is good for the righteous,   10
    for the fruit of his deeds he enjoys.
Alas, for the wicked, there is evil,   11
    for as his hands have done, it will be done to him.
My people's overseers are babes,   12
    and women rule over them.
My people, those who guide you mislead you
    and the course of your paths they confound.
The LORD is stationed to plead in court,   13
    and stands to judge peoples.

---

6. *this stumbling block under your hand.* There might be a distant play on words between *makhshelah*, "stumbling block," and *memshalah*, "government." In the general state of political disarray, government has turned into a stumbling block.

8. *For Jerusalem has stumbled.* This line pointedly picks up "stumbling block" from verse 6.

12. *My people's overseers are babes, / and women rule over them.* This line reverts to the evocation of a comprehensive absence of leadership that was announced at the beginning of the prophecy. In the patriarchal view—despite the exceptional instance of Deborah in Judges 4–5—women are no fitter than babes to govern.

14   The LORD shall come in judgment
                 with His people's elders and commanders.
            As for you, you have ravaged the vineyard,
                 what is robbed from the poor—in your homes.
15   Why should you crush my people
                 and grind down the face of the poor?
                      Word of the Master LORD of Armies.

16   And the LORD said:
            Since Zion's daughters are haughty,
                 and they walk with necks thrust forth
                      and with wanton eyes,
            walking with mincing steps
                 and jingling with their feet,
17   the Master shall blight the pates of Zion's daughters
                 and expose their private parts.
18   On that day the Master shall take away
                 the splendid ankle bells and the headgear

---

14. *As for you.* The emphatic use of the second-person plural pronoun, usually not stated before the conjugated form of the verb, is probably directed to the elders and commanders mentioned at the end of the preceding line of verse. This makes thematic sense of the removal of the leaders of the people that has been stressed from the beginning of the poem: these so-called leaders enrich themselves with goods robbed from the poor, grind down their faces, and so it is a leadership that must be revoked.

16. *with necks thrust forth.* The idea is that these elegant Jerusalemite women go about with their noses stuck up in the air.
    jingling with their feet. They are wearing some sort of ankle bracelets, which jingle as they walk in their mincing, seductive gait.

17. *expose their private parts.* Though some modern translations understand the rare Hebrew word *pot* as "head," a word close to it occurs elsewhere in the sense of "aperture" or "socket," and here indicates an orifice, as the King James Version understood ("secret parts"), in keeping with traditional Hebrew commentators. The verb used is a term for the exposing of nakedness. *Pot* is the word for "vagina" in modern Hebrew.

18–23. *the splendid ankle bells and the headgear / and the crescents and the pendants. . . .* This long catalogue of items of apparel and jewelry includes quite a few terms occurring nowhere else that are of uncertain meaning as well as some others that occur elsewhere which can be confidently identified (for example, "armlets," "veils," "shawls"). To understand the prophet's rage at these aristocratic women flirtatiously parading about in their expensive finery, one might imagine a contemporary social critic, dismayed and indignant over the plight of the homeless of New York, who sees the rich matrons of Manhattan walking along Madison Avenue in their designer dresses and coats, with shopping bags filled with more of the same.

and the crescents and the pendants   19
   and the bracelets and the veils
and the necklaces and the armlets   20
   and the sashes and the amulets and the charms,
the finger-rings and the nose-rings,   21
   the robes and the wraps and the shawls and the purses,   22
and the gowns and the draped cloths   23
   and the turbans and the capes.
For instead of perfume, rot shall be,   24
   and instead of sashes, rope,
and instead of beaten-work, baldness,
   and instead of rich nobles, girding of sackcloth,
     for instead of beauty, shame.
Your men shall fall by the sword,   25
   your valor, in battle.
And her gates shall mourn and lament,   26
   and stripped, she shall sit on the ground.
And seven women shall take hold of   4:1
   one man on that day,

---

24. *instead of perfume, rot.* There is a verbal violence in the strong antithesis between perfume and stinking "rot," which in the Hebrew, as in the English, is a monosyllable: *maq.*

   rope. The Hebrew *niqpah* occurs only here. Since Late Antiquity, it has been linked with a verbal root that means "to go around"—hence the translation "rope." But some translators see it in a different root and understand it to mean "blow."

   instead of beaten-work, baldness. This is what the Hebrew says, but it is a little odd because one would expect "baldness" to replace something like "fine tresses," not an ornament made of metal. Perhaps this is a metal ornament worn in the hair.

   for instead of beauty, shame. The Masoretic Text reads only "for instead of beauty." The Qumran Isaiah, however, as well as two ancient translations, shows a reading with the word "shame," which seems far more likely.

25. *Your men.* The Hebrew possessive suffix is a feminine plural, as the prophet is now angrily addressing the daughters of Zion directly, whereas until this point they have been referred to in the third person. He has announced that they will be stripped of their finery; now he tells them they will also be deprived of their men, who will perish in battle.

26. *stripped.* The Hebrew word is problematic. This form would ordinarily mean "she shall be clean."

4:1. The prophecy that began in 3:16 ends in this first verse of chapter 4.

   seven women shall take hold of / one man. With much of the eligible male population wiped out on the battlefield, there are no longer enough men to go around. The women forcibly grab the man they find, afraid to let him get away.

saying, "We shall eat our own bread,
   we shall wear our own cloak.
Only let your name be called upon us.
   Gather in our shame."

CHAPTER 4

2   On that day the LORD's shoot shall become
     beauty and glory,
and the fruit of the land
     pride and splendor
       for the remnant of Israel.
3   And who remains in Zion
     and who is left in Jerusalem,
"holy" shall be said of him
     each who is written for life in Jerusalem.
4   The Master shall surely wash the filth of the daughters of Zion,
     and Jerusalem's bloodguilt He shall cleanse from its midst
      with a wind of justice and a wind of rooting-out.
5   And the LORD shall create over all the sanctuary of Mount Zion

---

We shall eat our own bread, / we shall wear our own cloak. We do not even ask, they say to the man, that you provide material support for us, according to the accepted practice. All we want is that you redeem us from our unmarried state, which is a "disgrace" for nubile women, and that you let us take your name.

CHAPTER 4   2. *On that day the LORD's shoot shall become / beauty and glory.* Most translators and textual critics read this whole short chapter as prose, but the diction is manifestly poetic (*nogah,* "effulgence," for example, occurs elsewhere only in poetry), and it is possible to scan it as poetry, even though it is somewhat looser metrically than other Prophetic poems. "The LORD's shoot" would be the people of Israel to be redeemed after a period of devastation and tribulation that will leave a saving remnant ("who remains in Zion").

4. *the filth of the daughters of Zion.* The filth indicated by the Hebrew term is excremental. If this line does not directly refer to the prophecy about the daughters of Jerusalem that immediately precedes, it is at least an editorial warrant for placing this prophecy here.

   bloodguilt. The plural form of the word for "blood," which is used here, refers to bloodguilt, though it retains the concrete image of blood staining the hands of the killer (compare 1:15).

   justice . . . rooting-out. God will bring justice to the city, but the second term suggests that the implementation of justice involves purging the miscreants. The violence, as Joseph Blenkinsopp argues, suggests that the term *ruah* here is to be understood as a sweeping wind rather than as "spirit."

and over its solemn assemblies
a cloud by day
 and an effulgence of flaming fire by night,
  for over all the glory there shall be a canopy.
And a shelter it shall be   6
 as a shade by day from heat
  and a covert and refuge from pelting rain.

CHAPTER 5

Let me sing to My beloved   1
 the song of my lover for his vineyard.
A vineyard my beloved had
 on a hillside rich in soil.
And he hoed it and took off its stones,   2
 and planted it with choice vines.
And he built a tower in its midst,
 and a winepress, too, he hewed in it

---

5. *a cloud by day / and . . . fire by night.* This is an obvious invocation of the cloud by day and the pillar of fire by night that went before the Israelites in the wilderness: that miraculous divine protection is now to be re-created in the restored Jerusalem. The pillar of fire from Exodus here undergoes poetic elaboration as the writer adds both *nogah*, "effulgence," and *lehavah*, "flame."

 for over all the glory. This phrase is somewhat obscure. The least strained construction is that "glory" refers to the Temple and its solemn assemblies. The canopy that is over all the glory, providing shade and shelter, as the next verse spells out, is clearly an image of divine protection.

6. *from pelting rain.* The literal sense of the Hebrew is "from stream and from rain," but since there is no river in Jerusalem that could threaten it with a flood, this is probably a hendiadys meaning: rain that pounds down like a stream of water.

CHAPTER 5   1. *Let me sing to My beloved.* This Parable of the Vineyard would become an early warrant for reading the Song of Songs as an allegory of the love between God and Israel. The lover here is clearly God, and the vineyard over which the lover labors is the people of Israel. In the Song of Songs, the body of the beloved is represented metaphorically as a vineyard.

 on a hillside rich in soil. The translation of this phrase, following the proposal of Bleckinsopp, is conjectural. The literal sense of the Hebrew word is: "in a corner [or beam of light] son of oil." The conjectured translation builds on the association of oil with fruitfulness and assumes that the word for "corner" might extend to a plot of land.

2. *a tower.* This would probably be a watchtower from which one could survey the vineyard and protect it from predators.

And he hoped to get grapes
   but it put forth rotten fruit.

3   And, now, O dweller of Jerusalem
   and man of Judah,
judge, pray, between Me
   and My vineyard.

4   What more could be done for My vineyard
   that I did not do?
Why did I hope to get grapes
   and it put forth rotten fruit?

5   And now, let Me inform you, pray,
   what I am about to do to My vineyard:
take away its hedge, and it shall turn to waste,
   break down its fence, and it shall be trampled.

6   And I will make it a wild field,
   and it shall not be pruned nor raked,
     and thorn and thistle shall spring up.
And I will charge the clouds
   not to rain on it.

7   For the house of Israel is the vineyard of the Lord of Armies
   and the men of Judah are His delightful planting.
He hoped for justice, and, look, jaundice,
   for righteousness, and, look, wretchedness.

8   Woe, who add house to house,
   who put field together with field
till there is no space left

---

5. *take away its hedge, and it shall turn to waste.* The transparent referent of the unprotected vineyard that is trampled by wild beasts is the kingdom of Judah, shorn of defenses, which is overrun by invading armies.

6. *And I will charge the clouds / not to rain on it.* The weather conspires with wild beasts to destroy the vineyard.

7. *justice . . . jaundice . . . righteousness . . . wretchedness.* This translation proposes English equivalents for the Hebrew wordplay, where the meaning of the two second terms is somewhat different. The Hebrew is *mishpat,* "justice," *mispaḥ,* "blight," and *tsedaqah,* "righteousness," *tse'aqah,* "scream."

8. *Woe, who add house to house, / who put field together with field.* The social injustice against which the prophet inveighs is the consolidation of real estate—houses and fields—in the hands of the exploitative rich, who thus drive the peasantry from their possessions.

and you alone are settled, in the heart of the land.
In the hearing of the LORD of Armies: 9
   I swear, many houses shall turn to ruin,
      great and good ones with none living in them.
For ten acres of vineyard shall yield a single *bat,*   10
   and a *homer* of seed shall yield but an *ephah.*
Woe, who rise in the morning early   11
   to chase after strong drink,
who linger late in twilight,
   enflamed by wine.
Whose banquets are lyre and lute, timbrel and flute, and wine,   12
   and who do not regard the LORD's deeds,
      and the work of His hands do not see.
Therefore is My people exiled   13
   for lack of knowledge,
its honored men victims of famine
   and its masses parched with thirst.
Therefore Sheol has widened its gullet   14
   and gaped open its mouth beyond measure,
and her splendor and her hubbub have gone down,
   her noise and her revelers.

---

9. *In the hearing of the LORD of Armies.* The literal sense is: in the ears of the LORD of Armies. One must assume that the prophet himself, not God, speaks the lines that follow, beginning with this formula because he is pronouncing, with God as his witness, a solemn vow about the destruction to come.

10. *a single* bat . . . *an* ephah. These are two small units of solid measure, against "ten acres" (literally, "ten yokes") and a large measure, the *homer.*

11. *strong drink.* Since the Samson story appears to indicate that this drink, *sheikhar,* is derived from grapes but is different from wine, it probably means grappa. Archaeologists have discovered the apparatus for making grappa.

12. *who do not regard the LORD's deeds.* Since they spend their days drinking and carousing, from early morning until evening, they would be in a perpetual drunken stupor, scarcely in a condition to take note of the great things God has done.

13. *Therefore is My people exiled.* Verb tenses in ancient Hebrew poetry are fluid and at times ambiguous, and one suspects that the prophets purposefully exploited the ambiguity. The exile is so certain that it is as if it had already happened, or it is about to happen, or it will happen before too long.

14. *Sheol has widened its gullet.* Sheol, the underworld, often imagined as a great pit, is represented here as a kind of hungry monster swallowing those marked for destruction.
   her splendor. The feminine possessive refers to the people.

15 And humans are bowed low and man brought down,
and the eyes of the haughty are brought down.
16 And the LORD of Armies shall be raised up in justice
and the Holy One hallowed in righteousness.
17 And sheep shall graze as in their meadows
and goats shall feed in the ruins of the fatted.
18 Woe, who haul crime with the cords of falseness
and like the ropes of a cart, offense.
19 Who say: "Let Him hurry, let Him hasten His deed,
that we may see,
and let the counsel of the Israel's Holy One
draw near and come that we may see."
20 Woe, who say "good" to evil
and "evil" to good,
who turn darkness to light
and light into darkness,
turn bitter into sweet
and sweet into bitter.
21 Woe, wise in their own eyes
and in their own opinion discerning
22 Woe, mighty to drink wine
and men of valor to mix strong drink,
23 who declare the wicked innocent because of bribes
and righteous men's just cause deny.
24 Therefore, as a tongue of fire consumes straw

---

15. *and humans are bowed low.* This line picks up the refrain from the prophecy in chapter 2.

17. *and goats shall feed.* The Masoretic Text here reads *garim,* "sojourners," but this translation follows the Septuagint, which appears to have used a Hebrew text that read *gedayim,* "goats." (The Hebrew letters for *r* and *d* look quite similar.)

   in the ruins of the fatted. The Hebrew here is rather compressed, with *meihim,* "fatted," a word that generally refers to fatted animals, but the evident reference is to the overstuffed rich, who have gorged themselves on the resources of the poor.

19. *Let Him hurry.* This whole speech is an expression of the arrogant complacency of the evildoers: let God hurry and carry out His plans—we are not worried.

21. *in their own opinion.* The literal sense of the Hebrew is "before their own faces." The phrase is clearly parallel in meaning to "in their own eyes" in the first verset.

22. *mighty to drink wine / and men of valor to mix strong drink.* The heavy sarcasm is palpable: in this vehement denunciation, the prophet scarcely aims for subtlety.

and hay falls apart in flame,
  their root shall be like rot
    and their flower go up like dust.
For they have spurned the teaching of the LORD of Armies,
  and the utterance of Israel's Holy One they despised.
Therefore is the LORD incensed with His people,   25
  and has stretched out His hand and struck it.
And mountains have quaked,
  and their corpses are become like offal in the streets.
Yet His wrath has not abated
  and His arm is still stretched out.
And He shall raise a banner for nations from afar   26
  and whistle to one at the end of the earth,
    and, look, swiftly, quick, he shall come.
None tires, none stumbles among them,   27
  he does not slumber, does not sleep.
The belt round his loins does not slip open,
  and his sandals' thong does not snap.
His arrows are sharpened,   28
  all his bows are drawn.
The hooves of his horses are hard as flint

---

24. *as a tongue of fire consumes straw / and hay falls apart in flame.* The structure of this line is chiastic: in the first verset, fire is the grammatical subject, consuming the straw; in the second verset, the grammatical subject is the hay, disintegrating in the flame. The verb in the second verset usually means to go slack or become weak, but something like falling apart is required by the context.

26. *He shall raise a banner for nations from afar.* God is represented as a kind of general, giving the order for the invading armies to attack. The identity of the armies is left unstated, heightening the ominous effect, although Isaiah and his audience would surely have had the imperial forces of Assyria in mind.

27. *among them.* The Hebrew says "among him," but the sliding between singular and plural, especially for collective nouns, that is natural in Hebrew needs to be sorted out for English legibility.

28. *The hooves of his horses are hard as flint / and his wheels like the whirlwind.* This is one of many instances in which the poetic power of Prophetic verse pushes, perhaps not intentionally, in the direction of apocalypse. What the prophet means to do is to make frighteningly vivid through his poetry the terrible onslaught of foreign invaders that is about to overwhelm the kingdom of Judah. The hyperbolic force, however, of the language he uses is so strong that the attacking army begins to look apocalyptic—its troops unslumbering, the hooves of its horses like flint, the wheels of its chariots like the whirlwind.

and his wheels like the whirlwind.

29   He has a roar like the lion
        he roars like the king of beasts.
     He howls and seizes his prey,
        whisks it off and none can save.
30   And he shall howl against him on that day
        like the howling of the sea,
     and he shall peer toward the earth
        and, look, constricting darkness,
           and the light shall go dark in its clouds.

1   CHAPTER 6   In the year of the death of King Uzziah, I saw
the Master seated on a high and lofty throne, and the skirts of his robe

---

29. *He has a roar like the lion.* The representation of martial fierceness in the image of the
lion is conventional in ancient Near Eastern poetry, but the prophet makes the familiar
trope vivid in the way he highlights the roaring and then links it to the roaring of the sea.

30. *And he shall howl against him on that day.* Hebrew usage has a certain propensity to
multiply pronominal references: the initial "he" (merely indicated through the conjugated
form of the verb "shall howl") is of course the cruel enemy, whereas "against him" refers
to the people of Israel.
    and he shall peer toward the earth. Since what is seen is a dismaying landscape of disas-
ter, "he" would again have the unstated antecedent of the people of Israel.
    constricting darkness. The Hebrew is very compressed, but this is the most likely
meaning.
    and the light shall go dark in its clouds. Again, the poetic imagery is incipiently apoca-
lyptic: it is dark on the earth and dark in the heavens as well. This is a reversal of the first
moment of creation, when "let there be light" drives back the primordial darkness that
is over the face of the abyss. The suffix indicating "its" in the Hebrew is feminine and so
must refer to "the earth," the only feminine noun in this verse. The word for clouds, *'arifim,*
appearing only here, is high poetic diction, a designation linked with a verbal stem that
means to drip down, as the clouds yield rain.

CHAPTER 6   1. *In the year of the death of King Uzziah.* This might be 734 B.C.E.,
although the reignal chronology is disputed. In any case, the vision in the Temple in which
Isaiah is commissioned as prophet is clearly the beginning of his prophetic mission, and
this chapter would be the first thing he wrote.
    I saw the Master seated on a high and lofty throne. Since it was believed that there
was a correspondence between the Temple in Jerusalem and God's celestial palace, it is
understandable that Isaiah should have a vision of God enthroned in the Temple. God
apparently is imagined as having gigantic proportions, with the skirts of his robe filling
the entire interior of the Temple. The word translated here as "Temple," *heikhal,* generally
means "palace," and there appears to be a conflation between the two: the scene features
both a throne and an altar. One should note that this episode begins in prose, probably

filled the Temple. Seraphim were stationed over him, six wings for each ₂
one. With two it would cover its face, and with two it would cover its feet,
and with two it would hover. And each called out to each and said: ₃

> "Holy, holy, holy, is the LORD of Armies.
>   The fullness of all the earth is His glory."

And the pillars of the thresholds swayed from the voice calling out and the ₄
house was filled with smoke. And I said, ₅

> "Woe to me, for I am undone,
>   for I am a man of impure lips,
>   and in a people of impure lips do I dwell.
> My eyes have seen the King LORD of Armies."

And one of the seraphim flew down to me, in his hand a glowing coal in ₆
tongs that he had taken from the altar. And he touched my mouth and said, ₇

---

because it is a narrative report rather than the prophetic message proper. When dialogue
is introduced, the language switches to verse.

2. *Seraphim.* It is not entirely clear what these angelic attendants of God look like. Their
name shows the verb that means "to burn," and they might be angels of fire, but then why
would they need tongs to hold the burning coal? The root *saraf* is also associated with the
burning venom of serpents, and the Book of Kings registers the fact that at one point there
were icons of serpents in the Temple, leaving open the disquieting possibility that these
seraphim are winged snakes.

    cover its feet. Some think "feet" is a euphemism for the genitals, though that is not a
necessary inference.

    hover. The *piʿel* conjugation of the verb for flying, *ʿaf,* is used here, and this transla-
tion understands it to indicate hovering or fluttering without forward motion, since the
seraphim are, after all, "stationed," or "standing over" God. In verse 6, when one of the
seraphim swoops down to Isaiah, the primary conjugation (*qal*) of this verb is used, suggesting a different movement.

5. *I am undone.* The Hebrew verb could also mean "I am struck dumb," and a pun is probably intended.

    for I am a man of impure lips. As with Moses and Jeremiah, the prophet responds to the
call to prophecy by stating his unworthiness for the task. But here, pointedly, his unworthiness is implicated in that of his people: "and in a people of impure lips do I dwell."

7. *he touched my mouth.* Remarkably, what is entirely elided here is the excruciating pain of
having a burning coal pressed to the mouth. The role of pain in the initiation will be vividly
evoked in Pushkin's "The Prophet," a poem based on this chapter, in which the seraph rips
out the prophet's heart and replaces it with the burning coal.

"Look, this has touched your lips,
　　and your crime is gone, your offense shall be atoned."

8 And I heard the voice of the Master saying,

"Whom shall I send,
　　and who will go for us?"

And I said, "Here I am, send me."
9 And he said, "Go and say to this people:

'Indeed you must hear but you will not understand,
indeed you must see but you will not know.'
10　　Make the heart of this people obtuse
　　　　and block its ears and seal its eyes.
　　Lest it see with its eyes
　　　　and with its ears hear
　　and its heart understand
　　　　and it turn back and be healed."

11 And I said, "Till when, O Master?"
And he said,

---

8. *Here I am, send me.* The obvious implication is that, the prophet's lips having been cleansed, he is now ready to take up the mission. There is a linguistic note as well as a spiritual one in all of this: poetry, purportedly representing divine speech, is the prophet's vehicle; now, with his lips purified, he is in a condition to utter this elevated and powerful form of speech.

10. *Make the heart of this people obtuse / and block its ears and seal its eyes.* Since the heart is imagined as the seat of understanding, these are the three channels of perception. This particular message of God to the prophet is notoriously perplexing. Evidently, God does not want the people to understand, so that it will not change its ways and will not escape the dire punishment that it deserves. But if we see all this from Isaiah's point of view, the entire message is colored by his quite realistic fear that his prophetic mission is doomed to failure from the outset, that all his exhortations will not move the people to turn back from its evil ways. God's command, then, to make the heart of the people obtuse is a kind of preemptive justification by the prophet for the anticipated failure of prophecy.

11. *Till when, O Master?* The prophet is unwilling to contemplate the idea that the destruction will be total and final, and so he asks how long it will go on before God relents.

"Till towns are laid waste with no dwellers
and homes with no man
and the land is laid waste, a desolation.
And the Lord shall drive man far away 12
and abandonment grow in the midst of the land.
And yet a tenth part shall be in it and turn back. 13
And it shall be ravaged
like a terebinth and an oak
which though felled have a stump within them,
the holy seed is its stump.

CHAPTER 7   And it happened in the days of Ahaz son of 1
Jotham son of Uzziah king of Judah that Rezin king of Aram with Pekah
son of Remaliah king of Israel went up to Jerusalem to do battle against

---

Till towns are laid waste with no dwellers. God answers not by indicating any period of
time but by stating that first the land has to be devastated.

13. *a tenth part shall be in it and turn back.* This is an early articulation of the idea of the
saving—perhaps rather "saved"—remnant. This small group of survivors will "turn back"
to God, turn back from the disastrous acts of the majority.

And it shall be ravaged. The concluding clauses of this final verse are somewhat obscure.
The "it" here would have to refer not to the tenth part that will be saved but to the people
as a whole, who are destined to be ravaged.

like a terebinth and an oak / which though felled have a stump within them. Though
shalekhet, the word represented here as "felled," comes to mean "leaf-fall" in modern
Hebrew (it derives from a verb meaning "to fling away"), it most likely refers here to the
cutting down of the tree: while most of it is chopped down, it can regenerate from the stump
that remains, which would be the saving tenth part of the people.

the holy seed. In part because "holy seed," *zera' qodesh,* is an exilic expression, many
scholars conclude that this last clause, or even the entire final verse, is a later addition,
referring to the community of exiles who remain faithful to the covenant and are destined
to become the nucleus of the nation's regeneration.

CHAPTER 7   1. *And it happened.* As the text moves into narrative, it shifts from
poetry to prose.

*Rezin king of Aram with Pekah son of Remaliah king of Israel went up to Jerusalem to
do battle against it.* The northern kingdom of Israel entered into an alliance with Aram to
oppose Assyria, which was conducting a campaign (734–732 B.C.E.) in trans-Jordan, the
eastern Galilee, and along the Mediterranean coast. Their purpose in attacking Ahaz was
to force him to join their alliance.

2   it, but he was not able to battle against it. And it was told to the house of
David: "Aram has joined with Ephraim and made its heart and the heart of
3   its people sway like the trees of the forest before the wind." And the LORD
said to Isaiah, "Go out, pray, to meet Ahaz, you and Shear-Jashub your son,
to the edge of the conduit of the Upper Pool, by the road of Fuller's Field.
4   And you shall say to him, 'Watch yourself and be tranquil, do not fear and
let your heart not quail because of these two smoking tails of firebrands,
5   over the blazing wrath of Rezin and Aram and the son of Remaliah inasmuch as Aram, with Ephraim and the son of Remaliah, has devised evil
6   counsel against you: Let us go up against Judah and shake it, and we shall
break it into pieces for ourselves. And we shall set up within it the son of
Tabeel as king.'

7   Thus said the Master, the LORD:
                  It shall not happen and it shall not be,
8   that the head of Aram is Damascus,
                  and the head of Damascus is Rezin.
               [And in another sixty-five years
                  Ephraim as a people shall be smashed.]
9   And the head of Ephraim is Samaria,
                  and the head of Samaria is the son of Remaliah.

---

but he was not able to do battle against it. The obvious sense is that the invading forces
were unable to secure a decisive victory.

2. *made its heart . . . sway.* That is, struck terror in their hearts.

3. *Shear-Jashub.* Like other prophetic progeny, Isaiah's son has a symbolic name: it means
"a remnant shall come back."

4. *the blazing wrath.* The Hebrew *ḥori-'af* is a term for anger that suggests burning and thus
picks up the image of the smoking firebrands.

6. *son of Tabeel as king.* This would clearly be a puppet king. His patronymic suggests that
he was probably an Aramean.

7. *Thus said Master, the LORD.* As one would expect in a move to formal prophecy, the
language now switches from prose to poetry.

8. *And in another sixty-five years / Ephraim as a people shall be smashed.* This prophecy of
the destruction of the northern kingdom, which occurred in 721 B.C.E., looks very much
like a later interpellation, invited by the momentum of the prophecy of the interruption of
the reign of Rezin and of Pekah. The sixty-five-year span is nevertheless puzzling because
this prophecy would have been enunciated perhaps a dozen years before Assyria overwhelmed the northern kingdom.

If you trust not,
    you shall not hold firm."

And the LORD spoke again to Ahaz, saying, "Ask for a sign from the people 10,11
of the LORD your God, make it deep as Sheol or high above." And Ahaz 12
said, "I will not ask and I will not test the LORD." And Isaiah said, "Listen, 13
pray, O House of David! Is it not enough for you to weary men that you
should weary my God as well? Therefore the Master Himself shall give you 14
a sign: the young woman is about to conceive and bear a son, and she shall
call his name Immanuel. Curds and honey he shall eat till he knows how to 15
reject evil and choose good. For before the lad knows how to reject evil and 16
choose good, the land, whose two kings you despise, shall be abandoned.
The LORD shall bring upon you and your people and upon your father's 17
house days that have not come from the day Ephraim turned away from
Judah—the king of Assyria.

---

9. *If you trust not, / you shall not hold firm.* This cryptic declaration (the Hebrew involves
wordplay) is a little enigmatic, though it probably means that if Ahaz does not trust Isaiah
and hold out against Rezin and Pekah, he will come to a bad end.

13. *Isaiah said.* The Hebrew merely says "he said." The name has been substituted in order
to avoid confusion.

    to weary. The Hebrew verb sometimes means this, though it also means "to incapaci-
tate," which is not appropriate in this context. The development of the dialogue appears
to be as follows: Isaiah invites Ahaz to ask for a sign, however extravagant (verse 11); Ahaz
is afraid to put God to the test (verse 12); Isaiah answers that Ahaz is exasperating God by
his unwillingness to ask for a sign (verse 13); Isaiah further says that Ahaz will get a sign
whether he likes it or not (verse 14).

14. *the young woman.* Although this verse generated many centuries of Christological readings emphasizing the virgin birth, the Hebrew ʿalmah does not mean "virgin," but rather
"young woman," and in Proverbs the ʿalmah is represented engaged in sex. The "sign" here
is the name she gives the child, which means "God is with us." Nevertheless, the identity of
the young woman is unclear and has been much debated. She might be the prophet's wife
because there is precedent for prophets begetting symbolic sons, or she might be a woman
in the house of David.

15. *Curds and honey he shall eat.* From infancy, the child will be raised in sumptuous abundance, which, however, will be interrupted by the disaster that will sweep over the land.

17. *the king of Assyria.* This specification at the end of the sentence is syntactically awkward
and may have been added as an explanatory gloss. In any case, the prophecy of an Assyrian
onslaught that is an unprecedented disaster for the nation much better suits Sennacherib's
campaign against Judah in 701 B.C.E. than the events of 734–732 B.C.E. with which this
segment began.

18   And it shall happen on that day.
            The LORD shall whistle to the flies
                that are on the edge of Egypt's rivers
                    and to the bees that are in the land of Assyria,
19   and they shall all come and settle
            in the wadis of the unplowed fields,
        and in the crevices of the rocks
            and among all the thorns and thistles.
20   On that day the Master shall shave
            with a hired razor along the borders of the River Euphrates
                with the king of Assyria,
        the head and the pubic hair
            and the beard, too, it shall cut away.
21   And it shall happen on that day,
            a man shall nurture a calf and two sheep.
22   And it shall happen, from all the making of milk,
            he shall eat curds,
        for all who are left in the midst of the land
            shall eat curds and honey.
23   And it shall happen on that day,
            every place where there will be
                a thousand vines worth a thousand silver shekels
                    shall turn into thornbush and thistle.

---

18. *the flies / that are on the edge of Egypt's rivers / and to the bees that are in the land of Assyria*. The swarms of insects—perhaps killer bees in the case of Assyria—are metaphors for the invading armies. There were moments of Egyptian alliance with Assyria, but not in 701 B.C.E.

20. *with the king of Assyria*. This translation construes the king as the "hired razor" God uses to wreak destruction.
    the head and the pubic hair / and the beard. "Pubic hair" is literally "hair of the legs," but in this case "legs" does appear to be a euphemism for the genitals. Shaving of the head, beard, and pubic area is a way of humiliating prisoners, but here it also serves as a metaphor for destruction that is brutal and shaming but not total.

22. *for all who are left in midst of the land / shall eat curds and honey*. This sounds as though they are enjoying plenty, like the child Immanuel, but given the dire content of the three verses that follow, it probably means, in what may be an ironic twist, that they will live off the produce of their remaining livestock and what honey they can gather but will be unable to grow crops.

With bow and arrow one would come there,   24
    for thornbush and thistle the whole land shall be.
But the mountains that are worked with the hoe,   25
    there the fear of thornbush and thistle shall not come,
        and it shall be for oxen let loose and the trampling of sheep.

CHAPTER 8   And the LORD said to me, "Take for yourself 1
a large parchment sheet and write on it with a man's stylus: for Maher-
Shalal-Hash-Baz." And I enlisted for myself two trusty witnesses, Uriah the 2
priest and Zachariah son of Jeberechiah. And I drew close to the prophet- 3
wife and she conceived and bore a son. And the LORD said to me, "Call his
name Maher-Shalal-Hash-Baz. For before the lad knows how to say "father" 4
and "mother," the wealth of Damascus and the spoils of Samaria shall be
borne off to the king of Assyria." And the LORD spoke to me once again, 5

---

24. *With bow and arrow one would come there.* Vineyards will turn to brambles, and wild
beasts will roam there—hence the need for bow and arrow.

25. *there the fear of thornbush and thistle shall not come.* Though some understand this to
mean "you shall not come because of the fear of thornbush and thistle," the Hebrew lacks
any proposition that could be construed as "because of." The more likely sense would be:
unlike the flatlands, which will be covered with thornbushes and thistles, the mountain
slopes, while not amenable to cultivation, will provide pasture for free-roaming cattle.

CHAPTER 8   1. *a large parchment sheet.* "Parchment" is merely implied in the
Hebrew.
    a man's stylus. This is a literal representation of the Hebrew, which sounds a little odd.
Perhaps the phrase is meant to indicate an ordinary stylus used by human beings rather
than some magical or supernatural writing implement.
    Maher-Shalal-Hash-Baz. The name means "Hasten Booty Hurry Spoils." Hosea is
another prophet enjoined to give his offspring a symbolic name. The dire portent of this
name corresponds antithetically to the hopeful portent of the name Immanuel given to
the child prophesied in 7:14.

2. *two trusty witnesses.* Their purpose is to confirm the validity of the document with the
name that Isaiah has written.

3. *I drew close.* Isaiah, understandably, uses the most decorous of biblical idioms for sexual
intimacy since it might be unseemly for him to say he "knew" his wife or "lay with" her.
    the prophet-wife. Although the literal meaning of *nevi'ah,* the feminine form of the
word for "prophet," is "prophetess," she is given this designation only because she is the
spouse of a prophet.

4. *Damascus . . . Samaria.* These are the two allies, Aram and the northern kingdom of
Israel, that had attacked Jerusalem.

6 saying: "Inasmuch as this people has spurned the quietly flowing waters
7 of Shiloh and rejoiced in Rezin and the son of Remaliah, therefore, the
Master is about to bring up against them the great and mighty waters of
the Euphrates—the king of Assyria and all his glory.

And it shall rise up over its channels
    and go over all its banks
8   and pass through Judah, flooding and sweeping,
    up to the neck it shall reach.
And its outstretched wings
    shall fill your land, Immanuel.
9 Take note, O people, and be terror-stricken.
    Give ear, all far reaches of the earth.
Gird yourselves, and be terror-stricken,
    gird yourselves, and be terror-stricken.
10 Lay out counsel and it shall be overturned,
    speak a word and it shall not come to be,
      for God is with us."

11 For thus said the LORD to me with a strong hand, warning me not to go in
the way of this people, saying:

---

6. *and rejoiced.* The Hebrew syntax at this point is suspect: this single Hebrew word means, literally, "and rejoicing of." Proposed emendations remain unconvincing.

7. *the great and mighty waters of the Euphrates.* The antithesis with "the quietly flowing waters of Shiloh" is clear. The inhabitants of Jerusalem have not trusted in their own small kingdom, in the gentle brook Shiloh that flows through Jerusalem, but instead have turned to Samaria and Aram. For this, they will be overwhelmed by the mighty stream of the Assyrian empire.

8. *its outstretched wings.* The imagery of wings in the midst of flooding water is a little strange, but "wings" in biblical usage has a variety of metaphorical applications, and hence the loose application may not have seemed unnatural.
   Immanuel. This designation, apparently for the people of Judah, is ironic because God is scarcely with the people as it is overcome by the Assyrian forces. If the word at the end of verse 10, *ʿimmanuel,* is a statement ("God is with us") and not a name, it would reflect a pivot in the prophet's discourse: Assyria will sweep down over Judah, but the nations of the earth (verse 9–10) will be fear-stricken because, nevertheless, God is with His people. Yet the subsequent verses go on with a prophecy of doom.

9. *Take note.* This translation reads *deʿu* instead of the Masoretic *roʿu*, which would seem to mean "smash" (though some interpreters, by a stretch, understand it as "band together").

You shall not call a plot   12
to all that this people calls a plot,
    nor fear what it fears nor be terrified.
The LORD of Armies, Him shall you hallow,   13
    and He is your fear and your terror.
And He shall be a snare and a stone to strike against   14
    and a rock for stumbling
for the two houses of Israel,
    a trap and a snare for the inhabitants of Jerusalem.
And many shall stumble against them   15
    and fall and be broken
        and be snared and entrapped.

Wrap up the testimony, seal the teaching among My disciples. And I   16,17
shall await the LORD, Who hides His face from the house of Judah, and
I shall hope for Him. Here I am, and the children that the LORD gave me   18
as signs and portents in Israel, from the LORD of Armies Who dwells on
Mount Zion. And should they say to you, "Inquire of the ghosts and the   19
familiar spirits who chirp and murmur, shall not a people inquire of its
gods, from the dead for the living, for instruction and guidance?" They   20
indeed shall speak according to this word that has no dawn. And he shall   21
pass through it, stricken and hungry. And it shall happen when he hungers

---

14. *the two houses of Israel.* That is, both the northern and the southern kingdom.

16. *Wrap up the testimony, seal the teaching.* The evident reference is to the parchment scroll on which was written the child's name that is the dire portent. The Hebrew shows a strong alliteration between the two nouns, *te'udah* and *torah*, which this translation tries to emulate.

    among My disciples. The reference is a little obscure, and though this is the conventional rendering of the Hebrew noun, it could equally be translated as "My teachings."

19. *the ghosts and the familiar spirits who chirp and murmur.* Necromancy was, one may infer, a widespread practice in ancient Israel—so much so that King Saul was impelled to make it a capital crime (which he himself, in his last desperation, violated). It was believed that the spirits of the dead, when called up, emitted indistinct sounds, which the necromancer could then interpret as speech.

20. *this word that has no dawn.* The words of the purportedly murmurous dead are swathed in the dark of meaninglessness, and they will never have a dawn. This phrase became idiomatic in later Hebrew for anything hopeless or pointless.

21. *And he shall pass through it.* Given the grim fate of this person, "he" would refer to the inquirer of the spirits of the dead (or, alternately, to the "people" mentioned in verse 19). Although this sort of unmarked switch from plural to singular may be disorienting for the

that he shall be infuriated and curse his king and his gods, and turn his face
22 upward and to earth look down, and oh, distress and darkness, swooping
23 straits and uttermost gloom. For there is no swoop for him in straits. Now
the former has brought disgrace to the land of Zebulun and to the land of
Naphtali, and the latter brought honor to the Way of the Sea, across from
Jordan, Galilee of the nations.

CHAPTER 9

1   The people walking in darkness
        have seen a great light.
     Those dwelling in the land of death's shadow—
        light has beamed on them.
2   You have made great the nation
        and heightened its joy.
     They rejoiced before You

---

modern reader, it is fairly common in biblical usage. The "it" is feminine in the Hebrew
and probably refers to the land, a feminine noun, though the term does not appear in the
preceding verses.

22. *swooping straits.* The Hebrew of the received text, *me'uf tsuqah*, sounds equally bizarre.
The end of this verse and all of the next one, which concludes the chapter, look as though
they have been mangled in scribal transmission, and neither the ancient versions nor scholarly emendations provide much help.

23. *For there is no swoop for him in straits.* The translation candidly reflects the unintelligibility of the Hebrew.
    Now the former. Some interpreters think this is a reference to Pekah son of Ramaliah,
but, in the general textual murkiness of this verse, that is no more than a guess.
    the latter brought honor to the Way of the Sea. No convincing identification for "the
latter" has been established. The verb rendered as "brought honor" might also mean "dealt
heavily, oppressed," though if the previous verb in fact means "disgraced" (and not "was
lenient"), one would expect *hikhbid* here to be its precise antonym—the two verbs derive,
respectively, from roots that mean "light" and "heavy." In any case, no one has satisfactorily
resolved the enigma of the geographical references here and the military actions performed
in or on these regions.

CHAPTER 9   1. *The people walking in darkness / have seen a great light.* This is one
of the most arresting instances of antithetical parallelism in biblical poetry. The line is
starkly simple yet haunting. Second Isaiah would pick up this contrast between light and
darkness and develop it in a variety of elaborate ways. The line following here continues
the light-darkness antithesis in an interlinear parallelism.

as the joy in the harvest,
as people exalt
when they share out the spoils.
For its burdensome yoke   3
the rod on its shoulders,
the club of its oppressor—
You smashed, as on the day of Midian.
For every boot pounding loudly   4
and every cloak soaked in blood
is consigned to burning, consumed by fire.
For a child has been born to us,   5
a son has been given to us,
and leadership is on his shoulders.
And his name is called wondrous councillor,
divine warrior, eternal father, prince of peace,
making leadership abound and peace without end   6
on the throne of David and over his kingdom
to make it firm-founded and stay it up
in justice and righteousness, forever more.

---

3. *as on the day of Midian.* The probable reference is to Gideon's defeat of the Midianite oppressors reported in Judges 6–8.

4. *every boot.* The Hebrew *se'on* appears only here. A possible Akkadian cognate means "boot," and the parallelism with "cloak" argues for some item of apparel. Pounding boots and bloodied cloaks aptly serve as metonymies for a violently advancing army.

5. *a child has been born to us.* The child who is born with wondrous qualities and who is to assume leadership is the ideal king who will be a stay against all enemies and establish an enduring reign of peace.

   and leadership is on his shoulders. This expression reverses the rod of the oppressor on the shoulders in verse 3.

   wondrous councillor / divine warrior, eternal father, prince of peace. This string of epithets has been associated by many generations of Christian commentators and readers with Christ. What the prophet has in mind, however, is not "messianic" except in the strictly political sense: he envisages an ideal king from the line of David who will sit on the throne of Judah and oversee a rule of justice and peace. The most challenging epithet in this sequence is *'el gibor*, which appears to say "warrior-god." The prophet would be violating all biblical usage if he called the Davidic king "God," and that term is best construed here as some sort of intensifier. In fact, the two words could conceivably be a scribal reversal of *gibor 'el*, in which case the second word would clearly function as a suffix of intensification as it occasionally does elsewhere in the Bible.

The zeal of the Lord of Armies shall do this.

7   A word has the Master sent out in Jacob
        and it has fallen in Israel.
8   And all the people knew,
        Ephraim and the dwellers of Samaria,
            in pride and with a swelling heart, saying:
9   Bricks have fallen, and we shall build with hewn stone.
        Sycamores are cut down, and we shall replace them with cedars.
10 But the Lord shall raise Rezin's foes against him,
        and his enemies He shall stir up.
11 Aram from the east and Philistines from the west,
        and they shall devour Israel with all their mouth.
    Yet His wrath has not turned back.
        and His arm is still outstretched.
12 And the people has not turned back to Him Who struck it,
        and the Lord of Armies it has not sought out.
13 And the Lord shall cut off from Israel head and tail,
        branch and reed on a single day.
14 Elder and honored, they are the head,

---

6. *The zeal of the Lord of Armies shall do this.* This sentence is a kind of prose coda to the poetic prophecy. It underscores an important theological point: such an ideal ruler can come into being and sit on the throne of David only through God's zealous intervention.

8. *Ephraim and the dwellers of Samaria.* These are, of course, the inhabitants of the northern kingdom, who have allied themselves with Aram, as the mention of the Aramean king Rezin in verse 10 reminds us.

9. *Bricks have fallen, and we shall build with hewn stone.* There is probably an allusion to the Tower of Babel here. Babel was a byword for overweening human pride, as the story in Genesis 11 shows. These Israelites go beyond the builders of the Tower in their "pride and . . . swelling heart" by resuming their task of building after the brick structure has been razed and imagining that they can build it bigger and better with hewn stone (the building material of Canaan as against Mesopotamia).
    cedars. These are the tallest trees known in the region; they are used elsewhere as a symbol of arrogance (see chapter 15).

12. *And the people has not turned back.* The verb plays against the use of the same verb in a different sense in the previous verse: divine wrath "has not turned back" means that it has not relented, has not been withdrawn, whereas here "turned back" means "to repent," "to turn back to God."

14. *Elder and honored.* Some scholars view this whole verse as a gloss, though it could be original to the prophecy.

prophet and false teacher, they are the tail.
And the people's guides have misled,   15
    and its guided are confounded.
Therefore the Master shall not rejoice over its young men,   16
    and to its orphans and its widows shall show no mercy.
For it is wholly tainted and evil,
    and every mouth speaks scurrilous things.
For wickedness has burned like fire,   17
    thorn and thistle it has consumed.
And it has kindled the forest thickets,
    they went up in a surge of smoke.
In the anger of the LORD of Armies earth grew dark,   18
    and the people became like consuming fire,
        no man spared his fellow.
And they seized on the right and hungered,   19
    ate on the left and were not sated,
        the flesh of their fellow man they ate.
Manasseh does it to Ephraim   20

---

prophet and false teacher. As the second phrase makes clear, the prophet referred to is a false prophet. This provides a bridge to the misleading leaders of the next line.

16. *the Master shall not rejoice over its young men.* The verb here should not be emended, as some have proposed. In biblical poetry, young men (and virgins) often appear as the apt object of rejoicing, just as orphans and widows are the proverbial object of merciful concern (second verset).

17. *went up.* The Hebrew verb used appears only here. Abraham ibn Ezra and others construe it as going up in a column or spume. The term translated as "surge," *ge'ut,* supports this construction because when applied to water it means rising tide.

18. *grew dark.* This is still another term that occurs nowhere else, and so the meaning, proposed by many scholars, is necessarily conjectural.
    the people became like consuming fire. In this time of national catastrophe, social order breaks down and every man turns against his fellow.

19. *the flesh of their fellow man they ate.* The Masoretic Text reads "each man eats the flesh of his own arm." This is possible as a hyperbolic expression but looks rather strange. The Septuagint and one Targum read *re'o,* "his fellow man," instead of *zero'o,* "his arm," which sounds more likely and is also more in keeping with the previous verse. Cannibalism in times of siege is frequently mentioned in other biblical texts.

20. *Manasseh does it to Ephraim.* The Hebrew has no verb, only the accusative particle *'et.* But what is clearly indicated is that in this landscape of mutual savagery, such cannibalistic assault is what Manasseh does to Ephraim and vice versa. The reference is to civil strife within the northern kingdom and then to the war of the north on the south.

and Ephraim to Manasseh,
    together to Judah.
Yet His wrath has not turned back,
    and His arm is still outstretched.

CHAPTER 10

1 Woe, who inscribe crime's inscriptions
    and writs of wretchedness write,
2 to tilt from their cause the poor
    and rob justice from My people's needy,
  making widows their booty
    and despoiling orphans.
3 And what will you do for the day of reckoning,
    for disaster that comes from afar?
  To whom will you flee for help,
    and where will you leave your glory?
4 Only, they shall kneel beneath the captive,
    and beneath the slain they shall fall.

5 Woe, Assyria, rod of My wrath,
    in whose hand is a club—My fury.
6 Against a tainted nation I will send him,
    against the people of My anger I will charge him

CHAPTER 10   1. *writs.* Revocalizing the Masoretic *mekhatvim,* "indite," as *mikhtavim.*

2. *to tilt from their cause the poor.* The standard biblical idiom for perversion of justice is to tilt judgment or a case, but in this variation, the poor are the object of the verb, tilted away from their own legitimate cause or case.

3. *where will you leave your glory?* The interpretation sometimes proposed of the noun *kavod* as "body" is strained. The malefactors in their desperate flight must leave behind their "glory"—their fine houses and fields, all their accumulated substance.

4. *kneel beneath the captive.* Although emendations have often been proposed for this phrase, there is a coherent image here, if phrased a bit cryptically: these doomed people will be taken in captivity (presumably, by Assyrian invaders); some will fall under the feet of other captives in a forced march of those taken by the conquerors; others will perish among those killed in battles.

to take the booty and to seize the spoils,
　　and to turn it to trampling like mire in the streets.
But he shall not imagine so,　　　　　　　　　　　　　　　7
　　and his heart not so shall plot.
For destruction is in his heart,
　　to cut off nations, not a few.
For he shall say:　　　　　　　　　　　　　　　　　　　8
　　Are not my commanders all of them kings?
Is not Calno like Carchemish?　　　　　　　　　　　　　9
　　Is not Hamath like Arpad?
　　　Is not Samaria like Damascus?
As my hand has seized worthless kingdoms,　　　　　　　10
　　and their idols more than Jerusalem's or Samaria's,
why, as I have done to Samaria and its ungods,　　　　　11
　　so I will do to Jerusalem and its icons.
And it shall happen, when the Master carries out all His acts　12
　　against Zion and against Jerusalem,
I will reckon with the fruit of the swollen heart of Assyria's king
　　and with the grandeur of his haughty gaze.
For he has said:　　　　　　　　　　　　　　　　　　13
　　"Through the power of my hand I have done it,
　　　and through my wisdom, for I was discerning.
I have wiped out the borders of peoples
　　and their riches I plundered

---

7. *But he shall not imagine so.* The Assyrians collectively, or their king, do not realize that they are merely God's instrument for punishing His people; as the lines that follow spell out, they arrogantly assume it is all the consequence of their power.

8. *Are not my commanders all of them kings?* This is a peerless army of warrior-noblemen, in which every field commander is a king.

9. *Calno . . . Carchemish . . . Hamath . . . Arpad.* These are all cities to the east that have fallen to the Assyrian onslaught. Aram is the westernmost of them, and if it is conquered, that will surely be the fate of its Israelite ally Samaria.

10. *worthless kingdoms.* This translation follows the scholarly consensus that *'elil* in the singular here means "without value" or "insignificant," and not "idol."

11. *ungods.* Here we have the plural of *'elilim*, which appears often in the Bible and is probably a polemic antipagan derogatory coinage, playing on *'el*, "god," and *'al*, "not," or perhaps rather a mocking diminutive, "godlet."

and brought down to the dust those who dwelled there.
14   And my hand, as with a nest, has seized
      the wealth of peoples,
as one gathers abandoned eggs,
      all the earth I have gathered,
and none fluttered a wing,
      opened a mouth and peeped."
15   Should the axe boast over its wielder,
      the saw vaunt over him who plies it?
As though the rod had swung him who raised it,
      a club had raised the one not-wood!
16   Therefore shall the Master, LORD of Armies,
      send a wasting into his fatness,
and in his glory's stead a burning shall rage
      like the burning of fire.
17   And Israel's Light shall turn to fire
      and its Holy One to flame,
and it shall burn and consume his thorns
      and his thistles on a single day.
18   And the glory of his woods and his farmland
      from life-breath to flesh shall be destroyed,

---

13. *brought down to the dust.* The received text reads *ka'bir*, of doubtful meaning. The translation supposes instead *be'afar*, "into the dust." Bringing down into the dust is a recurrent biblical idiom and makes good sense here.

15. *Should the axe boast over its wielder.* These words begin God's rejoinder to the boast of the Assyrian king. The king is no more than a tool in God's hand, and the analogies of the axe and saw make the boasting transparently absurd.

    the one not-wood. This sounds a little awkward (perhaps even in the Hebrew), but the phrasing is to make a point: the club is inert, insensate wood, not conscious flesh and blood like its wielder.

16. *a burning shall rage.* This is both metaphor and literal referent: the invading army puts fields and towns to the torch.

17. *Israel's Light.* In context, this is an epithet for God.

18. *from life-breath to flesh.* This phrase, literally representing the Hebrew, seems odd in connection with a forest, but it is in all likelihood an idiomatic expression for the whole thing, through and through (a little like the English "body and soul"), and so perhaps may be extended to inanimate objects.

and shall be like a failing sick man.
And the remnant of his woods' trees shall be so few   19
   that a lad can write them down.

And is shall happen on that day, the remnant of Israel and the survivors of   20
the house of Jacob shall no longer lean on him who strikes them but shall
lean on the LORD, Israel's Holy One, in truth. A remnant shall come back, a   21
remnant of Jacob, to mighty God. For if your people Israel be like the sand   22
of the sea, but a remnant within it shall come back. Decreed destruction
sweeps down, vindication. For it is irrevocably decreed: the Master, LORD   23
of Armies, is about to do it in the midst of the land. Therefore, this said the   24
Master, LORD of Armies: "Do not be afraid, My people dwelling in Zion,
of Assyria, who strikes you with the rod, and raises his club against you
in the way he did to Egypt. For in just a little while, My wrath and fury   25
shall be utterly ended." And the LORD of Armies shall rouse against him   26
a scourge, like the striking down of Midian at the Rock of Oreb, and like
His rod over the sea, and bear him off like the way of Egypt. And it shall   27
happen on that day,

   his burden shall be removed from your shoulder
      and his yoke shall be shattered from your neck.

---

20. *him who strikes them.* Here the striker is not God but foreign powers.

21. *to mighty God.* It should be noted that the Hebrew phrase here, *'el gibor,* is the same
one attached to the ideal Davidic king in 9:5, but in this case the referent has to be God. It
is possible that the occurrence of the epithet here may have triggered a scribal reversal of
gibor 'el in 9:5.

22. *if your people Israel be like the sand of the sea.* This is the language of God's repeated
covenantal promise to Abraham in Genesis, but now only a small saving remnant is to
survive.

26. *like the striking down of Midian at the Rock of Oreb.* The story is told in Judges 7:25.
   His rod over the sea. The reference is to the parting of the Sea of Reeds (Exodus 14), and
the rod is raised by Moses.
   bear him off like the way of Egypt. In the account in Exodus, the entire Egyptian army
is drowned in the Sea of Reeds.
   like the way of Egypt. The Hebrew says merely "the way of Egypt." The reference appears
to be the Assyrian defeat of Egypt in more than one battle, and not on Egyptian soil.

He shall come up from the desert

28   come up to Ajath,

pass through Migron

      in Michmash place his gear.

29 He shall pass over a ford,

      Geva his lodging.

Ramah shall tremble,

      Saul's Gibeah flee.

30 With your voice give a piercing call, Bath-Gallim,

      Listen, O Laish, speak out, Anathoth.

31 Madmenah shall decamp,

      Gebim's dwellers take refuge.

32 That very day he shall stand at Nob,

      wave his hand against the Mount of Zion's Daughter,

        the hill of Jerusalem.

33 Look, the Master, LORD of Armies,

      hacks away the treetops with an axe,

and the lofty in stature are cut down

      and the tall ones brought low.

34 And he slashes the wood's thickets with iron,

      and Lebanon trees thunderously fall.

---

27. *He shall come up from the desert.* The received text is not intelligible at this point. It reads, literally, "a yoke from oil." The present translation supposes instead of these three Hebrew words, *'ol mipney-shamen*, a text that showed *'alah miyeshimon*. This is necessarily conjectural but more likely than the garbled Masoretic version. These words would then mark the beginning of a new prophecy, the scary description of the advance of the Assyrian invaders through the land. Their itinerary is spelled out in the place-names of the next two verses. The Assyrian army swoops down from the north, arriving at the capital city of Judah in verse 32. There is scholarly debate as to which Assyrian expedition is invoked. Blenkinsopp opts for the one of 713–711 B.C.E., a decade after the destruction of the northern kingdom.

33. *treetops . . . the tall ones.* The imagery here picks up the theme of bringing down the high and mighty that is prominent in chapter 2. The Lebanon trees of the concluding verse are part of this same pattern.

CHAPTER 11

And a shoot shall come out from the stock of Jesse,   1
    a branch shall bloom from his roots.
And the spirit of the LORD shall rest on him,   2
    a spirit of wisdom and insight,
a spirit of counsel and valor,
    a spirit of knowledge and fear of the LORD,
        his very breath in the fear of the LORD.
And not by what his eyes sees shall he judge,   3
    and not by what his ears hear shall he render verdict.
And he shall judge the poor in justice   4
    and render right verdict for the lowly of the land.
And he shall strike the land with the rod of his mouth,   5
    with the breath from his lips put the wicked to death.
And justice shall be the belt round his waist,
    faithfulness the belt round his loins.
And the wolf shall dwell with the lamb,   6

CHAPTER 11   2. *the spirit of the LORD shall rest on him.* There is a phonetic link between *ruaḥ,* "spirit," and *naḥah,* "rest," through the alliteration of the consonant *ḥet.* The choice of the verb is apt: the spirit descends gently on the ideal ruler to come. This noun is then repeated another three times in an emphatic anaphora.

his very breath. The Hebrew here is literally a verbal noun ("his breathing," "his smelling"?) that has somewhat perplexed interpreters, but the context indicates a sense like the one proposed in this translation. One should note that this verb reflects the same root as the reiterated word for "spirit."

3. *And not by what his eyes see.* This is reminiscent of God's words to Samuel, which have to do with making the right choice, that is, David, for the kingship: "For man sees with the eyes and the LORD sees with the heart" (1 Samuel 16:7). The ideal king breathes the spirit of the LORD, and that, rather than appearances, guides him in judgment.

5. *he shall strike the land with the rod of his mouth.* The formulation is a pointed oxymoron: striking the land and (in the second verset) killing the wicked are violent acts, but this king will somehow realize these ends necessary to justice through speech, in keeping with the spirit of the LORD that has rested on him.

justice . . . the belt round his waist. This extends the idea of the preceding line because a firmly encircled belt round the waist is what one wears going into battle.

6. *And the wolf shall dwell with the lamb.* The famous lines that begin with this phrase are a vivid reflection of the fondness for hyperbole manifested in Prophetic poetry. It is unlikely that the prophet literally envisaged a radical transformation of the order of nature in which carnivores would become pacific herbivores, but all this serves as a striking image for an ideal state when all violence will come to an end.

and the leopard lie down with the kid.
And the calf and the lion shall feed together,
a little lad leading them.

7 And the cow and the bear shall graze,
together their young shall lie,
and the lion like cattle eat hay.

8 And an infant shall play by a viper's hole,
and on an adder's den
a babe put his hand.

9 They shall do no evil nor act ruinously
in all My holy mountain.
For the earth shall be filled with knowledge of the Lord
as water covers the sea.

10 And on that day
the root of Jesse that is standing
shall become a banner for nations.
Nations shall seek him out,
and his resting place shall be glory.

11 And it shall happen on that day,
the Master shall pull in His hand once more
to take back His people's remnant

---

shall feed. The received text reads *umeri'*, "and a fatling," but two ancient versions provide warrant for *yimr'u*, "shall feed," and the context seems to require a verb.

7. *hay.* The Hebrew *teven* generally means "straw" (as in its repeated use for brickmaking in the Exodus story), but since straw is not edible, "hay" would be the plausible English equivalent here.

8. *put his hand.* The Hebrew verb occurs only here, and so the translation is purely an inference from the context.

10. *the root of Jesse that is standing.* The apparent sense is "that is still standing," i.e., that still remains and can be regenerated. But the syntax of the line is a little confusing: in the Hebrew "shall become" immediately follows "And on that day" and thus is distant from its probable predicate, "a banner for nations."

his resting place. This Hebrew term is often used for a place of settlement that is safe from enemies. Its choice here might be intended to resonate with the spirit of the Lord that "shall rest" on the ideal king.

11. *pull in His hand.* The Masoretic Text says *yosif*, "he will again," but this needs to be followed by an infinitive, and there is none in this line. The translation emends the verb to *ye'esof*, for which "hand" would be an idiomatic grammatical object.

that will remain from Assyria and Egypt
and from Patros and from Cush and from Elam
   and from Shinar and from Hamath and from the coastlands.
And He shall raise a banner to the nations,   12
   and gather the banished of Israel
and the dispersed of Judah He shall assemble
   from the four corners of the earth.
And the envy of Ephraim shall vanish,   13
   and the foes of Judah be cut off.
Ephraim shall not envy Judah,
   nor Judah be hostile to Ephraim.
And they shall swoop on the flank of the Philistines by the sea,   14
   together they shall plunder the Easterners.
Edom and Moab shall be subject to them,
   and the Ammonites under their sway.
And the LORD shall dry up the tongue of Egypt's sea   15
   and wave His hand over the Euphrates with His fierce wind
and strike it into seven wadis,
   that one may trod upon it dry-shod

---

from Assyria and Egypt. Although some scholars prefer to see this entire prophecy as a composition of the exilic period, it was Assyria and Egypt's hostility that were the concern of the Judahites in the later eighth century B.C.E.

12. *He shall raise a banner to the nations.* Earlier, God was raising a banner to far-off nations to attack Judah, but here the situation is reversed.

   the banished of Israel / and the dispersed of Judah. This might be taken as evidence of an exilic setting for this prophecy, but if it were written any time after 721 B.C.E., the prophet could have had in mind the grim fate of the northern kingdom as a signpost for what could happen imminently to the southern kingdom.

13. *Ephraim.* This is the northern kingdom of Israel.

14. *they shall swoop on the flank of the Philistines . . . / they shall plunder the Easterners.* The prophet envisages a united Israel and Judah striking enemies to the west, along the Mediterranean coast, and to the east, in Edom and Moab and perhaps even in Mesopotamia.

15. *the tongue of Egypt's sea.* This looks like an image for the Red Sea, which is tongue-shaped.

   His fierce wind. The first word *ba'yam*, occurring nowhere else, has defied etymological explanation, but the context suggests a sense like fierceness or power. The same word, *ruaḥ*, which means "spirit" above, here means "wind," and the antithesis between a gentle spirit and a fierce devastating wind is pointed.

   that one may trod upon it dry-shod. This clause completes a set of allusions to the miracle of the parting of the Sea of Reeds that runs through this and the next verse: the waving of the hand over the waters, the pushing back of the waters by a wind from

16   And it shall become a highway for His people's remnant
        that will remain from Assyria,
  as it was for Israel
     on the day it came up from the land of Egypt.

CHAPTER 12

1   And you shall say on that day:
     I acclaim You, O Lord, though You raged against me,
       Your wrath has withdrawn and You comforted me.
2   Look, God is my deliverance,
     I trust and fear not.
  For my strength and my power is Yah,
     and He became my deliverance.
3   And you shall draw water joyously
     from the springs of deliverance.
4   And you shall say on that day:
     "Acclaim the Lord, call upon His name.

God, walking where the sea was as on dry land. Here, of course, the drying up of the sea is a blight to the local inhabitants while the seabed becomes a highway for the saving remnant of Israel.

16. *that will remain from Assyria.* The Hebrew shows prominent sound-play: *'asher yisha'er me'ashur.*

CHAPTER 12   1. *I acclaim You, O Lord.* The language of this poem from the very beginning recalls the common formulas of the psalms of thanksgiving. The one important difference is that the thanksgiving psalms are usually recited by, or on behalf of, an individual—for example, after recovery from a grave illness—whereas in this poem the thanksgiving is collective or national. The editorial justification for inserting such a psalm at this point is that it comes immediately after the prophecy of national renewal and regeneration in chapter 11.

2. *my power.* This translation follows the scholarly consensus that *zimrah* means "power" or "might" and is a homonym for the more common word that means "song" or "hymn." It must be said, however, that in thanksgiving psalms the root *z-m-r*, which appears quite frequently, always has the sense of song. This entire line is a verbatim quotation from the Song of the Sea (Exodus 15:2), which is appropriate because the earlier text is one of the great poetic celebrations of national triumph through God's aid.

3. *the springs of deliverance.* Water sources are always precious in this arid region, as we are reminded in Exodus by the bringing forth of water from the rock for the thirsty people. However, this vivid poetic coinage—"the springs of deliverance"—is original to this text.

Make known His feats to the people,
    proclaim that His name is exalted.
Hymn to the LORD for He has wrought proudly,   5
    be it known through all the earth.
Shout loud, sing gladly, Zion's dweller,   6
    for great in your midst is Israel's Holy One."

CHAPTER 13   The portent about Babylon that Isaiah son of   1
Amoz saw in a vision.

On a bald mountain raise a banner.   2
    Lift up your voice to them, wave a hand,
        that they enter the gates of the princes.
I have charged the ones I have summoned,   3
    even called forth My warriors for My wrath,
        who exult in My pride.
The sound of a crowd on the mountains,   4

---

5. *be it known through all the earth.* This is a recurrent theme in biblical literature: God's powerful intervention in history on behalf of the people of Israel is a manifestation of His supreme dominion over all things, and the peoples of all the earth take note of it.

CHAPTER 13   1. *The portent about Babylon.* The word translated as "portent," *masaʾ,* has the literal sense of "burden," which is to say, a burden of prophetic pronouncement. Some render this as "oracle," though oracles tend to be murkier and also more strictly predictive. Babylon becomes an imperial power in the region that threatens, then destroys, the kingdom of Judah a century after Isaiah. Prophetic and other biblical books were conceived as open-ended affairs into which later materials could be introduced. Presumably, the editor felt that the portent about the doom of Babylon was in keeping with the outlook of Isaiah's prophecies concerning Assyria. The psalm placed as chapter 12 editorially marks the end of the first large unit of the book. The present chapter begins a series of prophecies about sundry foreign nations. Most of this material is later, although it is difficult to sort out the chronology of the various units.

2. *that they enter the gates of the princes.* "They" are the troops of the army invading Babylon.

3. *the ones I have summoned, / . . . My warriors for My wrath.* The political reference is unclear, though in verse 17 the Medes are mentioned as the ruthless invading army, and it was in fact the Persians—conflated with Media—who toppled the Babylonian empire in the fifth century B.C.E. These warriors enacting God's wrath sound rather like an apocalyptic, or at least supernatural, army.

4. *The sound.* The Hebrew word could also be read as an interjection, "hark," although "sound" makes at least as good sense in context.

the likeness of a vast people,
the sound of the din of kingdoms,
    nations assembling.
The LORD of Armies is mustering
    an army for war.
5   They come from a faraway land,
        from the end of the heavens—
the LORD with His anger's weapons,
    to destroy all the earth.
6   Howl, for the LORD's day is near,
        as shattering from Shaddai it shall come.
7   Therefore all hands shall go slack,
        every human heart shall quail.
8   They shall panic, and birth pangs shall seize them,
        like a woman in labor they shall shudder.
They shall gaze aghast at each other,
    their faces in flames.
9   Look, the LORD's day comes, ruthlessly,
        anger and smoldering wrath,
to turn the earth into desolation
    and expunge its offenses from it.
10   For the stars in the heavens and their constellations
        shall not shine with their light.
The sun shall go dark when it rises,
    and the moon shall not send forth its light.
11   And I will single out the world for its evil,
        against the wicked for their crime,
and put an end to the pride of the arrogant,
    bring low the overweening of tyrants.

---

5. *They come from a faraway land, / from the end of the heavens.* This may be merely a hyperbolic representation of an army coming from beyond the immediate region, but it again gives the invaders an apocalyptic look.

6. *shattering from Shaddai.* The more literal sense is "havoc" or "despoiling," but the translation emulates the sound-play of the Hebrew, *shod mishaddai.*

10. *the stars in the heavens . . . / shall not shine with their light.* This is still another striking instance in which poetic hyperbole becomes incipient apocalypse: the catastrophe about to overtake Babylon is cosmic, with the stars and the moon in the sky going dark and the sun rising without light.

I will make man scarcer than gold,   12
    human beings, than the gold of Ophir.
Therefore will I shake the heavens,   13
    and the earth shall quake from its base
in the anger of the Lord of Armies,
    on the day of His smoldering wrath.
And they shall be like a deer driven off,   14
    like sheep that are not gathered in.
Each man shall turn to his people,
    and each man shall flee to his land.
All who are found shall be stabbed,   15
    and all who are caught shall fall by the sword.
Their babes shall be smashed as they look,   16
    their homes shall be looted and their wives ravished.
I am about to rouse the Medes against them,   17
    who take no account of silver
        and have no desire of gold.
And with bows young men shall be pierced,   18
    and they shall not pity infants.
        Children they shall not spare.
And Babylon, splendor of kingdoms,   19
    the glorious pride of Chaldeans,
shall be as God's overthrowing
    of Sodom and Gomorrah.
She shall remain without settlers forever,   20

---

12. *the gold of Ophir.* Ophir, in the Red Sea region, was famous for its fine gold. In the Hebrew, a different word is used in this verset for "gold"; biblical Hebrew has several poetic synonyms for gold, but English has none.

14. *like a deer driven off, / like sheep.* These gentle and defenseless animals are the antithesis of the warriors that Babylonians once were, and by whom they are now overwhelmed.

15. *caught.* The meaning of the Hebrew verb is uncertain, and thus the translation is dictated by context. Elsewhere, this word means "swept away."

16. *babes . . . homes . . . wives.* The sheeplike men of Babylon are impotent to protect their most precious human and material possessions.
    as they look. Literally, "before their eyes."

18. *And with bows young men shall be pierced.* The Hebrew verb means "to smash," but that is not an action performed with a bow.

                have no dwellers for time without end.
              And the Arab shall not pitch his tent there,
                  nor shepherds bed their flocks there.
21   But wildcats shall lie down there,
                  and their homes shall be filled with owls.
              And ostriches shall dwell there,
                  and satyrs there shall dance.
22   And hyenas shall shriek in her palaces
                  and jackals in her mansions of pleasure.
              And it is close to come now.
                  Her days shall not draw on.

1   CHAPTER 14   For the Lord shall have pity on Jacob and again
shall choose Israel and set them down on their land, and the sojourner shall
2 join them and become part of the house of Jacob. And peoples shall take
them and bring them to their own place, and the house of Israel shall own
them on the Lord's lands as male slaves and slavegirls, and their captors
shall become their captives, and they shall hold sway over their taskmas-
3 ters. And it shall happen on the day the Lord relieves you of your pain and

---

20. *pitch his tent.* The Masoretic Text has *yahel,* "shine," but two manuscripts, followed by most scholars, show instead *ye'ehal,* "pitch a tent."

21. *wildcats.* The beasts in question have not been confidently identified; it is clear only that they are savage desert predators and probably emit a menacing sound.

   satyrs. The blurring of lines between the zoological and the mythological is character-istic of biblical poetry. These creatures may be something like goat-gods.

22. *in her palaces.* The Masoretic Text, patently defective here, reads *be'almenotav,* "in his widows," but three ancient versions reflect a text that showed *be'armenoteyha,* "in her palaces."

CHAPTER 14   1. *set them down on their land.* This formulation looks distinctly like the perspective of a prophet in the Babylonian exile.

   sojourner. That is, the resident alien, someone from a different ethnic stock who lives in the community of Israelites. This notion of non-Israelites joining the community of God's people is a recurrent theme in the late chapters of Isaiah.

2. *own them on the Lord's lands as male slaves and slavegirls.* The idea that in the return to Zion the former captors of the Israelites will become their menial servants is still another emphasis of Second Isaiah.

of your trouble and of the hard labor that was inflicted upon you, that you 4
shall take up this theme concerning the king of Babylon and say:

> How is the taskmaster ended,
>> arrogance is ended!
>
> The LORD has broken the wickeds' scepter,   5
>> the rod of rulers.
>
> He who struck down peoples in anger   6
>> with unrelenting blows,
>
> who held sway in wrath over nations,
>> pursued unsparingly.
>
> All the earth is calm and quiet,   7
>> bursts forth in song.
>
> The very cypresses rejoice over you,   8
>> the cedars of Lebanon:
>
> "With you now laid low,
>> the woodsman won't come up against us."
>
> Sheol below stirs for you   9
>> to greet your coming,

---

4. *you shall take up this theme concerning the king of Babylon.* It is by no means clear that this prose passage concluded here is by the same hand as the poem that now follows. In any event, it is quite possible that the poem exulting over the fall of the king of Babylon was actually composed at the moment when the Persians defeated the Babylonians and put an end to their empire. But some scholars think the introductory attachment of the poem to the king of Babylon is merely editorial and that the monarch could be Sargon, who was not buried in a tomb, or Sennacharib, who was assassinated.

    How is. The poem begins with the word *eikhah*, which usually signals the beginning of an elegy, but here instead it introduces an exultant poem celebrating the death of the tyrant.

5. *scepter / . . . rod.* The Hebrew terms can mean scepter, staff, rod, or even club, and this is a king who wielded his scepter like a club.

7. *All the earth.* The celebration of the tyrant's death is universal. This is the first of three senses in which the noun *'erets* will be used in the poem.

8. *the cedars of Lebanon / . . . you now laid low.* As elsewhere, the cedars of Lebanon are proverbial for their loftiness. These lines begin a thematic swinging between high and low that underlies the structure of the poem. The lofty trees are both literal and figurative. The tyrant cut down forests for his building projects and his siege-works, and, at the same time, the cedars and cypresses are metaphors for the great ones of the earth hacked down by the Babylonian king.

It rouses the shades,
    all the chiefs of the earth.
It raises from their thrones
    all the kings of the nations.

10   They all call out and say to you:
    "You, too, are stricken like us,
        like us you become.

11   Your pomp is brought down to Sheol,
    the murmur of your lutes.
Your bed is spread with worms,
    and your covers are maggots.

12   How are you fallen from the heavens,
    Bright One, Son of Dawn!
You are cut down to earth,
    dominator of nations!

13   And you once thought in your heart:
    'To the heavens will I ascend.
Above the eternal stars
    I will raise my throne

---

9. *It rouses the shades.* For the most part, Sheol in the Bible is imagined as a vast and deep pit that swallows those who have died, who thus know nothing but darkness and silence after their deaths. Here, however, the poet imagines an assembly of spirits of the dead, greeting the king, an idea loosely analogous to the representation of Hades in the sixth book of the Odyssey. It is hard to know if this whole picture reflects popular belief or is rather a useful—and vivid—poetic fiction.

    all the chiefs of the earth. They may have been chiefs when they were on earth, but *'erets* also means "underworld," and so what they may be is chiefs of the kingdom of death.

11. *your covers are maggots.* The Hebrew shows a brilliant pun: *tole'ah,* "maggots," also means "crimson cloth." The monarch who was used to sleeping under sumptuous dyed fabric now has a blanket of worms.

12. *How are you fallen from the heavens.* This verset encapsulates the up-down spatial thematics of the poem.

    Bright One, Son of Dawn. The appellation, of course, is heavily sarcastic; this is a sun that has set forever. The cosmic sweep of the language generated the idea among Christian interpreters that this figure is Lucifer (which means "light-bearer," in accordance with the Hebrew), that is, Satan.

    cut down. In the Hebrew, this is a term used for chopping down trees.

13. *To the heavens will I ascend.* This arrogant presumption links the tyrant with the Tower of Babel and many other biblical texts.

and sit on the mount of divine council,
in the far reaches of Zaphon.
I will climb to the tops of the clouds, 14
I will match the Most High.'
But to Sheol you were brought down, 15
to the far reaches of the Pit.
Those who see you stare, 16
they look at you:
'Is this the man who shook all the earth,
who made kingdoms shake,
who turned the world to wilderness, 17
and its towns destroyed,
his prisoners never released?'
All the kings of nations, 18
all lie honorably in their homes,
but you were flung from your grave 19
like a loathsome branch
clothed with the sword-slashed slain
who go down to the floor of the Pit
like a trampled corpse.
You shall not join them in burial, 20
for your land you laid waste
your people you slayed.

---

the mount of divine council, / in the far reaches of Zaphon. In Canaanite mythology, Mount Zaphon was the place of the council of the gods, like Olympus in Greek tradition.

15. *brought down, / to the far reaches of the Pit.* Instead of up, he goes down; instead of Mount Zaphon, the Pit.

18. *in their homes.* Many understand "homes" as "tombs" (compare the reference in Qohelet 12:5 to death as man's "everlasting home") with an eye to a neat contrast between honorable burial and being flung from the grave. But the Hebrew word does almost always mean "house" or "home," and the contrast may be between kings sleeping peacefully in their homes and the tyrant not even sleeping in the grave. But one cannot exclude the possibility that "homes" could be a wry epithet for the grave.

19. *to the floor of the Pit.* The Masoretic Text has *'avney bor*, "the stones of the Pit," which is a little puzzling. This translation reads with Blenkinsopp, *'adney bor*. The emended noun means "sockets," and in Job 38:6 it is used for the foundations of earth.

20. *for your land you laid waste.* This is the third sense of *'erets* displayed in the poem.

Let there be no lasting name
　　for the seed of evildoers!
21　Ready slaughter for his sons
　　for their father's crime.
Let them not rise to take hold of the earth,
　　and let the world be filled with towns."

22　And I will rise against them,
　　says the LORD of Armies,
and I will cut off from Babylon name and remnant,
　　kith and kin, says the LORD.
23　And I will make it a dwelling for herons,
　　and pools of water.
And I will sweep it with a broom of destruction.
　　says the LORD of Armies.

24　The LORD of Armies has vowed, saying:
　　As I have devised it, surely it shall be,
　　　and as I have planned, it shall come about:
25　To break Assyria in My land,
　　and on My mountains I will trample him.
And his yoke will be gone from upon them
　　and his burden gone from their back.

---

21. *Ready slaughter for his sons / for their father's crime.* Here sons are punished for the sins of fathers. In political terms, what is envisaged is a massacre of the whole royal line, a not infrequent practice when a king is overthrown.

　let the world be filled with towns. Once the destructive tyrant is gone, the world can be rebuilt.

22. *And I will rise against them.* This clearly begins a new prophecy, connected with the previous one by the theme of the destruction of Babylon.

　kith and kin. The literal sense of the Hebrew is "offspring and grandchildren."

23. *herons.* The identification of the *qipod* is uncertain. Elsewhere it appears to mean "hedgehog" (as in modern Hebrew), but hedgehogs do not live in marshlands.

24. *The LORD of Armies has vowed.* This is the beginning of a third distinct prophecy in this chapter, directed to the destruction of Assyria and so perhaps composed by Isaiah son of Amoz.

25. *To break Assyria in My land, / and on My mountains.* The Assyrian empire will be broken in the Judahite territory it has attacked and sought to conquer.

This is the plan framed for all the earth   26
    and this the hand outstretched over all nations.
For the LORD of Armies has devised it and who can thwart it?   27
    His hand is outstretched and who can turn it back?

In the year of the death of King Ahaz this portent was.   28

Rejoice not, Philistia, all of you,
    that the rod of him who struck you is broken.   29
For from the stock of a snake an asp shall come out,
    and its fruit a fiery flying serpent.
And the poor shall graze in My pastures,   30
    and the needy shall lie down in safety.
And I will kill your root with famine,
    your remnant it shall slay.
Howl, O gate, scream, O town,   31
    Philistia, all of you melts away.
For from the north smoke has come,

---

26. *the plan framed for all the earth.* It is noteworthy that the poem imagines the opposition between the people of Israel and the Assyrians in a global perspective, a design affecting all the earth and all nations.

28. *In the year of the death of King Ahaz.* This brief prose introduction marks the fourth prophecy included in this chapter, this one directed against the Philistines.

29. *the rod of him who struck you is broken.* Several Assyrian kings carried out campaigns against the Philistines along the Mediterranean coast, and there is scholarly debate about which one is referred to here.

    from the stock of a snake an asp shall come out. The probable reference is Assyria: though seemingly defeated, it will produce venomous successors. This understanding may be supported by the mention in verse 31 that destruction will come down from the north, the point of departure for the Assyrian forces.

    fiery flying serpent. Here *saraf* appears to carry its full serpentine mythological weight. See the comment on verse 2 in chapter 6 regarding seraphim.

30. *in My pastures.* The received text shows *bekhorey,* "firstborn of" (the poor), which makes little sense. Some Hebrew manuscripts have *bekharay,* "in My pastures," which works perfectly with the verb "graze."

31. *smoke.* The clear implication is the cloud of smoke (and probably dust) over the heads of the vast invading army. It is best to understand this as an evocative ellipsis: from the distance, as the enemy approaches, only the column of smoke is visible.

and none is alone in his ranks.
And what will he answer to a nation's envoys?—
32   that the LORD again has founded Zion,
and His people's poor shelter there.

1 CHAPTER 15   A portent concerning Moab.

Yes, in the night was Ar sacked,
Moab was undone.
Yes, in the night it was sacked,
Qir Moab was undone.
2   They went up to the temple of Dibon,
to the high places, to weep.
For Nebo and for Medbah
Moab wails.
Every head in it is shaved,
every beard is shorn.
3   In its streets they are girt with sackcloth,
on its roofs and in its squares.
All of them are wailing,
coming down in tears.
4   Heshbon and Elealeh cry out,
as far as Jahaz their voice is heard.
Therefore Moab's picked warriors cry,

---

and none is alone in his ranks. The Hebrew here is somewhat obscure, and there are some odd textual variants. The word translated as "ranks," *mo'adim*, usually means "appointed time." Perhaps here it might indicate "appointed forces."

32. *the LORD again has founded Zion.* The Hebrew merely says "has founded," but the implication is a new founding of Zion after the exile, just as the verb "build" is sometimes used to mean "rebuild." These final words clearly place this text among the prophecies of national restoration composed in the Babylonian exile.

CHAPTER 15   1. *in the night.* The Hebrew *beleyl* announces a kind of phonetic theme because it both alliterates and virtually rhymes with *yeyeilil,* "wails," which appears in verses 2 and 3 and then twice (in noun-form) in verse 8.
    Ar . . . Qir Moab. These are the first of a whole series of names of Moabite towns, invoked to suggest how sweeping is the destruction that overtakes the entire country.

2. *They went up to the temple of Dibon.* In their panic and despair, the Moabites spread out to their sundry cult-places in order to entreat their gods to help them.
    Every head . . . is shaved. Shaving the hair is a sign of mourning.

their life-breath broken up.
My heart for Moab cries out,   5
   those who flee her as far as Zoar
      and Eglath Shelishiyah.
For by the Ascent of Luhith,
   in weeping they go up.
For on the road to Horanaim
   they rouse disaster's cry.
For the Nimrim waters   6
   have become a desolation.
For the grass has withered,
   the vegetation gone,
      the green growth is no more.
Therefore the gains they have made and their stores   7
   they bear off to the Wadi of Willows.
For screaming encircles   8
   the region of Moab.
As far as Eglaim her wail,
   to Beer Eilim her wail,
For Dimon's waters are full of blood,   9
   yes, I will add still more against Dimon:
for Moab's survivors, a lion,
   for the remnant of the land.

---

4. *their life-breath broken up.* This verset is quite obscure, and the meaning of the Hebrew verb is especially doubtful.

5. *My heart for Moab cries out.* This is surely intended as sarcasm because the Israelite speaker is gladdened by the destruction of this traditional enemy of his people.

   they go up. The Hebrew has "he goes up." Vacillation between singular and plural is one of several sources of confusion in this poem.

7. *Therefore the gains they have made and their stores.* The Hebrew of this verset is crabbed, and hence any translation somewhat conjectural. What seems to be depicted is the Moabites fleeing from their towns before an unnamed enemy, carrying off whatever of their possessions they can manage to bring with them.

   the Wadi of Willows. Like many of the place-names in this prophecy, the watercourse in question has resisted identification.

9. *yes, I will add still more against Dimon.* The Hebrew of this verset as well as its connection with the second verset is obscure. Here is a literal rendering: Yes, I will set against [or upon] Dimon and its things.

   for Moab's survivors, a lion. Numerous emendations have been proposed here, especially for the last word, none very convincing. The language is certainly cryptic but may

CHAPTER 16

1   Send a lamb
        to the ruler of the land,
     from the wilderness crag
        to the Mount of the Daughter of Zion.
2   And like a wandering bird
        sent out from the nest,
     the daughters of Moab shall be
        at the fords of the Arnon.
3   Take counsel,
        weigh judgment.
     Make your shade like the night
        at high noon.
     Shelter those driven out,
        do not expose the displaced.
4   Those driven from Moab
        shall sojourn among you.
     Be a shelter for them
        against the marauder.
     For oppression is over,
        marauding has ended,
            the tramplers are gone from the land.
5   And a throne is set firm in kindness
        and on it shall sit in truth

---

make sense as it stands in the received text. We know from multiple biblical sources that lions proliferated in this region in the ancient period and were a menace to people and to their flocks. What the writer may have had in mind is that when the desperate Moabites flee from their towns as those towns are sacked by invaders, in the very place where they sought refuge they encounter lions and become their prey. In this understanding, the lions are what God "add[s] still more against Dimon."

CHAPTER 16   1. *Send a lamb / to the ruler of the land.* The Hebrew is very cryptic. This translation is based on the guess that the ruler of the land is the governing power in Judah and that the fugitive Moabites are obliged to turn to the Judahites for help. The lamb would be some kind of tribute. But whatever historical circumstance may be invoked here is highly uncertain. Verses 3–4 appear to be an injunction to take in Moabite refugees.

3. *Make your shade like the night.* "Shade" here is used in its frequent metaphoric sense of "protection."

5. *a throne is set firm in kindness / and on it shall sit in truth.* This line shows the device of the "break-up pattern" in which the two terms of a hendiadys are separated and placed in

> in the tent of David
>> one who judges and seeks justice
>> and is swift to do right.
>
> We have heard of Moab's pride,   6
>> so very proud,
> his pride and his proud anger.
>> Not so are his lies.
> Therefore shall Moab wail for Moab,   7
>> all of it shall wail.
> For the raisin cakes of Qir-Haresheth
>> you shall utter naught but moans.
> For the fields of Heshbon languish,   8
>> the vines of Sibmah.
> The notables of nations
>> pounded her tendrils.
> As far as Jazer they reached,
>> they strayed to the desert.
> Her shoots they pulled out,
>> they passed on to the sea.
> Therefore do I weep in the keening of Jazer,   9

---

the two halves of the line—here, *ḥesed*, "kindness" (or "loyalty") near the beginning of the first verset and *'emet*, "truth," at the end of the second verset. The apparent connection of this verse with the preceding lines is that with a king seeking justice sitting on the throne of Judah, the Moabite refugees can expect to receive succor.

6. *We have heard of Moab's pride.* Although this prophecy is linked with the previous one by the subject of Moab, the theme now is exulting over Moab's fall, with the keening for her disaster in verses 9–11 perhaps sarcastic.

Not so are his lies. The Hebrew noun here is problematic and many different solutions have been proposed.

7. *the raisin cakes.* Though some see these as an element in the cult, the mention in the next verse of the vineyards signifies where grapes for fine wine were grown and suggests that the raisin cakes, a different use of grapes, were simply part of the good times before disaster overtook Moab.

8. *The notables of nations.* Some interpreters understand *ba'aley goyim* as a place-name, which in terms of its form it could conceivably be. But since the lines that follow evoke an army wreaking havoc and sweeping down to the coast, it is more likely that the phrase, as rendered here, refers to invaders, or their commanders.

9. *Therefore do I weep.* It is ambiguous whether the speaker expresses sympathy for the plight of Moab or whether these lines are ironic.

> I drench you with my tears, Heshbon and Elealeh.
>   For over your fig and grain harvest
>   a shout has fallen away.
> 10 Joy and delight are gone from the farmland,
>   and in the vineyard no glad song or cheers.
>   No wine is in the presses,
>   the treader does not tread,
>   the shout is stifled.
> 11 Therefore my heart moans like a lyre for Moab,
>   my inward self for Qir-Heres.

12 And it shall happen that Moab will be seen unavailing on the high place,
13 and he will come to his sanctuary and achieve nothing. This is the word
14 that the LORD spoke concerning Moab in time past. And now the LORD
has spoken, saying, "In three years, like the years of a hired worker, Moab's
glory shall be debased, despite all the great crowd, and what is left—the
smallest bit, of no account."

1 # CHAPTER 17   A portent concerning Damascus.

> Damascus is to be no more a city
>   but shall become a heap of ruins.

---

a shout. This is an exclamation of joy, *heydad.*

12. *unavailing on the high place.* The Moabites will go to their site of worship, a hilltop altar
and sanctuary, to entreat their gods for help, but it will be unavailing.

13. *This is the word that the LORD spoke concerning Moab in time past.* The reference seems
to be to an earlier prophecy about the destruction of Moab (perhaps the one recorded in
chapter 15) that was not fulfilled. In a kind of temporal revision, the prophet now says that
the destruction will come in another three years.

14. *three years, like the years of a hired worker.* One might infer that there were contractual
arrangements—in all likelihood, for indentured servants—that fixed the term of service
for three years. Just as the hired worker awaits the end of his period of service and the
recompense and liberation that come at the end, the Israelites await the promised destruction of Moab.

CHAPTER 17   1. *Damascus.* This is the capital city of Syria, or Aram, with which
the northern kingdom of Israel allied itself. Hence a prophecy of the destruction of both,
as their bracketing in verse 3 emphasizes.

The towns of Aroer are abandoned,   2
　　become a place for flocks
　　　　that bed down there with none troubling them.
There is an end to the forts in Ephraim   3
　　and of kingship in Damascus.
And the remnant of Aram
　　shall be like what Israel's glory has become,
　　　　says the LORD of Armies.
And it shall happen on that day,   4
　　Jacob's glory shall turn gaunt
　　　　and the fat of his flesh become lean.

And as he was like one who gathers standing grain,   5
　　by armfuls gleaning,
he shall be like one gathering ears of grain
　　in the Valley of Rephaim,
only gleanings left him, as when an olive tree is beaten,   6
　　two or three berries at the top of the bough,
　　　　four or five on the branches of the fruit-tree
says the LORD God of Israel.

On that day man shall turn to his Maker and his eyes shall look to Israel's 7
Holy One. And he shall not turn to the altars, his handiwork that his   8
fingers made, and he shall not look to the cultic poles and the incense
altars. On that day his stronghold towns shall be like the abandoned sites 9
of Horesh and Amir that were abandoned because of the Israelites, and it
shall become a desolation.

---

4. *Jacob's glory shall turn gaunt.* Some interpreters try to make this verset more "logical" by rendering *kavod* as "body," a sense it probably does not have, or "weight," again a dubious sense, even if the related adjective *kaved* does mean "heavy." Poetic expression need not have this kind of neat consistency.

5. *And as he was like one who gathers standing grain.* Although this is the clear sense of this clause, it must be said that the syntax of this entire verse and the next one is quite crabbed.
　　the Valley of Rephaim. One infers from the context that this was a place that produced meager crops. It may be relevant that the place-name means Ghost Valley.

7. *On that day man shall turn to his Maker.* What leads him to turn away from the sites of idolatry to God is, as verse 8 makes clear, the destruction that will be wreaked on Israel.

10   For you have forgotten the God of your deliverance,
        and you have not recalled the Rock, your stronghold.
     Therefore did you plant your saplings for vegetal gods,
        sow the slip of an alien god.
11   The day you plant it, it will flourish,
        in the morn your sowing will blossom,
     but the roots become a heap on the ill-starred day,
        and grievous pain.

12   Woe, crowd of many peoples,
        like the roar of the seas they roar.
     and the clamor of nations
        like the clamor of mighty waters they clamor.
13   Nations like the clamor of many waters they clamor,
        but He rebukes them and they flee far away,
     driven like chaff in the hills before wind
        and like tumbleweed in the whirlwind.
14   At eventide, look—terror!
        Before morning it is no more.
     This is the lot of our despoilers
        and the fate of our plunderers.

---

10. *the Rock.* Though this is a common epithet for God in Psalms, the hardness of rock also forms a nice antithesis to the saplings and slips planted as part of the cult of nature gods.

    saplings for vegetal gods. The Hebrew seems to say "saplings of the pleasant ones," but *na'aman* is probably a designation for Tammuz, the god who dies annually and is reborn each spring. Blenkinsopp is a bit too specific, and too Greek, in translating this as "Adonis."

11. *but the roots become a heap on the ill-starred day.* Of the four Hebrew words of this verset, the only one whose meaning is certain is *beyom,* "on the day."

12. *Woe, crowd of many peoples.* This marks a new prophecy, concerning not Damascus but the many nations that have despoiled Israel. The identification of a specific historical event has proved elusive. Although some scholars are inclined to attribute this prophecy to Isaiah, one reason to be skeptical about the attribution is that the poetry is in no way on the level of the great poetry of the book's first chapters: both the simile of the roar of the seas and the wind-driven chaff (verse 13) are biblical clichés, and the verbatim repetition of the second half of verse 12 in the first half of 13 seems inert.

CHAPTER 18

Woe, land of the whirring wings   1
    that is beyond the rivers of Nubia!
That sends envoys into the sea,   2
    in vessels of reeds on the face of the water.
Go, swift messengers,
    to a rangy and smooth-skinned nation,
to a fearsome people from beyond,
    a gibberish nation and sowing defeat,
        whose land is cut through with rivers.
All the world's inhabitants and dwellers upon earth,   3
    when a banner is raised in the mountains, you shall see,
        and when the ram's horn blasts, you shall hear.
For thus said the LORD to me: 4
    I calmly look down from My dwelling place

CHAPTER 18   1. *land of the whirring wings.* Nubia (Cush in the Hebrew), along the upper reaches of the Nile in equatorial Africa, was known for its abundance of insects, a phenomenon attested to by Herodotus. The vessels of reeds mentioned in the next verse are equally part of the poem's evocation of the realia of a kingdom along the Nile.

2. *Go, swift messengers.* The messengers (*mal' akhim*) are evidently a different group from the envoys (*tsirim*) of the preceding line. It is not clear where the Nubian envoys are heading, and different attempts have been made to line up this passage with a particular moment in the political history of the late eighth century B.C.E. The swift messengers appear to be sent out from the kingdom of Judah to announce to the Nubians the disaster about to overtake them.

    a rangy and smooth-skinned nation. The Hebrew word translated as "rangy" is literally "pulled out" or "elongated," not the usual word for "tall." The term represented as "smooth-skinned" derives from a verbal stem that means either "polished" or "plucked." This would be an exoticizing way to describe the tall Africans with little body hair, even though their blackness is unmentioned.

    a gibberish nation. The Hebrew says "a *qaw-qaw* nation," this being an onomatopoeia for unintelligible sounds, always a scary aspect of foreigners.

    and sowing defeat. The Hebrew says merely "and defeat," but something like "sowing" or "inflicting" seems to be implied. This is in other words, a powerful nation.

3. *All the world's inhabitants.* The connection with the prophecy concerning Nubia may simply be that all the world's inhabitants are invited to witness the judgment God will wreak on Nubia.

    banner . . . ram's horn. Both are signals for rallying armies.

when the heat dazzles in the light,
  when the dew-cloud is in the harvest heat.
5   For before the harvest, when the blossom is gone,
  and the berry has ripened, becomes the bloom,
He shall cut away twigs with pruning hooks,
  lop off, take away the slack branches.
6   They shall be left together for the mountain vultures,
  and for the beasts of the land.
The vultures shall summer on them
  and all the beasts of the land winter on them.

7 All that time tribute shall be brought to the LORD of Armies from a rangy
and smooth-skinned people from beyond, a gibberish nation, and sowing
defeat, whose land is cut through with rivers, to the place of the name of
the LORD of Armies, Mount Zion.

1 # CHAPTER 19   A portent concerning Egypt.

The LORD is about to ride on a swift cloud
  and come down to Egypt.
And the ungods of Egypt shall shake before Him,
  and Egypt's heart inwardly quail.
2   And I will incite Egypt against Egypt,

---

4. *when the heat dazzles in the light.* This and all the seasonal indications that follow express
the temporal imminence of God's judgment.

5. *cut away twigs.* The entire agricultural metaphor points to the decimation of Nubia that
is to be inflicted by God.

7. *All that time.* It is unusual for a statement just expressed in poetry to be repeated verbatim
in prose. This could reflect an editorial addition to the text. In any case, the tribute brought
to the LORD is a prophecy that the Nubians will become subject to Judah.
    the place of the name of the LORD of Armies. The insertion of the superfluous "the name
of" reflects a Late Biblical tendency to qualify direct assertions about YHWH by introducing "the name of" as a kind of mediation. Thus it looks suspiciously like the intervention
of a later redactor.

CHAPTER 19   1. *ride on a swift cloud.* The mythological image of the deity mounted
on a cloud derives from Canaanite poetry and appears in several of the biblical psalms.

and each man shall battle his brother, each man his fellow,
town against town, kingdom against kingdom.
And Egypt's spirit shall be sapped within it,   3
and its counsel I will confound.
And they shall seek out the ungods and the shades
and the ghosts and the familiar spirits.
And I will hand Egypt over to a harsh master,   4
and a fierce king shall rule over them,
says the Master LORD of Armies.
And water shall be drained from the sea,   5
the river turn dry and parched.
And canals shall fall into neglect,   6
Egypt's watercourses drained and dried up.
Rush and reed shall wither,
laid bare at the Nile,   7
alongside the Nile,
And all that is planted by the Nile
shall wither, blow away, be no more.
And the fishermen shall lament and keen,   8
all who cast hooks into the Nile,
and those spreading nets on the water shall be forlorn.
And the flax workers shall be distraught,   9
carters and weavers turn pale.
And her foundations shall be crushed,   10
all who build dams be downcast.
The princes of Zoan are but fools,   11

---

2. *kingdom against kingdom.* This is sometimes interpreted as a clash between the Northern and Southern Kingdoms of Egypt. Others see here a reference to the different districts of Egypt ruled by different princes.

3. *the shades / and the ghosts.* Egypt was famous for its cult of the dead.

4. *the Master LORD of Armies.* The first epithet for God here aggressively picks up the "harsh master" at the beginning of the verse.

5. *And water shall be drained.* Biblical writers often look with envy on Egypt's abundant sources of irrigation from the Nile and elsewhere, which are a striking contrast to the land of Israel, dependent as it is on rainfall. This gives a special edge to the prophecy in the next verse of an Egypt "drained and dried up."

7. *laid bare at the Nile.* The translation reproduces the elliptic syntax of the Hebrew.

the wisest councillors of Pharaoh give witless counsel.
How can you say to Pharaoh:
  I am the son of sages,
    the son of ancient kings?
12 Where then are your sages?
  Let them tell you, pray, and let them know
    what the LORD of Armies devised against Egypt.
13 The princes of Zoan have been fools,
  the princes of Noph are deceived.
    The chiefs of her tribes have led Egypt astray.
14 The LORD has poured into her a twisted spirit,
  and they have led Egypt astray in all it does,
    as a drunkard strays into his vomit.
15 And there shall be nothing to do for Egypt,
  neither head nor tail, palm branch nor reed.

16 On that day, Egypt shall be like women, and tremble and fear from the
17 raised hand that the LORD of Armies raises against it. And the land of
Judah shall become a terror to Egypt. Whoever mentions it to them shall
be afraid because of the counsel of the LORD of Armies that He devises
18 against them. On that day, five cities in the land of Egypt shall speak the
language of Canaan and shall swear to the LORD of Armies. The City of the

---

11. *the wisest councillors . . . give witless counsel.* A verb appears to have dropped out in
the Hebrew, or perhaps "give" is meant to be implied. Egypt was renowned for exercising
wisdom, but here the wisdom fails.

15. *neither head nor tail, palm branch nor reed.* These are two different idioms with the
sense of through and through, from top to bottom, one expression referring to the human
body and the other to a plant.

16. *On that day.* These words begin a series of five "on that day" prose prophecies, regarded
by most scholars as later additions. One should keep in mind that the Prophetic books
grew by a process of sedimentation, later writers responding to earlier texts and composing
prophecies in their spirit.

17. *And the land of Judah shall become a terror to Egypt.* This bold statement of Judahite
triumphalism reflects no known or ever likely historical reality.

18. *the land of Egypt shall speak the language of Canaan and shall swear to the LORD of
Armies.* The language of Canaan is probably Hebrew. The notion that the Egyptians will
become worshippers of the God of Israel might have been encouraged by a time when there
was a large and vigorous diaspora community in Egypt, which would have been the case at
least as early as the fifth century B.C.E. Proposals to locate any of these prophecies as late
as the second century B.C.E. are unconvincing.

Sun it shall be said of one of them. On that day the altar of the Lord shall ₁₉
be in the midst of the land of Egypt and a pillar at its border to the Lord.
And it shall become a sign and a witness for the Lord of Armies in the ₂₀
land of Egypt that when they cry out to the Lord because of oppressors,
He sends them a deliverer and one who contests for them, and He shall
save them. And the Lord shall become known to Egypt, and the Egyptians ₂₁
shall know the Lord on that day, and they shall worship with sacrifice and
grain offering and make a vow to the Lord and fulfill it. And the Lord ₂₂
shall strike Egypt with plagues, plaguing and healing, and they shall turn
back to the Lord, and He shall hear their entreaty and heal them. On that ₂₃
day there shall be a highway from Egypt to Assyria, and Assyria shall come
into Egypt and Egypt into Assyria, and Egypt shall worship with Assyria.
On that day Israel shall be a third partner with Egypt and with Assyria, as ₂₄
a blessing in the midst of the earth. Which the Lord of Armies conferred, ₂₅
saying, "Blessed are My people Egypt and My handiwork Assyria and Israel
my estate."

CHAPTER 20   In the year Tartan came to Ashdod when ₁
Sargon king of Assyria sent him, and he battled against Ashdod and cap-

---

The City of the Sun. The Masoretic Text reads "the City of Destruction," *'ir heres,* but
some Hebrew manuscripts as well as several ancient translations read instead, more plausibly, *'ir ḥeres,* "the City of the Sun," which is probably the Egyptian Heliopolis. The scribal
error would have been caused by the fact that *ḥeres* is a rather rare synonym for "sun" and
by the context of destruction created in the previous prophecy.

21. *And the Lord shall become known to Egypt.* Here the utopian fantasy of the Egyptians
embracing the faith of Israel is made explicit.

22. *strike Egypt with plagues.* The writer of course has in mind the precedent of the Ten
Plagues, though in this case the afflictions impel the Egyptians to turn to YHWH.

23. *there shall be a highway from Egypt to Assyria.* This idea of a royal road joining the
two great warring empires that long threatened Israel and the creation of a God-fearing
triple partnership of Egypt, Assyria, and Israel to be a blessing to all the earth is the most
extravagant utopian fantasy of all the prophecies in this chapter. It is by no means clear
whether it is relatively early or late, although Assyria might not have been much of an issue
for a later writer.

CHAPTER 20   1. *In the year Tartan came to Ashdod when Sargon king of Assyria
sent him.* This notation refers to an actual historical event. In 714 B.C.E. the coastal city
of Ashdod rebelled against Assyria. Sargon dispatched a force against Ashdod under the
command of Tartan, and in 711 the rebellion was suppressed, its leader taken prisoner, and
the city reduced to subject status. All this leads one to suspect that precisely at this moment,

2 tured it. At that time the LORD spoke through Isaiah son of Amoz, saying,
"Go, and loosen the sackcloth from your loins and take off your sandals
3 from your feet." And so he did, going naked and barefoot. And the LORD
said, "As my servant Isaiah has gone naked and barefoot three years, it is a
4 sign and portent for Egypt and for Nubia. Just so shall the king of Assyria
drive off the captives of Egypt and the exiles of Nubia, lads and elders,
5 naked and barefoot with bare buttocks—the nakedness of Egypt. And they
shall be dismayed and ashamed of Nubia, in which they trusted, and of
6 Egypt, their glory. And the dweller of this coastland shall say on that day:
'Why, if it is thus with those we looked to, to whom we fled for help to be
saved before the king of Assyria, how shall we escape?'"

1 CHAPTER 21   A portent concerning the Desert of the Sea.

As storms sweep the Negeb
   from the desert he comes, from a fearsome land.

Isaiah undertook the symbolic act spelled out in the following verses, even though it is directed to the fate of Egypt and Nubia, not Ashdod.

2. *going naked and barefoot.* This kind of symbolic act performed by the prophet at God's behest occurs a number of times in Hosea and Ezekiel, but this is the sole instance in Isaiah.

4. *Just so shall the king of Assyria drive off the captives of Egypt and the exiles of Nubia.* It should be kept in mind that this was a period of repeated armed confrontation between Assyria and Egypt, with inner divisions in Judah between pro-Egyptian groups and those who sought to pursue accommodation with Assyria.
   captives . . . exiles. The Hebrew uses abstractions ("captivity," "exile") to indicate persons.
   with bare buttocks. It was unclear how complete Isaiah's "nakedness" was. Now, however, this detail is added that strongly emphasizes the shameful exposure of the Egyptians.
   the nakedness of Egypt. The term is used both literally and figuratively. The exiles stripped of their garments are literally naked, while "the land's nakedness," a phrase Joseph uses to his brothers referring to Egypt, means that which should not be exposed, or in this case, the shame of Egypt.

5. *in which they trusted.* The received text has *mabatam,* "their look," but the Qumran Isaiah reads *mivtaham,* "their trust." The scribal error was probably influenced by the appearance of *mabat* in the next verse.

CHAPTER 21   1. *the Desert of the Sea.* This sounds rather like an oxymoron, and attempts to explain it are uncertain. Perhaps the best scholarly guess is that it refers to a Mesopotamian marsh region, which would have been Assyrian territory at the time of Isaiah, or under Babylon later.
   from the desert he comes. The one coming would be the invader.

A harsh vision has been told me: 2
    the traitor betrays, the despoiler despoils.
Go up, Elam, lay siege, Media,
    all her groaning I have ended.
Therefore my loins are filled with shuddering.   3
    Pangs have siezed me, like birth pangs.
I am too contorted to hear,
    too dismayed to see.
My heart has gone astray,   4
    spasms dismay me.
My evening of revels
    has turned to terror.

From "lay the table" to "let the watchman watch,"   5
    from "eat and drink" to "rise, commander, burnish shield with oil."
For thus said the Master to me: 6
Go, post a watchman
    who will see and tell.
And he shall scc a rider,   7
    a pair of horsemen,
a rider on a donkey,

---

2. *go up, Elam, lay siege, Media.* The historical reference of this prophecy being unclear, all one can say is that these are two Mesopotamian peoples. Since Media–Persia overwhelmed Babylonia, it could be that the object of attack is Babylonia. Babylon is in fact mocked in the last line of this poem.

    all her groaning I have ended. The "her" would logically refer to Elam and Media, though those should have a plural referent (unless they are viewed collectively). Some scholars emend the Hebrew word for "groaning" to "joy," which would then be attached more neatly to the object of the invasion.

3. *Therefore my loins are filled with shuddering.* Here and in what follows the speaker of the prophecy appears to identify imaginatively with the kingdom about to be devastated.

5. *From "lay the table" to "let the watchmen watch."* The Hebrew lacks both "from" and to." This translation follows the proposal of the New Jewish Publication Society version.

    burnish shield with oil. The shields were leather, sometimes studded with metal. Rubbing the front surface with oil made them slippery and more of an obstacle to the enemy. In any case, the thrust of both lines is a switch from peaceful enjoyment to war.

6. *post a watchman.* Some interpreters take the watchman as a figure for the prophet, but this could as easily be an actual watchman who sees the mounted attackers approaching.

7. *a rider, / a pair of horsemen.* These lines pick up the point of view of the lookout, who first sees one rider, then more than one.

                a rider on a camel.
            And he shall listen intently,
                with great intentness.
8   And the seer shall call out:
            "On the Master's lookout
                I stand perpetually by day
                    and on my watch I am stationed all through the nights.
9   And look, it is coming—
                a man riding, a pair of horsemen."
            And He answered and said:
                "Babylon surely has fallen
                    and all its gods' idols He has dashed to the ground.
10   My threshing and what falls on the granary floor!"

What I heard from the LORD of Armies, the God of Israel, I have told you.

11   A portent concerning Dumah.
            To me someone calls from Seir:
                "Watchman, what of the night,
                    watchman, what of the night?"
12   The watchman said: "The morning comes,
                and night as well.

---

8. *And the seer shall call out.* The received text reads: "And he shall call out: A lion!" This is problematic if the danger is cavalry. The Qumran Isaiah has instead of "lion," *'aryeh*, "the seer," *haro' eh*, which is merely a reversal of consonants, and that looks more likely.

10. *My threshing and what falls on the granary floor.* This line is enigmatic, but because threshing and separating the grain from the chaff are often used in biblical poetry as a metaphor for the destruction of the wicked, that may be the intention here.

    What I heard from the LORD. This sentence is not part of the poem and functions as a prose epilogue to it.

11. *Dumah . . . Seir.* The kingdom referred to lies just to the east of ancient Israel: "Seir" is a poetic synonym for Edom, and "Dumah" could conceivably be a variation of Edom.

    watchman, what of the night? The Hebrew has a haunting musicality, *shomer mah milaylah / shomer mah mileyl*, and, understandably, the phrase would often reappear in later Hebrew poetry. But one must concede that this entire short prophecy is far too fragmentary to allow us to guess what it is about. The enigma is compounded by the last line of the prophecy, "If you would ask, do ask, / turn back, come." Linguistically, it should be noted that both the word for "ask" and the word for "come" are Aramaicisms, a usage that probably reflects a relatively late date, certainly well after the eighth-century B.C.E. setting of Isaiah.

If you would ask, do ask,
    turn back, come."

A portent in Arabia.   13
In the scrubland, in Arabia,
    you lodge, Dedonite caravans.
To meet the thirsty   14
    bring water.
The dwellers of the land of Tema
    greet the fugitives with bread.
For they are fugitives before the sword,   15
    before the drawn sword
and before the bent bow
    and before the crush of war.

For thus did the Master say to me: "In another year, like the year of a hired 16
worker, Kedar's glory shall be gone. And the remnant of the number of 17
Kedar's warrior bowmen shall dwindle, for the Lord God of Israel has
spoken."

---

13. *in Arabia.* It is puzzling that the chain of prophecies concerning foreign nations should reach as far to the southeast as Arabia (the vocalization of the name is peculiar), but Dedan and Tema, about to be mentioned, are definitely in the Arabian peninsula.

    scrubland. The Hebrew *ya' ar* usually means "forest," but there are no forests in Arabia, and here it seems likely that what is meant is a region where low bushes grow.

15. *fugitives before the sword.* Unfortunately, it is not feasible to say precisely who these pathetic war refugees are.

    the crush of war. The literal sense of the first of these two nouns is "heaviness," but surely something like "crush," or "brutal pressure" is meant.

16. *another year, like the year of a hired worker.* Earlier, it was three years like the years of a hired worker. Either there was an alternative for an indentured servant of a one-year contract, or there was a particular—perhaps, especially rigorous—way of computing the year in such arrangements with laborers.

    Kedar's glory. Roughly, Kedar is a biblical designation for the Arab people.

17. *the number of Kedar's warrior bowmen.* The Masoretic Text reads: "The number of bow, warriors of the Kedarites." This translation supposes a scribal transposition of the original order of words, so that *mispar giborey qeshet beney qedar* was turned into the syntactically dubious *mispar-qeshet giborey beney qedar*, a syntactic string for which the present note has provided a literal translation above.

CHAPTER 22   A Valley of Vision portent.

1

What is wrong with you that you go up,
  all of you, to the rooftops?

2   The bustling town is filled with shouts,
  the reveling city.
Your slain are not slain by the sword
  and not dead in battle.

3   All your captains have gone off,
  have fled far away.
All those of you who stayed have been taken captive,
  without bows have been taken captive.

4   Therefore have I said
  turn away from me,
    let me weep bitterly.
Do not rush to console me
  for the ruin of my People's Daughter.

5   For it is a day of turmoil and trampling and tumult
  for the Master, LORD of Armies,
in the Valley of Vision Kir crashes about

CHAPTER 22   1. *Valley of Vision.* Attempts to identify this place have been unavailing, though since this prophecy concerns Jerusalem, it seems likely that this is a valley in the vicinity of Jerusalem.

What is wrong with you that you go up, / . . . to the rooftops. Going up to the rooftops, perhaps to conduct parties in the fine weather, is part of the reveling of the city, unmindful of the disaster about to overtake it.

2. *Your slain are not slain by the sword.* The reference is unclear. Perhaps, with the military commanders having run off (verse 3), there has been internecine fighting among the remaining population, resulting in deaths.

3. *without bows.* The Hebrew seems to say "from bows" or "by bows," but the prefix *mi* sometimes has the sense of "without." This would accord with "your slain are not slain by the sword."

4. *my People's Daughter.* People, city, and land are often figured as a "daughter" or "young woman."

5. *turmoil and trampling and tumult.* The translation emulates the strong alliteration (but not the rhyming) of the Hebrew *mehumah umevusah umevukhah.*

Kir crashes about. This is again sound-play in the Hebrew: *qir meqarqer.* Kir, Shoa, and Elam are far to the east, and perhaps they are imagined—whether accurately or not—as contingents in the attacking Assyrian army.

and Shoa on the mountain.
And Elam bore the quiver   6
   in chariots of horsemen,
      and Kir bared the shield.
And your choicest valleys   7
   were filled with chariots,
and the horsemen pressed hard against the gates,
   and the cover of Judah was exposed.   8
And you looked on that day
   to the weapon-store of the Forest House.
And the breaches of the City of David   9
   you watched as they grew many,
      and you collected the waters of the Lower Pool.
And you counted Jerusalem's houses   10
   and demolished the houses to fortify the wall.
And a basin you made between the double walls   11
   for the waters of the Old Pool.
But you did not look to Him Who did it,
   and its Fashioner from afar you did not see.
And the Master LORD of Armies   12
   called on that day
for weeping and keening
   and shaved heads and the girding of sackcloth.

---

8. *the cover of Judah was exposed.* The term for "cover," *masakh,* is used for the cover of the Ark of the Covenant. This has led some scholars to a theological interpretation: God's protective cover has been taken away. Others see a reference to a fortress protecting the approach to Jerusalem.

the weapon-store of the Forest House. The Forest House was a cedar-paneled armory within the palace (see 1 Kings 7:2–5, where it is called the Lebanon Forest House). The weapons kept there appear to have been ornamental, but in the desperation of the siege, here they are taken up for use in combat.

9. *you collected the waters of the Lower Pool.* Under siege, maintaining a source of water was vital for survival. A tunnel was built—many still think, by Hezekiah, king at this time—to bring in the water of the Siloam brook into the city.

11. *Him Who did it, /. . . its Fashioner from afar.* The people who undertook these emergency measures in time of siege assumed it was their own doing and failed to recognize that God, unseen ("from afar"), was directing them.

12. *shaved heads.* Whether or not the Israelites made this pagan gesture of mourning part of their own practice, it is an inseparable part of the poetic language of mourning.

13   And, look—gladness and joy,
            killing of cattle and slaughtering of sheep,
        eating of meat and drinking of wine—
            "Eat and drink, for tomorrow we die."
14   And in my ears the LORD of Armies was revealed:
            "This crime shall not be atoned for you
                until you die," said the Master LORD of Armies.

15   Thus said the Master LORD of armies:
        Go in to this steward,
            Shebna, who is over the house.
16   What have you here and whom have you here
            that you hewed yourself here a tomb?
        Who hews a tomb on high
            carves into the cliff an abode for himself?
17   The LORD is about to shake you
            as one shakes a garment, and wrap you around,
18   He shall surely wind you round like a turban
            away to a spacious land.

---

13. *And, look—gladness and joy.* The Jerusalemites, instead of recognizing that they are facing catastrophe, continue their revels (going up to the rooftops), making the famous declaration that would become proverbial, "Eat and drink, for tomorrow we die."

14. *This crime shall not be atoned for you / until you die.* Many scholars conclude that this entire prophecy refers to Sennacherib's assault on Jerusalem in 701 B.C.E. After ravaging the countryside and destroying many of the towns (see chapter 1), his army laid siege against Jerusalem but then suddenly departed (see 2 Kings 19). If this is in fact the event in view here, Isaiah is taking the position that the city will yet feel the weight of a terrible divine justice.

15. *Thus said the Master LORD of Armies.* These words signal the beginning of a new prophecy, directed to Shebna, a high palace official ("who is over the house," that is, the house of the king or the palace). Shebna appears in the narrative of the siege in 2 Kings 19; however, there he is assigned a different title.

16. *hewed yourself here a tomb.* Tombs for the aristocracy were typically in niches or caves.

18. *wind you round like a turban.* Others understand this as "fling like a ball," but the Hebrew verb *ts-n-f* clearly means to wind round, not to fling, and the end of the previous line with the verb "to wrap" supports the sense of a garment. In light of this context, the translation of verse 17 adopts a proposed emendation of the Masoretic *gever*, "man," which appears after "shakes," to *begged*, "garment."

There shall you die,
>   and there the chariots of your honor
>   shall be the shame of your master's house.
>   And I will knock you away from your station   19
>   and from your stand you shall be torn.

And on that day I shall call to my servant Eliakim son of Hilkiah. And 20,21
I shall clothe him with your robe and bind him with your sash and give
your authority in his hand. And he shall become a father for the dwellers
of Jerusalem and for the house of Judah. And I shall place the key of the 22
house of David on his shoulder, and when he opens, none shall lock, and
when he locks, none shall open. And I shall affix him as a peg in a solid 23
place, and he shall be a seat of honor for his father's house. And they shall 24
hang upon him all the honor of his father's house, the offspring and the
sprouts, all the smallest vessels, from the basins to every kind of bowl. On 25
that day, said the LORD of Armies, the peg affixed in a solid place shall give
way and be cut down, and the load that was on it shall be destroyed, for
the LORD has spoken.

---

19. *your station / . . . your stand.* These terms are a direct reference to Shebna's position in
the palace bureaucracy.

21. *I shall clothe him.* The reference here to the robe and sash of royal office is surely meant
to pick up the negative garment metaphors of verses 17–18.
   a father. This is a term of political authority.

22. *the key . . . on his shoulder.* These ancient keys were very large, and usually wooden, so
placing a key on a shoulder, perhaps held by a strap, would make sense.
   the house of David. This is the royal palace.

23. *a seat of honor for his father's house.* These words are a pointed antithesis to the depiction of the exiled Shebna in verse 18, "the chariots of your honor / shall be the shame of
your mother's house."

24. *the offspring and the sprouts.* There is some doubt about the meaning of both Hebrew
nouns, especially the second one.

25. *the peg affixed in a solid place shall give way.* This entire verse is a blatant contradiction of the glowing prophecy concerning Eliakim's displacement of Shebna, and one must
conclude that a later editor, aware of a disaster that had befallen Eliakim, added these dire
words.

1 CHAPTER 23   A portent concerning Tyre.

> Wail, O Tarshish ships,
>   for their house is sacked.
> When they came from the land of Kittim,
>   it was revealed to them.
2 Be still, you coastland dwellers,
>   traders of Sidon.
> Your agents cross the seas
>   over the many waters.
3 Grain of Shihor, harvest of the Nile, her yield,
>   and she became the trade of nations.
4 Be ashamed, Sidon,
>   for the sea has said,
>   the stronghold of the sea:
> "I did not labor, did not give birth,
>   and I did not nurture young men,
>   nor raise up virgin girls."

CHAPTER 23   1. *for their house is sacked.* The Masoretic Text reads *mibayit*, "from within" (or "from a house"). This translation assumes that a scribe inadvertently transposed a *mem* at the end of the word, which would be a possessive plural suffix, to the beginning, and that the original text had *beytam*.

When they came from the land of Kittim, / it was revealed to them. Some scholars identify the land of Kittim with Cyprus, although that is not entirely certain. In any case, the Phoenicians were great seafaring merchants, as this poem repeatedly reminds us; what is envisioned here is that one such party of merchants, on their return from a Mediterranean voyage, discover that their city has been devastated.

2. *Be still.* Many interpreters argue that the meaning of this verb is "moan" or "howl," in consonance with "wail" at the beginning of the first line of the poem. A supposed Akkadian cognate is cited as evidence. But the word *domu* everywhere else means "to be still," or "silent," and there is no reason that the poet could not have imagined two antithetical responses to disaster—wailing and then dumbfounded silence.

Your agents. The translation emends *mil' ukh*, "they filled you," to *mal' akhayikh*, "your agents."

3. *Shihor ... Nile.* Both names refer to the same river. The second might be an editorial gloss on the first or a simple poetic apposition.

4. *I did not labor, did not give birth.* The point of this speech is not entirely clear, but since in prophecies of destruction, young men (*baḥurim*) and virgins (*betulot*) are often said to be killed, they being the icons of a people's pride and joy, what the sea may be saying is: I had no part in bringing these young men and women into the world and rearing them, so if they have perished, it is not my affair.

When Egypt heard of it,   5
　they shook as when hearing of Tyre.
Pass on to Tarshish,   6
　wail, you coastland dwellers.
Is this your reveling one,   7
　from days of yore, her ancient past,
whose feet led her
　to sojourn far away?
Who has counseled this   8
　against the crowned Tyre,
whose traders are nobles,
　her merchants notables of the land?
The Lord of Armies counseled it   9
　to profane the pride of all splendor,
　　to debase all notables of the land.
Pass through your land like the Nile,   10
　O Daughter of Tarshish—
　　there is no more a harbor.
His hand He stretched over the sea,   11
　He made kingdoms quake.
The Lord has charged concerning Canaan
　to destroy her strongholds.

---

5. *as when hearing of Tyre.* This probably means that "it" refers to the destruction of Sidon, the other chief Phoenician city, and that the report of the destruction of Tyre reached Egypt first.

7. *Is this your reveling one, / . . . whose feet led her / to sojourn far away?* Tarshish (verse 6) would have been one of the distant Mediterranean ports to the west plied by Phoenician ships. The Phoenicians in fact were great colonizers, establishing major centers in North Africa and as far away as Spain.

8. *crowned Tyre.* The Hebrew *maʿ atirah* is, more literally, "crown-wearing."

10. *Pass through your land like the Nile.* This might mean: just as the Nile runs through all of Egypt, Tyre is enjoined to pass through all her land.
　there is no more a harbor. The meaning of the word rendered as "harbor" is not entirely certain, but this sense seems likely. For Tyre, a coastal city dependent on seafaring trade, to be without a harbor is the ultimate sign of devastation.

11. *Canaan.* This reference may seem anomalous, but there is no textual warrant for changing it to the name of one of the Phoenician cities. It may simply be the case that the poet viewed the coastal stretch from Canaan north into Phoenicia as a single continuum, a notion echoed in the modern scholarly usage that speaks of a "Syro-Canaanite" culture.

12   And He said: You shall no longer revel,
            oppressed Virgin Daughter of Sidon.
        Rise, cross over to Kittim.
            There, too, you shall have no respite.
13   Look, the land of the Chaldeans,
            this is the people that is no more.
        Assyria founded it for ships,
            they put up their siege-towers,
        laid waste its citadels,
            turned it into ruins.
14   Wail, O Tarshish ships,
            for your stronghold has been sacked.

15 And it shall happen on that day that Tyre shall be forgotten for seventy
    years, like the days of a single king. At the end of the seventy years it shall
    be with Tyre as the song about the whore:

16   Take up a lyre, go round the town,
            forgotten whore.
        Play sweetly, many songs,
            so that you remember.

---

12. *There, too, you shall have no respite.* The distant regions that were either trading partners or sites of colonization for the Phoenicians now can offer them neither refuge nor
comfort.

13. *the land of the Chaldeans.* The switch of viewpoint to Mesopotamia is intended to offer
an object lesson to Sidon and Tyre: just as the Chaldeans became a "people that is no more,"
so now will be the fate of the Phoenicians. It must be said that scholarly attempts to tie in
this prophecy of the destruction of Tyre and Sidon with a particular historical event have
not been convincing, and it could be that this is all a kind of prophetic fantasy rather than
the report of an event.

15. *the song about the whore.* This is a rare moment when the prophet incorporates a piece
of the popular culture of his times into his text, though from the two lines quoted, it is
difficult to recover the narrative content of the song.

16. *forgotten whore.* The implication seems to be that she is a whore who has long been
neglected by her clients, perhaps because she is past her prime.
    Play sweetly many songs, / so that you remember. This image is clearly plaintive: the
forgotten whore is enjoined to play the lyre and sing songs—perhaps love songs—that will
help her recall the days gone by when she was much sought after.

And it shall happen at the end of the seventy years that God shall single 17
out Tyre, and she shall go back to her whore's pay and go whoring with
all the kingdoms of the world on the face of the earth. But her trade and 18
her whore's pay shall be consecrated to the LORD. It shall not be stocked
and shall not be stored, but her trade shall be for those dwelling before the
LORD, eating their fill, and for rich attire.

CHAPTER 24

> The LORD is about to sap the earth and strip it,   1
>> contort its face and scatter its dwellers.
> And the plain people shall be like the priest,   2
>> the slave like his master, the slavegirl like her mistress,
> the buyer like the seller, the lender like the borrower,
>> the creditor like him who seeks credit.
> Sapped, yes, sapped shall the land be,   3

---

17. *her whore's pay.* Despite the effort of most translations to bowdlerize this as "trade" or
"free," the unambiguous meaning of the Hebrew *'etnan* is payment received by a prostitute
for her sexual services. The Israelites, a nation of farmers and pastoralists in the earlier
biblical period, viewed the trade-based economy of their northern neighbors as an activity of shady dealing, a kind of prostitution. Tyre is imagined, after a canonical period of
seventy years following her destruction, renewing her former trade ties, returning to her
old whoring ways.

18. *But her trade and her whore's pay shall be consecrated to the LORD.* How this will come
about is in no way explained. Somehow, the again prosperous Tyre will funnel her profits
to Judah, enabling a life of luxury for the people dwelling in the LORD's presence (the sense
of "before the LORD"), which is to say, in the vicinity of the Jerusalem temple.

CHAPTER 24   1. *The LORD is about to sap the earth and strip it.* After the series of
prophetic pronouncements on the sundry foreign nations that began in chapter 13, these
words mark the beginning of a new large unit that runs to the end of chapter 27. In the
judgment of most scholars it is at the very least a century and a half later than Isaiah son of
Amoz, but this prophet is also a strong poet. His perspective at points is incipiently apocalyptic but lacks some of the features of full-fledged apocalypse that one finds in the very
late Daniel. Yet in keeping with this prophet's cosmic outlook, *'erets* here means "earth"
rather than "land." This is a poet who exhibits a vigorous inventiveness in emphatic sound-
play. Thus, "sap" and "strip" in this translation are only a pale approximation of *boqeq* and
bolqah in the Hebrew.

2. *And the plain people shall be like the priest.* As the catastrophe descends, all social and
economic distinctions are erased.

> and plundered, yes plundered,
>> for the LORD has spoken this thing.
4   The earth is bleak, has withered,
>> forlorn, the world has withered,
>>> the heights of the earth's folk forlorn.
5   And the earth is tainted beneath its dwellers,
>> for they transgressed teachings, flouted law,
>>> broke the eternal covenant.
6   Therefore has a curse consumed the earth,
>> and all its dwellers are mired in guilt.
> Therefore earth's dwellers turn pale,
>> and but a few humans remain.
7   The new wine is flat,
>> the vine forlorn,
>>> all the merry-hearted groan.
8   The gladness of timbrels is gone,
>> the revelers' clamor ended,
>>> the lyre's gladness has gone.
9   With no song do they drink wine,
>> strong drink turns bitter to its drinkers.
10   The futile city has been broken,
>> every house is closed to entrance.
11   A scream over wine in the streets,

---

4. *the earth . . . / the world.* The poetic parallelism of *ha'arets* and *tevel* (the latter term designates all the inhabited world) is linguistic evidence that the former term is used by this poet to mean "earth," not "land."

5. *the earth is tainted beneath its dwellers.* This is a recurrent biblical notion—that corrupt behavior pollutes the earth. It is perhaps because of this that the earth must be broken to pieces (verses 19–20).

6. *earth's dwellers turn pale.* The received text appears to say "are incensed" (*ḥaru*), but turning pale in terror is the appropriate response here, not anger. This translation reads, with the Qumran Isaiah, *ḥawru*, which means "to turn pale."

10. *The futile city.* The qualifier of "city" here, *tohu*, can mean "chaos," but its meaning extends to formlessness, pointlessness, futility; and something like "futile city" seems the most likely sense. Attempts to identify this place with a particular historical city have themselves proved futile, and it may be rather a paradigmatic or symbolic city where the earth's dwellers are engulfed by the catastrophe their actions have brought upon them.

11. *A scream over wine in the streets.* Wine is supposed to gladden the heart, but in this dire moment, it has turned bitter in the mouth and instead of rejoicing, there is terror.

on all joy the sun has set,
>   the earth's gladness has gone away.
In the town desolation remains,   12
>   and the gate is smashed to ruins.
For thus shall it be in the midst of the earth,   13
>   in the heart of the peoples,
as olives are beaten,
>   like gleanings as the harvest is done.

It is they who shall raise their voice, sing gladly,   14
>   in God's grandeur they shall shout out from the sea,
In the coastlands of the sea,   15
>   the name of the LORD, God of Israel.
From the edge of the earth,   16
>   we have heard songs: splendor to the righteous.
And I said: I have a secret, I have a secret—woe is me.
>   Traitors betrayed, in betrayal betrayed.
Terror and pitfall and trap   17
>   against you, dweller of the land!
And who flees from the sound of terror   18
>   shall fall into the pit
>   and who gets up from the pit shall be caught in the trap.
Shattered, the earth is shattered,   19
>   all broken to pieces the earth,
>   toppled, the earth has toppled.
Reeling, the earth reels like a drunkard   20

---

14. *It is they who shall raise their voice, sing gladly.* This line initiates a new prophecy: there will be another landscape of doom (verses 17ff.), but there is also a group in this scene that celebrates God's greatness.

16. *I have a secret.* While the meaning of this line is in dispute, the least strained construction is that *razi* is possessive declension of the Late Biblical *raz*, "secret." The secret would be the prophecy that follows.
   Traitors betrayed. The wording is a little obscure, but apparently the reference is to the reprehensible behavior of all those subject to divine retribution in the lines that follow.

17. *Terror and pitfall and trap.* The rich sound-play of the Hebrew is *paḥad wafaḥat wafaḥ.* One could come closer to this in the English with "terror and trip wire and trap," but the middle term has to be something one falls into, as is evident in the next line.

18. *And who flees from the sound of terror.* The prophet now turns the three alliterative nouns of the previous line into a miniature narrative in which all attempts to escape fail.

and rocks back and forth like a hut.
And its crime lies heavy upon it—
    it has fallen and no longer shall rise.

21 And it shall happen on that day,
        the Lord shall punish the heavenly hosts on high
            and the kings of earth on the earth.

22 They shall be rounded up as prisoners in a pit
        and locked up a dungeon,
            and after many days shall be punished.

23 And the moon shall be shamed
        and the sun disgraced,
    for the Lord of Armies has become king on Mount Zion and in Jerusalem,
        and before His elders is His glory.

CHAPTER 25

1 Lord, You are my God,
        I shall exalt You, acclaim Your name.
    For You have performed wondrous counsel,
        steadfast faithfulness from times long past.

2 For You turned a town into rubble,

---

21. *the Lord shall punish the heavenly hosts . . . / and the kings of earth.* Here the incipient apocalyptic perspective is especially clear. There is no logical reason that the heavenly hosts should be punished but perhaps a poetic reason: the global catastrophe will engulf heaven and earth alike.

23. *And the moon shall be shamed / and the sun disgraced.* This may be part of the scenario of punishing the heavenly host. Alternately, when the Lord of Armies is enthroned in all His glory in Jerusalem, the refulgence of His presence will put the sun and the moon to shame.
    on Mount Zion and in Jerusalem. This entire verset is metrically too long (with five or six stresses, depending on how one scans the Hebrew for "Mount Zion"). If one drops "Mount Zion," an acceptable four-stress verset emerges, and it could be that those two words were scribally inserted as a synonymous duplication of "Jerusalem."

CHAPTER 25   1. *I shall exalt You, acclaim Your name.* This is the formulaic language of a thanksgiving psalm. In keeping with the biblical literary practice, this may well have been editorially inserted here from another source. The psalm continues through verse 5.
    from times long past. This Hebrew word would ordinarily mean "from afar," but the context invites construing it in a temporal, not spatial, sense.

a fortified city to ruins,
　the arrogants' citadel, from a town,
　　it will never be built again.
Therefore a fierce people does You honor, 3
　a city of cruel nations reveres You.
For Your people a stronghold for the poor one, 4
　a stronghold for the needy when in straits,
a shelter from the downpour, a shade from the heat.
　For the spirit of the cruel is like a downpour on walls,
　　like heat in the desert. 5
The arrogants' uproar You subdued,
　the heat, with the shade of a cloud.
　　The chant of the cruel ones He answered.

And the LORD shall prepare a banquet for all the peoples on this moun- 6
tain, a banquet of rich food, a banquet of well-aged wines, rich food with
marrow, well-aged wines fine strained. And He shall swallow up on this 7
mountain the veil that covers all the peoples and the mantle cast over
all the nations. He shall swallow up death forever, and the Master LORD 8

---

2. *the arrogants'*. This translation reads, with two Hebrew manuscripts and the Septuagint,
zedim for the Masoretic *zarim*, "strangers." The same correction is made in verse 5.

　the arrogants' citadel, from a town. This translation follows the Hebrew. Either a phrase
has dropped out, or "turned into rubble" from the previous line is meant to do double duty
for this clause.

5. *The chant of the cruel ones He answered.* The received text is enigmatic here. Attempts to
render the concluding verb as "has silenced" are questionable: *ya'aneh* as it stands means
"answer," and a revocalization as *ye'aneh* doesn't work because that verb means "afflict,"
not "silence," and also requires a human object. Perhaps the "chant" is a battle chant, or a
triumphal song.

6. *And the LORD shall prepare a banquet for all the people on this mountain.* Here begins a
new, evidently eschatological section, first in prose. The mountain is probably Mount Zion,
and, as several commentators have observed, the banquet may recall the sacred feast on the
slopes of Mount Sinai with Moses and the seventy elders, which is marked by an epiphany.

　a banquet of rich food. This passage is probably the ultimate source for the Midrashic
idea of a grand banquet at the end of days in which the righteous will feast on the flesh of
the Leviathan and drink wine preserved from the time of creation.

8. *He shall swallow up death forever.* It is hard to determine the status as literal belief of these
ringing words. Standard biblical notions see death as inevitable and final. Prophetic discourse is given to extravagant hyperbole (the mountains dripping wine, the sower overtaking the reaper, and so forth), but then hyperbole may lead to new beliefs. Many generations

shall wipe the tears from every face, and His people's disgrace He shall
9 take off from all the earth, for the LORD has spoken. And it shall be said
on that day:

> Look, this is our God
>   in Whom we hoped, and He rescued us,
> This is our own God in Whom we hoped,
>   Let us exult and rejoice in His rescue.

10 > For the LORD's hand shall rest on this mountain,
>   and Moab shall be threshed beneath Him
>   as straw is threshed in a cesspool.

11 > And he shall spread his arms within it
>   as the swimmer spreads his arms to swim
>   and his pride shall be brought low
>   and his arms churn.

12 > The towering fortress of their walls He shall bring down,
>   bring it low, level it with the ground.

---

of Jews and Christians have taken these words literally, and the exquisite tenderness of the
clause that follows—"and the Master LORD shall wipe the tears from every face"—remains
deeply moving.

9. *And it shall be said.* The Hebrew appears to say "and he shall say," but the third-person
singular verb (like the *on* construction in French) is often used as the equivalent of a passive.

10. *as straw is threshed in a cesspool.* Straw was soaked in animal excrement, and the soggy
mixture was then trampled so that it could be used for fertilization. This is a deliberately
repellent and humiliating image to depict the fate of Israel's traditional enemy Moab.

11. *And he shall spread his arms within it.* Even though the Hebrew word for "cesspool" is
feminine and "within it" has a masculine ending, the reference seems to be to the cesspool.
This yields a rather nasty image of the flailing Moab trying to swim in a cesspool.

  churn. The Hebrew *'orbot* (what appears to be a noun attached to "arms") appears
nowhere else, and links to purported cognates in other Semitic languages are not convincing. This is another instance in which one is compelled to surmise the sense from the
context.

CHAPTER 26

On that day this song will be sung in the land of Judah: 1
A strong city is ours.
   Victory will be set—walls and ramparts.
Open the gates   2
   and let a righteous nation enter,
      keeping faith.
A steadfast nature You guard in peace   3
   for in You it trusts.
Trust in the LORD forever,   4
   for in Yah the LORD is an everlasting Rock.
For He has brought low the dwellers on high,   5
   the lofty city,
brought down, brought it down to the earth,
   leveled it with the dust.

The foot tramples it,   6
   the foot of the needy,
      the poor man's footsteps.

CHAPTER 26   1. *On that day this song will be sung.* The designation of the prophecy enunciated here as "song" signals from the beginning its celebratory, triumphalist character.

A strong city is ours. The nation, previously assaulted and overwhelmed, now possesses an impregnable city.

Victory will be set—walls and ramparts. The translation reproduces the rather crabbed formulation of the Hebrew. The verb appears to read "he will set," but third-person singular active verbs with no clear antecedent often serve in lieu of passives in biblical Hebrew. The general sense, despite the obscure wording, is clearly that the restored city will have strong ramparts that no enemy can conquer.

2. *Open the gates / and let a righteous nation enter.* This image looks as if it refers to the return to their city of a people who has been banished. In their righteousness, they are now worthy of this vindication and renewal.

4. *an everlasting Rock.* This metaphor, a stock image in Psalms, represents God as a stronghold and thus jibes with the references to powerful ramparts.

5. *brought low the dwellers on high, / the lofty city.* The lofty city that has been brought low is an obvious counterpoint to the strong city with its bristling ramparts.

6. *the needy, / the poor man's.* The rhetoric of prophecy in behalf of social justice is here intermingled with the prophecy of national renewal. Given the context, the "poor man" in

7   The path of the righteous is straight,
         a straight course for the righteous You pave.

8   The path of Your judgments
         we hoped for, O LORD.
      For Your name and repute
         are our utmost desire.

9   With my life-breath I desired You by night,
         with my spirit within me I sought You.
      For when Your judgments are on earth,
         the world's dwellers learn righteousness.

10   Should the wicked be spared, he does not learn righteousness,
         on earth he twists what is straight,
           and he does not see the LORD's majesty.

11   O LORD, when Your hand is raised,
         they do not look,
      let them look and be shamed by the zeal for the people,
         by the fire consuming Your foes.

12   O LORD, grant peace to us,
         for our every act You have wrought for us.

13   O Lord our God,
         masters besides You possess us.
           Your name alone we invoke.

14   The dead shall not live,
         nor shall the shades rise up.

---

this verse would appear to be a symbol of the people of Israel, weak and helpless in the face of powerful nations but now triumphing over them.

8. *For Your name and repute / are our utmost desire.* The practice of substituting God's "name" for the unmediated presence of the deity becomes especially pronounced in the Late Biblical period, but there are abundant precedents earlier. "Our" is added in the translation before "desire" for clarity.

10. *Should the wicked be spared, he does not learn righteousness.* What begins to emerge here is an eschatological differentiation between the wicked, who are beyond saving, and the righteous, who in a time to come will be singled out for renewal.

11. *when Your hand is raised.* Presumably, the divine hand is raised to punish the miscreants, but they pay no heed.

14. *The dead shall not live.* Although this is a standard biblical view, the emphasis here is on the dead who never heeded God in their lifetime: they have no hope of rising from the dust.

Therefore have You singled them out and destroyed them
    and expunged all remembrance of them.
You added to the nation, O LORD,   15
    You added to the nation, were honored.
        You enlarged all the limits of the land.
O LORD, in straits they sought You out.   16
    A whispered prayer of anguish was Your chastisement to them.
As a woman with child draws near to give birth,   17
    she shudders, she shakes in her pangs,
        so we were before You, O LORD.
We were with child, we shuddered, as if birthing the wind,   18
    no victories had we on earth,
        and the world's dwellers did not fall before us.
Your dead shall live, their corpses rise,   19
    the dwellers in the dust shall wake and sing gladly.
For Your dew is a dew of brightness,

---

16. *A whispered prayer of anguish was Your chastisement to them.* This whole verset is opaque in the Hebrew, and hence any translation is no more than a guess. *Tsaqun laḥash*, rendered here as "a whispered prayer of anguish," is especially obscure, although in later Hebrew it becomes a frequently invoked idiom with the sense of "heartfelt whispered prayer."

17. *As a woman with child draws near to give birth, / she shudders, she shakes in her pangs.* These two versets vividly illustrate the tendency in many lines of biblical poetry to produce a miniature narrative from one verset to the next: first, the pregnant woman is nearing term; then, she is in the midst of violent labor. The third verset, as is often the case in triadic lines, strikes out in a new direction instead of continuing the parallelism—here, spelling out the referent of the simile. The next line then further develops the applicability of the simile to its referent.

18. *and the world's dwellers did not fall before us.* The Hebrew merely says, rather enigmatically, "did not fall." "Before us" has been added in the translation as an interpretive guess.

19. *Your dead shall live.* The entire line of poetry flatly contradicts the declaration in verse 14 that the dead shall not live. The operative term of distinction is "Your." Is the prophet introducing a doctrine of the resurrection of the dead, which is generally not thought to emerge until the Book of Daniel? This is at least a possibility, and this is certainly the way this verse was later understood by communities of believers. But given the theme of national renewal that informs this entire prophecy, it may be more likely that what the poet has in mind is a rebirth of the nation, like Ezekiel's vision of the valley of dry bones.
    their corpses. The Masoretic Text has "my corpse," but two ancient versions show the more likely "their corpses."
    For Your dew is a dew of brightness. Dew is a component of the natural "irrigation" system in the land of Israel and hence an apt image for revivification.

and the netherworld releases the shades.

20   Go, my people, come into your chambers
                and shut your doors behind you.
            Hide but a moment
                until the wrath passes.

21   For the LORD is about to come out from His place
                to punish the crime of the dwellers on earth,
            and the earth shall lay bare its bloodguilt
                and no longer cover its slain.

CHAPTER 27

1   On that day the LORD shall punish
                with His fierce and great and mighty sword
            Leviathan the slippery serpent,
                Leviathan, the twisting serpent,
                    and shall slay the dragon that is in the sea.

---

the netherworld. In the context of "shades," 'arets has its occasional sense of the realm of the dead, even though it usually means "earth" or "land."

releases. The Hebrew verb means "to drop" and is the second odd use of that verb in this chapter.

20. come into your chambers. The sometimes proposed notion that this refers to the chambers of death is far-fetched. God's people are urged to take shelter within the shut doors of their houses until the divine wrath finishes its work of destruction.

21. to punish the crime of the dwellers on earth. The perspective looks global and hence eschatological. All who are guilty of murderous acts will now feel the fierce force of divine justice.

lay bare its bloodguilt / . . . no longer cover its slain. The language reflects the biblical notion that wrongfully shed blood pollutes the earth and needs to be "redeemed" by an act of retributive justice.

CHAPTER 27   1. On that day. Some take this verse to be the conclusion of the last prophecy in the previous chapter. Given its strikingly mythological character, however, it could be an independent fragment.

Leviathan the slippery serpent. The Hebrew epithet bariaḥ is not certain in meaning. It could derive from the verbal stem that means "to flee," hence "slippery." It is also the ordinary word for the bolt of a gate and so could conceivably refer to the serpent held under lock and key. The entire line invokes the Canaanite cosmogonic myth of Leviathan as the primordial sea monster that the weather god Baal must subdue in order for dry land, safe from the raging sea, to come into being.

On that day, 2
    a lovely vineyard, sing out to it!
I, the LORD, watch over it, 3
    moment by moment I watch it,
so that no harm come to it,
    night and day I watch over it.
No anger do I have. 4
    Should one give Me thorns and thistles,
I would stride out in battle against it.
    I would set it on fire.
If he clings to My stronghold, 5
    he makes peace with Me
        he makes peace with Me.

In days to come Jacob shall take root, 6
    Israel shall bud and flower,
        and the face of the world shall fill with bounty.

Has he been struck like the blow of his striker? 7
    Like the slaying of his slain was he slain?
In due measure, when He drove her out, He contended with her, 8
    He let loose His fierce blast on an east-wind day.

---

2. *a lovely vineyard.* This Song of the Vineyard is akin to the Parable of the Vineyard in chapter 5; in both cases, the vineyard is the people of Israel.

4. *Should one give Me thorns and thistles.* That is, if the people through its actions allow the vineyard to fall into ruins, God will burn out the noxious growths.

5. *If he clings to My stronghold.* The "he" would refer collectively to the people, and clinging to God's stronghold means keeping faith with Him. The result is peace with God instead of the battle mentioned in verse 4.

6. *In days to come.* The Hebrew says merely "coming" in the plural, but it is likely that "days" was inadvertently dropped from the text. This phrase is usually an introductory formula for a prophecy, which would make this verse a fragment, although it might also be taken as the conclusion of the prophecy that begins in verse 2.

8. *In due measure.* The Hebrew *besa'sa'h* is anomalous and its meaning is uncertain. This translation follows the Targum in relating it to *se'ah*, a dry measure.
    He drove her out. Though it may be disconcerting to the English reader, the Hebrew slides readily from referring to the Israelites as a collective "he" (verse 7) to a feminine pronominal suffix here (because the nation is often imagined symbolically as a woman).
    east-wind day. The east wind blowing from the desert generally signals disaster.

9   Therefore in this shall Jacob's crime be atoned,
         all this comes from removing his offense:
     When he turns all the stones of the altar
         into shattered stones of chalk—
             no cultic poles or incense altars shall stand.

10   For the fortified town is solitary,
         an abode deserted and abandoned, like the desert.
     There the calf grazes
         and there it lies down and gnaws away its boughs.
11   When its branches are dry, they are broken.
         Women come, light fires with them,
             for they are not a discerning people.
     Therefore its Maker shall show it no mercy,
             and its Fashioner shall not grant it grace.

12   And it shall be on that day:
     the Lord shall beat out the grain
         from the stream of the Euphrates to Egypt's river.
     And you shall be gathered in
         one by one, you Israelites.
13   And it shall be on that day

---

9. *all this comes.* More literally, "all the fruit of."

   the altar. As the third verset of this line makes clear, this is an altar dedicated to pagan worship, which therefore has to be shattered.

10. *gnaws away its boughs.* The boughs are a metonymy for the deserted town. Now women foraging for fuel (verse 11) come to pick up the dry broken branches to use as kindling.

11. *for they are not a discerning people.* In consonance with a recurrent pattern in triadic lines, this third verset breaks away from the semantic parallelism and instead provides an explanatory summary not only of the whole line but of the whole prophecy: this disaster has befallen the people because of its failure to see and understand God's ways.

12. *And it shall be on that day.* Once again, this formula signals the beginning of a new prophecy, one of national restoration and the punishment of Israel's enemies.

   from the stream of the Euphrates to Egypt's river. Assyria and Egypt were the two great imperial powers between which the kingdom of Judah was caught in Isaiah's time, the eighth century B.C.E.

a great ram's horn shall sound,
  and those lost in the land of Assyria shall come,
    and the dispersed in the land of Egypt
  and bow down to the LORD
    on the holy mountain, in Jerusalem.

CHAPTER 28

Woe, crown of the pride of Ephraim's drunkards,   1
  and a withered blossom his glory's splendor
    on the head of the fat-proud, stunned by wine.
Look, one powerful and strong for the Master,   2
  like a current of hail, a storm of destruction,
like a current of mighty rushing waters,
  He brings down to the earth.
Underfoot shall be trampled   3
  the crown of the pride of Ephraim's drunkards.
And his glory's splendor shall become a withered blossom   4

---

13. *a great ram's horn shall sound.* The ram's horn was blown at coronations and to announce the jubilee year: here it inaugurates a grand period of renewal after national tribulations. Traditional interpreters associated this verse with the messianic age.

and those lost in the land of Assyria. The Hebrew verb equally means "to be lost" and "to perish." It is distinctly possible that Isaiah, writing a century after the destruction of the northern kingdom of Israel and the exile of much of its population to Assyria, has that historical catastrophe in mind.

CHAPTER 28   1. *Woe, crown of the pride of Ephraim's drunkards.* Ephraim, the northern kingdom that was wiped out by Assyria in 721 B.C.E., is a somewhat puzzling presence at the beginning of this prophecy, which probably refers to the predicament of the southern kingdom, besieged by Assyria, twenty years later. Perhaps the complete desolation of Ephraim, whose leaders are seen as dissolute, is meant as a portent for Judah.

the fat-proud. The Hebrew spelling of *gey'* would lead one to understand it as "valley"— that is, "valley of the fat growth" or "valley of oils." It seems preferable to read it as *gei'*, "proud," in apposition with "stunned by wine" and referring to the drunkards.

2. *one powerful and strong for the Master.* The reference is probably Assyria, conceived as God's instrument for punishing Judah.

3–4. *the crown of the pride . . . / his glory's splendor.* There are evidently two idioms in this image—a crown which is trampled, and something like a floral wreath, which withers.

    on the head of the fat-proud,
    like a new fig before the harvest—
    who sees it will swallow it still in his hand.
5   On that day the LORD of Armies shall become
    a crown of splendor and a tiara of glory to His people's remnant,
6   and a spirit of justice for him who is seated in judgment
    and valor for those who drive back battle from the gate.
7   And these, too, blundered through wine
    and through strong drink went astray.
    Priest and prophet blundered through strong drink,
    were confounded through wine,
    went astray through strong drink,
    blundered with the seer,
    juddered in judgment.
8   For all the tables were covered with vomit,
    filth, with no space left.
9   To whom will they teach knowledge
    and to whom will they convey lessons?—

---

5. *a crown of splendor and a tiara of glory.* In these tightly woven lines, the undeserved or false crown adorning the drunkards is replaced by the true crown that God becomes for His people.

6. *a spirit of justice.* The drunkards, as the continuation of the prophecy makes vividly clear, pervert justice and distort values, and they are to be replaced by a just ruler.
    those who drive back battle from the gate. The city gate would be assaulted by besiegers, who are here repelled by valiant defenders.

7. *And these, too, blundered through wine.* The Judahites resemble their counterparts in Ephraim.
    strong drink. As elsewhere, *sheikhar,* which like wine is a product of the vine, probably indicates grappa.
    the seer. The Hebrew term clearly means this, not "vision," as many translations here have it, and it jibes with the reference to prophet and priest gone astray.
    juddered in judgment. The translation emulates the alliteration of the Hebrew, *paqu peliliyah.* The Hebrew verb does mean to shake, falter, be unsteady.

8. *For all the tables were covered with vomit.* The initial notion of drunkenness is now vividly joined by an evocation of the disgusting scene of wine-swilling debauchery.
    filth. The Hebrew term indicates excremental filth, so the physical effect of the debauches comes out of the body at both ends.

9. *To whom will they teach knowledge.* The most likely referent of "they" is the drunken priests, prophets, and seers, whose incoherent teaching would scarcely be suitable for newly weaned babes.

to the milk-weaned,
  to babes pulled from the breast?
For it is filth-pilth, filth-pilth,   10
  vomit-momit, vomit-momit,
    a little here, a little there.
For in a barbarous tongue   11
  and in alien language
    He shall speak to this people
to whom He said, "This is rest—leave it for the weary,   12
  and this is repose," and they did not want to listen.
And the word of the Lord became for them—   13
  filth-pilth, filth-pilth,
  vomit-momit, vomit-momit,
    a little here, a little here.
So that they should walk and stumble backward,
  and be broken, snared, and trapped.
Therefore, hear the word of the Lord,   14
  men of mockery,
rulers of this people
  who are in Jerusalem.
For you said, "We have sealed a covenant with Death,   15

---

10. *For it is filth-pilth, filth-pilth, / vomit-momit, vomit-momit.* Wildly divergent interpretations have been proposed for these words. The literal sense would seem to be: "precept precept, line line." But if precepts are at issue here, they are precepts that have been turned into gibberish by these drunkards. The phonetic kinship between *tsaw*, precept or command, and *tso'ah*, filth or excrement, and between *qaw*, line, and *qi'*, vomit, is surely not accidental. The translation seeks to convey both this correspondence and the effect of gibberish.

11. *For in a barbarous tongue / and in alien language / He shall speak to this people.* This is measure-for-measure justice: they have reduced any instruction they might offer to drunken babbling, and God will address them through the incomprehensible language of the Akkadian-speaking Assyrian conquerors.

13. *And the word of the Lord became for them— / filth-pilth, filth-pilth.* God's very word, which as leaders of the people they had the responsibility to convey to the people, has turned into grotesque nonsense syllables.

15. *We have sealed a covenant with Death.* The language here verges on the mythological (Mot, the word used here, is the Canaanite god of death). Some interpreters understand this as a reference to the party in Jerusalem that promoted an alliance with Egypt, known for its cult of the dead, against Assyria. That is possible, but the more evident point is that these perverse leaders have replaced God with the god of death, imagining that they will be safe from all dangers through these covenants with the deity of the netherworld.

and with Sheol we have made a pact.
No sweeping scourge that passes by
    will reach us,
for we have made falsehood our refuge
    and in lies we have taken shelter."
16   Therefore thus said the Master the LORD:
    I am about to lay a foundation stone in Zion,
        the stone for a tower,
a precious corner, a solid foundation.
    He who trusts shall have nothing to fear.
17   And I will make justice the measuring cord
    and righteousness the plumb line.
And hail shall sweep away the refuge of falsehood,
    and the shelter, water shall wash off.
18   And your covenant with Death shall be canceled,
    your pact with Sheol shall not come about.
The sweeping scourge that passes by—
    you shall be crushed by it.
19   As it passes it shall take you
    by day and by night,
and the conveying of lessons,
    shall be naught but horror.
20   For the couch is too short to stretch out on,
    and the blanket too narrow to cover one up.
21   For like Mount Perazim the LORD shall arise,

---

16. *I am about to lay a foundation stone in Zion.* This may look like a switch in direction, but it is not necessary to declare this a later editorial intrusion. In place of a city ruled by drunken idiots, God will establish a just, firm-founded city, while those who made a covenant with death will be swept away (verses 17–21).

19. *the conveying of lessons.* This phrase refers back to verse 9 and to the reduction of teaching to babble in the lines that followed it. Now, instead of gibberish, there will be terror.

20. *For the couch is too short to stretch out on.* This homey image represents the acute discomfiting helplessness of the miscreants when they are overtaken by divine judgment: they can neither lie without being cramped in the bed nor cover themselves.

21. *like Mount Perazim / . . . like Gibeon Valley.* These were places of victory, respectively, for David and for Joshua where God intervened on their behalf. Now He will intervene instead to effect a dire defeat of His people.

like Gibeon Valley He shall rage
to do His deed, strange is His deed,
   and to accomplish His work, alien His work.
And now, do not mock,   22
   lest your reins pull tight,
for direly decreed I have heard it
   from the Master, the LORD
     over all the earth.

Give ear and hear My voice,   23
   attend and hear My utterance.
Does the plowman plow all day to sow,   24
   break open and harrow his soil?
When he levels its surface,   25
   will he not scatter fennel and broadcast cumin
and set wheat in rows
   and barley in plots
     and spelt as a border?
For He guides him rightly,   26
   his God instructs him.
For fennel is not beaten with a threshing sledge   27
   nor does the cartwheel roll over cumin.
For fennel is beaten with a stick
   and cumin with a stick.

---

23. *Give ear and hear My voice.* This formal opening injunction clearly signals the beginning of a new prophecy.

24. *Does the plowman plow all day to sow.* These words initiate an extended simile—or perhaps it is meant to be a parable—that would have spoken directly to the ancient audience because of its agricultural imagery. Unfortunately, not all of the terms and agricultural procedures are transparent to modern readers. What compounds the difficulty is that the referent of the parable—the *nimshal* of the *mashal*—is barely hinted at.

25. *fennel.* This is one conjectural understanding of the Hebrew *qetsaḥ*.
   in rows. This translation reads *shurah* for the opaque *sorah* of the Masoretic Text.

26. *For He guides him rightly.* This would be the evident referent of the parable: God imbues the farmer with understanding so that he can raise his crops in proper fashion. Perhaps there is a more general implication that God implants in humankind the requisite wisdom to conduct all of its affairs. But it must be said that the Hebrew verb used here generally means "to discipline," not "to instruct."

28   Grain for bread is pounded,
                but the thresher does not thresh it forever.
            He runs over it with his cartwheel
                but his horses do not crush it.
29   This too from the LORD of Armies issues forth,
                He is wondrous in counsel, His wisdom is great.

CHAPTER 29

1   Woe, Ariel, Ariel,
                the city where David camped.
            Add year upon year,
                let festivals make their round.
2   And I shall cause distress to Ariel,
                and it shall turn into keening and crying,
                and it shall be to me as Ariel.
3   And I shall camp like David against it,

---

28. *Grain for bread.* "Grain for" is merely implied in the Hebrew.

  He runs over it. The verb here generally means "to panic," and so the translation, somewhat conjecturally, is dictated by the context.

29. *He is wondrous in counsel, His wisdom is great.* This concluding line is evidently meant to point the moral that all practical wisdom, like the know-how of the farmer who is careful to thresh his grain without polluting it, comes from God. It remains something of a puzzle why the editors chose to introduce a text of this sort in a series of prophecies about the political fate of the people of Israel.

CHAPTER 29   1. *Ariel.* Although the second verset makes it clear that this is an epithet for Jerusalem, wildly disparate proposals have been made for the etymology of the name. Perhaps the least strained is that it means "lion of God," which is to say, not an ordinary lion but some sort of heraldic lion; and a good candidate for that would be the cherubs carved over the Ark of the Covenant, which are more or less winged lions. By synecdoche, then, this carved beast in the Temple might have become an epithet for the city in which the Temple stood.

2. *And it shall be to Me as Ariel.* This third verset is a little enigmatic. The possible sense is: Ariel, once My protected sacred city, will now be for Me an Ariel of keening and crying.

3. *camp.* This sometimes military term is pointedly chosen because the reference is not to David's residence in the city but to his attack on it when he conquered it for the Jebusites.

and besiege it with a mound
   and lay siege-works against it.
And you shall be brought down, from the ground you shall speak,   4
   lower than the dust shall your utterance be,
and your voice shall be like a ghost from the ground,
   and from the dust your speaking shall chirp.
And the crowd of your strangers shall be like fine dust   5
   and like chaff blowing past the oppressors' crowd.
    And it shall happen at once, in a moment,
she shall be singled out by the Lord of Armies   6
   in thunder and earthquake and a great sound,
    tempest and whirlwind and tongues of consuming fire.
And it shall be like a dream, a night-vision—   7
   the crowd of all the nations arrayed against Ariel
and all her foes and the siege-works against her
   and those who distressed her.
And it shall be as the hungry man dreams he is eating,   8
   and wakes with an empty throat,
and as the thirsty man dreams he is drinking
   and wakes and is faint and his throat is parched,
so the crowd of all the nations shall be,
   arrayed against Mount Zion.

---

4. *from the dust your speaking shall chirp.* As several biblical texts suggest, there was a popular belief that the spirits of the dead communicated with the living by means of faint chirping sounds that might be interpreted by a necromancer.

5. *the crowd of your strangers.* These are the foreign armies attacking Jerusalem.

6. *she shall be singled out.* This verb *paqad* can mean to be singled out either for recompense, for benign attention, or for punishment. The storm imagery that immediately follows might lead one to apply the negative sense, but then in verse 7 it becomes clear that the people's enemies are the target of these foreign forces,

7. *And it shall be like a dream, a night-vision.* The horror of implacable enemies bent on the destruction of Jerusalem will vanish like a nightmare when the sleeper awakens. This image might accord with Sennacherib's siege of Jerusalem in 701 B.C.E., which was suddenly withdrawn.

8. *the hungry man / . . . the thirsty man.* In a rather peculiar move, the dream simile is now reversed: it is not Israel dreaming the nightmare of its destruction but the Assyrians dreaming of consuming the city who now awake and find that their hunger and thirst have not been satisfied.

9   Be dumbfounded, yes, dumbfounded,
                      be blinded, yes, be blinded.
                  They are drunk and not from wine,
                      stagger, and not from strong drink.
10   For the LORD has poured over you
                      a spirit of deep slumber,
                  and closed your eyes—the prophets,
                      and covered your heads—the seers.

11 And the vision of all things shall become to you like the words of a sealed book that is given to one who can read, saying, "Pray, read this," and he
12 says, "I cannot, for it is sealed," and the book is given to one who cannot read, saying, "Pray, read this," and he says, "I cannot read."

13   And the Master said,
                  Inasmuch as this people approached with its mouth
                      and with its lips honored Me
                        but kept its heart far from Me,
                 and their reverence for Me
                      was a commandment of men learned by rote,
14   therefore will I continue
                      to strike this people with wonder upon wonder,
                 and the wisdom of its wise men shall vanish
                      and the discernment of its discerners disappear.

15   Woe to those who burrow deep from the LORD
                      to hide their counsel,

---

9. *dumbfounded, / . . . blinded.* The prophet assumes, in consonance with general ancient belief, that the people needs the guidance of prophets and seers in order to see where it must go. In this case, false prophets have assumed the prophetic role, which is understood as a punishment from God sent against the people, causing general blindness.

11. *the words of a sealed book.* Some interpreters propose that this is the scroll of Isaiah's own prophecies. In any case, the book is sealed so that even the literate cannot read it, and how much more so the illiterate.

14. *wonder upon wonder.* While this word often has a positive sense of God's miraculous intervention in behalf of the people, here it obviously is used negatively for the perpetuation of a state of hopeless ignorance in the people.

15. *Woe.* As elsewhere, the introduction of this word, *hoy,* announces a new prophecy.

and their deeds are done in darkness,
    and they say, "Who sees us, who knows of us?"
You are perverse! 16
    Should the potter be reckoned as his clay,
        should the thing he made say of its maker, "He did not make me,"
           and the thing fashioned say of its fashioner, "He has no skill"?
Surely in just a while, 17
    Lebanon shall turn back into farmland
      and the farmland be reckoned as forest.
And the deaf on that day shall hear the book's words, 18
    and from darkness and gloom the eyes of the blind shall see.
Once more shall the lowly have joy in the LORD, 19
    and the needy exult in Israel's Holy One.
For the oppressor shall vanish, 20
    the mocker shall cease,
      and all those devoted to crime be cut off.
Who led people to offend through a word, 21
    ensnared the arbiter in the gate,
      perverted the innocent man's cause with lies.
Therefore thus said the LORD Who redeemed Abraham to the house of Jacob: 22
Not now shall Jacob be shamed,

Who sees us, who knows of us? These words express the delusion that it is possible to hide from God's all-seeing eyes.

16. *He has no skill.* The literal sense of the Hebrew is "He did not understand." The translation here, which makes the intention clear, is borrowed from Joseph Blenkinsopp.

17. *Lebanon shall turn back into farmland.* A day soon to come will witness radical transformations: the heavily forested Lebanon will become farmland, and the farmland a forest. These antithetical changes set the stage for what transpires in the human landscape in the verses that follow.

18. *the deaf . . . / the blind.* Especially because of the reference to hearing the book's words, which surely harks back to verse 11, the deaf and the blind are probably meant metaphorically: those who could neither hear nor read the words of the true prophet will now understand them.

19. *the lowly . . . / the needy.* The focus of this prophecy is not an attack by hostile armies but the perversion of social justice, which will now be restored.

21. *through a word.* Given the reference to courts of justice in the next two versets, the "word" here would be false testimony or perjury that deprives the innocent of his rightful cause.

and not now shall his face turn pale.

23   For when he sees his children,
                   My handiwork, in his midst,
               they shall hallow My name
                   and hallow Jacob's Holy One,
                       and the God of Israel they shall hold in awe.

24   And those whose spirit strayed shall know discernment,
                   and the grumblers shall learn their lesson.

CHAPTER 30

1   Woe, you wayward sons,
                   said the LORD,
               devising counsel, and not from Me,
                   clinging to molten images—
                       and not to My spirit,
               so as to compound
                   offense with offense.

2   Who head down to Egypt,
                   and have not asked My word,
               to shelter in Pharaoh's stronghold,
                   and take refuge in Egypt's shade.

3   And Pharaoh's stronghold shall turn into shame for you,

---

23. *they shall hallow My name.* It is noteworthy that the prophet conceives the hallowing of God's name not as a cultic act but as a restitution of social justice. Jacob's face no longer turns pale with shame because his society is no longer something to be ashamed of, and this is the true sanctification of God's name. The arc of this argument is completed in the next verse. The people that had been blind, that lacked the discernment to see the difference between right and wrong, will now come to its senses, again be discerning.

CHAPTER 30   1. *clinging to molten images.* The literal sense of the Hebrew is "making [or pouring] molten images."

2. *Who head down to Egypt.* Although the prophecy begins by inveighing against idolatry, it quickly switches to a political theme, and Isaiah may have associated the pursuit of foreign alliances with the worship of pagan gods. In any case, one should note that the prophet here and elsewhere assumes a vehement stance in a political debate: in the last years of the eighth century B.C.E., there was a party in Jerusalem that advocated an alliance with Egypt against the imminent military threat of the Assyrian empire, and Isaiah viewed this policy as a catastrophic error.
    Egypt's shade. As elsewhere, "shade" has the idiomatic sense of "protection."

and the shelter in Egypt's shade into disgrace.
Though his commanders were in Zoan,   4
    and his messengers reached Hanes,
whoever shames a people shall not avail them,   5
    neither for help nor for availing,
        but shall be shame and sheer disgrace.

The portent of the Beasts of the Negeb.   6
    In a land of straits and stress,
        a lion and maned beast from among them
    viper and flying serpent.
On the back of donkeys their wealth is borne
    and on camels' humps their treasures
        to an unavailing people.
And Egypt's help shall be useless and void.   7
    Therefore I call this:
        Her Arrogance Ended.

Now, come write it on a tablet with them   8
    and on a scroll its inscription,
and let it stand till the last day
    as a witness forever.
For it is a rebellious people,   9

---

4. *Though his commanders were in Zoan, / and his messengers reached Hanes.* Both these are Egyptian cities. A Judahite delegation actually traveled to Egypt to discuss a possible anti-Assyrian alliance.

6. *The portent of the Beasts of the Negeb.* The picturesque title of this prophecy (perhaps an editorial invention) invokes the beasts of the great southern desert through which the emissaries journey in order to reach Egypt. The first animals named are beasts of prey and thus suggest the dangers that the foolish delegates are running in order to conduct negotiations that will lead to nothing good.
    their wealth . . . / their treasure. The emissaries are bringing tribute—or perhaps rather a diplomatic bribe—in order to persuade Egypt to provide military assistance to Judah.

7. *Arrogance Ended.* The Masoretic Text reads *rahav hem shevet*, which would be literally: "arrogance [or Rahab] they to-sit." This cannot be right. The translation reads with many scholars *rohabam moshbat*, which is merely a respacing of the letters and a revocalization. The first word could either mean "arrogance" or be the proper name Rahab, a ferocious Canaanite sea beast, possibly here referring to Egypt.

8. *as a witness.* The received text reads *la'ad*, "forever," the same meaning as the next word in the text, but two Hebrew manuscripts and several ancient versions show *la'ed*, "as a witness."

deceitful sons,
sons who did not want to heed
the teaching of the LORD.

10   Who said to the seers, "You shall not see,"
and to the visionaries, "You shall not envision for us true things.
Speak smooth talk to us,
envision illusions.

11   Swerve from the way,
turn aside from the path.
Rid us of
Israel's Holy One."

12   Therefore, thus Israel's Holy One has said:
Inasmuch as you have spurned this word
and placed your trust in oppression and perversion
and leaned on it,

13   therefore this crime shall become for you
like a breach spreading down a high wall,
where all of a sudden the breaking point comes.

14   And its breaking like the breaking of a potter's jar,
relentlessly shattered,
and no shard will be found in its fragments
to carry fire from a hearth
or scoop water from a puddle.

15   For thus said the Master, the LORD, Israel's Holy One:
In quiet and stillness you shall be rescued,
in calm and trust shall your valor be,
but you did not want it.

16   And you said, "No, on a horse we shall flee."
Therefore shall you flee.
"And on a swift steed we shall ride."
Therefore shall your pursuers be swift.

17   A thousand before the shout of one,

---

13. *like a breach spreading down a high wall.* This image mingles metaphor with metonymy: a hidden flaw reaches a point where it suddenly causes a total breakdown, but the wall is also the actual structure that protects the city from invaders, who will now overrun it.

14. *like the breaking of a potter's jar.* The shift in metaphor is pointedly effective: the solid stone wall turns into a fragile earthenware jar that is easily broken to pieces. The smashing of the vessel into tiny fragments is vividly represented in the next line.

before the shout of five shall you flee,
till you are left like a flagpole on a mountaintop,
and like a banner on a hill.

And therefore the LORD shall wait to grant you grace,   18
and therefore He shall rise to show you mercy,
for a God of justice is the LORD.
happy all who wait for Him.
For the people shall dwell in Jerusalem,   19
nevermore shall weep.
He shall surely grant you grace at the sound of your crying,
when He hears it, He shall answer you.

And the Master shall give you   20
bread of straits and water of oppression.
But your Teacher shall no longer be concealed,
and your eyes shall see your Teacher,
and your ears shall hear a word behind you, saying: 21
This is the way, go upon it,
whether you turn to the right or the left.
And you shall defile the overlay of your silver idols   22
and the plating of your molten images of gold.
You shall scatter them like a woman in her uncleanness.

---

17. *before the shout of one, / before the shout of five.* Though it is more spectacular for a thousand to flee before the shout of a single person than five, the line follows the convention of biblical parallelism, where when a number is introduced in the first verset, it has to be increased in the second verset.

20. *your Teacher.* While other understandings are conceivable, the most likely reference is to God.

concealed. The verb *yikanef* is anomalous, but it may be related to the noun *kanaf,* the corner of a garment or a wing, perhaps suggesting a condition of lying under a fold.

21. *and your ears shall hear a word behind you.* The word coming from behind is a little puzzling, especially since the eyes that see the Teacher imply that He stands in front of the people. Perhaps God is in front and His prophet, to whom at last the people listens, urges them on from behind.

22. *And you shall defile.* That is, you shall make them unfit for worship.

You shall scatter them like a woman in her uncleanness. The verb "scatter" works better for the destroyed idols than for the menstruant woman, who in biblical law is certainly not "scattered" but rather kept at a distance in order to avoid physical contact with her.

Go out! You shall say to it.

23   And He shall give rain for your seed
            that you sow in the soil,
        and bread, the yield of the soil,
            and it shall be rich and fat.
        Your cattle shall graze on that day
            in a spacious pasture.

24   And the oxen and the donkeys that till the soil
            shall eat salted fodder
                that is winnowed with shovel and fan.

25   And there shall be on every high mountain
            and on every lofty hill
                streams, brooks of water,
        on the day of the great slaughter
            when towers fall.

26   And the light of the moon shall be like the light of the sun,
            and the light of the sun shall be sevenfold
                like the light of the seven days
        when the LORD binds up the breaking of His people
            and heals its smashing blow.

27   The LORD's name is about to come from afar,
            burning His wrath, heavy His burden,
        His lips are filled with fury,

---

25. *streams, brooks of water, / on the day of the great slaughter / when towers fall.* In a fusion of two motifs unusual in prophecies of redemption, the people restored to its glory will enjoy an abundance of fructifying freshets of water even as military catastrophe overwhelms the enemies that have dominated them.

26. *And the light of the moon shall be like the light of the sun.* This spectacular increase of natural light is a motif taken up by Second Isaiah and has led some scholars to conclude that at least this line was composed by him, which is a possible but not necessary inference. In any case, the striking hyperbole has invited eschatological readings, and "the light of the seven days" is clearly a mythological reference to the seven days of creation during which, according to some understandings, the light was more perfect. Creation begins with God's summoning light to replace the primordial darkness, so national restoration is imagined in cosmic terms as a kind of renewal of creation.

27. *The LORD's name.* The phrasing reflects a verbal practice that becomes pronounced in the Late Biblical period of interposing God's name as the active agent in order to avoid anthropomorphism.

His tongue, consuming fire.

His breath a sweeping stream   28
   crossing upward to the neck—
to shake nations in a ruinous sieve
   and a bridle on the jaws of peoples, leading them astray.
The song shall be for you   29
   like the night a festival is sanctified
and heart's joy like one who walks with the flute
   to come to the Lord's mountain, to Israel's Rock.
And the Lord shall sound His voice's majesty   30
   and show the downsweep of His arm
in furious wrath and tongues of consuming fire,
   cloudburst and torrent and hailstones.
For by the Lord's voice shall Assyria be terrified   31
   as He strikes with the rod.
And each swing of the club is punishment   32
   that the Lord shall lay down upon him
to the sound of timbrels and with lyres and with dance—

His tongue, consuming fire. These words concretize and intensify the "fury" of the first verset. They also incorporate a pun because of the intimations of tongues of fire.

28. *crossing upward to the neck.* The verb employed here is usually the one for a person crossing a stream, but here it indicates the water cutting the body in half and moving on upward to the neck.

   in a ruinous sieve. Some interpreters, striving to make the parallelism neat, cite a purported Arabic cognate for *nefet* that means "yoke." But this noun elsewhere clearly means "sieve," and the verb "to shake up" scarcely accords with a yoke. Biblical poetry sometimes switches metaphors between the first and second verset of a line.

29. *The song shall be for you.* This is the song of triumph and celebration when the enemy is destroyed and the people restored.

   like one who walks with the flute. This is the joyous procession at a pilgrim festival, in which the celebrants march up to the Temple mount to the accompaniment of musical instruments.

30. *tongues of consuming fire.* This is not the same Hebrew word as "tongue" in verse 27. The literal sense is "A flame of consuming fire."

32. *to the sound of the timbrels and with lyres.* As in verse 25, the joy of national restoration is mingled with a depiction in the second verset here of God's fearsome destruction of the enemy.

   and with dance. The Masoretic Text has *'uvemilḥamot*, "and with battles." The translation follows a commonly proposed emendation *uvemeḥolot*, "and with dances" (the plural has been changed to a singular in the translation for reasons of rhythm), a difference of one

in a swoop He does battle against her.

33 For Topheth was laid out long ago,
    it, too is readied for Molech,
its fire pit deep and wide,
    much fire and firewood.
The Lord's breath is like a torrent of brimstone
    burning within it.

CHAPTER 31

1 Woe, who go down to Egypt for help,
    who rely on horses
and trust in chariots because they are many,
    and in horsemen because they greatly abound,
and they have not looked to Israel's Holy One,
    nor have they sought out the Lord.
2 But He, too, is wise and will bring about harm,

Hebrew letter. Another possibility would be to move the word as it appears in the Masoretic Text to the second verset and have it read: "and in swooping battles He does battle against it." That, however, would produce a rhythmic imbalance of two stresses in the first verset and four in the second.

33. *Topheth.* This is the Valley of Ben-Hinnom in Jerusalem, where human sacrifice was offered. In later Hebrew usage, it became a term for "hell."

Molech. The Masoretic Text is vocalized to read *melekh*, "king," but it almost certainly is Molech, the pagan god to whom human sacrifices (usually children) were made.

The Lord's breath is like a torrent of brimstone / burning within it. The imagery aptly concludes the prophecy of the destruction of Israel's enemies: on the altar of Molech, human beings were devoted to the consuming flames; now God's fiery breath will burn up the Assyrians.

CHAPTER 31   1. *Woe, who go down to Egypt for help.* The prophet continues the vehement argument against seeking an alliance with Egypt that was put forth in the previous chapter. While *'ezrah* is a general term for "help," it often occurs in military contexts, and that connotation is obviously relevant here. The prophet will play sardonically on this word in the next two verses.

who rely on horses / and trust in chariots. Egypt was renowned for its horses and active in exporting them. There is probably also a reminiscence of the Exodus story, in which all of Pharaoh's horsemen with their chariots are engulfed in the Sea of Reeds.

2. *But He, too, is wise.* There is an implied opposition between God's wisdom and power and the purported sages and soothsayers of Egypt.

and His word He does not revoke.
And He shall rise up against the house of the evil ones
    and against those who help wrongdoers.
And Egypt is human and not a god,   3
    and their horses are flesh and not spirit.
And the LORD shall reach out His hand,
    and the helper shall stumble, the one helped shall fall,
        and both of them perish together.
For thus said the LORD to me: 4
    As the lion growls,
        the maned beast over its prey,
            when a shepherds' band gathers against it,
it fears not their voice
    nor is cowed by their clamor,
thus shall the LORD of Armies come down
    to marshal forces on Mount Zion and on its slope.
As birds fly above,   5
    so shall the LORD of Armies protect Jerusalem,
        protecting and saving, sparing and rescuing.

Turn back to Him from Whom you swerved far away, O Israelites. For on 6,7
that day every man shall spurn his ungods of silver and his ungods of gold
that your hands have made as offense.

    And Assyria shall fall by a sword not of man's,   8
        and a sword not a human's shall devour him.

---

4. *As the lion growls.* The lion is a stock image for martial fierceness in ancient Near Eastern poetry. Here it is applied to God, as the end of this verse makes clear.

    to marshal forces on Mount Zion. This whole line is ambiguous because the preposition *'al* could mean either "on" or "against" (for the latter construction, see the New Jewish Publication Society rendering, "to make war against the mount and hill of Zion"). But the idea of God's assaulting Mount Zion is hard to sustain because in the very next verse He is represented hovering protectively over Jerusalem. The marshaling of divine forces, then, would be God's driving off the enemies besieging Jerusalem. This might be a reference to the sudden departure of the besieging army in 701 B.C.E., though that is not certain.

5. *As birds fly above.* The switch of similes is pointed: if God is a fearless lion confronting Israel's enemies, He is also a gentle bird hovering protectively over His people.

8. *And Assyria shall fall by a sword not of man's.* The formulation, evoking the idea of a miraculous defeat of the Assyrian army, appears to accord with the account of the sudden flight of the Arameans (not the Assyrians) offered in 2 Kings 7.

> And he shall flee from the sword,
>> and his young men be put to forced labor.
9 And his rock from terror shall crumble,
>> and his commanders panic-stricken by the banner.
> Thus said the LORD,
> Who has a fire in Zion
>> and a furnace in Jerusalem.

CHAPTER 32

1 Yes, a king shall reign in righteousness,
>> and princes shall govern in justice.
2 Each shall be like a refuge from wind
>> and a shelter from the torrent,
> like freshets of water on parched earth,
>> like the shade of a great rock
>>> in an arid land.
3 And the eyes of those who see shall not be sealed,

---

9. *And his rock from terror shall crumble.* There are difficulties in the wording of this verset and the next one. The metaphor of rock or crag is often attached to God in Psalms, but it is not elsewhere linked with a human leader, as many interpreters of this verse claim. Perhaps here it is meant to designate the military power in which the Assyrians place their trust. The verb that is translated here as "crumble" because of the context actually means "to pass on," which does not sound appropriate for "rock."

his commanders panic-stricken by the banner. The wording is cryptic and many scholars have proposed emending the text. The text as we have it could be correct: the Assyrian commanders, seeing the banners of the army attacking them, are terrified.

a fire in Zion / and a furnace in Jerusalem. Given the defeat of the Assyrians that has just been evoked, this is a destructive fire: the Assyrians assaulting Jerusalem imagined they had surrounded a city that they would overwhelm, but God tends a blazing furnace within the city that consumes its enemies

CHAPTER 32   1. *a king shall reign in righteousness.* The theme of the just king instituting a reign of perfect harmony is picked up from chapter 11, whether by Isaiah himself or, as some scholars prefer to think, by a later prophet in the "Isaian tradition."

and princes shall govern in justice. The prophet envisages not only a righteous king but an entire royal bureaucracy of noblemen enacting justice.

3. *And the eyes of those who see shall not be sealed.* This whole line is an obvious reversal of the situation delineated in God's words to Isaiah in his dedication to the prophetic mission (6:9–10), when the prophet is enjoined to seal the eyes and stop up the ears of the people.

and the ears of those who hear shall listen,
and the heart of the rash shall come to understand,   4
    and the tongue of the stammerers speak eloquence.
The scurrilous man shall no longer be called noble,   5
    nor the villain named high-born.
For the scurrilous man speaks scurrility,   6
    and his heart performs misdeeds,
to carry out foul acts
    and speak wrongly of the LORD,
to leave the hungry man's throat empty
    and withhold drink from the thirsty.
The villain, his vessels are vile,   7
    he devises infamous things,
to do harm to the poor with lying speech,
    when the needy speak in court.
But the nobleman plans noble acts,   8
    and on noble acts he stands.

Women at ease, stand up,   9
    hear my voice.
Complacent young women,
    to my words give ear.
For within but a year,   10
    the complacent shall quake,

---

5. *The scurrilous man.* It is not entirely certain whether the Hebrew *naval* refers to turpitude or stupidity, or perhaps rather to a combination of the two. Blenkinsopp neatly describes this condition as "moral imbecility."

7. *The villain, his vessels are vile.* The translation emulates the wordplay in the Hebrew: *kelay kelaw ra'im.* More strictly, the initial noun means "miser."
    to do harm to the poor with lying speech. Although the thematic unity of this entire prophecy looks loosely associative, the connective logic is as follows: the just princes and monarch are to bring about a just judicial order that is very much lacking in a society where villains pervert justice; thus the nobleman with his noble acts invoked in the next verse has a crucially necessary role to play.

9. *Women at ease . . . / Complacent young women.* A female audience is addressed both because it is these women of Jerusalem who egregiously have been leading a self-satisfied life of luxury (compare chapter 3) and because it is the role of women to take up public keening in a time of disaster, which is about to come. The first of the two terms here is *nashim,* the second *banot,* and while *banot* (literally, "daughters") are definitely young women, there is no persuasive basis for the scholarly claim that *nashim* means "married women."

for the vintage is done with,
    no harvest shall come.

11   Tremble, you women at ease,
      quake, complacent ones.
Strip yourselves bare,
    put a cloth round your loins,

12   Beating on breasts
      over lovely fields,
        over fruitful vines.

13   On My people's soil
      thorn and thistle shall spring up,
for on all the houses of revelry,
    the merrymaking town,

14   the villa is abandoned,
      the town's hubbub left behind.
The citadel and the tower
    become bare places for all time,
wild asses' revelry,
    pasture for the flocks.

15   Till a spirit is poured on us from above,
      and the desert turns to farmland
        and farmland is reckoned as forest,

---

10. *the vintage is done with, / no harvest shall come.* Blenkinsopp suggests that this may refer to the devastation of the countryside of Judah by Sennacherib's invading army in 701 B.C.E.

11. *Strip yourselves bare, / put a cloth round your loins.* As the second verset clarifies, what the prophet has in mind is not a state of complete nakedness but the putting aside of fine clothing (again, see chapter 3) and binding sackcloth round the loins as a sign of mourning.

12. *Beating on breasts.* This is of course a gesture of mourning. The Hebrew participle is a masculine plural where it should be feminine. This may be a scribal error influenced by the word for "breasts," which is a masculine plural.

13. *for on all the houses.* The preposition here does not seem right for "houses" but may have been pulled into the discourse by its use with "soil" in the previous verse. It also might be an ellipsis for something like "curse."

15. *Till a spirit is poured on us from above.* This is the pivotal point of the prophecy: after the catastrophe in which the land is laid waste, God's spirit will envelop the people, instituting an era of justice and fructifying the devastated countryside.
    farmland is reckoned as forest. Though the forest does not produce crops, it is a place of dense verdant growth, and so it becomes hyperbolic of the efflorescence of the farmland. Throughout these lines, the prophet imagines a fusion of justice with the flourishing renewal of the land.

And justice abides in the desert,   16
    and righteousness dwells in the farmland.
And the doing of righteousness shall be peace,   17
    and the work of righteousness, safe and quiet forever.
And My people shall dwell in abodes of peace,   18
    in safe dwellings and tranquil places of rest.
And it shall come down as the forest comes down,   19
    and in the lowland the town shall come low.
Happy, you who sow near all waters,   20
    who let loose the ox and the donkey.

CHAPTER 33

Woe, plunderer, and you are not plundered,   1
    traitor, and they did not betray you.
When you are done plundering, you shall be plundered,
    when you finish betraying, they shall betray you.

O Lord, show us grace, in You we hope,   2
    be our arm every morning,
        yes, our rescue in a time of distress.
From the sound of a tumult peoples have fled,   3
    from Your loftiness nations have scattered.

---

19. *And it shall come down as the forest comes down.* This entire verse appears to be damaged beyond repair. The first word in the received text is *barad*, "hail" (though the vowel-points make it look like a verb), which makes no sense; it has been emended here in accordance with one Hebrew manuscript and two ancient versions to *yarad*, "shall come down," which at least yields semantic parallelism in the line. Even so, it is unclear what is being said, and attempts to explain the line or recover an original version that lies behind it have been unavailing.

20. *who let loose the ox and the donkey.* This is in keeping with the idea of planting alongside streams that provide abundant irrigation: there will be green pastures all around over which the oxen and donkeys may roam.

CHAPTER 33   1. *Woe, plunderer.* Some scholars take this verse to be the conclusion of the prophecy that runs to the end of chapter 32, but it may be an isolated fragment. The plunderer could refer to the Assyrian invader, whose destruction is prophesied in verses 10–13.

2. *O Lord, show us grace.* This initial formula, as many scholars have noted, is reminiscent of the psalms of supplication, but what follows in this poem scarcely constitutes a psalm.

4   And the spoil was gathered as locusts are gathered,
          like grasshoppers whirring, they whir over it.
5   Lofty is the LORD, for He dwells on high,
          He has filled Zion with justice and righteousness.
6   And He shall be the trust of your times,
          power to rescue, wisdom and knowledge,
               fear of the LORD, that is his treasure.

7   Look, the Arielites screamed in the streets,
          messengers of peace wept bitterly.
8   The highways are desolate,
          no wayfarer comes.
     He has broken the treaty,
          spurned the witnesses,
               made no account of man.
9   Mourning, forlorn, is the land
          He has shamed Lebanon, it withers.
     Sharon has become like a desert
          and Bashan and Carmel stripped bare.
10   Now will I rise, says the LORD,
          now will I loom, now be raised.
11   You shall conceive chaff, give birth to straw—
          My breath shall consume you in fire.

---

4. *as locusts are gathered, / like grasshoppers whirring, they whir over it.* This appears to be the general sense of the Hebrew even though the syntax is rather crabbed.

7. *the Arielites.* While some commentators understand this as a term for "messengers," it probably designates Jerusalemites, as in 29:1. The screaming and weeping, followed in the next verse with the evocation of the desolate countryside, reflect a moment when Jerusalem is sorely threatened by besiegers, and the best candidate for such a moment would be Sennacherib's assault on the city in 701 B.C.E. In that case, the one who has broken the treaty in the next verse would be Sennacherib.

8. *spurned the witnesses.* The Masoretic Text reads "spurned the cities ['*arim*]," but cities would be an odd object for the verb "spurned." The Qumran Isaiah reads '*edim*, "witnesses," and the translation adopts that reading.

10. *Now will I rise.* This is the turning point when God summons His power to rout the Assyrian forces

11. *You shall conceive chaff, give birth to straw.* The "you" (plural in the Hebrew) refers to the Assyrians. Conceiving chaff and giving birth to straw is an image of utter futility, and since these are both highly combustible materials, the metaphor also represents their absolute vulnerability to God's consuming fire.

And peoples shall be burnings of lime,   12
    thorns cut down that go up in fire
Hear, you who are far off, what I have done,   13
    and mark, you who are close, My might.

Offenders have feared in Zion,   14
    trembling has seized the tainted.
Who of us can abide the consuming fire,
    who of us can abide the eternal flames?
He who walks in righteousness, speaking truth,   15
    spurning oppression's profit,
who shakes his hands clean from holding a bribe,
    stops up his ears from hearing blood-schemes
        and shuts his eyes from looking at evil.
It is he who dwells on the heights,   16
    the fortress of crags his stronghold,
        his bread provided, his water secure.

A king in his beauty your eyes shall behold,   17
    they shall see a land stretched out to the distance.
Your heart shall murmur in awe,   18
    "Where is he who counts, where is he who weighs,
    where is he who counts the towers?"

---

14. *Offenders have feared in Zion.* This turn to the miscreants within Jerusalem marks the beginning of a new prophecy. It is possible that the appearance of consuming fire at the end of this verse led to the editorial decision to place this text here, after a prophecy that ends with consuming fire.

15. *He who walks in righteousness, speaking truth.* This list of ethical attributes has a catechistic look that recalls two different psalms in which similar questions are asked of the pilgrim ascending the Temple mount.

16. *he who dwells on the heights.* As the next verset makes clear, this would be a position of fortified security, although it is conceivable that there is also a kind of punning reference to the Temple mount.

17. *A king in his beauty.* This new prophecy harks back to Isaiah's evocation of an ideal king in chapter 11 and elsewhere.
    a land stretched out to the distance. The literal sense of the Hebrew is "a land of distances." The idea is that the divinely restored Zion will be a vast country.

18. *Where is he who counts.* It is quite unnecessary to suppose, as some scholars have done, that a census is envisaged. What the prophet has in mind is the splendid abundance of buildings and towers in the restored city, precisely as in Psalm 48:13—"Go around Zion,

19   A fearsome people you shall not see,
  a people with a tongue too unfathomable to grasp,
   a barbaric language beyond understanding.
20   Behold Jerusalem, our festival city,
  the tranquil dwelling, a tent not to be moved.
 Its pegs are not pulled up ever
  and all its cords never are snapped.
21   For there the LORD is mighty for us
  a place of rivers, wide streams,
 where no sailing craft can go
  nor mighty vessels pass,
22   For the LORD is our judge, the LORD our leader,
  the LORD is our king, He rescues us.
23   Your ropes have come loose,
  they cannot hold up their mast,
   they cannot unfurl the sail.
 Then were great spoils shared out,
  the very lame have taken plunder.
24   And he who dwells there won't say, "I am ill."
  The people who live there are pardoned of crime.

---

encircle it. / Count its towers"—which is also a poetic celebration of triumph over enemies who have attacked Jerusalem.

19. *a tongue too unfathomable to grasp, / a barbaric language beyond understanding.* Repeatedly in biblical poetry, one of the terrifying aspects of the enemy is that he speaks an unintelligible language.

20. *a tent not to be moved.* Even though Jerusalem is built up with stone houses, the traditional equation between "tent" and "habitation" is so strong that it can be introduced here, albeit with the pointed emphasis that this tent is as solid and permanent as a building.

21. *a place of rivers, wide streams.* There are no broad rivers in the land of Judah, but this is a kind of utopian fantasy. One recalls a line by the great Israeli poet Yehuda Amichai, "Jerusalem is the Venice of God."
 where no sailing craft can go. The context suggests that this means no invading fleets can enter.

23. *Your ropes have come loose.* The "you" would have to be Israel's enemies. This may explain why no sailing craft can enter these waters: the rigging of the ships is in disarray, and they cannot sail.
 the very lame have taken plunder. "Very" is added in the translation for clarification. The evident idea is that the defeat of the enemy will be so devastating that not just warriors but even the lame will plunder the armor and weapons that have been abandoned in panicked flight. This could accord with the description of the sudden flight of the Assyrian army that appears in 2 Kings 19.

CHAPTER 34

Draw near, O nations, to hear,   1
 and you peoples, hearken.
Let the earth and its fullness hear,
 the world and all its offspring.
For fury has the LORD against all nations, 2
 and wrath against all their army.
  He has destroyed them, consigned them to slaughter.
And their slain shall be flung away,   3
  their corpses shall give off a stench,
   and mountains shall melt from their blood.
All the heavens' array shall molder,   4
 and like a scroll the heavens roll up,
and all their array shall wither
 as the leaf withers on the vine
  and the withered fruit on the fig tree.

For My sword slaked its thirst in the heavens, 5
 look, on Edom it comes down,
  and on the people I doomed to destruction.

CHAPTER 34 2. *For fury has the* LORD *against all nations.* Although a specific national target of divine wrath will emerge in verse 5, the initial perspective is global and, in effect, apocalyptic: all the earth is summoned to listen to the dire prophecy (verse 1), and God's devastating judgment sweeps across the whole world.

3. *and mountains shall melt from their blood.* Other translations render the verb as "be drenched" or "flow," but it is worth retaining the literal sense of the Hebrew, which constitutes a strong hyperbole: the tide of blood, vast and corrosive, will melt the mountains.

4. *All the heavens' array shall molder.* The apocalyptic scope of the poetry is strikingly evident here: the swath of divine fury will encompass the very heavens, withering the stars, which as the army or host of the heavens correspond to the armies subjected to God's wrath in verse 2.
 as the leaf withers. The agricultural simile brings the distant and seemingly unassailable stars down to the familiar reality of transient things on earth, where a leaf or a date can wither overnight.

5. *Edom.* The appearance of Edom as the hated archenemy to be devastated by divine wrath suggests a relatively late date for this prophecy. Edom notoriously collaborated with the Babylonian invaders of Judah in 586 B.C.E., as Psalm 137 bitterly recalls.
 the people I doomed to destruction. The Hebrew noun rendered as "destruction" has a homonym that means "net," so the phrase might conceivably mean "the people caught in My net for judgment."

6   The LORD's sword is covered with blood,
          greased with suet
     from the blood of sheep and he-goats,
          from the suet of kidneys of rams.
     For a sacrifice the LORD has in Bozrah
          and a great slaughter in the land of Edom.
7   And wild oxen shall come down with them,
          and bulls with the steers.
     And their land shall slake its thirst with blood,
          and their soil shall be greased with suet.
8   For a day of revenge has the LORD,
          a year of retribution for Zion's cause.
9   And its rivers shall turn to pitch,
          its soil to brimstone,
               and its land turn to burning pitch.
10   Night and day it shall not go out,
          forever its smoke shall rise.
     For all generations it shall lie in ruins,
          for time without end none pass through it.
11   The hawk and the hedgehog shall take hold of it,
          and the owl and the raven shall dwell there,
               and He shall stretch over it the line of welter, the weight-stones of
          waste.

---

6. *For a sacrifice the* LORD *has.* In the poetic equivalent of a cinematic *faux raccord*, the verse that appears to begin with the sacrifice of sheep and he-goats now converts them into a metaphor for the slaughter of the Edomites.

   sacrifice . . . slaughter. As Blenkinsopp notes, the poet plays on the phonetic closeness between the two Hebrew terms, *zevaḥ* and *tevaḥ*.

   Bozrah. This is a prominent Edomite city.

7. *And wild oxen shall come down with them.* While the general sense of a massacre is clear, the formulation of this whole verse is rather opaque: the verb "come down" sounds odd; the reference of "with them" (the Edomites?) is uncertain; and given that the prophet has moved on from slaughtered animals to slaughtered Edomites, it is puzzling that he should revert here to animals.

9. *its rivers.* The land referred to here is clearly Edom.

11. *The hawk and the hedgehog.* In this verse and in verses 13–15 the only animals that can be identified confidently are the jackals and ostriches of verse 13. In any case, all these are beasts whose habitat is the desolate wilderness.

   the line of welter, the weight-stones of waste. The invocation of the "welter and waste"

Its nobles shall call out, "There is no kingship,"   12
    and all its princes be naught.
And thorns shall spring up in her citadels,   13
    in her fortresses nettle and briers,
and it shall turn into an abode of jackals,
    a courtyard of ostriches.
And wildcats shall meet hyenas,   14
    and the satyr shall call to its mate.
There Lilith shall rest
    and find repose for herself.
There the adder shall nest and lay eggs,   15
    hatch and brood in its shade.
There the buzzards shall gather,
    each one with its mate.
Inquire of the LORD's book and read,   16
    not one of these is absent,
      not one has missed its mate,
for the LORD's mouth has commanded,
    and His spirit has gathered them.

(*tohu wabohu*) of Genesis 1:2 is pointed: an activity of building will be undertaken but with the aim of irreversible destruction, restoring this land to the condition of primordial chaos.

12. *Its nobles shall call out, "There is no kingship."* Some scholars conclude that there is a missing clause here. This translation seeks to rescue the received text, deleting an initial "and" before "there."

13. *a courtyard of ostriches.* This translation reads *ḥatseir*, "courtyard," for the Masoretic *ḥatsir*, "grass." In this sense, it becomes an effective irony: a palace would have a courtyard; now, with the Edomite palaces in ruins, ostriches make these places their courtyard.

14. *the satyr . . . / Lilith.* As happens not infrequently in biblical poetry, there is an overlap between zoological and mythological entities: in the midst of the hyenas and jackals, goat-demons and a demonic goddess of the night make an appearance.

16. *Inquire of the LORD's book.* The most plausible reference, given the context of this prophecy, is to neither a celestial book nor a canonical text but the prophecy itself, which, after all, is presented to its audience as the word of God.
    not one of these is absent, / not one has missed its mate. "These" must be the noxious beasts listed in the preceding catastrophe. Every one of them will appear on the site of desolation where Edom once stood; every one will have its feral mate. The absolute fulfillment of the prophecy of the beasts in turn implies that every item in the prophecy of destruction set down in God's book will surely come about.

17   And He has cast for them a lot,
            His hand shared it out to them by measuring line.
        Forever they shall take hold of it,
            for all generations they shall dwell there.

CHAPTER 35

1   The deserts and parched land shall rejoice,
            the wilderness exult and bloom like the rose.
2   It surely shall bloom and exult,
            yes, exult and sing out in gladness.
        Lebanon's glory is given to it,
            the splendor of Carmel and Sharon.
        They shall behold the LORD's glory,
            the majesty of our God.
3   Strengthen the slackened hands,
            bolster the tottering knees.
4   Say to the fearful of heart:
            Be strong, do not fear.
        Look, your God in vengeance shall come,

---

17. *And He has cast for them a lot, / His hand shared it out to them by measuring line.* The effect of the imagery is literally sarcastic: dividing up an inheritance by lot (as in the Book of Joshua), measuring out plots of land with a line, are actions appropriate to carefully assigning property for human possession. Here, however, these actions are meant to give everlasting "property rights" in what once was Edom to all these wild beasts.

CHAPTER 35   1. *The desert and parched land shall rejoice.* This prophecy of a transformation of the desert into a lush land of blossoming flowers is a metaphor for the grand restoration of the defeated people of Israel. It is tempting to conclude, in particular because of the image of a highway in the wilderness (verse 8) that this prophecy is the work of Second Isaiah. That is not entirely certain, even though the notion (verse 10) of "those ransomed by the LORD" returning to Zion on a holy highway is certainly in accord with the language and themes of Second Isaiah.

    the rose. As with other biblical flora, the identity of this flower is uncertain (both crocus and asphodel have been proposed). This translation preserves the equivalent for *ḥavatselet* used by the King James Version both here and in the Song of Songs.

3. *Strengthen the slackened hands.* This entire exhortation to the people to be of good cheer, continuing in the next verse after having been downcast, speaks to the condition of exiles.

God's retribution shall come and rescue you.
Then shall the eyes of the blind be opened,   5
    and the ears of the deaf be unstopped.
Then shall the lame skip like a stag,   6
    and the tongue of the mute sing in gladness.
For water shall break forth in the desert
    and brooks in the wilderness.
The heat-scorched ground shall become a lake   7
    and the thirsty soil, springs of water.
Where a jackal's abode was, its lair—
    a courtyard for reeds and rushes.
And a highway shall be there,   8
    a holy way it shall be called.
No unclean one shall pass over it,
    but it shall be for him who goes on the way,
        and fools shall not wander there.
No lion shall be there,   9
    nor wild beasts go up on it.
        There the redeemed shall go.
Those ransomed by the LORD shall return   10
    and come to Zion with glad song,
joy everlasting on their heads,
    delight and joy they attain,
        and sorrow and sighing shall flee.

---

7. *The heat-scorched ground.* The Hebrew *sharav* actually means something like "heat scorch," but ground is metonymically implied as it is the ground, not the scorching air, that turns into a lake.

8. *but it shall be for him who goes on the way.* This clause and the next look textually suspect in the Hebrew, and so any translation is conjectural. A literal rendering here would be: and it is for them who goes [*sic,* singular verb] on the way.

    and fools shall not wander there. These are obviously meant to stand in contrast to the pure ones—Israel's exiles?—who are destined to go on the highway through the wilderness, but the use of the term "fools" is rather odd.

10. *come to Zion with glad song.* The invocation at the end of this prophecy of "glad song" (*rinah,* verbal stem *r-n-n*) and rejoicing marks a clear envelope structure with the beginning in verses 1–2. At the beginning, the desert is filled with glad song because it is blooming; now at the end, the exiles returning to Zion sing gladly as they walk on the highway through the desert.

1 CHAPTER 36   And it happened in the fourteenth year of
King Hezekiah, that Sennacherib king of Assyria went up against all the
2 fortified towns of Judah and took them. And the king of Assyria sent Rabshakeh from Lachish to Jerusalem to King Hezekiah with a heavy force.
And he took a stance at the conduit of the Upper Pool, on the road to the
3 Fuller's Field. And Eliakim son of Hilkiah who was appointed over the
house came out to him, together with Shebnah the scribe and Joah son of
4 Asaph the recorder. And Rabshakeh said to them, "Say, pray, to Hezekiah:
Thus said the great king, the king of Assyria: 'What is this great trust in
5 which you place trust? You thought, mere words are counsel and valor for
battle. Now, in whom did you trust that you should have rebelled against
6 me? Why, you have trusted in this shattered reed, in Egypt, which when a
man leans on it, enters his palm and pierces it. So is Pharaoh king of Egypt
7 to all who trust in him. And should you say to me, In the LORD our God we
trust, is it not He Whose high places and altars Hezekiah took away, and

---

CHAPTER 36   1. *And it happened in the fourteenth year of King Hezekiah.* The
prose narrative that begins here and runs to the end of chapter 39 replicates 2 Kings 18:13
through 2 Kings 20:19 with, for the most part, only minor textual differences and one added
unit, 38:9–20. Although some scholars have argued that the Book of Isaiah is the primary
source, copied by the editors of Kings, the reverse seems more likely. One indication that
the Isaiah text is secondary is that at quite a few points it slightly abbreviates the text in
Kings, dropping out a word, phrase, or even a clause that was not deemed strictly necessary.
The editorial decision to insert this narrative segment here at the end of the prophecies of
Isaiah son of Amoz (however much these include later writings) was evidently motivated by
a desire to round out the prophecies with some detailed historical context. The fourteenth
year of Hezekiah's reign is 701 B.C.E. Sennacharib's campaign in Phoenicia, Philistia, and
Judah in that year is elaborately documented in Assyrian annals and bas-reliefs.
    all the fortified towns of Judah. According to the Assyrian annals, the imperial forces
captured forty-six Judean towns—which may be an imperial exaggeration. The principal
one was Lachish, where Sennacharib is headquartered in the next verse. The Assyrians left
a vivid bas-relief of their archers, in characteristic high-pointed caps, assaulting this town.

2. *Rabshakeh.* Although this word is presented in the Hebrew text without a definite article,
as though it were a proper name, it is actually a title, "head steward." In Kings, this figure
is accompanied by two other Assyrian court officials who also have titles as names.

3. *who was appointed over the house.* That is, the palace.

6. *this shattered reed.* Reeds, of course, grow in abundance along the Nile.
    which when a man leans on it, enters his palm and pierces it. The metaphor is quite
realistic. The reed looks as if it could provide support, but it easily breaks when you lean
on it, and the jagged ends of the beak can pierce the skin. Rabshakeh's words neatly jibe
with Isaiah's political opposition to an alliance with Egypt.

he said to Judah and to Jerusalem: Before this altar you shall bow down in
Jerusalem?' And now, wager, pray with my master, king of Assyria, and 8
I shall give you two thousand horses if you can give yourselves riders for
them. And how could you turn away the agent of the least of my master's 9
servants and trust Egypt for chariots and horses? And now, was it without 10
the LORD that I have came up against this land to destroy it? The LORD said
to me, Go up against this land and destroy it." And Eliakim, and Shebnah 11
and Joah with him, said to Rabshakeh, "Speak, pray, to your servants Aramaic, for we understand it, and do not speak Judahite in the hearing of the
people who are on the wall." And Rabshakeh said, "Did my master send 12
me to you and to your master to speak these words? Did he not send me
to these men sitting on the wall—to eat their own turds and to drink their
own urine—together with you?" And Rabshakeh stood and called out in 13
a loud voice in Judahite and said, "Listen to the words of the great king,
the king of Assyria. Thus said the king, 'Let not Hezekiah deceive you, for 14
he will not be able to save you. And let not Hezekiah have you trust in the 15
LORD, saying, the LORD with surely save us, this city will not be given into
the hand of the king of Assyria.' Do not listen to Hezekiah, for thus said the 16

---

8. *I shall give you two thousand horses if you can give yourself riders for them.* Hezekiah's
attempted rebellion is so hopelessly pathetic, Rabshakeh says, that he could not even muster
sufficient cavalrymen were he given the horses.

9. *agent.* The Hebrew aptly uses an Assyrian imperial administrative title, *paḥat* (compare
the English "pasha," which has a shared linguistic background).

11. *Speak, pray, to your servants Aramaic.* Aramaic was the most widely shared language in
the lands of the Assyrian empire east of the Jordan, and so by the late eighth century B.C.E.
it had been adopted as the lingua franca. Thus, an educated Judahite court official would
have been fluent in Aramaic.
    do not speak Judahite. "Judahite," of course, is Hebrew. It is not explained how an Assyr-
ian court official had a command of Hebrew.

12. *Did he not send me to these men sitting on the wall.* The verb "send" is merely implied in
the Hebrew. Rabshakeh makes clear that his entire speech—itself a brilliant deployment of
political rhetoric—is precisely intended for the ears of the people. His purpose is to drive a
wedge between the rebellious Hezekiah and the people, convincing them that the uprising
is hopeless, and that, in fact, the fate of deportation to Assyria will be a happy one.

15. *let not Hezekiah have you trust in the LORD.* Rabshakeh appears to be shifting grounds.
First he claimed that it was YHWH Who sent the Assyrians against Judah (verse 10), which
was a way of conveying to the people the idea that their destruction was divinely ordained
and irreversible. Now he takes a different tack: no national god has ever prevailed against
the great king of Assyria.

king of Assyria: 'Make terms with me and come out to me, and each man
eat of his vine and each man of his fig tree, and each man drink the water
17 of his well. Until I come and take you to a land like your land—a land of
18 grain and new wine, a land of bread and vineyards. Lest Hezekiah mislead
you, saying the LORD will save us. Did the gods of the nations ever save
19 each its land from the hand of the king of Assyria? Where were the gods of
Hammath and Arpad? Where were the gods of Sepharvaim, and did they
20 save Samaria from my hand? Who is there of all the gods of these lands
that saved their land from my hand, that the LORD should save Jerusalem
21 from my hand?'" And they were silent and did not answer a word to him,
22 for it was the king's command, saying, "You shall not answer him." And
Eliakim son of Hilkiah, who was appointed over the house, and Shebnah
the scribe and Joah son of Asaph the recorder with him, came to Hezekiah,
their garments rent, and they told him Rabshakeh's words.

1 CHAPTER 37   And it happened when King Hezekiah heard,
that he rent his garments and covered himself in sackcloth and went into
2 the house of the LORD. And he sent Eliakim, who was appointed over the
house, and Shebnah the scribe and the elders of the priests, covered in
3 sackcloth, to Isaiah the prophet son of Amos. And they said to him, "Thus
said Hezekiah: 'A day of distress and chastisement and insult in this day.

For children have come to the birth-stool,
and there is no strength to give birth.

---

16. *Make terms with me.* The literal sense is "make a gift [or blessing] with me," but in
context, as Rashi and the King James Version after him understood, the expression means
to offer terms of surrender.

   each man eat of his vine and each man of his fig tree. The vine and the fig tree appear
in a repeated proverbial expression about peaceful and prosperous life. Eating from the
vine and the fig tree and drinking well-water are a vivid antithesis to the representation
of the starving besieged population eating its own excrement and drinking its own urine.

17. *a land like your land.* The catalogue of agricultural beauty that follows resembles the
recurrent list of all the good things of the Land of Israel. Rabshakeh in this fashion depicts
life in exile in Assyria as a new promised land.

CHAPTER 37   3. *For children have come to the birth-stool.* The poetic style makes
these words seem initially cryptic, but the obvious meaning is that the children about to
be born cannot emerge because when the mothers come to the birth-stool, they do not
have the strength to push the babies out. The delegation from the king may want to speak

Perhaps the LORD will have heard the words of Rabshakeh, whom his   4
master the king of Assyria sent, to defame the living God, and He will
chastise for the words that the LORD your God heard and you will offer
prayers for the remnant that still exists.'" And the servants of King Heze-   5
kiah came to Isaiah. And Isaiah said to them, "Thus shall you say to your   6
master: Thus said the LORD: 'Do not fear the words that you have heard,
with which the flunkies of the king of Assyria reviled Me. I am about   7
to send an ill spirit into him, and he shall hear a rumor and go back to
his land, and I shall make him fall by the sword in his land.'" And Rab-   8
shakeh went back and found the king of Assyria battling against Libnah,
for he had heard that he had journeyed on from Lachish. And he heard   9
about Tirhakah king of Cush, saying, "Look, he has sallied forth to do
battle with you." And he heard, and he sent messengers to Hezekiah,
saying, "Thus shall you say to Hezekiah king of Judah, 'Let not your god   10
in whom you trust deceive you, saying, Jerusalem will not be given into
the hand of the king of Assyria. Look, you yourself have heard what the   11
kings of Assyria did to all the lands, annihilating them—and will you be
saved? Did the gods of the nations save them, when my fathers destroyed   12
Gozan and Haran and Rezeph and the Edomites who are in Telassar?

---

to the prophet in his own characteristic language by first addressing him in a line of verse.
In any case, the line forcefully frames their message to Isaiah with an image of desperate
impotence that represents the plight of the people. The prophet in this narrative resembles
Elijah and Elisha in being seen by others as a holy man who has the power to intercede on
their behalf with God.

5. *And the servants of King Hezekiah came to Isaiah.* Their arrival was clearly implied by
the end of verse 2. Perhaps one should construe the verb as a pluperfect, though its form
does not indicate that.

6. *flunkies.* The Hebrew *ne'arim*, youths or people in a subservient status, is usually represented in this translation as "lads," but its use here by Isaiah, instead of the expected
'avadim, "servants," has a pejorative connotation.

7. *an ill spirit.* The Hebrew says only "a spirit," but since it induces fear followed by flight,
it appears to be a troubling spirit.
    he shall hear a rumor. What this might be is not spelled out. If the prophecy is to be
consistent with what is reported at the end of the chapter, it would be the news that his
army has been stricken with a plague.

9. *king of Cush.* Cush is Nubia, just south of Egypt and politically linked with it. Egypt was
a key player in the uprising against the Assyrian imperial forces, and so it is not surprising
that the Nubian king would oppose Sennacherib. The connection of this report with the
siege against Jerusalem is not entirely clear. Perhaps Sennacherib is impelled to finish off
Jerusalem quickly so that he can turn his forces to the south.

13 Where is the king of Hammath, and the kings of Arpad and the king
14 of Lair, Sepharvaim, Hena, and Ivvah?'" And Hezekiah took the letters
   from the hand of the messengers and read them, and he went up to the
15 house of the LORD, and Hezekiah spread them out before the LORD. And
16 Hezekiah prayed to the LORD, saying: "LORD of Armies, enthroned on
   the cherubim, You alone are God of all the kingdoms of earth. You it was
17 made heaven and earth. Bend Your ear and listen; open, LORD, Your eyes
   and see; and listen to the words of Sennacherib that he sent to insult the
18 living God. Indeed, LORD, the king of Assyria destroyed all the nations
19 and their lands and consigned their gods to fire, for they are not gods but
20 the work of human hands, wood and stone, and they destroyed them. And
   now, O LORD our God, rescue us from his hand, that all the kingdoms of
21 the earth may know that You alone are the LORD our God." And Isaiah
   son of Amoz sent to Hezekiah, saying, "Thus said the LORD God of Israel:
22 'Of which you prayed to Me about Sennacherib king of Assyria, this is the
   word of the LORD concerning him:

> She scorns you, mocks you,
>   the maiden, Zion's Daughter.
> She wags her head at you,
>   Jerusalem's Daughter.
23 Whom did you insult and revile,
>   and against whom have you lifted your voice,
>   and raised your eyes up high

---

14. *read them . . . spread them out.* The Hebrew has a singular object for these two verbs,
but the first part of the verse speaks of multiple letters.

16. *You alone are God of all the kingdoms of earth.* These words are a direct rebuttal of the
arrogant words of Rabshakeh in verse 12. Hezekiah will make his rejoinder to the Assyrian
boast still more explicit in verses 18–19.

18. *destroyed all the nations.* The received text has "lands," which looks like a dittography,
triggered by "land" at the end of the verse. The parallel passage in 2 Kings and some Hebrew
manuscripts show "nations."

22. *She scorns you, mocks you.* The "you" is of course Sennacherib. The personified Zion,
scorned by Sennacherib's spokesman, has nothing but contempt for the presumptuous
Assyrian king.
   She wags her head at you. In biblical poetry, this is a conventional gesture of scorn.

against Israel's Holy One?

By your messengers you insulted the Master   24
   and thought, "With my many chariots

I will go up to the heights of the mountains,
   the far reaches of Lebanon.

I will cut down its lofty cedars,
   its choicest cypresses,

and will come to its uttermost heights,
   and the woods of its undergrowth.

It is I who have dug and drunk   25
   the waters of foreigners

and dried up with the soles of my feet
   all Egypt's rivers.

Have you not heard from afar   26
   that which I did from time of old?

---

23. *raised your eyes up high / against Israel's Holy One.* Isaiah ups the ante of denunciation: Sennacherib's presumption in declaring that he will destroy the kingdom of Judah is cast as an assault on the God of heaven and earth.

24. *I will go up to the heights of the mountains, / the far reaches of Lebanon.* Although Sennacherib's campaign did include Phoenicia, here he is besieging Jerusalem. The mountains of Lebanon, however, are the proverbial loftiest heights in biblical poetry, and *yarketey levanon*, "the far reaches of Lebanon," contains an echo of *yarketey tsafon*, "the far reaches of Tsafon," the dwelling place of the gods. Sennacherib's declaration at this point sounds rather like that of the overweening king of Babylonia brought down to Sheol in chapter 14, which may allude to the text here. The cutting down of lofty cedars also figures in chapter 14.

   the woods of its undergrowth. The Hebrew *karmel* usually means "farmland," which would be anomalous on the Lebanon heights, but as Yehuda Feliks has noted, it can also mean "low shrubs." This would be the sparse vegetation in the mountaintops above the treeline.

25. *the waters of foreigners.* The Masoretic Text here says only "waters," and the translation follows the version of this line in 2 Kings 19:24. The phrase, slightly opaque, is part of Sennacherib's boast of conquest: he has seized the territories of nations and even sunk wells to exploit their water resources.

   and dried up with the soles of my feet / all Egypt's rivers. This is an antithetical act to the digging of wells—Egypt, blessed by the Nile, abounds in water. Here the Assyrian king makes himself, at least through hyperbole, a divine figure with the power to dry up rivers as he treads upon them.

   all Egypt's rivers. The translation reads *kol ye' orey mitsrayim* instead of the Masoretic *kol ye' orey motsar*, "all the waters of siege," which does not make much sense.

> I fashioned it, brought it to pass—
>> and fortified towns
>>> have turned into heaps of ruins.

27
> Their inhabitants, impotent,
>> are shattered and put to shame,
> become the grass of the field
>> and green growth,
> thatch on the roofs
>> by the east wind blasted."

28
> And your stayings and comings and goings I know
>> and your raging against Me.

29
> Because of your raging against Me
>> and your din that came up in My ears
> I will put My hook in your nose
>> and My bit between your lips,
> and will turn you back on the way
>> on which you came.

30 And this is the sign for you: eat aftergrowth this year, and in the second year stubble, and in the third year sow and harvest and plant vineyards
31 and eat their fruit. And the remnant of the house of Judah shall add root
32 beneath and put forth fruit above. For from Jerusalem shall come forth the surviving remnant from Mount Zion. The Lord's zeal shall do this.'
33 Therefore, thus said the Lord about the king of Assyria: 'He shall not enter this city and he shall not shoot an arrow there, and no shield shall
34 go before him, nor shall he raise a siege-work against it. In the way he
35 came he shall go back, and he shall not enter this city, said the Lord. And

---

27. *thatch on the roofs / by the east wind blasted.* The speech Isaiah attributes to Sennacherib concludes with a metaphor common in biblical poetry of the nations as mere grass, blasted by the hot wind blowing from the eastern desert.

29. *your din.* The received text has *sha' anenekha*, "your complacent one," for which this translation reads, with several ancient versions, *she' onkha*, "your din."
   I will put My hook in your nose / and My bit between your lips. Sennacherib has imagined himself as a god. Now the God of Israel describes him as a dumb helpless beast to be driven where God wants.
   turn you back. This is Isaiah's prophecy of Sennacherib's flight back to Assyria.

30. *eat aftergrowth this year.* The "you" now is Hezekiah, and the verb will then switch to the plural, referring to the people. Because the invading army has laid waste to the countryside, there will be no crops for two years—and yet, as a "sign," the Judahites will survive.

I will defend this city to rescue it, for My sake and for the sake of David
My servant.'" And the LORD's messenger went out and struck down in 36
the Assyrian camp, a hundred eighty-five thousand. And when they arose
early in the morning—look, they were all dead. And Sennacherib king of 37
Assyria pulled up stakes and went off and returned to Assyria and stayed
in Nineveh. And it happened as he was bowing down in the house of his 38
god Nisroch, that Adrammelech and Sarezer struck him down with the
sword, and they escaped to the land of Ararat. And Esharaddon his son
became king in his stead.

CHAPTER 38   In those days Hezekiah fell mortally ill, and 1
Isaiah son of Amoz the prophet came to him and said to him, "Thus said
the LORD: 'Charge your household, for you are about to die, and you will
not live.'" And Hezekiah turned his face to the wall and prayed to the 2
LORD. And he said, "Please, O LORD, recall, pray, that I walked before You 3
truthfully and with a whole heart and did what was good in Your eyes."
And Hezekiah wept copiously. And the word of the LORD came to Isaiah, 4

---

36. *And the LORD's messenger went out.* The parallel text in Kings begins with the phrase,
"And it happened on that night."

struck down in the Assyrian camp. The lifting of the siege is a historical event, though
the reason for it is uncertain. If the report is authentic, it might be because a plague swept
through the Assyrian camp. But one must say that the historian in 2 Kings has a vested
interest in presenting the event as a miraculous intervention, demonstrating God's commitment to protect Jerusalem (in contrast to Samaria, destroyed by an Assyrian king
twenty years earlier).

38. *Adrammelech and Sarezer struck him down with the sword.* The two figures named are
Sennacherib's sons. One gets the impression from the narrative report that the assassination took place directly after the emperor's return to Nineveh. In fact, Sennacherib was
murdered twenty years after the military campaign of 701 B.C.E. The writer, however, wants
to present this killing in the temple of a pagan god as an immediate fulfillment of Isaiah's
prophecy (verse 7) and a prompt retribution against the boasting conqueror depicted in
Isaiah's poem.

And Esharaddon his son became king in his stead. Esharaddon had been Sennacherib's
chosen successor. It was evidently this choice that led Adrammelech, abetted by one of his
brothers, to kill his father, hoping to seize the throne. One infers that he then discovered
no support in the court for his claim to the crown and thus was obliged to flee with his
brother to Ararat in the far north.

CHAPTER 38   1. *In those days Hezekiah fell mortally ill.* This chapter replicates 2
Kings 20, though with more extensive abridgment than in the preceding replication of
Kings and with the interpolation of a psalm of supplication not in 2 Kings 20.

5 saying, "Go and say to Hezekiah, 'Thus said the LORD God of David your
forefather: I have heard your prayer, I have seen your tears. I am about to
6 add to your days fifteen years. And from the hand of the king of Assyria I
7 will save you and this city, and I will defend this city. And this is the sign
8 for you that the LORD will do this thing which He has spoken. I am about
to turn back the shadow on the steps that has gone down on the Steps of
Ahaz with the sun ten steps backward.'" And the sun turned back ten steps
on the steps where it had come down.

9   A writ for Hezekiah king of Judah when he fell ill and revived from his
illness.

10   I thought, in the prime of my days I will pass away.
To the gates of Sheol am I consigned
    for the rest of my years.
11   I thought, I will not see Yah in the land of the living,
I will no more look on man, with the dwellers of the world.

---

5. *the* LORD *God of David your forefather.* This epithet serves as a reminder of God's commitment to preserve the Davidic dynasty, and Hezekiah is presented as a king who does what is right in the eyes of the LORD, like David his forefather.

6. *from the hand of the king of Assyria I will save you.* This clause could be an indication that Hezekiah's illness preceded the siege of Jerusalem, but the inference is not entirely certain because even after the lifting of the siege, Assyria would have remained a potential threat.

7. *And this is the sign.* At this point in the text in 2 Kings, Isaiah carries out what looks like an act of folk medicine by applying a clump of figs to Hezekiah's rash. Here that act is moved to the end of the chapter, where it appears to be out of place.

8. *I am about to turn back the shadow on the steps.* What is evidently in question is a kind of sundial, but one that is not a horizontal disk but rather a series of steps set into a wall, ten on the left side to show the shadow of the ascending sun and ten on the right side for the descending sun. A device of this sort has been found in Egypt. The King James Version and modern Hebrew understand *maʿalot* as "degrees," but these were probably actual steps, which is what the word usually means in biblical Hebrew.
    the Steps of Ahaz. The sundial in question proves to be a well-known marker in Jerusalem commissioned by King Ahaz.

9. *A writ for Hezekiah.* What follows is actually a psalm of supplication. Inserting poems from different sources was a common practice in biblical narrative or in the hands of the editors. The intention here is to give dramatic expression to the desperation of the king at death's door. While this psalm exhibits many of the formulaic features of supplications, the text that has come down to us is manifestly damaged, especially in its second half, sometimes reducing translation to guesswork, as will be duly noted at the relevant points.

10. *I will pass away.* Literally, "I will go," sometimes a euphemism for dying in biblical Hebrew.

My abode is pulled up and taken from me   12
   like the tent of a shepherd.
I have rolled up my life like a weaver,
   from the loom He cuts me away,
     from day to night You finish me.
I cried out until morning.   13
   Like a lion He broke all my bones,
     from day to night You finish me.
Like a swallow or swift I chirp,   14
   I moan like a dove.
My eyes are worn out looking high.
   O Master, I am oppressed, be my surety.
What can I speak, and He has said to me and done it?   15
   I toss fitfully all my years
     for the bitterness of my being.
O Master, for them who will live   16
   and all among them is my spirit's life,
     and You healed me and gave me life.
Why, instead of peace, it was bitter for me, bitter,   17
   but You held back my life
     from destruction's pit.
For You flung behind Your back all my offenses.
   For Sheol will not acclaim You,   18

---

12. *I have rolled up.* The verb *qiped* occurs only here, and so one is obliged to guess from the context what it might mean.

   You finish me. The verb, derived from a root that means "whole," looks as though it should have a positive connotation, but here it has to be negative.

13. *I cried out.* The received text reads *shiviti*, "I imagined," "I depicted," but the Targum reads *shiva'ti*, "I cried out," as does this translation.

14. *I am oppressed.* The received text has an imperative, "oppress me," which does not make sense.

15. *What can I speak, and He has said to me and done it?* Each of the Hebrew words here is understandable, but how they fit together is not entirely unclear.

16. *O Master, for them who will live / and all among them is my spirit's life.* The translation frankly mirrors the stubborn unintelligibility of both these clauses, which defy reconstruction.

18. *For Sheol will not acclaim You.* The declaration in this verse and the next is one that appears with some frequency in Psalms: only the living have the capacity to praise God, and so the speaker entreats God to sustain him in the land of the living.

> nor will Death praise You.
> Those who go down to the Pit
>   cannot hope for Your faithfulness.
19 The living, the living, he will acclaim you,
>   like me on this day.
> Father will make known to sons
>   Your faithfulness.
20 The LORD is here to rescue us,
>   and let us play music
> all the days of our life
>   in the house of the LORD.

21 And Isaiah said, "Let them fetch a clump of figs and smear it on the burning
22 rash, that he may revive." And Hezekiah said, "What is the sign that I will
go up to the house of the LORD?"

1 CHAPTER 39   At that time Merodach-Baladan son of Baladan
king of Babylonia sent letters and a gift to Hezekiah, for he had heard that
2 Hezekiah had fallen ill and regained strength. And Hezekiah rejoiced over the

---

20. *The LORD is here to rescue us.* The Hebrew says merely "The LORD to rescue us."

let us play music. Given that the music is to be played in the house of the LORD, this would be the music accompanying the singing of psalms of thanksgiving that would recount God's beneficence in rescuing the speaker from death.

21. *Let them fetch a clump of figs.* In Kings, this act of folk healing is performed immediately after Isaiah comes to visit the ailing Hezekiah. The fact that a textual displacement has occurred is reflected in the king's asking what the sign will be in the next verse. In the present chapter, this question should have occurred just before Isaiah's response to it in verse 7, "And this is the sign for you." That is precisely the order in 2 Kings 20.

22. *that I will go up to the house of the LORD.* Hezekiah is bedridden, so what he means by this question is: what is the sign that I will recover and again be able to participate in worship at the Temple? The version in 2 Kings 20:8 in fact makes this perfectly explicit: "What is the sign that the LORD will heal me and I will go up on the third day to the house of the LORD?"

CHAPTER 39   1. *At that time.* The narrative continues to replicate the text from the Book of Kings, with some minor divergences. The name Merodach-Baladan appears as Berodan-Baladan in the parallel passage in 2 Kings 20:12–19.

king of Babylonia. The Babylonians were threatened by the Assyrian empire to the north and so would have been eager to make common cause with the kingdom of Judah.

for he had heard. The translation reproduces the version in 2 Kings 20:12. The text here reads, illogically, "and he heard."

envoys and showed them all his house of precious things, the silver and the gold and the spices and the goodly oil and his armory and all that was found in his treasuries. There was nothing that Hezekiah did not show them in his house and in all his kingdom. And Isaiah the prophet came to Hezekiah ₃ and said to him, "What did these men say to you, and from where did they come to you?" And Hezekiah said, "From a distant land, from Babylonia." And he said, "What did they see in your house?" And Hezekiah said, "All ₄ that is in my house they saw. There was nothing that I did not show them of my treasuries." And Isaiah said, "Listen to the word of the LORD: 'Look, a ₅,₆ time is coming when everything that is in your house and that your fathers stored up till this day will be borne off to Babylonia. Nothing will remain,' said the LORD. 'And of your sons who will issue from you, whom you will ₇ beget, they will be taken, and they will become eunuchs in the palace of the king of Babylonia.'" And Hezekiah said to Isaiah, "The word of the LORD ₈ that you have spoken is good." And he thought, "For there will be peace and trust in my days."

---

2. *the envoys.* The received text has only "over them," and this identification is added in the translation for clarity.

6. *a time is coming when everything that is in your house . . . will be borne off to Babylonia.* This dire prophecy is presented as punishment for Hezekiah's imprudence in exposing all his treasures to the eyes of the Babylonian visitors. Many scholars think that the episode was added over a century later in an effort to explain the despoiling of Jerusalem during the reign of Johaiakim in 597 B.C.E. or in the final destruction of the city eleven years later, in 586.

7. *they will become eunuchs in the palace of the king of Babylonia.* Although *sarisim* sometimes may refer to court officials who are not necessarily castrated, one suspects that the core meaning of castration is invoked here: there could be no greater curse for a king than to have his sons turned into eunuchs, incapable of begetting offspring.

8. *The word of the LORD that you have spoken is good.* This response by Hezekiah to the grim prophecy is astonishing. On the surface, he seems to be saying to Isaiah that he accepts the word of the LORD, that it must be good because it is God's will. In the next sentence, however, he thinks to himself that what is good about it is that the disaster will not happen in his lifetime—something that in fact Isaiah has not clearly told him. This self-centered view of national catastrophe puts the virtuous Hezekiah in a somewhat questionable light. The narrative material taken from 2 Kings breaks off abruptly at this point, and the book resumes with the soaring poetry of the anonymous prophet of the Babylonian exile called by scholars Second Isaiah. The editorial placement of chapter 39 serves as a bridge to Second Isaiah because it involves a prophecy of the Babylonian conquest: after the devastating conquest and the exile of a large part of the Judahite population, the comforting words of Second Isaiah announce a glorious return from exile.

CHAPTER 40

1   Comfort, O comfort My people,
            says your God.
2   Speak to the heart of Jerusalem
            and call out to her,
        for her term of service is ended,
            her crime is expiated,
        for she has taken from the LORD's hand
            double for all her offenses.
3   A voice calls out in the wilderness:
            Clear a way for the LORD's road,
                level in the desert a highway for our God!
4   Every valley shall be lifted high
            and every mountain brought low,
        and the crooked shall be straight,
            and the ridges become a valley.
5   And the LORD's glory shall be revealed,

CHAPTER 40   1. *Comfort, O comfort My people.* The prophecies of Second Isaiah
begin abruptly, with no introductory formula such as "The word of the LORD came to me,
saying." If such introductory matter once existed, it would have been editorially deleted in
order to encourage the perception that these prophecies are a direct continuation of what
has preceded. Scholars have long puzzled over who is being addressed in the first verse. A
prevalent view that it is the members of the divine council seems unlikely because there
are no hints in the entire passage of a celestial setting. Others have proposed that these (the
Hebrew verb is a plural) are a group of prophets exhorted to comfort Israel, but there are no
such groups in the texts of the literary prophets. Groups of prophets appear only in the narrative books, where they are wandering bands of ecstatics. Perhaps it is simplest to assume
that those addressed are people in general, or even the nations, enjoined to comfort Israel. In
any event, the key word "comfort" at the very beginning of Second Isaiah sounds the great
theme of Second Isaiah's prophecies.

2. *her term of service.* The exile is imagined as a term of indentured servitude, or even a
prison sentence, which is now completed.

4. *the crooked shall be straight.* The power of this stark formulation is worth preserving literally, even though the phrase might mean "the rugged ground shall be leveled." The poet,
conjuring up the expanse of arid land, abounding in ravines and ridges and rough terrain,
that stretches between Babylonia and Judah, imagines a miraculous smoothing out of the
ground as a great highway is laid down for the return of the exiles.

and all flesh together see
   that the Lord's mouth has spoken.

A voice calls out, saying: "Call!"   6
   And I said, "What shall I call?"—
All flesh is grass
   and all its trust like the flowers of the field.
Grass dries up, the flower fades,   7
   for the Lord's wind has blown upon it.
     The people indeed is grass.
Grass dries up, the flower fades,   8
   but the word of our God stands forever.

On a high mountain go up,   9
   O herald of Zion.
Raise your voice mightily,
   raise it, do not fear.
Say to the towns of Judah:
   here is your God.
Look, the Master Lord shall come in power,   10
   His arm commanding for Him.
Look, His reward is with Him,
   His wages before Him.

---

5. *all flesh together see.* This universalizing phrase might be taken as an indication that all humanity is addressed at the beginning of the prophecy.

6. *A voice calls out.* This could well be a truncated version of the divine call to the prophet to take up his mission.

   trust. The Hebrew *ḥesed* here carries its sense of faithfulness or loyalty in meeting an obligation.

8. *Grass dries up, the flower fades.* The fondness of this poet for evocative repetition is evident here. In this case, it amounts to an incremental repetition, in which the increment is a strong antithesis to what has been repeated: "but the word of the Lord our God stands forever."

9. *here is your God.* God's vivid presence is manifest in the power and love with which He brings the exiles back to their land.

11
        Like a shepherd He minds His flock
           in His arm He gathers lambs,
               and in his lap He bears them, leads the ewes.

12
        Who with his hand's hollow has measured the waters,
           the heavens has gauged with a span,
        and meted earth's dust with a measure,
           weighed with a scale the mountains
           and the hills with a balance?

13
        Who has gauged the LORD's spirit,
           and what man told then His plan?

14
        With whom did He counsel, who informed Him,
           who taught Him the path of justice,
         taught Him knowledge
           and the way of discernment informed Him?

15
        Why, nations are a drop from the bucket,
           like the balance's dust are reckoned.
               Why, the coastlands He plucks up like dust.

16
        Lebanon has not enough fuel,
           and its beasts not enough for burnt offering.

17
        All the nations are as naught before Him,

---

11. *Like a shepherd He minds His flock.* This simile makes a lovely counterpoint to the previous verse: first God shows overwhelming force ("His arm commanding for Him") and now tender solicitude as the shepherd gathering lambs in His lap.

12. *Who with his hand's hollow has measured the waters.* With this prophecy, soaring poetry becomes the vehicle to convey God's magisterial role over all creation. It is perhaps at this point, most likely in the later sixth century B.C.E., that the universalist potential of biblical monotheism is fully realized. As several commentators have noted, there is a certain affinity here with the Voice from the Whirlwind in Job 38, though one cannot assume that either poet knew the other's work.

    weighed with a scale the mountains. Throughout these lines, there is a yawning gap between the paltry instruments of human measurement and the vastness of creation.

14. *With whom did He counsel.* This excludes not only puny humankind but also perhaps any traditional notion of a divine council from playing any part in creation.

15. *the balance's dust.* This strikingly picks up the imagery of measuring instruments from verse 12, pushing it further by likening humankind to the dust left on the pans of a balance after it has been used—which is to say, something that has no weight at all.

as nothing and void they are reckoned by Him.
And to whom would you liken God,   18
   and what likeness for Him propose?
The craftsman has shaped the idol,   19
   and the smith overlays it with gold
      and forges the links of silver.
Mulberry wood for the gift,   20
   wood that won't rot he chooses.
A skilled craftsman he seeks for himself
   to ready an idol that will not topple.
Do you not know,   21
   have you not heard?
Was it not told to you from the first,
   have you not grasped how the earth was founded?
He is enthroned on the rim of the earth,   22
   and its dwellers are like grasshoppers.
He spreads out the heavens like gauze
   and stretches them like a tent to dwell in.
He turns princes into nothing,   23
   earth's rulers He makes as naught.
Hardly planted, hardly sown,   24
   hardly their stem rooted in earth,
When He blows on them, they wither,
   and the storm bears them off like chaff.
And to whom would you liken Me   25
   that I be compared, says the Holy One?

---

17. *as nothing and void.* The second of the two Hebrew terms, *tohu*, takes us back to the primordial chaos (*tohu wabohu*) before creation.

19. *The craftsman has shaped the idol.* This would be a woodworker carving the idol, which would then be overlaid with precious metals. The focus on the manufacturing process that produces idols vividly conveys the futility of fashioning such material images of purported deities and stands in contrast to God, Who has no likeness (verse 18).

20. *Mulberry wood.* The Hebrew *mesukan* is obscure. This translation adopts one scholarly proposal, assuming that attention to craft materials fits in with the preceding verse, but there is no consensus on this.

22. *He spreads out the heavens like gauze.* This verset and the next are reminiscent of the splendid depiction of the grandeur of the Creator in Psalm 104.

26   Lift up your eyes on high,
           and see, who created these?
        He Who musters their host by number
           and all of them calls by name.
        Through abundant strength and mighty power,
           no one lacks in the ranks.

27   Why should you say, O Jacob,
           and speak, O Israel:
        My way is hidden from the LORD,
           my cause is ignored by my God?
28   Do you not know,
           have you not heard?—
        an eternal God is the LORD,
           Creator of the ends of the earth.
        He does not tire, is not weary,
           His discernment cannot be fathomed.
29   He gives vigor to the weary,
           and great power to those sapped of strength.
30   Lads may grow weary and tire,
           and young men may badly stumble.
31   But who wait for the LORD shall renew vigor,
           shall grow new pinions like the eagles,
        shall run and shall not tire,
           walk on and not be weary.

---

26. *He Who musters their host by number / and all of them calls by name.* This is a beautiful instance of the focusing or heightening that takes place between the first verset and the second in a line of biblical poetry: first, God musters the host of the heavens, the stars, as their supreme commander; then, going beyond what any terrestrial general could do, He is able to name each one of the vast multitude of the stars.

31. *grow new pinions like the eagles.* The phenomenon of molting and getting new feathers is here extended, probably as a deliberate hyperbole, to the growing of new wings. The Hebrew *'ever* is clearly a poetic term for "wing," and does not mean "feather," as some translations have it.

   shall run and shall not tire. God's inexhaustible nature is transferred to those who wait or hope for Him. If the prophet still has in mind his previous vision of a miraculous return to Zion, this idea here of a spectacular infusion of strength in the faithful would serve a double function: it would link up with the idea of a renewal of national strength after the crushing ordeal of the exile, and it could suggest that those marching over the long highway through the wilderness will not weary on the way.

CHAPTER 41

Be still for me, you coastlands,   1
   and let nations renew their vigor.
Let them draw near, then let them speak.
   Together let us come to trial.
Who has stirred up victory from the east   2
   called it to His feet?
He sets down before Him nations
   and holds sway over kings,
turns their sword into dust,
   like driven chaff their bow.
He pursues them, moves on safe and sound,   3
   He touches no path with His feet.
Who has enacted and done it,   4
   calling the generations from the first?—
"I the LORD am the first,
   and with the last ones it is I."
The coastlands have seen and feared,   5
   the ends of the earth have trembled,
     they have drawn near and have come.

CHAPTER 41   1. *and let nations renew their vigor.* This second verset is scarcely a parallel member to the first verset of this line. The general scholarly hypothesis that this is an inadvertent scribal duplication of 40:31a seems quite likely. Perhaps this was originally a triadic line, that is, "Be still for me, you coastlands," directly followed by "Let them draw near" and then "Together let us come. . . ."

come to trial. The trial, which is between advocates of the pagan gods and the one true God, runs through the chapter but will be followed explicitly in verses 21–24.

2. *Who has stirred up victory from the east.* Because of what is said in verse 4, this translation understands the reference to be to God, not to a king whom God is using as His instrument. But in all likelihood the historical event in view is the conquest of the Medes by Cyrus II in the years leading up to Persia's capture of Babylon in 539 B.C.E. That imminent victory is something this prophet would have looked forward to eagerly.

4. *calling the generations from the first.* This somewhat unusual characterization of God establishes an important theological theme for the whole prophecy: God has been present from the very beginnings of history; nations, caught up in their internecine struggles in what is no more than a fleeting historical moment, have by comparison no value or substance. Thus God goes on to make the ringing declaration of the next line: "I the LORD am the first, / and with the last ones it is I."

6 [Each man helps his fellow
   and to his brother says, "Be strong."
7 And the craftsman strengthens the smith,
   the hammer wielder—the anvil pounder.
  He says to the glue, "It is good,"
   and strengthens it with nails that it not totter.]

8 As for you, O Israel, My servant,
   Jacob, whom I have chosen,
    seed of Abraham My friend,
9 whom I took up from the ends of the earth
   and called forth from its nobles
  and said to you, "You are My servant,
   I have chosen you and have not despised you.
10 Do not fear, for I am with you,
   do not be frightened, for I am your God.
  I have sustained you, also have helped you,
   also have stayed you up with My triumphant right hand.
11 Look, they shall be shamed and disgraced,
   all who are incensed against you,
  they shall be as naught and shall perish,
   those who contend with you.
12 You shall seek them and shall not find them,
   those who battle with you.
  They shall be as naught and as nothing,

6–7. *Each man helps . . . it not totter.* The evocation of the enterprise of idol manufacture in this verse and the next seems out of place, and it is plausible that these lines were scribally misplaced from 40:18–20. These verses therefore are enclosed with brackets here.

9. *whom I took up from the ends of the earth.* Abraham was called by God to make his way from his native Mesopotamia to the land of Canaan. The prophet envisages a similar trajectory for the descendants of Abraham, exiled to Mesopotamia.

10. *My triumphant right hand.* The noun *tsedeq*, which usually means "righteousness" in either the judicial sense (the just cause in court) or the ethical sense, here and in verse 2 means "triumph" or "victory." In verse 2 the term is linked with God's feet, here with His mighty arm.

12. *as naught and as nothing.* These prophecies abound in synonyms for nothingness to represent the nonentity of both nations and their gods—*'ayin, 'efes, tohu,* and *'efa* (verse

those who war against you.
For I am the LORD your God,   13
    holding your right hand,
saying to you, Do not fear,
    I am helping you.
Do not fear, O worm of Jacob,   14
    men of Israel.
I am helping you, says the LORD,
    and your Redeemer, Israel's Holy One.
Look, I have made you a threshing board   15
    a new one, with double edges.
You shall thresh mountains and grind them to dust,
    and turn hills into chaff.
You shall winnow them—the wind shall bear them off,   16
    and the storm shall scatter them.
But you shall be glad in the LORD,
    in Israel's Holy One you shall exult.
The poor and the needy seek water and there is none,   17
    their tongues are parched with thirst.
I the LORD will answer them,
    God of Israel, I will not forsake them.
I will open rivers on the peaks   18
    and wellsprings in the valleys.

---

24)—although the anomalous last term may be a scribal error for *'efes* (in modern Hebrew, "zero").

14. *worm of Jacob.* This ostensibly insulting designation is used to represent Israel in defeat and exile as lowly and downtrodden.

15. *double edges.* The Hebrew term is commonly used to characterize a double-edged sword (a sickle-shaped sword with only one cutting edge was more common), and so this word turns the threshing board into a weapon.

17. *The poor and the needy.* This verset is too long metrically (it has five accents where the general limit is four), and so it seems likely that one of these two synonyms is a scribal interpolation.

18. *I will open rivers on the peaks.* The desert landscape envisioned here that is about to be transformed into a verdant garden is probably not the wilderness to be crossed on the return to Zion but rather the land of Judah itself, devastated by the Babylonian conquerors and then at least partly left uncultivated because much of the population was exiled.

I will turn desert into ponds of water
 and parched land into water sources.

19   I will put cedars in the desert,
         acacia and myrtle and wild olive tree.
   I will put cypress in the wilderness,
         box tree and elm together.

20   So they may see and know
         and take to heart and grasp together,
   that the hand of the LORD has done this,
         and Israel's Holy One has created it."

21   Bring out your case, says the LORD,
         make your brief, says Jacob's King.

22   Let them bring out and tell us
         that which will come about,
   the first things, what are they, tell,
         that we may pay heed and know the future,
            what is to come make us hear.

23   Tell the signs in advance
         that we may know that you are gods.
   Do either good or evil,
         that we may be frightened and fear as well.

24   Why, you are as naught
         and your deeds are as nothing—
            an abhorrence, who would choose you?

---

19. *box tree and elm.* The identification of these botanical items is a matter of guesswork.

20. *created.* The choice of verb is somewhat surprising, but "create" is probably used to suggest that the renewal of the land, after it has reverted to a state of chaos, is a kind of new creation.

21. *your brief.* The Hebrew noun derives from a root suggesting strength, so it might be taken to mean something like "strong arguments."

22. *Let them bring out and tell us / that which will come about.* What is at issue in this court case is a conflict between false, pagan prophets and the true prophets that God alone can inspire.
   that we may pay heed and know the future. This is sarcastic, a jibe directed at the false prophets: if you really have the gift of prophecy, tell us what the future will be.

24. *as naught / . . . as nothing.* A more literal reading would be "from naught . . . from nothing."

I have roused him from the north, he has come,   25
    from sunrise he invokes my name,
and he stomps on governors like mud,
    as a potter tramples clay.
Who has told from the first that we might know,   26
    from beforehand that we might say, he is right?
But none has told, none has announced,
    but none has heard Your sayings.
First for Zion, here they are,   27
    and for Jerusalem will I set a herald.
I looked but there was no man,   28
    among them none gave counsel,
        whom I could ask and have them answer.
Their deeds are nothing,
    mere wind and void their idols.

CHAPTER 42

Look, My servant, I have stayed him up,   1
    My chosen one, I have greatly favored.

---

25. *I have roused him from the north.* This new prophecy introduces a set of more strictly historical references. The Persian army threatening Babylonia in the sixth decade of the sixth century B.C.E. was advancing from the north, and the "he" in question is Cyrus II, the Persian emperor.

    from sunrise. This could be a geographical indication, but since the east conflicts with the just mentioned north, it is perhaps used in a temporal sense: from the beginning of each day this king invokes God's name.

26. *Who has told from the first.* These lines appear to pick up the theme of the failure of pagan prophecy from verses 21–24.

27. *First for Zion, here they are.* The Hebrew is rather cryptic here and may reflect a faulty text.

28. *among them none gave counsel.* This last verse continues the theme of the impotence and the abysmal ignorance of all pagan facsimiles of prophecy.

    mere wind. The use of "wind" to designate what is without body or substance is close to an anticipation of Qohelet ("herding the wind").

CHAPTER 42   1. *My servant.* The servant of the LORD, *'eved YHWH*, will become an important motif in the prophecies of Second Isaiah. Although some scholars have proposed that the reference here is to Cyrus II, it seems more likely, and more in keeping with

I have set My spirit on him,
    he shall bring forth justice to the nations.
2   He shall not cry out nor raise his voice
    nor let his voice be heard abroad.
3   A shattered reed he shall not break
    nor a guttering wick put out.
        In truth he shall bring forth justice.
4   He shall not gutter nor shall he be smashed
    till he sets out justice on earth
        and the coastlands yearn for his teaching.

5   Thus said God, the Lord,
    Creator of the heavens, He stretches them out,
      lays down the earth and its offspring,
    gives breath to the people upon it
      and life-breath to those who walk on it.
6   I the Lord have called you in righteousness
    and held your hand,
  and preserved you and made you
    a covenant for peoples and a light of the nations,
7   to open blind eyes,

---

later uses of this designation, that the servant is Israel, or perhaps an exemplary leader who will arise from the people. The idea in verses 2–3 that the servant will not raise his voice or so much as break an already shattered reed scarcely accords with Cyrus commanding a powerful conquering army.

    greatly favored. The adverb is added to intimate the intensifying effect of *nafshi*, not just "I" but "my very self."

2. *raise his voice.* The Hebrew merely says raise, but this is surely elliptical for "raise his voice," a common biblical idiom.

4. *nor shall he be smashed.* This received text appears to say "nor shall he run," *welo' yaruts*, but the verb is probably mistakenly vocalized and should be read *yeirots*, "be smashed."

6. *a covenant for peoples.* Literally, this should be a "people's covenant" as the received text shows, but the phrase is a little peculiar. The Qumran Isaiah instead of the Masoretic *brit-'am* reads *brit-'olam*, "an everlasting covenant."

7. *to open blind eyes.* This is not an eschatological granting of vision to the sightless but rather the imparting of the gift of sight to those who have been plunged in the darkness of a dungeon.

to bring out the captive from prison,
    those sitting in darkness from dungeons.
I am the LORD, that is My name,   8
    and My glory I will not give to another
        nor My acclaim to the idols.
The first things, look, they have happened,   9
    and the new things I do tell,
        before they spring forth I inform you.

Sing to the LORD a new song,   10
    His acclaim from the end of the earth,
you who go down to the sea in its fullness,
    you coastlands and their dwellers.
Let the desert and its towns raise their voice,   11
    the hamlets where Kedar dwells.
Let the dwellers of Sela sing gladly,
    from the mountaintops let them shout.
Let them pay honor to the LORD,   12
    and His acclaim in the coastlands let them tell.
The LORD sallies forth as a warrior,   13
    as a man of war he stirs up fury.
He raises the battle cry, even bellows,
    over His enemies He prevails.

---

to bring out the captive from prison. Here and elsewhere, prison is probably used metaphorically as an image of exile.

9. *The first things, look, they have happened, / and the new things I do tell.* Divinely inspired prophecy predicted the destruction of Zion and the consequent exile; now it will foretell a return from exile.

10. *Sing to the LORD a new song.* The beginning of this prophecy sounds like a psalm of acclamation or thanksgiving.

11. *Kedar.* These are Arab tribes whose habitat is in the desert area east of the Jordan.
    Sela. This is an Edomite town, also east of the Jordan.

13. *The LORD sallies forth as a warrior.* Like a good deal of biblical poetry, this line and the next draw on an old Canaanite poetic tradition that represents warrior-gods. In the present context, the God of Israel is about to do battle on behalf of His people, routing its enemies and restoring its grandeur.

14 "I have been silent a very long time,
      kept my peace, held Myself in check—
like a woman in labor now I shriek,
      I gasp and also pant.

15 I will wither mountains and valleys,
      and all their grass will I dry up.
And I will turn rivers into islands,
      and ponds will I dry up.

16 And I will lead the blind on a way they did not know,
      on paths they did not know I will guide them.
I will turn darkness before them to light,
      and rough ground to a level plain.
        These things will I do, I will not abandon them.

17 They have fallen back, are utterly shamed,
      who trust in idols,
who say to molten images:
      you are our gods.

18 O deaf ones, hear,
      O blind ones, look and see.

19 Who is as blind as My servant,
      as deaf as My messenger whom I send?
Who is as blind as Meshullam,

---

14. *I have been silent a very long time, / . . . held Myself in check.* These words answer a theological quandary that would have plagued the exiles: where is the God of Israel, why does He allow us to be reduced to this lowly state? What God says is that He has chosen to be silent and hold back, but that moment is now past.

like a woman in labor now I shriek. This simile marks the startling transition from God's silence and self-occultation to the moment when a new era is born, with birth pangs like a human birth. The verb here, *'ef'eh*, appears nowhere else, and so the translation is inference from context.

16. *I will lead the blind.* It is best to understand the blindness as entirely metaphorical.

rough ground to a level plain. This picks up the image in chapter 40 of a leveled highway in the desert.

19. *Who is as blind as My servant.* Again, this looks as if the reference is to the people of Israel or to a leader of the people. The servant has been blind until now because he has not been able to see the way of the LORD.

Meshullam. There is considerable dispute about the meaning of this word. It could conceivably be a noun meaning "the complete one" or "the one who is paid." It also has some currency elsewhere as a proper name, though no identification with any Meshullam mentioned in the Bible is plausible. As a poetic parallel to "My servant" and "My messen-

as deaf as the servant of the LORD?
You have seen much but do not watch,   20
    opened your ears but do not hear.
The LORD desires his vindication,   21
    that He make teaching great and glorious.
Yet it is a plundered and looted people,   22
    all of them trapped in holes,
        and hidden away in dungeons,
subject to plunder with none who can save,   23
    despoiled, and none says, "Give back."
Who among you gives ear to this,
    attends and heeds henceforth?
Who has subjected Jacob to plunder   24
    and Israel to despoilers?
Is it not the LORD against Whom they offended
    and did not want to walk in His ways
        and did not heed His teaching?
And He poured out upon them His fury,   25
    His wrath and the fierceness of battle,

---

ger," it most probably is a designation of the people, perhaps linked with the place-name "Shalem," a shortened form of Jerusalem.

20. *do not hear.* The received text has a third-person verb, but it is preferable to render this as a second-person verb, in keeping with the beginning of the line.

21. *that He make teaching great and glorious.* The teaching—*torah*, or law—is God's teaching, which the now vindicated Israel will be able to promulgate.

22. *Yet it is a plundered and looted people.* Even as the prophet announces a glorious national restoration, he is aware that the present condition of the people is that of a population which has been stripped of its precious possessions and driven into exile.

24. *Who has subjected Jacob to plunder.* Lest anyone imagine that the catastrophe of defeat and exile reflects some failure on the part of God, the prophet stresses that it is precisely God Who has brought all this about (a notion in keeping with the outlook of Deuteronomy).
    they offended. The Masoretic Text has "we offended," but the rest of the verse shows a third-person plural. This is a scribal error that may have been influenced by the frequent recurrence in biblical texts of "we offended against the LORD" or "we offended against You."

25. *upon them.* The Hebrew here and in the next verse has "him," such switches from plural to singular being fairly common in biblical usage.
    fury, / His wrath. The Masoretic cantillation markings put these two nouns together ("fury His wrath"), but both metrically and in regard to semantic parallelism, "His wrath" belongs at the beginning of the second verset.

and it seared them all round but they knew not,
        it burned them—they did not take it to heart.

CHAPTER 43

1   And now, thus said the LORD,
        your Creator, Jacob, and your Fashioner, Israel:
     Do not fear, for I have redeemed you.
        I have called you by name, you are Mine.
2   Should you pass through water, I am with you,
        and through rivers—they shall not overwhelm you.
     Should you walk through fire, you shall not be singed,
        and flames shall not burn you.
3   For I am the LORD, your God,
        Israel's Holy One, your Rescuer.
     I have made Egypt your ransom,
        Nubia and Saba in your stead.
4   As you are precious in My eyes,

---

it seared them all round but they knew not. There is an instructive element of shock in this image: the people is burning alive, suffering divine retribution, but it is so blind that it doesn't even realize it is on fire.

CHAPTER 43   1. *your Creator . . . and your Fashioner.* The prophet picks up the two terms for creation used, respectively, in the P version of the Creation story (Genesis 1–2:3), and in the J version (Genesis 2:4ff), the first, a word for creation *tout court,* the second a more anthropomorphic term for the fashioning of clay by a potter.

2. *Should you pass through water . . . / Should you walk through fire.* This image of coming out unscathed from extreme dangers speaks to the plight of an audience that has undergone the trauma of exile and captivity. The continuing power of these words of assurance is attested by Shmuel Hanagid, the great eleventh-century Hebrew poet of Granada, who was addressed with this verse in a dream and held it close as a kind of talisman during his dangerous campaigns as commander of Granada's army.

3. *For I am the LORD, your God.* This prophecy abounds in declarations like this one of God's name and identity as the only God. These may be a deliberate echoing of God's declaration to Moses at the burning bush.
    I have made Egypt your ransom, / Nubia and Saba in your stead. The people of Israel until now has been captive to Babylonia. The prophet anticipates that the conquering Cyrus will liberate them now and that these other peoples will be taken captive in their stead. This idea of one prisoner substituted for another is continued in the next verse: "I put people in your stead / and nations instead of your life."

you are honored, and I love you.
And I put people in your stead
  and nations instead of your life.
    Do not fear, for I am with you.   5
From the east I will bring your seed,
  and from the west I will gather you.
I will say to the north, "Give them up,"   6
  and to the south, "Do not withhold.
Bring my sons from afar
  and my daughters from the end of the earth,
all who are called by My name   7
  and for My glory I created them,
    I fashioned them, yes, I made them."

Bring out a blind people that yet has eyes   8
  and the deaf that yet have ears.
All the nations have gathered together,   9
  and the peoples have assembled.
Who among them will tell this
  and make us hear the first things?
Let them offer their witnesses and let them be right,
  let them hear and say the truth.
You are My witnesses, said the LORD,   10
  and My servant whom I have chosen,
so that you may know and trust in Me
  and understand that I am the One,
before Me no god was fashioned,

5–6. *From the east / . . . from the west / . . . / to the north / . . . to the south.* Attempts to give these lines a set of precise historical referents are misplaced. It is true that there were diaspora communities not only in Mesopotamia to the east but also in Egypt and elsewhere. But the point of invoking the four points of the compass is the sweep of poetic hyperbole: wherever God's people have been scattered, even at "the end of the earth," He will now gather them in.

8. *blind / . . . the deaf.* The metaphorical use of these terms is consistent with their previous use (see 42:16, 18–20); their figurative sense is made explicit here by the addition of "that yet has eyes / . . . that yet have ears."

10. *I am the One.* This could also be rendered as "I am He." It is perhaps the strongest of God's declarations of His uncontested status as God because of its sheer directness and simplicity.

and after Me none shall be.
11   I, I am the LORD,
         and besides Me there is no rescuer.
12   I Myself told and rescued and made it heard,
         and there is no foreign god among you,
            and you are My witnesses, said the LORD.
13   From the very first day I am the One,
         and none can save from My hand.
            I act, and who can reverse it?

14   Thus said the LORD,
         your Redeemer, Israel's Holy One:
      For your sake I have sent to Babylon
         and brought down all the bars
            and turned the glad song of Chaldeans to laments.
15   I am the LORD, your Holy One,
         Israel's Creator, your King.

16   Thus said the LORD,
         Who makes a way in the sea
            and a path in fierce waters,

---

11. *I, I am the* LORD, */ and besides Me there is no rescuer.* God is said to prove His divinity by rescuing His downtrodden people.

12. *I Myself told and rescued and made it heard.* These verbs indicate a process that probably refers in the first instance to the exodus from Egypt: God first assured Moses, "I am with you" (the verb "told" here), then carried out His promise by rescuing the Israelites from Egypt, then made sure that the story of liberation would be passed on to future generations.

14. *brought down all the bars.* The meaning of the Hebrew noun *barihim* is disputed, but given the fact that exile is repeatedly represented by this prophet as imprisonment, the most likely sense is the bars that bolt the doors of a prison. Although the verbal stem *b-r-h* does mean "to flee," there is no attested use in the Bible of *bariah* as "fugitive" (a mere grammatical possibility), a sense claimed by some for the word here.

   turned the glad song of Chaldeans to laments. The Masoretic Text has *'oniyot*, "ships," which does not make much sense, and the Chaldeans were scarcely a seafaring people. The translation revocalizes that noun as *'aniyot*, "laments."

16. *Who makes a way in the sea / and a path in fierce waters.* This is clearly a reference to the parting of the Sea of Reeds in Exodus 14–15. That recollection is continued in the next verse in God's leading chariot and horse to destruction.

Who leads out chariot and horse to destruction,   17
　　all the fierce forces.
They lay down to rise no more,
　　flickered out like a wick, were extinguished.
Do not recall the first things,   18
　　and what came before do not consider.
I am about to do a new thing,   19
　　now it will spring forth and you shall know it.
I will make a way in the desert,
　　paths in the wasteland.
The beast of the field shall honor Me,   20
　　the jackals and the ostriches,
for I have put water in the desert,
　　rivers in the wasteland
　　　to give drink to My people, My chosen.
The people that I fashioned for Me,   21
　　My acclaim they shall recount.

But not Me did you invoke, O Jacob,   22
　　for you are wearied of Me, O Israel.

---

17. *to destruction.* The Hebrew says only "leads out" (or "brings out"), but with the background of the story in Exodus, destruction is surely implied.

flickered out like a wick, were extinguished. In Exodus 15, the Egyptians sink in the water like a stone or like lead. Here the poet appears to be playing with similes, likening the sinking of the Egyptian in water to the contrasting image of a smoldering wick going out.

18. *Do not recall the first things.* Given the immediate context, these may be the events that occurred at the Sea of Reeds. Those were, it is implied, great signs and wonders, but the miracle God is about to perform is a wholly new thing.

19. *I will make a way in the desert.* The great highway in the desert that God will lay down for the return from exile is a symmetrical antithesis to the "way in the sea" (v. 16) He made for Israel in its first liberation from servitude. History is thus seen in a pattern of cyclical recurrences, with differences.

20. *The beast of the field shall honor Me.* That is, the miraculous nature of the return to Zion through the desert is to be confirmed by the fact that the very beasts of the wilderness will look in awe as God causes water sources to spring up in parched land for the sake of His people, and predators will not attack the returning exiles.

22. *But not Me did you invoke, O Jacob.* These words of castigation mark the beginning of a new prophecy.

23   You have not brought Me sheep for your burnt offerings
           and with your sacrifices you have not honored Me.
      I did not burden you with grain offerings
           nor weary you with frankincense.
24   You did not buy for Me cane with silver
           nor sate me with the fat of your sacrifices.
      But you burdened Me with your offenses,
           wearied Me with your crimes.
25   I, I wipe away your transgressions for My sake,
           and your offenses I do not recall.
26   Help Me recall, let us join in judgment,
           you, recount it, that you be proven right.
27   Your first father offended,
           and your spokesmen transgressed against Me.
28   So I profaned the sanctuary's princes
           and gave Jacob to destruction
               and Israel to reviling.

---

23. *You have not brought Me sheep for your burnt offerings.* This statement would most plausibly refer to the time when the Temple was still standing. But it is an unusual reference: more characteristic of the prophets in the idea (see 1:11–15) that the people offer sacrifices mechanically while persisting in acts of turpitude.

  I did not burden you with grain offerings. Grain offerings and incense would be the easiest kind of offering. God has not imposed anything burdensome on the people in requiring sacrifices, and yet they have neglected all these obligations.

24. *cane.* This is aromatic cane, *qaneh*, mentioned as an element of the incense used in the temple cult and also as one of the fragrances in the Song of Songs.

25. *I wipe away your transgressions.* This declaration of absolute remission of sins contradicts the castigation in the verses that precede and follow it. Conceivably, an editor introduced this line in an effort to mitigate the harshness of the condemnation. The contrast between "I do not recall" and the immediately following "Help me recall" might signal such an editorial effort.

27. *Your first father offended.* The reference is probably meant to be general and not to invoke Abraham: from as far back as can be recalled, your people has offended.

  spokesmen. The term probably means advocates in a trial.

28. *the sanctuary's princes.* These would be the priests in the national cult. What the entire line recalls is the destruction of Jerusalem.

CHAPTER 44

And now, listen, Jacob, My servant, 1
    and Israel whom I have chosen.
Thus said the LORD your Maker, 2
    your Fashioner in the womb, Who helps you:
Do not fear, My servant Jacob
    and Jeshurun whom I have chosen.
As I pour water on thirsty land 3
    and rivulets on dry ground,
I will pour My spirit on your seed
    and My blessing on your offspring.
And they shall sprout among the grass 4
    like willows by brooks of water.
This one shall say, "I am for the LORD," 5
    and another shall call upon Jacob's name,
and another shall write with his hand for the LORD
    and Israel's name he shall invoke.

Thus said the LORD King of Israel 6
    and its Redeemer, the LORD of Armies.
I am the first and I am the last—
    and besides Me there is no god.
Who is like Me? Let him call out, 7

CHAPTER 44   2. *Jeshurun.* This is a synonym for "Israel" used only in poetic texts. Although the name appears to derive from a root that means "straight," there are scholarly debates about its etymology.

5. *write with his hand for the LORD.* The received text says merely "write his hand," but several ancient translations show a preposition. Perhaps the phrase indicates signing a pledge of loyalty, but some interpreters understand it to mean that he shall write the name of the LORD on his hand.

7. *Who is like Me?* The context gives this rhetorical question a different meaning from "Who is like You among the gods" in the Song of the Sea in Exodus 15:11. There the implication is that there are other gods but that they scarcely measure up to the God of Israel. Here, God has just emphatically declared, "I am the first and I am the last— / and besides Me there is no god." The rest of the line, beginning with "Let him call out," clearly indicates that there is none capable of calling out.

let him tell it and lay it out to Me.
Who has made known from of old the signs
    and what is to come has told?
8 Do not be afraid and do not tremble.
    Have I not informed you and told?—
        And you are My witnesses.
Is there any god besides Me?
    Is there any Rock? None have I known.
9 Fashioners of idols, they are all mere wind,
    and their cherished things cannot avail,
and their witnesses cannot see
    nor know, and hence they are shamed.
10 Who fashioned a god and cast an idol
    to no avail?
11 Look, all his fellow workers shall be shamed,
    and the craftsmen, they are but men.
Let them all gather and stand,
    they shall fear and all be shamed.
12 The ironsmith with an adze
    works it with coals
and with hammers fashions it
    and works it with his strong arm.

Who has made known from of old the signs. The received text here looks garbled. It reads literally: "From My placing an everlasting people and signs." This translation accepts a widely proposed emendation, reading *mashmiʿa meʿolam ʾotiyot* instead of the Masoretic *misumi ʿam-ʿolam we ʾotiyot.* The "signs" are the omens of things to come: God's divinity is demonstrated by His power to tell future events through His prophets.

8. *Is there any Rock?* "Rock" (*tsur*) is a recurrent epithet for God in Psalms, based on God's role as a stronghold for His believers.

9. *Fashioners of idols.* The lengthy polemic against the manufacturers of idols that begins with these words is a hallmark of our prophet. No other biblical writer so scathingly reduces paganism to mere absurd fetishism. In the mid-twentieth century, the Israeli Bible scholar Yehezkel Kaufman used such prophecies to argue that the Israelites were so far removed from paganism that they failed to understand that idols were conceived merely as symbols of the gods they represented. One may question that view because polemic or satire is a literary vehicle that thrives on exaggeration: the prophet, in order to show vividly that idolators worship imagined entities, not real gods, represents them absurdly carving gods out of wood, using the leftover wood for fuel, and bowing down to their wooden carvings as to gods.

12. *with an adze.* The precise identity of several of the tools mentioned in this catalogue is uncertain.

Should he hunger, his strength will fail,
    should he not drink, he will grow faint.
The carpenter stretches a line,   13
    marks the outline with a stylus,
he makes it with a plane,
    marks the outline with a compass,
and makes it in the form of a man,
    human splendor to set in a temple,
cutting down cedars for it,   14
    taking plane trees and oak,
he picks from the trees of the forest,
    plants cedar, and the rain makes it grow.
And it turns into fuel for man,   15
    and he takes it and warms himself.
        He lights it and bakes bread and is sated.
He also makes a god and bows down,
    makes it an idol and worships it.
Half of it he burns in fire,   16
    on half he eats meat, he roasts it,
also warms himself, saying, "Hurrah!
    I have warmed myself, seen the fire."
And the rest he makes as a god, as his idol.   17
    He worships it and bows down
and prays to it and says,
    "Save me, for you are my god."
They do not know and do not discern,   18
    for their eyes are plastered over from seeing

Should he hunger. That is, the craftsman fashioning the idol is palpably subject to the human weakness of hunger and thirst, and hence it is preposterous to imagine that the image he produces is a god.

13. *human splendor to set in a temple.* By itself, the phrase "human splendor" sounds rather grand, but mere human splendor sitting in a temple as though it were a god becomes a satiric barb.

14. *plants cedar.* In this instance, the satire takes the process of manufacturing idols, all the way back to the planting of the tree that will later be cut down to provide wood for the statue.

15. *bakes bread . . . / makes . . . an idol.* This pairing is virtually a zeugma, the syntactic yoking together of disparate items: the same wood from which fuel is taken to bake bread also furnishes the material for an idol.

and their hearts from understanding.

19   None takes to heart,
      with no knowledge or discernment to say:
"Half of it I burned in fire
      and also baked bread on its coals,
         I roasted meat and ate it.
And the rest as an abhorrence I made,
      a block of wood I worshipped."

20   He herds ashes, a mocked heart has led him astray,
      and he shall not save his life,
         and he shall not say, "This is a sham in my right hand."

21   Recall these, O Jacob,
      and Israel, for you are My servant.
I fashioned you, you are My servant,
      Israel, do not forget Me.

22   I have wiped away your crimes like a cloud,
      and like the sky's mist your offenses.
         Turn back to Me, for I have redeemed you.

23   Sing gladly, O heavens, for the Lord has done it,
      shout out, you deeps of the earth.
Burst forth in glad song, you mountains,
      the forest and all trees within it,
For the Lord has redeemed Jacob,
      and shall glory in Israel.

---

19. *the rest as an abhorrence I made.* This is, of course, a polemic revision of the pagan's speech. The idol worshipper would never call his god an "abhorrence," but that is precisely the term, *to'evah,* that biblical writers frequently use to designate idols.

    a block of wood. The first verset uses an abstraction, "abhorrence"; now, in keeping with the general procedure of poetic parallelism, the second verset lets us know concretely what the abhorrence is.

20. *He herds ashes.* This is a pointed oxymoron: ashes cannot be herded, and if a wind blows on them, they fly away. The image is an anticipation of "herding the wind" in Qohelet.

22. *the sky's mist.* The Hebrew is simply another word for "cloud," but English has scant synonyms for "cloud," and the rare ones that come to mind (e.g., "thunderhead") are not right for this context.

23. *Sing gladly.* This entire verse, which evokes a cosmic celebration of God's glorious deeds in behalf of Israel, is reminiscent of quite a few psalms, and it is likely that the prophet-poet is remembering Psalms here.

Thus said the LORD your Redeemer,   24
   Who fashioned you in the womb:
I am the LORD, Maker of all,
   stretching out the heavens, I alone,
     laying down earth—who is with Me?
Overturning the omens of lies,   25
   making fools of soothsayers,
setting sages back on their heels
   and thwarting their devisings.
Confirming the word of His servant   26
   and fulfilling His messengers' counsel.
He says to Jerusalem, "You shall be settled,"
   and to Judah's towns, "You shall be rebuilt,
   and I will raise up her ruins."
He says to the Deep, "Dry up,   27
   and your streams I will make dry."
He says to Cyrus, "My shepherd!   28
   And all I desire he shall fulfill."
He says of Jerusalem, "It shall be rebuilt,"
   and to the Temple, "Your foundation shall be laid."

---

24. *Who fashioned you in the womb / . . . stretching out the heavens.* The bold movement of the poetry here from the tight confinement of the womb to the vast expanse of the heavens beautifully conveys God's magisterial power as Creator from the smallest things to the largest.

25. *the omens of lies.* The meaning of the second term, *badim,* is in dispute, although it could derive from the root *b-d-h,* which means to falsely invent or fabricate. In any case, here as above, the incapacity of pagan sages to forecast future events (which was a Babylonian specialty) is taken as a token of the nullity of their gods.

   their devisings. The literal sense is "their knowledge."

26. *His servant / . . . His messengers.* The reference is in all likelihood to God's prophets. Unlike the pagan soothsayers, the prophets have an authentic channel through which they can foretell future events.

28. *Cyrus.* For the first time, the Persian emperor whose armies are threatening Babylonia is mentioned by name. In the earlier prophetic poetry there are generalized references to foreign kings—those of Assyria in particular—serving as God's instrument, the rod of His wrath, but this text introduces a new order of specificity: a momentous change in history is unfolding, with the Babylonian empire, which destroyed the kingdom of Judah, under the shadow of destruction; and the Persian Cyrus is seen as God's shepherd, fulfilling a divine plan. The endgame of this plan is the return to Zion and the rebuilding of the Temple, invoked in the second half of this verse and in fact to be implemented by another Persian emperor, decades after the probable time of this prophecy.

CHAPTER 45

1   Thus said the Lord to His anointed one,
           to Cyrus, whose right hand I grasp,
       to hold sway over nations,
           and the loins of kings will I loosen,
       to open before him double doors,
           and the gates shall not be closed.
2   I will go before you,
           and rough places I will level,
       doors of bronze I will smash
           and iron bolts I will hack down.
3   And I will set before you treasures of darkness
           and hidden stores,
       so that you may know that I am the Lord
           Who calls your name, the God of Israel.
4   For the sake of My servant Jacob
           and Israel My chosen one,
       I called you by name,
           I named you when I had not known you.
5   I am the Lord and there is no other,

CHAPTER 45   1. *to His anointed one.* Some readers may find it startling that a Persian emperor should be designated God's "anointed one" (*mashiah*). One should keep in mind that in the first instance this is a political title, not a theological or eschatological one. Cyrus is God's anointed because he is a king whose legitimacy is confirmed or underwritten by God and as such a ruler who will play a role God has defined for what is to happen in history.

the loins of kings will I loosen. One again can detect the common pattern of biblical poetic parallelism: first the general concept ("hold sway over nations") and then in the parallel verset a concrete image—loosening the loins would be ungirding the loins that should be girded for battle, which is to say, disabling these royal enemies.

3. *treasures of darkness / and hidden stores.* The darkness here is pragmatic, not symbolic—the treasures have been hidden or buried in deep dark places, but now they will be brought to light to be appropriated by the conquering Cyrus.

4. *For the sake of My servant Jacob.* It is, of course, a peculiarly Israel-centered view of the world that Cyrus's conquests are imagined as coming about strictly to rescue the people of Israel from its exile.

I called you by name. Here this idiom has the sense of "to summon," as in the previous verse.

when I had not known you. As a foreign ruler, Cyrus would not have had any intimate relationship (the force of "to know" in the Hebrew) with YHWH.

besides Me there is no god.
So they may know from the sun's rising place to its setting,   6
   that there is none beside Me,
      I am the LORD and there is no other.
Fashioning light and creating darkness,   7
   making peace and creating evil.
      I am the LORD, making all these.
O, heavens, drip down from above,   8
   and skies, stream justice.
Let the earth open that it be fruitful with rescue
   and bring forth righteousness with it.
      I am the LORD. I created it.

Woe, who disputes with his Fashioner,   9
   a shard from the shards of the earth.
Shall the clay say to its Fashioner, "What are you doing?,
   and Your work has no hands."
Woe, who says to the father, "What did you beget?,"   10
   and to the woman, "Why do you labor?"
Thus said the LORD,   11
   Israel's Holy One and its Fashioner:
The signs have inquired of Me about My sons,
   and about the work of My hands they have charged Me.

---

7. *Fashioning . . .creating.* These are the two terms used for creation at the beginning of Genesis, respectively, in the J version (Genesis 2) and the P version (Genesis 1). The former term, *yotser*, is more concrete and, indeed, anthropomorphic, its primary reference being to the work of the potter with clay. This is a connotation that this poet repeatedly plays on, as in verse 9 below.

8. *O, heavens, drip down from above.* In this semiarid region dependent on rainfall, it is usually rain as a source of blessing that comes down from the sky in poetry, but here there is a metaphorical transformation of this primary notion: it is justice that rains down, fructifying human life.

9. *Shall the clay say to its Fashioner.* This line clearly harks back to Genesis 2, where God fashions the first human from the clay of the earth.

10. *Woe, who says to the father.* This line relates to the preceding one in a kind of *a fortiori* logic: just as it would be absurd for a person to deny that his father and mother had begotten him, it is even more preposterous that any human creature should deny that God is his Creator.

11. *The signs have inquired of Me.* It is unclear what these signs are. The Hebrew is as opaque as this translation and may reflect a defective text.

12   I made the earth
        and the humans upon it I created.
    It is I, My hands stretched out the heavens,
        and all their array I commanded.
13   It is I who roused him in justice
        and all his ways I made straight.
    He it is shall rebuild My city
        and release My exiles,
    not for a price and not for a payment,
        said the LORD of Armies.

14   This said the LORD:
    The profit of Egypt and Nubia's trade
        and the Sabeans, men of stature,
    shall pass over to you and be yours.
        They shall walk behind you, pass on in chains,
    and to you they shall bow,
        to you they shall pray:
    "In you alone is God,
        and there is none other save God."
15   Indeed, You are a God Who hides,

---

12. *I made the earth.* Just as God is the cosmic Creator, bringing into being heaven and earth, He also determines the direction of history, as the next verse will assert.

13. *It is I Who roused him in justice.* The "him" is Cyrus, who in this version is led to the conquest of Babylonia for the sole purpose of returning Israel from exile. As a matter of historical fact, the return to Zion took place eight decades after the fall of the Babylonian empire to the Persians.

14. *shall pass over to you and be yours.* "You" in this passage is feminine singular and so must refer to Zion, often represented in poetry as a woman.

    to you they shall bow, / to you they shall pray. This wording may sound somewhat suspect from a monotheistic point of view. It should probably be taken as an extravagant hyperbole—these peoples of the south will be so abjectly enslaved to the Israelites that they will prostrate themselves before them and worship them as though they were gods.

    In you alone is God. These words are best understood as the speech of the captives addressed to Israel and offering an explanation for their bowing down to their captors.

15. *Indeed, You are a God Who hides.* Many scholars view this verse as an interpolation, unrelated to what precedes or follows. If there is a connection it might be this: it is hard to detect the presence or earthly manifestation of God, but He dwells (or perhaps hides) within the people of Israel, where foreigners now discern Him through His conquering power.

God of Israel, Rescuer.
They were shamed and also disgraced   16
    all of them together,
they walk in disgrace,
    the crafters of idols.
Israel is victorious through the LORD,   17
    an everlasting victory.
You shall not be shamed and shall not be disgraced
    forever more.
For thus said the LORD,   18
    Creator of the heavens, He is God,
        Fashioner of earth and its Maker, He founded it.
Not for nothing did He create it,
    to dwell there He fashioned it.
        I am the LORD and there is no other.
Not in secret have I spoken   19
    in the place of a land of darkness.
I did not say to Jacob's seed,
    "In vain have you sought Me."
I am the LORD speaking justice,
    telling uprightness.

Gather and come,   20
    draw together,
        survivors of nations!
Those who bear the wood of their idols
    do not know
and who pray to a god
    that does not rescue.

---

17. *victorious . . . / victory.* Given the context of the subjugation of foreign peoples, the root *y-sh-ʿ*—elsewhere, "rescue"—probably has its military sense.

18. *Not for nothing.* The use of *tohu* amounts to a pun. Adverbially, it can mean "for nothing," "futilely," as it clearly does in the next verse. But as a noun, it designates the primordial chaos (in this translation of *tohu wavohu*, "welter and waste") that preceded creation, so what is also being asserted is that God did not create the earth to be mere chaos or void.

20. *Those who bear the wood of their idols.* The formulation glances back to the representation of idol manufacture in chapter 44, suggesting an image of the pagans carrying the wood out of which they will fashion their idols.

21   Tell it and bring it forth,
          even let them counsel together.
      Who made this known of yore,
          from of old told it?
      Am I not the LORD
          and there is no god beside Me,
      a righteous God and a Rescuer,
          there is none save Me.
22   Turn to Me and be rescued,
          all you ends of earth,
              for I am God and there is no other.
23   By Myself have I sworn,
          from My mouth has issued justice
              a word that will not be revoked:
      For to Me every knee shall bend,
          every tongue shall vow.
24   But through the LORD—of Me it was said—
          victory and strength!
      To Him shall they come and not be shamed,
          all who were incensed against Him.
25   Through the LORD shall they be victorious and praised,
          all the seed of Israel.

---

22. *all you ends of earth.* As elsewhere, *'afsey 'arets* is a metonymy since the object of the prophet's address is clearly the inhabitants of the ends of the earth.

23. *For to Me every knee shall bend, / every tongue shall vow.* This line would be incorporated in the *Aleinu* prayer at the end of the morning service, which affirms God's kingship over all things.

24. *of Me it was said.* There is no need to emend this clause, as has frequently been proposed. Although the verb appears to say "he said," the third-person singular is often used as the equivalent of a passive form of the verb.

   To Him shall they come and not be shamed. Even though "be shamed" is very often used for a condition of being defeated, here there is an image of those who have set themselves up as God's enemies ("all who were incensed against Him") obliged to come before God and accept His admonition in shame.

25. *victorious.* The root *ts-d-q* is associated with justice because its primary sense is winning a just case in court. But the concept of winning in a conflict also leads to its use to indicate winning in battle, which would appear to be the sense here.

CHAPTER 46

Bel has knelt, 1
  Nebo has cowered.
Their images you bore aloft
  become burdens for beasts and animals
    loaded to exhaustion.
They cowered, they knelt together, 2
  could not free the burden,
    and they themselves went into captivity.
Listen to me, O house of Jacob 3
  and all the house of Israel's remnant,
loaded heavy from birth,
  burdened from the womb.
And till old age it is I, 4
  till gray hair comes I Myself will bear it.
I have made it and I will carry,
  I will bear it and I will rescue.

To whom would you liken Me and make Me equal, 5
  compare Me that I be likened?

CHAPTER 46 1. *Bel has knelt, / Nebo has cowered.* These are Babylonian deities, and the cowering marks the defeat of Babylonia by Persia.

Their images you bore aloft / become burdens for beasts and animals. In the defeat, the images that were worshipped are loaded onto the backs of animals to be carried off in order to make use of any precious metals with which the idols may be overlaid.

2. *they themselves went into captivity.* This is a mocking representation of the Babylonian gods, impotent to save themselves (or their adherents), borne off as captives like a subjugated human population.

3. *loaded heavy from birth, / burdened from the womb.* These phrases obviously pick up the image of the beasts burdened with plundered idols from the previous verse. However, it is not clear with what the house of Jacob has been burdened from the womb. God's assertion in the next verse that He will now carry the burden suggests that it is the heavy load of national suffering, most recently manifested in the destruction of Jerusalem and the exile of a large part of its inhabitants.

4. *till old age.* God is with Israel from birth (verse 3) to old age.

5. *To whom would you liken Me.* These words sound a central theme of this prophet (compare 44:18ff). The verb of likening (*tedamyuni*) suggests *demut*, "image" or "likeness," which leads the poet in the following lines to evoke, as he has done before, the absurdity of manufacturing images that are then worshipped.

6   Who lavish gold from the purse
          and silver weigh out on the scale,
       hire a goldsmith that he make a god,
          they worship it, even bow down.
7   They carry it on shoulders, they bear it
          and set it down, it stands unmoving in its place.
       Though one cries out to it, there is no answer,
          from straits it does not rescue.

8   Recall this and be shamed,
          take it to heart, O criminals,
9   recall the first things of yore.
       For I am God, there is none other,
          God, and none is like Me.
10   Who tells from the beginning the end,
          and from old what is not yet done,
       Who says, "My counsel will be realized,
          and all My desire will I do."
11   Who calls the bird of prey from the east,
          from a distant land, the man of My counsel.

---

8. *be shamed.* The verb in the received text, *hit'oshashu*, appears to be based on a root that suggests strength, hence the New Jewish Publication Society rendering "stand firm." But that makes no sense in the context of a castigation. This translation adapts an emendation that has been proposed by several scholars, *hitboshashu*, which involves the changing of one consonant.

   take it to heart, O criminals. The denunciation appears to be a new note in these prophecies of Second Isaiah, which are predominantly prophecies of consolation. Joseph Blenkinsopp proposes that the prophet may have encountered resistance to his message and that these words reflect an element of antagonism between him and his audience.

9. *For I am God, there is none other.* The rejoinder to the doubts of the prophet's audience is an absolute theological truth: the deity in whose name the prophet speaks is the one and only God; this fundamental fact is what is entailed in "the first things of yore."

10. *Who tells from the beginning the end.* As before in these prophecies, the manifest evidence of YHWH's status as the one and only God is His proven power to predict the future through what is revealed to His true prophets. Thus God provides authorization for the authenticity of the words of His human spokesmen. It seems likely that what the exiled audience has doubted is the grand prediction of the restoration of Zion, which the prophet here goes on to affirm will be implemented through God's chosen instrument, Cyrus.

11. *the bird of prey from the east, / from a distant land, the man of My counsel.* Persia is actually to the northeast, but the poem need not be entirely precise about points on the compass. Cyrus is the man of God's counsel in the sense that he has been designated to carry out God's counsel or plan.

I have spoken and even will bring him,
    I have fashioned it, even will do it.
Hear Me, O bull-hearted,   12
    who are distant from victory.
I have brought My victory close—it is not distant,   13
    and My triumph shall not delay.
And I will set triumph in Zion,
    for Israel, my splendor.

CHAPTER 47

Go down and sit in the dust,   1
    Virgin Daughter of Babylon.
Sit on the ground with no throne.
    O Daughter of Chaldeans.
For no longer shall they call you
    tender and delicate.
Take up a hand mill and grind flour.   2
    Bare your tresses, strip your train.
        Bare your thigh, cross the rivers.

---

12. *bull-hearted.* The sense is "stubborn," but the strong image of "bull" implicit in the Hebrew *'abirim* is worth retaining. The audience of exiles, refusing to believe they will be returned to their land, are "bull-hearted." God now assures them through His prophet that the moment of national triumph is imminent and not distant, as the exiles may imagine.

CHAPTER 47   1. *Virgin Daughter of Babylon.* Others render this as "maid of Babylon." The personification of a people or a city as a woman is widespread in the Bible, especially in poetry. The term denoting virginity is worth retaining in translation because humiliating sexual exposure will follow.

Sit on the ground with no throne. Not only is she to be forced to sit in the dust, but now we are reminded that she was formerly seated on a throne as "mistress of kingdoms" (verse 5). This dire evocation of the crushing and stripping of Babylon is integral to this prophet's vision of the hated Babylonian empire falling to Persia.

2. *Take up a hand mill.* The once splendid queen is now to perform menial tasks.

Bare your tresses. Many interpreters insist that *tsamah* here and in the Song of Songs 4 means "veil," but Chana and Ariel Bloch have persuasively argued in their commentary on the Song that the verb used for "bare," *gali,* applies only to body parts, not to items of apparel, and *tsamah* in Song of Songs 4:1, 3 is part of a catalogue of body parts.

strip your train. Here a different verb is used, *hasaf,* which in fact applies to things worn.

Bare your thigh, cross the rivers. Blenkinsopp observes that she would have to hitch up her robes, thus exposing her thighs, in order to wade across rivers. The implied image is of a woman driven into exile.

3   Your nakedness shall be bared,
            your shame shall now be seen.
         Vengeance will I take
            and no man shall intercede.

4   Our Redeemer, the LORD of Armies is His name,
            Israel's Holy One.

5   Sit mute and come into the darkness,
            O Daughter of Chaldeans,
         for no longer shall they call you
            the mistress of kingdoms.

6   I was furious with My people,
            I profaned My estate
               and gave them into your hand.
         You showed them no mercy,
            on the elder you made your yoke very heavy.

7   And you thought, "Forever shall I be the mistress."
            You did not take these things to heart
               nor remember its outcome.

8   And now, hear this, pampered woman,
            dwelling secure,
         who says in her heart,
            "It is I and none besides me.
         I will not dwell a widow
            and will not know bereavement."

9   These two shall come upon you,
            in a flash, on a single day—
         bereavement and widowhood

---

3. *Your nakedness shall be bared.* This is an explicitly sexual term, referring to the pudenda.

    no man shall intercede. The Masoretic Text has "I will intercede," but the appropriate third-person form of the verb with the negative is reflected in the Septuagint.

4. *Our Redeemer.* This verse may be out of place.

6. *I was furious with My people / . . . You showed them no mercy.* This verse performs a theological balancing act. God was furious with Israel and punished them by allowing the Babylonians to defeat them, but the Babylonians enacted this historical role mercilessly, tormenting Israel with a heavy yoke, treating even the aged savagely. For this, Babylonia will now suffer severe retribution.

8. *bereavement.* The Hebrew word has the special sense of being bereaved of children. If Babylonia is personified as a woman, her people are her children.

shall come upon you in full measure
despite your many incantations
   and the great power of your spells.
But you trusted in your evil,   10
   you said, "No one sees me."
Your wisdom and your lore,
   it was this that made you stray.
And you said in your heart,
   "It is I and none besides me."
And evil shall come upon you,   11
   you shall never know dawn,
and disaster shall fall upon you,
   you shall not know how to ward it off,
and ruin shall suddenly come upon you,
   with you unwitting.
Stay, pray, with your spells   12
   and with your many incantations
      with which you toiled from your youth.
Perhaps you may avail,
   perhaps still tyrannize.
You are disabled despite all your counsels.   13
   Let the sky scanners, pray, stand and rescue you,
      those who see visions in the stars,
announcing them month after month,

---

9. *despite your many incantations / and the great power of your spells.* The Babylonians were famous for their expertise in soothsaying and divination, which is attested by the many texts of divination and spell casting that have been discovered.

10. *But you trusted in your evil.* "Evil" here is probably a denigrating summarizing term for all the skills of sorcery and divination ("Your wisdom and your lore") in which Babylonia placed its trust.

11. *You shall never know dawn.* The Hebrew says "its dawn," a feminine suffix with no clear referent. This is best taken as a follow-up to "come into the darkness" (verse 5)—the disaster about to overtake Babylonia is one long night of darkness without a dawn.

12. *Stay, pray, with your spells.* This is obviously sarcastic, with the introduction of the polite particle *na'*, "pray," heightening the sarcasm.

13. *the sky scanners.* This translation adopts the solution for *hovrey shamayim* proposed by both the New Jewish Publication Society version and Blenkinsopp. It should be noted that the Babylonians were not only astrological diviners but also rather sophisticated astronomers.

what is to come upon you.

14   Look, they have become like straw,
> fire burns them up,
>> they cannot save themselves from the flame.
> This is no coal to warm oneself,
>> no hearth by which to sit.

15   This have they become for you, with which you toiled,
> your traders since your youth:
> each man wanders on his own way,
>> there is no none to save you.

CHAPTER 48

1   Hear this, house of Jacob,
> who are called by the name of Israel
>> and came out from Judah's womb,
> and who invoke the God of Israel
>> neither in truth nor in righteousness.

2   For from the holy city they have been called
> and on Israel's God they have leaned—
>> the Lord of Armies is His name.

3   The first things of old have I told,

---

14. *they have become like straw.* "They" here would have to refer either to the astrologers or to the lore they deploy.

This is no coal to warm oneself, / no hearth by which to sit. There is no longer any question of domesticated fire for human benefit; instead, raging flames will consume everything.

CHAPTER 48   1. *house of Jacob, / who are called by the name of Israel.* Although it is a regular procedure in poetic parallelism to use "Jacob" (the primary term) in the first verset and "Israel" (the name to which "Jacob" was changed) in the second verset, the wording here looks as if it may be a gloss on the two names. Formerly "Israel" designated the northern kingdom, but since that kingdom was destroyed, the name has been attached to the Judahites as well, who now constitute the entire people. This adoption of the national name is further explained by the third verset, "who came out from Judah's womb."

and who invoke the God of Israel / neither in truth nor in righteousness. The end of this whole two-line sentence is a barbed reversal: the people of Judah, now calling itself "Israel," invokes the God of Israel—but falsely and hypocritically.

3. *The first things of old have I told.* As earlier, YHWH's authenticity as the one overmastering God is manifested in His power to foretell what will happen in the future through His prophets.

from My mouth they issued, I announced them,
    of a sudden I did it and they came about.
For I knew that you were hard,   4
    and your neck was iron sinews
        and your forehead brazen.
And I told you of old,   5
    before it came, I announced it to you,
lest you should say, "My idol did these.
    My carved and molten images ordained them."
You have heard—behold it all,   6
    and you, will you not tell?
I announced to you new things from hence
    and hidden things you did not know.
Now are they created and not long ago,   7
    before this day, and you have not heard.
        Thus you say, "Why, I did not know them."
You have never heard, you have never known,   8
    of old, your ear was never open.
For I knew you would surely betray,
    and from the womb you were called a rebel.
For My name's sake I will hold back My wrath   9
    and for My glory I will be restrained toward you
        so as not to cut you off.
Look, I have refined you but not as silver,   10
    I have purged you in the forge of affliction.
For My sake, for My sake, I do it,   11

---

4. *For I knew that you were hard.* The essential element of God's knowledge is His recognition of Israel's stubborn recalcitrance to live up to its covenantal obligations, which will inexorably bring about the national disasters predicted by the prophets.

7. *Now are they created.* The historical eventualities long predicted by the prophets are even now being shaped and happening.

8. *your ear was never open.* The reiterated theme of spiritual deafness and blindness is a notion that this prophet appears to have picked up from Isaiah 6.

9. *For My name's sake I will hold back My wrath.* The prophet invokes a recurrent biblical idea: that God's reputation in the world would suffer if He allowed Israel to be utterly destroyed, and for that reason He in the end spares Israel, despite its disloyalty.

10. *I have purged you in the forge of affliction.* This is the other component of God's plan for Israel: the people's treacherous behavior earns it punishment, and the punishment has a purging function, bringing the people to its senses about what it has done and leading it to change its ways.

for how could I be profaned?
   And My glory I will not give to another.

12   Listen to Me, O Jacob,
         and Israel, whom I have called.
      I am He, I am the first,
         and I am the last as well.
13   Indeed, My hand founded the earth,
         and My right hand spread out the heavens
      I summon them,
         they stand together.
14   Gather, all of you, and listen!
         Who among you has told these things?
      The LORD loves him, shall do his desire.
         against Babylonia, and his arm against the Chaldeans.
15   I, I have spoken, even called him,
         I have brought him and made his way prosper.
16   Draw close to me, and hear this:
         Not from the first did I speak in secret,
            from when it came into being, there I was.
      And now, the Master, the LORD,
         has sent me with His spirit.

---

11. *for how could I be profaned.* This whole line picks up the idea of verse 9: if God were to allow Israel to perish in exile, His name would be profaned, His glory surrendered, and so He is now prepared to intercede on behalf of his people.

14. *The LORD loves him.* The pronominal object of the verb here is Cyrus. It may seem extravagant to say that the LORD loves a foreign emperor, but the sense in context is that God, using Cyrus as the instrument in a divine historical plan, has chosen to give full support to Cyrus's imperial ambitions and to enable him to subdue Babylonia.

15. *even called him.* As often in biblical Hebrew, the multipurpose verb "call" has the sense of "summon," "single out for a mission."

16. *Not from the first did I speak in secret.* While there is no introductory formula, the next line of poetry makes it clear that the speaker of these words is the prophet, not God. From the moment of his dedication as prophet, he has spoken openly and plainly about what God has set out to do in history. These two lines of poetry constitute a kind of coda or closing frame to the prophecy spoken by God that begins in verse 12.
     has sent me with His spirit. The Masoretic Text reads "has sent me and His spirit," emended in this translation by substituting for the initial particle w^e ("and") the particle b^e ("with" or "in"). More elaborate emendations have been proposed but seem unnecessary.

Thus said the LORD, your Redeemer,   17
    Israel's Holy One:
I am the LORD your God,
    Who teaches you to avail,
        guides you on the way you should go.
Had you heeded My commands,   18
    your well-being would have been like a river
        and your bounty like the waves of the sea.
And your seed beyond number like sand   19
    and the offspring of your loins like its grains.
Its name before Me
    would not be cut off and not be destroyed.

Go out from Babylonia,   20
    flee from the Chaldeans.
With a sound of glad song tell,
    make this heard:
They have brought him out to the end of the earth.
    Say—the LORD has redeemed His servant Jacob.
And they did not thirst in the parched land where He led them.   21
    Water from a rock He made flow for them.
        There is no well-being, said the LORD, for the wicked.

---

18. *bounty.* The Hebrew *tsedaqah* has at least three meanings: "righteousness," "victory," and "bounty." In the present context, the third of these seems most likely.

19. *beyond number.* This idiom, often attached to "sand," is merely implied in the Hebrew.

20. *Go out from Babylonia.* This new prophecy makes explicit the vision of a return to Zion. That event in fact did not occur until almost a century later, and many of the exiles chose not to return.

21. *Water from a rock He made flow for them.* Though this line clearly invokes the miraculous providing of water to the Israelites in their wanderings in the wilderness, that divine intervention long ago is envisaged here as a miracle to be reenacted when the exiles make the long trek back from Babylonia to Judah.
    There is no well-being, said the LORD, for the wicked. The logical link of this third verset to the two preceding ones is weaker, and this may well be an interpolated sentence.

CHAPTER 49

1   Hear me, O coastlands,
       and listen, faraway nations.
    The Lord called me forth from the womb,
       from my mother's belly He invoked my name.

2   And He made my mouth a sharp sword,
       in the shadow of His hand He hid me,
    and He made me a well-honed arrow,
       in His quiver He sheltered me.

3   And he said to me, "You are My servant,
       Israel, in whom I glory."

4   And I had thought, "In vain have I toiled,
       for naught, for mere breath, my strength have I sapped.
    Yet my cause is with the Lord
       and my wages with my God."

5   And now the Lord has said,
       my Fashioner from the womb as a servant to Him,
    to bring back Jacob to him,
       and Israel shall be gathered to Him,
    and I shall be honored in the eyes of the Lord
       and my God shall be my strength.

6   And He said, "It is too little a thing that you are My servant,
       to raise up the tribes of Jacob
          and bring back Israel's survivors.
    I shall make you a light for the nations,
       that My rescue reach the end of the earth."

CHAPTER 49   2. *And He made my mouth a sharp sword.* The assertion in this line and the next that the prophet's discourse is a potent weapon may be a little surprising because the chief burden of his prophesies is a message of consolation. Perhaps, speaking in a situation of painful political powerlessness, he wants to assert that his poetry has power, even the power to devastate those who would resist it. One should note that there is a counterpoint between the first and second verset in each of these two lines: the first verset expresses the weaponlike power of the prophet's discourse, the second, his enjoyment of shelter provided by God, with the image of the quiver neatly combining shelter and weapon.

3. *You are My servant, / Israel.* The poem segues from the prophet to the people whose conscience and representative he is.

6. *I shall make you a light for the nations, / that My rescue reach the end of the earth.* The unheard-of act of bringing the exiled people of Israel back to its land is imagined as taking

Thus said the LORD,   7
    Israel's Redeemer, its Holy One,
to the despised one, reviled by nations,
    to the slave of rulers.
Kings shall see and rise,
    princes, and bow down,
for the sake of the LORD, Who is faithful,
    Israel's Holy One Who has chosen you.
Thus said the LORD: 8
    In an hour of favor I answered you
        and on a day of rescue I aided you.
And I fashioned you and made you a people's covenant
    to raise up the land,
        to inherit desolate estates.
Saying to the captives, Go out!   9
    to those in darkness, Come into the open!
Along the roads they shall feed
    and on all the heights—their pasture.
They shall not hunger and shall not thirst,   10
    and hot wind and sun shall not strike them
for He Who shows mercy to them shall lead them
    and by springs of water guide them.
And I will make all My mountains a road,   11
    and My highways shall rise.
Look, these shall come from afar,   12
    and, look, these from the north and the west,
        and these from the land of Sinim.
Sing gladly, heavens,   13
    and rejoice O earth,
        shout out, O mountains, gladly.

---

place in a cosmic arena: this spectacular intervention on behalf of the defeated people will be seen throughout the earth.

9. *Along the roads they shall feed.* This is a reprise of Second Isaiah's central vision of a grand journey through the wilderness back to Zion. Although in verse 11 it picks up the theme from chapter 40 of the rough terrain transformed into a level highway, the special emphasis here is on providing food and water for the returning exiles—something that would have been a practical concern for those anticipating a trek through desert-land over hundreds of miles.

12. *the land of Sinim.* Some read this as "the land Syene" (Aswan?), but the identification remains uncertain.

> For the LORD has comforted His people
> and shown mercy to His afflicted.

14
> Yet Zion says, "The LORD has forsaken me,
> and the Master has forgotten me."

15
> Does a woman forget her babe,
> have no mercy on the child of her womb?
> Though she forget,
> I will not forget you.

16
> Why, on My palms I have inscribed you,
> your walls are before Me always.

17
> Your children hasten.
> Those who ravaged you, destroyed you,
> shall leave you.

18
> Lift up your eyes all around and see—
> they all have gathered, have come to you.
> As I live, says the LORD,
> all of them like a jewel you shall wear
> and tie them on like a bride.

19
> As to your ruins and your desolate places

14. *Yet Zion says.* Zion is imagined as a woman (the verb is feminine), a common convention in biblical poetry for representing cities and countries. The poet, as we shall see, develops this feminine figure in an original way.

The LORD has forsaken me. This verb is one that would be used for a wife abandoned by her husband. The metaphor of God as husband and Israel as beloved wife is vividly articulated in Jeremiah 1; the poet here taps into this conventional trope.

15. *Does a woman forget her babe.* God assures Zion, who feels she has been rejected by Him, that His feelings for her are even stronger than those of a mother for her child. The elaboration of the simile leaves it ambiguous as to whether Zion is God's daughter or His bride. At the same time, the invocation of a mother's attachment to her baby lays the ground for the vision of restored children in verses 17–21.

17. *Your children hasten. / Those who ravaged you . . . / shall leave you.* This is a panorama of two-way traffic. The conquerors of Zion flee as Zion's children rush back.

18. *all of them like a jewel you shall wear.* The somewhat unusual image of children worn like a jewel may be motivated by a literary allusion. Benjamin Sommer has proposed that Second Isaiah explicitly has in mind Jeremiah 2:32: "Does a virgin forget her jewels, / a bride her knotted sash?" In our text, the forgetting is transferred from jewels to children, and "jewel"—the same Hebrew word, 'adi—becomes a metaphorical representation of the children. Since producing children was imagined in this culture as a woman's greatest fulfillment, it logically follows that they are her chief ornament, what she can glory in before the eyes of the world.

and your ravaged land—
now you shall scarcely have room for dwellers,
    and your destroyer shall go far away.
Yet shall they say in your hearing,   20
    the children of whom you were bereaved:
"The place is too crowded for me,
    make me room that I may dwell."
And you shall say in your heart: 21
    "Who gave birth for me to these,
when I was bereaved and barren,
    exiled and cast aside,
and these, why, who has raised?
    Why, I was left alone,
        these, from where have they come?"
Thus said the LORD: 22
Look, I will raise My hand to the nations,
    and to the peoples I will lift My banner,
and they shall bring your sons in their laps,
    and your daughters shall be borne on their shoulders.
And kings shall be your attendants   23
    and princesses your wet nurses.

---

20. *the children of whom you were bereaved.* This is an eloquent poetic paradox: as in a fairy-tale happy ending, the children who Zion had thought were lost forever now appear before her and announce that because there are so many of them, there is scarcely room for them all to dwell in the land to which they have returned.

21. *Who gave birth for me to these.* The poignant force of Second Isaiah's poetry of consolation is beautifully felt here. Zion had thought herself bereaved of all her children and hopelessly barren, never to replace them. Now she finds them swarming around her, and she expresses her amazement in simple, almost naïve exclamation: did some mysterious surrogate mother give birth to all of these for me, "these, from where have they come?" The last sentence is still more pared down in the Hebrew: "these, where are they?" One should note that the Hebrew verb for "gave birth" is, against biology, masculine. Either the final feminine *heh* was dropped in scribal transmission, or this is an instance in which the masculine singular verb serves as a passive ("by whom were these given birth").

22. *I will raise My hand to the nations.* In Isaiah 5:26, God raises a banner to marshal the armies from the ends of the earth that will attack Judah. In the reversal here, the military signal inaugurates the return from exile, which is wholly pacific, with the sons and daughters of Zion carried in the laps and on the shoulders of the rulers of nations.

23. *attendants.* The Hebrew *'omen* suggests "tutor," or perhaps even a kind of glorified babysitter.

Face to the ground they shall bow to you
 and lick the dust of your feet.
And you shall know that I am the Lord,
 all who hope for Me shall not be shamed.

24   Shall prey be taken from a warrior
      or captives of a tyrant be freed?
25   For thus said the Lord:
      even a warrior's captive shall be taken away
       and a tyrant's prey freed.
      And with your contender will I contend,
       and your children I Myself will rescue.
26   And I will feed your oppressors their own flesh,
       and as with wine they shall be drunk on their blood.
      And all flesh shall know
       that I am the Lord, your Rescuer,
        and your Redeemer, the strong one of Jacob.

Face to the ground they shall bow to you. After the humiliation of the subjugation in exile, the prophet puts forth a grand reversal in which kings and noblewomen lick the dust at the feet of the people of Israel.

24. *tyrant.* The Masoretic Text reads *tsadiq,* "righteous man" (or according to some, "victor"), but the Qumran Isaiah as well as two ancient versions have *'arits,* "tyrant," and this reading is supported by the fact that the terms "warrior" and "tyrant" recur in the next line of poetry in a pointed repetition.

25. *even a warrior's captive shall be taken away.* The terms of comparison are now made to refer directly to the condition of the people of Israel: though experience tells us that no one can snatch captives from a fierce warrior or prey from a tyrant, you, who have been captives and the prey of tyrants, will be freed.

    I Myself will rescue. For both verbs here ("contend" and "rescue"), the Hebrew introduces the personal pronoun "I," usually not needed for conjugated verbs, as a gesture of emphasis.

26. *And I will feed your oppressors their own flesh.* In the immediately preceding prophecy, the kings and princes of nations were reduced to nursemaids and attendants. Here, in an angrier turn of vengeful thinking, they are condemned to hideous starvation leading to cannibalism.

    all flesh shall know. In a move characteristic of both biblical poetry and biblical narrative prose, a word that has just been used in one sense—"flesh" as what constitutes together with "blood" the human body—is repeated in a very different sense: "all flesh" as a designation of all humankind.

CHAPTER 50

Thus said the LORD: 1
Where is the divorce writ of your mother,
   whom I have sent away,
      or to which of My creditors did I sell you?
Why, for your crimes you have been sold,
   and for your offenses your mother was sent away.
Why did I come and there was no one there, 2
   I called out and no one answered?
Is My hand too short to redeem,
   and is there no power in Me to save?
Why, when I roar, I dry up the sea,
   I turn rivers into desert.
Their fish stink where there is no water
   and die on parched ground.
I will clothe the heavens with blackness 3
   and make sackcloth their garment.

The Master, the LORD, has given me 4
   a skilled tongue,
      knowing how to proffer a word to the weary.

CHAPTER 50   1. *the divorce writ of your mother, / whom I have sent away.* The trope of the people of Israel as God's bride is now extended to the alienation of Israel from God, which is represented as divorce. The wife has been "sent away" (the technical verb used for divorcing a woman) because she has misbehaved—implicitly, because she has betrayed YHWH with other lovers, other gods. As the metaphor is developed, we see that she has been not only divorced but sold into slavery, a condition that jibes with that of the subjugated exiles.

2. *Why, when I roar, I dry up the sea.* Out of context, it may appear unseemly that God should boast of His divine powers. In the present context, the point is that Israel somehow has failed to take note of God's all-powerful nature: He certainly would have been able to save them, had they been worthy of it, and He also has the power to wreak devastating destruction, turning rivers into dry desert and enveloping the bright sky with darkness.

4. *has given me / a skilled tongue.* The prophet now speaks autobiographically. He has been granted the gift of language—he is after all a fine poet, and he is surely conscious of his ability. The phrase "a skilled tongue" is literally "the disciples' tongue," that is, a tongue that has been rigorously trained. The same Hebrew word appears in conjunction with "testimony" at the end of this verse, where it has been translated as "disciples."
   to proffer. The anomalous Hebrew verb is understood only by context here.

Morning after morning, He rouses my ear
   to listen as do the disciples.
5   The Master, the LORD, has opened my ear,
      for I, I did not rebel,
         nor did I fall away.
6   My back I gave to the floggers
      and my cheeks to those who plucked my beard.
         My face I did not hide
            from abasement and spittle.
7   But the Master, the LORD, has helped me,
      and so I was not disgraced,
   and so I set my face like flint
      and knew I would not be shamed.
8   My Vindicator is close.
      Who would contend with me, let us confront one another.
   Who would be my accuser in court,
      let him approach me.
9   Why, if the Master, the LORD, helps me,
      who can declare me wrong?
   Why, they all shall wear out like a garment,
      the moth shall eat them away.

---

5. *for I, I did not rebel.* Having been vouchsafed revelation ("the Master, the LORD, has opened my ear"), the prophet does not shirk the burden of his mission, even if he knows that his message will encounter harsh resistance.

6. *My back I gave to the floggers.* There is a long tradition of Christian interpretation that refers this entire verse to Christ. What the prophet is speaking about is his own experience: while most of his prophetic message has been a discourse of consolation, it is easy enough to imagine that his soaring vision of a splendid restoration to Zion would have been seen by many in his audiences as an outrageous pipe dream, an insult to their continuing plight as exiles, and some would have responded by mocking, insulting, even roughing up the prophet as he tried to address them.

   plucked my beard. "Beard" is merely implied in the Hebrew by the verb used and the reference in the Hebrew to "cheeks."

7. *and so I was not disgraced.* The prophet, knowing that he speaks for God and is supported by God, does not feel really shamed even in the midst of public humiliation, and he can set his face hard as flint even as it is spat upon and his beard torn.

8. *My Vindicator is close.* The prophet now represents his suffering vilification at the hands of his audience through a legal metaphor: whoever accuses him will be found wrong in a court of law.

Who among you fears the LORD,   10
    heeding the voice of His servant,
who has walked in darkness,
    no radiance for him,
let him trust in the name of the LORD
    and lean upon his God.
But all you who glow hot with fire,   11
    girded with firebrands,
walk by the blaze of your fire
    and by the firebrands you have lit.
From My hand this has come to you:
    in pain shall you lie down.

CHAPTER 51

Listen to me, pursuers of justice,   1
    seekers of the LORD.
Look to the rock you were hewn from
    and to the quarry from which you were cut.

---

10. *Who among you fears the LORD.* Now, in a kind of peroration to this prophecy, the prophet turns back to his audience.

who has walked in darkness. Darkness and light are obviously archetypal images, but this prophet is especially fond of them and rings the changes on them in his poetry. This particular verset might be a deliberate allusion to Isaiah 9:1: "The people walking in darkness / have seen a great light."

radiance. The Hebrew *nogah* is strictly poetic diction and suggests something grander than mere "light," which is the English equivalent used in most previous translations.

11. *But all you who glow hot with fire.* The poet now turns around the imagery of the light 180 degrees. Instead of the radiance God provides that liberates from darkness, there are those who prefer the light generated by their own fire. Whether this is simply arrogant self-reliance or the false light of fabricated gods is not clear. But this is a destructive source of light, its burning rather than its illumination salient in the language of these lines.

CHAPTER 51   1. *Look to the rock you were hewn from.* Although "rock" (*tsur*) in biblical poetry is often an epithet for God, the reference to Abraham and Sarah in the next verse suggests that the poet has in mind here the human forefather and foremother of the people of Israel. "Quarry" is never an epithet for God, and the fact that a rock juts up (and is a masculine Hebrew noun) while a quarry is a cavity in the ground (and a feminine Hebrew noun) further aligns the two metaphors with Abraham and Sarah respectively.

2   Look to Abraham your father
                  and to Sarah who spawned you.
For he was the one whom I summoned,
        and I blessed him and made him many.

3   For the Lord has comforted Zion,
         brought comfort to all her ruins
and made her desert like Eden,
        her wasteland like the garden of the Lord.
Gladness and joy are within her.
        thanksgiving and the sound of song.

4   Hearken to Me, My people,
        and My nation, give ear to Me.
For teaching from Me shall go out
        and My justice as a light to the peoples.

5   In an instant My triumph draws near,
        My rescue comes forth,
                and my arm shall rule over peoples.
The coastland shall wait for Me
        and count on My strong arm.

6   Lift up your eyes to the heavens,
        and look on the earth below.
Though the heavens be scattered like smoke,
        and the earth worn out like a garment,

---

3. *like Eden.* The references of this prophecy of national restoration keep moving back in time—first to the couple who were the founders of the nation and now to the lushness of the primordial garden.

5. *In an instant.* This phrase reflects in English the Hebrew verb *'argi'a*, which can mean to do something in an instant (*rega'*). In the Masoretic Text, this verb appears at the end of the previous verse, but it almost certainly serves here as part of a sequence of two successive verbs, the first in effect adverbially modifying the second—that is, *'argi'a 'aqriv*, "I will [do] in an instant, I will draw near."

    my arm shall rule over peoples. The arm in biblical idiom is repeatedly a metaphor for power, although the use of the plural here is unusual. The Hebrew here uses a plural, but the translation avoids "arms" in order not to suggest the sense of "weapons." At the end of this verse, "arm" occurs in the singular, and the translation has added "strong" in order to convey the idiomatic sense of the Hebrew.

6. *Lift up your eyes to the heavens, / and look on the earth below.* The poem now pushes its movement back in time from the Garden of Eden to the heavens and the earth that emerged at the very beginning of creation. Through all these eons, from Abraham and Sarah to Eden to the first moment of creation and forward to the imagined end of creation, God's beneficent power remains steadfast.

and its dwellers like gnats die out,
My rescue shall be forever,
   and My triumph shall not be shattered.
Listen to Me, knowers of justice,   7
   a people with My teaching in its heart.
Do not be afraid of the insults of men,
   and from their mockery do not quail.
For like a garment the moth shall consume them,   8
   and like wool the grub shall consume them.
But My triumph shall be forever
   and My rescue for ages to come.

Awake, awake, put on strength,   9
   O arm of the LORD.
Awake as in days of yore,
   ages long past.
Was it not You who hacked apart Rahab,
   who pierced the Beast of the Sea?
Was it not You who dried up the sea,   10

---

like gnats. The Hebrew *kemo-khen* appears to say "also thus," a dubious phrase before "die out" and after two strong similes ("like smoke," "like a garment") in the two preceding versets. This translation assumes a scribal error for *kemo kinim,* "like gnats."

7. *Do not be afraid of the insults of men.* These words attributed to God, spoken through the prophet, appear to assume a situation in which an embattled minority listen to the prophet and embrace his vision of a return to Zion. Others whom he may address either cynically dismiss his message as mere illusion or perhaps even show themselves ready to discard their national identity and deity and assimilate to the surrounding culture.

9. *Awake, awake.* As the feminine second-person verbs make clear, this new discourse is an apostrophe to the arm of the LORD, which, as we have seen, means His militant power.
   Rahab, / . . . the Beast of the Sea. These names locate the "days of yore" in the primordial era before creation came about. The Creation myth invoked, at least for the expressive purposes of poetry, is Canaanite, although this prophet of the sixth century B.C.E. would have been several centuries removed from its active circulation. In the Canaanite myth, the weather god Baal, replaced in Hebrew poetry by YHWH, subdues a ferocious sea monster, variously called Rahab, Leviathan, Yamm, or Tanin (rendered here as "the Beast of the Sea") in order for creation to take place.

10. *Was it not You who dried up the sea.* This verse ostensibly continues the archaic Creation story (and "the sea" could also be understood as Yamm, one of the names of the Beast of the Sea). That impression is reinforced by the use of "the great deep," a designation that refers to the primordial abyss. But in the next line of poetry, that Creation myth merges, in an effect like cinematic *faux raccord,* with the drying up of the Sea of Reeds—"Who turned the sea's depths into a road / for the redeemed to go over."

the waters of the great deep,
  Who turned the sea's depths into a road
    for the redeemed to go over?
11 And the Lord's ransomed shall return
    and come to Zion with glad song,
  everlasting joy upon their heads,
    gladness and joy they shall attain,
      and sorrow and sighing shall flee.

12 I, I am He Who comforts you.
    What troubles you that you should fear man who dies
      and the son of man who is no more than grass,
13 and you forget the Lord your Maker,
    Who stretches out the heavens and founds the earth,
  and you are in constant fear, all day long,
    of the oppressor's wrath, as he aims to destroy?
      But where is the oppressor's wrath?
14 He who crouches shall quickly be freed,
    and shall not die in the Pit,
      and his bread shall not lack.
15 As for Me, the Lord your God,
    Who treads the sea and its waves roar,
      the Lord of Armies is His name.
16 I have put My word in your mouth

---

11. *And the Lord's ransomed shall return.* In a second doubling of imagery with a leap forward in time, the "Lord's ransomed" at the Sea of Reeds are turned into a precursor for the people of the prophet's own time who are about to be ransomed from captivity and led not between walls of water but over desert terrain in the return to Zion.

13. *the oppressor's wrath.* While many scholarly attempts have been made to identify a specific historical oppressor, it is prudent to read this as a generalized reference to the oppression of the Babylonian exile.

14. *He who crouches shall quickly be freed.* The translation of this verse is somewhat conjectural, and the meaning of the initial verb is especially doubtful. The general sense, however, of someone—surely the people of Israel—suffering subjugation who is now to be liberated seems clear.

15. *Who treads the sea.* The Masoretic Text has as the verb here *rogaʿ*, but despite the contention of some scholars that this means "stir up," it actually means the opposite, "to quiet" or "to be subdued," (compare the occurrence of precisely this phrase in Job 25:12). The present translation reads instead *roqaʿ*, "to tread or stomp."

and in the shadow of My hand have covered you,
  stretching out the heavens and founding the earth
  and saying to Zion, "You are My people."

Awake, awake,   17
  rise up, Jerusalem,
you who have drunk from the hand of the LORD
  the cup of His wrath,
the chalice of poison
  you drank to the dregs.
There is none to guide her   18
  of all the sons she bore,
and none to hold her hand
  of all the sons she raised.
Two did I call down upon you—   19
  who will grieve for you?—
wrack and ruin, famine and sword
  how can I comfort you?
Your children have tainted, are lying   20
  at the head of every street
    like an antelope in a net,
filled with the wrath of the LORD,
  the rebuke of your God.
Therefore, pray hear this, afflicted woman,   21
  drunk but not from wine.
Thus said your Master the LORD   22
  and your God Who contends for His people:
Look, I have taken from your hand

---

16. *stretching out the heavens.* The received text shows *linto'a*, "to plant," but this is surely
a mistake for *lintot*, "to stretch out."

17. *the chalice of poison.* The usual translation of the term *tar'eilah* is "reeling" or "staggering" but it is more plausibly related to *ra'al*, which definitely means "poison" in postbiblical
Hebrew, as it may also do in Zechariah 12:2. This understanding is supported by the fact
that the word for "wrath" in "the cup of His wrath" also means "venom." The Hebrew for
"chalice" is two words, literally, "the cup of the chalice," and some think "cup" is a gloss on
the rare word for chalice, *quba'at*, but joining two synonyms in a construct form is elsewhere a means to intensify or heighten the sense of the noun, and that may be the case here.

20. *like an antelope in a net.* The identity of the beast is uncertain.

the cup of poison,
    the chalice of My wrath.
You shall no longer drink from it,
23   and I will put it in the hand of your oppressors
    who said to you, "Bow, that we may walk over you."
        and you made your back like the ground,
            like a street for passersby.

CHAPTER 52

1   Awake, awake,
        don your strength, O Zion.
    Don the garments of your glory,
        O Jerusalem, holy city.
    For no longer shall they enter you,
        the uncircumcised
            and the unclean.
2   Shake yourself from the dust, arise,
        sit on your throne, O Jerusalem.
    Loose the bonds round your neck,
        captive Daughter of Zion.

---

22. *the cup of poison, / the chalice of My wrath.* In an elegant reversal of terms, "cup" is now linked with "poison" and "chalice" with "My wrath," whereas in verse 17 it is the other way around.

23. *and you made your back like the ground, / like a street for passersby.* The second and third verset of this line vividly illustrate the impulse in biblical poetry to concretize semantic material introduced in the first verset as the line unfolds: first the oppressors command their victors to prostrate themselves so that they can step on them; then we get the concrete—and painful—image of the backs of the victims turned into a roadway upon which passersby tread.

CHAPTER 52   1. *Awake, awake.* This unit of text includes two prophecies, this one at the beginning and another near the end, that begin with a twice-repeated imperative verb in the second-person feminine singular addressed to Zion (the other is "Turn aside, turn aside," verse 11ff.). The repetitions are dictated by a powerful impulse of exhortation: Zion, long sunk in the dust and plunged in captivity, is urged to forget her sorrows and bestir herself to embrace her triumphant restoration.

2. *sit on your throne.* The Masoretic Text says only "Sit, O Jerusalem." The transition follows the Targum, which adds "on your throne," two Hebrew words that in all likelihood were dropped in a scribal error.

For thus said the LORD: For nothing were you sold and for no silver shall 3
you be redeemed. For thus said the Master LORD: To Egypt My people at 4
first went down to sojourn there, and then Assyria oppressed them for
no payment. And now, what do I have here, says the LORD, for My people 5
was taken for nothing. Those who ruled them howled, said the LORD, and
constantly all day long was My name reviled. Therefore shall My people 6
know My name. Therefore shall they know on that day that it is I Who
speak to them.

> How lovely on the mountains   7
>> the steps of the bearer of good tidings,
> announcing peace, heralding good things,
>> announcing triumph,
>>> saying to Zion: Your God reigns.
> Hark! Your watchmen raise their voice,   8
>> together they sing gladly.
> For with their very eyes they shall see
>> when the LORD comes back to Zion.
> Burst out in song, sing gladly together,   9
>> O ruins of Jerusalem,
> for the LORD has comforted His people,
>> He has redeemed Jerusalem.

---

3. *For nothing were you sold.* You were sold into slavery (this is the verb generally used for enslavement), but nobody paid a price for you—your captors simply took you into slavery. Enslavement here amounts to a hyperbole because the exiled Judahites were not necessarily enslaved, or, in any case, surely not all of them.

4. *To Egypt . . . then Assyria.* There is, then, a history of being subject to slavery that goes back to the beginnings of the nation: first Egypt, then Assyria (which "enslaved" the northern kingdom), and now Babylonia.

5. *howled.* The Hebrew verb suggests a kind of derisive yelp.

6. *shall they know on that day.* The repetition of the verb "know" either has been scribally omitted or is meant to be implied.

7. *How lovely on the mountains / the steps of the bearer of good tidings.* The poet makes a boldly poignant choice in using "lovely," the same word that is attached to the beautiful features of the beloved in the Song of Songs, for this is surprising in a reference to the feet of a messenger. The focus on the feet is because the messenger is running across the mountains to bring the good tidings.

8. *Your watchmen.* This probably continues the idea of the preceding verse—the watchmen, no doubt stationed on towers, see from afar the approach of the bearer of good tidings.

10   The LORD had bared His holy arm
            to the eyes of all the nations,
        and all the ends of the earth have seen
            the triumph of our God.

11   Turn aside, turn aside, come out from there,
            no unclean thing do touch.
        Come out from its midst,
            bearers of the LORD's vessels.
12   For not in haste shall you come out,
            nor in flight shall you go,
        for the LORD goes before you,
            and your rearguard is Israel's God.

13   Look, My servant shall prosper,
            be lofty, exalted, and very high.
14   As many were appalled by him,
            so marred beyond human his looks
                and his features unlike humankind's,
15   so he shall astound many nations,

---

10. *and all the ends of the earth have seen / the triumph of our God.* As before, the return to Zion is imagined as an event enacted in a global theater, the restoration of an exiled people to its land being, at least as the prophet sees it, an unprecedented historical event that manifests God's power.

11. *come out from there.* "There" has to be the condition of exile.

12. *for the LORD goes before you, / and your rearguard is Israel's God.* This is a purposeful paradox: as you march back to Zion, God both leads the way as vanguard and protects you from behind as rearguard.

14. *so marred beyond human his looks / and his features unlike humankind's.* This whole line vividly demonstrates the power of personification and hyperbole. Collective Israel is imagined as a person. In point of historical fact, the exiles, undergoing a fate that was by no means unprecedented, would scarcely have been perceived as having lost their humanity. In the poetic hyperbole, personified Israel, deprived of sovereignty, homeland, and place of worship, is envisaged as someone so degraded, humiliated, and abused by his condition in history that those who see him are appalled and can scarcely recognize a human form in this disfigured person.

15. *he shall astound many nations.* This is another instance in which the verb is anomalous, and so the translation is based on context.

kings shall seal their lips because of him,
for what was never told them they shall see,
and what they never heard they shall behold.

CHAPTER 53

Who could believe what we heard,   1
and to whom was the LORD's arm revealed?
He sprung up like a shoot before Him   2
and like a root from parched land.
He had no features nor decent appearance—
we saw nothing in his looks that we might desire.
Despised and shunned by people,   3
a man of sorrows and visited by illness.
And like one from whom the gaze is averted,
despised, and we reckoned him naught.

---

kings shall seal their lips. The literal sense of the Hebrew is "kings shall purse their mouths closed."

CHAPTER 53   2. *He sprung up like a shoot before Him.* This crucial prophecy carries over the representation of the Servant of the LORD in the third person that began with the last three verses of the previous chapter. Earlier, the Servant spoke of himself in the first person.

like a root from parched land. The objection that roots don't grow in parched land fails to see the context of the poetry. The point is that the Servant managed to flourish and carry out his prophetic mission in the most unpromising circumstances, addressing a hostile audience in the bleak condition of exile.

3. *Despised and shunned by people, / a man of sorrows and visited by illness.* Famously, these words and what follows were embraced by Christian interpreters from the formative period of Christianity onward as a prophecy of the Passion narrative and the Crucifixion. The emphasis on the Servant's bearing the sins of the people and becoming a kind of sacrificial lamb seemed especially relevant to the idea of Christ's dying for the sins of humankind. Illness, however, is not part of the story of Jesus. Virtually no serious scholars today see this as a prediction of the Passion, but it certainly provided a theological template for interpreting the death of Jesus. Debate persists about the identity of the Servant. A recurrent Jewish view sees him as a representation of collective Israel, but the details of the passage argue for the biography of an individual, and already in the Middle Ages Abraham ibn Ezra proposed that the Servant was the prophet himself. The speaker, then, would be one of the prophet's disciples, as Blenkinsopp suggests, eulogizing him after his death (see verse 8) on behalf of himself but also of a group of disciples (the "we" that is invoked here).

4   Indeed, he has borne our illness,
           and our sorrows he has carried.
       But we had reckoned him plagued,
           God-stricken and tormented.
5   Yet he was wounded for our crimes,
           crushed for our transgressions.
       The chastisement that restored our well-being he bore,
           and through his bruising we were healed.
6   All of us strayed like sheep,
           each turned to his own way,
       and the Lord brought down upon him
           the crimes of all of us.
7   Afflicted and tormented,
           he opened not his mouth.
       Like a lamb led to the slaughter
           and like an ewe mute before her shearers
               he opened not his mouth.
8   By oppressive judgment he was taken off,
           and who can speak of where he lives?
       For he was cut off from the land of the living
           for My people's crime, bearing their blight.
9   And his grave was put with the wicked,

---

6. *and the Lord brought down upon him / the crimes of all of us.* This reiterated idea, which later would nourish the central Christian story, is the solution to a psychological dilemma on the part of the speaker. He sees the Servant as a devoted and true prophet of God, yet the Servant has suffered unspeakably—plagued with illness, somehow physically disfigured, reviled and rejected by society, and finally condemned to an early death. The explanation for all this unwarranted suffering is that the Servant has acted as a surrogate for the people, taken upon himself the burden of the people's crimes. Thus, in a culture in which misfortune and sickness were usually seen as manifestations of divine punishment for wrongdoing (the view of Job's comforters), the wrongdoing is transferred to the people, and the righteousness of the prophet is actually confirmed by his suffering.

8. *By oppressive judgment he was taken off.* Textual obscurities begin to proliferate. "By oppressive judgment" is a somewhat conjectural translation, although "was taken off" probably refers to death. The translation of the second verse of this line is also by no means certain.
    bearing their blight. The literal sense of the Hebrew is "a blight for them," and "bearing" has been added as an interpretive guess.

and with evildoers his death,
for no outrage he had done
and no deceit in his mouth.
And the LORD desired to crush him, make him ill.   10
Would he lay down a guilt offering,
he would see his seed, have length of days,
and the LORD's desire would prosper through him,
from his toil he would see light,   11
be sated in his mind.
My servant shall put the righteous in the right for many,
and their crimes he shall bear.
Therefore I will give him shares among the many,   12
and with the mighty he shall share out spoils,
for he laid himself bare to death
and was counted among the wrongdoers,
and it is he who bore the offense of many
and interceded for the wrongdoers.

---

9. *and with evildoers his death.* The received text has "and with a rich man" (*'ashir*), which makes no sense either thematically or as a poetic parallelism. The translation is based on an emendation to *'osey ra'*. The word for "death" is an odd-looking plural form, but a proposed emendation from *bemotow* to *bamotow* is dubious because there is scant evidence that the latter term ever means "sepulchers," as scholars have claimed. In any case, the point of the line is that he was given a disgraceful burial.

10. *Would he lay down a guilt offering.* Again, the Hebrew is crabbed and the translation conjectural. It is also puzzling that after the Servant has been reported dead and buried, and a surrogate for Israel's sins, this conditional possibility of a long and happy life should be offered. Could this verse be a textual intrusion?

11. *see light.* There is no "light" in the Masoretic Text, but it appears both in the Qumran Isaiah and in the Septuagint.
be sated in his mind. The meaning of the two Hebrew words here is obscure.
My servant. The perspective now shifts, and it is God, not the disciple, who is speaking, but the idea that the Servant has borne the sins of the many is continued.

12. *Therefore I will give him shares among the many.* This is another somewhat perplexing declaration because the Servant is dead, and "he laid himself bare to death" appears to be a reiteration of that fact. Perhaps the reference is to a posthumous restoration of his reputation and to a posthumous acceptance of his prophecy by the many, though it is just conceivable that the words refer to reward in the afterlife. That was not an available alternative in previous biblical literature, but the beginnings of such an idea might be emerging at this late moment, as the polemic against it in Job and Qohelet appears to attest.

CHAPTER 54

1 Sing gladly, O barren one who has not given birth,
    burst out in glad song, exult, who has not been in labor,
 for the desolate one's children number more
    than the children of the one with a husband.

2 Spread wide the place of your tent,
    and let the curtains of your dwelling stretch out—
      do not stint.
 Lengthen your cords
    and strengthen your tent pegs.

3 For to the north and the south you shall burst forth,
    and your seed shall take hold of nations
      and shall settle desolate towns.

4 Do not fear, for you shall not be shamed,
    and you shall not be disgraced, for you shall not be dishonored.
 For the shame of your youth you shall forget,
    and the dishonor of your widowhood you shall no longer recall.

5 For he who takes you to bed is your Maker,
    the LORD of Armies is His name,
 and your redeemer is Israel's Holy One,

CHAPTER 54   1. *Sing gladly.* Although the natural association of song and joy is virtually idiomatic in biblical poetry, this prophet's repeated emphasis on song implicitly points to his own use of the medium of poetry to conjure up a joyous vision of the people restored to its land.

the one with a husband. The passive form *beʿulah* designates a woman who has a husband, *baʿal*, but it also has a sexual connotation because the active verb showing this root means "to cohabit," "to possess sexually." Thus, the *beʿulah* is the woman who has a bedmate, unlike "the desolate one." Compare verse 5, where the active verbal form *boʿalayikh* is translated as "he who takes you to bed."

2. *your tent.* While the actual habitations would of course have been stone houses, poetry, with its intrinsic attachment to archaic language, invokes the tent as the archetypal dwelling.

4. *the shame of your youth . . . / the dishonor of your widowhood.* As is often the case in biblical poetry, there is an implied temporal progression from the first verset to the second. First, Israel was a young bride who shamefully betrayed her husband. As a result, the bitter fate of widowhood was inflicted on her (God was "dead" to Israel), a condition that in this society was a humiliation because the woman was left without the sustaining support of the husband.

5. *he who takes you to bed . . . / your redeemer.* The widow again has a husband, who provides the "desolate one" with the gratification a woman needs. The parallel term "redeemer" is

God of all the earth He is called.
"For as a forsaken woman   6
   and pained in spirit the LORD called you
and a wife of one's youth who is spurned,"
   said your God.
"In a brief moment I forsook you   7
   but with great compassion will I gather you in.
In surge of fury I hid My face from you,   8
   but with everlasting kindness I have compassion for you,"
     said your redeemer, the LORD.
"For as Noah's waters is this to Me,   9
   as I vowed not to let Noah's waters go over the earth again,
so have I vowed
   not to be furious with you nor to rebuke you.
For though the mountains move   10
   and the hills totter,
My kindness shall not move from you
   nor My pact of peace totter,"
     said He Who has compassion for you, the LORD.

Afflicted, storm-tossed woman, uncomforted,   11
   I am about to lay your stones with turquoise.
And I will set your foundations with sapphires
   and make your battlements rubies   12
and your gates of beryl

---

used here less in a theological sense than in a social one—the "redeemer," *go'el*, is the man who marries the widow, thus redeeming her from her condition of abandonment. The Book of Ruth uses *go'el* precisely in this sense.

8. *with everlasting kindness.* The Hebrew noun *ḥesed* is a nexus of several related meanings. It can mean "kindness" or, as some render it, "love" (and the King James Version joins the two with "loving kindness"). It also suggests the "loyalty" or "faithfulness" of one party to another in a covenantal or conjugal relationship, and that sense is also obviously in play here. The connotation of "faithfulness" may be especially strong when "kindness" is used again in verse 10.

11. *I am about to lay your stones with turquoise.* Although this new prophecy begins with "Afflicted, storm-tossed woman," the focus of the vision of national restoration now shifts from the widowed and/or childless wife to the buildings of the city. The resplendent restored Jerusalem is to be built not out of stones but with precious jewels. The reader should be alerted that the precise identification of most of these precious stones, as elsewhere in the Bible, is uncertain. The dazzling bejeweled Jerusalem is obviously a poetic hyperbole, but it lays the ground for eschatological imaginings of Jerusalem as the glorious City of God.

and all your walls of precious stones.

13 And all your children—disciples of the LORD,
      and great the well-being of your children.

14 In righteousness shall you be firm-founded.
      Keep far from oppression that you need not fear
          and from terror that it not draw near you.

15 Why, none shall strike fear if it is not from Me,
      who would strike fear in you, before you shall fail.

16 Why, it is I Who created the smith,
      who fans the charcoal fire
    and makes the weapons for his deeds—
      but it is I Who created the Destroyer to wreak havoc.

17 Any weapon fashioned against you shall fail,
      any tongue that contends with you in court you shall show wrong.
    This is the estate of the LORD's servants,
      and their triumph through Me, says the LORD.

CHAPTER 55

1 Oh, every one who thirsts go to the water,
      and who has no silver,
          buy food and eat.
    Go and buy food without silver

---

15. *none shall strike fear if it is not from Me.* The Hebrew syntax is ambiguous, and the verb *gor* is anomalous, though it probably is related to the more familiar noun, *magor,* "terror," as this translation assumes.

16. *the weapons.* The all-purpose *keli* can also mean vessel, tool, or gear, but it is used in the very next verse in the sense of "weapon," and that is probably what it means here as well.

   the Destroyer to wreak havoc. The "Destroyer" would be the mythological agent who stalks through the land of Egypt in the terrible tenth plague, killing the firstborn. The intended relation of this verset to the preceding one is oppositional: man—himself created by God—forges his weapons in the workshop of the metalsmith, but God has the power to create a Destroyer who has an incomparably more devastating instrument of destruction. The image of God defending Israel with insuperable force complements the image of the jewel-studded Zion that precedes it: God promises to rebuild Jerusalem as a city of supernal splendor, and He then guarantees that no enemy will be able to assail the city.

CHAPTER 55   1. *Go and buy food without silver.* The water, food, milk, and wine are all metaphorical. What the metaphors suggest is that God's beneficence to His people will be unstinting and freely given with no price exacted for it. The Hebrew *kesef* is translated as "silver," not "money" as in other versions, because coins were not yet in general usage,

and at no cost, wine and milk.
Why should you weigh out silver for what is not bread   2
    and your substance for what does not sate?
Listen well to Me and eat goodly things,
    and you shall enjoy lavish fare.
Bend your ear and come to Me,   3
    listen and be revived,
and I will make with you a perpetual pact,
    the faithful kindness shown to David.
Look, I made him witness to the peoples,   4
    prince and commander of the peoples.
Look, to a nation you knew not you shall call,   5
    and a nation that did not know you shall run to you,
for the sake of the LORD your God
    and Israel's Holy One, for He made you glorious.
Seek the LORD where He is found,   6
    call to Him where He is near.
Let the wicked forsake his way   7
    and a wrongdoing man his devisings
and turn back to the LORD, and He will show mercy to him;
    and to his God, for He abundantly pardons.

---

and the use of the verb "weigh out" for "silver" in the next verse clearly indicates that what is imagined is silver weights. There is some question about the relation of this chapter to the fifteen preceding chapters of Second Isaiah. Joseph Blenkinsopp thinks that it is by a different hand and that it is intended as a bridge to the rest of the book, which, at least according to scholarly consensus, is the work of still another prophet. The evidence, however, is somewhat tenuous: the supposed stylistic differences of this chapter from the earlier ones are by no means clear-cut, and the claimed affinities with the Book of Proverbs are debatable.

3. *the faithful kindness shown to David.* The Hebrew says merely "the faithful kindness of David," but the clear sense is the faithful kindness, or staunch commitment to the divine promise, that God has shown to David. The poet is not necessarily speaking of a revival of the Davidic dynasty but is invoking God's commitment to David and his descendants as a model for how He remains committed to His exiled people.

4. *witness to the peoples, / prince and commander of the peoples.* This would have to be a reference to David's military dominance, his success in establishing a mini-empire (which biblical writers tend to exaggerate). As David was once a triumphant leader of the nation, Israel will again be triumphant. That notion is perfectly in keeping with the previous prophecies of a restored Israel to which kings and princes will be subservient. This idea is continued in the next verse, where nations from afar run to do Israel's bidding.

6. *Seek the LORD where He is found.* That is, you may have imagined that God was distant, hiding His face from you, but He is there close by, if only you seek Him.

8   For My devisings are not your devisings
            and your ways are not My ways,
                says the LORD.
9   For as the heavens are high over earth,
            so My ways are high over your ways
                and My devisings over your devisings.
10   For as the rain comes down upon earth
            and the snow from the heavens,
        and there it does not return
            but waters the earth
        and brings forth growing things
            and gives seed for the sower and bread to eat,
11   so is My word that comes out of My mouth,
            it does not return empty to Me
        but does what I desire,
            and makes prosper what I have sent.
12   For in joy shall you go out,
            and in peace you shall be led.
        The mountains and hills shall burst forth in glad song before you,
            and all the trees of the field shall clap their hands.
13   Instead of the thornbush a cypress shall grow.
            Instead of the nettle a myrtle shall grow.
        And it shall be a testimony for the LORD,
            a perpetual sign that shall not be cut off.

---

10. *For as the rain comes down upon earth / and the snow from the heavens.* The metaphor elaborated in this verse and then carried on to its referent in the next implies two ideas at once: just as the rain and snow cannot be turned back to the sky from which they come, God's pronouncements, once issued, cannot be reversed; but the rain and the snow fructify the earth, irrigating it so that it can yield life-sustaining produce, and in this prophecy of restoration, the word God issues is a word of bountifulness, with an effect like the rains of blessing, making things "prosper."

12. *For in joy shall you go out.* The going out clearly refers to going out from exile. This entire verse, with the mountains and hills bursting forth in song, as well as the initial poetic line of the next verse, is quite in keeping with earlier prophecies by Second Isaiah of a jubilant return to Zion.

13. *a testimony for the LORD.* The literal meaning of the noun used here is "name." The idea is that Israel's grand restoration will be a visible manifestation to all the nations of God's power and His loyalty to Israel.

   a perpetual sign that shall not be cut off. Once the people of Israel is again firmly established in Zion, there will be no further threats to the well-being of the nation, and this very continuity will bear lasting witness to God's greatness.

CHAPTER 56

Thus said the Lord: 1
Keep justice and do righteousness,
    for My rescue is soon to come
      and My triumph to be revealed.
Happy the man who does this   2
    and the son of man who holds fast to it,
keeping the sabbath, not profaning it
    and keeping his hand from doing all evil.
And let not the foreigner say,   3
    who joins the Lord, saying,
"The Lord has kept me apart from His people,"
    nor let the eunuch say, "Why, I am a withered tree."

CHAPTER 56   1. *Keep justice and do righteousness.* This moral exhortation, coupled with the urging to observe the sabbath in the next verse, strikes a new note in the Isaiah collection, one that some commentators have characterized as "sermonic." It is the strong consensus of biblical scholarship, with only a few dissenters, that Isaiah 56–66 is a later composition than Isaiah 40–55, and almost certainly the work of more than one prophet. The frequent allusions to the imminent Persian conquest of Babylonia in chapters 40–55 enable us to date it, or at least much of it, to the time just before the conquest in 539 B.C.E. The situation presupposed in chapters 56–66 is of the exiles already returned to their homeland—there are no further prophecies of the people triumphantly crossing the desert to Zion, and the issues engaged are the behavior of the people in their land and the nature of the community they constitute. The probable period for these prophecies is the early decades of the fifth century B.C.E., before the arrival from Babylonia of Ezra and Nehemiah in the middle of the century. Those responsible for these texts appear to have been familiar with Second Isaiah, but the often asserted claim that they were his disciples seems a little off the mark because they were separated from him by at least two generations.

3. *And let not the foreigner say.* This is another new note. There were foreigners living in the province of Judah, whether people who had settled there after the Babylonian conquest in 586 B.C.E. or those who may have been drawn to accompany the returning exiles from Mesopotamia. Some of these were attracted to the faith of the Judahites, and the prophet argues that such people should be freely admitted to the ranks of Israel. (At this point in time, there was nothing like a formal conversion ceremony.)

nor let the eunuch say, "Why, I am a withered tree." This declaration extends the prophet's program of inclusion. Eunuchs and men otherwise sexually maimed were prohibited from participation in the Temple cult. One therefore may infer that the "joining" the Lord envisaged here is not limited to the cultic (though sacrifices are mentioned in verse 7) but involves entering a community of observance—in particular, observance of the sabbath. The eunuch can produce no biological offspring, but in adhering to the covenant, he becomes part of a community vouchsafed the covenantal promise of a destiny to be as multitudinous as the stars in the sky and the grains of sand on the shore. This notion is spelled out in verse 5, "I will give them in My house and within my walls / a marker and a

4   For thus said the LORD:
         Of the eunuchs who keep My sabbath,
     and choose what I desire
         and hold fast to My covenant,
5   I will give them in My house and within My walls
         a marker and a name better than sons and daughters,
             an everlasting name will I give them that shall not be cut off.
6   And the foreigners who join the LORD
         to serve Him and to love the LORD's name,
             to become servants to Him,
     all who keep the sabbath, not profaning it
         and hold fast to My covenant,
7   I will bring them to My holy mountain
         and give them joy in My house of prayer.
     Their burnt offerings and sacrifices
         shall be welcome on My altar.
     For My house a house of prayer
         shall be called for all the peoples.
8   Thus said the Master the LORD,
         Who gathers Israel's dispersed:
             Still more will I gather for him besides those gathered.

9   All beasts of the field, come to devour,
         all beasts of the forest.

---

name better than sons and daughters." Offspring means permanence; here permanence is
being part of the covenanted people.

7. *For My house a house of prayer / shall be called for all the peoples.* Solomon's dedication
of the First Temple also emphasized prayer, but the designation here of the new Temple
as a house of prayer is noteworthy. The phrase "for all the peoples" reflects a universalist
perspective, but what it means in the context of foreigners joining the LORD is that God's
house becomes the house of prayer for all people when they embrace His laws.

8. *Still more will I gather for him.* Either this whole verse is a fragment, predicting another
wave of returned exiles and hence unconnected with what has preceded, or the clause refers
to the foreigners and eunuchs who are added to the community of Israel.

9. *All beasts of the field, come to devour.* These words mark the beginning of a new prophecy, one of castigation. It is usually assumed that the devouring beasts are a metaphorical
representation of Israel's enemies.

His watchmen are all of them blind,   10
    they do not know.
All of them are mute dogs
    who know not how to bark.
Dazed, they lie about,
    lovers of slumber.
But the dogs are fierce in appetite,   11
    they are never sated,
and they are the shepherds
    who know not understanding.
They all turn to their own ways,
    to their own gain, each and all.
"Come, let me take wine,   12
    and let us swill strong drink.
And it will be like this tomorrow,
    even still more than this."

---

10. *His watchmen are all of them blind.* The watchmen are the leaders of the people or, more specifically, its (false) prophets. The motif of the blind leadership is picked up from Second Isaiah.

    mute dogs. "Dogs" in biblical language is always a term of opprobrium—truly insulting for leaders or prophets. The muteness refers to their failure to rebuke the people as they should have done. There is scant evidence that watchdogs were used in ancient Israel; most of the biblical references to dogs conceive them as feral scavengers, not domesticated animals.

    Dazed. The verb *hozim* appears only here. In later Hebrew, based on an unlikely understanding of the meaning here, it suggests something like "to hallucinate" or "to entertain idle visions." Blenkinsopp proposes a possible pun on *ḥozim*, "to see visions."

11. *they are the shepherds.* Throughout the Bible and elsewhere in ancient Near Eastern literature, "shepherd" is a stock metaphor for "ruler."

12. *Come, let me take wine, / and let us swill strong drink.* The evocation of drunken leaders may allude to chapter 28. The word for "come" is an Aramaicizing usage that reflects the relatively late period of this text. In poetic parallelism, the more common term, *yayin*, "wine," always occurs in the first verset and *sheikhar*, "strong drink," in the second. But since *sheikhar*—in all likelihood, grappa—has a higher alcohol content, this order also follows the principle of intensification of parallel terms from the first verset to the second.

CHAPTER 57

1   The righteous one perishes,
        and no man takes it to heart,
    and loyal men are taken off
        with no one noticing,
            for through evil the righteous is taken off.
2   Yet he shall come in peace,—
        they shall rest on their couches—
            who walks straight before him.

3   As for you, draw near,
        sons of the sorcerer,
            seed of an adulterer and a whore.
4   Over whom are you gleeful,
        over whom do you gape with your mouth
            and stick out your tongue?
    Are you not children of crime,
        seed of lies?
5   Who go into heat over gods
        under every lush tree,
    slaughtering children in wadis

CHAPTER 57   1. *taken off.* More literally, "gathered," in all probability a euphemism
for dying, perhaps an elliptical form of the idiom "gathered to his fathers."

2. *they shall rest on their couches.* The Hebrew switches from singular to plural and then
back to singular (hence the bracketing off of this clause with dashes in the translation).
These words became part of the Jewish prayer for the dead.

3. *seed of an adulterer and a whore.* This verse, set in conjunction with verses 5–9, makes
a double use of sexual promiscuity. The prophet seems to assume that dabbling in pagan
magical rites is associated with violating the constraints of sexual morality, perhaps because
orgiastic rites are practiced. At the same time, promiscuity, as elsewhere in the Bible, is a
metaphor for abandoning YHWH, Israel's true husband, for dalliance with foreign gods.
For "a whore," the Masoretic Text shows a verb "and she went whoring," but several ancient
versions reflect the noun, *zonah.*

5. *Who go into heat over gods / under every lush tree.* See the previous comment on the
double use of sexuality. The phrase "under every lush tree" occurs in Jeremiah and elsewhere to indicate abandonment to paganism, and what may be in view here is the practice
of fertility cults under sacred trees.
    slaughtering children in wadis. The inveighing against child sacrifice, which began to
be widespread in the eighth century B.C.E., picks up the purely metaphorical aspect of the
language of sexual promiscuity just introduced.

under crevices in the rocks.
Your share is in the stones of the wadi,   6
   it is they that are your portion.
Even to them you poured libation,
   offered up grain offerings.
     Over these should I relent?
On a high and lofty mountain   7
   you put out your couch.
Even there you went up
   to offer sacrifice.
Behind the door and doorpost   8
   you have put your mark.
For away from Me you bared yourself,
   climbed up, made room on your couch.
And you sealed a pact with them,
   you loved bedding down with them,
     lust did you behold.
And you gave gifts of oil to Molech,   9
   and profusely put on your perfume,

---

6. *Your share is in the stones of the wadi.* Although the meaning is not certain, this may refer to sacred steles, *matseivot*, made of piles of stones. The wadis are where the abomination of child sacrifice is performed. It should be noted that throughout this passage, "you" is feminine singular: the female personification of the people, which also accords with the motif of sexual betrayal.

8. *you have put your mark.* The noun usually means "memorial." It would appear to be some sort of ritual marker of pagan worship, analogous to the words of Torah to be affixed to the doorpost according to the injunction in Deuteronomy.
   away from Me. The sense of the Hebrew preposition is not certain.
   climbed up, made room on your couch. "Climbing up" is the verb used in biblical idiom for getting into bed. The adulterous Israel is getting into bed with alien gods.
   lust did you behold. The Hebrew appears to say "a hand did you behold." Blenkinsopp's claim that *yad,* "hand," means "penis" is dubious: he cites two purported proof texts, Isaiah 56:5, where *yad* clearly means "memorial" or "marker," and Song of Songs 5:4–5, where *yad* clearly means "hand." This translation follows the proposal of the New Jewish Publication Society version that relates *yad* here to the verbal stem *y-d-d,* which means "to love." But this verset is metrically defective, having only two accents, so one suspects that there was originally a longer word here derived from *y-d-d* that a scribe contracted to *yad* either because he was unfamiliar with an unusual term or because of prudery.

9. *gave gifts.* The Hebrew *tashuri* ordinarily means "to espy," but that makes no sense here. This translation links it with the noun *teshurah,* "gift."
   Molech. The Masoretic Text shows *melekh,* "king," but the original text almost certainly read "Molech," the pagan deity to whom children were sacrificed.

and sent your envoys far off,
 as far down as Sheol.
10 On all your ways you wore yourself out,
 yet you never said, "I give up."
You found your own vigor
 and so you did not weaken.
11 Whom did you dread and fear
 that you should lie,
and Me you did not recall,
 you paid no heed?
Did I not keep silent and avert My gaze,
 yet Me you did not fear?
12 I will tell of your "triumph"
 and of your deeds,
  and they shall not avail for you.
13 When you cry out, let those gathered round you save you.
 But all of them the wind shall bear off,
  a mere breath take them away.
But who shelters in Me shall inherit the land
 and take hold of My holy mountain.

14 And He said, Build up, build up, clear a road,
 take away stumbling blocks from My people's road.

---

as far down as Sheol. The reference to the netherworld may be more than a hyperbole for great distances because it could refer to the worship of Mot, the Canaanite god of death.

13. *let those gathered round you save you.* This is another ambiguous reference. "Those gathered round" could mean the gods that the paganizing Israelites have collected, or it could refer to the adherents of the pagan cult. In all this, the denunciation of paganism in the Judahite community is a very different theme from what one finds in Isaiah 40–55. The aim of this later prophet is to purge the community of its wayward elements. A sharp division in the Judahites community is envisioned: those who have exerted themselves to go after strange gods (verses 9–10) will be borne off by the wind, while those who have been steadfast in their loyalty to YHWH will "inherit the land," which is to say, they will be the legitimate possessors of the Persian province of Yehud, now restored to the people of Israel.

14. *And He said.* Since the Hebrew of course has no capital letters, the verb here could refer to God, or it might be the prophet who is speaking.
 build up, clear a road. In Second Isaiah, the road or highway is a thoroughfare through the desert on which the exiles will pass on the way back to their land. It looks as though this later prophet, clearly familiar with both Isaiah and Second Isaiah, has picked up this image and turned it into a metaphor—as "road" or "way" often is used in the Bible—for the

For thus said the lofty and high One,   15
    Who dwells forever and holy His name:
Lofty and holy do I dwell
    and with him who is crushed and lowly in spirit,
to revive the spirit of the lowly
    and to revive the heart of those crushed.
For not for all times will I quarrel   16
    nor forever will I rage.
Though a spirit grows faint before Me,
    the life-breath—it is I Who made it.
For their crime of greed I raged   17
    and I struck them, hiding as I raged,
        and they went astray in the way of their heart.
Their ways will I see and heal them,   18
    will guide them and grant comfort to them and their mourners.
Creator of fruit of the lips,   19
    "Peace, peace, to the far and the near!"
        said the LORD, "And I will heal them."
But the wicked are like a roiled sea,   20
    for it cannot be still,
        and its waters roil with mud and muck.

"There is no peace," said my God, "for the wicked."   21

---

right way before God. The "stumbling block" would thus be the sort of scandalous behavior that has just been scathingly denounced.

15. *crushed.* Most translations render this as "contrite," but the Hebrew *daka'* is in the first instance a physical term: the condition of being pushed down.

16. *the life-breath—it is I Who made it.* The proposed understanding of this verse is as follows: a spirit may be on the point of failing, but I, God, as the Creator of all spirits, will show compassion and revive it.

19. *fruit of the lips.* This appears to be a kenning for "speech," though it does not occur elsewhere. The idea is that God, the Creator of the faculty of speech, has the power to pronounce these healing words of peace.

20. *But the wicked are like a roiled sea.* The prophet continues his notion of a radical split in the people between the faithful and the derelict. This divide has an incipiently sectarian look, preparing the way for the Book of Daniel and the Qumran texts.

21. *There is no peace.* This verse does not scan as a line of poetry and could be a kind of epilogue to the prophecy added editorially.

CHAPTER 58

1   Call out with full throat, do not stint,
         raise your voice like a ram's horn,
     and tell to My people its crime,
         and to the house of Jacob their offense.
2   And Me day by day let them seek,
         let them desire the knowledge of My ways
     like a nation that does what is right
         and its God's rule it does not forsake.
     Let them ask of Me rules of righteousness,
         God's closeness let them desire.
3   "Why did we fast and You did not see?
         We afflicted ourselves and You took no note?"
     In your fast-day you found pleasure
         while all your affairs you pursued?
4   For quarrel and strife you fasted
         and to strike with a wicked fist?

CHAPTER 58   1. *Call out with full throat.* This injunction is directed to the prophet, and what follows is the content of his clarion call.

2. *let them seek.* Verb tenses and verbal modes in biblical poetry are notoriously ambiguous. Many interpreters understand the verbs in this verse as present tense, but since what is stated contradicts the preceding proclamation of Israel's "crime" and "offense," translations based on this understanding have to preface the verse with "yet" or "to be sure," for which there is no warrant in the Hebrew. It makes better sense to construe all the verbs in this verse as cohortatives: would that they would seek God and the knowledge of His ways, in contrast to what they are actually doing.

3. *Why did we fast and You did not see?* Communal fasts were instituted in times of crisis—for example, during a famine or a plague—as one can see in Psalm 90. Members of the community not only refrained from eating but also adopted mourning practices such as the wearing of sackcloth and sprinkling ashes on the head. The underlying idea was that such practices of mortification would engage the compassion of the deity, and the disaster would end.

afflicted ourselves. This idiom, '*inuy nefesh,* is a synonym for fasting, and in rabbinic Hebrew the first of these two words would generate another noun for "fast," *ta'anit.*

In your fast-day you found pleasure / while all your affairs you pursued. The consideration of sincere versus hypocritical fasting led to the apt selection of this chapter to be chanted in the morning service for Yom Kippur, the great fast-day.

4. *to strike with a wicked fist.* The inveighing here and in the lines that follow against social injustice may reflect, as some scholars contend, the dire state of Judahite society in the early decades of the fifth century B.C.E., but it is difficult to link any of this to specific historical

Your fasting this day
>will not make your voice heard on high.
Will like this be the fast that I choose,   5
>the day a man afflicts himself,
to bow his head like a reed
>and bed down in sackcloth and ash?
Is it this that you call a fast,
>and a day pleasing to the LORD?
Is not this the fast that I choose—   6
>to unlock the shackles of wickedness,
>>and loosen the bonds of the yoke,
to set the downtrodden free—
>and to break every yoke?
Yes, to offer your bread to the hungry,   7
>and bring the wretched poor into your house.
When you see someone naked, you should clothe him,
>and your own flesh do not ignore.
Then shall your light break forth like the dawn   8
>and your healing quickly spring up.
And your vindication shall march before you,
>the LORD's glory shall be your rearguard.
Then shall you call and the LORD shall answer,   9
>cry out, and He shall say, "Here I am."
If you remove the yoke from your midst,
>the mocking finger and vicious speech.

---

circumstances. Exploitation of the poor, after all, and indifference to suffering are prevalent enough in virtually all societies, including affluent twenty-first-century America. That is precisely what imparts a sense of timeless relevance to this prophecy.

5. *afflicts himself.* A more idiomatic rendering would be "mortifies himself," although that, unfortunately, is rhythmically ponderous.

6. *the downtrodden.* The Hebrew *retsutsim* is usually translated as "oppressed," but the term requires a more physical English equivalent because the literal sense of the Hebrew is "smashed," "shattered."

7. *your own flesh.* The sense is "your fellow human being," who shares your condition as a creature of flesh and blood.

9. *Then shall you call.* The obvious antithesis is to the fasting supplicant who goes through the motions of prayer and calls to God while ignoring injustice.
   the mocking finger. The literal meaning is "extending of the finger." This idiom is not attested elsewhere, and so the translation is based on the context.

10   And you proffer your bread to the hungry,
         and sate the appetite of the afflicted.
       Then your light shall dawn in the dark,
         and your gloom shall be like the noon.

11   And the LORD shall guide you always
         and sate your appetite in arid land,
       and your bones He shall strengthen,
         and you shall be like a well-moistened garden
       and like a water source
         whose waters do not fail.

12   And from among you they shall rebuild the ancient ruins,
         foundations laid in times past you shall raise.
       And you shall be called repairer of the breach,
         restorer of paths for dwellers.

13   If you refrain from journey on the sabbath,
         from pursuing your affairs on My holy day,
       and call the sabbath a delight,
         the LORD's holy day, respected,
       and honor it by not following your ways,
         nor pursuing your affairs and speaking in vain.

14   Then shall you delight in the LORD,
         and I will mount you on the heights of the earth,
       and make you thrive with the estate of Jacob your father,
         for the mouth of the LORD has spoken.

---

12. *they shall rebuild the ancient ruins.* This formulation does seem to be directed to the challenges facing the Judahites in the early years of the return from exile.

    restorer of paths for dwellers. The Hebrew uses an infinitive, "to dwell," but since paths are not places of habitation, "for dwellers" may be the intended meaning.

13. *If you refrain from journey on the sabbath.* The literal sense of the Hebrew is "If you draw back your foot from the sabbath." This translation follows Blenkinsopp's proposal that "foot" stands in for "traveling," even though others think it suggests trampling the sabbath. In this period, the sabbath was becoming increasingly important, and prohibitions were evolving that would eventually issue in the elaborate rabbinic laws of the sabbath.

    speaking in vain. The Hebrew says, cryptically, "speaking a word." Since conversation on the sabbath was obviously not forbidden, the phrase may suggest something like what is indicated in this translation, though others think it has to do with business pronouncements.

14. *make you thrive.* The literal sense of the Hebrew verb is "feed you."

CHAPTER 59

Why, the LORD's hand is not too short to rescue,   1
    nor His ear too dull to hear.
But your crimes have parted   2
    you from your God,
and your offenses have hidden His face
    from you, so He does not hear.
For your palms are stained with blood   3
    and your fingers with crime.
Your lips speak lies,
    and your tongue utters wrong doing.
There is none who sues in righteousness   4
    or comes to court in good faith.
They trust in emptiness and speak falsehood,
    conceive trouble and bring forth vice.
Viper's eggs they hatch,   5
    and a spiderweb they weave.
Who eats their eggs will die,
    and when crushed an asp is hatched.
Their webs become no garment,   6
    and none covers up with what they make.
What they make are deeds of vice,
    and the work of outrage in their palms.

CHAPTER 59   2. *hidden His face.* The Hebrew merely says "face," but the clear reference is to God. The first two verses of this chapter are a strong articulation of a basic idea of prophetic theology: if you want to know why God appears to be absent, allowing the people of Israel to suffer grievously at the hands of its enemies, the explanation is that God has withdrawn His presence because of the people's offenses. Thus, one should not imagine that God in any way lacks the capacity to rescue Israel or to hear its prayers (verse 1); rather, the lack of divine intervention is solely the consequence of the people's own actions.

4. *There is none who sues in righteousness.* While the verb used generally means "to call" or "to call out," the parallel term in the second verset, *nishpat,* "comes to court," suggests a judicial meaning, and that is the understanding of most biblical scholars.

5. *Viper's eggs . . . / a spiderweb.* These two metaphors drawn from two of the more disagreeable members of the animal kingdom suggest two different negative consequences of the miscreant's acts—respectively, lethally poisonous effects and flimsy, useless insubstantiality.

7   Their feet run to evil
              and hurry to shed innocent blood.
           Their devisings, devisings of vice,
              wrack and ruin upon their paths.
8   The way of peace they do not know,
              and there is no justice where they go.
           They make their courses crooked—
              who treads on them knows not peace.

9   Therefore is justice far from us,
              and vindication does not reach us.
           We hope for light, but, look, darkness,
              for brightness, but we go in gloom.
10   We grope the wall like blind men,
              like the eyeless we grope.
           We stumble at noon as at twilight,
              among the robust like dead men.
11   All of us growl like bears,
              and like doves we ever moan.
           We hope for justice but there is none,
              for rescue,—it is far from us.
12   For many are our crimes before You,
              and our offenses bear witness against us.

---

7. *Their feet run to evil.* The function of the two lines of poetry that constitute this verse is to spell out in explicit moral terms the meaning of the metaphors of viper and spiderweb.

9. *Therefore is justice far from us.* These words initiate a new prophecy. Instead of the preceding castigation of the evildoers first in the second person and then in the third person, this text speaks in the first-person plural on behalf of a people plunged in disaster, for whom God will dramatically intervene (verses 16–20). The hook, surely visible to the eye of the editor, that connects the two prophecies is the pronouncement about the lack of justice at the beginning of the second prophecy.

10. *like blind men, / like the eyeless.* This line neatly illustrates how in the second verset in lines of biblical poetry some sort of epithet (or often metaphor) is substituted for the standard term (here, "blind") that appears in the first verset. "Eyeless" (more literally, "no-eyes") concretizes the condition of blindness. The line is also an elegant chiasm: we grope—blind men—the eyeless—we grope.
   the robust. The Hebrew *'ashamnim* appears only here, so the proposed meaning, linking it with the root *sh-m-n,* which can mean either "healthy" or "fat," is conjectural.

12. *For many are our crimes before You.* This, and what follows to the end of verse 15, is perfectly in accord with the theological notion of alienating God through evil actions that is expressed in verses 1–2, but here it constitutes a collective confession of sin.

For our crimes are with us,
    and our misdeeds, we know them.
Rebelling and denying the LORD   13
    and falling back from our God,
speaking oppression and waywardness,
    conceiving in the heart and uttering lying words.
And justice is made to fall back,   14
    and vindication stands off afar,
for truth stumbles in the square,
    and honesty cannot come in.
And truth is not to be found,   15
    who turns from evil is despoiled.
And the LORD saw, and it was evil in His eyes,
    for there was no justice.
And He saw that there was no man,   16
    and He was appalled, for none intervened.
But His own arm gave Him victory,
    and His triumph stayed Him up.
And He donned triumph as His armor   17
    and victory's helmet on His head.
And He donned clothes of vengeance as a garment,
    and wrapped round zeal like a robe.
As for their deserts, as for that, He requites,   18
    wrath for His foes, just deserts for His enemies,

---

14. *for truth stumbles in the square.* Since the square is the chief public place of the ancient city, usually facing the gates where courts of justice were held, the implication is that the entire society has violated the principles of justice.

16. *And He saw that there was no man.* At this point the prophet offers a new notion of God's saving power: the society is so thoroughly given over to injustice that there is scarcely hope that anyone will emerge who can turn things around, and consequently God Himself decides that He must intervene.

17. *And He donned triumph as His armor.* The prophet now draws on the ancient Canaanite imagery of the warrior-god, which appears with some frequency in biblical poetry.

18. *As for their deserts, as for that.* The Hebrew preposition *ke'al* is unusual, but the sense reflected in the translation seems likely, if not certain.
    wrath for His foes, just deserts for His enemies. All this continues the representation of God as a fierce warrior. If elsewhere in the Isaian corpus the enemies of Israel are conceived as God's instrument, they have, after all, devastated, exiled, and subjugated the covenanted people, and in doing so they have become God's enemies, on whom He will now wreak vengeance.

to the coastlands He exacts just deserts.

19   And they shall fear from the west the LORD's name,
            and from the sun's rising His glory.
        For He shall come like a pent-up river,
            for the LORD's breath drives it on.

20   And a redeemer shall come to Zion,
            and to those who turn back from crime in Jacob—
            said the LORD.

21 "As for Me, this is My covenant with them," said the LORD, "My spirit that is upon you and My word that I put in your mouth—they shall not depart from your mouth and from the mouth of your seed and from the mouth of the seed of your seed," said the LORD, "from now and for all time."

CHAPTER 60

1   Rise, O shine, for your light has come,
                and the glory of the LORD has dawned over you.

---

19. *they shall fear.* This translation agrees with Blenkinsopp that the verb is stronger than "revere," the choice of several modern versions: God the warrior, sweeping over vast regions like a torrential river, inspires fear from east to west.

20. *to those who turn back from crime in Jacob.* Despite the idea of a unilateral divine initiative of rescue articulated in verses 16ff., here at the end the prophecy asserts that the redemption will come only for those who turn back to God.

  said the LORD. This attribution of divine speech is introduced here to mark the end of the prophecy.

21. *As for Me.* What follows the prophecy is a prose epilogue. Some understand it as a formal conclusion to the whole section running from chapter 56 through chapter 59.

  My spirit that is upon you. The "you" is singular, but the claim that it refers to the prophet, with "your seed" indicating his disciples, is questionable. Similar formulations in Deuteronomy and elsewhere clearly indicate the spirit of God that will continue to invest the covenanted people for all time, and there is no warrant for the use of "seed" in the sense of "disciple" rather than as a term for biological offspring. "Seed" in precisely this sense repeatedly figures in the covenantal promises to Abraham.

CHAPTER 60   1. *Rise, O shine for your light has come.* Often thought of, with the next two chapters, as the core of Trito-Isaiah, this poem picks up the motif of transcendent light from Second Isaiah and transforms it into an enthralling poetic vision of Zion magnificently restored. This vision is dramatically developed in the next two verses, in which the whole earth is imagined engulfed in darkness, and Zion's brilliant dawn offers light for humankind.

For, look, darkness covers the earth,   2
    and thick mist, the peoples,
but nations shall walk by your light,   3
    and kings by your dawning radiance.
Raise your eyes all round and see—   4
    they all have gathered, come to you.
Your sons shall come from afar
    and your daughters dandled on the hip.
Then shall you see and gleam,   5
    and your heart shall throb and swell,
for the sea's bounty shall be yours,
    the wealth of nations shall come to you.
A tide of camels shall cover you,   6
    dromedaries from Midian and Ephah,
        they all shall come from Sheba.
Gold and frankincense they shall bear,
    and the LORD's praise they shall proclaim.
All Kedar's flocks shall be gathered to you,   7
    Nebaioth's rams shall serve you.
They shall be welcome offerings on My altar,
    and the house of My splendor I will make splendid.
Who are these who fly like a cloud   8
    and like doves to their cotes?
For Me the coastlands wait,   9

---

3. *your dawning.* The Hebrew verbal stem *z-r-ḥ* does not mean merely "to shine," as several translations show, but the breaking light of dawn, a pointed word choice because Zion's light is to come after the long dark night of the nations.

4. *Your sons shall come from afar.* The entire line builds on the image of Zion's sons and daughters being brought back to their homeland in Isaiah 49:14–21.
    dandled. The Hebrew verb, *'aman,* suggests caring for or tending to a child.

6. *A tide of camels.* The first noun here, *shif'ah,* indicates a flow or spate. The poetic image is of an endless flow of caravans of camels that is like a stream or tide.

7. *the house of My splendor I will make splendid.* This is not a redundancy. The Temple by rights is the house of God's splendor, but only when it is completely rebuilt and grandly refurbished will it achieve its status as the house of God's splendor.

8. *Who are these who fly like a cloud.* The obvious reference is to the exiles flocking back to their land. Although this and the next two verses reflect a clear connection with the sundry prophecies of the return to Zion in chapters 40–55, the difference is that the point of view here appears to be that of someone in Zion watching the crowd of returned exiles as it approaches.

and Tarshish ships are at the head
to bring your children from afar,
　　their silver and their gold are with them,
for the name of the Lord your God,
　　and Israel's Holy One, Who makes you splendid.

10　　And foreign sons shall build your walls,
　　and their kings shall serve you.
For in My fury I did strike you
　　and in My favor I have compassion for you.

11　　And they shall open your gates perpetually,
　　　　night and day they shall not close,
to buy you the wealth of nations,
　　and their kings as captives driven.

12　For the nation and the kingdom that does not serve you shall perish, and
the nation shall surely be destroyed.

13　　Lebanon's glory shall come to you,
　　　　cypress, fir, and box tree all,
to make splendid the place of My sanctuary,
　　and I will honor the resting place of My feet.

14　　And they shall go to you bent over,
　　　　the sons of your afflictions,
　　　　　　and all your revilers bow at the soles of your feet.
And they shall call you City of the Lord,

---

9. *Tarshish ships.* This is an exercise of poetic license to convey the idea of the exiles being brought from afar because in fact they would be coming overland from Mesopotamia, not from the west by sea.

10. *And foreign sons shall build your walls, / and their kings shall serve you.* This fantastic flourish is another motif picked up from chapters 40–55.

11. *And they shall open your gates perpetually.* As the next poetic line makes clear, the gates are open to bring in the wealth of nations. But normally, the gates of a city would be closed at least at night to guarantee its security, so what is envisaged here is a perfectly peaceful city that will never be attacked. This is still another instance in which the poem builds on hyperbole.

　　their kings as captives driven. The verb for "drive" is usually attached to animals or prisoners, so "as captives" is implied though not stated.

12. *For the nation and the kingdom.* This entire verse, which is in prose, looks like an editorial intervention meant to point the moral of the poem.

Zion of the Holy One.
Instead of your being forsaken,   15
    rejected, with none passing through,
I will make you an everlasting pride,
    a rejoicing for all times.
And you shall suckle the milk of nations,   16
    royal breasts you shall suckle,
and you shall know I am the LORD your Rescuer,
    and your Redeemer, Jacob's Mighty One.
Instead of bronze I will bring gold,   17
    and instead of iron I will bring silver
and instead of wood, bronze,
    and instead of stone, iron.
And I will set as your governance Peace
    and your overseers, Righteousness.
No more shall "outrage" be heard in your land,   18
    "wrack and ruin" within your borders.
And you shall call your walls Deliverance
    and your gates Praise.
No more shall the sun be your light by day,   19
    nor the moon's radiance shine for you,
but the LORD shall be your everlasting light
    and your God become your splendor.
No more shall your sun set,   20
    your moon shall not go down.

---

16. *And you shall suckle the milk of nations.* In 49:23 foreign princesses were to become the wet nurses of Judahite infants; here, that extravagant image is rerun metaphorically.

royal breasts. The Masoretic Text is vocalized to read *shod*, "booty," but the original word was almost certainly *shad*, "breast," either mistakenly vocalized by the Masoretes or altered by them because the image troubled them.

17. *governance.* The Hebrew *pequdah* is one of those biblical terms that can mean half a dozen different things, but in context, and with regard to the parallelism, this is the most likely sense here. Abraham Ibn Ezra sees it as an ellipsis for *'anshey pequdah*, "men of governance."

18. *outrage . . . / wrack and ruin.* These are conventional outcries in response to a disaster—for example, a person attacked by marauders.

19. *No more shall the sun be your light by day.* At the beginning of the poem, Israel's radiance lit up the world. Now, the heavenly luminaries are to be replaced by God, as an everlasting source of light. Again, poetic hyperbole points the way to eschatological vision.

But the Lord shall be your everlasting light,
   and your mourning days shall be done.

21 And your people, all of them righteous,
   shall forever possess the land,
the shoot I have planted,
   My handiwork in which to glory.

22 The least shall become a thousand,
   the smallest, a mighty nation.
     I, the Lord, in its due time I will hasten it.

CHAPTER 61

1 The Lord's spirit is upon me
   as the Lord has anointed me
to bring good tidings to the poor,
   to bind up the broken-hearted,
to proclaim freedom to the captives,
   to the prisoners, release,

---

21. *your people . . . / shall forever possess the land.* The land in question is of course the Land of Israel, and this is an especially pointed promise to a people that little more than a century earlier had been violently uprooted from its land.

22. *a mighty nation.* The Hebrew adjective can equally mean "multitudinous."

in its due time I will hasten it. The entire prophecy has conjured up the idea of a glorious national restoration. At the time it was delivered, in the early or middle decades of the fifth century B.C.E., the Judahite community was in disarray, the rebuilding of Jerusalem proceeding fitfully, inner divisions manifesting themselves, fears of armed attacks hovering over the Judahites. Thus the prophet is constrained to have God say that He will hasten the arrival of the grand restoration, but only in its due time.

CHAPTER 61   1. *The Lord's spirit is upon me . . . / to bring good tidings to the poor.* This prophet of the fifth century B.C.E. announces at the outset of the prophecy that he has been commissioned to bring a message of comfort, not castigation.

the poor. While many understand ʿanawim as "the humble," it can also be a variant form of ʿaniyim, "poor," and the prophet appears to be referring to people in a state of wretchedness.

to proclaim freedom to the captives. The first verb and noun here echo the language concerning the jubilee year in Leviticus 25:10, where Israelite slaves were restored to freedom. Efforts to link these lines with specific conditions in the fifth-century Judahite community are, however, no more than conjectures. Captivity is a recurrent poetic image for all sorts of states of subjugation, including its frequent use in chapters 40–55 as a metaphor for exile.

to proclaim a year of favor for the LORD   2
   and a day of vengeance for our God,
      to comfort all who mourn,
to set out for the mourners of Zion,   3
   to give them turbans instead of ashes,
joy's oil instead of mourning,
   a glorious wrap instead of gloomy spirit.
And they shall be called oaks of victory,
   God's planting in which to glory.
And they shall rebuild the ancient ruins,   4
   the desolate places of yore they shall raise up,
and renew the ravaged towns,
   and the desolate places of times long past.
And foreigners shall stand and tend your flocks   5
   and strangers be your farmers and keepers of your vineyards.
As for you, the LORD's priests you shall be called,   6
   our God's ministrants it shall be said of you.
The wealth of nations you shall enjoy
   and in their glory revel.
Instead of the shame twice over and disgrace   7
   they shall exult in their lot.
Therefore they shall possess their land twice over,
   everlasting joy shall be theirs.

---

3. *turbans instead of ashes.* The Hebrew features sound-play: "turban" (often the word means "splendor") is *pe'eir* and "ashes," *'eifer*, the same Hebrew consonants in a different order.

   joy's oil instead of mourning. Rubbing oneself with oil was part of the enjoyment of the good life, and mourners would refrain from this practice. Putting ashes on the head was a mourning rite.

4. *ancient ruins.* The ruins were made when Jerusalem was destroyed in 586 B.C.E., well over a century before this prophecy, and from the poet's perspective these ruins are "ancient," from "times long past."

6. *the LORD's priests you shall be called.* One should not take this declaration literally. The point is that all the people will now enjoy an intimate relationship with God in the Temple, rather in the spirit of all Israel's being "a kingdom of priests and a holy nation" (Exodus 19:6).

7. *they shall possess their land twice over.* This is a hyperbolic flourish: the people dispossessed of their land will now hold on to it with doubled security. The phrase might also refer to a second taking-possession of the land after the first one in Joshua's conquest.

8   For I, the LORD, love justice,
      hate robbery and vice,
  and I will truly pay their wages,
      an everlasting pact I will seal with them.
9   And their seed shall be known in the nations,
      and their offspring among the peoples.
  All who see them shall recognize
      that they are the seed the LORD has blessed.
10   I shall greatly rejoice in the LORD,
      my very being exult in my God.
  For He has clothed me with garments of triumph,
      has wrapped me with victory's cloak,
  as a bridegroom dons, priestlike, a turban
      and as a bride is adorned in fine clothes.
11   For as the earth brings forth its growth
      and a garden makes its plants flourish,
  so shall the LORD make victory flourish
      and praise before all the nations.

CHAPTER 62

1   For Zion's sake I will not be still,
      and for Jerusalem's sake I will not be quiet,
  till her triumph emerges like radiance
      and her deliverance burns like a torch,
2   and nations see your triumph
      and all kings, your glory.

---

8. *robbery and vice.* The Masoretic Text reads for the second noun *be'olah,* "in burnt offering," but this should be revocalized as *be'awlah.*

10. *For He has clothed me with garments of triumph.* The clothing metaphor, continued here until the end of the verse, picks up the "turban" and the "glorious wrap" from verse 3.
    as a bridegroom dons, priestlike, a turban. The Hebrew uses a verb, *yekhahein,* that literally means "to minister as a priest." The priests wore turbans and splendid robes and so serve as a model for fine attire.
    as a bride is adorned in fine clothes. "Fine" is implied in the Hebrew because the verb used is one for putting on ornaments.

And you shall be called a new name
    that the mouth of the LORD shall fix.
And you shall become a crown of splendor in the hand of the LORD   3
    and a regal diadem in the palm of your God.
No more shall be said of you "Forsaken"   4
    and of your land no more be said "Desolation."
For you shall be called "My Delight Is in Her"
    and your land, "The One Bedded."
For the LORD delights in you
    and your land shall be bedded.
As a young man beds a virgin,   5
    your sons shall bed you,
and a bridegroom's rejoicing over the bride
    shall your God rejoice over you.
On your walls, O Jerusalem,   6
    I have stationed watchmen.

CHAPTER 62   2. *And you shall be called a new name.* In the biblical world, as in many other cultures, the name was conceived as incorporating the essence of the person or object. The most striking illustration of this notion is Jacob's wrestling with the mysterious stranger in Genesis 32. He is given a new name, Israel, instead of his old one ("Jacob" is etymologically associated with crookedness or deception), while the stranger refuses to reveal his own name, saying it is a mystery. The prophet of these chapters is particularly preoccupied with changing names: Israel's disastrous destiny is about to be transformed into triumph, and the poetry marks this transformation by assigning a cluster of new names.

4. *My Delight Is in Her.* A transliterated version of the Hebrew for this name, Hephzibah, at one time had some currency among Bible-reading speakers of English.

The One Bedded. Again, the transliteration, Beulah, became an English name. Most translations render it as "espoused," but that is too formal and too decorous. This passive form of the verb *baʿal* does indicate a woman who has a husband (the noun *baʿal*), but it has a sexual connotation: Zion, the woman who has been forsaken, will now enjoy consummation again. The sexual implication of the term is clearly suggested in verse 5: "and a bridegroom's rejoicing over the bride / shall your God rejoice over you."

5. *your sons shall bed you.* This sounds inadvertently like incest (in the next line of poetry, it is rather God's relationship with Israel that is analogous to the bridegroom's relationship with the bride), but the intended idea is that the desolate land, personified as a woman, will be plowed and cultivated by its sons, as a young man is intimate with a virgin and makes her fruitful.

6. *watchmen.* Some take this to be a figure for the prophet and his disciples, but they may well be literal watchmen.

Through the day and through the night,
   they are never still.
You invokers of the LORD,
   do not fall silent,

7   and do not let Him fall silent
       till He sets Jerusalem firm, praise in the earth.

8   The LORD has vowed by His right hand
       and by His powerful arm:
I will no more give your grain
   to your enemies as food,
and foreigners shall not drink your new wine
   over which you toiled.

9   But those who garner it shall eat it,
       and they shall praise the LORD,
and those who gather it shall drink it
   in My holy courts.

10   Pass through, pass through the gates,
      clear the people's way.
Build up, build up the highway,
   clear away the stones,
      raise a banner over peoples.

11   Look, the LORD has made it heard
      to the end of the earth:
Say to Zion's Daughter,
   look, your rescue comes.
   Look, His recompense is with Him,

---

9. *those who gather it shall drink it / in My holy courts.* The point of this verse and the preceding one is not only that the people will no longer have the fruit of their agricultural labors stripped from them by invaders, but also that they will bring their grain and wine to celebrate God in His Temple. This is a sentiment very much in keeping with many of the Psalms.

10. *Build up, build up the highway.* This, like several other lines in the poetry of this prophet, is a pointed variation on the language of Second Isaiah (especially 40:3–4).

11. *Say to Zion's Daughter.* These are the words grandly confirming the restoration of Zion that God is about to proclaim throughout the earth.

   His recompense . . . / His wages. That is to say, God carries with Him the recompense He will now give to Israel.

and His wages are before Him.
And they shall call them "Holy People,"   12
    "The Redeemed Ones of the LORD."
And you shall be called "The One Sought Out,"
    "The City Unforsaken."

CHAPTER 63

Who is this coming from Edom,   1
    in ensanguined garments from Bosra?
The One glorious in attire,
    striding in His great power.
"I speak out in triumph,
    great for granting victory."
"Why is there red on your garments   2
    and your clothes like one treading a winepress?"

---

12. *And they shall call them "Holy People."* In the fervor of this vision, all the nations of the earth are caught up in this movement of assigning new names to the people of Israel because they see and attest to its splendid transformation.

CHAPTER 63   1. *Who is this coming from Edom, / is ensanguined garments from Bosra?* The first six verses of this chapter are the most vivid—and grisly—representation in biblical poetry of YHWH as a warrior-god. The image of God trampling the vineyard would be picked up in the Book of Revelation and then would be used at the beginning of "The Battle Hymn of the Republic."

Edom. If one may judge by Psalm 137, Edom took an eager role in collaborating with the Babylonian invaders in 586 B.C.E. and was thus singled out by the Judahites as a particular object of hatred. It is conceivable that this prophecy was composed not long after 586.

ensanguined. The adjective *hamuts* is unusual, and it is not the ordinary word for "red." It nevertheless refers through the color to the name "Edom," which is associated with *'adom*, "red," as one clearly sees in the naming of Esau in Genesis 25:30. In the story of the stealing of the blessing (chapter 27), Jacob puts on the "finery" that belongs to his brother Esau, but Yair Zakovitch proposes that the Hebrew word used for these, *hamudot*, is a scribal or editorial substitution for *hamatsot*, the adjective that occurs here.

glorious in attire. In a provocative leap, the blood-splattered garments are glorious attire.

2. *Why is there red on your garments.* The form of question and response between an anonymous observer (perhaps the prophet but not necessarily) and God is quite unusual in biblical poetry.

like one treading a winepress. The association between wine and blood is not only because of the color red but also because a kenning for wine in biblical poetry, inherited from the Ugaritic, is "blood of the grape" (see Genesis 49:11).

3   "In the vat I have trodden alone—
            of the peoples, no one was with Me,
        and I trampled them in My wrath,
            stomped on them in My fury,
        and their lifeblood splattered My garments,
            all My clothes I have befouled.
4   For it is vengeance day in My heart
            and My vindication's year has come.
5   And I looked, and there was no helper,
            and I stared—and there was no sustainer.
        But My own arm made Me triumph,
            and My wrath, it was this sustained Me.
6   And I trampled peoples in My wrath
            and made them drunk with My fury,
                and shed their lifeblood on the ground."

7   The LORD's acts of kindness I recall,
            the praises of the LORD.
        As for all that the LORD requited us,
            and the great bounty to the house of Israel
        whom He requited with His mercy
            and with His many acts of kindness.
8   And He said, "Why, they are My people,
            children who do not betray,"
                and He became their rescuer.
9   In all their distress was He distressed,

---

5. *But My own arm made Me triumph.* This is a very different view from that of Second Isaiah, in which Cyrus acts as God's agent in history, but this prophecy may antedate the advent of Cyrus by a century or more.

6. *made them drunk with My fury.* The metaphor of drunkenness is enhanced by the fact that the word for "fury" has a homonym that means "venom," a lethal liquid that can be imbibed.

7. *The LORD's acts of kindness I recall.* These words signal the beginning of a new poem with an entirely different theme. If we recall that "the LORD's acts of kindness," *ḥasdey YHWH*, is a recurrent motif in Pslams, the composition that begins here looks very much like a psalm—in this instance, a collective supplication that rehearses God's bounty to Israel in times past and prays for the renewal of divine intervention to save the people.

and the agent of His presence rescued them.
In His love and in His compassion He redeemed them,
    plucked them up and bore them all the days of yore.
But they rebelled and pained   10
    His Holy spirit,
and He became an enemy to them,
    He fought against them.
But He recalled the days of yore,   11
    drawing His people out from the water:
Where is He Who brought them up from the sea,
    the shepherds of His flock?
Where is He Who put in their midst
    His holy spirit?
Who led at the right hand of Moses   12
    with His glorious arm,
split the waters before them
    to make Him an everlasting name,
leading them through the deep;   13
    like a horse in the desert they did not stumble.
Like cattle in the valley You guided them,   14
    the LORD's spirit guided them.
So you led Your people
    to make You a glorious name.

---

11. *But He recalled the days of yore.* The recalling is stated as a completed fact, but that is somewhat confusing because in what follows God is repeatedly asked why He does not now come to the aid of Israel as He once did.

drawing His people out from the water. The Hebrew *mosheh 'amo* should not be construed as "Moses his people," which would make little sense. Instead, *mosheh* is used as a verb here, the verb with which the name of Moses is etymologized. This usage is clear because of the next line, "Where is He Who brought them up from the sea." But the poet interprets the Moses story as he invokes the miracle at the Sea of Reeds: the infant Moses drawn from the water is a prefiguration of Israel saved from the waters as the sea is split open.

13. *like a horse in the desert.* The odd-looking simile again alludes to the story of the Sea of Reeds: the Egyptian horses all drowned in the waters of the sea, whereas a horse on the dry surface of the desert—the antithesis of the sea—does not stumble.

14. *Like cattle in the valley You guided them.* The Masoretic Text reads "as cattle goes down in the valley," but three ancient versions have "You guided them" instead of "[it] goes down."

15   Look from the heavens and see,
                    from Your holy and glorious abode.
               Where are Your zeal and Your might?
                    Your deep feeling and your compassion
                    are held back from me.
16   Though Abraham did not know us
                    nor Israel recognize us,
               You, Lord, are our Father,
                    our Redeemer of yore is Your name.
17   Why should You make us stray, Lord, from Your ways,
                    why make our hearts callous to the fear of You?
               Turn back for the sake of Your servants,
                    the tribes of Your estate.
18   For a brief time Your holy people had possession—
                    our foes trampled Your sanctuary.
19   We become like ones You never ruled,
                    on whom Your name was not called.
               Would that You tore open the heavens, came down,
                    that the mountains melted before You,

---

15. *Your deep feeling.* The literal sense of the Hebrew is "the stirring [or roaring] of your innards." The innards or bowels were thought to be the seat of compassion, and for this odd reason, "bowels" in eighteenth-century English came to mean, through the literalism of the King James Version, "compassion."

16. *Though Abraham did not know us.* This is a rhetorical hypothesis contrary to fact: even if it were the case that Abraham did not know us, God would still be our Father.

17. *Why should You make us stray.* The theological reasoning is: since God causes all things, if we have strayed it must be somehow because He has decreed it, and so we are not entirely to blame.

18. *For a brief time Your holy people had possession.* The meaning of this whole verset is in doubt. Scholars have performed radical surgery on the received text, but their results are equally doubtful.

19. *the mountains melted before You.* The chapter ends on a comma because this sentence continues through the first verse of chapter 64, and the entire prophecy begun in verse 7 goes on until the end of chapter 64.

CHAPTER 64

as fire catches in brushwood,   1
   as fire makes water seethe,
to let Your name be known to Your foes,
   before You nations quake.
When You did fearsome things we had not hoped for,   2
   You came down, and before You the mountains melted.
They never had seen,   3
   they never gave ear,
no eye has seen a God besides You.
   He acts for those who wait for Him.
You struck him who delights in doing justice,   4
   who recalls You in Your ways.
Look, You raged, and so we offended,
   when You hid Yourself we transgressed.
We become all of us like an unclean thing,   5
   and like a filthy rag, all our merits.
And we all of us shriveled like leaves
   and our crimes bore us off like the wind.
And none called Your name   6

CHAPTER 64   1. *brushwood.* The Hebrew term appears only here, but the context suggests this sense.

to let Your name be known to Your foes. God's omnipotence is manifested on earth as He descends amid seismic upheavals in all His power.

2. *before You the mountains melted.* The language is reminiscent of the Song of Deborah. Compare Judges 5:5.

3. *He acts for those who wait for Him.* The switch from second-person to third-person reference to the same subject is characteristic biblical usage.

4. *You struck him who delights in doing justice.* This appears to be an abrupt transition on the argument of the poem. In times past, God showed His fearsome power in acting on behalf of Israel. Now, however, even those who pursue justice are the victims of His wrath. This negative construction of the verb *paga'*, which can mean either "to strike" (usually fatally) or "to encounter," is supported by the report of divine rage in the next line.

You raged, and so we offended, / when You hid Yourself we transgressed. This line extends the theological understanding of 63:17: Israel's transgressions are the consequence of God's rage and the hiding of His face rather than their cause.

5. *a filthy rag.* The Hebrew *'idim* is another word unique to this text, and the translation simply reflects the understanding of interpretive consensus.

nor roused himself to hold fast to You,
for You hid Your face from us,
and gave us over to our crimes.

7   Yet now, LORD, You are our Father,
we are the clay and You the Potter,
and Your handiwork all of us are.

8   Do not, O LORD, be so furious,
and do not forever recall crime.
Oh, look, pray, to Your people, all of us.

9   Your holy towns have become a desert,
Zion has become a desert, Jerusalem a desolate place.

10   Our holy house and our glory
in which our fathers praised You
has been consumed by fire
and all our precious things become a ruin.

11   For these will You hold back, O LORD,
be silent and gravely afflict us?

CHAPTER 65

1   I yielded oracles when they did not inquire,
I was found when they did not seek Me.
I said, "Here I am, here I am"
to a nation not called by My name.

---

6. *gave us over.* This translation reads instead of the Masoretic *watemugeinu* ("you melted us") *watemageinu,* a reading reflected in three ancient versions.

10. *Our holy house . . . / consumed by fire.* The language here clearly indicates that the Temple has not yet been rebuilt, and this poem may well have been written shortly after the destruction of 586 B.C.E. Scholars have noted several points of similarity in the language of this prophecy with Lamentations.

11. *For these will You hold back, O LORD.* This plea concludes the collective supplication: in light of the terrible devastation—Jerusalem turned into a desolate place, the Temple in ruins, the whole people cast off like a filthy rag—God must surely relent His fury and restore Zion. All this is very far from the upbeat vision of national redemption articulated by Second Isaiah and almost certainly reflects an earlier historical moment.

CHAPTER 65   1. *I yielded oracles.* The literal sense of the passive verb *nidrashti* is "I was sought out." But *darash* is the verb that has the technical sense of "inquire of an oracle," and that appears to be the meaning here: even though the people did not seek Me in any sense, including inquiry of My oracles, I was ready to vouchsafe them revelation.

I spread out My hands all day long   2
    to a wayward people
that walked on a way not good
    after its own devisings.
The people that vexes Me   3
    to My face perpetually,
offering sacrifice in the gardens,
    burning incense on the bricks,
sitting among the graves,   4
    in vigil stations passing the nights,
eating the flesh of pigs
    and broth of foulness in their pots,
saying, "Keep off,   5
    do not approach me, for I am not to be touched by you."
These are smoke in my nostrils,

---

2. *I spread out My hands.* This phrase continues the paradox of the previous verse because spreading out the hands is a gesture of prayer, and it is as though God, not the people, were praying.

3. *offering sacrifice in the gardens.* These are sacred gardens where nature gods, or fertility goddesses such as Asherah, were worshipped.

    burning incense on the bricks. We have no specific information about this cultic practice, although setting out incense on bricks for burning sounds plausible, and thus emending the received text seems unwarranted.

4. *sitting among the graves.* This looks like some sort of ancestor worship.

    vigil stations. The Hebrew *netsurim* is opaque, but it derives from a verbal stem that means to watch, or guard, hence this conjectural translation. What appears to be invoked is a practice of waiting through the night for some sort of epiphany of a god, perhaps a chthonic god because of the nocturnal setting.

    eating the flesh of pigs. This is, of course, prohibited, but the point is probably not just the dietary restriction but the consumption of pork in a pagan ritual.

    broth. The Masoretic Text shows *peraq*, a term not attested elsewhere, and this translation reads instead *meraq*. The vehement inveighing against a whole set of paganizing practices does not appear in the previous chapters, and pagan or syncretistic worship does not seem to have been an urgent issue either in Babylonian exile or in fifth-century B.C.E. Judah. One is led to the tentative inference that this is a prophecy dating from the last years of the Judahite monarchy, a time when, as other sources show, pagan practices were widespread.

5. *I am not to be touched by you.* The Hebrew *qedashtikha* is problematic. The reasoning behind this translation is: to be *qadosh*, "holy," is to be unapproachable except by designated priests. The speaker may be saying that I have assumed a condition of *qedushah*, holiness, by my participation in these rites, and so no profane person is allowed to come near me.

smoldering fire all day long.
6 Look, it is written before Me:
I will not be still
    till I have paid back,
        paid back into their laps,
7 their crimes and their fathers' crimes together—
    said the LORD—
that they burned incense on the mountains
    and on the hills reviled Me,
I will measure out their wages
    first in their lap.

8 Thus said the LORD:
As new wine is found in the cluster,
    and they say, "Do not destroy it
        for there is blessing in it,"
so will I do for My servants,
    not destroying everything.
9 And I will bring out seed from Jacob
    and from Judah as heir to My mountains,
and My chosen ones shall take hold of it,
    and My servants shall dwell there.
10 And Sharon shall become a pasture for flocks
    and the Achor Valley a bedding-down for cattle—

---

6. *Look, it is written before Me.* These introductory words are extrametrical. In the next verse, "said the LORD" is also extrametrical.

7. *on the mountains / . . . on the hills.* Though these terms are a formulaic word-pairing in the parallel structure of biblical poetry, their use here again points to nature worship, like the gardens in verse 3.
    first. The meaning of the Hebrew *ri'shonah* is unclear, and the translation mirrors that opaqueness.

8. *so will I do for My servants.* Here and in what follows, there is a distinction between those who are God's "servants" or His "chosen ones" and the rest of the people. Presumably, the servants are those who have not been spending their time burning incense in sacred gardens and sitting among graves. They are thus like the cluster of healthy grapes on the vine that also bears rotten fruit. Blenkinsopp sees in all this the beginnings of a sectarian perspective. Later, both the Book of Daniel and a good many of the Dead Sea Scrolls exhibit this division between those who will be saved and those who are irrevocably lost.

for My people who seek Me.

As for you, who forsake the LORD,   11
   neglecting My holy mountain,
who lay out a table for the good luck god
   and fill bowls of mixed wine for the god of fate.
I have destined you for the sword,   12
   and you all shall kneel to be slaughtered,
since I called and you did not answer,
   I spoke and you did not hear,
and you did what was evil in My eyes,
   and what I did not desire you chose.
Therefore, thus said the LORD: 13
Look, My servants shall eat
   and you shall hunger.
Look, My servants shall drink
   and you shall thirst.
Look, My servants shall rejoice
   and you shall be shamed.
Look, My servants shall sing gladly   14
   with a cheerful heart,
and you shall cry out for heart's pain

---

10. *for My people who seek Me.* This qualification is important: the splendidly restored countryside will not be for everyone but for those who seek God.

11. *neglecting My holy mountain.* The holy mountain is the site of the Temple. "Neglecting" (or, more literally, "forgetting") it means going to sacred gardens and graveyards to worship there.

   the good luck god. The Hebrew refers to him by name, Gad. The worship of Gad is attested in inscriptions in Phoenicia and in its North African colonies over many centuries.

   the god of fate. Again, a name is given in the Hebrew, Meni, and variations of this name for a god of fate or destiny appear in many extrabiblical sources.

12. *destined.* The Hebrew verb *maniti* plays sardonically on the just mentioned "Meni."

   I called and you did not answer. Normally, it is man's place to call out to God, but this reversal of roles is in keeping with the reversal in verses 1–2.

13. *Therefore, thus said the LORD.* This introduction is again extrametrical.

   My servants shall eat / and you shall hunger. This sharp antithesis between the fate of God's servants and the audience of paganizers that is rebuked vividly illustrates the split between those in the people who will be saved and those destined to come to a disastrous end.

and from a broken spirit howl.

15 And you shall leave your name as an oath to My chosen ones:
"May the Master, the LORD, put you to death!"
And My servants He shall call by another name.

16 Who blesses himself in the land
shall bless himself by the God of trust,
and who vows in the land
shall vow by the God of trust,
for the former troubles have been forgotten
and are hidden from My eyes.

17 For I am about to create new heavens
and a new earth,
and the former things shall not be recalled
and shall not come to mind.

18 But rejoice and exalt for all times,
that I am creating,
for I am about to create in Jerusalem
exultation and with it rejoicing.

19 And I will exult in Jerusalem
and rejoice in My people,
and no longer shall be heard within it
the sound of weeping and the sound of screams.

20 There shall not be there a tender babe or elder
who will not live out his days.

---

15. *And you shall leave your name as an oath.* What the miscreants will leave behind them is a name that will become the byword of a curse (in contrast to what is said in Genesis of Abraham, whose name is to be a blessing invoked by all). The words that follow here, "May the Master, the LORD, put you to death!," are the words of the curse, and they may have been completed by a name, "like So-and-so."

My servants He shall call by another name. Either there is a collective name for this group of paganizers that now must be replaced, or the individual paganizers bear names in general currency, and so new names are required.

16. *the God of trust.* This could be rendered as "the God of amen," but the word *'amen* derives from a root that suggests trust, dependability, confirmation.

17. *I am about to create new heavens / and a new earth.* Many interpreters read this literally as an eschatological statement, but it may be more plausible to understand it as poetic hyperbole: it is not that the order of nature will be radically transformed but that, in this Jerusalem now filled with joy and exultation, there will be a general sense of sweeping renewal.

For like a lad he shall die at a hundred,
    and who misses a hundred shall be thought accursed.
And they shall build houses and dwell in them   21
    and plant vineyards and eat their fruit.
They shall not build for another to dwell   22
    and shall not plant for another to eat,
for like the days of a tree My people's days,
    and the work of their hands shall My chosen outlive.
They shall not toil for naught   23
    nor give birth in panic,
for they are the seed blessed of the LORD,
    and their offspring are with them.
And it shall be, before they call, I will answer,   24
    while they still speak, I will hear.
The wolf and the lamb shall graze as one,   25
    and the lion like cattle eat hay
        and the serpent—dust, its food.
They shall do no evil and do no harm
    on all My holy mountain, said the LORD.

---

20. *like a lad he shall die at a hundred.* Not only will a person have an extravagantly long life span (easily two or three times the actual average longevity in ancient society), but he will come to his end after a century in all the vigor of his youth.

22. *They shall not build for another to dwell.* This of course would happen when the land was conquered. It is not, however, an inevitable inference that this prophecy is post-586 B.C.E., because the imminent prospect of being conquered and dispossessed was ominously evident through the last century and a half of the Judahite monarchy as Assyrian and then Babylonian armies threatened Jerusalem and other Judahite cities.

    and the work of their hands shall My chosen outlive. The verb used here means to "wear out," but the obvious sense is that they will live beyond the point where the things they make have fallen apart. Based on the formulation here, this verb would become idiomatic precisely in this sense in later Hebrew.

25. *The wolf and the lamb shall graze as one.* This entire verse is an obvious abbreviated reprise of Isaiah 11:6–9. Many scholars assume it is an editorial addition, though it is perfectly plausible that the prophet could choose to quote the earlier prophecy in order to round out his own picture of the ideal age.

    and the serpent—dust, its food. The serpent will no longer sink its fangs into human flesh or that of other animals. But these words also recall the curse on the primordial serpent, "and dust shall you eat" (Genesis 3:14).

CHAPTER 66

1   Thus said the LORD:
     The heavens are My throne
          and the earth is My footstool.
     What house would you build for Me
          and what place for My resting,
2   when all these My hand has made
          and Mine all these are?—
               said the LORD—
     But to this do I look, to the poor man
          and to the broken of spirit who trembles at My word.

3   Who slaughters an ox, who strikes down a man,
          sacrifices the sheep, breaks the neck of a dog,
     brings up in offering the blood of a pig,
          burns incense in token, blessing strange gods—
     they, too, have chosen their ways,
          in their abominations they have delighted.

CHAPTER 66   1. *The heavens are My throne . . . / What house would you build for Me.* These words are in keeping with a theme of Solomon's prayer at the dedication of the Temple (1 Kings 8), which may well have been composed in this post-exilic period. The point, as in Solomon's prayer, is not a categorical rejection of the Temple but resistance to the popular idea that it was literally God's house.

2. *to the poor man / and to the broken of spirit who trembles at My word.* The argument here is clearly against materialist notions of closeness to the deity. What a compassionate God wants is not a grand building but suffering humanity that is attuned to the divine word.

3. *Who slaughters an ox, who strikes down a man.* These words begin a new prophecy, which is a castigation of those given over to syncretistic or pagan forms of worship. The entire concluding chapter of Isaiah is made up of brief textual units only imperfectly connected with each other. This somewhat fragmented character may be the consequence of editorial process, in which remaining fragments of writing were drawn together at the end, as is the case in the last chapter of the Song of Songs. Some commentators think that the offensive rites listed here took place within the precincts of the Temple itself, although that is not altogether clear. In any case, all four versets here are structured as pairings of contradictions: a person slaughters an ox, which is acceptable, but kills a man (some think, in ritual slaughter); conducts the acceptable sacrifice of a sheep but also breaks the neck of a dog in a sacrificial rite; brings up in offering—a term usually set aside for grain offering—the blood of a pig.
     strange gods. The Hebrew *'awen* has the basic meaning of "wrongdoing" but is sometimes used as a pejorative epithet for pagan gods.

I, too, will choose their rank acts   4
    and what they fear I will bring upon them.
Because I called and none answered,
    I spoke and they did not listen,
and they did what was evil in My eyes,
    and in what I did not delight they chose.

Listen to the word of the LORD,   5
    you who tremble at His word.
Your brothers who hate you have said,
    who scorn you for the sake of My name:
"Let the LORD be honored,
    and we shall see your joy,"
        but they shall be shamed.
The sound of uproar from the town,   6
    a sound from the Temple,
the sound of the LORD,
    dealing punishment to His enemies.

Before she labors, she gives birth,   7
    before the birth pangs come upon her, she delivers a male.
Who heard the like of this,   8
    who has seen things like these?
Can a land go through birth in a single day,
    can a nation be born in a single breath?
For Zion went into labor,
    gave birth to her children.
Shall I cause labor and not bring about birth?   9

---

5. *you who tremble at His word.* This recurrent designation of the pious, as Blenkinsopp plausibly contends, probably refers to a sect or at least a group of true believers who resist the repellent practices of the paganizers enumerated in verse 3. The sense of a deep schism within the people is brought out in the next line, "Your brothers who hate you."

Let the LORD *be honored, / and we shall see your joy.* These words are uttered in biting sarcasm to those "who tremble at His word" by the people who hate them.

7. *Before she labors, she gives birth.* This begins still another prophecy. The "she" is Zion, and the image of childbirth is one picked up from Second Isaiah. To give birth without labor is to reverse the curse on Eve in Genesis, and it also suggests the miraculous swiftness with which the redemption is to be realized.

8. *in a single breath.* Literally, "in one time."

said the LORD.
Shall I bring about birth and block the womb?
said your God.

10   Rejoice with Jerusalem
            and all who love her exult in her.
        Be glad with her in gladness,
            all who mourn for her,
11   that you suck and be sated
            from her comforting breast,
        that you drink deep and know pleasure
            from her glorious teat.
12   For thus said the LORD:
        I am about to stretch out to her
            well-being like a river,
        and like a rushing brook
            the glory of nations,
        and your babes shall be borne on the hip,
            and on knees they shall be dandled.
13   As a man whose mother comforts him,
            so I Myself will comfort you,
                and you shall be comforted in Jerusalem.
14   And you shall see, and your heart shall rejoice,
            and your bones shall flourish like grass,
        and the LORD's hand shall be known to His servants,
            and He shall rage against His enemies.

---

11. *that you suck and be sated / from her comforting breast.* The metaphor of nursing infants builds on the birth imagery of the previous passage. The received text reads *shod*, "spoils," but this is certainly a scribal bowlderization of *shad*, "breast," just as it is in 60:16.

teat. The Hebrew *ziz* occurs in only one other place in the Bible, but in a sense that is inappropriate here. Both the poetic parallelism and a proposed Arabic cognate suggest that it means "breast" or "nipple."

12. *the glory of nations.* The context would indicate that "glory" here implies "wealth."
your babes shall be borne on the hip, / and on knees they shall be dandled. This line is a virtual citation of 60:4.

13. *comforts . . . / comfort . . . / comforted.* The triple insistence on this verb, following "her comforting breast" is an explicit allusion to the comforting, "Comfort. O comfort My people," at the beginning of chapter 40, bringing all of 40–66 to closure in an envelope structure.

14. *the LORD's hand.* As often elsewhere, "hand" suggests "power."

For, look, the LORD shall come in fire,   15
   and like the whirlwind His chariots,
to bring His anger to bear in fury
   and His rebuke in flames of fire.
For the LORD exacts justice in fire   16
   and with His sword against all flesh,
     and the slain by the LORD shall be many.

Those who consecrate themselves and purify themselves to enter the gar-   17
dens, following one in the center, eating the flesh of pigs, reptiles, and mice,
they shall come to an end together, says the LORD. As for Me, [I know] their 18a
acts and their devisings.

[A time] is coming to gather all nations and tongues, and they shall come 18b
and see My glory. And I will set a sign upon them and send from them sur- 19
vivors to the nations, to Pul and Lud, who draw the bow, Tubal and Javan,
the distant coastlands that have not heard of Me and have not seen My
glory, and they shall tell My glory among the nations. And they shall bring 20
your brothers from all the nations as an offering to the LORD on horses

---

16. *His sword against all flesh.* The phrase "all flesh," as in the Flood story (which may be a
relevant linguistic and thematic background here), means "all humankind." The objects,
then, of divine fury in this passage are by no means restricted to the paganizers in the
Judahite population but extend to all the nations that have violated God's law, whether by
oppressing Israel or in other ways.

17. *Those who consecrate themselves.* As the text moves from poetry to prose, the objects
of God's wrath again are those who engage in pagan rituals. One suspects that this verse
did not originally belong with what precedes it. "Consecrate" means to prepare oneself
ritually—perhaps through ablution and other acts of purification—to engage in the pagan
worship.
   following one in the center. Though "one" in the consonantal text is masculine, the
Masoretic marginal note changes it to a feminine. This might be a priestess ministering in
the cult, or it might be a vision of Asherah, the Canaanite fertility goddess, here worshipped
by those gathered round her in the sacred gardens.

19. *I will . . . send from them survivors to the nations.* In Second Isaiah, there is a vision of
acceptance of proselytes. This prophecy at the end goes a step further, imagining that those
among the nations who have finally seen God's glory wish to be sent out to the far reaches
of the known earth, as far as North Africa (Lud) and Greece (Javan) to bring the good news
of YHWH's universal dominion. This comes close to the project of a mission of conversion
in Acts and in the Pauline Epistles.

20. *they shall bring your brothers . . . as an offering.* "Offering," *minhah*, which means either
"grain offering" or "tribute," is used here metaphorically: the gentiles who bring back the
exiles to Zion will be as if bringing an offering to the Temple.

and chariots and covered wagons and on mules and on dromedaries to
My holy mountain in Jerusalem, said the LORD, as the Israelites bring a
21 grain offering in a pure vessel to the house of the LORD. And from them,
too, I shall take to be priests and Levites, said the LORD.

22   For as the new heavens and the new earth
              that I am making stand before Me, said the LORD
                  so shall stand your seed and your name.
23   And it shall be, from one month to the next
              and from one sabbath to the next,
        all flesh shall come
           to bow before Me, said the LORD.
24   And they shall go out and see
              the corpses of the people who rebelled against Me,
        for their worm shall never die
           and their fire shall not go out,
              and they shall be a horror to all flesh.

---

as the Israelites bring a grain offering. This clause explains the metaphor.

21. *I shall take to be priests and Levites.* This declaration, unless it is somehow figurative, is
a radical departure from earlier tradition, in which it is stipulated that only men from the
tribe of Levi are allowed to perform these functions, and certainly not proselytes.

22. *For as the new heavens and the new earth.* The book now concludes with an eschatological prophecy, again in poetry, that reprises the idea of a new creation put forth in 65:17.

23. *all flesh.* Once again, this expression means "all humankind," and so we have a universalist vision of all humanity coming to Jerusalem to worship God there. The precursor to
this prophecy is Isaiah 2:2–5.

24. *And they shall go out and see / the corpses of the people who rebelled against Me.* This
gloating—a sense implied by the verb "to see" followed in the Hebrew, as here, by the
preposition that means "in"—over the corpses of God's enemies, whether they are Judahite
paganizers or those of the nations who resisted God's word, is hardly an edifying note on
which to conclude the Book of Isaiah, as various commentators have noted. When these
verses were taken up as the prophetic reading or *haftarah* for the sabbath that falls on the
new moon, verse 23 was repeated after verse 24, in part to stress the conjunction of sabbath
and new moon but probably also to conclude the reading on an upbeat.

JEREMIAH

Introduction

O f all the prophets, Jeremiah is the one who conveys to us the most vivid sense of the man behind the words. For other prophets, we get at best a minimal notation of vocation (arborist, priest) and town of origin. However, Jeremiah, a priest from the town of Anathoth near Jerusalem who was active from the 620s B.C.E. until after the destruction of the kingdom of Judah in 586, tells us a good deal about himself because of his continual anguish over his prophetic calling. Many episodes of his life, moreover, are reported in narrative detail, for the most part probably by his amanuensis Baruch son of Neriah.

This was a trying moment for anyone to bring what he imperatively felt was God's word to the people of Israel. A century before the beginning of Jeremiah's mission, the northern kingdom of Israel had been overwhelmed by Assyrian invaders. A large part of the population was deported to sundry locations elsewhere in the Assyrian empire—this was when the so-called ten lost tribes were "lost"—and all vestiges of national sovereignty in the area once governed by the northern kingdom were eradicated. The extirpation of the northern kingdom was a national catastrophe that haunted its southern counterpart throughout the century and more that followed, since—given powerful military threats from foreign powers (for the first part of this period, the principal threat continued to be Assyria, then superseded by Babylonia)—the fate that had overtaken Israel could easily overtake Judah as well. In some of his prophecies, Jeremiah harbors the hope of a restored Israel reunited with a restored Judah, but one may justly describe this as a utopian fantasy, because by the late seventh century B.C.E. and early in the next century there were no visible remnants of the kingdom of Israel that could serve as the ground for such a restoration.

The other major event that stamped a strong mark on Jeremiah's prophecies was the sweeping religious reforms instigated by King Josiah beginning around 622 B.C.E. The playbook for these reforms was the text purportedly discovered during Josiah's renovation of the Temple and referred to in the account of its discovery in Kings as "the book of teaching [*torah*]," which is to say, the Book of Deuteronomy. The virtually unanimous scholarly consensus is that the book in question, or at least its core, was actually composed at this time to provide a textual warrant for the Josianic reforms. Its agenda incorporated two main points, one cultic and the other a theologically driven theory of historical causation. The previous four Books of Moses had assumed the legitimacy of the worship of God of Israel throughout the land; Deuteronomy now insisted that the cult could be practiced only "in the place that I will choose," which clearly meant Jerusalem. Sacrifice to YHWH on the "high places," the rural shrines, was excoriated as sheer paganism. The exclusive centralization of the cult was thus associated with Deuteronomy's persistent preoccupation with backsliding into paganism and with the notion that the worship of strange gods would lead directly to national disaster and exile as punishment for the people's failure to honor the covenant with its God.

All this is translated into Jeremiah's central message. While, like the other prophets, he on occasion castigates his audiences for egregious acts of social injustice and perversion of the legal system, his most repeated concern is with Judah's whoring after strange gods (the sexual metaphor is often flaunted) and the devastation of the nation that it will inevitably bring about. The English language aptly coined the noun "jeremiad"—a "complaining tirade," in the definition of the Oxford English Dictionary— because so often Jeremiah's prophecies are bitter denunciations of the people's wayward behavior accompanied by dire predictions that this will lead to scorched earth for the kingdom of Judah and exile for its inhabitants.

This sort of message, delivered at a time when Babylonian forces (597 B.C.E. and again in 587–586) were besieging Jerusalem, could not have made Jeremiah a very popular figure. The priests of his hometown of Anathoth, according to his own account, threatened to kill him. Zedekiah, the reigning monarch, had the scroll of his prophecies burned. (Jeremiah would promptly direct Baruch to make another copy.) Jeremiah was imprisoned more than once; in Jerusalem, his captors cast him into a deep, dried-up cistern with muck at the bottom, in the clear intention of leaving him there to die.

Against this background, one readily understands that Jeremiah saw his prophetic mission as a source of unending personal torment. Several of the prophets, beginning with Moses himself, express a sense of unworthiness to take up the prophetic calling. Thus Jeremiah: "Alas, O Master, LORD, / for, look, I know not how to speak, / for I am but a lad." (1:6). The reasonable inference is that Jeremiah was quite young when he first received the call, but in contrast to other prophets, tormented reluctance persists throughout his career. If at first he felt unworthy for the task, as he goes on to carry it out, subjected to vilification, death threats, and imprisonment, he repeatedly wishes he could free himself from the burden of prophecy; nevertheless, the searing consciousness that God demands it of him will not allow him to relinquish the prophetic role. The most striking expression of this dilemma is the great poem in chapter 20 that begins, "You have enticed me, O LORD, and I was enticed. / You are stronger than I, and You prevailed," and goes on to say, memorably, "I thought, 'I will not recall Him, / nor will I speak anymore in His name.' / But it was in my heart like burning fire / shut up in my bones." Jeremiah figures as a kind of prisoner of conscience: he is acutely aware that conveying his message of scathing castigation and impending doom at the very moment the Babylonian army is descending on Jerusalem will bring him nothing but humiliation and angry rejection, yet he feels he has no alternative other than to tell his people the bitter truth.

The lines in chapter 20 evoking Jeremiah's anguish over his prophetic calling are great poetry, and there are other strong and moving poems in the book. It must be said, however, that as a poet he does not exhibit a great deal of either the verbal virtuosity of Isaiah son of Amoz or the metaphoric brilliance of Second Isaiah. He is so intently focused on the message that artful articulation of the medium often seems less of a concern for him. Many of the poems use stereotypical phrases, and a considerable portion of the prophecies is delivered in prose. The prose seems especially prone to formulaic wording and to repetition, both within a single prophecy and between one prophecy and another. Jeremiah, like the other prophets, certainly exhibits a gift for elevated speech: it is the case for all the prophets that rhetorical power is inescapably part of effectively reporting the words of God to their audiences. But, by and large, one comes away from the collection of Jeremiah's prophecies not with a sense of deftly wrought verbal artifacts but rather with the existential and historical urgency of this particular prophet. Dark clouds of disaster lower over the kingdom of Judah. In Jeremiah's understanding, the disaster cannot be averted, for it is the ineluctable consequence of the people's violation of its covenant with God, its reckless infatuation with the gods and goddesses of a pagan cult, and the commission of acts of promiscuity and even human sacrifice entailed by that cult.

Politics is deeply implicated in this prophetic stance. The idea that Judah can parry the Babylonian threat by an alliance with Egypt is, in Jeremiah's eyes, a hopeless delusion. (This would prove to be an accurate political judgment.) The devastation of its towns, the exile of many of its inhabitants—the grim message that Jeremiah's countrymen did not want to hear—will surely come, and very soon. As a counterpoint, Jeremiah is also able to envisage a time when Babylonia itself will be destroyed and the people of Judah once more settled in peace and prosperity in its land. God would establish, in Jeremiah's pregnant phrase, a "new covenant" with His people. That upbeat message was dictated by an underlying theological assumption on the part of this harbinger of doom that, although God chastises Israel, His commitment to His people is for all time. But the vision of a radiant future remains a secondary emphasis in the somber prophecies of Jeremiah. The grand expression of such a vision would come a few decades after Jeremiah's lifetime in the poetry of the anonymous poet of the Babylonian exile whom scholars call Second Isaiah.

CHAPTER 1   The words of Jeremiah son of Hilkiah, of the 1
priests who were in Anathoth in the region of Benjamin, to whom the 2
word of the LORD came in the days of Josiah son of Amon king of Judah, in
the thirteenth year of his reign. And it continued in the days of Jehoiakim 3
son of Josiah until the end of the eleventh year of Zedekiah son of Josiah
king of Judah, until Jerusalem went into exile in the fifth month. And the 4
word of the LORD came to me, saying:

> Before I fashioned you in the belly I knew you, 5
>   and before you came out of the womb, I consecrated you.
>   A prophet to the nations I made you.
> And I said, "Alas, O Master, LORD, 6

CHAPTER 1   1. *The words of Jeremiah.* The term for "words," *devarim*, could also
mean "acts," though a continuity with "the word of the LORD" in the next verse might argue
against that sense here.

   Anathoth. This is a village near Jerusalem. Although Jeremiah is identified as a member
of the priestly caste there, what follows does not indicate that he was an officiant in the
Temple.

2. *in the thirteenth year of his reign.* This would be 626 B.C.E., four years before Josiah's
sweeping cultic reforms followed the purported discovery of the Book of Teaching (Deuteronomy) in the Temple. While some scholars have wondered why there is no direct
reflection of the Josianic reforms in Jerusalem's prophecies, it is noteworthy that he begins
with an indictment of imported pagan practices (see verse 16), unlike Isaiah, whose initial
emphasis is on social injustice. This stress on pagan practices may bespeak a Deuteroni-
mistic context.

3. *until Jerusalem went into exile.* This occurred in 586 B.C.E., roughly four decades after
the inauguration of Jeremiah's mission. There are, moreover, indications that he was not
entirely silent in the years immediately following the exile.

5. *I knew you, / . . . I consecrated you.* The sequence of verbs reflects the general pattern of
focusing in the second verset of a line of biblical poetry: first God has an intimate relationship with Jeremiah ("knew"); then He consecrates him as prophet. The third verset spells
out the nature of the consecration.

for, look, I know not how to speak,
     for I am but a lad."
7   And the LORD said to me,
          Do not say, "I am but a lad,"
     for wherever I send you, you shall go,
          and whatever I charge you, you shall speak.
8   Do not fear them,
          for I am with you to save you,
               said the LORD.

9   And the LORD reached out His hand and touched my mouth, and the LORD
10   said to me, "Look, I have put My words in your mouth. See, I have appointed
     you this day over nations and over kingdoms to uproot and to smash and
11   to destroy and to lay waste, to build and to plant." And the word of the
     LORD came to me, saying: "What do you see, Jeremiah?" And I said, "An
12   almond-tree wand do I see." And the LORD said to me, "You have seen well,
13   for I am vigilant with My word to do it." And the word of the LORD came
     to me a second time, saying: "What do you see?" And I said, "A seething

---

6. *I know not how to speak.* Jeremiah conforms here to a virtual *topos* of biblical prophecy. Moses and Isaiah before him first professed their inability to speak when God charged them with the prophetic mission.

   but a lad. The chronological range of the Hebrew *na'ar* slides from small child to young man. If Jeremiah is perhaps in his early twenties in 526 B.C.E., this would bring him into his sixties at the end of his career.

7. *And the LORD said to me.* Jeremiah's prophecies strikingly begin with a series of exchanges in dialogue between God and him, a feature that will continue in the prose section of this chapter.

8. *Do not fear them.* From the very start, a bitter antagonism is anticipated between Jeremiah and his audience. This theme will be developed in the military imagery of the concluding verses of the chapter.

9. *touched my mouth.* This dedication or empowering gesture is clearly reminiscent of Isaiah 6, where the seraph touches the prophet's mouth with a burning coal.

10. *to build and to plant.* After the prophecies of destruction, which will be preponderant as the items of destruction are preponderant in this sentence, there will be prophecies of restoration.

11. *What do you see, Jeremiah?* The question about the riddling vision resembles the question at the beginning of Amos. Both hinge on a pun (see the next note).

11–12. *An almond-tree wand . . . I am vigilant.* "Almond-tree" is *shaqed;* "vigilant" is *shoqed.*

pot I see, and it is turned to the north." And the LORD said to me, "From 14
the north shall the evil be broached on all the dwellers of the land. For I 15
am about to call forth all the clans of the kingdoms of the north," said the
LORD, "and they shall come and each set his throne at the entrance of the
gates of Jerusalem and against its walls all round and against all the towns
of Judah. And I will speak out My judgments against them, for all their evil 16
in that they forsook Me and burned incense to other gods and bowed down
to the work of their hands. As for you, you shall gird your loins and rise 17
and speak to them all that I charge you. Do not be broken-spirited before
them, lest I break you before them. As for Me, look, I have made you today 18
a fortress town and an iron pillar and walls of bronze against all the land,
against the kings of Judah and its nobles, against its priests and the people
of the land. And they shall battle against you but shall not prevail over you, 19
for I am with you," said the LORD, "to save you."

---

13. *it is turned to the north.* More literally, "it is facing the north." This wording has puzzled
interpreters because a pot has no front. Perhaps the least strained suggestion is Yair Hoffman's: the pot is sitting over a fire in a three-sided hearth, with the open side facing north.

14. *From the north shall the evil be broached.* The ominous nature of this prediction is
enhanced by the vagueness of the formulation. The enemy in the later sixth century B.C.E.
would have to be Babylonia, which is definitely more to the east than to the north, though
perhaps a northern invasion route is envisaged. The destroyer from the north also invokes
the dire memory of Assyria, which a century earlier descended from the north and annihilated the kingdom of Israel.

15. *each set his throne at the entrance of the gates of Jerusalem.* These are thrones because
kings command these daunting forces; what emerges is a rather surrealistic picture of kings
on their thrones sitting in siege against Jerusalem. It should be noted that many scholars,
including the editors of the *Biblia Hebraica*, read all or most of the section beginning with
verse 14 as poetry. To this translator, however, all these verses do not seem to be sufficiently
tight metrically to qualify as verse; however, as is often the case with high-rhetorical prose,
they exhibit loose approximations of the parallel structures of poetry.

16. *against them.* As the next clause makes clear, "them" refers to the Judahites, not to the
invading kings.

17. *Do not be broken-spirited.* The basic meaning of this verb is "to be afraid" but the next
clause plays on its other sense, "to be broken."

18. *a fortress town and an iron pillar and walls of bronze.* Here the military metaphor of
Jeremiah's oppositional stance is spelled out: God will make him an impregnable city,
with pillars not of stone but of iron and walls not of stone but of bronze. All this suggests
a prophet who is apprehensive from the start of a fierce struggle with those to whom he
has been sent.

1 CHAPTER 2   And the word of the LORD came to me, saying,
2 "Go and call out in the hearing of Jerusalem, saying, Thus said the LORD:

> I recalled for you the kindness of your youth,
>   your bridal love,
> your coming after Me in the wilderness,
>   in an unsown land.

3
> Israel is holy to the LORD,
>   the first fruits of His harvest.
> All who eat it bear guilt,
>   evil shall come upon them,
>   said the LORD.

4
> Listen to the word of the LORD, House of Jacob,
>   and all the clans of the House of Israel.

5
> Thus said the LORD:
> What wrong did your fathers find in Me
>   that they grew distant from Me
>   went after mere breath and turned into mere breath?

6
> And they did not say, "Where is the LORD,
>   Who brought us up from the land of Egypt

CHAPTER 2   2. *the kindness of your youth.* As elsewhere, the Hebrew *ḥesed* equally
implies loyalty in a relationship.

your bridal love. This image of Israel as bride, God as her spouse, later provided a powerful warrant for the allegorical reading of the Song of Songs.

your coming after Me in the wilderness, / in an unsown land. In the interlinear parallelism between this line and the preceding one, we are now given a concretization of the
bride Israel's loyalty and love: she did not hesitate to follow after her divine husband even
in the forbidding landscape of the Sinai desert.

3. *Israel is holy to the LORD.* The Hebrew also suggests something like "dedicated," "the
special possession of." Having shown her devotion in the wilderness, she becomes "holy
to the LORD."

4. *the house of Israel.* It is by no means necessary to conclude, as some scholars have, that
those words are addressed to the remnants of the northern kingdom of Israel, destroyed a
century earlier. With the northern kingdom gone forever, "Israel" began to be an alternative designation for the people of Judah, at least in literary usage. One sees the term used
this way in verse 14.

5. *went after mere breath and turned into mere breath.* "Mere breath," *hevel,* the term reiterated in Qohelet, is here a pejorative epithet for foreign gods, who have no real existence. The
cognate verb that is coined in this line expresses the idea that those who worship emptiness
turn themselves into emptiness.

and led us through the wilderness
    in a land of desert and pits,
in a land of parched earth and death's shadow,
    in a land where no man had gone,
        and where no human dwelled?"
And I brought you to a country of farmland   7
    to eat its fruit and its bounty,
and you came and defiled My land
    and My estate you made abhorrent.
The priests did not say, "Where is the LORD?"   8
    And those skilled in the Teaching did not know Me,
        and the shepherds rebelled against Me,
and the prophets prophesied for Baal,
    and after what cannot avail they went.
Therefore will I yet dispute with you—   9
    said the LORD—and with the sons of your sons will I dispute.
For pass through the isles of the Kittites and see,   10
    send out to Kedar and look carefully
        and see, has there been the like of this?
Has a nation given up its gods   11
    though they are ungods?
But My people exchange its Glory

---

6. *led us through the wilderness.* This clause plays back on Israel's going after God in the wilderness in verse 2.

7. *you came and defiled My land.* The formulation reflects an understanding that the land belongs to God, Who has bestowed it on the people as a bounty.

8. *those skilled in the Teaching.* The literal sense is "those who hold on to the Teaching," but that verb is used for anyone adept at a particular profession or skill.
    the shepherds. This is a fixed epithet for "rulers."
    what cannot avail. This is still another epithet for the nonentity of pagan gods.

9. *dispute.* The verb implies contestation in a court of law.

10. *the isles of the Kittites.* Many scholars think the reference is to Cyprus, though this may well be a more general invocation of the Greek islands far to the west of the Land of Israel.
    send out to Kedar. "Kedar" refers to Arab tribes, and so the line swings broadly from west to east and from sea to land.

11. *Has a nation given up its gods / though they are ungods?* The prophet here frames an *a fortiori* argument: in new lands that are known, from west to east, has a people switched gods, even though the gods they worship are not real? Yet Israel has exchanged its own glorious God for a set of illusions.

for what cannot avail.

12   Be appalled, O heavens, for this,
        be shocked, altogether, desolate—
           said the LORD.

13   For two evils My people has done:
        Me they forsook, the source of living waters,
      to hew for themselves cisterns, broken cisterns,
        that cannot hold the water.

14   Is Israel a slave, is he home-born chattel?
        Why has he become plunder?

15   Lions roar over him,
        lift up their cry,
      and they have made his land a desolation,
        his towns are ravaged with no dweller there.

16   The men, too, of Noph and Tahpanes
        shall smash your pate.

17   Is not this how you fare
        for forsaking the LORD your God
           when He led you on the way?

18   And now, why go in the way of Egypt
        to drink the waters of the Nile,
      and why go in the way of Assyria

---

12. *Be appalled, O heavens.* The Hebrew strengthens the emphasis through sound-play, *shomu shamayim.*

13. *cisterns, broken cisterns.* A cistern hewn in rock is a receptacle for the storage of water (perhaps rainwater) and not a water source or spring that continually flows. Its sides might be plastered but would be subject to cracks and breaks through which the water could leak out.

14. *Is Israel a slave.* Given the people's subjugation to foreign powers ("become plunder"), the prophet asks why such a fate should have befallen a freeborn people.

15. *Lions.* The Hebrew *kefirim* is the "young lions" of the King James Version, but that is merely part of the translators' desperate attempt to coin different terms for the five biblical synonyms for "lion." Presumably, the lions are a metaphor here for the invading foreign armies.

16. *Noph and Tahpanes.* These are prominent Egyptian cities. Jeremiah follows his predecessor Isaiah in thinking that any alliance with Egypt will in the end prove disastrous.

18. *why go in the way of Assyria.* We can infer that this prophecy was proclaimed before the final destruction of Assyria in 612 B.C.E. or shortly thereafter, at a moment when some circles in Judah imagined that an alliance with Assyria could save them from the onslaught of the Babylonians.

to drink the Euphrates' waters?
Let your evil chastise you   19
   and your rebellion reprove you,
and mark and see that it is evil and bitter,
   your forsaking the LORD your God.
The fear of Me is not upon you
   said the Master, LORD of Armies.
For of old you broke your yoke,   20
   you tore apart your bands,
     and you said, "I will not serve."
For on every high hill
   and under every lush tree
     you lean back, a whore.
And I, I planted you as a choice vine,   21
   a wholly true seed,
and how have you turned against Me
   into a wayward alien vine?
Though you scrub with natron   22
   and use abundant lye,
your crime is stained before Me,
   said the Master, the LORD.
How can you say, "I was not defiled,   23
   after the Baalim I have not gone"?

---

19. *Let your evil chastise you.* Some translators understand the noun *raʿah* here as "misfortune," but the parallelism with *meshuvotayikh*, which can only mean "rebellion" or "backsliding," argues against that construction. What the line rather says is: you have committed yourself to your wayward path, and that will eventually bring upon you dire consequences that may compel you to reflect on what you have done.

   it is evil. This phrase picks up on "evil" at the beginning of the verse.

20. *on every high hill / and under every lush tree.* These are places for worshipping nature gods, often in fertility rites, as the third verset suggests.

   you lean back, a whore. Jack R. Lundbom is probably right in proposing that the verb suggests a sexual position. The verset blends literal statement with metaphor: whoring is a recurrent metaphorical representation of idol worship (Israel's betrayal of her divine spouse), but literal sexual acts were performed in pagan rites in those bucolic settings.

22. *natron.* This is an English cognate, by way of the Greek, of the Hebrew *neter*, a sodium carbonate compound used in laundering.

   your crime is stained before Me. The image of the stain reverses Isaiah 1:18, "If your offenses be like scarlet, like snow shall they turn white."

23. *after the Baalim I have not gone.* This is a pointed antithesis to "your going after Me in the wilderness" in verse 2.

See your way in the valley,
    know what you have done.
A swift she-camel threading her way,
24   a wild ass at home in the wilderness,
sniffing wind in the lust of her appetite,
    her desire cannot be turned back.
All who seek her will not tire,
    in her season they will find her.
25 Keep your feet from walking bare
    and your throat from going dry.
And you give up hope, saying,
    "No, I love strangers,
      and after them I will go."
26 Like the shame of a thief when he is caught,
    thus the house of Israel acted shamefully,
they, their kings, and their nobles,
    and their priests, and their prophets.
27 They say to a tree, "You are my father,"
    and to a stone, "You gave birth to me."
For they have turned their backs to Me
    and not their faces.

See your way in the valley. Since Antiquity, many interpreters have seen here a reference to the Valley of Hinnom in Jerusalem, where child sacrifice was practiced.

23-24. *A swift she-camel . . . / a wild ass.* The image of idolatrous Israel as a whore is made more extreme now by likening the wayward people to animals in heat.

24. *sniffing wind in the lust of her appetite.* The female wild ass in heat sniffs for the scent of the male.
    All who seek her will not tire. In heat, she is easily accessible to any male that wants to couple with her.
    in her season. The literal sense is "in her month." The Septuagint shows "season," but that may be merely a translator's interpretation of "month."

25. *Keep your feet from walking bare / and your throat from going dry.* The probable reference is to lubricious Israel (throughout personified as a woman, with feminine grammatical forms used here), who runs barefoot after her lovers and cries out in lust until she is hoarse.
    you give up hope. Literally, "you say 'despair.'"

27. *to a tree, "You are my father," / and to a stone, "You gave birth to me."* Although trees were part of the cult of Asherah, the fertility goddess, and stones were often used for making the images of sundry male gods, the line is guided by grammatical gender—in Hebrew, "tree" is masculine and "stone" feminine.
    turned their backs. Literally, "turned their nape."

And when disaster befalls them, they say,
    "Arise and rescue us."
And where are your gods that you made for yourself?   28
    Let them rise and rescue when disaster befalls you.
For as the number of your towns
    were your gods, O Judah.
Why do you dispute with Me?   29
    All of you rebelled against Me, said the LORD.
In vain did I strike your sons,   30
    they did not accept reproval.
Your sword has consumed your prophets
    like a ravaging lion.
O you generation, see the word of the LORD!   31
    Was I a wilderness to Israel,
        a land of deep darkness?
Why did My people say, "We have broken loose,
    we will no longer come to you"?
Does a virgin forget her jewels,   32
    a bride her knotted sash?
Yet My people has forgotten Me,
    days without number.
How you make your way fair   33
    to seek love!
Thus, even to wicked women
    you have taught your ways.
In your skirts, as well, is found   34
    the lifeblood of the innocent poor.
Not in a hideout did I find them,
    but upon all of these.

---

30. *Your sword has consumed your prophets.* One may recall the slaughter of the prophets of YHWH by Ahab, and the murder of prophets by paganizing monarchs probably occurred in later reigns as well.

33. *How you make your way fair.* Literally, this could be "make your way good" or "do well in your way." This translation follows Rashi, who understands this as the woman primping and adorning herself in order to attract lovers.

34. *the lifeblood of the innocent poor.* Remarkably, this is the very first reference in the book to a sin of perpetrating injustice rather than a cultic trespass.
    a hideout. This is actually a tunnel dug in order to break into a house.
    but upon all of these. The reference is a little obscure. Perhaps the meaning is "all of these skirts," which would be splattered with the blood of the innocent.

35   And you said, "I am innocent.
         Why, His wrath has turned back from me."
      I am about to exact judgment from you,
         for your saying, "I did not offend."
36   Why do you cheapen yourself so much
         to change your way?
      By Egypt, too, you shall be shamed
         as you were shamed by Assyria.
37   For from this you shall come out
         with your hands upon your head.
      For the LORD spurns the ones you trust,
         and you shall not succeed through them.

CHAPTER 3

1   [And the word of the LORD came to me], saying:
      Look, should a man send away his wife,
         and she go from him and become another man's,
            can he go back to her again?
      Would not that land be wholly polluted?
         And you, you have whored with many lovers,
            and would you come back to Me? said the LORD.
2   Lift up your eyes to the bare heights and see.

---

36. *to change your way.* That is, to change your way from following the God of Israel to going after strange gods.

37. *For from this you shall come out.* In light of the immediately preceding line, "this" would have to be Egypt.
   with your hands upon your head. This is a gesture of despair or mourning.

CHAPTER 3   1. *saying.* This single word begins the Hebrew text of this chapter. Either it should be deleted, or, more likely, the introductory formula here presented in brackets was inadvertently omitted in scribal transmission.
   send away. This is the set term for divorce.
   can he go back to her again? According to the law in Deuteronomy 24:1–4, a man is not permitted to remarry his divorced wife.
   lovers. Though the Hebrew *re'im* usually means "companions," as it clearly does below in verse 20, the immediate context suggests the sense of "lovers," the same association for this noun clearly indicated in Hosea 3:1.

2. *to the bare heights.* These are probably the same locations as "the high hills" where fertility rites were conducted.

Where have they not lain with you?
On the roads you sat waiting for them
   like an Arab in the desert,
and you polluted the land
   through your whoring and through your evil.
And the showers were held back,   3
   and the latter rains did not come,
and a whore-woman's brow you had,
   you refused to be shamed.
Have you now not called Me, "My father,"   4
   You are the guide of my youth.
Will He bear a grudge forever,   5
   will He keep it for all time?
Look, you spoke and did evil things, and will you prevail?

And the LORD said to me in the days of King Josiah, "Have you seen what 6 Rebel Israel has done? She goes on every high mountain and under every lush tree and plays the whore there. And I thought, after she has done all 7 those, she will come back to Me, but she did not come back, and her sister, Judah the Treacherous, saw. And she saw that because Rebel Israel had 8

Where have they not lain with you? The passive Hebrew verb in the consonantal text, *shugalt*, is evidently a ruder term, euphemistically corrected in the Masoretic marginal note to the verb that means "to lie." Lundbom gets the flavor of the rudeness by translating the phrase as "where have you not been laid," but that expression sounds too colloquially modern.

On the roads you sat waiting for them. "Waiting for" is elliptically implied in the Hebrew, as Rashi notes. The story of Tamar and Judah in Genesis 38 leads one to infer that prostitutes often stationed themselves by the roadside to ply their trade.

like an Arab in the desert. The Arab is perhaps imagined sitting in his tent waiting for passing caravans in order to conduct commerce. Others see a reference to Arab marauders waiting to attack travelers.

4. *Have you not called Me, "My father."* These are the self-deluded words of Judah (still imagined in the second-person feminine singular as a woman), who has not truly turned back to God yet fancies that she has an intimate relationship with Him and that He will bear her no grudge.

5. *will you prevail?* The received text seems to say "And she will prevail," which does not make much sense. This translation emends the verb to a second-person feminine singular, like the two preceding verbs in this sentence, and construes it as a rhetorical question.

8. *And she saw.* The Masoretic Text has "And I saw," but both the Septuagint and the Peshitta show this more plausible reading, "And she saw."

committed adultery I sent her away and gave her a bill of divorce, yet Judah
9 the Treacherous did not fear, and she, too, went and played the whore. And
it happened that from all her whoring the land was polluted, and she com-
10 mitted adultery with stone and with tree. And yet, despite all this, Judah
the Treacherous did not turn back to Me with a whole heart but falsely,"
11 said the LORD. And the LORD said to me, "Rebel Israel has shown herself
12 more in the right than Judah the Treacherous. Go and call out these words
to the north and say, Turn back, Rebel Israel, said the LORD, and I will not
set My face against you, for I am faithful, said the LORD. I will not bear a
13 grudge forever. But know your crime, for against the LORD your God you
have rebelled, and you have scattered your ways among strangers under
14 every lush tree, and My voice you have not heeded, said the LORD. Turn
back, rebellious sons, said the LORD, for I have claimed possession of you
and have taken you, one from a town and two from a clan, and brought you

---

I sent her away and gave her a bill of divorce. The prophet, continuing his favored metaphor of the turn to pagan worship as sexual betrayal, represents the exile of the northern
kingdom as God's divorcing Israel.

9. *from all her whoring.* The received text seems to say "from the voice of her whoring,"
miqol zenutah. Many scholars emend this to *miqal zenutah,* claiming it means "from her
casual [or easy] whoring," but *qal* is an adjective that does not make syntactical sense as a
construct form with *zenutah.* This translation reads instead *mikol zenutah.*

11. *Rebel Israel has shown itself more in the right than Judah the Treacherous.* In this continuing allegory of the two sister-kingdoms, Judah is even worse than Israel—either because she
has the monitory example of exiled Israel before her eyes yet does not pay heed, or because
Jeremiah represents her as actually exceeding Israel in her paganizing promiscuity.

12. *call out these words to the north.* The likely location is not the kingdom of Israel, long
destroyed and its population largely replaced by people brought in from elsewhere in the
Assyrian sphere, but the northern reaches of the Assyrian empire, to which the inhabitants
of Israel have been exiled. This prophecy, enunciated a century after the destruction of the
northern kingdom, surely expresses what is no more than a utopian hope, for by Jeremiah's
time the exiles would have been assimilated into the surrounding peoples and would have
lost their national identity.
   Turn back, Rebel Israel. The Hebrew, *shuvah meshuvah yisra'el,* exhibits sound-play
(roughly like "turn back, backsliding Israel" in English). Verses 14 and 22 show a related
sound-play, *shuvu banim shovavim,* "Turn back, rebellious sons."

13. *you have scattered your ways.* The phrasing sounds a little odd, but the probable reference, as the medieval Hebrew commentator David Kimchi proposes, is to the many different gods that promiscuous Israel chose to worship.

14. *one from a town and two from a clan.* This looks like a version of the notion of the
saving remnant articulated by Isaiah. Only a small minority will be saved and brought
back to Zion.

to Zion. And I have given you shepherds after My own heart, and they have   15
shepherded you with knowledge and discernment. And it shall happen   16
when you multiply and are fruitful in those days, said the LORD, that they
no longer shall say 'the Ark of the LORD's Covenant' nor shall they bring it
to mind nor shall they recall it nor seek it out, nor shall it again be made. At   17
that time they shall call Jerusalem 'Throne of the LORD,' and all the nations
shall gather in it in the name of the LORD, in Jerusalem, and they shall not
go after the willfulness of their evil heart. In those days the house of Judah   18
shall go with the house of Israel, and they shall come together from the land
of the north to the land that I gave in estate to your fathers."

> As for Me, I said,   19
>   How shall I place you among children?
> I gave you a land of delight,
>   an estate of the greatest splendor of nations,
> and I said, You shall call Me "my Father,"
>   and you shall not turn back from Me.
> Yet, as a woman betrays her companion,   20
>   you have betrayed Me, O house of Israel,
>   said the LORD.
> A voice is heard on the bare heights,   21
>   the weeping supplications of Israel's children.
> For they have made their way crooked,
>   forgotten the LORD their God.

---

15. *shepherds.* As before, these are the rulers of the people.

16. *they no longer shall say "the Ark of the LORD's covenant."* The Ark Narrative in 1 Samuel 5–7 suggests that a fetishistic conception of the Ark as a magical object had currency among the people.

    nor shall it again be made. These words may indicate that the supposed original Ark had been removed from the Temple and lost, which one may infer from some biblical texts but not from others.

17. *they shall call Jerusalem "Throne of the LORD."* The Ark, crowned with carved cherubim, was in fact conceived as God's throne. In the new age, however, all Jerusalem will be a manifestation of God's presence, and hence there will be no need for a material cult-object like the Ark.

18. *the house of Judah shall go with the house of Israel.* This culminates the utopian fantasy that the northern kingdom will be restored—"from the land of the north," which is to say Assyrian exile—and will live in harmony with the southern kingdom.

21. *the weeping supplications of Israel's children.* They have realized the dire straits into which their actions have brought them.

22   Turn back, rebellious children—
              I will heal your rebellion.
           "Here we are, we have come to you,
              for You are the LORD and God.
           Indeed, falsehood is from the hills,
              the clamor of the mountains.
           Indeed, in the LORD our God
              is Israel's rescue.

23   And the shameful thing consumed
              the toil of our fathers from our youth,
           their sheep and their cattle,
              their sons and their daughters.

24   Let us lie down in our shame,
              and our disgrace be our cover,
                for the LORD our God we have offended,
           we and our fathers from our youth
              to this very day,
                and we did not heed the voice of the LORD our God."

CHAPTER 4

1   If you turn back, Israel, said the LORD,
              to Me you shall turn back,
           and if you remove your foul things
              from before Me and do not waiver,

2   I vow, as the LORD lives, in truth,
              in justice, and in righteousness,

---

22. *I will heal your rebellion.* This is best understood as an ellipsis: I will heal the terrible consequences of your rebellion. What follows is a confession of wrongdoing by the penitent rebels.

falsehood is from the hills, / the clamor of the mountains. The hills are where the pagan gods were worshipped. The clamor would refer to the throng of celebrants on the heights, raising their voices in the performance of their rites.

23. *the shameful thing.* The noun *boshet*, "shame" or "shameful thing," is regularly used as a pejorative substitution for "Baal." One sees this in theophoric names, where the *baal* suffix has been editorially changed to *boshet*, as in "Mephibosheth," originally "Mephibaal."

consumed / the toil of our fathers. As the next line makes clear, the wealth of the fathers, their sheep and their cattle, has been eaten up in sacrifices to Baal, and, what is worse, their sons and daughters have been offered in sacrifice as well.

that nations shall bless themselves through you,
  and through you shall they be praised.
For thus said the LORD to the men of Judah and Jerusalem: 3
  Till for yourselves tilled ground,
    and do not sow among thorns.
Be circumcised to the LORD   4
  and remove your hearts' foreskins,
    men of Judah and dwellers of Jerusalem,
lest My wrath come forth like fire
  and burn with none to quench it
    because of the evil of your acts.
Tell it in Judah,   5
  and in Jerusalem make it heard and say,
blow the ram's horn in the land,
  call out with full voice and say:
Assemble and let us come
  to the fortified towns.
Raise a banner toward Zion,   6
  take refuge, do not stand,
for I am about to bring harm from the north
  and a great disaster.
A lion has sprung from its thicket,   7
  and the ravager of nations has journeyed,

CHAPTER 4   2. *nations shall bless themselves through you.* This echoes God's promise to Abraham in Genesis 22:18.

  and through you shall they be praised. This probably means, as Rashi observes, that they
will consider it a merit for themselves to be associated with Israel

3. *Till for yourselves tilled ground.* As a prudent farmer cultivates cleared and tillable ground,
you should guide your acts in accordance with God's teaching and not give yourself over to
the futility of strange gods (the implicit referent of "thorns").

4. *Be circumcised to the LORD / and remove your hearts' foreskins.* This image anticipates
Paul's idea about the circumcision of the heart. Since the heart was thought of as the seat
of understanding, a membrane covering it would mean an unperceptive heart.

5. *blow the ram's horn.* One function of blowing the ram's horn was as a military signal,
either to assemble the troops or, as here, to sound a retreat.

6. *Raise a banner toward Zion.* The banner in this instance points to the direction to flee
to Zion as a fortified city.

7. *A lion has sprung from its thicket.* As elsewhere in biblical poetry, the lion is a set metaphor for a warrior or an army.

he has come forth from his place
　　to make your land desolate.
　　　　Your towns shall be ruined with no dweller.
8　　For this gird sackcloth,
　　　　keen and howl,
　　for the wrath of the LORD
　　　　has not turned back from him.
9　　And it shall happen on that day, said the LORD,
　　　　the heart of the king shall fail
　　　　　　and the heart of the nobles,
　　and desolate the priests shall be,
　　　　and the prophets shall be dumbfounded.
10　　And I said, "Alas, O Master, LORD!
　　　　Surely You have misled this people and Jerusalem,
　　saying, 'You shall have peace,'
　　　　but the sword has touched the throat."
11　　And at that time it shall be said
　　　　to this people and to Jerusalem:
　　a parching wind from the bare heights in the desert
　　　　going through My People's Daughter—
　　　　　　neither to winnow nor to sift.
12　　A full wind from these comes against Me.
　　　　Now will I speak judgments against them.
13　　Look, he comes up like the clouds
　　　　and like the whirlwind his chariots.
　　His horses are swifter than eagles—

---

9. *and desolate the priests shall be, / and the prophets shall be dumbfounded.* The translation reproduces the chiasm of the Hebrew, which has the expressive effect of sandwiching the priests and prophets between "desolate" and "dumbfounded."

10. *You shall have peace.* Although this could also mean "All will be well with you," the antithesis with the sword against the throat suggests that *shalom* here has the force of "peace."

11. *a parching wind.* The adjective *tsaḥ* in this instance does not mean "bright," as it does in the Song of Songs, but derives from *tseḥah* and *tsaḥiah*, terms that indicate a state of being parched.

　　neither to winnow nor to sift. This devastating wind blowing from the eastern desert— what is called from the Arabic the *khamsin*—allows nothing to grow and be harvested.

12. *from these.* The reference is obscure, and this single (Hebrew) word is not reflected in the Septuagint.

woe to us, for we are destroyed!

Cleanse your heart of evil, Jerusalem,   14
    so that you may be rescued.
How long will there lodge in your midst
    your wicked devisings?
For a voice proclaims from Dan   15
    and announces disaster from Mount Ephraim.
Make it known to the nations, look!   16
    Announce it concerning Jerusalem.
Watchers are coming from a faraway land,
    and they shall raise their voice against Judah's towns.
Like guards of the field they are against her all round,   17
    for she has rebelled against Me.
Your way and your deeds   18
    have done these to you,
this evil of yours, which is bitter,
    for it has touched your very heart.
My gut, my gut—I writhe,   19
    the walls of my heart,
my heart moans in me,
    I am not still,
for the ram's horn's sound I have heard,
    the blare of war.
Disaster upon disaster is called forth,   20
    for all the land is destroyed,
all at once my tents are destroyed,
    in a moment, my tent curtains.
How long shall I see the banner,   21

---

16. *Watchers.* The use of this term is ironic—the "watchers" are the invaders who have come to encircle Judah. The Hebrew *notsrim* may also pun on the verb *tsur*, "to besiege."

17. *Like guards of the field.* This simile continues the irony of "watchers"—people who guard a field to protect it from incursions—but these "guards" are besiegers.

19. *My gut, my gut.* Even though this is inelegant in English, it faithfully represents the Hebrew *me'ai me'ai.* The gut or intestine (the King James Version's "bowels") was thought to be the seat of emotion or compassion, but the expressive thrust here is that the prophet's innards and heart are pounding within him as he envisages the unfolding disaster.

21. *How long shall I see the banner.* This is the banner held aloft by the attacking army. There were no national flags in the ancient period, but military contingents had banners, like the armies in Japan's samurai era.

> hear the ram's horn's sound?
22   For My people are fools,
>   Me they did not know.
> Ignorant children are they,
>   and they are not discerning,
> they are wise to do evil,
>   but they know not how to do good.

23   I saw the earth, and, look, welter and waste,
>   the heavens, and their light was gone.
24   I saw the mountains and, look, they quaked,
>   and all the hills broke apart.
25   I saw, and look, there was no human there,
>   and all the fowl of the heavens had gone away.
26   I saw, and, look, the farmland was desert,
>   and all its towns were ruined

---

23. *I saw the earth, and, look, welter and waste.* This powerful prophecy is one of the most striking instances in which the hyperbole of Prophetic poetry pushes it toward apocalyptic vision, almost despite itself. What Jeremiah is imagining is the devastation of the land by foreign invaders, but by invoking the language of creation from Genesis 1, he conjures up a vision of reversing the very act of creation: if the world was once created out of welter and waste, when primordial darkness reigned over all, the process might be turned backward, everything reverting to its uncreated state. This vision is all the more vivid because the prophet reports it as though it were something he had actually witnessed with his own eyes, as he repeatedly insists on "I saw, and, look."

the heavens, and their light was gone. This reverses the "Let there be light" of Genesis 1. This is an anticipation of the apocalyptic note at the end of Alexander Pope's *Dunciad:* "Light dies before thy uncreating word."

25. *there was no human there.* In Genesis 1, the human—male and female—is the culminating product of creation.

all the fowl of the heavens. This is still another phrase from the Creation story. The vision has the effect of a science-fiction fantasy: not only is the earth turned back to primordial chaos with no remnant of human presence, but when the prophet looks up to the sky, it is mere vacancy, without birds.

26. *the farmland was desert, / and all its towns were ruined.* At this point, the vision segues from the global picture of the catastrophic reversal of creation to the historical picture of the land devastated by invaders. For this reason, *ha'arets* in this next verse could mean either "the earth" in consonance with the incipiently apocalyptic vision of verses 23–25, or "the land," in consonance with this verse, and perhaps a double meaning is intended. It is noteworthy that "all the earth shall mourn, / and the heavens above shall darken" in verse 28 reverts to the grim picture of the negation of creation.

before the Lord and before His blazing wrath.

For thus said the Lord: 27

A desolation shall all the earth be

    but I will not wreak utter destruction.

For this all the earth shall mourn,   28

    and the heavens above shall darken,

for I have spoken, I have laid plans,

    and I did not repent nor turn back from it.

From the sound of the horseman and archer   29

    all the town flees.

They have entered the crannies,

    gone up to the cliffs,

all the town is abandoned,

    and no man dwells in it.

As for you, the destroyed one, what have you done,   30

    that you dress up in scarlet,

        that you put on bangles of gold,

that you set off your eyes in kohl?

    For naught you make yourself lovely.

Your lovers despise you,

    your life they seek.

For I have heard a sound like a woman in labor,   31

    distress like one giving birth the first time,

        the voice of Zion's Daughter panting,

she stretches out her hands:

    "Woe to me, for my being goes faint before the killers!"

---

30. *the destroyed one.* The evident sense is "the one destined to be destroyed," foreseen and imagined as though it were already an accomplished fact. The Hebrew term is masculine but a feminine form is required, which may simply reflect a scribal lapse.

that you set off your eyes in kohl. The literal sense of the verb is "tear open." Rashi is probably right in proposing that outlining the eyes in dark kohl makes them appear to be larger (one is tempted to attribute his perception to the knowingness of an early French observer).

Your lovers. The Hebrew '*ogvim* has a strong sexual connotation, and so the meaning is close to "those who lust for you."

31. *a woman in labor, / . . . one giving birth the first time.* While the writhing of a woman in birth pangs is a conventional trope for suffering, it ends up being ironized here because the verse concludes in death instead of birth. The word "killers" is held back until the very end of the next poetic line.

CHAPTER 5

1   Roam through the streets of Jerusalem,
    and see, pray, and mark,
      and seek in her squares.
  If you find a man,
    if there be a man doing justice, seeking faithfulness,
      I shall forgive her.
2   But if, "as the Lord lives," they say,
    they swear falsely.
3   O Lord, Your eyes look for faithfulness.
    You struck them but they did not flinch,
      You made an end of them, they refused to take reproof.
  They made their faces harder than rock,
    they refused to turn back.
4   As for me, I said, they are but poor people,
    they are foolish,
  for they know not the way of the Lord,
    their God's justice.
5   Let me go to the great ones,
    and let me speak with them,
  for they know the way of the Lord,
    the justice of their God.
  But they together broke the yoke,
    they tore apart the bonds.
6   Therefore has the lion from the forest struck them,

CHAPTER 5   1. *If you find a man, / if there be a man doing justice.* Yair Hoffman detects an echo here of Abraham's dialogue with God in Genesis 18 over whether Sodom can be spared if ten just men can be found in it. That allusion mobilizes the trope of Israel as Sodom (compare Isaiah 1) and also makes the terms more generous: God would forgive Jerusalem if a single just man could be found there.

2. *But if, "as the Lord lives."* The habit of swearing in the Lord's name persists, even as the people abandon God.
   swear falsely. The Hebrew could also be rendered as "swear by a lie." Lundbom proposes that this "lie" refers to Baal.

3. *Your eyes look for faithfulness.* "Look" is merely implied.

5. *the great ones.* The Hebrew term suggests high social status and, probably, wealth.

the wolf of the steppes destroys them,
the leopard lies in wait at their towns,
all who come forth from there are ripped up.
For their crimes are many,
numerous their rebellions.
"Why, for this should I pardon you?   7
Your sons have forsaken Me
and sworn by ungods.
I sated them, yet they were adulterous,
and to the whore's house they trooped.
They were horses in heat rising early,   8
each man for his fellow's wife neighed.
For these shall I not exact judgment," said the Lord, 9
"and against a nation such as this not wreak vengeance?
Go up against her vine rows and ruin them,   10
but an utter end do not bring about.
Strip off her trailing branches,
for they are not the Lord's.
For the house of Israel and the house of Judah   11
have surely betrayed Me," said the Lord.
"They have been false to the Lord   12
and said, 'Not He.
And no harm will come upon us
and the sword and famine we shall not see.

---

6. *the lion . . . / the wolf . . . / the leopard.* All three beasts of prey are metaphors for an invading army.

7. *I sated them, yet they were adulterous.* Though God bestowed great bounty on the people, they betrayed Him. Since Israel is thought of as God's spouse, the adultery is its infatuation with alien gods, but the evocation of rampant lust in the next three lines is so vivid that one may see here a segue into a condemnation of actual sexual promiscuity.

8. *They were horses in heat rising early.* Two words in the Hebrew here are obscure, although the general reference to rampant sexuality is clear. The term *meyuzanim*, "in heat," does not appear elsewhere; some interpreters take it to refer to large sexual organs. *Mashkim*, "rising early," looks odd because it is singular and a plural form is required. If the present translation is correct, it would point to an eagerness of lust that impels these men to get up early in order to hop into bed with the wives of their fellow men.

12. *Not He.* These two words could also mean, "That's not it."

13   And the prophets are but wind,
     and there is no Word in them—
       thus shall be done to them.'
14   Therefore thus said the LORD God of Armies:
    Because you spoke this word,
      I am about to put My words in your mouth like fire
       and this people shall be wood it consumes.
15   I am about to bring against you a nation from afar,
     O house of Israel," said the LORD.
    "It is a nation of unfailing strength,
     a nation from of old,
   a nation whose tongue you do not know,
     nor understand what it speaks.
16   Its quiver—an open grave,
    all of them are warriors,
17   It shall devour your harvest and your bread,
     devour your sons and your daughters,
   devour your sheep and your cattle,
     devour your vines and your fig trees.
    I shall slash with the sword your fortress towns
     in which you trusted."

---

13. *And the prophets are but wind.* The Hebrew puns on *ruaḥ,* which means both "spirit"—what is supposed to imbue the prophets—and "wind."

thus shall be done to them. This clause is best understood as the conclusion of the arrogant words of the people: having said that the prophets have no divine word to convey, they now curse them.

14. *Because you spoke this word.* This is the false word dismissing the prophets, saying that "there is no Word in them." The measure-for-measure retribution will be a word of consuming fire placed by God in their mouths.

15. *a nation whose tongue you do not know.* As elsewhere in prophecies of assault by foreign forces, the terror is sharpened by the fact that the invaders speak an unintelligible language.

16. *Its quivers—an open grave.* This is a powerfully compressed image. The quiver is a grave because it holds death-dealing arrows, and its open cavity is a foreshadowing of the grave.

17. *devour your sons and your daughters.* The insistence through anaphora on "devour" conveys a strong sense of the comprehensiveness of the destruction. When "harvest" and "bread" are the object of this verb, it literally refers to eating. When the object is "your sons and your daughters," it means killing them. One should recall that in biblical Hebrew, the sword is said to "devour" or "eat" its victims.

slash with the sword. The Hebrew verb more literally means "smash" or "shatter."

"And even in those days," said the LORD, "I will not make an end of you. 18
And it shall happen when they say, 'For what has the LORD our God done 19
all these things to us?' You shall say to them, 'Because you forsook Me and
served alien gods in your own land, thus shall you serve strangers in a land
that is not yours.'"

Tell this in the House of Jacob,   20
    and let it be heard in Judah, saying:
Hear this, pray,   21
    ignorant, mindless people.
Eyes they have but they do not see,
    ears they have but they do not hear.
Is it Me you do not fear, said the LORD,   22
    before Me you do not quake?
For I set sand a boundary to the sea,
    an everlasting limit not to be crossed—
the waves tossed but could not prevail,
    they surged but could not cross it.
And this people had a wayward rebellious heart,   23
    they swerved away and went off.
And they did not say in their heart,   24
    "Let us fear, pray, the LORD our God,
Who gives rain, early and late rain in its season,
    the set weeks of harvest He keeps for us."
Your crimes turned aside these things,   25

---

19. *thus shall you serve strangers in a land that is not yours.* Here the prophecy of exile—
an imminent threat throughout Jeremiah's career—is made explicit. Serving strangers is
measure-for-measure retribution for serving alien gods.

21. *mindless.* Literally, "with no heart," the heart conceived as the seat of understanding.
    Eyes they have but they do not see, / ears they have but they do not hear. This is a
direct citation of Psalm 115:5–6. In the psalm, the reference is to idols, but here, after
the condemnation of the people's ignorance and mindlessness, it probably refers to the
people, who are too stupid to see that YHWH is the sole God of creation, as the next
verse spells out.

22. *I set sand a boundary to the sea.* This is a recurring motif in biblical poetry, appearing
often in Psalms and also in the Voice from the Whirlwind in Job. It ultimately harks back
to the Canaanite creation myth in which Yamm, the sea god, is subdued and restrained
from encroaching on the land.

23. *they swerved away and went off.* Again and again in biblical idiom, betraying God is
represented as swerving from a straight path.

and your offenses withheld the bounty from you.

26 For among My people wicked men are found,
    they watch as in a fowler's blind,
they set out an ambush,
    they capture men.

27 Like a cage full of fowl,
    so their homes are filled with deceit,
      therefore have they prospered, become rich.

28 They have fattened, have thickened,
    even passed beyond words of evil.
They did not judge a just case—
    the orphan's case, that he should do well,
      and the needy's judgment they did not judge.

29 For these shall I not exact judgment, said the LORD,
    against a nation such as this not wreak vengeance?

30 A frightful and fearsome thing
    has come about in the land:

31 The prophets have prophesied falsely,
    and the priests held sway alongside them,
and My people loved it so.
    But what will you do for its end?

CHAPTER 6

1 Seek shelter, you Benjaminites, from within Jerusalem,
    and in Tekoa sound the ram's horn,

---

26. *they watch as in a fowler's blind.* Of the three Hebrew words here, *yashur keshakh yequshim,* the only one that is certain in meaning is the last, "fowler's."

27. *their homes are filled with deceit.* Many interpreters understand the last word here to refer to what is gained through deceit, but the prophet wants to underline the actual activity of deception.

28. *have thickened.* The meaning of the unusual Hebrew verb is in dispute.

30. *A frightful and fearsome thing.* The idea is stronger in the Hebrew through the more pronounced alliteration, *shamah wesha'arurah.*

CHAPTER 6   1. *Seek shelter ... from within Jerusalem.* The Benjaminites have fled from adjacent territory to Jerusalem as a fortified city, but now Jerusalem itself is about to be assaulted, and they must flee elsewhere.
   in Tekoa sound the ram's horn. The Hebrew makes an untranslatable pun, *beteqo'a tiq'u.*

and on Beth Hakerem raise a signal fire,
for evil is in sight from the north
    and a great disaster.
Lovely and delicate   2
    did I imagine Zion's Daughter.
Against her came shepherds with their flocks,   3
        they pitched their tents all round,
            each shepherded his charge.
"Ready battle against her,   4
    arise and let us go up at noon.
Woe to us, for the day declines,
    for the shadows of evening stretch out!
Arise and let us go up by night,   5
    and let us lay waste to her citadels."
For thus said the LORD of Armies: 6
    Cut down the trees
        and build a siege-ramp against Jerusalem.
She is the city singled out,
    naught but oppression is in her midst.
As a well flows with water,   7
    so she has flowed with her evil.

Beth Hakerem. Like Tekoa, this is a village near Jerusalem. The literal translation, "House of the Vineyard," indicates it is a site of viticulture.

2. *did I imagine.* Though some interpreters understand the verb *damiti* to mean either "I destroyed" or "I silenced," the prophet is not the one doing the destruction, and so it is best to construe this verbal stem in the sense it has in the Song of Songs, "to imagine" or "to liken." That is, the speaker once thought Jerusalem to be a fair city, but matters have turned out differently.

3. *Against her came shepherds.* The "shepherds" are the kings commanding the divisions of the invading army. There is pointed irony in the elaboration of this pastoral metaphor to represent armed besiegers.

his charge. This is a guess at the meaning of the obscure Hebrew phrase, which literally means "his [or, perhaps, with his] hand."

4. *Ready battle against her.* These words and what follows are the speech of the invading forces.

Woe to us, for the day declines. They fear they will not have enough daylight to complete the taking of the city. But in the next verse, they resolve to go ahead and carry out a night attack.

6. *the trees.* The Hebrew *'etsah,* without a dot in the final *heh* that would indicate a possessive, is a collective noun for "trees."

build a siege-ramp. These were constructed from timber and packed-down earth.

"Outrage" and "plunder" are heard within her
    before Me perpetually sickness and plague.
8   Accept reproof, O Jerusalem,
    lest I loathe you,
lest I make you a desolation,
    an uninhabitable land.

9   Thus said the LORD of Armies:
They shall wholly glean as a vine
    the remnant of Israel.
Bring back your hand like a picker of grapes
    to the baskets.
10   To whom should I speak,
    and bear witness that they might heed?
Look, their ear is uncircumcised,
    and they are unable to listen.
Look, the word of the LORD has become for them
    a disgrace in which they do not delight.
11   And with the wrath of the LORD I am filled,
    I cannot hold it in.
Pour it on the babe in the street,
    and on the gathering of young men together,
for both man and woman shall be caught,

---

7. *"Outrage" and "plunder."* These two Hebrew words, *ḥamas* and *shod*, were exclamations that a person attacked or robbed would cry out, hence the verb "heard" here.

9. *They shall wholly glean as a vine / the remnant of Israel.* The subject of the verb is the invaders of Judah. The gleaning refers to going back and plucking whatever grapes are left over after the initial harvesting—these would be the remnant of Israel.

10. *their ear is uncircumcised.* As with the uncircumcised heart, the image is of an interfering membrane that prevents perception.

11. *I cannot hold it in.* This is a kind of confessional statement of the prophetic imperative: the prophet, identifying with God's perspective in observing the acts of his people, feels himself so overflowing with God's wrath that he is driven to express it angrily in his prophecies.

Pour it on the babe in the street. It of course sounds cruel to make toddlers playing in the street the object of divine wrath, but what the prophet has in mind is that the invading army, as was often the case, will perpetrate a general massacre: men, women, and even small children.

the elder with the one full of years.
And their homes shall be turned over to others,   12
   fields and wives together,
for I will stretch out My hand
   against the land's dwellers, said the LORD.
For from the least of them to their greatest   13
   all of them chase gain,
and from prophet to priest
   all of them work lies.
And they would heal My people's wound easily saying,   14
   "All is well, all is well," but it is not well.
They acted shamefully, for they performed abominations.   15
   They were not even ashamed,
     they did not even know how to be disgraced.
Therefore shall they fall among those who fall.
   When I exact judgment from them, they shall stumble—
     said the LORD.

Thus said the LORD: 16
Stand by the ways and see,
   ask for the paths of old,
what is the good way, and go on it,
   and find rest for yourselves.
     And they said: "We will not go."
And I set up watchmen for you—   17
   listen to the ram's horn's sound.
     And they said: "We will not listen."

---

the elder with the one full of years. The wording suggests some distinction between the two. Interpreters at least as far back as Rashi have understood "full of years" to mean "extreme old age," which is possible but not certain.

13. *chase gain.* A more literal indication of the Hebrew idiom would be "cut their slice," the probable origin of the expression being the cutting off of slivers of silver from an ingot.

16. *the ways . . . / the paths of old.* The prophet again invokes the standard Hebrew trope of the way as the regimen of proper conduct. The expression "paths of old" suggests that the right way has always been known, even though now the people neglects it, defiantly proclaiming, "We will not go."

17. *watchmen.* As elsewhere, these are the prophets.

18   Therefore, hear O nations,
            and note the testimony against them.

19 Hear, O earth, I am about to bring evil against this people, the fruit of their
    devisings, for they did not listen to all My words, and My teaching they
20 have spurned. Why do I need frankincense that comes from Sheba and the
    goodly fragrant cane from a faraway land? Your burnt offerings are not
    acceptable, and your sacrifices do not please Me.

21   Therefore, thus said the LORD:
        I am about to bring upon this people
            stumbling blocks, and they shall stumble on them.
        Fathers and sons together,
            a neighbor and his fellow shall perish.
22   A people is about to come from a land of the north,
            and a great nation is roused from the far corners of the earth.
23   Bow and javelin they grasp,
            they are ruthless and show no mercy.
        Their voice roars like the sea
            and on horses they ride,
        arrayed as one man for battle
            against you, O Zion's Daughter!
24   We heard the report of him—our hands went slack.
            Distress seized us, pangs like a woman in labor.
25   Do not go out to the field,

---

18. *note the testimony.* The Hebrew is rather obscure, but 'edah probably does not mean
"congregation" but "testimony."

20. *Why do I need frankincense.* This sounds rather like Isaiah 1:11.
    that comes from Sheba. Frankincense was an expensive imported item brought from
southern Arabia.

22. *from a land of the north.* Jeremiah repeatedly imagines the destruction descending from
the north. Here, that direction takes on an implicitly mythological coloration. "The far corners of the north [Zaphon]" is a repeated designation in biblical poetry for the Canaanite
mountain of the gods (Zaphon is both a proper name from the mountain and the direction
north). In a break-up pattern in the parallelism, *zaphon* appears at the end of the first verset
and "far corners of" at the end of the second.

23. *and on horses they ride.* The use of cavalry was relatively limited among the Israelites,
hence the mounted attackers seem all the more fearsome.

and on the road do not walk,
for the enemy's sword
    is terror all round.
My People's Daughter, gird sackcloth   26
    and wallow in the dust.
Observe mourning as for an only child,
    a bitter keening.
For the destroyer shall come
    all of a sudden against us.
An assayer I made you in My people [a fortress],   27
    that you should know and assay their way.
They all are wayward rebels,   28
    slanderers—bronze and iron—
        they all act ruinously.
The bellows puff, from the fire lead is consumed.   29
    In vain the refiner works,
        the impure matter is not drawn out.
Rejected silver they have been called,   30
    for the LORD has rejected them.

---

25. *the enemy's sword.* The translation follows Hoffman, who notes that the construction noun-to-noun often indicates a possessive, as here: *ḥerev le'oyev.*

27. *[a fortress].* This word is bracketed in the translation because it is probably an intrusive gloss. The word for "assayer" is close in form to a word that means "fortress," and the person responsible for the gloss probably understood it that way because God had promised to make Jeremiah a fortress against his enemies in 1:18. What is clear is that the image from here to the end of the chapter is of assaying and refining idolators, not of fortification.

28. *bronze and iron.* While the syntax seems a bit muddled, the idea is that the rebellious people is iron and bronze rather than silver.

29. *from the fire lead is consumed.* The received text reads *me'eshtam,* which would mean "from their fire," although the vocalization and grammar are wrong. This translation is based on an emendation to *me'esh titom,* literally "from the fire it [lead] comes to an end." Silver is found in lead ore; here the refining process doesn't work, and the silver is not separated from the lead.
    the refiner works. Literally, "the refiner refines."
    the impure matter. This could also mean "the evil ones."

30. *Rejected silver.* At the end of the refining, the silver has not been separated from the lead and so it must be rejected, as God rejects a people that has not cleansed itself of its human impurities.

1 CHAPTER 7   The word that came to Jeremiah from the LORD
2 saying: "Stand in the gate of the house of the LORD, and you shall call out
   there this word and say: 'Listen to the word of the LORD, all of Judah who
3 come through these gates to bow to the LORD. Thus said the LORD of Armies,
   God of Israel: Make your ways and your acts good, and I will have you dwell
4 in this place. Do not put your trust in lying words, saying: The LORD's
5 temple, the LORD's temple, the LORD's temple are these. Rather, if you truly
   make your ways and your acts good, if you truly do justice between a man
6 and his fellow, if you do not oppress orphan and widow and do not shed
7 innocent blood in this place nor go after other gods to your own harm, I
   will have you dwell in this place in the land that I gave to your fathers for all
8,9 time. Look, you put your trust in lying words that cannot avail. Would you
   steal and murder and commit adultery and swear by a lie and burn incense
10 to Baal and go after other gods that you did not know, and come and stand
   before Me in this house upon which My name has been called and say, We
11 are saved, only to do all these abominations? Has this house, on which My
   name has been called, become an outlaws' cave in your eyes? I Myself have

---

CHAPTER 7   2. *Stand in the gate of the house of the LORD.* The position is strategic:
crowds of worshippers, presumably having a fetishistic notion of the intrinsic efficacy of
the Temple (verse 3), would pass through this gate on their way to worship, "to bow to the
LORD."

3. *Make your ways and your acts good, and I will make you dwell in this place.* The people's
tenure in Jerusalem (and, implicitly, in Judah) is conditional upon honest behavior. This
idea is a Deuteronomistic emphasis.

4. *The LORD's temple, the LORD's temple, the LORD's temple.* The triple repetition reflects
something like a mantra recited by the people: this is the LORD's temple, and hence those
who enter it to worship have nothing to fear.
    are these. This phrase is a little obscure but probably refers to the multiple structures
of the Temple.

6. *if you do not oppress orphan and widow . . . nor go after other gods.* The prophet now
concretely defines "making your ways good," combining an imperative of social justice
with one of cultic loyalty.

7. *the land that I gave to your fathers for all time.* The last adverbial phrase shows a grand
flourish in the Hebrew—literally, "from everlasting to everlasting." This notion of an eternal gift of the land stands in dialectic tension with the idea that the gift is conditional.

8. *you put your trust in lying words.* These words, of course, are the triple "the LORD's temple."

9. *swear by a lie.* This would be to swear by a pagan god, most probably, Baal.

11. *an outlaws' cave.* Most translations render the word for the place as "den" in the interest
of English idiomatic usage. But the Hebrew term clearly means "cave," and caves, especially
abundant in the cliffs overlooking the Dead Sea, were favored sites for hideouts. There

even seen it, said the LORD. For go, pray, to My place which is in Shiloh, 12
where I first made My name dwell, and see what I have done to it because of
the evil of My people Israel. And now, inasmuch as you have done all these 13
deeds, said the LORD, and I spoke to you constantly and you did not listen,
and I called you, and you did not answer, I will do to this house on which 14
My name has been called, in which you put your trust, and to the place
that I gave to your fathers, as I did to Shiloh. And I will fling you from My 15
presence as I flung all your brothers, all the seed of Ephraim.' As for you, 16
[Jeremiah,] do not pray for this people, and do not lift up for them a chant
of prayer, and do not entreat Me, for I do not hear you. Do you not see what 17
they are doing in the towns of Judah and in the streets of Jerusalem? The 18
children gather wood, and the fathers light the fire, and the women knead
the dough to make cakes for the Queen of the Heavens and to pour liba-

---

is surely an intended contrast between the Temple, celebrated in the Book of Kings as a
magnificent architectural structure erected by Solomon, and a dark hollow in a cliff used
as a refuge by criminals.

12. *go, pray, to My place which is in Shiloh . . . and see what I have done to it.* Shiloh, which
figures importantly in the early chapters of the Book of Samuel, was a significant northern
sanctuary in the early Israelite occupation of the land. It was probably destroyed by the
Philistines in the middle of the eleventh century B.C.E.

14. *I will do to this house . . . as I did to Shiloh.* This is an especially bold and stark prophecy. Jeremiah, speaking scant years after Josiah's radical cleansing of the Temple and his
confirmation of its exclusive centrality, announces that the Temple, in which the people
complacently trust, is about to be destroyed.

15. *And I will fling you from My presence.* God's presence is in Zion, so this is a prophecy
of exile.

as I flung all of your brothers, the seed of Ephraim. "Ephraim" indicates the northern
tribes, which were exiled by the Assyrians in 721 B.C.E.

16. *As for you.* The Hebrew here switches from a plural "you" to a singular, indicating that
God is now no longer addressing the people but rather the prophet. Hence "Jeremiah" has
been added in brackets.

18. *The children gather wood, and the fathers light the fire, and the women knead the dough.*
This language represents idol worship as a family project, with both genders and all generations implicated.

to make cakes for the Queen of the Heavens. The Queen of the Heavens is the Assyro-
Babylonian fertility goddess Ishtar, associated with the evening star Venus. The Canaanite
equivalent is Astarte. The cult of astral deities was especially popular in the last two centuries of the First Temple period. There is archaeological evidence that sweet cakes, shaped in
the image of the goddess, were used in the cult of Ishtar. One should note that the Masoretic
Text has *melekhet*, "work of," instead of *malkat*, "queen of," but that is almost certainly a
pious euphemistic alteration by the Tiberian grammarians in order to avoid the suggestion
that there could be a Queen of the Heavens.

19 tions to other gods, so as to vex Me. Is it Me they vex, said the Lord. Is it
20 not themselves, to their own shame? Therefore, thus said the Master, the
   Lord: My anger and My wrath are about to pour forth upon this place,
   upon man and beast and upon the trees of the field and the fruit of the soil,
21 and it shall burn and not be quenched. Thus said the Lord of Armies, God
22 of Israel: Add your burnt offerings to your sacrifices, and eat meat. For I did
   not speak to your fathers nor did I charge them when I brought them out
23 from the land of Egypt about matters of burnt offering and sacrifice. With
   this word did I charge them saying, Heed my voice and I will be your God
   and you shall be a people for Me and go in all the way that I charged you,
24 so that it be well with you. But they did not heed and they did not bend
   their ear, and they went by their own counsels, in the willfulness of their
25 evil heart, and they went backward and not forward, from the day that
   your fathers came out of the land of Egypt to this day. And I sent you all
26 My servants, the prophets, day after day. But they did not heed Me and did
   not bend their ear, and they stiffened their necks, did more evil than their
27 fathers. And you shall speak to them these words and they shall not listen
28 to you, and you shall call to them, and they shall not answer you. And you
   shall say to them, This is the nation that would not heed the word of the
   Lord its God and would not accept reproof. Faithfulness is gone and cut
   off from their mouths."

29
        Shear your locks and fling them away,
           and raise a lament on the bare heights,
        for the Lord has rejected and abandoned
           the stock that called forth His fury.

20. *and it shall burn and not be quenched.* The Hebrew exploits the implication of heat in the word for "wrath," *ḥamah.* The image of wrath pouring forth suggests something like a tide of hot lava.

21. *eat meat.* Part of the sacrificial animals was reserved for human consumption.

22. *For I did not speak to your fathers nor did I charge them.* Some interpreters think these words reflect a view that sacrifices were not enjoined in the wilderness, only in the settled Land of Israel. But the main point seems to be in what the prophet goes on to say in the next verse, that any obligation of sacrifice was always secondary to heeding God's voice.

25. *And I sent you all My servants, the prophets, day after day.* Jeremiah repeatedly stresses the crucial spiritual authority of the prophets. It is with them that he identifies himself. Although he was born in the priestly caste, he accords no special weight of authority to the priests.

For the sons of Judah have done evil in My eyes, said the LORD, they have 30
placed their foul things in the house upon which My name was called, to
defile it. And they built the high places of Topheth, which are in the Valley 31
of Ben-Hinnom, to burn their sons and their daughters in fire, what I never
charged them and what never came to My mind. Therefore, look, a time is 32
coming said the LORD, when "Topheth" shall no longer be said nor "Valley
of Ben-Hinnom" but "Valley of the Killing," and they shall bury in Topheth
until there is no room. And the carcasses of this people shall be food for the 33
fowl of the heavens and for the beasts of the earth, with none to frighten
them away. And I will put an end in the towns of Judah and in the streets 34
of Jerusalem to the voice of gladness and the voice of joy, the voice of the
bridegroom and the voice of the bride, for a ruin the land shall become.

CHAPTER 8   At that time, said the LORD, they shall take out 1
from their graves the bones of the kings of Judah and the bones of its nobles
and the bones of the priests and the bones of the prophets living in Jerusa-

---

30. *they have placed their foul things in the house upon which My name is called.* There are
several reports in the Book of Kings that sundry Judahite monarchs—most egregiously,
Manasseh—actually introduced idols and a pagan cult into the Jerusalem temple.
    their foul things. As elsewhere, this is a scornful designation for idols.

31. *the high places of Topheth, which are in the Valley of Ben-Hinnom.* All that is known
about Topheth is that he is a god to whom child sacrifices in fire were offered. The vocalization of the name in Hebrew follows that of *boshet*, "shame," and so is probably an alteration
of the original pronunciation. The Valley of Ben-Hinnom is just to the west of what was
the ancient city of Jerusalem. The Hebrew name, *gei hinom*, through the Greek of the New
Testament, *gehenna*, came to be a term for hell. "Topheth" in later Hebrew equally was
used for hell.

32. *Valley of the Killing.* Because of the reference to piled-up unburied corpses, this name
records not the child sacrifice practiced in this place but the ghastly measure-for-measure
retribution to come, in which the masses of pagan sacrificers will be slaughtered.

34. *for a ruin the land shall become.* This movement of the prophecy—it will continue with
another movement in the next chapter—ends on a grim note of destruction: not only will
the Valley of Ben-Hinnom be piled up high with the corpses of the slaughtered, but the
entire land will be turned into a desolation.

CHAPTER 8   1. *they shall take out from their graves the bones.* Disinterring the
bones is a violation of the sanctity of the buried body and hence a shaming act.
    the kings . . . its nobles . . . the priests . . . the prophets. This sort of cumulative emphatic
series is often favored in Jeremiah's prose style. The prophets in question are false prophets, and the kings, nobles, and priests are the ones who have been guilty of reprehensible
practices.

2 lem. And they shall spread them out before the sun and before the moon
   and before all the array of the heavens that they loved and that they worshipped and after which they went and that they sought out and to which
   they bowed down. They shall not be gathered in nor shall they be buried.
3 Manure on the face of the soil they shall be. And death shall be preferable
   to life for all the remnant of those remaining from this evil clan in all the
4 remaining places where I will drive them, said the LORD of Armies. And
   you shall say to them, thus said the LORD:

> If they fall, will they not rise?
>> If they turn back, will they not turn?
5 Why is this people a rebel,
>> Jerusalem, everlasting rebellion?
> They have clung to deception,
>> refused to turn back.
6 I listened closely and have heard—
>> no honesty do they speak.
> No man regrets his evil,
>> saying, "What have I done?"
> They all go in their headlong course
>> like a horse rushing forward in battle.
7 Even the stork in the heavens
>> knows its seasons,
> and the turtledove, the swift, and the crane
>> keep the time of their coming.

---

2. *the sun . . . the moon . . . the array of the heavens.* This constitutes another cumulative
series. These are all objects of astral worship.
   They shall not be gathered. That is, gathered into the grave.

3. *all the remnant of those remaining . . . in all the remaining places.* Although many scholars
attribute the repetitions here to inadvertent scribal duplication (dittography), it is at least
as likely that the prophet wants to insist on the idea of "remaining" in order to convey a
sense of a scant few survivors, whose lot is even worse than that of all who have perished.

4. *If they turn back, will they not turn?* The formulation is reminiscent of a riddle; the probable sense is: if they turn back to offend, will they really turn back to God? The verb "turn
back" will be picked up with a negative attached to it in the next verse.

7. *Even the stork in the heavens.* The Land of Israel to this day is a place to which migratory
birds from the north came during the cold season. Thus God is seen to have implanted in
these birds the instinctual knowledge of when to migrate, but Israel lacks all knowledge of
the proper order of things set by God.

But my people does not know
    the justice of the LORD.
How could you say, "We are wise,   8
    and the LORD's teaching is with us"?
Why, look, but a lie
    has the scribes' lying pen made it.
The wise shall be shamed,   9
    they shall fear and be caught.
Look, the word of the LORD they rejected,
    and what wisdom do they have?
Therefore will I give their wives to others,   10
    their fields to dispossessors,
for from the least to the greatest
    they all chase gain,
from prophet to priest
    all of them work lies.
And they would heal the wound of My People's Daughter easily, 11
    saying, "All is well," but it is not well—
They are shamed,   12
    for abominations they have performed.
Therefore shall they fall among those who fall,
    in their time of reckoning they shall stumble,
        said the LORD.
I will surely sweep them up, said the LORD,   13
    There are no grapes on the vine
        nor figs on the fig tree,
and the leaf is withered,
    and I will give them to those they shall serve.

---

8. *but a lie / has the scribes' lying pen made it.* The prophet is referring either to written teachings that are turned into lies because they are ignored or, more likely, to false doctrines—perhaps reflecting pagan influences—that the scribes have written down.

10. *for from the least to the greatest.* Everything from this point to the end of verse 12 replicates 6:13–15, with a few minor variations.

13. *I will surely sweep them up.* The Hebrew involves a pun: first the infinitive *'asof*, which can mean "to gather," as in a harvest, a sense developed in the rest of the verse, and then *'asifeim*, "I will make an end of them."
    those they shall serve. The translation reads *ya'avdum*, with one Hebrew manuscript, instead of the Masoretic *ya'avrum* ("they will pass them"). But the syntax is still suspect.

14
"Why are we sitting here?
Gather, that we may enter the fortified towns
and be silent there,
for the LORD our God has silenced us
and made us drink venom-water,
for we have offended the LORD."

15
Hope for peace and there is nothing good,
for a time of healing, and, look, terror!

16
From Dan is heard his horses' snorts,
from the sound of his chargers' neighing
the whole earth shakes.
And they shall come and consume the land and its fullness,
the town and the dwellers within it.

17
For I am about to send against you
viper-serpents that cannot be charmed,
and they shall bite you, said the LORD.

18
I catch my breath from sorrow,
my heart within me aches.

19
Look, the sound of My People's Daughter crying out
from a faraway land:
"Is the LORD not in Zion,
is her King not within her?"—
Why did they vex Me with their idols,
with alien empty breath?

---

14. *Why are we sitting here?* These are the words of the Judahites who now find their land under assault and must seek refuge in fortified towns.

16. *From Dan is heard his horses' snorts.* Dan is in the far north of the Land of Israel—as elsewhere, the invading army descends from the north, its terrifying aspect heightened by its mounted troops attacking the Judahites, who have scant cavalry.

17. *viper-serpents that cannot be charmed.* There is a double meaning in the Hebrew. The word for "charm," *laḥash*, means "whisper" or "hiss," indicating the whispered formula recited to subdue the snake. But there are also vipers that have no hiss, and that thus issue no warning before they bite.

18. *I catch my breath from sorrow.* The verb here, *mavligiti*, is much in doubt, and many have proposed emendations. If the text is correct, it refers to the rare verb *havleig*, which appears in Job and in Psalms and may mean something like "to catch one's breath," although that is in no way certain. In any case, the form of the word is anomalous and seems ungrammatical.

19. *Why did they vex Me with their idols.* This is God's rejoinder to the people: if you want to know why neither the LORD nor the Davidic king is in Zion, consider your idolatry.

"The harvest has passed, the summer has ended,   20
    and we have not been rescued."
Over the breaking of my People's Daughter I am broken,   21
    I plunge in gloom, desolation has gripped me.
Is there no balm in Gilead,   22
    is there no healer there?
For why has no mending come
    to my People's Daughter?
Would that my head were water   23
    and my eye the font of tears,
that I might weep day and night
    for the slain of my People's Daughter.

CHAPTER 9

Would that I were in the wilderness, at a wayfarers' camp.   1
    I would forsake my people and go off from them.
For they are all adulterers,
    an assembly of traitors.

---

20. *The harvest has passed.* The people continues its desperate lament: time passes, and there is no sign of their being rescued from the plight of exile.

21. *Over the breaking of my People's Daughter.* The prophet now speaks in his own voice, not castigating the people but expressing his distress over the disaster that has befallen them. There is a certain oscillation in Jeremiah between angry denunciation of his fellow Judahites for their appalling acts and compassionate identification with them as they suffer the consequences of those acts

22. *Is there no balm in Gilead.* Scholars surmise that in the region of Gilead, to the northeast of the country, medicinal herbs were cultivated.
    no healer. The Masoretic *rofei'*, "healer," though it makes sense, may be a mistake through haplography (the preceding word ends in a *mem*, which could have been dropped here) for *marpei'*, "healing." That would make a neater parallel to "balm."
    mending. The evident sense of the Hebrew idiom is the formation of a scab over a wound.

CHAPTER 9   1. *I would forsake my people.* Jeremiah now expresses the other pole of his oscillating feelings toward his people. He had been devastated by the disaster befalling them; now he is so disgusted by their behavior that he wants to be as far away from them as possible.
    For they are all adulterers. Adultery is seized on as a kind of paradigm for all sorts of disloyalty and cheating—hence the parallelism with "betrayers."

2   They have drawn their tongue back
     on their bow of lies and not of truth.
  They have prevailed in the land,
     for they have gone on from evil to evil,
       and Me they have not known, said the LORD.
3   Each man, beware of his fellow,
     and trust not in any brother,
  for every brother deals crookedly,
     and every fellow man spreads slander.
4   And each man tricks his fellow,
     and truth they do not speak.
  They have taught their tongue to speak lies,
     they are worn out from wrongdoing.
5   Your dwelling is in the midst of deceit.
     In deceit they refused to know Me, said the LORD.
6   Therefore, thus said the LORD of Armies:
     I am about to smelt them and assay them,
       for what else would I do because of my People's Daughter?
7   Their tongue is a well-honed arrow,
     deceit they speak with their mouths.
  Peace a man speaks to his fellow,
     and inwardly lays an ambush.
8   For these shall I not reckon with them, said the LORD,
     from a nation like this shall I not be avenged?

9   Over the mountains I raise weeping and wailing,
     and over the wilderness pastures, lament,
  for they are laid waste, with no man passing through,

---

2. *They have drawn their tongue back / on their bow of lies.* The tongue as the instrument of vicious or lying speech is often thought of in biblical idiom as a weapon. The spreading of slander in the next verse develops this idea

4. *they are worn out from wrongdoing.* The two Hebrew words translated by this clause look textually suspect, and so the meaning is not certain.

5. *Your dwelling is in the midst of deceit.* The "your" is singular and thus refers to the prophet, who is condemned to live among a deceitful people.

6. *because of my People's Daughter.* This appears to be an ellipsis for "because of the crimes of my People's Daughter."

7. *with their mouths.* This seemingly unneeded specification after "speak" is introduced as a paired term with "tongue" in the first verset.

and they do not hear the sound of cattle.
From the fowl of the heavens to the beasts,
    all have wandered off, gone away.
And I will make Jerusalem heaps of stones,   10
    a den of jackals,
and the towns of Judah I will make a desolation
    with no dweller there.

Who is the wise man who would understand this, what the mouth of the   11
LORD spoke to him, that he might tell it?

Why is the land destroyed,
    laid waste like the wilderness with none passing through?

And the LORD said, "Because they forsook My teaching that I set before   12
them and did not heed My voice and did not go according to it. And they 13
went after the stubbornness of their heart and after the Baalim that their
fathers had taught them. Therefore, thus said the LORD of Armies, God   14
of Israel: I am about to feed this people wormwood and make them drink
venom-water. And I will scatter them among nations that neither they nor 15
their fathers have known, and I will send the sword after them until I have
made an end of them."

Thus said the LORD of Armies: 16
    Look to it and call to the keening women that they come
        and to the wise women send that they come.

---

9. *they do not hear the sound of cattle.* The wilderness pastures are personified through the
verb—the desolation is made more acute by the idea that the empty pastures can hear no
sound of living things.

11. *Why is the land destroyed.* A line of poetry is inserted in the middle of the prose prophecy
because this plaintive question amounts to a lament for the destroyed land.

13. *the Baalim that their fathers had taught them.* Instead of God's teaching, there was teaching of idolatry. The indication that it was taught by the forefathers means that it goes back
a long way in the history of the nation.

15. *nations that neither they nor their fathers have known.* The fact that these are utterly alien
nations, scarcely heard of in Judah, makes the condition of exile all the more terrifying.

16. *the keening women.* There are many indications in the Bible that there was a class of
professional keening women, *meqonenot,* in ancient Israelite society, as in many other
cultures, who performed public rites of wailing at times of bereavement and perhaps also
led the general populace in mourning, as the next verse may suggest. The "wise women"

17   Let them hurry and raise wailing for us,
         and let our eyes shed tears
            and our eyelids flow with water.
18   For the sound of wailing is heard in Zion:
         "How we are ruined,
            we are gravely shamed!
     For we forsook the land,
         they have flung us from our dwellings."
19   For hear, O women, the word of the LORD,
         and let your ear catch the word of His mouth,
     and teach your daughters wailing,
         and each woman her friend teach lament.
20   For death has come up through our windows,
         has entered our citadels,
     to cut off the babe from the street,
         the young man from the squares.
21   Speak thus, said the LORD:
     And the human corpses shall fall
         like manure on the face of the fields,
     and like the sheaf behind the reaper
         with none to gather it.

22   Thus said the LORD,
             Let the wise man not boast of his wisdom,

---

of the second verset are the keeners, and one may recall that "wise" in biblical idiom often
means "skilled in a craft," which here would be mourning.

18. *they have flung us from our dwellings.* The translation emends the Masoretic Text, which
reads, literally, "they have flung our dwellings," *hishlikhu mishkenoteinu,* to *hishilikhunu
mimishekenoteinu.*

20. *For death has come up through our windows.* Many commentators detect a mythological
reference here to Mot, the Canaanite god of death. That would certainly make the entrance
through the windows scarier.
    to cut off the babe from the street, / the young man from the squares. The preposition
"from" here does not indicate the place where the cutting off is done. Rather, since death
has climbed into the homes through the windows, the babes and young men perish in
their homes and will no longer be outside, where ordinarily small children might play and
young men congregate.

21. *like the sheaf behind the reaper / with none to gather it.* In the ordinary agricultural
process, the reaper would bind up the harvested ears of grain in sheaves, and afterward these would be gathered up. In this field full of corpses, there is no one to do any
gathering.

nor the warrior boast of his might.
Let the rich man not boast of his riches.
But in this may he who boasts boast:
understanding and knowing Me,
for I am the LORD doing kindness,
justice and righteousness in the land,
for in these I delight, said the LORD.

Look, a time is coming, said the LORD, when I will make a reckoning with 24
all who have circumcised foreskins, with Egypt and with Judah and with 25
Edom and with the Ammonites and with Moab and with all the desert
dwellers who have trimmed beards. For all the nations are uncircumcised,
but the house of Israel has an uncircumcised heart.

CHAPTER 10   Listen to the word that the LORD has spoken 1
about you, house of Israel. Thus said the LORD: 2

The way of the nations do not learn,
and from the signs of the heavens be not terrified,
for the nations are terrified by them.

---

24. *with all who have circumcised foreskins.* This phrase has caused some consternation among interpreters because what follows is a list of nations in which Judah appears after Egypt and before other traditional enemies. Circumcision may well have been practiced, at least in certain circles, by these sundry peoples—there is evidence, for example, that Egyptian priests were circumcised. But the writer seems to assume that many of these people were uncircumcised: "For all the nations are circumcised." The point, then, is that God will make no distinction between the uncircumcised and the circumcised in exacting retribution for offending behavior.

25. *the desert dwellers who have trimmed beards.* The "desert dwellers" are in all likelihood Arabs. Many translators conclude that the descriptive epithet refers to cut-off sidelocks, but the noun *pe'ah* can equally refer to "sidelock" and to "beard" (in an ellipsis for *pe'at zaqan,* "edge of the beard").

but the house of Israel has an uncircumcised heart. This is an idea that Jeremiah has already invoked (4:4)—that however obligatory circumcision may be as a mark of belonging to the community of Israel, what is more crucial is the circumcision of the heart, which is to say, possessing a capability of perception that responds to the demands of justice and sees the imperative truth of God's teaching.

CHAPTER 10   2. *and from the signs of the heavens be not terrified.* Astrology was a powerful presence in this period, in Babylonia and elsewhere. The prophet urges his audience to dismiss all supposed celestial portents.

3   For the nations' practices are mere breath,
         for the tree he cuts down from the forest,
             the craftsman's handiwork with an axe.
4   In silver and gold he embellishes it,
         with nails and hammer
             he secures it that it not totter.
5   Like a scarecrow in a patch of greens
         they do not speak, they are carried,
             for they cannot walk.
     Do not fear them, for they do no harm,
         nor is doing good any part of them.
6   Because none is like you, O LORD,
         great are You
             and great Your name in might.
7   Who would not fear You,
         King of nations?
             For to You it is fitting.
     For among all the nations' wise men
         and in all their regal state
             there is none like You.
8   And as one they are stupid and foolish,
         a doctrine of mere breath—it is but wood.
9   Hammered silver brought from Tarshish
         and gold from Uphaz,
             the craftsman's work and the hands of the smith,

---

3. *practices.* The Hebrew *ḥuqot* elsewhere means "statutes," but the context requires something on the order of "practices."

for the tree he cuts down from the forest. Jeremiah now imagines a kind of representative idolator (hence the singular form) who cuts down the tree, carves wood from it, and overlays it with silver and gold. The absurdity of attributing divinity to a material object fashioned through human craftsmanship would be picked up by Second Isaiah.

6. *Because none is like you, O LORD.* In antithesis to the absurdity of idol worship, the prophet launches on a kind hymn to God's greatness. The phrase "none is like you, O LORD" echoes the "Who is like You among the gods, O LORD" of the Song of the Sea (Exodus 15:11), but, significantly, "among the gods" is deleted because Jeremiah, at this relatively late moment, no longer imagines that there may be other, punier gods alongside YHWH.

7. *For to You it is fitting.* That is, to You is fear or reverence fitting.

8. *a doctrine of mere breath—it is but wood.* The doctrine, or guiding principle, is totally empty because it is based on the hopeless idea that wood can be a god.

  indigo and purple, their raiment,
    the work of skilled men, all of them.
  But the LORD is the God of truth,   10
    He is the living God and eternal King.
  From His fury the earth is shaken,
    and nations cannot contain His wrath.

Thus shall you say to them: gods that have not made the heavens and the 11
earth shall perish from the earth and from beneath these heavens.

  He makes the earth through His power,   12
    firmly founds the world through His wisdom,
      and in His discernment stretches out the heavens.
  As He sounds His voice—a roar of water in the heavens, 13
    and He brings up clouds from the end of the earth.
  Lightning for the rain He makes,
    and He brings out wind from His storerooms.
  Every human is too stupid to know,   14
    every smith is shamed by the idol,
  for the molten image is a lie,
    and there is no spirit in them.
  Mere breath are they, a work of mockery,   15
    in their judgment time they shall perish.

---

9. *indigo and purple, their raiment.* The idols were often dressed in fine clothing resembling royal raiment.

 skilled men. The Hebrew seems to say "wise men," but *ḥakhamim* is often a designation for people skilled in a craft, which is the likely sense here.

11. *Thus shall you say to them.* This entire verse is in Aramaic, being the only complete sentence in Aramaic in the Hebrew Bible apart from the Aramaic sections of Nehemiah and Daniel. There have been suggestions from Late Antiquity onward that Jeremiah is addressing the group of Judahites exiled to Babylonia in 597 B.C.E., who would have been constrained to speak in Aramaic to their pagan captors.

12. *He makes the earth through His power.* This celebration of God as Creator is reminiscent of many of the psalms.

14. *Every human is too stupid to know.* The prophet now swings back from the praise of God's mastering of the cosmic forces of the heavens to the foolishness of idol worship.

 there is no spirit in them. The Hebrew noun also means "breath," and both senses are probably intended here.

16   Not like these is Jacob's Portion,
            for He is the Fashioner of all things,
        and Israel is the tribe of His estate,
            the LORD of Armies is His name.

17   Gather from the ground your wares,
            you who dwell under siege.
18   For thus said the LORD:
        I am about to sling away the land's dwellers
            this time and bring them in straits, that they may find out.
19   Woe is me for my disaster,
            the blow against me is grievous,
        and I had thought:
            this is but illness and I shall bear it.
20   My tent is ruined and all my cords are ripped,
            my children have left me and are gone,
        no one pitches my tent again
            or sets up my tent curtains.
21   For the shepherds are stupid,
            and they have not sought the LORD.
        Therefore they have not prospered,
            and all their flock is scattered.
22   Hark, a sound, look, it comes
            and a great tumult from the land of the north,
        to make the towns of Judah
            a desolation, a jackals' den.
23   I know, O LORD,

---

16. *Jacob's Portion.* In the present context, this has to be an epithet for God. There is a reciprocity: God is Jacob's Portion and Israel is "the tribe of His estate."

17. *Gather from the ground your wares.* These words begin a new prophecy, a vision of destruction and exile. The word represented as "wares," *kinah,* is understood in this translation as deriving from *kena'ani,* "merchant," though others, proposing an Arabic cognate, think it means "bundle."

18. *this time.* The implication is that until now God has held back from condemning the people to exile but will no longer forbear.

20. *no one pitches my tent again.* This extending of the metaphorical image of destruction intimates that since the children are all gone, there is no one to set up the flattened tent.

21. *the shepherds.* As elsewhere, these are the leaders of the people.

that a person's way is not for him
  and not for a man walking to direct his own steps.
Correct me, LORD, but with justice,   24
  not in Your anger, lest You diminish me.
Pour out Your wrath on the nations   25
  that do not know you
and on the clans
  that do not call upon Your name.
For they have devoured Jacob and made an end of him,
  and have devastated his home.

CHAPTER 11 The word that came to Jeremiah from the 1
LORD, saying: "Listen to the words of this covenant, and you shall speak 2
to the men of Judah and to the dwellers of Jerusalem. And you shall say to 3
them, Thus said the LORD God of Israel: Cursed be the man who does not
heed the words of this covenant with which I charged your fathers on the 4
day I brought them out from the land of Egypt from the iron's forge, saying,
Heed My voice and do as all that I charge you, and be My people, and I

---

23. *a person's way is not for him.* The slightly puzzling formulation is best explained by
assuming that the verb "to direct" (or, more literally, "to make firm") just before the end
of the second verset does double duty for both parts of the line, yielding the sense "is not
for him to direct." The notion that a man's destiny is beyond his control fits in with the
monotheistic idea of an omnipotent God, but it has also often been articulated by ancient
and modern writers without any theistic assumption.

25. *Pour out Your wrath on the nations.* While the speaker—evidently the prophet identifying with the people—asks to be spared God's wrath in whatever punishment he may
have to suffer, he invites the full measure of divine fury to be administered to the nations
that have wreaked havoc on the people of Israel. It should be noted that "anger," *'af*, in the
previous verse and "wrath," *ḥeimah*, in this verse constitute a break-up pattern because the
two nouns are often idiomatically joined in a construct form, *ḥamat-'af*.

 For they have devoured Jacob and made an end of him. The Masoretic Text reads, "For
they have devoured Jacob and devoured him and made an end of him," but the second
"devoured" is in all likelihood a scribal duplication (dittography). It is absent in the parallel to this verse in Psalms 79:7 and also in the Septuagint and some Hebrew manuscripts.

CHAPTER 11 2. *this covenant.* This word and this concept figure importantly in
the prophecies of Jeremiah. It is possible that in this he is influenced by the Book of Deuteronomy, which is conceived as a kind of renewal of Israel's covenant with God.

4. *from the iron's forge.* This phrase appears in Deuteronomy 4:20, and Jeremiah is probably
quoting that text.

5 will be your God, so as to fulfill the vow that I made to your fathers to give
   them a land flowing with milk and honey as on this day." And I answered
6 and said, "Amen, O LORD." And the LORD said to me, "Call out all these
   words in the towns of Judah and in the streets of Jerusalem, saying, Listen
7 to the words of this covenant and do them. For I have surely warned your
8 fathers time after time, saying, Listen to My voice. But they did not listen
   and they did not bend their ear, and they went each in the stubbornness
   of his evil heart, and I brought upon them all the words of this covenant
9 that I charged to do and they did not do." And the LORD said to me, "A
   plot has been found out among the men of Judah and among the dwell-
10 ers of Jerusalem. They have turned back to the crimes of their first fathers
   who refused to listen to My words, and they have gone after other gods to
   serve them. The house of Israel and the house of Judah have breached the
11 covenant that I sealed with their fathers. Therefore, thus said the LORD, I
   am about to bring upon them an evil from which they will not be able to
12 escape, and they shall cry out to Me, but I will not listen to them. And the
   towns of Judah and the dwellers of Jerusalem shall go and cry out to the
   gods to whom they burn incense, but they shall surely not rescue them in
13 the time of their evil. For as the number of your towns the number of your
   gods has been, O Judah, and as the number of the streets of Jerusalem you
14 put up altars to the Shame, altars to burn incense to Baal. As for you, do

---

5. *Amen, O LORD.* Since God has just been cited pronouncing the words of a solemn vow,
the response of "amen"—that Hebrew term has the sense of "it is true"—is appropriate.

7. *For I have surely warned your fathers.* As elsewhere, Jeremiah sees the betrayal of the
covenant as behavior that goes all the way back to the early generations of the nation.

8. *And I brought upon them all the words of the covenant.* Part of the covenant, as Deuteronomy spells out, is a series of disastrous outcomes if the covenant is violated, and it is this
that is invoked in these words.

9. *A plot.* The Hebrew *qesher* usually refers to a political conspiracy, as in a plot to overthrow
the legitimate king. Here it is the divine King whom the plotters scheme to displace with
an alien god.

10. *the crimes of their first fathers who refused to listen to My words.* This amplifies the
notion of the guilt of the early generations introduced in verse 7.

11. *they will not be able to escape.* The literal sense of the verb is "go out."

13. *you put up altars to the Shame.* The Hebrew *boshet*, "shame," is repeatedly used as a
pejorative designation for Baal. Here this is especially clear because "the Shame" and "Baal"
appear in apposition.

not pray for this people and do not raise up for them a chant of prayer, for
I do not listen when they call to Me in the time of their evil."

> Why is My beloved in My house 15
>> when she carries out her schemes?
> The many, despite sacral flesh, shall pass on from you.
>> For in your evil you then exult.
> A lush olive tree, lovely in fruit and shape— 16
>> the Lord called your name.
> With a great roaring sound
>> He has set fire to it
>>> and its branches have fallen apart.

And the Lord of Armies Who planted you has spoken evil of you because 17
of the evil of the house of Israel and the house of Judah that they did to vex
Me, to burn incense to Baal.

---

14. *in the time of their evil.* The Masoretic Text reads "for [*be'ad*] their evil," but several
Hebrew manuscripts a well as four ancient versions read "in the time of [*be'et*]". The scribal
error was probably triggered by the use of *be'ad* earlier in the verse ("do not pray for this
people"). "Evil" in this phrase suggests "disaster" but is worth retaining as "evil" because
of the pointed reiteration of the term as the prophecy continues.

15. *Why is My beloved in My house.* The two lines of poetry that constitute this verse
swarm with difficulties, and the text is almost certainly corrupt, so any translation is
conjectural. As S. D. Luzatto, the eighteenth-century Italian Hebrew commentator wrote,
"There are many interpretations of this text, and they are all strained and unlikely." What
can be said with confidence is that the "house" is the Temple, and the "beloved" is Israel.
But "beloved" is masculine, whereas the rest of the line and the next line use feminine
singular forms.
    The many, despite sacral flesh, shall pass on from you. The translation is no more than
a guess. The "sacral flesh" refers to the flesh of the animal sacrifices offered in the Temple.
"Despite" does not appear in the Hebrew and has been added interpretively. The idea then
would be that however many sacrifices you offer, crowds of your people will pass on from
you—perhaps, in exile.
    in your evil. There is no "evil" in the Hebrew, and it has been added in an attempt to
give syntactic coherence to the phrase.

16. *A lush olive tree, lovely in fruit and shape.* This was Israel in its pristine state, or perhaps
as God first wanted to imagine it.

17. *Who planted you.* The verb used harks back to the metaphor of the olive tree.

18 And the LORD informed me and I knew,
  then did You show me their acts.
19 And I was like a docile lamb led to the slaughter,
  and I did not know that they had laid plans against me:
"Let us destroy the tree with its sap
  and cut him off from the land of the living.
   And his name will no more be recalled."
20 But, LORD of Armies, righteous Judge,
  Who tests the conscience and the heart,
let me see Your vengeance upon them
  for to You I lay out my case.

21 Therefore, thus said the LORD concerning the men of Anathoth who seek
your life, saying, "You shall not prophesy in the name of the LORD, or you
22 shall die by our hand." Therefore, thus said the LORD of Armies: "I am
about to exact judgment from them. The young men shall die by the sword,
23 their sons and their daughters shall die by famine, and there shall be no
remnant of them, for I will bring evil upon the men of Anathoth, in the
year of their judgment."

CHAPTER 12

1   Righteous are You, O LORD.
   When I dispute with you,

---

18. *And the* LORD *informed me and I knew.* These words begin a new prophecy, which is
autobiographical in context, dealing with the hostility toward Jeremiah exhibited by the
people of his hometown, Anathoth.

19. *Let us destroy the tree with its sap.* The received text reads *laḥmo*, "its bread," which by
a long stretch might be understood to refer to the fruit of the tree. It seems likely that the
original reading was *leiḥo*, "its sap," which involves the deletion of one consonant from the
Masoretic version. We need not doubt that Jeremiah is registering here an actual scheme
of the men of Anathoth to kill him. Anathoth was a town with a population of priests, and
perhaps, as Lundbom has proposed, they resented Jeremiah's upholding the exclusivity of
the Jerusalem cult. Or, they may have been catering to the paganizing bent of this populace,
which Jeremiah fiercely denounces.

20. *the conscience.* The literal sense of the Hebrew is "the kidneys," which were thought to
be the seat of the conscience.
 to You I lay out my case. Having addressed God as "righteous Judge," the prophet goes
on to use the language of judicial process.

my brief I will speak against You.

Why does the way of the wicked prosper,   2

all who deal treacherously rest tranquil?

You plant them, what's more, they strike root,

they spread out, what's more, they yield fruit.

Near are You in their mouth

and distant from their conscience.

As for You, LORD, You know me, You see me,   3

and You probe my heart that is with You.

Draw them out like sheep to the slaughter,

set them aside for the day of killing.

Till when will the land be bleak,   4

and the grass of every field wither?

From the evil of its dwellers

beasts and fowl are swept away,

for they thought, "He will not see our end."

For if you run with foot soldiers and they tire you,   5

how will you compete with horses?

And if in a peaceful land you flee,

CHAPTER 12   1. *my brief I will speak against You.* Even though the Hebrew word rendered as "against You" might be understood as "with you," the metaphorical context of an adversarial legal argument invites one to construe it as "against You."

2. *Why does the way of the wicked prosper?* This entire verse sounds rather like an early anticipation of Job, not only in its content but even in its language.

   they spread out. The Hebrew verb here would usually mean "they go," which is not right in context. The Septuagint, reading one consonant differently, shows, "they give birth." The idea that the wicked are a deep-rooted, fruit-bearing tree is an exact reversal of the imagery in Psalms (see Psalm 1), where that is the state of the righteous whereas the wicked are wind-blown chaff.

   their conscience. As before, the literal sense of the Hebrew is "their kidneys."

3. *Draw them out like sheep to the slaughter.* These are the wicked, the prophet imploring God to reverse matters and bring retribution upon the wrongdoers. Since he has just implicitly invoked his own innocence ("You know me, You see me"), it may be that Jeremiah has in mind his own predicament with the wicked—the men of Anathoth who have sought to kill him.

4. *He will not see our end.* The implication of these words is that God will pay no attention to the future condition of the speakers, which is to say, will never bring them to judgment.

5. *foot soldiers.* This is what the Hebrew *ragli* (here in the plural, *raglim*) always means elsewhere. The image, then, is of battle: if you can't keep up with foot soldiers on the battlefield, how will you contend with cavalry?

   flee. The received text has *boteaḥ*, "trust," which does not work in the *a fortiori* relation

what will you do in the Jordan's thickets?
6   For even your brothers and the house of your fathers,
               even they betrayed you,
                    they call after you in full voice.
           Trust them not
               when they speak to you good things.
7   I have forsaken My house,
               abandoned My estate,
           I have given My dearest one
               into her enemies' hands.
8   My estate has become for Me
               like a lion in the forest.
           She raised her voice against Me,
               therefore I do hate her.
9   Is My estate a blood-splattered vulture?
               Are the vultures circling round her?
           Go gather all beasts of the field,
               bring them to the devouring.
10   Many shepherds despoiled My vineyard,
               they trampled My plot.

---

of the first verset to the second. An old exegetical tradition, going back to the Aramaic Targum and several medieval commentaries and picked up by some modern scholars, understands the verb to mean "fall," which makes the meaning neat but for which there is slim philological evidence. This translation adopts a proposed emendation, reading *boreaḥ*, "flee," instead of *boteaḥ*.

the Jordan's thickets. The Hebrew says "Pride of the Jordan," and this appears to be the name for a twisting stretch of the river where there is dense overgrowth and so where one can easily stumble. The phrase occurs twice elsewhere in Jeremiah in this sense, 49:19 and 50:44.

7. My house, / . . . My estate. The house is the Temple and the estate is the Land of Israel.

9. a blood-splattered vulture. This phrase is a famous crux. The word *tsavuʿa* does mean "painted," as some understood it in later Hebrew, but is not used in this sense elsewhere in the Bible, and painting birds of prey would be a strange practice. Lundbom finesses this by translating it as "speckled." Others link it with the Hebrew word for "finger" and suggest that it refers to sharp claws. This translation follows Rashi and Kimchi, assuming that the relentlessness of the bird as a scavenger is emphasized. In later Hebrew, the phrase became a term for "hypocrite," with *tsavuʿa* by itself having that meaning. This usage was based on the idea that the bird was actually painted, passing itself off as something it was not.

10. Many shepherds. Elsewhere, "shepherds" refers to the leaders of the Judahite people, but some interpreters take it here as a reference to the generals of the allied armies that invaded Judah.

> They made My precious plot
>   a desolate wilderness.
> They have made her a desolation,   11
>   she mourns to Me, desolate.
> All the land is desolate,
>   for no man pays it heed.
> On all the bare heights in the wilderness   12
>   despoilers have come,
> for the Lord's sword has devoured from the end of the land
>   to the end of the land.
>   There is no peace for all flesh.
> They have sown wheat, and thorns they have reaped.   13
>   They fall ill to no avail.
> Be shamed by your harvests,
>   by the smoldering wrath of the Lord.

Thus said the Lord: "Concerning all My evil neighbors who encroach on 14 the estate that I conferred on My people Israel—I am about to uproot them from their land, and the house of Judah I will uproot from their midst. And 15 it shall be after I uproot them that I will turn back and show mercy to them and bring them back each to his estate and each to his land. And it shall 16 be, if they indeed learn the ways of My people to swear by My name—'as the Lord lives'—as they taught My people to swear by Baal, they shall be built up in the midst of My people. But if they do not heed, I will uproot 17 that nation, uprooting and destroying," said the Lord.

---

11. *desolate / . . . desolate.* Some form of this word is repeated four times in two verses in order to convey an emphatic sense of utter desolation.

13. *Be shamed by your harvests.* The harvests are metaphorical, in keeping with the wheat sown and the thorns reaped—they are the dire consequences of the people's actions.

14. *all My evil neighbors.* These are the sundry nations bordering on Judah, many of whom collaborated with the invading Babylonians. God calls them "My neighbors" because the Land of Israel is God's.

    I am about to uproot them from their land, and the house of Judah I will uproot from their midst. These are opposite actions: the hostile "neighbors" will now suffer the fate of exile, and the exiled Judahites will be plucked up and returned to their land.

16. *learn the ways of My people to swear by My name.* What the prophet envisages is a turning of the cultic tables. Previously, the Judahites had learned from their neighbors to invoke the name of Baal. Now, if those nations are not to undergo continuing exile, they must learn to invoke the name of YHWH, which implies accepting the God of Israel as the legitimate God of all.

1 CHAPTER 13   Thus said the LORD to me, "Go and buy yourself
2 a loincloth of linen and put it round your loins, and do not enter water." And
   I bought the loincloth according to the word of the LORD and put it round
3 my loins. And the word of the LORD came to me a second time, saying,
4 "Take the loincloth that you bought, which is round your loins, and rise, go
5 to Perath and hide it there in a crevice of the rock." And I went and hid it
6 in Perath as the LORD has charged me. And it happened at the end of many
   days that the LORD said to me, "Rise, go to Perath and take from there the
7 loincloth that I charged you to hide there." And I went to Perath and dug
   out and took the loincloth from the place where I had buried it, and, look,
8 the loincloth was ruined, it was not good for anything. And the word of the
9 LORD came to me, saying, "Thus said the LORD: So will I ruin the pride of
10 Judah and the great pride of Jerusalem. This evil people who refuse to heed
   My words, who go after the stubbornness of their heart and go after other
   gods to serve them to bow down to them, they shall be like the loincloth
11 that is not good for anything. For as the loincloth clings to a man's loins,
   so have I made all the house of Israel and all the house of Judah cling to
   Me, to be a people for Me, and for fame and for praise and for splendor,
12 but they did not heed. Thus said the LORD God of Israel, Every jar will fill
   with wine. And they shall say to you, 'Do we not know that every jar will

---

CHAPTER 13   1. *Go and buy yourself a loincloth of linen.* Jeremiah is now enjoined
to carry out a symbolic performative act, following the precedent of Hosea and to be continued by Ezekiel. These might be regarded as dramatic visual illustrations of the prophecies. A loincloth that has fallen apart, as this one will do, exposes the genitals, and in the
poetic prophecy that follows this prose prophecy, the skirts of the personified people will
be hitched up to expose her shame.

   and do not enter water. This slightly puzzling item in the instructions may be to ensure
that nothing in the fabric of the loincloth is in any way damaged before it is hidden in the
crevice.

4. *Perath.* This is a wadi located about two miles northeast of Anathoth.

9. *pride.* There is a certain disparity between the symbol and its referent because a loincloth is scarcely a person's "pride." The prophet may be thinking of the antithesis of pride,
shame, which is what a person suffers without a loincloth to cover his nakedness. In the
next verse, the disintegrated loincloth becomes the metaphor of the people itself, and the
body to which it once clung but no longer clings is God's.

12. *Every jar will fill with wine.* This bit of the prophecy is presented as a kind of riddle. The
people responds by saying that, of course, jars are made to be filled. God's rejoinder (verse
13) is to explain the jar as a riddling symbolic reference to the people, who will be filled
with drunkenness—which is to say, a condition of mental confusion and physical tottering
that is a prelude to collapse.

fill with wine?' And you shall say to them, 'Thus said the LORD: I am about 13
to fill all the dwellers of this land and the kings sitting on the throne of
David and the priests and the prophets and all Jerusalem's dwellers with
drunkenness. And I will smash them, each man against his brother and 14
the fathers and the sons together, said the LORD. I will not spare and will
not have pity and will show no mercy in ruining them.'"

Listen and give ear, do not be haughty,   15
   for the LORD has spoken:
Give glory to the LORD your God   16
   before He brings dark down
and before your feet are bruised
   on the twilight mountains.
And you shall hope for light, and He shall make it death's darkness,
   He shall turn it into thick gloom.
And if you do not heed it,   17
   my inmost self will secretly weep,
      because of pride, will constantly shed tears,
and my eyes will run with tears,
   for the LORD's flock is taken captive.
Say to the king and to the queen mother,   18
   sit down low,
for the diadem of your splendor
   has came down from round your heads.
The Negeb towns are shut,   19
   and there is none to open.
Judah is exiled, all of it,

---

14. *I will smash them.* This verse carries forward the metaphor of the jar, since the jar would
be earthenware and easily smashed.

15. *Listen and give ear.* Exhortations to listen are a conventional beginning of Prophetic and
other kinds of biblical poems.

16. *the twilight mountains.* This beautiful phrase continues the idea of darkness falling: as
the mountains are enveloped in the shadows of evening, one runs the danger of colliding
with rocks or stumbling into pitfalls in the mountainous terrain.

17. *because of pride.* The Hebrew *geiwah* is obscure. Though this translation links it with
ga'awah, "pride," that is no more than a guess. Others connect it with a rare word in Job
that might possibly mean "community."

18. *sit down low.* That is, descend from your exalted thrones.

is exiled utterly.
20   Raise your eyes and see
           the ones coming from the north.
        Where is the flock that was given to you,
           your splendid sheep?
21   What will you say when he appoints over you—
           and it was you who taught them—
              leaders to be a head?
        Will not pangs seize you
           like a woman in labor?
22   And should you say in your heart,
           "Why do these things befall me?"
        Through your many crimes your skirts were stripped,
           your heels ripped back.
23   Can a Nubian change his skin,
           a leopard its spots?
        Then you, too, might be able to do good,
           you who are learned in doing evil.
24   And I will scatter them like floating chaff
           to the desert wind.

---

20. *the ones coming from the north.* As elsewhere, these are the invading armies.

Where is the flock that was given to you. The "you" throughout this passage is feminine singular and so refers to the nation personified as a woman.

21. *What will you say when he appoints over you.* The reference is ambiguous. Rashi understood the appointer as God; Kimchi thought "he" refers to the enemy who, having conquered Jerusalem, chooses local governors for his own purposes, and that may be more likely.

and it was you who taught them. The most plausible meaning of this opaque clause is that if you resent these disagreeable leaders with whom you are saddled, you have only yourself to thank for fastening the administration of your society on morally dubious figures who can now be exploited by your conquerors.

22. *your heels ripped back.* The focus on the heels may seem puzzling. Women would have worn long robes, everything covered all the way down to the heels. The exposure of the heels then becomes a synecdoche for the exposure of the legs and most of the body. It should be noted that the verb here, *neḥmesu*, indicates a violent act or the perpetration of an outrage.

23. *Can a Nubian change his skin, / a leopard its spots?* This formulation—in traditional translations, *kushi* is rendered as "Ethiopian"—expresses a profound moral pessimism: just as these bodily features are ineradicable, your propensity for evil will never change, and so a national catastrophe is inevitable.

24. *like floating chaff.* Although *qash* usually means "straw," straw is not easily windblown, and so there seems to be a semantic slide from "straw" to "chaff." The image is akin to that of Psalms 1:4, where a different Hebrew word, *mots*, is used.

This is your lot, your measured portion from Me,   25
    said the Lord,
since you forgot Me,
    and put your trust in the lie.
And I, too, stripped back your skirts over your face   26
    and your shame was seen,
Your adulteries and your neighings,   27
    the depravity of your whoring,
on hills in the field
    I have seen your vile things.
Woe, to you, Jerusalem, you are not clean.
    How much longer will it be?

CHAPTER 14   That which was the word of the Lord to Jer- 1
emiah concerning matters of the droughts.

Judah moans,   2
    and her gates languish,
    they grow dark on the ground,

---

25. *the lie.* This may be, as some scholars have proposed, a pejorative epithet for Baal.

26. *stripped back your skirts over your face.* The relatively elliptical image of a woman stripped in verse 22 now becomes brutally explicit: her face covered by her own hitched up skirts, her entire naked body is exposed, and this looks like the sad condition of a woman about to be raped.

27. *your adulteries and your neighings.* While the latter term is often used for the noises made in revelry, it is also the word for a horse's neighing, and that is a metaphor adopted by Jeremiah to represent unbridled lust (see 5:8).

    the depravity. The Hebrew *zimah* is strongly associated with sexual depravity.

    on the hills in the field / I have seen your vile things. As elsewhere, the sexual imagery mingles literal and figurative senses. Idolatry is conceived as adultery, the betrayal by Israel of her divine Spouse, and the "vile things" are a fixed epithet for idols. But this pagan activity on the hilltops often involved a fertility cult with orgiastic rites.

    How much longer will it be? Though this is the evident sense of the final clause of the prophecy, the Hebrew syntax is rather crabbed. A literal rendering of the three Hebrew words would be: "after when still."

CHAPTER 14   1. *That which was the word.* The wording of this introductory formula is somewhat different from the usual "the word of the Lord came to."

2. *her gates . . . / grow dark on the ground.* "Gates" is a synecdoche for "towns." The verb "grow dark" (or "be dark"), *qadru,* is associated with mourning, and one sits on the ground in mourning.

and the scream of Jerusalem rises.

3   And their nobles sent their young ones for water.
           They came to the hollows, found no water,
       went back with empty vessels,
           were shamed and disgraced and covered their heads.

4   Because the soil cracked open,
           for there was no rain in the land,
       the farmers were shamed,
           they covered their heads.

5   For even the doe in the field gives birth then forsakes,
           for there is no grass.

6   And wild asses stand on the bare heights,
           they sniff the wind like jackals,
       their eyes go dead,
           for there is no herbage.

7   If our crimes bear witness against us,
           O LORD, act for the sake of Your name,
       for our rebellions are many,
           against You we offend.

8   Hope of Israel,
           its Rescuer in time of disasters,
       why should You be like a stranger in the land,
           like a wayfarer stopped for the night?

---

3. *their nobles sent their young ones.* The "nobles" (in other contexts, "mighty ones") send their "young ones," that is, their subalterns.

   the hollows. These are natural concavities in rock where rainwater would collect, when there is rain.

   covered their heads. This is a sign of grief. But the phrase is absent from the Septuagint, and it may be a scribal duplication of the phrase at the end of verse 4.

5. *For even the doe in the field gives birth then forsakes.* Lacking sustenance, the doe abandons her newborn faun.

6. *their eyes go dead.* More literally, "their eyes are finished." Later Hebrew traditions made this an idiom for pining or longing, and that could conceivably be its meaning here. But the sense may rather be that the eyes of the wild asses, faint with hunger, go dead as part of their failing state. Lundbom proposes that the lack of vegetal nutrients in fact leads to blindness in such animals.

8. *a stranger in the land / . . . a wayfarer stopped for the night.* The land is imagined to be God's land, His earthly abode, with the Jerusalem temple as God's house, but He has now come to seem alienated from the land and its people.

Why should you be like a man overwhelmed, 9
    like a warrior unable to rescue?
Yet you are in our midst, O Lord,
    and Your name is called upon us.
        Do not leave us.

Thus said the Lord to this people: "So did they love to stray. They did not 10
restrain their feet, and the Lord did not accept them with favor. Now shall
He recall their crime and make account of their offense." And the Lord 11
said to me: "Do not pray for this people for good things. Should they fast, 12
I will not listen to their chant of prayer, and should they offer up burnt
offering and grain offering, I will not accept them with favor, for by the
sword and by famine and by plague I will make an end of them." And I 13
said, "Alas, O Master, Lord, look, the prophets say to them, 'You shall not
see the sword, nor famine shall you have, but true well-being will I give you
in this place.'" And the Lord said to me, "Lies do the prophets prophesy 14
in My name. I did not send them nor did I charge them nor did I speak to
them. A vision of lies and a groundless divination and their own heart's
deceit do they prophesy to you. Therefore, thus said the Lord concerning 15
the prophets who prophesy in My name when I did not send them, and
they say, 'Sword and famine there shall not be in this land,' by the sword
and by famine these prophets shall perish. And the people to whom they 16
prophesy, they shall be flung into the streets of Jerusalem because of the
famine and the sword, and there will be no one to bury them—them, their
wives and their sons and their daughters—and I will pour out upon them
their own evil. And you shall say to them this word: 17

Let my eyes shed tears,
    night and day let them not cease
for in a great disaster is the Virgin Daughter of My people broken,

---

9. *Yet you are in our midst.* In the face of the perception of God's withdrawal, the prophet, on behalf of the people, asserts the traditional conviction that God dwells in the midst of His people.

13. *Alas, O Master, Lord, look, the prophets say to them.* Jeremiah reverts here to one of the central themes that preoccupies him, false prophecy. One may reasonably suppose that this is a reflection of autobiographical reality. People in this culture sought the guidance of prophets, and there appear to have been a good many such prophets in Jeremiah's time who told their audiences what they wanted to hear.

a very grievous blow.
18   If I go out to the field,
        look, those slain by the sword,
     and if I come to the town,
        look, those sickened by famine.
     For prophet and priest as well
        go round the land and know not where.
19   Have you wholly rejected Judah,
        by Zion are You repelled?
     Why have You struck us and we have no healing,
        we hope for peace and there is no good,
           for a time of healing, and, look, terror?
20   We know, LORD, our wickedness,
        the crime of our fathers, for we offended against You.
21   Do not spurn, for the sake of Your name,
        do not debase the throne of Your glory.
           Recall, do not breach Your covenant with us.
22   Can the empty breath of the nations yield rain,
        and the heavens, can they give showers?
     Are not You the one, O LORD,
        our God, and we hope in You?
           For it is You Who made all these."

---

18. *If I go out to the field, / look, those slain by the sword.* This entire verse reflects an arresting switch from the generalized symbolic image to concrete observation. First, we have
the quasi-allegorical figure of the Virgin Daughter of my people who has been shattered
by disaster. Then the meaning of the disaster is spelled out as the prophet goes out to the
field and sees it strewn with corpses, then enters the town and sees all around people dying
of famine.

   and know not where. Prophet and priest are supposed to be guides for the people. Now,
in the national catastrophe, they wander through the land, dazed, scarcely knowing where
they are going.

21. *Do not spurn . . . / do not debase.* Both verbs have as their object "the throne of Your
glory." That throne would be Jerusalem, or, more specifically, the Temple, so this is an
argument that God should not allow His own throne to be debased.

22. *the empty breath.* As elsewhere, this is a pejorative epithet for the idols or pseudo-gods
of the nations.

   yield rain. The reference reminds us that the entire prophecy addresses the disaster that
has befallen the land through a drought.

   the heavens, can they give showers? As a parallel to the first verset, this means: can the
heavens on their own, without God's action, produce showers?

CHAPTER 15   And the Lord said, "Even if Moses and Samuel ₁
were to stand before Me, I would have nothing to do with this people.
Send them away from Me and let them go out. And should they say to you, ₂
'Where shall we go out?,' you shall say to them: Thus said the Lord:

> Who for death—to death,
>   and who for the sword—to the sword,
>   and who for captivity—to captivity.

And I will set over you four clans, said the Lord, the sword to kill and ₃
the dogs to drag and the fowl of the heavens and the beasts of the earth
to devour and to destroy. And I will make them a horror for all the king- ₄
doms of the earth because of Manasseh son of Hezekiah, for what he did
in Jerusalem."

> For who will pity you, O Jerusalem,   5
>   and who will console you,
> and who will turn aside to ask
>   how you fare?
> You abandoned Me, said the Lord,   6
>   backward you did go,
> and I reached out My hand against you and destroyed you,
>   I could not relent.
> And I winnowed them with a winnowing fork   7

CHAPTER 15   1. *I would have nothing to do with this people.* The literal sense of the
Hebrew is: "My inward self [*nafshi*] is not toward this people."

2. *Where shall we go out?* Confronted with a decree of banishment—exile appears to be
implied—the people ask where they should go. The grim answer is: to death or captivity.
    Who for death—to death. The fate of the banished people is spelled out in lapidary
fashion, with the dire words repeated in quick sequence: death, sword, captivity.

3. *clans.* The word choice looks a little odd, though the prophet might have in mind the set
phrase "all the clans of the earth."
    the dogs to drag. One should recall that dogs in biblical Israel were semiferal scavengers,
not pets.

4. *because of Manasseh son of Hezekiah.* Manasseh was one of the most notorious of the
Judahite kings for instituting idol worship in the Temple ("for what he did in Jerusalem").
See 2 Kings 21.

in the gates of the land.
I bereaved, destroyed My people—
from their ways they did not turn back.

8   Its widows were more numerous to Me
than the sand of the seas.
I brought upon them, on mother and young man as well,
a despoiler at noon.
I let fall on them all of a sudden
alarm and panic.

9   Forlorn is she who bore seven,
she has gasped out her life-breath.
Her sun has gone down while it was still day.
She was shamed and disgraced.
And their remnant to the sword I will give
before their enemies, said the LORD.

10   Woe to me, my mother, that you gave birth to me,
a man of quarrel and a man of strife to all the land.
I have not loaned nor did they lend to me,
yet all of them curse me.

11   Said the LORD: "Have I not bolstered you for good?
Have I not made the enemy plead for your intercession

---

7. *in the gates of the land.* As before, this is probably a synecdoche for the towns of the land, though it should be noted that attacking forces would storm the gates.

8. *on mother and young man as well.* The Hebrew syntax is crabbed. It reads literally: "on mother young man." The Syriac shows "on mother and on young man." It is possible that the particle meaning "and" originally appeared before "young man" and was scribally omitted. That would yield the sense reflected in this translation.

   alarm. The translation, assuming a connection with the verbal stem that means "to rouse," is conjectural. The Hebrew ʿir elsewhere always means "town."

10. *Woe to me, my mother, that you gave birth to me.* These words mark the beginning of another autobiographical passage. (The translation, in order to distinguish between Jeremiah's first-person speech and God's words, puts the latter in quotation marks.) More than any other prophet, Jeremiah repeatedly complains about the destiny of bitter contention that his calling has imposed upon him. It were better, he says here, had he never been born.

   I have not loaned nor did they lend me. The giving and taking of loans could easily turn into a source of strife between lender and borrower. The prophet has done no such thing, yet he finds himself in perpetual conflict with those around him.

11. *bolstered . . . / made the enemy plead for your intercession.* Both verbs here are problematic and have generated wildly different understandings. This translation links the first term, *sheiritakha*, to a root associated with "armor," but that is at best an educated guess.

in a time of evil and a time of distress?
Can iron shatter iron   12
   from the north, or bronze?
Your wealth and your treasures   13
   I will turn to spoils, cost-free,
      for all your offenses, through all your regions.
And I will make you serve your enemies   14
   in a land you do not know.
For fire rages in My nostrils,
   against you it burns."
It is You Who knows, O LORD.   15
   Recall me and take account of me
      and avenge me of my pursuers.
Do not take me back in Your anger's slowness.
   Know that I bore disgrace for You.
Your words were found and I ate them,   16
   and your words became gladness for me
and my heart's rejoicing, for Your name was called upon me—
   the LORD God of Armies.
I did not sit in the gathering of revelers to make merry.   17
   Because of Your hand, alone I sat,
      for with wrath You filled me.
Why is my pain everlasting   18
   and my blow grievous, resistant to healing?

---

12. *iron / from the north.* Asia Minor was known for its high-quality iron. But in general, invaders in Jeremiah come from the north. The menacing note of this verse and what follows is a pointed antithesis to the positive declaration in verse 11: I stood by you against the enemy, but you failed to change your ways, and now I will bring disaster upon you.

14. *I will make you serve your enemies.* The received text has "I will make your enemies pass," *weha'avarti,* but the duplication of this verse in 17:4 as well as in many Hebrew manuscripts show *wa'avadti,* "I will make you serve." One should recall that the letters *resh* and *dalet* are close in form.

15. *Do not take me back in Your anger's slowness.* The force of the verb "take" here is unclear, but the gist of the line is that God should not be slow to anger in reversing Israel's fortunes and exacting retribution from its enemies.

16. *I ate them.* This prophetic eating of God's words looks like an anticipation of Ezekiel, who is enjoined to eat a scroll with God's words on it.

17. *Because of Your hand, alone I sat, / for with wrath You filled me.* This is still another vehement expression of Jeremiah's pained sense of isolation because of his prophetic mission.

You have surely been to me a dried-up spring,
 waters not to be trusted.

19 Therefore thus said the LORD:
 "If you turn back, I will bring you back,
  before Me you shall stand.
 And if you bring out what is precious from trash,
  you shall be as My mouth.
 It is they who shall turn back to you,
  and you shall not turn back to them.

20 And I will make you for this people
  a fortified wall of bronze.
 And they shall do battle against you
  and shall not prevail over you.
 For I am with you
  to rescue you and to save you, said the LORD.

21 And I will save you from the hand of the wicked,
  and redeem you from the clutch of the ruthless."

1 CHAPTER 16 And the word of the LORD came to me saying:
2 "You shall not take you a wife nor shall you have sons and daughters
3 in this place. For thus said the LORD concerning the sons and concerning the daughters born in this place and concerning their mothers who bore them and concerning their fathers who begat them in this land.
4 Deaths by illness shall they die. They shall not be lamented and shall

---

19. *If you turn back.* The "you" is masculine singular and so must refer to Jeremiah. Nevertheless, the meaning of the verb repeated here in two different conjugations is not entirely clear. Usually, "to turn back" means "to repent," but the prophet has no need to repent. Perhaps the reference is to his sense of distraught alienation because of his prophetic mission. That mission is clearly invoked in "you shall be as My mouth."

20. *a fortified wall of bronze.* The image of fortification, used twice before, reflects Jeremiah's sense of being embattled by enemies.

CHAPTER 16 2. *You shall not take you a wife.* This is perhaps the most drastic of the symbolic-prophetic acts that Jeremiah is asked to perform: the future will be so bleak that he must refrain from marrying and begetting children, for all will perish.

4. *illness . . . sword . . . famine.* Death comes from all directions—from the plague, from warfare, and from starvation.

not be buried. Manure on the face of the soil they shall become, and by
the sword and by famine they shall come to an end, and their carcasses
shall be food for the fowl of the heavens and the beasts of the earth. For 5
thus said the LORD: Do not go to the house of a wake and do not go to
lament and do not console them, for I have taken away My well-being
from this people, said the LORD, the kindness and the mercy. And great 6
and small shall die in this land. They shall not be buried and shall not
be lamented, nor shall one gash himself or shave his head for them. They 7
shall not break bread for them in mourning to console him for the dead,
and they shall not give him the cup of consolation for his father or for
his mother. Nor to the house of feasting shall you come to sit with them 8
to eat and to drink. For thus said the LORD of Armies, God of Israel: I 9
am about to stifle from this place before your eyes and in your days the
sound of gladness and the sound of joy, the sound of the bridegroom and
the sound of the bride. And it shall be when you tell this people all these 10
things and they say to you, 'For what did the LORD speak about us all
this great evil, and what is our crime and what is our offense that we have
offended against the LORD our God?' You shall say to them, 'Because your 11
fathers forsook Me, said the LORD, and went after other gods and served
them and bowed down to them, and Me did they forsake and My teaching
they did not keep. As for you, you did more evil than your fathers, and 12
here you are going each after the stubbornness of his evil heart so as not

---

5. *the house of a wake.* There is evidence—from the Ugaritic, from the Septuagint rendering
of this term, and from rabbinic literature—that the *beyt marzeaḥ* (etymology uncertain)
was a place where mourners gathered to drink and revel in celebration of the life of the
deceased. "Wake" seems the best modern English equivalent of this custom.

6. *nor shall one gash himself or shave his head.* These are actually pagan mourning practices
forbidden in the Torah. Either they survive as an archaic gesture in poetry, or they were
still widely practiced, despite the prohibition.

7. *They shall not break bread for them.* The reference is to a special meal for the mourner,
what in rabbinic Hebrew would be designated *se'udat havra'ah.*
    him. In keeping with common usage in biblical Hebrew, the passage switches back and
forth between singular and plural.
    the cup of consolation. This looks very much like a ritual cup of wine offered to the
mourner.

8. *the house of feasting.* This is an antithesis of "the house of a wake," although drinking—
for different purposes—characterized both. The Hebrew term for "feasting" in fact primarily suggests drinking, as in the Book of Esther.

13 to heed me.' And I will cast you from this land to a land you do not know,
neither you nor your fathers, and you shall serve there other gods day and
14 night, as I will show you no mercy. Therefore, look, days are coming, said the
LORD, when it shall no longer be said, 'As the LORD lives, Who brought up the
15 Israelites from the land of Egypt.' But rather, 'As the LORD lives, Who brought
up the Israelites from the land of the north and from all the lands into which
He drove them,' and I will bring them back to their country that I gave to their
16 fathers. I am about to send many fishermen, said the LORD, and they shall fish
them, and afterward I will send many hunters and they shall hunt them down
from every mountain and from every hill and from the crevices in the rocks.
17 For My eyes are on all their ways. They are not hidden from Me, and
18 their crime is not concealed from My eyes. And I will first pay back double
for their crime and their offense, for their profaning My land with the carcasses of their vile things. And their abominations have filled My estate."

19   The LORD is my strength and my stronghold,
                   and my refuge on a day of distress.
              To You the nations shall come

---

13. *I will cast you.* Here Jeremiah, who writes at the end of the First Temple period, uses what
amounts to a Late Biblical word, *hitil,* though in general his language is classical Hebrew.

14. *it shall no longer be said.* Commentators are divided as to whether the replacement
of "Egypt" by "the land of the north" is a prophecy of consolation—which is to say, the
redemption from exile will be even grander than the redemption from slavery in Egypt—or
a threat: that is, you are doomed to go into exile, a more bitter fate even than slavery in
Egypt. The prophet may well intend to suggest both these meanings.

16. *many fishermen . . . many hunters.* These are the troops of the invading army who will
pursue and kill the Judahites.
    they shall hunt them down . . . from every hill and from the crevices of the rocks. The
metaphor of the hunt now becomes literal fact as we see the fleeing Judahites running off
to the mountains and hills and, most vividly, hiding in crevices.

17. *They are not hidden from Me.* This picks up the hiding in crevices and caves: divine
surveillance sees all of Israel's crimes and all the places where they attempt to flee, and
directs their pursuers to hunt them down.

18. *the carcasses of their vile things.* Again, the "vile things" are idols, and they are represented pejoratively as "carcasses" because there is no life in them.

19. *The LORD is my strength and my stronghold.* The chapter now concludes with a psalm
celebrating God, here recognized as the true deity by the sundry nations. This poem could
be either a composition by Jeremiah in the spirit of Psalms or a noncanonical psalm that
has been inserted in the text.

from the ends of the earth and shall say:
But to lies our fathers were heir,
    mere breath that cannot avail.
Can a human make him a god,   20
    when these are not gods?
Therefore, I am about to show them,   21
    this time will I show them,
My hand and my power,
    and they shall know that My name is the LORD.

CHAPTER 17

Judah's offense is written   1
    with a pen of iron,
        incised with an adamantine point
on the tablet of their hearts
    and on the horns of their altars,
as their sons recall their altars and their sacred poles   2
    by lush trees,
        on high hills, on mountains in the open.
Your wealth, all your treasures,   3

---

21. *Therefore, I am about to show them.* The psalm incorporates three voices: first the speaker who proclaims that God is his stronghold; then the nations who confess the errors of their fathers and the futility of idol worship; and now at the end, God, announcing that he will manifest His power.

CHAPTER 17   1. *written / with a pen of iron, / incised with an adamantine point.* The writing in question is incised on a stone or clay tablet. The pen of iron has a point of very hard stone, *shamir,* for this purpose; *shamir* is perhaps diamond, though that identification is not certain.

    on the tablet of their hearts / and on the horns of their altars. Inwardly, the consciousness of their offense is indelible, whatever they outwardly profess. The altars should be sacred places but have been profaned by their acts, which would involve performing pagan rites on the altars. The altars usually had protuberances at their four corners, referred to as "horns." The received text has "your altars" but many Hebrew manuscripts show "their altars."

2. *as their sons recall.* The phrase is somewhat obscure and has been construed by some antithetically, making "sons" the object of the recalling. In the understanding of this translation, the verse is a direct continuation of the previous one: Judah's offense is manifested in the pagan altars and in the sons, perniciously taught by their fathers, who cling to all the paraphernalia of pagan worship.

I will turn into booty,
    your offending high places in all your regions.
4   And you shall let your estate slip away, on your own,
    that I gave to you.
And I will make you serve your enemies
    in a land you did not know.
For fire rages in My nostrils,
    forever shall it burn.

5   Thus said the LORD:
Cursed be the man who trusts in humans,
    and makes mortal flesh his strong arm.
6   And he shall be like an arid shrub in the desert,
    and he shall not see when good things come.
And he shall dwell in scorched places in the wilderness,
    a barren land that cannot be settled.
7   Blessed be the man who trusts in the LORD,
    and the LORD becomes his trust.
8   And he shall be like a tree planted by waters,
    and by a stream it sends forth its roots,
and it shall not see when the heat wave comes,
    and its leaves shall be lush,
and in a drought year it shall have no care
    and never cease from yielding fruit.
9   More crooked the heart than all things,

---

4. *And you shall let your estate slip away, on your own.* The wording is not entirely transparent, but this translation hews to the received text.

    And I will make you serve your enemies. These two lines of poetry replicate 15:14, with minor variations.

5. *humans.* Although *'adam* can be translated as "man," it is the generic term either for "person" or for "humankind" and is not limited to the male gender.
    strong arm. The Hebrew says merely "arm," an epithet for "strength."

6. *an arid shrub.* The exact identity of the plant named is not certain, but it should be noted that this Hebrew term *'ar'ar* clearly evokes *'ariri,* "barren," and alliterates with the next word in the Hebrew text, *'aravah,* "desert."
    barren land. Literally, "a salt land."

8. *And he shall be like a tree planted by waters.* The kinship of this entire verse with Psalm 1 has often been noted, though it is unclear whether Jeremiah was alluding to that psalm or simply deploying a stock comparison shared by his poem and the psalm.

it is grievously ill and who can fathom it?
I am the LORD who probes the heart,   10
    testing the conscience
and allotting to a man according to his ways
    according to the fruit of his deeds.
A partridge that hatched but did not lay   11
    is he who makes wealth but not in justice.
In the midst of his days it forsakes him,
    and at his end he becomes an abject man.
—The throne of glory is on high,   12
    from the first, the place of our sanctuary.—
Israel's hope is in the LORD.   13
    All who forsake You shall be shamed.
And those who swerve from You shall be cut off,
    for they forsook the source of living water, the LORD.
Heal me, O LORD, that I may be healed,   14
    rescue me, that I may be rescued

---

9. *More crooked the heart than all things.* While the adjective *'aqov* certainly suggests "deceitful," as many translations reflect, the root meaning of "crooked" is worth preserving. This is an etymology of Jacob's name, as the angry Esau reminds us in Genesis 27:36.

it is grievously ill. The crooked human heart is the manifestation of a pathological condition. Though Jeremiah may sometimes seem a ranter, on occasion he shows himself to be a shrewd moral psychologist.

10. *I am the LORD who probes the heart.* No human can fathom the deviousness of the heart, but God can.

conscience. As before, the literal sense is "kidneys."

11. *A partridge that hatched but did not lay.* At least in ancient understanding, the male partridge sits on the eggs (the noun and verb here are both masculine), which of course he could not have produced.

it forsakes him. The logical antecedent is "wealth."

an abject man. The Hebrew *naval* does not really mean "fool," as most translations continue to represent it. A *naval* is a scoundrel, a base fellow, someone in an abject state, and that is surely the dire end predicted for the person with ill-gotten wealth, not the condition of foolishness.

12. *The throne of glory.* This verse appears to be a fragment not directly connected with what proceeds or what follows and so it is marked off with dashes in the translation.

13. *those who swerve from You.* The translation reads *wesurekha* for the Masoretic *yesurey,* "torments of."

shall be cut off. The translation reads *yikareitu* for the Masoretic *yikateivu,* "shall be written."

for You are my praise.

15 Look, they say to me:
　　　Where is the LORD's word? Let it come.

16 As for me, I did not urge to be a shepherd following You,
　　　nor did I long for a day of disaster.
　　You Yourself knew my lips' utterance,
　　　in Your presence it was.

17 Do not become a terror to me.
　　　You are my refuge on an evil day.

18 Let my pursuers be shamed and I be not shamed.
　　　Let them be terrified and let not me be terrified.
　　Bring upon them an evil day
　　　and break them with a double breaking.

19 Thus said the LORD to me: "Go and stand in the People's Gate, through
which the kings of Judah come in and go out, and in all the gates of Jeru-
20 salem. And you shall say to them, 'Listen to the word of the LORD, O kings
of Judah, and all Judah, and all the dwellers of Jerusalem who come in
21 through these gates.' Thus said the LORD: Take care at the risk of your lives
and do not carry a burden on the sabbath day and bring it through the
22 gates of Jerusalem. And you shall not bring out a burden from your homes
on the sabbath day, nor any task shall you do. And you shall hallow the
23 sabbath day as I charged your fathers. But they did not listen and did not

---

15. *Look, they say to me.* These mockers are obviously the hostile Judahites to whom Jeremiah refers frequently.

16. *I did not urge to be a shepherd following You.* Although the translation proposed here
is a viable understanding of the Hebrew, the meaning of this clause has been disputed.
"Shepherd" would refer to the role of prophet. But a frequently proposed emendation of
that Hebrew word yields: "I did not urge to evil"—that is, the evil fate predicted for Israel.

18. *Let them be terrified.* The verb used can also mean "be shattered."

21. *do not carry a burden on the sabbath day and bring it through the gates of Jerusalem.*
Some scholars have claimed that the emphasis here on observance of the sabbath reflects
a sixth-century B.C.E. exilic setting, as in the late chapters of Isaiah. This is by no means a
necessary inference because the sabbath is, after all, part of the Decalogue, and its violation
in the Book of Exodus is considered to be a capital crime. The "burden" brought through
the gates would be produce from the surrounding countryside and perhaps also merchandise transported from abroad.

22. *nor any task shall you do.* Both the verb and the noun are the ones used in the prohibition of work on the sabbath in the Decalogue.

bend their ear, and they made their necks stiff so as not to listen and not
to take reproof. And it shall be, if you indeed listen to me, said the LORD, 24
not to bring your burden through the gates of this city on the sabbath day,
not to do on it any task, kings and nobles shall enter the gates of this city, 25
who sit on the throne of David and who ride in chariots or on horses, they
and their nobles, the men of Judah and the dwellers of Jerusalem, and the
city shall be dwelled in for all time. And they shall come from the towns 26
of Judah and from the environs of Jerusalem and from the land of Benjamin and from the lowlands and from the hill country and from the Negeb
bringing burnt offering and sacrifice and grain offering and frankincense
and bringing thanksgiving offering to the house of the LORD. And if you 27
do not listen to me to hallow the sabbath day and not to carry a burden
when you come through the gates of Jerusalem on the sabbath day, I will
light a fire in its gates and it shall consume the citadels of Jerusalem, and it
shall not be quenched."

CHAPTER 18   The word that came to Jeremiah from the 1
LORD, saying, "Rise and go down to the potter's house, and there I shall 2
let you hear My words." And I went down to the potter's house, and there 3
he was, attending to the task on the wheel. And if the vessel that he was 4
making in clay in the potter's hand was spoiled, he would go back and make
another vessel as it was fit in the eyes of the potter to make. And the word 5
of the LORD came to me saying: "Like the potter cannot I do with you, 6
house of Israel? said the LORD. Look, like clay in the hand of the potter, so

---

25. *who sit on the throne of David and who ride in chariots and on horses.* The translation
follows the Hebrew wording, which is distributive—that is, only the kings sit on the throne
whereas the nobles ride in chariots and on horses.

26. *the lowlands.* This refers to the coastal plain. Thus the four points of the compass in the
land are invoked: Benjamin to the north of Jerusalem, the hill country of its eastern region,
the Negeb to the south, and the lowlands to the west.

CHAPTER 18   2. *go down to the potter's house.* As many commentators have
observed, the verb used suggests that the potter's house was located in a lower part of the
city, perhaps in a valley, near a water source.

6. *like clay in the hand of the potter, so are you in My hand.* This entire sentence was
imported for an impressive liturgical poem in the Yom Kippur service. The symbolic use
of the potter harks back to the version of the creation of humankind in Genesis 2, where
God fashioned—the potter's verb *yatsar* is used—the human creature from the soil.

7 are you in My hand, house of Israel. One moment I speak about a nation
8 and about a kingdom, to uproot and to smash and to destroy. And if that
nation about which I spoke turns back from its evil, I will repent of the
9 evil that I planned to do to it. And another moment I speak about a nation
10 and about a kingdom to build and to plant, and if it does what is evil in
My eyes, not heeding My voice, I will repent of the good that I intended to
11 bestow on it. And now, pray, say to the men of Judah and to the dwellers of
Jerusalem, saying, Thus said the LORD: I am about to fashion evil against
you and devise a plan against you. Turn back, pray, each from his evil way
12 and make your ways and your actions good. But they said, 'It is hopeless,
for after our devising we will go and each of us will act in the stubbornness
of his evil heart.'"

13   Therefore thus said the LORD:
             Ask, pray, among the nations,
                 Who has heard things like these?
             A great frightfulness she has done,
                 the Virgin Israel.
14   Does the snow of Lebanon
                 leave the rock of the highland field?
             Do foreign waters dry up,
                 the cold flowing streams?
15   For My people has forgotten Me,

---

11. *to fashion.* Pointedly, the verb used is *yotser,* which as a verbal noun is the word for
"potter" that appears in the first part of this prophecy.

12. *It is hopeless.* The sense of the statement is: There is no point in hoping we will change
our ways, for we are set on them. Lundbom, amusingly but also relevantly, proposes that
the phrase means something like "we couldn't care less."

14. *Does the snow of Lebanon / leave the rock of the highland field?* As we are frequently
reminded in biblical poetry, there are mountains in the region of southern Lebanon bordering on the Land of Israel. On the heights, snow would be the equivalent of permafrost.
The point of the rhetorical question, then, is that the highland snow never leaves the rocks
on which it has accumulated, yet Israel has forsaken its God (also called "the Rock") to
which it should have clung.
    Do foreign waters dry up, / the cold flowing streams. This line has engendered conflict-
ing interpretations. The verb that appears in the received text, *yinatshu,* "be smashed,"
is scarcely appropriate for water and this translation accepts a widely used emendation,
yinashtu, which involves merely a reversal of two consonants. The poet is evidently still
thinking of Lebanon: its cold mountain streams never dry up, just as the snow on these
slopes never melts from the rocks. One detects a polemic thrust in the idea that these foreign waters continue to flow faithfully whereas Israel has betrayed its God.

to a lie they burn incense.
And they stumble in their ways,
    the paths of old,
to walk on paths
    of an unpaved way.
To make their land a desolation,   16
    an everlasting hiss.
Who passes over it shall be desolate
    and shall shake his head.
Like the east wind will I scatter them   17
    before the enemy.
The nape, not the face, I will see of them
    on the day of their disaster.

And they said, "Come, let us devise plans against Jeremiah, for teaching 18
shall not cease from the priest nor counsel from the wise man, nor oracle
from the prophet. Come, let us strike him with the tongue, and let us not
hearken to all his words."

Hearken, O Lord, to me,   19
    and listen to the sound of my quarrel.

---

15. *to a lie they burn incense.* The word translated as "to a lie" could also mean "in vain," but the context suggests that what the prophet has in mind is not simply the futility of burning incense but burning incense to a false god. The reference in the latter part of this verse to walking on wayward paths definitely accords with the sin of idolatry.

    they stumble. The Masoretic Text shows "they caused them to stumble," but one Hebrew manuscript and two ancient versions have the less cumbersome "they stumble."

16. *an everlasting hiss.* This is the sound of revulsion emitted when one sees something horrendous.

17. *Like the east wind will I scatter them.* The hot wind blowing from the deserts to the east of the Land of Israel is regularly said in biblical poetry to bring trouble.

    The nape, not the face, I will see of them. That is, they will be compelled to flee. Three ancient versions read "I will show them," which is merely a difference in vocalization.

18. *for teaching shall not cease from the priest.* Jeremiah, in confronting the people with his prophecies of disaster, evinces, in their view, the arrogance of displacing the more comforting teaching, counsel, and oracles of the established priests, wise men, and prophets.

    let us strike him with the tongue. This may suggest that the plot against Jeremiah was enacted through slander.

19. *my quarrel.* The Masoretic Text has *yerivai,* "my adversaries." The reading of the Septuagint, *rivi,* a difference of a single consonant, makes better sense.

20 Shall evil be paid back for good?
    For they have dug a pit for my life,
  Recall my standing before You
    to speak good of them,
  to turn back Your wrath from them.
21 Therefore, consign their children to famine,
    make them bleed from the sword,
  and let their wives be bereaved and widowed
    and their husbands slain by the sword,
      their young men struck down by the sword in battle.
22 Let screams be heard from their houses
    when You bring against them a sudden troop,
  for they dug a pit to trap me,
    and snares they laid for my feet.
23 And You, O LORD, You know
    all their counsel against me for death.
  Do not atone for their crime,
    and their offense before You do not blot out,
  and let them be made to stumble before You,
    in the hour of Your wrath act against them.

1 CHAPTER 19   Thus said the LORD: "Go and buy a potter's
earthenware flask, and [take] of the elders of the people and of the elders of
2 the priests, and go out to the Valley of Ben-Hinnom which is in the Gate of
3 the Potsherd, and call out there the words that I shall speak to you. And you

---

20. *they have dug a pit for my life.* Although the pit is in all likelihood metaphorical, the prophet is speaking, as he has before, about a real conspiracy to kill him. He will later be thrown into an actual pit.

my standing before You. The idiom implies intercession: the prophet actually pleaded to God on behalf of the people, and yet they now seek to kill him.

21. *make them bleed.* The literal sense of the verb is "make them pour."

22. *snares they laid for my feet.* The metaphor of snares is conventionally paired with the metaphor of the pit as two allied methods for trapping animals or birds. Because the snare is hidden (the literal meaning of this verb), it suggests the deviousness of the plot against the prophet.

23. *atone.* The verb also has the sense of "cover up."

CHAPTER 19   1. *[take].* There definitely seems to be a verb missing in the Masoretic Text (hence the brackets in the translation). "Take" appears in the Septuagint.

shall say: 'Hear the word of the LORD, kings of Judah and dwellers of Jerusalem. Thus said the LORD of Armies, God of Israel. I am about to bring such evil upon this place that whoever hears of it, his ears will ring. Inasmuch as 4 they have forsaken Me and made this place foreign and burned incense in it to other gods which neither they nor their fathers nor the kings of Judah knew, and they have filled this place with the blood of the innocent. And 5 they have built high places to Baal to burn their sons in the fire of burnt offerings to Baal, which I did not charge and of which I did not speak and which never came to My mind, therefore, look, days are coming, said the 6 LORD, when this place shall not be called Topheth and the Valley of Ben-Hinnom but the Valley of the Killing. And I will confound the counsel of 7 Judah and Jerusalem in this place and will bring them down by the sword before their enemies and by the hand of those who seek their life, and I will give their carcasses as food for the fowl of the heavens and the beasts of the earth. And I will make this city a desolation and a hissing. Whoever passes 8 by it shall be devastated and hiss over all its blows. And I will feed them the 9 flesh of their sons and the flesh of their daughters, and each man shall eat the flesh of his fellow man in the siege and in the straits that their enemies and those who seek their life shall press upon them. And you shall break 10 the flask before the eyes of the men who go with you. And you shall say to 11

---

4. *made this place foreign.* The clear implication of the context is that they have made it foreign by worshipping foreign gods there.

　they have filled this place with the blood of the innocent. As a rule, this phrase refers to murder, and perhaps occasionally to murderous exploitation, but given the location in the Valley of Ben-Hinnom, the "innocent" may well be the children sacrificed in this place.

5. *burnt offerings to Baal.* The linkage between Baal and human sacrifice is exceptional. Elsewhere, and especially in reference to the Valley of Ben-Hinnom, it is to Moloch that children are sacrificed.

6. *the Valley of the Killing.* As what follows makes clear, the killing is not the sacrificed children but the general slaughter that will be perpetrated here in retribution for this unspeakable crime.

7. *confound.* The literal sense of the Hebrew verb is "empty out."

9. *And I will feed them the flesh of their sons and . . . their daughters.* Although cannibalism under the duress of starvation in sieges is often invoked in the Bible, and evidently actually sometimes occurred, in this instance it is measure-for-measure justice: the paganizers murdered their own children in a macabre ritual; now they will be driven by extremity to eat their children.

10. *And you shall break the flask.* The fashioning of humankind in Genesis 2 was strongly analogized to the potter's artifact. Now, the patent frangibility of an earthenware flask becomes a vivid demonstration of the vulnerability of the people to destruction.

them, Thus said the LORD of Armies: So will I break this people and this city as the potter's vessel is broken and can no longer be made whole. And

12 in Topheth they shall bury till there is no room left to bury. Thus will I do to this place, said the LORD, and to its dwellers, to make this city like Topheth.

13 And the houses of Jerusalem and the houses of the kings of Judah like the place of Topheth shall be unclean, all the houses on the roofs on which they burned incense to all the array of the heavens and poured libations to

14 other gods.'" And Jeremiah came from Topheth where the LORD had sent him to prophesy, and he stood in the court of the house of the LORD and

15 said to all the people, "Thus said the LORD of Armies. God of Israel: I am about to bring upon this city and on all its towns the evil of which I spoke concerning it, for they have made their neck stiff not to heed my words."

1 CHAPTER 20   And Pashhur son of Immer the priest—he was the chief official in the house of the LORD—heard Jeremiah prophesying

2 these things. And Pashhur struck Jeremiah and put him in the stocks that

3 were in the upper Benjamin Gate which was in the house of the LORD. And it happened on the morrow that Pashhur let Jeremiah out of the stocks, and Jeremiah said to him, "Not Pashhur has the LORD called your name but

4 Terror-All-Around. For thus said the LORD: I am about to give you over to terror, you and all who love you, and they shall fall by the sword of your enemies, with your own eyes beholding, and all Judah will I give into the hand of the king of Babylonia, and he shall exile them to Babylonia and

5 strike them down with the sword. And I will give all that is stored in this

---

13. *the roofs on which they burned incense to all the array of the heavens.* The roofs were flat, making them readily appropriate settings for worship of astral deities.

14. *He stood in the court of the house of the LORD.* The temple court would have been an ideal place to address a large crowd. Moreover, by moving from the Valley of Ben-Hinnom to the temple precincts, Jeremiah makes clear that the prophesied destruction is not just for the Moloch worshippers but for all of Jerusalem, "the houses of Jerusalem and the houses of the kings of Judah like the place of Topheth."

CHAPTER 20   2. *struck.* This might be merely a slap in the face, but the verb used also could mean "beat."

   the stocks. The noun *mahpekhet* is some sort of device of confinement and perhaps also torture. Because it derives from a verbal stem that means "overturn," some have conjectured that it might be stocks in which a person is locked upside down. In any case, it is clear that Jeremiah undergoes very rough treatment at the hands of this establishment priest. But when he is freed, he remains unflinchingly defiant.

4. *all who love you.* The Hebrew term suggests both intimate friends and family.

city and all its gain and all its precious stuff and all the treasures of the king
of Judah I will give into the hand of their enemies, and they shall plunder
them and take them and bring them to Babylonia. As for you, Pashhur, and   6
as for all who dwell in your house, you shall go away in captivity and come
to Babylonia, and there you shall die, you and all who love you, as you have
prophesied lies to them.

> You enticed me, O LORD, and I was enticed.   7
>> You were stronger than I, and You prevailed.
> I became a laughingstock all day long,
>> all of them mocking me.
> For whenever I spoke, I screamed.   8
>> "Outrage and violence," I called.
> For the word of the LORD became to me
>> disgrace and contempt all day long.
> And I thought, "I will not recall Him,   9
>> nor will I speak anymore in His name."
> But it was in my heart like burning fire
>> shut up in my bones,
> and I could not hold it in,
>> I was unable.
> For I heard the slander of many;   10
>> "Terror all around!

---

7. *You enticed me, O LORD, and I was enticed.* The switch to poetry here signals the
beginning of a new prophecy. Its urgent autobiographical content is a trait that sets
Jeremiah apart from the other prophets. The verb represented as "enticed" could also
mean "seduced" in the sexual sense. Jeremiah was drawn into his prophetic calling
because he heard God addressing him, but prophecy has brought him nothing but
misery, as the harsh treatment at the hands of Pashhur that was just reported painfully
illustrates.

You were stronger than I, and You prevailed. The language here harbors an oblique hint
of rape, as in the report of the rape of Tamar in 2 Samuel 13:14.

8. *Outrage and violence.* These are the conventional words shouted by someone being
attacked by thieves or hooligans.

9. *But it was in my heart like burning fire.* The resolution to withdraw from prophecy
cannot, to Jeremiah's great anguish, be sustained because God's word—which is to say,
the overriding imperative to denounce the crimes of the people and warn them of the
impending disaster—is so powerful that he cannot hold it in: it bursts forth from him
like flames.

10. *Terror all around.* The words he has used in denouncing Passhur and predicting the
imminent destruction are mockingly quoted by the people of Jerusalem.

          Tell, let us tell on him."
All my intimates
   watch for my fall:
"Perhaps he will be enticed and we shall prevail over him,
   and we shall take our revenge of him."

11   But the LORD is with me as a fierce warrior,
   so my pursuers shall stumble and shall not prevail.
They shall be utterly shamed, for they shall not succeed,
   everlasting disgrace that shall not be forgotten.

12   LORD of Armies, probing the righteous,
   Who sees the conscience and the heart,
let me see Your vengeance against them,
   for to You I laid out my case.

13   Sing to the LORD,
   praise the LORD,
for he has saved the life of the needy
   from the hand of evildoers.

14   Cursed the day that I was born,
   the day my mother bore me,
      let it not be blessed.

15   Cursed the man who brought tidings
   to my father, saying,
"A male child is born to you,"

Tell, let us tell on him. This is a literal rendering of the Hebrew: what they have in mind is to inform against Jeremiah, identifying him as a traitor for his prophecies of doom.

   Perhaps he will be enticed and we shall prevail over him. These two verbs pointedly repeat the beginning of Jeremiah's personal complaint against God, which of course, they could not have heard. This is a very different enticement—an intent to draw Jeremiah into making statements that could be judged to be treasonous and thus cause him to be arrested and perhaps executed.

11. *But the LORD is with me as a fierce warrior.* This does not really contradict the opening lines of the poem. God has enticed the prophet to take up a calling that entails endless anguish, but this same God—after all, a God of truth and justice—will defend him against his malevolent enemies.

14. *Cursed the day that I was born.* This is surely the beginning of a new poem of complaint because the preceding verses are a confident proclamation that God will defend the oppressed. The language of this poem throughout is strikingly similar to the death-wish poem in Job 3. The similarities are so extensive that one must conclude that the Job poet, writing more than a century after Jeremiah, was familiar with this text and reworked it—brilliantly, it must be said—for his own purposes.

giving him great joy.
And let that man be like the towns   16
   that the Lord overturned and did not relent.
And let him hear screams in the morning,
   and battle shouts at the hour of noon.
Because he did not kill me in the womb,   17
   that my mother could be my grave
      and her womb pregnant for all time.
Why from the womb did I come out   18
   to see wretchedness and sorrow,
      and my days end in shame?

CHAPTER 21   The word that came to Jeremiah from the 1 Lord when King Zedekiah sent to him Passhur son of Malkiah and Zephaniah son of Maaseiah the priest, saying: "Inquire, pray of the Lord on 2 our behalf, for Nebuchadrezzar king of Babylonia is battling against us. Perhaps the Lord will do for us according to all His wonders, and he will withdraw from us." And Jeremiah said to them, "Thus shall you say to 3 Zedekiah: Thus said the Lord God of Israel: I am about to turn round the 4 weapons that are in your hands with which you do battle against the king

---

15. *giving him great joy.* The tone is bitterly sardonic: of course, the father would rejoice to hear that his wife had born him a son, but for the prophet that the infant has grown up to become, there is no scintilla of joy in the fact of his birth.

16. *And let that man be like the towns / that the Lord overturned.* The towns are Sodom and Gomorrah, with the verb "overturned," regularly used in connection with the cities of the plain, a clue to their identity. Jeremiah's anger at being born into a destiny of anguish is poetically displaced onto the man who brought the tidings of his birth, whom he curses.

18. *Why from the womb did I come out / to see wretchedness and sorrow.* The first verset appears in Job 3:11 in what looks like an approximate quotation. The noun "wretchedness," *'amal,* becomes a signature term in Job.

CHAPTER 21   2. *Inquire, pray, of the Lord.* This is a technical expression for inquiry of an oracle. What Zedekiah and his delegates are of course hoping for is a favorable oracle regarding the fate of the city, under siege by the Babylonians (most likely, in the period from 588 to 586 B.C.E., which would end in the conquest and destruction of Jerusalem).
   Nebuchadrezzar. In other biblical books this name often appears as Nebuchadnezzar, though the spelling with two *r*s used here is more faithful to the Akkadian. Hebrew transliterations of foreign names show a considerable degree of distortion.

4. *I am about to turn round the weapons that are in your hands.* That is, I am going to render your weapons ineffectual, forcing you to fall back into the city.

of Babylonia and against the Chaldeans who besiege you outside the wall,
5   and I will gather them inside the city. And I Myself will do battle against
you with an outstretched hand and a strong arm and with anger and with
6   wrath and with great fury. And I will strike down those who dwell in this
7   city, man and beast, in a great pestilence they shall die. And afterward,
said the LORD, I will give over Zedekiah king of Judah and his servants
and the people and those remaining in this city from the pestilence, from
the sword, and from the famine, into the hand of Nebuchadrezzar king of
Babylonia and into the hands of their enemies and into the hands of those
who seek their lives, and he shall strike them with the edge of the sword,
8   he shall not spare them and shall not pity and shall show no mercy. And to
this people you shall say; Thus said the LORD: I am about to set before you
9   the way of life and the way of death. Who stays in this city shall die by the
sword and by famine and by pestilence. And who goes out and goes over
to the Chaldeans besieging you shall live, and his life shall become booty.
10 For I have set My face against this city for evil and not for good, said the
LORD. Into the hand of the king of Babylonia it shall be given, and he shall
11 burn it in fire. And to the house of Judah, listen to the word of the LORD."
12   House of David, thus said the LORD:

> Render justice every morning,
>   and save the man robbed from the oppressor's hand.
>   lest My wrath spring out like fire
>   and burn with none to quench it

---

the Chaldeans. These are the dominant ethnic group in Babylonia.
I will gather them. The antecedent of "them" is the Chaldeans.

5. an outstretched hand and a strong arm. This is a variation of the phrase used in Deuteronomy 4:34 (where it appears as "a strong hand and an outstretched arm") to describe God's intervention against Egypt on behalf of the Israelites. Here, the application is pointedly reversed as God intervenes against Israel.

7. his servants. This noun, when attached to a king, almost invariably refers to his courtiers or attendants.
he shall strike them with the edge of the sword. Zedekiah's actual fate was perhaps worse than death: first he was forced to watch as his sons were murdered; then he was blinded and led off to captivity.

8. I am about to set before you the way of life and the way of death. This echoes Deuteronomy 30:19, where Israel is urged to "choose life." The allusion is ironic because in this case the choice is between death and a life of captivity and exile. The phrase in the next verse, "his life shall become booty," means booty to the Chaldeans.

12. House of David. The address is to the dynastic line, and "house of Judah" in the previous verse has the same meaning.

because of the evil of your acts.
Look, I am against you, valley dweller,   13
  rock of the plain, said the LORD,
those saying, "Who can come down upon us,
  and who can enter our dwellings?"
And I will exact judgment from you   14
  according to the fruit of your acts, said the LORD.
And I will light a fire in her forest,
  and it will consume all around her.

CHAPTER 22 Thus said the LORD: "Go down to the house of 1
the king of Judah, and you shall speak there this word. And you shall say, 2
Listen to the word of the LORD, king of Judah, who sits on the throne of
David, you and your servants and your people who enter these gates. Thus 3
said the LORD: Do justice and righteousness and release the robbed from
oppression, and the sojourner, the orphan, and the widow do not wrong
and do no violence to them, and do not shed the blood of the innocent in
this place. For if indeed you do this thing, kings in the line of David sitting 4
on his throne shall enter the gates of this house riding in chariots and on

---

13. *valley dweller.* The reference is not certain. Since the entire poem appears to have in
view the destruction of Jerusalem, as does the preceding prose prophecy, it is likely that
the valley dwellers live in Jerusalem, which does have valleys as well as steep hills. But the
next phrase, "rock of the plain," has not been satisfactorily explained.

14. *And I will light a fire in her forest.* Lundbom proposes that the reference is to the royal
palace, in which there was a hall called the Lebanon Forest House because of its extensive use of Lebanese cedar paneling. It seems more likely that what is to be burned is an
actual forest—there were wooded areas in and around Jerusalem—and "it will consume
all around her" thus plausibly invokes the destruction that extends beyond the city to the
surrounding countryside. Through this entire prophecy, one readily sees why Jeremiah
was a scorned or even hated figure in the eyes of his countrymen, here predicting the total
destruction of Jerusalem and the kingdom of Judah—a catastrophe that in fact was about
to occur—at the very moment the city was under siege.

CHAPTER 22 3. *Do justice and righteousness.* In the ancient Near Eastern polity,
it was ultimately the responsibility of the king to administer justice (as the fable of Solomon's judgment piquantly illustrates). Jeremiah, confronting the king, turns from his usual
theme of cultic transgressions to raise issues of legal, social, and economic justice.
  the sojourner. Throughout the Bible, this Hebrew word, *ger,* designates a resident alien,
who as someone without inherited land or the protection of a clan, is vulnerable, as are the
widow and the orphan.

4. *shall enter the gates.* The gates envisioned are the gates of the palace. The virtuous king,
his courtiers, and the people will troop proudly through these gates in a regal procession.

5 horses, the king and his servants and his people. And if you do not heed
   these words, by Myself do I swear, said the LORD, this house shall become
6 a ruin. For this said the LORD concerning the house of the LORD:

> You are Gilead to Me,
>   the Lebanon summit.
> But I will surely turn you to a desert,
>   uninhabited towns.
7 >   And I will summon against you destroyers,
>   each man with his weapons,
>   and they shall cut down the pick of your cedars,
>   and pile them on the fire.

8 And many nations shall pass by this city, and they shall say one to another:
9 'Why did the LORD do this to this great city?' And they shall say, 'Because
   they forsook the covenant of the LORD their God and bowed down to other
   gods and served them.'

10 > Do not keen for the dead,
>   and do not grieve for him.
> Keen constantly for him who goes,
>   for he will not come back and see
>   the land of his birth."

---

6. *You are Gilead to Me, / the Lebanon summit.* Both places are on heights with luxuriant
growth. The idea is that for God, Israel, or the Land of Israel, was a proud and fruitful place,
but now it will be turned into a desert.

7. *the pick of your cedars.* These may well be metaphorical cedars, emblems of the lofty and
eminent members of Judahite society, though some interpreters think the reference is to
the elaborate cedar paneling of the palace and the Temple.

8. *And many nations shall pass by this city.* This verse and the next one are a virtual citation
of Deuteronomy 29:23–25.

10. *Do not keen for the dead.* The Masoretic Text shows "a dead [man]," but that vocalization is almost universally corrected to yield "the dead." The particular dead person here,
according to long-standing scholarly consensus, is Josiah, who was killed by Pharaoh Neco
at Megiddo in 609 B.C.E. One should not keen for him because his fate of death is not so
dire as the fate of his son Shallum (more commonly called Jehoahaz, who was placed on
the throne by Neco after his father's death, reigned only scant months, and then was sent
down to Egypt as a prisoner). Thus Shallum-Jehoahaz is the one "who goes," never again to
see the land of his birth.

For thus said the LORD to Shallum son of Josiah reigning instead of Josiah   11
his father, "Who has gone out from this place shall not go back there again.
For in the place to which they exiled him he shall die, and this land he shall   12
not see again."

      Woe, who builds his house without righteousness   13
        and his upper chambers without justice.
      His fellow he makes work for nothing,
        and his wages does not give him.
      Who says, "I shall build me a massive house,   14
        with spacious upper chambers,
    and break open for it my windows,
      paneled in cedar,
        painted in vermillion."
      Would you be kings   15
        by competing in cedar?
      Did not your father eat and drink
        and do justice and righteousness?
          Then it went well for him.
      He defended the rights of the poor and the needy.   16
        Then it went well.
          Is not that to know Me? said the LORD.
      For your eyes and your heart   17
        are on naught but your gain

---

13. *Woe, who builds his house without righteousness.* The person excoriated is King Jehoia-kim, and so the house is a royal palace (biblical Hebrew regularly calls this structure not a "palace" but simply "the king's house"). *His fellow he makes work for nothing.* What is in view is the common practice of using forced labor for royal building projects.

14. *a massive house.* More literally, "a house of [great] measure." In the story of the spies in Num-bers, the Canaanites, perceived as giants, are called, literally in the Hebrew, "men of measure."
    my windows. Many correct this to "his windows" because the verb attached to it is in the third-person singular. But the received text actually makes sense: the grandiose king is still speaking, and the third-person verb serves as the equivalent of a passive ("my windows are broken open for it").

15. *by competing in cedar.* Here the cedar does appear to refer to the wood paneling of the palace: Do you need the conspicuous palatial furnishings of cedar to establish your king-ship in competition with surrounding monarchies?
    Did not your father eat and drink / and do justice. That is, your father contented himself with the simple satisfaction of food and drink while devoting himself to justice. Jehoiakim's father, Josiah, who oversaw the sweeping cultic reforms of 622 B.C.E., is regarded in the Book of Kings as one of the few morally exemplary kings.

and on shedding the blood of the innocent,
　　and on oppression and violence, to do it.

18 Therefore thus said the LORD to Jehoiakim son of Josiah king of Judah.

　　They shall not lament him,
　　　"Woe, my brother, woe, sister!"
　　They shall not lament him,
　　　"Woe, master, woe, his majesty!"
19　　In a donkey's burial he shall be buried,
　　　dragged and flung beyond Jerusalem's gates.

20　　Go up to Lebanon and cry out,
　　　and to Bashan, lift up your voice.
　　And cry out from Abarim
　　　for all your lovers are broken.
21　　I spoke to you when you were tranquil.
　　　You said, "I will not listen."
　　This is your way from your youth,
　　　for you did not listen to My voice.
22　　All your shepherds the wind shall herd,
　　　and your lovers shall go into captivity.
　　For then shall you be shamed and disgraced
　　　by all your evil.
23　　You who dwell in Lebanon,

---

18. *Woe, my brother, woe, sister!* These are the words of the lament that the people are enjoined not to say. That is equally true of the woe-saying in the next line.

19. *In a donkey's burial he shall be buried.* This prophecy conflicts with the report in 2 Kings 24:6 that Jehoiakim "lay with his fathers," an expression that indicates burial in the ancestral tomb. Either this is an unfulfilled prophecy, or there is something wrong with the notation in 2 Kings. Jehoiakim died at the time of the Babylonian siege in 598–597 B.C.E., but how he died is uncertain. Some have conjectured that he was assassinated in a palace coup.

20. *Lebanon . . . / Bashan . . . / Abarim.* These are all mountainous regions and hence aptly situated lofty places from which to cry out.

22. *All your shepherds the wind shall herd.* This reverses the repeated idiom for futility in Qohelet, "herding the wind." Here the wind does the herding, and the "shepherds" are the rulers of the people.
　　your lovers. That is, your false allies.

23. *You who dwell in Lebanon, / nesting among the cedars.* It is possible, as some claim, that the reference is to the cedar-paneled palace, although it may be more likely that the cedars

    nesting among the cedars,
   how will you groan when upon you come pangs,
     shuddering like a woman in labor?

"As I live," said the LORD, "Should you, Coniah son of Jehoiakim, king of 24
Judah, be a seal on My right hand, from there I would tear you away. And 25
I will give you into the hand of those who seek your life and into the hand
of those by whom you are terrified, and into the hand of Nebuchadrezzar
king of Babylonia and into the hand of the Chaldeans. And I will cast you 26
and your mother who bore you into another land where you were not born,
and there shall you both die. And the land to which they long to return, 27
there they shall not return.

    Is he a smashed, rejected pot,   28
     this man Coniah?
       Is he a vessel no one wants?
   Why have he and his seed been cast and flung
     into a land they did not know?
   Land, land, land,   29
     O hear the word of the LORD!
   Thus said the LORD: 30
   Write this person down as childless,
     a man who shall not prosper in his days.
   For no man sitting on David's throne shall prosper,
     nor rule again in Judah.

---

of Lebanon, here as elsewhere, are a stock metaphor for royal grandeur because of their
loftiness.

24. *Coniah.* This is a shortened form of Jeconiah.

   a seal on My right hand. Although "hand" is mentioned, the signet ring was worn on
the finger. Since it was used to seal important documents, a dignitary would always have
it with him.

26. *there shall you both die.* "Both" is added in the translation to indicate what is clear from
the plural form of the Hebrew verb, that both Coniah and his mother are being addressed.

30. *Write this person down as childless.* According to other sources, Coniah had several
sons, but the point appears to be that he is as good as childless because none of his sons
will inherit the throne.

   person . . . / a man. The two different words in the Hebrew text both mean "man." In the
next sentence, "no man" uses the same Hebrew word for "man" as in "a man."

   For no man sitting on David's throne shall prosper. This appears to proclaim the end of
the Davidic dynasty, but elsewhere Jeremiah speaks of its restoration. The evident sense is
that no one directly descending from Coniah will inherit the throne.

₁ CHAPTER 23   "Woe, negligent shepherds, who scatter the
₂ sheep of My flock, said the LORD. Therefore, said the LORD God of Israel,
concerning the shepherds who shepherd My people, you have let my flocks
scatter and dispersed them and did not attend to them. I am about to
₃ reckon with you for the evil of your acts, said the LORD. And I Myself will
gather the remnant of My flock from the lands to which I dispersed them,
and I will bring them back to their pasture, and they shall be fruitful and
₄ multiply. And I will raise up over them shepherds, and they shall shepherd
them, and they shall no longer fear nor be frightened, and none shall be
missing, said the LORD."

₅ Look, days are coming, said the LORD, when I will raise up a righteous
shoot for David,

> and a king shall reign and prosper,
>   and do justice and righteousness in the land.
₆ In his days Judah shall be rescued,
>   and Israel shall dwell secure.
> This is his name that they shall call him:
>   The-LORD-Is-Our-Righteousness.

₇ "Therefore, look, days are coming, said the LORD, when they shall no longer
say, 'As the LORD lives, Who brought up the Israelites from the land of

---

CHAPTER 23   1. *negligent shepherds.* The participle *me'abdim* could mean "destroying," but this verbal stem can signify either "to perish" or "to be lost," and since it is the
task of the shepherd to prevent any sheep in his flock from getting lost, the last meaning
seems more likely. A shepherd who allows sheep to go astray is negligent. As elsewhere, the
shepherds are the leaders of the people.

3. *And I Myself will gather the remnant of My flock.* This language casts God as a shepherd,
now stepping in to take up the task of the negligent shepherds who acted in such a way
through their misguided leadership that the people were "scattered" into lands of exile.
    they shall be fruitful and multiply. This phraseology borrowed from the beginning of
Genesis suggests that the return to Zion will be a kind of second creation.

4. *none shall be missing.* The multipurpose verb *paqad* is here pointedly used in the sense
of no sheep missing from the flock.

5. *a righteous shoot.* This phrase has currency as an epithet for the legitimate monarch not
only in the Bible but in the Ugaritic literature before it.

6. *This is his name that they shall call him.* The prophet is surely playing on the common
ancient Near Eastern practice of assigning a new name to the king when he assumed the
throne.

Egypt,' But 'As the LORD lives, Who brought up and led the seed of the 8
house of Israel from the land in the north and from all the lands to which
I dispersed them,' and they shall dwell on their soil."

Concerning the prophets: 9
My heart is broken within me,
    All my bones flutter.
I have been like someone drunken,
    like a man overcome by wine,
because of the LORD
    and because of His holy words.
For adulterers have filled the land,   10
    because of these the land is bleak,
        the desert pastures are dry.
And their running is for evil,
    and their valor is not so.
For prophet and priest, too, are tainted.   11
    Even in My house I found their evil,
        —said the LORD.
Therefore their way shall become for them   12
    like slippery ground in the dark.
They shall be thrust down and fall on it.
    For I will bring upon them evil,
        the year of their reckoning,
            —said the LORD.
And in the prophets of Samaria   13
    I have seen a senseless thing—
they prophesied by Baal
    and led astray My people Israel.
And in the prophets of Jerusalem   14

---

9. *I have been like someone drunken, /... because of the LORD.* Through the simile of a man
staggering from the effects of wine, Jeremiah takes up a recurrent theme that God's word
within him is so powerful and so dire that it shakes him to the core.

10. *adulterers.* It is not entirely clear whether the prophet is inveighing against sexual license
or whether the adultery in view is whoring after alien gods.

11. *Even in My house.* The house is the Temple, so the reference must be to corruption of
the cult of YHWH by pagan practices.

I have seen a frightful thing—
adultery and walking in lies,
and they strengthened the hands of evildoers
so none turned back from his evil.
They all have become to me like Sodom,
and its dwellers like Gomorrah.
15   Therefore thus said the LORD of Armies concerning the prophets:
I am about to feed you wormwood
and make you drink a poisoned draft,
for from the prophets of Jerusalem
a taint spreads out to all the land.
16   Thus said the LORD of Armies:
Do not heed the word of the prophets
who prophesy to you.
They deal emptiness to you.
Their own heart's vision they speak,
not from the mouth of the LORD.
17   They repeatedly say to those who despise the word of the LORD,
"It will go well with you,"
And to each who goes in the stubbornness of his heart,
"Evil will not come upon you."
18   For who has stood in the LORD's council
and seen and heard His words?
Who has attended to My word and heard it?

---

14. *a frightful thing.* This sounds more extreme than the "senseless thing" of the previous verse, and hence many commentators have inferred that the prophets of Jerusalem are condemned more sharply than the prophets of Samaria (which is to say, the now vanished northern kingdom). Jeremiah, regularly reviled by his fellow Judahites, is constantly outraged by the false prophets he sees around him, and this whole long passage to the end of the chapter is devoted to that theme.

16. *They deal emptiness to you.* The unusual verb, *mehablim,* is patently derived from *hevel,* "mere breath," "emptiness."

17. *to those who despise the word of the LORD.* The received text reads, improbably, "to those who despise Me the LORD has spoken." The translation here follows the reading reflected in the Septuagint and in the Targum Yonatan, which involves no consonantal changes, only a revocalization of two words.

18. *who has stood in the LORD's council.* Biblical poetry (as well as the frame-story of Job) repeatedly assumes the existence of a celestial council presided over by YHWH. The rhetorical question clearly conveys the idea that none of these false prophets could possibly have had access to the LORD's council.

Look, the tempest of the LORD!   19
    Wrath springs out and a whirling storm
        on the heads of the wicked it whirls.
The LORD's anger shall not turn back   20
    till it does and carries out
        what His heart has plotted.
In future days
    you shall surely grasp this.
I did not send the prophets,   21
    but they went running.
I did not speak to them,
    but they prophesied.
And had they stood in My council   22
    and heard My words about My people,
they would have turned them back from their evil way
    and from the evil of their acts.
Am I not a nearby God, said the LORD,   23
    and not a far-off God?
If a man should hide in secret places,   24
    would I not see him? said the LORD.
The heavens and the earth
    do not I fill? said the LORD.

I have heard what the prophets said prophesying in My name with lies, 25
saying, "I have dreamed a dream." How long will there be in the heart of 26
the prophets prophesying lies the deception of their heart? Who aim to 27

---

20. *In future days / you shall surely grasp this.* When God's devastating retribution descends,
you will have no choice but to finally understand His judgment.

22. *they would have turned them back from their evil way.* The fact that the people persisted
in its wrongful actions while listening to these prophets is, as it were, empirical proof that
these prophets could not have stood in the LORD's council.

23. *a nearby God.* In the present context, this designation is ominous rather than reassuring: God follows the people up close; they have no way of hiding from Him, as the next
verse spells out.

24. *The heavens and the earth / do I not fill?* God's presence is everywhere—in the faraway
sky but also throughout the earth, so there is no hiding from Him.

25. *I have dreamed a dream.* Dream interpretation would have been a common vehicle for
these popular prophets. Although dreams sometimes figure in the Bible as an instrument
of authentic revelation of future events (as in the Joseph story), the classical prophets,

make My people forget My name with their dreams that they recount to
28 each other, and their fathers forgot My name through Baal. The prophet
with whom there is a dream, let him recount the dream. And he with whom
My word is, let him speak words of truth. What does straw have to do with
29 grain? said the LORD. Is not My word like fire, said the LORD, and like a
30 hammer splitting rock? Therefore here I am against the prophets, said the
31 LORD, who steal My word from each other. Here I am against the proph-
32 ets, said the LORD, who take up their tongues and deliver an oracle. Here I
am against those who prophesy lying dreams, said the LORD, and recount
them and lead My people astray with their lies and with their inconstancy
when I did not send them nor charge them, and they surely will not avail
33 for this people, said the LORD. And should the people, or the prophet or
the priest ask you, saying, "What is the burden of the LORD?," you shall
say to them, "You are the burden," and I will abandon you, said the LORD.
34 As to the prophet or the priest or the people who will say "The burden of

---

depending on "the word of the LORD" that they repeatedly hear, do not have recourse to
dreams.

28. *What does straw have to do with grain?* This sounds very much like a proverbial saying,
to the effect: what does something worthless have to do with good edible stuff? The referents of the saying have already been spelled out—lying prophets and prophets who speak
the truth.

29. *Is not My word like fire . . . and like a hammer splitting rock?* Jeremiah had previously
likened God's word to fire that shut up in his bones, an image that expressed his own
tormented experiential sense of the divine message within him. Now he focuses on the
outward effect of God's word, which is fearsome and devastating. There may be an associative link between the fire and the hammer because of the spark that would leap out from
the struck rock, or perhaps even because of hammers in the forge.

30. *who steal My word from each other.* Not only do they speak lies but they also steal from
each other the lying words. "My word" is virtually sarcastic—what they claim to be My word.

31. *who take up their tongues.* More literally, "who take their tongues." It is an odd but actually pointed use of the verb: this delivery of purely manufactured oracles involves forced
effort, a kind of heavy lifting performed with the tongue.

33. *What is the burden of the LORD?* The Hebrew *masa'*, "burden" has two meanings—
burden, portent, or content of a prophecy, and a load to be carried. The passage will play
these two meanings against the other, but it is clear that in the question posed in this verse,
"burden" is used in its prophetic sense.
     You are the burden. The Masoretic Text reads *'et-mah-masa'*, which yields something
unintelligibile: accusative-particle-what-burden. A simple redistribution of consonants
produces *'atem hamasa'*, "you are the burden," and this reading is confirmed by the Septuagint and the Vulgate. The question about the burden of prophecy, then, in the mouths
of the followers of false prophets is turned back against them in a response that stigmatizes
them as the real burden.

the LORD," I will reckon with that man and with his household. Thus shall 35
you say each man to his fellow and each man to his brother, "What has the
LORD answered and what has the LORD spoken?" But "the burden of the 36
LORD" you shall no longer mention, for "the burden" becomes each man's
own word, and you overturn the words of the living God, the LORD of
Armies, our God. Thus shall you say to the people, "What has the LORD 37
answered you, and what has the LORD spoken?" And if you all say "the 38
burden of the LORD," thus said the LORD, inasmuch as you have said this
word, "the burden of the LORD" when I sent to you saying you shall not say
"the burden of the LORD," therefore, I will surely lift you as a burden and 39
abandon you from My presence and the city that I gave to you and to your
fathers, and I will give you everlasting shame and everlasting disgrace that 40
will not be forgotten.

CHAPTER 24   The LORD showed me, and, look, two baskets 1
of figs were set out before the LORD's temple after Nebuchadrezzar king of
Babylonia had exiled Jeconiah son of Jehoiakim king of Judah from Jerusalem and the nobles of Judah and the craftsmen and the smiths and brought
them to Babylonia. In one basket were very bad figs that could not be eaten 2

---

36. *But "the burden of the LORD" you shall no longer mention.* The mouthing of this phrase
about prophetic revelation when there is no revelation is an odious act and the very phrase
should be banned. There is no real prophetic burden, only "each man's word" that he has
invented as pseudo-prophecy.

38. *if you all say.* "All" has been added in the translation to indicate what the Hebrew verb
makes clear, that a group is being addressed.

39. *I will surely lift you as a burden.* The Masoretic Text has *nashiti nasho'*, which would
mean "I will surely forget you." But some Hebrew manuscripts as well as two versions of
the Septuagint and the Vulgate read *nasa'ti naso'*, "I will surely lift you." It is definitely
in accord with Jeremiah's style to insist on this already repeated verbal stem inscribed in
the word for "burden," here turning it into an expression of measure-for-measure justice.

40. *I will give you everlasting shame.* It is worth keeping the Hebrew repetition of the verb
used at the end of the previous sentence because the repetition makes a point: Once I gave
you this city in an act of generosity; now I will give you instead shame and disgrace.

CHAPTER 24   1. *showed me.* Very literally, this verb means "caused me to see." It
is regularly used for prophetic passages involving vision.
     after Nebuchadrezzar king of Babylonia had exiled Jeconiah. This took place in 597
B.C.E., a decade before the final destruction of Jerusalem.
     the craftsmen and the smiths. These workers, respectively in wood and stone and in
metal, were presumably deported in order to prevent the manufacture of arms in Judah.

3 because they were so bad. And the LORD said to me, "What do you see, Jeremiah?" And I said, "Figs. The good figs are very good and the bad figs
4 are very bad, which cannot be eaten because they are so bad." And the word
5 of the LORD came to me, saying, "Thus said the LORD God of Israel: Like these good figs, so will I recognize for good the exiles of Judah whom I sent
6 away from this place to the land of the Chaldeans. And I will set My eyes on them for good and bring them back to this land and rebuild them and
7 not destroy and plant them and not uproot. And I will give them a heart to know Me, for I am the LORD. And they shall be a people for Me, and I Myself will be God for them, for they shall turn back to Me with all their
8 heart. And like the bad figs that cannot be eaten because they are so bad, thus will I make Zedekiah king of Judah and his nobles and the remnant of Jerusalem remaining in this land and those dwelling in the land of Egypt.
9 And I will make them a horror for evil to all the kingdoms of the earth, a disgrace and a byword and a taunt and a curse in all the places where
10 I will scatter them. And I will send against them sword and famine and pestilence until they come to an end on the land I gave to them and to their forefathers."

1 CHAPTER 25   The word that came to Jeremiah concerning Judah in the fourth year of Jehoiakim son of Josiah king of Judah, which
2 was the first year of Nebuchadrezzar king of Babylonia, which Jeremiah

---

3. *What do you see, Jeremiah?* This is God's formulaic question after He has shown a vision to a prophet.

7. *a heart to know.* As elsewhere, the heart is conceived as the seat of understanding.

8. *the remnant of Jerusalem remaining in this land.* As Lundbom notes, this prophecy reverses conventional expectations: it is the Judahites who were exiled who will prove to be the saving remnant, whereas those who remained in the kingdom of Judah will be like the bad figs, unfit for consumption and hence destined to be thrown away.

9. *And I will make them a horror.* The prophecy of destruction in this verse and the next is entirely composed of stereotypical phrases that express humiliation (verse 9) and destruction (verse 10). One might justifiably say that this is boilerplate prophecy, at least in stylistic terms. It may be that prose prophecy lends itself to this tendency, whereas the pressure to formulate parallel terms and metaphors in the poetic prophecy more often, though not invariably, leads to original expression.

CHAPTER 25   1. *in the fourth year . . . of Nebuchadrezzar king of Babylonia.* This would be 599 B.C.E., six years after the Babylonian army defeated the Egyptians in the decisive battle of Carchemish, thus threatening to dominate the entire Fertile Crescent.

the prophet spoke concerning all the people of Judah and all the dwellers of Jerusalem, saying: "From the thirteenth year of Josiah son of Amon king 3 of Judah to this day it is twenty-three years that the word of the LORD has come to me, and I have spoken to you, constantly speaking, but you did not listen. And the LORD constantly sent you His servants the prophets, 4 but you did not listen, and you did not bend your ear to listen, saying: Turn 5 back, pray, each from his evil way and from the evil of your acts, and dwell on the land that the LORD gave to you and to your fathers for all time. And 6 do not go after other gods to serve them and to bow down to them, and do not vex Me with the work of your hands, and I will do no harm to you. But you did not listen to Me, said the LORD, so as to vex Me with the work 7 of your hands for your harm. Therefore, thus said the LORD of Armies, 8 inasmuch as you have not listened to My words, I am about to send for 9 and take all the clans of the north, said the LORD, and for Nebuchadrezzar, My servant, king of Babylonia, and I will bring them against this land and against its dwellers and against all these nations round about, and I will destroy them and make them a desolation and a hissing and everlasting ruins. And I will put a stop among them to the sound of gladness and 10 the sound of rejoicing, the sound of the bridegroom and the sound of the bride, the sound of millstones and the light of the lamp. And all this land 11 shall become a ruin and a desolation, and these nations shall serve the king of Babylonia seventy years. And it shall happen at the end of the seventy 12

---

5. *saying: Turn back.* In this sprawling sentence, all the words of this verse have to be the essential content of the message that the prophets who were constantly sent by God brought to the people.

for all time. The Hebrew shows a grand rhetorical flourish—literally "from everlasting to everlasting." Although the taking away of the land might seem to contradict this notion of its eternal donation to Israel, the Hebrew idiom actually suggests something short of eternity, on the order of "from a very long time ago to a very long time to come."

7. *harm.* As in the previous sentence, the Hebrew *ra'* means both "evil" and "harm."

9. *against all these nations round about.* Nebuchadrezzar's campaign was in fact not just against Judah but against the sundry small kingdoms of trans-Jordan, and against Philistia, Phoenicia, and Egypt.

10. *the sound of millstones and the light of the lamp.* The former are not large millstones but hand mills used domestically by women on a regular basis to grind grain. The lamp (a small earthenware oil lamp) would have been used in these domestic settings when the sun went down.

11. *these nations shall serve the king of Babylonia seventy years.* This number is formulaic, though much would be made of it later, as the Book of Daniel illustrates.

years, I will reckon with the king of Babylonia and with all that nation, said
the LORD, for their crime, and with the land of the Chaldeans, and I will
13   turn it into an everlasting desolation. And I will bring upon that land all
My words that I have spoken about it, and that are written in this book that
14   Jeremiah prophesied about all the nations. For they too shall serve many
nations and great kings, and I will pay them back according to their acts
15   and according to the work of their hands. For thus said the LORD God of
Israel to me, "Take this cup of wine, of wrath, from My hand, and make all
16   the nations to whom I send you drink it. And they shall drink and retch
17   and go mad before the sword that I send among them." And I took the cup
from the hand of the LORD and made all the nations to whom the LORD
18   had sent me drink, Jerusalem and the towns of Judah and its kings and its
nobles, to turn them into a ruin, a desolation, a hissing, and a curse, as on
19   this day, Pharaoh king of Egypt and his servants and his nobles and all his
20   people, and all the mixed stock and all the kings of the land of Uz and all
the kings of the land of the Philistines and Ashkelon and Gaza and Ekron
21,22 and the remnant of Ashdod, Edom and Moab and the Ammonites, and all

---

12. *I will reckon with the king of Babylonia.* As elsewhere in biblical prophecy, there is a double calculus here. God calls the Babylonian emperor "My servant" because he is the instrument of divine punishment against Judah. Yet, the havoc that he wreaks is a "crime," and in the end he will have to pay for it. This notion is elaborated in verse 14.

15. *this cup of wine, of wrath.* The Hebrew syntax is slightly odd. It seems to say: this cup of wine, the wrath. In this translation, the words are understood as standing in apposition: "this cup of wine, [this cup] of wrath."

16. *And they shall drink and retch and go mad before the sword.* The prophecy in effect telescopes two different images: the cup of wrath is a figure for the destruction that will overtake the Babylonians; the sword is then a synecdoche for the onslaught of the army that will overwhelm Babylonia.

17. *And I took the cup from the hand of the LORD.* This is a bold and quite uncommon move: the metaphoric cup of wrath seems to become an actual cup that the prophet takes from God's hand. Such quasiphysical proximity between God and prophet is altogether unusual. But since the cup is, after all, symbolic, the prophet's taking it from the hand of the LORD finally must be understood as a purely figurative act, and that understanding is confirmed by his making the nations drink from it, an act that could not be literally performed.

19. *Pharaoh king of Egypt.* These words launch a sweeping catalogue of the surrounding nations marked for destruction (the agency of destruction being the Babylonian army that in fact advanced across the entire region)—Egypt to the south, the Philistines along the coast to the west, Tyre and Sidon to the north, and the sundry kingdoms east of Jordan going all the way to Dedan, Tema, and Buz in the Arabian peninsula and to Media in the far northeast.

the kings of Tyre and all the kings of Sidon and the kings of the coastland
that is beyond the sea, and Dedan and Tema and Buz and all whose hair is   23
cropped, and all the kings of Arabia and all the kings of mixed stock who   24
live in the desert, and all the kings of Zimri and all the kings of Elam and all   25
the kings of Media, and all the kings of the north, near and far to each other   26
and all the kingdoms of the world that are on the face of the earth. And
King Sheshak shall drink after them. And you shall say to them, Thus said   27
the LORD of Armies God of Israel: Drink and get drunk and vomit and fall
down, and you shall not rise because of the sword that I send among you.
And it will happen, if they refuse to take the cup from your hand to drink,   28
you shall say to them: Thus said the LORD of Armies, 'You shall surely
drink.' For, look, in the city on which My name was called I begin to wreak   29
harm, and will you be declared innocent? You shall not be declared innocent, for I call a sword against all the dwellers of the earth, said the LORD
of Armies. As for you, prophesy to them all these things and say to them: 30

> The LORD roars from on high,
>> and from His holy dwelling He raises His voice.
> He roars fiercely against His abode,
>> a shout like grape-treaders rings out
>> to all the dwellers on earth.

---

26. *And King Sheshak shall drink after them.* The name "Sheshak" has long been understood
as a coded reference to Babylon (Hebrew *bavel*), in which the last letter of the Hebrew alphabet is substituted for the first, the second from the last letter for the second in the alphabet,
and so forth. It remains unclear why the code was used.

27. *Drink . . . and fall down, and you shall not arise because of the sword.* In this instance,
the metaphorical act (drinking from the cup of wrath) and the literal event (falling by the
sword) are linked sequentially: the nations, fallen drunk after imbibing the potent wine,
are unable to protect themselves against the sword.

28. *if they refuse to take the cup from your hand to drink.* Given the metaphorical status
of the cup, this would have to mean that they will refuse to accept Jeremiah's prophecy
of doom. But they cannot escape the prophesied end—"You shall surely drink"—and the
prophet goes on to articulate its terrible inevitability by casting it in poetry (verse 30ff.).

30. *the LORD roars from on high.* The poetic representation of the warrior as a fierce lion
is conventional and would have been immediately recognized by the ancient audience.
　　His abode. This is the earth, which in biblical parlance belongs to God
　　a shout like grape-treaders. The shout, *heydad*, of the treaders would be a shout of joy,
or perhaps, as some scholars have suggested, a rhythmic chant or song. But here it becomes
a shout that spells destruction.

31 The uproar comes to the end of the earth,
    for a dispute has the Lord with the nation,
He exacts justice from all flesh,
    the wicked He gives to the sword
      —said the Lord.
32 For thus said the Lord of Armies:
    Look, evil goes out
      from nation to nation,
and a great storm is stirred up
    from the far corners of the earth.

33 And on that day the slain of the Lord shall be from one end of the earth to the other. They shall not be lamented nor gathered in nor buried. They shall become dung on the face of the earth.

34 Wail, you shepherds, and scream,
    wallow, you lords of the flock.
For your time to be slaughtered has come,
    and I will smash you like a precious vessel, and you shall fall.
35 And flight shall be lost for the shepherds,
    and escape for the lords of the flock.
36 Hark, the scream of the shepherds
    and the howling of the lords of the flock,
      for the Lord is ravaging their pasture.
37 And the peaceful meadows shall be silent
    before the burning wrath of the Lord.

---

31. *a dispute.* The Hebrew term suggests a legal dispute.

34. *you shepherds.* As before, shepherds are the leaders of the people.
   I will smash you. The grammatical form of the Hebrew verb is anomalous, seemingly combining a verbal conjugation and a noun formation, but the meaning is not in doubt.

35. *the shepherds / . . . the lords of the flock.* These two epithets, repeated three times in three verses, become a kind of anaphora that insistently conveys the dire fate of the Judahite leaders.

37. *And the peaceful meadows shall be silent.* Even though some interpreters construe the verb as "shall be destroyed" (a phonetically similar verbal stem), "silent" makes better sense. The meadows, once filled with the lowing of flocks, are now deadly silent. This ominous silence is a complementary counterpoint to the screams and wailing of the people's shepherds.

Like a lion, He has left his lair,   38
        for their land has become a desolation,
before the oppressive sword,
        and before His burning wrath."

CHAPTER 26   At the beginning of the kingship of Jehoiakim   1
son of Josiah king of Judah this word came from the LORD, saying: Thus   2
said the LORD, "Stand in the court of the house of the LORD, and you shall
speak concerning all the towns of Judah who come to bow down in the
house of the LORD the words that I have charged you to speak to them.
Omit not a word. Perhaps they will listen and each man will turn back from   3
his evil way and I shall repent of the evil that I am planning to do to them
because of the evil of their acts. And you shall say to them: Thus said the   4
LORD, If you listen to Me to go in My teaching that I set before you, to listen   5
to the words of My servants the prophets whom I have constantly sent to
you—but you did not listen! And I will make this house like Shiloh, and this   6
city I will make a curse for all the nations of the earth." And the priests and   7

---

38. *Like a lion, He has left His lair.* The lion that was implied in the roaring at the beginning
of the poem is now made explicit, forming an envelope structure.

    before the oppressive sword. The Masoretic Text shows "before the oppressive wrath,"
but *ḥaron,* "wrath," is probably an inadvertent scribal duplication of that word in the second
verset here. Several Hebrew manuscripts as well as the Septuagint and the Targum read
ḥerev, "sword." The word represented here as "oppressive," *yonah,* looks like the noun
that means "dove," which makes no sense in the present context. Some Hebrew exegetes
understood it to mean "enemy," but without much philological warrant. It is most plausibly
linked with the verbal stem *y-n-h,* which means to "oppress," and the word here would be
a participle modifying "sword," not a noun.

CHAPTER 26   2. *Stand in the court of the house of the LORD.* It is likely that the
occasion is one of the three pilgrim festivals, when huge crowds would flock to the Temple
from all around the country. The clause "who come to bow down [that is, to worship] in
the house of the LORD" suggests pilgrimage.

4. *If you listen to Me.* One would expect a positive clause completing this conditional statement: if you listen, I will not harm you. Instead, the statement breaks off in the middle—
"but you did not listen"—because the people's refusal to change its ways is already perceived
as an accomplished fact.

6. *I will make this house like Shiloh.* Shiloh was a central sanctuary in the north (see the early
chapters of 1 Samuel) that was destroyed by the Philistines in the eleventh century B.C.E. It
appears to have become incised in the national memory as a once sacred site that was violated and laid waste, and Jeremiah invokes it in this sense as a grim precedent for Jerusalem.

the prophets and all the people heard Jeremiah speaking all these words in
8 the house of the Lord. And it happened when Jeremiah finished speaking
all that the Lord had charged him to speak to all the people, the priests and
the prophets and all the people seized him, saying, "You are doomed to die.
9 Why did you prophesy in the name of the Lord, saying, 'Like Shiloh shall
this house be, and this city shall be destroyed with none dwelling there'?"
10 And all the people crowded round Jeremiah in the house of the Lord. And
the nobles of Judah heard of these things, and they went up from the king's
house to the house of the Lord and sat at the entrance of the new gate of
11 the house of the Lord. And the priests and the prophets said to the nobles
and to all the people, saying, "A death sentence for this man! For he has
12 prophesied about this city as you have heard with your own ears." And
Jeremiah said to all the nobles and to all the people, saying, "The Lord
sent me to prophesy about this house and about this city all the words that
13 you have heard. And now, make your ways and your acts better and listen
to the voice of the Lord, that the Lord repent of the evil that He spoke
14 concerning you. As for me, here I am in your hand. Do to me what is good
15 and what is right in your eyes. But you must surely know that if you put

---

8. *You are doomed to die.* These words (rendered by many, following the King James version, as "you shall surely die") are the set formula for pronouncing a death sentence. Before this point, Jeremiah had repeatedly stated that his life was in danger because of his prophecies, beginning with a conspiracy against him by the people of his hometown, Anathoth. Now the threat is explicit and imminent. One should recall that at this moment toward the end of the seventh century B.C.E. Judah was gravely menaced by the Babylonian army. One might imagine a preacher in California in 1942, when there were fears of a Japanese invasion, repeatedly declaring that the land would be laid waste for the evil of its ways and that Los Angeles and San Francisco would be turned into rubble by a cruel enemy coming from across the great ocean. Such a person would surely have been arrested for treason and perhaps subjected to capital punishment. The anger against Jeremiah is scarcely surprising.

9. *all the people crowded round Jeremiah.* This detail suggests that they may be ready to lynch the prophet. The historicity of this entire episode seems likely.

10. *the house of the Lord.* The Masoretic Text lacks "the house of," but it appears in many Hebrew manuscripts as well as in four different ancient versions. The nobles have been in the palace, a plausible location for them, but when they hear of what has happened in the temple court, they hasten there.

11. *as you have heard with your own ears.* This must mean, as you have heard the report of what he said.

14. *As for me, here I am in your hand. Do to me what is good and what is right in your eyes.* Throughout this stark confrontation, Jeremiah exhibits steady resolution. He has

me to death, you lay innocent blood on yourselves and on this city and on its dwellers, for in truth did the LORD send me to speak in your hearing all these words." And the nobles and all the people said to the priests and to the   16
prophets, "This man has no death sentence, for he has spoken to us in the name of the LORD." And men of the elders of the land arose and said to all   17
the assembly of the people, saying, "Micah the Morashthite did prophesy in   18
the days of Hezekiah king of Judah, and he said to all the people of Judah, saying, Thus said the LORD of Armies:

> Zion shall be plowed like a field,
>> and Jerusalem shall become rubble heaps,
>>> and the Mount of the House, high places in the forest.

Did Hezekiah king of Judah and all Judah really put him to death? Did he   19
not fear the LORD and entreat the LORD, and the LORD repented of the evil that he had spoken concerning them? And should we do great evil against our own selves? And also there was a man prophesying in the name of the   20
LORD, Uriah son of Shemaiah from Kiriath-Jearim, and he prophesied concerning this city and concerning this land like all the words of Jeremiah. And King Jehoiakim heard his words, and with him all his warriors and   21
all his nobles, and the king sought to put him to death, and Uriah heard and was afraid and fled and came to Egypt. And King Johaiakim sent his   22

---

just reiterated the burden of his prophecy, and if the people refuse to listen, he is prepared to submit to his fate.

15. *for in truth did the* LORD *send me.* This is the crux of Jeremiah's self-defense: he does not deserve to die because he has spoken his dire prophecies with the full authority of God. In the ancient society, this is an argument that many would have found persuasive, because they shared the assumption that God in fact had messages for the people that he conveyed through prophets (our California analogue would not have fared so well with an argument of this sort).

16. *And the nobles and all the people said to the priests and to the prophets.* The aristocracy and the common people rebuke the priests and the "establishment" prophets, both groups being Jeremiah's rivals in imparting instruction to the populace.

17. *men of the elders of the land.* The relevant point of this designation is not their actual age but their status as recognized authorities or sages.

20. *And also there was a man prophesying in the name of the* LORD, *Uriah son of Shemaiah.* Unlike Micah, whose prophecies became part of the canon, there is no written record of Uriah's prophesies, and all that is known of him is what is reported here. His fate proved to be the opposite of Micah's.

23   men to Egypt, Elnathan son of Achbor and men with him, to Egypt. And
     they took Uriah out of Egypt and brought him to King Jehoiakim, and he
     struck him down with a sword, and they flung his corpse into the graves
24   of the common people." Yet the hand of Ahikam son of Shaphan was with
     Jeremiah not to give him into the hands of the people to put him to death.

1   CHAPTER 27   At the beginning of the kingship of Jehoiakim
     son of Josiah king of Judah this word came to Jeremiah from the LORD,
2   saying: Thus said the LORD, "Make for yourself bands and yoke bars, and
3   you shall put them on your neck. And you shall send them to the king of
     Edom and to the king of Moab and to the king of the Ammonites and to the
     king of Tyre and to the king of Sidon in the hand of the messengers coming
4   to Jerusalem to Zedekiah king of Judah. And you shall charge them to their
     masters, saying, Thus said the LORD of Armies, God of Israel, thus shall you

---

23. *And they took Uriah out of Egypt and brought him to King Jehoiakim.* At this point,
Judah was allied with Egypt, and consequently there was no difficulty about extradition.

and they flung his corpse into the graves of the common people. The report of this humiliating death of the prophet—"flung" suggests that the corpse was not given proper burial—
is clearly invoked by the elders as a shameful act that should not be repeated.

24. *Yet the hand of Ahikam son of Shaphan was with Jeremiah.* Shaphan was a royal scribe,
a high court position. He played an important role in the discovery of the Book of Teaching
in the Temple around 622 B.C.E. Ahikam, then, would have been a well-placed official who
provided support for Jeremiah within the royal court.

not to give him into the hands of the people to put him to death. First the people crowded
around Jeremiah with murderous intent (verse 9). Then they appear to have accepted,
together with the nobles, Jeremiah's defense that he was truly sent by the LORD (verse 16).
Now, they are again represented as a threat to the prophet. This volatility of sentiment is a
realistic rendering of mob psychology.

CHAPTER 27   1. *At the beginning of the kingship of Jehoiakim.* Although this is the
reading of the Masoretic Text, the name of the king appears to be a scribal error, for these
events occur during the reign of Zedekiah, and it is he who is mentioned in what follows.

2. *Make for yourself bands and yoke bars.* This is another symbolic act that the prophet is
called on to perform. "Yoke" in biblical usage is a recurrent image for subjugation (and
the very English word "subjugation" means "being under the yoke"). The repeated verb
"serve" in this prophecy, which can also mean "work" or "worship," has its political sense,
"to be subject to."

3. *Edom . . . Moab . . . the Ammonites . . . Tyre . . . Sidon.* A conference of these kings took
place in Jerusalem in 594–593 B.C.E. to consider an alliance that would resist Babylonian
domination. Jeremiah's message is that any such resistance will prove futile.

say to your masters: I Myself made the earth, humankind and beast, over 5
the face of the earth, with My great power and with My outstretched arm,
for him who was right in My eyes. And now, I Myself have given all these 6
lands into the hands of Nebuchadnezzar My servant, king of Babylonia,
and even the beasts of the field I have given to him to serve him. And all 7
the nations shall serve him and his son and his son's son until the time of
his land comes—he, too—and many nations and great kings shall make
him serve. And it shall be, that the nation and the kingdom that does not 8
serve him, Nebuchadnezzar king of Babylonia, and that does not put its
neck in the yoke of the king of Babylonia, by the sword and by famine and
by pestilence will I reckon with that nation, said the Lord, until I make
an end of them by his hand. As for you, do not listen to your prophets and 9
to your sorcerers and to your dreams and to your soothsayers and to your
wizards who say to you, saying, 'You shall not serve the king of Babylonia.'
For lies do they prophesy to you so as to take you far from your land, for I 10
will scatter you and you shall perish. And the nation that puts its neck in 11
the yoke of the king of Babylonia and serves him I will leave on its land,
said the Lord, and it will till it and dwell upon it." And to Zedekiah king 12
of Judah I spoke according to these words, saying, "Bring your neck into
the yoke of the king of Babylonia and serve him and his people, and live.
Why should you die, you and your people, by the sword and by famine and 13
by pestilence, as the Lord has spoken of the nation that does not serve the
king of Babylonia? And do not listen to the words of the prophets who say 14
to you, saying: 'You shall not serve the king of Babylonia,' for lies do they
prophesy to you. For I have not sent them, said the Lord, and they prophesy 15

---

5. *I Myself made the earth.* God's status as creator of all things on earth implies that it is
absolutely within His power to decide which nations will be masters and which subjugated.

7. *until the time of his land comes.* History is viewed, quite realistically, as a cycle of shifting
conquest and defeat. For now, Nebuchadrezzar reigns supreme, but a time will come when
his nation will fall to another empire—in point of historical fact, it would be the Persians.

8. *until I make an end of them by his hand.* Throughout this vision of history, emperors are
merely the instruments of God's purpose.

10. *For lies do they prophesy to you so as to take you far from your land.* It is Jeremiah's
political view that exile can be avoided if Judah accepts vassal status under Babylonia. This
notion is spelled out in the next verse.

14. *And do not listen to the words of the prophets . . . for lies do they prophesy to you.* This
entire prophecy abounds in repetitions and sounds a little prolix. The rhetorical looseness
may be encouraged by the prose medium.

lies in My name, so that I will scatter you and you shall perish, you and
16 the prophets who prophesy to you. And to the priests and to all the people
I have spoken, saying, Thus said the LORD: do not listen to your prophets
who prophesy to you, saying, 'Look, the vessels of the house of the LORD
are now soon to be brought back from Babylonia,' for lies do they prophesy
17 to you. Do not listen to them. Serve the king of Babylonia and live. Why
18 should this city become a ruin? And if they are prophets, and if the word
of the LORD is with them, let them entreat, pray, the LORD of Armies that
the vessels remaining in the house of the LORD and in the house of Judah
19 not come to Babylonia. For thus said the LORD of Armies concerning the
pillars and the basins and the stands and concerning the rest of the vessels
20 remaining in this city, which Nebuchadnezzar did not take when he exiled
Jeconiah king of Judah from Jerusalem to Babel with all the aristocrats of
21 Judah and Jerusalem. For thus said the LORD of Armies God of Israel concerning the vessels remaining in the house of the LORD and in the house of
22 the king of Judah and Jerusalem: To Babylonia shall they be brought, and
there shall they be until the day I attend to them and bring them up and
return them to this place."

1 CHAPTER 28   And it happened in that year, at the beginning of
the kingship of Zedekiah king of Judah, in the fourth year, in the fifth month,
that Hananiah the prophet son of Azzur, who was from Gibeon, said to me
in the house of the LORD before the eyes of the priests and all the people,

---

16. *Look, the vessels of the house of the LORD are now soon to be brought back.* A portion of
the temple valuables had been carted off by the Babylonians when they took the Judahite
king Jeconiah into exile, as is stated in verse 20.

19. *the pillars and the basins and the stands.* This constitutes a small catalogue of the sacred
furniture that is destined to be looted and taken away to Babylonia if the Judahites persist
in their futile resistance to the invading forces.

22. *To Babylonia shall they be brought.* This prophecy of the despoliation of the Temple
was fulfilled in the final defeat and destruction of 586 B.C.E., seven or eight years after the
enunciation of this prophecy. The added note that a time will come when the vessels will be
brought back to Jerusalem sets the stage for the prophecies of the return to Zion of Second
Isaiah, who was active in the Babylonian exile a few decades after Jeremiah. Centuries later,
the author of the episode of the writing on the wall in Daniel will still be pondering the
violation of the transfer of the sacred vessels into Babylonian hands.

CHAPTER 28   1. *in the house of the LORD before the eyes of the priests and all the
people.* This confrontation between true and false prophet is staged for maximum public
exposure—in the Temple, when priests and a throng of people are assembled for worship.

saying: "Thus said the LORD of Armies, God of Israel, saying, I have broken 2
the yoke of the king of Babylonia. In another two years I will bring back 3
to this place all the vessels of the house of the LORD that Nebuchadnezzar
king of Babylonia took from this place and brought to Babylonia. And 4
Jeconiah son of Johaiakim king of Judah and all the exiles of Judah who
came to Babylonia I will bring back to this place, said the LORD, for I will
break the yoke of the king of Babylonia." And Jeremiah the prophet said 5
to Hananiah the prophet before the eyes of the priests and before the eyes
of all the people standing in the house of the LORD. And Jeremiah said, 6
"In truth, thus shall the LORD do, the LORD shall fulfill your words that
you prophesied, to bring back the vessels of the house of the LORD and all
the exiles from Babylonia to this place. But listen, pray, to this word that 7
I speak in your hearing and in the hearing of all the people. The prophets 8
who were before me and before you from times of old and prophesied concerning many lands and concerning many great kingdoms for war and for
evil and for pestilence. The prophet who prophesies peace, when the word 9
of the prophet comes about, it will be known of the prophet that the LORD
truly sent him." And Hananiah the prophet took the yoke bar from the neck 10
of Jeremiah the prophet and broke it. And Hananiah said before the eyes 11

---

2. *Thus said the LORD of Armies.* The false prophet uses the same messenger-formula as the true prophet, claiming to convey the words of God.

5. *Jeremiah the prophet said to Hananiah the prophet.* The two are given the same epithet as they vie to demonstrate which of them is the authentic prophet.

6. *In truth, thus shall the LORD do.* What sounds like an affirmation is actually a biting challenge, as if to say: Let us see if the LORD will really fulfill your words. Alternatively, Jeremiah may mean that at some point the sacred vessels will be returned, but not as you say, and not in two years.

8. *prophesied . . . for war and for evil and for pestilence.* The prophets of old invoked here go back to Amos in the eighth century B.C.E., a century and a half before Jeremiah. The claim he makes is not that the only true prophecies are prophecies of doom but rather that, given the course of historical events and the misbehavior of Israel and other nations, the doomsayers are usually the ones who prophesy truly, whereas those who predict that all will end well are likely to be merely courting the approval of their audiences.

9. *when the word of the prophet comes about, it will be known of the prophet that the LORD truly sent him.* Obviously, peace and good historical outcomes occasionally happen, but given the historical circumstances—a powerful empire threatening to overwhelm Judah—the positive scenario is unlikely, and only if it really happens will the prophecy be authenticated.

10. *And Hananiah the prophet took the yoke bar . . . and broke it.* As Hananiah now makes clear, two can play at the game of symbolic act. Jeremiah bears the yoke to demonstrate

of all the people, saying, "Thus said the Lord: So will I break the yoke of
Nebuchadnezzar king of Babylonia in another two years from the neck of
12 all the nations." And Jeremiah the prophet went on his way. And the word
of the Lord came to Jeremiah after Hananiah the prophet had broken the
13 yoke bar from Jeremiah's neck, saying: "Go and say to Hananiah, saying,
Thus said the Lord: the wooden yoke bars you have broken, and you shall
14 make in their stead iron yoke bars. For thus said the Lord of Armies,
God of Israel: An iron yoke I have put on the neck of all these nations to
serve Nebuchadnezzar king of Babylonia, and they shall serve him. And the
15 beasts of the field as well I have given to him." And Jeremiah the prophet
said to Hananiah the prophet, "Listen, pray, Hananiah. The Lord has not
16 sent you, and, as for you, you have made this people trust in a lie. Therefore,
thus said the Lord: I am about to send you away from upon the earth. This
17 year you shall die, for you have spoken rebellion against the Lord." And
Hananiah the prophet died that year in the seventh month.

1 CHAPTER 29   And these are the words of the missive that
Jeremiah the prophet sent from Jerusalem to the rest of the elders of the

---

Judah's necessary subjugation to Babylonia; Hananiah now tries to show that this political
yoke is about to be broken.

11. *And Jeremiah the prophet went on his way.* Jeremiah's silence and his withdrawal from
the scene of confrontation are, at least for the moment, ambiguous. He may even think
that Hananiah's theatrical gesture of breaking the yoke bar could prove to have predictive
force. But then the word of the Lord comes to him again (verses 12–13), giving the lie to
Hananiah's gesture and affirming that unbreakable yoke bars of iron are now to replace
the wooden ones.

14. *all these nations.* Judah's subjugation to Babylonia is a necessary part of Babylonia's
imperial domination of nations all around.

16. *This year you shall die.* Hananiah's premature death is both punishment for his misleading the people with false prophecy and an almost immediate refutation of his prophecy—
instead of the predicted liberation and restoration, the prophet himself dies.

CHAPTER 29   1. *the missive.* Although the Hebrew *sefer* often has the sense of
"book," it can designate anything set down in writing on a scroll. In this instance it clearly
refers to a letter, but it is a communication of public and prophetic import, hence the
more formal translation choice of "missive." But what is Jeremiah doing in this sending of
missives to the exiles in Babylonia? One might think he has enough on his hands with a
contentious populace and a hostile king in Judah. This entire episode must be read in the
context of Jeremiah's confrontation with the false prophet Hananiah, recorded in the previous chapter. For Jeremiah, everything in his prophetic mission is at stake in distinguishing
between true and false prophecy. Hananiah had predicted that the exiles would return to

exiles and to the priests and to the prophets and to all the people whom
Nebuchadrezzar had exiled from Jerusalem to Babylonia, After King Jeco- 2
niah and the queen mother and the eunuchs, the nobles of Judah and the
craftsmen and the smiths had gone out from Jerusalem, by the hands of 3
Elasah son of Shaphan and Gemariah son of Hilkiah whom Zedekiah king
of Judah had sent to Nebuchadnezzar king of Babylonia, saying: "Thus said 4
the LORD of Armies, God of Israel, to all the exiles whom I exiled to Babylonia: Build houses and dwell in them and plant gardens and eat their fruit. 5
Take wives and beget sons and daughters, and take wives for your sons and 6
give your daughters to husbands and let them bear sons and daughters,
and multiply there and do not dwindle. And seek the welfare of the city to 7
which I exiled you and pray for it to the LORD, for through its welfare you
shall have welfare. For thus said the LORD of Armies, God of Israel: Let not 8
your prophets who are in your midst delude you, or your soothsayers, and
do not listen to your dreams that you dream. For with lies do they proph- 9
esy to you in My name. I have not sent them, said the LORD. For thus said 10
the LORD: When seventy years are fulfilled for Babylonia, I will single you

---

their land in just two years. One infers that he had counterparts in Babylonia itself who
were deluding the people with similar rosy predictions. Against this, Jeremiah wants to
make it perfectly clear to the exiles that they will have a long residence in Babylonia before
any return can take place (verses 5–7).

2. *the craftsmen and the smiths.* As is also noted in 2 Kings, Nebuchadnezzar took pains to
exile skilled workers in order to ensure that the Judahites would not have the capacity to
manufacture weapons.

6. *multiply there and do not dwindle.* The first verb echoes the "be fruitful and multiply"
of the Creation story. With the prospect of a long stay in Babylonia ahead of them, the
exiles are enjoined to settle into the place, conduct normal lives, establish a flourishing
community. In the event, when the opportunity of return was afforded after the Persian
conquest of Babylonia, many in this community chose to stay there—it is at this point that
Israel becomes both a people in its land and a diaspora community.

7. *seek the welfare of the city to which I exiled you.* The exiles do not exactly become patriotic
naturalized Babylonians, but given their long-term stay in this place, they are enjoined to
pray for the prosperity and safety of the city that is, after all, their habitat as well.

8. *that you dream.* Though the form of the Hebrew verb looks a little odd, it seems strained
to construe it, as some have, to mean "cause to dream."

10. *When seventy years are fulfilled for Babylonia.* This would take us to the 520s, about a
decade after the destruction of the Babylonian empire by Persia. But the number of seventy
is clearly formulaic, a way of indicating that the return to Zion will not occur for some three
generations. In the Book of Daniel, this prophecy will be given a novel interpretation in
which seventy is understood to be seventy units of seven years, thus bringing it more or
less to the time when Daniel was written.

11 out and bring about My good word to return you to this place. For I surely
know the plans that I have devised for you, said the LORD, plans for peace
12 and not for evil, to give you a future and hope. And you shall call Me and
13 go and pray to Me, and I will listen to you. And you shall look for Me and
14 find Me when you seek Me with all your heart. And I will be found by you
and restore your fortunes, and I will gather you from all the nations and
from all the places where I scattered you, said the LORD, and I will bring
15 you back to the place from which I exiled you. For you thought, the LORD
16 has raised up prophets for us in Babylonia. For thus said the LORD concerning the king seated on the throne of David and concerning all the people
17 dwelling in this city, your brothers who did not go out with you in exile. For
thus said the LORD of Armies: I am about to send against them sword and
famine and pestilence, and I will make them like the ghastly figs that are
18 so bad that they cannot be eaten. And I will pursue them with sword and
famine and pestilence and make them a horror to all the kingdoms of the
earth, an imprecation and a desolation and a hissing and a disgrace among
19 all the nations where I have scattered you. Because they have not heeded
My words, said the LORD, that I sent to them through My servants the
prophets, repeatedly sending, and you did not heed them, said the LORD.
20 As for you, heed the word of the LORD, all the exiles whom I sent from
21 Jerusalem to Babylonia. Thus said the LORD of Armies, God of Israel, concerning Ahab son of Kolaiah and Zedekiah son of Maaseiah, who prophesy
lies to you in My name. I am about to give them into the hand of Nebuchadnezzar king of Babylonia, and he shall strike them down before your

---

11. *to give you a future and hope.* Jeremiah thus does not cast himself merely as a doomsayer
but rather as a prophet who envisages national restoration at a later moment in history.

16. *For thus said the LORD concerning the king seated on the throne of David.* Jeremiah is not
really switching subjects, as it might momentarily seem. If the false prophets in Babylonia
predict an imminent return to Zion, one has only to look to the true prophecy pronounced
about those who remain in Judah: instead of a national restoration, things will become
much worse, with the Judahite populace to be utterly devastated by sword and famine and
plague.

19. *My words . . . that I sent to them through My servants the prophets.* This is Jeremiah's
great recurring theme: prophecy is God's chief channel of communication with His people,
and the people's persistent refusal to heed its true prophets is the inexorable cause of the
disaster about to overtake it.

20. *heed the word of the LORD, all the exiles whom I sent from Jerusalem.* The catastrophe
that is about to engulf the homeland should be an object lesson to the exiles.

eyes. And a curse shall be taken from them for all the exiles of Judah who   22
are in Babylonia, saying, 'May the LORD make you like Zedekiah and like
Ahab, whom the king of Babylonia roasted in fire.' Inasmuch as they did a   23
scurrilous thing in Israel and committed adultery with the wives of their
fellow men and spoke a lying word in My name with which I did not charge
them. As for Me, I know and am witness, said the LORD. And to Shemaiah   24
the Nehelamite you shall say, saying: Thus said the LORD of Armies, God of   25
Israel, saying: Inasmuch as you have sent missives in your name to all the
people who are in Jerusalem and to Zephaniah son of Maaseiah the priest
and to the priests, saying, 'The LORD made you priest instead of Jehoiash   26
the priest to serve as official in the house of the LORD for every madman
playing the prophet, and you were to put him in stocks and in the pillory.
And now, why did you not rebuke Jeremiah the Anothite, who played the   27
prophet to you? For thus did he send to us in Babylonia, saying, It will be   28
a long time. Build houses and dwell in them, and plant gardens and eat
their fruit.'" And Zephaniah the priest read this missive in the hearing of   29
Jeremiah the prophet. And the word of the LORD came to Jeremiah, saying,   30
"Send to all the exiles, saying, Thus said the LORD concerning Shemaiah   31
the Nehelamite: Inasmuch as Shemaiah prophesied to you when I did not
send him and made you trust in a lie, therefore, thus said the LORD, I am   32
about to make a reckoning with Shemaiah the Nehelamite and with his
seed. No man of his shall dwell among this people, and he shall not see the

---

22. *a curse shall be taken from them.* This reverses the more common linguistic practice in
which someone's name is invoked as part of a blessing by future generations.

   roasted. The verb is unusual, perhaps meant to convey the horror of the burning.

23. *Inasmuch as they did a scurrilous thing in Israel and committed adultery with the wives
of their fellow men.* "Scurrilous thing," *nevalah,* often refers to a sexual offense. That added
note may be a bit surprising in a denunciation of false prophets. One suspects Jeremiah
is referring to known facts: these so-called prophets are actually lascivious men guilty of
scandalous acts.

25. *you have sent missives in your name.* The sender of the missives is Shemaiah.

27. *why did you not rebuke Jeremiah the Anothite, who played the prophet to you?* Prophecy
is sometimes viewed in the biblical world as a form of madness (compare "every madman"
in the previous verse), especially, as here, when the verb for prophecy appears in the reflexive conjugation, which implies giving into an ecstatic frenzy. Why, then, Shemaiah asks
Zephaniah the priest, did he not treat Jeremiah as a lunatic and throw him in the stocks?
The content of Jeremiah's missive to the exiles, quoted in the next verse, is cited as evidence
of his madness.

good that I do for My people, said the Lord, for he has spoken rebellion against the Lord."

1 CHAPTER 30   The word that came to Jeremiah from the
2 Lord, saying: "Thus said the Lord God of Israel, Write you these words
3 that I have spoken to you on a scroll. For, look, days are coming, said the
   Lord, when I will restore the fortunes of My people Israel and Judah, said
   the Lord, and bring them back to the land that I gave to their fathers, and
4 they shall take hold of it." And these are the words that the Lord spoke
5 concerning Israel and concerning Judah. For thus said the Lord:

> A voice of terror we have heard,
>   fear and not peace.
6 Ask, pray, and see,
>   if a male is giving birth.
> Why do I see every man,
>   his hands on his loins like a woman in labor
>   and every face turned sickly green?
7 Woe, for great is that day,
>   there is nothing like it,
> and a time of distress for Jacob,
>   but from it he shall be rescued.

CHAPTER 30   3. *For, look, days are coming . . . when I will restore the fortunes of My people.* These words, signaling a prophecy of national redemption after the destruction, are taken by many scholars to mark the beginning of a distinctive subunit in Jeremiah that scholarship labels the Book of Restoration.

    restore the fortunes. More literally, "restore the former state."

5. *A voice of terror we have heard.* After the summary prophecy of national restoration in verse 3, there is a switch to poetry, which serves as a vehicle to make vividly clear the great tribulation that is to precede the restoration.

6. *Why do I see every man, / his hands on his loins like a woman in labor.* The convulsions of childbirth are a standard trope in biblical poetry for shuddering and pain. In this instance, the familiar simile is represented through a startling image: males, who could not possibly be experiencing birth pangs, writhe in pain with their hands on their loins, their faces sickly green, as though they were in labor.

7. *but from it he shall be rescued.* Only in the last verse of the last line of the poem is the move from anguish to redemption announced.

"And it shall happen on that day, said the LORD of Armies, I will break his 8
yoke from upon his neck, and his bands I will snap, and strangers shall no
longer make him serve. But they shall serve the LORD their God and David 9
their king whom I will raise up for them.

> As for you, do not fear, My servant Jacob,   10
>> —said the LORD—
>> and do not be afraid, O Israel,
> for I am about to rescue you from afar
>> and your seed from the land of their captivity,
> and Jacob again shall be at ease,
>> be tranquil, with none to make him tremble.
> For I am with you, said the LORD, to rescue you,   11
>> for I will make an end of all the nations
>>> where I have scattered you.
> But of you I will not make an end,
>> I will surely chastise you in justice,
>> I will surely not acquit you.
> For thus said the LORD.   12
>> your shattering is grievous,
>>> grave is your blow.
> None considers your case for a cure,   13
>> no healing of the wound do you have.

---

8. *from upon his neck.* The Masoretic Text has "your neck," but the Septuagint shows the
third person—perhaps only an understandable regularization of the Hebrew by the Greek
translators.

9. *David their king.* The ruler of the restored monarchy is to be a kind of new version of
David, who is imagined to be the ideal king.

11. *I will surely chastise you in justice, / I will surely not acquit you.* These two verses are
an explanatory qualification of the initial verset in this triadic line: Unlike My treatment
of your oppressors, I will not entirely destroy you; however, I will first submit you to just
chastisement, for I cannot ignore your crimes.

12. *your shattering is grievous, / grave is your blow.* These words follow from the reference
to chastisement in the previous verse: the people is condemned to acute suffering (verses
12–15) before the redemption comes (verses 16–22).

13. *healing of the wound.* The first of the two Hebrew nouns here clearly means "healing";
the second is generally thought to refer to the scab that forms over a wound in the process
of healing.

14 All your lovers have forgotten you,
        you they do not seek.
    For an enemy's blow I struck you,
        a ruthless punishment
    for all your crimes,
        your many offenses.
15 Why should you cry out for your shattering,
        your grievous pain,
    for all your crimes, your many offenses?
        I have done these to you.
16 Therefore all who devour you shall be devoured,
        and all your foes, they all shall go as captives,
    and your plunderers shall become plunder,
        And all your despoilers I will turn into spoil.
17 For I will bring healing to you
        and cure you of your blows, said the LORD,
    though they called you "outcast,"
        "Zion, whom no one seeks."
18 For thus said the LORD:
        I am about to restore the fortunes of Jacob's tents
            and show mercy to his dwellings,
    and the city shall be rebuilt on its mound,
        and the citadel sit in its rightful place.
19 And a song of thanksgiving shall issue from them

14. *All your lovers.* The probable reference is to the nations with whom Judah sought to create alliances.

an enemy's blow. God struck the people a blow so hard that it is as if He were acting as an enemy.

16. *Therefore all who devour you shall be devoured.* This is the pivotal point of the prophecy. The logical force of "therefore" is that after you have suffered these terrible blows and thus paid for your crimes, your enemies will get their comeuppance and you will be restored to your former state.

18. *and the city shall be rebuilt on its mound.* The mound or *tell* (it has become a modern archaeological term) is the heap of soil and rubble where the city once stood, which is now to underpin the rebuilding of the city.

19. *And a song of thanksgiving shall issue from them.* This and the lines that follow mark a dramatic progression: first we see the inanimate structures of the city rising again; now we

and the sound of celebrants,
and I will make them multiply, they shall not dwindle,
    give them honor, they shall not be paltry.
And his sons shall be as before,   20
    his community before Me firm-founded,
        and I will reckon with all who oppress him.
And his leader shall be from within him,   21
    and his ruler shall come forth from his midst.
I will bring him close and he shall approach Me,
    for who would presume to approach Me?
        said the LORD.
And you shall become My people;   22
    as for Me, I will be your God.

Look, the LORD's storm goes forth in wrath,   23
    a whirling tempest,
        it comes down on the head of the wicked,
until He does and until He fulfills
    His heart's devisings.
        In the days afterward you shall grasp it.

At that time, said the LORD, I will be God for all the clans of Israel and they 24
shall be My people.

---

have the rebuilt city filled with joyful human beings, chanting songs of thanksgiving to the accompaniment of musical instruments ("the sound of celebrants").

21. *And his leader shall be from within him.* Instead of foreign rulers, or rulers put in place by alien dominators, as in fact the Babylonians did, an authentic—presumably Davidic—king from the midst of the people will assume the throne.

for who would presume to approach Me. This is a recurring motif in a variety of biblical texts—that it is dangerous, often fatal, to approach God or His sanctuary uninvited. Here, however, God encourages the Judahite leader to approach.

23. *Look, the LORD's storm goes forth in wrath.* This entire verse may be a fragment unconnected with what precedes or follows because the image of wrathful destruction scarcely accords with the prophecy of jubilant restoration just annunciated. It is conceivable that because the destruction is said to come down on "the head of the wicked," it refers back to the devouring of the devourers in verse 16, but if that is so, the placement of these lines here looks odd.

1 CHAPTER 31   Thus said the LORD:

> The people, survivors of the sword,
>   have found favor in the wilderness,
>   Israel going to find rest.

2 From afar the LORD appeared to me:
>   With everlasting love do I love you,
>   therefore did I draw you in kindness.

3 Yet will I rebuild you and you will be built,
>   O Virgin Israel,
> Yet shall you deck yourself with your timbrels
>   and go out in the celebrants' dance.

4 Yet shall you plant vineyards on Samaria's hills,
>   the planters shall plant and eat the fruit.

5 For a day is to come when watchmen call out
>   on Mount Ephraim:
> Rise and let us go up to Zion,
>   to the LORD our God.

6 For thus said the LORD:
>   Sing out in joy for Jacob,
>   shout jubilant at the head of nations.
> Proclaim, praise and say,
>   the LORD has rescued your people,
>   the remnant of Israel.

7 I am about to bring them from the land of the north,

CHAPTER 31   1. *The people, survivors of the sword, / have found favor in the wilderness.* For the sake of English coherence, the translation reverses the order of the two Hebrew versets.

Israel going to find rest. Throughout this prophecy, the meaning of the term "Israel" that is used has been debated by scholars. Some understand it in its traditional sense as a name for the northern kingdom. While that is possible, it may not be likely that Jeremiah, writing well over a century after the destruction of the northern kingdom, was still hoping for a return of the exiled ten tribes. By this point, then, "Israel" may have become an interchangeable term with "Judah," and meaning "Judah."

2. *therefore did I draw you in kindness.* The verb here is probably dictated by an image of God's leading the people through the wilderness on the way back from exile. The noun *ḥesed,* which can also mean something like "loyalty," is better rendered here as "kindness" (or perhaps even "tenderness") because of the affirmation of love in the parallel verset.

3. *Yet shall you deck yourself with your timbrels.* The timbrel, played by the young women as they danced in celebration, is of course not exactly an ornament, but held by the hip of the dancer, it is imagined as ornamenting her in her dance.

and I will gather them from the corners of the earth.
The blind and the lame are among them,
    she with child and the woman in labor,
        a great assembly shall come back here.
In weeping shall they come,   8
    in supplications will I lead them,
I will make them walk by brooks of water,
    on a straight way where they shall not stumble,
For I am father to Israel,
    And Ephraim is my firstborn.
Listen to the word of the Lord, you nations,   9
    and tell in the coastlands far off and say:
He who scattered Israel shall gather it
    and guard it as a shepherd his flock.
For the Lord has ransomed Jacob   10
    and redeemed him from the hand of one stronger than he.
And they shall come and sing gladly on Zion's heights   11
    and shall shine with the Lord's bounty,
for the grain and the new wine and the oil,
    and for the flocks and the cattle.
And their life-breath shall be like a watered garden,

---

7. *The blind and the lame are among them, / she with child and the woman in labor.* The return from exile will be so comprehensive that even those barely capable of walking—the blind and the lame, the pregnant and the parturient—will join "the great assembly." It is noteworthy that between these two versets there is a move from physical impairment to bringing life into the world, which is thus a kind of miniature intimation of the whole process of national restoration.

8. *In weeping shall they come, / in supplications will I lead them.* Both versets refer unambiguously to return, not to going out from Zion. An argument to understand the term rendered as "supplications" to mean "compassion" rests on shaky grounds. The probable meaning, in keeping with the interpretation of several medieval exegetes, is that as the people returns, it weeps and implores God to forgive it for its previous misdeeds.

    I will make them walk by brooks of water. The terrain that the people must cross in their long trek from exile in the east is largely parched desert, so leading them along watercourses is a necessary part of the redemption. Second Isaiah will pick up this motif.

11. *their life-breath.* The tricky Hebrew noun is the multivalent *nefesh.* It does not mean "soul," as many translators continue to render it. The core meaning is "life-breath" and, by extension, "life," but the latter would be misleading here because it could suggest "a lived life." *Nefesh* also often implies "essential self." It sometimes means "throat" or "gullet" (by metonymy because the throat is a passageway for the breath), and that is the probable sense in verse 13, where the satisfaction of appetite is invoked.

and they shall no longer be in pain.

12   Then shall the virgin rejoice in dance
       and young men and elders together,
    and I shall turn their mourning to gladness
       and comfort them and give them joy for their sorrow.

13   And I will wet the priests' gullet with richness,
       and My people shall be sated with My bounty
           —said the Lord.

14   Thus said the Lord:
       A voice in Ramah is heard,
         lament and bitter weeping.
    Rachel weeps for her sons
       She refuses to be comforted
         for her sons, for they are no more.

15   Thus said the Lord:
       Hold back your voice from weeping
         and your eyes from tears,
    for there is a reward for your labor—said the Lord—
       and they shall come back from the enemy's land,

16   and there is hope for your future—said the Lord—
       and the sons shall come back to their place.

17   I have surely heard
       Ephraim rocking with grief:

---

12. *the virgin . . . / young men.* This is a fixed pair in biblical poetry, often associated with joyfulness. She is referred to as a virgin simply on the assumption that young women as yet unmarried would preserve their virginity, though nothing is really made of the abstention from sexual intercourse.

14. *A voice in Ramah is heard.* Ramah is a site just north of Jerusalem associated with Rachel, but it means "height," and so it is also possible to render this as "on the height."
   for they are no more. The Hebrew shows a singular, dictated by a pointed allusion to "is no more" referring to Rachel's son Joseph, a word first uttered by the ten brothers to the man they see as the vizier of Egypt, then by their father, who laments that "Joseph is no more" and "Simeon is no more." He is wrong in both cases, which here provides an intimation that the sons for whom Rachel weeps will return.

15. *said the Lord.* It should be kept in mind that this formula for assigning speech is often extrametrical in poetry and sometimes may reflect an editorial intervention.

16. *their place.* The literal sense is "their border," which often, by metonymy, means "territory."

You chastised me and I was chastised
    like an untrained calf.
Bring me back, that I may come back,
    for You are the LORD my God.
For after I turned back I repented,   18
    and after I became aware I struck my thigh.
I was ashamed, indeed, disgraced,
    for I bore the reproach of my youth.
Is not Ephraim a dear son to Me,   19
    a delightful child?
For even as I speak against him,
    I surely recall him.
Therefore does My heart stir for him,
    I will surely show him mercy, said the LORD.
Set yourself markers,   20
    put up road signs for yourself,
pay heed to the highway,
    the way where you walked,
Turn back, O Virgin Israel.
    Turn back to these towns of yours.
How long will you slip away,   21
    rebellious daughter?
For the LORD has created a new thing on earth—
    the female goes round the male.

Thus said the LORD of Armies, God of Israel: "Yet shall they say this thing 22
in the land of Judah and in its towns when I restore their fortunes: May the
LORD bless you, righteous abode, holy mountain. And farmers and those 23

---

18. *I struck my thigh.* This is obviously a gesture of grief or regret.

19. *does My heart stir for him.* The literal sense of the Hebrew is "innards" or "bowels," imagined as the seat of compassion.

20. *road signs.* The Hebrew *tamrurim,* of uncertain etymology, appears only here, and thus the meaning is surmised from the poetic parallelism.

21. *the female goes round the male.* This is the literal sense of the Hebrew, and the claim of some scholars that the verb here means "protect" is dubious. Following the castigation of the young woman as a "rebellious daughter" who "slips away," the clause might be sarcastic: it is the way of the world for the male to court the female, but in this case of the wayward daughter the roles are scandalously reversed.

journeying with the flock shall dwell in Judah and all its towns together.
24 For I have given full drink to the thirsty gullet, and every being in pain I
25 have sated." For this have I awoken and seen, and my sleep had been sweet
26 to me. "Look, days are coming, said the LORD, when I will sow the house of
27 Israel and the house of Judah with human seed and seed of beast. And as I
was zealous over them to uproot and smash and lay ruin and destroy and
harm, so will I be zealous over them to build and to plant, said the LORD.
28 In those days, they shall no longer say:

> The fathers ate unripe fruit
> and the sons' teeth were blunted.

29 Instead, a man shall die through his own crime, and every person eating
30 unripe fruit, his teeth shall be blunted. Look, days are coming, said the
LORD, when I will seal with the house of Israel and with the house of Judah
31 a new covenant. Not like the covenant that I sealed with their fathers on
the day I held their hand to bring them out of the land of Egypt, as they

---

24. *I have given full drink to the thirsty gullet.* This appears to be still another instance in which *nefesh* refers to "gullet" or "throat." The verb here, which suggests "watering" or "providing abundant drink" is the same one attached to the garden in verse 11 and to the priests' gullet in verse 13.

    every being in pain. This is again *nefesh*, and the translation guesses that here it means "being" or "self," although it could again mean "gullet."

25. *For this have I awoken and seen.* These words are probably the prophet's, not God's, especially because the deity is said neither to slumber nor to sleep.

    and my sleep had been sweet to me. The prophet evidently has enjoyed a pleasing dream of national restoration, and now he awakes to find that it is true.

26. *I will sow the house of Israel.* This may seem like a mixed metaphor, but "house of" as a term for "people of" or "kingdom of" is so formulaic that no suggestion of a built structure is conveyed.

28. *The fathers ate unripe fruit / and the sons' teeth were blunted.* This is obviously a proverbial saying with the sense: if the fathers behave badly, their offspring will suffer. In the future, Jeremiah promises, this will no longer be true. Most translations render the first Hebrew noun, *boser*, as "sour grapes," but with little warrant. In fact, it is eating unripe fruit, which is still hard, that blunts the teeth, something unripe grapes would not do. The time-honored translation of the verb in the second verset is "set on edge," but it actually means to "become blunt."

30. *a new covenant.* This Hebrew phrase, *brit hadashah,* famously became the designation for the Christian Scriptures ("New Testament"). What it refers to in Jeremiah's prophecy is a new covenant between God and Israel, to be fully internalized ("inscribed" on the heart), that will replace the covenant violated by Israel.

broke My covenant, though I was master to them, said the LORD. But this is 32
the covenant that I shall seal with the house of Israel after those days, said
the LORD: I have put My teaching in their midst, and on their heart I have
inscribed it, and I will be their God and they shall be My people. And they 33
shall no longer teach each to his fellow man and each to his brother, saying,
'Know the LORD.' For they shall all know Me from the least of them to their
greatest, said the LORD, for I will forgive their crime, and their offense I
will no more recall."

> For thus said the LORD,   34
>   Who makes the sun for light by day,
> the laws of moon and stars
>   for light by night,
> roiling the sea, and its waves do roar
>   —the LORD of Armies is His name.
> Should these laws be set aside   35
>   from before Me? said the LORD.
> Then Israel's seed would cease
>   to be a nation before Me forever.
> Thus said the LORD: 36
> Should the heavens be measured above
>   and the earth's foundations fathomed below,
> only then would I reject all Israel's seed
>   for all that they did, said the LORD.

Look, days are coming, said the LORD, when a city for the LORD shall be 37
built from Hananel Tower to the Corner Gate. And the measuring line shall 38

---

33. *For they shall all know Me.* In the coming era of the new covenant, every person in
Israel will be inwardly informed of what God expects, and no teachers or external force
will be required.

34. *the laws of moon and stars.* The world is created with set guiding principles, "statutes"
or "laws," *ḥuquot*—the cycle of day and night (there is a reminiscence of Genesis 1:14–15),
the movement of the tides. The universe is orderly, and just as its laws are immutable, God's
commitment to the continuation of Israel will never waver (verse 35).

36. *for all that they did.* Israel has compiled a long bill of offenses, and for this they have
suffered a national disaster, but whatever their crimes, God remains steadfast in sustaining
their existence as a nation.

37. *from Hananel Tower to the Corner Gate.* These and the places mentioned in the next
two verses are markers of the perimeter of Jerusalem, thus conveying to the audience of the

39 again go out before it to the Hill of Gareb and swing down to Goah. And all
the Valley of Corpses and the Ashes and all the fields to the Kidron Wadi,
to the corner of the Horse Gate, shall be holy to the LORD. It shall not again
be uprooted and shall not be destroyed for all time.

1   CHAPTER 32   The word that came to Jeremiah in the tenth
year of Zedekiah king of Judah, which is the eighteenth year of Nebu-
2 chadrezzar. Then were the forces of the king of Babylonia besieging
Jerusalem, and Jeremiah the prophet was imprisoned in the court of the
3 guard which was in the house of the king. As Zedekiah king of Judah had
imprisoned him, saying, "Why do you prophesy, saying, 'Thus said the
LORD: I am about to give this city into the hand of the king of Babylonia,
4 and he shall capture it. And Zedekiah king of Judah shall not escape
from the hand of the Chaldeans but shall surely be given into the hand
of the king of Babylonia, and he shall speak to him mouth to mouth and
5 see him eye to eye. And to Babylonia he shall take Zedekiah, and there
he shall be until I single him out, said the LORD. Though you do battle
6 against the Chaldeans, you shall not succeed.'?" And Jeremiah said, "The
7 word of the LORD came to me, saying: Look, Hanamel the son of Shallum
your uncle is coming to you, saying, 'Buy for yourself my field which is

---

prophecy a concretely defined sense of the dimensions of the city that is now to be rebuilt
and never again to be destroyed.

CHAPTER 32   1. *in the tenth year of Zedekiah.* This is 587 B.C.E., the year before
the destruction of Jerusalem by the Babylonians. Hence the notation of the siege in the
next verse.

2. *Jeremiah the prophet was imprisoned.* If one recalls that he was repeatedly prophesying
destruction and exile in the midst of the war with the Babylonians, he would certainly have
been seen as guilty of sedition, so the imprisonment is hardly surprising.
  the court of the guard. The literal sense is "the court of the target." It is possible that this
area within the palace precincts was sometimes used for target practice by the royal guard.

4. *he shall speak to him mouth to mouth and see him eye to eye.* The captive king of Judah
is to be confronted—we would say "face-to-face"—by the Babylonian emperor. This may
well have happened.

5. *until I single him out.* The Hebrew verb *paqad* is appropriately ambiguous. It could mean
either "make a reckoning with him" or "single him out to redeem him," although the former
meaning is more likely.
  the Chaldeans. Throughout this passage, this designation is interchangeable with
"Babylonians."

in Anathoth, for yours is the right of redemption to buy.' And Hanamel 8
the son of my uncle came to me according to the word of the LORD, to
the court of the guard, and said to me, 'Buy for yourself my field which is
in Anathoth, which is in the region of Benjamin, for yours is the right of
inheritance and yours is the redemption. Buy it for yourself.' And I knew
that it was the word of the LORD. And I bought the field which is in Ana- 9
thoth from Hanamel the son of my uncle and weighed out to him the silver,
seventeen silver shekels. And I wrote it in a scroll and sealed it and had it 10
witnessed and weighed the silver on the scales. And I took the sealed scroll 11
of purchase, the injunction and the stipulations, and the open copy. And I 12
gave the scroll of purchase to Baruch son of Neriah son of Mahseiah before
the eyes of Hanamel son of my uncle and before the eyes of the witness who
signed the scroll of purchase before the eyes of all the Judahites sitting in
the court of the guard. And I charged Baruch before their eyes, saying, 13
Thus said the LORD of Armies, God of Israel: 'Take these scrolls, this sealed 14
scroll of purchase and this open scroll, and put them in an earthenware jar
so that they may last many days.' For thus said the LORD of Armies, God 15
of Israel, 'Yet shall houses and fields and vineyards be bought in this land.'

---

8. *for yours is the right of inheritance and yours is the redemption.* The legal procedure here is
similar to what is evident in the Book of Ruth. Hanamel appears to be in need of money—in
this period, silver ingots that are weighed out, not coin—and thus turns to a kinsman to
"redeem" the property, which thus will not be lost to the family. But the economic transaction in this instance is directed by God with the purpose of having the prophet purchase
the land as a symbolic act, signifying that after the impending destruction a time will come
when the Judahites will again possess their lands.

11. *And I took the sealed scroll of purchase . . . and the open copy.* This was standard procedure. The official document was signed, witnessed, and sealed, and an unsealed copy of it
was made that could be referred to if a need arose to review the terms of the transaction.
  scroll of purchase. Since what is involved is a sale of property, this is of course a deed, but
the translation preserves the sense of the Hebrew, which keeps in view the material scroll
on which the agreement is written and does not use a specialized term for deed.

12. *Baruch son of Neriah.* Baruch, who will appear later in the narrative, is a scribe and
Jeremiah's personal secretary.
  Hanamel son of my uncle. The Masoretic Text omits "son of," which is almost certainly
a scribal slip.
  before the eyes of all the Judahites sitting in the court of the guard. This formulation
suggests that Jeremiah's place of confinement was not a prison cell but some sort of open
space on the palace grounds to which people had ready access.

14. *put them in an earthenware jar.* The jar, which then would have been tightly sealed, was
a means of preservation, as we know from the Dead Sea scrolls, which were preserved in
such jars for more than two thousand years.

16 And I prayed to the LORD after I gave the scroll of purchase to Baruch son
17 of Neriah, saying: Alas, O Master LORD! Look, You made the heavens and
   the earth through your great power and with Your outstretched arm. Noth-
18 ing is beyond you, doing kindness for the thousands and paying back the
   crime of the fathers into the lap of their sons after them, great and mighty
19 God, LORD of Armies is His name. Great in counsel, grand in acts, Whose
   eyes are open on all the ways of humankind to give to each man according
20 to his ways and according to the fruit of his deeds. You Who set out signs
   and wonders in the land of Egypt to this day in Israel and in humankind,
21 and You have made You a name as on this day. And You brought out Your
   people Israel from the land of Egypt in signs and wonders and with a strong
22 hand and with an outstretched arm and with great terror. And You gave
   them this land that You vowed to their fathers to give to them, a land
23 flowing with milk and honey. And they came and took hold of it, but they
   did not heed Your voice and did not go by Your teachings. All that You
24 charged them to do they did not do, and all this evil befell them. Look, the
   siege-ramps have come against the city to capture it, and the city is given
   into the hands of the Chaldeans battling against it—because of the sword
   and the famine and the pestilence. And that which You spoke has come
25 to be, and here You see it. And You, You said to me, O Master LORD, 'Buy
   for yourself the field with silver and summon witnesses when the city is
26 given into the hands of the Chaldeans.'" And the word of the LORD came
27 to Jeremiah, saying: "Look, I am the LORD, God of all flesh. Can anything
28 be beyond Me? Therefore, thus said the LORD: I am about to give this city
   into the hand of the Chaldeans battling against this city and into the hand

---

18. *paying back the crime of the fathers into the lap of their sons.* This of course contradicts
the affirmation in the previous chapter that no longer will the teeth of the sons be blunted
after their fathers eat unripe fruit. Perhaps Jeremiah has in mind the imminent exile, knowing that generations will languish in a foreign land before they can return.

24. *because of the sword and the famine and the pestilence.* This reiterated chain of disasters
is actually related to the conditions of siege: the sword enforces the siege; with the city cut
off, famine ensues; in the crowded conditions of the besieged city, with an inadequate water
supply, contagion spreads.

25. *And You, You said to me.* This is a cry of outraged disbelief: in light of the comprehensive
disaster now enveloping the city, how could God have issued instructions for the purchase
of land?

27. *Can anything be beyond Me?* This is a reiterated formula in the Bible (see, for example,
Genesis 18:14). Since God is all-powerful and can do all things, an eventual reversal of the
fortune of disaster awaiting Israel is surely not beyond Him. However, before God comes

of Nebuchadrezzar king of Babylonia, and he shall capture it. And the 29
Chaldeans battling against this city shall come and set this city on fire and
burn it, with the houses and the roofs on which they burned incense to
Baal and poured libations to other gods so as to vex Me. For the Israelites 30
and the Judahites have been doing naught but evil in My eyes from their
youth, for the Israelites have been vexing Me with the work of their hands,
said the Lord. For to My anger and to My wrath this city has been to Me 31
from the day they built it to this day, so as to remove it from before Me, for 32
all the evil of the Israelites and the Judahites that they have done to vex Me,
they, their kings, their nobles, their priests, and their prophets, the men of
Judah and the dwellers of Jerusalem. They turned their backs to Me, and 33
not their faces. I taught them constantly, but they have not heeded to accept
discipline. And they put their foul things in the house on which My name 34
was called, to defile it. And they built the high places for Baal which are in 35
the Valley of of Ben-Hinnom to consign their sons and their daughters to
Molech, which I did not charge them and which never came to My mind
to do this abomination, so as to make Judah offend. And so now, thus said 36
the Lord God of Israel concerning this city of which you said, It is given
into the hand of the king of Babylonia by the sword and by famine and by
pestilence. I am about to gather them from all the lands where I scattered 37
them in My anger and in My wrath and in great fury, and I will bring them
back to this place and make them dwell secure. And they shall be My people 38
and I will be their God. And I will give them a single heart and a single 39
way to fear Me always, so that it will be well with them and with their sons
after them. And I will seal with them an everlasting covenant, that I not 40
turn back from them so that I do good for them, and My fear I will put in
their heart, that they do not swerve from Me. And I will rejoice over them 41
to do good for them, and I will plant them on this land truly, with all My
heart and with all My being. For thus said the Lord: As I brought upon 42
this people all this great evil, so I am about to bring upon them all the
good that I am speaking of them. And the field shall be bought in this land 43
about which you say, 'It is a desolation without human beings and beasts; it

---

to the promise of restoration (verse 37ff.), He launches on a lengthy indictment of Israel,
listing the sins that are about to lead to a catastrophe for the nation.

33. *turned their backs.* The body part in the Hebrew is literally "nape."

43. *And the field shall be bought in this land.* Finally, after sixteen verses, God comes to
Jeremiah's incredulous question about the purchase of the field, reassuring him that after

44 is given into the hands of the Chaldeans.' Fields they shall buy with silver,
writing on scrolls and sealing and summoning witnesses, in the region of
Benjamin and in the environs of Jerusalem and in the towns of Judah and
in the towns of the hill country and in the towns of the lowland and in the
towns of the Negeb, for I will restore their fortunes, said the LORD."

1 **CHAPTER 33**   And the word of the LORD came to Jeremiah
2 again while he was still shut up in the court of the guard, saying, "Thus said
3 the LORD, Who fashions it to bring it about, the LORD is His name. Call out
to Me that I may answer you and tell you great and lofty things you did not
4 know. For thus said the LORD God of Israel concerning the houses of the
city and the houses of the kings of Judah torn down before the siege-ramps
5 and before the sword, those coming to do battle with the Chaldeans, but
to fill them with human corpses whom I struck down in My wrath and in
6 My anger as I hid My face from this city for all their evil. I am about to
grant them a cure and a healing, and I will heal them and reveal to them a
7 wealth of true peace. And I will restore the fortunes of Judah and the for-
8 tunes of Israel and rebuild them as before. And I will cleanse them of their
crimes with which they offended against Me and with which they rebelled

---

the devastation of the whole Judahite countryside, the land will again be settled and properties will be bought.

44. *Fields they shall buy with silver, writing on scrolls and sealing and summoning witnesses.*
In reprising the conditions of Jeremiah's own purchase of land, these words evoke a time to
come in which full normalcy will be restored to the country and all the regular procedures
for transfer of property will be firmly in place.

CHAPTER 33   2. *Who fashions it to bring it about.* The feminine pronominal object
of both verbs refers to the plan or design in history that God is about to bring to fulfillment.

3. *lofty.* The Hebrew *betsurot* usually means "fortified," but by extension it could suggest
"looming high," and there is no need to emend it to the more predictable *netsurot,* "hidden."

4. *torn down before the siege-ramps.* The probable reference is to a strategy of razing houses
in close proximity to the city walls, either to prevent their being set on fire from the siege-
ramps above them or to allow the defenders more room to maneuver. It is doubtful that
the palace would have been close to the wall, so "the houses of the kings of Judah" would
be royal properties beyond the palace.

5. *but to fill them with human corpses.* The strategy of razing the houses is doomed to failure, and the cleared space merely becomes a killing ground.

6. *true peace.* The Hebrew reads "peace and truth," a phrase understood in this translation
as a hendiadys.

against Me. And it shall become for Me a joyous name, praise and glory, to ₉
all nations of the earth, who shall hear of all the good that I do for them.
They shall fear and tremble over all the good and all the peace that I do
for them. Thus said the Lord: Again shall be heard in this place of which ₁₀
you say, it is in ruins, without humans and without beasts, in the towns
of Judah and in the streets of Jerusalem that are desolate, without humans
and without beasts—the voice of gladness and the voice of joy, the voice of ₁₁
the bridegroom and the voice of the bride, saying 'Give thanks to the Lord
of Armies, for the Lord is good, for His kindness is everlasting,' as they
bring a thanksgiving offering to the house of the Lord, for I will restore the
fortunes of the land as before, said the Lord. Thus said the Lord of Armies: ₁₂
Again shall there be in this ruined place without humans and beasts as
well and in all its towns a pasture for shepherds resting their flocks. In the ₁₃
towns of the hill country, in the towns of the lowland and in the towns of
the Negeb and in the region of Benjamin and in the environs of Jerusalem,
again shall the flocks pass under the hands of him who counts them, said
the Lord. Look, days are coming, said the Lord, when I will fulfill the ₁₄
good word that I spoke concerning the house of Israel and the house of
Judah. In those days and at that time I will make a righteous shoot flourish ₁₅
for David, and he shall do justice and righteousness in the land. In those ₁₆
days Judah shall be rescued and Jerusalem shall dwell secure, and this is
what it shall be called: The-Lord-Is-Our-Righteousness. For thus said the ₁₇

---

9. *And it shall become for Me.* The implied subject of the feminine verb is the nation.

11. *the voice of gladness and the voice of joy, the voice of the bridegroom and the voice of the bride.* The words of this evocation of joy in the land after its devastation would be incorporated in the traditional Jewish marriage ceremony.

for the Lord is good, for His kindness is everlasting. These words echo a recurrent formula in Psalms. This is especially appropriate because the jubilant Judahites are then said to be bringing a thanksgiving offering to the Temple (which will be rebuilt after its destruction).

13. *again shall the flocks pass under the hands of him who counts them.* This is a practice invoked both in biblical narrative and in biblical poetry: an important responsibility of the shepherd is to count his sheep in order to make sure that none is missing. Should the count not be full, he is obliged to search for the missing sheep.

15. *I will make a righteous shoot flourish for David.* This picks up a prominent theme from Isaiah, that in the grand national restoration to come, an ideal king from the Davidic line will arise who will bring about a reign of perfect justice.

16. *The-Lord-Is-Our-Righteousness.* The idea of assigning epithets or names to Jerusalem that express its new status of rightness with God will be abundantly deployed in Second Isaiah.

LORD: no man of David seated on the throne of the house of Israel shall be

18   cut off. And of the levitical priests no man shall be cut off for all time from
before Me who offers up burnt offering and who burns grain offering and

19   performs sacrifice." And the word of the LORD came to Jeremiah, saying,

20   "Thus said the LORD: Should you break My covenant with the day and My

21   covenant with the night, that day and night come not in their time, only
then would My covenant with David My servant be broken, that he have

22   a son reigning on his throne, and the levitical priests, My ministrants. As
the array of the heavens cannot be counted nor the sand of the sea, so will I
multiply the seed of David My servant and the Levites who minister to Me."

23,24   And the word of the LORD came to Jeremiah, saying: "Have you not seen
what this people has spoken, saying, 'The two clans that the LORD chose
He has rejected.' My people they have spurned from being again a nation

25   before them. Thus said the LORD: As I have surely set out My covenant with

26   day and night, the laws of the heavens and the earth, so will I not reject
the seed of Jacob and David My servant to take rulers from his seed, from

---

17. *no man of David seated on the throne of the house of Israel shall be cut off.* At this historical moment, when the kingdom of Judah is about to be destroyed, Jeremiah provides an urgent emphasis that the divinely elected line will continue for all time. At least in this context, "Israel" is clearly interchangeable with "Judah" and cannot refer to the lost northern kingdom.

18. *And of the levitical priests no man shall be cut off.* The Temple priesthood and the Davidic monarchy are a single package—as the reform of Josiah around 622 B.C.E. stressed—and hence the continuity of both is guaranteed.

20. *Should you break My covenant with the day and My covenant with the night.* The rhetorical argument is made through a pointed extension of the term "covenant." As a rule, a covenant is a pact agreed upon between two conscious parties. Here, however, the fixed laws of nature—implicitly, fixed by God—whereby night follows day in an unvarying order are represented as a "covenant." Only if this covenant could be broken would the covenant between God and David, God and priesthood, be abrogated.

24. *The two clans that the LORD chose He has rejected.* The Hebrew *mishpaḥot,* "clans" or "families," is given an extended sense here to refer to the two kingdoms of Israel and Judah. One has already been destroyed and the other is on the brink of destruction: hence, the judgment that God has rejected both. It is not immediately clear who "this people" is that makes such a judgment. The second part of the verse, "My people they have spurned from being again a nation before them," suggests that it is a foreign people that imagines that Israel will never again have a place among the nations.

25. *the laws of the heavens and the earth.* "Laws" is now added to "covenant," making clear that the laws of nature constitute an eternal pact between God and creation. It is characteristic of the biblical conception of nature that its laws or regulating principles are imagined not as intrinsic to it or automatic but divinely ordained.

the seed of Abraham, Isaac, and Jacob, for I will restore their fortunes and show them mercy."

CHAPTER 34   The word that came to Jeremiah from the 1 LORD when Nebuchadrezzar king of Babylonia and all his force and all the kingdoms of the land of his dominion and all the peoples were doing battle against Jerusalem and against all its towns, saying, "Thus said the 2 LORD God of Israel: Go and say to Zedekiah king of Judah and say to him, Thus said the LORD: I am about to give this city into the hand of the king of Babylonia, and he shall burn it in fire. And you, you shall not escape from 3 his hand, for you shall surely be caught and be given into his hand, and your eyes shall see the eyes of the king of Babylonia, and his mouth shall speak to your mouth, and you shall come to Babylonia. But listen to the 4 word of the LORD, Zedekiah king of Judah. Thus said the LORD: You shall not die by the sword. In peace you shall die, and like the incense burnings 5 of your fathers the former kings who were before you, so shall they burn incense for you. And 'Woe, master' shall they lament for you, for it is the word I have spoken, said the LORD." And Jeremiah the prophet spoke to 6 Zedekiah king of Judah all these words in Jerusalem. And the force of the 7 king of Babylonia was doing battle against Jerusalem and against all the remaining towns of Judah, against Lachish and against Azekah, for these were left of the towns of Judah, fortress towns.

The word that came to Jeremiah from the LORD after King Zedekiah sealed 8 a covenant with the people who were in Jerusalem, to proclaim a release for

---

CHAPTER 34   1. *all the kingdoms . . . of his dominion and all the peoples.* This is a realistic notation: vassal kings and vassal populations were obliged to join the imperial forces in the military campaign.

5. *In peace you shall die.* In the event, this was a highly qualified peace. The captive Zedekiah was forced to watch the murder of his sons, and then the Babylonians blinded him.

    the incense burnings. The Hebrew says only "burnings," but cremation was not an option in ancient Israel, and there is evidence that burning incense was sometimes part of funeral rites.

7. *Lachish.* Lachish was the principal fortified city of Judah after Jerusalem, and a quantity of written and archaeological evidence has survived bearing on its siege and capture.

8. *to proclaim a release.* This is the idiom used for the release of slaves in the jubilee year. Setting free slaves in a time of siege had a certain practical logic: the slaves could no longer work in the fields; their owners could be relieved of the responsibility of feeding them when food was scarce during the siege; and perhaps the freed slaves could have been conscripted to fight.

9 them, for every man to set free his male Hebrew slave and every man his
10 Hebrew slavegirl, that no man should enslave a Judahite, his brother. And
all the nobles and all the people who had entered the covenant listened to
set free every man his male slave and every man his slavegirl so as not to
11 enslave them anymore, and they listened and set them free. But they went
back afterward and brought back the male slaves and the slavegirls whom
they had set free, and they forced them to be male slaves and slavegirls.
13 And the word of the LORD came to Jeremiah from the LORD saying, "Thus
said the LORD God of Israel: I Myself sealed a covenant with your fathers
on the day I brought you out from the land of Egypt from the house of
14 slaves, saying, At the end of seven years you shall send away each man his
Hebrew brother who was sold to you and served you six years, and you
shall set him free from you. But your fathers did not listen to Me and did
15 not bend their ear. And you should turn back today and do what is right in
My eyes to proclaim a release, each man to his fellow, and you should seal
16 a covenant before Me in the house upon which My name is called. But you
turned back and profaned My name, and you brought back each man his
male slave and each man his slavegirl whom you had set wholly free, and
17 you forced them to be male slaves and slavegirls for you. Therefore, thus
said the LORD: You, you did not listen to Me to proclaim a release, each man
to his brother and each man to his fellow. I am about to proclaim a release
for you, said the LORD, to the sword and to pestilence and to famine, and I
18 will make you a horror to all the kingdoms of the earth. And I will make the
men trespassing My covenant, who did not fulfill the words of the covenant
that they sealed before Me like the calf that they cut in two and passed
19 between its parts, the nobles of Judah and the nobles of Jerusalem, the

9. *his brother.* Although the term is obviously used in an extended sense to indicate belonging to the same ethnic group, its implication of close kinship is used pointedly.

11. *But they went back afterward.* This may have been during the early months of 587 B.C.E., when the Babylonians temporarily lifted the siege, an event alluded to in verse 21. This act of reclaiming the slaves reflects not only the bad faith of the Judahites but also their previous inclination to ignore the injunction (Exodus 21:2, Deuteronomy 15:1–2) that a Hebrew slave had to be set free at the end of seven years. He was thus less a slave than an indentured servant. God invokes the violation of this law in verse 14.

16. *set wholly free.* This translation understands the added Hebrew term *lenafsho* as an intensifier of the condition of freedom. Others think it means "according to his desire."

18. *like the calf that they cut in two and passed between its parts.* This is a covenant-making ritual well attested in the ancient Near East and reflected in Abraham's covenant with God

eunuchs and the priests and all the people of the land who passed between
the parts of the calf. And I will give them into the hand of their enemies   20
and into the hand of those who seek their life, and their carcasses shall be
food for the fowl of the heavens and the beasts of the earth. And Zedekiah   21
king of Judah and his nobles I will give into the hand of their enemies and
into the hand of those who seek their life and into the hand of the force of
the king of Babylonia that is withdrawing from you. Look, I am about to   22
give the command, said the Lord, and I will bring them back to this city
and they shall do battle against it and capture it and burn it in fire, and
the towns of Judah I will turn into a desolation, with none dwelling there."

CHAPTER 35   The word that came to Jeremiah from the   1
Lord in the days of Jehoiakim son of Josiah king of Judah saying, "Go to   2
the house of the Rechabites and speak to them and bring them to the house
of the Lord to one of the chambers and give them wine to drink." And I   3
took Jaazaniah son of Jeremiah son of Habazziniah and his brothers and
all his sons and all the house of the Rechabites. And I brought them to the   4
house of the Lord to the chamber of the sons of Hanan son of Igdaliah man

---

in Genesis 15. The evident idea was that if a party to the pact violated it, his fate should
be like that of the cloven animal. The verb "cut" picks up the Hebrew idiom for sealing a
covenant, which is literally "to cut a covenant." The verse incorporates another pun because
"pass between" and "trespass" are the same Hebrew verb.

21. *that is withdrawing from you.* See the comment on verse 11. Zedekiah is not to imagine
that the lifting of the siege means he and his kingdom will escape from the onslaught of
the Babylonians.

22. *Look, I am about to give the command . . . and I will bring them back to this city.* God
now makes it perfectly explicit that the Babylonian withdrawal is temporary and that He
will soon call back the invading army to complete its work of destruction. Since we can
assume that this prophecy was pronounced by Jeremiah early in 587 B.C.E., he either would
have surmised from the strategic situation that this must be a temporary measure or would
have been led to that conclusion by his deep conviction that the destruction of the city had
been divinely decreed and was inevitable.

CHAPTER 35   2. *the Rechabites.* This clan, which has the look of a sect and (perhaps,
as some scholars conclude) of a distinct ethnic group, first appears in 2 Kings 10, when its
"father" or founder, Jonadab (there spelled Jehonadab), joins forces with Jehu in his ruthless extirpation of Baal worshippers. They are extreme pietists, taking on themselves the
abstention from drinking wine, like the nazirites, and also a nomadic way of life. When
Jeremiah is enjoined to give them wine to drink, this is obviously devised as a test to see if
they still are faithful to the vows imposed by their first father, Jonadab.

of God, which is by the chamber of the nobles which is above the chamber
5 of Maaseiah, guardian of the threshold. And I set before the sons of the
house of the Rechabites pitchers filled with wine, and cups, and I said to
6 them: "Drink the wine." And they said, "We will not drink wine, for Jonadab son of Rechab our father charged us saying, you shall not drink wine,
7 you and your sons, for all time. And no house shall you build nor seed shall
you sow nor vineyard shall you plant, and you shall not have them, but in
tents shall you dwell all your days, so that you may live many days on the
8 face of the land where you sojourn. And we heeded the voice of Jonadab
son of Rechab our father in all that he charged us, not to drink wine all our
9 days, we, our wives, our sons, and our daughters. And not to build houses
10 for our dwelling, nor to have vineyard and field and seed. And we have
dwelled in tents and heeded and done as all that Jonadab our father charged
11 us. And it happened when Nebuchadrezzar king of Babylonia came up to
the land that we said, Come, and let us come to Jerusalem from before
the Chaldean force and from before the force of Aram and let us dwell in
12,13 Jerusalem." And the word of the LORD came to Jeremiah, saying, "Thus
said the LORD of Armies, God of Israel: Go and say to the men of Judah
and to the dwellers of Jerusalem, Will you not accept correction to heed
14 My words, said the LORD? The words of Jonadab son of Rechab have been
fulfilled, who charged his sons not to drink wine, and they have not drunk
till this very day, for they heeded the command of their father. Yet I Myself
15 have spoken to you continually, and you have not heeded Me. And I sent to
you all My servants the prophets, continually sent them, saying: Turn back,
pray, each from his evil way and make your acts good and do not go after
other gods to serve them, and dwell on the land that I gave to you and to
16 your fathers. But you did not bend your ear and you did not heed Me. For

---

11. *when Nebuchadrezzar king of Babylonia came up to the land.* Although the Rechabites dwell in tents as nomads, the Babylonian invasion forces them to take refuge in Jerusalem. This sets the stage for Jeremiah's invitation to them to come to the Temple, where he puts wine before them.

14. *The words of Jonadab son of Rechab have been fulfilled.* The point of the test by wine of the Rechabites is now revealed: their unswerving commitment to the restrictions imposed by their ancestor provides a stark contrast to the general behavior of the Judahites, who, though bound by a much less demanding code of laws coming directly from God, flagrantly violated it.

15. *And I sent to you all My servants the prophets.* This is a recurrent theme in Jeremiah: it is not as though the people were ignorant of what God required of them, for He repeatedly sent prophets to remind them, but they ignored the prophets. Jeremiah, of course, sees himself as the most recent, and perhaps the most painfully resisted, of God's emissaries.

the sons of Jonadab have fulfilled their father's command that he charged
them, but this people has not heeded Me. Therefore, thus said the LORD 17
God of Armies, God of Israel, I am about to bring upon Judah and upon
all the dwellers of Jerusalem all the evil of which I spoke concerning them
inasmuch as I spoke to them and they did not heed, and I called them and
they did not answer. And concerning the house of Rechabites, Thus said the 18
LORD of Armies, God of Israel: Inasmuch as you have heeded the command
of Jonadab your father and kept all his commands and have done as all that
he charged you, therefore, thus said the LORD of Armies, God of Israel, no 19
man of Jonadab son of Rechab shall be cut off from serving Me for all time."

CHAPTER 36   And it happened in the fourth year of Jehoia- 1
kim son of Josiah that this word came to Jeremiah from the LORD, saying,
"Take for yourself a book-scroll and write on it all the words that I have 2
spoken to you concerning Israel and concerning Judah and concerning all
the nations from the day that I spoke to you, from the days of Josiah, to
this day. Perhaps the house of Judah will listen to all the evil that I plan to 3
do to them so that they may turn back each from his evil way, and I shall
forgive their crime and their offense." And Jeremiah called to Baruch son 4
of Neriah, and Baruch wrote from the mouth of Jeremiah all the words

---

17. *I am about to bring upon Judah and upon all the dwellers of Jerusalem all the evil of which
I spoke.* As elsewhere in his prose prophecies, Jeremiah relies heavily on repeated formulas.

CHAPTER 36   1. *In the fourth year of Jehoiakim.* This is 605 B.C.E., when Nebuchadrezzar defeated the Egyptians at Carchemish and consequently threatened the lands
to the west.

2. *Take for yourself a book-scroll.* The Hebrew construct form is *megilat-sefer. Megilah* is
a scroll; *sefer* is any written document, and in some contexts it can also mean scroll. Here
it is actually a book because it contains some two decades of Jeremiah's prophecies, and
perhaps that is why the double form is used. The physical existence, moreover, of the book
as a scroll will be highlighted as the story unfolds.

4. *Baruch wrote from the mouth of Jeremiah.* "From the mouth" obviously means "from the
dictation," but this translation preserves the physical concreteness of the Hebrew idiom.
The present chapter offers a rare perspective on the mechanics of transmission of biblical prophecy. Baruch, elsewhere given the epithet of "scribe," was probably a professional
scribe, but he also served as Jeremiah's personal amanuensis, in all likelihood not for pay
but out of devotion to the prophet. Jeremiah may well have had some form of abbreviated
written notations of his earlier prophecies, though we should not exclude the possibility
that he knew them all by heart. (One recalls the instance of the great Russian poet Osip
Mandelstam, who for years did not dare to commit his poems to writing during Stalin's
reign of terror but memorized them all, as did his wife.)

5 of the Lᴏʀᴅ that he had spoken to him on a book-scroll. And Jeremiah charged Baruch, saying: "I am confined. I cannot come to the house of the
6 Lᴏʀᴅ. And you instead shall come and read out from the scroll that you have written from my mouth all the words of the Lᴏʀᴅ in the hearing of the people in the house of the Lᴏʀᴅ on the fast-day, and you shall also read
7 it out in the hearing of all Judah who come from their towns. Perhaps their supplication will fall before the Lᴏʀᴅ and they will turn back each from his evil way, for great are the anger and the wrath that the Lᴏʀᴅ has spoken
8 concerning this people." And Baruch did as all that Jeremiah had charged him to read out from the book the words of the Lᴏʀᴅ in the house of the
9 Lᴏʀᴅ. And it happened in the fifth year of Jehoiakim son of Josiah king of Judah, in the ninth month, all the people in Jerusalem and all the people
10 coming from the towns of Judah proclaimed a fast before the Lᴏʀᴅ. And Baruch read out from the book the words of the Lᴏʀᴅ in the house of the Lᴏʀᴅ in the chamber of Gemariah son of Shaphan the scribe in the upper court at the entrance to the gate of the house of the Lᴏʀᴅ in the hearing
11 of all the people. And Micaiah son of Gemariah son of Shaphan heard all
12 the words of the Lᴏʀᴅ from the book. And he went down to the house of the king to the chamber of the scribe, and, look, all the nobles were sitting there, Elishama the scribe and Delaiah son of Shemaiah and Elnathan son of Achbor and Gemariah son of Shaphan and Zedekiah son of Hananiah
13 and all the nobles. And Micaiah told them all the words that he had heard when Baruch had read out from the book in the hearing of the people.
14 And all the nobles sent to Baruch Jehudi son of Shelemiah son of Cushi, saying, "The scroll from which you read in the hearing of the people, take it in your hand and go." And Baruch son of Neriah took the scroll in his
15 hand and came to them. And they said to him, "Sit down, pray, and read it
16 in our hearing." And Baruch read it out in their hearing. And it happened when they heard all the words, that they turned in fear to each other, and

---

5. *I am confined.* As before, this indicates some sort of confinement on the palace grounds in which he has a certain amount of freedom of movement and visitors had access to him.

6. *the fast-day.* Given the Babylonian military threat, it is likely that a general fast had been proclaimed in order to implore God for help.

9. *in the ninth month.* This would be Kislev, corresponding to December—hence the winter chambers and the burning brazier in what follows.

13. *And Micaiah told them all the words.* Despite the phrase "all the words," this has to mean that he told them the general sense of Jeremiah's prophecies because he scarcely would have been expected to have memorized the entire book as he listened.

they said to Baruch, "We will surely tell all these words to the king." And 17
Baruch they asked, saying, "Tell us, pray, how did you write all these words
from his mouth?" And Baruch said to them, "With his mouth he read out 18
to me all these words, and I wrote it in the book with ink." And the nobles 19
said to Baruch, "Go, hide, you and Jeremiah, that no man know where you
are." And they came to the king in the court, and the scroll they laid aside 20
in the chamber of Elishama the scribe, and they told all these words in the
hearing of the king. And the king sent Jehudi to take the scroll from the 21
chamber of Elishama the scribe, and Jehudi read it out in the hearing of
the king and in the hearing of all the nobles standing in attendance upon
the king. And the king was sitting in the winter house in the ninth month, 22
and fire in the brazier before him was burning. And it happened, as Jehudi 23
read three or four columns, he would cut them out with a scribe's knife
and fling them into the fire that was in the brazier until the entire scroll
was consumed in the fire that was in the brazier. And the king and all his 24
servants hearing all these words were not afraid and did not rend their

---

17. *how did you write all these words from his mouth?* The courtiers express amazement at
Baruch's ability to produce this long text. He responds (verse 18) by explaining that it was
a simple matter of dictation, the prophet reading or reciting out loud and the scribe tran-
scribing everything with pen and ink on the scroll. It is possible that Baruch possessed a
special skill of rapid writing. Elsewhere in the Bible, a "rapid scribe's pen" is an idiom for
the work of a skilled scribe.

19. *Go, hide.* They immediately understand that these prophecies predicting the imminent
destruction of the kingdom will be regarded as seditious by the king and could endanger
the lives of both the prophet and the scribe.

22. *the winter house.* This is probably palace chambers exposed to the sun and hence better
suited for residence in the cold months.
    the brazier. The Hebrew *'aḥ* is an Egyptian loanword. Although in later Hebrew it came
to mean "hearth" or "fireplace," ancient palaces had neither hearths nor chimneys, so this
would have to be a freestanding brazier.

23. *he would cut them out with a scribe's knife and fling them into the fire.* It is not entirely
clear whether the scroll was papyrus or parchment. Many scholars favor papyrus because it
would have burned more readily. In that case, the "scribe's knife" would be the instrument
used for cutting out sheets of papyrus. But *ta'ar,* the word used here for "knife," elsewhere
means "razor," and it derives from a verbal stem that means "to raze" or "remove to the
roots." Such an instrument could be used to scrape away words or letters on parchment as
a kind of eraser.

24. *were not afraid.* They did not take the dire warnings of the prophecies to heart but
instead dismissed them, demonstrating their view of the nullity of the prophet's words by
burning them.

25 garments. And though Elnathan and Delaiah and Gemariah implored the
26 king not to burn the scroll, he did not listen to them. And the king charged
    Jerahmeel the king's son and Seraiah son of Azriel and Shelemiah son of
    Abdel to take Baruch the scribe and Jeremiah the prophet, but the LORD
27 had hidden them. And the word of the LORD came to Jeremiah after the
    king had burned the scroll and the words that Baruch had written from
    the mouth of Jeremiah, saying, "Again, take for yourself another scroll and
    write on it all the former words that were in the first scroll that Jehoiakim
28 king of Judah burned. And concerning Jehoiakim king of Judah, you shall
    say: Thus said the LORD, You burned this scroll, saying, 'Why did you write
    in it, saying, the king of Babylonia shall surely come and lay waste to this
29 land and make man and beast cease from it?' Therefore, thus said the LORD
    concerning Jehoiakim king of Judah: No one of his shall sit on the throne of
    David, and his carcass shall be flung to the parching heat by day and to the
30 frost by night. And I will reckon his crime against him and against his seed
    and against his servants and bring down on them and on all the dwellers
    of Jerusalem and on the men of Judah all the evil that I spoke concerning
31 them, yet they do not heed. And Jeremiah had taken another scroll and had
    given it to Baruch son Neriah the scribe, and he wrote on it all the words
    of the book that Jehoiakim had burned in the fire, and many words of the
    sort were added.

---

26. *but the* LORD *had hidden them.* Obviously, it was Jeremiah and Baruch who hid themselves, but the narrative report seeks to attribute the agency to God, as though there were
divine intervention on behalf of the two men.

27. *take for yourself another scroll and write on it all the former words.* The story vividly illustrates the futility of censorship. The scroll has been consumed in fire, column by column.
Yet the words of the scroll persist in the mind of the prophet, and he is again enjoined to
dictate them to his able scribe. Neither Jeremiah nor Baruch is intimidated by the threat
of royal action against them.

29. *his carcass shall be flung.* Pointedly, the same verb, "flung," that was used for tossing the
pieces of the scroll into the fire is now part of a grim prophecy of the king's fate.

30. *his servants.* As is almost invariably the case in royal contexts, this general term here
indicates "courtiers."

31. *and many words of the sort were added.* In a gesture of defiance of the king's attempt
to eradicate these prophecies, not only are they again written down verbatim, but in this
second scroll, additional prophecies with the same message of destruction are included.

CHAPTER 37   And King Zedekiah son of Josiah became 1 king instead of Coniah son of Jehoiakim, as Nebuchadrezzar king of Babylonia had made him king in the land of Judah. And he and his servants 2 and the people of the land had not heeded the words of the LORD that he spoke through Jeremiah the prophet. And King Zedekiah sent Jehucal 3 son of Shelemiah and Zephaniah son of Maaseiah the priest to Jeremiah the prophet, saying, "Pray for us to the LORD our God." And Jeremiah 4 was coming and going in the midst of the people, and they had not put him in prison. And Pharaoh's force had gone out from Egypt, and the 5 Chaldeans besieging Jerusalem heard of them and withdrew from Jerusalem. And the word of the LORD came to Jeremiah the prophet, saying, 6 "Thus said the LORD God of Israel, thus shall you say to the king of Judah 7 who is sending you to Me to seek Me: Look, Pharaoh's force coming out to you to help is turning back to its land, Egypt. And the Chaldeans shall 8 turn back and battle against this city and capture it and burn it in fire. Thus said the LORD: Do not deceive yourselves, saying, 'The Chaldeans 9 will surely go away from us,' for they shall not go away. Though you strike 10 down the whole Chaldean force battling against you and there remain men run through, each in his tent, they shall rise up and burn this city in fire." And it happened when the Chaldean force withdrew from Jeru- 11 salem before Pharaoh's force, that Jeremiah went out from Jerusalem to 12 go to the region of Benjamin to hide there in the midst of the people.

CHAPTER 37   1. *Coniah.* This is a shortened form of Jeconiah.

as Nebuchadrezzar king of Babylonia had made him king. Nebuchadrezzar had removed Jeconiah from the throne and put Zedekiah in his place, assuming he would serve submissively as a vassal king, which did not prove to be the case.

3. *Pray for us to the LORD our God.* The usual linguistic protocol is to say "the LORD your God" when addressing a prophet. The king evidently wants to emphasize his solidarity with Jeremiah—they share the same God. His attitude toward the prophet is ambivalent: he regards him as someone who has direct access to God but dismisses his prophecies of doom, even judging them to be seditious.

4. *and they had not put him in prison.* Not yet, but this would very soon happen.

10. *and there remain men run through.* This is a hyperbole used for dramatic effect: even should you slaughter the Chaldeans, the very men you have stabbed with your swords will rise up from their tents and complete the assault against your city.

12. *to hide there.* The verb *ḥalaq* usually means "to share," and so many interpreters understand this to say that Jeremiah was going on personal business, to realize a share in an inheritance coming to him. The conduct of such business in a time of siege is unlikely. Hoffman cites an Akkadian cognate that means "to hide" or "to flee," and that sounds plausible here: Jeremiah may be fleeing from a fate of death when the city falls to the Babylonians.

13 And as he came to the gate of Benjamin, there was a prison warden there
    named Irijah son of Shelemiah son of Hananiah, and he caught Jeremiah
14 the prophet, saying, "You are going over to the Chaldeans." And Jeremiah
    said, "That is a lie! I am not going over to the Chaldeans." But he did not
    listen to him, and Irijah caught Jeremiah and brought him to the nobles.
15 And the nobles were furious with Jeremiah and struck him and put him
    into the place of confinement, the house of Jonathan the scribe, for they had
16 turned it into a prison. So did Jeremiah come to the house of the pit and to
17 the cells, and Jeremiah stayed there many days. And King Zedekiah sent
    and took him, and the king questioned him secretly in his house and said,
    "Is there any word from the LORD?" And Jeremiah said, "There is—into
18 the hand of the king of Babylonia you shall be given." And Jeremiah said
    to King Zedekiah, "How have I offended you and your servants and this
19 people that you should have put me in prison? And where are your prophets
    who prophesied to you, saying, the king of Babylonia shall not come against
20 you and against this land? And now, listen, pray, my lord the king, let my
    supplication fall before you and do not turn me back to the house of Jona-
21 than the scribe and let me not die there." And Zedekiah gave the command,

---

13. *And as he came to the gate of Benjamin.* This would be the gate in the wall of Jerusalem
leading to the territory of Benjamin. All this takes place during the brief period when the
Babylonians lifted the siege.

  a prison warden. The Hebrew *ba'al pequdot* is linked with *beyt hapequdot,* one of several
terms for "prison."

  You are going over to the Chaldeans. Given Jeremiah's history of grimly predicting a
Babylonian victory, he would readily be suspected of desertion to the enemy.

14. *brought him to the nobles.* The nobles (*sarim*) are royal officers, evidently superior to
the prison warden.

16. *So did Jeremiah come to the house of the pit and to the cells.* The use of "house of the pit"
for "prison"—"pit" for prison also occurs in the Joseph story—suggests that it was a harsh
place of confinement. Ḥanuyot, "cells," appears only here. In postbiblical Hebrew, it came
to mean "shops," but at least one Semitic cognate indicates that it had the ancient meaning
of "cell" or "dungeon."

17. *Is there any word from the LORD?* Zedekiah still clings to Jeremiah as a privileged source
of knowledge of God's intentions, but the answer to his question is a repetition of the
prophecy of destruction.

20. *let me not die there.* Either he fears that he could not long survive in the harsh conditions of the prison pit at the house of Jonathan the scribe, or he is afraid that the nobles
overseeing that place are so furious with him that they will end up killing him if he stays
there in their charge.

and they placed Jeremiah in the court of the guard and gave him a loaf of bread each day from the Baker's Street, till there was no longer any bread in the city. And Jeremiah stayed in the court of the guard.

CHAPTER 38   And Shephatiah son of Mattan and Gedaliah 1 son of Pashshur and Jucal son of Shelemiah and Pashhur son of Malkiah heard the words that Jeremiah was speaking to the people, saying, "Thus said 2 the LORD: He who dwells in this city shall die by the sword and by famine and by pestilence, and he who goes out to the Chaldeans shall live, and his life shall be booty but he shall live. Thus said the LORD: This city shall surely 3 be given into the hand of the king of Babylonia's force and he shall capture it." And the nobles said to the king: "Let this man be put to death, for he is 4 surely weakening the hands of the men of war remaining in this city and the hands of the people to speak to them words of this sort, for this man does not seek the welfare of this people but rather harm." And King Zedekiah said, 5 "Here he is in your hand, for the king can do nothing with you." And they 6 took Jeremiah and flung him into the pit of Malchiah the king's son, which is in the court of the guard, and they lowered Jeremiah with ropes. And in the

---

21. *they placed Jeremiah in the court of the guard and gave him a loaf of bread each day.* As we have seen before, this amounts to a kind of house arrest on the palace grounds in which Jeremiah is given some freedom of movement and access to visitors. The provision of a daily loaf reflects the king's concern for Jeremiah, especially because food supplies would have been very scarce during the siege, as the next clause, "till there was no longer any bread in the city," clearly indicates.

CHAPTER 38   4. *Let this man be put to death, for he is surely weakening the hands of the men of war.* This response of the nobles—who are probably high royal officials—is hardly surprising. Jerusalem is engaged in a bitter fight for its survival, and this prophet repeatedly and vehemently announces that all is lost, a kind of speech that could easily be regarded as treasonous.

   the men of war remaining in this city. The phrasing may suggest that a substantial number of the warriors have deserted to the enemy, which is basically what Jeremiah has been urging. Compare verse 19.

5. *for the king can do nothing with you.* These words reflect a real power struggle in the court during the siege. The king is disinclined to harm Jeremiah because he regards him as an authentic prophet, but he feels that he is unable to resist the angry resolution of his nobles, who, after all, see dangerous sedition in Jeremiah's prophecies.

6. *they lowered Jeremiah with ropes.* This report qualifies "flung" in the previous clause. The pit must have been quite deep—perhaps twenty feet or more—to necessitate the lower-

7 pit there was no water, only muck, and Jeremiah sank into the muck. And
   Ebed-Melech the Cushite, a eunuch, heard, and he was in the king's house,
   that they had put Jeremiah in the pit, and the king was sitting in the Ben-
8 jamin Gate. And Ebed-Melech came out from the king's house and spoke
9 to the king, saying, "My lord the king, these men have done evil in all that
   they have done to Jeremiah the prophet, in that they have flung him into
   the pit, and he could die on the spot of hunger, for there is no more bread in
10 the city." And the king charged Ebed-Melech the Cushite, saying, "Take in
   your charge from here thirty men and raise up Jeremiah the prophet from
11 the pit before he dies." And Ebed-Melech took the men in his charge and
   came into the king's house beneath the treasury, and he took from there
   worn rags and worn clothes and sent them to Jeremiah in the pit with ropes.
12 And Ebed-Melech the Cushite said to Jeremiah, "Pray, put the worn rags
   and clothes under your armpits beneath the ropes," and so did Jeremiah
13 do. And they pulled Jeremiah up with the ropes and brought him up out of
14 the pit, and Jeremiah stayed in the court of the guard. And King Zedekiah
   sent and took Jeremiah the prophet to him by the third entrance which

---

ing with ropes. The nobles do not want to kill Jeremiah outright, but rather to leave him to
perish at the bottom of the dank pit.

   there was no water, only muck. During the winter months, such a pit would serve as a
reservoir for rainwater, but it is now midsummer, so only a residue of muck at the bottom
remains.

7. *Ebed-Melech the Cushite.* A Cushite is a Nubian. One assumes that this is an accurate
historical identification, but it is ironic that a foreigner should take the initiative to save
the prophet.

9. *he could die on the spot of hunger.* This is new information: the nobles intended to let
Jeremiah die by not providing him any food from the scarce resources.

10. *thirty men.* Obviously, just two or three would have sufficed to haul Jeremiah up out of
the pit. In all likelihood, this reflects a countermove by the king to the nobles' assertion of
power. Thirty men would ensure that no one could easily interfere with the rescue, and it
is even possible that these men are armed.

11. *the treasury.* This may be a storeroom because it contains rags.

12. *put the worn rags and clothes under your armpits beneath the ropes.* The rags are to serve
as padding so that Jeremiah will not be cut or abraded by the ropes under his arms as he
is pulled up.

13. *Jeremiah stayed in the court of the guard.* This is his previous place of confinement, where
he enjoyed relative freedom of movement.

14. *And King Zedekiah sent and took Jeremiah the prophet to him.* The king's motive in
accepting Ebed-Melech's advice and defying the nobles to save Jeremiah becomes clear:

is in the house of the LORD, and the king said to Jeremiah, "I am asking
something of you. Do not hide the thing from me." And Jeremiah said to 15
Zedekiah, "Should I tell you, would you not surely put me to death? And
should I counsel you, you would not heed me." And King Zedekiah secretly 16
swore to Jeremiah, "As the LORD lives, Who made this life of ours, I will
not put you to death and I will not give you into the hand of the men who
seek your life." And Jeremiah said to Zedekiah, "Thus said the LORD God 17
of Armies, God of Israel: If you indeed go out to the commanders of the
king of Babylonia, you shall live and this city shall not be burned, and you
and your household shall live. And if you do not go out to the commanders 18
of the king of Babylonia, the city shall be given into the hand of the Chaldeans, and they shall burn it in fire, and you yourself shall not escape from
their hand." And King Zedekiah said to Jeremiah, "I am worried about the 19
Judahites who have gone over to the Chaldeans, lest they give me into their
hands and they abuse me." And Jeremiah said, "They will not give you over. 20
Heed, pray, the voice of the LORD that I speak to you, that it be well with
you, and you live. But should you refuse to go out, this is the word that the 21
LORD has shown me. Look, all the women who have remained in the house 22
of the king of Judah are to be brought out to the commanders of the king
of Babylonia, and, look, they say:

> 'They deceived you and prevailed over you,
>   the men who were your intimates.
> Your feet have sunk in mud,
>   They have fallen back.'

---

he continues to regard the prophet as a crucial channel of God's intentions, and in this
moment of national crisis, he wants to know what those may be.

17. *If you indeed go out to the commanders of the king of Babylonia.* Jeremiah counsels surrender, a piece of advice that may well have followed from his unblinking assessment of the
military situation rather than from a directive by God.

19. *the Judahites who have gone over to the Chaldeans.* These deserters, opposed to Zedekiah's policy of armed resistance to the Babylonians, would have seen him as their enemy.

22. *They deceived you and prevailed over you.* To drive home his point, Jeremiah attributes
two lines of poetry to the women of the royal house being led out to the Babylonians, presumably to become their sex slaves.
     Your feet have sunk in mud. Although this clause approximates the metaphorical rep-
resentation of dire distress in Psalms, it also obviously resonates with Jeremiah's plight in
the muck at the bottom of the pit.

23 And all your wives and your children are to be brought out to the Chaldeans, and you yourself shall not escape from their hand, for in the hand of the king of Babylonia you shall be caught, and this city shall be burned in
24 fire." And Zedekiah said to Jeremiah "Let no man know these things, and
25 you shall not die. And should the nobles hear that I have spoken with you and come to you and say to you, 'Tell us, pray, what you spoke to the king. Do not conceal it from us, and we will not put you to death, what the king
26 spoke to you.' You shall say to them, 'I was laying my supplication before
27 the king not to send me back to the house of Jonathan to die there.'" And all the nobles came to Jeremiah and asked him, and he told them according to these words that the king had charged him, and they ceased speaking
28 with him, for the thing had not been heard. And Jeremiah stayed in the court of the guard till the day Jerusalem was captured. And it happened, when the city was captured. . . .

1 CHAPTER 39   In the ninth year of Zedekiah king of Judah in the tenth month Nebuchadrezzar king of Babylonia and all his force came
2 to Jerusalem and besieged it. In the eleventh year of Zedekiah in the fourth
3 month on the ninth of the month the city was breached. And all the com-

---

24. *Let no man know these things.* Zedekiah does not want to compound his own political difficulties vis-à-vis members of his court by having it known that, beyond the act of saving Jeremiah, he has been the willing audience to the prophet's grim pronouncements that the nobles would regard as seditious.

27. *and he told them according to these words that the king had charged him.* Here we have an instance of a prophet lying, though one must say that it is a lie intended to save the king from a gravely compromising predicament in this complicated play of political forces.

28. *And it happened, when the city was captured. . . .* The Hebrew cannot mean "And he was there when the city was captured," as some have claimed. Rather, this is a clause that breaks off. S. D. Luzzatto, the eighteenth-century Italian Hebrew exegete, proposes that the actual place of this clause is at the beginning of 39:11. This does make syntactic and semantic sense as follows: "And it happened, when the city was captured, that Nebuchadrezzar king of Babylonia charged concerning Jeremiah through Nebuzaradan the high chamberlain, saying."

CHAPTER 39   1. *In the ninth year of Zedekiah.* According to the notation here and in the next verse, the siege lasted about a year and a half, from the winter of 587 B.C.E. to midsummer 586.

2. *in the fourth month on the ninth of the month.* This is the ninth of Av, traditionally marked by Jews as a fast-day to commemorate the destruction of Jerusalem and the Temple.

manders of the king of Babylonia came and sat in the central gate—Nergal-Sarezer, Samgar-Nebo, Sarsechim the chief eunuch, Nergal-Sarezer high magus, and all the rest of the commanders of the king of Babylonia. And it happened when Zedekiah king of Judah and all the men of war saw them, they fled and went out by night from the city through the king's garden, through the gate of the double walls, and he went out toward the Arabah. And the Chaldean force pursued them and overtook Zedekiah in the desert country of Jericho and took him and brought him up to Nebuchadrezzar king of Babylonia at Riblah in the region of Hamath, and he spoke harshly with him. And the king of Babylonia slaughtered Zedekiah's sons before his eyes in Riblah, and all the aristocrats of Judah the king of Babylonia slaughtered. And the eyes of Zedekiah he blinded, and he bound him in bronze fetters to bring him to Babylonia. And the king's house and the people's houses the Chaldeans burned in fire, and the walls of Jerusalem they shattered. And the rest of the people who remained in the city and those who had gone over to him and the rest of the people remaining Nebuzaradan the

---

3. *Nergal-Sarezer.* This name occurs twice in this verse, which must be a scribal duplication. Note as well that, understandably, all the Akkadian names in this list are somewhat distorted by the Hebrew transliteration.

high magus. The Hebrew is *rav-mag,* and as with other titles of the officials here, the precise function is uncertain.

4. *they fled and went out by night from the city through the king's garden.* The spatial indication in this clause suggests that they used some sort of secret exit, as many commentators have proposed.

the Arabah. This is the north-south rift through which the Jordan runs. They are fleeing to the south, perhaps trying to reach Egypt.

5. *the desert country of Jericho.* The Hebrew uses a plural of Arabah, which could refer either to the north-south rift or, as here, to a kind of terrain.

Riblah. This is far to the north, in Syria, where the Babylonian emperor was contending with other enemies.

he spoke harshly with him. Literally, "he spoke judgments with him." This translation understands the plural noun *mishpatim* to have an adverbial sense.

7. *And the eyes of Zedekiah he blinded.* This was, sad to say, a common treatment of prisoners of war in the ancient Near East. But Nebuchadrezzar has added to it a sadistic gesture: first he slaughters Zedekiah's sons "before his eyes," and with this last horrific sight lingering in the mind of the Judahite king, he has him blinded. Nebuchadrezzar wants to make clear to all that he does not tolerate the rebellion of vassal kings.

8. *the people's houses.* The Hebrew reads "the people's house," which sounds like a public institution, one that actually did not exist in ancient Israel. This translation adopts David Kimchi's plausible proposal that the noun is collective.

10 high chamberlain exiled to Babylonia. And from the poor people who had
nothing Nebuzaradan the high chamberlain left in the land of Judah and
11 gave them vineyards and plots of land on that day. And Nebuchadrezzar
king of Babylonia charged concerning Jeremiah through Nebuzaradan
12 the high chamberlain, saying, "Take him, and keep your eye on him, and
13 do him no harm, but as he speaks to you, do for him." And Nebuzaradan
the high chamberlain and Nebushazbaz the chief eunuch and Nergal-
sarezer the high magus and all the officers of the king of Babylonia sent,
14 they sent and took Jeremiah from the court of the guard, and they gave
him over to Gedaliah son of Ahikam son of Shaphan to bring him out to
the house, and he dwelled in the midst of the people.

15 And to Jeremiah the word of the Lord had come when he was detained in
16 the court of the guard, saying, "Go and say to Ebed-Melech the Cushite,
saying: Thus said the Lord of Armies, God of Israel, I am about to bring
My words to this city for evil and not for good, and they shall happen before
17 you on that day. And I will save you on that day, said the Lord, and you
18 shall not be given into the hand of the men by whom you are terrified. But
I will surely let you escape, and you shall not die by the sword and your life
shall be your booty, for you trusted in Me, said the Lord."

---

9. *the high chamberlain.* The literal sense of the Hebrew title is "chief butcher," though it is
obvious that the term was extended far beyond its origins to indicate some sort of important political or military function. Potiphar in Genesis 39 bears the same title.

10. *gave them vineyards and plots of land.* This redistribution of property to the destitute
was calculated to enlist their loyalty to the conquerors.

12. *do him no harm.* Nebuchadrezzar accords Jeremiah special treatment because he has
heard—probably from the Judahite deserters—that the prophet had been preaching capitu-
lation to the Babylonians.

14. *Gedaliah.* He would then be appointed by Nebuchadrezzar to serve as governor of the
conquered province.
    the house. Many commentators, medieval and modern, conclude that this is Gedaliah's
house.

17. *the men by whom you are terrified.* These would be the men who wanted to fight to the
bitter end and so sought to kill Jeremiah, whom Ebed-Melech saved, as a traitor.

18. *and your life shall be your booty.* It will not be the booty of others. This is a way of saying
that you will escape with your life.

CHAPTER 40   The word that came to Jeremiah from the ₁
LORD after Nebuzaradan the high chamberlain sent him off when he took
him—and he was bound in fetters—in the midst of all the exiles of Jerusalem and Judah who were exiled to Babylonia. And the high chamberlain ₂
took Jeremiah and said to him, "The LORD your God spoke of this evil
concerning this place. And the LORD brought to pass and did as He had ₃
spoken, for you offended against the LORD and did not heed His voice,
and this thing happened to you. And now, I release you today from the ₄
fetters that are on your hands, and if it be good in your eyes to come with
me to Babylonia, come, and I will keep my eye on you. And if it be not
right in your eyes to come with me to Babylonia, do not. See, all the land
is before you. To wherever is good and right in your eyes to go, there go."
And yet he did not turn back. "And turn back to Gedaliah son of Ahikam ₅
son of Shaphan, whom the king of Babylonia appointed over the towns of
Judah and stay with him in the midst of the people, or wherever is right in
your eyes to go, go." And the high chamberlain gave him a food allotment
and provisions and sent him off. And Jeremiah came to Gedaliah son of ₆
Ahikam at Mizpah, and he stayed with him in the midst of the people
remaining in the land.

CHAPTER 40   1. *The word that came to Jeremiah from the LORD.* This introductory phrase has puzzled interpreters because what follows is not a prophecy but a narrative
report. The least strained explanation is that of S. D. Luzatto: in 1:3, Jeremiah's prophecies
were said to continue "until the exile of Jerusalem"; the opening phrase here introduces his
acts and prophecies after the exile has begun.

he was bound in fetters. This is an outright contradiction of the report in the preceding
chapter that Nebuchadrezzar gave orders that Jeremiah be sent to stay with Gedaliah at
Mizpah, unhampered and unharmed. Various attempts at harmonization of the two stories
have been made, but it looks as though the text has combined two contradictory sources.
See the comment on verse 6.

2. *The LORD your God spoke of this evil.* The high chamberlain's speech must be a historical fiction because it is hard to imagine that a Babylonian official would invoke this pious
Yahwistic language.

5. *And yet he did not turn back.* This brief clause, which interrupts the speech of the Babylonian commander, looks grammatically suspect: *we'odenu l'o-yashuv* (the verb in the
imperfect should be *we'odenu l'o-shav*). The entire clause may be a clumsy gloss.

6. *And Jeremiah came to Gedaliah.* Only now is the contradiction of verse 1 with chapter
39 resolved.

7 And all the commanders of the troops who were in the field heard, both they and their men, that the king of Babylonia had appointed Gedaliah son of Ahikam over the land and that he had left with him men, women, and children, some of the poor of the land who had not been exiled to Babylo-
8 nia. And they came to Gedaliah at Mizpah, Ishmael son of Nethaniah and Johanan and Jonathan sons of Kareah, and Seraiah son of Tanhumeth, and the sons of Eiphai the Netophathite, and Jezaniah son of Maacathite, they
9 and their men. And Gedaliah son of Ahikam swore to them, saying, "Do not be afraid to serve the Chaldeans. Stay in the land and serve the king
10 of Babylonia, and it will go well with you. As for me, here I am staying in Mizpah to stand in attendance before the Chaldeans who come to us, and you, gather wine and summer fruit in your vessels, and dwell in your
11 towns of which you have taken hold." And also all the Judahites who were in Moab and in Ammon and in Edom and in all the lands had heard that the king of Babylonia had left a remnant for Judah and had appointed over
12 them Gedaliah son of Ahikam son of Shaphan. And the Judahites turned back from all the places where they were scattered and came to the land of Judah to Gedaliah at Mizpah, and they gathered wine and summer fruit in
13 great abundance. And Johanan son of Kareah and all the commanders of
14 the troops who were in the field had come to Gedaliah at Mizpah. And they said to him, "Do you actually know that Baalis king of the Ammonites has sent Ishmael son of Nethaniah to kill you?" But Gedaliah son of Ahikam

---

7. *all the commanders of the troops who were in the field.* The crucial phrase here is "in the field." The Judahite troops in Jerusalem would have been killed or captured when the city was breached, but there remained forces of resistance in open areas well beyond the city.

9. *Stay in the land and serve the king of Babylonia, and it will go well with you.* Gedaliah's counsel is entirely in keeping with Jeremiah's: resistance is futile and flight self-defeating; if the remaining Judahites cooperate with the Babylonian conquerors, they will be treated generously.

10. *gather wine and summer fruit.* Some commentators see a problem here because wine is not "gathered." The idiom is no more than an ellipsis: gather grapes, which will be turned into wine.
    your towns of which you have taken hold. The verb suggests seizing something not previously possessed. Many of the towns may have been emptied out as their population fled from the Babylonians, and those who remained, perhaps roaming over the countryside in bands, took over the towns.

14. *Baalis king of the Ammonites has sent Ishmael son of Nethaniah to kill you.* The Ammonites were one of the trans-Jordanian peoples that resisted the Babylonians. Their king would thus want to kill Gedaliah as a collaborator with the Babylonians. Some have proposed that he had an eye to taking over the kingdom of Judah.

did not believe them. And Johanan son of Kareah secretly said to Geda- 15
liah at Mizpah, saying, "Let me go, pray, and strike down Ishmael son of
Nethaniah, and no man will know. Why should he kill you, and all Judah
gathered round you will disperse, and the remnant of Judah will perish?"
And Gedaliah son of Ahikam said to Johanan son of Kareah, "Do not do 16
this thing, for you speak a lie about Ishmael."

CHAPTER 41   And it happened in the seventh month that 1
Ishmael son of Nethaniah son of Elishama of the royal seed and the king's
officers and the men with him came to Gedaliah son of Ahikam at Mizpah,
and they broke bread together there at Mizpah. And Ishmael the son of 2
Nethaniah rose up, together with the ten men who were with him, and
they struck down Gedaliah son of Ahikam son of Shaphan by the sword,
and they put him to death, whom the king of Babylonia had appointed
over the land. And all the Judahites who were with him, with Gedaliah at 3
Mizpah, and the Chaldeans who were found there, the men of war, Ishmael
struck down. And it happened on the second day after Gedaliah had been 4
put to death that no man knew. And men came from Shechem and from 5
Samaria, eighty men with beards shaved and rent garments and slashed

16. *Do not do this thing, for you speak a lie about Ishmael.* Gedaliah is no doubt recoil-
ing from the idea of authorizing an assassination, which could scarcely have remained a
secret, as Johanan claims. But he also appears to be by temperament an accommodationist,
unwilling to imagine either that the Babylonians will deal harshly with those who remain
in Judah or that a fellow Judahite might harbor murderous intentions toward him. He will
pay with his life for his naïveté.

CHAPTER 41   1. *of the royal seed.* This is a politically significant notation. Gedaliah
is the grandson of Shaphan, a court scribe, and not a member of the dynastic family. Ishmael
thus regards him as both usurper and a quisling, while his own biological connection to the
royal line may have encouraged him to make a move for the throne, once he has eliminated
Gedaliah and at such time as there might be a possibility to shake off the Babylonian yoke.
　　the king's officers. These words do not appear in the parallel passage in 2 Kings 25:25,
and they are probably an erroneous insertion here because Ishmael's contingent of ten men
is all that is mentioned in what follows.
　　they broke bread together. This act of fellowship indicates Ishmael's strategy of deception. Gedaliah would surely have had many more than ten men around him, even including Chaldean soldiers, but he and those with him are taken by surprise by Ishmael and
his ten killers.

5. *eighty men with beards shaved and rent garments and slashed bodies.* These are all signs
of mourning. Slashing the body is explicitly prohibited in the Torah, but popular practice
is quite another matter. The mourning, of course, is for the destruction of the Temple.

bodies, grain offerings and frankincense in their hand, to bring to the
6 house of the LORD. And Ishmael son of Nethaniah went out toward them
from Mizpah, walking along weeping, and it happened when he met them,
7 he said, "Come to Gedaliah son of Ahikam." And it happened when they
came into the town that Ishmael son of Nethaniah slaughtered them and
8 flung them into the cistern, him and the men who were with him. But ten
men were found among them who said to Ishmael, "Do not put us to death,
for we have hidden stores in the field, wheat and barley and oil and honey."
9 And he desisted and did not put them to death with their brothers. And
the cistern into which Ishmael had flung all the corpses of the men whom
he had struck down because of Gedaliah, it was the one that King Asa had
made on account of Baasha king of Israel. Ishmael son of Nethaniah filled
10 it with the slain. And Ishmael took captive all the rest of the people who
were in Mizpah, the daughters of the king and all the people remaining at

---

grain offerings and frankincense in their hand, to bring to the house of the LORD. Since
they know that the house of the LORD is no longer standing, this would have to be a pilgrimage to the site of the destroyed Temple, where they hope to participate in some sort of
rite with the grain offering and the incense, though animal sacrifice would be not possible
without the Temple and its altar.

6. *walking along weeping.* He pretends to share their mourning.
    Come to Gedaliah. In this way he lures them into Mizpah, concealing his murder of
Gedaliah.

7. *Ishmael son of Nethaniah slaughtered them.* The likely motive for this act of mass murder
is to make sure, lest any of the pilgrims passing by Mizpah get word of what has happened
there, that no report of the assassination be made. Ishmael's unflinching ruthlessness is
clearly evident.

8. *we have hidden stores in the field.* It should be kept in mind that the Judahite population
has been under siege, and so food supplies are very scarce. Ishmael would have to keep these
men alive so that they could lead him to the storage pits or other places of concealment
where they had left the provisions.

9. *the cistern into which Ishmael had flung all the corpses.* Merely wanting to get the bodies
out of sight, he compounds the brutality of the murders by denying his victims a proper
burial.
    the one that King Asa had made on account of Baasha king of Israel. This was in a time
of war between the southern kingdom ruled by Asa and the northern kingdom. The cistern
was probably dug to provide a water supply if Baasha were to besiege Mizpah.
    Ishmael son of Nethaniah filled it with the slain. This grisly detail offers a concrete image
of the magnitude of the slaughter.

10. *the daughters of the king.* The king's sons were executed by Nebuchadrezzar, but evidently his daughters were allowed to take refuge with Gedaliah at Mizpah.

Mizpah whom Nebuzaradan the high chamberlain had left with Gedaliah son of Ahikam. And Ishmael son of Nethaniah took the captives and went to cross over to the Ammonites. And Johanan son of Kereah and all the 11 commanders of the troops who were with him heard of all the evil that Ishmael son of Nethaniah had done. And they took all the men and went to 12 do battle with Ishmael son of Nethaniah, and they found him by the great pool which is at Gibeon. And it happened when all the people who were 13 with Ishmael saw Johanan son of Kereah and all the commanders of the troops, they rejoiced. And all the people whom Ishmael had taken captive 14 from Mizpah swung round and turned back and went over to Johanan son of Kereah. But Ishmael son of Nethaniah had escaped from Johanan 15 with eight men and had gone over to the Ammonites. And Johanan son of 16 Kereah and all the commanders of the troops who were with him took the rest of the people whom he had brought back from Ishmael son of Nethaniah from Mizpah, who had struck down Gedaliah son of Ahikam—the males, men of war, women and children and eunuchs whom he brought back from Gibeon. And they went and stayed at Geroth Chimham, which is 17 by Bethlehem, on the route down to Egypt from before the Chaldeans, for 18 they feared them, for Ishmael son of Nethaniah had struck down Gedaliah son of Ahikam, whom the king of Babylonia had appointed over the land.

---

12. *the great pool.* The literal sense of the Hebrew is "many waters," but in 2 Samuel 2:13 it is a pool at Gibeon alongside which a battle in the civil war takes place.

14. *And all the people whom Ishmael had taken captive from Mizpah swung round and turned back.* As captives, they were scarcely willing allies of the murderous Ishmael, so it is hardly surprising that they should go over to the other side at the first sign of a strong opposing force. Ishmael, confronted by superior numbers and compelled to flee, is in no position to retain them.

15. *with eight men.* Two of the ten are now missing. Either they have defected or, if Gedaliah's people offered some resistance, they have been killed in the course of the slaughter.

16. *and eunuchs.* This is the first mention of their presence in this group. Their probable function is as attendants to the king's daughters.

17. *on the route down to Egypt.* The literal sense is "to come to Egypt." The people who sheltered at Mizpah now conclude that it is not safe for them to remain in Judah, and so they prepare to go to Egypt, Babylonia's adversary. The second half of this sentence, which appears in the next verse, explains that because Gedaliah, appointed by the Babylonians, has been murdered (together with a contingent of Chaldean military men), they are afraid that they may be held accountable, perhaps suspected as survivors to be accomplices of Ishmael.

1 CHAPTER 42   And all the commanders of the troops of
Johanan son of Kareah and Jezaniah son of Hoshaiah and all the people
2 from the least to the greatest approached, and they said to Jeremiah the
prophet, "Let our supplication, pray, fall before you and pray for us to the
LORD your God for all this remnant, for we remain few of many, as your
3 own eyes see us. And let the LORD your God tell us the way in which we
4 should go and the thing we should do." And Jeremiah the prophet said to
them, "I have heard. I am about to pray to the LORD your God according
to your words, and it shall be, whatever word the LORD answers you I will
5 tell you, I will not hold back anything from you." And they had said to
Jeremiah, "May the LORD be a true and faithful witness against us if we
do not do according to all the word that the LORD our God will send you
6 concerning us. Whether good or bad, we will heed the voice of the LORD
our God to Whom we are sending you, so that it will go well with us, that we
7 heed the voice of the LORD our God." And it happened at the end of ten days
8 that the word of the LORD came to Jeremiah. And he called to Johanan son
of Kareah and to all the commanders of the troops who were with him and
9 to all the people from the least to the greatest. And he said to them, "Thus
said the LORD God of Israel to Whom you sent me to lay your supplication
10 before Him: If you indeed dwell in this land, I will build you and will not
destroy, and I will plant you and will not uproot, for I have repented of the
11 evil that I have done to you. Do not fear the king of Babylonia of whom you

---

CHAPTER 42   3. *And let the LORD your God tell us the way in which we should go.*
After the murder of Gedaliah and the contingent with him at Mizpah, which included
Chaldeans, this group of Judahites is fearful that the Babylonians may hold them responsible and exact retribution from them, and they seek guidance about what to do. One
suspects that they are actually determined to flee to Egypt—"the way" could even mean
"the route"— and are seeking prophetic confirmation of this decision. Following biblical
protocol in addressing a man of God, they refer to the deity as "the LORD your God."

4. *I am about to pray to the LORD your God.* This usage, identifying the LORD as the God of
the petitioners, is unusual and may be intended to make a point: The LORD is in fact your
God as well as mine, and so you had better do whatever He commands.

5. *the LORD our God.* They here assent to Jeremiah's attaching God to them.

7. *And it happened at the end of ten days.* Such a period of waiting for word from God is
unusual. Perhaps Jeremiah is struggling before he delivers an oracle that he knows they
don't want to hear. Perhaps he wants to keep them in suspense before delivering the difficult prophecy.

10. *If you indeed dwell in this land, I will build you and will not destroy.* God's message as
Jeremiah conveys it is emphatic and unambiguous: these Judahites must now stay in their
land. But unlike the prophet's previous counsel that it was futile to resist the Babylonians,
this imperative is scarcely based on a sober assessment of the political situation. There is

are afraid. Do not fear him, said the Lord, for I am with you to rescue you and to save you from his hand. And I will grant you mercy and he shall be 12 merciful to you and bring you back to your land. And if you say, 'We will 13 not dwell in this land,' not heeding the voice of the Lord your God, saying 14 'No. Rather we shall go to the land of Egypt where we shall not see war nor hear the sound of the ram's horn nor hunger for bread, and there shall we dwell.' And now listen to the word of the Lord, remnant of Judah. Thus 15 said the Lord of Armies, God of Israel: if you indeed set your face to go to Egypt and go to sojourn there, the sword that you fear shall overtake you 16 in the land of Egypt, and the famine about which you worry shall catch up with you in Egypt, and there shall you die. And all the people who set their 17 face to go to Egypt to sojourn there shall die by the sword and by famine and by pestilence, and you shall have no remnant or survivor from the evil I bring upon you. For thus said the Lord of Armies, God of Israel: As My 18 anger and wrath have poured forth on the dwellers of Jerusalem, so shall My wrath pour forth upon you when you go to Egypt, and you shall become an imprecation and a desolation and a curse and a disgrace, and you shall not see this place again. The Lord has spoken concerning you, remnant of 19 Judah. Do not go to Egypt. You surely know that I have warned you today. For you have misled yourselves, for you, you sent me to the Lord your God, 20

---

surely no objective evidence that they have no reason to fear the king of Babylonia (verse 11), or that they will now be granted a grand national restoration.

14. *we shall go to the land of Egypt.* Throughout this passage, the Hebrew uses "come," but the directional logic of English usage requires "go."

nor hear the sound of the ram's horn. One of the chief uses of the ram's horn, which emits a shrill, piercing sound, was as a call to battle.

15. *sojourn.* The Hebrew verb implies temporary residence, but even this, in Jeremiah's view, is to be strictly avoided.

17. *shall die by the sword and by famine and by pestilence.* This is the triad of means of destruction that recurs repeatedly in Jeremiah's prophecies.

18. *As My anger and wrath have poured forth on the dwellers of Jerusalem.* The entire kingdom has been devastated by the invasion, not just the capital city, but Jerusalem, its temple razed to the ground, its houses put to the torch, is the epitome and synecdoche of the general destruction.

20. *for you, you sent me.* Jeremiah stresses the second-person pronoun *'atem* by inserting it before the conjugated verb, which would not normally require a pronoun: it was you yourselves who took the initiative to send me to inquire of the Lord on your behalf, promising that you would strictly follow His dictates. Now, would you dare to ignore what God has emphatically told you to do? In the event, as we learn from the narrative report that immediately follows in the next chapter, they in fact reject what Jeremiah has conveyed to them as the word of the Lord.

saying, 'Pray for us to the LORD our God, and according to all that the LORD
21 our God says, so tell us and we will do it.' And I have told you today, and
you did not heed the voice of the LORD your God and all of which he sent
22 me to you. And now, you surely know that by the sword, by famine, and by
pestilence you shall die in the place that you desire to go to sojourn there."

1 CHAPTER 43   And it happened when Jeremiah finished
speaking to the people all the words of the LORD their God which the LORD
2 their God had sent to them, all these words, that Azariah son of Hoshaiah
and Johanan son of Kareah and all the arrogant men said to Jeremiah, "You
speak a lie! The LORD our God did not send you, saying, 'You shall not go
3 to Egypt to sojourn there.' But Baruch son of Neriah is inciting you against
us so as to give us into the hand of the Chaldeans to put us to death or to
4 exile us to Babylonia." And Johanan son of Kareah, and all the commanders of the troops and all the people with him, had not heeded the voice of
5 the LORD to dwell in the land of Judah. And Johanan son of Kareah, and
all the commanders of the troops with him, took all the remnant of Judah
who had come back from all the nations where they were dispersed to
6 sojourn in the land of Judah—the men and the women and the children
and the king's daughters and every living person whom Nebuzaradan the
high chamberlain had left with Gedaliah son of Ahikam, and Jeremiah the
7 prophet and Baruch son of Neriah. And they came to the land of Egypt, as
far as Tahpanes, for they had not heeded the voice of the LORD.

8,9 And the word of the LORD came to Jeremiah in Tahpanes, saying, "Take in
your hand large stones and bury them in mortar in the brickwork that is

---

CHAPTER 43   1. *all the words of the LORD their God.* This narrative report continues
the procedure of the preceding textual unit in affirming that YHWH is the God of these
people—the very people who have rejected God's word delivered by Jeremiah.

3. *Baruch son of Neriah is inciting you against us.* This is a surprising accusation. It may
be founded merely in a paranoid suspicion that someone must have misled the prophet on
whom they were counting to confirm their decision about going to Egypt. The alternative
possibility is that they are loath to accuse Jeremiah directly and so make his amanuensis
responsible for what he has done.

6. *and Jeremiah the prophet and Baruch son of Neriah.* These two crucial figures are left
till the very end of the list of those who were taken down to Egypt. The implication would
seem to be that Jeremiah and Baruch were taken against their will.

at the entrance of the house of Pharaoh in Tahpanes before the eyes of the
Judahite men. And you shall say to them: Thus said the LORD of Armies, 10
God of Israel. I am about to send and take Nebuchadrezzar My servant,
king of Babylonia, and I will put his throne over these stones that I have
buried, and he shall stretch out his splendor over them. And he shall come 11
and strike the land of Egypt—who for death to death and who for captivity to captivity and who for the sword to the sword. And he shall set fire 12
to the houses of the gods of Egypt, and he shall burn them and take them
captive and wrap round the land of Egypt as a shepherd wraps himself in
his garment, and he shall go out from there in safety. And he shall smash 13
the obelisks of the House of the Sun that is in the land of Egypt, and the
houses of the gods of Egypt he shall burn in fire."

---

9. *the house of Pharaoh in Tahpanes.* Tahpanes, near the northern border of Egypt, was not
the capital city, but there may have been some sort of royal palace there.

10. *Nebuchadrezzar My servant.* What this epithet indicates is that the Babylonian emperor
is God's instrument in history, which in the present instance involves the conquest of
Egypt.

    he shall stretch out his splendor over them. The noun *shafrir* appears only here. Because
of the verb "stretch out," some think it means "canopy" or "pavilion," but it reflects a
Hebrew root that indicates beauty, and so the general term "splendor" may be the safest
translation.

12. *he shall set fire.* The Masoretic Text has "I will set fire," but the Septuagint, the Syriac,
and the Vulgate all show the third-person singular, making Nebuchadrezzar the subject of
the verb. It is, of course, possible that the original text simply switched from God's human
agent to God.

    take them captive. It was common to cart off the gods of a conquered land. Presumably,
the wooden ones were burned and those with precious metals were taken away.

    wrap round the land of Egypt. This slightly odd image is meant to indicate Nebuchadrez-
zar's total domination of the country. The comparison to the shepherd wrapping himself
in his garment suggests that the Babylonian conqueror will take warmth and comfort from
appropriating the entire land.

13. *obelisks.* The Hebrew *matseivot* in Canaanite and Israelite settings refers to steles, sacred
piles of stones, but in the Egyptian context these would have to be obelisks, which in fact
have been found at this site in archaeological excavations.

    the House of the Sun that is in the land of Egypt. The qualifying clause is introduced
because there is a place in Canaan that bears this same name in Hebrew, *Beyt Shemesh.*
The Septuagint renders this as "Heliopolis [Sun City] which is in On." There was a cult of
sun worship at On.

1 CHAPTER 44   The word of the Lord that came to Jeremiah concerning all the Judahites dwelling in the land of Egypt, dwelling in Migdol and in Tahpanes and in Noph and in the region of Pathros, saying,
2 "Thus said the Lord of Armies, God of Israel: You have seen all the evil that I brought upon Jerusalem and upon all the towns of Judah, and look,
3 they are a ruin to this day and none dwells in them because of their evil that they did to Me, to go to burn incense to serve other gods which neither
4 you nor your fathers knew. And I sent to you all My servants the prophets, continually sent, saying, 'Pray, do not do this abhorrent thing that I hate.'
5 But they did not heed and did not bend their ear to turn back from their
6 evil, not to burn incense to other gods. And My wrath and My anger poured out and burned through the towns of Judah and through the streets of
7 Jerusalem, and they became a ruin and a desolation as on this day. And now, thus said the Lord God of Armies, God of Israel: Why are you doing this great evil to yourselves to cut off from you man and woman, infant and suckling, from the midst of Judah, so as not to leave for yourselves a
8 remnant, to vex Me with the work of your hands, to burn incense to other gods in the land of Egypt where you came to sojourn, so as to cut off for yourselves and so that you become a curse and a disgrace among all the
9 nations of the earth? Have you forgotten the evils of your fathers and the evils of the kings of Judah and the evils of their wives and your own evils

---

CHAPTER 44   1. *concerning all the Judahites dwelling in the land of Egypt.* There was an expatriate Judahite population in Egypt before 586 B.C.E., and this wording here—with "all the Judahites" and "dwelling," the term for permanent settlement—suggests that Jeremiah is addressing all these people, not just the group with whom the prophet had been brought down.

Noph. This is the Egyptian city generally called Memphis.

3. *to burn incense.* The ritual act of burning incense, though part of most cults, is particularly associated with the worship of the Assyrian goddess Ishtar (known in Greek as Astarte), which was widespread among the Israelites in the last two centuries before the destruction. This identification will be made clear later in the prophecy, where Ishtar is named by her epithet "Queen of the Heavens."

6. *burned through the towns of Judah and through the streets of Jerusalem.* The Hebrew word for "wrath" suggests heat, and so the transformation into burning, which is actually what the invaders have done, is direct.

9. *the evils of the kings of Judah.* As is clear in the Book of Kings, several Judahite monarchs encouraged pagan practices, even introducing them into the temple precincts.

the evils of their wives. Again by the account of the Book of Kings, the wives, some of them foreigners, were sometimes especially active in pagan worship, and the cult of Ishtar had a strong attraction for women.

and the evils of your own wives that they did in the towns of Judah and in the streets of Jerusalem.? They have not been contrite to this day and 10 they have not feared, and they have not walked by My teaching and by My statutes that I set before them and before their fathers. Therefore, thus said 11 the LORD of Armies, God of Israel: I am about to set My face against you for evil to cut off all of Judah. And I will take the remnant of Judah who set 12 their face to go to the land of Egypt to sojourn there, and all shall come to an end in the land of Egypt. They shall fall by the sword and come to an end by famine. From the least to the greatest, by sword and by famine they shall die, and they shall become an imprecation and a desolation and a curse and a disgrace. And I will reckon with those dwelling in the land of Egypt, as 13 I reckoned with Jerusalem, by the sword and by famine and by pestilence. And there shall be no fugitive and no survivor for the remnant of Judah 14 coming to sojourn there in the land of Egypt to go back to the land of Judah to which they long to go back to dwell there, for they shall not go back except as fugitives." And all the men knowing that their wives were burning 15 incense to other gods and all the women standing, a great assembly, and all the people dwelling in the land of Egypt, in Pathros, answered Jeremiah, saying, "The word that you have spoken to us in the name of the LORD—we 16 will not heed you. For we will surely do every word that comes out of our 17 mouth, to burn incense to the Queen of the Heavens and to pour out libations to her, as we have done, we and our fathers, our kings and our nobles, in the towns of Judah and in the streets of Jerusalem, and we ate our fill of bread, and we were good, and evil we did not see. And ever since we stopped 18 burning incense to the Queen of the Heavens and pouring out libations to

---

10. *contrite.* The basic meaning of the Hebrew term is "crushed," but a convincing exegetical tradition going back at least to Rashi links it with contrition, or a crushed spirit.

11. *set My face.* The idiom here indicates measure-for-measure justice to be meted out to the people who "set their face to go to the land of Egypt" (verse 12).

14. *except as fugitives.* This of course contradicts the statement at the beginning of the verse that "there shall be no fugitive and no survivor." Either an editor or perhaps Jeremiah himself seeks to qualify the total grimness of the prophecy of destruction.

16. *we will not heed you.* The people's response is unrepentant defiance.

17. *we ate our fill of bread, and we were good, and evil we did not see.* The people present an empirical theological justification for their worship of Ishtar: over the many decades that they observed her cult, they were never in want. After the religious reforms of Josiah, beginning in 622 B.C.E., the cult was suppressed, and then disaster after disaster came upon them, culminating in the destruction of the kingdom.

her, we have lacked everything, and by the sword and by famine we have
19 come to an end. And when we burn incense to the Queen of the Heavens
and pour out libations to her, is it without our husbands that we have made
20 cakes for her, framing her image and pouring out libations to her?" And
Jeremiah said to all the people, including all the men and all the women
21 and all the people who answered in speech, saying, "Why, the incense that
you have burned in the towns of Judah and in the streets of Jerusalem, you
and your fathers, your kings and your nobles and the people of the land,
22 that is what the LORD recalls and brings to mind. And the LORD shall no
longer bear it because of the evil of your acts, because of the abominations
that you have done, and your land has become a ruin and a desolation and
23 a curse with no dweller as on this day because you have burned incense
and have offended the LORD and have not heeded the voice of the LORD,
and by His teaching and His statutes and His precepts you have not gone.
24 Therefore has this evil befallen you as on this day." And Jeremiah said to all
the people and to all the women: "Listen to the word of the LORD, all Judah
25 that is in the land of Egypt. Thus said the LORD of Armies, God of Israel,
saying, you and your women, who have spoken with your mouths and with
your hands you have fulfilled it, saying, 'We will surely carry out our vows
to burn incense to the Queen of the Heavens and to pour out libations to
her.' Then indeed fulfill your vows, you women, and carry out your vows.
26 Therefore listen to the word of the LORD, all Judah who dwell in the land

---

19. *And when we burn incense to the Queen of the Heavens . . . is it without our husbands.*
Although the verb is masculine, the content of the clause indicates that the women are
speaking, and a certain freedom in grammatical gender is sometimes observable in biblical
Hebrew. The women are saying that they always had the support and perhaps participation
of their husbands when they worshipped Ishtar.

   made cakes for her. This was a prominent part of the cult. Archaeologists in fact have
found numerous clay molds with the image of a naked female, presumably, Ishtar. The verb
rendered as "framing her image" appears to refer to this practice, and Rashi, long before
the advent of archaeology, understood it precisely in this way. The people appear to report
the specific details of the cult of the Queen of the Heavens with relish.

21. *Why, the incense that you have burned . . . that is what the LORD recalls.* Jeremiah flings
their own words back in their face: you take such pleasure in recalling how you have burned
incense to Ishtar, but it is precisely this that God will bring to mind to punish you.

24. *and to all the women.* They are singled out for mention because of their special attachment to the cult of the Queen of the Heavens.

25. *fulfill your vows, you women.* Although the beginning of the verse refers to "you and
your women," the verbs used sarcastically here are conjugated in the feminine, and so
"you women" has been added in the translation to make it clear that Jeremiah is addressing the women.

of Egypt. Look, I vow by My great name, said the LORD, that My name shall no longer be called by the mouth of any man of Judah, saying, 'As the LORD lives,' in all the land of Egypt. Look, I am vigilant over them for evil 27 and not for good, and all the men of Judah who are in the land of Egypt shall come to an end by the sword and by famine until they are no more. And the fugitives of the sword shall come back from the land of Egypt to 28 the land of Judah as a handful of men. And all the remnant of Judah who have come to the land of Egypt to sojourn there shall know whose word shall be fulfilled, Mine or theirs. And this is the sign for you, said the LORD, 29 that I am reckoning with you in this place, so you may know that My word concerning you shall surely be fulfilled for evil. Thus said the LORD: I am 30 about to give Pharaoh Hophra king of Egypt into the hand of his enemies and into the hand of those who seek his life as I gave Zedekiah king of Judah into the hand of Nebuchadrezzar king of Babylonia, his enemy and the one who sought his life."

CHAPTER 45   The word that Jeremiah the prophet spoke to 1 Baruch son of Neriah as he wrote these words in a book from the mouth of Jeremiah in the fourth year of Jehoiakim son of Josiah king of Judah,

---

26. *My name shall no longer be called by the mouth of any man of Judah.* In all likelihood, the cult of Ishtar among the Judahites was not an exclusive practice but part of syncretistic worship, so that people might well still invoke the name of YHWH in their vows even as they burned incense to the Queen of the Heavens. God now announces that He will put an end to this hypocrisy—presumably, by destroying all the paganizers, as the verse goes on to say.

28. *And the fugitives of the sword shall come back from the land of Egypt.* This is the same contradiction of the prophecy of total destruction that is noted above in verse 14.

29. *And this is the sign for you.* If the Pharaoh who is the protector of the refugees from Judah is killed, their dream of a safe haven in Egypt will be shattered.

30. *I am about to give Pharaoh Hophra king of Egypt into the hand of his enemies.* Even though the enemies are not specified, the prime candidate would be Babylonia. Some classical sources say that Hophra (Apries) came to a violent end, but not at the hand of Nebuchadrezzar, who did not invade Egypt until 568 B.C.E., two years after Hophra's death.

CHAPTER 45   1. *The word that Jeremiah the prophet spoke to Baruch son of Neriah.* After the narrative of Jeremiah's probably unwilling descent into Egypt and his confrontation with his countrymen there, the text goes back to the fourth year of Jehoiakim, which would be 605 B.C.E., almost two decades earlier. This brief chapter may have been intended editorially as a kind of concluding frame for all the preceding narrative material, especially if, as is often inferred, Baruch is the author of these narratives.
    as he wrote these words in a book from the mouth of Jeremiah. "From the mouth of," as

2,3 saying, "Thus said the LORD God of Israel concerning you, Baruch: You
said, 'O woe is me, for the LORD has added sorrow to my pain. I am weary

4 with my groaning, and no rest have I found.' Thus shall you say to him:
Thus said the LORD. Look, what I built I will destroy. What I planted I will

5 uproot—all of that land is Mine. As for you, do you seek great things for
yourself? Do not seek, for I am about to bring evil upon all flesh, said the
LORD, but I will give you your life as booty in all the places where you go."

1 CHAPTER 46   Which was the word of the LORD to Jeremiah

2 concerning the nations. For Egypt, concerning the force of Pharaoh Neco
king of Egypt that was by the River Euphrates at Carchemish, which Nebuchadrezzar king of Babylonia struck down in the fourth year of Jehoiakim
king of Judah.

---

before, means "from the dictation of." The book of prophecies that Baruch is writing out
could not be the one burned by Zedekiah because that happened considerably later. The
reasonable inference is that this is a first installment of the prophecies of Jeremiah, perhaps
chapters 1–20 in the canonical collection.

3. *O woe is me.* The language here is close to poetry—specifically the poetry of lament—
although the sentence does not quite scan as formal verse. The cause for the woe may be
the dire content of the prophecies.

   I am weary with my groaning. Approximate parallels of this language appear in Psalms
6:7 and 69:4.

4. *all of that land is Mine.* The Masoretic Text reads, abruptly, "all of that land," prefaced
by an accusative particle but without a verb. The Targum Yonatan translates as "all of the
Land of Israel, for it is Mine," but it is uncertain whether this is based on a Hebrew text that
showed this reading or is simply an interpretive clarification.

5. *As for you, do you seek great things for yourself?* This is not a time for personal ambition
(which would not have been out of place on the part of a scribe) when the entire country
is about to be laid waste. Against the background of the preceding chapters, Baruch's fate,
with the national hierarchy where he might have risen in ruins, will be to go with a group
of exiles to Egypt and, in all likelihood, to chronicle the conflict there between the prophet
and the other exiles.

   I will give you your life as booty in all the places where you go. As before, this expression
means: I will enable you to survive, but you can count on little more than that. "All the
places where you go" probably intimates the future destiny of exile.

CHAPTER 46   2. *by the River Euphrates at Carchemish.* The battle at Carchemish would determine much of Near Eastern history for decades to come. Pharaoh Neco
headed north in 609 B.C.E. in an effort to aid the Assyrians, who were waging a losing war
against the Babylonians. The Judahite King Josiah tried to stand in his way and was killed
in battle by Neco. In 605, the Egyptian and Babylonian armies clashed at Carchemish, and
the Egyptians were routed, as this prophecy reports.

Ready the buckler and shield   3
   and move forward to battle.
Harness the horses   4
   and mount, O riders.
Take your station in helmets,
   burnish the lances,
      gird on the chain armor.
Why did I see them panicked,   5
   falling back, their warriors crushed and fled,
      they do not turn back, terror all around?
         said the LORD.
The swift does not flee   6
   nor the warrior escape.
To the north by the River Euphrates
   they stumbled and fell.
Who is this rising like the Nile,   7
   like the streams his waters swell?
Egypt like the Nile rises,   8
   and like streams the waters swell.
And he said, "I will rise, will cover the earth,
   will destroy town and its dwellers."
Rise up, O horses,   9
   and chariots, go wild!
Let the warriors come out,
   Cush and Put handling the buckler
      and the Ludim who bend the bow.

---

3. *Ready the buckler and shield.* All these words of military exhortation are best under-stood as addressed by God—"the word of the LORD"—to the Egyptian army, which is being urged to head into the battle where it will meet its destruction. "Buckler," *magen,* is generally thought to be a small round shield and "shield," *tsinah,* a larger rectangular one.

7. *Who is this rising like the Nile, / like the streams his waters swell?* The Nile does periodi-cally overflow its banks. As the principal source of water for Egypt, it serves here as an apt image of the overweening Egyptian expeditionary force that aspires to "cover the earth."

9. *Rise up, O horses.* The verb in this instance, playing back against the rising of the Nile, probably refers to the rearing up of the horses.
   Cush and Put . . . / Ludim. Cush is Nubia, at one point a conqueror of Egypt. Put is probably Lybia and the Ludim are probably the Lydians, a people of Asia Minor. All these foreigners would be mercenaries fighting in the Egyptian ranks, and mercenaries ("hired troops") are explicitly mentioned in verse 21.
   the Ludim who bend the bow. The implication is that the Lydian contingent were skilled

10   And that day is the Master's, the LORD of Armies,
        day of vengeance to take revenge of His foes.
     And the sword shall consume and be sated
        and drink its fill of their blood.
     For a sacrifice has the Master, LORD of Armies,
        in the land of the north by the River Euphrates.
11   Go up to Gilead and get balm,
        O Virgin Daughter of Egypt.
     In vain you devised many cures—
        there is no healing for you.
12   The nations heard of your infamy,
        and the earth is filled with your screaming,
     for warrior stumbled against warrior,
        together the two of them fell.

13   The word that the LORD spoke to Jeremiah the prophet about the coming of Nebuchadrezzar king of Babylonia to strike the land of Egypt.

14   Tell it in Egypt and make it heard in Migdol,
        and make it heard in Noph and Tahpanes.
     Say, take your station and ready yourself,
        for the sword consumes all round you.
15   Why are your heroes swept away?

---

archers. "Bend the bow" is literally "trod the bow" because one foot was needed to pull back these large bows.

10. *sacrifice.* Much to the point of the present line, the Hebrew noun can also mean "slaughter."

11. *Go up to Gilead and get balm.* The northern region of Gilead was famous for its medicinal herbs. The injunction for Egypt to go up there is obviously sarcastic, for as the next line spells out, she will not heal from the grievous wounds she has suffered at the hands of the Babylonians.

12. *for warrior stumbled against warrior.* This is an image of their panicked flight as they are routed on the battlefield.

13. *the coming of Nebuchadrezzar king of Babylonia to strike the land of Egypt.* While Josephus and some other ancient sources report a Babylonian invasion of Egypt in the late 580s B.C.E., the historicity of this event is now widely doubted. It seems more likely that Jeremiah, after the Egyptian defeat at Carchemish, is projecting the prospect of a devastating Babylonian assault on the Egyptian homeland.

15. *your heroes.* The Hebrew *'abirim* can mean "bulls," "steeds" (its sense in the Song of Deborah, Judges 5, and here in 47:3), or, because of the association of both animals with

They do not stand, for the LORD thrust them down.
He made many stumble, even fall.   16
    Each man said to his fellow,
"Rise up, let us go back to our people
    and to our birth land before the oppressive sword."
There they called Pharaoh king of Egypt   17
    "an uproar that missed the set time."
As I live, said the King,   18
    LORD of Armies is His name,
like Tabor among the mountains
    and like Carmel by the sea he shall come.
Prepare yourself gear of exile,   19
    O dweller, Daughter of Egypt.
For Noph shall become a desolation,
    shall be razed with none there to dwell.
O beautiful heifer in Egypt—   20
    a gadfly from the north comes, it comes.
Her hired troops, too, in her midst   21

---

physical strength, something like "powerful warriors." This last sense seems the most likely here especially because of the reference to not standing and being pushed down in the next line. Lundbom thinks the term refers to Apis, the Egyptian bull god, which is ingenious but not persuasive.

16. *Rise up.* The imperative verb, *qumah,* is particularly appropriate here because they—not their horses or their bull god—have been knocked down on the battlefield.

17. *an uproar that missed the set time.* Although the meaning of this phrase is in dispute, it is best understood as a mocking designation of the Pharaoh who has failed to defend his land: he makes a big noise, but he does not arrive at the right time and place to rescue his people.

18. *the King / LORD of Armies.* The monarchic epithet for God is purposefully chosen as a contrast to "Pharaoh king of Egypt" in the preceding line.
    like Tabor . . . / like Carmel. Since neither of these mountains can move, the reference must not be to "he [the invader] shall come," but to "the King, / LORD of Armies," who stands lofty over all the nations like these two mountains over the surrounding landscape.

19. *gear of exile.* This would presumably be minimal changes of clothing, cooking utensils, and other wherewithal for everyday life on the move.

20. *gadfly.* The Hebrew *qerets* occurs only here, but it probably relates to a verbal stem that means to break off or pinch and is thus linked with the bite of the gadfly. That, in turn, is a metaphor for Nebuchadrezzar.

21. *Her hired troops.* See the second comment on verse 9.

> were like stall-fed calves.
> They, too, turned away,
>   fled together, they did not stand.
> For the day of disaster came upon them,
>   the time of their reckoning.

22 Her voice like a snake as it goes.
>   For in a force they shall go
> and with axes come against her
>   like hewers of wood.

23 They have cut down her forest, said the LORD,
>   yes, it cannot be fathomed,
> for they are more numerous than locusts,
>   and they are beyond number.

24 The Daughter of Egypt was shamed,
>   given into the hand of the people of the north.

25 The LORD of Armies has said: "I am about to make a reckoning with Amon of No and with Pharaoh and with Egypt and with its gods and with its kings
26 and with Pharaoh and with all who trust in him. And I will give them into the hand of those who seek their life and into the hand of Nebuchadrezzar king of Babylonia and into the hand of all his servants. But afterward she shall dwell as in days of old."

---

like stall-fed calves. The fatted calves are led directly from the confining stall to be slaughtered, with no chance to escape.

22. *Her voice like a snake as it goes.* Crushed by defeat, the Egyptians can emit no more than the rustling sound of a snake crawling over the ground. This is an obvious antithesis to the "uproar" made by Pharaoh.

23. *They have cut down her forest.* Since Egypt has no forests, this is either an extension of the metaphor of woodcutting for destruction or possibly a reference to the wood-paneled interiors of Egypt's palaces.
it cannot be fathomed. The "it" is in effect explained in the next line: the invading force is so vast that it cannot be fathomed.

25. *with its kings.* The slightly puzzling plural might refer to a succession of Egyptian monarchs destined to suffer under the yoke of foreign domination.
with Pharaoh. This replicates the phrase at the beginning of the series, so one of them may be a scribal duplication.

26. *But afterward she shall dwell as in days of old.* This final positive note may be based on the prophet's realistic assessment of the geopolitical situation: Babylonia will not be able to sustain its conquest of Egypt indefinitely.

And now, do not fear, My servant Jacob,   27
    nor be panicked, Israel.
For I am about to rescue you from afar
    and your seed from the land of captivity,
and Jacob once more shall be quiet
    and tranquil with none making him tremble.
As for you, do not fear, My servant Jacob—   28
      said the LORD—
    for I am with you.
I will make an end of all the nations
    where I have dispersed you,
but of you I will not make an end,
    yet I will chastise you in justice,
      will surely not leave you unblamed.

CHAPTER 47   Which was the word of the LORD to Jeremiah 1
the prophet concerning the Philistines before Pharaoh struck down Gaza.
    Thus said the LORD;   2

Look, waters come up from the north
    and turn into a sweeping torrent,
and they shall sweep through the land and its fullness,
    the town and those dwelling within it,
and men shall shout,
    all the land's dwellers howl.

---

28. *but of you I will not make an end, / yet I will chastise you in justice.* This is a balancing act of prediction that the prophet performs elsewhere. Unlike other nations, which are destined to be utterly destroyed, Israel will survive; nevertheless, because of its repeated offenses against God, it must first be brought to judgment and pay the bitter price of defeat and captivity ("chastisement") for what it has done.

CHAPTER 47   1. *before Pharaoh struck down Gaza.* In the prophecy that follows, it is Babylonia ("waters come up from the north") that attacks the Philistines, but there is some warrant for concluding that an Egyptian incursion into Philistine territory took place at some point in the last decade of the seventh century B.C.E.

2. *torrent.* The usual sense of the Hebrew *naḥal* is "wadi," but the poetic image is based on the fact that the dry gulches of wadis are filled during the heavy winter rains with rushing torrents.

3   From the sound of his stallions' pounding hooves,
      from the clatter of his chariots, the roar of his wheels
    fathers turn not to the sons
      because of slackness of hands
4   for the day that comes to ravage
      all the Philistines,
    to cut off from Tyre and Sidon
      every survivor, helper.
    For the LORD ravages the Philistines,
      the remnant of the isle of Crete.
5   Shaved pates have come upon Gaza,
      Ashkelon is demolished.
    Remnant of the Anakites,
      how long will you gash yourselves?
6   Woe, O sword of the LORD,
      till when will you be unquiet?

---

3. *From the sound of his stallions' pounding hooves.* Here the poetry switches from the metaphor of the sweeping torrent to a literal representation of the Babylonian chariot corps galloping against the Philistines.

slackness of hands. "Hand" in biblical idiom is often a term for "strength," and so "slackness of hands" means weakness, incapacity.

4. *Tyre and Sidon.* These are principal Phoenician cities, farther up the coast from the five Philistine cities, which also sit on the shore of the Mediterranean. There is archaeological evidence of abundant commercial contact between the Philistines and the Phoenicians, and some sort of political alliance may also have been in place.

every survivor, helper. The verbal noun "helper" often appears in military contexts and could conceivably have a technical sense of "ally."

5. *Shaved pates.* Though the literal sense is "baldness," the clear reference is to shaving the head as a sign of mourning. The gashing at the end of this verse is another act of mourning. Israelites are prohibited from following both these practices, although there are grounds to suspect that they often ignored the prohibition.

Remnant of the Anakites. The received text, which seems to say "remnant of their valley," *she'erit 'imqam,* does not make much sense (and there are no valleys along the coastal area where the Philistines lived). The proposal of some scholars, citing a purported Ugaritic cognate, that *'imqam* means "their strength" has no warrant elsewhere in the biblical corpus. This translation follows the Septuagint, which reads *she'erit ha 'anaqim,* the Anakites being in biblical lore an archaic race of giants (perhaps ancestors of Goliath).

6. *Woe, O sword of the LORD, / till when will you be unquiet?* Babylonia is imagined as the "sword of the LORD," carrying out His purposes in history—here, wreaking vengeance on Israel's historic enemies, the Philistines. Even though the prophet is no friend of the Philistines, as he envisages the terrible onslaught against them, he is aghast and so asks in this apostrophe how long it will continue.

Slip back into your sheath,
   rest and be still.
How can it be quiet   7
   when the Lord has commanded it?
To Ashkelon and to the seashore,
   there He has posted it.

CHAPTER 48   Concerning Moab, thus said the Lord of 1
Armies, God of Israel.

Woe to Nebo, for it is ravaged,
   Kiriathaim is shamed, is captured.
      The stronghold is shamed and shattered.
The Praise of Moab is no more.   2
   In Heshbon they plotted harm against her:
"Come, let us cut her off as a nation
   Madmein, too, you shall be mute.
      After you the sword shall go."
A sound of outcry from Horonaim—   3
   wrack and great ruin.
Moab is broken,   4
   her young make heard an outcry.
For on the Ascent of Luhith   5
   weeping upon weeping goes up.
For in the Descent of Horonaim
   a distressed outcry of shattering they hear.
Flee, save your lives,   6
   and become like Aroer in the desert.

---

7. *How can it be quiet / when the Lord has commanded it?* This is the rejoinder to the horrified "how long" of the two previous lines. It is God's will to extirpate Philistia, and so the horrific destruction must continue.

CHAPTER 48   1. *Nebo . . . / Kiriathaim.* Nebo was the mountain in trans-Jordan on which, according to Deuteronomy, Moses delivered his farewell address. Kiriathiam means "twin city." In the list of Moabite towns that follows, some of the sites have been identified by archaeologists; others remain unknown.

2. *Madmein.* The conventional English transliteration, Madmen, unfortunately looks like a designation of the insane.

7   For, as you put trust
          in your works and in your treasures,
               you, too, shall be caught,
     and Chemosh shall go out into exile,
          his priests and his nobles together.
8   And the ravager shall come to each town,
          no town shall escape.
     And the valley shall perish,
          and the plain be destroyed,
               as the LORD said.
9   Make a marker for Moab,
          for she surely shall go out,
     and her towns shall become a desolation
          with no dweller within them.
10   Cursed be he who deceives when he does the LORD's task,
          and cursed be he who holds back his sword from blood.
11   Moab was tranquil from his youth
          and settled in his lees,
     and was not poured from jug to jug,
          nor in exile did he go.
     Therefore his flavor stood in him
          and his fragrance did not change.

12   Therefore, look, days are coming, said the LORD, when I will send him men
13   to tip him over, and they shall pour out his jugs and shatter his flasks. And

---

7. *Chemosh shall go out into exile.* Chemosh is the principal god of Moab. In conquest, local idols were often borne off by the conquerors, although this clause probably has a secondary meaning, suggesting that the deity is exiled with his worshippers.

9. *Make a marker for Moab.* The Hebrew noun here, *tsits,* means either "tassel," "diadem," or "blossom." Attempts to make the sense of "diadem" work here are strained, as is the claim that the term means "wing." This translation follows the Septuagint, which reads *tsiyun,* "marker."

10. *the LORD's task.* As verse 2 made clear, the LORD's task is the ruthless implementation of the destruction of Moab.

12. *I will send him men to tip him over.* These would be the invading Babylonians, about to devastate and exile Moab after its long period of relative tranquillity, "settled in his lees" (verse 11). The breaking of the (clay) vessels both continues the metaphor of the wine in jugs and evokes the actual destruction of Moab, when its towns and possessions are smashed.

Moab shall be shamed of Chemosh as the house of Israel was shamed of
Bethel, their trust.

> How can you say, "We are warriors   14
>   and men of valor for battle"?
> Moab is ravaged, gone up from its towns   15
>   and its choicest young men gone down to the slaughter
>   —said the King, LORD of Armies is His name.
> Moab's disaster is close to come,   16
>   and its harm is very swift.
> Console him, all who are round him   17
>   and all who know his name.
> Say, how is the staff of strength broken,
>   the splendid rod!
> Go down from glory, sit in thirst,   18
>   O dweller, Daughter of Dibon.
> For Moab's ravager has gone up against you,
>   laid waste to your fortresses.
> By the wayside stand and look out,   19
>   O dweller of Aroer.
> Ask him who flees and him who escapes,
>   Say "What has happened?"
> Moab is shamed, for she is shattered.   20
>   Wail and cry out.
> Tell it in Arnon
>   that Moab is ravaged.

---

13. *as the house of Israel was shamed of Bethel.* The prophet, hewing to the view of the Deuteronomistic History, conceives the northern kingdom's sanctuary at Bethel, with its bull-shaped icons of YHWH, as a place of idolatry and hence a cultic equivalent of pagan Moab.

15. *Moab is ravaged, gone up from its towns.* There is no good textual warrant for emending the passive verb *shudad* to read *shoded,* "ravager." The land has been ravaged, and its people "go up," which has the sense of "withdraw," from the towns where they lived. The going up has a pointed antithesis in the second verset, when the young men are said to have "gone down to the slaughter."

17. *all who know his name.* This idiom suggests an intimate relationship and hence is a parallel term to "all who are round him."

18. *sit in thirst.* The Moabite towns, like the one mentioned here, Dibon, were surrounded by desert—hence the sitting in thirst as the fate of the exiles.

21 And judgment has come to the plain land, to Holon and to Johzah, and
22,23 to Maphaath and to Dibon and to Nebo and to Beth-Diblathaim and to
24 Kiriathaim and to Beth-Gamul and to Beth-Maon and to Kerioth and to
Bozrah and to all the towns of Moab, far and near.

25   The horn of Moab is hacked down
          and his arm is broken, said the LORD.
26   Make him drunk, for over the LORD he vaunted,
          and Moab shall dabble in his vomit
          and he, too, shall become a mockery.
27   For was not Israel a mockery to you?
          Was he found among the thieves,
          for as you spoke against him, you shook your head?
28   Leave the towns and dwell among the rocks,
          O dwellers of Moab,
      and be like the dove that nests
          on the brink of a pit.
29   We have heard the pride of Moab,
          very proud,
      his haughtiness, headstrong, his pride,
          and his overweening heart.

---

25. *The horn of Moab.* As almost everywhere in biblical poetry, "horn" is an epithet for "strength," an idiom deriving from the goring power of a bull or ram. "Arm" in the second verset is equally a term for strength, though one that comes from human anatomy.

26. *dabble in his vomit.* The Hebrew verb usually means "to clap" and so here probably means to "dabble" or "splash about."

   he, too. It should be noted that Moab is referred to sometimes as a masculine agent, because the noun is masculine, and sometimes in the feminine, because lands are imagined as women. Such gender switching is fairly common in biblical poetry.

27. *For was not Israel a mockery to you?* Here, "Israel" probably means the northern kingdom. Moab mocked it when the Assyrians destroyed it, but now the same fate has overtaken Moab.

   Was he found among the thieves. Moab treated Israel as though it were a criminal who deserved what had befallen it.

   for as you spoke against him. The literal sense of the Hebrew is "for as your words against him." Either *devareykha,* "your words," should be emended to *dabrekha,* "your speaking," or it may simply have the same sense as *dabrekha.*

   you shook your head. This is a gesture of mockery.

29. *his haughtiness, headstrong, his pride.* The Hebrew makes the point emphatic through strong alliteration: *govho uge'ono wega'awato.* This translation reproduces only two-

I know, said the LORD, his rage and his lies are not right, not right have 30
they done. Therefore over Moab I wail, and over all Moab I cry out, for the 31
men of Kir-Heres I moan.

> More than the weeping for Jazer I weep for you,   32
>   O vine of Sibmah.
> Your branches passed over the sea,
>   to the sea, to Jazer they reached.
> On your summer fruit and on your vintage
>   the ravager has fallen.
> And joy and gladness are taken away   33
>   from the farmland, from the land of Moab,
> and wine from the presses I made cease,
>   none treads with a shout,
>   the shout is no shout.

From Heshbon's cry to Eleaheh to Jahaz they raised their voices, from Zoar 34
to Horonaim, Eglath-Shelishiah, for the waters of Nimrim have become
a desolation. And I have caused to cease for Moab, said the LORD, offer- 35
ing up on the high places and burning incense to his gods. Therefore My 36
heart moans for Moab like pipes and, for the men of Kir-Heres like pipes
it moans, for the abundance they made—it has vanished.

---

thirds of the alliteration. A more literal rendering is: his haughtiness and his arrogance
and his pride.

30. *his lies are not right, not right have they done.* The Hebrew syntax is obscure and the
meaning far from certain.

32. *Your branches passed over the sea.* Given that Moab is in the trans-Jordanian region,
the sea would be the Dead Sea.

33. *none treads with a shout, / the shout is not a shout.* The shout in question, *heydad,* is the
rhythmic shout or perhaps chant that the grape-treaders call out as they trample the grapes.
This would be a joyous shout, but here there is no vintage, and either no one shouts (first
verset), or there is no shout of joy (second verset).

36. *like pipes.* Most translations represent this as "flutes," but the term refers to a shepherd's
simple wooden pipes, which emit a rustic, piercing sound.
    for the abundance they made—it has vanished. The Hebrew text here looks defective, so
the translation is merely a guess.

37   For every pate is shaved,
    and every beard is shorn,
on all the hands are gashes
    and over loins is sackcloth.

38 On all the roofs of Moab and in her squares all is lament, for I have broken
39 Moab like an unwanted vessel, said the LORD. How she is shattered! O, wail!
How Moab has turned its back in shame, and Moab has become a mockery
40 and a fright, said the LORD. For thus said the LORD,

    Look, like an eagle he soars,
        and spreads his wings against Moab.
41   Kerioth is captured
        and the strongholds are seized,
    and the heart of Moab's warriors on that day
        is like the heart of a woman in pangs.
42   And Moab is destroyed as a people,
        for it vaunted over the LORD.
43   Terror and pitfall and trap
        against you, O dweller of Moab, said the LORD.
44   Who flees from the terror
        shall fall into the pit,
    and who gets up from the pit
        shall be caught in the trap.
    For I will bring against her, against Moab,
        the year of their reckoning, said the LORD.
45   In the shadow of Heshbon they stopped,
        those fleeing without strength,
    for fire has come out from Heshbon

---

37. *For every pate is shaved, / and every beard is shorn, / on all the hands are gashes, / and over loins is sackcloth.* Every one of these items is a sign of mourning.

40. *like an eagle he soars.* The "he" is Nebuchadrezzar, whose armies are about to lay waste to Moab and the other trans-Jordanian kingdoms and then to Judah.

41. *the strongholds.* It is possible that the Hebrew *hametsudot* is a place-name.

43. *Terror and pitfall and trap.* This whole line of poetry, together with the next two, constitutes a direct citation of Isaiah 24:17–18. The Hebrew exhibits rich alliterative wordplay only faintly mirrored in the single alliteration of this translation (*paḥad wafaḥat wafaḥ*).

and a flame from within Sihon,
and consumed the brow of Moab
and the pate of the raucous ones.
Woe to you, O Moab,   46
Chemosh's people has perished.
For your sons are taken captive
and your daughters are in captive state.
But I will restore the fortunes of Moab   47
in the days after, said the LORD.
Thus far the judgment of Moab.

CHAPTER 49   Concerning the Ammonites, thus said the   1
LORD:

Does Israel have no sons,
does he have no heir?
Why has Milcom dispossessed Gad,
and his people has dwelled in Gad's towns?
Therefore days are coming, said the LORD,   2

---

45. *from within Sihon.* This appears to be what the Hebrew text says. But it is possible that the preposition *mibeyn* simply reflects a scribal reversal of consonants and that the original word was *mibeney,* "from the sons of."

46. *Chemosh's people.* Chemosh being the tutelary god of Moab, "Chemosh's people" is a poetic epithet—situated in the second verset, as such epithets almost invariably are—for the Moabites.

47. *But I will restore the fortunes of Moab.* It may seem a bit odd that Jeremiah would stipulate restoration for this traditional enemy of his people. Some scholars say that such stipulation at the end of a prophecy of destruction is more or less formulaic, but Jeremiah may have in mind a geopolitical consideration: if the Babylonian conquest of Judah is eventually to be reversed and the kingdom of Judah reestablished, such restoration would also be extended to Judah's neighbors to the immediate east.

CHAPTER 49   1. *Does Israel have no sons, / does he have no heir?* The line is clearly framed on the legal assumption of the patriarchal society that it is the sons who inherit from the father. But it also plays on the other meaning of the verb *yarash,* which is "to take hold of," as in conquest.
Milcom. He is the patron god of Ammon. The Masoretic Text reads *malkam,* "their king," but three ancient versions show "Milcom," and most modern scholars concur that this is the correct reading.

when I will make Rabbah of the Ammonites hear
    the trumpet blast of war,
and she shall become a desolate heap,
    and her villages shall be burned in fire,
and Israel shall dispossess those who dispossessed her
    —said the LORD.

3   Wail, O Heshbon, for Ai has been ravaged,
    scream, O daughters of Rabbah,
gird sackcloth and lament,
    and run about among the sheep pens,
for Milcom shall go into exile,
    his priests and his nobles together.

4   Why should you boast of the valleys?
    —Your valley oozes sickly, wayward daughter
who trusts in her treasures:
    "Who can come against me?"

5   I am about to bring upon you terror
    —said the Master, LORD of Armies—
from all sides round you,
and you shall be dispossessed, each before him,
    with none taking in the wanderer.

---

2. *Rabbah of the Ammonites*. This capital city stood on the site of present-day Amman, and all of the foreign nations mentioned in this chapter are trans-Jordanian kingdoms, with the exception of Elam, which is in Persia.

her villages. Though the literal sense of the Hebrew is "her daughters," this is a term regularly used for the small outlying towns or hamlets in the vicinity of a city, and the city itself is sometimes given the epithet of "mother."

3. *daughters of Rabbah*. In this instance, "daughters" must refer to the young women of the city, who take up the role of keening women, wailing and lamenting.

for Milcom shall go into exile. As in verse 1, the Masoretic Text has *malkam*, "their king."

4. *Your valley oozes sickly*. The claim of some scholars that ʿemeq, "valley," either here or in the preceding verset, means "strength," is far-fetched. The Ammonites took pride in their fertile valleys (first verset). Now, however, the valley "flows" or "oozes," *zav*. While this verb is the one that is used in the recurrent phrase "a land flowing with milk and honey," it is also used for suppurations of the body, and that is the more likely sense here, because what the context suggests is a contrast between the valley about which the Ammonites once boasted and its present woeful state.

5. *the wanderer*. Here and below, this term is used as a loose synonym for an "exile" or "fugitive."

And afterward I will restore the fortunes of the Ammonites,   6
said the LORD.

Concerning Edom. Thus said the LORD of Armies: 7
    Is there no longer wisdom in Teman?
        Counsel is lost to the discerning,
            their wisdom is brought down.
Flee, turn round, sit low,   8
    O dwellers of Dedan!
For Esau's disaster have I brought upon him,
    the time when I reckon with him.
If grape harvesters came to you,   9
    would they not leave gleanings?
If thieves in the night,
    they would despoil just what they need.
For I have stripped Esau,   10
    have laid bare his hidden places,
and he cannot be concealed,
    his seed and brothers are ravaged
        and his neighbors—he is no more.
Leave your orphans with me, I will sustain them,   11
    and your widows, rely on me!

---

6. *I will restore the fortunes of the Ammonites.* See the comment on 48:47.

7. *Teman.* This place-name also means "south." A tradition going back to Late Antiquity locates it near Petra in present-day Jordan, but the precise identification remains uncertain.

8. *sit low.* The odd phrasing of the Hebrew is, literally, "deepen sitting." The likely reference is sitting or living (the verb means both) in a lowly, humble condition.
    Esau's disaster. Esau is the purported founding father of the people of Edom.

9. *would they not leave gleanings? / . . . they would despoil just what they need.* In the normal order of things, grape harvesters leave some small grapes, and even thieves (the second verset is a kind of *a fortiori*) leave behind what they cannot use. Edom's condition, on the other hand, will be grimmer, for the ravaging invader will take everything. In point of historical fact, Edom allied itself with the Babylonian invaders (see Psalm 137), and only two decades later would it become the target of a Babylonian assault.

11. *I will sustain them.* Literally, "I will make them live."

12 For thus said the LORD, "Look, those who are not wont to drink the cup will surely drink, and as for you, you shall not go scot free, you shall not go
13 scot-free, for you surely shall drink. For by Myself do I vow, said the LORD, that a desolation, a disgrace, a ruin, and a curse shall be Bosra, and all its towns shall be everlasting ruins."

14   A report I have heard from the LORD,
             and an envoy among the nations is sent:
         Gather and come against her
             and rise up for battle.
15   For, look, I have made you least among the nations,
             spurned by humankind
16   The horror you imposed deceived you,
             the arrogance of your heart.
         Dweller in crevices of the rock,
             who seizes the height of the hill,
         though you raise high your nest like the eagle,
             from there I will bring you down, said the LORD.

17 And Edom shall become a desolation. All who pass by her shall be shocked
18 and hiss at her blows. Like the overturning of Sodom and Gomorrah and its neighbors, said the LORD, no man shall dwell there and no human being sojourn within her.

---

12. *those who are not wont to drink the cup.* The cup in question is the cup of poison or destruction, so the reference is to a people that had been accustomed to live in security.

14. *an envoy among the nations is sent.* The most likely identity of the envoy is the prophet himself, here bringing this message of doom to the sundry nations east of Judah.

15. *I have made you least among the nations.* "You" is Edom.

16. *The horror you imposed deceived you.* The Hebrew simply says "your horror deceived you." Though other interpretations have been proposed, this translation assumes that the reference is to the fear that a once powerful Edom inspired in its neighbors and hence "you imposed" has been added by way of clarification.
    Dweller in crevices of the rock, / who seizes the height of the hill. The Edomites were prone to take strategic advantage of the rocky mountainous terrain around their towns. These elevated military positions, however, will not avail against the devastating force of the invaders: "though you raise high your nest like the eagle, / from there I will bring you down."

18. *no man shall dwell there and no human being sojourn within her.* Jeremiah's prophecies of doom make abundant use of stereotypical phrases such as this one.

> Look, as a lion comes up   19
>   from the Jordan's thicket to a secure pasture,
> so in a flash I will rush him off from her,
>   and who is the young man I could appoint over her,
> for who is like Me, who can fix a time for Me,
>   who the shepherd that can stand against Me?
> Therefore hear the counsel of the LORD   20
>   that He conceived against Edom
> and the plans that He devised
>   against the dwellers of Teman—
> they shall surely drag them off, the young of the flock,
>   they shall surely desolate their pastures.
> From the sound of their falling the earth shook   21
>   the sound of a scream at the Reed Sea was heard.

Look, as the eagle goes up and soars and spreads its wings over Bosra, the 22 heart of the warriors of Edom on that day shall be like the heart of a woman in travail.

> Concerning Damascus.   23
>   Be shamed, Hamath and Arpad,
>   for an evil report they have heard.
> They quailed in a sea of unease,
>   they cannot be quiet.
> Damascus has gone slack,   24
>   turned back to flee,

---

19. *I will rush him off from her.* The received text here is puzzling because what is envisaged is someone attacking Edom. It is possible that the "him" refers to the fleeing inhabitant of Edom, but it may be more likely that the initial *mem* of the preposition here is a scribal error and that one should read *'aleyha*, "against her."

who is the young man I could appoint over her. This somewhat obscure formulation, in light of what is said in the next line, may mean: what able-bodied man could I appoint to take charge of the conquest of Edom when I Myself will do it?

the shepherd. As repeatedly elsewhere, this is an epithet for the king.

23. *Concerning Damascus.* The prophecies against the nations now move northward to Syria and its capital, Damascus.

a sea of unease. The Masoretic Text shows a syntactically problematic reading: *bayam de'agah*, "in the sea unease." This translation revocalizes the first word as *beyam*, yielding a construct state between the two nouns, "a sea of unease."

and trembling has seized her,
  distress and pangs gripped her like a woman in labor.
25   "How is the city of praise forsaken,
  the town of my joy!"

26 Therefore shall her young men fall in her streets and all the men of war shall be silent on that day, said the LORD of Armies.

27   And I will light a fire in the wall of Damascus,
    and it shall consume the citadels of Ben-Hadad.

28 Concerning Kedar and the kingdom of Hazor that Nebuchadrezzar king of Babylonia struck down, thus said the LORD:

      Arise, go up to Kedar,
    and ravage the Easterners.
29   Their tents and their flocks shall be taken,
    their curtains and all their gear.
    And their camels they shall bear off for themselves,
    and they shall call them: Terror All Round.
30   Flee, wander far, sit low,
    O dwellers of Hazor, said the LORD.

---

25. *How is the city of praise forsaken, / the town of my joy!* This is best construed as the quotation of a lament (the initial "how is" is the formula for beginning a lament) spoken by an inhabitant of Damascus. It is such a person who would call it "the city of praise," "the town of my joy." It should be noted that the verb "forsaken" in the Hebrew is preceded by *lo'*, which usually means "no" or "not" but here functions as a marker of emphasis, as it does in rhetorical questions (is it not . . . ?).

27. *Ben-Hadad.* This is a hereditary name for the kings of Syria.

28. *Kedar.* This is an umbrella term for nomadic tribes to the southeast of ancient Israel, perhaps extending as far as the Arabian peninsula. The nomadic character of this population is signaled in the next verse in the reference to "tents," "flocks," and "curtains" (that is, tent curtains).

29. *And their camels they shall bear off for themselves.* This verset and the next exhibit the fluidity of pronominal reference that often characterizes biblical Hebrew. The antecedent of the initial "their" has to be the peoples of Kedar, whereas "they shall bear off for themselves" must refer to the Babylonian troops who seize the camels of Kedar as booty.

For Nebuchadrezzar king of Babylonia has conceived counsel against you,
    and devised plans against you.
Arise, go up against a tranquil nation   31
    dwelling safely, said the LORD.
No double doors nor bolt he has,
    Alone do they dwell.
And their camels shall become spoil,   32
    and their crowd of cattle become booty.
And I will scatter them to every wind,
    the men of cropped hair,
        and from all sides I will bring their disaster
            —said the LORD.
And Hazor shall become a jackals' den,   33
    an everlasting desolation.
No man shall dwell there,
    and no human being sojourn within her.

Which was the word of the LORD to Jeremiah the prophet at the beginning of 34
the kingship of Zedekiah king of Judah, saying,

"Thus said the LORD of Armies: I am about to break the bow of Elam, the   35
prime of their valor. And I will bring against Elam four winds from the four 36
corners of the heavens and I will scatter them to all these winds, and there
shall be no nation where the dispersed of Elam will not go.

And I will shatter Elam before their enemies   37
    and before those who seek their life,
and I will bring harm upon them,
    My smoldering wrath, said the LORD.
And I will send the sword after them
    until I make an end of them.

---

31. *Arise, go up against a tranquil nation.* The preceding imperative to flee was addressed to the inhabitants of Hazor. The present command, however, must be to the Babylonian forces, urging them to attack this people that had before been secure and had not felt the necessity to protect itself with bolted doors in its city walls.

35. *I am about to break the bow of Elam.* Some ancient sources indicate that the Elamites were renowned archers.

38   And I will set My throne in Elam
          and destroy from there king and nobles, said the Lord.

39   And it will happen in the days after
          that I will restore the fortunes of Elam."

1   **CHAPTER 50**   The word that the Lord spoke concerning Babylonia, concerning the land of the Chaldeans, through Jeremiah the prophet.

2   Tell among the nations and make it heard,
          and raise a banner, make it heard, do not conceal it.
       Say: Babylonia is captured, Bel is shamed, Merodach shattered.
          Her idols are shamed, her foul things shattered.

3   For a nation from the north has gone up against her,
          and it shall make her land a desolation,
       and there shall be no dweller in it,
          from man to beast, they shall wander, go off.

4   In those days and in that time, said the Lord,
          the Israelites and the Judahites shall come together,
       weeping as they walk shall they go,

---

38. *I will set My throne in Elam.* The formulation is unusual. God will depose the king and nobles of Elam (second verset) and reign there instead. The theological idea behind this line is that God is the ruler of all nations, determining their fate, so that if He decides to destroy faraway Elam, He Himself will be king there, as He is king of all the earth.

39. *And it will happen in the days after / that I will restore the fortunes of Elam.* As with the other prophecies concerning the sundry nations, the prediction of doom concludes with this stereotypical pronouncement about a future restoration. History is a continual cycle of conquests and devastations, but in the course of events, most nations are not obliterated, only ravaged and then eventually restored.

CHAPTER 50   2. *Bel . . . Merodach.* There are two names for the patron deity of Babylonia. The latter also appears as "Marduk."
    her foul things. As elsewhere in biblical usage, *gilulim* is a deliberately insulting epithet for "idols" that invokes *gelalim,* "turds."

3. *a nation from the north.* Babylonia's traditional enemies—most recently, the Assyrian empire, which it conquered—came from the north, so this is neither a prediction nor a late reflection of Persia's successful assault on Babylonia half a century after Jeremiah.

4. *the Israelites and the Judahites shall come together.* This is another moment when Jeremiah cherishes the idea of a restored Israel reunited with a restored Judah, though by his

and the LORD their God they shall seek.
Zion shall they ask, 5
    their faces turned this way.
"Come!" and they shall join the LORD
    in an everlasting covenant never forgotten.
Lost sheep my people were. 6
    Their shepherds led them astray.
To the mountains they led them astray,
    quick to the hills they went,
        they forgot their resting place.
All who found them devoured them, 7
    and their foes said, "We bear no guilt
as they offended the LORD,
    the righteous pasture and their father's hope, the LORD."
Wander from the midst of Babylon 8
    and from the land of the Chaldeans.
They shall go out and become like he-goats
    before the flock.
For I am about to rouse and bring up against Babylonia 9
    an assembly of great nations from the land of the north,

---

own time, a century and a half after the destruction of the northern kingdom of Israel by the Assyrians, scant trace of it remained.

weeping as they walk. This is a very different picture of the return to Zion from the one in the prophecies of Second Isaiah, where the returning exiles are jubilant and triumphant. Here, they weep because they have been shattered by the experience of exile, and they are even uncertain about how to get back to Zion, asking for directions (verse 5).

5. *"Come!" and they shall join the LORD.* The Syriac reads somewhat more smoothly, "Come, and let us join the Lord."

6. *To the mountains they led them astray, / quick to the hills they went.* The probable reference is to sites in the mountains and hills where they worshipped nature gods, led by false leaders ("shepherds").

their resting place. The Hebrew noun is a term for the place where animals bed down and so continues the metaphor of the people as lost sheep.

7. *All who found them devoured them.* Sheep wandering over the hills with no proper shepherd would be vulnerable to predators.

8. *Wander from the midst of Babylon.* The prophet exhorts the inhabitants of Babylonia to flee before the arrival of the murderous invaders. The Hebrew *bavel* can refer either to the country, Babylonia, or to its principal city, Babylon, and the latter sense is perhaps more likely here.

and they shall array against her, from there she shall be captured.
His arrows like those of a death-dealing warrior,
he does not turn back empty.

10 And the Chaldeans shall become spoil,
all their despoilers shall be sated, said the LORD.

11 For you rejoiced, for you exulted,
O plunderers of My estate.
For you stomped like a heifer threshing,
and you neighed like stallions.

12 Your mother is greatly shamed,
she who bore you is disgraced.
Look, the last among nations—
wilderness, parched land, and desert.

13 Because of the LORD's fury she shall not be settled,
and all of her shall be a desolation.
All who pass by Babylonia shall be shocked
and hiss at all her blows.

14 Array against Babylonia all round,
all who bend the bow.
Shoot at her, spare no arrow,
for she has offended against the LORD.

15 Shout against her all around.
She gave up, her bastions have fallen,
her walls have been destroyed.
For the LORD's vengeance it is, take vengeance of her,
as she did to you, do to her.

16 Cut off the sower from Babylonia
and the sickle wielder in harvesttime.
From the oppressive sword

---

9. *a death-dealing warrior.* The Hebrew *mashkil,* unusual in this conjugation, literally means "causing bereavement." Some Hebrew manuscripts and three ancient versions read *maskil,* "cunning."

12. *the last among nations.* The phrase *'aḥarit goyim* plays antithetically on the more common collocation, *re'shit goyim,* "first among nations." Babylonia's standing has been entirely reversed.

15. *She gave up.* The literal sense is "she gave her hand," but since "hand" often means "power," giving up is the likely meaning.

            each man shall turn to his people
                and each man shall flee to his land.
        Israel is a scattered flock—   17
            lions have harried him.

First the king of Assyria devoured him and then the last one, Nebuchadrezzar king of Babylonia, crunched his bones. Therefore, thus said the LORD   18
of Armies, God of Israel: I am about to reckon with the king of Babylonia
and with his land as I reckoned with the king of Assyria.

        And I will bring back Israel to his pasture,   19
            and he shall graze on Carmel and in Bashan,
                and on Mount Ephraim and in Gilead he shall be sated.
        In those days and in that time, said the LORD,   20
            Israel's crime shall be sought and it shall be gone,
                and Judah's offenses—and they shall not be found.
            For I will forgive those I let remain.

        Against the land of Merathaim,   21
            go up against her.
        And against the dwellers at Pekod,
            ruin and utterly destroy them
                said the LORD,
            and do as all I have charged you.
        Hark! War is in the land   22
            and a great shattering.
        How hacked and broken   23
            is the hammer of all the earth.
        How become a desolation
            Babylonia among the nations.

---

16. *each man shall turn to his people.* The evident assumption is that there was a multiethnic
population in Babylonia, whether through immigration or the attachment of mercenaries
to the army.

21. *the land of Merathaim / . . . the dwellers at Pekod.* Although these are actual regions of
Babylonia, the prophet is also clearly playing on the seeming echoes in the names of Hebrew
words: Merathaim could suggest to the Hebrew ear either "rebellion" or "bitterness" and
Pekod, "reckoning."

23. *the hammer of all the earth.* In all likelihood this is an epithet for the mighty Babylonian
emperor. Jeremiah would have been thinking of Nebuchadrezzar.

24 I laid a snare for you and you were captured,
        O Babylonia, and you did not know.
    You were found and also caught,
        for you provoked the LORD.

25 The LORD opened his armory
        and brought out the weapons of His wrath,
    for the LORD of Armies has a task
        in the land of the Chaldeans.

26 Come against her from all sides,
        open her granaries.
    Pile her up like heaps and utterly destroy her.
        Let her have no remnant.

27 Put all her bulls to the sword,
        let her go down to the slaughter.
    Woe to them, for their day has come,
        the time of their reckoning.

28 Hark! The fugitives flee
        from the land of Babylonia
    to tell in Zion
        the vengeance of the LORD our God,
            the vengeance for his people.

29 Summon archers against Babylonia
        all who bend the bow.
    Camp against her all around,
        let her have no fugitives.
    Pay her back for her acts,
        as all that she did, do to her,
    for she was arrogant toward the LORD
        toward Israel's Holy One.

---

25. *The LORD opened his armory.* At several points in biblical poetry, a virtually mythic image occurs of YHWH as a warrior-god with a storehouse of weapons in the sky saved for a cosmic battle.

for the LORD of Armies has a task / in the land of the Chaldeans. This is a striking instance in which instead of the usual semantic parallelism in the second half of the line of poetry, a surprise is sprung. The word "task" in itself might seem innocuous, but when it is followed by "in the land of the Chaldeans," and after the mention of weapons of wrath, the task turns out to be a grim mission of destruction throughout Babylonia.

28. *to tell in Zion / the vengeance of the LORD.* This is a piquant fantasy of revenge. Not only do the inhabitants of Babylonia flee as their kingdom falls, but they flee to Zion, where they can bear witness before the Judahites of the full extent of vengeance God has exacted from those who destroyed His temple.

Therefore shall her young men fall in her squares, and all her men of war 30
shall be silent on that day, said the LORD.

Here I am against you. Arrogance,   31
    said the Master, LORD of Armies.
For your day has come,
    the time when I reckon with you.
And Arrogance shall stumble and fall,   32
    with none to raise him up,
and I will light a fire in his towns
    and it shall consume all round him.

Thus said the LORD of Armies: 33

The Israelites were oppressed
    and the Judahites, together,
and all their captors held on to them,
    refused to set them free.
Their redeemer is strong,   34
    the LORD of Armies is His name.
He shall surely take up their cause
    so as to bring quiet to the land
        and make the dwellers of Babylonia quake.
A sword against the Chaldeans, said the LORD,   35
    and against Babylonia's dwellers
        and against her nobles and her sages.
A sword against the soothsayers, exposed as fools.   36
    A sword against her warriors, that they be shattered.
A sword against her horses and her chariots.   37

---

31. *Here I am against you. Arrogance.* The poem now moves into a quasi-allegorical mode. Babylonia, or perhaps its king, is represented as the very personification of arrogance.

34. *Their redeemer is strong.* Despite the salvific resonance of the English noun "redeemer," *go'el* is less a theological term than a legal term. The *go'el* is the kinsman who sets right a wrong that has been done to one of his close relatives. Its very use implies a kind of kinship between God and Israel.

35. *A sword against the Chaldeans.* In a rhetorical move relatively rare in biblical poetry, this prophecy builds on an insistent anaphora, virtually every line beginning with "A sword against . . ." The effect is to powerfully convey a sense of the inexorable, comprehensive destruction that is about to sweep over Babylonia.

A sword against the mixed race in her midst,
   that they turn into women.
A sword against her treasures,
   that they be looted.

38   A drought against her waters, that they dry up,
        for she is a land of idols,
           and through the gods they fear, they madden.

39   Therefore wildcats and hyenas shall dwell there,
        and ostriches shall dwell within her,
     and she shall be uninhabited forever,
        and shall not be settled for all time.

40   Like God's overturning of Sodom
        and Gomorrah and its neighbors, said the LORD.
     No man shall dwell there
        and no human sojourn in her.

41   Look, a people is coming from the north,
        a great nation,
     and many kings shall be roused
        from the far corners of the earth.

42   Bow and lance they wield,
        they are cruel and show no mercy.
     Their voice roars like the sea,
        and on horses they do ride,

---

38. *A drought against her waters.* The Hebrew for "drought" here is *ḥorev,* which, as many commentators have observed, puns on *ḥerev,* "sword." A sword, of course, would be an odd weapon to use against water, hence the punning substitution of "drought."

   and through the gods they fear, they madden. The Hebrew says merely "the terrors," though the firm consensus of interpreters, medieval and modern, is that the reference is to their deities—hence "gods" in the translation. (One epithet for God in Genesis is "Fear of Isaac"). The maddening may be their behavior in ecstatic pagan rites, as some medieval commentators have proposed, or it could mean that they become wildly distraught in the crisis of destruction because their gods can in no way help them.

39. *wildcats and hyenas.* All that is certain about the identity of these two groups of beasts is that they are indigenous to wasteland terrain.

41. *from the far corners of the earth.* In the geographical perspective of the ancient Hebrews— which encompasses India but nothing as distant as the Far East—the lands to the north of the Mesopotamian valley qualify as "the far corners of the earth."

42. *and on horses they do ride.* The detail about mounted troops adds to the general sense of terrific clamor and speed in the attacking army, and the horses may have been especially scary to an Israelite audience whose armies were thin in cavalry.

arrayed as one man for battle—
    against you, Daughter of Babylonia.
Babylonia's king heard the report of them,   43
    and his hands went slack.
A pang seized him,
    travail like a woman in labor.
Look, as a lion comes up   44
    from the Jordan's thicket to a secure pasture,
so in a flash I will rush him off from her,
    and who is the young man I could appoint over her,
        for who is like Me, who can fix a time for Me?
Therefore hear the counsel of the LORD   45
    that He conceived against Babylonia
and the plans that He devised against the land of the Chaldeans—
    they shall surely drag them off, the young men of the flock,
        they shall surely desolate their pastures.
And from the sound of "Babylonia is captured" the earth shook,   46
    and a scream was heard in the nations.

CHAPTER 51

Thus said the LORD: 1

I am about to rouse against Babylonia
    and against the dwellers of Leb-Kamai
        a destroying wind.

44–45. *Look, as a lion comes up.* These two verses approximately replicate 49:19–20. See the comments on those verses.

46. *the sound of "Babylonia is captured."* The two Hebrew words that immediately follow "the sound" (or "the sound of") are most plausibly understood as the words cried out when the realization of Babylonia's defeat is grasped (hence the quotation marks in the translation). This is how Lundbom understands it. All are dumbfounded, or perhaps aghast, at the fall of the powerful empire—hence all the earth shakes, the outcry is heard among all the nations.

CHAPTER 51   1. *Leb-Kamai.* This ostensible name is actually a cipher for Chaldea based on the simple system of substituting the last letter of the alphabet for the first, the second-to-last letter for the second, and so forth. The same cipher is manifested in verse 41, where "Sheshak" stands in for *Bavel,* "Babylon." No one has satisfactorily explained why

2   And I will send strangers to Babylonia and they shall scatter her,
          and they shall devastate her land,
      for they are all around against her
          on an evil day.
3   Let not the bowman bend his bow,
          and let him not put on his armor,
      and spare not her young men.
          Utterly destroy all her army.
4   And the slain shall fall in the Chaldeans' land,
          and the ones run through in her streets.
5   For Israel and Judah are not widowed
          of their God, the LORD of Armies,
      but their land was filled with guilt
          before Israel's Holy One.
6   Flee from the midst of Babylonia;
          each man, save your life,
              do not be wiped out through her crime.
      For it is vengeance time for the LORD,
          requital He pays back to her.
7   A golden cup was Babylonia in the LORD's hand

---

ciphers should be used in a text that, after all, constantly refers to Babylonia and Chaldea by their actual names.

3. *Let not the bowman . . . / let him not put on.* The Masoretic Text has a puzzling vocalization of the initial word in these clauses, *'el,* "to," but many Hebrew manuscripts and several ancient versions show *'al,* "let not." The idea is that resistance on the part of the Babylonians is futile.
   and spare not her young men. This clause equally begins with *'al,* but the verb now is second-person plural, so the prophecy turns from the Babylonians to their attackers.

5. *For Israel and Judah are not widowed.* The Hebrew *'alman*—this masculine form appears only here, although the feminine *'almanah,* "widow," is very common—should be construed as an adjective. That is, Israel is the bride and God the husband, as in Jeremiah's opening prophecy in chapter 1. The masculine form is dictated by the fact that either "Israel" or "Judah" can be treated as a masculine noun.

6. *Flee from the midst of Babylonia.* While some interpreters understand this imperative differently, it is probably an injunction to the exiles to flee the land of their captivity as it is about to be devastated.
   each man, save your life. Though the Hebrew actually says "his life," the imperative verb requires the second person for idiomatic coherence in English.

7. *A golden cup was Babylonia.* The gold, as many commentators have noted, invokes Babylonia's fabled wealth.

making all the earth drunk.
From her cup the nations drank,
 and so the nations maddened.
Of a sudden Babylonia fell and was broken.   8
 Wail over her.
Take balm for her hurt,
 perhaps she will be healed.
We sought to heal Babylonia but she was not healed.   9
 Leave her, and let us go each to his land.
For her judgment has touched the heavens,
 and mounted to the sky.
The LORD has brought forth our just cause.   10
 Come and recount in Zion
  the deed of the LORD our God.
Hone the arrows,   11
 fill the quivers!
The LORD has roused the spirit of the kings of Media
 for His design is against Babylonia to destroy it,
for it is the vengeance of the LORD
 the vengeance for His temple.
Against the walls of Babylon raise a banner,   12
 reinforce the watch,
set out the watchmen,
 ready the ambushers.
For the LORD has devised and also done
 that which He spoke for Babylon's dwellers.
You who settle by many waters,   13

---

making all the earth drunk. The contents of the golden cup are evidently terrifying—Babylonia has delivered a cup of the wine of destruction to the nations, driving them into a frenzy.

8. *Take balm for her hurt.* As the next verse makes clear, this is ironic.

11. *the vengeance for His temple.* This is a recurring note in Jeremiah. Although Babylonia may have served as God's instrument in punishing Judah, it bears the indelible guilt of having destroyed God's own house, and for this it will pay a severe price.

12. *the walls of Babylon.* As elsewhere, this translation distinguishes between Babylonia, the nation, and Babylon, the city. Given the reference to the city walls here, "Babylon" seems more appropriate. The Hebrew *Bavel* can mean either.

13. *many waters.* Babylon was located on the banks of the Euphrates, and also had canals and smaller streams as well as an artificial lake.

    abundant in treasures,
  your end has come,
    the measure for your ill-gotten wealth.

14 The LORD of Armies has sworn by Himself:
  I will surely fill you with people like locusts,
    and they shall raise a joyous shout over you.

15 Who makes the earth through His power,
  firmly founds the world through His wisdom,
    and through His discernment stretches out the heavens.

16 When He sounds His voice—the roar of waters in the heavens,
  and He brings up the clouds from the end of the earth.
Lightning for the rain He has made,
  and He brings forth the wind from His treasure stores.

17 Every human is ignorant without knowledge,
  every goldsmith is shamed by his idol,
for his molten image is false,
  no breath is in them.

18 They are emptiness, work of delusion,
  at the time of their reckoning they shall perish.

19 Not like these is Jacob's Portion,
  for He fashions everything,
and Israel is the tribe of His estate—
  the LORD of Armies is His name.

20 You were a mace for Me,
  weapons of battle,
and I smashed nations with you
  and laid waste kingdoms with you.

---

your ill-gotten wealth. The Hebrew *betsa'* has the literal sense of "slice" or "cut" but strongly suggests illegitimate profits.

14. *a joyous shout.* This is the cry *heydad* called out or chanted by grape-treaders. Here it is the invading armies treading on the Babylonians in a harvest of blood.

16. *the roar of waters.* One should keep in mind that in the Hebrew cosmology, there are waters above the visible "slab," *raqi'a,* of the sky, and when it rains, as in the Flood story, they come down through the open casements of the heavens.

19. *Jacob's Portion.* This is an ad hoc epithet for God, stressing His intimate connection with Israel.

20. *You were a mace for Me.* Elsewhere in Prophetic poetry, powerful empires figure as God's "rod," but here that metaphor is intensified in the image of the smashing battle-mace.

And I smashed with you horse and rider   21
   and smashed with you chariot and its rider.
And I smashed with you man and woman   22
   and smashed with you elder and lad
      and smashed with you young man and virgin.
And I smashed with you shepherd and his flock   23
   and smashed with you farmer and his team,
      and smashed with you satraps and prefects.
And I will pay back Babylonia   24
   and all the dwellers of Chaldea
for their evil that they did
   in Zion before your eyes, said the LORD.
Here I am against you, a destroying mountain   25
   —said the LORD—
      that destroys all the earth,
and I will stretch out My hand against you
   and roll you down from the crags
      and make you a burnt-out mountain.
And they shall not take from you a cornerstone   26
   nor a stone for the foundations,
      for you shall be an everlasting desolation, said the LORD.
Raise a banner on the earth,   27
   sound the ram's horn in the nations.
Marshal nations against her,
assemble kingdoms against her,
   Ararat, Minni, and Ashkenaz.

---

21. *horse and rider / . . . chariot and its rider.* These phrases are a reminiscence of the Song of the Sea (Exodus 15), in which Pharaoh's horses and riders are destroyed by God.

23. *shepherd . . . / farmer . . . / satraps and prefects.* The swathe of destruction perpetrated by the Babylonian king swept all the way from ordinary peasants to high government officials.

25. *a destroying mountain.* Though the image of an inert mountain as an agent of destruction may seem a little strange, the mountain is meant to invoke the massive solidity and towering stature of the Babylonian empire.
   a burnt-out mountain. This seems to imply that the "destroying mountain" was a volcano—now extinct.

26. *And they shall not take from you a cornerstone.* The rocky mountain is useless even as a quarry for building stones.

27. *Ararat, Minni, and Ashkenaz.* These are kingdoms to the far north, in Asia Minor and

    Appoint against her an officer,
        bring up horses like locusts swarming.
28   Marshall nations against her,
        Media and her satraps and all her prefects
        and all the lands of their dominion.
29   And the earth shall shake and shudder,
        for the Lord's plan against Babylonia has risen,
    to turn the land of Babylonia
        into a desolation with no one dwelling.
30   The warriors of Babylonia have ceased fighting,
        they sit in the strongholds.
    Their valor is sapped, they turn into women.
        They have set fire to her dwellings,
           broken are her bolts.
31   Runner to meet runner dashes
        and herald to meet herald
    to tell to the king of Babylonia
        that his city is captured from end to end.
32   And the forces have been seized,
        and the marshes they have burned with fire,
           and the men of war are panicked.

33 For thus said the Lord of Armies, God of Israel:

    The Daughter of Babylonia is like a threshing floor when it is trod—
        in a little while her harvesttime shall come.

---

northwestern Iran. Ashkenaz would later be taken up as the designation for the lands where the Jews settled along the Rhine, although that of course is not its biblical meaning.

30. *they sit in the strongholds.* The clear implication is that they are afraid to go out to the battlefield.

31. *Runner to meet runner dashes / and herald to meet herald.* The dramatic effect of this structure of repetition is to convey a sense of frantic rushing to and fro by the messengers bringing news of the disaster that is engulfing Babylonia.

32. *the marshes they have burned with fire.* There were marshes along the Euphrates with bushes growing that could be set on fire by the invaders.

33. *in a little while her harvesttime shall come.* This second verset moves from a simile ("like a threshing floor," which is to say, stomped upon) to an implied but directly related metaphor: the harvesttime for Babylonia is the harvest of death and destruction.

Nebuchadrezzar king of Babylonia has devoured me, has stunned me,   34
    set me out like an empty vessel, swallowed me like the sea monster.
He has filled his belly with my delicacies,
    he has dispossessed me.
The outrage against me and my flesh be upon Bablyonia   35
    says the dweller of Zion,
and my blood be upon the dwellers of Chaldea,
    says Jerusalem.

Therefore thus said the LORD: 36

I am about to take up your cause
    and will exact vengeance for you,
and I will drain her sea
    and dry up her fount.
And Babylonia shall turn into heaps of ruins,   37
    a den of jackals,
desolation and target of hissing
    with no one dwelling.
Together they shall roar like lions,   38
    growl like lion cubs.
In their heat I will set out their drink   39

---

34. *Nebuchadrezzar king of Babylonia has devoured me.* The poem now switches from the report of Babylonia's destruction to the cry of dismay of Zion, devastated by the Babylonians and now eager to see the unfolding devastation of their hated enemies.

    sea monster. This is an allusion to the fearsome sea monster (*tanin*) of Canaanite mythology.

36. *take up your cause.* This is a frequently used idiom of legal advocacy.

    I will drain her sea / and dry up her fount. There is, of course, no actual sea in Babylonia, but the reference may be to its artificial lake. "Fount" appears to be a collective image for all the many water sources of Babylonia.

37. *target of hissing.* "Target" is merely implied.

38. *growl.* The Hebrew verb *na'ar* appears only here, but the parallelism compels a sense like "growl." In later Hebrew, this would be the verb used for a donkey's braying, but lions do not bray.

39. *In their heat.* There is debate about the reference of "heat," but the probable sense is sexual or quasisexual: they are filled with imperative desire for strong drink.

    and make them drunk so that they be merry. The drunken merriment proves to be illusory: the cup God offers them is lethal, as the next line of poetry spells out. What would ordinarily be a wine-induced slumber or stupor turns out to be the sleep of death.

and make them drunk so that they be merry,
   and they shall sleep an eternal sleep,
     and they shall not awake, said the LORD.

40 I will bring them down like lambs to the slaughter,
   and like rams with he-goats.

41 "How has Sheshak been taken and caught,
    the praise of all the earth!
How has she become a desolation,
   Babylonia among the nations.

42 The sea has gone up over Babylonia,
    in the surge of its waves she is covered.

43 Her towns have become a desolation,
   parched land and desert,
a land where no man dwells,
   and no human passes through it."

44 And I will reckon with the Daughter of Babylonia
   and take what she has swallowed from her mouth,
and nations shall no longer flow to her,
   the very wall of Babylon has fallen.

45 Go out from her midst, O my people,
   and each man, save your life
     from the smoldering wrath of the LORD.

46 And lest your heart quail and you fear for the rumor heard in the land, and the rumor shall come that year and afterward in the next year a rumor, and outrage is in the land, and ruler against ruler.

47   Therefore, look, days are coming

---

42. *The sea has gone up over Babylonia.* In verse 36, Babylonia's literal body of water was drained. Now, in what may be a deliberate poetic counterpoint, we have a metaphorical sea, representing Babylonia's enemies, which overwhelms the country. The metaphorical character of this sea of invaders is underscored in the next verse when the whole country is turned into "parched land and desert."

44. *and take what she has swallowed from her mouth.* The clear implied image is of Babylonia as a beast of prey. "What she has swallowed" would be both the captive Judahites and the temple treasures that the Babylonians looted and brought back to their land.

45. *each man, save your life.* See the comment on verse 6.

46. *the rumor shall come that year and afterward in the next year a rumor.* The repetitive structure conveys a sense of panicked upheaval. Babylonia is convulsed; ruler strives against ruler; rumors of disaster abound.

when I will reckon with the idols of Babylonia,
and all her land shall be shamed,
   and all her slain shall fall within her.
And they shall cry for joy over Babylon,   48
   the heavens and the earth and all that is in them.
      For from the north shall come against her the ravagers, said the LORD.
Babylonia, too, shall fall   49
   O slain of Israel,
yes, as before Babylonia did fall
   the slain of all the earth.
Fugitives of the sword,   50
   go, do not stand.
Recall from afar the LORD
   and let Jerusalem come to mind.
We were shamed, for we heard reproach,   51
   disgrace had covered our face.
For strangers came
   against the sacred places of the house of the LORD.
Therefore, look, days are coming, said the LORD,   52
   when I will reckon with her idols
      and through all her land those being slain shall groan.
Though Babylonia go up to the heavens,   53
   and though she bolster her stronghold on high,
      from Me shall come ravagers, said the LORD.
Hark! screaming from Babylonia,   54
   and a great shattering from the land of the Chaldeans!
For the LORD is ravaging Babylonia,   55
   has put an end to her great voice.
And their waves roar like mighty waters,

---

50. *Fugitives of the sword, / go, do not stand.* This urging of the exiles to flee Babylonia as it is enveloped by bloody destruction is of a piece with the imperative in verse 6 and verse 45.

52. *those being slain shall groan.* The Hebrew appears to say "the slain shall groan," but dead men do not groan, so a reference to those in the throes of dying is inevitable.

53. *Though Babylonia go up to the heavens.* The formulation is reminiscent of the mockery of the king of Babylonia in Isaiah 14. There, too, he is said to aspire to mount to the heavens in his overweening arrogance.

55. *has put an end to her great voice.* This would be the boastful or imperious voice of the once dominant Babylonia.

   their waves. The referent of this metaphor of destruction is spelled out here: "they" are "the ravagers."

        the din of their sound rings out,

56   for the ravager has come against her, against Babylonia.
        and her warriors are captured,
          their bows are shattered,
        for a God of requital is the LORD,
          He surely shall pay back.

57 And I will make her nobles and her sages, her satraps and her prefects drunk, and they shall sleep an everlasting sleep and not awake, said the
58 King, LORD of Armies is His name. Thus said the LORD of Armies: the walls of broad Babylon shall surely be razed and her high gates shall be set on fire. And peoples shall strive for naught, and nations against the fire, and shall be wearied.

59 The word with which Jeremiah the prophet charged Seriah son of Neriah son of Mahseiah when he went with Zedekiah king of Judah to Babylonia
60 in the fourth year of his reign. And Seriah was minister of tribute. And Jeremiah wrote down in a single scroll all the harm that would come upon
61 Babylonia, all these words written concerning Babylonia. And Jeremiah said to Seraiah, "When you come to Babylonia and see, you shall read
62 aloud all these words. And you shall say, 'LORD, You Yourself spoke concerning this place to cut it off, so there should be in it no human dweller
63 nor even a beast, for it should be an everlasting desolation.' And it shall

---

57. *drunk, and they shall sleep an everlasting sleep.* Sleep, of course, is one effect of drunkenness, but here the sleep is everlasting because the chalice is a chalice of poison.

58. *nations against the fire, and shall be wearied.* The formulation is a little odd, but the context makes its meaning clear: peoples will exhaust themselves trying to save Babylonia, but the fires they try to put out will be too much for them.

59. *Seraiah son of Neriah.* The patronymic tells us that he is the brother of Jeremiah's loyal secretary Baruch.
   minister of tribute. The received text reads *sar menuḥah,* which would mean "minister of rest," but the more likely reading is *sar minḥah,* the minister appointed to oversee the payment of tribute, *minḥah.*

61. *read aloud all these words.* Jeremiah has remained in Judah, and then is forced to join the group of Judahites that goes down to Egypt. He thus is obliged to send Seraiah as his spokesman to read out loud his written words that he, as prophet, would ordinarily have delivered orally himself.

62. *LORD, You Yourself spoke concerning this place.* The sentence Seraiah is enjoined to say is a kind of authentication of the written words he has read out: it is God Himself Who has pronounced this message of the destruction of Babylon.

be, when you finish reading aloud this book, you shall tie it to a stone and fling it into the Euphrates. And you shall say, 'So shall Babylonia sink and 64 not rise because of the harm that I am about to bring upon her.' And they shall be wearied."

Thus far the words of Jeremiah.

CHAPTER 52   Twenty-one years old was Zedekiah when he 1 became king, and his mother's name was Hamutal daughter of Jeremiah from Libnah. And he did what was evil in the eyes of the LORD as all that 2 Jehoiakim had done. For because of the LORD's wrath, it was against Jeru- 3 salem and Judah, till He flung them from His presence. And Zedekiah rebelled against the king of Babylonia. And it happened in the ninth year 4 of his reign, in the tenth month, on the tenth of the month, Nebuchadrez-zar king of Babylonia came—he and all his forces—against Jerusalem and

---

63 *you shall tie it to a stone and fling it into the Euphrates.* This is the last in the series of symbolic-predictive acts that punctuate the Book of Jeremiah. In this case, the meaning of the act is crystal-clear.

64. *And they shall be wearied.* Many scholars think that these words—actually, a single word in the Hebrew—are an inadvertent scribal duplication of the last word of verse 58. It is also possible that the repetition is deliberate, intended to mark an envelope structure between the end of that final prophecy of destruction and the end of the collection of the prophecies of Jeremiah.

Thus far the words of Jeremiah. This is a formal indication of the conclusion of Jeremiah's book. The single chapter that follows is not ascribed to him. It is no longer "the words of Jeremiah" but instead a narrative report of the fall of Jerusalem—a dire event repeatedly predicted by Jeremiah—that replicates, with minor variations, 2 Kings 24:18–25:30.

CHAPTER 52   1. *Twenty-one years old was Zedekiah.* The conclusion of the Book of Jeremiah, as noted above, largely replicates the conclusion of the Book of Kings, begin-ning with 2 Kings 24:18. The obvious rationale is that the principal burden of Jeremiah's prophecies has been the imminent destruction of Jerusalem and the exile of the Judahites, which is now presented as a historical report. Some of this material also appears in 39:1–10.

3. *And Zedekiah rebelled against the king of Babylonia.* As usual, the writer provides no political explanation—in this case, for the fact that Zedekiah, having been installed by Nebuchadrezzar in 597 B.C.E. as vassal king, now decides to rebel. We have seen earlier in the book that there were sharp divisions within the kingdom of Judah between a pro-Egyptian faction and one advocating accommodation with Babylonia. Zedekiah at this moment, counting on Egyptian support, joined an alliance of trans-Jordanian kingdoms plotting to overthrow Babylonian rule in the west. Egypt did not provide support, and the rebellion failed to materialize. The consequence was Nebuchadrezzar's assault on Jerusa-lem and the destruction of the kingdom of Judah in 586 B.C.E.

5 camped against it and built siege-towers all around it. And the city came
6 under siege till the eleventh year of King Zedekiah. In the fourth month on
   the ninth of the month the famine was severe in the city and there was no
7 bread for the people of the land. And the city was breached, and all the men
   of war fled and went out of the city by night through the gate between the
   double walls which is by the king's garden, and the Chaldeans were upon
8 the city all around. And they went through the Arabah. And the Chaldean
   force pursued the king and overtook him on the plain of Jericho, and all his
9 forces scattered from around him. And they seized the king and brought
   him up to the king of Babylonia at Riblah, and he pronounced judgment
10 against him. And the king of Babylonia slaughtered Zedekiah's sons before
11 his eyes, and also all the nobles of Judah he slaughtered in Riblah. And
   the eyes of Zedekiah he blinded, and he bound him in bronze fetters,
   and the king of Babylonia brought him to Babylonia and put him in the
12 house of detention. And in the fifth month on the seventh of the month,
   which was the nineteenth year of King Nebuchadrezzar king of Babylonia,
   Nebuzaradan the high chamberlain stood in attendance before the king
13 of Babylonia in Jerusalem. And he burned the house of the LORD and the
   house of the king and all the houses of Jerusalem, and every great house he
14 burned in fire. And all the walls of Jerusalem all around did the Chaldean
15 force that was with the high chamberlain shatter. And some of the poorest of the people and the rest of the people remaining in the city and the
   turncoats who had gone over to the king of Babylonia and the rest of the

---

6. *bread.* As elsewhere, this word is a synecdoche for food in general.

9. *he pronounced judgment against him.* This would scarcely have been a proper trial but
summary judgment of a vassal king who had proved himself a traitor.

11. *the house of detention.* The Hebrew *beyt hapequdot* is an unusual term for a prison or
place of confinement, but the meaning is clear.

13. *every great house.* These are the houses of the nobility, as the Aramaic translation, *batey
revavaia,* properly registers.

14. *And all the walls of Jerusalem all around did the Chaldean force . . . shatter.* Destroying
the walls rendered the city totally indefensible, eradicating any possibility that it could
continue to be the capital of an independent state.

15. *the turncoats.* Literally, "those who fell," a term that occurs earlier in Jeremiah. One
should recall that there was a strong group among the Judahites (including Jeremiah) who

artisans Nebuzaradan the high chamberlain exiled. And of the poorest of 16
the land Nebuzaradan left to be vine-dressers and field workers. And the 17
bronze pillars that were in the house of the LORD and the stands and the
bronze sea that was in the house of the LORD the Chaldeans smashed and
bore off their bronze to Babylonia. And the pails and the scrapers and the 18
snuffers and the ladles and the bronze vessels with which one ministered
they took. And the fire-pans and the sprinkling bowls and the snuffers and 19
the pails and the lampstands and the ladles and the scrapers, whatever was
of gold and whatever was of silver, the high chamberlain took. The two 20
pillars, the sea, the twelve bronze bulls that were under the stands that
King Solomon had made for the house of the LORD—all these vessels were
beyond measure in their bronze. And the pillars were eighteen cubits high 21
each pillar, and a thread of twelve cubits encircled it, and its thickness four
fingers, hollow. And there was a bronze capital on it, and the height of a 22
single capital was five cubits, with meshwork and pomegranates on the
capital all around. Everything was bronze, and like these were the second
pillar and the pomegranates. And there were ninety-six pomegranates 23
to a side, a hundred all the pomegranates over the meshwork all around.
And the high chamberlain took Seraiah the head priest and Zephaniah the 24
assistant priest and the three guards of the threshold. And from the city 25
he took one eunuch who was the official over the men of war and seven
men who attended in the king's presence, who were in the city, and the
scribe of the army commander who mustered the people of the land who

---

thought that the rebellion was ill-advised, and so it is not surprising that some of these
should defect to the Babylonians.

the artisans. The Hebrew *he'amon* appears to be a collective noun for "artisans." The
parallel text in Kings reads *hehamon,* "the masses."

17. *And the bronze pillars.* This catalogue of precious vessels seized by the Babylonians
reverses everything reported in 1 Kings 6–7 about the splendid furnishings for the Temple
and palace that Solomon caused to be fashioned. Everything that the grand first king after
David built or made is either reduced to rubble or taken off by the enemy.

the bronze sea. This is a large cast-metal pool mentioned in 1 Kings 7:23 and elsewhere.

20. *beyond measure.* More literally, "beyond weighing."

24. *And the high chamberlain took Seraiah the head priest and Zephaniah the assistant
priest.* The obvious intention is to prevent a renewal of the cult. The usual term for high
priest (in the Hebrew, "great priest") is not used but rather "head priest," *kohen haro'sh.*

26 were in the city. And Nebuzaradan the high chamberlain took them to the
27 king of Babylonia at Riblah. And the king of Babylonia struck them down
   and put them to death in Riblah in the land of Hammath. And he exiled
28 Judah from its land. This was the people that Nebuchadrezzar exiled in the
29 seventh year—three thousand twenty-three Judahites. In the eighteenth
   year of Nebuchadrezzar—from Jerusalem, eight hundred thirty-two per-
30 sons. In the twenty-third year of Nebuchadrezzar, Nebuzaradan the high
   chamberlain exiled seven hundred forty-five Judahites; all the persons
31 were four thousand six hundred. And it happened in the twenty-seventh
   year of the exile of Jehoiakim king of Judah in the twelfth month on the
   twenty-seventh of the month, that Evil-Merodach in the year he became
   king lifted up the head of Jehoiakim king of Judah and brought him out
32 from the prison house. And he spoke kindly to him and gave him a throne
33 above the thrones of the kings who were with him in Babylonia. And he
   changed his prison garments, and Jehoiakim ate bread perpetually before

---

27. *And the king of Babylonia struck them down and put them to death.* No Geneva convention obtains for these ancient prisoners of war, and since they constitute the nation's
military and sacerdotal elite, Nebuchadrezzar wants to eliminate them entirely.

28. *This was the people that Nebuchadrezzar exiled.* This enumeration of the exiles does not
appear in the parallel passage in Kings.
   in the seventh year. This is Nebuchadrezzar's seventh reignal year, 597 B.C.E., when he
put down the Judahite rebellion, made King Jehoiakim a captive and exile, and installed
Zedekiah as vassal king.

29. *In the eighteenth year.* This would be 587 or 586 B.C.E., a one-year discrepancy evident
between this and the mention of "the nineteenth year" in verse 12.

30. *In the twenty-third year.* This would be 582 B.C.E., the year of the assassination of Gedaliah (not mentioned in this chapter), an act of insurrection that provoked an additional
deportation of Judahites.
   all the persons were four thousand six hundred. This amounts to a rather small number
of exiles, even if the general population of Judah was not large.

31. *lifted up the head.* This idiom is borrowed from the Joseph story, where it is applied
to the release from prison of Pharaoh's vizier. The change of garments in verse 33 recalls
Joseph's change of garments after Pharaoh takes him from prison to occupy a high place
in the royal court.

32. *gave him a throne above the thrones of the kings who were with him.* This is probably a
nationalistic flourish of the writer's because it is unlikely that Jehoiakim would have been
granted a higher status than other kings held in Babylonian captivity.

33. *Jehoiakim.* The Hebrew says merely "he," and the proper noun has been added in order
to avoid confusion of pronominal reference.

him all the days of his life. And his provision was a perpetual provision 34
given him by the king of Babylonia day after day till his dying day, all the
days of his life.

---

34. *And his provision was a perpetual provision . . . day after day.* This verse is also the last
verse of the Book of Kings. Its editorial inclusion here is an attempt to mitigate the national
catastrophe that Jeremiah has repeatedly predicted and that is reported in this chapter.
The concluding image intimates a hopeful possibility of future restoration: a Davidic king
is recognized as king, even in captivity, and is given a daily provision appropriate to his
royal status. As he sits on his throne elevated above the thrones of the other captive kings,
the audience of the story is invited to imagine a scion of David again sitting on his throne
in Jerusalem.

EZEKIEL

■ ■ ■

Introduction

Ezekiel is surely the strangest of all the prophets. Well before the appearance of the so-called writing prophets in the middle of the eighth century B.C.E., figures known as prophets, *nevi'im*, at least as they are represented in the narratives, were identified as people given to ecstatic states when they were inhabited by the divine spirit. All of the prophets appear to have felt that they heard God speaking, the speech sometimes accompanied by visual revelations, in what would have amounted to paranormal experiences. Prophets were sometimes perceived as altogether transgressing the borders of sanity. "The prophet is witless, / the man of spirit crazed," Hosea proclaims, having in mind the way Israel's waywardness had driven the prophet to wild distraction. Yet even against this background, Ezekiel is an extreme case.

He was a Jerusalem priest, in all likelihood part of the group of an exiled elite that was deported to Babylonia with King Jehoiachin in 597 B.C.E., a decade before the destruction of Jerusalem and the more general exile. His entire activity as a prophet took place in Babylonia, with many of the prophecies introduced by a careful notation of day, month, and year. (Although biblical scholars, as they are wont to do, once sought to ascribe many of these prophecies to a later period, the current consensus is that they were in fact composed by Ezekiel, probably on the dates he cites, but of course the editing could have been done considerably later.) Unlike Jeremiah, who was also from a family of priests, Ezekiel often exhibits distinctively priestly concerns—with purity and impurity, with the Temple and its architectural configurations, and with the regimen of sacrifices. But what most distinguishes Ezekiel is that so much of the prophesying is conducted in a condition that looks like God-intoxicated derangement. He is by no means a master of literary craft, like Isaiah, and most of his prophecies are composed in prose that exhibits a weakness for repetition. His power as a prophet stems from the hallucinatory vividness and utter originality of his visions.

The book begins with the grand theatrical effect of his vision of the divine chariot—fire flashing, radiance all around, the face of a different living creature on each of the four sides of a dazzling structure with mysterious wheels beneath that appears to hover in the air. Elsewhere in the Bible, "the glory of the Lord" designates an overpowering radiant manifestation of God's presence, but we are told that it cannot really be seen. When Moses asks God to show him His glory, God tells him that he cannot look upon it head-on but, hidden in the crevice of a rock, may glimpse only its afterglow as it passes by. Ezekiel, by contrast, is vouchsafed a full and detailed vision of the divine apparatus, which he calls "the glory of the Lord." There is nothing quite like this elsewhere in the Bible, and Ezekiel's first chapter would accordingly become the inspiration for the development of Jewish mysticism in Late Antiquity.

There are quite a few arresting visions in Ezekiel's book, the most memorable of them being the vision of exiled Israel's national restoration in the Valley of the Dry Bones (chapter 37). This was a man whose mind swarmed with potent images, many of them cast as figures in allegories, which are the most effective vehicle of his prophecies. One senses that these images were not contrived or invented but manifested themselves imperatively in the imagination of the prophet. While the idea of the spirit descending on an elected person is common in biblical literature, including many of the narratives, again and again in this book the prophet attests to being seized, sometimes violently, by the spirit. In Hebrew, as in several other languages, the same word means both "spirit" and "wind," but for Ezekiel the latter meaning is often salient, even if the former sense may also be implied: repeatedly, he is "borne off" by the wind to a place of vision (often Jerusalem), or, in tandem with this idea, the heavy "hand of the Lord" comes down on him, as in the beginning of the vision of the Dry Bones, "The hand of the Lord was upon me, and He took me out by the wind of the Lord and set me down in the valley."

All this powerful seizure by visionary experience is associated in Ezekiel with a variety of bizarre behaviors that would seem to reflect some kind of psychological disturbance. Other prophets feel they are commanded by God to perform symbolic-prophetic acts. Jeremiah, for example, is enjoined to go down to the potter's workshop, to purchase a plot of land, and to do other acts that are more or less ordinary actions which are given symbolic or illustrative significance. But the acts that Ezekiel reports God has ordered him to carry out are not normal ones: he eats a scroll, he constructs a model of Jerusalem with a brick and an iron pan, he lies on one side for three hundred ninety days and then forty days on his other side without the capacity to turn over. This last instance is the most egregious. It is fairly plausible that Ezekiel actually did this, and lying on one side for more than a year in "bonds," he says, imposed by God looks very much like an extreme symptom of hysterical paralysis.

Among the themes of Ezekiel's prophecies, the most striking expression of neurosis is his troubled relation to the female body. Real and symbolic bodies become entangled with each other. In biblical poetry, a nation, and Israel in particular, is quite often represented as a woman. God's covenant with Israel—see Jeremiah 1—is imagined as a marriage, and so the bride Israel's dalliance with pagan gods is figured as adultery or whoring. This is a common trope in biblical literature, but the way Ezekiel articulates it is both startling and unsettling.

The most vivid instance of this psychological twist in Ezekiel is the extended allegory of whoring Israel in chapter 16. The allegory here follows the birth of the nation in Canaan—represented with stark physicality in the image of the infant girl naked and wallowing in the blood of afterbirth, then looked after by a solicitous God—to her sexual maturity and her betrayal of God through idolatry. The focus throughout is on Israel as a female sexual body. Thus, the prophet notes (as does no other biblical writer) the ripening of the breasts and the sprouting of pubic hair. The mature personification of the nation is a beautiful woman, her beauty enhanced by the splendid attire God gives her (this is probably a reference to national grandeur and to the Temple). Yet, insatiably lascivious, she uses her charms to entice strangers to her bed: "you spilled out your whoring" (given the verb used and the unusual form of the noun, this could be a reference to vaginal secretions) "upon every passerby." Israel as a woman is even accused of harboring a special fondness for large phalluses: "you played the whore with the Egyptians, your big-membered neighbors." She is, the prophet says, a whore who asks no payment for her services. "You befouled your beauty," he inveighs, "and spread your legs for every passerby." All this concern with female promiscuity is correlative with Ezekiel's general preoccupation with purity and impurity.

It is of course possible to link each of these sexual details with the allegory of an idolatrous nation betraying its faith. But such explicitness and such vehemence about sex are unique in the Bible. The compelling inference is that this was a prophet morbidly fixated on the female body and seething with fervid misogyny. What happens in the prophecy in chapter 16 is that the metaphor of the lubricious woman takes over the foreground, virtually displacing the allegorical referent. Ezekiel clearly was not a stable person. The states of disturbance exhibited in his writing led him to a series of remarkable visionary experiences, at least several of which would be deeply inscribed in the Western imagination, engendering profound responses in later poetry and in mystical literature. At the same time, there is much in these visions that reminds us of the dangerous dark side of prophecy. To announce authoritatively that the words one speaks are the words of God is an audacious act. Inevitably, what is reported as divine speech reaches us through the refracting prism of the prophet's sensibility and psychology, and the words and images represented as God's urgent message may sometimes be distorted in eerie ways.

CHAPTER 1   And it happened in the thirtieth year, in the ₁
fourth month on the fifth of the month, that I was among the exiles by the
Kebar Canal, and I saw divine visions. On the fifth of the month, which ₂
was the fifth year of the exile of King Jehoiachin, the word of the LORD ₃
came to Ezekiel son of Buzi the priest in the land of the Chaldeans, by the
Kebar Canal, and the hand of the LORD was upon him there. And I saw, ₄
and, look, a storm wind was coming from the north, a great cloud, and
fire flashing, and radiance all round it, and from within it like the appear-

---

CHAPTER 1   1. *in the thirtieth year.* What this refers to has stumped scholars. One
proposal is that it is the thirtieth year of Ezekiel's life.

divine visions (or, "visions of God") But most of the vision here is devoted to the divine
"chariot," with the figure of God introduced only toward the end, so "divine" may be a
more apt translation.

2. *the fifth year of the exile of King Jehoiachin.* He was exiled with a substantial group of
Judahites, by Nebuchadnezzar in 597 B.C.E., when Judah was reduced by Babylonia to a
vassal state. The clear implication is that Ezekiel was among those deported to Babylonia
in 597. The beginning of his prophecy overlaps with the last decade of Jeremiah's prophecy;
he would have been a generation younger, Jeremiah having begun his mission in the 620s.

3. *the word of the LORD came to Ezekiel.* Since the book begins in the first person and then
continues here in the first person, this third-person reference to the prophet may reflect
an editorial intervention.

4. *a storm wind was coming from the north, a great cloud, and fire flashing, and radiance all
round it.* These accoutrements of epiphany are traditional in the Bible: in many different
texts, from Exodus to Psalms, God reveals himself in fire and lightning and cloud. Nevertheless, this prophecy is strikingly innovative in form. First, it combines the pyrotechnic
paraphernalia of divine revelation with imagery evidently borrowed from sundry Mesopotamian sources—the wheeled throne, the four faces of the creatures like the four faces
of the Babylonian god Marduk, the iconic animals. Isaiah in his dedication scene (Isaiah
6) glimpses the skirts of God's robe filling the Temple and sees seraphim, but there is no
direct description of God and no elaborate imagining of a celestial vehicle. One should
also note that this elevated vision is cast in prose, but it is a visibly poetic prose marked by
hypnotic cadences. The words do not scan as poetry, yet some of the diction is poetic. The
reiterated term for "radiance," *nogah,* for example, ordinarily appears only in poetic texts.
Thus, Ezekiel has devised a prophetic prose-poetry that has scant precedents.

like the appearance. The preposition here could also mean "the color of."

5   ance of amber from within the fire. And from within it the likeness of four
living creatures, and this was their look—the likeness of a human being
6,7 they had. And each had four faces and four wings to each of them. And
their legs were straight legs, and the soles of their feet like the soles of a
8   calf's foot, and they glittered like the look of burnished bronze. And there
were human hands beneath their wings on their four sides. And the faces
9   and the wings of the four of them were joined to each other. Their wings
10 did not turn as they went; each went straight ahead. And the likeness of
their faces—the face of a human and the face of a lion on the right of the
four of them, and the face of a bull to the left of the four of them, and the
11 face of an eagle to the four of them. And their faces and their wings were
separated from above for each—two were joined for each and two covered
12 their bodies. And each went straight ahead: wherever the spirit was to go,
13 they would go; they did not turn as they went. And the likeness of the
creatures, their look, was like burning coals of fire, like the look of torches
going back and forth among the creatures, and the fire had a radiance, and
14 from the fire lightning came forth. And the creatures were racing back and
15 forth like the look of sparks. And I saw the creatures, and look, one wheel
16 was on the ground by the creature on its four sides. The look of the wheels
and their fashioning were like chrysolite, and a single likeness the faces of

---

amber. This translation adopts one traditional equivalent for the Hebrew *ḥashmal,* but
its precise identity is elusive. It would seem to be some sort of precious stone that is orange,
yellow, or reddish in color.

5. *likeness.* This word, *demut,* and its complementary term, *mar'eh,* "look" or "appearance,"
are insisted on again and again in this vision as well as in several visions that follow. The
prophet wants to make clear that his report of what he has seen is of something that can be
represented only by analogy: these are likenesses, appearances, analogs of things known
to humankind, but not literally those things.

8–9. *And the faces and the wings of the four of them were joined to each other.* As the vision
proceeds, it becomes progressively difficult to sort out visually what these creatures and
the moving composite they make up look like. (Two and a half millennia of exegetes have
labored in vain to work out all the details.) A certain bewilderment may well have been
Ezekiel's intention. There are abundant repetitions of phrases through the passage, some
of them probably quite deliberate in order to create an incantatory effect, although at least
a couple of them seem to be the product of scribal inadvertence.

10. *lion . . . bull . . . eagle.* These are all heraldic beasts associated with royalty or divinity.
The fourth face is human.

11. *two covered their bodies.* Evidently, for modesty as with the wings of the seraphim in
Isaiah 6.

14. *sparks.* The Hebrew *bazak* appears only here, but it clearly indicates some sort of flashing light. In rabbinic Hebrew, it serves as a synonym for "lightning."

them had, and their look and their fashioning as when a wheel is within a
wheel. On their four sides as they went they would go. They did not turn as 17
they went. As for their rims, they were high and they were fearsome, and 18
their rims were filled with eyes, all round the four of them. And when the 19
creatures went, the wheels went with them, and when the creatures lifted
up above the ground, the wheels lifted up. Wherever the spirit was there to 20
go, there they went [there the spirit to go], and the wheels lifted up along
with them, for the spirit of the creature was in the wheels. When they went, 21
they would go. When they stood still, they would stand still, and when they
lifted up above the ground, the wheels would lift up along with them, for
the spirit of the creature was in the wheels. And there was a likeness over 22
the heads of the beasts—a platform like the appearance of the fearsome ice
stretched over their heads above. And beneath the platform their wings 23
stood straight and toward each other, each had two covering them, covering their body. And I heard the sound of their wings like the sound of many 24
waters, like the sound of Shaddai, as they went, like the sound of an uproar,

---

16. *as when a wheel is within a wheel.* The most likely reference is to concentric wheels.

18. *they were high and they were fearsome.* More literally, "they had height and they had
fearsomeness." The fearsome aspect of the wheels may be because they are then said to be
studded, nightmarishly, with eyes. The meaning of the eyes remains mysterious. Some
commentators claim they were a manifestation of all-seeing divine omniscience. Perhaps
the primary effect is that they are disorienting and disturbing: these are wheels like none
ever encountered by human gaze.

19. *when the creatures went, the wheels went with them.* The wheels are not physically
attached to the creatures, but their movements are synchronized with them through a
shared "spirit."

20. *[there the spirit to go].* This bracketed phrase, with its tenuous syntactic connection with
the rest of the sentence, definitely looks like a mistaken scribal repetition.

21. *when they lifted up above the ground, the wheels would lift up along with them.* This
four-sided moving structure, with wheels below and a kind of platform above, is what led
tradition to call it a "chariot," *merkavah*. To moderns, it may seem like a bizarrely composite hovering helicopter.

22. *a platform.* The Hebrew *raqiʿa* indicates a flat, pounded-out surface (it is derived from
a verbal root that means to "pound" or "to stomp"). In Genesis 1, it is the word used for the
vault of the heavens (more traditionally, "firmament"), so here it figures as a constructed
equivalent of the sky. Structurally, the *raqiʿa* amounts to a beaten slab.

24. *many waters.* This phrase, recurring often in biblical literature, refers to the primordial
sea or deep, with mythological overtones. Compare, for example, Psalm 93:4.
    like the sound of an uproar, like the sound of an armed camp. All this emphasis on
sound, after the exclusive focus on visual elements, sets the stage for God's speech, which
is introduced at the end of the chapter.

like the sound of an armed camp. When they stood still, their wings grew
25 slack. And there was a sound above the platform that was over their heads.
26 When they stood still, their wings slackened. And above the platform that
was over their heads, it was like the look of sapphire stone—the likeness of
a throne, and above the likeness of the throne, like a human form upon it
27 above. And I saw like the appearance of amber, like the look of fire within
it all round—from the look of his loins above and from the look of his loins
28 below I saw like the look of fire with radiance all round. Like the look of
the rainbow that is in the clouds on a day of rain, this was the look of the
radiance all round, the look of the likeness of the glory of the LORD. And I
saw and fell on my face and heard a voice speaking—

1 CHAPTER 2   And He said to me, "Man, stand on your feet
2 and I shall speak with you." And a spirit entered me as He spoke to me and
3 stood me on my feet, and I heard what was spoken to me. And He said to
me, "Man, I am sending you to the Israelites, to the rebellious nations that
have rebelled against Me, they and their fathers have revolted against Me
4 to this day. And to the brazen-faced hard-hearted sons I am sending you,

---

28. *the look . . . of the glory of the* LORD. Never before in biblical literature has God's "glory,"
kavod, been given such visual realization.

CHAPTER 2   1. *Man.* The Hebrew *ben-'adam,* "human being," is the characteristic form through which God repeatedly addresses Ezekiel. As several commentators
have noted, it places the prophet in an antithetical relation to the "creatures" of the divine
chariot, who are not mortal humans. The translation avoids rendering the term as "son
of man" because, after the Gospels, that designation took on Christological connotations.

2. *And a spirit entered me as He spoke to me and stood me on my feet.* Ezekiel is thus like
the wheels in the divine vision, which are inhabited by a spirit that directs them. Ezekiel
appears to exert less human agency than the other prophets, and that could well be a manifestation of his distinctive psychology as prophet.
    and I heard what was spoken to me. Some understand this as "one speaking to me."
The Hebrew shows a reflexive form of the verb "to speak," with no visible subject, perhaps
reflecting reticence about saying "God."

3. *the rebellious nations.* The designation of the Israelites as "nations" in the plural is peculiar. Some think it refers to the tribes, but they are not elsewhere called "nations." Perhaps
the plural is meant to encompass both the northern kingdom of Israel and the southern
kingdom of Judah. While the northern kingdom had long been destroyed, the verbal phrase
"have rebelled against Me" invokes past actions, and Ezekiel may also be imagining a virtual presence of the vanished kingdom, as Jeremiah sometimes does.

and you shall say to them, 'Thus said the Master, the LORD.' As for them, 5
whether they listen or not, they are surely a house of rebellion, but they
shall know that a prophet has been in their midst. As for you, man, do not 6
fear them and do not fear their words, for they are thorns and thistles to
you, and among scorpions you dwell. Do not fear their words and do not be
terrified by them, for they are a house of rebellion. And you shall speak My 7
words to them, whether they listen or not, for they are a house of rebellion.
As for you, man, listen to what I speak to you. Be not rebellious like the 8
house of rebellion. Open your mouth and eat what I give you." And I saw, 9
and, look, a hand was stretched out to me, and, look, in it was the scroll of
a book. And He unrolled it before me, and it was written on both sides and 10
written in it—dirges, lament, and woe.

CHAPTER 3   And He said to me, "Man, what you find, eat. 1
Eat this scroll and go speak to the house of Israel." And I opened my mouth 2
and He fed me this scroll. And He said to me, "Man, your belly you shall 3
feed and your innards you shall fill with this scroll that I give you." And I

---

4. *Thus said the Master, the* LORD. This is the so-called messenger-formula with which
many prophecies begin. No words of prophecy follow, though the last words of this chapter
indicate the content of the prophecy.

5. *but they shall know that a prophet has been in their midst.* The anticipation, shared by
Isaiah and Jeremiah, that the people may not heed the prophet, is parsed in a different way
here: perhaps the people will choose to ignore the prophet's admonitions, but they will not
escape a strong and troubling sense of the urgent authenticity of his message.

6. *thorns and thistles.* Many translations render the first term as "nettles" (only an approximate meaning is known), but the Hebrew shows a forceful alliteration—*saravim, salonim*—
that deserves to be emulated in the English.

8. *Open your mouth and eat what I give you.* Other prophets are bid to perform symbolic
acts, but this one is extreme, and characteristic of Ezekiel. He has just been told not to be
rebellious like his countrymen; now he is asked to show his total submission by ingesting
a scroll. Again, this appears to reflect Ezekiel's aberrant psychology. God does not inform
him what he is to eat until the mysterious hand appears with the scroll.

10. *it was written on both sides.* As Menachem Haran has noted, this means the scroll was
papyrus, not parchment, because the way animal skins were prepared for scrolls in this
period precluded writing on both sides. It would, of course, be considerably easier to ingest
papyrus than parchment.

CHAPTER 3   3. *Man, your belly you shall feed and your innards you shall fill with
this scroll.* Such specification indicates that the prophet is not merely meant to chew the

4 ate, and it became sweet as honey in my mouth. And He said to me, "Man,
5 come! Go to the house of Israel and speak to them My words. For not to
   a people of an unfathomable language and an obscure tongue do I send
6 you—but to the house of Israel. Not to many peoples of impenetrable language and obscure tongue whose words you would not understand. Surely
7 had I sent you to them, they would have listened to you. But the house of
   Israel does not want to listen to you, for they do not want to listen to Me,
8 for all the house of Israel are hard-browed and hard-hearted. Look, I have
   made your face hard against their faces and your brow hard against their
9 brows. Like diamond harder than flint I have made your brow. You shall
   not fear them and shall not be terrified by them, for they are a house of
10 rebellion." And He said to me, "Man, all My words that I shall speak to
11 you—take into your heart and with your ears listen, and come! go to the
   exiles, to the sons of your people, and speak to them and say to them: Thus
12 said the Master, the LORD, whether they listen or not." And a wind lifted
   me, and I heard behind me the sound of a great roar: "Blessed be the LORD's
13 glory from its place," and the sound of the creatures' wings touching each

---

papyrus scroll but to swallow and digest it. It seems quite likely that Ezekiel believed he
had been commanded to perform this difficult symbolic act and in fact carried it out. His
report that the taste of the papyrus in his mouth was sweet as honey leads one to infer that
he was a person susceptible to aberrant or perhaps abnormal states.

5. *a people of an unfathomable language and an obscure tongue.* The literal sense is "deep
of language and heavy of tongue." Elsewhere in Prophetic texts, the unintelligibility of the
language of the conquerors is part of their fearsome aspect. Here, it becomes part of an *a
fortiori* statement: had the prophet been sent to peoples speaking a barbaric foreign tongue,
they would have listened to him; but when he is sent to the Israelites, addressing them in
their shared mother tongue, Hebrew, they refuse to listen because of their stubbornness.
    but to the house of Israel. The "but" is merely implied in the Hebrew.

8. *I have made your face hard against their faces and your brow hard against their brows.*
Rimon Casher has proposed that the repetition throughout these verses of ḥazak ("hard,"
and elsewhere usually "strong") may be a play on the root of Ezekiel's name, yeḥezq'el ("God
will make strong").

9. *You shall not fear them . . . for they are a house of rebellion.* The causal logic here is that
because they are rebels, they are destined to be punished by God, and so there is nothing
to fear from them, however they may threaten the prophet.

12. *And a wind lifted me.* We repeatedly see this prophet as a passive subject of prophecy,
being lifted, borne off, stood on his feet, by divine powers.
    Blessed be the LORD's glory from its place. One often proposed emendation reads instead
of barukh, "blessed," berum, "in the rising of," which yields not a line of dialogue but a
narrative report about the divine chariot: "When the LORD's glory rose up from its place."

other and the sound of the wheels over against them and the sound of a
great roar. And a wind lifted me and took me, and bitter did I go, with   14
an incensed spirit, and the hand of the LORD was strong upon me. And   15
I came to the exiles at Tel Abib who dwelled by the Kebar Canal, where
they dwelled, and I sat there seven days, desolate in their midst. And it   16
happened at the end of seven days that the word of the LORD came to me,
saying, "Man, I have made you a lookout for the house of Israel. When you   17
hear a word from My mouth, you shall warn them from Me. When I say   18
to a wicked man, 'You are doomed to die,' and you have not warned him
and have not spoken to warn the wicked man against his wicked ways to
keep him alive, that wicked man shall die for his crime but his blood I will
requite of you. As for you, when you warn the wicked man and he does not   19
turn back from his wickedness and from his wicked way, it is he who shall
die for his crime and you, you shall have saved your own life. And when the   20
righteous man turns back from his righteousness and does wrong, and I put
a stumbling block before him, he shall die, for you did not warn him. For
his offense he shall die, and his righteousness shall not be recalled, but his
blood I will requite of you. And you, when you have warned the righteous   21
man not to offend and he has not offended, he shall surely live, for he has
taken warning, and you, you shall have saved your own life."

This emendation is encouraged by the fact that in paleo-Hebrew script the letters *mem* and
kaf look fairly similar, so a scribe could easily have erred. The emended reading flows more
smoothly into the next verse and a half reporting the ascent of the divine chariot, but the
Masoretic Text has been retained in this translation because it has become prominently
enshrined in the Hebrew liturgy.

14. *bitter did I go, with an incensed spirit.* The prophet's disturbed emotional state reflects
his troubled sense that the prophetic mission will be very arduous, perhaps impossible.

15. *Tel Abib.* Though this looks like a Hebrew name, "mound of the sprouting season," and
modern-day Tel Aviv drew the name from here, it is actually Akkadian and means "mound
of the flood."
     where they dwelled. This might be a scribal duplication.

17. *lookout.* The lookout or watchman, as can be inferred from the appearance of the term in
narrative contexts, was someone posted on an elevation to look for the approach of hostile
forces. Thus, the prophet is appointed to look out for imminent disaster triggered by Israel's
bad behavior and to warn them, as a watchman would.

18. *but his blood I will requite of you.* This is a much grimmer formulation of the burden of
prophecy than that given to other prophets: Ezekiel is obliged to work under an imminent
death sentence if he fails to adequately warn the transgressors.

22 And the hand of the Lord was upon me there, and He said to me, "Arise,
23 go out to the valley, and there will I speak to you." And I arose and went out
   to the valley, and, look, the Lord's glory was standing there, like the glory
24 I had seen by the Kebar Canal, and I fell on my face. And a spirit entered
   me and stood me on my feet and spoke to me and said to me, "Come, shut
25 yourself within your house. And now, man, they have put cords on you and
26 bound you with them, that you not go out in their midst. And your tongue
   I will make cleave to your palate that you be mute, and you shall not be a
27 reprover to them, for they are a house of rebellion. But when I speak to you
   I will open your mouth, and you shall say to them: 'Thus said the Master,
   the Lord: Who listens shall listen, and who does not shall not, for they are
   a house of rebellion.'"

1 CHAPTER 4   And you, man, take you a brick and put it
2 before you and incise on it the city of Jerusalem. And you shall lay a siege

---

22. *the valley.* Although some render this as "plain," the Hebrew term clearly derives from
a verbal stem that means "rift" or "split," and it refers to a valley—in the case of Jordan, the
riverbed and the surrounding banks.

23. *the* Lord's *glory was standing there.* Repeatedly in Ezekiel, "the Lord's glory" (or "majesty") refers to the divine "chariot" described in chapter 1.

24. *And a spirit entered me and stood me on my feet.* As before, Ezekiel is a virtual puppet
of the divine spirit. This is an idea that will be picked up in Daniel.
    shut yourself within your house. Some have seen this as a contradiction of the previous
injunction to the prophet to "warn" Israel, compounded by the fact that in the next verse
God says He will impose a condition of complete muteness on the prophet. But such oscillations should not surprise us, especially if we assume that all these divine instructions have
some relation to the psychology of this particular prophet. In that case, at one moment he
feels an absolute imperative to reprove the people, a responsibility he needs to carry out
on the pain of death. At another moment, despairing of the very possibility of in any way
changing the course of action of these stubborn rebels against God, he shuts himself up in
his house and sinks into a condition of total silence.

25. *they have put cords on you and bound you with them.* Since the prophet has already
shut himself up in his house, it is unclear why anyone would feel the necessity to bind
him in cords in order to prevent him from going outside. Perhaps this statement should
be construed as a metaphor: "they" (the people) have through their actions imposed on
the prophet a condition of isolated withdrawal, as though they had bound him with cords.

CHAPTER 4   1. *take you a brick and . . . incise on it the city of Jerusalem.* Bricks were
the building material of choice in the Mesopotamian valley, whereas stone was more commonly used in the mountainous region of Judah. (Compare the use of bricks in the story

against it and build against it a siege-work and throw up a ramp against it and set an armed camp against it and put against it battering rams all round. And you, take you an iron pan and make it an iron wall between you ₃ and the city. And you shall set your face toward it, and it shall be besieged, and you shall lay siege against it. It is a sign for the house of Israel.

And you, lie down on your left side and put the guilt of the house of Israel ₄ upon it. For the number of days that you lie on it you shall bear their guilt. As for Me, I have made for you the years of their crime as the number of ₅ days, three hundred ninety days, and you shall bear the guilt of the house of Israel. And you shall complete these and lie down again on your right ₆ side and bear the guilt of the house of Judah forty days, each day for a year

---

of the Tower of Babel, Genesis 11.) The incising would have been done before the firing of the brick. A brick with a depiction of the Babylonian city of Napur was actually discovered in an archaeological dig.

2. *And you shall lay a siege against it.* This appears to be a model of a siege with the appropriate siege-works, not an image also incised on the brick. The proclivity for symbolic acts is brought to an elaborate extreme here.

3. *an iron wall between you and the city.* Now, in the playing with models and symbols, Ezekiel takes on the role of God (!), estranged from the city, a condition represented by the interposed iron wall.

4. *For the number of days that you lie on it you shall bear their guilt.* This is another instance in which the borderline between symbolic act and psychological aberration in Ezekiel is blurred. If, as seems likely, he actually performed this act, he would have been in a state of paralysis (hysterically induced?), lying on one side, for almost thirteen months. The idiom "bear guilt" has several different meanings in biblical usage, but the most likely one here is that the prophet symbolically takes on himself the guilt—the word can also indicate "punishment"—of his offending people.

5. *three hundred ninety.* This number of years, if one calculates from the erection of the Temple around 970 B.C.E., takes us forward to 580 B.C.E., which falls within the period of Ezekiel's prophecy in Babylonia. Moshe Greenberg observes that, in accordance with the viewpoint of the Deuteronomist, the existence of the "high places" outside of Jerusalem throughout this period would define the entire span of nearly four centuries as a time when guilt was incurred.

6. *lie down again on your right side and bear the guilt of the house of Judah forty days.* Forty is a formulaic number, but it is difficult to reconcile it with the figure of 390 or to imagine what it could refer to historically. Many scholars plausibly conclude that the lying on the right side is a secondary interpolation, and that "the house of Israel" in verse 5 refers to the entire people of Israel, and then is made to indicate the northern kingdom only by this inconvenient add-on that introduces a reference to the southern kingdom. Surely more than a year would have been enough for the prophet to continue in this paralytic state.

7 I have made it for you. And to the siege of Jerusalem you shall set your face
8 with your arm laid bare, and you shall prophesy against it. And, look, I
have put cords on you, that you not turn over from side to side until you
9 complete the days of your siege. And you, take you wheat and barley and
beans and lentils and millet and emmer and put them in a single vessel
and make them into bread for yourself the number of days that you lie on
10 your side, three hundred ninety days you shall eat it. And your food that
you shall eat, by weight, twenty weights a day, from one day to the next you
11 shall eat it. And water by measure you shall drink, the sixth of a *hin*, from
12 one day to the next you shall drink. And a barley loaf you shall eat, and
13 it shall be baked on the turds of human excrement before your eyes. And
the Lord said, "Thus shall the Israelites eat their bread defiled among the
14 nations where I will scatter them." And I said, "Alas, O Master, Lord, look,
my throat is undefiled, and carrion and torn animal carcasses I have not
eaten from my youth until now, nor has foul meat come into my mouth."
15 And He said to me, "Look, I give you cattle dung instead of human turds,
16 and you shall make your bread upon that." And He said to me, "Man, I am

---

7. *your arm laid bare.* The bared arm is a token of the use of force.

8. *I have put cords on you.* As in 3:25, these are not literal cords: the prophet, feeling unable
to move from this position lying on his side, understands that he has been immobilized
by God.

9. *wheat and barley and beans and lentils and millet and emmer.* Although one American
Christian group actually markets bread purportedly made from this recipe, it is in fact siege
bread, made not from wheat but from a combination of grains and legumes because of the
lack of sufficient wheat supplies. The Talmud reports an experiment in which the bread
was made with these ingredients and a dog would not touch it.

10. *twenty weights a day.* By some calculations, this is no more than eight ounces—a very
scant daily ration.

12. *it shall be baked on the turds of human excrement before your eyes.* Dried animal dung
was commonly used for fuel, but not human excrement. Thus the baking manifests the
condition of the exiles constrained to live in an "unclean" (or "defiled") land, which is
how foreign territory was conceived. The "your" of "your eyes" is plural and is addressed
to the exiles, not the prophet.

14. *my throat is undefiled.* While the prohibition against consuming the meat of carrion
and animals torn up by predators is incumbent on all the people, Ezekiel as a priest would
have taken special care to preserve the condition of ritual purity.

15. *cattle dung instead of human turds.* Seeing the prophet's visceral revulsion, God offers
a compromise, but the bread is still baked on filth.

about to break the staff of bread in Jerusalem, and they shall eat bread by
weight and in disgust, and water by measure and in desolation they shall
drink, so that they want for bread and water and each man and his brother   17
be desolate, and they shall rot in their guilt."

CHAPTER 5   And you, man, take you a sharp blade, a barber's   1
razor, take it for yourself, and pass it over your head and your beard, and
take you a scales and divide it. A third you shall burn in fire within the city   2
when the days of the siege are done. And you shall take a third and strike
it with a blade all round her, and a third you shall scatter to the wind. And
a sword will I unsheathe after them. And you shall take from there a bit   3
and wrap it in the skirts of your garment. And from it you shall take more   4
and fling it into the fire and burn it in fire. From it fire shall go out to the
whole house of Israel. Thus said the Master, the LORD: This is Jerusalem,   5
in the midst of the nations I set her, with lands all round her. And she   6
rebelled against My laws for wickedness more than the nations, and against
My statutes more than the lands that are all round her. For they spurned
My laws and did not follow My statutes. Therefore, thus said the Master,   7

---

16. *break the staff of bread in Jerusalem.* Bread is a "staff" because it supports or sustains life,
and in biblical Hebrew, as in many other languages, it is a synecdoche for food in general.
The obvious reference is to the condition of near starvation in time of siege, and so this
element of the prophecy is linked with the model siege of verses 1–3. The phrase "break the
staff of bread" is taken from the dire prediction of disaster in Leviticus 26 if Israel abandons
God's ways, and other phrases from that passage in Leviticus are invoked here.

CHAPTER 5   1. *a sharp blade.* The noun *ḥerev* usually means "sword." The choice of
the term here, as several commentators have noted, is in order to point forward to the use
of the same word in the sense of "sword" near the end of the next verse.

2. *A third you shall burn in fire within the city.* The city in question is the design of the city
that has been incised on the brick. The destruction of the cut hair in three equal parts is
thus a continuation of the symbolic modeling of the destruction of Jerusalem.

5. *This is Jerusalem.* In this speech, God is pointing to the image of the city incised on the
brick and expounding its meaning.

6. *she rebelled against My laws.* The noun *mishpatim* can mean "judgments," "laws," "rules."
The English equivalent "laws" is used here because "judgments" is not right for the context,
but as the passage continues, the cognate *shefatim,* which means "judgments" in the sense
of "punishment," is insisted on.

the LORD: Inasmuch as you have raised a clamor more than the nations
that are all round you, My statutes you did not follow, My laws you did
not keep, and like the laws of the nations that are all round you, you did not
8   do. Therefore, thus said the Master, the LORD: Look, I on My part am now
against you, and I will carry out judgments in your midst before the eyes
9   of the nations. And I will do what I have not done and the like of which I
10 will not do again because of all your abominations. Therefore, fathers shall
eat sons within you and sons shall eat their fathers, and I will perform
11 judgments against you and scatter your remnant to every wind. Therefore,
as I live, said the Master, the LORD, because you have defiled My sanctuary
with all your disgusting things and with all your abominations, I on My
part will surely shear, and My eye shall not spare, and I, too, will show no
12 pity. A third of you shall die by pestilence and come to an end within you
by famine, and a third shall fall by the sword all round you, and a third will
13 I scatter to every wind, and I will unsheathe the sword after them. And My
anger shall come to an end, and I will put to rest My wrath against them,
and I will repent, and they shall know that I the LORD have spoken in My
14 passion when I bring to an end My wrath against them. And I will make

---

7. *raised a clamor.* The verb strongly implies rebellion.

like the laws of the nations that are all round you, you did not do. This is an extreme
element in Ezekiel's castigation of Judah. The surrounding nations, though they had no
covenant with God, observed at least some basic guidelines or laws (*mishpatim,* also "judgments") of civilized behavior, but even these minimal constraints on behavior you ignored.

10. *fathers shall eat sons within you and sons shall eat their fathers.* Although the horror of
cannibalism in time of siege is frequently invoked in the Bible—see especially Leviticus
26, an important intertext to this one—the idea of reciprocal cannibalism between the
generations is an added ghastly twist.

11. *your disgusting things and with all your abominations.* Both terms are repeatedly used in
the Bible for pagan idols. Ezekiel has in mind the fact that more than once idols were actually introduced into the Jerusalem sanctuary. The language here and again further in this
passage borrows from the denunciations in Deuteronomy 32, the so-called Song of Moses.

12. *I will unsheathe the sword after them.* In the bleakly schematic terms of Ezekiel's prophecy of the three thirds, after a third die by pestilence and famine and a third fall to the
sword, the third who flee ("scatter[ed] to every wind") will also perish by the sword. The
unusual usage of the preposition "after" is intended to indicate that the scattered ones are
in flight, pursued by the sword.

13. *My anger shall come to an end.* This is a qualified consolation. God's anger will come to
an end only after He has thoroughly devastated the people.

passion. The Hebrew *qin'ah* has a core meaning of "jealousy" (and in English we speak
of "jealous passion"), a sense not altogether irrelevant here because God is so often imagined as Israel's spouse.

you a ruin and a reproach among the nations that are all round you, before
the eyes of every passerby. And she shall be a reproach and a revilement, 15
an object lesson and a fright to the nations all round you when I carry out
judgments in anger and in wrath and in chastisements of wrath. I the Lord
have spoken. When I let loose My deadly arrows—famine—against them, 16
which become a destroyer, which I will let loose against them to destroy
them, and famine will I add against them and break their staff of bread.
And I will let loose against you famine and vicious beasts, and they shall 17
bereave you, and pestilence and bloodshed shall pass through you, and the
sword will I bring against you. I the Lord have spoken.

CHAPTER 6   And the word of the Lord came to me, saying, 1
"Man, set your face to the mountains of Israel and prophesy to them, And 2,3
say, 'Mountains of Israel, hear the word of the Master, the Lord. Thus said
the Master, the Lord, to the mountains and to the hills, to the gullies and
to the valleys: I am about to bring the sword against you, and I will destroy
your high places, and your altars shall be desolate and your incense stands 4
broken, and I will make your slain fall in front of your vile things. And I 5

---

15. *judgments.* Here *shefatim* is used. In verse 8 the cognate *mishpatim* is used in the same
sense as *shefatim*, which means "punishment."

16. *deadly.* More literally, "evil."

17. *against you.* The switch from third person (plural) to second person (still plural), or the
other way around, is fairly common in biblical usage.
  vicious beasts. Again, the literal sense is "evil beasts." Such attacks by beasts of prey
would occur because the countryside of Judah would be devastated and depopulated,
allowing dangerous carnivores to proliferate.
  bloodshed. The Hebrew says merely "blood," which constitutes a somewhat unusual
employment of the word.

CHAPTER 6   2. *set your face to the mountains of Israel.* The apostrophe to the
mountains and the hills and the valleys that begins in the next verse amounts to a rhetorical displacement of an address to the people of Israel that worshipped idols in these
nature settings. The sword that is about to come against the mountains and hills is actually
directed, in a metonymic slide, against the places of pagan worship and finally against the
worshippers.

3. *high places.* These elevated altars were often placed on hilltops outside towns, but they
could also be located in valleys (hence the "the gullies and the valleys" earlier in this verse).

4. *I will make your slain fall.* The metonymic slide is completed here: "your high places"
could still refer to the hills and mountains, but "your slain" means the slain of the people
of Judah.

will put the corpses of the Israelites in front of your vile things, and I will
6 scatter your bones all round your altars. Through all your settlements the
towns shall be reduced to ruins and the high places made desolate so that
your altars lie in ruins and be desolate, and your vile things shall be broken
and destroyed and your incense stands be cut down, and your handiwork
7 wiped out. And the slain shall fall in your midst, and you shall know that
8 I am the LORD. And I will leave some of you, when you are fugitives of the
9 sword among the nations, when you are scattered in the lands. And your
fugitives shall recall Me among the nations where they were captive, that
I have broken their whoring heart that swerved from Me and their eyes
whoring after their vile things, and they shall loathe themselves for the
10 evils that they did, for all their abominations. And they shall know that I,
the LORD, not for nothing did I speak to them this evil.'"

11 Thus said the Master, the LORD: "Strike with your palm and stamp with
your foot and say, Alack! for all the evil abominations of the house of Israel.
12 Who by the sword, by famine, or by pestilence shall fall. He who is far off by
pestilence shall die, and he who is near by the sword shall fall, and he who
remains and is besieged, by famine shall die, and I will bring My wrath to
13 an end against them. And you shall know that I am the LORD when their
slain are in the midst of their vile things all round your altars on every

---

5. *your vile things.* As elsewhere, this is a pejorative (even probably excremental) epithet
for idols.
　scatter your bones all round your altars. This act renders the area ritually impure.

8. *And I will leave some of you.* The Hebrew merely says "And I will leave" and it is textually problematic. It is absent in the Septuagint, and its deletion yields a smooth-reading
sentence here: "When you are fugitives of the sword among the nations, when you are
scattered in the lands, your fugitives shall recall Me...."

9. *I have broken their whoring heart.* The Hebrew appears to say "I am broken," *nishbarti.*
Many interpreters, medieval and modern, understand this to mean, "I am brokenhearted,"
but there are no other instances where the verb "to break" is used elliptically in this manner
to mean "brokenhearted." Either this is a case in which the passive form takes an active
sense, or, more likely, it is a scribal error for the active form, *shavarti,* triggered by the
similar form of the immediately preceding verb *nishbu,* "were captive."

12. *He who is far off . . . he who is near . . . he who remains.* This tripartite division spells
out the meaning of the symbolic prophetic act of dividing the hair into three parts (5:1–4).
　I will bring My wrath to an end. The verb "bring to an end," *kilah,* is susceptible to two
interpretations, but these come down to the same idea: it means either "I will utterly implement all My wrath" or "having entirely carried out the aims of My wrath, it will come to
an end, be spent."

high hill, on all the mountaintops, and under every lush tree and under
every leafy oak, the places where they offered a pleasing odor to all their
vile things. And I will stretch out My hand against them and make the land 14
an utter desolation from the desert to Diblah through all their settlements.
And they shall know that I am the LORD.

CHAPTER 7   And the word of the LORD came to me, saying: 1
"And you, man, thus said the Master, the LORD, concerning the country 2
of Israel:

> An end, the end has come
>> upon the four corners of the earth.
> Now the end is upon you,   3
>> and I have let loose My wrath against you
> and exacted judgment of you by your ways
>> and laid upon you all your abominations.
> And My eye shall not spare you   4
>> nor will I show pity,
> for your ways will I lay upon you,
>> and your abominations shall be in your midst,

---

13. *where they offered a pleasing odor to all their vile things.* The formulation incorporates
a pointed polemic contradiction: the "pleasing odor" is the standard phrase for incense,
presumed to be pleasing to the gods, or to God; but a stench attaches itself to *gilulim,* "vile
things," because of the association of the term with dung.

14. *an utter desolation.* In the Hebrew, this sense is conveyed by joining two different nouns
derived from the same root, *shemamah* and *meshamah.*
   Diblah. This is probably the same site as Riblah, the town on the edge of Syrian territory where Nebuchadnezzar set up headquarters during his campaign against Judah and
surrounding lands. The desert here marks the south and Diblah the far north.

CHAPTER 7   2. *An end, the end has come / upon the four corners of the earth.* This
is the first prophecy in Ezekiel unambiguously cast as poetry. Perhaps Ezekiel sensed an
appropriate match between the incantatory force of the poetic medium and the apocalyptic reach of the prophetic message (note the hypnotic insistence on "the end" at the very
beginning of this prophecy). Although what follows concentrates on the judgment of the
people of Israel, "the four corners of the earth" embraces the entire world, as if to say: the
catastrophe about to overtake Israel will engulf all humanity.

3. *exacted judgment.* Though the verb relates to the root concept of "judgment," its sense
in context is close to "punish."

and you shall know that I am the LORD.

5   Thus said the Master, the LORD:

6   One evil, an evil about to come,
       the end has come, is roused against you, yes, it comes!

7   The gyre has come round against you,
       O dweller in the land.
   The time has come, the day is near,
       an uproar, no cheers in the mountains.

8   Now soon I will pour out My anger against you,
       and bring My wrath to an end against you,
   And judge you by your ways
       and lay upon you all your abominations.

9   And My eye shall not spare,
       nor will I show pity,
   by your ways I will lay upon you
       and your abominations shall be in your midst,
         and you shall know that I am the LORD.

10   Here is the day, here it comes,
       the gyre has turned around,
         the staff blooms, arrogance flowers.

11   Outrage rises as a staff of wickedness—
       not of them nor of their crowd,
         not of them, and no lament in them.

12   The time has come, the day arrived.

---

4. *you shall know that I am the* LORD. This is a virtual refrain in Ezekiel. The idea behind it is that until now the people, pursuing its refractory ways, behaved as though YHWH did not exist, but as they bear the terrible punishment for their acts, they will be forced to recognize His existence and power.

7. *the gyre.* The Hebrew *tsefirah* is a rare term. It has most plausibly been linked by both medieval and modern commentators with a root that indicates something round, here perhaps a cycle of time. Because of the unusualness of the Hebrew term, this translation uses "gyre" (the same element one finds in "gyroscope"), a word famously deployed by the poet W. B. Yeats for an apocalyptic turn in the cycle of time.

     no cheers in the mountains. Following many interpreters, this translation understands *hed* as a shortened variant form of *heydad,* the cry of joy of grape harvesters.

10. *the staff blooms, arrogance flowers.* As has often been noted, this is a sardonic reversal of the blooming of Aaron's staff (Numbers 17:23), which was a sign of divine election.

11. *not of them nor of their crowd, / not of them, and no lament in them.* The Hebrew is one long string of fused phonemes, perhaps a sign that the text has been garbled, perhaps an intended poetic effect. It sounds like this: *lo'-meihem welo' meihamonam welo' mehamei-hem welo'-nohah bahem.*

Let not the buyer rejoice nor the seller mourn,
 for there is wrath against all her crowd.
For the seller to his sold goods shall not come back,   13
 though they be still alive,
for the vision against all her around shall not turn back,
 each alive in his crime shall not hold fast.
They have sounded the horn and readied all things,   14
 but none goes to the battle,
  for My wrath is against all her crowd.
The sword is outside,   15
 pestilence and famine within.
Who is out in the field by the sword shall die,
 and he in the town, famine and pestilence consume him.
And their refugees flee   16
 and come to the mountains,
like doves of the valleys
 they all moan in their crime.
All hands go slack,   17
 and all knees run with water.
And they shall gird sackcloth,   18
 and shudders cover them.
On every face is shame,
 and all their heads are shaven.

---

12. *Let not the buyer rejoice nor the seller mourn.* In ordinary circumstances, the buyer would rejoice at having acquired something he wanted and the seller mourn for having lost something he was obliged to part with. Now, however, all exchanges of property become meaningless because everyone is about to be swept up in the general destruction.

13. *though they be still alive.* The Hebrew here is a little obscure.

14. *readied all things.* Given the sounding of the horn and the reference to battle in the next verset, this means readied weapons for war.

16. *like doves of the valleys.* There is a species of dove that nests among the rocks and crevices of valleys. Greenberg proposes that *ge'ayot,* "valleys," puns on *hogot,* the moaning sound made by doves.

17. *all knees run with water.* This refers to urinating in terror. The line thus neatly illustrates the general pattern in which the second verset in a line concretizes or intensifies what is stated in the first verset: "slack hands" is a very common idiom for weakness, but then we see the shameful evidence of fear in urine running down the knees.

18. *all their heads are shaven.* As elsewhere, the shaving of the head is a sign of mourning, prohibited to the Israelites, but much in evidence in the language of poetry.

19   Their silver they fling into the streets,
            and their gold becomes unclean.
        Their silver and their gold cannot save them
            on the day of the wrath of the Lord.
        Their gullets shall not be sated
            nor their innards shall they fill,
                for a stumbling block their crime has become.
20   And their lovely ornaments of which they were proud,
            they made of them images of their loathsome abominations,
                therefore will I make them unclean.
21   And I will give them into the hand of strangers as booty
            and to the wicked of the earth as spoils, and they shall defile her.
22   And I will turn My face from them,
            and they shall defile My treasure,
                and brutes shall enter her and defile her.
23   Forge a chain,
            for the land is filled with blood-justice
                and the city is filled with outrage.
24   And I will bring the most evil of nations,
            and they shall take hold of your homes;
        and I will end the pride of the strong,
            and their sanctuaries shall be defiled.
25   Terror comes!
            They shall seek peace and it shall not be.

---

19. *Their silver they fling into the streets.* This is in keeping with the pointlessness of buying and selling in verse 12. Wealth is now utterly useless because, as the next line goes on to say, it cannot save them.

22. *and they shall defile My treasure.* Since the defiling by "brutes" that follows has a feminine object, God's "treasure" is in all likelihood the city of Jerusalem, regularly represented as a feminine singular.

23. *blood-justice.* The collocation *mishpat-damim* in the Hebrew is unusual, but the parallel with "outrage" (others, "violence") clearly indicates it is a perversion of justice that victimizes the innocent. The plural form of "blood" used here almost always indicates unjust or murderous violence.

25. *Terror comes!* The word for "terror," *qefadah,* is unusual but appears to relate to a root that means "to bristle." Note that "comes," a verb prominent at the beginning of this prophecy, is repeated as a kind of key word, stressing the terrible imminence of the end.

Disaster upon disaster shall come,   26
     and rumor after rumor shall be.
And they shall seek vision from a prophet,
     but teaching shall be gone from the priest
       and counsel from the elders.
The king shall mourn,   27
     and the prince don desolation.
The hands of the people of the land shall panic.
     By their way will I do with them,
       and by their judgments will I exact judgment of them.
And they shall know that I am the LORD.

CHAPTER 8   And it happened in the sixth year in the sixth   1 month on the fifth of the month, I was sitting in my house, and the elders of Judah were sitting before me, and the hand of the Master, the LORD, fell upon me there. And I saw and, look, a likeness like the look of fire, from the   2 look of his loins and below fire, and from his loins and above like the look of brilliance, like the color of amber. And He reached out the form of a hand   3

---

26. *rumor after rumor.* These are clearly rumors of disaster.

    vision from a prophet, / . . . teaching . . . from the priest / . . . counsel from the elders. These are the three sources of authority in ancient Israelite society: the prophet is the vehicle of vision; the priest offers instruction, perhaps from a written text; the elders, with their accumulated wisdom, proffer counsel. In the dire end-time, a manifestation of the punishment of the people will be that all sources of authority and guidance will be taken away.

27. *don desolation.* After the mourning of the king, we might have expected the formulaic "don sackcloth," so "desolation" comes as a small but striking surprise. Ordinarily, of course, princes would put on regal raiment.

    by their judgments. The multipurpose *mishpatim* can also mean something like "practices" or "modes of behavior."

CHAPTER 8   1. *in the sixth year.* This would be the sixth year of Jehoiachin's exile (and Ezekiel's), or 591 B.C.E.

    the hand of the Master, the LORD, fell upon me. The usual idiom is "came [or was] upon me." This more physical formulation is scarcely accidental: as before, Ezekiel is a passive vessel acted upon vigorously, almost violently, by God.

2. *a likeness like the look.* As in the vision of the celestial chariot, Ezekiel is careful to interpose a whole set of qualifying terms indicating that what he sees in the vision is not the thing itself but a resemblance or analogical image of things familiar to humankind.

    like the look of fire. The Septuagint, instead of *'esh,* "fire," reads *'ish,* "a man."

and took me by a lock of my head, and a wind bore me between the earth
and the heavens and brought me to Jerusalem through divine visions to the
entrance of the gate of the inner court facing northward where the icon of
4 the provoking provocation is set. And, look, there was the glory of the God
5 of Israel like the sight that I had seen in the valley. And He said to me, "Man,
raise your eyes toward the north." And I raised my eyes toward the north,
and, look, from north of the altar gate, this icon of provocation was in the
6 entranceway. And He said to me, "Man, do you see what abominations they
are doing, which the house of Israel are doing here to go far from My sanctu-
7 ary? And you will yet see greater abominations." And He brought me to the
8 entrance of the court, and I saw, and, look, there was a hole in the wall. And
He said to me, "Man, pray, break through the wall." And I broke through the
9 wall, and, look, there was an entrance. And He said to me, "Come and see
10 the evil abominations that they are doing here." And I came and saw and,
look, every form of creeping thing and beast, disgusting things, and all the
11 foul things of the house of Israel were incised on the wall all around. And

---

3. *a wind bore me between the earth and the heavens and brought me to Jerusalem.* The
sense of the prophet as the passive object of divine action continues here. The basis of this
whole vision appears to be some sort of hallucinatory experience in which the prophet, who
has very recently been lying immobilized for more than a year, senses that he is physically
borne off to Jerusalem, if only in a divine vision. As an exiled priest, the Temple there was
very much on his mind, and now he envisages, or is made to witness, the pagan abominations practiced in this holy space.

the gate of the inner court. "Court" is implied in an ellipsis in the Hebrew.

the icon of the provoking provocation. The unusual word for "icon," *semel,* is an appropriate borrowing from the Cannanite, where it indicates the statue of a god. The prophet
refuses to name a particular god but instead uses an elliptical epithet of opprobrium, "the
provoking provocation." The verbal stem from which that designation derives suggests
"jealousy," which makes sense here because God is a "jealous" God, indignant when Israel
goes whoring after other deities.

7. *there was a hole in the wall.* This is the oddest moment in Ezekiel's vision of the abominations in the Temple. It suggests a kind of prophetic voyeurism. There is a hole through
which he might almost peek into the vile pagan rites practiced within the chambers of
God's temple. In order actually to see them, however, he must enlarge the hole and break
through the wall.

10. *every form of creeping thing and beast, disgusting things, and all the foul things of the
house of Israel were incised on the wall.* There is an effective segue here from living creatures
prohibited as food and regarded with disgust to the "foul things"—which is to say, idols—
equally felt to be disgusting by the prophet. It is questionable whether there was a practice
of incising the images of pagan gods on the temple walls, but it is a forceful representation
of how deeply paganism had penetrated into the most sacred space of the nation.

seventy men of the elders of Israel, with Jaazaniah son of Shaphan standing in the midst of them, were standing before these, each with his incense
pan in his hand, and a dense cloud of incense was rising. And He said to   12
me, "Do you see, man, what the elders of the house of Israel are doing in
the dark, each in the chambers of his sculpted images, for they say, 'The
LORD does not see us. The LORD has abandoned the land.'" And He said to   13
me, "You shall yet see greater abominations that they are doing." And He   14
brought me to the entrance of the gate of the house of the LORD that was to
the north, and, look, women were sitting there keening for Tammuz. And   15
He said to me, "Do you see, man? You will yet see greater abominations
than these." And He brought me to the inner court of the house of the   16
LORD, and, look, between the great hall and the altar were some twenty-five
men, their backs to the LORD's temple and their faces eastward, and they
were bowing down eastward to the sun. And He said to me, "Do you see,   17
man? Is it too light a thing for the house of Judah to do the abominations

---

11. *seventy men of the elders of Israel.* This assembly of the canonical seventy elders, evidently led by one of the eminent figures of the court aristocracy, amounts to the group's
celebrating a kind of black mass, at least in the eyes of the prophet.

    dense cloud. The first of these two nouns, *'atar,* appears only here, but it is probably
related to a Syriac word that means "fume." As elsewhere, when two synonymous nouns
are joined in the construct form, the effect is an intensification of their meaning, hence
"dense cloud" in this translation. Compare the very similar construction in Exodus 19:9,
'av-he 'anan, "the utmost cloud."

12. *Do you see, man, what the elders of the house of Israel are doing in the dark.* Although
the elders go on to say that the LORD does not see them, they may be hedging their bets
or are perhaps fearful that some groups in the community of Judah—certainly prophets
such as Jeremiah and Ezekiel—would vehemently object to what they are doing. The fact
that they worship strange gods in their private chambers seems to contradict the pagan
assembly in the Temple depicted here. Perhaps as a rule they practice their pagan rites in
the darkness of their chambers but here have exceptionally joined together to celebrate the
cult of strange gods within an inner hall of the Temple, still hidden from the eyes of the
general populace but not from the prophet, who has enlarged the hole in the wall so that
he can see everything.

14. *women were sitting there keening for Tammuz.* Tammuz is a deity imported from Babylonia (the Akkadian name is Dumuzi). Like Adonis, he is a vegetation god thought to die
and descend into the underworld after the dying of vegetation at the end of the spring.
Women in ancient Near Eastern societies were assigned the role of keening for the dead,
and so they took over the cultic function of keening for Tammuz.

16. *bowing down eastward to the sun.* Worship of the sun god and other astral deities,
because of Assyrian influences, became widespread in the last two centuries of the First
Commonwealth.

they have done here that they should fill the land with outrage and repeatedly vex Me? And here they are reaching out the vine branch to My nose.
18 And I on My part will act in wrath and My eye shall not spare them nor
will I show pity, and they shall call out in My hearing with a loud voice but
I will not listen to them."

1 **CHAPTER 9**   And he called out to me in a loud voice, saying,
"Bring near those appointed over the city, each with his weapon of destruc-
2 tion in his hand." And, look, six men were coming by the way of the upper
gate, which faces to the north, and each had his mace in his hand, and a man
in their midst was dressed in linen with a scribe's case at his waist. And they
3 came and stood by the bronze altar. And the glory of the LORD had ascended
from the cherub on which it had been to the threshold of the house, and He
4 called out to the man wearing linen with a scribe's case at his waist. And
the LORD said to him, "Pass through the city, in the midst of Jerusalem, and
trace a mark on the foreheads of the men groaning and moaning over all

---

17. *reaching out the vine branch to My nose.* The Masoretic Text says "their nose," but this is
an explicit "scribal correction," introducing a kind of euphemism in order not to say something offensive relating to God. But the meaning of the expression is elusive. The attempt
by some to link *zemorah,* "vine branch," with a homonymous root that means "strength"
is far-fetched—the clear meaning of the word is "vine branch." Some have imagined, perhaps fancifully, that it reflects the worship of a phallic deity. But, as Greenberg observes,
the prophet at this point has moved on from pagan rituals to a condemnation of moral
turpitude—"they . . . fill the land with outrage." The most reasonable assumption is that
the branch extended toward the nose is some sort of insulting gesture.

CHAPTER 9   1. *those appointed.* Though the Hebrew term suggests "officials," or
"appointed ones," Greenberg notes that this same root is also associated with punishment
or retribution, and so he renders it more grimly as "executioners."

2. *mace.* This specification of the identity of the "weapons of destruction" points to an
especially bloody and brutal implementation of the command of destruction—not with
sword thrusts, but with the bashing of heads.
    a man in their midst was dressed in linen. This makes a total of seven, the sanctified
number. He wears linen like the priests (in Daniel, by extension, angels will be dressed in
linen).
    a scribe's case. He will use his pen and ink to make the marks on the foreheads of those
to be saved.

4. *trace a mark on the foreheads.* The word for "mark," *taw,* is the last letter of the Hebrew
alphabet. In paleo-Hebrew script, the form of this letter was an X. The saving mark on the
forehead recalls the mark that saves Cain from retribution.
    groaning and moaning. The translation imitates the Hebrew sound-play, *hane'enahim
wehane'enaqim.*

the abominations done in her midst." And to these He said in my hearing, 5 "Pass through the city after him and strike, let your eye not spare, nor show pity. Elder, young man and virgin, little ones and women you shall slay, 6 destroying. But do not approach any man upon whom is the mark. And from My sanctuary you shall begin." And they began with the elders who 7 were in front of the house. And He said to them, "Defile the house and fill 8 the courts with corpses. Go forth." And they went forth and struck in the city. And it happened as they were striking that I remained, and I fell on my 9 face and cried out and said, "Woe, O Master, LORD, are You destroying all the remnant of Israel as You pour out Your wrath on Jerusalem?" And He 10 said to me, "The crime of the house of Israel and Judah is very, very great, and the land is filled with bloodguilt and the city filled with injustice, for they have said, 'The LORD has abandoned the land, and the LORD does not see.' And I on My part, My eye shall not spare nor will I show pity. I will 11 bring their ways down on their head." And, look, the man dressed in linen 12 with the case at his waist brought back word, saying, "I have done as You have charged."

---

5. *let your eye not spare, nor show pity.* These fierce phrases are a refrain through this whole large prophecy, repeatedly attached to God, but here to His agents.

6. *Elder, young man and virgin, little ones and women you shall slay.* Although other prophets foresee a comprehensive disaster that will sweep over the entire people, Ezekiel is distinctive in imagining an active undertaking of genocidal killing by executioners commanded by God.

7. *the elders who were in front of the house.* Presumably, these are the paganizing elders, previously seen within the Temple, who now have come out in front of it.

8. *Defile the house and fill the courts with corpses.* Corpses intrinsically defile a place. The command to defile the Temple is shocking, but as Greenberg notes, it has already been defiled by the abomination of idol worship and hence is no longer a fit place for the worship of YHWH.

9. *are You destroying all the remnant of Israel.* Some interpreters have taken this to contradict the saving of those marked on the forehead. In fact, it makes emotional sense: Ezekiel, confronted in his vision with the bloody spectacle of the Temple courts filled with corpses, and men, women and children bludgeoned to death with maces everywhere, is devastated and feels as if the entire people were being wiped out.

10. *The crime of the house of Israel and Judah is very, very great.* Ezekiel's God is perhaps the most implacable of the many versions of God in the Hebrew Bible.

1 **CHAPTER 10**   And I saw and, look, on the platform that was upon the heads of the cherubim—like the sapphire stone, like the look
2 of the likeness of a throne was seen upon them. And He said to the man dressed in linen, and said, "Come between the wheels beneath the cherubim and fill your hands with fiery coals from between the cherubs and cast
3 them over the city." And he came in before my eyes. And the cherubim were standing at the right side of the house as a man enters, and the cloud filled
4 the inner court. And the glory of the Lord rose up over the cherub on the threshold of the house and filled the house, and the house was filled with
5 the radiance of the glory of the Lord. And the sound of the cherubim's wings could be heard as far as the outer court, like the sound of El Shaddai
6 when He speaks. And it happened when He charged the man dressed in linen, saying, "Take fire from within the wheelwork from among the cheru-
7 bim," he came and stood by the wheel. And the cherub reached out his hand from between the cherubim to the fire that was between the cherubim and carried it and gave it into the hands of the man dressed in linen, and he took
8 it and went out. And there appeared on the cherubim the form of a human
9 hand beneath their wings. And I saw, and, look, there were four wheels by the cherubim, a single wheel by each cherub, and the look of the wheels was
10 like the color of chrysolite. And their look, a single likeness for the four of
11 them, as a wheel is within a wheel. When they go, to their four sides they do go, they do not turn as they go, but to the place where the head turns,
12 toward it they go, they do not turn as they go. And all their flesh and their backs and their hands and their wings and the wheels were filled with eyes

---

CHAPTER 10   1. *like the look of the likeness of a throne.* Ezekiel's proclivity for interposing words negating the literalness of the nouns attached to the divine apparition is especially pronounced here.

2. *cast them over the city.* Throwing the fiery coals over the city is obviously either a symbolic prefiguration or the actual implementation of the fiery destruction that will engulf Jerusalem.

5. *El Shaddai.* This is an archaic—and hence usually poetic—designation of God that emphasizes His terrific power, though the etymology of the second word is disputed.

6. *he came and stood by the wheel.* Since in the next verse it is one of the cherubim who gives him the fiery coals, the man dressed in linen stops short of carrying out the command. David Kimchi plausibly suggests that he was afraid to reach into the wheelwork.

7. *gave it into the hands of the man.* No explanation is offered as to how his hands would not have been scorched. Contrast Isaiah 6:6, where a seraph needs tongs for the fiery coal.

all round the four of them, their wheels. As to the wheels, in my hearing 13
they were called wheelwork. And each one had four faces. The face of one 14
was a cherub's face, and the face of the second was a human face, and of
the third, a lion's face, and of the fourth, an eagle's face. And the cherubim 15
rose up—these were the creatures that I had seen by the Kebar Canal. And 16
when the cherubim went, the wheels went along with them, and when the
cherubim lifted their wings to rise from the ground, the wheels did not
turn either from alongside them. When they stood still, they, too, stood 17
still, and when they rose, they, too, rose, for the spirit of the creatures was
in them. And the glory of the LORD went forth from the threshold of the 18
house and stood over the cherubim. And the cherubim lifted their wings 19
and rose from the ground before my eyes as they went forth, and the wheels
were opposite them. And they stood still at the entrance of the eastern gate
of the LORD's house. And the glory of the God of Israel was upon them
from above. These were the creatures that I had seen beneath the God of 20
Israel at the Kebar Canal, and I knew that they were cherubim. Each one 21
had four faces, and each one had four wings, and a likeness of human
hands was beneath the wings. And the likeness of their faces—these were 22
the faces that I had seen by the Kebar Canal, the same look. Each straight
ahead they did go.

---

12. *four of them, their wheels.* The ostensible apposition here looks awkward and "their wheels" may not belong. It must be said that there are several junctures in this description of the celestial chariot where the text looks garbled. This might even reflect a confusion on the part of the ancient scribes about what precisely was going on in this bewildering vision.

13. *As to the wheels . . . they were called wheelwork.* The puzzling fact is that both *'ofanim,* "wheels," and *galgal,* "wheelwork," mean "wheel." This translation follows Greenberg and the New Jewish Publication Society version in using "wheelwork" for the collective noun *galgal,* but that may be no more than a strategy of desperation.

14. *The face of one was a cherub's face.* The description here diverges from the description in chapter 1. There, each of the creatures had four different faces. Here each appears to have four similar faces with the differences showing from one creature to the next. The face of the bull, moreover, in chapter 1 is replaced here by the face of a cherub (unless, as some have claimed, cherubs had bull faces). These discrepancies may derive from the fact that Ezekiel had two parallel but not entirely identical visions of the same celestial apparatus, or they may reflect struggles in the process of transmitting this difficult vision.

15. *these were the creatures.* Though the Hebrew uses a singular noun, the context requires understanding it as a collective noun.

22. *the same look.* The Hebrew here sounds odd: *mar'eyhem we'otam* would be literally "their looks and them." The translation is thus somewhat speculative.

1 CHAPTER 11   And the wind bore me and brought me to the
eastern gate of the house of the LORD facing eastward, and, look, in the
entrance of the gate were twenty-five men, and I saw in their midst Jaaza-
2 niah son of Ezer and Pelatiah son of Benaiah, officials of the people. And
He said to me, "Man, these are the men plotting wrongdoing and devising
3 evil counsel in this city, thinking, 'Soon is not the time to build houses.
4 It is the pot and we are the meat.' Therefore prophesy concerning them,
5 prophesy, man." And the spirit of the LORD fell upon me, and He said; "Say,
thus said the LORD: So have you thought and what comes to your mind I
6 know. You have left many slain in this city and filled its streets with the
7 slain. Therefore, thus said the Master, the LORD: Your slain that you put
within it, they are the meat and it is the pot, and you will I bring out from
8 within it. You feared the sword, and a sword I will bring against you, said
9 the Master, the LORD. And I will bring you out from within it and give you
10 into the hand of strangers and exact punishment from you. By the sword
you shall fall, at the border of Israel I will punish you, and you shall know
11 that I am the LORD. It shall not be a pot for you nor shall you live within it
12 as meat. At the border of Israel I will punish you. And you shall know that
I am the LORD in Whose statutes you did not go and My laws you did not

---

CHAPTER 11   1. *twenty-five men.* These are evidently the same twenty-five mentioned in 8:16 who were worshipping the sun.

3. *Soon is not the time to build houses.* The plotters belong to the party resisting Babylonia,
and so they think that all efforts should be channeled into constructing fortifications, not
building houses.

  It is the pot and we are the meat. The sense of this rather odd metaphor is: it (the city)
is the pot that contains us, and we are the good meat within the pot. But the metaphor
undermines its own arrogant assertion because meat in a pot over a fire is destined to be
cooked and consumed.

6. *You have left many slain in this city.* The preceding account of the turpitude of these
Jerusalemites concentrated on their attachment to idolatry. Now, however, they are casti-
gated as murderers.

7. *Your slain . . . they are the meat and it is the pot, and you will I bring out from within it.*
God now reverses the self-congratulatory metaphor of the perpetrators of crime. Their
victims are the true elite ("the meat"), and the victimizers will be cast out of the pot (that
is, the city) as matter unfit for consumption.

10. *By the sword you shall fall, at the border of Israel.* The miscreants will be cast very far
from the city in which they thought they might find safety. What the prophet may have in
mind concretely is that they will flee Jerusalem in the face of the Babylonian invaders, only
to be caught and killed at the border.

do, but like the laws of the nations that were all round you did you do." And 13
it happened as I prophesied that Pelatiah son of Benaiah died, and I fell on
my face and cried out in a loud voice and said, "Woe, O Master, the LORD,
You are making an utter end of the remnant of Israel."

And the word of the LORD came to me, saying, "Man, your brothers, your 14,15
next of kin, and all the house of Israel to whom the dwellers of Jerusalem
have said, 'Go away from the LORD. To us the land has been given as an
inheritance.' Therefore, say, Thus said the Master, the LORD: Though I have 16
taken them far away among the nations and though I have scattered them
among the lands and became for them but a bare sanctuary in the lands
where they came, therefore say, Thus said the Master, the LORD: I will gather 17
you from the peoples and bring you together from the lands where you were
scattered, and I will give you Israel's soil. And they shall come there and 18
take away from it all its disgusting things and all its abominations. And I 19

---

12. *like the laws of the nations that were all round you did you do.* Here the reference appears
to be to idolatry. One should keep in mind that the Hebrew *mishpatim* means both "laws"
and "practices" or "behavior."

13. *Woe, O Master, the LORD, You are making an utter end of the remnant of Israel.* This sentence could also be construed as a tormented question (Are you making . . . ?). It may seem
puzzling that Ezekiel should be distressed over the death of Pelatiah, who is after all one
of the ringleaders of the men "devising evil counsel." All we know about Pelatiah is that he
was some sort of high-ranking official, but this may have been enough to make his sudden
death a cause of distress for the prophet. That is, if the leaders of the people suddenly begin
to drop off in this fashion, is God about to wipe out the whole people?

15. *your brothers, your next of kin.* The designation "next of kin" is adopted from Greenberg.
The literal sense is "your redemption people," that is, the people who because of their kinship are legally obliged to redeem property that has been somehow alienated from a person.
(Compare the "redeeming kin" in the Book of Ruth.) The mention in the next verse of God's
having "taken them far away among the nations" indicates that these are the exiles. The
self-satisfied residents of Jerusalem want to dissociate themselves from their exiled brothers, claiming exclusive rights to the land: "Go away from the land. To us the land has been
given as an inheritance."

16. *but a bare sanctuary.* The Hebrew expression *miqdash me'at* was taken by later tradition as a reference to the synagogue, but this text well antedates the institution of the
synagogue. The idea seems to be that in the exile, in the absence of a temple, God provides
only minimal indications—perhaps through prophecy?—of His continuing closeness to
Israel.

17. *Israel's soil.* Here, and in the next chapter, the reference seems to be to the land, but the
suggestion of soil to be tilled in the Hebrew term is worth retaining.

will give them a single heart, and a new spirit I will put in your midst, and
I will take away the heart of stone from their flesh and give them a heart of
20 flesh. So that they go by My statutes and keep My laws and do them, and
21 they shall be a nation for Me and I will be their God. But those whose heart
goes after their disgusting things and their abominations, I have laid their
22 ways on their head, said the Master, the LORD." And the cherubim lifted
their wings, with the wheels alongside them, and the glory of the LORD
23 was over them from above. And the glory of the LORD ascended from the
24 midst of the city and stood on the mountain that is east of the city. And a
wind bore me and brought me to Chaldea, to the exiles, in the vision, in
the divine spirit, and the vision that I had seen ascended away from me.
25 And I spoke to the exiles all the words of the LORD that He had showed me.

1 CHAPTER 12   And the word of the LORD came to me saying,
2 "Man, in the midst of the house of rebellion you dwell, who have eyes to
see but do not see, ears to hear but do not hear, for they are a house of
3 rebellion. And you, man, make for yourself exile's gear and go into exile
by day before their eyes, and go into exile from your place to another place

---

19. *give them . . . put in your midst.* As elsewhere, the switching back and forth between
third person and second person reflects ancient Hebrew usage.

21. *But those whose heart goes after their disgusting things.* The beginning of this clause in
the Masoretic Text reads, incomprehensibly, "But to the heart [*we'el lev*] of their disgusting
things." The translation reflects a widely accepted emendation grounded in the Targum
Yonatan, *we'eleh 'aharey.*

24. *in the vision, in the divine spirit.* By stipulating these phrases, Ezekiel again emphasizes
that all the sights he has been vouchsafed to see in Jerusalem were a visionary experience,
not a bodily one. Since the same noun, *mar'eh* (literally, "what is seen"), is then used for
the celestial chariot that rises into the sky above the prophet, the implication is that it,
too, is not a literal, physical entity, but a visionary reality that reveals something about the
nature of the deity.

CHAPTER 12   2. *who have eyes to see but do not see, ears to hear but do not hear.*
The people's resistance to the prophetic message is a recurrent theme in the prophecies (see
especially Isaiah's dedication scene, Isaiah 6). But this clause also recalls the language of
Psalm 115:5–6, where it is applied to idols—as if to say, these stupidly obtuse people are no
better than dumb carvings of wood.

3. *exile's gear.* These would be the basic implements of daily survival wrapped up in a pack
and carried on the shoulder. Assyrian bas-reliefs depict precisely this image of exiles driven
off by Assyrian troops.
    go into exile . . . before their eyes. Ezekiel is addressing a group of exiles in Babylonia in

before their eyes. Perhaps they will see that they are a house of rebellion. And you shall take out your gear as exile's gear by day before their eyes. ₄ And you, you shall go out at evening before their eyes as the going out to exile. Before their eyes, break through the wall and take out your gear ₅ through it. Before their eyes you shall shoulder the burden. In the gloom ₆ you shall take it out. Your face you shall cover and you shall not see the land, for I am making you a portent for the house of Israel." And so did I ₇ do as I was charged. I took out my gear as exile's gear by day, and at evening I broke through the wall by hand in the gloom. I took it out, I shouldered the burden before their eyes. And the word of the LORD came to me in the ₈ morning, saying, "Man, have not the house of Israel, the house of rebellion, ₉ said to you, 'What are you doing?' Say to them, Thus said the Master, the ₁₀ LORD: The prince is this burden in Jerusalem and all the house of Israel who are in their midst. Say, I am your portent. As I have done, so it will ₁₁ be done to them. In exile in captivity they shall go. And the prince who is ₁₂ in their midst shall shoulder the burden in the gloom, and he shall go out, they shall break through the wall to bring out gear through it. His face he shall cover, so that he not see the land with his eyes. And I will cast My ₁₃ net over him, and he shall be caught in My toils. And I will bring him to Babylonia, to the land of the Chaldeans, but he shall not see it, and there

the late 590s B.C.E., but his symbolic act prefigures a much more comprehensive exile that in fact will take place in 586.

4. *you shall go out at evening.* Although this looks like a contradiction of his going out into exile by day, the intention may be to suggest the encompassing nature of the departure into exile—by day, *yomam,* and in the evening, *ba 'erev,* as well.

5. *break through the wall.* This peculiar detail is an odd echo of the prophet's breaking through the wall of the Temple in 8:8 in order to witness the abominations performed inside. Perhaps an equivalence is suggested between discovering the shame within the chambers and the shame of exile outside. There may be an intimation here of something surreptitious in the flight into exile. Perhaps more pertinent, he is asked to do damage to the house he is leaving, with no expectation that he will return to it.

6. *Your face you shall cover and you shall not see the land.* Some interpreters take this as a gesture of hiding because of the humiliation of exile. The second clause, however, suggests that the aim is to cover the eyes so that the exile will not look on the homeland he is forced to abandon.

10. *The prince is this burden.* The Hebrew shows a pun: *hanasi',* "the prince" (etymologically, "the one borne up"), and *hamasa',* "the burden."

13. *he shall not see it.* Many interpreters, medieval and modern, take this as a reference to the last Judahite king, Zedekiah, who was blinded before he was brought to Babylonia (the

14 shall he die. And all that is around him, his allies and all his divisions, I will
15 scatter to every wind, and the sword I will unsheathe after him. And they
shall know that I am the LORD when I disperse them among the nations and
16 scatter them in the lands. And I will leave of them a handful of men from
the sword, from the famine, and from pestilence, that they may recount all
their abominations among the nations where they have come. And they
shall know that I am the LORD."

17,18 And the word of the LORD came to me, saying, "Man, your bread you shall
eat quaking, and your water you shall drink in upheaval and in unease.
19 And you shall say of the people of the land, Thus said the Master, the LORD,
concerning the dwellers of Jerusalem on the soil of Israel: their bread they
shall eat in unease, and their water they shall drink in desolation, so that its
land be desolate of what fills it, because of the outrage of all who dwell in it.
20 And the settled towns shall be in ruins, and the land shall be a desolation,
and you shall know that I am the LORD."

21,22 And the word of the LORD came to me, saying, "Man, what means this
proverb for you on the soil of Israel, saying, 'Long days will pass and vision
23 will vanish'? Therefore, say to them, Thus said the Master, the LORD: I have
put an end to this proverb, and they shall no longer recite it in Israel. Rather,
speak to them, 'The time has drawn near for every vision to come about.'
24 For there shall no longer be any empty vision or soothing divination within
25 the house of Israel. For I the LORD, I will speak the word that I speak and

---

medieval exegetes see this as a prophecy that was fulfilled, the moderns as a prophecy *ex eventu*, after the fact). Even if this clause does refer to Zedekiah's fate, it does not follow that the preceding verses about the exile of the king reflect that fate, because the terms are rather general. Even the wording here could simply stem from the prophet's knowledge that it was a common practice to blind vassal kings who had rebelled.

22. *what means this proverb for you.* The "you" is plural in the Hebrew, so in contrast to other passages that begin with the vocative "man," it is not the prophet but the people that is addressed.

    Long days will pass and vision will vanish. Time will go on, and the prophet's vision of impending doom will not come to pass.

23. *The time has drawn near for every vision to come about.* This reversal of the popular proverb that dismisses prophecy has in view the prophecies of doom pronounced by Ezekiel, Jeremiah, and a few others, "every vision" being a kind of ellipsis for prophecies of doom.

24. *For there shall no longer be any empty vision or soothing divination.* It now emerges that the people, while rejecting the prophecies of imminent disaster, embraced false prophets

it shall be done. It shall no longer be drawn out, but in your days, O house
of rebellion. I will speak a word and do it, said the Master, the LORD." And 26
the word of the LORD came to me, saying, "Man, look, the house of Israel 27
say, 'The vision that he sees, of many days hence and of faraway times he
prophesies.' Therefore say to them, Thus said the LORD: All My words shall 28
no longer be drawn out. I will speak a word and it shall be done,'" said the
Master, the LORD.

CHAPTER 13   And the word of the LORD came to me, saying, 1
"Man, prophesy to the prophets of Israel who prophesy, and say to these 2
prophets out of their own heart, Listen to the word of the LORD. Thus said 3
the Master, the LORD: Woe to the scoundrel prophets who follow their own
spirit and have seen nothing. Like foxes among the ruins, O Israel, your 4
prophets have become. You did not go up in the breaches and build a barrier 5
around the house of Israel to stand in battle on the day of the LORD. They 6

---

who assured them nothing amiss would happen. This is a theme emphatically displayed
in Jeremiah.

25. *It shall no longer be drawn out.* This translation reproduces the literal force of the
Hebrew, which obviously means "to be delayed."

27. *of many days hence and of faraway times he prophesies.* This is a somewhat different
formulation of dismissal of the prophecy from the proverb cited in verse 22. According to
the proverb, with the passage of time it will be seen that the prophecy is entirely groundless.
Here, the deniers say that these predictions of doom may someday be fulfilled, but that
time is so distant that it is of no concern to them. Ezekiel, we should recall, is at this point
prophesying no more than five years before the final destruction of the kingdom of Judah,
so in fact his prediction will come about very soon and not in "faraway times."

CHAPTER 13   2. *prophets out of their own heart.* The idiom "out of their own heart,"
which occurs elsewhere, indicates things that are purely a person's invention.

3. *follow their own spirit.* Greenberg renders "spirit" here as "whims." It is obviously a parallel to "their own heart" in verse 1.

5. *the breaches.* This image picks up the simile of the foxes among the ruins from the previous verse: foxes could make their way through the breach in the stone walls protecting
vineyards and planted fields to wreak havoc within. Thus, the prophets, who should have
protected the people, are themselves predators.
    to stand in battle on the day of the LORD. As elsewhere in the Prophets, "the day of the
LORD" is the day when God comes to exact retribution from Israel for its offenses. The
prophets, then, in this battle metaphor, should have defended Israel and warded off punishment from God by warning the people about its waywardness.

saw empty visions and false divinations, saying, 'the Lord said,' when the

7 Lord did not send them, and they expected to fulfill their word. Why, you have seen an empty vision and a false divination you have spoken, saying,

8 'the Lord said,' when I did not speak. Therefore, thus said the Master, the Lord: Inasmuch as you have spoken emptiness and have seen false visions,

9 therefore, here I am against you, said the Master, the Lord. And My hand shall be against the prophets who see empty visions and perform false divinations. They shall not take part in the council of My people and shall not be written in the writ of the house of Israel and shall not come to the soil of

10 Israel. And you shall know that I am the Lord. Surely because they misled My people, saying, It is well, when it was not well. The people was building a

11 mere partition, and they daubed it with plaster. Say to the daubers of plaster that it will fall. When pounding rain comes—and you—hailstones fall and

12 a storm wind that splits things apart, and, look the wall shall fall. Why, it

13 shall be said to you, Where is the plaster that you daubed? Therefore, Thus said the Master, the Lord: I will split things apart with a storm wind in My wrath, and pounding rain in My anger shall there be and hailstones in

14 wrath for utter destruction. And I will wreck the wall on which you daubed plaster and bring it down to the ground, and its foundation shall be laid bare. And it shall fall and you shall be utterly destroyed within it, and you

---

9. *shall not come to the soil of Israel.* This phrase is an indication that Ezekiel is excoriating a group of false prophets in the Babylonian exile.

10. *The people was building a mere partition.* The subject of the verb in the Hebrew is simply "it," but its antecedent has been introduced in the translation in order to avoid confusion. The Hebrew word *ḥayits*, represented in this translation as "mere partition," occurs only here; however, it patently derives from a root that suggests demarcating inside from outside. Both the etymology and the context indicate that it is a rather flimsy barrier, hence the addition of "mere" in the translation.

    they daubed it with plaster. Many interpreters conclude that the word for "plaster," *tafel* (elsewhere a term for "insipid"), designates an inferior form of plaster, mixed with straw. But smearing plaster over a wall—especially if it is a shaky wall—would scarcely strengthen it against breaches, no matter what kind of plaster was used.

11. *When pounding rain comes—and you.* The "and you" definitely looks out of syntactic place and may reflect a scribal error.

13. *Thus said the Master, the Lord.* Rimon Kasher proposes that Ezekiel's constant use of this introductory formula could be polemic: Ezekiel has been sent by God and is faithfully quoting God's actual words, in contrast to the false prophets.

    split things apart. The splitting verb is chosen in reference to the wall.

    hailstones. The Hebrew *'elgavish* is not the usual word for "hail" and may reflect poetic diction.

shall know that I am the LORD. And I will exhaust My wrath upon the wall 15
and upon those who daubed it with plaster, and I will say to you: the wall is
gone and those who plastered it are gone, O prophets of Israel who prophesy 16
concerning Jerusalem and see a vision of well-being for her when there is no
well-being, said the Master, the LORD. And you, man, set your face toward 17
the daughters of your people who babble prophecy out of their own heart,
and prophesy about them. And you shall say, Thus said the Master, the 18
LORD: Woe, you who sew cushions for all the joints of the arms and make
padding for the head of every stature to entrap lives. Would you entrap the
lives of My people and your own lives preserve? And you profane Me to My 19
people with handfuls of barley and morsels of bread to proclaim death for
people who will not die and to proclaim life for people who will not live, as
you lie to My people, who listen to lies. Therefore thus said the LORD: Here 20
I am against your cushions with which you entrap lives like birds. And I
will tear them from your arms and set free the people whom you entrapped
like birds. And I will tear off your cushions and save My people from your 21
hands, and they shall no longer be in the toils in your hand. And you shall
know that I am the LORD. Inasmuch as you have struck the heart of the 22
innocent man with lies, when I did not cause him grief, and strengthened
the hands of the wicked man to preserve him that he turn not back from
his evil way to preserve his life. Therefore, no longer shall you see empty 23

---

15. *I will exhaust My wrath.* The Hebrew employs the same verbal stem that appears in "utter destruction" and "utterly destroyed."

17. *daughters of your people who babble prophecy out of their own heart.* Having dealt with the male prophets, Ezekiel now is commanded to turn to the women. They are not so much prophets as soothsayers or fortune-tellers, and consequently the verb for prophesying is used here in the reflexive conjugation, which has the connotation of going into ecstatic fits, a nuance represented in this translation by the addition of "babble."

18. *cushions . . . padding.* We have only an approximate sense of the meaning of both these nouns, and the same is true of their function. They appear to be the trappings of rites of divination performed by these women, but the specifics remain elusive.
    all the joints of the arms. This same phrase in Jeremiah means "armpits," but here the whole arm seems to be involved, as verse 21 indicates.

19. *with handfuls of barley and morsels of bread.* These are used in the superstitious ritual, either as instruments of divination—in Mesopotamia, flour was cast on water for this purpose—or as offerings to the gods.

22. *to preserve his life.* This is the same verb that is used in verse 19 in the sense of "proclaim life." These soothsaying women, instead of making baseless proclamations about who is destined to live, should have been warning the wicked man to turn back from his path of evil in order to save his life.

visions and no longer perform divinations, and I will save My people from
your hands, and you shall know that I am the LORD."

1   CHAPTER 14   And men of the elders of Israel came to me and

2,3 sat down before me. And the word of the LORD came to me, saying, "Man,
these men have brought to mind their foul things, and the stumbling block
of their crime they have set before them. Shall I respond in an oracle to

4   them? Therefore, speak to them and say to them, Thus said the Master, the
LORD: Every man of the house of Israel who brings to mind his foul things
and puts before him the stumbling block of his crime and comes to the
prophet, I the LORD will answer him as he comes with his many foul things,

5   so as to catch the house of Israel in their thoughts, as they all have fallen

6   back from Me with their foul things. Therefore say to the house of Israel,
Thus said the Master, the LORD: Turn back, and turn away from your foul

7   things, and turn your face away from all your abominations. For every man
of the house of Israel and of the sojourner who sojourns in Israel who falls
back from Me and brings to mind his foul things and puts the stumbling
block of his crime before him and comes to the prophet to ask an oracle of

8   him, I the LORD will answer him Myself. And I will set My face against that
man and desolate him as a sign and a byword, and I will cut him off from

9   the midst of My people, and you shall know that I am the LORD. And the
prophet who will be enticed and will speak a word, it is I the LORD Who
enticed that prophet, and I will reach out My hand against him and destroy

---

CHAPTER 14   1. *came to me and sat down before me.* The only reason they would
come to the prophet would be to hear an oracle from him. This very expectation enrages
Ezekiel because he is aware that while seeking instructions about the intentions of
YHWH—hedging their bets, one might say—their thoughts are taken up with other gods.

3. *their foul things, and the stumbling block of their crime.* It is characteristic of Ezekiel's
polemic style that he often will not bring himself to refer to false gods as "gods" or "idols"
but instead substitutes pejorative epithets—*gilulim,* "foul things," a word that recalls the
Hebrew term for "turds," and "stumbling block of their crime." (For this reason, translations that render *gilulim* as "idols" or "fetishes" dilute the force of the original.)
    Shall I respond in an oracle to them? The verb *darash* is the technical term for inquiry
of an oracle, which is precisely what the elders have come to do.

7. *I the LORD will answer him Myself.* The "answer" that God says He will deliver is not the
communication of an oracle but withering punishment.

9. *And the prophet who will be enticed and will speak a word, it is I the LORD Who enticed
that prophet.* The theology behind this statement is somewhat convoluted. The evident idea
is that these false prophets have habitually been speaking "out of their own heart," which
surely suggests human initiative. Given that behavior, God will now proceed to "entice"

him from the midst of My people. And they shall bear their punishment,   10
he who seeks an oracle and the prophet, with like punishment. So that the   11
house of Israel no longer stray from Me nor be defiled by all their transgressions, and they shall be My people, and as for Me, I will be their God, said
the Master, the LORD."

And the word of the LORD came to me, saying, "Man, when a land offends   12, 13
against Me, to commit betrayal, I will stretch out My hand against her and
break her staff of bread and let loose against her famine and cut off from
her man and beast. And these three men shall be within her, Noah, Daniel,   14
and Job. They in their righteousness shall save their lives, said the Master,
the LORD. Should I send vicious beasts through the land and they bereave   15
her and she become a desolation with no passerby because of the beasts,
these three men within her—by My life, said the Master, the LORD—shall   16
surely save neither sons nor daughters. They alone shall be saved, and the
land shall be a desolation. Or should I bring the sword against that land   17
and say, The sword shall pass through the land and I will cut off from her
man and beast, these three men within her—by My life, said the Master, the   18
LORD—shall not save sons and daughters but they alone shall be saved. Or   19
should I let loose pestilence against that land and pour My wrath on her in
blood to cut off from within her man and beast, and Noah, Daniel, and Job   20
are within her—by My life, said the Master, the LORD—they shall surely
save neither son nor daughter. They in their righteousness shall save their

---

(or "seduce") such a prophet to continue pronouncing false prophecies so that he will be
ripe for punishment.

11. *they shall be My people, and as for Me, I will be their God.* This recurring statement
expresses Ezekiel's expectation that after the national cleansing of terrible retribution,
Israel's wholeness will be restored.

14. *Noah, Daniel, and Job.* It is now clear to all scholars that here Daniel does not refer to
the protagonist of the Book of Daniel. One should note that the consonantal text allows us
to pronounce this name as *Dan'el.* In the Ugaritic Epic of Aqhat, there is a righteous judge
named *Dan'el.* These three figures, then, are three legendary righteous men, none belonging to the people of Israel. Job's presence among the three reflects the fact that a story about
a righteous man named Job was current in the region well before the composition of the
Book of Job. The non-Israelite identity of the three is in keeping with the generalizing force
of the declaration, "when a land offends against Me," which is to say, any land.

16. *these three . . . shall surely save neither sons nor daughters.* In Ezekiel's implacable moral
vision, God follows a more stringent standard of justice than he does in the story of Sodom
and Gomorrah. There, he agreed to save the cities of the plain if there were ten righteous
men within them, and in the implemented destruction, Lot was able to save his two daughters. Here, only the three righteous men will survive, and their own children will perish.

21 lives. For thus said the Master, the LORD: How much more so when I have
    let loose against Jerusalem My four evil scourges, the sword and famine and
22 vicious beasts and pestilence, to cut off from her man and beast. And, look,
    there shall be left in her a remnant that is brought out, sons and daughters.
    Here they are going out to you. And you shall see their way and their deeds
    and be consoled for the evil that I brought upon Jerusalem, all that I have
23 brought upon her. And they shall console you when you see their way and
    their deeds, and you shall know that not for naught did I do all that I did
    against her," said the Master, the LORD.

1 CHAPTER 15   And the word of the LORD came to me, saying,
2 "Man, what will come of the vine stock, the vine branch, of all the trees
3 of the forest? Will wood be taken from it to use for any task? Will a peg
4 be taken from it to hang upon it any vessel? Look, it is given to the fire to
    be consumed, its two ends the fire consumes and its inside is reduced to

---

21. *How much more so.* This formula for an *a fortiori* condition, *'af ki,* is applied here
because if any offending land is subject to the unremitting scourge of divine punishment,
an offending Jerusalem, which was God's chosen city, will all the more be punished.

22. *there shall be left in her a remnant that is brought out, sons and daughters.* This is the
surprise turn of God's compassion for Israel. By all rights, since the sons and daughters of
all other lands would not be spared, we might expect that Jerusalem's sons and daughters
would perish. God, however, will not allow the covenanted people to be utterly destroyed,
and so, after the terrible devastation, the sons and daughters survive to go out of the city
and join the earlier exiles in Babylonia as the nucleus of national regeneration.

23. *And they shall console you when you see their way and their deeds.* Although many claim
that *'alilot,* "deeds," has a negative sense in Ezekiel, the present context invites the opposite
inference: the exiles will be consoled when they see these sons and daughters behaving as
Israelites should and thus bringing hope for the future. There may even be an intended
contrast between the paganizing elders of the previous prophecy and the young exiles here.

CHAPTER 15   1. *And the word of the LORD came to me.* In this instance, the formula
introduces a parable instead of the usual message of castigation. Because the borders of the
parable are quite distinct, the chapter concludes with the end of the parable, not attaching
to it any other kind of prophecy. This makes the present chapter the shortest in the book.

2. *the vine stock.* The Hebrew *'ets-hagefen* could mean either "wood of the vine," as some
versions represent it, or "tree of the vine." The grapevine, of course, is not exactly a tree,
though its branches are made of woodlike material. The point of the parable is that, unlike
the wood of real trees, the branches of the vine cannot be made into anything. This translation adopts from Greenberg "vine stock" as a solution.

4. *it is given to the fire to be consumed.* You can't make anything out of vine branches, but
you can feed a fire with them if they are sufficiently dry.

ash. Can it serve for any task? Look, when it was whole, it could be used 5
for no task. How much more so when fire consumes it and it is reduced
to ash. Could it still be used for any task? Therefore, thus said the Master, 6
the LORD: Like the vine stock among the trees of the forest that I give to
the fire to consume, so have I given the dwellers of Jerusalem. And I will 7
set My face against them. From the fire they shall come out, but the fire
shall consume them. And you shall know that I am the LORD when I set
My face against them. And I will make the land a desolation inasmuch as 8
they have betrayed," said the Master, the LORD.

CHAPTER 16   And the word of the LORD came to me, saying, 1
"Man, make known to Jerusalem her abominations. And you shall say, Thus 2, 3
said the Master, the LORD to Jerusalem: Your origins and your birthplace
are from the land of the Canaanite. Your father was an Amorite and your
mother a Hittite. As to your birth, on the day of your birth, your navel cord 4
was not cut nor were you washed smooth in water nor were you rubbed with

---

5. *How much more so.* The logic of the *a fortiori* statement is evident: if the branches were
useless for anything when they were whole, once they are burned there is nothing left of
them except ashes.

6. *Like the vine stock . . . so have I given the dwellers of Jerusalem.* Given the aggressively
didactic purpose of this parable, its meaning is now clearly spelled out. Comparisons of
Israel to a vineyard or a vine were traditional (see the Parable of the Vineyard in Isaiah 5),
but here the comparison is tilted hard against Israel. Just as the vine is useless in comparison to the wood of real trees, the people of Israel has demonstrated its own worthlessness
by its treacherous behavior, and hence all that it is good for is to be consumed by fire. The
fire is quite literal because conquered cities were put to the torch.

7. *From the fire they shall come out.* The critical consensus is that the first fire is the partial
destruction of Jerusalem when Jehoiachin was exiled in 597 B.C.E. A greater destruction
is to come.

CHAPTER 16   3. *Your origins and your birthplace are from the land of the Canaanite.* The point is that the people of Israel is not to think of itself as altogether unique—it is
just one of the Canaanite peoples (Amorites and Hittites are ethnic groups repeatedly numbered among the seven that constitute the population of Canaan). One wonders whether
this statement might reflect a historical tradition that the origins of Israel were not in a
Hebrew slave population escaped from Egypt but among the indigenous peoples of Canaan.
That, in fact, is the view of modern scholarship.

4. *your navel cord was not cut.* This emphasis on addressing the physical care of the newborn prepares us for the focus on the physicality of the mature woman who will develop
from this infant.
  nor were you rubbed with salt. There was a practice—still sometimes observed among

5 salt nor were you swaddled. No eye had pity on you to do even one of these
to show mercy to you, but you were flung out into the field in the disgust you
6 caused on the day of your birth. And I passed by you and saw you wallowing
in your blood, and I said to you, 'In your blood live,' and I said to you, 'In
7 your blood live.' Myriad as the plants of the field I made you, and you grew
and came of age and put on the finest jewels. Your breasts were ripe and your
8 hair sprung up, but you were stark naked. And I passed by you and saw you,
and, look, your time was the time for lovemaking. And I spread My skirt
over you and covered your nakedness, and vowed to you and entered a cov-
9 enant with you, said the Master, the LORD, and you became Mine. And I
washed you in water and rinsed your blood from upon you and rubbed you
10 with oil. And I dressed you in embroidered cloth and shod you in ocher-dyed
11 leather and turbaned you in linen and covered you with silk. And I bedecked
you with jewels and put bracelets on your arms and a necklace round your

Bedouins—of rubbing the baby's body with a mixture of olive oil and salt in the belief that
it toughened the tender skin.

5. *you were flung out into the field in the disgust you caused.* It is hard to relate these details
of the neglect of the newborn babe to the actual history of Israel, except, perhaps, through
some general sense that the origins of the people were humble and unpromising. The point
seems to be that God now takes up the neglected and rejected child and nurtures her, bringing her to flourishing womanhood.

6. *wallowing in your blood.* This would be the blood of childbirth that had not been wiped
away.
　In your blood live. Despite being covered with blood, you will now live. There may be a
suggestion that the future history of Israel will be marked by bloodshed but that the people
will nevertheless survive. The repetition of these words might be a scribal duplication.

7. *Myriad.* Although many interpreters understand this simply to mean "growing" or
"sprouting," the set meaning of the Hebrew term is "myriad," and this surely could be a
reference to the proliferation of the people, the allegory of the daughter slipping from the
allegorical vehicle to its tenor or referent, the history of Israel. This will occur again at
another point in the prophecy.
　your hair. The context suggests that this is pubic hair.

8. *your time was the time for lovemaking.* The infant girl has passed puberty, and God (seen
before as a kind of foster father) will now take her as His bride—"I . . . vowed to you and
entered a covenant with you . . . and you became Mine." But the focus on her sexuality will
then be given an explosive development.

9. *And I washed you in water and rinsed your blood from upon you.* These acts appear to
repair the neglect of the infant, as though the blood of birth were still on her. But the blood
now may well be the blood from the onset of menstruation.

10. *I dressed you in embroidered cloth.* In the allegory, this whole catalogue of finery refers
to the splendor of Jerusalem and its Temple that God bestowed on His people.

neck. And I put a ring on your nose and earrings on your ears and a splendid 12
diadem on your head. And you were bedecked with gold and silver, and your 13
attire was linen and silk and embroidered cloth. Fine flour and honey and
oil you ate, and you became very, very beautiful and fit to be a queen. And a 14
name for you went out among the nations for your beauty, for it was consummate through My splendor that I set upon you, said the Master, the LORD.
And you trusted in your beauty and played the whore with your name, and 15
you spilled out your whoring upon every passerby—his it was. And you took 16
from your garments and made yourself tapestried high places and played
the whore on them. Such things should never be. And you took your splen- 17
did ornaments, from My gold and from My silver that I gave to you, and
made for yourself male images and played the whore with them. And you 18
took your embroidered garments and covered them, and My oil and My
incense you set before them. And My bread that I gave you, the fine flour 19
and honey and oil that I fed you, you set before them as a fragrant odor, and
so it was, said the Master, the LORD. And you took your sons and your 20
daughters whom you had born Me and sacrificed them to these as food. And

---

15. *And you trusted in your beauty and played the whore.* The image of unfaithful Israel
as a whore betraying her Spouse by dalliance with alien gods is common in the Prophets,
appearing in Hosea, Isaiah, and Jeremiah. No other prophet, however, focuses at such
length and so concretely as does Ezekiel on the physical aspects of promiscuity. One detects
here an expression of Ezekiel's distinctive psychology, which appears to involve some sort
of morbid obsession with the female body in its sexual aspect. The word "whore" and its
derivatives are repeated again and again.

you spilled out your whoring upon every passerby. Because of the unusual choice of the
verb "spill out," the reference may well be to vaginal secretions as a metonomy for "whoring." Such a reference is made explicit in verse 36.

16. *tapestried high places.* This is a crossover from allegorical vehicle to tenor: the woman
Zion was adorned in finery; here she takes embroidered cloth to decorate the altars of
pagan worship.

Such things should never be. The Hebrew wording at this point is somewhat cryptic, so
the translation is an educated guess.

17. *made for yourself male images and played the whore with them.* The whoring is again the
following of a pagan cult, but in the allegorical vehicle there is a suggestion of autoeroticism
in this playing with male—probably phallic—images.

18. *covered them.* That is, covered the idols.

My oil and My incense. The oil and incense that should have been used for the worship
of YHWH in the Temple were devoted to pagan deities.

20. *And you took your sons and your daughters.* Child sacrifice, which on the evidence
of the Prophets was actually practiced in ancient Israel, is regarded as one of the greatest
obscenities of the pagan cult.

21 as though your whorings were not enough, you slaughtered My sons and
22 gave them over to these. And with all your abominations and your whorings
you did not recall the days of your youth when you were stark naked, wal-
23 lowing in your blood you were. And it happened after all your evil—woe, oh
24 woe to you—said the Master, the LORD, that you built yourself mounds and
25 made yourself a height in every square. At every crossroad you built your
height, and you befouled your beauty and spread your legs for every passerby
26 and multiplied your whorings. And you played the whore with the Egyptians, your big-membered neighbors, and multiplied your whorings to vex
27 Me. And, look, I set My hand on you and cut back your daily portion and
gave you into the gullet of those who hate you, the Philistine girls shocked
28 by your lewd way. And you played the whore with the Assyrians insatiably,
29 and you played the whore with them, yet were not sated. And you multiplied
your whorings as far as the trader-land, Chaldea, but even in this you were
30 not sated. How hot was your ardor, said the Master, the LORD, when you did
31 all these, the acts of a willful whore, Building your mound at every crossroad
and making your height in every square, but you were not like a whore, for
32 you scorned a whore's pay. Adulteress, who takes strangers instead of her
33 husband! To every whore they give pay, but you, you gave your pay to all

---

24. *mounds . . . a height in every square.* These structures are different from the hilltop altars or "high places" mentioned so frequently, but they are clearly constructed sites for pagan worship.

26. *the Egyptians, your big-membered neighbors.* As is often the case of different peoples living in proximity, fantasies spring up about the sexual potency or endowments of the neighboring group. Here, the prophet excoriates the lasciviousness of the Daughter of Zion by asserting that she was drawn to the Egyptians by the supposed large size of their male members. This complements the image of playing the whore with phallic icons.

27. *the Philistine girls shocked by your lewd way.* Even the young women of Philistia, reputed to be far from virtuous, are shocked by your lasciviousness.

29. *but even in this you were not sated.* This reiterated emphasis clearly suggests that the Daughter of Zion is what used to be called a nymphomaniac, before that term was discredited.

30. *How hot was your ardor.* The meaning of both the adjective and the noun is not altogether clear. This translation follows Greenberg's philological analysis and adopts his English rendering of the phrase. The heat of ardor is certainly in keeping with the thematic emphasis of the prophecy as a whole.

31. *for you scorned a whore's pay.* You did not give yourself to other men for pay, which at least would have had a commercial logic, but gratuitously, out of sheer perversity.

32. *instead of her husband.* Some construe this phrase to mean "while under her husband's authority."

your lovers and bribed them to come to bed with you in your whoring all
around. And you became the contrary of women in your whoring, and after 34
you none will play the whore so, when you gave a whore's pay and no
whore's pay was given you but the contrary. Therefore, whore, listen to the 35
word of the LORD. Thus said the Master, the LORD: Inasmuch as your wet- 36
ness poured out and you laid bare your nakedness in your whoring with
your lovers and with all the foul things of your abominations, as by the
blood of your children that you gave to them, therefore I am about to gather 37
all your lovers to whom you were sweet, and all whom you loved with all
whom you hated, and I will gather them against you from all around and
lay bare your nakedness to them, and they shall see all your nakedness. And 38
I will condemn you with the punishment of adulteresses and women who
shed blood and give you over to blood, wrath, and jealousy. And I will give 39
you into their hand, and they shall wreck your mound and raze your
heights, and they shall strip your garments from you and take your splendid ornaments and leave you stark naked. And they shall bring up a crowd 40

---

33. *you gave your pay to all your lovers and bribed them to come to bed with you.* The
unbridled lust of Israel is such that she paid to get sex from all her alien lovers. This reduces
them to gigolos and may imply that she has lost her extraordinary beauty through all her
whoring.

36. *your wetness poured out and you laid bare your nakedness in your whoring.* The initial
noun *nehushteikh* resembles the Hebrew word for "bronze" (hence the New Jewish Publication Society renders it as "brazen effrontery"). But contemporary scholarship has made
a convincing case that it is an Akkadian loanword that means "vaginal lubrication." This
not only fits the focus on the bodily manifestations of female sexuality, but also is likely
because of Ezekiel's location in Babylonia, where Akkadian was used—he might well have
been inclined to borrow a term for which there was no good Hebrew equivalent.
     as by the blood of your children that you gave to them. The wording of this reference to
child sacrifice, the greatest of pagan abominations, loops back to the wallowing in blood of
the infant Daughter of Zion, which is now seen as a foreshadowing of her future behavior.

37. *I will . . . lay bare your nakedness to them, and they shall see all your nakedness.* This is
a piece of measure-for-measure justice: she has spread her legs for every passerby; now she
will be shamefully exposed to all eyes, not only to her former lovers but to those whom
she despised.

38. *women who shed blood.* Here, again, there is a shuttling between tenor and vehicle.
"Adulteress" belongs to the figurative representation of paganism as whoring, whereas the
bloodshed refers literally to child sacrifice.

39. *they shall strip your garments from you . . . and leave you stark naked.* This was in fact
a known punishment for an adulteress in many regions of the ancient Near East. The allegorical reference would be to the stripping away of the splendor of Jerusalem, razed by its
conquerors, and to the divestment of national sovereignty.

41 against you and stone you and hack you to pieces with their swords. And
    they shall burn your houses in fire and inflict punishment upon you before
    the eyes of many women, and I will stop you from being a whore, nor
42 whore's pay shall you give anymore. And I will let My fury against you
    come to a rest, and My jealousy of you shall turn away, and I will be tran-
43 quil and no longer be vexed. Inasmuch as you did not recall the days of
    your youth nor quake before Me in all these things, I on My part, look, I
    have set out your way first, said the Master, the LORD. Have you not done
44 lewdness in addition to all your abominations? Look, whoever pronounces
45 a byword says about you, 'Like mother, like daughter.' You are your moth-
    er's daughter, showing contempt for her husband and her children. And
    you are your sister's sister, who showed contempt for their husbands and
46 their children. Your mother is a Hittite and your father is an Amorite. And
    your big sister is Samaria—she and her daughters—who dwells on your
    left, and your little sister who dwells on your right is Sodom and her daugh-
47 ters. Did you not go in their ways and perform their abominations? Very
48 soon, you will have acted more ruinously than they in all your ways. By
    My life, said the Master, the LORD, surely Sodom and her daughters have
49 not done as you and your daughters have done. Here was the crime of

---

40. *stone you and hack you to pieces.* This was an actual practice: stoning to death followed
by mutilation of the corpse.

42. *My jealousy.* Given the whole context of sexual betrayal, the Hebrew *qin'ah* surely means
"jealousy" and not "passion," as many have claimed.

44. *Like mother, like daughter.* The point of invoking this proverb here is that Israel's waywardness is a long-standing practice, not something invented by the current generation.
Authorized by the convention of representing cities and nations as women, Ezekiel continues through this section of the prophecy in his sharply gender-focused denunciation,
invoking mothers and daughters and sisters.

45. *Your mother is a Hittite and your father is an Amorite.* This line from the very beginning
of the prophecy is repeated here because Ezekiel will go on to say that the people of Judah
resembles its neighbors in evil, only it is worse than they.

46. *your big sister is Samaria.* "Big" and "little" here refer not to age but to the size of the
territory of each of these kingdoms.
    she and her daughters. The Hebrew builds on an untranslatable pun: "daughters" also
means the villages or hamlets around a city, the implied metaphor being that the city is
the mother.
    on your left . . . on your right. Left and right are, respectively, north and south, the imag-
ined point of orientation being someone facing the east (one word for "east" also means
"front" or "forward").

48. *surely Sodom and her daughters have not done as you and your daughters have done.*
The idea that Israel could turn into Sodom had some currency early in biblical literature

Sodom and her daughters: the pride of satiety of bread and the ease of
tranquillity she and her daughters had, and she did not support the hand
of the poor and the needy. And they were haughty and performed abomi- 50
nations before Me, and I removed them when I saw it. And Samaria, barely 51
half your offenses she committed, and you did more abominations than
these, and you made your sister look innocent through all your abominations that you performed. Even you, bear your disgrace for advocating for 52
your sister through your offenses in which you were more abominable than
they and they more innocent than you. And even you, be shamed and bear
your disgrace for making your sister look innocent. And I will restore their 53
fortunes, the fortunes of Sodom and her daughters and the fortunes of
Samaria and her daughters, and the fortunes of your captives in their
midst, so that you bear your disgrace and be disgraced by all that you have 54
done in giving comfort to them. And your sisters, Sodom and her daugh- 55
ters, shall be restored to their former state, and Samaria and her daughters
shall be restored to their former state, and you and your daughters shall be
restored to your former state. Was not Sodom, your sister, a word of scorn 56
in your mouth on the day of your pride, before your evil was exposed? Now 57
[you are] a disgrace to the daughters of Aram and all her environs, to the

---

(compare Judges 19 and Isaiah 1). Ezekiel, however, pushes the notion further by contending
that Israel is worse than Sodom. In verse 49, it is explained that Sodom's crime consisted
in neglecting the needy through her complacent satisfaction with her own affluence. This
scarcely accords with the representation of the Sodomites as vicious sexual predators in
Genesis 19, but the prophet probably wants to reserve sexual misbehavior exclusively for
his castigation of his own people.

51. *and you made your sister look innocent.* Zion's offenses are compounded by the fact that
they were so unspeakable that even the crimes of her neighbors to the north and south came
to look innocent by comparison.

52. *bear your disgrace for advocating for your sister.* This is a rhetorical conceit: by setting a
standard of evil that her neighbors could not equal, Judah became an inadvertent advocate
for them.

55. *And your sisters, Sodom and her daughters . . . and Samaria and her daughters shall be
restored to their former state, and you and your daughters shall be restored to your former
state.* The prophet now gives his argument another peculiar twist. "Restoring the former
state" (the idiom that appears in verse 55) is equally used to express the national restoration
of the people of Israel after its punishment. Here, however, in keeping with "your mother
is a Hittite and your father is an Amorite," this restoration is not unique for Judah but part
of a general pattern in the region.

56. *a word of scorn.* More literally, "a rumor."

57. *[you are] a disgrace to the daughters of Aram.* The bracketed words do not appear in the
Hebrew but are necessary for intelligibility and may have been dropped in scribal transmis-

58 daughters of the Philistines who loathe you all around. You have borne
59 your lewdness and your abominations, said the LORD. For thus said the
   Master, the LORD: I will do unto you as you have done when you despised
60 the oath to violate the covenant. But I on My part will recall My covenant
   with you in the days of your youth and establish for you an everlasting
61 covenant. And you shall recall your ways and be ashamed when you receive
   your big sisters and your little sisters and I give them to you as daughters,
62 though they are not of your covenant. And I Myself will establish the cov-
63 enant with you, and you will know that I am the LORD. So that you recall
   and be shamed, and you shall be unable to open your mouth again because
   of your disgrace when I atone for you for all that you have done," said the
   Master, the LORD.

1 CHAPTER 17   And the word of the LORD came to me, saying,
2,3 "Man, pose a riddle and frame a parable for the house of Israel. And you
   shall say to them, Thus said the Master, the LORD: The great eagle, great-
   winged, broad of pinion, full-plumaged, richly colored, came to Lebanon

---

sion. Some critics emend "Aram" to "Edom" (graphically similar in Hebrew) because the
Edomites became eager allies of the Babylonian invaders.

60. *But I on My part will recall My covenant with you.* Even though Israel has been a faith-
less, adulterous wife, God remains committed to the everlasting covenant He has sealed
with His people.

61. *though they are not of your covenant.* This clause reflects two rather cryptic Hebrew
words, and the sense is uncertain.

63. *you shall be unable to open your mouth.* The literal sense is "you shall have no opening
of the mouth."

CHAPTER 17   2. *pose a riddle and frame a parable.* There is a semantic overlap
between the two nouns here, *ḥidah* and *mashal,* and the bracketing of them at the beginning of the Book of Proverbs suggests that sometimes they were nearly synonymous.
Ḥidah, as in the Samson story, does point to an enigmatic saying that requires decipher-
ing. *Mashal* has a wider range of meanings, from allegorical "parable," as here, to "proverb"
and to "poetic burden," as in Balaam's oracles. Some scholars view the text that follows
as formal verse, but it doesn't scan very well, though it does employ a good many loosely
parallel sentence structures. The poetic function, as is often the case in Ezekiel, would
appear to be manifested not prosodically but chiefly in the use of allegorical imagery, the
vehicle of the *mashal.*

3. *The great eagle . . . came to Lebanon.* The eagle is Nebuchadnezzar. Lebanon with its lofty
cedars is, perhaps somewhat confusingly, Zion.
    richly colored. The Hebrew uses the term that usually means "embroidered cloth."

and took the crown of the cedar. Its topmost tendril he plucked and brought 4
it to the land of Canaan, set it down in the city of traders. And he took from 5
the seed of the land and put it in a seed-field, a slip by many waters, he set
it down as a willow. And it flourished and became a vine, spreading in low 6
stature, its branches turned toward him and its roots to be beneath him.
And it became a vine, and it produced branches and sent forth boughs.
And there was another great eagle, great-winged, abundant in plumage, 7
and, look, this vine wrapped its roots around him and sent its boughs out
to him to be watered in the bed where it was planted. In the goodly field, by 8
many waters it was planted, to put forth branches to bear fruit, to become
a majestic vine. Say, Thus said the Master, the LORD: Will it thrive? Will he 9
not break off its roots and rot out its fruit that it wither, and all the leaves it
sprouted will wither? And not with great power nor with many troops will
it be pulled up by its roots. And, look, it is planted—will it thrive? Will it 10
not surely wither when the east wind touches it? On the bed where it grew,
it will wither."

---

4. *Its topmost tendril he plucked.* This is the Judahite king Jehoiachin, taken captive and
exiled by Nebuchadnezzar to Babylonia in 597 B.C.E.

    brought it to the land of Canaan. Like "Lebanon," this is a confusing reference because
"Canaan" in the historical allegory has to mean Babylonia. Ezekiel is probably punning
on the secondary meaning of "Canaanite" as "merchant," making this phrase semantically
parallel with "the city of traders."

5. *the seed of the land.* The phrase indicates the royal seed, and the reference is to Zedekiah,
whom Nebuchadnezzar installs as a vassal king.

    a slip. The noun *qaḥ* occurs only here, but it is attested in three Semitic languages as a
tree growing alongside streams, perhaps a variety of willow.

6. *its branches turned toward him and its roots to be beneath him.* Both these details are
tokens of Zedekiah's vassal status.

7. *another great eagle.* "Another," *aḥer,* is the plausible reading of the Septuagint instead of
the Masoretic *eḥad,* "one." The second eagle is the Egyptian Pharaoh. The vine wrapping
its roots around him indicates Zedekiah's seeking an alliance with Egypt.

8. *In the goodly field, by many waters it was planted.* Nebuchadnezzar had seen to it that his
vassal would enjoy comfortable circumstances and the majesty of kingship.

9. *Will he not break off its roots.* The "he" is Nebuchadnezzar, and we may assume that this
prophecy antedates the actual destruction of Judah in 586 B.C.E.

    not with great power. Ezekiel assumes that the Babylonians will not require a massive
force to overwhelm Jerusalem.

10. *the east wind.* In biblical literature, the east wind, blowing from the desert, brings
trouble. Nebuchadnezzar comes from the east.

11,12 And the word of the LORD came to me, saying, "Pray, say to the house of
       rebellion: Do you know what these are? Say! Look, the king of Babylonia
       has come to Jerusalem and taken her king and her nobles and brought them
   13 to him in Babylonia. And he has taken one of the royal seed and sealed
       with him a pact and made him swear an oath, and he has taken away the
   14 leaders of the land, to make it a lowly kingdom, that it not be raised up,
   15 to keep his pact that it might endure. But he rebelled against him, send-
       ing his messengers to Egypt to give him horses and many troops. Will he
       thrive? Will he who does these things escape? Will he break the pact and
   16 escape? By My life, said the Master, the LORD, in the place of the king who
       made him king, whose oath he spurned and whose pact with him he broke,
   17 within Babylonia he shall surely die. And not with a great force nor with a
       large assembly shall Pharaoh deal with him in battle, piling up ramps and
   18 building siege-works to cut off many lives. But he has spurned the oath and
       broken the pact, and look, he gave his hand to it, but all these things he did.
   19 He shall not escape. Therefore, thus said the Master, the LORD: By My life,
       My oath that he has spurned and My pact that he has broken, I will put on

---

12. *Do you know what these are?* Now the meaning of the parable, the *nimshal* of the *mashal,*
is spelled out.

   the king of Babylonia has come to Jerusalem. These are the events of 597 B.C.E., so now
it is clear that "Lebanon" is Zion.

13. *And he has taken one of the royal seed.* This is Zedekiah.

   made him swear an oath. The particular category of oath, *'alah,* is one in which a curse
is pronounced on the party of the oath should he violate it.

14. *that it might endure.* There is an ambiguity as to whether "it" refers to the pact or the
kingdom.

16. *within Babylonia he shall surely die.* This will prove to be the fate of Zedekiah, first
blinded by Nebuchadnezzar and then brought captive to Babylonia. This is a reasonable
prediction in light of Ezekiel's understanding that it is folly to rebel, so one need not construe this as an *ex eventu* prophecy.

17. *And not with a great force nor with a large assembly shall Pharaoh deal with him in battle.*
The ostensible historical reference is puzzling, and many critics assume that "Pharaoh"
is a mistaken addition, the original reference being to Nebuchadnezzar, as in the parallel
statement in verse 9.

19. *My pact that he has broken.* The Hebrew *brit* can mean either "pact," which seems the
appropriate sense for the political context of the verses above, or the more theological "covenant." To preserve the parallelism of this passage with the preceding one, "pact" is again
used here in the translation. However, the clear implication is that just as Zedekiah has
broken his pact with Nebuchadnezzar, he has violated his covenant with God, and hence
the punishment inflicted on him by Babylonia is also God's punishment.

his own head. And I will spread My net over him, and he shall be caught 20
in My toils. And I will bring him to Babylonia and will come to judgment
with him there for his betrayal of Me. And all his fugitives in all his battal- 21
ions shall fall by the sword, and those left shall be scattered to every wind."

Thus said the Master, the Lord: "I Myself will take from the lofty crown of 22
the cedar, from its topmost branches, a tender one I will pluck, and I Myself
will plant it on a high and steep hill. On the mount of the height of Israel 23
I will plant it, and it shall bear branches and put forth fruit and become a
majestic cedar, and every winged bird shall dwell beneath it, in the shade of
its boughs they shall dwell. And all the trees of the field shall know that I, 24
the Lord, have brought low the high tree, have raised high the lowly tree,
have made the moist tree wither and made the withered tree bloom. I, the
Lord, have spoken and have done it."

CHAPTER 18   And the word of the Lord came to me, saying, 1
"What is wrong with you, who recite this proverb on the soil of Israel, 2
saying:

> The fathers ate unripe fruit
>   and the sons' teeth were blunted.

By My life, said the Master, the Lord, there shall be none reciting this 3
proverb in Israel. Look, all lives are Mine, the life of the father and the son 4
alike are Mine. The person offending, it is he shall die. And should a man 5

---

22. *I Myself will take from the lofty crown of the cedar . . . and I Myself will plant it on a high and steep hill.* God performs the same figurative action as the conquering Nebuchadnezzar, but now it is an act of restoring the kingdom of Judah.

23. *put forth fruit.* The cedar does not bear fruit, so this is a miraculous fulfillment.

CHAPTER 18   2. *The fathers ate unripe fruit / and the sons' teeth were blunted.* This phrase is also quoted in Jeremiah 31:28, attesting to its circulation as a popularly invoked saying. Most translations read "unripe grapes," with little warrant, for the term can mean any unripe fruit. Presumably, the hardness of the unripe fruit is what blunts the teeth (and that would scarcely work for grapes). The proverb as Ezekiel quotes it reflects the absurdity of thinking that the sons suffer for the crimes of the fathers because, obviously, no one could suffer the ill effects of someone else's imprudence in biting down on unripe fruit.

6 be righteous and do what is just and right, he did not eat on the mountains nor lift his eyes to Israel's foul things, and he did not defile his fellow
7 man's wife nor was intimate with a menstrual woman. And no man did
he wrong; what is pawned in debt he returned; he did not rob; his bread he
8 gave to the hungry and the naked he covered with clothes. He did not lend
with advance interest nor accrued interest. He pulled his hand back from
9 wrongdoing; he enacted true justice between one man and another. By My
statutes he walked, and My laws he kept to act in truth. He is righteous, he
10 shall surely live, said the Master, the LORD. And should he beget a brutish
11 son, who sheds blood, and who does none of these things, and he did none
of these things but ate on the mountains and defiled his fellow man's wife,
12 wronged the poor and the needy, robbed, did not return what was pawned
13 and to the foul things lifted his eyes—abomination he did. He lent with
advance interest and took accrued interest. He surely shall not live—all
these abominations he did. He is doomed to die, his bloodguilt is upon him.
14 And look, should he beget a son who sees all the offenses of his father, sees
15 and does not do the like, on the mountains he does not eat nor does he lift
his eyes to the abominations of the house of Israel. He does not defile his
16 fellow man's wife, nor does he wrong any man. He takes nothing in pawn,

---

6. *he did not eat on the mountains.* Since the clause that immediately follows mentions idolatry, the reference here is almost certainly to a sacrificial feast that was part of a pagan cult.

he did not defile his fellow man's wife. The prophet moves without transition from cultic
transgressions to sexual ones. In the next verse, he will go on to the economic wrongs,
making all three categories part of a single package.

8. *advance interest nor accrued interest.* The first term, *neshekh,* has the literal sense of
"bite": hence, a chunk taken out from the loan extended. The second term, *tarbit,* etymologically suggests compounding or multiplying.

9. *By My statutes he walked, and My laws he kept.* Like a good many other phrases in this
chapter, all this will be repeated. Repetition appears to be part of the prophet's rhetorical
strategy of didactic insistence in conveying the message that each person is solely responsible for the consequences of his acts.

10. *who does none of these things.* In the Hebrew, there is an intrusive *'aḥ,* "brother," which
is almost certainly a mistaken scribal duplication of the two middle consonants in the word
that immediately follows, *me'eḥad,* "one of."

11. *he did none of these things but ate.* The wording is somewhat confusing, especially after
the last clause of the previous verse. It is possible that a negative before the verb has been
dropped out in the previous verse.

15. *on the mountains he does not eat.* The repetitiousness is especially pronounced here and
through to the end of verse 17.

nor does he rob. His bread he gives to the hungry, and the naked he covers
with garments. He draws his hand back from harming the poor, neither 17
advance interest nor accrued interest does he take. He performs My laws,
in My statutes he walks. He shall not die for his father's crime—he shall
surely live. As for his father, should he have committed fraud, robbed a 18
brother, and what was not good should have done among his people, look,
he shall die for his crime. And should you say, 'Why does the son not bear 19
the crime of the father?' When the son has done justice and righteousness and kept My statutes and performed them, he shall surely live. The 20
offending person, it is he who shall die. The son shall not bear the father's
crime, and the father shall not bear the son's crime. The righteousness of
the righteous man shall be on him, and the wickedness of the wicked man
shall be on him. And the wicked man who turns back from all his offenses 21
that he did and keeps all My statutes and does justice and righteousness,
he shall surely live, he shall not die. All his wrongs that he did shall not be 22
recalled against him. Through his righteousness that he has done he shall
live. Do I really desire the death of the wicked, said the Master, the LORD, 23
and not instead his turning back from his ways, that he may live? And when 24
the righteous man turns back from his righteousness and does wrong like
all the abominations that the wicked man did, will he do this and live? All
his righteousness that he did shall not be recalled for him when he betrays
and in his offense that he commits. For them he shall die. And should 25
you say, 'The way of the Master does not measure up,' listen, pray, house
of Israel. Does My way not measure up? Why, your way does not measure
up! When the righteous man turns back from his righteousness and does 26

---

20. *bear the . . . crime.* This Hebrew idiom clearly means "bear the consequences of the
crime." In fact, *'awon,* "crime," is often used interchangeably for "punishment" as well.

22. *All his wrongs that he did shall not be recalled against him.* This element of Ezekiel's
doctrine of divine justice surely addresses the condition of his audience of exiles. According to theological principle, their plight of exile is a consequence of their evil acts, and the
prophet has been insistently castigating them for their behavior. But a person who turns
away wholeheartedly from his misdeeds will qualify for God's protection.

24. *And when the righteous man turns back from his righteousness.* The system is symmetrical: just as the wicked man has the power to reverse his fortunes, the righteous man can
undo all the merit he has earned by slipping from the straight and narrow path to do evil.

25. *does not measure up.* There has been some dispute among interpreters about the meaning of the verb *yitakhen.* The clear biblical sense of this verbal stem is "to measure." (Compare Isaiah 40:12: "and the heavens has gauged [*tiken*] with a span.") The idea seems to be
that in the eyes of Israel, God's way makes no sense, has no good measure.

27 wrong, he shall die for it. For his wrong that he has done he shall die. And when the wicked man turns back from his wickedness that he has done
28 and does justice and righteousness, he shall preserve himself in life. And if he sees and turns back from all his trespasses that he committed, he shall
29 surely live, he shall not die. And should the house of Israel say, 'The way of the Master does not measure up,' do My ways not measure up? Why, it
30 is your ways that do not measure up! Therefore each according to his ways will I judge you, O house of Israel, said the Master, the LORD. Turn back altogether from your trespasses, and they shall not be a stumbling block of
31 crime for you. Fling away from you all your trespasses that you have committed and make you a new heart and a new spirit. Why should you die,
32 O house of Israel? For I do not desire anyone's death, said the Master, the LORD, but turn back and live."

1 CHAPTER 19   And you, sound this lament over the princes
2 of Israel, and say,

> What a lioness your mother
>   among lions!
> She crouches among young lions,

---

31. *Fling away from you all your trespasses that you have committed and make you a new heart and a new spirit.* A vivid image informs this sentence: a person's trespasses weigh down on his very body—the Hebrew literally means "fling away from upon you." Once this weight of evil acts is flung away, a person can regenerate from within, making a new heart and spirit for himself.

32. *anyone's death.* More literally, "the death of him who dies."

CHAPTER 19   1. *sound this lament.* What follows are two allegorical prophecies, one involving lions and the other a vine. Unlike the allegories that have preceded, this pair is cast in poetry because it is a "lament," *qinah*, and it follows—loosely, it should be said—the lament meter of three accents in the first verset and two in the second.

the princes of Israel. These are the last kings of Judah, though precise identification of monarchs will become problematic.

2. *your mother.* After the plural "princes," the poem switches to the singular, evidently having in mind one particular king.

She crouches among young lions. The fierce lion is a stock figure for monarchs in biblical poetry (as in many other cultures), being linked in the Blessing of Jacob (Genesis 49:9) with the royal tribe of Judah. But this proud image of the royal line will be quickly subverted here.

    she rears her cubs.

She raised up one of her cubs,   3
    he became a young lion
and learned to go after prey,
    a human did he eat.

And nations heard of him,   4
    in their pit he was caught,
and they brought him down in hooks
    to the land of Egypt.

And she saw that she waited in vain,   5
    her hope was lost.
And she took another of her cubs,
    made him a young lion.

And he walked about among lions,   6
    he became a young lion.
And he learned to go after prey,
    a human did he eat.

And he harrowed their bastions,   7

---

3. *a young lion.* It is the translator's despair that there are five different words for "lion" in biblical Hebrew, and the distinctions among them are unclear. "Young lion" for *kefir* is the solution of the King James Version, perhaps in part because of this passage, even though elsewhere *kefir* is indistinguishable in meaning from the four other terms for "lion."

4. *pit.* The Hebrew *shaḥat* everywhere else means "pit," and so there is not much justification for rendering it here as "net," which many modern interpreters do. Lions were sometimes trapped in pits, and then a restraining net was cast over them, which seems to be the case in verse 8.

    they brought him down in hooks / to the land of Egypt. The one Judahite king who was carried off to Egypt was Jehoahaz son of Josiah and Hamutal. What remains somewhat problematic about this identification is that he reigned only three months before his deportation by Pharaoh Neco, which makes the representation of his ravening power in the previous verse look a bit odd. Perhaps any king once enthroned was imagined to be a fierce lion.

5. *she took another of her cubs.* At this point, the identification becomes ambiguous: two of Hamutal's sons reigned successively, Jehoiachin and Zedekiah.

7. *harrowed.* The Hebrew seems to say "knew." Many interpreters, medieval and modern, understand it in the sexual sense, meaning "rape" (although, despite its sexual sense, it is not a verb used for rape). Its object in the received text is *'almenotaw,* "their [literally, its] widows." All this seems improbable. *'Almenotaw* has been emended here to *'armenotaw,* "their bastions." The verb is understood in the sense in which it is used in Judges 8:16. The verb as it appears in Judges is in a different conjugation, but the Masoretic vocalization here may be mistaken.

and their towns he destroyed.
And the land and its fullness were dumbfounded
    by the sound of his roaring.

8   And nations set upon him,
    all the provinces round about,
and cast their net upon him,
    in their pit he was caught.

9   And they put him in a neck iron with hooks
    and brought him to the king of Babylonia,
        brought him in toils;
so that his voice would no more be heard
    on the mountains of Israel.

10   Your mother was like a vine
    planted by waters,
fruitful and branching
    from many waters.

11   And she had mighty boughs,
    for the scepters of rulers.
And its stature rose on high
    to be among the clouds.
And it was seen in its height
    with all its branches.

12   But it was torn from its roots in fury,
    to the ground it was flung,
and the east wind withered its fruit,

---

9. *brought him to the king of Babylonia.* This makes Jehoiachin, who was exiled to Babylonia in 597 B.C.E., the most likely candidate for the historical reference.

   so that his voice would no more be heard / on the mountains of Israel. This line neatly joins vehicle and tenor: the captured lion will no longer strike terror in the terrain around him; the king of Judah will no longer exercise authority in his land.

10. *Your mother was like a vine.* The received text seems to say "Your mother like a vine in your blood." This translation emends *bedamkha,* "in your blood," to *damta,* "was like." Rashi understands it this way without emendation.

   like a vine. As the lion is a traditional image of the king, the vine is a traditional image of the people of Israel.

11. *And she had mighty boughs / for the scepters of rulers.* The branches of the vine are thick and strong, producing powerful kings.

12. *But it was torn from its roots in fury.* While the prophetic mode uses verbs that imply a completed action, this is a prediction of the final destruction of the kingdom.

it fell apart and withered,
> her mighty bough the fire consumed.
And now she is planted in the desert,   13
> in a parched and thirsty land.
And a fire springs out from her boughs,   14
> consumes her fruit
and no mighty bough is there within her,
> a scepter for ruling.
—This is a lament, and has become a lament.

CHAPTER 20   And it happened in the seventh year, in the 1
fifth month, on the tenth of the month, men of the elders of Israel came to
inquire of the Lord and sat down before me. And the word of the Lord 2
came to me, saying, "Man, speak to the elders of Israel and say to them, 3
Thus said the Master, the Lord: To inquire of Me do you come? By My life,
I will not respond to your inquiry, said the Lord. Will you judge them, will 4
you judge, man? Make known to them all the abominations of their fathers.
And say to them, Thus said the Master, the Lord: On the day I chose Israel, 5

---

13. *the desert.* The reference must be to the land of exile.

14. *And a fire springs out from her boughs.* No explanation is offered for the sudden appearance of fire in the vine, either here or in verse 12. The image may be used automatically because fire is a constant image of destruction, or the historical referent—the destruction of Jerusalem, put to the torch by the invaders—may have seeped into the allegorical image.

CHAPTER 20   1. *in the seventh year, in the fifth month.* As before, the reckoning is from the beginning of the exile of Jehoiachin, so the year is 591 B.C.E. The fifth month is Av, which occurs in midsummer.
    came to inquire of the Lord. Though several theories have been proposed about the nature of the oracle they were seeking, there is no clear indication of what it might have been.

3. *I will not respond to your inquiry.* Given what is presumed to be the reprehensible behavior of the elders, God—or perhaps one should say, His spokesman the prophet—will issue no oracle but instead will castigate them for their misdeeds.

4. *all the abominations of their fathers.* Ezekiel, himself taken into exile with the Judahite king and nobles and seeing the imminence of a much more comprehensive exile and national disaster, here undertakes an extensive revision of the history of Israel. In his perception, the people's reprehensible behavior is by no means limited to recent generations but goes all the way back to its origins in Egypt and is indelibly stamped in the national character.

I raised My hand to the seed of the house of Jacob and made Myself known
6 to them in the land of Egypt, saying, I am the LORD your God. On that day
I raised My hand to them to bring them out of the land of Egypt to a land
that I had searched out for them, flowing with milk and honey, a splendor
7 for all the lands. And I said to them: Let each man fling away the loathsome
things that are before his eyes, and do not be defiled with the foul things of
8 Egypt. I am the LORD your God. But they rebelled against Me and did not
want to heed Me. Each man did not fling away the loathsome things that
were before his eyes, and they did not forsake the foul things of Egypt. And
I thought to pour out My wrath upon them, to exhaust My anger against
9 them in the land of Egypt. But I acted for the sake of My name, that it not be
profaned in the eyes of the nations in whose midst they were, as I had made
10 Myself known before their eyes, to bring them out of the land of Egypt. And
I brought them out of the land of Egypt and brought them into the wilder-
11 ness. And I gave them My statutes and made My laws known to them, that
12 a man should do them and live through them. And My sabbaths, too, I gave
to them to be a sign between Me and them, to know that I am the LORD who
13 hallows them. And the house of Israel rebelled against me in the wilderness.
They did not follow My statutes, and they spurned My laws, that a man
should do them and live. And My sabbaths they profaned grievously, and I

---

5. *I raised My hand.* This is the gesture of someone taking a solemn vow (still used in courtrooms in our own society).

6. *to a land that I had searched out for them.* In this version, the episode of the twelve spies sent by Moses to search out the land is elided in order to emphasize God's extravagant bountifulness to Israel.

8. *Each man did not fling away the loathsome things.* The idea that the Hebrews in Egypt were wallowing in the idolatrous practices of their Egyptian enslavers is nowhere hinted in Exodus.

9. *But I acted for the sake of My name.* This notion that God spared wayward Israel in order not to compromise His reputation among the nations is no more than hinted at in the Wilderness narrative, but Ezekiel gives it special prominence because in his dour view Israel has scarcely any redeeming features that would intrinsically justify its national survival.

12. *And My sabbaths, too, I gave to them to be a sign between Me and them.* In the late monarchic period and on into the era of exile, there was an increasing emphasis on the centrality of the sabbath, as attested in passages in Jeremiah and Trito-Isaiah as well as in Ezekiel. The portability of the sabbath as a community-affirming observance may have made it especially appealing in a time when the Temple was no longer accessible.

13. *And My sabbaths they profaned grievously.* In Exodus, it is one man who violates the sabbath, but Ezekiel accuses the whole people of such violation.

thought to pour My wrath against them in the wilderness. But I acted for the 14
sake of My name, not to profane it in the eyes of the nations before whose
eyes I had brought them out. And I on My part raised My hand to them in 15
the wilderness not to bring them to the land that I had given, flowing with
milk and honey, a splendor to all the lands, inasmuch as they spurned My 16
statutes, they had not followed them, and My sabbaths they had profaned,
for after the foul things their heart had gone. But My eye had pity for them 17
not to destroy them, and I did not make an end of them in the wilderness.
And I said to their children in the wilderness: Do not follow the statues of 18
your fathers and do not keep their laws and do not be defiled with their foul
things. I am the LORD your God. Follow My statutes and keep My laws and 19
do them. And hallow My sabbaths, that they be a sign between Me and you 20
to know that I am the LORD your God. And the sons rebelled against Me, 21
My statutes they did not follow and My laws they did not keep to do them,
which a man does and lives through them. My sabbaths they profaned.
And I thought to pour out My wrath on them, to exhaust My anger against
them in the wilderness. But I pulled back My hand and acted for the sake 22
of My name not to profane it in the eyes of the nations before whose eyes I
had brought them out. I on My part raised My hand to them in the wilder- 23
ness to disperse them among the nations and to scatter them in the lands.
Inasmuch as they did not do My laws and they spurned My statutes and 24
they profaned My sabbaths and their eyes went after the foul things of their
fathers. And I on My part gave them statutes that were not good and laws 25
through which they would not live. And I defiled them with their gifts when 26

---

18. *Do not follow the statues of your fathers . . . and do not be defiled with their foul things.*
Given that the Israelites, in Ezekiel's revision of the national narrative, persisted in their
Egyptian idolatry in the wilderness, they had no right to be brought into the land flowing
with milk and honey. God nevertheless allows them to survive and come into the land,
both for the sake of the divine name and because He chooses to give the next generation
an opportunity—which they will reject—to turn away from the misdeeds of their fathers.

22. *and acted for the sake of My name not to profane it in the eyes of the nations.* As in the
long prose prophecy of chapter 18, this prophecy is marked by didactic repetition.

25. *And I on My part gave them statutes that were not good.* This is a startling theological
idea. In part it flows from the general assumption that since God is ultimately responsible for everything that happens, if Israel adopts perverse practices, it is because God has
decreed it. A dynamic of punishment, however, is detectable here: if Israel stubbornly clings
to pagan abominations, God will compound the guilt of the people by encouraging them
to persist in their waywardness.

26. *gifts.* In this context, the term means "sacrifices," gifts to a deity.

they passed every womb-breach in sacrifice, so that I might desolate them,
27 so they might know that I am the Lord. Therefore speak to the house of
Israel, man, and say to them, Thus said the Lord: In this, too, your fathers
28 insulted Me in betraying Me. And I brought them to the land that I had
raised My hand to give them, and they saw every high hill and every thick-
branched tree and offered their sacrifices there and put their vexing offerings there and set their fragrant odors there and poured out their libations
29 there. And I said to them, What is the high place to which you come? And
30 its name has been called *high place* to this day. Therefore, say to the house
of Israel, Thus said the Master, the Lord: Are you defiled in the way of your
31 fathers, and do you whore after their loathsome things? And in bringing
up your gifts, in passing your children through the fire you are defiled for
all your foul things to this day. And shall I respond to your inquiry, house
of Israel? By My life, said the Master, the Lord, I will not respond to you.
32 And what occurs to your mind, it shall surely not come about, that you say,
'We shall be like the nations, like the clans of the lands, to serve wood and
33 stone.' By My life, said the Master, the Lord, with a strong hand and with
an outstretched arm and with outpoured wrath, I will surely reign over you.
34 And I will bring you out from the peoples and gather you from the lands
where you were scattered with a strong hand and with an outstretched hand
35 and with outpoured wrath. And I will bring you to the desert of peoples and

---

they passed every womb-breach in sacrifice. The prophets of this era so often inveigh against child sacrifice that one may reasonably infer it was actually widespread. "Womb-breach" is a term borrowed from Exodus as an epithet for the firstborn.

29. *What is the high place to which you come?* The Hebrew exhibits a derisive false etymology: "high place" is *bamah;* "what" is *mah;* the first syllable of "come" is *ba.* (James Moffatt, with some ingenuity and a little strain, conveys this in English as: "What is this high place you hie to?) The implication of the ad hoc etymology is that the very name *bamah* reflects the fact that it is something alien, scarcely comprehensible.

31. *And shall I respond to your inquiry.* This phrase loops back to the beginning of the proph-ecy (verse 3), suggesting that the elders do not deserve any oracular revelation because they are the representatives of an idolatrous people.

34. *And I will bring you out from the peoples . . . with a strong hand.* Momentarily, this sounds like a promise to bring them out from exile, but that illusion is shattered as God goes on to say that the people will be brought out into the desert to be destroyed (and note how "outpoured wrath" is held back until the end of the sentence).

35. *the desert of peoples.* This is the great Syrian desert to the west of Babylonia and contigu-ous with several countries.

come to judgment with you there face-to-face. As I came to judgment with 36
your fathers in the desert of the land of Egypt, so will I come to judgment
with you, said the Master, the LORD. And I will make you pass under the 37
rod and bring you into the bonds of the covenant. And I will purge from 38
you the rebels and those who trespass against Me. I will bring them out of
the land of their sojourning, but to the soil of Israel they shall not come,
and you shall know that I am the LORD. And you, house of Israel, thus said 39
the Master, the LORD: Each man go, worship his foul things, and afterward,
if you do not heed Me. . . . But My holy name you shall no longer profane
with your gifts and with your foul things. But on My holy mountain, on the 40
mountain of the height of Israel, there shall all the house of Israel worship
Me, all of it in the land. There will I favor them, and there will I require your
offerings and your choice donations with all your sacred things. By a fra- 41
grant odor I will show favor to you when I bring you out from the peoples,
and I will gather you from the lands where you were scattered, and I will be
hallowed through you before the eyes of the nations. And you shall know 42
that I am the LORD when I bring you to the soil of Israel, to the land for
which I raised My hand to give it to your fathers. And you shall recall there 43
your ways and all your acts through which you were defiled, and you shall

---

36. *As I came to judgment with your fathers in the desert of the land of Egypt.* This is a mysterious reference, and it may be that Ezekiel is caught up here in the rhetorical momentum
of his invective, reaching to invoke a historical parallel to the present moment. Egypt in
the ancient period didn't have a desert, and if it is the "desert" at the Sea of Reeds, Israel
was saved there, not brought to judgment.

37. *And I will make you pass under the rod.* This is the notion of the shepherd counting his
sheep. But "rod" also suggests punishment.

    the bonds. The Hebrew *masoret* looks as though it were the word for "tradition," though
in its syntactical position that word would have been vocalized as *mesoret.* Most scholars
plausibly conclude that it is an elliptical spelling of *ma'asoret,* a noun derived from the verb
'asar, which means "to bind."

38. *I will purge from you the rebels.* Ezekiel's vision is quite implacable: before any return
to Zion, the exiles will be taken out into the desert where many of them—implicitly, the
majority—will be destroyed.

39. *Each man go, worship his foul things.* This is obviously sarcastic.

    and afterward, if you do not heed Me. . . . The only way to save the received text is to
assume, as several scholars have proposed, that a clause has dropped out that would have
stipulated the dire consequences of not heeding God. The words that follow swivel around
to imagine an Israel that puts aside the idolatrous ways of its fathers and returns to worship
God in the proper place, on Mount Zion.

44 be disgusted with yourselves for all your evils that you did. And you shall know that I am the LORD when I deal with you for the sake of My name, not according to your evil ways and your ruinous acts, O house of Israel," said the Master, the LORD.

1 CHAPTER 21   And the word of the LORD came to me, saying,
2 "Man, set your face to the way of Teman and proclaim to the south, and
3 prophesy to the wooded region of the Negeb. And you shall say to the wooded region of the Negeb: hear the word of the LORD. Thus said the Master, the LORD: I am about to light a fire in you, and it shall consume in you every moist tree and every dry tree. The white-hot flame shall not go
4 out, and every face shall be scorched by it from south to north. And all flesh
5 shall see that I the LORD kindled it, it shall not go out." And I said, "Woe,
6 O Master, LORD, they say to me, 'Is he not just reciting parables?'" And the
7 word of the LORD came to me, saying, "Man, set your face to Jerusalem and proclaim concerning the sanctuaries and prophesy concerning the soil of
8 Israel. And you shall say concerning the soil of Israel, Thus said the LORD: Here I am against you, and I will take out My sword from its sheath and
9 cut off from you the righteous and the wicked. Inasmuch as I have cut off from you the righteous and the wicked, My sword shall come out from its

---

43. *you shall be disgusted with yourselves for all your evils that you did.* A psychological manifestation of the people's true repentance is that it experiences deep revulsion in thinking of its past behavior—a revulsion clearly shaped by the prophet as he castigates Israel for its idolatry.

CHAPTER 21   2. *Teman . . . the south . . . Negeb.* The Hebrew uses three different words that mean "south." Although the territory of Judah is to the west of Ezekiel's location in Babylonia, what this prophetic injunction has in view is a destruction of Judah that will begin from the south and sweep up through the north.

3. *the wooded region.* It is unclear whether the Negeb once had a wooded region. Some think this may be an area of low shrubs, but the next verse speaks of trees.
   The white-hot flame. The joining of two Hebrew synonyms in the construct form (literally, "fire of flame") is an intensifier.

5. *Is he not just reciting parables?* The adverb "just" has been added in the translation to bring out the sense of the Hebrew—that the people think the prophet is merely spinning out parables that have no relation to reality.

8. *cut off from you the righteous and the wicked.* The phrase essentially means "everyone." It is a severe form of divine justice, in direct contradiction to the exchange between Abraham and God over the destruction of Sodom and Gomorrah in Genesis 18.

sheath against all flesh from south to north. And all flesh shall know that I   10
am the LORD. I have taken out My sword from its sheath, it shall no more
turn back. And you, man, groan with shuddering loins and bitterly groan   11
before their eyes. And should they say to you, 'Why are you groaning?,' you   12
shall say, 'For the tidings that have come.' And every heart shall quail and
all hands go slack and every spirit grow weak and all knees be wet. Look, it
has come and has happened, said the Master, the LORD."

And the word of the LORD came to me, saying, "Man, prophesy and say,   13,14
Thus said the LORD:

> A sword, a sword is whetted
>   and also it is burnished,
> to wreak slaughter it is whetted,   15
>   that it gleam it was burnished
> [Or we rejoice for the rod, my son, spurning all blood.]
> And it was given to be burnished,   16
>   to be grasped in the hand.
> For this the sword was whetted
>   and for this was burnished
>   to be put in the hand of a killer.
> Scream and howl, O man,   17
>   for it was against My people,

---

11. *shuddering loins.* More literally, "broken loins."

12. *all knees be wet.* As above (7:17), the expression derisively indicates people wetting themselves in terror.

14. *A sword, a sword is whetted.* The sword is often used in biblical language as a metonymy for "military force" or "destructive power." The special effectiveness of the poetry here is that it builds on this ordinary sense of "sword" but focuses with unusual concreteness on the weapon, unsheathed, whetted, burnished, and gleaming.

15. *Or we rejoice for the rod.* This entire bracketed sentence is unintelligible, even though each separate word is understandable. In the Hebrew, neither the syntax nor the grammar makes sense. It is hard to believe that Ezekiel could have written this sentence, at least in the form we have, though how these words got into the text is a mystery.

16. *to be put in the hand of a killer.* The spooky power of these lines is heightened by cloaking the identity of the killer in anonymity, but he is no doubt the fierce Babylonian emperor Nebuchadnezzar.

17. *for it was against My people.* The "it" is feminine and refers to the sword, a feminine noun.

it was against all Israel's princes.
Felled by the sword were My people,
  so clap upon the thigh.
18 [For he probes and what if the rod, too, spurning shall not be?] said the
  LORD.
19 And you, man, prophesy
  and strike palm against palm.
Let the sword do double work and triple,
  it is a sword for the slain,
a sword for many slain,
  driving into them,
20 so that the heart faint
  and stumbling blocks abound.
At all their gates I set
  slaughter by the sword
Ah, it is made to gleam,
  burnished for the slaughter.
21 Stay whetted! Lay about on the right and the left!
  Where do you turn?
22 And I, too, will strike palm against palm
  and let My wrath come to rest."

23,24 And the word of the LORD came to me, saying, "And you, man, set out for
yourself two ways for the coming of the sword of the king of Babylonia
from one land. The two of them shall go out, and clear away a space, and the
25 crossroad of the way of the city, clear it. Set out a way for the coming of the
sword against Rabbah of the Ammonites and against fortified Jerusalem

---

18. *For he probes and what if the rod.* This bracketed sentence has the same problems of
intelligibility as the one in verse 15 and incorporates some of the same cryptic phrases.

21. *Where do you turn?* This question reinforces the sense of the sword slashing on every
side.

22. *let My wrath come to rest.* After the sword has done its terrible work, God's wrath against
Israel will be completely spent, setting the stage for restoration.

24. *two ways for the coming of the sword of the king of Babylonia.* This prose prophecy, following the poetic one, more or less spells out the meaning of the oracle of the sword—here
the sword comes together with its wielder, the king of Babylonia, across known geographical space. The two ways are evidently the trajectories to Rabbah of the Ammonites in trans-
Jordan and to Jerusalem.

in Judah. For the king of Babylonia has stood at the fork of the road, at the 26
crossroad of the two ways, to perform divination, to shake out arrows, to
inquire of the household gods, to inspect the liver. On its right lobe, was 27
the omen of Jerusalem, to set up battering rams, to scream murder with
full throat, to raise the voice in shouting, to set up battering rams against
the gates, to pile up ramps, to build siege-towers. And it seemed in their 28
eyes like an empty divination—they had oaths sworn to them, but it was a
remembering of guilt for them to be caught. Therefore, thus said the Master, 29
the LORD: Inasmuch as you have remembered your guilt as your trespasses
are laid bare, for your offenses to be seen in all your acts, inasmuch as you
have been remembered, you shall be caught in a grip. And you, profane in 30
wickedness, O prince of Israel, whose day has come at the end-time of the
guilt! Thus said the Master, the LORD: Take off the turban and lift off the 31
diadem. This is not this—raise up what is low and bring down what is high.

---

26. *to perform divination, to shake out arrows.* It was a regular practice in military campaigns in the ancient Near East to seek guidance through an oracle or divinatory devices
in order to choose the proper route or strategy. The shaking out of arrows for divination involved writing alternatives—here, those might be "Rabbah" and "Jerusalem" on
the shafts of different arrows. Inspecting patterns in animal livers was a very common
divinatory procedure.

27. *On its right lobe.* The Hebrew says only "on its right," but the clear reference is to the
liver.

28. *And it seemed in their eyes like an empty divination.* The grammatical subject here refers
either to Ezekiel's audience of exiles or to the population in Judah. If it is the latter, they
were imagined as somehow having got wind of the Babylonian divination.
     they had oaths sworn to them. This is obscure. It might mean that the Judahites were
confident in their safety because they thought God had sworn to protect them for all time.
     it was a remembering of guilt for them to be caught. Perhaps: their confidence was a trap,
involving their guilt or crime, in which they would be caught. The collocation "remembering of guilt" appears in Numbers 5:15 in the passage about the woman suspected of adultery,
and the echo may be intended to suggest Israel's whoring after other gods.

29. *you have remembered your guilt.* Or, "have called to mind your guilt"—that is, caused
it to be remembered.

30. *profane in wickedness.* The phrase could also mean "corpse of uncleaness," although
that sense seems unlikely.
     the end-time of the guilt. The literal order of the Hebrew is "the time of the end of the
guilt [or punishment]." The obvious sense is: the time when you will have to pay for the
guilt you have incurred.

31. *This is not this.* The three Hebrew words are a little obscure but probably mean: things
as they are will no longer be the same.

32 Ruins, ruins, ruins will I make it. This, too, has not come about, until the
33 coming of him who has the judgment and will grant it to him. And you,
    man, prophesy and say, Thus said the Master, the LORD, to the Ammonites
    concerning their disgrace, and you shall say, 'A sword, a sword unsheathed
34 for slaughter, perfectly burnished to gleam, when empty visions were seen
    for you, when false divinations were cast for you concerning the necks of
35 the profane wicked whose day has come at the end-time of guilt.' Put it
    back in its sheath; in the place where you were created, in the land of your
36 origin I will judge you. And I will pour out on you My anger, the fire of My
    fury I will fan against you and give you into the hand of hotheaded men,
37 craftsmen of destruction. You shall be fuel for the fire. Your blood shall be
    in the land. You shall not be recalled. For I the LORD have spoken."

1 CHAPTER 22   And the word of the LORD came to me, saying,
2 "And you, man, you shall surely judge the city of bloodshed and make
3 known to her all her abominations. And you shall say, Thus said the Master,
   the LORD: O city shedding blood in its midst, to cause her time to come, and

---

32. *until the coming of him who has the judgment and will grant it.* This is another crabbed formulation, though the most likely reference is to Nebuchadnezzar, who is to be the instrument of divine judgment.

33. *the Ammonites.* Their capital city, Rabbah, is one of the two targets of the Babylonian assault.

34. *when empty visions were seen for you.* The Ammonites evidently trusted in false oracles that they would be saved from the Babylonians.
  concerning the necks of the profane wicked. The Ammonites believed that the prophecy of destruction pertained only to the Judahites.

35. *Put it back in its sheath.* Once the ordained project of destruction has been completed, the sword must be sheathed again, for the Babylonian rampage cannot go on indefinitely. On the contrary, while they have served as God's punishing instrument, they will now have to pay for their own excess of cruelty.
  in the land of your origin I will judge you. It is the fate of conquering Babylon to become the victim of its conquerors.

36. *hotheaded men.* The Hebrew is probably a pun. *Bo 'arim* can mean "ignorant" or "crude," but it also means "burning." Since fire is prominent in the immediate context, burning or heated temperament is probably the more salient meaning.

CHAPTER 22   3. *in its midst.* This phrase (a single word in the Hebrew) and one variant are constantly repeated in this prophecy, emphasizing the idea that the corruption has penetrated to the very heart of the city.

she makes foul things for herself in defilement. In your blood that you shed 4
you are guilty, and in your foul things that you make you are defiled, and
you bring your days close and come to the end of your years. Therefore do I
make you a disgrace to the nations and a revilement to all the lands. Those 5
near and those far shall revile you, O defiled in name, great in disorder.
Look, the princes of Israel, each with his strong arm, were within you so as 6
to shed blood. Father and mother they treated with contempt within you. 7
Toward the sojourner they acted oppressively in your midst. Orphan and
widow they wronged within you. My holiness you despised and My sab- 8
baths you profaned. Slanderers there were within you so as to shed blood, 9
and they ate on the mountains among you. Lewdness they did in your
midst. A father's nakedness was laid bare within you. The menstruant's 10
defilement they took by rape within you. And each man did an abomina- 11
tion with his fellow man's wife, and each defiled his daughter-in-law in
lewdness, and each took his sister, his father's daughter, by rape. They took 12
bribes within you, so as to shed blood. Advance interest and accrued interest you took, and you got ill gain from your fellow men through oppression.
And Me you have forgotten, said the Master, the LORD. And look, I have 13
struck My palm over your ill-gotten gain that you acquired and over your
bloodguilt that was in your midst. Will your heart stand the test, will your 14
hands be strong, in the days I am about to set against you? I am the LORD.

---

4. *you bring your days close and come to the end of your years.* The obvious reference is
to the time of judgment; but the preposition rendered as "to" here, *'ad,* is unusual, and a
number of Hebrew manuscripts show instead *'et,* "the time of." The phrase "the end" does
not appear in the Hebrew but is assumed here to be implied.

7. *Father and mother . . . sojourner . . . Orphan and widow.* Although the prophet has begun
with the sin of idolatry ("foul things"), he now moves on to violations of the familial order
and the perpetration of social injustice. From this he will go on (verses 10–11) to acts of
sexual indecency, something that appears to have particularly enraged him.

9. *Slanderers . . . so as to shed blood.* Slander is used as a weapon to condemn the innocent
to death or to provoke acts of violence against them, either out of simple hatred or in order
to seize the property of those whose blood is shed.
    they ate on the mountains. As before, the reference is to a pagan ritual meal.

10. *The menstruant's defilement they took by rape.* Sex with a menstruating woman is forbidden even when there is mutual consent. Here the prophet assumes that she would not
agree to have sex during her period, so she is taken by force, two taboos thus violated in one
fell swoop. The same situation pertains to the rape of the sister in the next verse.

11. *his father's daughter.* In a polygamous marriage, she might well be only his half sister,
but this is still incest.

15 I have spoken and I have done. And I will disperse you among the nations and scatter you in the lands, and I will wipe out your defilement from you.
16 And you shall be dishonored before the eyes of the nations, and you shall know that I am the LORD."

17,18 And the word of the LORD came to me, saying, "Man, the house of Israel has become dross to me. They are all bronze and tin and iron and lead, in
19 a kiln of silver dross they are. Therefore, thus said the Master, the LORD: Inasmuch as they all have become dross, therefore will I gather them into
20 Jerusalem, a gathering of silver and bronze and iron and lead and tin into the kiln to fan fire upon it for smelting. So will I gather My anger and My
21 wrath and fan the fire and smelt you. And I will gather you in and fan the
22 fire of My fury upon you, and you shall be smelted within it. As silver is smelted within a kiln, so shall you be smelted, and you shall know that I, the LORD, have poured out My wrath upon you."

23,24 And the word of the LORD came to me, saying, "Man, say to her: You are
25 an unclean land. She was not rain-washed on the day of anger. The plot of her prophets is in her midst. Like a roaring lion rending prey they devoured

---

18. *dross.* What follows might possibly be an elaborated allusion to Isaiah 1:22, "your silver has turned to dross." In any case, it exemplifies Ezekiel's penchant for adopting quasipoetic strategies in his prose prophecies. The metaphor of silver cheapened by dross is extended through verse 21.

19. *Inasmuch as they all have become dross.* What follows is an image of measure-for-measure justice: the people have debased their intrinsic value, turned silver into dross; now God will take together all this debased metal and burn it away in a fiery kiln.

20. *fan the fire and smelt you.* Since one of several synonyms for "anger" that are used here, ḥeimah, "wrath," is derived from a root that means "heat," the anger jibes nicely with the metaphor of the burning furnace.

21. *you shall be smelted within it.* As smelting is a process that burns away impurities, the suggestion is that the base elements of the people will be destroyed but a virtuous core will remain.

25. *The plot of her prophets.* The general meaning of the noun qesher (literally, "knot") is "plot" or "conspiracy." There is not much warrant to render it as "gang," as does the New Jewish Publication Society. The Septuagint, however, reads 'asher nesi'eha, "that her princes," which is attractive because it eliminates the duplication of "prophets" in verse 28 in this catalogue of miscreants.

lives; treasure and riches they took, they made her widows many in her midst. Her priests outraged My teaching and profaned My sacred things. 26 They did not distinguish between sacred and profane, they did not teach the difference between clean and unclean. They averted their eyes from My sabbaths, and I was profaned in their midst. Her nobles in her midst were 27 like wolves rending prey, to shed blood, to destroy lives, so as to take ill-gotten gain. And her prophets daubed the walls with plaster, seeing empty 28 visions and divining lies, saying, 'Thus said the Master, the LORD' when the LORD had not spoken. The people of the land committed oppression and 29 robbed and wronged the poor and the needy and oppressed the sojourner lawlessly. And I sought from them a man to mend the fence and stand in 30 the breach before Me for the sake of the land so as not to destroy it, and I found none. And I poured out My anger upon them, in the fire of My 31 fury I made an end of them. Their way I paid back on their head," said the Master, the LORD.

CHAPTER 23   And the word of the LORD came to me, saying, 1

"Two women were there,   2
        daughters of one mother.
And they played the whore in Egypt, in their youth,   3

---

they made her widows many. This is the obvious consequence of killing the husbands.

26. *They did not distinguish between sacred and profane . . . between clean and unclean.* This is the special responsibility of the priests, as Ezekiel, himself a priest, was keenly aware.

28. *And her prophets daubed the walls with plaster.* This covering up of cracks in the figurative wall of the people is inspired by the elaboration of that image in 13:10ff.

30. *a man to mend the fence and stand in the breach.* That man would be the authentic prophet, who speaks truth to the people and acts to turn them from their evil ways and thus averts God's assault on the city through the very breaches that the people have made. Ezekiel, of course, is speaking about Jerusalem while himself prophesying in Babylonia. There is no recognition here of his older contemporary Jeremiah, surely a man who tried to stand in the breach. Ezekiel would have known, or at least heard about, Jeremiah before he himself was exiled in 597 B.C.E.

31. *Their way I paid back on their head.* The translation follows the contours of the Hebrew idiom (still more literally, "gave on their head"), which implies payback for misdeeds.

> they played the whore there.
> Their breasts were squeezed
> and there were their virgin teats fondled.

4 And their names were Oholah, the elder, and Oholibah, her sister. And they
became Mine and bore sons and daughters, and their names were Samaria,
5 Oholah, and Jerusalem, Oholibah. And Oholah played the whore while she
6 was Mine, and she was hot for her lovers, the warriors of Assyria, clothed
in indigo, satraps and governors, all of them lovely young men, horsemen
7 riding steeds. And she gave her whoring to them, the pick of Assyria all of
them, and in everything she was hot for, in all their foul things, she was
8 defiled. And her whoring from Egypt she did not abandon, for they had
lain with her in her youth, and they fondled her virgin teats and spilled
9 their whoring upon her. Therefore did I give her into the hand of her lovers,

---

CHAPTER 23   3. *Their breasts were squeezed and there were their virgin teats fondled.* As in chapter 16, Ezekiel takes the conventional metaphor of whoring as an image of
idolatry (and also of alliances with foreign powers) and pushes it to a level of sexual explicitness as does no other biblical writer. Nowhere else in the Bible does one find this sort of
direct reference to fondling breasts in sexual play, and nowhere else does one encounter
an evocation of a concupiscent woman allured by the largeness of the male sexual organ
(verse 20). There are passages in this prophecy where the allegorical referent of idolatry
virtually disappears as the sexual foreground is flaunted. Ezekiel looks distinctly like a
man morbidly obsessed with the female body and with female sexuality, exhibiting a horrified fascination with both. The word in the second verset of this line, *dad,* is represented
by some as "nipple," but on dubious grounds. It is a phonetic cousin of *shad,* the standard
word for "breast." It occurs only here and in Proverbs 5:19, where it does not seem to mean
"nipple" either. In any case, "fondling" (the more general sense of the verb is "knead") does
not work well for nipples, although it is appropriate for breasts.

4. *Oholah . . . Oholibah.* No entirely convincing explanation for the choice of these names
to designate, respectively, Samaria and Judah, has emerged. Both names have a component
that suggests "tent," *'ohel,* and names close to these appear elsewhere in the Bible.

5. *while she was Mine.* Literally, "beneath Me," that is, under My authority—a phrase used
for adulterous wives. Ezekiel invokes the familiar trope that Israel is wedded to God.

7. *all their foul things.* In this polemic designation of idols, the referent of the metaphor
briefly breaks through the sexual foreground of the figure.

8. *her whoring from Egypt she did not abandon.* Ezekiel persists in his notion that the
Israelites first became idolators in Egypt, and, having become accustomed to the practice,
never let go of it.
    spilled their whoring upon her. In her case, "whoring" indicates her promiscuous readi-
ness to give herself to all comers. In the case of the lovers, because the noun is the subject
of the verb "spill," there is a clear suggestion that it means "semen."

into the hand of the Assyrians for whom she was hot. They laid bare her   10
nakedness. Her sons and her daughters they took, and her they slew with
the sword. And she became a byword for women, and they exacted punishment upon her. And her sister Oholibah saw, and she made her hot lust   11
more ruinous than hers and her whoring more than her sister's whoring.
For the Assyrians she was hot, satraps and governors, warriors clothed to   12
perfection, horsemen riding steeds, lovely young men all of them. And I   13
saw that she was defiled—a single way for the two of them. And she went   14
further with her whoring, and she saw men etched on the wall, images of
Chaldeans etched with vermillion, girded with belts around their waists,   15
wrapped turbans on their heads, the look of captains all of them had, the
image of the sons of Babylonia, Chaldeans, the land of their birth. And she   16
was hot for them, for what her eyes saw, and she sent messengers to them
in Chaldea. And the sons of Babylonia came to her for lovemaking and   17
defiled her with their whoring. And she was defiled by them and disgusted
by them. And she laid bare her whoring and laid bare her nakedness, and   18
I was disgusted by her as I was disgusted by her sister. And she played the   19
whore still more to recall the days of her youth when she played the whore
in the land of Egypt. And she was hot for their consorts, whose flesh was   20
the flesh of donkeys and whose members were like the members of stallions. And you went back to the lewdness of your youth when your teats   21
were fondled by the Egyptians, your youthful breasts squeezed. Therefore,   22

---

10. *They laid bare her nakedness.* Usually, this idiom is used for incest. Here, it has a literal
sense (they stripped her naked as an object of sexual exploitation) and a figurative one (she
was utterly without defenses). What is represented by the figure is the destruction of the
northern kingdom by Assyria.

12. *lovely young men all of them.* The warriors are good-looking, muscular young men,
inciting the desire of Oholibah. They will, of course, destroy her.

14. *she saw men etched on the wall.* The peoples of Mesopotamia had a sophisticated art of
bas-relief, sometimes outlining the figures in vermillion, as here. Oholibah is at once drawn
to the visual art, to the heroic male figures it depicts, and to the pagan culture it embodies.

20. *their consorts. Pilagshim,* a loanword that elsewhere refers to concubines, here must
refer to male lovers, an application encouraged by the fact that the plural ending of the
word looks like a masculine plural.
  the members. The noun *zirmah,* which occurs only here, is derived from a verbal stem
that means "to flow." It seems formally analogous to *shufkhah,* a term for the penis derived
from a verb that means "to pour." In both cases, the use to indicate the male member would
be through metonymy. It is possible, however, that *zirmah* has the sense of the noun (not
the verb) "ejaculate." It is also possible that "flesh" in this verse is a euphemism for "penis."

Oholibah, thus said the Master, the LORD: I am about to rouse your lovers
against you, by whom you were disgusted, and I will bring them against you
23 all around. The Babylonians and all the Chaldeans, Pekod and Shoa and
Koa, all the Assyrians, those lovely young men, satraps and governors all
24 of them, captains and marshaled fighters, riders of horses all of them. And
they shall come against you, charger and chariot and wheel in an assembly
of troops, buckler and shield and helmet. They shall set about against you
all around, and I will set judgment before them, and they shall punish you
25 with their judgments. And I will set My jealousy against you, and they
shall deal with you in wrath. Your nose and your ears they shall lop off,
and those left after you shall fall by the sword. They shall take your sons
26 and your daughters, and those left after you shall be consumed by fire. And
I will strip off your garments, and they shall take your splendid apparel.
27 And I will end your lewdness and your whoring from the land of Egypt,
and you shall not lift up your eyes to them, and Egypt shall you no more
28 recall. For thus said the Master, the LORD, I am about to give you into the
hand of those you hate, into the hand of those by whom you were disgusted.
29 And they shall deal with you in hatred and take all your gain and abandon
you stark naked, and your whoring nakedness and your lewdness and your
30 whoring shall be laid bare—the doing of these to you in your whoring after
31 the nations, for your being defiled by their foul things. In the way of your
sister you went, and I have given her cup in your hand."

32   Thus said the Master, the LORD:
                               Your sister's cup you shall drink,

---

22. *your lovers . . . by whom you were disgusted.* It now emerges that the promiscuous Oholibah, having given herself to all these lovers, has discovered that they, or at least some of
them, are distasteful.

23. *Pekod and Shoa and Koa.* These are obviously Babylonian ethnic groups, though precise
identification, at least for the last two, is uncertain.

25. *Your nose and your ears they shall lop off.* Such mutilation was actually sometimes
practiced against conquered populations, but in the sexual metaphor, the once alluring
Oholibah will be hideously disfigured.

28. *those you hate . . . those by whom you were disgusted.* The evident idea is that these were
foreign lovers with whom she had dalliances and then after the fact was revolted by them.

31. *her cup.* The cup or chalice of destruction or poison is such a stock image for the prophets that Ezekiel merely has to mention "cup" and the whole idea is evoked. Samaria was
destroyed, and now it is the turn of Judah.

> deep and wide.
> It shall be a laughingstock and scorn.
>   Much does it hold.
> With drunkenness and sorrow you are filled,   33
>   the cup of devastation and desolation,
>   your sister's cup, Samaria.
> And you shall drink it to the dregs,   34
>   and its shards you shall grind,
>   and your breasts you shall cut off.
> For I have spoken, said the Master, the LORD.

Therefore, thus said the Master, the LORD: "Inasmuch as you forgot Me and 35
flung Me behind your back, even you shall bear your lewdness and your
whoring." And the LORD said to me, "Man, will you judge Oholah and 36
Oholibah and tell them their abominations? For they committed adultery 37
and there is blood on their hands, and they committed adultery with their
foul things, and also their sons whom they bore for Me they gave over to be
consumed. This besides they did to Me: they defiled My sanctuary on that 38
day and My sabbaths they profaned. And they slaughtered their children 39
to their foul things and came into My sanctuary on that day to profane it
and, look, so did they do within My house. And even more, they sent for 40
men coming from afar, to whom a messenger was sent, and, look, they
came to you who bathed, put kohl around your eyes, and decked your self
with jewels. And you sat on a sumptuous bed with a table set before it, and 41

---

32. *It shall be a laughingstock.* An emendation of the suffix of the verb here would yield
"you shall be."

33. *devastation and desolation.* The Hebrew wordplay is *shamah ushemamah.*

34. *your breasts you shall cut off.* This ghastly self-mutilation follows the lopping off of ears
and more above and provides a violent denouement to the breasts fondled by Egyptian
lovers.

38. *they defiled My sanctuary on that day.* Ezekiel seems to have in mind a particular event
in which a pagan cult was brought into the Jerusalem temple. A certain day in the reign of
Manasseh might be a candidate for the reference.

40. *they came to you who bathed, put kohl around your eyes, and decked your self with jewels.*
While Ezekiel may have in mind Judah's seeking foreign alliances, the sexual metaphor
once more occupies the foreground: like the seductress in Proverbs 7, Jerusalem prepares
the bed where she will receive her lovers with rich fabrics, and lays out a feast for their
enjoyment. All of this points to burning incense and offering sacrifices to strange gods
in the Temple.

42 you put My incense and My oil on it. And the sound of a singing throng
was in it, and to many men [you sent]. Drink was brought from the desert,
and they put bracelets on their arms and splendid diadems on their heads.

43 And I said to her worn out from adultery: now let them whore in her whor-

44 ing. And she—. And they came to bed with her as one comes to bed with
a whore-woman, so did they come to bed with Oholah and Oholibah, the

45 lewd women. And righteous men, they shall judge them by the law of adulteresses and by the law of those who shed blood, for they are adulterers and

46 there is blood on their hands. For thus said the Master, the LORD: Bring up

47 against them a crowd and make them a horror and an object of scorn. And
let the crowd stone them and cut them apart with their swords. Their sons
and their daughters let them slay, and let them burn their houses in fire.

48 And I will put an end to lewdness in the land, and all the women shall learn

49 a lesson and not do like your lewdness. And they shall put your lewdness
upon you, and you shall bear the offenses of your foul things. And you shall
know that I am the Master, the LORD."

1 CHAPTER 24   And the word of the LORD came to me in the

2 ninth year in the tenth month on the tenth of the month, saying, "Man,
write you the name of the day, this very day. The king of Babylonia has laid

---

42. *a singing throng.* This translation emends the Masoretic *shalew,* "tranquil," to *shirim,*
"songs."

  bracelets on their arms. The suffix for "their" is feminine and hence refers to the women
waiting for the foreigners. The Hebrew also veers from the second person to third person,
as happens frequently in biblical usage.

43. *her worn out from adultery.* Through all her promiscuity, she has become a worn-out,
faded thing, no longer alluring to men.

  And she— This (a single Hebrew word) dangles at the end of the sentence, and it looks
as if something has been lost in the text.

47. *let the crowd stone them and cut them apart with their swords.* Although this is a prophecy of the destruction of the kingdom of Judah, what remains in the foreground at the end
is the image of the insatiable adulteress, stoned to death and hacked to pieces.

CHAPTER 24   1. *in the ninth year in the tenth month.* This computes to January
587 B.C.E., which means that the final conquest of Jerusalem is only a year and a half in
the future. Ezekiel could well have had word in Babylonia of the expeditionary force sent
to take Jerusalem.

siege against Jerusalem on this very day. And speak a parable to the house 3
of rebellion and say to them, Thus said the Master, the LORD:

> Put the pot on the fire
>> and pour water into it, too.
> Gather in it the cuts of meat, 4
>> every good cut,
> thigh and shoulder,
>> with choice bones fill it.
>>> take the choice of the flock. 5
> And burn the wood under it, too,
>> let it boil away,
>>> and its bones, too, will be cooked within it.

Therefore, thus said the Master, the LORD: Woe, city of bloodshed, pot with 6
its filth within it, and its filth has not left it. Empty it cut by cut. No lot has
fallen on it. For her blood has been within it. On bare rock she put it, she 7
did not spill it on the ground to cover it with dirt. To raise up wrath, to 8
wreak vengeance I have put her blood on bare rock so as not to be covered.
Therefore, thus said the Master, the LORD: Woe, city of bloodshed. I on My 9

---

2. *has laid siege.* An unusual verb is used here that has the more common sense of "lean
on" or "support."

3. *speak a parable.* The fluid sense of the Hebrew *mashal* is in this instance close to "veiled
saying." That is, an image of uncertain reference is developed through the lines of poetry;
then its meaning is spelled out in the prose that follows.

4. *Gather in it the cuts of meat, / every good cut.* The poetic parable unfolds through a false
lead: it seems as though what is being evoked is the preparation of a sumptuous meat meal,
but then the explication of the images will turn them into a portent of total destruction.

6. *pot with its filth within it.* Only now are we told that there is something disgusting in
this pot of cooking meat.

No lot has fallen on it. This brief sentence is rather cryptic. Since lots were sometimes
used to single out the guilty person in a crowd (see, for example, the story of Achan in
Joshua 7), the meaning may be that here no lots were cast because everyone was guilty and
everyone would be punished.

7. *For her blood has been within it.* In this prophecy, Ezekiel targets bloodshed rather than
idolatry as the crime for which the city is condemned. Child sacrifice, of course, combines
the two.

to cover it with dirt. This violates the injunction to cover spilled blood. Blood splashed
on bare rock is painfully conspicuous, as is the crime of Judah in the eyes of the prophet.

10 part will make the pyre blaze. Pile on the wood, kindle the fire, let the meat
11 be consumed, stir the broth, and let the bones be charred. And set it empty
   over its coals, that it grow hot and its copper heat up and its uncleanness
12 melt within it, its filth be purged, but it will not leave it—the abundance
13 of its filth, in the fire is its filth. In your lewd uncleanness, inasmuch as
   I cleansed you but you were not clean of your uncleanness, you shall no
14 longer be clean until I have set My wrath upon you. I the LORD have spoken.
   It has come and I have done it. I will not revoke and will not show pity and
   will not repent. By your ways and by your acts they have judged you, said
   the Master, the LORD."

15,16 And the word of the LORD came to me, saying, "Man, I am about to take
   from you by plague what is dear in your eyes, but you shall not lament
17 and you shall not keen and no tear shall you shed. Groan silently. Perform
   no mourning for the dead. Wear your head-cloth, put your sandals on
   your feet, and do not cover your moustache, and do not eat the bread of
18 other men." And I spoke to the people in the morning, and my wife died
19 in the evening, and the next morning I did as I had been charged. And

---

10. *let the meat be consumed, stir the broth, and let the bones be charred.* In the poem, it seemed as if a proper meal were cooking in the pot. Now it emerges that the contents of the pot are to be cooked to death—the meat boiling until there is nothing left, the bones entirely charred. As the next verse spells out, only the destruction of the unclean matter within the pot will cleanse it, which is to say, the defilement of the people of Judah can be eradicated only by fiery annihilation.

12. *but it will not leave it.* The first Hebrew word of this verse, *te'unim,* is unintelligible, and the second word, *ḥel'at,* makes no syntactic sense. This translation assumes an erroneous scribal duplication here—*te'unim* repeating and expanding the penultimate word of the previous verse, *titom,* and *ḥel'at* repeating the last word of that verse, *ḥel'atah.*

13. *My wrath.* The word for "wrath" suggests "heat," and thus picks up the image of the burning pot.

14. *It has come.* "It" is the catastrophe.

16. *what is dear in your eyes.* It is not at first revealed to Ezekiel that the dear possession to be taken away is his wife. This is the first mention of the marital status of this prophet so morbidly obsessed with female sexuality. One may assume that the loss of his wife by plague is a biographical fact, but it is turned here into a portent of the destiny of the nation.

17. *Wear your head-cloth.* Going bareheaded was one of the practices of mourning.
   do not cover your moustache. This is an odd-sounding gesture of mourning, but it is attested elsewhere (Leviticus 13:45).
   do not eat the bread of other men. As in later Jewish practice, it was customary for mourners not to prepare their own food but to be fed by members of their community.

the people said to me, "Will you not tell us what these things that you are doing mean for us?" And I said to them, "The word of the LORD came to 20 me, saying, Say to the house of Israel, Thus said the Master, the LORD: 'I 21 am about to profane My sanctuary, the pride of your strength, what is dear in your eyes, what is cherished in your heart, and your sons and your daughters whom you abandoned shall fall by the sword. And you shall do 22 as I have done: you shall not cover your moustache nor shall you eat the bread of other men. And your head-cloth shall be on your head and your 23 sandals on your feet. You shall not lament and you shall not keen, and you shall rot in your crimes and moan to one another. And Ezekiel shall be 24 a portent for you. As all that he did, you shall do when it comes, and you shall know that I am the Master, the LORD. And you, man, on the day I 25 take from them their stronghold, the joy of their splendor, what is dear in their eyes, their heart's longing, their sons and their daughters, will not 26 on that day a fugitive come to you to let you hear with your own ears? On 27 that day your mouth shall open to the fugitive and you shall no longer be mute, and you shall become a portent for them, and they shall know that I am the LORD.'"

CHAPTER 25   And the word of the LORD came to me, saying, 1 "Man, set your face to the Ammonites and prophesy about them. And say 2,3

---

21. *I am about to profane My sanctuary.* Because God determines all things in this theological perspective, it is He Who decrees that the Babylonians should profane the Temple.

and your sons and your daughters whom you abandoned. What is suggested is that the panicked parents fled the city, leaving their children behind.

24. *And Ezekiel shall be a portent for you.* At this point, God, as it were, interrupts Ezekiel's address to the exiles in order to comment on the meaning of the prophet's acts.

25. *their heart's longing.* The literal sense of the Hebrew is "their being's longing." (The same is true of "cherished in your heart" in verse 21.) The multipurpose noun *nefesh* is used here and in verse 21.

26. *a fugitive come to you to let you hear with your own ears.* Ezekiel has been constantly prophesying the destruction of Jerusalem, but now he will be confronted with an eyewitness account of the actual horror.

CHAPTER 25   2. *set your face to the Ammonites and prophesy about them.* Ezekiel now turns his attention from Israel to the surrounding peoples that have been hostile toward Israel, each now predicted to have its comeuppance. Four different peoples are singled out in this chapter, and the language used is stereotypical, varying only slightly from one prophecy to the next.

to the Ammonites, 'Listen to the word of the Master, the LORD. Thus said the master, the LORD: Inasmuch as you have said hurrah concerning My sanctuary when it was profaned and concerning the soil of Israel when it was desolated and concerning the house of Judah when they went into exile,

4 therefore am I about to give you to the Easterners as an inheritance, and they shall set up their encampments within you and place their dwellings

5 within you. They shall eat your fruit and they shall drink your milk. And I will turn Rabbah into a camel pasture and the Ammonite towns into a

6 place where sheep bed down, and you shall know that I am the LORD. For thus said the Master, the LORD: Inasmuch as you have clapped your hands and stamped your feet and rejoiced in all your utmost spite over the soil of

7 Israel, therefore, look, I have stretched out My hand against you and have made you spoil for the nations and have cut you off from among the peoples and made you perish from among the lands. I have destroyed you. And you shall know that I am the LORD.'"

8 Thus said the Master, the LORD: "Inasmuch as Moab and Seir have said,

9 'Look, the house of Judah is like all the nations,' therefore will I expose the flank of Moab, its towns every one of them, the splendor of the land—

10 Beth-Jeshimoth, Baal-Meon, and Kiriathaim to the Easterners, besides the Ammonites, I will give it as an inheritance, that the Ammonites be not

11 recalled among the nations. And against Moab will I wreak punishment, and they shall know that I am the LORD."

---

3. *Listen to the word of the Master, the* LORD. One may regard this direct address to the Ammonites as a kind of rhetorical fiction since it is virtually inconceivable that Ezekiel actually will speak to them.

you have said hurrah. The guilt of the Ammonites is in their open expression of schadenfreude at the destruction of Jerusalem. Given the context, it looks as if this sequence of prophecies was pronounced after 586 B.C.E.

4. *the Easterners.* These are nomadic tribes, chiefly Arab, living in the desert area east of the Jordan. Their nomadic character is indicated in their setting up "encampments," not towns, in the conquered area of Ammon. The erasure of the urban nature of Ammon is spelled out in the next verse.

7. *I have destroyed you.* This phrase (a single Hebrew word) looks out of place syntactically and is a superfluous repetition of what immediately precedes.

10. *besides the Ammonites.* The evident sense is that Moab as well as Ammon will be given to the eastern tribes.

Thus said the Master, the Lord, "Inasmuch as Edom has taken vengeance   12
on the house of Judah and incurred guilt and wreaked vengeance upon
them, therefore thus said the Master, the Lord: I will stretch out My hand   13
against Edom and cut off from her man and beast and turn her into ruins,
from Teman to Dedan they shall fall by the sword. And I will set My ven-   14
geance against Edom through the hand of My people of Israel, and they
shall act against Edom according to My anger and according to My wrath;
and they shall know My vengeance, said the Master, the Lord."

Thus said the Master, the Lord, "Inasmuch as the Philistines have acted in   15
vengeance and wreaked vengeance in utmost spite as a destroyer, in age-
old enmity, therefore, thus said the Master, the Lord: I am about to stretch   16
out My hand against the Philistines and I will cut off the Cherithites and
destroy the remnant of the seacoast. And I will wreak great vengeance upon   17
them in punishing wrath, and they shall know that I am the Lord when I
exact vengeance from them."

CHAPTER 26   And it happened in the eleventh year on the   1
first of the month, the word of the Lord came to me, saying, "Man, inas-   2

---

12. *Edom has taken vengeance.* Unlike the previously mentioned peoples, who gloated over
the fall of Judah, Edom actually allied itself with the Babylonians and played an active role
in Judah's destruction. The anger against the Edomite collaboration with the Babylonian
invaders is sharply registered in Psalm 137.

13. *from Teman to Dedan.* Though both are obviously Edomite towns and are mentioned
elsewhere, their exact location has not been determined.

15. *the Philistines.* They were perennial enemies of the Israelites from the period of the
Judges onward, a fact noted in the phrase "age-old enmity."

16. *the Cherithites.* That is, the Cypriots. According to biblical tradition, the origin of the
Philistines, who certainly came from the Greek sphere, was Cyprus.
    the remnant of the seacoast. The Philistines, associated with the Sea Peoples who are
mentioned in Egyptian sources, arrived via the Mediterranean in the thirteenth century
B.C.E. and remained largely confined to a strip of territory close to the seacoast.

CHAPTER 26   1. *the eleventh year on the first of the month.* In the received text, the
name of the month is missing. The eleventh year of Ezekiel's exile brings us to 586 B.C.E.,
probably after the destruction of Jerusalem (although that would depend on the month),
as the cries of schadenfreude noted here would seem to indicate. It could be that the month
is the eleventh month, omitted by haplography, which would put this prophecy after the
fall of Jerusalem.

much as Tyre has said concerning Jerusalem 'Hurrah! The doors of the
peoples are broken. It has come round to me. Let me be filled from the city
3   in ruins.' Therefore, thus said the Master, the LORD: Here I am against you,
Tyre, and I will bring up against you many nations as the sea brings up its
4   waves. And they shall ruin the walls of Tyre and destroy her towers, and
5   I will sweep away her earth from her and turn her into bare rock. A place
for spreading fishnets she shall be within the sea, for I have spoken, said
6   the Master, the LORD, and she shall become spoil for the nations. And her
daughter-villages that are in the field shall be slain by the sword, and they
7   shall know that I am the LORD. For thus said the Master, the LORD: I am
about to bring against Tyre Nebuchadrezzar, king of Babylonia, from the
north, a king of kings, with horses and with chariots and with horsemen
8   and an assembly and many troops. Your daughter-villages in the field he
shall slay with the sword, and he shall set against you siege-towers and build
9   against you siege-ramps and put up against you shields. And his assault
catapults he shall set against your walls, and your towers he shall raze to
10 ruins. In the rush of his horses he shall cover you with their dust. From
the sound of horsemen and wheels and chariots your walls shall shake as
11 he enters your gates as through the entrance of a breached town. With his
horses' hooves he shall trample all your streets. Your people he shall slay
with the sword, and the pillars of your strength he shall bring down to

---

2. *Let me be filled from the city in ruins.* In this dialogue attributed to the Phoenician city of
Tyre, the city imagines herself looting the riches of Jerusalem that are left among the ruins.

3. *as the sea brings up its waves.* The simile is strategically chosen because Tyre is situated
on an island.

4. *turn her into bare rock.* The flourishing island-city, after the invading army has swept
over it, is imagined as desolate bare rock in the sea.

6. *daughter-villages.* The Hebrew *banot* means both "daughters" and the villages adjacent
to a town. This translation adopts the solution of the Jewish Publication Society version by
representing both meanings hyphenated. The slaying, of course, works better for "daughters" than for "villages."

7. *a king of kings.* This is a title that had currency in Akkadian. As a Hebrew idiom, it has
the force of a superlative, "the supreme king."

8. *put up against you shields.* The whole sequence of assault here is realistic. First, arrows
are shot into the city from the height of siege-towers. Then troops rush up to the top of
the walls on the ramps they have built, protecting themselves with serried rows of shields.

11. *With his horses' hooves he shall trample all your streets.* This vivid depiction of Nebuchadrezzar's army swarming through the streets of Tyre and destroying everything in
sight was not realized historically. The Babylonian siege of Tyre went on for a very long
time—according to Josephus, for thirteen years—but the city was never taken.

the ground. And they shall loot your wealth and plunder your wares and destroy your walls, and your precious houses they shall raze, and your stones and your timber and your earth they shall plunge into the water. And I will bring an end to the murmur of your songs, and the sound of your lyres shall be heard no more. And I will turn you into bare rock, a place for spreading fishnets she shall be. She shall not be built again. For I the LORD have spoken, said the Master, the LORD. Thus said the Master, the LORD, to Tyre: Why, from the sound of your collapse, in the groaning of the slain, in the killing within you, the coastlands shall shudder. And all the princes of the seacoast shall come down from their thrones and take off their robes, and their embroidered garments they shall strip. They shall don shuddering. On the ground they shall sit, and they shall shudder moment by moment and be desolate over her. And they shall sound an elegy over you and say to you: 12 13 14 15 16 17

> How you have perished, O settled from the seas,
>   the celebrated city
> that was strong in the sea,
>   she and her dwellers,
> who struck with terror
>   all dwelling in her.
> Now will the coastlands shudder   18
>   on the day of your collapse,
> and the coastlands that are by the sea
>   are dismayed by your demise.

12. *And they shall loot your wealth and plunder your wares.* Ezekiel's language is nicely calibrated for Tyre. It was a mercantile city par excellence, its ships plying the Mediterranean. An unusual word is chosen for "wares," *rekhulet,* a term derived from the more common *rokhel,* "trader."

your stones and your timber and your earth. These are all building materials, especially for city walls.

14. *I will turn you . . . She shall not be built again.* The weaving between second person and third person is common in biblical usage.

16. *all the princes of the seacoast.* The Hebrew is literally "princes of the sea," but the obvious reference is to the kingdoms by the sea or islands just offshore, such as Tyre.

They shall don shuddering. In a shrewd metaphorical move, the Tyrian princes, having shed all their finery, clothe themselves not in garments but in shudders.

On the ground they shall sit. This is a gesture of mourning as well as of dethronement.

17. *settled from the seas.* The preposition "from" probably indicates that people have come by the sea to settle in Tyre.

19 For thus said the Master, the LORD: When I turn you into a city in ruins, like cities that were never settled, when I bring up over you the deep and 20 many waters cover you, I will bring you down with the dwellers of the Pit, to the people of yore, with those who go down to the Pit, so that you shall 21 not be settled and you shall not show splendor in the land of the living. I will turn you into horror, and you shall be sought and never found again, said the Master, the LORD."

1 CHAPTER 27   And the word of the LORD came to me, saying, 2,3 "And you, man, sound a lament for Tyre. And say to Tyre, which sits at the gateways to the sea, trader to peoples, to many coastlands, thus said the Master, the LORD:

> Tyre, you said,
>   'I am perfect in beauty.'
4 In the heart of the seas are your borders.
>   Your builders perfected your beauty.
5 With cypress from Senir they built you—
>   all your panels.

---

19. *like cities that were never settled.* While the ruins suggest that a city once stood here, the devastation is so complete that it is as if there had never been a settlement in this place.

20. *I will bring you down.* There is a pointed antithesis between bringing up the deep in the previous clause and bringing down the inhabitants of the city to the netherworld. Though drowning is a set trope for dying in biblical poetry, it is especially relevant to Tyre, an island washed by the waves.

   you shall not show splendor. The wording of the Hebrew is a little difficult. It might seem to say, "I will give you (*wenatati*) splendor," which does not make much sense. But the verb here could also be an archaic form of the second-person feminine singular, which is how it is understood in this translation, and the "not" of "you shall not be settled" could carry over to this verb that immediately follows.

21. *I will turn you into horror, and you shall be sought and never found again.* The meaning of "horror" is unpacked in the second clause: Tyre's extinction will be so absolute an ending that no trace of her will remain.

CHAPTER 27   3. *trader to peoples.* This epithet announces the central theme of the prophecy. The Phoenicians were famous as a maritime and mercantile people, developing trade routes far to the west in the Mediterranean and establishing colonies as distant as Carthage (present-day Tunisia) and Spain. Ezekiel will evoke the breadth and splendor of this mercantile empire as he forecasts its destruction.

5. *Senir.* A mountainous region mentioned in the Song of Songs 4:8 as adjacent to Mount Hermon to the north of Israel.

Cedar from Lebanon they took
   to make masts for you.
Of oak from Bashan they made your oars,   6
   your planks they made of ivory
      inlaid in boxwood from the coastlands of Kittim.
Embroidered linen from Egypt   7
   were your sails
      to be for you a banner.
Indigo and crimson from the isles of Elisha
   were your canopy.
The dwellers of Sidon and Arvad   8
   were rowers for you.
Your skilled men, O Tyre, were within you,
   they were your mariners.
Gebal's elders and skilled men   9
   were within you repairing the crafts.
All the ships of the sea and their sailors
   were within you to traffic in your wares.
Peras and Lud and Put   10
   were in your forces, your men of war.
Buckler and helmet they hung in you,
   it is they who gave your glory.

---

to make masts for you. At this point it becomes clear that the perfected beauty of Tyre is not chiefly in the structures of the city but in its ships, which become a kind of metonymy for the city that sends them far to the west.

6. *your planks they made of ivory / inlaid in boxwood.* Whether this description reflects the reality of Tyre's merchant fleet or not, it represents the ships as not merely utilitarian vessels but as extravagantly luxurious constructions ("Your builders perfected your beauty" [verse 4]), with decks inlaid with ivory, sails made of embroidered Egyptian linen, and canopies of regal indigo and crimson cloth to shade the travelers.

7. *the isles of Elisha.* This may be Cyprus.

8. *Your skilled men.* The noun *ḥakham* usually means "wise man," but it also has a general sense of someone skilled in a craft or trade.

10. *Lud and Put.* Although some want to identify Lud with Lydia in Asia Minor, both places are probably located in Africa, in proximity to Egypt, in the region of modern Libya. In Ezekiel's vision, the reach of Tyre extends on the west to the Greek sphere, on the south to North Africa, on the east to Arabia and Mesopotamia.

it is they who gave your glory. The clear sense is that the army of Tyre was manned by mercenaries from these sundry far-off lands.

11 Men of Arvad and Helech were within your walls all around, and the Gam-
    marites were on your towers. Their shields they hung on your walls all
12 around, it is they who perfected your beauty. Tarshish traded with you.
    From all the great wealth of silver, tin, and lead, they deposited your goods.
13 Javan, Tubal, and Meshech, they traded with you in human beings and
14 copper vessels; they gave your wares. From Beth-Targemah, horses and
15 horsemen and mules, they deposited your goods. The men of Dedan traded
    with you, many coastlands were traders under you. Ivory tusks and ebony
16 they gave back as your tribute. Aram traded with you and all the things
    you made in malachite, purple cloth and embroidery and linen and coral
17 and agate they gave for your deposited goods. Judah and the land of Israel
    traded with you in the wheat of Minnith and Paggo, and honey and oil
18 and balm they gave for your wares. Damascus traded with you in all the
    things you made, from all the great wealth of Helbon wine and white wood.
19 Vedan and Javan of Uzal for your deposited goods gave forged iron, cassia,
20 and cane. For your wares it was. Dedan traded with you in saddle cloths
21 for riding. Arabia and all the princes of Kedar were traders under you. Fat
22 sheep and rams and he-goats of theirs were your trade. The traders of Sheba
    and Raamah traded with you in the choicest of all spices and precious

---

11. *Men of Arvad.* One should note that Ezekiel readily slips from poetry—virtually required
by the *qinah,* the lament form—into prose, with no real change in content. This is not a
prophet who is entirely comfortable in verse.

   Gammarites. The received text shows "Gammadites," but the known place-name is
Gomer (the Hebrew letters for *r* and *d* are rather similar in shape, and there are many scribal
confusions in the transcription of the two).

   it is they who perfected your beauty. In this instance, the perfected beauty is linked not
to the ships but to the city walls displaying the highly polished shields (compare Song of
Songs 4:4).

12. *Tarshish.* Though frequently mentioned in the Bible, Tarshish has not been confidently
identified, locations as different as Asia Minor, North Africa, and Spain having been proposed. All that is certain is that it is far to the west.

13. *Javan.* This name, which looks like the two that come after it, appears in the Table of
Nations in Genesis, and is a Hebrew transliteration—*yawan*—of Ion or Ionia.

15. *were traders under you.* The literal sense is "were trade of your hand." Since "hand"
implies power, responsibility, oversight, it is assumed in this translation that the word
suggests superiority in the trade relationship.

16. *malachite.* As elsewhere in the Bible, the identification of this and other precious stones
in this verse is conjectural.

19. *cassia, and cane.* These are both aromatic substances.

stones and gold, they gave for your deposited goods. Haran and Canneh 23
and Edom, the traders of Sheba, Assyria, and Cilmad traded with you. They 24
traded with you in fine raiment, in indigo robes and bright-colored rugs
bound in cords and packed tight among your wares. Tarshish ships were 25
in the service of your trade.

> And you were full and became greatly ladened
>   in the heart of the seas.
> Into many waters they brought you,   26
>   those rowing for you.
> The east wind broke you
>   in the heart of the seas.

Your wealth and your deposited goods, your wares, your sailors, the repair- 27
ers of your ships and the supervisors of your wares and all your men of war
who were within you and all your assembly that was within you shall fall
into the heart of the seas on the day of your downfall.

> At the sound of the scream of your mariners   28
>   the breakers shall toss.
> And they shall come down from their ships,   29
>   all who wield the oar,
> sailors, all the sea's mariners
>   shall stand on the ground.
> And they shall make their voices heard over you   30

---

25. *Tarshish ships.* As elsewhere, this is probably a designation not of ships built in Tarshish
but of a particular kind of vessel constructed for long voyages.

26. *The east wind broke you.* The previous line initially seems to continue the evocation of
Tyre's dominance as a trader city over vast regions. Now, however, in a sudden transition,
the prosperous city, emblematized by a ship, is shattered in the heart of the seas by an east
wind, which in the Bible generally brings bad things.

28. *At the sound of the scream of your mariners / the breakers shall toss.* Tyre's grandeur had
been represented in this lament chiefly through the splendor of her sea vessels. Now the
ships are shattered, engulfed by waves, and the crewmen terrified.

29. *shall stand on the ground.* This final verset seems rather flat for the depiction of a disaster at sea, conveying merely a sense of the sailors leaving the ship to stand on dry land.
The move may be dictated by the desire to represent the sailors in the next three verses as
assuming all the grief-stricken postures of mourning.

and scream bitterly,
    and put dust upon their heads,
        in ashes they shall wallow.
31   And they shall shave their heads over you
        and gird sackcloth
    and keen over you most bitterly,
        a bitter dirge.
32   And their sons shall sound over you a lament
        and lament over you:
    Who is like Tyre for silence
        within the sea?

33   When your deposited goods went out from the seas, you sated many peoples with your great wealth, and with your wares you enriched the kings
of the earth.

34   When you were broken on the seas,
            into the waters' depths your wares
                and all your assembly within you fell.
35   All the coastland dwellers
            were shocked over you,
        and their kings were horrified,
            and their faces were contorted.
36   Traders among the peoples
            hissed over you.
        You are become a horror,
            and you exist no more, forever."

---

31. *they shall shave their heads over you.* Less familiar than the ashes and sackcloth, this is
a gesture of mourning.

32. *Who is like Tyre for silence / within the sea?* The meaning of *kedumah*, "for silence," is
somewhat doubtful, but *dumah*, "silence," is an epithet for the realm of death.

35. *their faces were contorted.* Though the Hebrew verb here, deriving from the word for
thunder, sometimes suggests "anger," that does not seem appropriate for this context.

36. *Traders among the peoples / hissed over you.* This is the final turn in Tyre's reversal of
fortunes. The many peoples of the region had enjoyed multiple trade relations with Tyre
and had been willing to assume the role of subordinate partners in trade. Now these very
partners in commerce are both shocked by and contemptuous of Tyre (both implied by
the hissing).

CHAPTER 28   And the word of the Lord came to me, saying, 1
"Man, say to the prince of Tyre, Thus said the Master, the Lord: Inasmuch 2
as your heart was haughty and you said, 'I am a god, enthroned like a god.
I have sat in the heart of the seas.'—but you are human and not a god, and
you thought your heart like the heart of a god! Why, you are wiser than 3
Daniel. In all obscure things none can match you! Through your wisdom 4
and through your discernment you have gained wealth, and you have gathered gold and silver in your treasure houses. Through all your wisdom in 5
your trading you have made your wealth great, and your heart became
haughty through your wealth. Therefore, thus said the Master, the Lord: 6
Inasmuch as you have thought your heart like the heart of a god, therefore 7
am I about to bring against you strangers, the fearsome ones of the nations,
and they shall unsheathe their swords against the beauty of your wisdom
and profane your splendor. To the Pit they shall bring you down, and you 8
shall die the deaths of the slain in the heart of the seas. Will you really say, 'I 9
am a god' before your killer? But you are human and not a god in the hand
of him who slays you. The death of the uncircumcised you shall die by the 10
hand of strangers, for I have spoken," said the Master, the Lord.

CHAPTER 28   2. *the prince of Tyre.* Why Ezekiel should have directed all these
prophecies of doom against Tyre is not entirely evident. The Phoenicians had been trading partners of the kingdom of Judah since the time of Solomon, and they were in no way
allied with the Babylonians, as were the hated Edomites. The prophet's objection to Tyre,
as emerges in the second part of this verse and in what follows, appears to have been theological rather than political: this prosperous maritime kingdom, enjoying luxurious wealth
from its trading activities, had in the prophet's view committed the primal transgression
of imagining that it was godlike.

   your heart. Again, one must remember that the heart was thought of as the seat of
intellection, which leads to the indictment of Tyre's pride in its wisdom in the next verse.

3. *wiser than Daniel.* This is, of course, not the Daniel of the later biblical book but a wise
and virtuous figure of Ugaritic—and, presumably, Canaanite—legend. It might be noted
that though the Masoretic vocalization asks us to pronounce the name "Daniel," the consonantal text shows *dan'el* (without the *yod* after the *nun*), which is how the name appears
in the Ugaritic.

10. *The death of the uncircumcised you shall die.* This dire fate must be understood in light
of the relatively widespread practice of circumcision among the peoples adjacent to ancient
Israel. The act enjoined on Abraham and his descendants was not an innovation; what
was new was the meaning imposed on the act. It is noteworthy that of all the surrounding
groups, only the Philistines are given the repeated epithet "uncircumcised," and the Philistines were not a Semitic people, having arrived on the eastern shore of the Mediterranean
from the Greek realm in the thirteenth century B.C.E.

11,12   And the word of the LORD came to me, saying, "Man, sound a lament over
        the king of Tyre and say to him, Thus said the Master, the LORD: Man,
13   you are the sealer of the plan, full of wisdom, perfect in beauty. In Eden
        the garden of God you were. Every precious stone was in your raiment—
        carnelian, chrysolite, and amethyst, beryl, lapis lazuli, and jasper, sap-
        phire, turquoise, and emerald and gold crafted to beautify you and your
14   groves within you. On the day you were created they were made. You were
        a cherub anointed and sheltering. And I set you on a holy mountain. A
15   god you were. Among stones of fire you walked about. Unblemished you
        were in your ways from the day you were created until wrongdoing was
16   found in you. Through all your trading, you were filled with acts of out-
        rage and offended, and I profaned you, not to be on the mountain of God,
        and made you wander, O sheltering cherub, far from the stones of fire.
17   Your heart grew haughty through your beauty. You ruined your wisdom

---

13. *In Eden the garden of God you were.* The prophet here chooses a somewhat surprising
rhetorical strategy. In order to represent—hyperbolically—the perfect splendor enjoyed by
Sidon, which will now be violently shorn from it, he imagines the king of Sidon living an
angelic life in the Garden of Eden.

Every precious stone was in your raiment. The list of precious stones is the same as those
on the breastplate of a high priest. In both cases, the precise identification of most of the
stones is not possible. There is nothing whatever about bejeweled garments in the Garden
story in Genesis—the first two humans walk about naked—so this is either a free elaboration on the part of Ezekiel or the reflection of a different tradition about Eden.

crafted to beautify you and your groves. The meaning of the entire string of phrases is
doubtful.

14. *You were a cherub anointed and sheltering.* The Hebrew phrase is obscure, especially the
word here conjecturally translated as "anointed." In the Garden story, the only cherub mentioned appears at the moment of expulsion, wielding a fiery sword to block the way to Eden.

a holy mountain. There is no reference to a mountain in the Eden of Genesis, but perhaps Ezekiel introduces one here because of the conception of a mountain as the dwelling
place of the gods in Syro-Canaanite tradition.

A god you were. This is, of course, an audacious assertion. It probably should be seen as
a translation into poetic-mythological hyperbole of Tyre's notion that it is a god.

Among stones of fire you walked about. Although this is meant to express the godlike
invulnerability of the Edenic Sidon, it is still another detail never hinted at in the canonical
Garden story. It could be a poetic invention, but one suspects that Ezekiel was tapping a
tradition about Eden that has not survived elsewhere.

16. *I profaned you, not to be on the mountain of God.* "To be" is merely implied in the
Hebrew.

17. *Your heart grew haughty through your beauty.* Just as Ezekiel rages against the seductive
allure of the female body, the very presence of beauty—the finely wrought aesthetic objects
made possible through Sidon's wealth—seems to him a snare that catches its possessor in
pride and arrogant self-regard.

together with your splendor. I flung you to the ground; before kings I set
you to be stared at. From all your crimes, through the wrongdoing of your   18
trading, you profaned your sanctuaries, and I brought out fire from within
you—it consumed you. And I turned you into ashes on the ground before
the eyes of all who saw you. All who knew you among the peoples were   19
shocked over you.

> You are become a horror,
>   and you exist no more, forever."

And the word of the Lord came to me, saying, "Man, set your face to   20,21
Sidon and prophesy concerning her. And say, Thus said the Master, the   22
Lord: Here I am against you, Sidon, and I will be honored in your midst,
and they shall know that I am the Lord when I carry out punishments
within her, and I will be hallowed in her. And I will send against her pes-   23
tilence and blood in her streets, and the slain shall fall within her by the
sword against her all around, and they shall know that I am the Lord.
And the house of Israel shall no longer have stinging thistles and painful   24
thorns from all around them who despise them, and they shall know that
I am the Lord."

Thus said the Master, the Lord: "When I gather in the house of Israel from   25
the peoples where they were scattered, I will be hallowed through them in
the eyes of the nations, and they shall dwell on their soil that I gave to My
servant Jacob. And they shall dwell on it secure and build houses and plant   26
vineyards when I carry out punishments against all who despise them all
around them, and they shall know that I am the Lord."

CHAPTER 29   In the tenth year, in the tenth month, on the   1
twelfth of the month, the word of the Lord came to me, saying, "Man,   2

---

22. *I will be honored in your midst.* God is honored, hallowed, by manifesting His overwhelming power to destroy a kingdom intoxicated with its own grandeur.

24. *And the house of Israel shall no longer have stinging thistles and painful thorns.* Historically, it is not clear how the Phoenicians were such tormentors of Israel, though Ezekiel
seems persuaded that this was the case.

CHAPTER 29   1. *In the tenth year.* This would be 587 B.C.E., roughly half a year
before the conquest of Jerusalem.

set your face to Pharaoh king of Egypt and prophesy concerning him and
3 concerning all of Egypt. Speak and say, Thus said the Master, the LORD:

> Here I am against you, Pharaoh,
>> king of Egypt,
> the great crocodile
>> crouching in its rivers,
> who said, 'My Nile is mine,
>> and I made it for myself.'

4   I will put the hooks in your jaws
>> and make the fish of your rivers cling to your scales
> and bring you up from your rivers,
>> and all the fish of your rivers shall cling to your scales.

5   And I will abandon you in the desert,
>> you and all the fish of your rivers.
> On the surface of the field you shall fall,
>> you shall not be gathered nor taken up.
> To the beasts of the earth and to the fowl of the heavens
>> I will give you to be eaten.

6   And all the dwellers of Egypt shall know
>> that I am the LORD
> inasmuch as they have been

---

2. *Pharaoh king of Egypt.* Like Jeremiah, Ezekiel saw a proposed alliance with Egypt against Babylonia as a self-destructive illusion, but Pharaoh, like the king of Tyre, is also excoriated for his overweening idea that he is a god.

3. *the great crocodile.* Although this same Hebrew word in Genesis and Psalms refers to a mythological sea beast, here it is the crocodile, whose habitat is the Nile, and who also is an emblem for Pharaoh. The "scales" or armor plates of the beast belong to the crocodile.

    its rivers. The Hebrew is the plural of *ye'or,* an Egyptian loanword designating the Nile. In biblical poetry it often has the general sense of "rivers," although here the probable reference is to the seven tributaries of the Nile. "Rivers" in the following lines is again the plural of *ye'or.*

4. *make the fish of your rivers cling to your scales.* This is a double disaster: the crocodile (Pharaoh) will be hauled out of the Nile after being caught with hooks, and the fish of the Nile—a vital source of sustenance for the Egyptians—will be hauled out with the crocodile, to die on dry land.

5. *And I will abandon you in the desert.* This is, of course, a place without water where neither the crocodile nor the fish can survive.

    you shall not be gathered nor taken up. The probable reference is to being collected for burial. Not only will the crocodile-Pharaoh perish in the desert, but it will suffer the ignominy of denied burial and becoming food for scavengers.

a reed staff to the house of Israel.

When they grasp you with the palm, you shatter,   7
    and you crack every shoulder among them.
And when they lean on you, you break,
    and you wrench all loins among them.

Therefore, thus said the Master, the LORD: I am about to bring the sword   8
against you, and I will cut off from you man and beast. And the land of   9
Egypt shall become a desolation and a ruin, and they shall know that I am
the LORD, inasmuch as he said, 'The Nile is mine and I made it.' Therefore,   10
here I am against you and against your Nile and its offshoots, and I will
turn the land of Egypt into ruins, desolate parched ground, from Migdol
to Seyene and to the border of Nubia. No human foot shall pass over it, and   11
no beast's foot shall pass over it, and it shall be unsettled for forty years.
And I will make the land of Egypt a desolation among desolate lands, and   12
its ruined cities shall be a desolation for forty years, and I will disperse
Egypt among the nations and scatter them among the lands. For thus said   13
the Master, the LORD: At the end of forty years I will gather Egypt from
the peoples where they were dispersed. And I will restore the fortunes of   14
Egypt and bring them back to the land of Patros, to the land of their origins,

---

6. *a reed staff.* The slender reed will of course break when a person tries to lean on it.

7. *When they grasp you.* The "you" is the reed, made clear in the Hebrew because it is masculine singular, like the word for "reed."

   you crack every shoulder. When the reed breaks, the shoulder of the person leaning on
it as though it were a solid staff is wrenched. This is an image of the illusory trust in any
alliance with Egypt.

   you wrench all loins. Though the Hebrew *ha'amadta* looks as though it meant "made
stand," there is a reversal of consonants here (something Rashi already understood), and
the meaning is the same as *ham'adta*—literally, "cause to stumble."

10. *your Nile and its offshoots.* While this is the same plural form for the word for "Nile" that
is translated above as "rivers," the pointed reference to "The Nile is mine" at the end of the
previous verse is crucial, so the word "Nile" needs to be repeated. A very literal rendering
would be "your Niles," but of course there is only one Nile.

   desolate parched ground. Egypt, watered by the Nile and its tributaries, was famous in
the region for its lushness. Now it will become a desert.

   from Migdol . . . to the border of Nubia. Migdol is on the northern border of Egypt, Nubia
(Cush in the Hebrew) to its south.

11. *unsettled for forty years.* The formulaic number forty is invoked.

14. *And I will restore the fortunes of Egypt.* This amounts to an ironic use of this familiar
phrase. When the fortunes of Israel are restored, it is returned in splendid triumph to its
land. Egypt will be returned to its land, but only in a pitifully reduced state.

15 and they shall be there a lowly kingdom. Among the kingdoms she shall be lowly and shall no longer be raised up over the nations, and I will diminish
16 them, that they not hold sway over the nations. And they shall no longer be for the house of Israel a place to trust, recalling crime when they turned toward them. And they shall know that I am the Master, the LORD."

17 And it happened in the twenty-seventh year, in the first month, on the first
18 of the month, that the word of the LORD came to me, saying, "Man, Nebuchadrezzar king of Babylonia has made his forces labor mightily against Tyre. Every head is bald and every shoulder scraped. But no gain did he and
19 his forces get from all the labor that he spent upon it. Therefore, thus said the Master, the LORD: I am about to give Nebuchadrezzar king of Babylonia the land of Egypt, and he shall carry away her abundance and take her
20 spoil and seize her plunder, and she shall be gain for his forces. His wages for which he labored I will give him, the land of Egypt, for what they did to
21 Me, said the Master, the LORD. On that day I will make a horn sprout for the house of Israel, and to you I will give freedom to speak in their midst, and they shall know that I am the LORD."

---

17. *in the twenty-seventh year.* This would be 571 B.C.E., making this the latest of all the precisely noted dates in Ezekiel.

18. *Nebuchadrezzar . . . has made his forces labor mightily.* Much earlier, Ezekiel had predicted the fall of Tyre. The siege had been very protracted (according to Josephus, thirteen years, but perhaps even longer), hence the laboring mightily of the troops.

Every head is bald. Although elsewhere this is translated as "shaven," here it is not a sign of mourning but an indication that the soldiers are worn (or perhaps simply aged) through the long siege.

19. *she shall be gain for his forces.* The conquest of Egypt becomes a kind of consolation prize for the Babylonians. Unable to take Tyre, they are compensated—at least they have "gain" for their labors—by the opportunity to plunder Egypt.

20. *for what they did to Me.* The phrase is cryptic. It could mean "for what the Egyptians did in offending Me"; it could also mean "for what the Babylonians did in acting on My behalf."

21. *make a horn sprout.* As throughout biblical literature, the horn—whether bull's or ram's horn—is an idiom for "strength."

to you I will give freedom to speak. The literal sense of the Hebrew is "opening of the mouth." The idea is that in the restored Israel the prophet will be able to speak without inhibition, and everyone will listen to him.

CHAPTER 30   And the word of the LORD came to me, saying, 1
"Man, prophesy and say, Thus said the Master, the LORD: 2

Wail 'woe' for the day.
  For the day is near and the night is near for the LORD.   3
A day of cloud, a day of nations it shall be.
  And a sword shall come against Egypt,   4
    and there shall be shuddering in Nubia
  when the slain fall in Egypt
    and they take off her abundance, and her foundations shall be ruined.
Nubia and Put and Lud and all the mixed throng   5
  and Cub and the people from the land of the pact,
    they shall fall by the sword.
Thus said the LORD: 6
The supporters of Egypt shall fall,
  and the pride of her strength shall come down.
From Migdol to Seyene
  by the sword they shall fall within her
    —said the Master, the LORD.
And they shall be desolate among desolate lands,   7
  and its towns among ruined towns shall be.
And they shall know that I am the LORD   8
  when I set fire to Egypt,
    and all who help her are broken.

CHAPTER 30   3. *A day of cloud.* Given the context of impending catastrophe, this is more than just a cloudy day. The day when God exacts retribution is here (compare verse 18), as in several other prophets, a day when the sky goes ominously dark.

4. *shuddering in Nubia / when the slain fall in Egypt.* The Hebrew features wordplay: "shuddering" is *ḥalḥalah,* "the slain" is *ḥalal.*

5. *Nubia and Put and Lud and all the mixed throng / and Cub.* These are all neighboring lands (though Cub has not been indentified) that were either allied with Egypt or provided mercenaries to the Egyptians.
  the people from the land of the pact. The reference is somewhat obscure, but as part of a list of allies of Egypt, it probably indicates a country that had some sort of military pact with the Egyptians.

6. *From Migdol to Seyene.* As before, this is from north to south within Egypt.

8. *all who help her.* As with the "supporters" in verse 6, this is a term often used for those who provide military aid.

9   On that day messengers shall go out before Me in ships to strike secure
    Nubia with terror, and there shall be shuddering in them on the day of
10 Egypt, for look, it is coming. For thus said the Master, the LORD: I will
    bring an end to the abundance of Egypt by the hand of Nebuchadrezzar
11 king of Babylonia. He and his troops with him, the fearsome ones of the
    nations, are to be brought to lay ruin to the land, and they shall unsheathe
12 their swords against Egypt, and they shall fill the land with the slain. And
    I will turn the rivers into dry land and give over the land into the hand of
    evil men, and I will make the land and its fullness desolate by the hand of
13 strangers. I, the LORD, have spoken. Thus said the Master, the LORD: I will
    destroy the foul things and bring an end to the ungods from Noph, and no
    prince shall there be from the land of Egypt, and I will set fire to the land
14 of Egypt. And I will make Patros desolate and set fire to Zoan, and I will
15 execute punishments in No. And I will pour out My wrath upon Sin, the
16 stronghold of Egypt, and cut off the abundance of No. And I will set fire to
    Egypt. Sin shall surely shudder, and No shall be breached, and Noph, the
17 foes by day. The young men of Aven and Pi-Beseth shall fall by the sword,
18 and the cities shall go into captivity. And in Tahpanhes the day shall go
    dark when I break there the staffs of Egypt. And the pride of her strength
    shall end within her. As to her, a cloud shall cover her, and her daughters

---

9. *there shall be shuddering in them on the day of Egypt.* This formulation conveys the idea
that as retribution comes down on Egypt, it will engulf her neighboring allies as well.

12. *I will turn the rivers into dry land.* Again, "rivers" is literally "Niles," meaning the Nile,
its tributaries, and its canals.

14. *No.* This is a city in northern Egypt that at times served as a capital. "No" is a variant of
"Noph": the Hebrew sometimes uses one form and other times the other (e.g., in verse 16
below, as well as in Jeremiah 2:16).

15. *the abundance of No.* It should be noted that both here and in verses 4 and 10 above, the
term *hamon*, "abundance" or "wealth," can also mean "crowd."

16. *and Noph, the foes by day.* The translation reproduces the obscurity of the Hebrew.
Perhaps a preposition ("from," "by") was dropped.

18. *Tahpanhes.* Another prominent Egyptian city; like No, there are variant spellings in
the Hebrew. This translation reflects that, sometimes using the spelling Tahpanes (e.g.,
Jeremiah 2:16).
    go dark. The Masoretic Text reads *ḥasakh*, "hold back," but many Hebrew manuscripts
show the more plausible *ḥashakh*, "go dark."
    when I break there the staffs of Egypt. The staff is an emblem of sovereignty.

shall go into captivity. And I will execute punishments in Egypt, and they 19
shall know that I am the LORD."

And it happened in the eleventh year in the first month on the seventh of 20
the month that the word of the LORD came to me, saying, "Man, I have 21
broken the arm of Pharaoh king of Egypt, and, look, it has not been bound
up to heal, to put a dressing on it to bind it for strengthening it to grasp a
sword. Therefore, thus said the Master, the LORD: Here I am against Pha- 22
raoh king of Egypt. I will break his arms, the strong one and the broken one
and make the sword drop from his hand. And I will disperse Egypt among 23
the nations and scatter them among the lands. And I will strengthen the 24
arms of the king of Babylonia and put My sword in his hand, and I will
break the arms of Pharaoh, and he shall groan as the slain groan before
Me. And I will strengthen the arms of the king of Babylonia, but the arms 25
of Pharaoh shall drop. And they shall know that I am the LORD when I put
My sword in the hand of the king of Babylonia and he reaches it out against
the land of Egypt. And I will disperse Egypt among the nations and scatter 26
them among the lands, and they shall know that I am the LORD."

---

20. *the eleventh year.* This takes us back to 587 B.C.E. This historical moment, just before
the final destruction of Jerusalem, seems to have been a time when Ezekiel was repeatedly
moved to pronounce prophecies about the nations.

21. *I have broken the arm of Pharaoh.* The prophecy is a striking instance of the rhetorical
strategy of resuscitating a dead metaphor. Repeatedly, "arm" is a term for "strength" or
"power." That is what it means here, but the literal sense of the word becomes salient: the
arm is broken; it has been given no medical attention to heal it; dangling broken, it can no
longer grasp a sword; then the other arm is broken, and the damaged one is broken a second
time. The devastation of Egypt as a military power in this way is made painfully vivid.

22. *make the sword drop from his hand.* In keeping with the literalization of the metaphor
of the arm, Pharaoh's broken, pain-wracked arm, incapable of holding a sword, lets it drop
from his grip.

24. *And I will strengthen the arms of the king of Babylonia and put My sword in his hand.*
This is the final turn of the metaphor of the arm: while Pharaoh's broken arms dangle,
unable to wield any weapon, God makes Nebuchadnezzar's arms strong and ready to grasp
the sword. "My sword" does not refer to a divine or magical weapon but simply invokes the
idea that the Babylonian king is acting on God's behalf, or at God's bidding.

26. *And I will disperse Egypt among the nations and scatter them among the lands.* One again
sees the pronounced tendency in Ezekiel's prose prophecies to deploy formulaic language
and frequent repetition.

1 CHAPTER 31   And it happened in the eleventh year in the third month, on the first of the month, that the word of the LORD came to me, saying,

2   "Man, say to Pharaoh king of Egypt and to his throng:
          Whom were you like in your greatness?
3   Look, Assyria was a cedar in Lebanon,
     lovely in branches, a shady wood,
        and lofty in stature,
           among the clouds its crest.
4   Water made it grow,
        the deep raised it high,
     led its rivers round where it was planted
        and sent out its channels
           to all the trees of the field.
5   Therefore did its stature grow higher
        than all the trees of the field,
     and its boughs became many,
         its branches grew long
           from the many waters in its duct.
6   On its boughs nested
        all the fowl of the heavens,
     and under its branches
        all the beasts of the field spawned,
     and in its shade dwelled
        all the many nations.

CHAPTER 31   1. *in the eleventh year in the third month.* This would be June 587 B.C.E.

3. *Look, Assyria was a cedar in Lebanon.* Assyria had been the paradigmatic image of the towering, overweening imperial power that was brought down to the dust. The body of this prophecy will focus on the grandeur and downfall of Assyria, but it is all intended to serve as a monitory image of the fate that will now overtake arrogant Egypt.

4. *the deep.* Although *tehom*, "the deep," often refers to the cosmic abyss of waters (as at the beginning of Genesis), here it indicates the groundwater that nurtures the tree.

5. *boughs . . . branches.* One might note that Ezekiel uses four different Hebrew words (one borrowed from the Aramaic) for "branches" in the course of this prophecy.

6. *in its shade dwelled / all the many nations.* The introduction of "many nations" is a clear indication that the towering tree is an image of Assyria's imperial grandeur.

And it was lovely in its great size   7
    in the length of its branches,
for its roots were
    by many waters.
Cedars did not match it   8
    in the garden of God.
Cypresses did not equal
    its boughs,
and plane trees did not have
    the like of its boughs.
No tree in the garden of God
    was like it in its beauty.
Lovely did I make it   9
    in all its boughs,
and all the trees of Eden envied it,
    which were in the garden of God.

Therefore, thus said the Master, the LORD: Inasmuch as it grew high in   10
stature, and its crest was set among the clouds, and its heart became lofty
through its height, I will give it into the hand of the fiercest of nations. He   11
shall surely do to it according to its wickedness. I have banished it. And   12
strangers, the most fearsome of nations, shall cut it off and abandon it in the
mountains and in all the valleys. Its boughs shall fall and its branches shall
break in all the watercourses of the earth, and all the peoples of the earth
shall come away from its shade and abandon it. In the place of its downfall   13

---

8. *Cedars did not match it / in the garden of God.* As in the prophecy concerning Egypt in chapter 28, Ezekiel pushes his hyperbole to the limit by bringing Eden into the picture, saying that even the perfect cedars of God's garden were not the equal of this grand tree.

10. *it grew high.* The Masoretic Text reads "you grew high," and perhaps the switch from second person to third person in this verse was accepted usage for Ezekiel, but it would be confusing in English. The Syriac shows the third person here, but there is no way of knowing whether it used a Hebrew text with the third person or whether the translators were regularizing the Hebrew.

11. *I have banished it.* This clause (a single word in the Hebrew) looks syntactically disjunct and may reflect a scribal error.

12. *its branches shall break in all the watercourses of the earth.* Previously, the many watercourses nurtured the tree and caused it to grow high. Now, the broken branches float down the streams, manifestly unable to be sustained in life by the water.

all the fowl of heavens shall dwell, and on its branches all the beasts of the
14 field shall be, so that no trees by water be lofty in their stature and they not
set their crests among the clouds, and no well-watered trees stand up to
them in their height. For they are all given over to death, to the netherworld,
15 in the midst of humans who go down to the Pit. Thus said the Master, the
LORD: On the day it went down to Sheol, I dried up, covered the deep over
it, and held back its rivers, and the many waters were blocked. And I made
Lebanon grow dark over it, and all the trees of the forest languished over
16 it. With the sound of its downfall I shook nations, when I brought it down
to Sheol with those who go down to the Pit, and in the netherworld all the
trees of Eden, the choicest and the best of Lebanon, all well-watered, took
17 comfort. They, too, went down with it to Sheol, to the slain by the sword,
18 its helpers who had dwelled in its shade in the midst of nations. To whom
were you like in such glory and grandeur among the trees of Eden? But you
were brought down with the trees of Eden to the netherworld. Among the
uncircumcised you lie with those slain by the sword. This is about Pharaoh
and all his throngs," said the Master, the LORD.

---

13. *on its branches all the beasts of the field shall be.* The tree has been shattered and the
broken branches lie on the ground. Instead of birds nesting in the living branches, earth-
bound animals crouch over them.

14. *well-watered trees.* The Hebrew says literally "water-drinking trees."
    For they are all given over to death. The fact that trees, like human beings, die is an
indication that empires, too—the grandest of trees—come to an end.

15. *I dried up, covered the deep over it.* The wording is a little confusing. Ordinarily, the
deep is an inexhaustible source of water. Here, however, the deep is dried up—or, perhaps
alternatively, its waters are "blocked"—so that when the great tree of the Assyrian empire
descends into the netherworld, the "deep" or abyss that covers it serves to reinforce its
withered state.

16. *when I brought it down to Sheol . . . all the trees of Eden . . . took comfort.* The somewhat
complicated symbolic plot is as follows: Because trees, like humankind, are mortal, even
the trees of Eden have gone down to Sheol. Now, when they see that the great tree of the
Assyrian empire, which they were said to have envied, has joined them in the realm of
death, they rejoice; the tree that towered over them has now been reduced to their equal.

17. *the slain by the sword, its helpers.* As is often the case with Ezekiel's handling of allegorical figures, the referent here obtrudes into the allegorical image: "the slain by the sword"
are fallen soldiers, and "helpers" would be Assyria's military allies or mercenary troops.

18. *Among the uncircumcised you lie.* See the note on 28:10.
    This is about Pharaoh and all his throngs. This notation at the very end of the prophecy
betrays a certain awkwardness in the deployment of the allegory. The entire extended
image of the towering tree has been a representation of the grandeur of the Assyrian
empire. Now, however, the prophet must remind his audience that in fact Pharaoh is like
Assyria in his greatness and that the whole prophecy is really about Pharaoh.

CHAPTER 32   And it happened in the twelfth year, in the ₁
twelfth month, on the first of the month, that the word of the LORD came
to me, saying, "Man, sound a lament over Pharaoh, king of Egypt, and say ₂
to him:

> To a lion among nations were you likened,
>   but you were like a crocodile in the seas
>   churning through your rivers,
>   muddying waters with your feet,
>   trampling their rivers.

Thus said the Master, the LORD: I will cast over you My net in the assembly ₃
of many peoples and bring you up in My toils. And I will abandon you on ₄
the ground and cast you on the surface of the field. And I will settle upon
you all the fowl of the heavens and sate from you the beasts of the earth.
And I will put your flesh on the mountains and will fill the valleys with ₅
your blood. And I will water the earth with what floods from you, from ₆
your blood on the mountains, and the channels shall fill from you. And I ₇
will cover the heavens with your going dark, and I will darken their stars.
I will cover the sun with cloud, and the noon shall not shine its light. All ₈
the sources of light in the heavens will I darken upon you. And I will set
darkness over your land, said the LORD. And I will vex the heart of many ₉

CHAPTER 32   1. *in the twelfth year, in the twelfth month.* This sets the prophecy in
585 B.C.E., some months after the destruction of the kingdom of Judah.

2. *To a lion among nations were you likened.* The metaphor of the conquering king as a
lion is conventional throughout the Near East and appears frequently in biblical poetry.
    but you were like a crocodile in the seas. The crocodile, while perhaps fearsome, has little
of the grandeur of the lion and is confined to his aqueous habitat ("the seas" here are the
Nile and its tributaries). It can be caught with nets (verse 3), and when it is flung on dry
land far from the water (verse 4), it cannot long survive.

5. *with your blood.* The Masoretic *ramutekha* is opaque. Some interpreters derive it from
r-m-h, a verbal stem that means "to throw," and so take it to indicate the body of Pharaoh
thrown away in open country. Because that interpretation seems strained, this translation
follows the Septuagint in reading *damkha,* "your blood," which aptly matches "your flesh"
in the first half of this sentence.

6. *what floods from you.* The single Hebrew word here is problematic, and so the translation is conjectural.

7. *I will darken their stars.* Although apocalyptic darkness is often part of prophecies of
God's day of judgment, the elaboration of engulfing darkness has special resonance here
in relation to Pharaoh because it recalls the plague of darkness that descended on Egypt.
"I will set darkness over your land" in verse 8 is an especially pointed allusion to Exodus.

peoples when I bring your breaking among the nations, upon nations that
10   you never knew. And I will shock many peoples over you, and their kings
shall be horrified by you when I let My sword fly over their faces, and they
11   shall tremble constantly, each for his life, on the day of your downfall. For
thus said the Master, the LORD:

> The sword of the king of Babylonia shall come upon you.
12   By the swords of warriors will I make your throng fall.
> Fearsome among the nations they all are,
> and they shall plunder the pride of Egypt,
> and all her throng shall be destroyed.
13   And I will destroy all their cattle
> from alongside many waters,
> and no more shall human foot muddy them,
> and the hooves of cattle shall not muddy them.
14   Then will I sink their waters
> and lead their rivers like oil
> —said the Master, the LORD.
15   When I make the land of Egypt a desolation
> and the land and its fullness become desolate,
> when I strike down the dwellers there,
> they shall know that I am the LORD.
16   It is a lament, and the daughters of Egypt lament it,
> they shall lament it over Egypt,
> and over all their throng they shall lament it."
> —said the Master, the LORD.

17   And it happened in the twelfth year, on the fifteenth of the month, the word
18   of the LORD came to me, saying, "Man, weep over the throng of Egypt and
bring it down, you and the daughters of the nations:

---

10. *when I let My sword fly over their faces.* The horrendous power of God's act of destruction is so sweeping that the surrounding peoples fear for their own lives, even though the wrath is not directed at them.

14. *lead their rivers like oil.* When poured, oil advances in a slow trickle.

16. *the daughters of Egypt lament it.* As elsewhere in the Bible, women figure as designated keeners crying over deaths.

18. *you.* This translation reads 'atah, "you," instead of the Masoretic 'otah, "her."

The mighty to the netherworld
    with those who go down to the Pit.
More lovely than who were you? Go down!   19
    and be laid with the uncircumcised.
Among the slain by the sword they shall fall.   20
    The sword is let loose. They have pulled down her and all her throngs.
The mightiest warriors speak to him   21
    from Sheol, together with his allies:
The uncircumcised have come down, they lie,
    those slain by the sword.
Assyria is there and all her assembly,   22
    round her all her graves.
All of them are slain,
    fallen by the sword,
whose graves have been put   23
    in the far reaches of the Pit.
And her assembly is round her gravesite,
    all of them are slain,
        fallen by the sword,
who had sown terror
    in the land of the living.
Elam is there and all her throng   24
    round her gravesite.
All of them are slain,
    fallen by the sword,
who came down uncircumcised
    to the netherworld,
who had sown terror
    in the land of the living,
and they bear their disgrace
    with those who go down to the Pit.
Amidst the slain   25
    they made her a place to lie

---

19. *be laid with the uncircumcised.* This again appears as a shameful fate. Circumcision was practiced in Egypt's priestly class, and there may have been a difference between a circumcised elite and uncircumcised masses.

23. *who had sown terror.* The literal sense of the Hebrew verb here is "had given." This is not a collocation that occurs elsewhere.

> with all her throng
>> round her graves.
> All of them are uncircumcised,
>> fallen by the sword.
> For they had sown terror
>> in the land of the living,
> and they bear their disgrace
>> with those who go down to the Pit.

26 Meshech and Tubal are there and all their throng
>> round their graves.
> All of them are uncircumcised,
>> pierced by the sword.
> For they had sown terror
>> in the land of the living.

27 And they shall not lie with the warriors,
>> those fallen of the uncircumcised
> who came down to Sheol with their weapons of war
>> and put their swords beneath their heads,
> and their crimes were upon their bones,
>> for the terror of the warriors was upon the land of the living.

28 As for you, in the midst of the uncircumcised you are broken,
>> and you lie with those slain by the sword.

---

25. *with all her throng.* The "her" refers to Elam, in Persia, following the common biblical usage in which nations are represented in the feminine singular because of an implied personification of the nation as a woman.

26. *Meshech and Tubal.* These are peoples of Asia Minor, always paired together in the Bible. The Hebrew text does not have an "and" here and treats the two as a feminine singular, but they are in fact two distinct peoples.
   pierced by the sword. There is a slight variation here in this highly repetitious text. In previous instances, the phrase was *ḥaleley ḥerev,* "slain by the sword," whereas here a passive verb, *meḥuleley,* is used instead of the noun.

27. *And they shall not lie with the warriors.* That is, they shall be denied the dignity of a warrior's burial.
   who came down to Sheol with their weapons of war / and put their swords beneath their heads. This line invokes the widespread practice, abundantly confirmed by archaeology, in the Near East (and, indeed, elsewhere) of burying warriors with their weapons.

28. *you are broken.* This verb is often used for defeat or catastrophe, but here it probably indicates that the corpse in the grave is damaged or mutilated through violent death.

Edom is there and all her kings and all her princes, who despite their valor ₂₉
were put with those slain by the sword—they lie with the uncircumcised
and with those who go down to the Pit. The princes of the north are all of ₃₀
them there and all the Sidonians, who have come down with the slain in
their terror, shamed of their valor, and they lie with the uncircumcised,
with those slain by the sword, and bear their disgrace with those who go
down to the Pit. Pharaoh sees them and regrets all her throng. Pharaoh ₃₁
and all his force are slain by the sword, said the Master, the LORD. For he ₃₂
had sown terror in the land of the living and was laid down in the midst
of the uncircumcised with those slain by the sword—Pharaoh and all her
throng"—said the Master, the LORD.

CHAPTER 33   And the word of the LORD came to me, saying, ₁
"Man, speak to the sons of your people and say to them: When I bring the ₂
sword against a land, the people of the land take one man from their best
and make him a lookout for them. And when he sees the sword coming ₃
against the land, he blows the ram's horn and warns the people. And who- ₄
ever hears the sound of the ram's horn and does not heed the warning and

---

30. *The princes of the north.* Although "north" is used freely by the prophets to designate
distant enemy powers, the mention here of the Sidonians makes this a reference to the
Phoenicians.

31. *Pharaoh sees them.* Witnessing all these rulers who have descended to the netherworld
in disgrace, Pharaoh is compelled to recognize that he shares their dire fate.
    all her throng. As in the previous usages here, the feminine "her" refers to the nation,
Egypt.
    Pharaoh and all his force. This is virtually a formulaic phrase, occurring in a variant
form in the destruction of the Egyptian army at the Sea of Reeds in Exodus 15.

32. *he had sown terror.* The Masoretic Text shows a first-person singular verb, but three
ancient versions, more plausibly, have the third person.

CHAPTER 33   2. *a lookout.* The same metaphor for the role of the prophet is used in
3:17. Although this term could also be rendered as "watchman," the connotation is clearly
military: he is the person posted in a tower or on a height to look out for and warn the people
of approaching armies, as the prophet sees and warns of impending disaster.

3. *when he sees the sword coming against the land.* This passage makes effective use of synecdoche: "the sword" clearly refers to the military force wielding swords, but the concrete
image of a destructive sword descending upon the city is palpable.
    the ram's horn. The ram's horn, with its sharp, penetrating sound, was used both to
muster troops and to warn of an attack.

5   the sword comes and takes him, his blood is on his own head. The sound of
    the ram's horn he heard but he did not heed the warning, his blood is upon
6   him. But he who heeds the warning shall save his life. And the lookout who
    sees the sword coming and does not blow the ram's horn and the people is
    not warned, and the sword comes and takes lives from them, the person is
7   taken in his crime, but his blood will I demand of the lookout. And you,
    man, I have made you a lookout for the house of Israel, and you shall hear a
8   word from My mouth and warn them from Me. When I say to the wicked:
    Wicked man, you are doomed to die, and you have not spoken to warn the
    wicked man of his way, he, the wicked man, shall die for his crime, but his
9   blood I will seek out from you. And you, when you warn the wicked man of
    his way to turn back from it, and he does not turn back from it, he shall die
10 for his crime, but you shall save your life. And you, man, say to the house
    of Israel: Thus you have said, saying, 'Why, our trespasses and our offenses
11 are upon us, and we rot in them, and how shall we survive?' Say to them: By
    My life, said the Master, the LORD, I do not desire the death of the wicked
    but rather the turning back of the wicked from his way, that he may live.
    Turn back, turn back from your evil ways, for why should you die, O house
12 of Israel? And you, man, say to the sons of your people: The righteousness
    of the righteous shall not save him on the day of his trespass, and in the
    wickedness of the wicked he shall not stumble on the day he turns back
    from his wickedness. And the righteous cannot live by virtue of it on the
13 day of his offense. When I say of the righteous, he shall surely live, and he
    trusts in his righteousness and does wrong, all his righteousness shall not
14 be recalled, and for the wrong that he has done, he shall die. And when I say
    to the wicked, you are doomed to die, and he turns back from his offense
15 and does justice and righteousness, if he gives back what is pledged, pays for
    what is robbed, goes by the statutes of life, not doing wrong, he shall surely

---

6. *the person is taken in his crime, but his blood will I demand of the lookout.* The offending person (the Hebrew says merely "he"), not having been warned by the prophet, will be
punished by death, but the prophet, because he has failed to fulfill his calling, will bear
responsibility for that death, and retribution will be exacted from him. Verse 8 essentially
repeats this idea in slightly different language, Ezekiel's penchant for repetition again in
view.

11. *I do not desire the death of the wicked.* More than any other prophet, Ezekiel is repeatedly
concerned with questions of divine justice and penitence. This sentence, for understandable reasons, was later incorporated in the liturgy for the Day of Atonement.

12. *And the righteous cannot live by virtue of it.* The "it," though a little distant from its
antecedent, refers to "the righteousness of the righteous."

live, he shall not die. All his offenses that he committed shall not be recalled 16
for him. He has done justice and righteousness—he shall surely live. And 17
should the sons of your people say, 'The way of the Master does not measure
up,' it is they whose way does not measure up. When the righteous turns 18
back from his righteousness and does wrong, he shall die for it. And when 19
the wicked turns back from his wickedness and does justice and righteousness, for it he shall live. And you have said, 'The way of the Master does not 20
measure up.' Each man of you will I judge for his ways, O house of Israel."

And it happened in the twelfth year of our exile in the tenth month on the 21
fifth of the month, a fugitive came to me from Jerusalem, saying, "The city
has been struck down." And the hand of the LORD was upon me in the 22
evening before the fugitive came, and He opened my mouth, and I was no
longer mute. And the word of the LORD came to me, saying, "Man, these 23,24
dwellers among the ruins on the soil of Israel are saying, 'Abraham was but
one, and he took hold of the land, and we are many. To us has the land been
given as an inheritance.' Therefore, say to them, Thus said the Master, the 25
LORD: Over blood you eat, and your eyes you lift up to your foul things, and

---

16. *All his offenses that he committed shall not be recalled for him.* In Ezekiel's vision of
divine justice, a person lives in a condition of constant existential choice: the wicked man
can reverse the dire consequences of all his previous trespasses by deciding to do what is
right, and the righteous man can cancel all the good effects of his acts of justice by sliding
into acts of wickedness. The next four verses, hewing to Ezekiel's characteristic style, go
on to repeat this idea.

21. *a fugitive came to me from Jerusalem.* Since the notation of date at the beginning of
the verse places this prophecy in 585 B.C.E., this would be a year after the destruction of
Jerusalem.

22. *And the hand of the LORD was upon me . . . and He opened my mouth.* As elsewhere,
Ezekiel represents his prophetic experience as a kind of bodily seizure by God in which
he is virtually a passive instrument. One suspects that, more than the other prophets, he
underwent extreme ecstatic states. He seems to imply here that prior to the night before the
arrival of the fugitive, he had been plunged in a condition of muteness. By his own account,
he had certainly prophesied several times in the period before and after the final conquest
of the kingdom of Judah. It may be the case that he alternated between times of ecstatic
prophecy and times of total silence.

24. *these dwellers among the ruins.* This phrase suggests that Ezekiel had already heard of
the destruction of Jerusalem.

25. *Over blood you eat.* Consuming blood, or eating "over" blood, is explicitly prohibited
(see Leviticus 19:26). There could also be a reference here to some sort of magical rite, as
the invocation of idolatry in the next phrase might suggest. But then the end of the verse

26 you shed blood. And shall you take hold of the land? You took your stand
   with your sword. You performed abominations, and each man defiled his
27 fellow man's wife. And shall you take hold of the land? Thus shall you say
   to them, Thus said the Master, the LORD: Those who are among the ruins
   shall surely fall by the sword, and those on the surface of the field I will give
   to the beasts as food, and those in the fortresses and in the caves shall die
28 by pestilence. And I will turn the land into a desolation and a devastation,
   and the pride of its strength shall come to an end, and the mountains of
29 Israel shall be desolate with no passerby. And they shall know that I am
   the LORD when I turn the land into a desolation and a destruction for all
30 their abominations that they did. And you, man, the sons of your people
   who speak to each other about you by the walls and at the entrances of the
   houses, and one speaks to another, a man to his kinsman, saying, 'Come,
31 pray, and hear what is the word coming forth from the LORD.' They shall
   come to you as the people are wont to come, and My people shall sit before
   you and hear your words, but these they do not do, for in the lust in their
32 mouths they act, after their gain their heart goes. And look, you are for

---

mentions shedding blood, so the blood forbidden to be eaten perhaps puns on the idea of
murder—you eat as you are immersed in bloodshed.

27. *among the ruins . . . on the surface of the field . . . in the fortresses and in the caves.* This
constitutes a panorama of where the survivors of the destruction of Jerusalem are to be
found: some remain among the ruins of the city; some have fled to the open field; some have
taken refuge outside the city in fortresses (whether actual fortresses or simply mountain
crags) and caves.

28. *a desolation and a devastation.* The wordplay in the Hebrew is *shemamah umeshamah.*

30. *by the walls and at the entrances of the houses.* This is a realistic picture of people con-
gregating on the streets outside their homes to speak to one another.
   one speaks to another, a man to his kinsman. Since both phrases mean the same thing,
this is probably one of those instances in which scribal tradition has incorporated in the
text two alternate versions of the same phrase.
   Come, pray, and hear what is the word coming forth from the LORD. As elsewhere, the
people, despite the tension between them and the prophet, are anxious to hear from him
what God's word is, especially at this grim moment when they know that their homeland
has been destroyed.

31. *as the people are wont to come.* Literally, "as the coming of the people."
   the lust in their mouths. While the expression sounds a bit strange (the Septuagint has
instead "the lies of their mouth"), it is probably authentic, leading to the reference to "a
song of lust" in the next verse. The people are scarcely ready to take in the word of the LORD
spoken by the prophet, immersed as they are in concupiscence and greed ("after their gain
their heart goes").

them a song of lust, lovely in sound and deftly played. And they hear your
words but do not act on them. And when it comes—look, it comes—they 33
shall know that a prophet was in their midst."

CHAPTER 34   And the word of the LORD came to me, saying, 1
"Man, prophesy against the shepherds of Israel. Prophesy, and say to them, 2
to the shepherds, Thus said the Master, the LORD: Woe, shepherds of Israel
who were shepherding them. Will not the shepherds shepherd the flock?
You eat the suet and wear the wool, slaughter the fat one. The flock you do 3
not shepherd. You did not strengthen the weak ones, and the sick ones you 4
did not heal nor bind up the one with a broken limb nor bring back the
one that had wandered nor did seek out the one that was lost. And by force
you held sway over them with crushing labor. And they scattered without 5
a shepherd and became food for all the beasts of the field [and they were
scattered]. My flock has strayed through all the mountains and on every 6
high hill, and over the face of the earth has my flock scattered, and none
searches and none seeks for them. Therefore, listen, O shepherds to the 7
word of the LORD. As I live, said the Master, the LORD: My flock has surely 8
become plunder, and My flock has become food for all the beasts of the field

---

32. *you are for them a song of lust, lovely in sound and deftly played.* The prophet speaks
God's imperative words, but all his listeners are capable of hearing is the sort of lewd song
accompanying their own profligacy to which they are habituated.

33. *And when it comes—look, it comes.* The meaning "it" invoked is the disaster of which
Ezekiel has prophesied—at this dark moment, a disaster compounding the catastrophe of
material defeat.

CHAPTER 34   2. *the shepherds of Israel.* Since the equation between shepherds and
leaders is a fixed trope, the prophet's audience would immediately know about whom he
was talking.

3. *You eat the suet.* The shepherds prey on their flocks, picking off the best sheep to feed
their appetite, instead of looking after them.

4. *And by force you held sway over them with crushing labor.* As elsewhere, Ezekiel has
some difficulty in keeping apart his metaphor and its referent. "Hold sway" and "crushing
labor" direct us to the actual exploitation of the people by their leaders and are not phrases
appropriate to shepherds and flocks.

5. *[and they were scattered].* These words—only one word in the Hebrew—are bracketed
because they seem to be an inadvertent scribal repetition of the beginning of the verse.
The flock has just been said to be eaten by predators, so they could not now be scattered.

without a shepherd, and My shepherds have not sought out My flock, and
9 the shepherds herded themselves, but My flock they did not herd. There-
10 fore, O shepherds, listen to the word of the LORD. Thus said the Master, the
    LORD: Here I am against the shepherds, and I will demand My flock from
    their hand and stop them from herding the flock, and the shepherds shall
    not herd themselves anymore, and I will save My flock from their mouths,
11 and they shall not be food for them. For thus said the Master, the LORD:
12 Here I am, and I will seek out My flock and sort them. As a shepherd sorts
    his herd when there are ones that are separated within his flock, so will
    I sort My flock and save them from all the places where they were scat-
13 tered on the day of cloud and gloom. And I will bring them out from the
    peoples and will gather them from the lands and bring them to their soil
    and herd them on the mountains of Israel by watercourses and in all the
14 places of settlement of the land. On good pastures will I herd them, and on
    the mountains of the height of Israel their fold shall be. There shall they lie
    down in a good fold and feed in a rich pasture on the mountains of Israel.
15 I Myself will herd My flock, and I Myself will bed them down, said the
16 Master, the LORD. The lost one will I seek out, and the strayed one will I
    bring back, and the one with the broken limb will I bind up, and the weak
    one will I strengthen, but the fat and the strong I will destroy. I will herd it

---

10. *I will save My flock from their mouths.* Though this expression looks back to the consumption by the shepherds of the choicest sheep mentioned in verse 3, the formulation
also suggests that the shepherds themselves have been like the ravening beasts of the field
preying on the flocks.

11. *sort them.* The Hebrew verb refers to the shepherd's activity of surveying and counting
his flock, seeing which sheep may be missing, which injured or ailing and hence needing
special attention. This meaning is spelled out in the next verse.

12. *the day of cloud and gloom.* This is the day Jerusalem was conquered. The scattered
flock, then, are the Judahites who either fled the city or were driven into exile. Exile is
clearly the more salient sense.

13. *watercourses.* A reliable source of water is always necessary for the population to prosper.

16. *but the fat and the strong I will destroy.* This is another instance in which Ezekiel does
not quite manage his metaphorical vehicle. These two terms are feminine and so must
be part of the flock, *ts' on,* which is a feminine noun. But the reference is clearly to the
predatory leaders, so at this point the shepherds have become part of the flock. Their
metaphorical identity as belonging to the flock is spelled out in the next verse: "I am about
to judge between sheep and sheep, between rams and he-goats." A partial justification for
this confusion is that God is now the shepherd and hence all Israel is the flock, but the
switch is nevertheless awkward.

in justice. And you are My flock. Thus said the Master, the LORD: I am about 17
to judge between sheep and sheep, between rams and he-goats. Is it not 18
enough for you that you graze in the good pasture, and what is left of your
pasture you trample with your feet, and you drink pools of water, and what
is left you muddy with your feet? And My flock feeds on what your feet have 19
trampled, and what your feet have muddied they drink. Therefore, thus said 20
the Master, the LORD, to them: Here I am, and I will judge between the fat
sheep and the lean, inasmuch as you have shoved against flank and shoul- 21
der and gored with your horns all the weak ones till you scattered them
abroad. And I will rescue My flock, and they shall no longer be plundered, 22
and I will judge between sheep and sheep. And I will set up over you a single 23
shepherd, and he shall herd them. My servant David, he shall herd them,
and he shall be their shepherd. And I the LORD will be their God and My 24
servant David a prince in their midst. I the LORD have spoken. And I will 25
seal a covenant of peace with them and put an end to vicious beasts in the
land, and they will dwell secure in the wilderness and sleep in the forests.
And I will make them a blessing round My hill, and I will bring down the 26
rain in its season, rains of blessing they shall be. And the trees of the field 27

---

18. *pools of water.* The literal sense is "sinking of water."

19. *My flock feeds on what your feet have trampled.* Previously, the leaders were predatory
shepherds devouring the sheep. Now they are greedy sheep, taking all the good grass and
water for themselves and leaving scarcely anything fit to eat or drink for the rest of the
flock.

21. *gored with your horns all the weak ones.* Now it emerges that the leaders are not pacific
sheep but rather rams and he-goats (see verse 17) that attack the sheep.

23. *a single shepherd.* Throughout this prophecy, God has been addressing a plurality of
leaders—shepherds. In the restored Israel, there will be a single shepherd, a righteous king.

My servant David. This is surely a reference to a legitimate monarch from the line of
David. While the actual narrative of David's rise and reign in the Book of Samuel presents a decidedly mixed record, in the Book of Kings the retrospective references to David
represent him as an ideal king, God's "servant," and Ezekiel is clearly drawing on that
background.

he shall herd them. There is a nice convergence here of metaphor and literal reference
because David began as an actual shepherd and then became the leader of his people.

25. *they will dwell secure in the wilderness and sleep in the forests.* The "peace" of the covenant implies security and tranquillity, so that the people of Israel feel safe even in dangerous places.

26. *round My hill.* The Masoretic Text has "and round My hill," but the Septuagint plausibly
deletes the "and." The hill is Mount Zion.

shall yield their fruit, and the land shall yield its produce, and they shall
be secure upon their soil, and they shall know that I am the LORD when I
break the shafts of their yoke and save them from the hand of their enslav-
28 ers. And they shall no longer be plunder for the nations, and the beasts of
the field shall not devour them, and they shall dwell secure with none to
29 make them tremble. And I will set up for them an esteemed planting, and
they shall no longer be swept away by famine in the land, and they shall no
30 longer suffer the disgrace of the nations. And they shall know that I am the
LORD your God with them, and they are My people, the house of Israel, said
31 the Master, the LORD. And you My flock, the flock of My pasture, you are
human beings. I am your God, said the Master, the LORD."

1 CHAPTER 35   And the word of the LORD came to me, saying,
2,3 "Man, set your face to Mount Seir and prophesy concerning it. And say to
it, Thus said the Master the LORD:

Here I am against you, Mount Seir,
    and I will reach out My hand against you
        and turn you into a desolation and a devastation.
4   Your towns I will make a ruin,
        and you shall be a desolation,
            and you shall know that I am the LORD.

5 Inasmuch as you harbored age-old enmity and made the Israelites bleed
6 with the sword in the time of their disaster, in the end-time of guilt. There-

---

31. *And you My flock, the flock of My pasture, you are human beings.* Once again, this looks
awkward: Ezekiel, as if he were not altogether sure that his audience would understand
that the flock all along has been the people of Israel, feels obliged to say at the end of the
prophecy that what he is talking about is not sheep but human beings.

CHAPTER 35   2. *Mount Seir.* This mountainous region in trans-Jordan was the
territory of the Edomites.

5. *you harbored age-old enmity.* Hostile relations between Israel and Edom marked much
of the period of the First Commonwealth.
    made the Israelites bleed with the sword in the time of their disaster. Edom allied itself
with Babylonia and played an eager role in the destruction of Jerusalem, as Psalm 137
vehemently recalls.
    in the end-time of guilt. Ezekiel understands Israel's violation of its covenant with
God as the cause of national disaster, so the moment when Jerusalem is destroyed is the

fore, as I live, said the Master, the Lord, I will surely turn you into blood, and blood shall pursue you. In blood did you hate, and blood shall surely pursue you. And I will turn Mount Seir into a desolation and a devasta- 7 tion and cut off from it anyone passing through or returning. And I will 8 fill its mountains with its slain. Your hills and your valleys and all your watercourses—the slain by the sword shall fall in them.

> An everlasting desolation will I make you,   9
> and none shall dwell in your towns,
> and you shall know that I am the Lord.

Inasmuch as you thought, 'The two nations and the two lands shall be 10 mine, and we shall take hold of them.' But the Lord was there. Therefore, 11 as I live, said the Master, the Lord: I will act according to your anger and according to your zeal as you acted from your hatred of them, and I will become known through them as I judge you. And you shall know that I 12 am the Lord. I have heard all your jibes that you said of the mountains of Israel, saying, 'A desolation! They have been given to us for food.' And you 13 were arrogant toward Me in your speech, and piled up words against Me. I

---

end-time when the people are doomed to pay the collective price for the guilt they have incurred.

6. *I will surely turn you into blood, and blood shall pursue you.* The Hebrew is terrifically compact and the meaning thus not entirely certain. What stands out is the triple insistence on "blood" in this verse. It is a way of emphasizing Edom's bloodguilt: they shed the blood of Israelites, and now a fate of blood will befall them, bloodthirsty enemies will pursue them. The Hebrew for "blood," *dam,* may play on *Edom.*

   In blood did you hate. The Hebrew is literally "Blood did you hate," and so the translation is somewhat conjectural.

10. *The two nations and the two lands.* These are Judah and Israel.

11. *your hatred of them.* That is, your hatred of Judah and Israel.

   I will become known through them. This is a recurrent biblical theme: God's fame is manifested to the nations as He shows His power through the destruction of the enemies of Israel.

12. *A desolation!* In this instance, the word appears to refer not to a landscape turned to desert but to a landscape emptied of human inhabitants. Thus the Edomites imagine that they will find or extract food on the mountains of Israel.

13. *you were arrogant toward Me in your speech.* Literally, "You were big against Me with your mouth."

   piled up. This translation takes the unusual verb *he 'etarta* to derive from the Aramaic root *'-t-r,* which indicates abundance or riches.

14 have heard. Thus said the Master, the LORD: When all the earth rejoices, I
15 will turn you into a desolation. Like your joy over the estate of the house of
Israel for its becoming desolate, so will I do to you. Mount Seir shall be a
desolation and all Edom, all of it, and they shall know that I am the LORD."

1 CHAPTER 36   And you, man, prophesy to the mountains of
2 Israel and say, Mountains of Israel, heed the word of the LORD. Thus said
the Master, the LORD: "Inasmuch as the enemy said of you, 'Hurrah! The
3 age-old high places have become an inheritance for us,' therefore, prophesy
and say, Thus said the Master, the LORD: Surely inasmuch as to devastate
and trample you all round, that you become an inheritance for the remnant
of the nations and come up on the tip of the tongue and in the people's slan-
4 der, therefore, hear the word of the Master, the LORD. Thus said the Master,
the LORD, to the mountains and to the hills and to the watercourses and
to the valleys and to the desolate ruins and to the deserted towns that had
become a scorn and mockery for the remnant of the nations that were all
5 round. Therefore, thus said the Master, the LORD: I have surely spoken in
the fire of My zeal concerning the remnant of the nations and concerning
all Edom that made My land an inheritance for themselves with the joy
6 of every heart and with spite so as to take its fields in plunder. Therefore,
prophesy concerning the soil of Israel and speak to the mountains and to
the hills and to the watercourses. Thus said the Master, the LORD: Look, in

---

14. *When all the earth rejoices.* The probable reference is to the general rejoicing when Israel is restored to its land.

CHAPTER 36   1. *prophesy to the mountains of Israel.* Ezekiel effects an interesting rhetorical switch here: the prophecy of consolation, instead of being directed to the conquered Judahites, is addressed to the mountains that have been occupied by the conquerors. This becomes a means of focusing the idea of the restoration of the land and its soil.

2. *The age-old high places.* Given the preceding invocation of mountains, the term here must refer to natural heights, not to hilltop altars.

3. *trample.* The verb *sha'af* can mean "to pant" or "intensely aspire to," but it has a homonym that means "to trample" or "to crush," and that is the more likely sense here.

4. *to the desolate ruins and to the deserted towns.* The series of places addressed by the prophet moves effectively from the natural landscape to the devastated places where the Judahites once lived.
   scorn. The Masoretic Text shows *baz,* which usually means "plunder." Either this should be revocalized as *buz,* "scorn," or *baz* may also have the sense of "scorn."

My zeal and in My wrath I have spoken inasmuch as you have borne the disgrace of nations. Therefore, thus said the Master, the LORD: I Myself 7 have raised My hand—the nations that are all round you shall surely bear their disgrace. And you, O mountains of Israel, you shall put forth your 8 branches and bear your fruit for My people Israel, for soon shall they come. For here I am for you, and I will turn to you, and you shall be tilled and 9 sown. And I will multiply humankind upon you, the whole house of Israel, 10 all of it, and the towns shall be settled and the ruins shall be rebuilt. And 11 I will multiply upon you man and beast, and they shall multiply and be fruitful, and I will settle you as you were before and do well by you more than in your beginnings, and you shall know that I am the LORD. And I will 12 lead humankind upon you, My people, and they shall take hold of you, and you shall become for them an estate, and you no longer shall make them bereaved. Thus said the Master, the LORD: Inasmuch as they say of you, 'You 13 are a man-eater, and a bereaver of your nations you are,' therefore, you shall 14 no longer eat man, and you shall no longer bereave your nations. You no longer shall stumble, said the LORD. And I will no longer let the disgrace 15 of the nations be heard against you, and the taunts of the people you shall

---

7. *I Myself have raised My hand.* As elsewhere, the raising of the hand is a gesture for making a solemn vow.

10. *I will multiply humankind upon you.* The mountains have been shorn of human population by the devastating conquest. Now they will again abound with people. The verb "multiply" and the term for "humankind," *'adam,* obliquely recall the Creation story: the national restoration is to be a second Genesis.

11. *man and beast.* The Hebrew again uses *'adam,* "humankind," but the translation preserves the proverbial collocation "man and beast."
    and they shall multiply and be fruitful. This is the most explicit echo in this chapter of the beginning of Genesis.

12. *you no longer shall make them bereaved.* The Judahites through their acts have brought disaster upon the nations and triggered widespread bereavement in the conquest by the Babylonians, but this will no longer be the case.

13. *You are a man-eater.* This continues the idea of the previous verse: Israel's evil acts have had murderous consequences for its own population.
    your nations. This evidently refers to Judah and Israel. This usage of the term is unique to Ezekiel.

14. *You no longer shall stumble.* If the first two consonants of the verb are reversed, as a few Hebrew manuscripts show, this would read "You no longer shall make bereaved," both here and in verse 15.

no longer hear, and you shall no longer make your nations stumble," said the Master, the LORD.

16,17 And the word of the LORD came to me, saying, "Man, the house of Israel dwell on their land and defile it through their way and through their acts.

18 Like the defilement of the menstruant has their way been before Me. And I poured out My wrath upon them for the blood they shed on the land and for

19 their foul things by which they defiled it. And I scattered them among the nations, and they were dispersed among the lands. According to their way

20 and their acts have I judged them. And they came to the nations where they came and profaned My holy name when it was said to them, 'These are the

21 people of the LORD, and from His land they have gone out.' But I had pity for My holy name that the house of Israel had profaned among the nations

22 where they had come. Therefore, say to the house of Israel, Thus said the LORD: Not for your sake do I act, house of Israel, but for My holy name that

23 you have profaned among the nations where you have come. And I will hallow My great name profaned among the nations that you profaned in their midst, and the nations shall know that I am the LORD, said the Master,

24 the LORD, when I am hallowed through you before their eyes. And I will take you from the nations and gather you from all the lands and bring you

25 to your soil. And I will cast upon you clean water, and you shall be cleansed

---

17. *Like the defilement of the menstruant.* Although in biblical law the menstruant does impart ritual defilement, it is characteristic of Ezekiel's troubled relation to the female body that he should invoke menstruation as the paradigmatic instance of defilement.

18. *for the blood they shed on the land.* This item reflects an associative connection with the menstrual blood.

    their foul things. The excremental connotation of this pejorative epithet for idols is activated here because idolatry defiles or pollutes the land.

20. *profaned My holy name.* The people of Israel are supposed to be in the land God gave them as an inheritance. The mere fact of their exile is a profanation of God's reputation, for it suggests to the nations that His power has failed.

22. *Not for your sake do I act, house of Israel, but for My holy name.* This is an odd theological twist, but it has an antecedent in the Wilderness narrative when God is tempted to wipe out Israel and is dissuaded by Moses. God decides to redeem Israel not for any merit in the people but because He does not want His standing in the eyes of the nations to be compromised.

24. *your soil.* The obvious sense of the Hebrew *'adamah* here and above is "land," but the prophet, in using this term instead of *'erets*, emphasizes the arable soil that will again be

of all your defilements, and of all your foul things I will cleanse you. And I 26
will give you a new heart, and a new spirit will I put within you, and I will
take away the heart of stone from your body and give you a heart of flesh.
And My spirit I will put within you, and I will act so that you go by My 27
statutes and keep My laws, and you shall do it. And you shall dwell in the 28
land that I gave to your fathers, and you shall become My people, and I will
be your God. And I will rescue you from all your defilements, and I will call 29
forth the grain and make it abundant, and I will not set famine upon you.
And I will make the fruit of the tree abundant and the yield of the field so 30
that you no longer bear the disgrace of famine among the nations. And you 31
shall recall your evil ways and your acts that were not good, and you shall
be disgusted by your crimes and by your abominations. Not for your sake 32
do I act, said the Master, the LORD. Let it be known to you—be ashamed
and remorseful for your ways, O house of Israel." Thus said the Master, the 33
LORD: "On the day I cleanse you of all your crimes and settle the towns, and
the ruins are rebuilt, and the desolate land is tilled after having been deso- 34
late before the eyes of every passerby, they shall say, 'That desolate land has 35
become like the garden of Eden, and the ruined and desolate and ravaged
towns are settled, fortified.' And the nations that shall remain all round 36
about you shall know that I the LORD have rebuilt the ravaged towns, I have
sown the desolate land. I the LORD have spoken and have done it." Thus said 37

---

cultivated. Moshe Greenberg makes the same translation choice in his rendering of the
first twenty chapters of the book.

25. *of all your foul things I will cleanse you.* Once more, the suggestion of filth in *gilulim,*
the term used for "idols," is clearly activated.

26. *I will take away the heart of stone from your body.* The Hebrew term rendered as "body"
is the same word as "flesh" in "heart of flesh" at the end of this verse. Although "flesh" is
its more common meaning, it is sometimes used for "body," and that is the less confusing
sense here.

27. *And My spirit I will put within you.* In Ezekiel's view, the perversity of the people is such
that a kind of spiritual surgery is required: first its heart of stone has to be replaced by a
heart of flesh, and then it can be infused with God's spirit.

30. *so that you no longer bear the disgrace of famine among the nations.* A suffering nation,
stricken with famine and other collective disasters, is viewed with contempt by other
nations as a pitiful entity that must somehow be unworthy.

35. *settled, fortified.* Fortification is the emblem of a secure city.

the Master, the LORD: "For this, too, will I be sought out for the house of
38 Israel to do for them—I will multiply humans like sheep. Like consecrated
sheep, like the sheep of Jerusalem on its festivals, so shall the ruined towns
be filled with human sheep, and they shall know that I am the LORD."

1 CHAPTER 37   The hand of the LORD was upon me, and He
took me out by the wind of the LORD and set me down in the valley, and
2 it was filled with bones. And He made me pass by them all around, and,
look, they were very many on the surface of the valley, and, look, they were
3 very dry. And He said to me, "Man, can these bones live?" And I said, "O
4 Master, LORD, it is You Who knows." And He said, "Prophesy to these
5 bones and say to them, 'O dry bones, listen to the word of the LORD. Thus

---

37. *will I be sought out.* The passive form of this verb suggests that the people seek God and,
now favorably disposed, He allows Himself to be found.

38. *Like consecrated sheep, like the sheep of Jerusalem on its festivals.* The reference is to
sheep brought to be sacrificed in the Temple. At least according to the hyperbolic account
in Kings, which Ezekiel probably knew, thousands upon thousands of sacrificial animals
were brought to Jerusalem on the occasion of the festivals. The simile is not entirely apt
because, even though it conveys the idea of a very large number, the sheep were destined
to be slaughtered, which is hardly what the prophet means to suggest about the people.

CHAPTER 37   1. *He took me out by the wind of the LORD.* Throughout this prophecy,
Ezekiel plays on the different senses of *ruaḥ*, which can mean "spirit," "wind," and "breath."
While many translators render the term here as "spirit," the sense of "wind" fits much
better with Ezekiel's repeated pattern of being borne off physically by a palpable divine
force. Compare 11:24, where it is precisely a wind that carries him to the place of revelation.

2. *and, look, they were very dry.* The remains of these dead are at a very great remove from
life: they are not corpses but disarticulated bones and very dry, suggesting that the deaths
occurred much earlier. This is an obvious way of amplifying the miraculous restoration
to life.

3. *Man, can these bones live?* This prophecy is probably the most famous one in Ezekiel.
Early Jewish and Christian interpreters took it as a prophecy of the resurrection of the dead,
but it is quite doubtful that this is what Ezekiel meant. The scattered dry bones of the long
dead are a symbolic image of the people of Israel in exile, its national existence violently
ended by the conquest and destruction of the kingdom of Judah. The miraculous return to
life of the bones figures the restoration of national existence in the homeland.

4. *Prophesy to these bones.* The startling extremeness of the prophecy of the bones is dramatically evident in the command to the prophet to address, as surely no prophet in the
real world ever did, a message to dry bones.

said the Master, the LORD, to the dry bones: I am about to bring breath into
you and you shall live. And I will lay sinews over you and bring up flesh   6
over you and stretch over you skin. And I will put breath in you, and you
shall live, and you shall know that I am the LORD.' " And I prophesied as   7
I was charged, and there was a sound as I prophesied and, look, a clatter,
and the bones came together, one bone to another. And I saw, and, look,   8
upon them were sinews, and flesh came up, and skin stretched out over
them from above, but there was no breath in them. And He said to me: 9
"Prophesy to the wind, prophesy, man, and say to the wind, 'Thus said the
Master, the LORD: From the four winds, come, wind, and blow into these
slain that they may live.' " And I prophesied as He had charged me, and   10
the breath came into them and they lived, and they stood up on their feet,
a very very great legion. And He said to me, "Man, these bones are all the   11
house of Israel. They say, 'Our bones are dry and our hope is lost. We have
been cut off.' Therefore prophesy and say to them, Thus said the Master, the   12
LORD: I am about to open your graves, and I will bring you up, My people,
from your graves and bring you to Israel's soil. And you shall know that I   13
am the LORD when I open your graves and when I bring you up from your
graves, My people. And I will put My breath in you, and you shall live, and   14
I will set you on your soil, and you shall know that I the LORD have spoken
and have done it," said the LORD.

---

5. *breath.* Here *ruaḥ* has to mean "breath," not "wind" or "spirit."

7. *and the bones came together, one bone to another.* This weird self-assembling of the disarticulated bones became the basis for the language of the famous Negro spiritual about
this prophecy.

9. *From the four winds, come, wind.* The initial "winds" here has still another meaning:
the four directions, or the four corners of the earth. In Genesis, God blows the breath of
life into the inert clay of the first human. Here it is the four winds that perform this act
of vivification, giving it a global scope that jibes with the implied idea that the exiles have
been scattered to the four corners of the earth.
      slain. Now we learn that these dead have met a violent end.

10. *legion.* The Hebrew *ḥayil* usually means "military force" (hence the King James Version's "army"). Here it probably indicates the great number of the revived, but to translate
it "multitude," as some modern versions do, erases the martial connotation, that this vast
number of the conquered dead has become a large army. "Legion" in English actually has
both meanings.

12. *I am about to open your graves.* Ezekiel appears to have forgotten that the bones are
scattered on the surface of the valley. Now the dead have been buried and will rise from
their graves.

15,16 And the word of the LORD came to me, saying, "And you, man, take you
one stick and write upon it 'For Judah and for Israel joined to him,' and take
another stick and write on it 'For Joseph, the stick of Ephraim, and for the
17 Israelites and all the house of Israel, joined to him.' And put them together
each to each as a single stick for you, and they shall be one in your hand.
18 And when the sons of your people say to you, saying, 'Will you not tell us,
19 what are these to you?,' speak to them, Thus said the Master, the LORD: I
am about to take the stick of Joseph, which is in the hand of Ephraim, and
those joined with him, the tribes of Israel, and I will set upon it the stick
of Judah and make them a single stick, and they shall be one stick in My
20 hand. And the sticks upon which you shall write shall be in your hand
21 before their eyes, and speak to them, Thus said the Master, the LORD: I am
about to take the Israelites from among the nations where they have gone,
22 and I will gather them from all around and bring them to their soil. And I
will make them a single nation in the land on the mountains of Israel, and
a single king shall be their king, and they no more shall be two nations,
23 and no more shall they be divided into two kingdoms. And they shall no
more be defiled by their foul things and by their vile things and by all their
trespasses. And I will rescue them in all the places of their habitation where
they offended, and I will cleanse them, and they shall be My people, and
24 I will be their God. And My servant David shall be king over them, and

---

16. *take you one stick.* The Hebrew *'ets* means "tree," "wood," or "stick." Some modern interpreters see these as wooden tablets because we know that such tablets were sometimes used
to write on. However, the joining together of the two to make one works better for sticks
than for tablets, and in Numbers writing is inscribed on staffs, something close to sticks.
   Judah . . . Joseph. These indicate the southern and northern kingdoms, sundered after
the death of Solomon.

18. *Will you not tell us, what are these to you?* Unlike the visionary-allegorical prophecy of
the dry bones, this is a rather traditional, and didactic, symbolic-prophetic show-and-tell.
Its meaning is fairly apparent even before Ezekiel goes on to explain it.

22. *I will make them a single nation.* This is a utopian prophecy because by Ezekiel's time
there was no real trace of the northern kingdom, destroyed a century and a half earlier by
the Assyrians.
   on the mountains of Israel. Ezekiel, originating in Jerusalem, repeatedly imagines
a mountainous landscape for his homeland, though in fact it extended to valleys and
lowlands.

23. *in all the places of their habitation.* Many manuscripts show instead of the Masoretic
moshvoteyhem, "their habitations," *meshuvoteyhem,* "their rebelliousness."

24. *And My servant David shall be king over them.* The reference is not to some sort of
reincarnation of David but to a legitimate heir to the Davidic dynasty who embodies the
ideal qualities attributed to him in the Book of Kings.

they shall all have a single shepherd. And by My laws they shall go, and
My statutes they shall keep and do them. And they shall dwell in the land   25
that I gave to My servant Jacob, where your fathers dwelled, and they shall
dwell in it, they and their children and their children's children evermore,
and My servant David shall be prince over them evermore. And I will seal   26
with them a covenant of peace, an everlasting covenant shall there be with
them, and I will set them [as a blessing] and multiply them, and I will set
My sanctuary in their midst evermore. And My dwelling place shall be over   27
them, and I will be their God and they shall be My people. And the nations   28
shall know that I am the LORD hallowing Israel when My sanctuary is in
their midst evermore."

CHAPTER 38   And the word of the LORD came to me, saying,   1
"Man, set your face to Gog in the land of Magog, supreme prince of Meshech   2
and Tubal, and prophesy about him. And say, Thus said the Master, the LORD: 3
Here I am against you, Gog, supreme prince of Meshech and Tubal. I will   4
lead you and put hooks in your jaws, and I will bring you out and all your
force out, horses and riders, all of them clothed to perfection, a great assembly, with buckler and shield, all of them wielding swords. Persia, Nubia, and   5

---

26. *I will set them [as a blessing].* The received text has only "I will set them," but it looks
as if a predicate or adverbial qualifier such as the one supplied in brackets has dropped
out of the text.

27. *My dwelling place.* This is a synonym for "sanctuary" in the preceding verse, and both
terms refer to the Temple, which, restored, is to manifest God's greatness in the world.

CHAPTER 38   2. *Gog in the land of Magog.* The Hebrew syntax could also be construed as "Gog of the land of Magog." Both names, which look quite foreign in the Hebrew,
are mystifying and as such have encouraged the mythological readings of this prophecy
prevalent in both Christian and Jewish tradition. Gog is sometimes linked by scholars with
a King Gugu of Lydia in Asia Minor. Ezekiel does not appear to be referring to a historical
figure—in contrast, for example, to Second Isaiah's references to Cyrus—and may have
embraced the name for its sheer strangeness. What is important is that Gog comes from
the far north, the direction from which destruction traditionally descends upon Israel, as
is repeatedly evident in Jeremiah.
    supreme prince. The literal sense is "prince of the chief," but when two synonyms are
joined in a construct form, the effect is to indicate a superlative.
    Meshech and Tubal. This kingdom, mentioned previously by Ezekiel, is in Asia Minor.

3. *Here I am against you.* Although Gog is sent by God on a mission of conquest, he is
yanked along with hooks in his jaws and will come to a bad end.

5. *Persia, Nubia, and Put.* This suggests a vast array of mercenaries assembled by Gog from
Persia in the east down to Nubia and Put south of Egypt.

6 Put with them, all with shields and helmets. Gomer and all its divisions,
Beth-Torgemah from the far reaches of the north with all its divisions, many
7 peoples are with you. Be ready, and ready yourself and all your assembly
8 gathering round you, and become their guard. After many days you shall
be mustered, at the end of years you shall come to a land brought back from
the sword, and gathered in from many peoples on the mountains of Israel
that had become a perpetual ruin, and it was brought out from the peoples,
9 and they all dwell secure. And you shall come up like a storm, like a cloud,
to cover the land you shall be, and all your divisions and the many peoples
10 with you. Thus said the Master, the LORD: On that day things shall come
11 to mind for you, and you shall conceive a plan of evil. And you shall say: I
will go up against a land of unfortified towns, I will come upon the tranquil
folk dwelling secure, all of them dwelling without walls, neither bolt nor
12 double doors do they have, to plunder and to loot, to put your hand against
resettled ruins and against a people gathered from the nations, abounding
13 in herds and possessions, dwelling in the heartland. Sheba and Dedan and
the traders of Tarshish and all its leaders shall say to you, 'Have you come
to loot, have you assembled your throng to bear off silver and gold, to take
14 herds and possessions, to plunder a great plunder?' Therefore, prophesy,
man, and say to Gog, Thus said the Master, the LORD: On that day, when My

---

7. *assembly.* This general term is repeatedly used by Ezekiel in a military sense.

8. *a land brought back from the sword.* The population of Judah, driven off by the sword,
has now been brought back to its land.

9. *And you shall come up like a storm.* One of the peculiar features of this strange prophecy
is that the people of Israel, after having been restored from bitter exile to their land, are to
be subjected to still another horrendous assault.

11. *a land of unfortified towns.* The Judahites returned from exile are so confident of their
safety that they leave their towns unfortified, with no walls and "neither bolt nor double
doors."

11–12. *I will come upon the tranquil folk . . . to put your hand against resettled ruins.* The
switch here from first person (Gog speaking) to second person (Gog addressed) is fairly
common in biblical usage.

12. *the heartland.* The Hebrew phrase *tabur ha'arets* occurs only here and in Judges 9:37.
The Septuagint understood the obscure *tabur* to mean "navel," and in that sense it was
ensconced in later Hebrew.

13. *its leaders.* The literal sense is "its lions," leaving a margin of doubt about the meaning. The translation follows an interpretive tradition going back to Late Antiquity, which
essentially takes this as a metaphor for "leaders."

people Israel dwells secure, shall you not know? And you shall come from 15
your place, from the far reaches of the north, you and the many peoples
with you, all of them riding horses, a great assembly and a vast force. And 16
you shall come up against My people Israel; like a cloud to cover the land,
in the days afterward, you shall be. And I will bring you against My land
so that the nations may know Me as I am hallowed through you, O Gog."
Thus said the Master, the LORD: "Are you the one of whom I spoke in former 17
days through My servants, the prophets of Israel who were prophesying in
those days for years, to bring you upon them? And it shall happen on that 18
day when Gog comes against the soil of Israel, said the Master, the LORD,
My wrath shall mount in My nostrils. And in My zeal, in the fire of My 19
fury I have spoken: surely on that day there shall be a great earthquake on
the soil of Israel. And the fish in the sea and the fowl in the heavens shall 20
quake before Me, and the beasts of the field and every crawling thing that
crawls on the earth, and every human who is on the face of the earth, and
the mountains shall be destroyed and the cliffs shall fall, and every wall
shall fall to the ground. And I will call forth the sword against him in all My 21
mountains, said the Master, the LORD. Each man's sword shall be against
his brother. And I will wreak punishment upon him through pestilence 22

---

14. *shall you not know?* As what follows makes clear, you will come to know the power of
the God of Israel.

16. *as I am hallowed through you, O Gog.* It is Gog's defeat, despite the overwhelming might
of all his forces, that is to hallow God by making manifest God's power.

17. *Are you the one of whom I spoke.* No actual mention of Gog appears in any of the earlier
prophets, but he is represented here as the realization of the sundry vague prophecies of a
dire enemy descending on Israel from the distant north.

18. *My wrath shall mount in My nostrils.* The second term here, *'af,* is a synonym for "wrath"
because smoke or fire is imagined to be exhaled from the nostrils of the infuriated deity.
Here, the idiom is returned to its physical base, and God is imagined breathing fire (fire is
mentioned at the beginning of the next verse).

20. *the fish in the sea and the fowl in the heavens . . . the beasts of the field and every crawling
thing.* These terms all recall the Creation story in Genesis 1. It is as though the earthquake
that will shake the whole land of Israel will be so cataclysmic that the work of creation
itself will be undone. Such language strongly encouraged the apocalyptic reading of this
prophecy, linking Gog with the cosmic upheavals of the end of days.

21. *And I will call forth the sword against him.* It had seemed as though the cataclysm was
directed against Israel, but now it emerges that Gog and his vast army will be panicked
and destroyed.

and through blood and through pelting rain and hailstones; sulfurous fire
will I rain down on him and on his divisions and on the many peoples that
23 are with him. And I will be magnified and hallowed, and I will become
known before the eyes of many nations, and they shall know that I am the
LORD."

1 CHAPTER 39   And you, man, prophesy concerning Gog and
say, "Thus said the Master, the LORD: Here I am against you, Gog, supreme
2 prince of Meshech and Tubal. I will lead you and take you along and bring
you up from the far reaches of the north and bring you to the mountains of
3 Israel. And I will strike your bow from your left hand and will make your
4 arrows drop from your right hand. On the mountains of Israel you shall
fall, and all your divisions and the people that are with you. I will make
you food for carrion birds, every winged thing, and for beasts of the field.
5 On the surface of the field you shall fall, for I have spoken, said the Master,
6 the LORD. And I will send fire against Magog and against those who dwell

---

22. *sulfurous fire.* The literal sense is "fire and sulfur," but this is most likely a hendiadys.
In any case, Gog's army is devastated both by fierce natural forces and by violent internal
divisions. (Compare verse 21, "Each man's sword shall be against his brother.")

23. *I will be magnified and hallowed.* The two Hebrew words here, *wehitgadalti wehitqad-
shti,* expressing God's glorification through the sweeping defeat of Gog's army, are picked
up as the first two words of the Kaddish, which is a prayer for the establishment of God's
kingdom on earth.

CHAPTER 39   2. *I will lead you and take you along.* This whole verse repeats the
scenario of the previous chapter. However, the verb translated as "take you along" is unique
to this text, so its meaning must be inferred from the context and from a possible Semitic
cognate. The salient difference in this second account of Gog's expedition to the land of
Israel is that there is a much more detailed focus on his devastating defeat.

6. *I will send fire against Magog.* In this version, not only will Gog's vast invading army
be devastated on the mountains of Israel but also a second prong of divine destruction
will be directed toward Gog's distant homeland and toward its allies or colonies ("the
coastlands"). It is worth noting that this entire vision of Israel's triumph over its enemies
is quite different from anything in the other Prophets. The characteristic Prophetic vision
is of Israel restored to its land and dwelling in peace and prosperity after the bitter experience of defeat and exile. Only Ezekiel imagines that the people again ensconced in its land
and living in tranquillity will be assaulted by a fearsome invading power which, however,
will be utterly destroyed. Perhaps Ezekiel, himself an exile who had witnessed the dominant force of the Babylonian empire, and who also had in mind the earlier dominance of
the Assyrians, could not easily conceive a simple peaceful national restoration. History
was felt as a continuing cycle of violent imperial aggressions. In this prophetic version,
an ultimate—virtually mythological—aggressor is drawn to the land of Israel where God

secure in the coastlands, and they shall know that I am the LORD. And My 7
holy name I will make known in the midst of My people Israel, and I will
no longer let My holy name be profaned, and the nations shall know that I
am the LORD, the Holy One in Israel. Look, it has come and now it is, said 8
the Master, the LORD, it is the day of which I spoke. And the dwellers of 9
Israel's towns shall go out and light fires with the weapons, the bucklers
and shields, with the bows and with the arrows and with the clubs and
with the spears, and they shall light fires with them for seven years. And 10
they shall not carry off wood from the field nor cut down trees from the
forests, for with weapons they shall light fires. And they shall plunder their
plunderers and loot their looters, said the Master, the LORD. And it shall 11
happen on that day that I will give Gog a burial place there in Israel, in
the Valley of Those Who Pass Through, east of the sea, and it blocks those
who pass through. And they shall bury Gog there with all his throng and
call it the Valley of the Throng of Gog. And the house of Israel shall bury 12
them so as to cleanse the land, for seven months. And all the people of the 13
land shall do the burying, and the day I am granted glory shall be a famous
thing for them, said the Master, the LORD. And perpetually appointed men 14
shall separate those who pass through the land, burying those who pass
through, the ones left on the surface of the land, to cleanse it. At the end
of seven months they shall probe it. And those who pass through the land 15
shall pass through, and should someone see a human bone, he shall build
by it a marker till the buriers bury it in the Valley of the Throng of Gog.

---

will bring about his total destruction, at last making Israel genuinely secure. Through this
scenario, all the nations of the earth finally "shall know that I am the LORD."

9. *they shall light fires with them for seven years.* What is intended here is an extravagant
hyperbole: the huge mass of arms left by the extinct army of Gog, mostly made of combustible materials (leather shields stretched on wooden frames, spears with wooden shafts,
bows and arrows and clubs) is sufficient to provide firewood for seven years, obviating the
need to bring wood from the forests.

11. *the Valley of Those Who Pass Through.* The meaning of the name is a little ambiguous.
It would seem to refer to the searchers for corpses mentioned in verse 14 who pass through
the land looking for dead enemy soldiers. But in verse 14 the same word is also attached
to the invaders.
   it blocks those who pass through. Perhaps the blockage is because of the vast quantity of
corpses piled up in the valley.

12. *so as to cleanse the land.* Corpses are a source of ritual contamination.

14. *perpetually appointed men.* "Appointed" is merely implied.
   At the end of seven months they shall probe it. That is, they shall check to make sure no
corpses have been left unburied.

16 And the name of the town, too, is Throng. And they shall cleanse the
17 land. And you, man, Thus said the Master, the LORD: Say to the birds,
every winged thing, and to all the beasts of the field—Gather and come,
assemble from all around for My sacrificial feast that I am about to sacrifice for you, a great sacrificial feast on the mountains of Israel. And
18 you shall eat flesh and drink blood. The flesh of warriors you shall eat,
and the blood of princes of the earth you shall drink, rams, lambs, and
19 he-goats, bulls, all of them fatlings of Bashan. And you shall eat suet to
satiety and drink blood to drunkenness, from My sacrificial feast that
20 I have prepared for you. And you shall be sated at My table with horse
and chariot, warrior and every man of war, said the Master, the LORD.
21 And I will set out My glory among the nations, and all the nations shall
see My judgment that I have done and My hand that I set against them.
22 And all the house of Israel shall know that I am the LORD their God from
23 that day onward. And the nations shall know that for their crime the
house of Israel went into exile, because they betrayed Me and I hid My
face from them and gave them into the hand of their foes, and they all
24 fell by the sword. According to their defilement and according to their
25 trespasses I dealt with them and hid My face from them. Therefore, Thus
said the Master, the LORD: Now will I restore the fortunes of Jacob and

---

16. *And the name of the town, too, is Throng.* Evidently, there was a town in proximity to
the valley.

17. *sacrificial feast.* This is a macabre idea—that the corpses to be consumed by scavengers
and carrion birds are a grand sacrificial feast prepared for them by God. As the preceding
reference to a discovered bone indicates, the bones picked clean by the scavengers would
then still need to be buried.

18. *rams, lambs, and he-goats.* Since there would not be large flocks at hand, all these are
metaphors for the sumptuous feast of corpses that the scavengers will enjoy.

20. *horse and chariot.* The chariot is obviously not edible but it goes along with "horse" as
part of a fixed pair.

23. *And the nations shall know that for their crime the house of Israel went into exile.* This is
an essential theological point for Ezekiel: Israel went into exile because of neither the sheer
military power of its enemies nor any weakness in its God, but as a punishment—now come
to an end—for betraying its God.
    they all fell by the sword. As is often the case, Ezekiel's language is not entirely precise.
By no means all of the people were killed by the Babylonians: some stayed in Judah while
many others were exiled rather than killed.

show mercy to the house of Israel and be zealous for My holy name. And 26
they shall forget their disgrace and all their betrayal that they committed
against Me when they dwell secure upon their soil with none to make
them tremble, when I lead them back from the peoples and gather them 27
from the lands of their enemies. And I will be hallowed through them
before the eyes of many nations. And they shall know that I am the LORD 28
when having exiled them among the nations I gather them in upon their
soil and do not leave any of them there anymore. And I will not hide My 29
face from them anymore, as I have poured out My spirit upon the house
of Israel," said the Master, the LORD.

CHAPTER 40   In the twenty-fifth year of our exile, at the 1
beginning of the year on the tenth of the month in the fourteenth year
after the city was struck, on that very day, the hand of the LORD was upon
me, and He brought me there. In divine vision He brought me to the land 2
of Israel and set me down on a very high mountain, and upon it was like
the shape of a city on the south. And He brought me there, and, look, a 3
man, his appearance like the appearance of bronze, and a linen tassel in
his hand, and a measuring rod, and he was standing in the gate. And the 4
man spoke to me: "Man, see with your eyes and with your ears hear and
pay mind to all that I show you, for in order that it should be shown you
have you been brought here. Tell all that you see to the house of Israel."

---

28. *and do not leave any of them there.* Ezekiel's vision of a total return of the exiles to Zion
was not fulfilled, as many of them chose to stay in Babylonia. From this point onward, the
Jews would remain in part a diasporic people.

CHAPTER 40   1. *the twenty-fifth year of our exile.* This locates the present prophecy in 572 B.C.E., as the text goes on to note, fourteen years after the destruction of the
Jerusalem temple.
    the hand of the LORD was upon me, and He brought me there. This formulation is in line
with others in Ezekiel in which the visionary experience is registered as a virtual physical
transportation from one place to another. But the term "divine vision" indicates this is a
mental experience.

2. *like the shape of a city.* As in Ezekiel's visions from chapter 1 onward, what he sees is
represented not as the thing itself but as a semblance to or analogue of the real thing.

3. *a man.* As the next phrase makes clear, "the man" is in fact a divine emissary. Daniel will
pick up this usage from Ezekiel.

5   And, look, there was a wall outside the house all around, and in the man's
    hand a measuring rod six cubits and a handsbreadth in length, and he
    measured the depth of the building's wall to be one rod and the height one
6   rod. And he entered that gate facing toward the east and went up its steps
    and measured the threshold of the gate to be one rod in depth and the inner
7   threshold one rod in depth. And each recess was one rod high and one rod
    deep, and there were five cubits between the recesses, and the threshold of
8   the gate alongside the gate's hall from within was one rod. And he measured
9   the gate's hall from within to be one rod. And he measured the gate's hall
    to be eight cubits and its pillars two cubits, and the gate's hall was within.
10 And the recesses of the gate facing east were three on each side, a single
    measure for the three of them and a single measure for the pillars on each
11 side. And he measured the depth of the gate entrance to be ten cubits. The
12 height of the gate was thirteen cubits. And there was a partition in front of
    the recesses of one cubit, one cubit the partition on each side, and the recess
13 was six cubits on each side. And he measured the gate from the ceiling of
    the recess to the ceiling of the opposite recess, the depth was twenty-five

---

5. *there was a wall outside the house.* Throughout, "the house" is the house of God—that
is, the Temple. To the modern reader, it is certainly odd that Ezekiel's book should end
with nine chapters devoted to an intricate account of the architecture of the Temple and
the procedures of the sacrificial cult. There is nothing quite like this in any of the other
Prophets. There is no reason, however, to question the status of these chapters as an authentic production by Ezekiel. One should remember that he was a Jerusalem priest deported
from the city where the Temple stood in the early, partial exile of 597 B.C.E. Now, a quarter
of a century later, and fourteen years after the Temple was demolished in the conquest of
Jerusalem by the Babylonians, he undertakes a kind of imaginative reconstruction of the
Temple, and then of the cult, painstakingly laying out its sundry structures, gate by gate,
hall by hall, recess to recess. For him, this amounts to a prophecy of consolation. All this, it
must be said, is rather bewildering to follow, although various commentators have sought
to provide charts and floor plans based on Ezekiel's notations. There is, to begin with, a
problem of architectural terms, many of which are uncertain in meaning. (The same is
true of the account of Solomon's temple in Kings.) At least a few terms actually fluctuate
in meaning. The two Hebrew words that usually mean "width" and "length" at first appear
to indicate "depth" and "height," but later in the chapter they revert to their ordinary
meaning. But even if we could be certain of all the architectural terms, the lineaments of
the Temple are hard to make out. This commentary therefore will not attempt to elucidate
the picture of the Temple. It should also be noted that Ezekiel's description of the Temple
does not altogether jibe with the one in the Book of Kings, nor does his account of the cult
entirely match other biblical formulations. One must assume that he either was writing
from imperfect memory of the Jerusalem scene he had left two and a half decades earlier or
was projecting what he conceived as an ideal image of the Temple and the worship within it.

    he measured the depth. The device of having all the measurements done by the divine
emissary is a way of confirming their unvarying accuracy.

cubits, entrance facing entrance. And he measured the columns to be sixty 14
cubits, and the column of the gate's court all around. And in front of the 15
gate was the entranceway, in front of the inner wall of the gate, fifty cubits.
And the recesses had latticed windows, and toward their pillars inside the 16
gate all around, and so it was for the halls, windows all around inside,
and on each pillar palm designs. And he brought me to the water court, 17
and look, there were chambers and a pavement fashioned for the court
all around, thirty chambers for the pavement. And the pavement was up 18
to the side of the gates and opposite the width of the gates was the lower
pavement. And he measured the depth from in front of the lower gate in 19
front of the inner court from outside to be a hundred cubits, the east and
the north sides. And the gate that was facing north of the outer court, he 20
measured its height and its depth. And its recess was three cubits on each 21
side, and its pillars and its hall were as the measure of the first gate, fifty
cubits long and twenty-five cubits wide. And its windows and its pillars and 22
its palm designs as the measure of the gate facing out, and on seven steps
they would go up to it with its pillars before them. And the inner court had 23
a gate opposite the gate to the north and to the east, and he measured from
gate to gate to be a hundred cubits. And he led me to the south side, and, 24
look, there was a gate on the south side. And he measured its pillars and its
halls according to these measures. And there were windows in its halls all 25
around like these windows, fifty cubits long and twenty-five cubits wide.
And there were seven steps going up to it, and its hall was in front of them, 26
and its pillars had palm designs on each side. And the inner court had a 27
gate on the south side. And he measured from gate to gate on the south side
to be a hundred cubits. And he brought me to the inner court through the 28
south gate, and he measured the south gate to be as these measures. And 29
its recesses and its pillars and its halls were as these measurements, and its
halls had windows all around, fifty cubits long and twenty-five cubits wide.
And the halls all around were twenty-five cubits long and five cubits wide. 30
And the outer court had a hall with its pillars, and eight steps going up. And 31
he brought me to the inner court on the east side and measured the gate
to be as these measurements. And its recesses and its pillars and its halls 33
were as these measurements, and its halls had windows all around, fifty
cubits long and twenty-five cubits wide. And the outer court had halls and 34
palm designs on its pillars on each side and eight steps going up. And he 35
brought me to the north gate and measured as these measures. Its recesses, 36
its pillars and its halls and the windows it had all around, fifty cubits long
and twenty-five cubits wide. And there were pillars for the outer court and 37
palm designs on the pillars on both sides and eight steps going up. And 38

there was a chamber with its entrance in the hall of the gates. There they
39 would wash the sacrifice. And in the hall of the gate were two tables on each
side on which to slaughter the burnt offering and the offense offering and
40 the guilt offering. And on the flank outside the hall of the gate's entrance to
the north were two tables and on the other flank of the hall of the gate two
41 tables. Four tables there were on each side of the flank of the gate—eight
42 tables on which they did the slaughtering. And four tables of hewn stone
for the burnt offering, one and a half cubits long and one and a half cubits
wide and one cubit high. Upon them they would set the utensils with which
43 they slaughtered the burnt offering and the sacrifice. And the spits, one
handsbreadth, were set in the house all around, and upon the tables was the
44 flesh of the sacrifice. And outside the inner gate were the chambers of the
nobles, in the inner court that was by the flank of the northern gate, and
they faced to the south, one by the flank of the eastern gate, facing to the
45 north. And he spoke to me: "This is the chamber that faces to the south for
46 the priests who keep the watch of the house. And the chamber that faces
to the north is for the priests who keep the watch of the altar. They are the
sons of Zadok from the sons of Levi who drew near to the LORD to serve
47 Him." And he measured the court to be a hundred cubits in length and a
hundred cubits in width, square, and the altar was in front of the house.
48 And he brought me to the hall of the house and measured the hall to be five
hundred cubits on each side, and the width of the gate was three cubits on
49 each side. The hall was twenty cubits long and eleven cubits wide, and one
went up to it by steps. And there were columns by the pillars on each side.

1 CHAPTER 41   And he brought me into the great hall and
measured the pillars to be six cubits wide on each side, the width of the
2 pillar. And the width of the entrance was ten cubits, and the supports of
the entrance five cubits on each side. And he measured its length to be forty

---

38. *There they would wash the sacrifice.* For Ezekiel the priest, the Temple is vital not only
as a splendid architectural structure but because within it animal sacrifices can be offered
daily—sacrifices that had been totally interrupted for the past fourteen years.

46. *who drew near to the LORD.* The verb here is used in its technical cultic sense: one who
"draws near" is the priest who is authorized to enter into the sacred space of the Temple.

CHAPTER 41   2. *And the width of the entrance was ten cubits, and the supports
of the entrance five cubits on each side.* Most modern translations seek to impart coherence to this whole account of the layout of the Temple by choosing terms familiar in our
own architecture—"vestibules," "ledges," "porticoes," and the like—and rearranging the

cubits and its width twenty cubits. And he came within and measured the   3
pillars of the entrance to be two cubits and the entrance two cubits and the
width of the entrance seven cubits. And he measured its length to be twenty   4
cubits and the width twenty cubits facing the great hall. And he said to me,
"This is the Holy of Holies." And he measured the wall of the house to be six   5
cubits and the width of the flank four cubits all around the house. And the   6
flanks, one on top of another were thirty-three, and in the indentation of
the wall of the house for the flanks all around to be fastened, and they were
not fastened in the wall of the house. And it became wider as it went round   7
higher and higher on the flanks, for the house turned all around higher and
higher. Therefore the width of the house was greater above. And thus did
we go up from the bottom level to the top level through the middle level.
And I saw that the house had a raised pavement all around, the founda-   8
tions of the flanks, a full rod's length, six cubits. The width of the flank's   9
wall on the outside was five cubits, and there was a walkway between the
flanks of the house. And between the chambers it was twenty cubits wide   10
all around the house. And the entrance of the flank for the walkway, one   11
entrance to the north and one entrance to the south, and the width of the
place of the walkway was five cubits all around. And the structure facing   12
the open space at the western corner was seventy cubits wide, and the wall
of the structure was five hundred cubits wide all around, and its length was
ninety cubits. And he measured the house to be a hundred cubits long, and   13
the open space and the structure and its walls a hundred cubits long. And   14
the width of the façade of the house and the open space to the east was a
hundred cubits. And he measured the length of the structure facing the   15
open space which was to the west with a passage on both sides, a hundred
cubits. And the inner great hall and the halls of the court, the thresholds   16
and the latticed windows and the passages around the three of them opposite the threshold, there was an overlay of wood all around from the ground
to the windows, and the windows were covered. Up above the entrance as   17
far as the inner house and outside on the entire wall all around, on the inner

---

tangled syntax. But, in fact, even if we knew the precise meaning of these architectural
terms, which we do not, Ezekiel's report of spatial entities and their dimensions is quite
bewildering. The clarity, then, of the modern translation is illusory, and the present translation is meant to replicate the bewilderment conveyed in the Hebrew. Verses 7 and 8 are a
particularly striking instance of the impenetrability of Ezekiel's description, but there are
problems of comprehension throughout.

11. *the walkway.* The Hebrew *munaḥ* is one of the most elusive of the many architectural
terms used, so this translation, like everyone else's, is no more than a guess.

18 and on the outer, were carvings. And it was fashioned with cherubim and
   palm designs on both sides, and the palm design had a lion's face on one
19 side fashioned for the entire house all around. And the palm design had
   a human face on one side and a lion's face on the other, fashioned for the
20 entire house all around. From the ground to above the entrance there were
   cherubim and the fashioned palm designs, and on the wall of the great hall.
21 And the great hall had four doorposts, and facing the sanctum a look like
22 the look of the altar, of wood, three cubits high and twelve cubits its length,
   and it had corners, and its length and its walls were of wood. And he spoke
23 to me: "That is the table that is before the LORD." And the great hall and the
24 sanctum had two doors. And the doors had two door panels, panels swing-
25 ing open, two for each door. And fashioned for them on the doors of the
   great hall were cherubim and palm designs like the ones fashioned for the
   walls, and there was a wooden beam in the front of the hall on the outside.
26 And the windows were latticed, and there were palm designs on both sides
   on the supports of the hall and the flanks and the beams.

1 CHAPTER 42   And he took me out to the outer court. The
   way was to the north. And he brought me to the chamber that is opposite
2 the open space and that is opposite the structure to the north. Its façade was
3 a hundred cubits, the northern entrance, and the width fifty cubits. Opposite the twenty cubits of the inner court and opposite the pavement of the
4 outer court was a passage. The façade of the passage had three levels. And
   in front of the chambers a walkway ten cubits wide to the inner court and a
5 hundred cubits long, and their entrances were to the north. And the upper
   chambers were cut back, for the passages could not [fit?] in them from the
6 lowest levels and from the middle levels of the structure. For they were

---

CHAPTER 42   1. *And he brought me to the chamber that is opposite the open space
and that is opposite the structure to the north.* The bafflements of Ezekiel's floor plan of the
Temple continue to proliferate, and no attempt will be made here to sort them out. Verses
5–6 are especially egregious. Rashi, perhaps the greatest of medieval Hebrew exegetes and
an acute close reader, frankly confessed, "I was unable to understand at all these three
phrases: What are these *'atiqim* [in the guess of this translation, "passages"], and how do
they fit [eat?] from the lowest levels and from the middle ones, and the reason he gives, that
they were triple-tiered and had no columns, I was unable to understand." We shall follow
Rashi in throwing up our hands in despair.

5. *[fit?].* As indicated in the previous note, the Hebrew word represented in the translation
within brackets and with a question mark is altogether opaque: *yokhlu* looks like a defective
spelling of the word that means "eat," but that makes no sense whatever, and so one can
only guess about the meaning.

triple-tiered, and they did not have columns like the columns of the courts. Therefore space was taken from the lowest levels and from the middle levels from the ground. And there was a barrier from the outside facing the cham- 7 bers through the outer court to the front of the chambers fifty cubits long. For the length of the chambers of the outer court was fifty cubits, and at 8 the front of the great hall a hundred cubits. And below these chambers an 9 entrance from the east where one enters from the outer court, in width like 10 the barrier of the court to the north facing the open space. And facing the structure were chambers. And the way in front of them was like the shape 11 of the chambers on the northern side, both their length and their width and according to their arrangements were their exits and their entrances, and like the entrances of the chambers that were on the southern side, an 12 entrance at the head each way, a way in front of the barriers to the garden on the east side where one entered. And he said to me, "The northern cham- 13 bers and the southern chambers that are in front of the open space—they are the holy chambers in which the priests who are close to the LORD shall eat the holiest offerings. There shall they set the holiest offerings and the grain offering and the offense offering and the guilt offering, for the place is holy. When the priests come, they shall not go out from the sanctum to 14 the outer court, and there they shall lay down their garments in which they minister, for they are consecrated, and they shall put on other garments, and they shall draw near to what is the people's area." And he finished the 15 measurements of the inner house and brought me out through the gate that faces to the east and measured it all around. He measured the eastern 16 side with the measuring rod to be five hundred cubits by the measuring rod all around. He measured the northern side to be five hundred cubits 17 by the measuring rod all around. He measured the southern side to be five 18 hundred cubits by the measuring rod. He turned round to the western side, 19 measured it to be five hundred cubits by the measuring rod. On four sides 20 he measured it. It had a wall all around five hundred cubits long and five hundred cubits wide to separate the holy from the profane.

CHAPTER 43   And he led me to the gate, the gate that faces 1 the eastern way. And, look, the glory of the God of Israel was coming from 2

CHAPTER 43   2. *the glory of the God of Israel.* This phrase marks the beginning of another of Ezekiel's epiphanies. The "glory" is the dazzling manifestation of the divine presence before the eyes of the prophet. It is possible that the glory here is identical with the divine chariot of chapter 1, but there is no unambiguous indication in the text that this is the case.

the eastern way, and its sound was like the sound of many waters, and the
3 earth shone from His glory. And it was like the look of the sight that I had
seen, like that sight that I had seen when I came to pronounce the destruction of the city, and sights like the sight I had seen by the Kebar Canal. And
4 I fell on my face. And the glory of the LORD came into the house through
5 the gate that faced the eastern way. And a wind bore me up and brought me
6 to the inner court, and, look, the glory of the LORD filled the house. And
7 I heard it speaking to me, and a man was standing by me. And he said to
me, "Man, the place of My throne and the soles of My feet where I dwell in
the midst of the Israelites forever! Nor shall the house of Israel defile My
name anymore—they and their kings—with their whoring and with the
8 corpses of their kings, their high places, when they set their threshold by
My threshold and their doorpost by My doorpost, with the wall between
them and Me, and they defiled My holy name with their abominations
9 that they did, and I made an end to them in My wrath. Now let them put
far from Me their whoring and the corpses of their kings, and I will dwell

---

3. *that sight that I had seen when I came to pronounce the destruction of the city.* The Hebrew
says merely "when I came to destroy the city," but the prophet is not the agent of destruction, so it is assumed in this translation that he is referring to his prophecies of destruction
in chapters 8–11.

    and sights like the sight I had seen by the Kebar Canal. This phrase does take us back to
the vision in chapter 1, which is located on the banks of the Kebar Canal.

5. *the glory of the LORD filled the house.* This clause is reminiscent of the epiphany in
Isaiah 6. Here, as throughout these chapters, "the house" means "the house of the LORD,"
which is to say, the Temple.

6. *speaking to me.* The Hebrew, at least as it is vocalized in the Masoretic Text, does not
actually say "speaking," *medaber,* but uses an unusual reflexive form of this verb, *midaber,*
which would appear to suggest a kind of mediated activity of speech rather than direct
address to the prophet. The somewhat paraphrastic but semantically correct solution of
the New Jewish Publication Society translation is "speech addressed to me."

7. *the place of My throne.* The noun phrase here is preceded by the accusative particle
'et, leading us to expect a verb, but none appears in this sentence. Some understand the
'et as indicating emphasis. This translation replicates the syntactic incompleteness of the
Hebrew. It should be noted that the "man" addressing Ezekiel is now clearly God.

    with their whoring and with the corpses of their kings. As elsewhere, the probable refer-
ence of "whoring" is idolatry. The "corpses of their kings" refers to the practice of the last
several Judahite kings of using the Garden of Uzza, in proximity to the Temple, as a royal
burial ground. Corpses impart ritual defilement. The threshold and doorposts of the next
verse would thus be the threshold and doorposts of the royal mausoleums.

in their midst forever. You, man, tell the house of Israel about the house, 10
and let them be ashamed of their crimes, and let them measure its design.
And if they are ashamed of all that they have done, inform them of the plan 11
of the house and its design and its exits and its entrances and all its plan
and all its regulations [and inform them of all its designs and all its rules]
and write them before their eyes that they may observe all its design and
all its regulations and do them. This is the regulation for the house on the 12
mountaintop, all its boundaries all around are holy of holies. Look, this is
the regulation for the house. And these are the measurements of the altar in 13
cubits, a cubit and a cubit and a handsbreadth, and the trench a cubit deep
and its boundary at its edge all around one span and its depth one cubit.
And this is the structure of the altar. From the trench in the ground to the 14
lower level it is two cubits, and one cubit wide, and from the small level to
the large level, four cubits and a cubit wide. And the altar hearth is four 15
cubits, and from the altar hearth to above the horns on the altar four. And 16
the altar hearth is twelve cubits long by twelve cubits wide, square on its
four sides. And the level section is fourteen cubits long by fourteen cubits 17
wide on its four sides, and the boundary around it is half a cubit, and it has
a trench a cubit all around, and its steps face the east." And he said to me, 18
"Man, thus said the Master, the LORD: These are the statutes of the altar on
the day it is made, to offer up on it a burnt offering and to cast blood upon
it. And you shall give these to the levitical priests who are the seed of Zadok, 19
who may draw near to Me, said the Master, the LORD, to minister unto

---

10. *let them measure its design.* For Ezekiel, there is a seamless connection between grand
visions of a restored temple and a restored monarchy with the cubit-by-cubit measurements
of the Temple that is to be rebuilt. It is as if, as he contemplates the Temple that has been in
ruins for two decades, the reality of its rebuilding becomes palpable for him by his tracing
all the details of its measurements that the builders are to follow.

11. *[and inform them of all its designs and all its rules].* Although Ezekiel's prose is prone
to repetition, the repetition in this instance is so excessive that one suspects the bracketed
clause to be an inadvertent scribal duplication.

13. *a cubit and a cubit and a handsbreadth.* As before, the indications of the measurements
and the architectural terms are bewildering.

18. *the altar on the day it is made.* This phrase clearly indicates that this is a plan which the
builders are to implement as they proceed with the reconstruction of the destroyed temple.

19. *And you shall give these to the levitical priests.* Now Ezekiel moves from architectural
instructions to instructions about the sacrifices to be performed within the rebuilt temple.

20 Me, a bull from the herd for an offense offering. And you shall take from
   its blood and put it on the four horns of the altar and at the four corners
   of the level section and on the boundary all around, and you shall purify
21 and purge it. And you shall take the bull of the offense offering and burn it
22 in the set place of the house outside the sanctuary. On the second day you
   shall sacrifice an unblemished he-goat as an offense offering, and they shall
23 purify the altar as they purified with the bull. When you finish purifying,
   you shall sacrifice an unblemished bull from the herd and an unblemished
24 ram from the flock. And you shall sacrifice them before the Lord, and the
   priests shall cast salt upon them and offer them up as a burnt offering to the
25 Lord. Seven days you shall do a goat for offense offering each day and a bull
26 from the herd and a ram from the flock. Unblemished shall they be. Seven
27 days they shall purge the altar and make it clean and consecrate it, and the
   days shall be completed. And it shall happen from the eighth day onward
   that the priests shall do their burnt offerings and their well-being sacrifices
   on the altar, and I will accept them favorably, said the Master, the Lord."

1 CHAPTER 44   And he brought me back through the outer
2 gate of the sanctuary facing eastward, but it was closed. And the Lord said
   to me, "This gate shall be closed. It shall not be opened, and no man shall
   enter it, for the Lord God of Israel has entered it, and it has become closed.
3 The prince, he, the prince—it is he who shall sit in it to eat bread before the
   Lord. By the way of the gate hall he shall come in and by its way he shall
4 go out." And He brought me through the gate of the north in front of the
   house, and I saw and, look, the glory of the Lord filled the house, and I fell
5 on my face. And the Lord said to me, "Man, pay mind and see with your
   eyes and with your ears hear all that I speak to you about all the statutes
   of the house of the Lord and about all its regulations, and you shall pay
6 mind to the entrance of the house and to all the exits of the sanctuary. And
   you shall say to the rebels, to the house of Israel, Thus said the Master, the

---

20. *the four horns of the altar.* The ancient altars had hornlike protuberances, probably
symbolizing power, at their four corners.

27. *from the eighth day onward that the priests shall do their burnt offerings.* After seven
days during which the rebuilt altar is purified and sanctified, the priests will take up their
set regimen of regular offerings.

CHAPTER 44   6. *And you shall say to the rebels, to the house of Israel.* Until this
point, the prophet seemed to be focused on laying out all the regulations of the use of the

LORD: Enough for you of all your abominations, house of Israel, when you 7
bring foreigners, uncircumcised of heart and uncircumcised of flesh, to
be in My sanctuary to profane My house when you offer up the food, suet,
and blood, and they violate My covenant with all their abominations! And 8
you have not kept My holy watch, but you have set them for yourselves as
keepers of My watch in My sanctuary. Thus said the Master, the LORD: No 9
foreigner uncircumcised of heart and uncircumcised of flesh shall enter My
sanctuary, no foreigner who is among the Israelites, but only the Levites, 10
who went far away from Me when Israel strayed, as they strayed from Me
after their foul things, and they shall bear their punishment. And they shall 11
minister in My sanctuary, in appointed office, at the gates of the house,
ministering in the house. They shall slaughter the burnt offering and the
sacrifice for the people, and they shall stand before them to minister to
them. Inasmuch as they ministered to them before their foul things and 12
became a stumbling block of crime for the house of Israel, therefore I have
sworn concerning them, said the Master, the LORD, that they shall bear
their punishment. And they shall not approach Me to serve as priests to 13
Me, to approach all My consecrated things, to the Holy of Holies. And they
shall bear their disgrace and their abominations that they did. And I will 14
make them keepers of the watch of the house in all its service and in all that

---

Temple. Now, however, a theme of castigation is introduced: before the destruction of the
First Temple, its sanctity had been repeatedly violated in ways that Ezekiel will spell out;
in the restored Temple, things must be set right.

7. *when you bring foreigners, uncircumcised of heart and uncircumcised of flesh, to be in
My sanctuary.* Ezekiel appears to refer to an actual practice of using foreigners to perform
menial tasks in the Temple. In his view, the state of ritual unfitness of someone who is
uncircumcised is correlative to a state of spiritual or moral unfitness ("uncircumcised of
heart").
    they violate My covenant. The verb here might conceivably have a causative sense: "they
cause My covenant to be violated."

8. *My holy watch.* This is the Temple cult with all its intricate procedures designed to preserve the sanctity of the place and of the service.

10. *but only the Levites, who went far away from Me.* The Levites, because of their pedigree,
will be allowed back in the sanctuary, but because they were complicit in the sins of Israel,
they are to be demoted in function as the prophet will spell out. The verb, "went far away,"
raḥaqu, is the antonym of *qarvu,* "drew close," the technical term used for the officials who
can enter the sanctuary.

11. *They shall slaughter the burnt offering and the sacrifice for the people.* The sacerdotal
function of these Levites is limited to preparing the sacrifices for the people, but they are
barred from the Holy of Holies as punishment for their past acts.

15 they do within it. But the levitical priests, the sons of Zadok, who kept the
    watch of My house when the Israelites strayed from Me, they shall draw
    near to minister to Me and stand before Me to offer up suet and blood, said
16 the Master, the LORD. They shall enter My sanctuary and they shall draw
17 near to My table to minister to Me, and they shall keep My watch. And it
    shall happen when they enter the gate of the inner court, they shall wear
    linen garments, and no wool shall be upon them when they minister in the
18 gates of the inner court and within. Linen headdresses shall be on their
    heads and linen trousers shall be on their loins, and they shall not gird what
19 causes sweat. And when they go out to the outer court, to the outer court,
    to the people, they shall remove their garments in which they have minis-
    tered and lay them in the sacred chamber and don other garments, lest they
20 consecrate the people through their garments. Their heads they shall not
    shave, nor shall they let their hair grow long. They shall surely trim their
21 hair. And no priest shall drink wine when he comes into the inner court.
22 Nor shall they take for themselves a widow or a divorced woman as wife but

---

15. *the levitical priests, the sons of Zadok, who kept the watch of My house.* It is not clear
whether Ezekiel had reliable knowledge that the Zadokite priests were not complicit in
compromising the sanctity of the cult or whether he is merely inclined to see them as a
legitimate priestly elite for genealogical reasons.
   stand before Me. This idiom has both its literal meaning and the sense of "to serve."

16. *They shall enter My sanctuary.* This is in contrast to the Levites, who are to remain in
the court of the Temple.
   My table. This is an epithet for the altar.

17. *they shall wear linen garments.* This is in keeping with the stipulations about priestly
dress in Leviticus. Perhaps linen was thought of as a purer fabric than wool because it did
not come from an animal. In any case, a linen garment would have been cooler, less likely
to induce sweating, a concern stated at the end of the next verse.

19. *to the outer court, to the outer court.* The repetition may be a scribal error (dittography).
   lest they consecrate the people through their garments. This appears to be an idea peculiar
to Ezekiel: Just as ritual uncleanness is imparted by contact with an unclean object, sacredness is imagined to be imparted by contact with anything that has been consecrated. For
Ezekiel, who is after all a priest and preoccupied with drawing the boundaries between the
sacred and the profane, it is essential that the condition of consecration not spread among
the people. Hence the consecrated garments must be removed and left inside the sacred
chamber.

20. *trim their hair.* More literally, "trim their head."

22. *Nor shall they take for themselves a widow or a divorced woman.* In Leviticus, this
prohibition is for the high priest, not for the whole priestly caste. The motive is to ensure
the genealogical purity of the priestly line. Perhaps it is feared that the widow or divorced

only a virgin from the seed of the house of Israel, or a widow who is widow
of a priest they may take. And My people they shall teach, what is between 23
sacred and profane and between unclean and clean they shall inform them.
And concerning a legal dispute they shall stand to judge by My laws and 24
judge it. And My teachings and My statutes in all My appointed times they
shall keep, and My sabbaths they shall hallow. And no human corpse shall 25
they approach because of the uncleanness, but for a father or a mother or
a son or a daughter or a brother or a sister who is unmarried they may
become unclean. And after he has become clean, they shall count seven 26
days for him. And on the day he comes into the sanctuary, into the inner 27
court, to minister in the sanctuary, he shall offer his offense offering, said
the Master, the LORD. And it shall be an estate for them. I am their estate. 28
And you shall not give them a holding in Israel. I am their holding. As to 29
the grain offering and the offense offering and the guilt offering, they shall
eat them, and whatever is consecrated in Israel shall be theirs. And the best 30
of all first fruits and all gifts whatsoever shall be the priests', and the best of
your kneading troughs you shall give to the priests so as to settle blessing
on your home. No carrion nor preyed-upon animal, whether fowl or beast, 31
shall the priests eat."

---

woman might have conceived by her first husband, before that marriage was ended by
death or divorce. Alternately, her sexual contact with a man not of the priestly line might
have been thought of as contaminating.

24. *My appointed times.* This is a fixed idiom for the festivals.

26. *And after he has become clean, they shall count seven days for him.* After the priest has
cleansed himself through the prescribed ablutions, he must wait seven days before again
entering the sanctuary.

27. *his offense offering.* This is one of the many indications in the biblical corpus that the
ḥataʾt is not a "sin offering," as it is usually translated. The priest has committed no sin.
He has merely been in a state of ritual uncleanness, which would be an offense or violation
of the sacred space of the sanctuary.

28. *I am their estate . . . I am their holding.* The priest needs no crop-producing tribal territory because his sustenance is provided through the animal and grain offerings brought
to the Temple.

31. *No carrion nor preyed-upon animal . . . shall the priests eat.* These are taboo to all Israelites, but there is contextual justification for mentioning them here for the priests: their
food comes from the best of what the Israelites bring, and thus it is all the more unthinkable
that they would ever resort to carrion and animals torn by beasts of prey.

1 CHAPTER 45   And when you cast lots for the land as estate,
you shall give a donation to the LORD, sacred from the land, twenty-five
thousand cubits long and ten thousand cubits wide. It is to be sacred
2 through all its boundary all around. From this, for the sanctuary, shall be
five hundred cubits square all around, and fifty cubits for an open space all
3 around it. And by this measure you shall measure it: twenty-five thousand
cubits long and ten thousand cubits wide, and within it shall be the sanctu-
4 ary, the holy of holies. It shall be sacred from the land for the priests who
minister in the sanctuary, who draw near to minister to the LORD, and
it shall be for them a place for houses and a consecration for the sanctu-
5 ary. And twenty-five thousand cubits long and ten thousand cubits wide
shall be for the Levites who minister in the house. Theirs it shall be as
6 a holding, twenty chambers. And the city's holding you shall give—five
thousand cubits wide and twenty-five thousand cubits long corresponding
7 to the sacred donation. It shall be for the whole house of Israel. And for
the prince on both sides of the sacred donation and to the city's holding
facing the sacred donation and facing the city's holding from the western
side westward and from the eastern side eastward and the length corresponding to one of the sections from the western border to the eastern
8 border for the land. It shall be a holding in Israel for him, and My princes
shall no longer cheat My people, and the land they shall give to the house
of Israel by their tribes.

CHAPTER 45   1. *cast lots for the land.* The idiom used here harks back to Joshua,
where a system of casting lots is used in order to divide up the tribal territories.

a donation to the LORD. The area designated is to be set aside for the Temple, the Levites,
and the priests.

4. *It shall be sacred from the land.* That is, it shall be set off from the rest of the land as
consecrated ground.

5. *twenty chambers.* This is the reading of the Masoretic Text, *'esrim leshakhot,* but it is
puzzling what chambers are doing out in this open area. Perhaps one should adopt the
Septuagint's reading, which is *'arim lashavet,* "towns in which to dwell."

7. *And for the prince.* Throughout, "the prince" is the king.

8. *My princes shall no longer cheat My people.* With these clear demarcations of what area
belongs to the crown, what to the priests and Levites, and what to the people, royal expropriation of lands belonging to the people will cease.

Thus said the Master, the LORD: "Enough for you, princes of Israel. Put 9
aside outrage and plunder and do justice and righteousness. Take away
your banishments from My people, said the Master, the LORD. Just scales 10
and a just *ephah* and a just *bat* shall you have. The *ephah* and the *bat* shall 11
have a single measure, the *bat* to contain a tenth of a *homer,* the *ephah* a
tenth of the *homer* shall its measure be. And the shekel shall be twenty 12
gerahs. Twenty shekels, twenty-five shekels, fifteen shekels shall the *minah*
be for you. This is the donation that you shall make: a sixth of an *ephah* 13
from each *homer* of wheat and a sixth of an *ephah* from each *homer* of
barley. And the regulations for oil, the oil by the *bat*, a tenth of a *bat* for 14
each *kor,* ten *bats* are a *homer,* [for ten *bats* are a *homer*]. And one sheep 15
from the flock from every two hundred from Israel's well-watered pastures
as a grain offering and as a burnt offering and as well-being sacrifice to
atone for them, said the Master, the LORD. All the people of the land shall 16
be with the prince of Israel for this donation. And upon the prince shall be 17
the burnt offerings and the grain offerings and the libation on the festivals
and on the new moons and on the sabbaths. On all the appointed times of

---

9. *outrage and plunder.* This could be construed as a hendiadys, having the sense "outrageous plunder."

Take away your banishments. The grammatical form of the noun that derives from the
verbal stem meaning "to banish" is peculiar, but, given the context of royal exploitation of
the people, the probable sense is eviction of people from lands that have been expropriated
by the crown.

10. *a just* ephah *and a just* bat. The *ephah* is a dry measure, the *bat* a liquid measure. The
homer, as is spelled out at the end of the next verse, is a dry measure ten times the size of
an *ephah.*

12. *shekel.* This word means "weight"—its cognate is used in several other Semitic
languages—and it is not, as in later usage, a coin. Although equivalents in modern measurements are often proposed by scholars for all these terms of weight and volume, there
appears to have been some fluctuation of their values in different times and regions.

14. *[for ten* bats *are a* homer]. This clause is bracketed because it appears to be an inadvertent duplication of the immediately preceding clause.

15. *well-watered pastures.* The Hebrew *mashqeh* usually means "offering drink," so the
translation is a surmise based on context.

17. *And upon the prince shall be the burnt offerings.* Since it is the duty of the priests, not
of the king, to perform the actual rite of sacrifice, this must mean that it is the prince's
obligation to oversee the arrangements for the sacrifices and to make sure they are done in
the appropriate ways at the appropriate times.

the house of Israel he shall do the offense offering and the grain offering and the burnt offering and the well-being sacrifice to atone for the house of Israel."

18 Thus said the Master, the LORD: "In the first month, on the first of the month, you shall take an unblemished bull from the herd and purify the 19 sanctuary. And the priest shall take from the blood of the offense offering and put it on the lintel of the house and on the four corners of the level 20 space on the altar and on the lintel of the gate of the inner court. And thus shall you do on the seventh of the month for the errant man and for 21 the unwitting, and you shall purge the house. In the first month, on the fourteenth day of the month, you shall have the Passover, a festival of seven 22 days. Flatbread shall be eaten. And the prince shall do for himself and for 23 all the people of the land an offense-offering bull. And the seven days of the festival he shall do a burnt offering to the LORD, seven unblemished bulls and seven unblemished rams each day of the seven days and an offense 24 offering of a he-goat each day. And a grain offering, an *ephah* for each bull 25 and an *ephah* for each ram he shall do, and oil, a *hin* for each *ephah*. In the seventh month, on the fifteenth day of the month, on the festival he shall do like these for seven days, the offense offering and the burnt offering and the grain offering and the oil alike."

1 CHAPTER 46   Thus said the Master, the LORD: "The gate of the inner court facing eastward shall be closed during the six workdays,

---

18. *the first month.* This is Nissan, approximately corresponding to April.

purify the sanctuary. This was done by sprinkling the blood of the slaughtered bull on the altar. The blood, as Jacob Milgrom puts it, was thought of as a kind of detergent.

19. *on the lintel of the gate of the inner court.* In Leviticus, the rite of purification was restricted to the altar. Ezekiel, preoccupied as he is with purity, extends it here to the inner court.

20. *for the errant man and for the unwitting.* These would be people who without intending to do so have brought ritual uncleanness into the sacred zone of the Temple. The impurity has to be purged.

25. *In the seventh month, on the fifteenth day of the month.* This is the month of Tishrei, corresponding to September–October. The festival in question is the fall holiday of Succoth. Between the two festivals mentioned here, Passover is the holiday that affirms belonging to the community of Israel, whereas Succoth, which takes place at the completion of the work of harvesting, is the holiday for which the greatest number of pilgrims came to Jerusalem.

and on the sabbath day it shall be open and on the day of the new moon it
shall be open. And the prince shall come through the gate hall from outside 2
and stand by the lintel of the gate, and the priest shall do his burnt offerings and his well-being sacrifices, and he shall bow down on the threshold
of the gate and go out, and the gate shall not be closed until evening. And 3
the people of the land shall bow down before the LORD at the entrance of
that gate on sabbaths and on new moons. And the burnt offering that the 4
prince shall offer to the LORD on the sabbath day shall be six unblemished
sheep and an unblemished ram. And a grain offering, an *ephah* for each 5
ram, and for the sheep, a grain offering, the gift of his hand, and oil, a *hin*
to the *ephah*. And on the day of the new moon, an unblemished bull from 6
the herd and six sheep and a ram. Unblemished shall they be. And an *ephah* 7
for each bull and an *ephah* for each ram he shall do as a grain offering, and
for the sheep, as his hand may attain, and oil, a *hin* to the *ephah*. And when 8
the prince enters, through the gate hall he shall enter and by way of it he
shall go out. And when the people of the land enter before the LORD on 9
the appointed times, who enters through the northern gate to bow down
shall go out through the southern gate, and who enters through the southern gate shall go out through the northern gate, and he shall not go back
through the gate by which he entered, but straight ahead of him he shall
go out. As for the prince, in their midst when they enter he shall enter, and 10
where they go out he shall go out. And on the festivals and on the appointed 11
times the grain offering shall be an *ephah* for each bull and an *ephah* for
each ram and for the sheep the gift of his hand, and oil, a *hin* to the *ephah*.
And should the prince do a freewill offering, whether burnt offering or 12
well-being sacrifices, a freewill offering to the LORD, he shall open the gate
facing eastward and do his burnt offering and his well-being sacrifices as
he does on the sabbath day, and he shall go out and close the gate after he

CHAPTER 46   1. *on the sabbath day it shall be open and on the day of the new moon
it shall be open.* The obvious reason for opening the gate, as becomes clear in the next verse,
is so that the prince can enter through it.

2. *and he shall bow down.* As is usually the case in ritual contexts, this verb carries both its
literal sense and, through a kind of synecdoche, designates the act of worship.

7. *as his hand may attain.* This idiom, taken from the sacrificial laws of the Torah, indicates
a category of offering in which the number or quantity is not fixed but determined by the
economic capacity of the person who brings it to the Temple.

9. *who enters through the northern . . . shall go out through the southern gate.* It is not clear
whether this instruction has some ritual or symbolic justification or is simply a means of
regulating foot traffic within the Temple.

13 has gone out. And a yearling unblemished sheep he shall do on the sabbath day, a burnt offering to the LORD for the day, each morning you shall do it.
14 And a grain offering you shall do together with it, each morning, the sixth of an *ephah,* and oil, the third of a *hin,* to sprinkle on the fine flour, a grain
15 offering to the LORD, an everlasting perpetual statute. And they shall do the sheep and the grain offering and the oil every morning, a perpetual
16 burnt offering. Thus said the Master, the LORD: Should the prince give a gift to one of his sons, it shall be his estate, to his sons shall their holding
17 be, it comes in estate. And should he give a gift from his estate to one of his servants, it shall be his till the year of release and shall go back to the
18 prince. His estate must surely belong to his sons. And the prince shall not take from the estate of the people to cheat them of their holding. From his own holding he shall bequeath to his sons, so that My people be not scattered each man from his holding."

19 And he brought me into the entrance that is on the side of the gate to the sacred chambers for the priests that face northward, and, look, there was
20 a place in the far corner to the west. And he said to me, "This is the place in which the priests prepare the guilt offering and the offense offering, where they bake the grain offering so as not to bring it out to the outer
21 court to consecrate the people." And He took me out to the outer court

---

13. *each morning you shall do it.* The switch from "he" (the prince) to "you" (singular) is slightly disorienting, but it may reflect the fluidity with which biblical Hebrew switches grammatical person, rather than being the result of a scribal error.

14. *oil, the third of a* hin, *to sprinkle on the fine flour.* The reason for this instruction is culinary rather than strictly ritual: the grain offering is to be baked, and so the flour needs to be suffused with oil to make it into dough.

16. *it shall be his estate.* That is, the gift shall become the inheritance of the son to whom it has been given.

17. *one of his servants.* In royal contexts, "servants" usually means "courtiers." A royal gift to a courtier for exemplary service rendered would be fairly common.
    the year of release. This might be the jubilee year. In any case, it is a set year in which slaves are freed and property that has been assigned to others reverts to its original owners. Thus the king's gift to his courtiers, unlike the gift to his sons, is not permanent.

18. *so that My people be not scattered each man from his holding.* As in earlier biblical literature, Ezekiel envisages an agrarian society in which stability and prosperity are contingent on possessing arable land. It is for this reason that the king is sternly prohibited from expropriating land from his subjects.

20. *so as not to bring it out . . . to consecrate the people.* As before, consecration is conceived as a kind of contagious condition. The consecrated grain offering must be prepared by the priests within their chambers and should not come in contact with the people.

and made me pass by the four corners of the court, and, look, there was an
enclosure in each corner of the court. In the four corners of the court there 22
were enclosures without roofs, forty cubits long and thirty cubits wide the
measure of each of the four corners. And there was a row of bricks within 23
all around for the four of them, and cooking utensils fashioned beneath
the rows all around. And He said to me, "These are the kitchens where the 24
ministrants of the house cook the sacrifices of the people."

CHAPTER 47   And he brought me back to the entrance of 1
the house, and, look, water was coming out from under the threshold of
the house to the east, for the front of the house was on the east, and the
water was going down from the right side of the house from south of the
altar. And he took me out through the gate to the north and turned me 2
around outside the gate on the way facing eastward, and, look, water was
seeping from the right side. When the man came out to the east, there was 3
a line in his hand, and he measured out a thousand cubits and made me
cross through the water, ankle-deep water. And he measured out a thou- 4
sand cubits and made me cross through the water, knee deep water, and
he measured out a thousand cubits and made me cross through waist-deep

---

21. *an enclosure.* This is the same Hebrew word that is rendered as "court" at the beginning
of this verse, but it has a secondary sense of "enclosure."

22. *each of the four corners.* The Masoretic Text reads "in each of the four of them
mehuqats'ot." This last word is not intelligible and in fact is marked by the Masoretes with
dots over it, a way of indicating that a word is textually suspect. This translation adopts the
emendation proposed by Rimon Kasher, *le'arba'at hamiqtsqa'ot.*

23. *a row of bricks.* The Hebrew merely says "row," but what is indicated is a low inner wall
of bricks or perhaps of stones.

CHAPTER 47   1. *water was coming out from under the threshold of the house.* In the
midst of all the technical reports of temple floor plans and sacrifices, to be followed later
in this chapter by a listing of the borders of the land, Ezekiel offers the last of his entirely
original visionary experiences. At first blush, this looks like it might be merely some underground spring beneath the Temple from which water is seeping, but the miraculous nature
of the flow of water quickly becomes apparent.

2. *seeping.* The verb *mefakim* occurs only here. The probable root is *p-k-h,* and it has been
suggested that it is related to the noun *pakh,* a jar from which liquid would pour out in a
thin stream.

3. *there was a line in his hand.* The line for measuring looks back to the elaborate measurements of the Temple carried out by "the man" earlier, but in this case he will measure only
the extent of the stream, which deepens after every thousand cubits.

5 water. And he measured out a thousand cubits—a stream which I could
   not cross for the water was surging, water to swim in, a stream that could
6 not be crossed. And he said to me, "Do you see, man?" and he led me and
7 brought me back to the bank of the stream. When I came back, look, on the
8 bank of the stream were very many trees on both sides. And he said to me,
   "This water is going out to the eastern area and will go down to the Arabah
   and enter the sea, the sea of filthy water, and the water shall become clean.
9 And it shall be that every living creature that swarms, all that enters there
   in the double stream shall live, and there shall be very many fish there, for
   this water has entered there and it has become clean. And all that enters
10 there in the stream shall live. And it shall be that fishermen shall stand over

---

5. *a stream which I could not cross.* The familiar pattern, manifested in quite a few biblical stories and in folktales outside the Bible, is three (or in some instances, three plus one) with a difference at the end: in this case, an intensification from one to three (the deepening water), concluding in the unfordable depth of the stream. The pattern thus conveys the miraculous character of the vision—water seeping out from under the Temple somehow turns into a deep surging stream.

7. *very many trees.* While the Hebrew uses a singular form, it is clearly a collective noun. The abundant trees alongside the stream are a foreshadowing of the vision of fruitfulness in the culmination of this prophecy.

8. *This water is going out to the eastern area and will go down to the Arabah.* The water flows downhill from Mount Zion eastward to the Arabah, the rift of the Jordan Valley. From there it will continue downward to the Dead Sea, which is more than 435 feet below sea level and the lowest place on the face of the earth.

the sea. This lowercased body of water is the Dead Sea, in contrast to the uppercased Sea in verse 17, which is the Mediterranean. The Mediterranean, referred to in verse 10 in the Hebrew as the Great Sea, constitutes the sea par excellence for the Land of Israel—hence the capital S.

the sea of filthy water. The designation is somewhat imprecise, motivated by the awareness that the saline content of the Dead Sea is so high that nothing can live in it.

become clean. The literal sense of the Hebrew verb is "be healed," but the biblical term for healing is often used for restoring a person or substance to a condition of wholeness. "Clean" water is water in which life can now survive. This meaning is spelled out in the last sentence of the next verse: "And all that enters there in the stream shall live."

9. *every living creature that swarms.* The phrasal echo of the Creation story evokes the idea of abundant proliferating life-forms and perhaps of Eden itself.

the double stream. The vocalization of this noun in the Hebrew is a doublative form. This could be a scribal error, but perhaps it might be meant to intensify "stream."

there shall be very many fish there. This is the focus of Ezekiel's vision of an eschatological restoration of the devastated homeland: the Dead Sea, where nothing can live, will be transformed by these miraculous waters seeping out from the Temple into fresh water pullulating with life, suggesting a new Eden.

it from Ein-Gedi to Ein-Eglaim, a place for spreading nets. There shall be
fish of all kinds, like the fish of the Great Sea, very many. Its swamps and   11
its marshes shall not become clean—for salt shall they be set aside. And by   12
the stream, on its bank, on both sides every fruit-bearing tree shall spring
up. Their leaf shall not wither, their fruit shall not cease. They shall yield
new fruit month after month, for their water comes out from the sanctuary,
and their fruit shall be for eating and their leaf for healing."

Thus said the Master, the LORD: "These are the boundaries by which you   13
shall inherit the land for the twelve tribes. For Joseph—two portions. And   14
you shall inherit it, each man like his fellow, as I have sworn to give it to
your fathers, and this land shall fall in lots to you as an estate. And these are   15
the boundaries of the land: at the northern end from the Great Sea by way
of Hethlon, Lebo-Hamath, Zedad, Beratah, Sibraim, which is between the   16
border of Damascus and the border of Hamath, Hazer-Hatticun, which is
on the border of Hauran. And the boundary shall be from the Sea to Hazer-   17

---

10. *from Ein-Gedi to Ein Eglaim.* Ein Gedi is an oasis overlooking the northern reaches of
the Dead Sea (*ein* means "spring"), and Ein-Eglaim is presumably somewhere to the south
in this same region.

    a place for spreading nets. The establishment of marine life in this hitherto lifeless body
of water also provides sustenance to the people living nearby.

11. *for salt shall they be set aside.* The Dead Sea was no doubt drawn on as a source of salt,
and since salt is a necessary substance, the marshlands along its borders will be excluded
from the cleansing and continue to provide salt.

12. *every fruit-bearing tree.* This is another phrase that recalls the Creation narrative.

    They shall yield new fruit month after month. Complementing the miracle of the
cleansed waters, the trees along the banks of the stream will be miraculously fruitful, not
just in one season but month after month. This, too, is an edenic motif.

    their leaf for healing. In fact, leaves, especially from the Dead Sea region, were often
used as herbal medication.

13. *These.* For the Masoretic *geh,* which is not comprehensible, we read here with the ancient
versions *zeh,* "this" or "these."

    These are the boundaries. Ezekiel's prophecy of national restoration now returns to its
preoccupation with measurements and demarcations—in this case, the sundry boundaries of the land.

    For Joseph—two portions. The tribe of Joseph is the exception because it comprises two
half-tribes, Ephraim and Manasseh.

15. *Lebo-Hamath.* The received text says only Lebo, not a place-name, but the Septuagint
has Lebo-Hamath, and the second component of this name evidently was displaced to the
beginning of the next verse, where it does not belong.

Enan, north of the border of Damascus, and the border of Hamath to the
18 north. This is the northern limit. And the eastern limit is from Hauran to
Damascus and from Gilead to the Land of Israel, the Jordan a border. To
19 the eastern sea you shall measure. And this is the eastern limit. And the
southern limit is south of Tamar to the waters Meriboth-Kadesh, along the
20 wadi to the Great Sea. This is the southern limit. And the western limit is
the Great Sea, the border as far as opposite Lebo-Hamath. This is the west-
21 ern limit. And you shall share out this land for yourselves for the tribes of
22 Israel. And it shall be that you shall let lots fall in estate for yourselves and
for the sojourners who sojourn in your midst who have begotten children
in your midst. And they shall become for you like the native-born of the
Israelites. With you they shall share in estate in the midst of the tribes of
23 Israel. And it shall be that in the tribe in which the sojourner sojourns,
there you shall grant his estate, said the Master, the LORD."

1 **CHAPTER 48**   And these are the names of the tribes: From
the northern end by the way of Hethlon, Lebo-Hamath, Hazar-Enan, the
border of Damascus to the north, and from the eastern side to the west—
2 Dan, one. And by the boundary of Dan from the eastern end to the western

---

18. *the eastern sea.* This is the Dead Sea, the Mediterranean being the western sea.

22. *and for the sojourners who sojourn in your midst.* In Joshua, the sojourners, or resident
aliens, are not given territory, so this is an innovation of Ezekiel's. It may reflect a demo-
graphic reality in which there was a substantial population of resident aliens and in which
the tribes as distinctive entities had largely disappeared.

    who have begotten children in your midst. Ezekiel stipulates that the sojourners would
have to be longtime residents in the Israelite community.

CHAPTER 48   1. *And these are the names of the tribes.* For modern readers, this
catalogue of the tribal territories, including a delineation of the sectors of Jerusalem, is
likely to be an uninspiring conclusion to a book of prophecy. One suspects that for Ezekiel,
on the contrary, these dry listings were inspiring because they constituted a geometrical
representation of a vision of national restoration. It should be noted that almost none
of this corresponds to the historical realities of the land but is rather an eschatological
imagining of the land. All the demarcations are symmetrical—equal borders for each of
the tribes; Jerusalem is divided into symmetrical sectors for the priests, the Levites, the
king, and the common people; the four walls of the city with gates named for three tribes
on each side.

    Dan. Another manifestation of the eschatological character of Ezekiel's report of tribal
borders is that it is careful to include all twelve tribes, even though the ten northern tribes
had ceased to exist a century and a half before this prophecy.

end—Asher, one. And by the boundary of Asher from the eastern end to 3
the western end—Naphtali, one. And by the boundary of Naphtali from 4
the eastern end to the western end—Manasseh, one. And by the boundary 5
of Manasseh from the eastern end to the western end—Ephraim, one. And 6
by the boundary of Ephraim from the eastern end to the western end—
Reuben, one. And by the boundary of Reuben from the eastern end to the 7
western end—Judah, one. And by the boundary of Judah from the eastern 8
end to the western end there shall be a donation that you shall set aside—
twenty-five thousand cubits in width and length like one of the portions
from the eastern end to the western end, and the sanctuary shall be within
it. The donation that you shall set aside for the LORD is to be twenty-five 9
thousand cubits long and ten thousand cubits wide. And for these shall 10
the sacred donation be: for the priests on the north twenty-five thousand
cubits long and to the west ten thousand cubits wide and to the east ten
thousand cubits wide and to the south twenty-five thousand cubits long,
and the LORD's sanctuary shall be within it, for the consecrated priests of 11
the sons of Zadok, who kept My watch, who did not stray when the Israelites strayed as the Levites strayed. And it shall be a donation to them from 12
the donation of the land, holy of holies, by the territory of the Levites. And 13
the Levites are opposite the territory of the priests, twenty-five thousand
cubits long and ten thousand cubits wide, the whole length twenty-five
thousand cubits and the whole width ten thousand cubits. And they shall 14
not sell any of it nor shall they exchange nor shall it be transferred. It is
the best of the land, sacred to the LORD. And the remaining five thousand 15
cubits in width by twenty-five thousand in length is profane ground for the
city for dwellings and for open fields, and the city shall be within it. And 16

---

2. *Asher, one.* The evident sense of "one" is "one share in the division of the land." The
unvarying repetition of this formula for each of the twelve tribes conveys the idea that
each receives an equal portion—again, in contradiction to the preceding historical reality.

8. *And by the boundary of Judah . . . there shall be a donation that you shall set aside.* For
Judah, there is a break in the series of formulaic repetitions because Jerusalem is in the
tribal territory of Judah, and so here the prophet reverts to his delineation of the borders
of sacred space around the Temple. "Donation," which elsewhere in the Bible refers to a
kind of sacrifice, is throughout these concluding chapters a large plot of land reserved for
priestly use.

and the sanctuary shall be within it. In Ezekiel's priestly vision, the city and the whole
land are centered around the sanctuary.

15. *open fields.* Israelite cities had open fields, *migrashim,* around them, chiefly used to
pasture herds and cultivate crops.

these are its measurements: on the north side four thousand five hundred cubits and on the south side four thousand five hundred cubits and on the east side four thousand five hundred cubits and on the west side four

17 thousand five hundred cubits. And there shall be an open field for the city to the north, two hundred fifty cubits, and to the south, two hundred fifty cubits and to the east, two hundred fifty cubits and to the west, two

18 hundred fifty cubits. And the remaining area in length opposite the sacred donation shall be ten thousand cubits on the east and ten thousand cubits on the west, and it shall be opposite the sacred donation. And its produce

19 shall be for bread for the city workers. And the city workers shall work in

20 it from all the tribes of Israel. The whole donation, twenty-five thousand cubits by twenty-five thousand cubits square, you shall set aside as a sacred

21 donation in addition to the city's holding. And what is remaining is for the prince on both sides of the sacred donation and of the city's holding, facing the twenty-five thousand cubits of the donation to the eastern and western borders facing the twenty-five thousand cubits on the western border opposite the tribal portions. This is the prince's, and the sacred donation

22 and the sanctuary of the house shall be within it. And the Levites' holding and the city's holding shall be within what is the prince's between the territory of Judah and the territory of Benjamin. For the prince it shall be.

23 As for the remaining tribes, from the eastern end to the western end: Ben-

24 jamin, one. And by the territory of Benjamin from the eastern end to the

25 western end: Simeon, one. And by the territory of Simeon from the eastern

26 end to the western end: Issachar, one. And by the territory of Issachar from

27 the eastern end to the western end: Zebulun, one. And by the territory of

28 Zebulun from the eastern end to the western end: Gad, one. And by the territory of Gad to the southern end, the boundary shall be from Tamar

29 to the waters of Meribath-Kodesh, to the wadi, as far as the Great Sea. This is the land that you shall cast in lots for the tribes of Israel, and these are

---

18. *bread for the city workers.* As elsewhere, bread is a synecdoche for food.

19. *And the city workers shall work in it from all the tribes of Israel.* Because Jerusalem is the site of both the Temple and the royal bureaucracy, its maintenance is an obligation of the entire people, the exaction of labor being a kind of taxation.

23. *As for the remaining tribes.* Having detailed the sundry divisions within Jerusalem triggered by the mention of Judah, the prophet now returns to his formulaic catalogue of tribal boundaries.

29. *This is the land that you shall cast in lots . . . said the Master, the* LORD. This sentence uses two rather different formulations: the verb at the beginning, which suggests the casting of

its portions, said the Master, the Lord. And this is the span of the city: 30
from the eastern side four thousand five hundred cubits in measure. And 31
the gates of the city are after the names of the tribes of Israel: three gates
on the north—the Gate of Reuben, one; the Gate of Judah, one; the Gate of
Levi, one. And on the eastern side, four thousand five hundred cubits and 32
three gates—the Gate of Joseph, one; the Gate of Benjamin, one; the Gate
of Dan, one. And the southern side, four thousand five hundred cubits and 33
three gates—the Gate of Simeon, one; the Gate of Issachar, one; the gate of
Zebulun, one. The western side, four thousand five hundred cubits. Their 34
gates are three—the Gate of Gad, one; the Gate of Asher, one; the Gate of
Naphtali, one. All around it is eighteen thousand cubits. And the name of 35
the city from that day shall be "The Lord Is There."

---

lots, harks back to the procedure said to be used for the division of the land in Joshua, but
the Lord's "saying" how the land should be divided implies the symmetrical, preordained
plan of division evident here.

30. *And this is the span of the city.* Having finished with the tribal territories, Ezekiel returns
to his overriding preoccupation with the dimensions of the city, his vision constantly centered on Jerusalem.

35. *And the name of the city from that day shall be "The Lord Is There."* This concluding
flourish underscores the grand eschatological character of this vision of the restored city
and land: in the rebuilt, carefully demarcated, symmetrical Jerusalem, with the sanctuary
at its center, the very name of the city will express God's constant presence in the place
where He has chosen to dwell.

THE TWELVE
MINOR
PROPHETS

∎ ∎ ∎

Introduction

T he Twelve Minor Prophets are "minor" only in regard to the quantity of their writings that have come down to us. In fact, in Hebrew they are simply called "the Dozen," with no mention of minor. The longest among these books, Hosea and Zechariah, are barely a sixth the length of Isaiah, Jeremiah, or Ezekiel, and some of these Prophets show only three, two, or even one chapter. (The brevity might reflect the temporal brevity of their missions, in contrast to the three major prophets, each of whom was active for decades.) One of the twelve, moreover, Jonah, doesn't really belong. The Book of Jonah was put in this group because it is a very short text about a prophet; however, in fact it is not, like the others, a book of prophecies but rather a fable about prophecy featuring a fictitious prophet, and as such it really should have been placed in Ketuvim, the miscellaneous writings. (Consequently, it will be accorded its own introduction here.) "Minor," then, has nothing to do with the resonance or power of these Prophets, and at the very best, Hosea and Amos are among the greatest biblical Prophets, though their books weigh in, respectively, at fourteen and nine chapters according to the conventional chapter divisions.

Hosea and Amos are the first of the so-called literary prophets, and it is a mystery why in the eighth century B.C.E. Hebrew prophets should have begun to cast their messages in writing—chiefly, in poetry. There are frequent appearances of prophets in the early biblical narratives—Samuel, Nathan, Elijah, and Elisha are the most familiar names, and quite a few others enter the sundry stories. These prophets are said to exert a certain divinatory power; some are reported to work miracles; and most assume a role of moral castigation, which, however, is usually directed to rulers, not to the general populace. There is no indication that any of these early figures used writing as a medium for their prophecies. Then, probably in the 760s B.C.E., a cattle herder and arborist from a small village near Jerusalem makes his way from the kingdom of Judah to the northern kingdom of Israel and begins to inveigh, in powerful poetry, against the moral and economic crimes of its inhabitants. While some of the other prophets come from a priestly background, it is noteworthy that the first among

them is of peasant stock, and yet literate, which might offer a clue about
the dissemination of literacy in this culture. He evinces a mastery of the
parallelistic form of Hebrew verse, which lends itself to strong emphasis
through interechoing utterances; and he uses this form, among other purposes, to convey to his audience the urgent imperative of the prophetic
calling:

> Do two walk together
>> if they have not first agreed?
> Does the lion roar in the forest
>> unless it has taken prey?
> Does the maned beast put forth its voice from its lair
>> if it has not made a catch? . . .
> A lion roars,
>> who does not fear?
> The Master, the LORD, speaks.
>> Who cannot prophesy? (Amos 3:3–4 and 8)

Amos provides a bit of autobiographical information in responding
to a challenge from a northern priest. About others of the Twelve Minor
Prophets we know less, or nothing at all. Hosea, who probably prophesied
in the generation after Amos, is definitely from the northern kingdom,
and some of his writing appears to reflect traditions about the patriarchs
that diverge from those that appear in Genesis, the larger part of which
was written and certainly edited in the south. He is enjoined to marry a
whore, but whether this is an actual biographical fact or merely a symbolic
gesture is not entirely certain. About Joel nothing is known, and the dating
of his four chapters is elusive. Of Obadiah, represented by a single chapter, all that is inferable is that because of his angry doomsaying against
Edom, he probably wrote during the last years of the kingdom of Judah,
when the Edomites were active collaborators with the Babylonians in their
onslaught against Jerusalem. The ordering of the twelve is not strictly
chronological, and thus Micah, the next in sequence after Obadiah and
Jonah, would have been active after the destruction of the northern kingdom in 721 B.C.E. and also after the incursion of Sennacherib into Judah
in 701 B.C.E., both reflected in his writing. One famous passage, 4:1–5, the
exalted vision of teaching going out from Zion and the nations grinding
their swords into plowshares, is nearly identical with Isaiah 2:2–4, and may

well be the insertion of a later editor, although it is at least possible that Micah was Isaiah's source. Scholars have detected other late materials in his text, which is common for any Prophetic book longer than a couple of chapters. In any case, Micah's noble vision of the LORD requiring justice and humility more than spates of animal sacrifice puts him early in the line of prophets that set ethical behavior above the Temple cult as Israel's primary responsibility.

Nahum (three chapters) is another prophet about whom precious little is known. His book is followed in the canonical order by Habakkuk. Here, again, there are three brief chapters with little indication of historical context. The invocation of a threat from the Chaldean army suggests a date not long before the destruction of the kingdom of Judah by the Babylonians in 586 B.C.E., but even that has been disputed by some scholars. Zephaniah, the next book in the canonical order, has a superscription reporting that he was active during the reign of King Josiah (640–609 B.C.E.). Some have inferred that he wrote before Josiah's sweeping reforms in 622 B.C.E. He fulminates about the imminent Day of the LORD, which is also a motif in other Prophets, and which is imagined to be realized when Jerusalem will be destroyed. Haggai and Zechariah are the latest of the Twelve who can be confidently dated. They prophesied in the later decades of the fifth century B.C.E. and were part of the early community of those who had returned to Jerusalem from Babylonian exile after the enabling edict of the Persian emperor Cyrus issued in 538 B.C.E. Both Haggai and Zechariah are concerned with the project of rebuilding the Temple and establishing safeguards for its ritual purity. Both ally themselves with Zerubbabel, the Persian-appointed governor of the province of Yehud (formerly the kingdom of Judah) and Joshua the high priest. This concentration on the practical task of restoring the Temple reflects a reduction of the grand moral sweep of many of the earlier prophets.

Malachi, the concluding book of the Twelve Minor Prophets, again three relatively short chapters, takes its title not from the proper name of a prophet but rather from a general designation: the Hebrew means "my messenger," and quite a few times the prophets are elsewhere referred to as God's messengers. This text also appears to be post-exilic, but, even in its brevity, it is uncertain whether it is the work of a single writer. In any case, it does provide an apt conclusion to the collection of all the prophets by invoking Elijah, the iconic prophet of the preliterary era, in a promise of a restorative, not destructive, Day of the LORD.

Look, I am about to send to you
    Elijah the prophet
before the coming of the day of the LORD,
    great and fearsome.
And he shall bring fathers' hearts back to sons
    and the sons' hearts to their fathers. (Malachi 3:23–24)

    This is not altogether as upbeat as it initially sounds because this last poetic line of the book is triadic, and its third verset reads as follows: "lest I come and strike the land with utter destruction." That is, if people know what is good for them, they will embrace Elijah's project of bringing fathers' hearts back to sons. Otherwise, the usual prophetic warning of disaster remains in place. In any case, this conclusion of the Book of Malachi, of which much has been made by both Jewish and Christian tradition, vividly illustrates the enduring power of the Minor Prophets. Each works on a small scale; many of these texts tend to be fragmentary; most of them are stripped of the enhancing sense of historical context that Isaiah, Jeremiah, and Ezekiel give us. But despite all this, these little books incorporate moments of soaring poetry and visionary illumination that still speak to the heart and to the religious imagination.

Hosea

CHAPTER 1   The word of the LORD that came to Hosea son of 1
Beeri in the days of Uzziah, Jotham, Ahaz, Hezekiah, kings of Judah and
in the days of Jeroboam son of Joash king of Israel. When the LORD began 2
to speak to Hosea, the LORD said to Hosea:

> Go, take you a wife of whoring
> and children of whoring,
> for the land has surely whored
> away from the LORD.

And he went and took Gomer daughter of Diblaim, and she conceived 3
and bore him a son. And the LORD said to him: "Call his name Jezreel, for 4

CHAPTER 1   1. *in the days of Uzziah, Jotham, Ahaz, Hezekiah, kings of Judah.* These
monarchs reigned from the middle of the eighth century B.C.E. to the later decades of that
century. Given that Hosea was a prophet of the northern kingdom, this notation probably
reflects the presence of a later Judahite editor who wanted to place the prophecies in a time
frame more familiar to his Judahite audience.

and in the days of Jeroboam son of Joash king of Israel. It has puzzled scholars why only
Jeroboam is mentioned because there were several kings of Israel during this period, most
of them reigning rather briefly.

2. *When the LORD began to speak.* The literal sense is "in the beginning of the LORD's
speaking"—the grammatical structure is the same as "When God began to create" at the
beginning of Genesis, although a different word for "beginning" is used there.

take you a wife of whoring. Some commentators think she may have been a cult-
prostitute rather than a whore for profit, but this notion may well be merely an effort to
mitigate the shocking character of what Hosea is commanded to do.

for the land has surely whored. While the Hebrew verb looks like a future, verb tenses
are fluid in biblical poetry, and God is surely objecting to trespasses already committed.

4. *Call his name Jezreel.* Many set out this whole passage as poetry, but it does not really
scan.

soon I will make a reckoning for the blood of Jezreel against the house of
5 Jehu and put an end to the kingdom of the house of Israel. And it shall be
6 on that day I will break the bow of Israel in the Valley of Jezreel." And she
   conceived again and bore a daughter. And He said to him: "Call her name
   Lo-Ruhamah, for I will no more show mercy to the house of Israel nor will
7 I forgive them in any way. But to the house of Judah I will show mercy
   and rescue them through the LORD their God, but I will not rescue them
8 through bow and sword and in battle with horses and with horsemen." And
9 she weaned Lo-Ruhamah and conceived and bore a son. And He said: "Call
   his name, Lo-Ami, Not My People, and I will not be yours."

1 CHAPTER 2   And the number of the Israelites shall be like the
   sand of the sea that cannot be measured and cannot be counted, and it shall
   happen, instead of its being said of them, "You Are Not My People," it shall
2 be said of them, "Children of the Living God." And the people of Judah and

---

I will make a reckoning for the blood of Jezreel against the house of Jehu. Jehu, usurping
the throne, killed Jezebel and carried out a mass execution of those loyal to her (2 Kings
9–10). The Book of Kings represents these bloody acts as authorized by God, but Hosea
appears to have had a very different view of them.

5. *I will break the bow of Israel in the Valley of Jezreel.* This could be a specific reference to
the Assyrian army that repeatedly threatened Israel in this period.

6. *Lo-Ruhamah.* This inauspicious name means "Not Shown Mercy." One hopes that this
whole story of marrying a whore and blighting two of the three offspring with dire names
was a Prophetic fiction, not something Hosea actually did, but there is no way of knowing.
   nor will I forgive them in any way. The Hebrew does not show a negative, but this translation assumes that "no" is carried over from the first clause as a double-duty term.

7. *But to the house of Judah I will show mercy.* It is possible that Hosea, as a prophet of the
northern kingdom, draws this contrast to make a didactic point to his audience, even
though some scholars infer that this is an insertion by a Judahite editor.

9. *and I will not be yours.* This brief concluding clause is perfectly coherent as it stands in
the Masoretic Text, but some interpreters are inclined to infer that a word was dropped:
"I will be *your God.*"

CHAPTER 2   1. *And the number of the Israelites shall be like the sand of the sea that
cannot be measured.* These words manifestly introduce a new prophecy, one of national
restoration, after the doomsaying of the first chapter. They pointedly invoke the language
of God's grand promise to Abraham in Genesis.

2. *And the people of Judah and the people of Israel shall gather together.* Some scholars detect
here the hand of the Judahite editor who envisages the reunification of the southern and

the people of Israel shall gather together and set over them a single chief, and they shall go up from the lands, for great is the day of Jezreel.

> Say to your brothers, "My People,"   3
> and to your sisters, "She Is Shown Mercy."
>
> Bring a case against your mother, bring a case,   4
> for she is not My wife,
> and I am not her husband.
> Let her take off her whoring from her face
> and her adultery from between her breasts,
> lest I strip her naked   5
> and set her out as the day she was born.
> And I will turn her into a desert
> and make her like parched land
> and let her die of thirst.
> And to her children I will show no mercy,   6
> for they are the children of whoring.
> For their mother played the whore,   7
> she who conceived them acted shamefully.

---

the northern kingdoms (presumably, after the northern kingdom was destroyed), though it is certainly possible that Hosea could have imagined a reunited nation as part of his utopian vision of the future.

they shall go up from the lands. The received text shows "land," but "to go up from the land" is a phrase that would imply leaving the country, as in Exodus 1:10. The New Jewish Publication Society's rendering, "rise up from the ground" is philologically possible but strained. This translation assumes the original text had a plural, "lands," implying return from the lands of exile.

4. *Bring a case against your mother.* The language of a court case is used because she has committed adultery and so deserves to be hauled before a judge.

Let her take off her whoring from her face. This expression is a metonymy: she has put kohl around her eyes, reddened her lips, and set a ring in her nose, to ply her whore's trade.

and her adultery from between her breasts. This is a parallel metonymy: she has put a sachet of fragrance between her breasts (compare the Song of Songs 1:13) to make herself more alluring to her lovers.

5. *And I will turn her into a desert.* As often happens in biblical poetry, the prophet switches from one set of images—Israel as a promiscuous female body—to another—the barren desert as a representation of national ruin.

7. *their mother . . . / she who conceived them.* While these two terms are conventional in poetic parallelism, the second one, intimating the physical act in which conception takes place, underscores the wife's sexual betrayal of her husband.

> For she said, "Let me go
>> after my lovers
> who give me my bread and water,
>> my wool and my flax,
>>> my oil and my unguents."

8
> Therefore I am about to hedge in your way with thorns
>> and raise a wall for her,
>>> and she shall not find her paths.

9
> And she shall run after her lovers
>> and shall not catch them,
>>> and she shall seek them and not find them.
> And she shall say, "Let me
>> go back to my first husband,
>>> for it was then better for me than now."

10
> And she did not know
>> that it was I who gave her
>>> the new grain and the wine and the oil,
> and silver I showered upon her
>> and gold that they fashioned for Baal.

11
> Therefore will I turn back and take away
>> My new grain in its time
>>> and My wine in its season
> and reclaim My wool and My flax

---

my bread and water, / my wool and my flax, / my oil and my unguents. Zeev Wisman aptly notes that there is a progression here from the basic elements of food and drink to the materials needed to clothe the body to the more luxurious substances used to gratify the body and make it attractive. The last word here, rendered by some as "drink," means "balm" in Proverbs 3:8 and "unguents" seems right for this context.

8. *your way . . . / for her.* The switch in grammatical person is common in biblical usage.

9. *And she shall run after her lovers / and shall not catch them.* This line should be taken together with the preceding one: her way is blocked and bristles with thorns, and she cannot see where she should go; desperately running after her lovers, she finds herself lost and trapped. All this leads her to the realization expressed in the next line that she was better off with her husband.

10. *it was I who gave her.* The word for "I," *'anokhi,* is placed before the verb for emphasis: she had thought that her lovers provided all her needs (verse 7), but it was actually God.
   silver I showered upon her. The literal sense of the verb is "multiplied" or "made abundant."
   that they fashioned for Baal. God had bestowed national prosperity on Israel, including precious silver and gold, but these were then used by the Israelites to fashion idols for Baal.

that would cover her nakedness.
And now, I will lay bare her shame   12
   before the eyes of her lovers,
      and no man shall save her.
And I will put an end to her rejoicing,   13
   to her festivals, her new moons, and her sabbaths
      and all her appointed times.
And I will wither her vines and her fig trees   14
   of which she said, "They are a whore's pay for me
      that my lovers gave to me."
And I will turn them into scrubland,
   and the beasts of the field shall devour them.
And I will make a reckoning against her for the days of the Baalim   15
   to whom she burned incense,
and she put on her nose-ring and her jewelry
   and went after her lovers,
      but Me she forgot, said the LORD.

Therefore, I am about to beguile her   16
   and will lead her to the wilderness
      and speak to her very heart.
And I will give her from there her vineyards   17
   and the Valley of Achor an opening to hope,
and she shall sing out there as in the days of her youth,

---

12. *her shame.* This is an equivalent of "her nakedness" at the end of the preceding line.

13. *festivals . . . new moons . . . sabbaths.* All these nouns are singular in the Hebrew but with a collective sense.

15. *the days of the Baalim.* The probable reference is to festival days when the Baalim were worshipped.

16. *Therefore.* It should be noted that this word (*lakhen*) is used by Hosea as a transitional term rather than one of causation to mark the beginning of a new prophecy.
   beguile. Although this Hebrew verb elsewhere means "to entice" or "to seduce," here it clearly has a positive sense, suggesting tenderness.

17. *the Valley of Achor an opening to hope.* The Hebrew *'akhor* suggests "trouble," but in the bright future this very place with its dark associations will become the entranceway to hope.
   sing out. The Hebrew verb *'anah* also often means "to answer," but a clearly attested sense is "to speak out" or "to sing out." That is the compelling sense here. The third verset, which invokes the moment of exodus from Egypt, probably means to make us recall the Song of the Sea that Moses and Miriam sing to celebrate God's triumph over Egypt.

as on the day she came up from the land of Egypt.

18   And it shall be, on that day, said the Lord,
        she shall call Me "my Husband"
          and no longer call Me "my Baal."

19   And I will take away the names of the Baalim from your mouth,
        and they shall no more be recalled by their name.

20   And I will seal a pact with them on that day,
        with the beasts of the field and with the fowl of the heavens
          and the creeping things of the earth.
     And bow and sword and battle
        will I break from the earth,
          and I will make them lie down secure.

21   And I will betroth you to Me forever,
        I will betroth you in right and in justice
          and in kindness and in mercy.

22   And I will betroth you in faithfulness,
        and you shall know that I am the Lord.

23   And it shall be on that day,
        I will answer, said the Lord,
     I will answer for the heavens,
        and they shall answer for the earth.

24   And the earth shall answer for the new grain

---

18. *she shall call Me "my Husband" / and no longer call Me "my Baal."* This line turns on an untranslatable pun: *ba'al* is one of two Hebrew words for "husband," but it is also the name of the principal Canaanite deity; the Hebrew synonym, *'ish,* is the word translated here as "husband."

19. *the names of the Baalim.* What is referred to is invoking the name of the deity in worship or in vows. Plurals are used because Baalim (*im* is the masculine plural suffix) can refer not to Baal alone but to a plurality of Canaanite deities.

20. *a pact . . . / with the beasts of the field.* A kind of edenic harmony will be imposed on nature, so that even ravening beasts and birds of prey will be pacific. Peace in nature will be coordinated with peace among men, as the next line spells out.

21. *I will betroth you to Me forever.* The prophet now reverts to the marriage metaphor, forseeing that the wretchedness of adultery will be replaced by a faithful union. The triple repetition of "I will betroth you" sounds very much like a performative speech-act, God pronouncing the wedding vows.

23. *I will answer for.* "Answer for" is probably the best English equivalent here for the Hebrew verb that means "to answer" (in each instance followed by a direct object in the Hebrew). The idea is that all the constituents of nature will be harmoniously joined in mutual responsibility, giving each to each.

> and for the wine and for the oil,
> and they shall answer for Jezreel.
> And I will sow her for Me in the land   25
> and show mercy to Lo-Ruhamah,
> and I will say to Lo-Ami, "You are My people,"
> and he shall say, "You are my God."

CHAPTER 3   And the Lord said to me, "Again, go love a 1
woman beloved by a companion yet an adulteress, like the love of God
for the Israelites when they turn to other gods and to lovers of cups of the
grape." And I loved a lusting woman. And I hired her for myself with fifteen 2
weights of silver and a *homer* of barley and a *letekh* of barley. And I said to 3
her, "Many days you shall dwell with me. You shall not play the whore and
you shall be no man's, and I, too, shall not come to bed with you. For many 4
days shall the Israelites dwell without king and without commander and

---

25. *I will sow her.* This declaration—a single Hebrew word   immediately follows "Jezreel"
at the end of the previous line: *yizr'e'el / uzer'atiha* and so is clearly a play on the etymology of the name, which means "God will sow." The very valley that in the first chapter was
associated with crimes because of all the blood that was shed there is now to live up to its
name by becoming a place of fecund growth.

You are my God. The Hebrew has only "my God," but the verb "to be," according to
standard usage, is implied, and "my God" by itself would sound like an exclamation rather
than an affirmation.

CHAPTER 3   1. *said to me, "Again.* It should be noted that the Masoretic cantillation
markings attach "again" to the words introducing God's speech, "And the Lord said to me
again," and that reading is possible.

a companion. This probably means her husband, but it could conceivably indicate a
devoted lover.

And I loved a lusting woman. The Hebrew of the received text looks quite suspect. The
literal sense of the last two words is "raisin cakes" (though others think that the meaning is
"grape cups"). The Revised English Bible tries to rescue some sense from this by translating
"the cakes of the raisin offered to idols." The present translation adopts the emendation
proposed by Tur-Sinai: instead of the Masoretic *ohavey 'ashishey 'anavim,* he reads *wa'ohav
'eshet 'agavim.*

2. *a* homer *of barley and a* letekh *of barley.* A *letekh* is half a *homer,* so the repetition appears
to be a way of saying, "a *homer* and a half of barley."

3. *shall not come to bed.* A verb of sexual intimacy is implied in the elliptical Hebrew.

4. *the Israelites dwell without king and without commander.* This is a prophecy of the loss
of national sovereignty and of exile.

without sacrifice and without sacred pillar and without ephod and without

5 teraphim. Afterward, the Israelites shall turn back and seek the LORD their
God and David their king, and they shall revere the LORD and His bounty
in the latter days."

CHAPTER 4

1   Hear the word of the LORD, O Israelites,
        for the LORD has a brief
            against the dwellers of the land.
    For there is no truth and there is no trust
        and there is no knowledge of the LORD in the land.
2   Falsely swear and murder
        and steal and commit adultery.
            They burst bonds—and blood spills upon blood.
3   Therefore the land does languish,
        and all those dwelling within it are bleak.
    With the beasts of the field and the fowl of the heavens
        and with the fish of the sea, too—they shall perish.
4   But let no man inveigh
        and let no man rebuke
            when your people inveighs against priest.

---

without ephod and without teraphim. Both are divinatory devices.

5. *David their king.* Many scholars conclude that the reference to David was inserted by the Judahite editor, although it is perhaps possible that Hosea as a prophet of the northern kingdom envisaged a utopian future in which the two kingdoms would reunite under the divinely elected Davidic dynasty.

CHAPTER 4   1. *trust.* The Hebrew term *ḥesed* is usually represented in this translation as "kindness," but it also often implies loyalty in a covenant or relationship, and that is clearly the salient meaning here.

2. *They burst bonds.* The Hebrew says merely "burst" (which could also mean "break through" or "spread out"), but what the verb appears to imply here is reprobate behavior, and thus "bonds" has been added for clarification.
    blood spills upon blood. Literally, "blood touches blood."

4. *when your people inveighs against priest.* The Hebrew of this clause is obscure and looks as though it has been scrambled in scribal transmission. It reads literally: "and your people is like the quarrels [or inveighings] of a priest." The general idea of the whole line would seem to be: offer no criticism when your people inveighs against the priests, for they deserve it.

And you stumbled by day,   5
    and the prophet, too, stumbled by night,
    and I will destroy your people.
My people is destroyed without knowledge,   6
    for you—you rejected knowledge,
and I rejected you from being priest to Me.
    And you forgot your God's teaching—
    I will forget your sons on My part.
As they increased, they offended against Me,   7
    I will exchange their honor for disgrace.
My people's offense offerings they eat,   8
    and they long for its crimes.
And it shall be, people and priest alike,   9
    I will make a reckoning with them for their ways,
        and for their acts I will pay them back.
And they shall eat yet not be sated,   10
    play the whore yet not burst bonds.
For they have forsaken the LORD
    to keep on whoring and drinking   11
        and new wine that takes away the mind.
My people asks oracles of a tree,   12
    and his rod tells him what to do.
For a spirit of whoring made them stray,

---

5. *you.* The probable reference is to the priest, matched by the mention of the prophet in the next verset. Both have betrayed their calling of providing moral instruction to the people.

7. *As they increased.* Others take this to mean "most of them."

8. *My people's offense offerings they eat, / and they long for its crimes.* The priests had a substantial portion of the sacrificial animal set aside for their own consumption. Here they are represented as wanting the people to transgress more and more because that would bring them more offense offerings to eat.

10. *play the whore yet not burst bonds.* The second verb is the same verb that is used in verse 2. In the understanding behind this translation, the meaning would be: they were promiscuous without ever attaining the immoral freedom of total libertinage, just as they ate (perhaps even stuffed themselves) without being sated. Others, looking toward the sense of "spread out" that the verb sometimes has, think the reference is to lack of progeny from their promiscuous couplings.

12. *his rod tells him what to do.* This would be a divining rod. The words "what to do" are added in the translation to make clear that this is an activity of seeking guidance parallel to the asking of an oracle in the first verset.

and they played the whore against their God.
13   On the mountaintops they sacrificed,
      on the hills they offered incense,
    beneath the oak and the poplar,
      and the terebinth of goodly shade.
    Therefore their daughters go whoring,
      and their daughters-in-law are adulterous.
14   I will make no reckoning with your daughters for whoring
      and with your daughters-in-law who are adulterous.
    For they themselves go off with the whores
      and with the cult-harlots they sacrifice,
        and a people undiscerning comes to grief.
15   If you go whoring, Israel,
      let Judah not be held guilty
    And do not come to Gilgal
      nor go up to Beth-Aven,
        and do not swear, "As the LORD lives."
16   For like a wayward cow
      Israel was wayward.
    Now shall the LORD herd him
      like a sheep in an open field?

---

against their God. The literal sense of the Hebrew preposition is "from under," the word "under" suggesting "authority."

13. *On the mountaintops they sacrificed, / on the hills.* These terms, and the small catalogue of trees that follows, suggest worship of nature gods, often accompanied by fertility rites— hence the invocation of the whoring daughters in the next line.

14. *I will make no reckoning with your daughters.* They are not accountable because they have been led astray by their fathers; the "they themselves" who go off whoring are the fathers.

15. *let Judah not be held guilty.* Again, this is often seen as an intervention of the Judahite editor, though the inference is not inevitable.

   do not come to Gilgal. Gilgal was a well-known cultic site in the north, near the Jordan.

   nor go up to Beth-Aven. Beth-Aven, which means "house of sin," is probably not the actual place-name but a polemic substitution for Bethel, one of the two principal cultic sites of the northern kingdom.

16. *Now shall the LORD herd him / like a sheep in an open field?* If Israel behaves like a cow that swerves from the way that she should go (occasionally they were used as draft animals), how could one expect God to allow it the freedom of a sheep pacifically grazing in an open field?

Ephraim is stuck fast to idols.   17
   Let him be!
When their swilling is over,   18
   they go on to whore.
      They love the disgrace of their defenders.
The wind bundles them in its wings,   19
   and their altars are shamed.

CHAPTER 5

Hear this, you priests,   1
   and listen, house of Israel,
and the house of the king, bend your ear,
   for against you is the judgment.
For a trap you have been to Mizpah,
   and an outspread net against Tabor,
and have dug a deep pit at Shittim,   2

---

17. *Let him be.* This is a little obscure but it probably means that since Ephraim has become so addicted to idolatry, there is no point in trying to rebuke or dissuade him—let him wallow in his vile cult.

18. *When their swilling is over.* The Hebrew implies that they have recovered from their drunken stupor—now they are ready for sex with a whore.

   They love the disgrace of their defenders. This clause is obscure and may have suffered textual damage. First, the two words represented as "they love," *'ahavu heivu,* look strange (they might mean "they love, give"), and the second word may be a dittography triggered by the last two syllables of the preceding word. It is also not clear who the defenders are, and the Hebrew says "her defenders." The conclusion of many traditional Hebrew commentators that the reference is to the leaders of the people is as good a guess as any.

19. *The wind bundles them in its wings.* The wind will carry off the profligate drunkards and fornicators. This is an image similar to the one in Psalm 1 where the wicked are borne off like chaff, but the notion here of being bundled in the wings of the wind evokes the helpless passivity of the practitioners of vice carried away to their destruction.

CHAPTER 5   1. *for against you is the judgment.* Although others understand the polyvalent Hebrew term *mishpat* differently, the most likely meaning is: You are about to be sentenced, or brought to justice, for your crimes.

2. *Shittim.* The Masoretic Text shows an obscure word, *seitim,* but most scholars conclude this is a mistake for the well-attested place-name Shittim, which would make it, plausibly, the third in a series of place-names here.

> but I am chastisement for them all.
>
> 3 I know Ephraim,
>   and Israel is not hidden from Me.
>   For now you have whored, Ephraim,
>   Israel is defiled.
>
> 4 Their acts do not let them
>   turn back to their God.
>   For the spirit of whoring is within them,
>   and the LORD they do not know.
>
> 5 And Israel's pride bore witness against him,
>   and Israel and Ephraim stumble in their crime.
>   Judah, too, has stumbled with them.
>
> 6 With their sheep and their cattle they go
>   to seek out the LORD.
>   But they do not find Him.
>   He slipped away from them.
>
> 7 The LORD they betrayed,
>   for alien sons they bore.
>   Now the new moon shall consume them,
>   together with their fields.
>
> 8 Sound the ram's horn at Gibeah,
>   the trumpet at Ramah.
>   Shout out at Beth-Aven:
>   "After you, Benjamin!"
>
> 9 Ephraim shall be a desolation

---

5. *Israel's pride bore witness against him.* Literally, "bore witness in his face." While the verb here can also mean "to answer" or "to call out," what is clearly involved is testimony of a crime, continuing the judicial image of verse 1.

6. *With their sheep and their cattle.* These are the sacrificial animals they bring with them when they go to seek the LORD.

7. *for alien sons they bore.* This could mean either sons estranged from God because they have been raised in alien ways or sons begotten with foreign women.

   Now the new moon shall consume them. This clause is mysterious. Many emendations have been proposed for "new moon," *ḥodesh,* but none is very convincing. Perhaps the reference is to the new moon celebrations, tainted with pagan practices that will turn into catastrophes when God carries out judgment against these people.

8. *After you, Benjamin.* Since the sounding of the ram's horn and trumpet is a marshaling of troops for battle, this may indicate a rallying of the tribes, north and south, to face the invader.

on the day of stern rebuke.
Among the tribes of Israel
   I have faithfully made it known.
The nobles of Judah have become   10
   like those who move boundaries.
Upon them I will pour
   My wrath like water.
Exploited is Ephraim,   11
   and crushed in justice,
For he undertook to go
   after an empty thing.
And I am like the moth to Ephraim   12
   and like rot to the house of Judah.
When Ephraim saw his sickness   13
   and Judah his running sores,
Ephraim went off to Assyria
   and sent out to King Jareb.
But he cannot cure you
   and will not give you healing.
For I am like a lion to Ephraim   14
   and like the king of beasts to the house of Judah.
I, I will maul the prey and go off,
   bear it away and no one will save it.
I will go, return to My place,   15
   until they sense their guilt and seek Me,
      when in straits they shall search for Me.

---

10. *like those who move boundaries.* Moving stone boundary markers in order to lay claim to land that belongs to someone else is strictly forbidden (see Deuteronomy 27:17). The nobles of Judah are accused of expropriating land, though not necessarily by shifting boundary markers. Why Judah is introduced here is not entirely clear.

11. *after an empty thing.* As elsewhere, the referent is idolatry.

13. *King Jareb.* This term is obscure. It might be a proper name, as tentatively assumed in this translation, or it might be a peculiar formation from the verbal stem that means "to quarrel" or "to contest." The context, however, suggests turning to a person in power for help.

15. *I will go, return to My place.* This is an interesting biblical intimation of the idea of *deus absconditus*. God, in His anger against Israel, withdraws from them to His celestial abode, where He will await the moment they recognize their guilt and seek Him out before He will return to Israel.

CHAPTER 6

1   Come let us return to the Lᴏʀᴅ,
         for He mauled but He will heal us,
         He struck but He will bind up.
2   He will revive us after two days,
         on the third day raise us up,
         that we may live in His presence,
3   and that we may know, pursue knowing the Lᴏʀᴅ.
         Like daybreak His emergence is sure,
     and He will come to us like the rain,
         like the latter rain He will shower the earth.
4   What shall I do for you Ephraim,
         What shall I do for you, Judah,
     When your trust is like a morning cloud,
         like early dew that melts away?
5   Therefore have I hacked among your prophets,
         slain them with the utterances of My mouth,
             and your sentence will come out like light.
6   For trust did I want and not sacrifice
         and knowledge of God more than burnt offerings.

CHAPTER 6   1. *Come let us return to the Lᴏʀᴅ.* These words, until the end of verse 3, are the speech of the Israelites, imagining that their present suffering will be of brief duration and that God will heal their wounds and revive them. God's angry rejoinder begins in verse 4.

3. *like the latter rain He will shower the earth.* As often happens in the Bible, there is a pun hiding close to the surface. God's instruction to humankind (the word translated as "shower" also means "instruct") is life-giving, like the rain. But the verb for "teach" or "instruct," *yoreh,* is also a homonym of the noun that means "former rain," often paired with *malqosh,* "latter rain." One should also note that in these two lines God is compared first to the sun, then to the rain—both giving life to earth.

4. *like a morning cloud, / like early dew.* These two similes pick up the invocation of vivifying rain in the speech of the Israelites (verse 3), but with the meaning turned entirely around: the moisture-bearing clouds and dew quickly dissipate, like the purported trust of the Israelites.

5. *your prophets.* Given the two verbs of destruction, these would have to be false prophets.
    like light. The Masoretic Text lacks the particle that means "like," but this single letter, *kaf,* has probably been dropped through haplography because the immediately preceding Hebrew word ends in a *kaf.*

But they like humankind breached the covenant,   7
   there they betrayed Me.
Gilead is a town of criminals,   8
   covered with tracks of blood.
And like gangs who lie in wait for a man   9
   is the band of the priests.
They murder on the road to Shechem.
   Why, debauchery they perform!
In the house of Israel I have seen a horror.   10
   There the whoring is Ephraim's,
     Israel is defiled.
Judah, too, He sets a harvest for you.   11

CHAPTER 7

When I would restore the fortunes of My people,   6:11b
   and I would heal Israel,   1
Ephraim's crime is laid bare
   and the evils of Samaria,
for they have acted in lies;
   the thief comes within
     and the gang raids outside.
And let them not say in their heart   2

---

7. *like humankind.* This sounds a bit odd, but it may express the idea that humankind has a proclivity for treachery, as David Kimchi proposed. Others emend *ke'adam* to *be'adam*, "in Adam" (or Admah), construing the word as a place-name. This would make better sense of "there" in the second verset.

9. *They murder on the road to Shechem.* This is a bitter irony because Shechem was supposed to be one of the towns of refuge where an unintentional manslaughterer could flee.

11. *Judah, too, He sets a harvest for you.* This whole clause is puzzling. One reading proposed by a number of interpreters is that God has prepared a harvest of retribution for offending Judah. In any case, this looks like an orphaned verset because there is no matching second verset. The three Hebrew words that follow in the canonical chapter division in all likelihood belong to the beginning of the next chapter, and that is how they are treated in this translation.

CHAPTER 7   6:11b. *When I would restore the fortunes of My people.* God would like to show favor to His people, but Israel continues in its waywardness.

  that I have recalled all their evil.
  Now their deeds have turned them around—
   before My face they are.
3 In their evil they gladden the king,
   and with their deceits, the nobles.
4 All of them are adulterers,
   like a burning oven.
  The baker ceases from stirring,
   from kneading the dough till it rises.
5 On the day of our king
   the nobles made him sick with poisoned wine.
   He had set his hand with the scoffers.
6 For they drew near in their ambush,
   their hearts like an oven.
  All night their leader sleeps,
   in the morning he burns like a tongue of flame.

---

2. *I have recalled all their evil.* The evident sense is: let them not think I have done registering all their evil, for there is still more.

Now their deeds have turned them around. The image is of miscreants who have turned their backs on God or have hidden from Him. Now, their evil deeds turn them around and they are exposed to God's head-on gaze.

3. *In their evil they gladden the king.* This is best understood as pillorying the king for his complicity with them, delighting in their evil acts.

4. *like a burning oven.* The simile of the burning oven, which will be elaborated, is chosen because of the association of heat with sexual desire—in Hebrew, as in other languages, to be in heat is one of the idioms for sexual readiness.

The baker ceases from stirring. Because the oven of desire is stoked, the baker is presumed to have finished his task of preparing the dough and now puts it in the heated oven. But the stirring, the kneading, and the fermenting of the dough do not appear to have a further figurative referent.

5. *the day of our king.* This term has no equivalent elsewhere but probably designates the king's birthday or a similar celebration for the monarch.

the nobles made him sick with poisoned wine. The court atmosphere roils with vicious conspiracies, the king no better than his murderous nobles. All this may well reflect the recent history of the northern kingdom, which was marked with assassinations and coups.

He had set his hand with the scoffers. Although the meaning is not altogether clear, this probably indicates that the king had been involved with dubious characters, thus providing a motive for his assassination.

6. *their hearts like an oven.* Now the referent of the oven simile shifts from adulterers to conspirators, hot to carry out their plot against the king.

They all grow hot like an oven   7
    and devour their judges
All of their kings have fallen,
    none among them calls to Me.
Ephraim among the nations—   8
    it is he who mingles.
Ephraim is like a loaf
    not turned over.
Strangers consumed his strength,   9
    but he did not know.
His hair turned suddenly gray,
    but he did not know.
And Israel's pride bore witness against it,   10
    yet for all that they did not seek him.
And Ephraim became like a   11
    foolish senseless dove.
To Egypt they called,
    to Assyria went.
Where they go   12
    I will spread My net upon them.
Like the fowl of the heavens I will bring them down.
    I will bind them as their kinfolk listen.
Woe to them for they have wandered from Me.   13

---

7. *All of their kings have fallen.* The plural here does seem to evoke the bloody court history
of the northern kingdom.

8. *Ephraim among the nations— / it is he who mingles.* This is in all likelihood a critique of
the repeated quest for foreign alliances on the part of the northern kingdom.
    like a loaf / not turned over. The simile now dispenses with the oven and imagines a
round flat loaf of bread baked on coals (as present-day Bedouins still bake their *pittah*),
which, not having been turned over, is burned on the bottom and unbaked on the top.

11. *like a / foolish senseless dove.* It is a dove that lacks the homing instinct a dove (or
pigeon—the Hebrew term covers both) should have. Thus Ephraim seeks out Egypt and
Assyria.

12. *My net.* Nets were often used to trap fowl. The metaphor of fowling picks up the foolish
dove in verse 11.
    I will bind them. The translation reads, with many scholars, *'e'surem* for the Masoretic
ayesirem, "I will afflict them," which doesn't make much sense in context and shows grammatically anomalous vowel-points in the received text.
    as their kinfolk listen. The Hebrew is obscure and the translation conjectural.

Disaster for them, as they rebelled against Me!
Shall I redeem them
    when they have spoken against Me lies?
14 And they did not cry out to Me from their heart,
        but they wailed upon their couch,
    over grain and new wine they gashed themselves,
        they swerved away from Me.
15 I braced, I strengthened their arm,
        but against Me they plotted evil.
16 They go back to what is worthless,
        they are like a faulty bow.
    Their nobles shall fall by the sword
        because of their angry tongue,
            which is their mockery in the land of Egypt.

CHAPTER 8

1 A ram's horn to your lips!
    —he is like an eagle against the LORD's house.
    For they have breached My covenant
        and rebelled against My teaching.

---

14. *they gashed themselves.* The Masoretic Text has *yitgoraru,* meaning uncertain. This translation reads, with the Septuagint, *yitgodadu,* the shape of the Hebrew letters for *r* and *d* being quite similar. Gashing oneself was a form of imprecating the gods, as in the story of the prophets of Baal at Mount Carmel in 1 Kings 18.

15. *I braced.* The received text says "I afflicted," *yisarti,* but this translation, like that of the New Jewish Publication Society, reads instead *yisadti,* which can mean "to make firm."

16. *to what is worthless.* The Hebrew has two unintelligible monosyllabic words, *lo' 'al* (not above?). The translation reads with the Septuagint and the Syriac *labliya'al.*
    which is their mockery in the land of Egypt. There is debate over the meaning of this last cryptic clause, but the sense could be that the Egyptians regard the rash angry speech of the Israelite nobles as a butt of mockery. Some think the reference is to an attempt to seek an alliance with Egypt that becomes a target of ridicule.

CHAPTER 8   1. *to your lips.* Literally, "to your palate."
    he is like an eagle against the LORD's house. The clause is obscure. The probable referent is an invader of the kingdom of Israel—hence the sounding of the ram's horn as an alarm. In that case, "the LORD's house" would have to be the northern kingdom and not, as it usually means, the Temple.

To Me they cry out—   2
   "We know you, O God of Israel!"
Israel rejects what is good—   3
   an enemy shall pursue him.
They set up kings but not through Me,   4
   installed nobles but without My knowledge.
From their silver and their gold
   they made themselves idols,
     that they might be cut off.
Your calf rejects you, Samaria,   5
   My wrath against them flares.
     How long will they fail to be clean?
And it—a craftsman made it,   6
   and it is not a god.
For shards it shall become,
   the calf of Samaria.
For they sow the wind   7
   and harvest a storm.
Standing grain that has no sprouts,
   it will not make flour.
If perhaps it should make some,
   strangers shall swallow it up.
Israel has been swallowed,   8
   now they become among the nations
     like a vessel no one wants.
For they have gone up to Assyria,   9
   a wild ass on its own is Ephraim,
     they have made courtship's plea.

---

2. *We know you, O God of Israel.* The Hebrew word order is scrambled. This declaration, made by the people, is clearly a deluded one.

4. *that they might be cut off.* Their idolatrous ways will lead to their destruction.

5. *Your calf.* This is the icon used for worship in the northern kingdom. It corresponds to the cherubim in the southern kingdom. It was viewed by the Judahite writers as an idol.

9. *a wild ass.* The wild ass figures in biblical poetry as a creature that cannot be tamed, living solitary in the wilderness. Israel's seeking an accommodation with Assyria (represented here as a courtship) manifests its proclivity to go it alone, ignoring both prudent counsel and God's instruction.

10   Though they give gifts among the nations,
          now will I gather them up,
      and they will soon tremble
          from the burden of kings and nobles.
11   For Ephraim made many altars
          an offense they were for him,
              altars to offend.
12   I wrote for him My many teachings—
          like something strange they were viewed.
13   The sacrifices I gave they slaughtered,
          it was flesh, and they ate.
              The LORD did not accept them favorably.
      Now will their crime be recalled,
          and a reckoning made for their offense.
              They shall go back to Egypt.
14   And Israel forgot his Maker
          and he built palaces.
      And Judah made many fortified towns,
          but I set fire to his towns,
              and it consumed his citadels.

CHAPTER 9

1   Do not rejoice, O Israel,
              no exulting like the peoples.

---

10. *give gifts.* The Hebrew says only "give," and "gifts" is supplied as a guess. These could be courtship gifts.

   now will I gather them up. Though this phrase is often used for gathering exiles to return to Zion, here it would appear to mean "gather up for destruction."

13. *it was flesh, and they ate.* They viewed the sacrifices not as a means of expressing devotion to God but merely as a source of meat meals.

   accept them favorably. The object of this verb is the sacrifices.

   They shall go back to Egypt. This should probably be understood figuratively: they shall return to a condition of slavery. The likely candidate for enslavers would be the Assyrians.

CHAPTER 9   1. *no exulting.* The received text reads *'el-gil,* "to exulting," emended here to *'al-gil,* "no exulting."

For you went whoring from your God,
　　you loved a whore's pay
　　　　on every new grain threshing floor.
Threshing floor and winepress know them not,   2
　　and new wine shall deny them.
They shall not dwell in the land of the LORD,   3
　　and Ephraim shall go back to Egypt
　　　　and in Assyria eat unclean things.
They shall pour no wine libation to the LORD,   4
　　and their sacrifices shall not please Him.
Like mourners' bread it shall be to them,
　　all who eat it become unclean.
For their food is for their gullet,
　　it shall not enter the house of the LORD.
What will you do for the appointed day,   5
　　for the day of the LORD's festival?
For, look, they go off from destruction.   6
　　Egypt gathers them in,
　　　　Memphis buries them.
The treasure house for their silver
　　the thistle shall inherit,

---

on every new grain threshing floor. These would be sites where pagan rites took place.

2. *Threshing floor and winepress know them not.* The Masoretic Text shows *lo' yir'em,* "did not shepherd them," but this translation reads, with the Septuagint, *lo' yed'aem,* "knew them not." The idea is measure-for-measure justice: the Israelites worshipped alien gods in these places; now threshing floor and winepress will give them no yield.

3. *Ephraim shall go back to Egypt.* See the third comment on 8:13.

4. *all who eat it become unclean.* Mourners' food would be ritually unclean because it has been in contact with the dead.
　　For their food is for their gullet. In bringing animals to sacrifice, their chief interest is in consuming the meat of the part of the animal that is not devoted to the offering.

5. *the appointed day.* The Hebrew term is a synonym for "festival."

6. *they go off from destruction.* This is one of many obscure phrases in this chapter. Given the reference to Egypt and to the Egyptian city of Memphis in the next two versets, it probably means that they flee the devastation of their own land (by the Assyrians) to take refuge in Egypt, where they die.

the thorn is in their tents.

7   The days of reckoning have arrived,
         the days of retribution have arrived.
             Israel shall know it.
     The prophet is witless,
         the man of spirit crazed
     by all your crimes,
         all your hate.

8   The lookout of Ephraim,
         the prophet with my God—
     a snare is laid in all his ways,
         hate in the house of his God.

9   They have acted most ruinously
         as in the days of Gibeah.
     He shall recall their crime,
         make a reckoning for their offense.

10   Like grapes in the wilderness
         I found Israel.
     Like the first fruit on the fig tree when it appears
         I saw your fathers
     Yet they came to Baal Peor
         and devoted themselves to a shameful god
             and became vile things like what they loved.

---

7. *all your hate.* The hatred is directed against the prophet, driving him to distraction.

8. *The lookout.* Elsewhere in the Prophets, this noun is a synonym for "prophet," and that would seem to be the case here.

9. *as in the days of Gibeah.* At Gibeah (Judges 19), the local Benjaminites gang-raped a woman to death, fulfilling what Sodom only sought to do, as the elaborate allusions to the Sodom story there remind us. Gibeah thus becomes the paradigm of a wholly depraved society.

10. *Like grapes in the wilderness / I found Israel.* The discovery of grapes in the largely barren wilderness is gratifying. Israel at the beginning of its wilderness wanderings could delight God in this way.
     when it appears. More literally, "at its first."
     Yet they came to Baal Peor. The cherished Israelites quickly abandoned their God to join in a pagan orgy at Baal Peor (see Numbers 25:1–5.)
     a shameful god. The Hebrew *boshet* means "shame" and is regularly used as a polemic substitution for "Baal," especially in theophoric suffixes.
     like what they loved. The Hebrew is cryptic but may refer to the idols.

Ephraim—their glory shall fly off like a bird,   11
    from birth and from the womb and from conception.
For should they raise their sons,   12
    I would bereave them of humankind,
for woe to them indeed
    when I swerve away from them.
Ephraim as I saw him—   13
    a palm frond planted in a meadow.
      But Ephraim brings out his sons to the slayer.
Give them, LORD,   14
    what should you give?
Give them a miscarrying womb
    and shriveled breasts.
All their evil at Gilgal,   15
    for there did I hate them.
For the evil of their deeds
    I will banish them from My house.
I will no longer love them.
    All their nobles are knaves.
Ephraim is stricken,   16
    their root is dry,
      they cannot make fruit.
    Even when they give birth,

---

11. *from birth and from the womb and from conception.* This series goes back in time from birth to the womb from which the infant is born to conception nine months earlier. The curse of infertility and child mortality is spelled out in the next verse.

13. *a palm frond.* The Hebrew *tsor* seems to refer to "Tyre," the Phoenician city, but both a talmudic source and many modern scholars link it to a term that means "palm frond," which makes far better sense as something planted in a meadow. Ephraim was seen by God as a luxuriant plant, but his own actions led to the killing of his sons (or "children") by invaders.

14. *Give them a miscarrying womb / and shriveled breasts.* This picks up the curse of dying infants from verses 11–12. Even if the mother doesn't miscarry, her shriveled breasts will spell doom for the infant.

15. *All their evil at Gilgal.* The phrase lacks both preposition and verb. Gilgal was where the people demanded of Samuel that he put a king over them (1 Samuel 12). Unless Hosea has some different association with Gilgal in mind, he seems to be saying that the establishment of the monarchy was in itself a rejection of God's kingship.
    All their nobles are knaves. This imitates the Hebrew wordplay, *sareyhem sorerim.*

I will put to death the precious ones of their womb.
17 My God shall reject them,
     for they did not heed Him,
      and they shall be wanderers among the nations.

CHAPTER 10

1 A blighted vine is Israel,
     his fruit is just the same.
When his fruit was abundant,
     he made abundant altars.
When it was good in his land,
     they made goodly cult-pillars.
2 Their heart is divided—
     now they bear guilt.
He shall break the back of their altars,
     ravage their cultic pillars.
3 For now they say,
     "We have no king,
for we have not feared the LORD,
     and a king—what can he do to us?"

---

16. *I will put to death the precious ones of their womb.* Once again, the reiterated grim theme of infant mortality is struck.

17. *My God shall reject them.* Until this point, God has been speaking in the first-person singular. It is possible that this switch to the third person, the prophet now speaking about God, is meant to mark the end of the prophecy. Some critics, basing themselves on the Septuagint, prefer to read "their God."

CHAPTER 10   1. *is just the same.* More literally, "is equal to it," revocalizing the verb *yeshaveh* as *yishveh*.
    When it was good in his land. When the land flourished and yielded its abundance, the Israelites used the bounty they had garnered from the land to build lavish pagan altars.

2. *He shall break the back of their altars.* The subject of the verb is God. The verb itself is an unusual and vivid choice: its general meaning is "to behead" or "break the neck."

3. *We have no king.* This speech attributed to the people may reflect the political predicament of the northern kingdom, which was plagued by a series of coups and assassinations.
    for we have not feared the LORD, / and a king—what can he do to us? There is an *a fortiori* logic here: we have not feared the LORD, so why should we fear a king? The Israelites have embraced a rule of anarchy, rejected the authority of monarchs and of the divine King.

They have spoken words,   4
    empty oaths,
        sealed a pact,
and justice blooms like poison weeds
    in the furrows of the field.
The calf of Beth-Aven they fear,   5
    the dwellers of Samaria.
For his people mourns for it,
    and his priests for it.
They wail over their glory,
    for it has departed from them.
It, too, shall be brought to Assyria,   6
    a tribute to King Jareb.
Ephraim shall be disgraced
    and Israel shamed by its counsel.
Samaria shall be destroyed and her king,   7
    like foam upon the water.
And the high places of Aven are ravaged,   8
    the offense of Israel.
Thorn and thistle shall spring up
    upon their altars.
And they shall say to the mountains, "Cover us,"
    and to the hills, "Fall upon us."
From the days of Gibeah Israel offended,   9

---

5. *Beth-Aven*. As before, this is a pejorative distortion of Bethel.

For his people mourns for it. The antecedent is the calf icon at Bethel.

his priests. The term used, *kemarim*, usually refers to officiants in a pagan cult, in contrast to *kohanim*, priests of God.

They wail. The received text has *yagilu*, "they exult." This translation adopts a widely proposed emendation, *yeililu*. The mistake, if it is a mistake, might have been triggered by the word for "departed" (or "exiled") in the second verset, *galah*, "for it has departed from them." There is an echo here of the report of the loss of the Ark to the Philistines in 1 Samuel 4:22.

6. *King Jareb*. See the comment on 5:13.

7. *and her king*. The translation adds "and" for the sake of coherence.

8. *And they shall say to the mountains, "Cover us."* The inhabitants of Samaria, in their terror of the destruction overtaking them, extravagantly beg of the mountains and hills to cover them.

9. *the days of Gibeah*. See the comment on 9:9.

there they took their stand.
"War will not overtake them in Gibeah
     against the wrongdoers."

10   As I wish will I harness them
          and peoples shall gather against them
               as they are harnessed to their two shafts.
11   And Ephraim is a trained calf
          that loves to thresh,
     and I passed over its goodly neck,
          yoked Ephraim that he would plow,
     [Judah] that Jacob would harrow.
12   Sow for yourselves in righteousness,
          reap in faithfulness.
     Till for yourselves tilled ground,
          and it is time to seek the LORD
               until He comes and teaches you righteousness.
13   You have plowed wickedness,
          wrongdoing do you reap.
     You have eaten denial's fruit
          for you trusted in your own way,

---

there they took their stand. The meaning of the Hebrew is uncertain, although the ordinary verb for "stand" is used.

War will not overtake them in Gibeah. This should perhaps be construed as the speech
of the inhabitants of Gibeah, imagining that they will be safe from evil enemies. In the
story that follows the gang-rape in Judges 19, an alliance of the tribes in fact attacks Gibeah
and the whole tribe of Benjamin and comes close to exterminating them. This will be the
fate of the northern kingdom.

10. *harness them.* The vocalization of the Hebrew word is anomalous, and some see a different verb here. "Harness," however, makes good sense in conjunction with the image of
the plowing calf in what follows.

11. *passed over its goodly neck.* The implied object of the verb is "yoke."
[Judah]. This word is bracketed because it does not make sense in context and may well
be the interpolation of the Judahite editor.

12. *and it is time to seek the LORD.* Once the (metaphoric) field has been planted in righteousness and reaped in faithfulness, the time will be ripe to seek the LORD.
teaches you righteousness. A pun is hidden in the verb "teaches," *yoreh,* because it has a
homonymous noun, "former rain," which would fructify the planted field.

13. *denial's fruit.* The phrase also suggests disappointing or false fruit that cannot really
be eaten.
in your own way. The Masoretic Text makes perfectly good sense, but it is worth noting
that the Septuagint seems to have used a Hebrew text that read *berikhbekha,* "in your

in all your warriors.

And the clamor shall rise in your people   14
   and all your fortresses shall be ravaged
like Shalmaneser's ravaging
   at Beth-Arbel on the day of battle—
     mothers with children were ripped apart.
Thus is it done to you, Bethel,   15
   because of your utter evil.
At daybreak the king of Israel
   will indeed be destroyed.

CHAPTER 11

For Israel was a lad and I loved him,   1
   and from Egypt I called to My son.
They called to them,   2
   yet they went off from them.
To the Baalim they sacrificed,
   and to the idols they burned incense.
Yet I taught Ephraim to walk,   3
   took him by his arms,

---

chariots," instead of *bedarkhekha,* "in your own way." This yields a better parallelism with "warriors" in the second verset.

14. *the clamor.* This is the loud noise of the attacking army.

   like Shalmaneser's ravaging. The Hebrew shows merely "Shalman," not an attested name. It seems likely that this is an abbreviated version of "Shalmaneser," the Assyrian emperor.

   Beth-Arbel. Nothing is known about this place and the evidently savage fighting that took place there.

15. *Thus is it done to you.* This translation construes the third-person singular verb as an equivalent of the passive. It could also be understood as "He [God] does to you." A third, rather less likely, possibility adopted by others is to construe the whole clause as "Thus does Bethel do to you."

CHAPTER 11   2. *They called to them.* This is the first of the many obscurities with which this chapter swarms. Those calling may be God's agents, but that is not quite clear. The veering from singular to plural compounds the difficulty.

3. *I taught Ephraim to walk.* The unusual conjugation of the verb based on the root meaning "foot" has been variously interpreted, but taking Ephraim by the arms suggests holding a small child who is just learning to walk.

   but they did not know that I had healed them.
4 With human cords I tugged them,
       with bonds of love,
   and I became to them
       like those who lift an infant to their cheeks,
          and I bent over them and fed them.
5 No! He turned back to the land of Egypt,
       and Assyria was his king,
          for they refused to come back to Me.
6 And the sword shall swoop down on his towns
       and destroy his limbs
          and devour because of their counsels.
7 And My people cling to rebellion against Me.
       When they call him on high,
          he does not rise up.
8 How can I give you over, Ephraim,
       surrender you, Israel?
   How can I make you like Admah,
       set you like Zeboiim?
   My heart churns within me,
       My compassion altogether is stirred.
9 I will not act in My blazing wrath,
       I will no more destroy Ephraim.
   For I am God and not a man,
       the Holy One in your midst,
          and I do not desire to root out.

---

4. *like those who lift an infant to their cheeks.* The entire phrase is obscure. This translation takes the noun *'ol* not to mean "yoke," as it does elsewhere, but to be a shortened form of *'olal*, "infant," continuing the imagery of the preceding verse.

6. *And the sword shall swoop down.* Again, the translation is conjectural, not just for this verset but for the entire line.

7. *When they call him on high, / he does not rise up.* The Hebrew here is quite opaque.

8. *How can I give you over, Ephraim.* This marks a turning point: although Israel has provoked God, He is unwilling to consign it to destruction.
     Admah, / ... Zeboiim. These are two of the cities of the plain mentioned in Genesis 10:19 that are destroyed together with Sodom and Gomorrah.

9. *and I do not desire to root out.* The received text reads *welo' 'avo' be'ir,* "I will not come into a town," which does not make much sense. The translation supposes the emendation *welo' 'oveh ba'er.*

After the Lord they shall go,   10
    like a lion He shall roar.
When He roars,
    the sons shall hasten from the west.
They shall hasten like a bird from Egypt,   11
    like a dove from Assyria's land
        and I will settle them in their homes, said the Lord.

CHAPTER 12

Ephraim encircled Me in denial,   1
    and the house of Israel in deceit.
But Judah still stays with God
    and with the holy ones is faithful.
Ephraim herds the wind   2
    and chases the east wind all day.
Lies and plunder he multiplies
    and seals a pact with Assyria,
    oil to Egypt is brought.

And the Lord has a case against Judah   3
    to make a reckoning with Jacob for his acts,
        by his deeds He shall pay him back.
In the womb he cheated his brother,   4

---

10. *hasten.* Even though the Hebrew verb usually means "to tremble" (as in 1 Samuel 21:2), it is also used in the sense of "hasten."

from the west. It is not clear why the sons should be in the west.

CHAPTER 12   1. *But Judah still stays with God.* The meaning of the verb *rad* (and its verbal root as well) is uncertain, and the translation is a surmise from the context.

the holy ones. Who these are is obscure. Some claim that this is a plural of majesty, referring to God, but that seems questionable.

2. *herds the wind.* This is the earliest occurrence of this vivid metaphor for futility that will be abundantly used in Qohelet.

chases the east wind. Bad things come from the east wind, blowing from the desert.

oil to Egypt is brought. Olive oil, an important product of the Land of Israel, would be exported to Egypt, implying both a commercial and a political relationship and thus a parallel to the pact with Assyria.

4. *he cheated his brother.* The verb *'aqav* is a negative etymology of the name Ya'aqov, Jacob, and the one invoked by Esau when he discovers that Jacob has stolen his blessing. The birth

> and with his power he strove with God.
> 5 He strove with the Messenger and prevailed—
> he wept and pleaded with him.
> At Bethel he did find him,
> "And there he spoke with us."
> 6 And the LORD God of Armies,
> the LORD is what He is called.
> 7 As for you, to your God you shall turn back,
> faithfulness and justice keep,
> and hope for your God always.
> 8 A huckster in whose hand are cheating scales
> loving to exploit!
> 9 And Ephraim said,
> "Why I have grown rich,
> found power for myself.
> All my gains do not expose for me
> a crime that is an offense."
> 10 But I am the LORD your God
> from the time of the land of Egypt

---

narrative of the twins in Genesis 25 actually provides a more neutral etymology, relating it to *'aqev,* "heel," which would make it mean "grab the heel." Thus Hosea represents Jacob (which is to say, Israel) as a cheat from the womb, in keeping with the people's behavior in the prophet's time.

he strove with God. This is what the Hebrew says. The next line "corrects" this to a divine messenger or angel.

5. *he wept and pleaded with him.* This clause presents a rather different picture of the struggle with the divine adversary from the one in Genesis 32. Unlike the story in Genesis, the adversary here is reduced to tears and pleading.

At Bethel he did find him. In context, this has to mean that the mysterious stranger found Jacob at Bethel. Again, this differs from the tradition in Genesis, where the nocturnal encounter is at the Jabbok ford, whereas at Bethel, in Jacob's flight to Aram, he had the epiphany of the angels ascending and descending on a ramp (or ladder).

And there he spoke with us. The import of this clause is unclear. Perhaps the people of Israel are represented as confidently declaring that God spoke to them at Bethel through Jacob. Bethel was a principal cult-site of the northern kingdom.

8. *A huckster.* This is a denunciation of Israel, using the noun *kena'an*—elsewhere, Canaan—to mean "trader" or "huckster," evidently as a pejorative.

9. *found power for myself.* The same term, *'on,* that was used to explain Jacob's conquest of God or angel is again invoked.

10. *from the time of the land of Egypt.* "The time of" is merely implied in an ellipsis.

Once more will I settle you in tents
    as on the festival days.
And I spoke to the prophets,   11
    and I framed many visions
        and through the prophets showed forth images.
If Gilead does wrong,   12
    they become an empty thing.
At Gilgal they offered bulls.
    Their altars, too, are like heaps of ruins
        in the furrows of the field.
And Jacob fled to the field of Aram,   13
    and Israel labored for a woman,
        and for a woman he guarded the flocks.
But by a prophet the LORD brought up Israel from Egypt,   14
    and by a prophet it was guarded.
Ephraim was bitterly vexing,   15
    and his bloodguilt shall be set upon him,
        and his Master shall pay him back for his shame.

CHAPTER 13

When Ephraim spoke in trembling,   1
    he was a prince in Israel,

Once more will I settle you in tents. This is best understood as a restoration of the idyllic early days, although some see it as a punishment. Or, since "the festival days" are mentioned, it could refer to pilgrims at the crowded Succoth festival staying in improvised tent accommodations.

13. *for a woman he guarded the flocks.* This is another ellipsis, the Hebrew saying only "he guarded." The reference is to Jacob's working for Laban for seven years as payment of a bride-price for the woman he loved, Rachel.

14. *But by a prophet.* The prophet is Moses. There is an antithesis here: Jacob labored for a woman, but it was by Moses (in Hebrew, the same preposition as "for") that God rescued the Hebrews from slavery. Thus, the pedigree of the people as a whole is finer than the pedigree of Jacob-Israel.

it was guarded. The guarding of the people by a prophet is a nobler thing than the guarding of the flocks by Jacob.

CHAPTER 13   1. *spoke in trembling.* The context suggests that it is trembling before God, when Ephraim was still God-fearing.

but he was guilty with Baal and died.
2   And now they continue to offend
            and make themselves molten images
        from their silver in their form as idols,
            all of it craftsmen's work.
        To them they say:
            sacrifices of man, calves to be kissed.
3   Therefore shall they be like a morning cloud
            and like early dew that melts away,
        like chaff whirled out from the threshing floor
            and like smoke from a chimney.
4   Yet I am the LORD your God
            ever since the land of Egypt,
        and no God save Me shall you know
            and no rescuer except for Me.
5   I knew you in the wilderness
            in a parched land.
6   When they grazed and they were sated,
            they were sated and grew proud.
                Therefore they forgot Me.
7   And I will become to them like a lion,
            like a leopard I spy on the way.
8   I will meet them like a bear robbed of her cubs
            and rip the sinews round their heart.
        And I will devour them there like a lion,

---

but he was guilty with Baal and died. Although this sounds like a flat statement, it must mean that Ephraim's pagan ways caused many of the people to perish.

2. *in their form.* The Masoretic Text reads *ketevunam,* "according to their discernment" (?), but the Septuagint *ketavnitam* makes much better sense. *Tavnit* is a term often used for the form or image of an idol.

To them they say. Perhaps these are denouncers of the idolatrous people of Ephraim, though this is not entirely clear.

sacrifices of man. This is another opaque phrase. It could possibly mean "human sacrifices," but there are no indications elsewhere that Ephraim practiced human sacrifice.

calves to be kissed. These are the icons that figured in the cult of YHWH in the northern kingdom.

6. *grew proud.* Literally, "their heart was high."

8. *like a lion.* Here the poem uses another of the five biblical terms for "lion," not the same word as in verse 7.

the beasts of the field shall tear them apart.
You are ruined, O Israel,   9
    for who will come to your aid?
Where is your king, then?   10
    Let him rescue you in all your towns.
And your leaders to whom you said,
    "Give me a king and nobles."
But I will give you a king in My wrath   11
    and take him away in My anger.
Ephraim's crime is bundled up,   12
    hidden, his offense.
Birth pangs come upon him,   13
    and the child is not wise.
For now he shall not last
    on the birth-stool for children.
From Sheol shall I ransom them,   14
    from death shall I redeem them?
Where are your words, O Death,
    where your scourge, O Sheol?

---

9. *for who.* The Masoretic Text has "me," *bi,* but two ancient versions show "who," *mi.*

10. *Where is.* The received text has *'ehi,* "I will be," but this is generally corrected to *'ayeh* (a simple reversal of consonants).

    Give me a king and nobles. As before, Hosea follows the line of the prophet Samuel in viewing the popular demand for a king as a presumptuous mistake.

12. *bundled up, / hidden.* These words may anticipate the birth imagery of the following lines.

13. *and the child is not wise.* This formulation may suggest that the child born is defective.

    now. The Hebrew *'et* usually means "time," but here it appears to be the equivalent of a related word *'atah.*

    he shall not last. Literally, "he shall not stand"—that is, "he shall not survive."

14. *From Sheol shall I ransom them, / from death shall I redeem them?* Some interpreters construe this as a positive declaration by God, that He will ransom Ephraim from death. But this makes no sense in light of the language of utter devastation deployed in the next verse, so it is best to understand it as a rhetorical question with the implied answer "no."

    Where are your words, O Death. Some critics revocalize *devareyka,* "your words," as *devrekha,* "your pestilence," yielding a neater parallelism with the second verset. As in verse 10, *'ehi* at the beginning of each of the two versets here is emended to *'ayeh.* If, as this translation assumes, the preceding line of poetry comprises two rhetorical questions, then the meaning of the two questions here is: where is your scourge, Death?—bring it to bear on these miscreants.

Regret is hidden from My eyes.
15   Though he put forth fruit in meadows,
         the east wind shall come, the LORD's wind.
            from the desert rising up.
      And his fountain shall dry up
         and his spring shall arid be.
      It shall ravage treasure,
         every precious vessel.

CHAPTER 14

1   Samaria is guilty,
         for it rebelled against its God.
      They shall fall by the sword,
         their infants shall be smashed,
            and their pregnant women split apart.
2   Turn back, O Israel, to the LORD your God,
         for you have stumbled in your crime.
3   Take words with you
         and turn back to the LORD.
      Say to Him, "All crime You shall forgive.
         And take what is good,
            and we shall offer our speech instead of bulls.
4   Assyria will not rescue us,
         on horses we shall not ride.
      And we shall say no more 'our God'

---

15. *It shall ravage treasure.* The antecedent of "it" is probably the devastating east wind rising from the desert. The alternative would be that the image of the wind is now dropped and that the pronoun, which could also mean "he," refers to the invader.

CHAPTER 14   1. *their infants shall be smashed, / and their pregnant women split apart.* It is a sad historical fact that such barbaric practices are repeatedly attested to in biblical literature.

3. *Take words with you.* This slightly odd formulation probably conveys the idea that words are to be the vehicles of repentance—not animal sacrifices or grain offerings but words spoken from the heart.
   All crime You shall forgive. The Hebrew word order is "All you shall forgive crime," which is either a scribal error or nonstandard syntactical usage.
   we shall offer our speech instead of bulls. This picks up and explicates "Take words with you."

to our handiwork,
    as in You alone the orphan is shown pity."
"I will heal their rebellion,   5
    I will love them freely,
        for My wrath has turned back from them.
I will be like dew to Israel.   6
    He shall blossom like the lily
        and strike root like Lebanon.
His branches shall go forth   7
    and his glory be like the olive tree,
        and his fragrance like Lebanon.
Those who dwell in his shade shall come back,   8
    they shall give life to new grain,
and like the vine they shall blossom.
    His fame is like Lebanon wine.
Ephraim—'Why more should I deal with idols?   9
    I have answered and I espy Him
I am like the lush cypress.
    from me your fruit is found.'"

---

5. *I will heal their rebellion.* God now responds to the words of penitent Israel. Although "heal" may seem an unusual verb to attach to "rebellion," the condition of "rebellion" is conceived as a sickness. Compare the imagery of illness in Isaiah 1:5–6.

My wrath has turned back from them. This is God's matching response to Israel's turning back (verse 3) to Him.

6. *I will be like dew to Israel.* Twice earlier, the simile of dew was used to evoke Israel's melting away. Now, with Israel likened to a flowering plant and a tree, the dew is fructifying.

strike root like Lebanon. In the pattern of second-verset intensification common in biblical poetry, the line moves from a flowering bush to a deep-rooted tree. "Lebanon" is a poetic ellipsis for "trees of Lebanon," a heavily forested region, as the ancient audience would immediately have understood.

8. *like the vine they shall blossom.* They raise crops—"they shall give life to new grain"—and themselves flourish like the growing vine.

9. *I have answered and I espy Him.* Some interpreters contend that these words and everything that follows in this verse are spoken by God. But the verb *shur*, "to espy" or "to make out from a distance," is more appropriate for Israel to God than the other way around. The comparison, moreover, to a verdant tree is often used for a resurgent Israel or for a righteous person but not for God.

from me your fruit is found. The "you" here would be anyone seeking fruit, which the flourishing Israel can provide.

10
> Who is wise and can grasp these things,
> discerning, and can know them?
> For straight are the ways of the Lord,
> and the righteous shall walk on them,
> but rebels shall stumble on them.

---

10. *Who is wise and can grasp these things.* The language of this concluding verse is entirely constituted of formulas from Wisdom literature. The inevitable conclusion is that this is a coda added by an editor that asks us to contemplate the moral wisdom of this collection of Hosea's prophecies.

rebels shall stumble on them. While the clause is formulaic (and the noun here could also be represented, as many translations do, as "sinners"), the editorial choice of a formula with "stumbles" makes a nice envelope structure with "stumbled" in verse 2 at the beginning of the prophecy.

Joel

CHAPTER 1   The word of the LORD that came to Joel son of 1
Pethuel.

> Hear this, you elders,   2
>   and give ear, all dwellers of the land.
> Has its like happened in your days
>   and in the days of your fathers?
> Recount it to your children   3
>   and to your children's children
>   and to their children in a generation to come.
> What remained from the locust the grasshopper ate,   4
>   and what remained from the grasshopper the swarmer ate
>   and what remained from the swarmer the grub did eat.
> Wake up, you drunkards and weep,   5
>   and wail, all drinkers of wine,
>   for the fermented juice that is cut off from your mouth.

CHAPTER 1   3. *a generation to come.* Literally, "another generation."

4. *the locust.* Plagues of locusts, an instance of which figures in the Ten Plagues, were known catastrophic events in the Near East. Vast swarms of the voracious insects would eat everything in their path, leaving the fields bare of produce. Joel uses four different Hebrew synonyms for "locust," and all the English versions, including the present translation, flounder to find or invent four equivalents. Some scholars think these four terms indicate four stages in the metamorphosis of the insect, but that is uncertain. Three of the four Hebrew words show a transparent etymology: *gazam* (the word rendered here as "locust"), "to cut back"; *'arbeh,* "multitude"; and *ḥasil,* "to finish off or destroy." The last, *yeleq,* might conceivably be linked with *laqaq,* "lick."

5. *drunkards . . . / drinkers of wine.* This is not a denunciation of drunkenness, as one finds, for example, in Isaiah. Rather, the prophet is invoking all the hedonists who delighted in the pleasures of drinking and now, with the vineyards stripped bare by the locusts, will have nothing to drink.

6   For a nation has come up against my land,
          vast and countless.
     Its teeth are the teeth of a lion,
          the maned beast's jaws it has.
7   It has turned my vine to a desolation
          and my fig tree into shards.
     It has stripped it bare,
          its branches are gone white.
8   Howl like a virgin girt in sackcloth
          over the husband of her youth.
9   Grain offering and libation are cut off
          from the house of the LORD.
     The priests mourn,
          the ministers of the LORD.
10   The field is ravaged,
          the soil mourns,
     for the new grain has been ravaged,
          the new wine dried up,
              the oil is bleak.
11   The farmers are shamed,
          the vintners wail
     over wheat and over barley,
          for the field's harvest is gone.
12   The vine has dried up
          and the fig tree is bleak.

---

6. *For a nation has come up against my land.* In this instance, the invading nation is a metaphorical representation of the locusts.

   Its teeth are the teeth of a lion. The prophet revels in a poetic paradox. In biblical poetry, warriors are often compared to ravening lions. Here, the gnawing insects are tiny, with nothing like lion's teeth, but the effect of their vast voracious numbers is as devastating as the rending fangs of a lion.

9. *Grain offering and libation are cut off.* With the standing grain and the vines utterly consumed by the locusts, there is nothing left to bring to the Temple.

10. *the oil is bleak.* While in context this probably means something like "gone bad," there is a persistent personification in this prophecy that is worth preserving.

11. *The farmers are shamed.* The Hebrew verb in this conjugated form is a homonym of "dried up" in verse 10, and the pun seems quite deliberate. "Dried up" at the beginning of the next verse is the same word, thus carrying a subsurface secondary meaning of "shamed."

Pomegranate, also palm tree and quince,
    all the trees of the field are sear,
for joy has dried up
    from the sons of man.
Gird and lament, you priests,   13
    wail, ministrants of the altar.
Come, spend nights in sackcloth,
    ministrants of my God.
Pronounce a fast,   14
    proclaim convocation.
Gather the elders,
    all the land's dwellers,
to the house of the LORD your God
    and cry out to the LORD.
Alack for the day,   15
    for the day of the LORD is near,
      and like a shattering from Shaddai it comes.
Why, before our eyes   16
    food is cut off
from the house of our God,
    rejoicing and exultation.
The seeds have rotted   17
    beneath their clods.

---

12. *quince.* The Hebrew *tapuaḥ*, appearing only here and in the Song of Songs (2:3), does not mean "apple," as it is often translated, because there were no apple trees in the ancient Near East. "Quince" is an educated guess, although others opt for "apricot."

joy has dried up. This is the fourth occurrence of this verb, again with a likely double meaning.

13. *Gird.* This verb is an ellipsis for "gird sackcloth."

15. *like a shattering from Shaddai it comes.* The Hebrew wordplay, approximated in this English version, is *shod* (literally, "devastation," "ravaging") *mishaday*. "Shaddai" is an archaic name for God, of uncertain etymology, largely restricted to poetry.

16. *rejoicing and exultation.* The verb "cut off" does double duty for "food" and for these two nouns. The festivals in the Temple were times of joyous celebration as pilgrims came from throughout the land to offer sacrifices and to partake in the festive feasts. Now, there is nothing to bring as offering ("food") and no occasion for joy.

17. *The seeds have rotted.* The point of view now swivels away from the desolate Temple, deprived of the wherewithal for the celebration of the festivals, to the fields across the country lying in ruins.

The storehouses are desolate,
   the granaries ruined,
      for the new grain has dried up.

18   How the livestock groans,
   the herds of cattle are confounded,
for there is no pasture for them,
   the flocks of sheep are desolate.

19   To you, O Lord, I call,
   for fire consumed the wilderness meadows.
     and a flame burned all the trees of the field.

20   The beast of the field, too,
   yearns for You.
For the channels of water are dry.
   Fire consumed the wilderness meadows.

CHAPTER 2

1   Blow the ram's horn in Zion,
   sound the alarm on my holy mountain.
Let all the land's dwellers shake,
   for the day of the Lord comes, yes, nears.

2   A day of darkness and of gloom,
   a day of clouds and dense fog.
Like dawn spread out on the mountains—

---

18. *the flocks of sheep are desolate.* The verb here is another reflection of Joel's fondness for introducing double meanings through similarities of sound. The verb *ne'ashmu* would ordinarily mean "to be guilty," but it seems to be a deliberate distortion of *nashamu*, "to be desolate," thus intimating a shadow of personifying guilt in the depiction of the desolate animals.

19. *for fire consumed the wilderness meadows.* At this point, it becomes clear that another disaster, distinct from the locusts, has swept over the land. The drying out of the new grain (verse 17) and of the watercourses (verse 20) are the result of drought, and as residents of California know, in a drought the tinder-dry fields and forests are wont to catch fire.

20. *The beast of the field, too, / yearns for You.* Joel is probably recalling Psalm 42:2: "As a deer yearns for streams of water, / so I yearn for You, O God." The elided term "water," associated with God, is activated through the allusion.

CHAPTER 2   2. *Like dawn spread out on the mountains.* This is another striking poetic paradox. Dawn is a positive idea, but here the appearance of the millions of locusts

a vast and numerous people.
Its like has never been
   and after it will be none like it
      through years of generations without end.
Before it fire consumes   3
   and behind it a flame burns hot.
Like the Garden of Eden was the land before it,
   and behind it desolate desert,
      nor does anything escape it.
Like the look of horses is its look,   4
   like horsemen so they race.
Like the sound of chariots   5
   on the mountaintops they bound.
Like the sound of fiery flame
   consuming straw,
like a vast troop
   arrayed for battle.
Before it peoples tremble,   6
   all faces lose their luster.
Like warriors they race,   7
   like men of war they scale the walls.
Each goes ahead on his way
   and they do not bend their paths,
and each does not press against his fellow,   8

---

on the eastern horizon—a dark mass and not bright like the dawn—is altogether sinister, sharing with dawn only the attribute of being spread out over the mountains.

3. *Before it fire consumes / and behind it a flame burns hot.* This metaphor effects a kind of synthesis of the plague of locusts in 1:1–14 and the drought with wildfire depicted in 1:15–20. The total devastation brought about by the army of locusts is like the destruction wrought by an uncontrolled fire that reduces everything in its path to scorched earth.

4. *Like the look of horses is its look.* At this point, the poem begins a different metaphorical representation of the locusts, as an army with its cavalry racing in the vanguard.

5. *Like the sound of fiery flame.* This line of poetry splices the metaphor of wildfire into the dominant metaphor of an invading army.

6. *all faces lose their luster.* The second noun here, *pa'rur,* has been much disputed. The most likely construction, proposed in the Middle Ages by Abraham ibn Ezra, is that it is related to *pe'er,* "splendor," with a doubling of the final consonant.

7. *bend.* The Hebrew verb in question occurs only here, but the idea of making the path swerve, first proposed in Late Antiquity, seems likely.

every man goes on his road,
and through the outer wall they pounce,
     they do not suffer wounds.
9   In the town they raise a clamor,
          they race upon the walls,
     they go up in the houses,
          through the windows they come like a thief.
10   Before it the earth shudders,
          the heavens shake,
     sun and moon go dark
          and stars their radiance withdraw.
11   And the LORD sends forth His voice
          before His force,
     for very great is His camp,
          for vast are those who do His command.
     For great is the day of the LORD,
          and who can endure it?
12   And now, too, said the LORD,
          turn back to Me with all your heart,
               in fasting and weeping and mourning,
13   and rend your heart, not your garments,
          and turn back to the LORD your God,
     for He is gracious and compassionate,
          slow to anger and abounding in kindness
               and relenting over evil.

---

8. *the outer wall.* The Hebrew *shelaḥ* elsewhere can mean "weapon," and some interpreters understand it in that sense here, but a proposed Akkadian cognate indicating an outer wall may be more plausible in context.

　　suffer wounds. This translation assumes that *yivtsaʻu* is the equivalent of *yiftsaʻu,* the verb for being wounded.

9. *they go up in the houses, / through the windows they come like a thief.* Here the metaphor of an invading army segues into the actual penetrative movement of the locusts.

11. *before His force.* One must keep in mind that the locusts are not imagined as a natural phenomenon but as an army summoned by God to punish the wayward people.

13. *for He is gracious and compassionate.* The prophet here invokes the doxology of divine attributes that first appears in Exodus 34:6–7. The Book of Jonah quotes a version of this same formula.

　　relenting. The Hebrew verb means to change one's mind after having determined to follow a particular course of action.

Who knows? He may once more relent   14
   and leave blessing after Him,
      grain offering and libation to the Lord your God.
Blast the ram's horn in Zion,   15
   pronounce a fast,
      proclaim convocation.
Gather the people,   16
   dedicate an assembly,
summon the elders,
   gather the babes,
      the sucklings at the breast.
Let the bridegroom come out from his chamber
   and the bride from her wedding canopy.
Between the great hall and the altar   17
   let the priests weep,
let the Lord's ministrants say,
   "Have pity, Lord, on Your people,
and do not let Your estate be disgraced
   for nations to rule over them.
Why should they say among the peoples,
   'Where is their God?'
And let the Lord be zealous for His land   18
   and show mercy for His people."

---

14. *blessing . . . / grain offering and libation.* After neither has been possible because of the devastation of the land (1:13), the fields will return to being fruitful.

15. *Blast the ram's horn in Zion.* This picks up, word for word, the beginning of the prophecy, but now the ram's horn sounds not as an alarm but as a summons to a national convocation of penitence through which the evil will be reversed.

16. *the babes, / the sucklings at the breast.* These two versets illustrate the general poetic pattern in which the synonym in the second verset concretizes the matching term in the first verset.

   Let the bridegroom come out from his chamber. As other biblical uses of "chamber" in connection with man and woman indicate, this is the chamber in which the bridegroom consummates his marriage. But the urgency is so great that he must leave it.

   the bride from her wedding canopy. More decorously, she is linked with the wedding ceremony rather than with the marriage bed. Or perhaps we are invited to imagine that he has been waiting in the bedchamber for her to leave the canopy and join him.

17. *Have pity, Lord.* The words here, continuing through the end of verse 18, are the language of the collective supplication addressed to God in this penitential rite.

19   And the LORD answered and said to His people,
            I am about to send to you
        new grain and new wine and oil
            and you will be sated with them.
        And I will no more make you
            disgraced among the nations.
20   And the northerner I will put far from you
            and scatter him to a parched and desolate land,
        his face to the eastern sea
            and his end to the western sea.
        And his stench shall go up
            and his foul odor go up,
                for he has done enormities.
21   Do not fear, O land,
            exult and rejoice,
                for the LORD has done enormous things.
22   Do not fear, O beasts of the field,
            for the wilderness meadows sprout grass,
        for the tree yields its fruit,
            the fig tree and vine put forth their wealth.
23   And children of Zion,
            exult and rejoice
                in the LORD your God.
        For he has given you the early rain as bounty

---

20. *the northerner.* This is a slightly odd designation for the locusts, which would have come from the east and the south. It is in all likelihood influenced by the disposition throughout Prophetic poetry to see invaders as descending from the north.

the eastern sea. This is the Dead Sea.

the western sea. This is the Mediterranean.

for he has done enormities. Very literally, this would be "for he has greatly done." Some think it refers to God, but, coming as it does at the end of the description of the rotting hordes of locusts, it more likely refers to the terrible destruction they have caused which now brings about their own deserved extinction.

21. *for the LORD has done enormous things.* The same phrase is used again, but now in an antithetical sense: God has "greatly done" in reversing the destruction wrought by the locusts.

22. *the wilderness meadows sprout grass.* Now the ravaged fields and plantations are restored to fruitfulness.

23. *as bounty.* Although the Hebrew *tsedaqah* usually means "righteousness," it also has this sense (compare, for example, Judges 5:11, "His bounties [*tsidqot*] for unwalled cities in Israel"), and that meaning is the apt one here.

and brought down the rain for you,
    early rain and latter rain as before.
And the threshing floors shall fill with grain   24
    and the vats overflow with new wine and oil.
And I will pay you back for the years   25
    that the grasshopper ate,
        the swarmer, the grub, and the locust,
My great force that I sent against you.
And you shall eat, be continuously sated,   26
    and you shall praise the name of the LORD your God
Who has done wondrously for you,
    and My people shall not be shamed evermore.
And you shall know that I am in the midst of Israel,   27
    and I am the LORD your God, there is none else,
        and My people shall not be shamed evermore.

CHAPTER 3   And it shall happen afterward: 1

I will pour My spirit upon all flesh,
    and your sons and your daughters shall prophesy.
Your elders shall dream dreams,
    your young men see visions.
And even upon male slaves and slavegirls   2

---

as before. The received text has *bari'shon,* "in the first," but one Hebrew manuscript and three ancient versions show *kari'shon,* "as before."

25. *the grasshopper . . . / the swarmer, the grub, and the locust.* The prophet now recapitulates the initial list of different kinds of locust, although in a different order.

26. *and My people shall not be shamed evermore.* This grand pronouncement, repeated in the next verse at the very end of this prophecy is an incipiently eschatological flourish: after the ghastly devastation of the land, the people return with all their hearts to God, upon which He undertakes to grant them a splendidly restored prosperity and security that will never again be interrupted.

CHAPTER 3   1. *And it shall happen afterward.* Rashi, Kimchi, and most modern interpreters take this to be an indication of the end-time, but it is a rather quotidian expression, as if one were to say "the day after tomorrow" or "in a month or so." Could it be an indication that Joel thought the end-time was very close?

2. *And even upon male slaves and slavegirls.* There is, then, to be no social limitation to the gift of prophecy—it will envelop all.

in those days will I pour My spirit.

3   And I will set portents in the heavens and on earth,
           blood and fire and columns of smoke.
4   The sun shall turn into darkness
           and the moon into blood
       before the coming of the day of the LORD,
           great and fearful.

5   And all who call in the name of the LORD shall escape. For on Mount Zion
there shall be a remnant, as the LORD has said, in the survivors whom the
LORD calls.

1   CHAPTER 4   For, look, days are coming and that time when
I will restore the fortunes of Judah and Jerusalem.

2   And I will gather all the nations
               and bring them down to the Valley of Jehoshaphat
           and come to judgment with them there
               over My people and Israel, My estate,

---

3. *blood and fire and columns of smoke.* What begins as an ostensibly benign vouchsafing
of prophecy to all here turns violent and, indeed, ominous.

4. *The sun shall turn into darkness.* Even though this seems to be the prediction of a solar
eclipse, it is clearly represented as a frightening supernatural event.

   and the moon into blood. Under certain atmospheric conditions, the moon does have
a reddish appearance but, again this is imagined as a supernatural occurrence—blood in
the sky answering to the blood and fire on earth, harbinger of the terrifying "day of the
LORD" that is invoked in the next line of poetry.

5. *And all who call in the name of the LORD shall escape.* The vision becomes properly
apocalyptic, a reflection of Joel's Late Biblical location. As in the conclusion of the Book
of Daniel, there will be a great cataclysm in which many will perish and only the elect who
cling to God will be saved.

   the survivors whom the LORD calls. Some interpreters, with an eye to the beginning of
the verse, understand this as "the survivors who call to the LORD." The verb, however, is
in the singular, and the prophet is probably registering a familiar biblical idea that when
people call sincerely to God, He will call to them in return.

CHAPTER 4   2. *the Valley of Jehoshaphat.* The name means "The LORD judges,"
and the prophet immediately plays on *shafat,* "judges," as he says "come to judgment,"
nishpateti.

> whom they scattered among the nations,
>> and they divided up their land.
> And over My people they cast lots   3
>> and bartered a boy for the price of a whore
>>> and sold a girl for wine which they drank.
> And also what are you to Me, Tyre and Sidon   4
>> and all the provinces of Philistia?
> Are you paying back against Me?
>> If you are paying back against Me,
>>> swiftly, quick will I pay it back on your head.
> As My silver and My gold you took,   5
>> and My goodly treasures you brought to your palaces,
> and the people of Judah and the people of Jerusalem   6
>> you sold to the Greeks
>>> to put them far from their frontiers.
> I am about to raise them from the place   7
>> where you sold them
>>> and pay you back upon your head.

---

3. *bartered a boy for the price of a whore / and sold a girl for wine.* The captive Judahite children are treated as cheap merchandise, sold for the price of a quick bout of sex or a flask of wine.

4. *Tyre and Sidon / . . . Philistia.* In this concluding prophecy, Joel casts his net of condemnation over most of the surrounding nations—the Phoenicians to the north, the Philistines (in fact, no longer a political entity) on the southern strip of the Mediterranean coast, and, farther on, Egypt to the south and Edom to the east. No mention is made of Persia or any great eastern empire.

5. *My silver and My gold.* The reference is to the treasures of the Temple. The despoliation of the Temple was perpetrated by the Babylonians in 586 B.C.E., which would have been considerably before Joel's probable time. It seems that he has bundled together exile, exploitation, and the remembered plunder of the Temple as an amalgam of the victimization of Judah by the sundry nations.

6. *sold to the Greeks.* Some interpreters take this as an indication that Joel wrote after the conquest of the Near East by Alexander the Great in the late fourth century B.C.E. This is not a necessary inference because there were trading connections with the Greeks earlier, and Greece, *yawan* ("Ion"), is mentioned as a known entity in the Table of Nations in Genesis 10.

7. *I am about to raise them from the place / where you sold them.* Joel is presumably prophesying in Judah to a Judahite audience at some point after the return to Zion in the middle of the fifth century B.C.E. There was, however, a substantial diaspora population in this Second Temple period, and it is this that he appears to have in mind.

8   And I will sell your sons and your daughters
        into the hands of the Judahites,
   and they shall sell their captives to a distant nation.
        For the Lord has spoken.

9   Proclaim this among the nations,
        assemble for battle.
   Raise the warriors,
        let all the men of war
           come forth, go up.
10   Grind your plowshares into swords
        and your pruning hooks into spears.
          The weak shall say: I am a warrior.
11   Hasten and come,
        all nations round about, and gather.
          There bring down, O Lord, your warriors.
12   The nations shall be roused and come up
        to the Valley of Jehoshaphat.
   For there will I sit to judge
        all the nations round about.
13   Wield the sickle,
        for the harvest is ripe.
   Come, go down,
        for the winepress is full.
   The vats overflow,
        for their evil is great.

---

9. *assemble for battle.* This has the look of an apocalyptic war, when a final reckoning will be made with all the nations.

10. *Grind your plowshares into swords / and your pruning hooks into spears.* This is an obvious—and grim—reversal of the famous verse in Isaiah 2:4 that envisions a wondrous era of peace.
     The weak shall say: I am a warrior. This has a double meaning of "I am mighty."

11. *There bring down, O Lord, your warriors.* The meaning of this line—especially the verb—is somewhat uncertain.

12. *the Valley of Jehoshaphat, / . . . sit to judge.* The same play on the "judge" component of the name as in verse 2 is evident here.

13. *for their evil is great.* Only at the end of these three lines of poetry does it become clear that the ripe harvest, the full winepress, and the overflowing vats are allegorical figures

Crowds upon crowds   14
　　in the Valley of Doom,
for near is the day of the LORD
　　in the Valley of Doom.
Sun and moon go dark   15
　　and the stars withdraw their light.
And the LORD from Zion roars   16
　　and from Jerusalem sounds His voice,
　　　　and the heavens and the earth shudder.
But the LORD is a refuge to His people.
　　and a stronghold to the Israelites.
And you shall know that I am the LORD your God   17
　　Who dwells in Zion, My holy nation,
and Jerusalem shall be holy,
　　no more shall strangers pass through it.
And it shall happen on that day: 18
　　the mountains shall drip fermented juice
　　　　and the hills run with milk
　　and all the channels of Judah
　　　　run with water.
And a spring shall issue from the house of the LORD
　　and water the Wadi of Acacias.
Egypt shall become a desolation   19
　　and Edom a desolate wilderness

---

for the harvest of death that is about to be reaped in retribution for the evil the nations have done.

14. *the Valley of Doom.* The verbal stem *ḥ-r-ts*, appearing here in the name *ḥaruts*, means to pronounce judgment or issue a verdict. It seems to be a poetic synonym for the Valley of Jehoshaphat.

17. *no more shall strangers pass through it.* In Joel's historical moment, this may indicate the status of the province of Yehud as a vassal entity within the Persian empire, lacking the autonomy to exclude foreigners. Joel might also be harking back to memories of the conquest of Jerusalem by the Babylonians.

18. *the mountains shall drip fermented juice / and the hills run with milk.* Joel is recalling Amos 9:13, although he changes the second verset. In Amos it is: "and all the hills shall melt." The entire verse here runs the gamut of sustaining liquids, from wine to milk to water.
　　And a spring shall issue from the house of the LORD. This appears to be a direct reference to the miraculous spring gushing forth from the Temple in Ezekiel 47.

for the outrage done to the Judahites
    in whose land they shed the blood of the innocent.

20   And Judah shall be settled forever
    and Jerusalem for all generations.

21   Shall I acquit for their blood? I will not acquit.
    And the LORD dwells in Zion.

---

20. *Judah shall be settled forever.* This marks a strong antithesis to the desolation of Egypt and Edom in the preceding verse.

21. *Shall I acquit for their blood? I will not acquit.* The formulation is cryptic and has engendered different understandings. The assumption reflected in this translation is that "their blood" refers back to "the blood of the innocent" in verse 19. The first clause here is then construed as a rhetorical question. God will certainly not acquit those who have shed the blood of His innocent people—Judah will dwell peacefully for all time, but those who once victimized it will remain an eternal desolation.

Amos

CHAPTER 1   The words of Amos, who was among the sheep- 1
breeders of Tekoa, who saw visions concerning Israel in the days of Uzziah
king of Judah and in the days of Jeroboam son of Joash king of Israel, two
years before the earthquake. And he said: 2

> The LORD from Zion roars
>   and from Jerusalem puts forth His voice,
> and the shepherds' meadows wither,
>   and the peak of Carmel dries up.
> Thus said the LORD: 3
> For three trespasses of Damascus

CHAPTER 1   1. *Tekoa.* This is a village in the vicinity of Jerusalem. There is no
evidence for a Tekoa in the north, although some scholars have sought to place Amos
there because he later identifies himself as a trimmer of sycamore trees, not known to be
cultivated in the southern region. The case remains convincing that Amos was a Judahite
who undertook a prophetic mission to the northern kingdom.

two years before the earthquake. This was obviously a well-remembered event. There is
some archaeological evidence for such a seismic event around 770 B.C.E. or slightly later.
It is not clear whether Amos's prophesying begins or ends then, though beginning may be
more likely.

3. *For three trespasses of Damascus / and for four.* In context, *pesha ʿaim* means something
like "atrocities" or "crimes against humanity," but this translation respects the stylistic
decorum of the Hebrew, which hews to general terms that may take on a distinctive coloration according to context. There are neither three nor four trespasses listed here that
a reader can count. Rather, this is a common biblical idiom, occurring several times in
Proverbs, with the sense, "a certain few, and even one more." Because the three and four
together add up to a formulaic seven, some have proposed that they indicate a totality.
There is no way of knowing whether these dire prophecies about the surrounding nations
were actually the beginning of Amos's message, but they certainly would have provided
a means of drawing in the Israelite audience with something they wanted to hear before
the prophet launched on a denunciation of that very audience. The formulaic repetition of
these lines for one nation after another generates a kind of hypnotic drumbeat.

and for four I will not turn it back—
for their threshing Gilead
    with iron threshing boards.
4 And I will set fire to the house of Hazael,
    and it shall consume the citadels of Ben-Hadad,
5 and I will break the bolt of Damascus
    and cut off dwellers from Aven Vale
        and him who holds the scepter from Beth-Eden.
And the peoples of Aram shall be exiled to Kir, said the LORD.
6 Thus said the LORD:
For three trespasses of Gaza
    and for four I will not turn it back—
for their inflicting a total exile
    to hand over to Edom.
7 And I will set fire to Gaza's wall,
    and it shall consume her citadels.
8 And I will cut off dwellers from Ashdod
    and him who holds the scepter from Ashkelon,
and I will bring My hand against Ekron,
    and the Philistines' remnant shall perish.
9 Thus said the LORD:
For three trespasses of Tyre
    and for four I will not turn it back—
for their inflicting a total exile,

I will not turn it back. The object of the verb is left unspecified, perhaps deliberately and ominously, but it would have to be something like "retribution" or "wrath."

Gilead. This is an area in the northeastern sector of the kingdom of Israel.

4. *the house of Hazael.* Hazael and Ben-Hadad designate the royal house of Aram, the capital of which is Damascus.

5. *break the bolt.* The bolt is the heavy iron bar that secures the gates of the city.

Kir. This is a city in the far north, perhaps near Armenia.

6. *Gaza.* In Amos's time, Gaza was the principal Philistine city, though three others are mentioned in the following lines. The view has now swung from north to south.

for their inflicting a total exile. The identity of those exiled is unspecified. In any case, uprooting an entire population means putting an end to its national existence and hence is viewed as a war crime.

9. *Tyre.* This is the principal Phoenician city, so the perspective moves north again, along the Mediterranean coast.

handing over to Edom,
> and they did not recall the pact of brothers.
And I will set fire to Tyre's wall 10
> and it shall consume her citadels.
Thus said the LORD: 11
> For three trespasses of Edom,
> > and for four I will not turn it back—
for his pursuing his brothers with the sword
> and stifling his compassion,
and he bore a grudge ceaselessly
> and kept up his wrath unending.
And I will set a fire in Teman, 12
> and it shall consume the citadels of Bosra.
Thus said the LORD: 13
For three trespasses of the Ammonites
> and for four I will not turn it back—
for their splitting open the pregnant women of Gilead
> so as to expand their borders.
And I will light a fire on the wall of Rabbah, 14
> and it shall consume her citadels
with trumpet blast on the day of battle
> and with a storm on the tempest day.
And their king shall go into exile, 15
> he and his nobles together
> —said the LORD.

---

11. *Edom.* Now we are in the southeast, across the Jordan.

his brothers. Since Esau, Jacob's brother, is the purported ancestor of the Edomites, the Israelites would be their "brothers."

stifling his compassion. Because of the unusual verb, which usually means "lay ruins to" or "destroy," some scholars have suggested that the phrase has the sense of "destroying his [Israel's] wombs," an alternative term for splitting open pregnant women.

bore a grudge. The Masoretic Text reads *wayitrof . . . 'apo,* "and his anger ravaged," but three ancient versions reflect *wayitor* (dropping the last consonant of the verb), and Jeremiah 3:5 shows precisely this poetic parallelism of *n-t-r / sh-m-r.*

13. *so as to expand their borders.* This is an explanation for the savagery perpetrated on the pregnant women. Not only are they murdered, but their offspring are as well, so there will be no one left in the future to lay claim to the territory. This looks very much like genocide.

14. *Rabbah.* The capital city of Ammon.

¹ CHAPTER 2   Thus said the Lord:

For three trespasses of Moab,
 and for four, I will not turn it back—
  for his burning the bones of Edom's king into lime.
² And I will set fire to Moab,
 and it shall consume the citadels of Kerioth,
and Moab shall die in an uproar,
 in shouts and the sound of the ram's horn.
³ And I will cut off the leader from her midst
 and all her nobles I will slay with him
  —said the Lord.
⁴ For three trespasses of Judah,
 and for four, I will not turn it back—
for their spurning the Lord's teaching,
 and His statutes they did not keep,
and their false things led them astray,
 after which their fathers had gone.
⁵ And I will set a fire in Judah,
 and it shall consume Jerusalem's citadels.
⁶ Thus said the Lord:
For three trespasses of Israel,
 and for four, I will not turn it back—
for their selling the just man for silver

CHAPTER 2   1. *burning the bones.* Desecrating a corpse was seen as a violation of human dignity and thus is included in the list of war crimes.

4. *For three trespasses of Judah.* While some scholars claim that the introduction of Judah is a later editorial interpolation, it makes perfect sense that this Judahite prophet, moving from pronouncements of doom on the surrounding nations to Israel, would include a denunciation of the trespasses of his own kingdom before arriving at his main target, the northern kingdom of Israel.

 their false things. This is an epithet for idols, which makes this a very different kind of transgression from the crimes against humanity. Some see here Deuteronomistic language, thus attributing this text to a much later date than that of Amos, but this identification is not convincing, even if the anti-idolatry theme resembles Deuteronomy.

6. *for their selling the just man for silver / and the needy for sandals.* When Amos turns to the transgressions of Israel, his concern is injustice and exploitation of the vulnerable. Coming after the catalogue of crimes against humanity perpetrated by the surrounding nations, perversions of justice are in effect also represented as crimes against humanity. "The just man," *tsadiq,* may here carry its legal sense—the person who deserved to be declared right, given justice, in a court of law. In that case, selling him for silver would mean taking a bribe

and the needy for sandals.
Who trample the head of the needy   7
   in the dust of the ground
     and pervert the way of the poor.
And a man and his father go to the same girl
   to profane My holy name.
And on pawned garments they stretch out,   8
   alongside every altar,
and wine bought with funds from fines
   they drink in the house of their God.
Yet I had destroyed the Amorite before them,   9
   who is tall as the height of cedars
     and sturdy as the oaks.
And I destroyed his fruit above
   and his roots below.
And I brought you up from the land of Egypt   10
   and led you in the wilderness forty years.
     to take hold of the Amorite's land.
And I raised up from your sons to be prophets   11
   and from your men to be nazirites.
     Is it not so, O Israelites ? said the Lord.
But you gave the nazirites wine to drink   12
   and to the prophets you charged, "Prophesy not!"

---

so that he is given an unfavorable ruling. Selling the needy for sandals means selling such a person—perhaps into slavery—for something of relatively minor value.

7. *a man and his father go to the same girl.* One understanding that has had considerable currency is that they both go to the same cult-prostitute, but this is not certain. The word for "girl," *na'arah*, means "a nubile young woman," with no special indication of her profession or sexual activity. The choice of the term here is pointed: a *na'arah* could conceivably be an appropriate sexual partner for a young man, but a son and father sharing her is an abomination—in fact, a kind of incest.

9. *Yet I had destroyed the Amorite before them.* Israel has done all these unspeakable acts even though historically it was the beneficiary of God's manifest generosity that enabled it, against all odds, to conquer the land.

who is tall as the height of cedars. The gigantic stature of the Canaanites is registered in Numbers 13 and elsewhere.

12. *But you gave the nazirites wine to drink.* The nazirites take a vow of abstention from alcohol, thus constituting a kind of elite of holiness within the people. The likely motive for giving them wine is not sheer perversity but reflects an indiscriminate abuse of alcohol in the Israelite population, of the sort Isaiah would denounce a few decades after Amos.

13   I am about to halt you where you are
                as the wagon overflowing with grain halts.
14   And flight shall elude the swift,
                and the strong shall not summon his power,
                        and the warrior shall not escape with his life.
15   And the bowman shall not stand,
                and the fleet-footed shall not escape,
                        and the horseman shall not escape with his life.
16   And whose heart is staunch among the warriors
                naked shall flee on that day—said the LORD.

1   CHAPTER 3   Hear this word that the LORD has spoken concerning you, O Israelites, concerning the entire clan that I brought up from
Egypt, saying:

2   Only with you was I intimate
                of all the clans of the earth.
           Therefore will I make a reckoning with you
                for all your crimes.

---

13. *halt you.* Although this Hebrew verb would later mean something like "to weigh down," its likely biblical sense is "to bring to a stop, to impede."

14. *And flight shall elude the swift.* The failure of flight follows directly from the "halting" of the previous line. The three lines of poetry beginning here—the first two are triadic—are all the more effective as a representation of a catastrophe overtaking the nation because there is no direct mention of an invading army: all we see is the swift and the strong and the martially skilled in the army of Israel flailing and unable to escape.

15. *the horseman shall not escape with his life.* The whole line exhibits a striking pattern of intensification from one verset to the next. First, the stationary bowman is unable to withstand the onslaught of the enemy; then, the swift-footed soldier is not fast enough to escape; finally, even the horseman on his mount cannot get away.

16. *naked shall flee on that day.* While the literal sense of "naked" is possible, the likely meaning is that the brave warrior, now terrified by the overwhelming force of the enemy, will strip himself of his armor and throw away his weapons in order to flee.

CHAPTER 3   1. *clan.* The Hebrew *mishpaḥah* slides from a clan proper to larger groups. It may be used here to underscore the mutual belonging of the Israelites.

2. *was I intimate.* The literal sense of the verb is "know," which famously has in some contexts a sexual connotation but here is employed to suggest a special close relationship.

Do two walk together   3
    if they have not first agreed?
Does the lion roar in the forest   4
    unless it has taken prey?
Does the maned beast put forth its voice from its lair
    if it has not made a catch?
Does a bird fall into a trap on the ground   5
    when there is no snare for it?
Does a trap spring up from the soil
    and fail to make a catch?
Is the ram's horn sounded in the town   6
    and the people do not tremble?
Is there harm within the town
    and the LORD has not done it?

For the Master, the LORD, does nothing without revealing His secret to His   7
servants, the prophets.

A lion roars   8
    Who does not fear?
The Master, the LORD, speaks.
    Who cannot prophesy?

---

3. *Do two walk together.* These words initiate an extended anaphoric series arriving at a compelling conclusion that will not be revealed until verse 8. Everything in nature and in human affairs exhibits a pattern of cause and effect, including the call to prophecy.

4. *Does the lion roar in the forest.* It should be observed that all of the instances cited involve either the inspiring of fear or the creating of an entrapment: the call to prophecy is scary, and it locks the person called in a trap.

6. *Is the ram's horn sounded in the town.* The shrill piercing notes of the ram's horn were used to sound the alarm in moments of military crisis.
    Is there harm within the town / and the LORD has not done it? God is introduced at the end of the series, preparing the ground for the introduction of prophecy.

7. *For the Master, the LORD.* This prose verse breaks the poetic series and, in the way it makes explicit the point of all the images, it looks like an editorial interpolation.

8. *A lion roars. / Who does not fear?* The poem in this way loops back to its beginning, making an envelope structure. Then God and prophecy will be added in the next line.
    The Master, the LORD, speaks. / Who cannot prophesy? This is an idea invoked by other prophets—most strikingly, by Jeremiah. Prophecy is not experienced as a choice. The prophet feels it as an overwhelming imperative coming from God.

9 Let it be heard in the citadels of Ashdod and in the citadels of the land of
Egypt, and say: Gather on the mountains of Samaria and see the many
upheavals within it and the oppressed in its midst.

10   And they do not know how to do what is right, said the Lord, who store
up outrage and plunder in their citadels.

11   Therefore, thus said the Master, the Lord:

> A foe goes round the land.
> > He shall take down from you your strength,
> > > and your citadels shall be despoiled.

12   Thus said the Lord:
> > As the shepherd may save
> > > from the lion's mouth
> two shank bones or an earlobe,
> > so shall Israel be saved.
> You who sit in Samaria
> > by the head of a bed or at the end of a couch,

13   listen and bear witness against the house of Jacob,
> > said the Master, the Lord God of Israel.

14   For on the day I make a reckoning
> > for Israel's trespasses
> I will make a reckoning with the altars of Bethel
> > and the horns of the altar shall be hacked off,

---

9. *Let it be heard in the citadels of Ashdod and in the citadels of the land of Egypt.* Philistia and Egypt are summoned to serve as witnesses of the shame of Samaria.

10. *who store up outrage and plunder.* An expressive ellipsis is put into play: what the Israelites store up in their citadels is the ill-gotten wealth amassed from acts of outrage and plunder. After the prose introduction of verses 9 and 10, the prophecy swings back into poetry, beginning with "A foe goes round the land."

11. *A foe goes round the land.* The received text reads *tsar wesaviv,* "a foe and around." This translation presupposes an emendation to *tsar yesoveiv.*

12. *save / from the lion's mouth.* The verb here incorporates the sense of "to pull out from."
   so shall Israel be saved. Only a few bloody scraps will be left.
   the head of a bed or at the end of a couch. There are philological grounds for thinking that the first term, *pe'ah,* means "head of the bed" here (elsewhere, it means "corner"). The second term is obscure, and so the translation leans on the poetic parallelism. Sitting on the bed may allude to the indolence of the aristocrats of the northern kingdom.

14. *the horns of the altar.* The four corners of altars had hornlike protuberances, symbolic of power.

and they shall fall to the ground.
And I will strike down the winter house   15
  together with the summer house,
and the houses of ivory shall be destroyed
  and the great houses swept away
    —said the Lord.

CHAPTER 4

Listen to this word,   1
  you cows of Bashan who are on Mount Samaria,
who exploit the poor,
  who crush the needy,
who say to their husbands,
  "Bring, that we may drink."
The Master, the Lord, has sworn by His holiness   2
  that days are coming upon you
when you shall be borne off in baskets
  and the last of you with fishhooks,

---

15. *the winter house / together with the summer house.* Many think these are the winter and summer palaces of the king, but members of the wealthy class could well have enjoyed such luxuries.

the houses of ivory. The houses were not built of ivory but decorated inside with ornamental ivory panels, some of which have been unearthed by archaeologists.

the great houses. The adjective here usually means "many" but can also mean "great," and the target of the destruction is clearly not the habitations of the general populace but the grand homes of the aristocracy.

CHAPTER 4   1. *you cows of Bashan who are on Mount Samaria.* The region of Bashan was famous for its cattle, but these well-fed cows are in Samaria. The prophet addresses the women with this vitriolic epithet not because they are fat but because all they do is indolently satisfy their appetite, like cows grazing in a pasture. It should be noted that because Hebrew verbs are conjugated according to gender, all the verbs that follow remind us of the female identity of those excoriated.

Bring, that we may drink. The pampered wives of Samaria are worse than cows because they have an appetite not only for nutrients, like their bovine counterparts, but for wine.

2. *baskets / ... fishhooks.* Both Hebrew words occur only here. Some scholars think both are terms for baskets used by fishermen; others think both are kinds of hooks.

3   and through the breaches each woman shall go out straight ahead,
              and you shall be flung on the refuse heap—said the LORD.

4   Come to Bethel and trespass,
              to Gilgal and continue to trespass,
         and bring the next morning your sacrifices
              and on the third day your tithes.
5   And burn a thanksgiving offering of leavened bread
              and proclaim freewill offerings, make them heard.
         For so have you loved,
              O Israelites—said the Master, the LORD.
6   And I on My part have given you
              cleanness of teeth in all your towns
                   and want of bread in all your places,
         but you did not come back to Me,
              said the LORD.
7   And I on My part withheld from you the rain
              with still three months till the harvest,
         and I rained on one town
              but on another town did not rain.

---

3. *through the breaches.* The use of this noun implies that the walls of the city have been broken through by invaders.

   the refuse heap. The meaning of the Hebrew *harmon* is uncertain, and it could even be a place-name. This translation adopts one scholarly conjecture.

4. *Come to Bethel and trespass.* This verse and the next are strongly sarcastic. None of the ritual acts mentioned, to be performed at the two principal cult centers of the northern kingdom, is in itself illegitimate, but the offense is in going through the steps of ritual when the worshippers have been exploiting the poor, perverting justice, and wallowing in ill-gotten gains. Amos is not expressing a principle of opposition to the cult but, like Isaiah after him, is objecting to the conjunction of what Isaiah calls "crime and convocation," of approaching the altar with hands stained with blood.

6. *cleanness of teeth.* This is an original coinage of Amos's. It of course does not have anything to do with dental hygiene but evokes a mouth in which there is no food, as "want of bread" in the next verset makes clear. The line reverses the usual pattern, in which the standard term appears in the first verset and a metaphorical or poetic equivalent in the second, because the prophet means to confront his audience with a small enigma at the beginning of the line that is spelled out at the end.

7. *with still three months till the harvest.* Lack of rain three months before the harvest would be devastating for the crops.

   I rained on one town / but on another town did not rain. It is unclear whether such selective distribution of rainfall could have actually occurred, but the prophet's statement of

One field would have rain,
    but the field without rain would dry up.
And two or three towns would wander   8
    to a single town to drink water,
        and would not slake their thirst.
But you did not turn back to Me, said the LORD.
I struck you with blight and with mildew.   9
    Ruins were your gardens and your vineyards,
and your fig trees and your olive trees the locusts devoured.
    But you did not turn back to Me, said the LORD.
I let loose the pestilence against you as in Egypt.   10
    I slew your young men by the sword with your captured horses
        and made your camps' stench rise in your very nostrils.
But you did not turn back to Me, said the LORD.
I overthrew you   11
    as God overthrew Sodom and Gomorrah,
and you became like a brand saved from burning.
    But you did not turn back to Me, said the LORD.
Therefore, this will I do to you, Israel,   12
    because this will I do to you,
        prepare to meet your God, O Israel.
For, look, He fashions the mountains and creates the wind   13
    and tells man what is his thought,
turns dawn into darkness

---

it is meant to convey the idea that God exercises absolute power to bless or blight human populations according to His will.

9. *Ruins were your gardens.* The Masoretic Text reads *harbot,* "to multiply," which does not make much sense. This translation is based on an emendation of that word to *ḥorvot,* "ruins."

10. *with your captured horses.* This phrase suggests that the "young men" are fighters who have been defeated in battle, their mounts taken by the victors and they themselves put to the sword.

11. *overthrew.* This is a set verb beginning with the account in Genesis 19 of the destruction of Sodom and Gomorrah for the total devastation of a town or a nation.

13. *For, look, He fashions the mountains and creates the wind.* The doxology of this concluding verse is continuous with what precedes: the powerful God that Israel must prepare to meet is the cosmic Creator Who controls all the forces of the earth. This verset makes strategic use of the verbs for creation that appear, respectively, in Genesis 2 and 1: for the solid mountains the potter's concrete word "fashion," *yotser,* is used; for the wind, the more spiritual *borei',* "create."

and treads on the earth's high places.
The Lord God of Armies is His name.

1 CHAPTER 5 Listen to this word that I bear about you as a dirge, O house of Israel.

2   She has fallen, no more shall rise,
           the Virgin of Israel.
        She is abandoned on her soil,
           none lifts her up.
3   For thus said the Master the Lord:
           The town that goes out a thousand
               shall be left a hundred
           and that goes out a hundred
               shall be left ten—for the house of Israel.
4   For thus said the Lord to the house of Israel:
        Seek Me and live
5   and seek not Bethel
        and to Gilgal do not come
           and to Beersheba do not pass on.
        For Gilgal shall go in exile
           and Bethel shall turn into evil.
6   Seek the Lord and live,
           lest the house of Joseph flare like fire
               and consume Bethel with none to quench it.

CHAPTER 5   2. *She is abandoned on her soil.* This wording suggests that the kingdom has been conquered and Israel is now left on her own soil at the mercy of the invaders.

3. *The town that goes out a thousand.* This might suggest a military sortie because the verb "go out" is sometimes used in that sense, but this is not entirely certain here.

5. *Bethel / . . . Gilgal . . . / Beersheba.* The first two, as noted above, are the principal cultic sites of the northern kingdom. Beersheba is far to the south, hence the need to "pass on" (through the kingdom of Judah). It would seem that some sort of cult was conducted at Beersheba, but we have scant information about it.

    Gilgal shall go into exile...Bethel . . . evil. The Hebrew sound-play is *hagilgal galoh yigaleh* and *beit-'el . . . 'awen.*

6. *flare.* This Hebrew verb generally is used for the "descent" of the spirit, but perhaps it also indicates any kind of sudden movement.

You who turn justice into wormwood   7
   and righteousness bring to the ground—

He makes the Pleiades and Orion   8
   and turns death's darkness into morning
      and day He darkens to night,
  calls to the waters of the sea
     and pours them over the land.
        The LORD is His name.
He flashes destruction on the strong,   9
   and destruction comes down on the fortress.

They hated the reprover in the gate,   10
   and the truth speaker they despised.
Therefore, as you trampled upon the poor man,   11
   and a payment of grain you exacted from him,
hewn-stone houses you have built,
   but you shall not dwell in them.
Lovely vineyards you have planted,
   but you shall not drink their wine.
For I know that your trespasses are many   12
   and numerous your offenses—
foes of the righteous, takers of bribes,
   you pervert the needy's case in the gate.
Therefore the prudent on that day shall fall silent,   13
   for it is an evil time.
Seek good and not evil,   14
   that you may live.

---

7. *You who turn justice into wormwood.* This prophecy appears to break off after these two versets, which lack a predicate.

8. *He makes the Pleiades and Orion.* These words begin another doxology celebrating God's greatness, but it manifestly interrupts the castigation of Israel of the preceding lines, which is resumed again in verse 10. This makes it look suspiciously like an editorial glitch.

10. *the reprover in the gate.* The square in front of the city gate was where courts of justice were held (compare verse 15) and it would also be an appropriate setting for the prophet to reprove or harangue the people.

11. *hewn-stone houses.* These are grand houses, which have already been the subject of Amos's ire (3:15).

> And so may the Lord God of Armies be with you,
>> as you have said.
15
> Hate evil and love good
>> and set out justice in the gate.
> Perhaps the Lord God of Israel
>> may grant grace to Joseph's remnant.

16
> Therefore thus said the Lord,
>> the God of Israel, the Master:
> In all the squares—lament,
>> and in all the streets they say "alas."
> And they shall call the farmer to mourning,
>> and to lament, those expert in weeping.
17
> And in all the vineyards there is wailing
>> as I pass in your midst, said the Lord.

18
> Woe, who long for the day of the Lord!
>> Why should you need the day of the Lord?
>>> It is darkness and not light.
19
> As a man flees from a lion
>> and a bear blocks his way,
> and he enters the house
>> and leans his hand on the wall,
>>> and a snake bites him.

---

16. *And they shall call the farmer to mourning, / and to lament, those expert in weeping.* The idea of summoning the farmers to join in the mourning may be meant to indicate that the entire people, not just the inhabitants of the towns, will be involved. The line exhibits a neat chiastic structure—farmer (a), mourning (b), lament (b′), those expert in weeping (a′). The second group would be professional keeners, who are usually women—although the verb here is masculine.

18. *Woe, who long for the day of the Lord.* The background to this idea must be inferred. It appears to be a popular eschatological belief that a grand era is coming when God will elevate Israel and make it triumphant among the nations. Some of the later prophecies of national restoration—as, for example, in Second Isaiah—may have drawn on such traditions of folk belief. In any case, Amos makes emphatically clear that such expectations are a delusion and that the day of the Lord will be a day of dire retribution for Israel's sins.

19. *a bear blocks his way.* The verb can mean "meet" or "encounter" but also "strike" or "attack." Since, however, the man escapes the bear and makes it to his house, it does not seem that the bear actually assaults him.

Why, the day of the LORD is darkness and not light,   20
   pitch black, and no radiance in it.

I hate, I spurn your festivals   21
   and smell no fragrance in your convocations.
Should you offer up to Me burnt offerings   22
   or grain offerings, I will not accept them;
      nor will I look on the well-being sacrifice of your fatted calves.
Take away from me the noise of your singers,   23
   nor will I listen to the melody of your lutes.
But let justice well up like water   24
   and righteousness like a steady stream.
Did you bring Me sacrifices and grain offering   25
   in the wilderness forty years, house of Israel?
And you shall bear away Sikkuth your king and Kiyyun,   26
   your icons, your star gods that you made for yourselves,
and I will exile you beyond Damascus,   27
   said the LORD, God of Israel in His name.

---

21. *I hate, I spurn your festivals.* As before, God's revulsion from the Israelite cult is because it is conducted by people whose moral behavior is vicious.

   smell no fragrance. The Hebrew says merely "I will not smell." The incense burned on the altar and the burnt offerings themselves were thought—perhaps literally—to be a pleasing fragrance to the LORD.

23. *the noise of your singers, / . . . the melody of your lutes.* The prophet now moves from smell to sound: both vocal music (the chorus of the Levites) and instrumental music were part of the Temple service.

24. *like water / . . . like a steady stream.* The simile of water of course expresses the idea of an uninterrupted and abundant flow of justice, but it is also associated with a process of cleaning after the morally contaminated odors and music of the suspect cult.

25. *in the wilderness forty years.* As with later prophets—most notably, Jeremiah—the Wilderness era is imagined as a kind of idyll, when God and Israel were secluded together.

26. *Sikkuth . . . Kiyyun.* These are actual deities, initially Assyrian and later taken over by the Babylonians. The vocalization of both names has been deliberately distorted by the Masoretes to make them sound like *shiqutz,* "abomination." The original names were Sakkut and Keivan.

   your king. This is surely sarcastic.

27. *I will exile you beyond Damascus.* This is somewhere unspecified, far to the northeast. In fact, when the inhabitants of the northern kingdom were exiled by the Assyrians in 721 B.C.E., this was the general direction in which they were taken.

CHAPTER 6

1   Woe, you complacent in Zion
               and you trusting ones on Mount Samaria,
         eminent among the first of nations,
               and the house of Israel came to them.
2   Pass on to Calneh and see,
               and go from there to great Hammath,
                    and go down to the Philistines' Gath.
         Are you better than these kingdoms,
               is your territory larger than theirs?
3   You who dismiss the evil day
               but bring on disaster and outrage;
4   who lie on ivory-inlaid beds
               and lounge on their couches
         and eat the lambs from the flock
               and calves from the stall,
5   who pluck on the lute,

CHAPTER 6   1. *you complacent in Zion.* The reference to Zion—which is to say, Jerusalem, the capital of the southern kingdom—is something of a puzzle because Amos's mission has been to the northern kingdom. Some scholars want to see this as the interpolation of the Judahite editor, but if one removes this verset, there is no longer a line of parallelistic poetry. We should not exclude the possibility that Amos had in view a similar group of smugly self-satisfied people in his home kingdom, even if he was addressing a northern audience.

the first of nations. This appears to be a designation—perhaps sardonic—for Israel.

the house of Israel came to them. The meaning is not transparent, but the sense may be that the people would come for guidance to the elite of the nation, the "eminent."

2. *Calneh.* A distant city in Syria.

great Hammath. A city in central Syria.

is your territory larger than theirs? The received Hebrew text reads, "is their territory larger than yours?," but the context surely requires that these terms be reversed.

3. *but bring on disaster and outrage.* The first of these two nouns in the Masoretic Text is *shevet,* "dwelling" or "sitting," which makes little sense. This translation assumes, as do many scholars, that this is a scribal error for either *shever* or *shod,* either of which suggests disaster.

4. *who lie on ivory-inlaid beds.* Amos, a farmer and pastoralist, is no doubt repelled by the indolent life of luxury he observes among the northern aristocratic class, but he also has in mind the exploitation of the vulnerable that is the source of the wealth.

like David they devise song's instruments.
Who drink from bowls of wine   6
   and with the finest oils anoint themselves
     and are not distressed by Joseph's disaster.
Therefore now shall they be exiled at the head of exiles,   7
   and the lounging feasts shall be no more.
The Master, the LORD, has sworn by His life,   8
   said the LORD, God of Armies:
I loathe the pride of Jacob,
   and his citadels I hate,
     and I will hand over the town and its fullness.

And it shall happen that if ten men are left in a house, they shall die. And   9,10
a handful of men shall remain to carry out the bones from the house. And
one shall say to him who is in the far corners of the house, "Is anyone still
with you?" And he shall say, "None." And he shall say, "Hush!" so as not to
mention the name of the LORD.

---

5. *like David they devise song's instruments.* The tone is sarcastic. David's legendary skill as
a lyre player and "sweet singer" was by this time ensconced as an item of popular culture.

6. *Who drink from bowls of wine.* Pointedly, they are said to drink not from flasks but from
large bowls.
   and with the finest oils anoint themselves. Rubbing the body with oil was one of the
pleasures of the good life, as in Homer's Greece. But the verb *mashaḥ,* "anoint," is generally
reserved for sacral or royal use of oil, so its employment here adds to the invective.
   Joseph. The house of Joseph, one should recall, is an equivalent for the house of Israel.

7. *at the head of exiles.* That is, they shall lead the rest of the people into exile, a bitterly
ironic turn of their leadership.

10. *And a handful of men shall remain.* The first three words of the Masoretic Text, *unas'u
dodo umesarfo,* are not intelligible, and there is no grammatical agreement between the
initial verb and the two words that follow. A literal rending would be: and they shall-carry
his-uncle and-his-*mesaref,* the meaning of this last noun remaining unknown. The present
translation adopts the reading of the Septuagint, which evidently had a Hebrew text with
three different (and intelligible) Hebrew words: *wenish'aru metey mispar.*
   to him who is in the far corners of the house. Apparently, there is a single survivor,
huddled, perhaps hiding, in a remote corner of the house.
   so as not to mention the name of the LORD. People often greeted each other in the name
of the LORD, as Boaz does with his laborers in Ruth 2:4. The speaker wants to make sure
this will not happen in this place of death and devastation, for that would be a violation of
the sanctity of the divine name.

11   For, look, the LORD commands,
                and He shall strike the great house into splinters
                and the small house into shards.
12   Can horses race on rock,
                can one plow with an ox in the sea?
            For you have turned justice into poison
                and the fruit of righteousness into wormwood.
13   You who rejoice over Lo-Dabar,
                who say, Why, with our strength
                we have captured Karnaim.
14   But I am about to raise against you, house of Israel,
                said the LORD, God of Armies, a nation.
            And they shall harry you
                from Lebo-Hammath
                to the Wadi of Arabah.

1   **CHAPTER 7**   Thus did the Master, the LORD show me: And,
    look, He was creating locusts at the beginning of the sprouting of the late
2   grain, and, look, it was the late grain after the king's reaping. And so,
    after they had finished devouring the green growth of the land, I said, "O

---

12. *can one plow with an ox in the sea?* The received text reads *'im-yaharosh babeqarim,* "can
one plow in the mornings?" A small, widely accepted emendation breaks out the last word
into two, *babaqar yam,* yielding the meaning shown in this translation.

13. *Lo-Dabar.* This is a town in the northern part of Gilead, but the name could also be
understood to mean "nothing," and a pun is clearly intended.
    Karnaim. A town in the Bashan region. Both Gilead and Bashan were part of the north-
ern kingdom but at times were contested.

14. *a nation.* Though the verb "raise against" occurs at the beginning of this verse, its object,
as a kind of ominous revelation, is withheld to the very end of the sentence.
    from Lebo-Hammath / to the Wadi of Arabah. Lebo-Hammath is in the Lebanon valley;
the Wadi of Arabah is far to the south, in the rift descending from the Sea of Galilee to
the Dead Sea.

CHAPTER 7   1. *Thus did the Master, the LORD show me.* These words, which will
be repeated as a formula, initiate a series of four prose prophecies that come in the form of
visions (the Hebrew verb for "show" is literally "cause to see").
    And, look. This word, *wehineh,* is regularly used to introduce what is seen in a dream
and thus underscores the generic connection between vision and dream.
    after the king's reaping. Part of the earlier harvest was set aside for fodder for the king's
herds and horses.

Master, LORD, pray forgive! How will Jacob stand, for he is small?" The 3
LORD repented concerning this. "It shall not be," said the LORD. Thus did 4
the LORD show me: And look, the Master, the LORD was calling forth to
contend with fire, and it consumed the great deep and consumed the fields.
And I said, "O Master, LORD, pray cease. How will Jacob stand, for he is 5
small?" The LORD relented concerning this. "This, too, shall not be," said 6
the Master, the LORD. Thus did the LORD show me: And, look, the Master 7
was stationed by a wall built with a plumb line, and in His hand was a
plumb line. And the LORD said to me; "What do you see, Amos?" And I 8
said, "A plumb line." And the Master said to me, "I am about to place a
plumb line in the midst of My people Israel. I will no longer forgive them."

> And Isaac's high places shall be desolate,   9
>   and Israel's sanctuaries shall become ruins,
>   and I will rise against the house of Jeroboam with a sword.

And Amaziah the priest of Bethel sent to Jeroboam king of Israel, saying, 10
"Amos has plotted against you in the midst of the house of Israel. The land
cannot bear all his words." For thus has Amos said: 11

> By the sword Jeroboam shall die,
>   and Israel shall surely be exiled from its soil."

---

4. *it consumed the great deep and consumed the fields.* This would be a truly catastrophic
fire, not only burning the fields (a natural event when a wildfire spreads) but drying out the
groundwater beneath the surface of the earth (in effect, an apocalyptic event).

7. *plumb line.* This is the traditional understanding of *'anakh,* which appears only here.
Some have disputed its meaning, claiming it might be a term for "axe" because it becomes
here an instrument of destruction. "Plumb line," however, makes perfectly good sense. The
wall is a plumb-line wall ("built" is merely implied) because it is properly constructed as
a perfect vertical. God will use a plumb line to measure out inexorable judgment against
Israel. Compare 2 Kings 21:13: "I will stretch over Jerusalem the line of Samaria and the
weight [the "plumb" of the plumb line] of the house of Ahab, and I will wipe out Jerusalem."

10. *And Amaziah the priest of Bethel sent to Jeroboam.* This narrative episode interrupts the
sequence of four visionary prophecies.
    Amos has plotted against you. Given the recent history of court conspiracies and coups
in the northern kingdom, Amaziah readily represents the prophet as a political subversive.

11. *By the sword Jeroboam shall die, / and Israel shall surely be exiled from its soil.* Amaziah
steps up the actual words of Amos's prophecy (verse 9), putting in his mouth an explicit
prediction of the death of Jeroboam and of Israel's exile.

12 And Amaziah said to Amos, "Seer, go, flee to the land of Judah and there
13 eat bread and prophesy there. But in Bethel you shall no longer prophesy,
14 for it is the king's sanctuary and a royal house." And Amos answered and
    said to Amaziah, "No prophet am I, nor the son of a prophet am I, but a
15 cattle herder am I and a tender of sycamore fruit. And the LORD took me
    from going after the flock, and the LORD said to me 'Go, prophesy to My
16 people Israel.' And, now, hear the word of the LORD, you who say, 'You shall
17 not prophesy to Israel and shall not preach to the house of Isaac.' Therefore
    thus said the LORD:

> Your wife shall play the whore in the town,
>   and your sons and your daughters shall fall by the sword,
>   and you shall be shared out with a measuring line,
>   and you shall die on unclean soil,
>   and Israel shall surely be exiled from its soil."

---

12. *there eat bread.* Modern translations have often eliminated the concreteness of this idiom by rendering it as "There earn your living" or some equivalent, but English has its own idiomatic use of "bread" as "sustenance" (for example, "breadwinner"). In fact, Rashi may be correct in saying "in language of contempt he spoke to him—there they will give you crusts of bread as payment for prophesying to them."

14. *No prophet am I, nor the son of a prophet.* Amos responds directly to the remark about eating bread. He says that he is no professional prophet of the sort that expects payment for prophesying. The expression "son of a prophet" refers to the disciples who constituted the following of such a prophet. What he is invoking is the phenomenon registered in Samuel and Kings of career prophets surrounded by their disciples (who are called "sons of the prophet") and who cultivate ecstatic states, often with the aid of musical instruments. Amos, by contrast, is a simple herdsman and farmer driven to prophesy by a call from God.

   a tender of sycamore fruit. The sycamore yields a figlike fruit, and the unusual verb used here, *boles,* may refer to a well-attested practice of scratching the surface of the fruit in order to facilitate its ripening.

17. *Your wife shall play the whore in the town.* Some interpreters want to understand the verb *tizneh* as "be raped" (or substitute another verb that has this meaning), but that seems questionable. The priest's shame will be compounded when his wife decides to give herself to the invading troops, either because she simply has her eye on the main chance or because she wants to avert any harm that might come to her.

   you shall die on unclean soil. The "unclean soil" is of course the soil of the foreign land to which the exiles will be deported. This carries a special barb for Amaziah because he is a priest, enjoined to preserve ritual purity, and no sacrifices can be offered on unclean soil.

CHAPTER 8   Thus did the Master, the LORD, show me: And, 1
look, a basket of summer's-end fruit. And He said to me, "What do you 2
see, Amos?" And I said, "A basket of summer's-end fruit." And the LORD
said to me:

> The end has come upon My people Israel.
>   I will no longer forgive them.
> And the palace's songstresses shall howl   3
>   on that day, said the LORD:
>   "Many the corpses flung everywhere. Hush!"

> Hear this, who trample the needy,   4
>   destroying the poor of the land,
> saying, "When will the new moon be over, that we may sell grain,   5
>   and the sabbath, that we may trade in wheat?
> to use a short *ephah* measure and an oversize shekel-weight
>   and to tilt cheating scales,
> to buy the indigent with silver   6
>   and the needy for the price of sandals,
>   and we may sell chaff as grain."

CHAPTER 8   2. *summer's-end fruit*. The Hebrew puns on *qayits*, "summer" and
qeits, "end." Since many fruits do not ripen until late in the summer, *qayits* might even
actually mean "summer's end."

3. *songstresses*. The Masoretic Text has *shirot*, "(long) songs," but most scholars prefer to
read, as does this translation, *sharot*, "songstresses."
    Many the corpses flung everywhere. Hush! These are probably the women's words. This
does not scan as a line of poetry and the Hebrew syntax is ambiguously terse. The received
text has *hishlikh*, "he flung," but the context requires a passive form, *hoshlakh*. The Masoretes linked this verb with "hush," but flinging is an action more appropriate to abandoned
corpses.

5. *trade*. The verb here usually means "open" and probably refers to opening sacks of grain.
    a short ephah *measure and an oversize shekel-weight*. Giving the buyer a short *ephah* (a
dry measure) would be shortchanging him. The oversize weight for the shekel would mean
paying more in silver than the actual stipulated silver weight.

6. *sell chaff as grain*. This loops back to the grain transactions at the beginning of their
speech. Obviously, they would not actually have spoken this catalogue of their cheating
practices—it is rather the prophet who exposes their intentions, putting the words in their
mouths.

7   The Lord has sworn by the Pride of Jacob:
           I will never forget their acts.
8   For this should not the earth shudder
           and all its dwellers mourn?
       It shall rise, altogether, like the Nile,
           heave and sink like the Nile of Egypt.
9   And it shall happen on that day, said the Lord,
           I will make the sun set at noon
               and darken the earth on a day of light.
       And I will turn your festivals into mourning
           and all your songs into lament,
       And lay sackcloth on all loins
           and every head a shaved pate.
       And I will make her as the mourning for an only child
           and her end as a bitter day.

10   Look, days are coming, said the Lord,
           when I will let loose famine in the land,
       not famine for bread
           and not thirst for water
               but for hearing the words of the Lord.
11   And they shall wander from sea to sea,
           and from the north to the east they shall roam
       to seek the Lord's word,
           but they shall not find it.

---

7. *the Pride of Jacob.* Though elsewhere this expression refers to the people of the northern kingdom, here it would have to be God.

8. *rise . . . like the Nile.* There are tides in the Nile and periods of flooding. The earth in this image will have the instability of water.

9. *every head a shaved pate.* This is a practice of mourning forbidden in Deuteronomy 14:1, evidently because of its association with paganism. It appears, however, with some frequency in poetry, either as a linguistic fossil or because it was actually common in popular religion.

   I will make her. The nearest antecedent for this pronoun is "the earth" at the beginning of this verse, although it is possible that the reference is to Israel, often represented as a woman.

11. *from sea to sea.* This probably means from the Mediterranean to the Dead Sea, though from the Mediterranean to the Red Sea is also possible.

On that day the lovely virgins shall faint   12
   and the young men, too, with thirst.
Who swear by the Guilt of Samaria   13
   and say, "As your God lives, Dan,"
     and "As the way to Beersheba lives."
They shall fall and rise no more.

CHAPTER 9

I saw the Master stationed by the altar, and He said: 1
Strike the capitals that the thresholds shake.
   I will split them on the heads of them all,
     and who is left of them I will slay with the sword.
   None from them shall be able to flee,
     and no survivor from them shall escape.
Were they to dig down to Sheol,   2
   from there My hand would take them,
and were they to ascend to the heavens,

---

12. *the lovely virgins / . . . the young men.* These are young people in their prime, and the pride and joy of the nation. If even they faint away, one may infer that elders and children will scarcely be able to withstand the distress of this famine for the word of the Lord. Thus the idea of such a famine is made vividly concrete because people grow faint and perish, as if they were deprived of actual food and water.

13. *Who swear by the Guilt of Samaria.* The received text makes sense as it stands: the worship of the icons of the calves in Dan and Bethel is guilty worship. Some scholars, however, propose emending the Hebrew word for "guilt" so that it reads as the name of a pagan deity.
   As the way to Beersheba lives. Here the oath is taken in the name of the way because a long pilgrimage to the south is involved in order to reach the cultic center in Beersheba. This is the second mention of this center—compare 5:5.

CHAPTER 9   1. *Strike the capitals.* The imperative here is puzzling because it makes the prophet the agent of destruction, a role that prophets do not play. Some medieval Hebrew commentators propose that this command is delivered to an angel (not mentioned in the text) and not to Amos. An alternative would be to emend the verb to "I will strike," changing *hakh* to *'akh.*
   I will split them. The received text has "he will split them." See the previous comment.

2. *Were they to dig down to Sheol.* This sequence of lines to the end of verse 3 is strongly reminiscent of Psalms 139:7–12. Both the passage in Psalms and this one articulate a vision of God as an all-seeing cosmic deity from Whom there can never be escape. The theater of retribution against Israel is thus dramatically widened.

from there I would bring them down.
3   And were they to hide on the peak of Carmel,
        I would search them out there and take them.
     And were they to take cover from My eyes on the floor of the sea,
        from there I would summon the Serpent and it would bite them.
4   And should they go in captivity before their enemies,
        from there I will summon the sword and it would slay them.
     And I will put My eye on them
        for evil and not for good.

5   And the Master, LORD of Armies,
        Who but touches the earth and it melts
           and all dwellers upon it mourn,
     and it all goes up like the Nile,
        and sinks like the Nile of Egypt.
6   Who builds in the heavens His lofts
        and His vault upon earth He founds.
     Who calls forth the waters of the sea
        and pours them over the earth—the LORD is His name.

7   Are you not like the Cushites to Me,
        O Israelites? said the LORD.

---

3. *the Serpent.* This is a mythological entity, not the serpent of the Garden story but the monstrous Leviathan of Canaanite tradition. Here the once menacing sea god answers the LORD's bidding.

5. *Who but touches the earth and it melts.* This verse and the next are still another doxology celebrating God's overwhelming power, with language reminiscent of several psalms. The editorial motivation for the placement of the doxology here is the vivid evocation in verses 2–4 of God's cosmic omniscience in pursuit of all who seek to flee.

6. *vault.* The translation is a guess for *'agudah,* a term that may be architectural because it derives from a verbal stem that means "to bind together."

7. *Are you not like the Cushites to Me.* The Cushites are the Nubians, perhaps invoked here because as black Africans, they would seem to be an ultimate other to the Israelites (a presence of individual Nubians among the Israelites is attested to in several biblical narratives, with no suggestion of racial prejudice). The idea, then, is that God oversees all nations and peoples, however different they might seem from Israel. But from what follows in the next line of poetry, one would expect a mention of God's having brought the Cushites to Nubia from another land, and that is absent.

Did I not bring up Israel from the land of Egypt
   and the Philistines from Crete
      and Aram from Kir?
Look, the eyes of the Master, the LORD,   8
   are upon the offending kingdom,
and I will destroy it
   from the face of the earth.
But I will surely not destroy the house of Jacob, said the LORD.
For I am about to command,   9
   and I will shake up the house of Israel in all the nations
as one shakes in a sieve
   and no pebble shall fall to the ground.
By the sword shall die   10
   all the offenders among My people
who say "The evil shall not
   approach and come close to us."

Israel from the land of Egypt. Nubia borders on Egypt to the south, so its mention in the preceding line provides an associative preparation for the introduction at this point of Egypt.

the Philistines from Crete / and Aram from Kir. The Philistines in fact migrated to the eastern shore of the Mediterranean from somewhere in the Greek realm, perhaps actually from Crete. Nothing is known about a migration of Arameans from Kir, far to the northeast in Mesopotamia, but the reference here may reflect factual knowledge about such origins in Amos's time. In any case, the point of these references is to say that God oversees the migration of all peoples and that the movement of Israel from Egypt to Canaan is not unique.

8. *the eyes of the Master . . . / are upon the offending kingdom.* The offending kingdom must be Israel. Thus, the God Who moves peoples from one territory to another does not grant special privileges or guarantee permanent residence to Israel if it turns itself into an offending kingdom.

But I will surely not destroy the house of Jacob. The prophet has just represented God as saying He will destroy the offending kingdom from the face of the earth. Although it is possible that he wants to qualify that sweeping declaration, one suspects that the mitigation of the prophecy of destruction is an editorial addition—especially since this entire sentence does not scan as poetry.

9. *no pebble shall fall to the ground.* This is a little confusing. Does it mean that the whole people, good and bad, will be shaken in the sieve of exile and destroyed? A possible solution is that the "pebble"—"the offenders" of the next line—will remain in the sieve while the grain, which has smaller particles, will fall through the holes and be saved.

11   On that day I will raise up
          the fallen shelter of David
      and I will stop up its breaches
          and its ruins will I raise
          and rebuild it as in days of yore,
12   so that they take hold of the remnant of Edom
          and all the nations on which My name has been called,
          said the LORD, Who does this.
13   Look, days are coming, said the LORD,
          when the plowman shall overtake the reaper
          and the treader of grapes the sower of seed.
      And the mountains shall drip fermented juice,
          and all the hills shall melt.
14   And I will restore the fortunes of My people Israel,
          and they shall rebuild desolate towns and dwell there
          and plant vineyards and drink their wine.
      And they shall make gardens
          and eat their fruit.
15   And I will plant them on their soil,
          and they shall no more be uprooted from their soil
          that I have given them, said the LORD your God.

---

11. *the fallen shelter.* The Hebrew noun *sukah* is strategically chosen. It is the shelter or hut erected in a field for someone watching over the crops. Thus, unlike a fortress or a palace, it is easily knocked down.

   David. This invocation of the Davidic dynasty appears to suggest a hope on the part of the prophet that in future times the united kingdom will be restored.

12. *all the nations on which My name has been called.* Edom and other regions east of the Jordan were conquered by David and made part of a mini-empire. David's taking possession of these lands is what is meant by God's name being called on these nations. Now the empire will be restored.

13. *the plowman shall overtake the reaper.* The whole line is a hyperbole for an era of extravagant agricultural fertility.

   and all the hills shall melt. Those who see in this an image of fields of waving grain betray a lack of understanding of how biblical poetry works. First, the mountains "drip" new wine because the yield of the vineyards is so abundant. Then, in an intensification in the second verset, the hills produce such a flow of wine that they veritably melt.

15. *And I will plant them on their soil, / and they shall no more be uprooted from their soil.* The prophecy pointedly concludes by underscoring through the terms chosen a continuity between the flourishing vineyards and gardens and the people flourishing on the soil. The Hebrew *'adamah* means "soil" but has an extended sense of "land," and both meanings are brought into play here.

Obadiah

CHAPTER 1   The vision of Obadiah. Thus said the LORD 1
concerning Edom:

A report we have heard from the LORD,
  and an envoy among the nations was sent.
    Rise and let us rise against her for battle.
Look, I have made you last among the nations,   2
  you are utterly spurned.
Your heart's arrogance deceived you   3
  who dwell in the clefts of the rock,
    in your abode on high,
who say in your heart,
  "Who can bring me down to the ground?"
Should you go high as the eagle   4
  and should you nest among the stars,
    from there I would bring you down, said the LORD.
Should thieves come to you,   5
  plunderers in the night,

CHAPTER 1   1. *concerning Edom.* Obadiah's exclusive subject is the outrages Edom has committed against Judah and the retribution it will receive for its hateful acts. The inference is compelling that he witnessed Edom's collaboration with the Babylonians in the dire events of 586 B.C.E. Jeremiah, Second Isaiah, and, most vividly, Psalm 137, register responses to these same acts of Edom.

A report we have heard. Much of this passage through verse 6 replicates Jeremiah 49:14–16, although the order of verses is different and there are some discrepancies between the two texts. Either Obadiah drew from Jeremiah (perhaps the most likely explanation) or the other way around, or both writers used a common source.

3. *who dwell in the clefts of the rock.* Edom is in part a mountainous region, referred to as "Mount Seir" and also (here only) as "Edom's mountain."

how you would be destroyed!
   They would take but what they needed.
Should grape harvesters come to you,
   would they not leave gleanings?

6   How Esau has been stripped,
   his hidden places laid bare!

7   To the border they have sent you off,
   all the men allied with you.
They deceived you, prevailed against you,
   all the men in league with you.
Who ate bread at your table
   have laid a trap beneath you.
     There is no discerning in him.

8   Why, on that day, said the LORD:
   I shall destroy the sages from Edom
     and discerning from Esau's mountain.

9   And your survivors shall be terror-stricken, Teman,
   that every man be cut off from Esau's mountain.

10   For the slaughter, for the outrage against your brother Jacob,
   shame shall cover you, and you shall be cut off forever.

11   On the day you stood aloof,

---

5. *how you would be destroyed.* This is somewhat puzzling because the point is that the thieves would take only what they needed. One solution would be to read this clause as a question, although that would clash with the exclamatory "how" at the beginning of the next verse.

7. *all the men allied with you.* This is measure-for-measure justice: Edom betrayed its brother Israel; now it will be betrayed by its allies.

   Who ate bread at your table. The Hebrew shows merely "your bread," but the text looks defective because this one word is not sufficient prosodically to constitute a verset. The translation assumes that the line originally read *'okhley laḥmekha,* literally, "the eaters of your bread," a biblical idiom for dependents or vassals.

   There is no discerning in him. The masculine pronoun refers to Edom. Such switches from third person to second person are common biblical usage.

8. *discerning from Esau's mountain.* This is part of a new prophecy, inserted at this point because the "discerning" at the end of the previous prophecy is picked up in the opening line here.

9. *Teman.* A principal city of Edom.

10. *For the slaughter.* The received text puts this single Hebrew word at the end of the previous verse, but it makes better sense here.

on the day strangers seized his wealth
and aliens entered his gates,
　　and for Jerusalem they cast lots,
　　　and you were as one of them.
And do not gloat on your brother's day,　　　　　　　　　　12
　　on the day of his downfall.
And do not rejoice over the Judahites
　　on the day of their destruction.
And do not boast
　　on the day of distress.
Do not enter My people's gate　　　　　　　　　　　　　　13
　　on the day of their disaster.
Do not gloat on your part
　　over the evil that befalls him on the day of his disaster.
And do not stand at the crossroads　　　　　　　　　　　　14
　　to cut off his fugitives
and do not hand over his survivors
　　on the day of distress.
For near Is the day of the LORD　　　　　　　　　　　　　15
　　against all the nations.
As you have done, it shall be done to you.
　　Your requital shall come back on your head.
For as you drank on My holy mountain,　　　　　　　　　　16
　　all the nations shall drink ever more.

---

11. *On the day you stood aloof.* As the next three versets make clear, this is the day of the conquest of Jerusalem.

　for Jerusalem they cast lots. They cast lots in order to divide up the city in shares for the conquerors.

12. *And do not gloat.* The literal sense of the word is "see in," a set idiom for witnessing the downfall of one's enemy with schadenfreude. This series of sentences is cast as negative imperatives, but the implication is that this is what Edom in fact did and should never have done.

14. *And do not stand at the crossroads / to cut off his fugitives.* The indictment of Edom moves from his simply gloating over the downfall of Judah to his taking an active part in the onslaught by killing those who attempt to flee.

16. *For as you drank on My holy mountain.* The "you" of the preceding verse is in the singular and clearly refers to Edom. This "you" is plural and probably refers to the Judahites: they have drunk the poison chalice (*kos hatarʿeilah*—that term is elliptically implied but not mentioned) on the day Jerusalem ("My holy mountain") was destroyed, and now the turn of the nations is coming to drink that cup to its bitter dregs.

They shall drink and babble
　　and be as though they never had been.
17　　But on Mount Zion there shall be a remnant,
　　　　and it shall be sacrosanct,
　　　　　and the house of Jacob shall dispossess their dispossessors.
18　　And the house of Jacob shall be a fire
　　　　and the house of Joseph a flame,
　　and the house of Esau shall be straw,
　　　　and they shall ignite them and consume them.
　　And the house of Esau shall have no survivor,
　　　　for the LORD has spoken.

19　And they shall take hold of Esau's mountain and the lowland of the Phi-
　　listines and the field of Ephraim and the field of Samaria, and Benjamin—
20　Gilead. And this force of exiles of the Israelites that is among the Canaanites
　　as far as Zarephath and the exiles of Jerusalem who are at Sepharad—they
21　shall take hold of the Negeb towns. And rescuers shall go up Mount Zion
　　to exact judgment against Esau's mountain, and the kingdom shall be the
　　LORD's.

---

babble/ . . . never had been. The Hebrew deploys an untranslatable pun: *laʿu . . . loʾ hayu.*

18. *no survivor.* This is condign justice for the people who cut down the survivors of Judah.

20. *Zarephath.* This is a Phoenician town about nine miles south of Sidon. In the Middle Ages, it would be adopted as the designation for France, a usage carried over into modern Hebrew.
　　Sepharad. This is Sardis in Asia Minor. In the Middle Ages, it would be used as the name for Spain, another usage preserved in modern Hebrew. Obadiah appears to have mapped out a plan in which groups of Judahites exiled to different regions would be assigned different territories in the return to Zion.

21. *And rescuers shall go up Mount Zion to exact judgment against Esau's mountain.* The military strategy is somewhat opaque, the point being to set mountain over against mountain. Perhaps what is implied is that the forces of Judah will assemble on their own lofty mountain and then proceed to attack Mount Seir.

Jonah

Introduction

W e know nothing about the author of the Book of Jonah or his geographic location, and only a rough approximation can be made
of the time of the book's composition. The main evidence for dating is
linguistic: there are quite a few turns of phrase that indicate this is Late
Biblical prose, a kind of Hebrew not written until after the return from the
Babylonian exile in the fifth century B.C.E. The book's universalist theology
probably also argues for a relatively late date because one does not find this
sort of rigorously world-embracing monotheism until Second Isaiah, the
anonymous sixth-century prophet of the Babylonian exile. It is possible
that the book's author drew on an earlier folktale, as some scholars have
conjectured, although there is no way of proving that, and the fabulous elements of the story in their very extravagance have the look more of literary
invention than of a naïve folk imagination.

The name Jonah son of Amittai is drawn from a passing reference in 2
Kings 14:25 to a prophet so designated who delivered God's word during
the reign of Jeroboam II and about whom nothing more than that is said.
Since our story, which has no clear historical moorings, apart from the
vague invocation of Assyria, was almost surely composed centuries later
(despite some unconvincing dissent on the issue of dating from a few
biblical scholars), the protagonist is surely not identical with the prophet
mentioned in 2 Kings. The writer may have adopted the name because the
patronym *amittai* suggests *'emet*, "truth," in Hebrew. The first name, *yonah*,
means "dove," which could have an ironic application here because this
Jonah is an unwilling agent who ends up averting a punitive cataclysm, in
approximate analogy to Noah's dove, which signals the restoration of life
after a punitive cataclysm. Alternately, the writer might simply have chosen

this particular prophet's name as a convenient hook on which to hang a fable about prophecy precisely because nothing more is known about the prophet in question.

While the Hebrew narratives composed in the First Temple period utilize heterogeneous materials, they exhibit a great deal of uniformity in regard to narrative conventions and the general purposes for which narratives are framed. By contrast, what characterizes the narratives of the Late Biblical period is a vigorous experimentation with genre and an impulse to move beyond the governing procedures of earlier biblical narrative. Perhaps the most distinctive hallmark of Jonah's relatively late composition is that it tells a story altogether unlike those of earlier biblical literature. The recalcitrance of the prophet is a recurring feature of the classic call narratives of the prophets, as with Jeremiah, Isaiah, and Moses himself, but nowhere else do we have a person summoned to prophecy who actually tries to flee to the other end of the known world. Similarly, though one prophet, Amos, is sent from his home in Judah to prophesy in the northern—and not very friendly—kingdom of Israel, the two realms are still, after all, within the family, while only in Jonah is a man called to deliver a prophecy to the general populace of an altogether foreign, and hostile, nation.

The two instances just mentioned offer a clue to Jonah's relation to its literary antecedents. It picks up certain hints or precedents from earlier biblical narrative but pushes them to an extreme where they play a role in what amounts to a different genre. The narratives originating in the First Temple period, despite exhibiting some miraculous events and some spectacular episodes of divine intervention, are by and large "history-like," as Hans Frei has aptly called them, from the Patriarchal Tales to the stories of David and the later kings. Jonah, on the other hand is a manifestly fabulous tale. Though earlier Hebrew narrative offers one anomalous instance of a talking animal, Balaam's she-ass, that is the exception that proves the rule, an invention introduced to sharpen the satire on the pagan soothsayer who is blind to what his visionary beast can plainly see. Jonah's fish does not speak, but it follows God's instructions dutifully, first swallowing Jonah and then, when it gets the word, vomiting him up on dry land. Its capacity, moreover, to keep Jonah three days in the dark wet prison of its innards is an even more fantastic contrivance than according Balaam's ass the momentary gift of speech. This peculiar performance of the fish, serving as God's obedient instrument, is in keeping with the cattle and sheep in Nineveh, bizarrely required to don sackcloth and fast together with the human beings, and, in the deliberately ambiguous wording of the Hebrew, seen as if consciously covering themselves with sackcloth and as if crying out to God along with the human denizens of Nineveh.

All this has led scholars to scramble for labels to describe Jonah. It has been called everything from a Menippean satire to an allegory, but none of these identifications of Jonah is entirely convincing. I would see Jonah as its own kind of ad hoc innovative narrative. It aims to recast traditional Israelite notions of prophecy in a radically universalist framework. The prophets of Israel all work in an emphatically national context. Their messages are addressed to the people of Israel, often with explicitly political concerns, and the messages are manifestly directed to the fate of the nation—its imminent destruction by foreign powers if it fails to mend its evil ways, the fulfillment of its hope for national restoration after the disaster has occurred. The medium of the prophets is generally poetry, where all the powerful expressive resources of the Hebrew language could be summoned to convey the prophetic vision to the people. This may be one reason that Jonah is accorded no verbal prophetic message, only that single brief prediction of catastrophe which, if one is supposed to think of such considerations, he would have spoken not in Hebrew but in Akkadian. Jonah engages with no Israelites in the story. First he has an exchange with the polytheistic mariners, then he addresses the Ninevites, and his closest connection is with two presumably insensate living things, a very large fish and a leafy plant. The God with whom he has such difficulties because of his Israelite nationalist mind-set is not chiefly the God of Israel but the God of the whole world, of all creatures large and small. He is not a God you can pin down to national settings. Although He initially addresses Jonah somewhere within the land of Israel—perhaps even in Jerusalem, where the Temple, evoked in chapter 2, stands—His fullest dialogue with Jonah is on a promontory overlooking Nineveh. While He does rebuke Jonah as the God of earlier Hebrew narratives and poems rebukes wayward people, the rebuke itself is oddly formulated, in keeping with the wonderful strangeness of this book. God exercises magisterial control over storm winds, fish, livestock, and plants, as well as over human beings of all tribes and nations, and He asks the recalcitrant prophet why he should "have pity" for an ephemeral plant but not for a vast city of clueless human beings and their beasts. It is beautifully appropriate that the story ends with the beasts, and with a question. It is in no way clear how Jonah will respond to this question. Will God's challenge lead him to a transformative insight about God's dominion over all things and all peoples, or will it prove to be a challenge that is quite beyond the myopia of his ingrained prejudices? The trembling balance of this concluding ambiguity perfectly focuses the achievement of the Book of Jonah both as an enchanting story and as the shaking up of an entire theological world.

CHAPTER 1   And the word of the LORD came to Jonah son 1
of Amittai, saying, "Get up, go to Nineveh the great city, and call out 2
against it, for their evil has risen before Me." And Jonah got up to flee to 3
Tarshish from before the LORD to Jaffa and found a ship coming from
Tarshish, and he paid its fare and went down with them to go to Tarshish
from before the LORD. And the LORD cast a great wind upon the sea, and 4
there was a great storm on the sea, and the ship threatened to break up.

CHAPTER 1   1. *came to Jonah.* The literal meaning of the Hebrew verb is "was to
Jonah."

2. *Nineveh the great city.* The entirely fabulous proportions of its vastness will become
clear in chapter 3. Although there are a couple of rare instances in the Book of Kings of
an Israelite prophet's going on a mission to a foreign country, the call to go to Nineveh is
anomalous and hardly historical. Nineveh, the capital of the Assyrian empire, no longer
existed by the likely time of Jonah's composition; however, it is remembered as the power
that entirely destroyed the northern kingdom of Israel and later seriously threatened the
southern kingdom of Judah as well. To send a Hebrew prophet to Nineveh would be rather
like sending a Jewish speaker to deliver moral exhortation to the Germans in Berlin in 1936.
While Jonah's words to God in 4:2 make it clear that he does not want to undertake the
mission because he foresees that the Ninevites will repent and that God will forgive them,
he might well also be afraid to go to Nineveh.

3. *And Jonah got up to flee.* For a brief moment, he might seem to be heeding God's command
to get up and go to Nineveh, but this momentary illusion is broken by the infinitive "to flee."
    Tarshish. This location, mentioned in a variety of biblical texts, has been identified
with a variety of places from Asia Minor to Spain. In any event, it is far to the west, in the
opposite direction from Nineveh.
    Jaffa. This port city, more or less on the site of present-day Tel Aviv, was probably not
under Israelite control. The rest of Jonah's story will unfold entirely among foreigners.
    went down. We are not informed about Jonah's hometown, but it would likely be up in
the hill country, perhaps even in Jerusalem, for Israelite habitation in the coastal plain was
sparse. First Jonah goes down to Jaffa, then into the ship. His trajectory is a series of goings
down as he is cast into the sea and then into the belly of the fish.

4. *the ship threatened to break up.* The term *ḥishvah* reflects a root that in earlier biblical
Hebrew means "to plan," "to devise," or "to reckon." Jack Sasson argues that it is a deliberate
personification and thus he renders it as "expected," but "threatened" is personification
enough and more idiomatic in context.

5 And the sailors were afraid, and each man cried out to his god, and they
   cast the gear that was in the ship into the sea to lighten their load. And
   Jonah had come down into the far corners of the craft and had laid down
6 and fallen deep asleep. And the captain approached him and said, "What
   are you doing deep asleep? Call out to your god. Perhaps the god will give
7 some thought to us, that we may not perish." And they said to each other,
   "Let us cast lots that we may know on whose account this evil is upon us."
8 And they cast lots, and the lot fell on Jonah. And they said to him, "Tell us,
   pray, you on whose account this evil is upon us, what is your work and from
   where do you come? What is your land, and from what people are you?"
9 And he said to them, "I am a Hebrew and the LORD God of the heavens do I
10 fear, Who made the sea and the dry land." And the men feared greatly, and
   they said to him, "What is this you have done?" For the men knew that he
11 was fleeing from before the LORD, for he had told them. And they said to

---

5. *the sailors were afraid.* Their fear will mark this entire episode, taking on a new meaning at its end.

to lighten their load. The literal sense of the Hebrew is "to lighten from upon them."

Jonah had come down. This is the third occurrence of this thematically fraught verb,
marked here as a pluperfect (subject before the verb, verb in the *qatal* form).

the far corners of the craft. This is presumably the hold, but the phrase *yarketey hasefi-
nah* plays on *yarketey bor*, "the far corners of the Pit" (that is, death), and perhaps also, as
James Ackerman has proposed, on *yarketey tsafon*, "the far corners of Tsafon" (the dwelling
place of the gods in Canaanite mythology).

6. *will give some thought to us.* The Hebrew *yit'ashet* is unique to this text. The translation
follows the proposal of some medieval exegetes that is related to *'eshtonot*, "thoughts."

7. *Let us cast lots.* The lot is a divinatory device, especially for determining guilt. See Joshua
18:6 and 1 Samuel 14:41–42.

8. *you on whose account.* The "you" is merely implied in the Hebrew.

what is your work. Most passengers would have been merchants, but Jonah has brought
no merchandise on board. The noun has the specific connotation of a designated task, so
they may be asking Jonah what he is up to.

What is your land. Jaffa, probably a polyglot city where traders embarked and disem-
barked, would give them no clue as to the national identity of this passenger.

9. *I am a Hebrew.* This is regularly the designation used by foreigners for Israelites and
so it makes sense that Jonah would choose it to identify his nationality to the ship's crew.

and the LORD God of the heavens do I fear, Who made the sea and the dry land. Although
this declaration of faith serves the thematic purposes of this story, the effect is almost
comic: Jonah, who has run away from God's command, as if a geographic escape from God
were possible, now announces his reverence for the universal God of sky, sea, and earth.
His declaration would surely at first have baffled the polytheistic sailors, for whom there
would have been a separate deity for each of these realms.

him, "What shall we do that the sea calm for us?" For the sea was storming
more and more. And he said to them, "Lift me up and cast me into the sea   12
that the sea calm for you, for I know that on my account this great storm
is upon you." And the men rowed to get back to the dry land and were not   13
able, for the sea was storming upon them more and more. And they called   14
out to the LORD and said, "Please, O LORD, pray let us not perish on account
of the life of this man, and do not exact from us the blood of the innocent,
for You, O LORD, as You desire You do." And they lifted up Jonah and cast   15
him into the sea, and the sea ceased from its fury. And the men feared the   16
LORD greatly and offered sacrifices to the LORD and made vows.

---

11. *For the sea was storming more and more.* As the story continues, there is an indication
in the verbal form used, *holekh weso'er*, of a constant increase in the intensity of the storm,
which was powerful to begin with.

12. *Lift me up and cast me into the sea.* Jonah means simply that if they get rid of his jinxing
presence on board, the storm will cease to pound the ship. The crew, however, may well
have construed this as casting an offering to appease the raging sea god.

13. *And the men rowed to get back to the dry land.* They are reluctant to follow Jonah's
instructions, which they of course understand as condemning him to almost certain death.
But rowing toward the shore (the ship would have been equipped with both oars and sails)
is a strategy of desperation because in a fierce storm, approaching the shore would have
most likely led to a catastrophic shipwreck.

14. *And they called out to the LORD.* They may not have been transformed into monotheists, but Jonah's testimony to them has clearly convinced them that in the present dire
circumstances, the LORD, YHWH, is a powerful deity who controls the urgent situation.
    let us not perish on account of the life of this man. This may mean that they do not want
to be the target of God's punishing wrath together with Jonah, who is on the ship with
them. But the reference to the blood of the innocent in the next clause may rather suggest
that they are praying not to be condemned for killing Jonah by throwing him overboard.

16. *And the men feared the LORD greatly.* This is exactly the phrase used for their fear of the
storm in the verse 10. Now it appears in its other meaning of showing reverence through
worship (the sacrifices and vows at the end of this verse) for a deity, even though the first
sense of terror still lingers—they revere the LORD because they have witnessed His fearsome power in the terrible storm and in His causing it to suddenly stop. Again one needn't
assume that they have become perfect monotheists, like the Aramean general in 2 Kings
miraculously cured of his skin disease, for they might simply be recognizing that Jonah's
deity is the one who has manifested fearsome control over the storm that almost destroyed
them. In any case, the turning of the hearts of these pagans to the God of Israel anticipates
the response of the Ninevites to Jonah's message.
    offered sacrifices to the LORD and made vows. There is some evidence that ships in the
ancient world actually carried animals which could be sacrificed on board at urgent or
propitious moments. The "vows" are pledges to offer further, votary sacrifices after their
safe return to land.

1 **CHAPTER 2**   And the Lord set out a great fish to swallow
Jonah, and he was three days and three nights in the innards of the fish.
2,3 And Jonah prayed to the Lord his God from the innards of the fish. And
he said:

> "I called out from my straits
>   to the Lord, and He answered me.
> From the belly of Sheol I cried out—
>   You heard my voice.
4 You flung me into the deep, in the heart of the sea,
>   and the current came round me.
> All your breakers and waves
>   streamed over me.

CHAPTER 2   1. *And the Lord set out.* This term (*m-n-h*) recurs in the subsequent
story, highlighting God's supervisory control over all living constituents of creation:
animal, vegetable, and human.

   a great fish. Although this could conceivably be a whale, as traditional understandings of the story imagine—perhaps most vividly in *Moby-Dick*—the Hebrew employs the
unspecific generic term for sea creature.

   three days and three nights. Many events in biblical narrative are said to occur in precisely this time span. What is distinctive here is the emphatic addition of three nights to
three days, inviting us to envisage Jonah's terror imprisoned in the dark belly of the big
fish three long nights and three long days, during which he of course has no way of distinguishing between day and night.

   2. *the Lord his God.* Now, as if to confirm Jonah's declaration of faith to the mariners, the
Lord is reported to be his God.

   3. *I called out from my straits / to the Lord, and He answered me.* As is the regular practice
in biblical narrative, a poem is inserted that was originally composed for another context
(compare Hannah's thanksgiving psalm, 1 Samuel 2:1–10). This poem is a psalm of thanksgiving, exhibiting many of the formulas and metaphors of that genre. It fits the narrative
situation somewhat imperfectly because, while it is introduced as Jonah's prayer from the
belly of the fish, it is not actually a plea for deliverance but the rendering of thanks to God
for having already delivered the speaker, as this opening line at once makes clear. The
image of almost drowning in the depths of the seas as a metaphor for near death (often
because of a grave illness) is conventional in thanksgiving psalms, but here it is made to
apply literally to Jonah's desperate aqueous plight. Not surprisingly, the inserted psalm
makes no mention of being swallowed by a fish because the maws of gigantic fish do not
figure in thanksgiving psalms. Nevertheless, the poem does incorporate several relevant
points of connection with Jonah's story.

   You heard my voice. Having first referred to God in the third person, the speaker now
intimately addresses Him directly.

   4. *All your breakers and waves / streamed over me.* This vivid image of drowning invokes,
as noted, a conventional trope of the thanksgiving psalm.

And I thought: 5
  I am banished from before Your eyes.
Yet again will I look
  on Your holy temple.
Water lapped about me to the neck,   6
  the deep came round me,
    weed was bound round my head.
To the roots of the mountains I went down—   7
  the underworld's bolts against me forever.
But You brought up my life from the Pit,
  O Lord my God.
As my life-breath grew faint within me,   8
  the Lord did I recall,
and my prayer came unto You,
  to Your holy Temple.
Those who look to vaporous lies   9
  will turn away from their mercy.

---

5. *And I thought: / I am banished from before Your eyes.* Death is the ultimate separation from God in the biblical worldview. But the psalm also provides a geographical orientation for Jonah's story: fleeing God's presence, which has its territorial focus in the Jerusalem Temple on Mount Zion, Jonah finds himself in the watery depths, at the antipodes from God's holy place. He has manifestly "gone down" (compare verse 7, "to the roots of the mountains I went down") from Jerusalem.

Yet again will I look / on Your holy temple. The speaker expresses faith against odds that he will live and return to worship God in His temple. Jonah, who has fled from the divine presence, now affirms the desire to return and enjoy it.

6. *weed was bound round my head.* This strong image of the head entrammeled in seaweed amplifies the conventional metaphor of sinking into the depths. The clause is rhythmically compact and assonant in the Hebrew—*suf havush lero'shi*—an effect the translation tries to emulate.

7. *underworld's . . . / the Pit.* Because the sea as a site of drowning is the metaphorical equivalent of death, the poem naturally moves from the watery abyss to the underworld, just as it began by placing the speaker in "the belly of Sheol."

8. *my prayer came unto You, / to Your holy Temple.* The Temple is where prayer is most readily heard by God. We have here a cosmic reach from the roots of the mountains, the bottom of the sea, to the Temple on Mount Zion.

9. *Those who look to vaporous lies.* This phrase replicates a phrase that occurs in Psalm 31:7.

will turn away from their mercy. The wording in the Hebrew is cryptic and has encouraged diverse interpretations. The least strained, which this translation seeks to register, is that the idol worshippers (clearly the referent of "those who look to vaporous lies") at some point will be compelled to recognize that the purported deities from whom they seek mercy

10   And I with a voice of thanksgiving
                let me sacrifice to You.
            What I vowed let me pay.
            Rescue is the LORD's."

11   And the LORD spoke to the fish, and it vomited Jonah onto the dry land.

1 CHAPTER 3   And the word of the LORD came to Jonah a
2 second time, saying, "Get up, go to Nineveh the great city, and call out
3 to it the call that I speak to you." And Jonah got up and went to Nineveh

---

are mere illusions, and thus they will abandon their futile worship. The possessive pronoun "their" (in Hebrew merely a suffix) attached to "mercy" would refer to the idolators. In all this, as both medieval and modern commentators have noted, there is some relevance to Jonah and the sailors: each of the mariners calls upon his own God, but to no avail; after hearing Jonah's words, they implore YHWH instead, Who in the end saves them.

10. *And I with a voice of thanksgiving.* One of the conventions of the thanksgiving psalm is to announce thanks or acclamation (*todah*, which is also the designation of the thanksgiving sacrifice) at the end of the poem.

    let me sacrifice . . . / let me pray. Existing translations render this as a simple future, but that misses the nuance of the Hebrew because both verbs show the suffix that is the marker of the optative mode. What the speaker declares is that he *wishes* to offer sacrifice. Presumably, we will carry out his desire, but that is different from a simple statement of the future tense.

11. *And the LORD spoke to the fish.* Just as He assigns the fish to swallow Jonah at the beginning of the episode, now He gives word to the fish to spew out Jonah. God's omnipresent control of all things is again manifest.

    vomited. As Sasson observes, this unpleasant verb is perfectly appropriate for a kind of indignity to which Jonah is subjected in the very act of being rescued.

CHAPTER 3   2. *Get up, go to Nineveh the great city, and call out to it.* God repeats verbatim His initial command to Jonah, rightly anticipating that after Jonah's terrifying experience of God's power on the ship and in the belly of the fish, the prophet will now be prepared to carry out the mission. The one small difference from the opening words of chapter 1 is that instead of the preposition *'al,* "against," God uses *'el,* "to," perhaps suggesting that Jonah's message may not have an altogether hostile purpose. If that is so, it is a clue Jonah does not pick up, as we shall see.

3. *And Jonah got up and went to Nineveh.* All we know about his location is that, after having been spewed out by the big fish, he is somewhere on the eastern coast of the Mediterranean. In a move characteristic of biblical narrative, his journey to Nineveh, which would have taken weeks, is compressed into four Hebrew words, with all circumstantial detail suppressed.

according to the word of the LORD. And Nineveh was a great city of God's, a three days' walk across. And Jonah began to come into the city, one day's walk, and he called out and said, "Forty days more, and Nineveh is overthrown." And the people of Nineveh trusted God, and they called a fast and donned sackcloth, from the greatest of them to the least. And the word reached the king of Nineveh, and he rose from his throne and took

4

5

6

---

a great city of God's. The Hebrew has been variously understood as "a great city to God," "a great city before God," and even as "a super-great city" (with *'elohim* serving merely as an intensifier). But this preposition, *l*ᵉ, often means "belonging to" in biblical Hebrew (including many inscriptions on pottery, seals, and the like). That meaning makes sense in terms of the theology of the book: Nineveh, like everything else in the world, is God's possession, and thus God is appropriately concerned about the behavior of its inhabitants and their fate.

a three days' walk across. "Across" is merely implied in the Hebrew. But the dimensions of the city vividly reflect the fabulous nature of the story: clocking roughly three miles an hour, a walker could cover as much as thirty miles in a day. A city ninety miles across would be considerably larger than contemporary Los Angeles, and, needless to say, no actual city in the ancient Near East could have been anywhere near that big. This three days' walk also has the consequence that it will take Jonah three days—a formulaic unit in biblical narrative, as we have seen in the instance of the sojourn in the fish's belly to proclaim his message throughout the city.

4. *Forty days more, and Nineveh is overthrown.* The number is formulaic, as in the forty days of the Flood, the forty days Moses spends on the mountain, and the forty years of wandering in the wilderness. Unless we are to construe Jonah's prophecy as a highly elliptical report, it is unconditional: in forty days, Nineveh is to be utterly devastated (and Jonah uses the participial form, not the future, to heighten the immediacy), with the verb "overthrown" the same one that is applied to Sodom. But, as the next verse makes clear, the people of Nineveh understand this dire prediction as implying a reversal of the disaster if they change their ways.

5. *And the people of Nineveh trusted God.* That is, they trust God's word delivered by Jonah that they will be annihilated unless they turn back from their evil ways. This translation avoids the use of "believe" for the Hebrew term because the general meaning of this word in the Bible—as opposed to the postbiblical usage of *he'emin*—suggests an act of trust, not belief. One should not imagine that the Ninevites have become monotheists, but rather that they have taken seriously the word of YHWH that He is prepared to destroy the city. The claim of some scholars that this verb when followed by the preposition *b*ᵉ means "believe" does not stand up under analysis. The few cases where it occurs with this preposition are at best ambiguous, and in Micah 7:5, the usage is unambiguously a statement about trust, not belief: "Do not trust in evil," and then in the poetic parallelism, "nor place confidence (*tivteḥu*) in a leader."

6. *And the word reached the king of Nineveh.* First, a wave of penitence sweeps through the populace as Jonah continues his three days' walk through the city, crying out his grim prophecy, then word of it comes to the king in his palace.

7   off his mantle and covered himself in sackcloth and sat upon ashes. And he
    had it proclaimed and he said in Nineveh: "By the authority of the king and
    his great men, saying, man and beast, cattle and sheep, shall taste nothing.
8   They shall not graze and they shall not drink water. And man and beast
    shall cover themselves with sackcloth, and they shall call out to God with
    all their might, and every man of them shall turn back from his evil way
9   and from the outrage to which they hold fast. Who knows? Perhaps God
    will turn back and relent and turn back from His blazing wrath, and we
10 shall not perish." And God saw their acts, that they had turned back from
    their evil way, and God relented from the evil that He said to do to them,
    and he did not do it.

---

his mantle. Elsewhere the noun *'aderet* can be any sort of mantle or cloak, but here it is
clearly a royal mantle with the designation perhaps playing on the word *'adir,* "majestic,"
that might be discerned in its root.

7. *had it proclaimed.* Literally, "caused to be shouted."

   By the authority. The term *mita'am* is appropriate for the introduction of a royal decree
and also is one of the reflections in our text of Late Biblical Hebrew.

   man and beast, cattle and sheep, shall taste nothing. The bracketing, a virtual equation,
of man and beast becomes a thematic thrust of the story. It is, of course, bizarre that a fast
should be imposed on animals, another reflection of the fabulous character of the story,
and that bizarreness will be heightened in the next verse.

   graze. Although this word ordinarily apply only to the animals, here it seems, almost
comically, to refer to humans as well.

8. *And man and beast shall cover themselves with sackcloth.* The translation closely follows the wording of the Hebrew, which intimates an image, against all logic, of the beasts
voluntarily covering themselves with sackcloth. In the next clause, even though "call out"
should refer to the humans only, its syntactical placement comes close to inviting us to
imagine the beasts calling out as well. All this amounts to a kind of hyperbolic farcical
representation of the penitence of Nineveh: after Jonah's message, the city is so caught up
in a profound impulse of penitence that a fast with sackcloth is imposed on beasts as well
as on human beings.

   turn back. The verb *shuv,* repeated three times in two verses, becomes the thematic
focus of this episode: the people turn back from evil, and God then turns back from His
baleful intentions.

10. *God relented from the evil that He had said to do to them.* "Evil" here means "harm," as
often elsewhere in biblical usage, but it is a measure-for-measure response to the evil of the
Ninevites, and thus the translation follows the repetition of the word in the Hebrew. As in
the previous episode, God is seen first as a wrathful God—sending the terrible storm that
threatens the sailors' lives as well as Jonah's—and then as a merciful God—rescuing Jonah
from the belly of the fish to give him a second chance as a prophet, and now canceling the
decree to destroy Nineveh.

CHAPTER 4   And the thing was very evil for Jonah, and he 1
was incensed. And he prayed to the LORD and said, "I beseech You, LORD, 2
was it not my word when I was still in my land? Therefore did I hasten to
flee to Tarshish, for I knew that You are a gracious and compassionate God,
slow to anger and abundant in kindness and relenting from evil. And now, 3
LORD, take my life, pray, from me, for better my death than my life." And 4
the LORD said, "Are you good and angry?" And Jonah went out of the city 5
and sat down to the east of the city and made himself a shelter there and
sat under it in the shade till he might see what would happen in the city.
And the LORD God set out a *qiqayon* plant, and it rose up over Jonah to be 6

CHAPTER 4   1. *And the thing was very evil for Jonah.* Various translations seek
to reconcile this clause with English idiomatic usage by representing Jonah here as
"dejected," "depressed," or "displeased." But the repetition of the term *ra'ah*, "evil," is
important for the writer's purpose. When the Ninevites decide to turn away from evil,
their very repentance so upsets Jonah that it becomes, ironically, an evil—which is to say,
a bitter vexation for him.

2. *hasten.* The basic meaning of the Hebrew *qidem* is to anticipate something by acting
before it can happen. As Sasson notes, there is an interplay between this term and *miqedem*,
"to the east of," in verse 5 as well as with the "east wind," *ruaḥ qadim*, in verse 8.
     You are a gracious and compassionate God, slow to anger and abundant in kindness.
These words are a direct quotation of Exodus 34:6. One may infer that by the late moment
of the writing of Jonah, the Torah was already canonical and these words were familiar as
a kind of doxology. Jonah, knowing God's compassionate nature from such an authoritative text, did not want to undertake the prophetic mission because he did not want to be
an instrument in saving Israel's hated archenemies from destruction. At this late point
in the story, he remains an unreconstructed Israelite nationalist, in contradiction to the
universalist outlook of the book.

3. *take my life.* Facing the galling fact that he has enabled the despised Ninevites to survive,
which was God's intention all along but not his, Jonah does not want to go on living. This
becomes the story of a prophetic mission that is a great success (unlike those of the historical prophets), with the success being intolerable to the prophet.

4. *Are you good and angry?* God's response in this first exchange with Jonah is scarcely a
response, only a provocation that leaves Jonah simmering.

5. *till he might see what would happen in the city.* Jonah hopes that either the Ninevites will
yet abandon their repentance and suffer cataclysmic destruction, with him as a privileged
spectator, or he will be confirmed in what he must see as God's perverse compassion as
he watches Nineveh prosper. Jonah must be situated on a hilltop or promontory, so he has
gone up after the repeated and emphatic going-downs. The verb "to go up" will be repeated
in this episode, but it is not attached to Jonah.

6. qiqayon *plant.* The term appears only in this passage. The King James Version renders
this as "gourd," which is as good as anybody's guess; however, since the plant has not been

a shade over his head to save him from his evil plight. And Jonah rejoiced
7 greatly over the *qiqayon*. And God set out a worm as dawn came up on the
8 morrow, and it struck the *qiqayon* and it withered. And it happened, as the
sun rose, that God set out a slashing east wind, and the sun struck Jonah's
head, and he grew faint and wanted to die, and he said, "Better my death
9 than my life." And God said to Jonah, "Are you good and angry over the
10 *qiqayon*?" And he said, "I am good and angry, to the point of death." And
the LORD said, "You—you had pity over the *qiqayon*, for which you did not
toil and which you did not grow, which overnight came and overnight was
11 gone. And I, shall I not have pity for Nineveh the great city, in which there
are many more than one hundred twenty thousand human beings who do
not know between their right hand and their left, and many beasts?"

---

confidently identified, it seems prudent to preserve the Hebrew name in the translation.
Why does Jonah need the *qiqayon* if he has already set up a shelter to give him shade? The
most reasonable explanation is that the shelter, assembled no doubt from the materials he
could scrape together from what was on hand, provided rather imperfect shade whereas
the *qiqayon*, miraculously sprung up overnight, offered luxuriant foliage.

7. *God set out.* God in this story repeatedly assigns elements of nature to do His bidding,
alternately protecting and destroying.

8. *slashing.* The adjective *ḥarishit* occurs only here. Because it appears to recall the verb
heḥerish, "to be silent," one understanding, which becomes ensconced in later literary
Hebrew, is that it means "silent" here. But that scarcely accords with the present context
because the wind—the hot wind called the *hamsin* that blows from the eastern desert—has
an obviously devastating effect. The translation guesses, picking up a cue from some of the
medieval Hebrew exegetes, that the adjective is related to the verb *ḥarash*, "to plow" and
perhaps by extension "to shear or cut through something."
    the sun struck Jonah's head. What happened to the shade of the shelter? Sasson plausibly
suggests that the shelter was swept away by the powerful east wind.

9. *Are you good and angry over the* qiqayon? God repeats the words he spoke in the earlier
exchange, adding "over the *qiqayon*."
    I am good and angry, to the point of death. Jonah bounces back to God the provoking
words He has just spoken, adding, in a pattern of incremental repetition, "to the point of
death."

10.*You—you had pity for the* qiqayon. God points an emphatic vocative finger at Jonah
by using the second-person singular pronoun, normally not required in front of the conjugated verb. With similar pronominal emphasis, He contrasts "I, shall I not" at the beginning of the next verse. The choice of the verb "pity" is pointedly not quite appropriate. Jonah
not does pity the plant for withering; rather, he is furious that he has been stripped of its
vitally necessary shade. His "pity" for the *qiqayon* is by no means disinterested, whereas
God's pity for all the living creatures of Nineveh flows from His compassion.

Micah

CHAPTER 1   The word of the LORD that came to Micah the 1
Morashtite in the days of Jotham, Ahaz, Hezekiah, kings of Judah, which
he saw in visions concerning Samaria and Jerusalem.

> Listen, all you peoples,   2
>   hearken, earth and its fullness,
> that the Master, the LORD, be witness against you forever,
>   the Master from His holy temple.
> For the LORD is about to come out from His place,   3
>   and go down and tread on earth's high places,
> and the mountains shall melt beneath Him   4
>   and the valleys split open,
> like wax before the fire,
>   like water pouring down a slope.
> For Jacob's trespass all this has happened   5
>   and for the house of Israel's offenses.
> What is Jacob's trespass
>   if not Samaria?
> And what Judah's high places
>   if not Jerusalem?

CHAPTER 1   2. *Listen, all you peoples, / hearken, earth and its fullness.* The beginning of Micah's prophecies is close to the formulaic beginning of long poems (compare
Isaiah 1 and Deuteronomy 32), although instead of invoking the heavens and the earth, it
invokes the sundry peoples of the earth.

5. *For Jacob's trespass all this has happened.* Because the imagery of the preceding lines has
expressed a global upheaval, Micah appears to be making a theologically novel point—that
the offenses of Israel are so grave that they will trigger a cataclysm that will roil the whole
earth.

    Judah's high places. Micah's chief emphasis will be on social injustice, but this is a refer-
ence to cultic disloyalty, the "high places" being the rural hilltop shrines. The Septuagint,
however, reads here "offense" instead of "high places."

6   And I will make Samaria a ruined heap in the field,
      a place for the planting of vineyards.
    And I will pour down her stones to the valley
      and her foundations I will lay bare.

7   And all her idols shall be shattered,
      and all her whore's pay burned in fire,
        and all her icons I will make a desolation.
    For from a whore's pay she amassed it,
      and to a whore's pay it shall revert.

8   For this would I lament and would wail,
      I would go naked and bare.
    I would raise a lament like the jackals
      and mourning like the ostriches.

9   For grievous is her wound,
      for it has come as far as Judah,
    has reached My people's gate,
      as far as Jerusalem.

10   Tell it not in Gath,
      surely do not weep.
    In Beth-Leaphrah
      wallow in the dust.

---

6. *And I will make Samaria a ruined heap in the field.* Jotham, the first of the three kings under whom Micah prophesied, began his reign in 758 B.C.E. The last of the three, Ahaz, ended his reign in 698 B.C.E. While there is no way of knowing when in this span Micah began and completed his prophetic mission, the mention in this prophecy of the future destruction of Samaria would have to occur before its conquest by Assyria in 721 B.C.E.

a place for the planting of vineyards. Where once a city stood, there will be only a flat field suitable for such planting.

I will pour down her stones to the valley. The unusual verb for "pour" is the same one used at the end of verse 4 and is surely meant to pick up the image of water pouring down a slope.

8. *ostriches.* This is what the Hebrew term used here generally means, though some scholars think it may indicate a kind of screech owl.

9. *it has come as far as Judah, / has reached My people's gate.* Micah uses the Prophetic past in his verbs—that is, events predicted are represented as though they had already been accomplished, perhaps just now (hence the present perfect in this translation). Reaching the gate is a clear indication of an invading army coming up to the walls of the city.

10. *Tell it not in Gath.* This line is an obvious citation of David's lament over the deaths of Saul and Jonathan (2 Samuel 1:20).

surely do not weep. In keeping with the preceding verset, this would mean: don't show your grief outwardly lest your enemies see it.

In Beth-Leaphrah / wallow in the dust. The Hebrew puns on the name of the place and 'afar, "dust."

Pass on, you who dwell in Shapier   11
    Did not Zaanan's dweller go out in shame?
Lament in Beth-Ezel.
    He shall take his station from you.
Though the dweller of Maroth   12
    had hoped for good,
evil came down from the LORD
    to the gate of Jerusalem.
Harness the steed to the chariot,   13
    you who dwell in Lachish.
It is the source of offense for Zion's Daughter
    for in you are found the trespasses of Israel.
Therefore give parting gifts   14
    for Moresheth-Gath.
Achziv's houses betray
    the kings of Israel.
Yet will I bring to you the dispossessor,   15
    you who dwell in Mareshah.
As far as Adullam he shall come—
    the glory of Israel.
Shave the pate and shear your hair   16
    over your pampered children.

---

11. *He shall take his station from you.* The "he" is the invader, but the wording of the Hebrew is obscure.

13. *Lachish.* Lachish was a major fortified Judahite town, destined to be destroyed by Sennacharib in 701 B.C.E. That conquest is celebrated in a famous Assyrian bas-relief. The inhabitants of Lachish are enjoined to harness their chariots in order to flee the town.

    for in you are found the trespasses of Israel. The nature of these trespasses is not spelled out. Some interpreters have surmised that these would be linked to Lachish's confidence in its own military strength, but that is not clear.

14. *parting gifts.* The use of the Hebrew *shiluḥim* is probably ironic. Ordinarily, it means "betrothal gifts," but the verbal stem suggests "sending away," and here that would be into exile.

    Achziv's houses betray. The Hebrew puns on "Achziv" and *'akhzav,* "betrayal," a word used especially for wadis that flow with water during the winter rains and then "betray" by turning dry in the summer.

15. *the glory of Israel.* This phrase modifies Adullam, a town linked with Lachish and evidently thought of, because of its military strength, as redounding to the national glory.

16. *over your pampered children.* A more literal rendering would be "the children of your pleasures."

Make yourself bald as an eagle,
    for they are gone from you into exile.

CHAPTER 2

1   Woe, who plot crime
                        and work evil on their couches.
                     In the morn they do it,
                        for they have the power.
2   They covet fields and rob them,
                        houses, and bear them away.
                     They exploit a man and his home,
                        a person and his estate.

3 Therefore, Thus said the Lord: I am about to plot evil against this clan, that you shall not be able to pull out your necks from it, and you shall not
4 walk with high heads, for it is an evil time. On that day this theme shall be sounded about you, and sobbing shall be sobbed. One shall say:

                     Ravaged, we are ravaged.
                        My people's portion is passed to another.
                     How it is taken away from me,
                        to a miscreant our fields are shared out!

5 Therefore there shall not be among you any who casts a lot by cord in the Lord's assembly.

CHAPTER 2   3. *plot evil.* The word that usually means "evil" carries its related sense of "harm" here, but it is worth repeating as "evil" because it reflects a measure-for-measure response to "plot crime" and "work evil" in verse 1.

    you shall not be able to pull out your necks from it. What is elliptically implied is the image of a restraining yoke.

4. *sobbing shall be sobbed.* This deliberately odd phrasing echoes the Hebrew, which in fact shows a triple occurrence of a single verbal stem: *wenahah nehi nihyah.*

    How it is taken away from me. The initial "how" is the formal sign of a lament, occurring here atypically not in the first line of the lament but in the second. It should be noted that both versets of this line as well as the second verset of the preceding line employ a third-person singular verb as the equivalent of a passive, which is fairly common biblical usage.

5. *any who casts a lot by cord.* This is a procedure for dividing territory, but in the destruction there will be no territory to divide.

"Do not preach—they preach.   6
    They shall not preach these things.
    Shame shall not overtake us.
What is said of the house of Jacob—   7
    will the LORD's patience be short,
        are these His acts?
Will not His words do well
    with him who goes upright?"
But against My people   8
    an enemy arises.
From him without cloak
    you strip the mantle,
from those who pass by thinking themselves safe
    returning from the war.
My people's wives you drive out   9
    from their luxurious homes.
From their infants you take away
    My glory for all times.
Rise up and go,   10
    for this is not a resting place.

---

6. *Do not preach.* These words, and what follows through the end of verse 7, are spoken by Micah's recalcitrant audience. As abundantly elsewhere, there is acute tension between the prophet and those he addresses, who do not want to hear the harsh things he has to say.

7. *What is said of the house of Jacob.* The Hebrew wording is obscure.
    Will not His words do well / with him who goes upright? The translation, in accordance with the Septuagint, reads "His words" instead of the Masoretic "my words." What the prophet's challengers are expressing is a confidence that they are the ones who go upright and that God will be patient with them and reward them.

8. *against.* The translation assumes that the anomalous *'etmul* should be broken into *'et*, the accusative particle, and *mul*, "opposite," but the meaning remains questionable.
    From him without cloak. The enigmatic *mul* recurs here, and the translation is again conjectural.
    thinking themselves safe. The Hebrew uses an ellipsis, saying only "safe."

9. *My people's wives you drive out.* The "enemy" of the previous verse is clearly the enemy within, who strips of their remaining garments those who can barely cover themselves and despoils people returning from battle who imagine themselves safe. Here they expropriate the homes of once pampered wives (perhaps now widowed).
    My glory. This term sounds somewhat odd in context. It would have to indicate something like security and prosperity, as the women are driven from their homes with their infants.

Because she has defiled herself,
    dire destruction shall descend.
11   Were a man to go
      after wind and cheating lies,
    "I would preach to you
      for wine and for strong drink."
        He would be this people's preacher.

12   I will surely assemble Jacob, all of you.
      I will surely gather Israel's remnant.
    I will make him like sheep in the pen,
      like a flock within the fold.
        They shall bustle with people.
13   He who makes the breach shall go up before them,
      they shall break out and pass through the gate and go out there.
    And their king shall pass through before them,
      the Lord at their head.

CHAPTER 3

1   And I said:
    Listen, pray, chieftains of Jacob
      and captains of the house of Israel.
    Is it not yours
      to know what is right?

---

10. *she has defiled herself.* The reference is to the collective nation, Judah.

    dire destruction shall descend. Although this is the clear gist of the three Hebrew words, the syntax is somewhat problematic.

11. *I would preach to you.* These are the words of the prophet sarcastically representing the intention of his hostile audience. The third verset, "He would be this people's preacher," would thus suggest that someone who exhorts his audience to get drunk would be the fitting preacher for such people.

12. *They shall bustle with people.* The unspecified "they," the subject of a feminine plural verb, has to refer to the towns (feminine in Hebrew) of Judah.

13. *He who makes the breach.* Since this is a prophecy of national restoration after a dispersal (verse 12), the breach would be in a wall enclosing the exiles. The same verb is used for "break out" in the next verset, but it is slightly puzzling that they then go out through a gate, not a breach in the wall. Perhaps passing through the gate is to be understood as "passing, as if through a gate," which would indicate a very wide breach.

Haters of good and lovers of evil,   2
   who flay their skin from them
      and their flesh from their bones.
Who devour My people's flesh   3
   and strip their skin from them
      and crack open their bones.
And they cut it like flesh in the pot
   and like meat in the cauldron.
Then shall they cry to the LORD,   4
   and He shall not answer them.
He shall hide His face from them at that time
   as they did evil through their acts.

Thus said the LORD concerning the prophets who lead My people astray; 5 who bite with their teeth and proclaim peace, and as to him who gives nothing for their mouths, they declare war against him.

Therefore shall it be night for your vision   6
   and darkness for you for divining,
and the sun shall set on the prophets,
   and the day turn to gloom upon them.
And the seers shall be shamed   7
   and the diviners disgraced,
and all of them cover their moustaches,

CHAPTER 3   2. *who flay their skin from them / and their flesh from their bones.* This pair of versets is a startling instance of intensification and specification of material from the first verset to the second and third. Initially, we get the general terms of hating good and loving evil, then this horrific image of flaying and cannibalism.

3. *crack open.* The verb *patseaḥ* is a devastating strategic choice: what it suggests is cracking open the bones in order to suck the marrow.
   like flesh. the Masoretic Text has *ka'asher*, "as," but the Septuagint shows *keshe'eir*, "like flesh" (a simple reversal of the two middle consonants), which seems far more likely.

5. *who bite with their teeth.* This image of voraciousness is in all likelihood motivated by the editorial placement of this prophecy here, immediately after the metaphorical use of cannibalism in the previous prophecy.

6. *night for your vision.* These false prophets pretended to see into the future or exercise clairvoyance; now they will be enveloped in the darkness of a prophetic eclipse.

7. *cover their moustaches.* This bizarre-sounding phrase refers to a mourning practice in which the face was covered down to the upper lip. Compare Ezekiel 24:17.

for there shall be no response from God.
8   And yet, I have been filled with power,
with the spirit of the LORD,
with justice and valor,
to tell to Jacob his trespass
and to Israel his offense.
9   Hear this, pray, chieftains of the house of Jacob
and captains of the house of Israel,
who despise justice
and everything straight they twist,
10   Who build Zion with bloodshed
and Jerusalem with wickedness.
11   Her chieftains judge with bribes,
and her priests instruct for payment,
and her prophets divine for silver
and on the LORD they lean, saying,
"Is not the LORD in our midst?
No harm will come upon us."
12   Therefore, because of you,
Zion shall be plowed like a field,
and Jerusalem become heaps of ruins
and the Temple mount a high forest.

---

8. *And yet, I have been filled with power.* Having excoriated the false prophets, Micah now sets himself antithetically as a prophet actually imbued by the spirit of YHWH.

11. *Her chieftains judge with bribes.* Having previously represented the leaders of the people preying cannibalistically upon those they rule, Micah now translates the metaphor into literal acts: the judges pervert justice by taking bribes; the priests fulfill their role as teachers—perhaps, unreliable teachers—only for gain; and the prophets turn themselves into merchants of divination.

on the LORD *they lean.* While merely pursuing the accrual of wealth, these purported spiritual leaders claim to enjoy the full benevolent support of God in what they do.

12. *a high forest.* Some have questioned the meaning of *bamot ya'ar,* literally, "high places of a forest." The first of these two nouns can designate a topographical height and is also used for the rural altars despised by the Deuteronomist. The New Jewish Publication Society version renders the phrase in the latter sense, imagining that the holy Temple will be turned into a simple pagan hilltop shrine, but that seems unlikely. There are some biblical instances in which the two nouns joined in a construct state show a reversal of the semantic relation between the two. In this perspective, *bamot ya'ar* would mean the same as *ya'ar bamot,* "a forest of high places," which is to say, a high forest. Since the Temple was built on a mountain, after being razed, it would be replaced by the wild growth of a "high forest."

CHAPTER 4

And it shall happen in future days   1
   that the mount of the LORD's house shall be firm-founded
     at the top of the mountains and lifted over the hills.
And the people shall flow to it,
   and many nations shall go and say: 2
Come, let us go up to the mount of the LORD,
   and to the house of Jacob's God,
that He may teach us of His ways
   and that we may walk in His paths.
For from Zion shall teaching come forth
   and the LORD's word from Jerusalem.
And He shall judge among many peoples   3

CHAPTER 4   1. *And it shall happen in future days.* The first four verses of this chapter duplicate Isaiah 2:2–4, constituting the most extensive such duplication between two prophets. There are only minor differences (e.g., when Isaiah says "nations," Micah says "peoples"). Different explanations have been offered for the duplication: that Micah borrowed from Isaiah, that Isaiah borrowed from Micah, that both drew on a common source, that a later editor inserted the passage in both books. This last alternative seems the least likely; and an unknown common source is merely a conjectural hypothesis. These two prophets were roughly contemporaneous, but given the fact that Isaiah was the more prominent figure—see, for example, the narrative in 2 Kings 20, where the king turns to him at a moment of crisis—it may be more plausible that Micah took from Isaiah. Scrolls of the prophecies evidently had some circulation in the prophet's lifetime. One point where there are two small additions as well as a substituted term in Micah may provide a clue: verse 3 reads "And He shall judge among many peoples / and be arbiter to vast nations from far away." In Isaiah it is: "And He shall judge among the nations / and be arbiter for many peoples." Micah adds "many" in the first verset, heightens "many" to "vast" in the second, and inserts "far away" at the end. By and large, this kind of amplification is a telltale sign of adopting and "improving" a preexisting text. Otherwise, since there are no substantive divergences between the two passages, the comments on Isaiah will be repeated here.

in future days. Older translations represent this Hebrew phrase as "in the end of days," giving it an emphatically eschatological meaning it does not have. The Hebrew *'aḥarit*, derived from the word that means "after," refers to an indefinite time after the present.

2. *the mount of the LORD.* Mount Zion in Jerusalem is imagined as a kind of second Sinai, from which God's teaching will go out.

3. *many peoples.* The universalist note struck here is new. It will be elaborated and expanded in the visions of the anonymous prophet of the Babylonian exile whose writing is appended to the Book of Isaiah, beginning with chapter 40.

    and be arbiter to vast nations from far away.
    And they shall grind their swords into plowshares
       and their spears into pruning hooks.
    Nation shall not raise sword against nation,
       nor shall they learn war anymore.

4   And they shall dwell each man beneath his vine
       and beneath his fig tree, with none to make him tremble,
         for the mouth of the LORD of Armies has spoken.

5   For all the peoples shall walk
       each in the name of his god.
    But we shall walk
       in the name of the LORD our God
         forevermore.

6   On that day, said the LORD:
    I will gather the lame one,
       and the outcast I will take in
         and to whom I did harm.

7   And I will make the lame one a remnant
       and the failing one a vast nation,
    and the LORD shall reign over them
       on Mount Zion, from hence and forever.

Nation shall not raise sword against nation. God's teaching from Zion, then, is to have the effect of inaugurating a reign of universal peace. There is an imaginative boldness, or perhaps rather the courage of desperation, in this vision because it was articulated at a historical moment of continual warfare among imperial powers when the land of Israel itself was threatened with destruction by Assyria.

learn war. Fighting was a skill that required training, as noted in Psalms and elsewhere.

4. *And they shall dwell each man beneath his vine.* This evocation of an era of tranquillity and peace is stereotypical and does not appear in the Isaiah passage.

5. *For all the peoples shall walk / each in the name of his god.* This sentence, which appears to express the idea that polytheism will persist, however much the nations take instruction from Zion, is not present in Isaiah.

But we shall walk / in the name of the LORD our God / forevermore. This line, too, has no direct equivalent in Isaiah, though it may have been inspired by the use of the same verb in the concluding line of the Isaiah passage: "O house of Jacob, / come, let us walk in the LORD's light."

7. *the failing one.* The Masoretic *nahala'ah* is obscure. Two ancient versions appear to read *nahalah* or *nil'ah,* and either of those terms could be rendered as "failing."

And you, watchtower of the flock,   8
    rampart of Zion's Daughter,
to you shall come the former kingdom,
    and the kingship of Jerusalem's Daughter shall arrive.
Now, why should you scream so loud?   9
    Is there no king in you?
Is your councillor gone,
    that pangs seize you like a woman in labor?
Writhe and groan,   10
    Zion's Daughter, like a woman in labor,
for now will you go from the city
    and dwell in the field.
And you shall come as far as Babylonia.
    There you shall be saved.
There shall the LORD redeem you
    from the clutch of your enemies.
And now many nations   11
    have gathered against you, saying:
      "Let her be tainted, that we may gloat over Zion."
But they do not know   12
    the plans of the LORD,
and they do not understand His counsel,
    for He has gathered them like a sheaf on the threshing floor.
Rise and thresh, Zion's Daughter!   13
    For I will make your horn like iron
      and your hooves I will make like bronze,
and you shall grind down many peoples,

---

8. *come . . . / arrive.* The two Hebrew words appear in immediate sequence in the first verset, leaving the second verset without a verb. This translation assumes that one of the verbs should be moved to the second verset.

10. *groan.* The meaning of the Hebrew verb is obscure.
    And you shall come as far as Babylonia. This is not a prophecy of the Babylonian exile. In the eighth century B.C.E., the threat was Assyria, and there were amicable relations between Judah and Babylonia. Thus it figures here as a place of refuge.

11. *gloat.* As before, this translation represents a Hebrew idiom that means to look upon with schadenfreude.

13. *I will make your horn like iron.* Although "horn" is idiomatic for "strength," here the dead metaphor is revived by the addition of the hooves in the next verset. Thus Zion's Daughter is turned into an ox or bull performing the threshing.

and I will devote to the LORD their riches
  and their wealth to all the earth's Master.

14   Now gash yourself, gashing's Daughter
       they have laid a siege against us.
     With a rod they strike on the cheek
       the judge of Israel.

CHAPTER 5

1   And you, Bethlehem of Ephrath,
      the least of Judah's clans,
    from you shall one come forth for Me
      to be ruler of Israel
    whose origins are from ancient times,
      from days of yore.
2   Therefore shall He give them over
      till the time the woman in labor bears her child,
    and the rest of his brothers shall come back
      with the Israelites.
3   And he shall stand and shepherd them by the might of the LORD,
      by the pride of the name of the LORD his God.
    And they shall dwell secure,
      for then shall he be great to the ends of the earth.

---

14. *Now gash yourself.* This verse clearly does not belong to the preceding passage, which is a prophecy of triumphal redemption, whereas this is a prophecy of doom. The gashing is a mourning practice, forbidden by biblical law but licit as poetic expression.

  gashing's Daughter. The phrase *bat-gedud* is peculiar. Normally, *gedud* means "troop," but immediately following the verb *titgodedi* here, it would have to refer to gashing. Perhaps a pun is intended: Zion's Daughter, now mourning, has become "the troop's daughter," subject to the ravages of the invading forces.

CHAPTER 5   1. *Bethlehem.* This is David's hometown, and so the idea of a ruler coming forth from this place is a signal of the future continuity of the Davidic dynasty.

2. *give them over.* The Hebrew says, somewhat enigmatically, merely "give them," but this is probably an ellipsis for "give them into the hands of their enemies." The kingdom of Judah, then, is to be subjugated until a crucial moment of transition, when the ideal Davidic ruler will be born.

3. *dwell secure.* "Secure" is merely implied.

  for then shall he be great to the ends of the earth. It is highly unlikely that this is a proph-

And thus shall be the peace: 4
   Assyria shall not enter our land
      nor tread in our citadels.
And we shall set up against him seven shepherds
   and eight princes of the peoples,
and they shall smash the land of Assyria with the sword   5
   and the land of Nimrod in its gateways.
And they shall save us from Assyria
   should he enter our land
      and should he tread within our borders.
And the remnant of Jacob shall be   6
   in the midst of many peoples
like the dew from the LORD,
   like gentle rain upon the grass,
as he shall not place hope in man
   nor expectation in humankind.
And the remnant of Jacob shall be   7
   in the midst of many peoples
like a lion among forest beasts,
   like a young lion among the flocks of sheep
that passes through and tramples
   and tears apart with none to save.
Your hand shall loom over your foes   8
   and all your enemies be cut off.

---

ecy of global empire commanded by the Davidic king. Rather, his reign will be so glorious that the fame of it will reach the ends of the earth.

4. *seven shepherds / and eight princes of the peoples.* The numeric progression from first verset to second is a familiar convention of biblical poetry. The seven shepherds and eight princes are in all likelihood foreign rulers allied with Judah. "Princes of the peoples" is literally "princes of humankind," which would mean "non-Judahites."

7. *like a lion among forest beasts.* The "beasts" are deer and other forest creatures vulnerable to the fierce predation of the lion. In any case, there is a striking contradiction between the imagery of this verse and the preceding one. First, the people of Israel is figured as a gentle blessing—dew and rain—for all the nations. Now it is depicted as a furious force destroying nations. Some have tried to reconcile the contradiction temporally: first Judah will be a militant power, then, after its victory, a beneficent presence. But if that is the prophet's intention, it remains puzzling that the dew image should precede the lion image.

9   And it shall happen on that day, said the LORD:
         I will cut off your horses from your midst,
             and I will destroy your chariots.
10   And I will cut off the towns of your land
             and reduce to ruins all your fortresses.
11   And I will cut off sorcery from your hands,
             nor soothsayers shall you have.
12   And I will cut off your idols
             and your cultic pillars from your midst.
         And no more shall you bow down
             to the work of your hands.
13   And I will uproot your cultic poles from your midst,
             and I will destroy your icons.
14   And I will act in anger and in vengeful wrath
             toward the nations that did not heed.

---

9. *And it shall happen on that day.* This is clearly a new prophecy, not of redemption but of doom. The editorial signal for inserting it here is probably the occurrence of the verb "cut off" in the second line of this prophecy, which picks up the use of the same verb at the end of the preceding prophecy.

11. *sorcery from your hands.* "From your hands" (the Hebrew uses a singular) probably means "that you possess," although it may also refer to the actual manipulation of divinatory instruments in the hands of the soothsayer. For this reason, the translation renders the idiom literally.

12. *idols / . . . cultic pillars.* The castigation of paganism is somewhat unusual for Micah, whose main focus is on social injustice.

13. *I will destroy your icons.* The Masoretic Text reads "I will destroy your towns ['*areykha*]." This looks rather odd in a catalogue of destruction of pagan cultic objects and may well be an inadvertent scribal replication of the destruction of "towns" in verse 10. This translation assumes the original text reads '*atsabeykha,* "your icons."

14. *I will act in anger . . . / toward the nations.* This last verse does not seem to belong to a prophecy about the devastation of idolatrous Israel. It may have been added editorially in order to mitigate the grimness of the prophecy of doom. Alternately, the prophet might be saying that the same dire fate which will overtake Israel awaits the nations that do not heed God's word.

CHAPTER 6

Listen, pray, to what the LORD has said.   1
   Rise, plead a case before the mountains,
      and let the hills hear your voice.
Hear, O mountains, the case of the LORD,   2
   and you mighty pillars of the earth.
For the LORD has a case against His people,
   and with Israel He would dispute.
"My people, what have I done to you,   3
   and in what did I do you in? Testify against Me!
For I brought you up from the land of Egypt,   4
   and from the house of slaves I redeemed you,
and sent before you
   Moses, Aaron, and Miriam.
My people, recall, pray, what Balak king of Moab devised   5
   and what Balaam son of Beor answered him,
from Shittim to Gilgal,
   that the LORD's bounties would be known."

With what shall I come before the LORD   6
   bow to the most high God?
Shall I come before Him with burnt offerings,
   with yearling calves?
Is the LORD pleased with thousands of rams,   7

CHAPTER 6   1. *the mountains, /... the hills.* These are conventionally exhorted to listen to the discourse at the beginning of biblical poems. Here, they are called upon to act as witnesses in a legal contestation between God and the Judahites.

3. *do you in.* The basic meaning of this verbal stem in its intransitive form is "to be unable." Some opt here for its secondary meaning, "to exhaust."

5. *Balak.* His story is told in Numbers 22–24. Balak hired Balaam as a professional seer to put a hex on Israel but instead, following God's bidding, Balaam blessed them.
   from Shittim to Gilgal. These are, respectively, the last way station of the Israelites east of the Jordan and their first encampment after crossing the Jordan.

6. *With what shall I come before the LORD.* Although some interpreters prefer to link this with what precedes, it looks like a new literary unit.

7. *Is the LORD pleased with thousands of rams.* There is a pattern of intensification in these lines: first, simply burnt offerings and yearlings; then, in a hyperbolic flourish, thousands of rams and tens of thousands of streams of oil; and, in the crowning extravagance, child sacrifice—the most a person can give.

myriads of streams of oil?
Shall I give Him my firstborn for my trespass,
  the fruit of my loins for my offense?
8 It was told to you, man, what is good
  and what the LORD demands of you—
only doing justice and loving kindness
  and walking humbly with your God.

9 The voice of the LORD calls out to the town,
  and a man of insight shall see Your name.
    Heed the rod—and who brought it about?
10 Can there yet be in the house of the wicked
  treasures of wickedness
    and an accursed short *ephah*?
11 Could I declare innocent who has wicked scales
  and in his pouch cheating weight-stones?
12 Whose rich are filled with outrage
  and those who dwell in her speak lies

---

8. *It was told to you.* The Hebrew seems to say "he told you," and almost all interpreters assume the implied subject of the verb is God. But third-person singular verbs are often used as the equivalent of the passive, and the passive makes smoother sense in this line, obviating the necessity to have "the LORD" here tell what the LORD demands in the next verset.

only doing justice and loving kindness / and walking humbly with your God. This is a succinct and especially beautiful expression of the view Micah shares with Isaiah that ethical behavior is far more important than the mechanics of sacrificial rites.

9. *a man of insight shall see Your name.* From this point through to verse 14, textual problems abound. "A man" is added in this translation as an interpretive guess. The expression "see Your name" might mean something like "recognize Your power," but it remains obscure.

Heed the rod. One surmises this is "the rod of wrath" that recurs in Prophetic literature.

who brought it about. This may mean that the addressee is responsible for the disaster that has overtaken the people, but that is conjectural.

10. *Can there.* The Hebrew *ha'ish*, with no medial *yod*, is odd, but Shmuel Vergon has made a persuasive case that it is archaic orthography for *hayeish*, and he cites a clear instance of this spelling in 2 Samuel 14:19 ("there is ['ish] no turning right or left").

short ephah. The literal sense is "an *ephah* of thinness," that is, a measure used to shortchange the buyer.

11. *Could I declare innocent.* This translation reads, with the Vulgate, *ha'azakeh*, the transitive form of the verb, instead of the Masoretic *ha'ezkeh*, "could I be innocent."

and their tongue in their mouth is cheating.

And I on My part have made you ill, have smitten you,   13

    made you desolate for your offenses.

As for you, you shall eat and not be sated   14

    and your filth shall be within you.

She will conceive and not give birth

    and what she bears, to the sword I will give.

As for you, you shall sow and not reap.   15

    You, you shall trample the olives and not use the oil,

        get fermented juice and not drink the wine.

And the practices of Omri are kept   16

    and all the acts of the house of Ahab,

        and you go by their counsels,

so that I turn you into a desolation

    and those who dwell in her into hissing,

        and My people's disgrace you shall bear.

CHAPTER 7

Alas for me,   1

    as I have become like the leavings of summer fruit,

        like the last gleanings of the vintage—

there is no cluster for eating,

---

14. *your filth.* The Hebrew term *yeshaḥ* occurs only here. This is the meaning scholars have proposed on the basis of an Arab cognate: the victim of the curse gets no satisfaction from what he eats and is unable to evacuate.

    She will conceive. The grammar also allows this to be construed as "you will conceive," but because the person addressed has been masculine, it may be preferable to understand this as an unspecified woman (your wife).

15. *trample the olives.* Olives, of course, are pressed, not trampled, but this is probably a simple extension of the idiom used for grapes.

    get fermented juice. The verb is merely implied.

16. *Omri.* Along with Ahab, Omri is one of the monarchs of the northern kingdom singled out in the Book of Kings for his abominations.

    and My people's disgrace you shall bear. It is possible, though not entirely certain, that Micah is drawing a distinction between the person addressed in the prophecy, a stand-in for the whole group of malefactors who have lied and cheated and used false scales and measures, and "My people," who have been victimized, reduced to disgrace, by this group.

no ripe figs that my palate has longed for.
2   The faithful has vanished from the land,
        and the upright among men is gone.
     They all lie in wait to shed blood,
        each man hunts his brother with a net.
3   For evil their hands are skilled.
        The noble and the judge ask payment.
     The great one speaks the disaster he wants,
        and they pervert it for him.
4   Their good is like a thornbush,
        no straighter than a hedge.
     The day those who look for You, of Your reckoning, has come.
        Now shall their confounding take place.
5   Do not trust in a friend,
        nor place confidence in a leader.
     From her who lies in your lap
        guard your lips.
6   For the son reviles the father,
        the daughter rises against her mother,
        the daughter-in-law against her mother-in-law—

CHAPTER 7   1. *my palate.* Although *nafshi* might simply be an intensive alternative for the first-person pronoun, the context of a desire to eat suggests that it carries its other sense of either "throat" or "appetite." Hence "palate" is proposed here as a readable English equivalent.

2. *with a net.* Nets were used for catching birds and, of course, also for catching fish.

3. *For evil their hands are skilled.* The Hebrew wording is odd, and thus the translation is only an educated guess.
    The great one speaks the disaster he wants. Again, the Hebrew is opaque, and the text may be corrupt. This sentence does not properly scan as a line of poetry.
    pervert it for him. The object would probably be a case in law. "For him" is added in the translation.

4. *no straighter than a hedge.* In modern horticulture, hedges are usually straight, but what is envisioned here is an informal hedge made of brambles.

5. *guard your lips.* The literal sense is "guard the openings of your mouth."

6. *the daughter-in-law against her mother-in-law.* The inclusion of this item suggests that in ancient Israel, as in many other societies, the mother-in-law exercised authority over her son's wife.

a man's enemies are the people of his household.
But I look for You,   7
   I await the God of my rescue
      May the LORD hear me.

Rejoice not, O my enemy.   8
   Though I fall, I will arise.
Though I sit in darkness,
   the LORD is a light for me.
The LORD's wrath I will bear   9
   for I have offended against Him,
till He takes up my case
   and renders Me justice.
He shall bring me out to the light,
   I will see His vindication.
And my enemy shall see   10
   and shame shall cover her,
who has said to me,
   "Where is the LORD your God?"
I will gloat over her—
   now she shall be trampled
      like the mud of the streets.
The day for rebuilding your walls,   11
   that day the borders shall widen,
that day—and to you shall it come,   12
   from Assyria and the towns of Egypt
and from Egypt to the Euphrates

---

8. *Rejoice not, O my enemy.* In the Hebrew, all the verbs and nouns are in the feminine singular, reflecting the representation of the enemy people as a female figure. This conventional mode of representing a nation becomes a means of dramatizing the relation between Israel and its enemies: the hostile nation is a woman who would gleefully mock Israel in its downfall but who is destined to be humiliated and trampled upon.

10. *I will gloat over her.* As before, this translation conveys the general sense of the idiom that is literally "my eyes will see in her."

11. *the borders.* The Hebrew *ḥoq* usually means "limit," "fixed measure," or "statute," but the vision of a utopian expansion of the kingdom of Judah in the next two lines argues for the sense of "border."

and from sea to sea and mountain to mountain.

13   And the earth shall become a desolation
        with its dwellers, as the fruit of their acts.

14   Shepherd Your people with Your staff,
        the flock of Your estate,
      that dwells secure in the forest
        in the midst of the farmland.
      They shall feed in Bashan and Gilead
        as in days of yore.

15   As the days when you came out from the land of Egypt,
        I will show him wonders.

16   Nations shall see and be shamed
        of all their valor.
      They shall put hand over mouth,
        their ears shall be deafened.

17   They shall lick the dust like a snake,
        like the crawlers on the ground.
      They shall be shaken out from their enclosures
        to the Lord our God.
          They shall dread and fear You.

18   Who is a God like You dismissing crime
        and forgiving trespass for the remnant of His estate?
      He does not cling forever to His wrath,

---

13. *And the earth shall become a desolation.* If in fact this verse belongs at the end of this prophecy of a grand expansion of Judah, it would mean that nations across the known earth will be subject to cataclysmic devastation as Judah triumphs.

15. *I will show him wonders.* The first-person verb means that God is now speaking. Many scholars prefer to emend this phrase to an imperative: "Show him wonders."

16. *their ears shall be deafened.* It is obvious why they should cover their mouths—because in the face of God's great wonders there is nothing they could possibly say. Why they should be deafened is less clear. Perhaps it is because of the great uproar in the cataclysm God brings upon the nations.

17. *their enclosures.* This noun, derived from the verbal stem that means "to close," is not the ordinary term for "fortress," but that seems to be its meaning here.

18. *Who is a God like You dismissing crime.* After prophecies that sharply accuse Judah for its sundry misdeeds, the collection of Micah's writing fittingly ends with a celebration of YHWH as a forgiving God.

for He desires kindness.
Again He shall have mercy on us.   19
  he shall cleanse our crimes.
And You shall fling into the depths of the sea
  all our offenses.
Grant truth to Jacob,   20
  kindness to Abraham,
as You swore to our fathers
  in ancient days.

---

19. *he shall cleanse our crimes.* The verb in the received text, *yikhbosh* means something like "suppress" or even "squash." This translation reads instead *yekhabeis,* the same Hebrew consonants with different vowel-points.

  our offenses. The Masoretic Text has "their offenses," but three ancient versions as well as some Hebrew manuscripts read "our offenses."

20. *truth . . . / kindness.* This is a common instance of the so-called break-up pattern, where a known collocation—in this case, "truth-and-kindness," i.e., faithful, unswerving kindness—is broken up and distributed between the two versets.

Nahum

CHAPTER 1   A portent concerning Nineveh, the book of the   1
vision of Nahum the Elkoshite.

> A jealous and vengeful God is the Lord;   2
>   vengeful, the Lord and master of wrath.
> The Lord is avenged of His foes,
>   and bears a grudge against His enemies.
> The Lord is slow to anger and great in power,   3
>   but the Lord surely does not acquit.
> In tempest and whirlwind His way,
>   and a cloud is the dust at His feet.
> He rebukes the sea and it dries up,   4
>   and all rivers He turns to dry land.
> Bleak are Bashan and Carmel,
>   and Lebanon's blossom is bleak.
> Mountains shake before Him,   5
>   and the hills melt.
> The earth lies in ruins before Him,

CHAPTER 1   1. *A portent concerning Nineveh.* Unlike the other prophets, Nahum concentrates exclusively on the impending fate of Judah's enemy and includes no rebuke of his own people. The focus on the imminent destruction of the capital city of Assyria would place these prophecies close to 616 B.C.E., when Nineveh was conquered by the Medes and the Babylonians.

3. *surely does not acquit.* He exacts retribution against His enemies.

4. *He rebukes the sea.* There is a kind of *a fortiori* argument here: if God is so powerful that he can dry up the sea and wither Bashan, Carmel, and Lebanon, He can surely overwhelm Assyria.

5. *The earth lies in ruins.* The Masoretic Text reads "the earth bears," *watisa',* but two ancient versions reflect, more plausibly, *watisha',* which in the Hebrew involves merely moving the dot over the letter *shin* from the left side to the right.

the world and all who dwell in it.

6   Before His fury who can stand,
            and who can arise in His smoldering ire?
        His wrath pours out like fire,
            and the rocks are shattered by it.

7   The LORD is a good stronghold on a day of distress,
            and He embraces those who trust Him.

8   And in his sweeping torrent He puts an end to His foes,
            and His enemies the dark pursues.

9   What could you plot against the LORD?
            An utter end He brings about—
                not twice shall the foe arise.

10   For like tangled thorns—
            as they swilled they were besotted—
                they were consumed like heaps of dry straw.

11   From you has come forth
            one who plots evil against the LORD,
                a worthless councillor.

12   Thus said the LORD:
        Though they be joined in a pact and many,
            yet shall they be done with and gone.
                I afflicted you but will afflict you no more.

---

8. *His foes.* The received text reads, incomprehensibly, *meqomah*, "her place," but both the ancient Greek and Latin versions used texts that evidently have *beqamav*, literally, "those who rise against him."

9. *What could you plot against the LORD?* The "you" (plural) is clearly the Assyrians.

   not twice shall the foe arise. The noun here, *tsarah*, usually means "distress," and so, if one adheres to the received text, it could mean that Judah will not find itself in straits a second time. But it could be a collective noun for "foe" or perhaps might be corrected to *tsar*. Given the surrounding emphasis on the destruction of the enemy, "foe" seems the likely meaning.

10. *as they swilled they were besotted.* This verset interrupts the metaphor of combustible thorns, switching from figure to its referent, which would be the drunken Assyrian army unprepared to defend itself.

   like heaps of dry straw. The Hebrew seems to say "like dry straw full," but this translation assumes that the sense is "like a fully packed heap of dry straw."

12. *joined in a pact.* The Hebrew *shleimim* usually means "complete," but the related *shlomim* can mean "party to a pact or alliance"; either *shleimim* may mean that as well, or it could be revocalized as *shlomim*.

And now I will break his shaft from upon you   13
    and snap your cords.
And the LORD has charged concerning you: 14
    There shall be no seed of your name anymore.
        I will cut off from the house of your god
            idol and molten image.
I will lay out your grave,
    for you are of no account.

CHAPTER 2

Look, upon the mountains   1
    are the feet of the herald
        announcing good tidings.
Celebrate, Judah, your pilgrim feasts,
    fulfill your pledges.
For no more shall the base man pass through you—
    he is cut off altogether.
The battering ram has come up against you.   2
    Put up a watch. Look out to the road.
        Brace yourself, flex all your strength.
For the LORD has brought back the pride of Jacob   3
    like the pride of Israel.
For marauders have blighted them
    and have ruined their branches.

---

13. *shaft . . . / cords.* The image is of a harnessed draft animal.

14. *concerning you.* The lines that follow make clear that the person addressed is the Assyrian emperor.

CHAPTER 2   1. *pledges.* The "pledges" or "vows" are pledges to offer particular sacrifices in the Temple, and for this reason they are paired with "pilgrim feasts."

2. *The battering ram has come up against you.* After the preceding verse, there is some ambiguity as to whether "you" is Judah or Assyria, but the sequence of lines that follows makes it clear that it is Assyria (or Nineveh) that is about to be destroyed.

    Put up a watch. Look out to the road. These exhortations are ironic: no measure of self-defense will avail the besieged Nineveh.

3. *For the LORD has brought back the pride of Jacob.* This would be a corollary of the destruction of Assyria.

4   His warriors' shields are reddened,
  the soldiers are stained crimson.
Like torch-fire are the chariots
  on the day they are made ready,
   and the cypress shafts are poisoned.
5   Through the streets the chariots run wild,
  they rumble through the squares.
Their look is like torches,
  like lightning they race.
6   He calls out his staunch men—
  they stumble as they go.
They rush to the wall,
  and mantlets are set up.
7   The gates of the rivers are opened
  and the palace is swept away.
8   And the mistress is brought out, exiled,
  and her slavegirls moan like doves,
   beating on their chests.
9   And Nineveh in time past was like a pool of water,
  but now they flee.
   "Stop! Stop!" but none turns round.
10   Loot the silver, loot the gold!

---

4. *reddened, / . . . stained crimson.* Several modern translations have understood this as the color of the shields and of the warrior's garments. But the first of these two Hebrew words means "reddened," not "red," and in light of the havoc of battle evoked in the next few lines, it makes far better sense to see this as a depiction of the fighters and their shields splattered with gore.

 the cypress shafts. That is, the shafts of the spears.

6. *mantlets.* The mantlet, *sokheikh,* is a movable shelter devised to protect the besiegers as they approach the walls.

7. *The gates of the rivers are opened.* The evident reference is to moats around the city.

8. *And the mistress is brought out, exiled.* The Masoretic Text is not coherent here. It begins with a masculine verb, *wehutsav,* "and it was stationed, set up," followed by two feminine verbs. This translation is based on a frequently proposed emendation, but without great confidence, and there are no ancient versions that reflect it.

9. *like a pool of water.* The implication is a tranquil pool of water. Perhaps we are invited to imagine Nineveh once securely surrounded by its moats.

10. *Loot the silver, loot the gold.* The poem, after having addressed "Stop! Stop!" to the fugitives (or having quoted words addressed to them), turns to exhort the conquerors.

and there is no end to the horde,
    treasure of every precious vessel.
Stripped and distraught and despoiled,   11
    fainting heart and buckling knees
and shuddering in all loins,
    and all faces lose their luster.
Where now is the den of the lions,   12
    the cave of the king of beasts?
There the lion walked, the maned beast there,
    the lion's cub, with none to make them tremble.
The lion tearing prey for its cubs   13
    and breaking necks for his lioness,
he filled his lair with prey
    and his den with torn-apart flesh.
Here am I against you,   14
    said the LORD of Armies.
I will burn up your chariots in smoke,
    and your maned beasts the sword shall devour,
and I will cut off from the earth your prey,
    nor shall the sound of your envoys be heard again.

CHAPTER 3

Woe, city of bloodshed,   1
    all of it deceit.
Filled with plunder,

---

11. *Stripped and distraught and despoiled.* The Hebrew sound-play is more intense: *buqah umevuqah umevulaqah.* The basic meaning of the recurring root is to be hollowed out, emptied, but the replicated sounds go beyond lexical meaning.

13. *breaking necks.* The usual meaning of this verb is "to strangle," but lions don't strangle. This translation follows the solution of the Revised English Bible.

14. *your maned beasts the sword shall devour.* These two concluding lines obviously pick up the metaphor of the lion from verses 12–13, the lion being a standard trope for a warrior exercising martial prowess. An apt understanding of this line is reflected in the battle poems of Shmuel Hanagid, the great medieval Hebrew poet of Granada, who uses the same word for "lions," *kefirim,* as an epithet for "warriors."

CHAPTER 3   1. *plunder.* The Hebrew *pereq* in this context means "something ripped apart" and thus is a parallel to "prey" in the next verset.

prey never gone from it.

2   The sound of the whip
      and the sound of the wheel's clatter,
galloping horse
      and chariot bounding.

3   Rearing charger
      and blade of the sword
        and flash of the spear,
and many the slain
      and the press of the corpses—
there is no end to the bodies,
      they stumble on the bodies.

4   Because of all the whoring of the whore,
      the beguiling sorceress,
who ensnares nations with her whoring
      and clans with her spells,

5   here am I against you, said the Lord of Armies—
      I will lay bare your skirts over your face
and show nations your nakedness
      and kingdoms your shame.

6   And I will fling foul things upon you
      and make you vile and make a spectacle of you.

7   And it shall be that all who see you
      shall shrink from you and say:
"Nineveh is ravaged!
      Who will grieve for her,
and where can I seek

---

2. *The sound of the whip / and the sound of the wheel's clatter.* Nahum's power as a poet is especially manifested in his ability to evoke battle scenes—in this case, the invading army with all its accoutrements charging through the streets of Nineveh.

3. *they stumble on the bodies.* The Hebrew says "their bodies," meaning the bodies of their own people.

4. *the whore.* This is the female personification of Nineveh.

5. *I will lay bare your skirts over your face.* The condign punishment for the promiscuous woman is to publicly expose her sexual parts. This is a recurrent trope in the Prophets. Compare, for example, Ezekiel 16:37.

6. *I will fling foul things upon you.* The whoring Nineveh is first shamefully exposed and then has filth piled on her.

comforters for her?"
Are you better than No-Amon 8
   that sits by the Nile,
      water all around her,
that has a sea as a rampart,
   water is her wall?
Nubia the vast 9
   and Egypt without end,
Put and the Lybians
   were her allies.
Yet she, too, went captive into exile. 10
   Her babes, too, were smashed
      at every street corner,
and for her notables they cast lots
   and all her great men were shackled in chains.
You, too, shall be drunk, 11
   you shall be overcome.
      You, too, shall seek a stronghold against the enemy.
All your fortresses are figs, 12
   ripe fruit.
If they are shaken, they fall
   into the mouth of the eater.
Look, your people are women 13
   in your midst for your enemies.

---

8. *No-Amon.* This is the major city of northern Egypt.

   that has a sea as a rampart. A canal cut from the Nile ("that sits by the Nile") is used as a moat to surround the city.

   water is her wall. The Masoretic Text reads *miyam,* "from the sea," but a simple revocalization of those three consonants to *mayim* yields the more coherent "water."

9. *Nubia . . . / Put and the Lybians.* These are all contiguous nations presumed here to have been allied with No-Amon.

11. *You, too, shall be drunk.* The trope of the poison chalice is so common that the simple verb "be drunk" is sufficient to convey its presence to the audience.

12. *All your fortresses are figs.* The prophet exhibits a boldness of metaphoric imagination in turning fortresses—solid stone structures—into ripe figs that fall from the branches when they are shaken.

   they fall / into the mouth of the eater. This image conveys the ease with which Nineveh's bastions will be taken: a little shake, and the fruit falls right into the mouth of the eater, with scarcely any effort involved.

The gates of your land are wide open.
  Fire has consumed their bolts.
14 Siege water draw for yourself,
  reinforce your fortresses.
Come into the mud
  and trample the clay,
    grasp the brickwork.
15 There shall fire consume you,
  the sword shall cut you off,
    shall consume you like locusts.
Be as many as locusts,
  be as many as grasshoppers.
16 You had merchants more numerous
  than the stars of the heavens—
    locusts spread out and flew off.
17 Your commanders were like grasshoppers
  and your officers like swarms of locusts
that settle on stone fences
  on a cold day.
When the sun rises, they go off,
  and where their place is no one knows.

---

13. *Fire has consumed their bolts.* The Hebrew says "your bolts," altered in the translation to "their" in order to make clear that these are the bolts used to bar the gates of the city walls. This is an instance in which the relation of second verset to first is explanatory: the gates are wide open because their wooden bars have been burned away. Fire was often used in the assault on cities.

14. *Siege water.* This is evidently water used in the making of bricks to reinforce the ramparts, as the next line indicates.

15. *consume you like locusts.* That is, as locusts consume everything before them. The locust simile will then be put to a different use.

16. *merchants.* Nineveh is mentioned as a great commercial center. But its trade relations with other countries may also be associated with the "whoring."
  stars . . . / locusts. First, the huge number of merchants is compared to the stars, a conventional biblical simile. But in the next verset, their numerousness moves from the lofty stars to swarms of nasty locusts that spread out over all the earth and then fly off, so the representation of the now vanished merchants is hardly flattering. In the next verse, Nineveh's military commanders are represented in the same harsh light.

Your shepherds have slumbered, Assyrian king,   18
    your staunch men are asleep,
        your people scattered over the mountains, none gathering them.
There is no healing for your disaster,   19
    your wound is grievous.
All who hear the report of you
    clap hands over you.
For over whom has not passed
    your constant evil?

---

18. *Your shepherds.* As elsewhere, this means "leaders"—probably, the military officers.
    are asleep. The received text shows *yishkenu,* "dwell," but this is probably a scribal error
for *yashnu,* an emendation that involves merely dropping the middle consonant.

19. *All who hear the report of you.* This is obviously the report of Nineveh's downfall,
depicted in the preceding lines.
    clap hands. The clapping is an expression of delighted schadenfreude.

Habakkuk

CHAPTER 1   The portent that Habakkuk the prophet saw in   1
a vision.

How long, O Lord, shall I cry out,   2
    yet You do not listen?
I scream "outrage" to You,
    and You do not rescue!
Why do You show me mischief,   3
    and You look upon wretchedness?
Plunder and outrage are before me,
    quarrel and contention I bear.
Therefore teaching fails,   4
    and justice never comes forth.
For the wicked surrounds the righteous.
    Therefore perverted justice comes forth.
See among the nations and look,   5
    and be altogether astonished.
For a deed is being done in your time,
    you would not believe it were it told.
For I am about to raise up the Chaldeans,   6
    the harsh and headlong nation
that goes to the wide reaches of the earth

CHAPTER 1   2. *How long, O Lord.* These initial words of complaint are borrowed directly from the psalms of supplication.

3. *You look upon.* This is the set meaning of this verb, but it is possible that here it is used, unusually, in a causal sense: "You have made [me] look upon."

6. *the Chaldeans.* These are the Babylonians.
   the harsh and headlong nation. The Hebrew uses internal rhyme as well as alliteration: *mar wenimhar.*

to take hold of dwellings not theirs.
7   Fearsome he is and frightful,
from him his rule and his majesty come forth.
8   And his horses are swifter than leopards
and quicker than the wolves of the steppes.
And his horsemen spread out,
his horsemen come, they fly from afar,
like a vulture pouncing on prey.
9   All of them come for outrage,
devastation is before them,
and they gather captives like the sand.
10   And he is scornful of kings,
and rulers are a mockery for him.
He mocks every fortress,
piles up earth and captures it,
11   then passes on like the wind
and attributes his might to his god.
12   Are you not of old, O Lord,
my holy God? You shall not die!
Lord, You have arraigned him for justice
and Rock, You set him aside for censure.

---

7. *from him his rule and his majesty come forth.* Although the gist of this clause is clearly that the Chaldeans are an imposing and powerful nation, the wording of the Hebrew is a little obscure, and this translation replicates the grammatical structure of the original.

8. *the wolves of the steppes.* While the Hebrew might appear to say "the wolves of evening," in this context *'erev* probably is a shortened poetic form of *'aravah,* "steppe."

9. *devastation.* The Hebrew *megamah* appears only here, and its meaning is uncertain. Some scholars have linked it with the rabbinic root *g-m-m,* which means "to cut," and thus it might have something to do with destruction. The likelihood of such a meaning is reinforced by the parallelism. Modern Hebrew, drawing on a different understanding of the term, uses *megamah* to mean "direction" or "tendency."

10. *piles up earth.* The reference is to ramps built of earth that were used to assault a besieged city.

11. *attributes.* The Masoretic Text reads *we'asheim,* "guilty," but the Qumran Pesher Habakkuk shows the more likely *wayasem.*

12. *Are you not of old, O Lord.* The prophet, just having mentioned the false god of the Chaldeans, now invokes the eternity of the God of Israel.
  You shall not die. The Masoretic Text shows "We shall not die," but this is a *tiqun sofrim,* a euphemistic scribal correction so as to eliminate the necessity of saying "God shall not die," when all know that death is not a category that applies to God.

Too pure of eyes to see evil,   13
    and You cannot look on wretchedness,
Why do You look upon traitors and stay silent,
    when the wicked destroys one more righteous than he?
And You make humankind like the fish of the sea,   14
    like creeping things that have no ruler.
They are all brought up with a line,   15
    swept up in a net,
and he gathers them in his trawl,
    therefore he rejoices and exalts.
Therefore he sacrifices to his net   16
    and burns incense to his trawl,
for through them his share is rich,
    and his food is fat.
Thus does he ever unsheathe his sword   17
    to slay nations with no pity.

CHAPTER 2

On my watch let me stand,   1
    and let me take my station at the watchtower and look out

---

14. *You make humankind like the fish of the sea.* The prophet now launches an extended metaphor of fish caught in a net to convey the helplessness of humanity in the face of the forces of destruction that God unleashes in history.

that have no ruler. The fish might seem to differ from human communities—which have kings to offer them a modicum of protection from predatory nations, while the fish have no monarch, government, or army to parry the ensnaring nets of the fishermen—but in the end that is the plight of humans as well.

16. *Therefore he sacrifices to his net.* It is unclear whether this reflects any actual cultic practice of ancient fishermen or is merely a poetic hyperbole. In any case, it picks up "attributes his might to his god" from verse 11.

17. *unsheathe his sword.* The received text has "his net," *ḥermo*, but the Qumran Pesher Habakkuk reads *ḥarbo*, "his sword." This is more likely both because the verb *yariq* is one used for unsheathing swords and the second verset is concerned with slaying nations, not with catching fish. The error in transcription probably occurred when a scribe inadvertently reproduced a word from the fish metaphor here in the concluding line, which actually moves from the metaphor to its referent.

CHAPTER 2   1. *On my watch let me stand.* Although the prophet here is on the lookout for God's response to his complaint, he draws on a familiar trope of the prophet as watchman of Israel.

     to see what He will speak to me
       and what He will respond to my complaint.
2   And the Lord answered me and said:
     Write the vision, make it clear on the tablets,
       so that one may read it readily.
3   For there is yet a vision for the appointed time
       and a witness for the end who is not false.
     Though it tarries, wait for it,
       for it shall surely come, it shall not delay.
4   Look, the spirit within him is callous, not upright,
       but the righteous man lives through his faithfulness.
5   How much more so the arrogant treacherous one who presumes
       and who does not prosper,
     who gapes open his maw like Sheol
       and like death he is never sated.
     And he rounds up for himself all the nations,
       gathers in to him all the peoples.
6   Will not all these an adage pronounce against him,
       verses and maxims against him, and say:
     Woe, who amasses what is not his—for how long?—
       and weighs himself down with debt.
7   Will not your creditors suddenly rise

2. *so that one may read it readily.* The literal sense is: so that he may run in reading it.

3. *For there is yet a vision.* Some prefer to emend *'od,* "yet," to *'eid,* "witness," yielding a neat parallelism with the second verset, a vision for the appointed time, the end. This phraseology was picked up by Daniel and imbued with apocalyptic meaning, but the reference here is simply to the time when Babylonian domination will come to an end, as is made clear in the verses that follow.

4. *callous.* The meaning of *'uplah* is uncertain, but it probably relates to a root that means "to wrap," and so the surmise reflected in this translation is that it indicates being enveloped, impervious to true perception.
   the righteous man lives through his faithfulness. The probable sense of "lives" here is "survives and thrives."

5. *who presumes.* The translation reads *heihin* instead of the Masoretic *hayayin,* "the wine."
   And he rounds up for himself all the nations. At this point it becomes evident that the referent of the insatiable figure is the Babylonian empire.

6. *weighs himself down with debt.* Babylonia has incurred "debt" by seizing from the nations what does not belong to it and which it thus "owes" to them.

and those who will shake you will awake?
For as you despoiled many nations,   8
    the remnant of nations shall despoil you
for the bloodshed of people and the outrage of lands,
    the town and all who dwell in it.
Woe, who takes illicit gain,   9
    through evil, to his house
to set his nest on high
    to be saved from the clutch of harm.
You have counseled shame for your house   10
    when you maimed many peoples
      and gravely offended.
For a stone from the wall shall shriek   11
    and a wooden beam answer it:
Woe, who builds a town with bloodshed   12
    founds a city with wrongdoing.
Is it not from the LORD of Armies?   13
    And peoples shall strive for the fire
      and nations for naught shall be wearied.
For the earth shall be filled   14
    with knowing the LORD's glory
      as water covers the sea.

Woe, who gives drink to his friend,   15
    adding venom and making him drunk
      so as to look on his nakedness.

---

9. *illicit gain*. The Hebrew *betsaʿ* is literally "a slice cut off"—evidently, from an ingot of silver in a cheating practice.

    house / . . . nest. The exploiter, which is to say, the Babylonian empire, carts off his loot to his home (Babylonia), foolishly imagining he will be safe within his house.

10. *maimed*. The translation of this Hebrew verb is conjectural.

13. *And peoples shall strive for the fire*. What they strive for will be consigned to destruction. This entire verse approximately duplicates Jeremiah 51:58.

15. *venom*. Given the context of drinking, this sense for *ḥeimah* rather than "wrath" seems probable.

    his nakedness. The Hebrew, veering between grammatical persons, has "their nakedness."

16   You shall be sated with shame instead of glory.
                 You, too, drink and expose yourself.
            The cup of the LORD's right hand shall come round to you,
                 and noxious shame instead of your glory.
17   For the outrage of Lebanon shall cover you,
                 and the plunder of beasts shall dismay you
            for the bloodshed of people and the outrage of lands,
                 the town and all who dwell in it.
18   What will the idol avail when its fashioner carves it,
                 the molten image that gives false oracles,
            Though its fashioner puts his trust in it,
                 making speechless ungods.
19   Woe, who says to wood, "Awake,"
                 "Bestir" to lifeless stone.
            "It will give oracles." Look, it is inlaid with gold and silver
                 and no spirit is there within it.
20   But the LORD is in His holy palace.
                 Hush before Him all the earth!

---

16. *expose yourself.* This is the plausible understanding of the verb *he'areih* (instead of the Masoretic *he'areil*, of obscure meaning), reflected in the Targum Yonatan and in at least one medieval interpreter. What is involved is measure-for-measure justice.

noxious shame. The unique *qiqalon* looks as if it is a portmanteau word coined by Habakkuk from *qi'*, "vomit," and *qalon*, "shame" (the same word that is used near the beginning of this verse).

17. *the outrage of Lebanon / . . . the plunder of beasts.* The reference is to the many trees from the Lebanon forests cut down by the Babylonians for their building projects and the animals slaughtered for their consumption.

18. *gives false oracles.* This could be rendered as "teaches falsely," but the cultic context makes the sense of oracle likely. The denunciation of idol worship in this verse and the next, reminiscent of passages in Second Isaiah and elsewhere, is not entirely in keeping with the prophecy of the downfall of Babylonia. It is possible that the prophet sees the devotion to inert wood and stone as part and parcel of the unreflective and misguided character of the Babylonian empire.

20. *But the LORD is in His holy palace.* This evocation of God's majesty as He dwells in His celestial abode is calculated as a strong contrast to the witless idolators: instead of lifeless stone and wood, here is the God of heaven and earth, and all the earth is struck with silent awe in His presence.

CHAPTER 3   A prayer of Habakkuk the prophet, on the ₁
shigyonot.

LORD, I have heard the report of You,   ₂
    am in awe, O LORD, of your acts.
In these very years revive them,
    in these very years make them known.
        In anger, remember to show mercy.
God shall come from Teman   ₃
    and the Holy One from Mount Paran.   selah.
His majesty covers the heavens,
    and His splendor fills the earth.
And the radiance is like light.   ₄
    Beams from His hand He has,
        and there His might is hidden.
Before Him pestilence goes,   ₅
    and plague comes forth at His feet.
He halts, and He makes the earth rock,   ₆
    looks, and makes nations leap,

CHAPTER 3   1. *A prayer.* This is actually a psalm, celebrating the power of YHWH as a warrior god. It looks very much like an editorial coda attached to Habakkuk's prophecies, perhaps because whoever assembled the text felt that these brief poems needed a kind of rounding out. Some of the references are mythological and archaic, leading one to suspect this could be a much older poem. At several points the text looks badly scrambled, either because a scribe did not understand all of its archaic language or he tried to alter its mythological content.

the shigyonot. As is often the case in the Book of Psalms, the identity of this musical instrument is not known, although the verbal stem could suggest a rhapsodic or elevated state.

2. *In these very years revive them.* The argument is as follows: we have heard tell of Your great deeds on behalf of Israel in the past; now, in this moment of crisis, is the time to renew these deeds.

3. *selah.* This is a musical notation, again of unknown character, that often appears in Psalms.

4. *the radiance is like light.* The Hebrew *nogah* is poetic diction and often used for some sort of supernal light. Thus the poet explains that the *nogah* has the quality of what we usually identify as light.

Beams from His hand. While *qarnayim* usually means "beams of light," here it probably indicates lightning bolts, wielded as a weapon by the warrior-god in many mythologies. That would explain the reference to hidden might in the next verset.

and the age-old mountains crumble,
   the ancient hills collapse.
     The ancient marches are His.
7   The tents of Cushan are shattered,
   shaken the tent curtains of Midian's land.
8   With Neharim is the LORD incensed,
   against Neharim Your wrath, against Yamm Your fury,
when You ride Your horses,
   Your chariots of victory.
9   Laid bare is Your bow,
   and the seven Rods of Eimar.   selah.
You split the earth with rivers.
10   The mountains see you, shudder.
A stream of water surges.
   The deep sends forth its voice.
     The sky swears solemnly.
11   Sun and moon stand still at the zenith
   by the light of Your arrows they go,
     by the radiance of the gleam of Your spear.
12   In wrath You stride across earth,
   in fury You trample nations.
13   You sally forth to Your people's rescue,
   to the rescue of Your anointed.

---

6. *The ancient marches.* The term *halikhot* can mean "ways," "goings," or "processions." Given the martial context here, it probably refers to God's marching fearsomely across the earth.

8. *Neharim . . . / Yamm.* Although in other contexts these two words can mean, respectively, "rivers" and "sea" (the usual plural of the former is *neharot*), here they hark back to Canaanite mythology, where they figure as different names for the primordial sea monster that must be subdued by Baal (in Israelite literature, by YHWH).

9. *the seven Rods of Eimar.* The Hebrew has *'omer,* "saying," but the scribe has either erased or was ignorant of the mythological reference that has been identified by Umberto Casutto: in Ugaritic literature, Baal wields two rods called Eimar with which he strikes Nahar or Yamm.

10. *The sky swears solemnly.* This is a little puzzling. The literal sense of the Hebrew is "the sky raised its hand," which is a gesture for taking a solemn oath. Perhaps the sky is swearing to witness, or participate in, the cataclysmic events unfolding.

11. *Sun and moon stand still.* They stand still in astonishment, but also their light is not needed because the radiance of God's weapons lights up the world.

You smash the top of the wicked's house,
>   You raze the foundation down to bedrock.   selah.
You pierce the head with a rod.   14
>   His troops storm in their glee to scatter me
>   as one devours the poor in ambush.
You made Your horses tread in the sea—   15
>   the great waters were roiled.
I heard and I quaked within,   16
>   at the sound my lips quivered.
Rot comes into my bones
>   and I quake where I stand.
Will You rest on the day of distress
>   when a people comes up to assault us?
For the fig tree does not bud,   17
>   and there is no yield from the vines.
The olive tree's crop is shriveled
>   and the fields do not grow grain.
The sheep are gone from the fold,
>   and no cattle are in the barns
But I in the LORD will exult,   18

---

13. *down to bedrock.* The Masoretic Text has *tsaw'ar*, "neck," but razing has to move downward, not upward, so this is in all likelihood a mistake for *tsur.* The error would have been triggered by the fact that the word translated as "top" in the preceding verset has the more common meaning of "head."

15. *You made Your horses tread in the sea.* This maneuver continues the cosmogonic battle between YHWH and Yamm that was invoked above.

16. *I quaked within.* Literally, "my belly quaked."
    Rot comes into my bones. This sounds odd, but the idea is probably that the bones became squishy, as though they had been eaten away by rot.
    Will You rest. The Masoretic Text has "I will rest," which would be peculiar, given the speaker's terror at this moment. The translation adopts the proposal of Yitzhak Avishur that the Masoretic reading is a *tiqun sofrim*, a scribal euphemism, to avoid an expression that might seem to impugn God's majesty.

17. *For the fig tree does not bud.* Some take this entire verse as a reference to a plague of locusts because of a certain similarity to the language of Joel, but it is perfectly plausible that the fields and the livestock would be devastated by an invading army, "when a people comes up to assault us" (verse 16).

18. *But I in the LORD will exult.* As in many of the psalms, there is a sharp reversal at the end: After the evocation of a landscape of terror, the speaker affirms his confidence in God's rescuing power.

           will rejoice in the God of my rescue.

19   The LORD Master is my strength,
           He makes my feet like the gazelle's
           and has me tread upon the heights.

For the lead player, on stringed instruments.

---

19. *He makes my feet like the gazelle's / and has me tread upon the heights.* The language here is close to Psalms 18:34, which is a victory psalm. It seems that the celebration of YHWH as warrior god has slid into the proclamation of a human victor who praises God for giving him strength on the battlefield.

    For the lead player, on stringed instruments. This is actually a superscription for introducing a psalm, not a formula for concluding it. One suspects that this chapter was copied from a noncanonical manuscript of psalms and that the copyist inadvertently included at the end a line that in fact belonged to the next psalm in the manuscript.

Zephaniah

CHAPTER 1   The word of the LORD that came to Zephaniah 1
son of Cushi son of Gedaliah son of Amariah son of Hezekiah in the days
of Josiah son of Amon king of Judah.

> I will surely sweep away everything   2
>   from the face of the earth, said the LORD.
> I will surely sweep away man and beast,   3
>   sweep away the fowl of the heavens and the fish of the sea—
>   with stumbling blocks for the wicked.
> And I will cut off humankind
>   from the face of the earth, said the LORD.

CHAPTER 1   1. *Zephaniah son of Cushi son of Gedaliah son of Amariah son of Hezekiah.* No other prophet is given such a long pedigree, and the reason for it is by no means
apparent. Two items are problematic: "Cushi" means "Nubian," which would be odd for
an Israelite first name, and "Hezekiah" could be the name of the Judahite king, as some
commentators, traditional and modern, have proposed, but that remains questionable.

in the days of Josiah. His reign was from 640 to 609 B.C.E., so that would make Zephaniah an approximate contemporary of Isaiah. Zephaniah's angry denunciation of idolatry
in Jerusalem suggests that he prophesied before the sweeping reforms of Josiah, which
began in 622.

2. *I will surely sweep away everything.* Zephaniah's great power as a prophet-poet is in his
evocations of the landscape of disaster.

from the face of the earth. Although presumably the impending destruction is to fall
upon the inhabitants of the kingdom of Judah, the prophet's language makes the disaster
sound global. In the next verse, he will pointedly echo the language of the Creation story,
implying a reversal of creation itself ("man and beast, / . . . the fowl of the heavens and the
fish of the sea"). This is an instructive instance in which the language of Prophetic poetry,
with its commitment to hyperbole, pushes beyond its intended subject to an incipiently
apocalyptic horizon.

3. *with stumbling blocks for the wicked.* These words fit into the prophecy rather awkwardly
and may be an editorial gloss.

4   And I will reach out My hand against Judah
         and against all who dwell in Jerusalem.
     And I will cut off from this place
         the remnant of Baal,
     the name of the pagan priests with the priests,
5   and those bowing on the roofs to the array of the heavens
     and those bowing and swearing to the Lord
         and yet swearing by Milcom,
6   and those falling back from the Lord
         and who did not seek the Lord
         and did not search for Him.
7   Hush before the Lord!
         —for the day of the Lord is near.
     For the Lord has readied a slaughter,
         has invited His guests.
8   And on that day there shall be a slaughter for the Lord,
         and I will make a reckoning with the nobles
             and with the sons of the king
         and with all who don
             the garb of the foreigner.
9   And I will make a reckoning with all who hop
         over the threshold on that day,

---

4. *the remnant of Baal, / the name of the pagan priests.* The two Hebrew words *she'ar* and *shem,* "remnant" and "name," are a hendiadys meaning "any remnant at all" and they appear here in the two versets in what scholars call a break-up pattern. That explains the slight oddness of "the name of the pagan priests." The term for "pagan priests," *kemarim,* designates celebrants of alien cults. Its bracketing here with *kohanim,* "priests," suggests that the officiants of the cult of YHWH were joining forces with their pagan counterparts in syncretistic practices, as the Book of Kings reports.

5. *those bowing on the roofs to the array of the heavens.* There is abundant evidence that in the seventh century B.C.E. worship of astral deities, through Assyrian influence, had become widespread in Israel.
     Milcom. The Masoretic Text has *malkam,* "their king," but this is almost certainly a scribal substitution in order not to mention the name of the pagan deity.

7. *a slaughter.* The Hebrew means both "slaughter" and "feast," and Zephaniah intends the former while playing on the latter as he goes on to represent God inviting guests to the slaughter-feast.

8. *all who don / the garb of the foreigner.* The prophet probably associates the use of foreign attire with pagan practices.

9. *all who hop / over the threshold.* This appears to have been a pagan practice when entering sanctuaries. An etiology for it is offered in 1 Samuel 5:5.

who fill the house of their Master
    with outrage and deceit.
And it shall happen on that day—   10
    the sound of outcry from the Fish Gate
        and wailing from the Mishneh
            and a great disaster from the hills.
Wail, you who dwell in the Ravine,   11
    for the people of traders is destroyed,
        all weighers of silver are cut off.
And it shall happen at that time—   12
I will search out Jerusalem with lamps
    and make a reckoning with the men
        who sit still on their lees
saying in their hearts,
    "The LORD does neither good nor evil."
And their wealth shall become plunder   13
    and their homes a desolation,
and they shall build homes and not dwell in them
    and plant vineyards and not drink their wine.
The great day of the LORD is near,   14
    near and very swift.
The sound of the day of the LORD is bitter,
    on it the warrior shrieks.
A day of wrath is that day,   15
    a day of distress and discomfort,
a day of devastation and desolation,
    a day of darkness and deep dusk,

---

10. *the Mishneh.* This is a quarter in Jerusalem. The name means "the addition" or "the annex."

11. *the Ravine.* This would have to be a valley running through Jerusalem, perhaps the Valley of Ben-Hinnom, just west of the walls of the city.

    the people of traders. The epithet sounds derisive and may point to sharp trading practices.

14. *on it the warrior shrieks.* Even the battle-hardened fighter will be terrified.

15. *A day of wrath is that day.* The power of this prophecy of doom is focused in the anaphoric insistence on "day" throughout these lines. It is the day of the LORD, now heightened (in verse 14) to "the great day of the LORD" rushing down bitter and swift on the kingdom of Judah.

    distress and discomfort. The Hebrew sound-play is *tsarah umetsuqah.*

    devastation and desolation. The Hebrew sound-play is *sho'ah umesho'ah.*

and a day of cloud and fog.

16   a day of ram's horn and trumpet blast
            against the fortress towns
                and against the lofty corner-towers.

17   And I will bring humankind into straits,
            and they shall walk about like the blind,
                for they have offended against the LORD.
        And their blood shall be spilled like dust
            and their flesh like turds.

18   Neither their silver nor their gold
            shall avail to save them.
        On the day of the wrath of the LORD
            all the land shall be consumed in His zealous fire,
        for a ghastly end
            shall He make of all who dwell in the land.

CHAPTER 2

1   Gather yourselves, O gather,
            nation undesired,

2   before the decree is born—
            the day slips by like chaff—
        before it comes upon you,
            the day of the LORD's fury.

3   Seek the LORD,

---

17. *And their blood shall be spilled like dust / and their flesh like turds.* The similes are purposefully unpleasant. Liquid blood turns into dry dust as it might be spilled, say, from a shovel. Solid flesh becomes turds dropping to the ground. The word used for "flesh," *leḥum,* is not the standard term but poetic diction, its initial consonant alliterating with the double *l* sound of *gelalim,* "turds."

CHAPTER 2   1. *Gather yourselves.* This verbal stem is generally used for the gathering of firewood and the like. Here it might suggest that the people have fallen apart, become disparate sticks or limbs, and need to be pulled together.

   undesired. Though other meanings have been proposed, this verb elsewhere clearly means "to long for."

2. *the day slips by like chaff.* The day is moving rapidly down on Judah, like wind-borne chaff.

all you humble of the land
   who have fulfilled His law.
Seek justice, seek to be humble.
   Perhaps you will be sheltered on the day of the LORD's fury.
For Gaza shall be abandoned   4
   and Ashkelon a desolation.
Ashdod shall be banished at noon,
   and Ekron be uprooted.
Woe, you who dwell in the coastal region,   5
   nation of Cherithites.
     The word of the LORD is against you.
Canaan, land of the Philistines,
   I will destroy you with none dwelling there.
And the coastal region shall become   6
   meadows for shepherd's feasts and sheep pens.
And it shall become a region   7
   for the remnant of the house of Judah.
On these they shall graze their flocks,
   in the houses of Ashkelon at evening they shall bed down,
for the LORD their God shall single them out
   and restore their fortunes.

I have heard the insult of Moab   8
   and the jibes of the Ammonites,
who insulted My people
   and gloated over their lands.
Therefore, as I live, said the LORD of Armies, God of Israel: 9
   Moab shall be like Sodom

---

4. *Gaza shall be abandoned / . . . Ekron be uprooted.* The Hebrew exhibits untranslatable wordplay for both of these: *'azah 'azuvah* and *'eqron te'aqeir.*

5. *Cherithites.* This probably means "Cypriots," Cyprus being the approximate or putative place of origin of the Philistines.

7. *they shall bed down.* Because the verb used is for the bedding down of animals, the reference is still to the flocks. But, in the fluidity of pronominal reference characteristic of biblical Hebrew, "them" in the next line is the Judahites, not their flocks.

8. *gloated.* The Hebrew says merely "made big," but this is in all likelihood an ellipsis for "made their mouths big," which is to say "gloated." The same verb is used in verse 10, where it clearly has the sense of "gloated."

and the Ammonites like Gomorrah—
   nettle growth and salt mine
    and a desolation for all time.
The remnant of My people shall despoil them,
   and the remains of the nation inherit them.

10 This comes to them for their pride because they insulted and gloated over
11 the people of the LORD of Armies. Fearsome is the LORD over you, for
He holds sway over all the gods of the earth, and all the coastlands of the
nations shall bow to Him, each man in his place.

12   You, too, Cushites,
                   are slain by My sword.
13   And He shall reach out His hand in the north
                   and destroy Assyria
             and make Nineveh a desolation,
                   parched land like the desert.
14   And flocks shall bed down in her midst,
                   all the beasts of the nations.
             Both jackdaw and owl
                   on her capitals shall roost.
             The screech owl shall hoot in the window,
                   the raven on the threshold,
                       for the cedarwood is laid bare.

---

11. *holds sway.* The verb *razah* in the received text is problematic. The meaning of this root
is "thin," and so some imagine that it means YHWH has "shriveled" the gods of the nations,
but that sounds odd, and nowhere else does this verbal stem occur as a transitive verb with
a direct object. It is more plausible to emend it to *radah* (*d* and *z* being phonetically close
and interchangeable between Hebrew and Aramaic).

12. *Cushites.* These are the Nubians, dwelling south of Egypt. God's reaching out to the
north in the next verse makes this a geographically comprehensive assault on the nations.

14. *jackdaw . . . owl / . . . screech owl.* As elsewhere, the precise identification of these wild
birds is uncertain.
    the raven. Here it is assumed in the translation that *ḥorev,* which has a far more common
homonym that means "dry place," is the equivalent of *'orev,* "raven."
    the cedarwood is laid bare. The meaning of the two Hebrew words is not entirely certain.
The unusual noun *'arzah* is assumed to be derived from *'erez,* "cedar," and would thus refer
to the cedarwood paneling of Nineveh's palatial buildings. The verb *'eirah* means "he laid
bare," but as elsewhere, the third-person masculine singular is probably the equivalent of
the passive.

This the merry city,   15
   dwelling secure,
saying in her heart,
   "I and none besides me,"
how has she become a desolation,
   a bedding-down place for beasts!
All who pass by her shall hiss,
   wag a mocking hand.

CHAPTER 3

Woe, sullied and besmirched,   1
   oppressive city!
She heeded not the voice,   2
   did not accept reproof.
In the Lord she did not trust,
   nor drew near to her God.
Her nobles within her   3
   are roaring lions
Her judges are wolves of the steppes,
   they gnawed all the bones by morning.
Her prophets are unsteady,   4
   men of treachery.
Her priests profaned the holy,
   did outrage to the teaching.
The Lord is righteous in her midst,   5

---

15. *wag a mocking hand.* The literal meaning of the Hebrew is simply "wag their hand," but in biblical parlance this is a gesture of mockery or contempt, and so "mocking" has been added in the translation in order not to baffle the English reader.

CHAPTER 3   2. *She heeded not the voice, / did not accept reproof.* This entire verse reflects a tendency here to rely on formulaic language.

3. *they gnawed all the bones by morning.* The literal sense of the Hebrew is "they did not gnaw by morning"—that is, they had finished gnawing.

4. *Her priests profaned the holy, / did outrage to the teaching.* The two main functions of the priests are to perform the cult within the Temple scrupulously and to provide proper instruction to the people. In both of these tasks, they have failed miserably.

He does not do wrong.
Morning after morning He brings His justice to light—
    it never lacks.
        But the wrongdoer knows no shame.

6   I have cut off nations,
    their corner-towers are devastated.
I have destroyed their streets
    with none passing by.
Their towns are demolished,
    with no men, without dwellers.

7   I said, "If you but fear Me,
    if you accept reproof,
her abode will not be cut off,
    all that I had summoned against her."
Yet they continued acting ruinously
    in all their deeds.

8   Therefore, wait for Me, said the LORD,
    for the day I rise as witness,
for My judgment is to gather in nations,
    to assemble kingdoms,
to pour out My wrath upon them,
    all my smoldering anger.
For in My zealous fire
    all the earth shall be consumed.

9   For then will I transform peoples
    with a pure language
for them all to call in the name of the LORD,
    to serve Him with single intent.

---

6. *I have cut off nations.* This is another verse composed entirely of formulaic language.

8. *For in My zealous fire / all the earth shall be consumed.* This is another instance in which the orientation of Prophetic poetry toward hyperbole pushes a statement about judging the nations into language that is incipiently apocalyptic.

9. *a pure language.* There is an interesting idea here that perverse or harmful behavior is entrammeled with a corruption of language—a notion George Orwell would develop in a celebrated essay written during World War II about how Nazi totalitarianism had subverted the German language. Thus, the gift of a pure language is necessary so that the peoples can truly call to God.

From beyond the rivers of Cush   10
   they who entreat Me, whom I dispersed,
     shall bring My tribute.
On that day: 11
You shall not be shamed by all your acts
   in which you trespassed against Me,
for then will I remove from your midst
   those merry with your pride,
and no longer shall you be haughty
   on My holy mountain.
And I will leave in your midst   12
   a poor and lonely people,
     and they shall shelter in the LORD's name.
They shall do no wrong   13
   nor speak lies,
and there shall be in their mouth
   no tongue of deceit,
but they shall graze and bed down,
   and none shall make them tremble.

Sing gladly, Daughter Zion,   14
   shout out, Israel.
Rejoice and delight with whole heart,
   O Daughter Jerusalem.
The LORD has set aside your judgments   15
   removed your enemy.
The King of Israel, the LORD, is in your midst.
   You need no longer fear evil.
On that day shall it be said to Jerusalem: 16

---

10. *Cush.* As elsewhere, this is Nubia, south of Egypt.

12. *a poor and lonely people.* This is an obvious antithesis to the haughty and the proud invoked in the previous verse. The sins of Judah are associated with the arrogance and self-importance of its ruling class, which will be replaced by the simple people who preserve the true values of the nation.

13. *there shall be in their mouth / no tongue of deceit.* This picks up the idea of the need for a transformation of language as a precondition of moral transformation.
   they shall graze and bed down. Both verbs invoke the familiar metaphor of the people as a flock to be led by a faithful shepherd, the just king.

Do not fear, O Zion,
    let not your hands fall slack.
The LORD your God is in your midst,
    a rescuing warrior.
He delights over you with rejoicing,
    He renews His love,
        He exults over you with glad song.

17   Those sorrowing from lack of festivals, bearing her disgrace,
    I will gather from you.
I am about to deal with all your tormentors at that time.

18   And I will rescue the lame,
        and the scattered I will gather,
and I will make them a glorious name
    through all the land of their shame.

19   At that time I will bring you,
        at that time gather you,
for I will make you a glorious name
    among all the peoples of the earth
        when I restore your fortunes before your eyes.
—said the LORD.

---

16. *He renews His love.* The Masoretic Text reads *yaḥarish be'ahavato,* "He is silent in His love," but it is unclear why the living God should be silent. The translation follows the reading of the Septuagint, which appears to have used a Hebrew text that showed *yeḥadesh 'ahavato* (the Hebrew graphemes for *r* and *d* being quite close).

17. *Those sorrowing from lack of festivals.* This rather awkward English phrase translates two compact Hebrew words, *nugey mimo'eid.* What they mean is not altogether certain, but it is most plausible to understand the prefix *mi,* which usually means "from," in its other sense of "without." The sorrowful ones, then, are sad because they have been deprived access to the Temple to celebrate the pilgrim festivals.

19. *when I restore your fortunes before your eyes.* The prophecies of Zephaniah begin with a vision of doom threatening the kingdom of Judah, the terrible "day of the LORD." They end here with a promise of restoration after exile. Either this chapter is by the hand of a prophet writing after 586 B.C.E., as some scholars conclude, or Zephaniah is following out the logic of the scenario he has been sketching: first catastrophe will overtake the kingdom, resulting in its destruction and the exile of its people; then the people will be restored to its land.

Haggai

CHAPTER 1   In the second year of King Darius in the sixth 1
month, on the first day of the month, came the word of the LORD through
Haggai the prophet to Zerubbabel son of Shealtiel, the prefect of Judah, and
to Joshua son of Jehozadak the high priest, saying, Thus said the LORD of 2
Armies, saying, "This people have said, 'The time has not come, the time
for rebuilding the house of the LORD.'" And the word of the LORD came 3
through Haggai the prophet, saying: "Is this the time for you to sit in your 4
paneled houses when this house is in ruins?" And now, thus said the LORD 5
of Armies, "Pay mind to your ways. You have sown much and brought in 6
little, eaten, but were not sated, drunk, but not to intoxication; were clothed,
but without warmth from it. And he who earns wages earns for a purse with
holes." Thus said the LORD of Armies, "Pay mind to your ways. Go up to 7,8
the mountain and bring timber and build the house, and I will be pleased

---

CHAPTER 1   1. *In the second year of King Darius.* This is 520 B.C.E. Small groups of
exiles have returned, under the initial authorization of Cyrus, to the kingdom of Judah,
now the Persian province of Yehud. As Haggai immediately makes clear, little progress as
yet has been made in rebuilding the Temple.

Zerubbabel . . . the prefect . . . Joshua . . . the high priest. These are the principal secular
authority and the principal religious authority, respectively. Haggai's mission, unlike that
of the earlier prophets, is to the leaders, not to the people, and only through the leaders to
the general populace.

2. *The time has not come, the time for rebuilding.* The Hebrew syntax is somewhat distorted,
and similar problems will occur as the book progresses.

6. *You have sown much and brought in little.* The comprehensive catalogue initiated by
these words suggests that these are metaphorical assertions to the following effect: whatever you have done has been futile and has given you no satisfaction. Nevertheless, in the
background of these assertions are the dire material circumstances of the returned exiles
at this moment.

8. *Go up to the mountain and bring timber.* Solomon's temple was built with fine cedarwood
imported from Lebanon. In the present reduced circumstances, such luxurious materials
are not an option, so the people are asked to cut down trees from a local mountain.

9   with it, that I may be honored, said the LORD. You have sought much and,
    look, there was little and brought it home, and I blew it away. Because of
    what, said the LORD of Armies? Because of this house that lies in ruins
10 while you rush off each to his home. Therefore, the heavens have held back
11 dew from you, and the earth has held back its yield. And I called forth a
    drought upon the land and upon the mountains and upon the new grain
    and upon the new wine and upon the new oil and upon what the soil brings
    forth and upon man and upon beast and upon all the effort of your hands."
12 And Zerubbabel son of Shealtiel, and with him Joshua son of Jehozadak the
    high priest and all the remnant of the people, heeded the voice of the LORD
    and the words of Haggai the prophet as the LORD their God had sent him,
13 and the people feared the LORD. And Haggai, the LORD's messenger, on the
    LORD's mission, said to the people, saying, "I am with you, said the LORD."
14 And the LORD roused the spirit of Zerubbabel son of Shealtiel prefect of
    Judah and the spirit of Joshua son of Jehozadak the high priest, and the
    spirit of all the remnant of the people, and they came and performed the
15a tasks in the house of the LORD of Armies their God, on the twenty-fourth
    day of the sixth month,

1:15b,1 CHAPTER 2   in the second year of Darius in the seventh
        month, on the twenty-first of the month, the word of the LORD came
2   through Haggai the prophet, saying, "Say, pray to Zerubbabel son of Sheal-
        tiel the prefect of Judah and to Joshua son of Jehozadak the high priest

---

9. *I blew it away.* The intention behind the choice of this verb is unclear. It is the verb generally used for blowing on a fire, as with a bellows.

11. *I called forth a drought upon the land.* The failure to rebuild the Temple is conceived as
a collective sin that brings disaster upon the land, in a way analogous to the presence of
Oedipus, the incestuous parricide, bringing a plague on Thebes.

13. *the LORD's messenger.* Although this is basically how the role of the prophet is conceived,
the use of the term is rare. It will, however, be picked up as the fictive name of the prophet
Malachi, "my messenger."

14. *roused the spirit.* This is a different formulation from the "descent" of the spirit on
prophets and judges. It suggests the instilling of motivation and morale.

15a. *on the twenty-fourth day of the sixth month.* This is when they begin work on the
Temple. The second half of this brief verse actually belongs at the beginning of the next
chapter, where it has been moved in this translation, and which explains why this chapter
ends with a comma.

and to the remnant of the people, saying, 'Who among you remains who ₃
saw this house in its former glory? And how do you see it now? Is it not as
nothing in your eyes?' And now, be strong, Zerubbabel, said the LORD, and ₄
be strong, Joshua son of Jehozadak the high priest, and be strong, all the
people, said the LORD, and act, for I am with you, said the LORD of Armies.
Remember this word that I sealed with you when you came out of Egypt ₅
and My spirit was standing in your midst. Do not fear. For thus said the ₆
LORD of Armies: Soon I will shake the heavens and the earth and the sea
and the dry land. And I will shake the nations, and the precious things of ₇
all the nations shall come, and I will fill this house with glory, said the LORD
of Armies. Mine is the silver and mine the gold, said the LORD of Armies. ₈
Great shall be the glory of this house, the latter more than the former, said ₉
the LORD of Armies, and in this place I will bestow peace, said the LORD
of Armies."

On the twenty-fourth of the ninth month in the second year of Darius, ₁₀
the word of the LORD came to Haggai the prophet, saying, "Thus said the ₁₁
LORD of Armies: Inquire, pray, teaching of the priests, saying, If a man car- ₁₂
ries sacrificial flesh in the skirt of his garment and touches with his skirt

---

CHAPTER 2   3. *Who among you remains who saw this house in its former glory?*
There could be a few in Haggai's audience who had actually seen the First Temple, but they
would be very old because sixty-seven years had passed since its destruction.

Is it not as nothing in your eyes? The foundation for the Temple, according to the Book
of Ezra, had been laid during the reign of Cyrus, but the work did not go forward, so what
met the eye was a half-finished foundation and no structure above it.

5. *Remember.* In the received text, this verse begins with the particle *'et*, which ordinarily is
placed before the direct object of a verb, but there is no verb. It is assumed in this translation
that a verb such as "remember" was dropped from the text.

7. *I will shake the nations.* Through the authorization of Cyrus, exiles had returned from
Babylonia, but their material existence was meager and their Davidic ruler was merely a
functionary of the Persian empire. Against this background, Haggai envisages a grand
triumphal moment when all the nations will be shaken and their riches flow to Zion.

the precious things of all the nations shall come. When the Temple was destroyed, its
precious vessels were carried off by the conquerors.

9. *peace.* Others construe this as "well-being" or "prosperity."

11. *Inquire, pray, teaching of the priests.* From what follows, it becomes clear that the "teaching," *torah,* that the priests are to provide involves issues of religious law, what the rabbis
later would call *halakhah.* In this case, however, the teaching becomes an analogy for the
condition of the people in its relation to God.

bread or stew or wine or oil or any food, is it sanctified? And the priests

13 answered and said, 'No.'" And Haggai said, "If someone unclean from a corpse touches any of these, does it become unclean?" And the priests

14 answered and said, "It becomes unclean." And Haggai answered and said, "So is this people and so is this nation before Me, said the LORD, and so is

15 all the work of their hands and what they sacrifice there—it is unclean. And now, put your mind, pray, to it; from this day forward, from before stone

16 was put upon stone in the LORD's Temple, from when they were coming to a heap of twenty measures and it was ten, coming to the wine vat to draw out

17 fifty measures from the winepress and it was twenty, I smote you with blight and with mildew and with hail—all the work of your hands—and there was

18 none with you for Me, said the LORD. Put your mind, pray, to it: from this day forward, from the twenty-fourth day of the ninth month, from the day

19 that the foundation of the LORD's Temple was laid, when the seed was still in the granary, and the vine and the fig tree and the pomegranate tree and the olive tree had not yet borne fruit, from this day will I grant blessing."

20 And the word of the LORD came again to Haggai on the twenty-fourth of

21 the month, saying, "Say to Zerubbabel the prefect of Judah, saying, 'I am

22 about to shake the heavens and the earth, And I will overturn the thrones

---

14. *So is this people . . . before Me.* At first, it may seem puzzling that Haggai should proclaim the uncleanness of the people before God when he has just urged them to devote themselves to the rebuilding of the Temple and has reported that God had roused a spirit within them. The answer to the ostensible contradiction may be in the phrase "what they sacrifice there." Although "there" is left vague, if the people have been sacrificing—and worship without sacrifice would be difficult for ancient Israelites to imagine—this would have to take place on improvised altars, for there was as yet no temple. Such unauthorized sacrifices would then be the source of impurity.

16. *when they were coming to a heap of twenty measures and it was ten.* This harks back to 1:6: "You have sown much and brought in little." The Hebrew shows only numbers in this verse but "measure," or perhaps a specific unit of measure, is implied.

18. *from this day forward.* As the work of rebuilding the Temple moves ahead, a new era is launched. Now there will again be people for the LORD, and the sundry blights that had stricken the community will come to an end.

   the day that the foundation of the LORD's temple was laid. Rashi's explanation in light of the earlier foundation work is apt: "They were now beginning again to add to the first foundation that had been built in the time of Cyrus."

19. *not yet.* This translation reads 'od, "yet," for the Masoretic 'ad, "until."

21. *I am about to shake the heavens and the earth.* The passage that begins here is a kind of concluding recapitulation of 2:6–9. In this instance, explicit battle imagery is introduced—the overturning of chariots and horses and riders.

of kingdoms, and I will destroy the strength of the kingdoms of the nations, and I will overturn chariot and its riders, and horses and their riders shall go down, each by the sword of his fellow. On that day, said the LORD of 23 Armies, I will take you, Zerubbabel son of Shealtiel, My servant, said the LORD, and I will set you as a seal, for you have I chosen,'" said the LORD of Armies.

---

22. *each by the sword of his fellow.* What is suggested is a general panic in the armies of the nations in which confusion and mutual slaughter take place.

23. *I will set you as a seal.* The expression is elliptical. The ellipsis is elucidated in Song of Songs 8:6: "Set me as a seal on your heart, / as a seal on your arm."

for you have I chosen. While neither "king" nor "anointed" appears in the text—might Haggai have feared these could be politically dangerous terms?—the strong implication is that Zerubbabel, as a descendant of the line of David now presiding over the rebuilding of the Temple, is the chosen heir to David's throne.

Zechariah

CHAPTER 1   In the seventh month, in the second year of 1
Darius, the word of the Lord came to Zechariah the prophet son of
Berechiah son of Iddo, saying, "The Lord was very furious with your 2
fathers. And you shall say to them, Thus said the Lord of Armies: Turn 3
back to Me, said the Lord of Armies, that I may turn back to you, said the
Lord of Armies. Do not be like your fathers to whom the former prophets 4
called saying, Thus said the Lord of Armies: Turn back, pray, from your
evil ways and from your evil acts. But they did not listen to Me, said the
Lord. Your fathers, where are they?" "And the prophets, did they live 5
forever?" "But My words and My statutes that I charged to My servants 6
the prophets, did they not overtake your fathers?" And they turned back
and said, "As the Lord of Armies aimed to do to us according to our ways
and according to our acts, so He has done with us."

On the twenty-fourth day of the eleventh month, which is the month of 7
Shebat, in the second year of Darius, the word of the Lord came to Zecha-

---

CHAPTER 1   4. *the former prophets.* Zechariah has in mind especially Jeremiah but
probably also Isaiah, Ezekiel, and perhaps others. He thus inserts himself at this late date,
520 b.c.e., in the long line of prophecy. It was the failure of the earlier generations to listen
to their prophets that brought upon them the national catastrophe, and he implores his
own audience to make a new start by listening to him.

5. *And the prophets, did they live forever?* This is best construed as the people's rejoinder
to Zechariah: if their forefathers are now gone, so are the prophets who inveighed against
them.

6. *As the Lord of Armies aimed to do to us.* The people now concede the justice of the
prophet's argument: not only our fathers but we as well have suffered for our acts, as our
present reduced condition bears witness, and we are thus ready to change our ways.

7. *On the twenty-fourth day of the eleventh month.* This is just two months after the foundation work for the Temple had begun, with Haggai's exhortation to Zerubbabel and Joshua.

8   riah the prophet son of Berechiah son of Iddo, saying, "I saw at night, and,
    look, there was a man riding on a bay horse, and he was standing among
    the myrtles that are by the deep, and behind him were bay, sorrel, and
9   white horses. And I said, 'What are these my lord?' And the messenger
10 speaking to me answered, 'I shall show you what these are.' And the man
    standing among the myrtles answered and said, 'It is these that the LORD
11 has sent to go about the earth.' And they answered the LORD's messenger
    who was standing among the myrtles and they said, 'We have gone about
12 the earth, and, look, all the earth dwells tranquilly.' And the LORD's mes-
    senger answered and said, 'O LORD of Armies, how long will You show no
    mercy to Jerusalem and to the towns of Judah against which You have been
13 wrathful now seventy years?' And the LORD answered the messenger who
14 was speaking to me good words, comforting words. And the messenger
    who was speaking to me said to me, 'Call out, saying, Thus said the LORD
15 of Armies: I have been greatly zealous for Jerusalem and for Zion. And I
    am very greatly furious with the nations resting quiet; as I was but a little
16 furious yet they piled on the harm. Therefore, thus said the LORD, I have
    turned back in mercy to Jerusalem, and a building line shall be stretched
17 over Jerusalem. My house shall be built in her.'" Call out again, saying,
    Thus said the LORD of Armies: "Again shall my towns spread out from
    bounty, and again shall the LORD comfort Zion, and again shall He choose
    Jerusalem."

---

8. *I saw at night, and, look.* Though the word "dream" does not appear, this is manifestly a
dream-vision, using the formulaic language that reports the beginning of a dream.
    a bay horse. While this is the realistic color for a horse, the Hebrew *'adom* could also
mean, more surrealistically, "red." This would be the color of blood, perhaps a prelude to
God's fury with the nations expressed in verse 15.
    standing among the myrtles that are by the deep. These details may be evocative but
their purpose is mystifying.

9. *the messenger.* Now the mysterious "man" on the bay horse is explicitly identified as a
divine messenger. The Book of Daniel will use "man" in this same sense.

10. *to go about the earth.* The horses, then, are themselves agents of the divine, sent to see
what is happening on earth. In a moment, they will speak, delivering their reconnaissance
report.

15. *as I was but a little furious yet they piled on the harm.* God had used them as an instrument to punish Israel, but in their vicious treatment of the conquered people, they exceeded
all limits. The literal sense of "they piled on harm" is "they helped for harm [or, for evil]."

16. *a building line.* These were lines used to assure the straight rectilinear contours of the
building.

CHAPTER 2   And I raised my eyes and saw and look, there 1
were four horns. And I said to the messenger speaking to me, "What are 2
these?" And he said to me, "These are the horns that scattered Judah, Israel,
and Jerusalem." And the LORD showed me four smiths. And I said, "What 3,4
have these come to do?" And he said, saying, "These are the horns that scattered Judah, so no man could raise his head, and these have come to rattle
them, to hurl down the horns of the nations that bore horns against the
land of Judah to scatter it." And I raised my eyes and saw, and, look, there 5
was a man and in his hand a measuring cord. And I said, "Where are you 6
going?" And he said to me, "To measure Jerusalem, to see what is its width
and what is its length." And, look, the messenger speaking to me was going 7
out and another messenger was coming out to meet him. And he said to 8
him, "Run, speak to that lad, saying: 'Jerusalem shall dwell as an unwalled
city because of all the people and beasts within her. And I will be for her, 9
said the LORD, a wall of fire all around, and for glory will I be within her.
Away, away, flee from the land of the north, said the LORD, for like the four 10

CHAPTER 2   1. *four horns.* Throughout biblical literature, horns are an image of
power—in this instance, destructive power.

2. *scattered.* This verb, generally used for the winnowing of grain, is one of several somewhat odd choices of verb in this passage. It obviously refers to the exiling of the Judahites.

    Judah, Israel. Three centuries have passed since the exile of the population of Israel,
the northern kingdom, but Zechariah preserves, as do other prophets, a utopian hope for
its restoration.

3. *smiths.* They are probably ironsmiths, who could fashion weapons to hack horns.

4. *rattle.* As in verse 2, this is an unusual word choice. The verb generally means "to shake"
or "to strike with terror." One might have expected a verb like "to cut down."

    to hurl down. This verb usually means "to cast stones."

7. *the messenger speaking to me was going out and another messenger was coming out to meet
him.* The apparatus of the vision becomes complicated: it seems that there are teams, or
perhaps hierarchies, of divine messengers.

8. *speak to that lad.* The probable referent is Zechariah, the recipient of all these prophetic
messages. "Lad" would not necessarily indicate his age but rather his (necessarily) subservient position in relation to the celestial messengers.

    an unwalled city. Every important city in the ancient Near East had walls to protect it
against enemies. Jerusalem, however, will have no walls because its spectacular expansion
cannot be contained within walls. Instead, God will be a wall of fire all around it.

10. *Away, away.* The Hebrew *hoy* usually means "woe," but here it has to be an interjection
of urging. This is the solution of at least two modern translations.

    flee. This imperative is prefixed by the particle that means "and." Either that is a scribal
error, or, as Kimchi proposes, a word such as "go out" was dropped.

11 corners of the heavens did I spread you out, said the Lord. Away, Zion,
12 escape, you who dwell with the Daughter of Babylon.' For thus said the
   Lord of Armies Whose glory sent me to the nations that despoil you. For
13 he who touches you touches the apple of His eye. For I am about to swing
   My hand against them, and they shall be spoil for their slaves, and you shall
14 know that the Lord of Armies sent me. Sing gladly and rejoice, Daughter
15 of Zion, for I am coming and will abide in your midst, said the Lord. And
   many nations shall join the Lord on that day and become My people, and
   I will abide in your midst, and you shall know that the Lord of Armies
16 sent me to you. And the Lord shall bestow upon Judah its portion on the
17 holy soil and again choose Jerusalem. Hush, all flesh before the Lord, for
   He has stirred from His holy abode!'"

1 CHAPTER 3   And he showed me Joshua the high priest standing before a messenger of the Lord, and the Adversary was standing on

---

11. *Away, Zion, escape.* One could also construe this as "to Zion escape," with the particle
for "to" omitted by ellipsis.

12. *Whose glory sent me.* The Masoretic Text reads, enigmatically, "after glory He sent me."
This translation adopts a frequently proposed emendation.

   the apple of His eye. The Midrash Tanhuma lists this as a scribal euphemistic correction for "the apple of My eye," introduced to avoid anthropomorphism. But if, as in several
modern languages, "apple of the eye" is an idiom for what is most precious to a person, its
use would not necessarily imply that God has an eye with a pupil.

13. *sent me.* The first person, which at the beginning of this verse was God, now refers to
the prophet. Such unmarked transitions are common biblical usage.

14. *will abide in your midst.* This is in all likelihood a reference to the Temple, in the process
of being rebuilt, for the Temple was conceived as God's terrestrial abode, His "house."

15. *And many nations shall join the Lord on that day.* The idea of a universal acceptance of
YHWH as God strikes a new note in this passage. It is in keeping with a theme in Third
Isaiah.

17. *Hush, all flesh before the Lord.* "All flesh" means "all humankind" and so continues the
idea of a conversion of the nations introduced in verse 15.

CHAPTER 3   1. *the Adversary.* This is the *satan* (note the definitive article, indicating someone filling a role rather than a proper name), not to be confused with the
later mythological Satan. In Job, this translation renders the term as "the Adversary," but
"accuser" would also work here to pick up the link with the cognate verb at the end of this
sentence. The Accuser, a kind of prosecuting attorney who belongs to the divine entourage
("the sons of God" in Job), carries out the task of calling attention to the sundry trespasses
of the people, but now he is rebuked because God is ready to remove the guilt of the people.

his right to accuse him. And the LORD said to the Adversary, "The LORD 2
rebuke you, Adversary, the LORD, Who has chosen Jerusalem, rebuke you.
Is not this a brand saved from the fire? And Joshua was clothed in foul gar- 3
ments and was standing before the messenger. And he spoke out and said 4
before all those standing before him, saying, "Remove the foul garments
from him." And he said to him, "See, I have taken away your guilt from you
and dressed you in fine raiment." And he said, "Let them put a pure diadem 5
on his head." And they put a pure diadem on his head and dressed him in
fit garments with the LORD's messenger standing by. And the LORD's mes- 6
senger warned Joshua, saying, "Thus said the LORD of Armies: If you walk 7
in My ways and if you keep My watch, and also if you oversee My house and
also guard My courts, I will let you come and go among these attendants.
Listen, pray, Joshua, high priest, you and your companions sitting before 8
you, for they are men who have had a portent that I am about to bring My
servant, Branch. For, look, the stone that I set before Joshua, on a single 9
stone are seven eyes. I am about to engrave its engraving, said the LORD of
Armies, and I will wipe away the guilt of this land on a single day. On that 10

---

3. *foul.* The Hebrew word is associated with excrement. It is not that the high priest is
personally culpable, but as chief sacerdotal officiant for the people, the residue of all their
heinous acts clings to him.

4. *all those standing before him.* The idiom means "standing in attendance."

5. *fit garments.* "Fit" is merely implied in the Hebrew, but that must be the sense.

7. *if you oversee My house and also guard My courts.* This injunction to see to the maintenance of the Temple anticipates its rebuilding, which at this moment has just begun.

I will let you come and go among these attendants. This is an extraordinary promise
because the attendants are divine beings.

8. *men who have had a portent.* The literal sense is "men of a portent." But it is hard to
see how Joshua's priestly colleagues could be the portent, as they are represented in most
translations. The rendering here follows the Babylonian Talmud, Sanhedrin 93A, which
says "for whom a portent was performed." Perhaps they have witnessed Joshua's change
from foul garments to fine raiment, which would be the portent.

My servant, Branch. The Hebrew term for "Branch," *tsemaḥ,* has clear dynastic associations. There is a debate among interpreters as to whether this refers to an eschatological
Davidic ruler or to Zerubbabel, but the latter seems more likely because the grand restoration appears to be imminent. Political considerations may have led Zechariah to suppress
his name.

9. *seven eyes.* These will recur in a different context in chapter 4.

wipe away. The verbal stem *m-w-sh* indicates "removal," but it does not appear elsewhere in this conjugation as a transitive verb. The Hebrew *mashti* could be a mistake for
maḥiti, the verb usually employed for the expunging of guilt.

day, said the LORD of Armies, you shall invite, each man his fellow, to come under the vine and under the fig tree."

1 CHAPTER 4   And the messenger speaking to me came back
2 and woke me as a man wakes from his sleep. And he said to me, "What do you see?" And I said, "I have seen, and, look, a lampstand all of gold and a bowl on its top, and its lamps were on it, seven pipes for the lamps on its top.
3 And there were two olive trees by it, one to the right of the bowl and one to
4 its left." And I spoke out and said to the messenger speaking to me, saying,
5 "What are these, my lord?" And the messenger speaking to me answered
6 and said, "Why, you know what these are." And I said, "No, my lord." And he answered and said to me, saying, "This is the word of the LORD to Zerubbabel, saying, Not by might and not by power but by My spirit, said the
7 LORD of Armies. What are you, great mountain? Before Zerubbabel you become a plain. And he shall bring out the capstone—shouts of 'lovely,
8,9 lovely' for it." And the word of the LORD came to me, saying, "Zerubbabel's hands laid the foundation for this house, and his hands shall complete it,
10 and you shall know that the LORD of Armies sent me to you. For who has

---

10. *to come under the vine.* "Come" is supplied in the translation for idiomatic coherence in English. Sitting under the vine and under the fig tree is a proverbial expression for a time of peace and prosperity. Only later would it take on an eschatological meaning, as in the mention of Jesus sitting under the fig tree in the first chapter of John's gospel.

CHAPTER 4   1. *woke me as a man wakes from his sleep.* There is a pointed ambiguity in this statement because all of these visions convey a sense of things seen in a dream. He awakes, then, from one dream to another.

2. *a bowl.* This is probably a receptacle for the oil.
    seven pipes. The oil would be conducted through these pipes.

6. *Not by might and not by power but by My spirit.* These memorable words have great resonance, but how do they follow from the vision of the golden lampstand? The golden lampstand, with its seven burning oil lamps, is to be a focal point in the Temple, its light a token of God's radiant presence in His house, in the midst of His people. Thus the rebuilding of the Temple, in difficult material conditions and perhaps with some resistance from the Persian imperial power, will be consummated through God's spirit, which is symbolized in the lampstand. The idea of imposing obstacles that are set as naught is spelled out in the next verse.

7. *And he shall bring out the capstone—shouts of "lovely, lovely" for it.* What is imagined here is the completion of the rebuilding of the Temple, with Zerubbabel setting the capstone in place and the assembled people bursting out in cheers.

despised the day of small things? They shall rejoice and see the stone of separation in Zerubbabel's hand. These seven are the eyes of the LORD that roam through all the earth." And I spoke out and said to him, "What are 11 these two olive trees on the right of the lampstand and on its left?" And I 12 spoke out again and said to him, "What are these two branches of the olive trees that are by the golden tubes emptying out the gold?" And he said to 13 me, saying, "Why, you know what these are." And I said, "No, my lord." And he said, "These are the two men consecrated with oil who attend upon 14 the Master of all the earth."

CHAPTER 5   And again I raised my eyes and saw and, look, 1 a flying scroll. And he said to me, "What do you see?" And I said, "I see a 2 flying scroll, twenty cubits long and ten cubits wide." And he said to me, 3

---

10. *For who has despised the day of small things?* This rather crabbed formulation probably means: you who have dismissed the humble beginning of the construction as unimpressive will be filled with joy when you witness its completion by Zerubbabel.

the stone of separation. The Hebrew, *ha'even habedil,* is enigmatic ("the tin stone"?). Most scholars emend the second word to *hamavdil,* "separating." It could be identical with the capstone, *'even haro'shah,* though it is not clear what it separates—perhaps, two large sections of the roof.

12. *I spoke out again.* Perhaps Zechariah is obliged to repeat his question by the divine messenger because the initial formulation is insufficiently specific.

the golden tubes emptying out the gold. The entire lampstand is golden, but the color of the fine olive oil is also golden. The tubes presumably empty out into the receptacles of the seven lamps.

14. *the two men consecrated with oil.* The literal sense is "the two sons of oil." It should be recalled that "sons" has many broad applications in biblical Hebrew. The word for "oil" used is not the common *shemen* but *yitshar,* perhaps adopted as a literary effect or perhaps an encoding device, so as not to make too explicit a reference to anointing. The two men are Zerubbabel and Joshua, so the anointing of the former would be royal, not sacerdotal.

CHAPTER 5   1. *and, look, a flying scroll.* By this point, it is evident that Zechariah's mode of prophecy is essentially different from that of his predecessors. They occasionally experience enigmatic visions that are then explained, but their principal vehicle is direct address—castigations for trespasses, predictions of doom, prophecies of consolation— usually cast in poetry. Zechariah, by contrast, witnesses a series of puzzling visions shown him by a divine emissary, and they seem to become progressively more bizarre, as this chapter abundantly illustrates.

2. *twenty cubits long and ten cubits wide.* This computes to roughly thirty-three feet by seventeen feet, making this a decidedly supernatural scroll.

"This is the imprecation going out to all the land. Whoever steals, as on one
side of it, has not been condemned, and whoever swears, as on the other
4 side of it, has not been condemned. I have brought it out, said the LORD of
Armies, and it shall enter the house of the thief and the house of him who
swears falsely in My name and lodge within his house and make an utter
5 end of it, with its timbers and with its stones." And the messenger speaking
to me came out and said to me, "Raise your eyes, pray, and see what is this
6 going out." And I said, "What is this?" And he said, "This is a measuring
basin going out." And he said, "This is their crime through all the land."
7 And, look, an ingot of lead was being lifted, and there was a certain woman
8 seated in the basin. And he said, "This is Wickedness," and he flung her
9 down within the basin and flung the lead stone over its opening. And I
raised my eyes and saw and, look, two women were going out, and there
was wind in their wings, and they had wings like the wings of a stork. And
10 they lifted the basin between the earth and the heavens. And I said to the
11 messenger speaking to me, "Where are they taking the basin?" And he said

---

3. *going out.* This verb recurs insistently throughout the visions here. It conveys a sense of
mysterious visual objects emerging before the eyes of the prophet, as well as of the agencies
of divine judgment (as here) or divine scrutiny going out over the land.

    as on one side of it . . . as on the other side of it. The Hebrew formulation is terse and
somewhat opaque, but the probable sense is that the injunctions against theft and false
swearing are written on the two sides of the huge scroll—another manifestation of its
supernatural character. Until now, the violators of these injunctions have gone scot-free,
but that is about to change.

6. *a measuring basin.* The Hebrew reads *'efah,* the most common unit of dry measure, but
this object is clearly a receptacle that is one *'efah* in capacity.

    This is their crime. The Masoretic Text has *'eynam,* "their eye," but two ancient ver-
sions and one Hebrew manuscript show the more likely *'awonam.* The *'efah,* then, either
is associated with their crooked practices, using a false measure, or indicates the measure
of justice that will now be applied to them.

7. *an ingot of lead was being lifted.* This probably means that the ingot of lead was covering
the basin. Lead on a measuring basin would make it yield a falsely large weight and so might
be associated with cheating by means of a crooked *'efah.*

8. *flung the lead stone over its opening.* In this fashion, Wickedness is now trapped within
the basin.

9. *two women.* The enigma of the vision is compounded. After the woman embodying wickedness, we have two winged women—clearly divine agents and not ordinary women—who
are to carry off the basin.

to me, "To build a house for it in the land of Shinar, and it shall be founded, and they shall set it down there on its firm place."

CHAPTER 6   And again I raised my eyes and saw and, look, 1 four chariots were going out from between two mountains, and the mountains were mountains of copper. The first chariot had bay horses and the 2 second chariot black horses. And the third chariot had white horses and 3 the fourth chariot dappled, spotted horses. And I spoke out and said to the 4 messenger speaking to me, "What are these, my lord?" And the messenger 5 answered and said to me, "These are the four winds of the heavens going out from standing in attendance before the Master of all the earth in which the 6 black horses go out to the land of the north and the white ones have gone out to the western sea, and the dappled ones have gone out to the land of the south, and the red ones have gone out and sought to go about on the earth. 7

11. *To build a house for it in the land of Shinar.* Shinar is the archaic name for Babylonia, and the designation used at the beginning of the story of the Tower of Babel, in Genesis 11:2. Many commentators conclude that Wickedness is transported to Shinar because that is the location of humankind's transgressive presumption in seeking to build a tower with its top in the heavens.
    they shall set it down. The Masoretic Text has a hybrid and grammatically impossible vocalization, *wehuniḥah*, but the Septuagint shows *wehiniḥuha*, a grammatically correct form that is reflected in this translation.

CHAPTER 6   1. *two mountains . . . mountains of copper.* It is probably wise not to translate these details into any symbolism. The gap between the two mountains provides a dramatic entrance point for the chariots, and the fact that the mountains are copper highlights their supernatural character.

5. *the four winds of the heavens.* Though this is the idiomatic expression for "the four corners of the heavens" ("wind" can mean "direction" in Hebrew), the literal sense needs to be preserved in this case because the four chariots rushing off in four directions appear to be the embodiment of the winds, which have been "standing in attendance" before God.

6. *to the western sea.* As elsewhere, this is the Mediterranean. The Masoretic Text reads *'el-'aḥareyhem,* "to after them," which is ungrammatical and also confusing. This translation supposes that the original reading was *'el hayam ha'aḥaron* or an equivalent phrase.

7. *the red ones.* The received text has *ha'amutsim,* "the spotted ones," but this is a synonym for "the dappled ones," who have already been accounted for, and the red horses seem to have disappeared. The translation therefore reads *ha'adumim,* "the red ones."
    have gone out and sought to go about on the earth. This is somewhat puzzling because one would expect that these horses would head off in the fourth direction. Some scholars

And he said, 'Go, go about on the earth,' and they went about on the earth."
8 And He summoned me and spoke to me, saying, "See, the ones going out to the north have pleased Me in the land of the north."

9,10 And the word of the LORD came to me, saying, "Take from the exiles, from Hildi and from Tobiah and from Jediah, who have come from Babylonia, and as for you, on that day you shall come to the house of Josiah son of
11 Zephaniah. And you shall take silver and gold and make diadems and put
12 one on the head of Joshua son of Jehozadak the high priest. And you shall say to him, saying, "Thus said the LORD of Armies, saying: Here is the man named Branch, and from his place it shall branch out, and he shall build
13 the LORD's Temple. And he shall build the LORD's Temple, and he shall assume majesty, and he shall sit on his throne and rule. And the priest shall be by his throne, and there shall be a counsel of harmony between the
14 two of them. And the diadems shall be in the LORD's Temple as a memorial, for Tobiah and Jedaiah and Hen son of Zephaniah. The far-away shall come and build in the LORD's Temple, and you shall know that the LORD of Armies has sent me to you. And it shall happen, if you heed the voice of the LORD your God."

---

correct the phrase to "had gone out to the east," but there is only a logical warrant for the emendation, not a textual one.

8. *the ones going out to the north have pleased Me.* It is from the north that the destruction comes, and this is probably a prophecy of doom.

10. *Take from the exiles.* The object of the taking does not appear until the beginning of the next verse. It seems that some of the returning exiles brought substantial riches with them.

11. *diadems.* The Hebrew ʿatarot is not the word generally used for royal crowns, and the high priest would be wearing a diadem, not a crown.
    put one. "One" is merely implied in the Hebrew.

13. *the priest shall be by his throne.* The preposition could also mean "on," but priests do not have thrones, and this translation follows an interpretation proposed by Kimchi and many others.
    there shall be a counsel of harmony between the two of them. This prophecy of smooth cooperation between Zerubbabel and Joshua probably reflects a sense that there might be some tension between them. Zerubbabel is of the Davidic line but an appointee of the Persian rulers, whereas Joshua is the legitimate heir to the high priesthood with no foreign intervention. Zechariah repeatedly elevates Zerubbabel's importance as Davidic ruler.

14. *The far-away.* The most likely reference is to returning exiles (who have already provided silver and gold for the Temple). Zechariah may be seeking to promote a unity of purpose between those who have remained in Jerusalem and those who have recently come back from Babylonia.

CHAPTER 7   And it happened in the fourth year of King 1
Darius that the word of the LORD came to Zechariah on the fourth of the
ninth month, Kislev. And Beth-El Sar-Ezer and Regen-Melech and his men 2
had sent to entreat the LORD, saying to the priests who were in the house of 3
the LORD of Armies and to the prophets, saying, "Shall I weep and practice
abstinence in the fifth month as I have done for years?" And the word of 4
the LORD of Armies came to me, saying, "Say to the people of the land and 5
to the priests, saying, 'Though you fasted and mourned in the fifth month
and the seventh these seventy years, have you actually fasted for Me? And 6
if you eat and if you drink, are you not the ones who eat and you the ones
who drink? Are not these the words that the LORD proclaimed through 7
the former prophets when Jerusalem was dwelling tranquil and her towns
round about her and the Negeb and the lowland dwelled tranquil?' "

And the word of the LORD came to Zechariah, saying, "Thus said the LORD 8,9
of Armies, saying: Judge true justice, and do kindness and mercy each man

---

CHAPTER 7   2. *Beth-El.* Though this was the location of one of the two principal
sanctuaries of the northern kingdom, it cannot be a place-name here, and it is also not used
as a designation for the Temple (its literal meaning is "house of God"). On the evidence of
documents from the Jewish community of Elephantine in Egypt from this period, it was
also used as a man's name.

3. *the fifth month.* This is the month of Av, when the destruction of the First Temple occurred.

5. *in the fifth month and the seventh.* The latter would be the fast commemorating the assassination of Gedaliah, who was appointed governor of Judah after the Babylonian conquest.
Neither of these fasts, of course, has any basis in the Torah, and so the people understandably want a directive from God ("to entreat the LORD," verse 2) through the Temple priests
and the Temple prophets about whether these fasts should be observed.
     have you actually fasted for Me? God has not enjoined these fasts, and they are no more
than a human initiative to express collective grief, which is not the thing God wants.

6. *are you not the ones who eat and you the ones who drink?* Eating and drinking, like abstention, are a human affair that does not really concern God.

7. *Are not these the words that the LORD proclaimed through the former prophets.* The words
are not spelled out, but Zechariah would have in mind such prophecies as the one in Isaiah
1, where God proclaims that He does not want people to trample through the courts of the
Temple when their hands are filled with blood.
     dwelled tranquil. "Tranquil" does not appear here in the Hebrew. Either it was dropped
in scribal transmission or "tranquil" in the preceding clause was meant to do double duty.

9. *Judge true justice.* Although this appears to be a new prophecy, the editorial logic of its
placement here is that these demands for social justice are God's "words," what He wants
rather than fasts.

10 with his fellow. And do not exploit widow and orphan, sojourner and poor
11 man, and do not plot evil in your heart, each man against his fellow." But
they refused to listen and turned their backs in defiance, and their ears they
12 stopped up from hearing. And they made their heart adamantine against
hearing the teaching and the words that the Lord of Armies had sent with
His spirit through the former prophets, and there was a great fury from
13 the Lord of Armies. "And just as He had called and they would not hear,
14 so shall they call and I will not hear, said the Lord of Armies. And I will
whirl them out over all the nations that they did not know, and the land
behind them shall be desolate of passersby. They turned a precious land
into a desolation."

1 CHAPTER 8   And the word of the Lord of Armies came,
2 saying, "Thus said the Lord of Armies: I have been very jealous for Zion,
3 and with great wrath I have been jealous for her. Thus said the Lord: I have
come back to Zion and abided within Jerusalem, and Jerusalem shall be
called the City of Truth, and the Mountain of the Lord, the Holy Moun-
4 tain. Thus said the Lord of Armies: Again shall old men and old women
sit in the squares of Jerusalem, each with his staff in hand because of their
5 many years. And the squares of the city shall be filled with boys and girls
6 playing in her squares. Thus said the Lord of Armies: Does it seem beyond
the remnant of this people in these days? So it would be beyond Me, said

---

14. *And I will whirl them out over all the nations.* Given Zechariah's role promising a Davidic
restoration and urging the rebuilding of the Temple, it is unlikely that he could be addressing this blistering prophecy of exile to his contemporaries. Rather, this would be a citation
of God's pronouncement of doom on the rebellious generation seven decades earlier. This
situation of the prophecy in the historical moment leading up to 586 B.C.E. is spelled out
in the last sentence here, which uses a past tense (the so-called converted future) for its
report of turning the land into a desolation. The grandparents of Zechariah's audience,
then, ignored God's teaching and consequently reduced their land to ruins. Now the people
of Zechariah's time, inhabiting the ruins, have been summoned to the task of rebuilding.

CHAPTER 8   3. *Jerusalem shall be called the City of Truth.* Zechariah here follows
the practice of Third Isaiah, who attributes new names to Jerusalem in keeping with its
dramatically transformed nature in the restoration of Zion.

4. *each with his staff in hand because of their many years.* In the new era of peace and prosperity, the city will be filled with people who will have lived to a ripe old age. The complement to this multiplication of elders is the children playing in the squares.

6. *Does it seem beyond the remnant of this people in these days?* This rhetorical question is
addressed to those who might doubt the capacity of the people to complete the project of

the LORD of Armies. Thus said the LORD of Armies: I am about to rescue 7
My people from the land of the east and from the land of the sunset, and I
will bring them, and they shall abide in Jerusalem and be My people and
I will be their God in truth and in righteousness. Thus said the LORD of 8
Armies: May your hands be strong, you who hear in these days these words
from the prophets who are in the time the foundation of the house of the
LORD of Armies was laid for the Temple to be rebuilt. For before these days 9
the wages of man was naught and the wages of beast was nothing, and for
him coming and going there was no peace from the foe, and I set each man
against his fellow. And now not as in the former days am I to the remnant 10
of this people, said the LORD of Armies. For the peaceful sowing—the vine 11
shall give its fruit and the land shall give its yield and the heavens shall give
their dew, and I will bestow on the remnant of this people all these. And it 12
shall be, as you were a curse among the nations, house of Judah and house
of Israel, so will I rescue you and you shall become a blessing. Do not fear,
and may your hands be strong. For thus said the LORD of Armies: As I 13
devised to do harm to you when your fathers infuriated me, said the LORD

---

rebuilding the Temple. It is surely not beyond God to conceive such a consummation, and
it should not be beyond the people. One might note that many scholars view the recurrent
phrase "the remnant of this people" as a designation for those who remained in Judah after
its conquest by the Babylonians.

7. *I am about to rescue My people from the land of the east.* The plausible inference from
these words is that a substantial population of exiles from Judah remained in Babylonia
after Cyrus's decree permitting return, and this seems historically very likely. "The land
of the sunset" is added to convey the sense "everywhere."

8. *May your hands be strong.* These words, which will be repeated in verse 12, are an exhortation to those engaged in the arduous effort of rebuilding the Temple, as the reference to
the rebuilding in the second part of this verse makes clear.

   these words from the prophets. The reference is probably to Haggai and to Zechariah
himself.

9. *the wages of man was naught and the wages of beast was nothing.* Man reaped no profit
for his labor, and there was no food for his beasts of burden.

   and for him coming and going there was no peace from the foe. Although other identifications have been proposed, the language sounds like a reference to siege. The same Hebrew
phrase (literally, "going out and coming in") is used to describe the besieged Jericho in
Joshua.

   I set each man against his fellow. If these lines in fact refer to Jerusalem besieged by the
Babylonians, what this formulation reflects is the bitter divisions within the people during
that moment of crisis. Jeremiah, one recalls, was the object of a murderous conspiracy.

12. *a curse . . . a blessing.* Zechariah invokes common biblical usage, in which "curse" means
a byword of calamity and "blessing" the opposite.

14 of Armies, and I did not repent, so I have again devised in these days to
15 do good for Jerusalem and for the house of Judah. Do not fear. These are
the things that you should do: Speak truth, each man to his neighbor, and
16 render truth and justice in your gates. And do not plot evil in your hearts,
each man against his fellow, and do not love a false vow, for all these do I
hate, said the Lord."

17,18 And the word of the Lord of Armies came to me, saying, "Thus said the
Lord of Armies: the fast of the fourth month and the fast of the fifth month
and the fast of the tenth month shall become a rejoicing for the house of
Judah and gladness and good festivals. And love truth and peace."

19 Thus said the Lord of Armies: "Peoples and the dwellers of many towns
yet shall come, and the dwellers of one town shall go to another, saying,
'Let us go to entreat the Lord and to seek the Lord of Armies—I, too,
20 shall go.' And many peoples and vast nations shall come to seek the Lord
21 in Jerusalem and to entreat the Lord." Thus said the Lord of Armies: "In
those days ten people from all the tongues of the nations shall grasp the
border of a Jew's garment, saying, 'Let us go up with you, for we have heard
that God is with you.'"

---

18. *the fast of the fourth month.* This reversal of a whole series of fasts addresses the question
of the people in Jerusalem as to whether they should continue to keep two particular fasts.

   good festivals. This rather odd use of "good" with "festivals" may be influenced by the
Late Biblical *yamim tovim,* "good days," for "festivals," which occurs in Esther and becomes
standard in rabbinic Hebrew.

   And love truth and peace. Abraham ibn Ezra aptly observes that what God really wants
of His people is not the awkward practice of fasts but the love of truth and peace, a life of
ethical behavior.

19. *Peoples and the dwellers of many towns yet shall come.* This vision of the nations coming
to seek out the God of Israel is in keeping with a recurrent theme in Third Isaiah and may
well be influenced by him.

21. *ten people from all the tongues of the nations shall grasp the border of a Jew's garment.*
This vivid image conveys the sense of throngs of foreigners desperate to join the people
with whom God dwells. The term *yehudi,* "Jew," never appears in earlier biblical literature,
although it occurs frequently in Esther, which also belongs to the Persian period. *Yehudi* is
palpably moving toward the meaning of "Jew" because it is now hard to speak of a "Judahite" (Hebrew, *ben yehudah*), given that the kingdom of Judah no longer exists, having been
replaced by the Persian province of Yehud.

CHAPTER 9   A portent.

The word of the LORD in the land of Hadrach, and Damascus is His resting place, for toward the LORD is the eye of humankind and all the tribes of Israel. And Hamath, too, borders on it, Tyre and Sidon, though they have ₂ great wisdom.

> And Tyre built herself a fortress   3
> > and piled up silver like dust
> > > and finest gold like sand in the streets.
>
> Look, the LORD shall beggar her   4
> > and strike her wealth down into the sea,
> > > and she shall be consumed by fire.
>
> Ashkelon shall see and be afraid   5
> > and Gaza greatly tremble
> > > and Ekron, for her stronghold has failed.
>
> And a bastard shall be enthroned in Ashdod,   6
> > and I will cut off the Philistines' pride.

CHAPTER 9   1. *A portent.* The very anomaly of this "heading" signals that we have moved on to a new unit of prophecies. In regard to both style and subject matter, these last chapters of the book are quite different from the prophecies of Zechariah, and the mention of Javan (which is to say "Ion," or Greece) in verse 13 is a possible indication that this text was composed after the conquest of the region by Alexander the Great in 332 B.C.E., more than a century after the time of Zechariah. Although the first two verses are in prose, these prophecies continue in poetry, unlike the prose writing of Zechariah.
     Hadrach. This is a city in Syria north of Damascus.

2. *though they have great wisdom.* The "wisdom," in keeping with one prevalent sense of the Hebrew *ḥokhmah,* is their skill in shipbuilding and in the construction of buildings, perhaps especially fortifications, as the next verse suggests. While these Phoenician cities are famed for their "wisdom," they are doomed to fall through the sovereign decree of the God of all the earth.

4. *beggar her.* If one construes the Hebrew verb as deriving from a different root, it might mean "dispossess her," but the mention in the preceding line of silver and gold argues for the sense of "beggar."
     her wealth. The Hebrew *ḥayil* has three different meanings—"wealth," "wall," and "military force"—and one must concede that any of these three senses would work here. This translation opts for "wealth" because of the invocation of silver and gold.

5. *Ashkelon . . . / Gaza . . . / Ekron.* These are Philistine cities, like Tyre and Sidon on the Mediterranean coast but considerably to the south. When the Philistines hear of the fall of the Phoenician towns, they are seized with panic.

7   And I will take away the blood from his mouth
        and the disgusting things from between his teeth,
    and he, too, shall remain for our God
        and become like a friend in Judah
            and Ekron like the Jebusite.
8   And I will camp at My house against armies,
        against any who pass by,
    and no more shall oppressors pass over them,
        for now I have seen their affliction.
9   Greatly exult, Zion's Daughter,
        shout for joy, Jerusalem's Daughter.
    Look, your king shall come to you,
        victor and triumphant is he,
    a lowly man riding on an ass,
        on a donkey, the foal of a she-ass.
10 And I will cut off the chariots from Ephraim
        and the horses from Jerusalem,
    and the bow of battle shall be cut off,
        and he shall parley for peace with the nations,

---

7. *take away the blood from his mouth / and the disgusting things from between his teeth.* The consumption of blood is explicitly forbidden in the Torah. The "disgusting things" are probably pork, a staple of the Philistine diet, as the evidence of bones uncovered in Philistine sites indicates. The Philistines, in this utopian scenario, will put aside their odious practices and join the people of Israel.

    a friend. The Hebrew *'aluf,* which also means "guide," does have the sense of "friend" or "companion."

    Ekron like the Jebusite. The Jebusites, after their city Jerusalem was conquered by David, appear to have had amicable relations with the Israelites.

8. *I have seen their affliction.* The Masoretic Text has "I have seen with My eyes" (*be'eynay*), but the Septuagint seems to have used a Hebrew text that showed *be'onyam,* "their affliction," and that makes better sense.

9. *a lowly man riding on an ass.* This is the surprising switch: though a victor, the king comes as a lowly man. In the earlier biblical period, donkeys were actually the mount of royalty, but at this late moment, horses would have been used. The introduction of the ass here anticipates the elimination of horses from Jerusalem in the next verse.

10. *I will cut off the chariots from Ephraim / and the horses from Jerusalem.* Ordinarily, this language would signal a prophecy of doom. Here, however, it conveys the idea that the implements of warfare will be cast aside because the ideal ruler will be able to "parley for peace with the nations."

and they shall rule from sea to sea
    and from the Euphrates to the ends of the earth.
You, too, through the blood of the covenant,   11
    I have freed your prisoners from the waterless pit.
Go back to the fortress,   12
    you prisoners of hope.
This very day proclaiming,
    double I will give back to you.
For I have bent Me Judah as a bow,   13
    strong Ephraim as an arrow.
And I have roused your sons, O Zion,
    against your sons, O Javan,
        and made you as a warrior's sword.
And the Lord shall be seen over them,   14
    and His arrow come out like lightning,
and the Master, the Lord, shall blast the ram's horn
    and go forth in the storms of the south.
The Lord of Armies shall defend them,   15
    and the slingstone shall consume and conquer
and drink blood like wine
    and be filled like ritual basins,
        like the corners of an altar.

---

from sea to sea. Although this could mean from the Dead Sea to the Mediterranean, given the expansive dimensions of the province of rule, it may instead refer to the Mediterranean and the Persian Gulf, far to the south.

11. *through the blood of the covenant.* In all likelihood, this is the blood of the covenant of circumcision. Because Israel has remained faithful to its covenant with God, He will now liberate its captives.

12. *the fortress.* The Hebrew word might instead be a place-name, Bitsaron.
    you prisoners of hope. This evocative phrase so caught the imagination of the great medieval Hebrew poet Judah HaLevi that he used it several times in his poems.

13. *I have bent Me Judah as a bow, / strong Ephraim as an arrow.* This follows from the idea that horses and chariots are put aside, for Judah itself now is embodied as a weapon.

14. *blast the ram's horn.* This is a call to battle.

15. *drink blood like wine.* The Masoretic Text has "drink and roar [*hamu*] like wine," but the Septuagint reads *dam*, "blood," which is more plausible. Drinking blood like wine is a topos of ancient Hebrew martial poetry.
    like ritual basins, / like the corners of an altar. Blood was collected in basins as part of the animal sacrifices, and it was also sprinkled at the four corners of the altar.

16   And the Lord shall rescue them on that day—
  His people like sheep—
   for they are crown jewels that gleam on His soil.
17   How goodly and how lovely
  the young men like new grain
   and the virgins like lush new wine.

CHAPTER 10

1   Ask of the Lord rain
  in the season of the latter rains.
The Lord makes lightning
  and drenching rain.
He gives to every man
  the grass of the field.
2   For the household gods spoke deceit,
  and the sorcerers envisioned lies,
and vain dreams do they speak,
  with mere breath they console.
Therefore they have strayed like sheep,
  wandered, for there is no shepherd.
3   Against the shepherds I am incensed
  and with the he-goats I will make a reckoning.
For the Lord of Armies has singled out His flock,
  the house of Judah,

---

16. *His people like sheep.* Though the syntactic placement is a little odd, the clear sense is that God will rescue Israel as a shepherd rescues his sheep.

17. *lush.* The Hebrew uses a verb, *yenoveiv,* that means something like "to bring forth produce."

CHAPTER 10   1. *drenching rain.* In the Hebrew, two synonyms, *metar-geshem,* are joined in the construct state, signifying intensification.

2. *the household gods.* These domestic icons, *terafim,* were used for divination.
 wandered. The Masoretic Text reads *ya'anu,* "answered" or "were afflicted." This translation supposes a reversal of consonants and reads instead *yanu'u.*

3. *the shepherds.* This stock epithet for "leaders" picks up the sheep metaphor of the previous line. In the second verset, "he-goats" is another fixed epithet for leaders.
 make a reckoning /... singled out. The same verb, *paqad,* is used for both, but because it has both a positive and a negative meaning, divergent English equivalents are necessary.

and made them like a stallion, His glory in battle.

From them the cornerstone and from them the tent peg, 4
from them the bow of battle,
from them all commanders together.

And they shall be as warriors 5
trampling the mud of the streets in battle,
and they shall battle, for the LORD is with them,
and they shall put the horsemen to shame.

And I will make the house of Judah mighty, 6
and the house of Joseph I will make victorious.

And I will restore them, for I have mercy upon them,
and they shall be as though I never forsook them,
for I am the LORD their God and will answer them.

And Ephraim shall be like a warrior, 7
and their heart shall rejoice as from wine,
and their children shall see and rejoice,
their heart shall exult in the LORD.

I will whistle to them and gather them, 8
for I will ransom them, and they shall increase as before.

And I will sow them among the peoples, in far places they shall recall Me, 9
and they shall thrive with their children and return.

And I will bring them back from the land of Egypt 10
and from Assyria I will gather them.

---

4. *cornerstone . . . tent peg, / . . . bow.* These are all metaphors for the leaders or champions of the people. At the end of the line, the literal referent of all these is introduced in "commanders." It should be noted that the Hebrew term used for "commander," *nogeis,* generally has a negative meaning ("taskmaster," "overseer"), but that cannot be the case here. The shift in meaning may reflect the fluidity of Late Biblical Hebrew.

5. *trampling the mud of the streets in battle.* It is not entirely evident why the warriors should be trampling mud. Perhaps this is intended as an image of conquest—the troops stomp through the streets of the conquered city, overwhelming all that stands in their way. It is also possible that an object of the verb has dropped out (the literal sense of the Hebrew is "in the mud of the streets") and that the original text read: "trampling *the slain like* the mud of the streets."

8. *I will whistle to them.* Whistling appears elsewhere as a signal for the marshaling of troops, a sound that may have been produced with some sort of wooden whistle.
they shall increase as before. More literally, "they shall increase as they increased."

9. *sow.* The idea is that the exiles are planted far and wide in order to flourish.

10. *And I will bring them back from the land of Egypt / and from Assyria.* This invocation of lands to the south and to the far northeast is meant to express the comprehensiveness of

And to the land of Gilead and Lebanon I will bring them,
   and still it shall not suffice for them.
11   And he shall pass through the sea against the foe
   and strike waves in the sea,
and all the depths of the Nile shall dry up,
   and the pride of Assyria be brought down,
   and the scepter of Egypt shall vanish.
12   And I will make them mighty in the LORD,
   and in His name they shall go about
   —said the LORD.

CHAPTER 11

1   Open, O Lebanon, your doors,
   that fire consume your cedars.
2   Wail, O cypress,
   for the cedar has fallen,
   as the majestic ones are ravaged.
Wail, O Bashan oaks,
   for the dense forest is taken down.
3   Hark! The wailing of shepherds,
   for their majesty is ravaged.
Hark! The roar of lions,
   for Jordan's bends are ravaged.

---

the ingathering of exiles. In the fourth century B.C.E. there was a substantial diaspora community in Egypt. Assyria no longer existed, but it had become a byword for distant exile.

11. *And he shall pass through the sea against the foe.* The "he" would be Israel, transformed by God into a mighty warrior. But the three Hebrew words of this verset, *weʿavar bayam tsarah,* are cryptic. One possible literal rendering would be: "And he shall pass through the sea [in?] straits." Given the militant context, the last of these three words has been construed as a collective noun meaning "foe," and "against" is assumed to be implied by ellipsis.

CHAPTER 11   1. *Open, O Lebanon, your doors.* There is a double meaning here. These are the doors of the kingdom within which are the great stands of cedar; and they are the gates of the city within which are buildings with sumptuous cedarwood paneling.

2. *dense forest.* Though *batsir* usually means "vintage," a forest is not a vineyard, and hence in this instance the word may reflect the verbal stem that means "fortified" or, by implication, "impenetrable."

3. *shepherds, / . . . lions.* As in many other lines of poetry, these are the leaders (in the case of the lions, perhaps military commanders).

Thus said the LORD my God: "Look after the sheep to be slaughtered, 4
whose buyers will slaughter them and bear no guilt and whose sellers will 5
say, 'Praise the LORD, and I will get rich.' And their shepherds show no pity
for them. For I will no longer show pity for the dwellers of the land, said 6
the LORD, and I am about to deliver every man into the hand of his fellow
and into the hand of his king, and they shall grind up the land, and I will
not save it from their hand." And I looked after the sheep to be slaughtered 7
for the sheep traders, and I took me two staffs. One I called Pleasantness
and the other I called Bruising, and I looked after the sheep. But I got rid 8
of the three shepherds in a single month and lost patience with them, and
they on their part were disgusted with me. And I said, "I will not look after 9
you." The sheep dying will die, and the missing will go missing, and those
rescuing, each will eat the other's flesh. And I took my staff Pleasantness and 10
broke it apart to annul my covenant that I had sealed with all the peoples.
And on that very day it was annulled, and the sheep traders watching me 11
knew that it was the word of the LORD. And I said to them, "If it is good 12
in your eyes, give me my wages, and if not, don't." And they weighed out

---

4. *the sheep to be slaughtered.* The prophet continues the metaphor of the leaders as shepherds and the people as their flock. Here, the flock is bought and sold and slaughtered
with impunity.

7. *the sheep traders.* The received text reads *aniyey hatso'n,* "the poor of the sheep," but pov-
erty seems an odd attribute for sheep. The Septuagint, which appears to have used a Hebrew
text that had *likhena'aney hatso'n,* "for sheep traders," is followed in this translation.
    Bruising. The Hebrew *hovlim* reflects one of two homonymous verbal stems, one mean-
ing "to bruise" and the other "to bundle together." Some translations opt for the latter and
render the name as Unity. But there is a biblical notion of antithetical staffs, one for mercy
and one for punishment, and the present translation assumes that this is reflected here.

8. *the three shepherds.* They are introduced without explanation.

9. *I said.* It appears that the prophet is now speaking, not God.
    each will eat the other's flesh. The metaphor of the flock now takes a fantastic, and grisly,
turn: the herbivore sheep, reflecting the nature of the people they represent figuratively,
turn into voracious carnivores consuming each other's flesh.

10. *my covenant that I had sealed with all the peoples.* The reference is by no means transparent. First, since it would be strange for Zechariah to have a covenant with all the peoples,
he may have segued into speaking on behalf of God, such slippage being not uncommon in
biblical usage. But the content of the covenant is unclear. It might be a tacit agreement—not
at all like God's covenant with Israel—that the peoples are not to destroy Israel. "Pleasantness" might then be linked with this covenant through its pacific connotation.

12. *If it is good in your eyes.* That is, if you accept my breaking of the staff, even though as
a shepherd I would need it.
    give me my wages. In the metaphor of the flock, the prophet, observing what is happen-
ing to the flock, is represented as someone hired by the sheep traders.

13 my wages, thirty silver shekels. And the LORD said to me, "Fling it into the
    potter's kiln," this majestic sum that I was worth to them. And I took the
    thirty silver shekels and flung them into the potter's kiln at the house of
14 the LORD. And I broke apart my second staff, Bruising, to annul the broth-
15 erhood between the house of Judah and the house of Israel. And the LORD
16 said to me once again, "Take you the gear of a foolish shepherd. For I am
    about to raise up a shepherd in the land of the missing sheep. The lad shall
    not count them nor seek for them, and the injured he shall not heal nor the
    immobile one sustain, but the fat one he shall eat and break off their hooves."

17   Woe, O useless shepherds,
                              forsakers of the sheep.
                        Let a sword be over his arm
                              and over his right eye.
                        Let his arm entirely wither
                              and his right eye go utterly dark.

1 CHAPTER 12   A portent.

The word of the LORD concerning Israel, said the LORD, Who stretches out
the heavens and founds the earth and fashions the spirit of man within

---

13. *the potter's kiln.* The Hebrew noun *hayotseir* is opaque. Many interpreters understand
it as though it were *ha'otsar,* "the treasury," but there is scant evidence for interchangeability between those two terms, despite a limited phonetic similarity, and the violent verb
"fling" for putting something in a treasury would be surprising. *Yotseir* means "potter,"
and perhaps here, through metonymy, it refers to the potter's kiln, where the weights of
silver would be smelted.

14. *to annul the brotherhood between the house of Judah and the house of Israel.* This is still
another anomalous detail in this enigmatic prophecy, because the northern kingdom of
Israel ceased to exist three centuries before this prophet wrote.

15. *a foolish shepherd.* His foolishness is spelled out in the next verse.

16. *The lad.* This word, *na'ar,* is used because it was often young men (alternately, subalterns) who tended the flocks, as we see at the beginning of David's career in 1 Samuel 16.
Again, the reference is to the king.
    the immobile one. The Hebrew *hanitsavah* is unclear. It would ordinarily mean "one
who is standing," hence the guess of this translation.

him. I am about to make Jerusalem a bowl of poison to all the peoples round 2 about, and Judah, too, shall be caught in the siege against Jerusalem. And 3 it shall happen on that day that I will make Jerusalem a burdensome stone for all the peoples. All who lift her burden shall surely be scraped, while all the nations of the earth gather against her. On that day, said the LORD, I will 4 strike every horse with confusion and its rider with madness, but upon the house of Judah I will open My eyes, while all the horses of the peoples I will strike with blindness. And the leaders of Judah shall say in their heart, "The 5 dwellers of Jerusalem are strength for me through the LORD their God." On that day I will make the leaders of Judah like a flaming brazier among 6 wood and like a flaming torch among sheaves, and they shall consume on the right and on the left all the peoples round about, and Jerusalem shall again dwell in its place. And the LORD shall rescue the tents of Judah first 7 so that the glory of the house of David and the glory of Jerusalem's dwellers shall not surpass Judah. On that day, the LORD shall defend Jerusalem, and 8 the faltering among them on that day shall be like David and the house of

CHAPTER 12   2. *I am about to make Jerusalem a bowl of poison.* The besiegers will imagine that they are about to overwhelm Jerusalem, but instead they themselves will be destroyed.

Judah, too, shall be caught in the siege. There is no "caught" in the Hebrew, but this translation follows the precedent of two other modern English versions in adding it in order to avoid the impression that the kingdom of Judah is to take part in the siege against Jerusalem. Though one can lay siege only to a city, not to a kingdom, the obvious sense is that Judah, too, will be attacked by invaders.

3. *a burdensome stone.* This is a complementary metaphor to the bowl of poison. The stone is too heavy to be lifted (by the invaders), and those who attempt it will only injure themselves.

4. *I will strike every horse with confusion.* Now the two metaphors are translated into military facts: the enemy's horses will run amok and then go blind, and their riders will lose their minds, and thus the invading army will fall into fatal disarray.

5. *strength for me.* The Hebrew *'amtsah,* a familiar verbal stem but an anomalous form, is best construed as a noun.

6. *a flaming brazier . . . a flaming torch.* This is the third figurative representation of Jerusalem's destructive force and the most violent of the three.

7. *And the LORD shall rescue the tents of Judah first.* The prophet introduces a somewhat surprising political note here: even though Jerusalem is the capital, it should not think of itself as the exclusively important domain of God's people, and, to that end, He will rescue the regions outside Jerusalem first. But the next verse offers a counterbalance to this statement.

9   David like a god, like the LORD's messenger at their head. And on that day
10 I will set about to destroy all the nations coming against Jerusalem. And
    I will pour out upon the house of David and upon Jerusalem's dwellers a
    spirit of grace and graciousness, and they shall look upon those who were
    stabbed and mourn for them like the mourning for an only child, and
11 they shall grieve bitterly for them as one grieves bitterly for a firstborn. On
    that day the mourning in Jerusalem shall be as great as the mourning for
12 Hadad-Rimmon in the Valley of Megiddo. And the land shall mourn clan
13 by clan, the house of Nathan by itself and their women by themselves, the
    clan of the house of Levi by itself and their women by themselves, the house
14 of Shimei by itself, and their women by themselves, all the remaining clans,
    clan by clan by itself, and their women by themselves.

1   CHAPTER 13   On that day shall a spring be opened for the
    house of David and for Jerusalem's dwellers for the cleansing of offense and
2   impurity. And it shall happen on that day, said the LORD of Armies, that I
    will cut off the names of the idols from the land, and they no longer shall

---

8. *like a god.* The Hebrew uses the polyvalent *'elohim,* which can mean "God," "god," or
"divine being." The first of these three senses should be excluded because it would be too
extravagant, and theologically inadmissible, to say that the house of David was like God.

10. *grace and graciousness.* Two cognates appear in the Hebrew, *ḥein* and *taḥanunim.* While
the latter elsewhere means "supplications," the present context suggests that here it has
sense close to *ḥein.*
    look upon. The Masoretic Text has "look to Me ['*eilay*], revocalized here as '*eiley* ["to"
or "upon"].
    mourn for them like the mourning for an only child. It is puzzling that a prophecy prom-
ising the destruction of Judah's enemies and the pouring out of a spirit of grace upon the
people should conclude in this wave of desperate mourning. The least complicated explanation is Rashi's: in the battle to defend the city, many have fallen by the sword, and so the
triumph is darkened by a deep sadness over these terrible losses.

11. *as great as the mourning for Hadad-Rimmon.* These are two Canaanite gods, here conflated, as they may have been in popular religion. The mourning indicates that Hadad-
Rimmon was a dying god, like Tammuz and like the Greek Adonis, whose annual descent
into the underworld was marked by rites of grief.

CHAPTER 13   1. *for the cleansing of offense and impurity.* "Cleansing" is merely
implied in the Hebrew through ellipsis.

2. *the names of the idols.* Not only will the idols be destroyed but their very names will be
expunged—thus, "they no longer shall be recalled." One should note that invoking the
name of a deity in a vow was considered to be a very weighty act.

be recalled, and the prophets, too; and the spirit of uncleanness I will take
away from the land. And it shall happen that should a man still prophesy,   3
his father and his mother, his begetters, shall say, "You shall not live, for you
have spoken lies in the name of the LORD." And his father and his mother
shall stab him for his prophesying. And it shall happen on that day that the   4
prophets shall be shamed, each of his visions when he prophesies, and they
shall not wear a hairy mantle in order to deceive. And he shall say, "I am   5
no prophet. I am a tiller of the soil, for the soil has been consigned to me
from my youth." And one shall say to him, "What are these wounds on your   6
chest?" And he shall say, "Because I was struck in the house of my lovers."

> Sword, rouse against My shepherd,   7
>   against My companion man
>   —said the LORD of Armies.
> Strike the shepherd
>   and let the sheep be scattered,

---

the prophets These are false prophets, as the mention immediately afterward of "the
spirit of uncleanness" makes clear.

3. *his father and his mother, his begetters.* This extreme case highlights the terrible gravity
of the crime of false prophecy: his own parents condemn him to death and then carry out
the sentence.

for his prophesying. An alternate construction of this single Hebrew word is "when he
prophesies."

4. *a hairy mantle.* There is some indication that the early prophets (that is, earlier than the
so-called Literary Prophets) wore hairy mantles, and so this would be the outward show
of his status as a prophet.

5. *I am no prophet. I am a tiller of the soil.* Confronted with the charge of false prophecy,
which is a capital crime, he pretends to have nothing to do with prophecy but to be only
a simple farmer.

for the soil has been consigned to me. The noun in the received text is *'adam*, "man" or
"humankind," but this is probably an error for *'adamah*, "soil," the final *heh* having been
lost through haplography because it is also the first letter of the next word.

6. *What are these wounds on your chest?* His own body bears evidence against him. The
wounds would be gashes, self-inflicted or made by others, as one sees with the prophets of
Baal in 1 Kings 18:28, in a pagan rite to rouse the attention of a deity.

Because I was struck in the house of my lovers. Most translators render the last word
as "friends," but its general meaning is "lovers." The usage is probably influenced by the
common representation in Prophetic literature of pagan deities as "lovers" of the adulterous
Israel. The wounds do not reflect any homosexual sadomasochistic practice but rather the
cultic excesses of a pagan ritual.

7. *My shepherd.* Once again, the shepherd is the king.

and I will bring My hand back against the shepherd lads.
8   And it shall happen throughout the land,
                  said the Lord,
            two-thirds within it shall be cut off, perish,
                  and a third shall be left within it.
9   And I will bring the third into fire
                  and purge them as silver is purged
                  and try them as gold is tried.
            He shall call out in My name.
                  As for Me, I will answer him.
                  And he shall say, "The Lord is my God."

1 **CHAPTER 14**   Look, a day is coming for the Lord when what
2 is despoiled from you shall be shared out in your midst, and I will gather
all the nations against Jerusalem for battle. And the city shall be captured
and the houses looted and the women ravished. And half the city shall go
3 out in exile, but the rest of the people shall not be cut off from the city. And
the Lord shall sally forth and do battle with those nations as on the day
4 He fought, on the day of battle. And His feet shall stand on that day on the
Mount of Olives, which faces Jerusalem from the east. And the Mount of
Olives shall split in half, from east to west, into a very great valley, and half
5 the mountain shall shift to the north and half to the south. And the valley
of My mountains shall be blocked, as the valley of the mountains reaches

---

the shepherd lads. The Hebrew *tso'arim* means "assistant shepherds," which would refer figuratively to people in the royal court and administration.

9. *He shall call out.* As often happens in biblical usage, the pronouns switch from plural to singular, Israel now imagined as a collective.

CHAPTER 14   2. *the city . . . the houses . . . the women.* The panorama of conquest moves inward, and intensifies, in concentric circles: first the city falls, then the homes are ransacked, and—worst of all—within the homes the women are raped.
      but the rest of the people shall not be cut off. This prepares the ground for the great pivot, in which the Lord sallies forth as a warrior-god to route the enemies.

4. *the Mount of Olives, which faces Jerusalem from the east.* The enemies would have come from the east.
      And the Mount of Olives shall split in half. God's principal weapon in this battle is a cataclysmic earthquake.

5. *shall be blocked.* The Masoretic Text reads *wenastem,* "and you shall flee," but the strong scholarly consensus is that the word should be revocalized to show *wenistam,* as it does in some Hebrew manuscripts and in three ancient versions.

as far as Azal, and it shall be blocked as it was blocked by the earthquake in
the days of Uzziah king of Judah. And the LORD my God shall come, all the
holy ones with Him. And it shall happen that on that day there shall be no 6
daylight nor chill moonlight. And it shall be a single day—it shall be known 7
to the LORD—neither day nor night, and it shall be, at eventide there shall
be light. And it shall happen on that day, fresh waters shall come out from 8
Jerusalem, half of them toward the eastern sea and half of them toward the
western sea, in summer and in winter it shall be. And the LORD shall be king 9
over all the earth. On that day the LORD shall be one and His name one. All 10
the land shall become as a plain, from Geba to Rimmon south of Jerusalem,
but the city shall rise high and sit in her place, from the Benjamin Gate to
the site of the Former Gate as far as the Armor Gate and from Hanamel
Tower as far as the king's winepress. And they shall dwell within her, and 11
no more shall there be devastation, and Jerusalem shall dwell secure. And 12
this shall be the plague with which the LORD shall strike all the peoples that
marshaled against Jerusalem: their flesh shall rot as they stand on their feet,
and their eyes shall rot in their sockets, and their tongues shall rot in their
mouths. And it shall happen on that day, the panic from the LORD among 13
them shall be great, and every man shall seize his fellow, and his hand shall
be raised against the hand of his fellow. And Judah, too, shall do battle 14
in Jerusalem, and the wealth of the nations round about shall be gathered
in—gold and silver and very many garments. And so shall there be a plague 15

---

all the holy ones. These would be the divine entourage.
   with Him. The Masoretic reading is "with you," but almost all the ancient versions have
"with Him."

6. *there shall be no daylight nor chill moonlight.* This is the construction of many modern
versions, but the Hebrew is cryptic.

8. *fresh waters shall come out from Jerusalem.* Jerusalem thus becomes a source of fructi-
fication for all its distant environs. The vision may be inspired by the stream flowing out
from the Temple in Ezekiel 47.

10. *the city.* The Hebrew says only "she," but "the city" is added in the translation in order
to avoid the impression that it is the land that rises high.

12. *And this shall be the plague.* The prophet is not content with the evocation of Jerusalem
dwelling secure but goes on to describe the ghastly fate of its enemies.
   their flesh. The Hebrew uses a masculine singular throughout the plague passage, but
this is basically a collective noun, hence the plural in the translation.

14. *Judah, too, shall do battle in Jerusalem.* Hebrew usage also allows one to construe this
as "do battle against Jerusalem," and a few scholars have proposed a background of bitter
enmity between the population in Jerusalem and the inhabitants of the outlying districts,
but this seems unlikely.

against horse and mule and camel and donkey and every beast that will be
16 in those camps, like this plague. And it shall happen that all who remain of
the nations coming up against Jerusalem shall go up year after year to bow
to the King, the LORD of Armies, and to celebrate the Festival of Booths.
17 And it shall happen that he who does not go up from the clans of the earth
to Jerusalem to bow to the King, the LORD of Armies, no rain shall fall on
18 him. And if the clan of Egypt does not go up and does not come, upon them
shall be the plague with which the LORD shall strike all the nations that do
19 not go up to celebrate the Festival of Booths. This shall be the punishment
for the offense of Egypt and for the offense of all the nations that do not go
20 up to celebrate the Festival of Booths. On that day there shall be on the bells
of the horses "Holy to the LORD," and the pails in the house of the LORD shall
21 be like the basins before the altar. And every pail in Jerusalem and in Judah
shall be "Holy to the LORD of Armies." And all those offering sacrifice shall
come and take from them and cook in them, and there shall no longer be a
merchant in the house of the LORD of Armies on that day.

---

15. *like this plague.* That is, the plague in which the living body rots.

16. *all who remain of the nations . . . shall go up year after year to bow to the King, the LORD of Armies.* This passage picks up the idea proclaimed in Third Isaiah that all the nations will embrace the worship of YHWH. It is for this reason that God here is given the epithet King, for He is king of all the earth.

the *Festival of Booths.* This is the fall festival, which, because it was celebrated after the labor of harvesting was completed, drew the largest throngs of pilgrims. Evidently, the obligation of the sundry nations is just this festival and not all three pilgrim festivals.

17. *who does not go up . . . to bow to the King.* Unlike the parallel passages in Third Isaiah, this call to universalism is accompanied by a threat to those who do not comply.

18. *the clan of Egypt . . . upon them shall be the plague.* The withholding of rain is not a threat to Egypt because it has the Nile as its water source, so the Egyptians will be punished by plague.

19. *the punishment for the offense.* "Punishment" is merely implied in the Hebrew.

20. *Holy to the LORD.* This is the formulaic phrase that indicates consecration to the Temple. The horses will no longer serve as mounts for battle but will be part of the sacred service.

the *pails in the house of the LORD shall be like the basins before the altar.* The intention of this statement is obscure. Since the next verse goes on to say that all the pails (others translate the Hebrew term as "pots"—in the kingdom will be inscribed with the words dedicating them to the sanctuary, perhaps the meaning may be that even receptacles commonly used for mundane purposes will be devoted to the service of God.

21. *there shall no longer be a merchant in the house of the LORD.* The presence of merchants was required in order to exchange gold and silver for chattel that could be offered as sacrifice. Jesus, it will be remembered, objected to such commercial activity in the Temple and drove out the money changers. It would appear that this prophet was actuated by that same impulse of purism or zealotry.

Malachi

CHAPTER 1   A portent: the word of the LORD through Malachi.   1

> I have loved you, said the LORD,   2
>   and you said, "How have you loved us?"
> Is not Esau Jacob's brother? said the LORD.
>   And I loved Jacob,
> but Esau I hated,   3
>   and I made his mountains a desolation
>   and his estate—for the desert jackals.
> Should Edom say, "We are beggared,   4
>   but once more we will build the ruins,"
> thus said the LORD of Armies:
>   They shall build but I will destroy,
> and they shall be called the region of wickedness
>   and the people the LORD cursed for all time.
> And your own eyes shall see and you shall say,   5
>   "May the LORD be great beyond the region of Israel."
> A son honors his father,   6
>   and a slave his master,
> but if I am a father,
>   where is My honor,

CHAPTER 1   1. *Malachi.* In contrast to many of the other prophets, no father's name is given, and no indication of the years of his prophecy is offered. This suppression of identifying context lends support to the inference that "Malachi" is not actually a name but a common noun designating a role, "My messenger."

3. *but Esau I hated.* Esau is Edom, and the bitter lingering memory of the Edomites' collaboration with the Babylonians in the destruction of Jerusalem informs these lines.

5. *May the* LORD *be great beyond the region of Israel.* This idea that God's kingship will be reverentially recognized by the nations of the earth is picked up in verse 11.

and if I am a master,
   where is the fear of Me?
said the LORD of Armies to you,
   priests who despise My name.
      And you said, "How have we despised Your name?"

7   Bringing on My altar
   defiled food,
     and you say, "How have we defiled You?"
When you say the LORD's table
   is despised,

8   and when you bring a blind beast to sacrifice—
   "there is nothing wrong."
And when you bring a lame and sickly beast—
   "there is nothing wrong."
Offer it, pray, to your prefect.
   Will he be pleased with you or favor you?
     said the LORD of Armies.

9   And now, entreat, pray,
   God, that He be gracious to us
From your hand this was.
   Will He show favor to you?
     said the LORD of Armies.

10   Who then among you would close double doors
   and not light fire on My altar in vain?

---

6. *priests who despise My name.* The prophecy began by addressing the people of Israel. Now attention is focused on the priests and their abuse of the Temple cult. Since the prophet assumes that the Temple service is being conducted, his own discourse would have to occur at some point after the completion of the rebuilding of the Temple around 514 B.C.E.

How have we despised Your name? This articulation of the prophecy through challenge and response (compare verse 2) is characteristic of Malachi.

8. *blind . . . / lame . . . sickly.* All such maimed animals are forbidden as offerings in the sacrificial cult. The priests may be passing off cheaply acquired beasts of this sort while keeping the sound animals for their own consumption.

your prefect. The Hebrew word used here, *peḥah*, is a loanword taken from the Persian (compare the English "pasha," which entered the language through a Turkish intermediary) and is thus linguistic evidence of the setting of this prophecy in the Persian period.

10. *close double doors / and not light fire on My altar.* Given the egregious abuse of the Temple cult, what needs to be done is to close the doors of the sanctuary and stop lighting the lampstands on the altar.

I have no desire of you,
  said the Lord of Armies,
    and with grain offering from your land I will not be pleased.
For from the sun's rising to its setting   11
  great is My name among the nations,
and in every place incense is offered to My name
  and pure grain offering,
for great is My name among the nations,
  said the Lord of Armies.
But you profane it   12
  when you say, "The Master's table is defiled,
    and the food on it despised."
And you say, "How tiresome,"   13
  and you insult Me, said the Lord of Armies.
And you bring the stolen and the lame and the sickly,
  and you bring the grain offering.
Will I be pleased with it from your hand?
  said the Lord.

And cursed be the schemer who has in his flock a sound male but pledges   14
and sacrifices a damaged one to the Master. For I am a great king, said the
Lord of Armies, and My name is fearsome among the nations.

---

11. *in every place incense is offered to My name / and pure grain offering.* While the offerings in the Jerusalem temple are contaminated, elsewhere the nations serve God with pure
sacrifices. One must construe the assertion either as a rhetorical maneuver or as a monotheistic fantasy.

12. *when you say, "The Master's table is defiled."* The priests, of course, would not actually
make such an open declaration of their own contempt for the sacred altar, but the prophet
attributes to them words that expose the effect of their actions.
  the food on it despised. The received text includes a word, *nivo* ("its fruit"?), that has not
been translated because it is syntactically awry and looks like a scribal error. It may be a
dittography triggered by the next word in the text, *nivzeh.*

13. *How tiresome.* The Masoretic Text shows an odd formation, *matla'ah,* and this translation follows many critics in breaking it into two words, *mah tela'ah.*

14. *a sound male.* "Sound" is merely implied in the Hebrew.
  My name is fearsome among the nations. The prophet reverts here to the idea introduced
in verse 11 that the sundry nations fear and worship Him with the appropriate sacrifices
while the priests in Jerusalem offer up tainted beasts.

1,2 CHAPTER 2   And now, for you is this command, O priests. If
you do not heed and do not pay mind to give honor to My name, said the
LORD of Armies, I will let loose the curse among you and make your bless-
3 ings curses, yes, make them curses, for you do not pay mind. I am about to
rebuke your seed and scatter dung on your faces, the dung of your festival
4 offerings, and it shall carry you off to where it is. And you shall know that
I have sent you this command, for My covenant to be with Levi, said the
5 LORD of Armies. My covenant has been with him, life and peace, and I have
given them to him—fear, and he did fear Me, and before My name he was
6 awestruck. A teaching of truth was in his mouth, and no wrong was found
on his lips. In peace and in uprightness he walked with Me, and many did
7 he bring back from crime. For the lips of the priest preserved knowledge,
and teachings they sought from his mouth, for he was the messenger of the
8 LORD of Armies. Yet you yourselves swerved from the way; you made many
stumble through rulings. You made a ruin of the covenant of the Levite,
9 said the LORD of Armies. And I on My part made you despised and lowly
to every people, as you have not been keeping My ways, and you have been
showing favoritism in rulings.

10   Do we not all have one father,
                   did not one God create us?
          Why should we each betray our brothers
                   to profane the covenant of our fathers?

CHAPTER 2   2. *give honor to My name.* This phrasing reflects a tendency in the
Second Temple period to substitute God's "name" for direct references to the deity.
     make your blessings curses. The literal sense is "curse your blessings," but this is the
obvious meaning. An important function of the priests was to bless the people.

3. *your seed.* It is not entirely clear whether the reference is to the offspring of the priests or
to anything, literal or figurative, that they plant.
     scatter dung on your faces. Though shameful and disgusting for anyone, this is particu-
larly disgraceful for priests, who are obliged to remain in a condition of purity.
     it shall carry you off to where it is. The translation reflects the obscurity of the Hebrew.
What might be intended is the dung-heap, but it remains puzzling how dung scattered on
a face could carry a person off.

6. *A teaching of truth.* An important responsibility of the priests was to provide instruction (*torah*) to the people concerning the laws and moral imperatives they were obliged to
observe. But the term also has the sense of judicial ruling, as in verses 7, 8, and 9.

9. *showing favoritism in rulings.* This perversion of justice is precisely what a judge is
enjoined not to do.

Judah has betrayed, and an abomination was done in Israel and in Jerusa- 11
lem. For Judah profaned the LORD's sanctity that He had loved and coupled
with the daughter of an alien god. May the LORD cut off for the man who 12
does this, a witness and answerer from the tents of Jacob and bringer of
grain offering to the LORD of Armies. And this, besides, did you do: cause 13
to cover with tears the LORD's altar, with weeping and groans, because
there is no more turning to the grain offering or accepting with favor from
your hand. And you say, "Why?" Because the LORD bore witness between 14
you and the wife of your youth. It was you who betrayed her when she was
your friend and your covenanted wife. And did not one do [right], who 15
has exceeding spirit? And what does the one seek?—seed of God. And you
should guard yourselves with your spirit and not betray the wife of your
youth. For I hate divorce, said the LORD God of Israel, and one who covers 16

---

11. *coupled with the daughter of an alien god.* The prophet here, like Ezra, inveighs against
mixed marriages, though he may be referring simply to sexual relations with foreign
women. Calling such a woman "daughter of an alien god" is a way of stressing the involvement of non-Israelite women in paganisim.

12. *a witness and answerer.* The received text says 'er, "one awake," which this translation,
following one version of the Septuagint, emends to 'ed. Given the parallelism with "bringer
of grain offering to the LORD," this would then refer to a priestly function—perhaps, bearing witness in legal matters.

13. *cause to cover with tears.* While the literal sense of the Hebrew is simply "cover with
tears," this could not be the act of the priests, for that would suggest profound contrition.
Rather, by consorting with alien women, the priests impel God to reject their offerings on
the altar, and thus the people they serve are stricken with despair and weep in the Temple.

14. *It was you who betrayed her when she was your friend and your covenanted wife.* Since
the next verse explicitly mentions divorce, one must conclude that the prophet actually
rejects divorce as a "betrayal" of one's wife. This view puts aside the legislated provision
for divorce in the Torah. It is an attitude adopted by Jesus in Matthew.

15. *And did not one do [right].* The entire sentence is obscure. Some interpreters think
that "one" refers to God, but that seems strained. The understanding reflected in this
translation is: although many among you have betrayed your spouses by divorcing them
(and perhaps taking foreign women as mates), there is one—implicitly, a few—among you
of "exceeding spirit" who does the right thing. (The word "right" has been added speculatively, in brackets.) What this person seeks is the "seed of God," which would be pure
Israelite offspring. If in fact this whole passage is addressed to the priests, it may be that
Malachi objects only to divorce among priests, not to divorce in general. The wording,
however, at the beginning of the next verse, "For I hate divorce, said the LORD," does sound
like a generalizing statement.

16. *I hate divorce.* Unfortunately, the "I" is lacking in the Hebrew text, opening up a window
of ambiguity as to what these words mean.

his garb with outrage, said the LORD of Armies. And you shall guard your-
17 selves with your spirit and not betray. You have wearied the LORD with
your words, and you say, "How have we wearied Him?" In your saying,
"All evildoers are good in the eyes of the LORD, and them He desires," or,
"Where is the God of justice?"

CHAPTER 3

1   I am about to send My messenger,
        and he shall clear the way before Me.
In a trice He shall enter His Temple,
        the Master Whom you seek,
and the covenant's messenger whom you desire,
        look, he comes, said the LORD of Armies.
2   And who can bear the day of His coming
        and who can stand when He appears?
For He is like the smelter's fire
        and like the launderers' lye.
3   And the smelter shall sit and purify silver,
        and purify the sons of Levi,
and refine them like gold and silver,
        and they shall become grain offerings to the LORD in righteousness.
4   And the grain offering of Judah and Jerusalem
        shall be sweet to the LORD
            as in days of yore and in former years.
5   But I will approach you for judgment,

---

17. *You have wearied the* LORD. This verse might be the introduction to the prophecy
recorded in the next chapter because the malfeasance now is not divorce but a general
perversion or rejection of divine justice.

CHAPTER 3   1. *My messenger.* Although this is the designation of the prophet
responsible for the book (*mal'akhi*), here the obvious reference is to a divine messenger
who will herald God's entrance into the Temple.

2. *the day of His coming.* Because of the fiery power of the one who comes, it is most probably God, even though grammatically the pronominal references might be attached to the
divine messenger.
    the smelter's fire / . . . the launderers' lye. Malachi may have borrowed these images of
purification from Isaiah.

and I will be a swift witness
   against sorcerers and against adulterers
      and against those who swear falsely,
   and against those who extort the hired man's wages,
      who wrong widow and orphan and sojourner
and do not fear Me,
   said the LORD of Armies.
For I am the LORD, I have not changed,   6
   and you, sons of Jacob, have not come to an end.
From your fathers' days you swerved from My statutes   7
   and you did not keep them.
Turn back to Me, that I may turn back to you,
   said the LORD of Armies.
      But you said, "How shall we turn back?"
Can a human cheat God?   8
   For you are cheating Me.
And you said, "How did we cheat You?"
   —in tithes and in donations.
Despite the curse with which you are cursed,   9
   Me you cheat, the whole nation.
Bring the whole tithe   10
   to the treasure house
      that there be provision in My house.

---

5. *But I will approach you for judgment.* While this sharp antithesis to what precedes could signal the beginning of a new prophecy, it could also be a dialectic swing within a continuous prophetic utterance: God will restore the purity of the Levites when He comes back to the Temple, but He will also make a reckoning with the sundry wrongdoers in Israel.

against those who extort the hired man's wages. Until now, Malachi has been concerned chiefly with the corruption of the Temple cult, but now he moves into the denunciation of the sundry social injustices familiar from the First Commonwealth prophets.

8. *How did we cheat You?* Malachi again invokes his favored form of dialogic challenge and response.

in tithes and in donations. Now he returns to the dominant theme of abuse of the cult. In this instance, the object of critique is the failure to deliver tithes and donations to the Temple—or, perhaps, shortchanging in the delivery.

9. *Despite the curse.* The people palpably suffer as punishment for their misdeeds but still persist in them.

10. *that there be provision in My house.* The tithe was not currency—this was still not a money economy—but a tithe of agricultural products and livestock, hence "provision."

and test Me, pray, in this,
  said the LORD of Armies.
I will surely open for you
  the casements of the heavens
and shower upon you
  blessings without end.

11 And I will rebuke for you the devourer,
  and it shall not ruin for you the fruit of the soil,
nor shall the vine of the field lose its yield,
  said the LORD of Armies.

12 And all the nations shall call you happy,
  for you shall be a land desired,
   said the LORD of Armies.

13 Your words against Me have been harsh,
  said the LORD.
   And you said, "How did we speak against You?"
14 You said, "It is for naught to serve God,
  and what profit if we keep His watch
   and if we walk downcast because of the LORD of Armies?
15 And now we see the arrogant happy,
  evildoers actually flourish,
   actually test God and escape."
16 Then did the LORD-fearers speak together,
  each man to his neighbor,
   and the LORD hearkened and He heard,

I will surely open for you / the casements of the heavens. Approximately the same phrasing occurs at the beginning of the Flood in Genesis 7:11. In Genesis, it designates a devastating deluge, but here it is rain that fructifies the land.
 shower upon you. More literally, "empty out upon you."

11. *the devourer.* This is an epithet for the locust, as becomes clear in what immediately follows.

14. *if we walk downcast because of the LORD of Armies.* The Hebrew represented here as "downcast" suggests something like "gloomy." The idea is contrition in the presence of God, which, according to these naysayers, is pointless.

15. *And now we see the arrogant happy.* This subversive perception by the rebellious people turns out to be quite similar to the recurrent argument against the traditional moral calculus articulated in the Book of Job.

and a book of remembrance was written before Him
    for the Lord-fearers who value His name.
And they shall become for Me, said the Lord of Armies,   17
    a treasure on the day that I prepare.
And I will have pity on them
    as a man has pity
        on his son who serves him.
And you shall turn back and see   18
    between righteous and wicked,
between him who serves God
    and him who does not serve Him.
For, look, the day is coming,   19
    burning like a kiln,
when all the arrogant and all the evildoers shall be straw.
    And the day that is coming shall set them ablaze,
        said the Lord of Armies,
            shall not leave them root or branch.
But to you who fear My name shall dawn   20
    a sun of righteousness with healing in its wings,
and you shall go forth and become plump
    like stall-fed calves.
And you shall trample the wicked, for they shall be ashes   21
    beneath the soles of your feet

---

17. *the day that I prepare.* This is the prophetic Day of the Lord, when the evildoers will be punished and the righteous redeemed.

    his son who serves him. What is envisaged is a stable social order in which sons dutifully serve their fathers. Malachi will give the theme of the union of fathers and sons a grand flourish in his concluding prophecy.

18. *him who serves God.* The service of son to father is now transposed into the service of God by man. At the beginning of the book (1:6), God identifies Himself as father to humankind.

19. *shall not leave them root or branch.* Though "root or branch" is idiomatic for "all of it," these are combustible materials, like the straw just mentioned.

20. *a sun of righteousness with healing in its wings.* This beautiful phrase takes advantage of the multivalent Hebrew *kenafayim*, "wings" and also "hems of a garment." The dawning sun of righteousness has wings either because of the radiant beams around it or because it sails through the sky. The Near Eastern sun can be blistering and lethal, as we are often reminded in the Bible, but this sun instead gives restorative warmth and brightness.

21. *trample.* The unusual word used in the Hebrew generally means "knead."

on the day that I prepare,
    said the Lord of Armies.

22   Recall the teaching of Moses My servant
            that I charged him on Horeb,
                for all Israel, statutes and laws.
23   Look, I am about to send to you
            Elijah the prophet
        before the coming of the day of the Lord,
            great and fearsome.
24   And he shall bring fathers' hearts back to sons
            and the sons' hearts to their fathers—
                lest I come and strike the land with utter destruction.

---

22. *Horeb.* This is another name for Sinai.

23. *I am about to send to you / Elijah the prophet.* This verse inaugurates a rich legendary tradition in which Elijah is imagined as the harbinger of the messiah. Elijah would appear to be a different harbinger from the "messenger" mentioned in 3:1, and it is by no means certain that these concluding verses are from the same hand as the rest of the book. Whether this text is drawing on an already existent folk tradition is a matter of speculation. Elijah, because of the stories of his miraculously aiding common people, would have been a likely candidate for a folk hero, and his seclusion on Mount Horeb (1 Kings 19:8ff.), where he is vouchsafed an epiphany, aligns him with Moses, who is invoked in the previous verse.

24. *lest I come and strike the land with utter destruction.* This grim warning, immediately after the vision of perfect harmony between fathers and sons, seems a discordant note on which to conclude the book. The framers of Jewish tradition recognized the discordance and ruled that when this passage was chanted in synagogue, one must end by going back to repeat from the preceding verse the lines about the coming of Elijah.